PRACTICAL ENQUIRE WITHIN

A Practical Work that will Save Householders and Houseowners Pounds and Pounds Every Year

Volume V

DIY

'Do It Yourself', also known as DIY, is the method of building, modifying, or repairing something without the aid of experts or professionals. It is undertaken by a wide variety of people, for many different reasons – but what links them all, is a desire to improve their material surroundings and skills.

The term 'do-it-yourself' has been associated with consumers since at least 1912, primarily in the domain of home improvement and maintenance activities. It only came into common usage around the 1950s however. Back in the mid-twentieth century, DIY referred specifically to the new trend for people undertaking home improvements and various other small craft and construction projects, both as a creative-recreational and as a cost saving activity.

In the present day, DIY can also refer to music, radio, magazines and the arts and crafts movement – in that it offers an alternative to modern consumer culture's emphasis on relying on others, to satisfy needs. It also includes crafts such as knitting, crochet, sewing, handmade jewellery and ceramics, as well as the general environmental movement towards 'Recycle, Reuse and Reduce.' Painting and decorating is also a particularly prevalent form of home and aesthetic improvement.

Aside from its appearance in 1912, DIY as a broader concept has a much longer history. Italian archaeologists unearthed the ruins of a sixth century BCE Greek structure in southern Italy that came with detailed assembly instructions. It has since become known as an 'ancient IKEA building'! The find was a temple-like construction discovered at Torre Satriano, near the southern city of Potenza; a region where local people mingled with Greeks who settled along the southern coast of Sicily from the eighth century BCE onwards. Professor Christopher Smith, director of the British School at Rome, said that the discovery was 'the clearest example yet found of mason's marks of the time. It looks as if someone was instructing others how to mass-produce components and put them together in this way.'

Much like the instruction booklets, various sections of the luxury building were inscribed with coded symbols showing how the pieces slotted together. The characteristics of these inscriptions indicate they date back to around the sixth century BCE, which tallies with the architectural evidence suggested by the decoration. Although close to the modern conception of DIY, this find cannot properly be termed a 'do it yourself' though – as the building was actually built by Greek artisans coming from the Spartan colony of Taranto in Apulia (Southern Italy).

The DIY movement is a re-introduction (often to urban and suburban dwellers) of the old pattern of personal involvement and use of skills in upkeep of a house or apartment, making clothes; maintenance of cars, computers, websites; or any material aspect of living. In the 1970s, DIY spread through the North American population of college and recent-graduate age groups. In part, this movement involved the renovation of affordable, rundown older homes. But it also related to various projects expressing the social and environmental vision of the 1960s and early 1970s. The young visionary Stewart Brand, working with friends and family, and initially using the most basic of typesetting and page-layout tools, published the first edition of *The Whole Earth Catalogue* (subtitled *Access to Tools*) in late 1968.

The first *Catalogue*, and its successors, used a broad definition of the term 'tools'. There were informational tools, such as books (often technical in nature), professional journals, courses, classes, and the like. There were specialized, designed items, such as carpenters' and masons' tools, garden tools, welding equipment, chainsaws, fibreglass materials and so on; even early personal computers. Often copied, the *Catalogue* appealed to a wide cross-section of people in North America and had a broad influence.

For decades, magazines such as *Popular Mechanics* and *Mechanix Illustrated* offered a way for readers to keep current on useful practical skills and techniques. DIY home improvement books began to flourish in the 1970s, first created as collections of magazine articles. *Time-Life*, *Better Homes and Gardens*, and other publishers soon followed suit. In the mid-1990s, DIY home-improvement content began to find its way onto the World Wide Web. HouseNet was the earliest bulletin-board style site where users could share information. Beyond magazines and television, the scope of home improvement DIY continues to grow online, and in the true spirit of DIY, many homeowners blog about their experiences – taking knowledge away from organisations, and into the hands of individual people.

As is evident from this short introduction to the practice of DIY, it is an aspect of human endeavour with a surprisingly long history. We will always need to make and improve the spaces in which we live and work, and DIY provides the means with which everyday people can do just this. It is hoped that the current reader enjoys this book on the subject – and it encouraged to undertake some DIY of their own.

Woodworking

Woodworking is the process of making items from wood. Along with stone, mud and animal parts, wood was one of the first materials worked by early humans. There are incredibly early examples of woodwork, evidenced in Mousterian stone tools used by Neanderthal man, which demonstrate our affinity with the wooden medium. In fact, the very development of civilisation is linked to the advancement of increasingly greater degrees of skill in working with these materials.

Examples of Bronze Age wood-carving include tree trunks worked into coffins from northern Germany and Denmark and wooden folding-chairs. The site of Fellbach-Schmieden in Germany has provided fine examples of wooden animal statues from the Iron Age. Woodworking is depicted in many ancient Egyptian drawings, and a considerable amount of ancient Egyptian furniture (such as stools, chairs, tables, beds, chests) has been preserved in tombs. The inner coffins found in the tombs were also made of wood. The metal used by the Egyptians for woodworking tools was originally copper and eventually, after 2000 BC, bronze - as ironworking was unknown until much later. Historically, woodworkers relied upon the woods native to their region, until transportation and trade innovations made more exotic woods available to the craftsman.

Today, often as a contemporary artistic and 'craft' medium, wood is used both in traditional and modern styles; an excellent material for delicate as well as forceful artworks. Wood is used in forms of sculpture, trade, and decoration including chip carving, wood burning, and marquetry, offering a fascination, beauty, and complexity in the grain that often shows even when the medium is painted. It is in some ways easier to shape than harder substances, but an artist or craftsman must develop specific skills to carve it properly. 'Wood carving' is really an entire genre itself, and involves cutting wood generally with a knife in one hand, or a chisel by two hands - or, with one hand on a chisel and one hand on a mallet. The phrase may also refer to the finished product, from individual sculptures to hand-worked mouldings composing part of a tracery.

The making of sculpture in wood has been extremely widely practiced but survives much less well than the other main materials such as stone and bronze, as it is vulnerable to decay, insect damage, and fire. It therefore forms an important hidden element in the arts and crafts history of many cultures. Outdoor wood sculptures do not last long in most parts of the world, so we have little idea how the totem pole tradition developed. Many of the most important sculptures of China and Japan in particular are in wood, and the great majority of African sculptures and that of Oceania also use this medium. There are various forms of carving which can be utilised; 'chip carving' (a style of carving in which knives or chisels are used to remove small chips of the material), 'relief carving' (where figures are carved in a flat panel of wood), 'Scandinavian flat-plane' (where figures are carved in large flat planes, created primarily using a carving knife - and rarely rounded or sanded afterwards) and 'whittling' (simply carving shapes using just a knife). Each of these techniques will need slightly varying tools, but broadly speaking, a specialised 'carving knife' is essential, alongside a 'gouge' (a tool with a curved cutting edge used in a variety of forms and sizes for carving hollows, rounds and sweeping curves), a 'chisel' and a 'coping saw' (a small saw, used to cut off chunks of wood at once).

Wood turning is another common form of woodworking, used to create wooden objects on a lathe. Woodturning differs from most other forms of woodworking in that the wood is moving while a stationary tool is used to cut and shape it. There are two distinct methods of turning wood: 'spindle turning' and 'bowl' or 'faceplate turning'. Their key difference is in the orientation of the wood grain, relative to the axis of the lathe. This variation in orientation changes the tools and techniques used. In spindle turning, the grain runs lengthways along the lathe bed, as if a log was mounted in the lathe. Grain is thus always perpendicular to the direction of rotation under the tool. In bowl turning, the grain runs at right angles to the axis, as if a plank were mounted across the chuck. When a bowl blank rotates, the angle that the grain makes with the cutting tool continually changes between the easy cuts of lengthways and downwards across the grain to two places per rotation where the tool is cutting across the grain and even upwards across it. This varying grain angle limits some of the tools that may be used and requires additional skill in order to cope with it.

The origin of woodturning dates to around 1300 BC when the Egyptians first developed a two-person lathe. One person would turn the wood with a rope while the other used a sharp tool to cut shapes in the wood. The Romans improved the Egyptian design with the addition of a turning bow. Early bow lathes were also developed and used in Germany, France and Britain. In the Middle Ages a pedal replaced hand-operated turning, freeing both the craftsman's hands to hold the woodturning tools. The pedal was usually connected to a pole, often a straight-grained sapling. The system today is called the 'spring pole' lathe. Alternatively, a two-person lathe, called a 'great lathe', allowed a piece to turn continuously (like today's power lathes). A master would cut the wood while an apprentice turned the crank.

As an interesting aside, the term 'bodger' stems from pole lathe turners who used to make chair legs and spindles. A bodger would typically purchase all the trees on a plot of land, set up camp on the plot, and then fell the trees and turn the wood. The spindles and legs that were produced were sold in bulk, for pence per dozen. The bodger's job was considered unfinished because he

NEWNES
PRACTICAL
ENQUIRE WITHIN

A PRACTICAL WORK THAT WILL
SAVE HOUSEHOLDERS AND
HOUSEOWNERS POUNDS AND
POUNDS EVERY YEAR

How to Lay a Stair Carpet

The laying of stair carpets is a task which must be done in every household periodically, and for this reason alone it is important to set about the job in the best way possible. Not only can a considerable amount of time and energy be saved, but a neater and altogether smarter staircase is the result.

Calculating Length Required.

If you are setting up house for the first time, or moving into a house where new carpeting will be necessary, the first step is to calculate the length of material required. You will probably find that 14½ inches of carpeting are necessary for the tread and riser of each stair, and it is also very important to allow an additional 18 inches which, when the carpet is quite new, should be laid along the floor at the top of the stairs. The standard widths of stair carpet are 18 inches, 22½ inches and 27 inches; and if the width of the stairs is not more than 2 feet 6 inches, a width of 18 inches or 22½ inches will be sufficient for the carpeting, if the stairs are stained and polished at the sides. With regard to costs, 3s. 11d. a yard for an 18-inch width and 4s. 11d. a yard for a 22½-inch width should be average prices for Wilton carpeting.

Don't Choose a Thick Carpet if there are Bends in Your Stairs.

The first points to decide are the kind and quality of the carpeting and the nature of the holders to be used for keeping it in place. Especially where there are bends in the stairs to be negotiated it is not advisable for the carpet to be too thick, as it will have to be folded, and for this reason an Axminster, with its rather deep, luxurious pile, is not entirely to be recommended. It is often better to select a short pile Wilton or a hair carpet, which will be found to possess excellent wearing properties combined with comparative thinness.

Felt Pads for Softness.

Additional softness and silence under foot is obtained by the use of felt pads laid on each stair tread beneath the carpet. Alternatively, carefully folded brown paper or newspaper could be used, but the felt pads specially intended for this purpose are quite inexpensive and very serviceable. The price of stair pads should range from about 6s. a dozen to 9s. a dozen, according to their width.

Carpet Holders.

With regard to carpet holders, brass stair rods are, of course, out of date. Instead you can get oak stair rods,

Fig. 1.—Stair Carpet neatly kept in position by means of Clipper Holders.

triangular in section, which are every bit as serviceable as brass ones, while at the same time no sort of cleaning is necessary. With all stair rods, how-

Fig. 1A.—How the Clipper Holds the Carpet.

ever, there is always a possibility that one of the rods may work loose and trip somebody up when going down

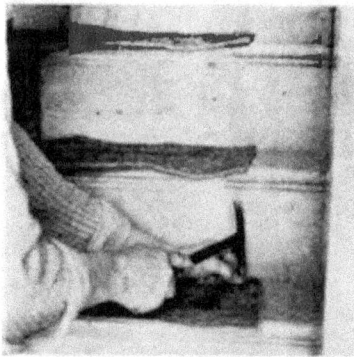

Fig. 2.—Laying the Stair Pads, allowing them to Overhang the Nosing by about 1 inch.

Two or three tacks placed along the back will keep the pads in position.

stairs. Probably the best means of keeping the carpet in position is the clipper type of holder, which is simply slipped on to a special single-screw bracket at each side of the carpet just at the base of each riser. These clippers hold the carpet absolutely taut and are flush with the edge of the carpet, leaving nothing sticking out to trap dust or catch on the duster (see Fig. 1). They cannot work loose and cause a fall, and at the same time they are easily removable.

The charm of most stair carpets has in the past been lost, and the elegance of both plain and figured carpets ruined by the employment of stair rods to keep the carpet in place.

Stair rods have been employed because no other satisfactory method of holding a carpet down has been available, and their ugliness was not even questioned.

No one, however, would tolerate unsightly lines drawn across the upholstery of their furniture or across their curtains, their wallpapers, or even the carpet of their rooms, and yet they fail to notice the incongruity of the straight line of a rod across their stair carpet at every step.

If the harmonious entity of a plain staircase and a plain carpet with its unbroken continuity is ruined by the interruption of stair rods, how much more is a beautiful patterned one ruined by rods? Stair carpet clippers, by non-interference with the appearance of a carpet, give one the full benefit of the colour, texture or pattern without any spoliation of one's ideas.

The simplicity of a clippered stair carpet is something that must be seen to be believed—one soon comes to realise why a new carpet, when laid in position on the stairs, does not quite come up to the expectations of the purchaser—it is because the whole conception is spoiled by the ugly lines of the rods.

Labour Saving.

Carpet clippers, for this reason, are making a very big contribution towards beautifying the home, but this is not all, they are tremendous labour-savers, as not only do they banish for ever the weekly or fortnightly cleaning of stair rods, but they enable the complete staircase to be cleaned and dusted much more quickly and much more thoroughly.

The best examples do not project over the edge of the carpet, thus it is a simple matter to wipe down the woodwork at the sides, and, moreover, the whole surface of the stair carpet is open to treatment by brush or vacuum cleaner, leaving no hiding places for dust or fluff.

HOW TO LAY A STAIR CARPET

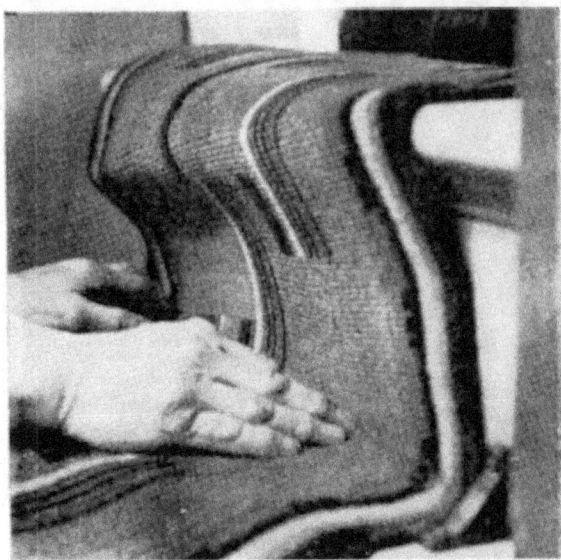

Fig. 3.—Start laying the Stair Carpet from the Top.
Allow about 18 inches at the top, so that the carpet can be gradually moved downwards to ensure obtaining the maximum of wear.

Fig. 4.—How to deal with a Bend.
Set the carpet out roughly, place the rods in position, and start adjusting and pleating the carpet.

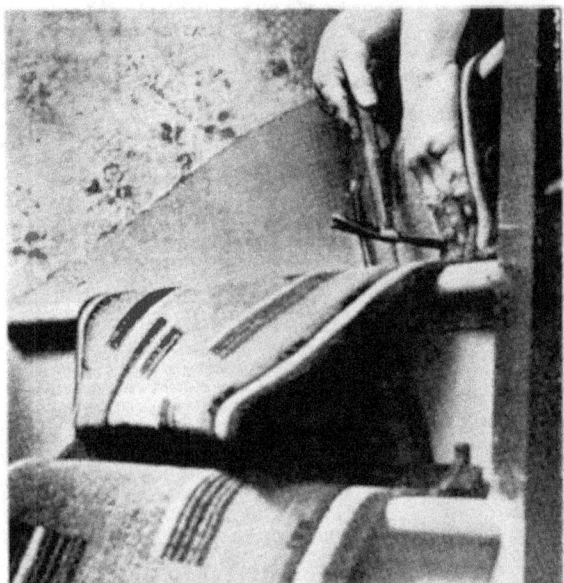

Fig. 5.—Push the Carpet well back to the Rod Line of the Tread after allowing sufficient to come over to make the Pleat.
When finishing off tack the carpet at the top line of the rod as shown.

Fig. 6.—Before finishing off, get the Carpet for the Straight Stairs to follow in Position.
Any surplus can then be taken up by pleating.

The fact that clipper stair carpet holders are out of the way of the feet, results in them rarely being kicked and scratched, and cleaning is therefore abolished. The carpet laid down firmly in the first instance cannot move, as the clippers hold it firmly— they move outwards to release carpet, instead of upwards, as did some of the earlier makes of holders, and for this reason resist all efforts of the stair carpet to creep and become baggy at each tread. Clipper stair carpet holders are made in one piece, thus there are no hinges, springs or catches to go wrong.

With their use a stair carpet can be released from top to bottom in under two minutes with a slight thumb pressure on each clipper.

Fixing the Carpet Holders.

Whether one decides on rods or clippers, however, the first step is to screw the eyes for the rods or the holders for the clippers in position before the carpet is laid. If rods are preferred, the eyes should be fixed at the angle between tread and riser, just beyond the outside edge of the carpeting, and holders for clippers should be fixed at the bases of the risers, just within the edge of the carpeting, so that the carpet will be laid over them.

HOW TO LAY A STAIR CARPET

Where to Start when Laying the Carpet.

In laying the carpet one has always to begin at the head of the stairs. The 18 inches or so of spare carpeting additional to that needed to cover the stairs themselves should be tacked down on the first floor landing, with a pair of stair pads beneath it, using, for preference, brass-headed carpet tacks. The entire length of carpeting should be unrolled and laid loosely over the stairs, and the stair pads placed in position on each tread. If preferred the pads can all be nailed in position before laying the carpet in place. The first riser at the top of the stairs should be covered by pulling and pressing the carpet down firmly and securing it with the first stair rod or pair of clippers. Now make sure that the stair pad on the first tread is correctly in position, covering the nosing of the stair, bring the carpet down the next riser, adjust the next stair pad and fix the carpet with rod or clippers as before.

If the stairs run straight from top to bottom one has only to continue this process until the bottom of the stairs is reached, but a complication arises if the stairs include a bend. This is generally the case with modern houses, where space is limited and the stairs take up as little room as possible.

How to Negotiate a Bend—1. Cutting.

There are two ways of negotiating a bend in the stairs. The first is to cut out a V-shaped piece from the carpeting and make a seam, so that the carpeting is made to follow the curve of the stairs. This has the advantage of extreme neatness if done well, but the method is laborious and requires great accuracy. Moreover, the carpet must ever afterwards be laid so that it occupies practically the same position, and there is no way of equalising the wear.

2. Folding.

For this reason it is better, as well as easier, to fold the carpet neatly and tack it against the riser. The fold has to be made, of course, on the inner side of the bend of the stairs, and if the bend is at all abrupt a fold will have to be made at each riser in order to keep the carpet central on the stairs. This should be done on each stair before fixing the carpet down with the rod or clippers.

Why 18 Inches is Laid at Top of Stair.

The reason for the additional 18 inches of carpeting laid at the top of the stairs has not yet been explained. Stair carpeting should be taken up every year at spring cleaning time, and it should be re-laid each year so that a different part of the carpet comes in for the severest wear. The hardest wear is always encountered just above the stair nosings, so when the carpet is relaid after the first year one should begin by laying only 12 inches along the first floor landing instead of 18 inches. Consequently the carpeting which had previously covered the nosings and treads will now have twelve months rest covering the risers, and there will be a piece of about 6 inches along the floor at the foot of the stairs—concealed, of course, by a mat. In this way, by altering the position slightly every year, the entire length of carpeting can be given equal wear.

This would, of course, be impossible without the additional 18-inch strip provided at the outset, and it enables the carpeting to be kept in good condition five or six times as long.

In addition to being relaid annually the stair carpet should be swept and cleaned at least once or twice a week —daily if there are many in the family. There are people who prefer doing the stairs with a dustpan and a fairly stiff brush, but an electric cleaner, with a curtain and upholstery attachment, is an efficient labour-saving alternative.

HEAT-RESISTING HANDLE

Metal handles on cooking utensils are apt to become too hot to be grasped when in use. Asbestos string wound round, as shown in Fig. 1, will overcome this trouble.

The method of winding the string on the handles is as follows: Commence as is shown in A of Fig. 2, and lap the string round, pulling it tight at each turn. When within

Fig. 1.—Heat-resisting Handles.

about six turns of the end, place a stick of wood on the handle and wind the remaining turns round both the handle and, with stick, pass the end of the string back, as shown in B. Remove the stick and tighten up each of these last six turns separately. Finally pull up the end of the string, as in C, and cut off the surplus.

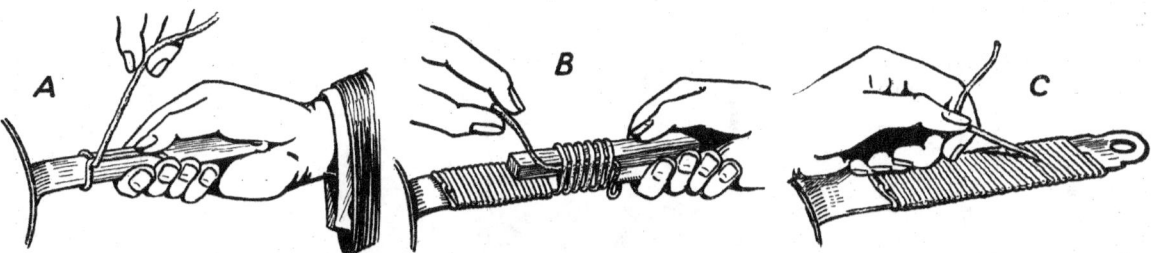

Fig. 2.—Method of Winding String round Handle.

Re-upholstering Occasional Chairs

Fig. 1.—A Canework Chair in need of Repair.

Fig. 2.—The Chair complete with Renewed Back and Seat.

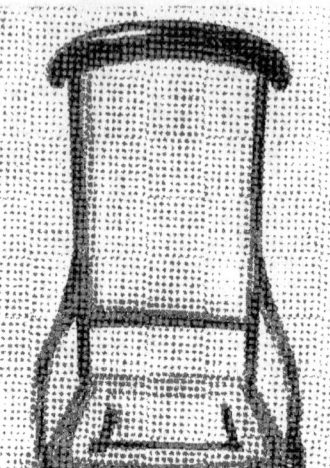

Fig. 3.—Back and Seat prepared for Upholstering.

OCCASIONAL chairs are upholstered in several ways, and the method of dealing with them must be adapted accordingly.

We will deal first with a canework chair, and will describe how the broken canework can be removed entirely and the chair given a simple upholstery treatment. Fig. 1 shows such a chair before the repairs were undertaken; Fig. 2 shows the finished job.

The chair illustrated was a birch chair that had been stained and varnished to imitate mahogany. If the finish is at all shabby, it is advisable to smooth it down with glasspaper and stain afresh with aniline stain powder, Bismarck and brown, in lac polish, afterwards polishing with a rubber and brush in the usual way.

Removing the Old Cane.

The old cane should be cut out entirely, and in the seat place, pieces of tacking wood (tough spruce) are fitted, fixing them with glue and screws. Pieces of tacking wood should also be fixed in the back space on the lower curved rail and on the uprights; but not on the top back rail. This is wide enough to spare an inch behind the cane for tacking the upholstering work, a line being marked accordingly. Lines should also be marked on the seat rails one inch from the outline. The chair is now as shown in Fig. 3.

Webbing Seat Frame and Back.

The next thing is to web the seat frame, using No. 12 English web, fixed with ½-inch webbing tacks. Three strips of webbing are placed each way and stretched taut. The back frame is also webbed, but instead of stretching the webbing taut leave it slack enough to conform with the curves of the uprights and rails.

Canvas is next tacked over the webbing the same way, doubled in about an inch on the edges and fixed with ordinary ½-inch tacks.

The Stuffing.

A light stuffing of wool flock is then packed evenly on the back to be covered by a scrim canvas doubled in and tacked about ½-inch from the marked lines. The centre part is stitched through with thin twine to keep the stuffing permanently in position. The seat is treated in a similar manner, but it is convenient to tack the scrim along at the back edge before putting on the flock. When drawn over and tacked, it is stitched and made even by adding a little more flock and a layer of sheet wadding. It is then ready for the final covering, as described later.

OTHER TYPES OF CHAIRS

We come now to other types of

Fig. 4.—Seat and Back Webbed to support Stuffed Work.

chairs and the methods of re-covering them.

The simplest form is that known as "pin-cushion upholstery" and consists of bands of webbing nailed to the seat frame, then covered with hessian, stuffed with flock, horsehair or other material and covered with linen, the result being a rather flat plain cushioned seat as shown in Fig. 6.

The second group are similarly prepared, but the upholstery is much thicker, stands up well above the frame and generally has a rolled edge.

The third group includes all kinds of chairs with spring upholstery, that is, those in which springs are used to give greater resiliency and comfort.

Materials.

The only materials needed will be sufficient tapestry or other upholstery covering material to cover the chairs, and a corresponding amount of gimp. For a single chair allow about ½ yard of material and 2 yards of gimp, but several chairs can be re-covered with proportionately less material, as it can be cut up to greater advantage. A few tin-tacks about ½ to ⅝ inch long, and some black upholsterers' "gimp pins" and a few yards of wadding, complete the list of necessaries.

Preliminary Work.

Commence by removing the old gimp and covering—by prising out the pins and tacks which hold it to the frame and at the same time take note of the way the cover was turned in at the edges and was nailed to the seat frame.

Next turn the chair upside down and remove the canvas outer covering sufficiently to reveal the webbing. If the latter is at all slack, unfasten one end of each web, draw it tight and refix it with stout tin-tacks. Only do one web at a time and take care to pull up the web as tightly as possible, then refix the canvas covering.

Turn the chair right way up and examine the linen cover and the general shape of the seat stuffing. Should there be hollow places, get a strong packing needle, a steel knitting needle or something of the kind; push it through the covering at the hollow place and work up the stuffing by turning the needle about, thus stirring up the stuffing and filling out the hollow.

Cutting and Fitting the Cover.

Lay the new covering material flat on a table and pick out a central feature of the pattern, then lay the old cover flat upon it—with the original outer face upwards. Centre it upon the selected feature, then cut out the new material to the shape of the old piece.

Turn in the edges at the part which comes to the seat back, then tack it temporarily to the seat frame, spread a layer of wadding over the seat, then lay the cover neatly over it, tack the cover temporarily at the sides and front, drawing the material as tightly as possible but avoiding all creases or puckers. When the cover is nicely in position fasten it permanently with tin-tacks spaced about 1½ inches apart. Next fix the gimp to cover the joint between the covering and the seat frame, tacking it every inch or so with the gimp pins, thus completing the re-covering of a chair with pin-cushion upholstery.

Re-covering an Upholstered Seat.

Chairs with deeply upholstered seats should be dealt with along similar lines except that, when examining the seat stuffing, remove the outer linen cover and see if the upholstery has slackened near the edges; if so it can be improved by "blind stitching." To do this obtain a long needle—preferably an upholsterer's needle—and some strong

Fig. 5.—Chair Back and Seat being Stuffed.

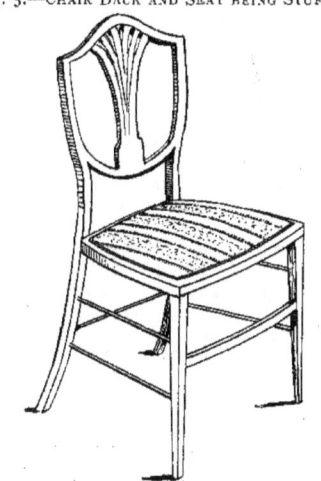

Fig. 6.—Chair with Pin-Cushion Upholstery.
This type is the simplest to re-cover.

twine. Commence by fastening the end of the twine to the scrim covering near the frame, then thrust the needle upwards and backwards through the stuffing, as in Fig. 7, draw it tight and make a short stitch about ¾ inch long through the seat covering, then thrust the needle down again and out near the seat frame, as shown in Fig. 8, repeating these processes all round the seat. While the stitching is in progress, press the upholstery into shape with the left hand.

When fixing the new cover take care to set the pattern properly with some central feature in the middle of the seat, also lay a sheet of wadding over the old inner cover before fixing the new covering.

Fix the back, front and sides so that the cover is held firmly, then carefully pleat the corners, tack them neatly, then finish off the tacking of the cover and fix the gimp as before.

Rexine, leather or other materials can be used in the same way for re-covering, but in such cases it is best to finish off with banding of similar material and oxidized copper studs, that is, nails with large cup-like heads.

Re-covering Spring Seat Chairs.

Special points to observe when re-covering occasional chairs with spring upholstery are to place heavy weights on the springs to compress them while tightening the webbing—if the latter is in need of it. As this class of furniture is generally twice stuffed, that is, has a first or lower stuffing with a "roll" edge, and a distinct second or upper layer of stuffing, it is quite practicable to remove the second or upper stuffing by removing the outer cover. Then teaze or shake out the stuffing material and replace it, carefully repacking it evenly into place.

Should the "roll" be deficient or crushed out of shape it can be revived by pinching it into shape with the fingers and making it firm by stitching

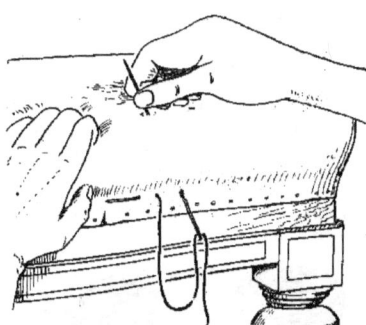

Fig. 7.—Stitching the Seat Stuffing.
This is done to stiffen the front and make the seat more shapely.

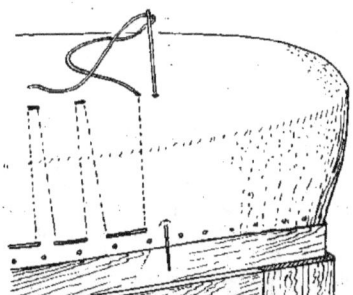

Fig. 8.—Completing the Stitching.
The stitch is made upwards from near the frame and downwards from the seat towards the frame.

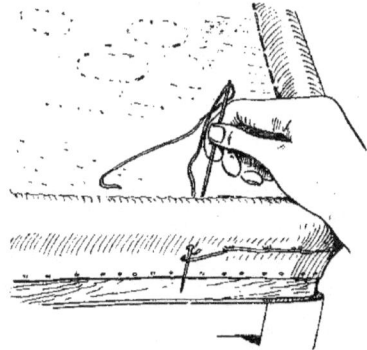

Fig. 9.—Stitching the Roll.
Sprung seats usually have a roll or ridge of stuffing which can be tightened by stitching through from back to front.

RE-UPHOLSTERING OCCASIONAL CHAIRS

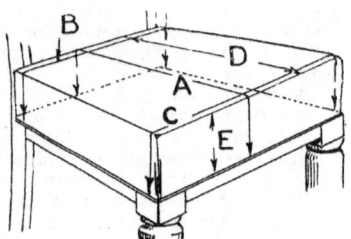

Fig. 10.—Where to Measure a Chair Seat. Measurements are taken at places shown by the letters.

through the canvas covering, as shown in Fig. 9, drawing the stitches tightly so as to compress the stuffing and make it firm and shapely.

Re-cover in the manner before described, and finish off neatly with gimp or banding as required.

To measure a seat take the dimensions as shown in Fig. 10 at the places indicated by the letters A, B, C, etc. Next double over the covering material as in Fig. 11, along the centre line—from front to back of the part that is to be used for the chair cover, then measure along the centre line the length, A, from back frame to front frame. Mark the distance, E, that is, the depth of the seat, then measure off and mark the distance, D, that is, length of seat from front to back.

Then measure and mark off half the distances B and C, that is, half of the amount obtained by measuring the width of the seat plus twice the depth of upholstery. Allow an extra ½ to ¾ inch or so for turnings all round, then cut the material and try it on the seat; if all is correct use it as a pattern for the remaining seat covers if more than one chair is being re-covered.

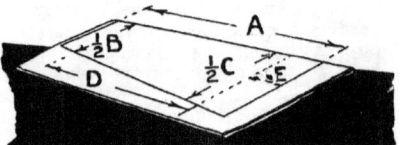

Fig. 11.—Measuring the Covering. The measurements obtained from the chair seat are transferred to the folded material.

HOW TO SHAPE WIRE

BY "shaping wire" is meant thinning it down to the required size and shape. Such work is done in making silverware and small pieces of jewellery from silver wire, in which case a fairly stout gauge wire, about 18 S.W.G., may be kept in stock, and lengths of it may be drawn down to the required size and shape through a suitable draw-plate.

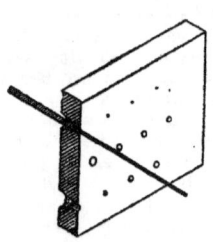

Fig. 1.—Section of Wire, Draw-plate, showing the Conical Holes.

Draw-plates for shaping to circle, square, triangular, oval, and other shaped sections may be obtained. An example of a draw-plate for drawing wire to circular section is shown in Fig. 1. The plate is provided with graduated conical holes, which are measured in millimetres. A plate giving a largest hole of 4 mm. will be found serviceable for silver-work. It will be necessary to provide a strong vice to hold the draw-plate, but, if this is not convenient, the draw-plate may be held between blocks of wood screwed to a board, as shown in Fig. 2.

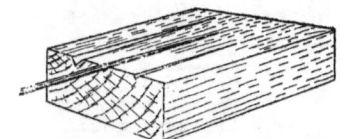

Fig. 3.—The Block used in Tapering the End of the Wire before Drawing.

Before Shaping Wire.

Before drawing a length of wire, it is as well to note that the wire is increased over twice its length after being pulled through a hole in the plate; it will be realised that a very short original length after passing through several holes will make a lengthy wire in the end. To begin with the wire should be filed to a long tapered point, so that a sufficient length passes through the hole to enable a good grip being made with pliers. The best way to do this is to place the wire on a block of wood and rotate it with the fingers of the left hand while it is being filed. It is an advantage to prepare a block with a few tapered grooves made with a triangular file; this will serve for several diameters and will make the tapering, as shown in Fig. 3, much easier.

How to Draw Wire.

The usual method of holding the wire in drawing it through a plate is

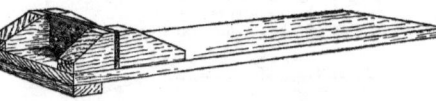

Fig. 2.—A Board for Holding the Draw-plate on a Bench.

to use hand tongs, shown in Fig. 4; but a pair of flatnose cutting pliers can be used. Fill up all the holes in the draw-plate with tallow, and as soon as the wire has been drawn all the used holes should be filled again; this precaution prevents rust forming in the hole which, in time, will ruin the plate.

Care must be taken in gripping the wire and holding the plate so that the pull through can be carried out without a jerk. A stoppage during the process may result in a breakage. It will be found that the operation of tapering the end is necessary after each new length has been drawn. In drawing long lengths, the board holding the

Fig. 4.—Hand Tongs used in Drawing Wire.

plate should be secured with cramps so that there is no need to hold it.

Annealing the Wire.

When the wire has been drawn through three or four holes it should be annealed. The wire is wrapped round the fingers to form a coil and then lightly bound with iron binding wire, as indicated at Fig. 5. The small coil is now placed on a charcoal or carbon block. These blocks, measuring about 5 × 3 × 1¼ inches, cost about 1s., and are indispensable for the work. A smoky flame is now played over the wire to blacken it and then the heat is increased until the black disappears and the silver becomes white. During the heating the silver becomes red hot, but, as it is rather difficult to detect the colour, the method suggested is an effective one.

Fig. 5.—How to Bind the Wire before Annealing.

Installing an Electric Bell and Indicator System

An electric bell and indicator system suitable for a dwelling-house is not difficult to install, and the convenience obtained from it will amply repay the cost of the installation.

If the house is supplied with electricity for lighting and power from alternating current mains, the bell and indicator system may be energised through a bell transformer. This method is more reliable and satisfactory than using a battery of cells, and will not greatly add to the cost of the job.

Lead-covered twin bell wire for the various wiring runs will make a lasting and satisfactory job. The wire will be run on the surface where possible to do so, but certain of the runs will be run under the ground floor so as to make a sightly job and reduce cutting of the decorations and plaster to a minimum.

Admission to below the ground floor is obtained through the traps, which may be easily cut in the floor at a convenient position, and there is usually enough space below the floor joists to allow of fixing the wiring runs on their lower faces.

The Materials and their Approximate Cost.

Twin lead-covered bell wire, each wire insulated with rubber and a double layer of paraffined cotton, 12s. per 50-yard coil.

One 5-hole pendulum indicator, 12s. 6d.

One watertight front-door bell push, 2s.

Two bakelite wall pushes, 1s.

Two pear suspension pushes, 2s.

Two wall rosettes, 1s.

One bell, 2s.

One bell transformer and clock connector fuses, 7s. 6d. Or three No. 2 Leclanché cells, 2s. each.

One gross box buckle wiring clips, 2s.

One gross box brass fixing pins, 1s.

If a bell transformer is used it should be mounted on a 6 × 6-inch polished block and connected to the main fuses with a suitable length of 1/·044-inch twin cab-tyre cable.

The Positions for the Bell, Indicator, Pushes, and Battery or Transformer.

The positions suggested for the various pushes are indicated on the ground floor and upstairs plan; these may vary according to the actual requirements.

The push for the front door is on the right door jamb and at a suitable height, say, 4 feet from floor level, and at this point drill a ¼-inch hole through the jamb, taking care not to splinter the wood as the twist bit cutting edge emerges from the hole.

Fig. 1.—An Electric Bell with Cover Removed.
The adjusting screw which controls the tension of the platinum point contact is shown at A.

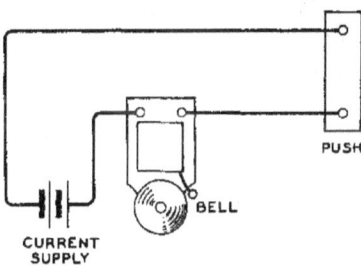

Fig. 2.—Simple Circuit Diagram showing how Bell, Push and Current Supply are connected.

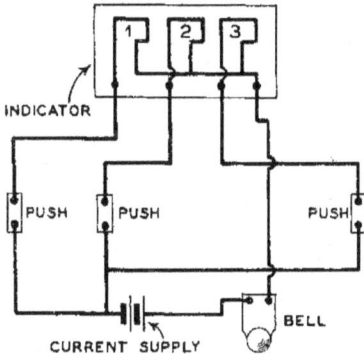

Fig. 3.—Simple Circuit Diagram showing Method of connecting Bell, Push, Current Supply and Indicator.
Only three pushes are shown here.

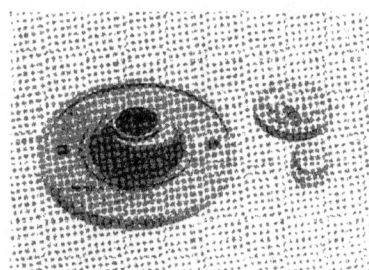

Fig. 4.—The Parts of a Bell Push.
On the left is the cover, while on the right are the terminals for the wires and spring at the top, and the press button.

If a barrel type push is used, the hole should be drilled for a depth equal to the length of the barrel with a twist bit which has the same diameter as the barrel, and the hole then completed with a ¼-inch twist bit to allow of admission of the wiring to the terminals of the push.

In each of the bedrooms a wall rosette is fixed on the skirting board which is adjacent to the head of the bed.

The push in the bathroom is fixed so that it may be conveniently operated by anyone using the bath; the adjacent wall is drilled in two places and rawlplugs fitted. The push may then be securely fixed with rawlplug screws to the wall, the height of the push from floor level should be about 2 feet 6 inches.

In the dining-room the push may be fixed by the side of the fireplace, the actual place depending upon the wiring run to it. The wire may be concealed in the plaster by carefully cutting the paper and turning over the cut edges, then chase out the plaster for a depth and width of ¼ inch to accommodate the wire. When the wire is fixed in position and connected to the push, the channel may be filled with plaster of Paris flush to the surface of the wall. The cut edges of the paper may be turned back again and fastened in position with Cloy or other suitable paste.

The Trap to give Admission to Below-the-ground Floor.

The trap consists of about three short pieces of floor board which lie together between two adjacent floor joists; these boards may be removed by taking out the screws which secure their ends to the joists, and when removed there will be a rectangular hole in the floor large enough to allow a person to go through and get underneath the ground floor. The position of this trap may be where the electric light, gas, or water mains come through the ground floor for connection to the meter, or stop tap in the case of water mains.

The Wiring runs from the Pushes on the Ground Floor.

Drill ¼-inch holes through the ends of the floor boards from below the ground floor at the positions where the wires will pass through the floor. At the front door the hole will be immediately below the door jamb on which the push will be fixed; in the dining-room the hole will emerge into the plaster behind the skirting board immediately below the push position on the wall. The plaster behind the skirting board is cut away with a ¼-inch wood chisel or a long thin-bladed screwdriver so that a clear passage is obtained from below the

INSTALLING AN ELECTRIC BELL AND INDICATOR SYSTEM

Fig. 5.—Typical arrangement of Fuses and Transformer for Mains Supply. The method of wiring is shown in Fig. 6.

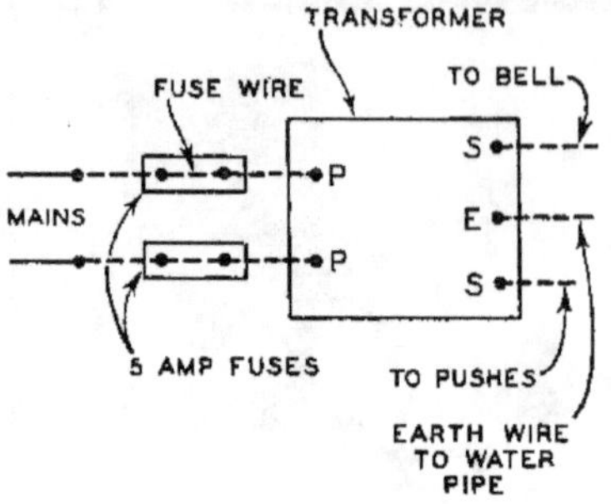

Fig. 6.—Simple Diagram showing the Connections from the Mains to Fuses and Transformer.

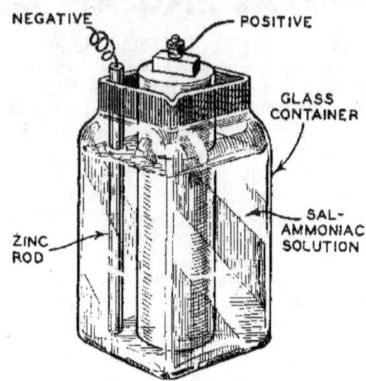

Fig. 7.—Details of a Leclanché Cell which can be used instead of a Transformer.

floor to the upper edge of the skirting board. Where the wires from the front door and the dining-room will come up into the kitchen, a suitable hole is drilled; this position may be conveniently below the indicator, which will be fixed on the kitchen wall, and the wires may be brought up behind the skirting board similar to the method adopted in the dining-room.

A hole will be drilled through the wall dividing the kitchen from the dining-room, underneath the floor, for the passage of the wires.

Leave a short piece of wire called a "fish" wire in each of the passages for the wires to the dining-room and front-door pushes from below the floor to the upper edge of the skirting board; these wires are used to pull the wiring runs through from beneath the floors to their respective terminating points.

The line of the wiring runs are now marked off across the lower edges of the floor joists underneath the floors, and buckle clips fixed with brass pins at each marked position.

Fixing the Wiring.

Measure the length of the wiring required for the two runs from the pushes to the indicator position, allowing a yard extra in each case for terminal connections, bends in the run, etc. Cut off from the coil of twin lead-covered wire the measured lengths, taking precautions not to kink or damage the lead covering or the wires when taking off the lengths, and make each length into a neat coil.

Take the coils below the floor and at the front-door position fasten the end of the wiring for this position to the end of the fish wire. This end is now pulled through the floor until there is sufficient length to reach the push position on the door jamb. The end of the wiring for the dining-room push is treated in a similar manner. The ends which

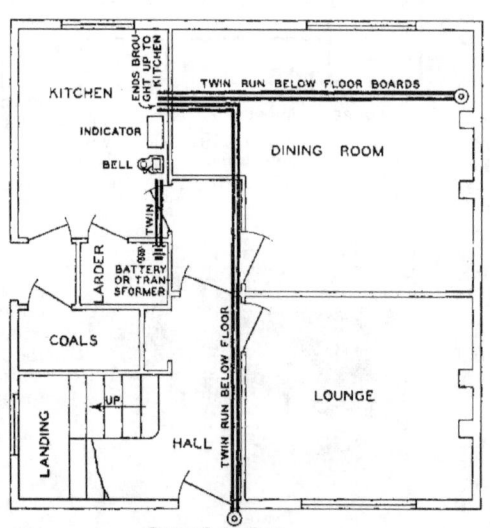

Fig. 8.—Suggested Positions for Pushes, Bell, Indicator; Battery or Transformer, and Run of Wires.

have been pulled through are neatly coiled up until they are run up to their respective pushes.

The wiring from the front door is now fixed with the buckle clips into position across the joists up to the point where the run from the dining-room will meet it, and the wiring from the dining-room is similarly fixed up to this point.

The free ends of the two lengths of wiring are threaded through the hole which has been cut in the division wall and then pulled through into the kitchen with the fish wire.

The wires are fixed together up to the point where they pass up into the kitchen with buckle clips. The whole of the wiring run should be stretched taut when fixing in position; the ends which pass into the kitchen are coiled up neatly until the connection to the joint box and indicator is made.

The Wiring Runs from the Bedroom Floor Pushes.

Drill a $\frac{1}{4}$-inch hole through the wall at the upper edge of the skirting board in No. 1 and No. 2 bedrooms, where the rosettes will be fixed; these holes will give an outlet for the wiring runs into the passage which leads to the various bedrooms. In the passage at a point which is adjacent the bathroom cupboard, drill a $\frac{1}{2}$-inch hole through the wall at the upper edge of the skirting board and another $\frac{1}{2}$-inch hole from the cornice of the kitchen ceiling above the door, through the kitchen ceiling and the floor of the bathroom cupboard. A clear passage is now obtained for the wiring runs from the push positions to the indicator position in the kitchen.

The holes through the walls should be drilled with a brace and

INSTALLING AN ELECTRIC BELL AND INDICATOR SYSTEM

a metal twist drill; if a wall drill and hammer are used there is a danger of displacing the plaster and possibly a brick, where the wall is only single brick thickness.

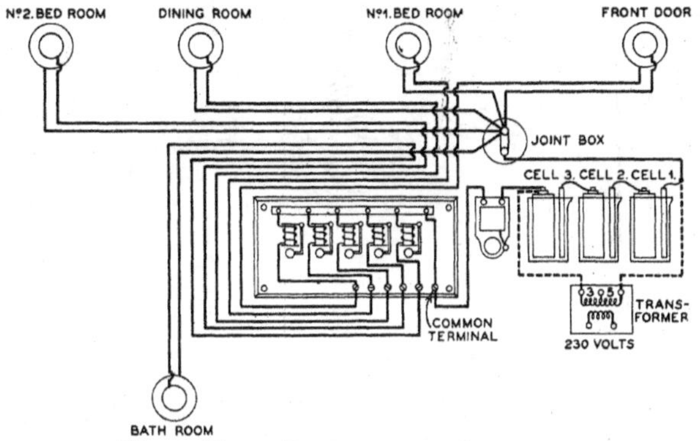

Fixing the Wiring.

Buckle clips are fixed at intervals of 18 inches along the upper edges of skirting boards and round the door architraves, which lie in the line of route of the three wiring runs, to the point where the runs pass through the bathroom cupboard floor into the kitchen below.

The runs are measured up, and the measured lengths are cut off from the coil of twin wire and carefully coiled up.

One end of each of the coils for No. 1 and No. 2 bedrooms are threaded through the holes from the passage into the bedrooms and pulled through into the rooms for a length of 1 foot.

The wiring is carefully laid along the upper edges of the skirting boards and round the door architraves, and fastened into position with the buckle clips; take care not to fracture the lead sheath and the wires when bending round corners, any sharp edges of wood over which the wires pass should be rounded with a chisel. The remaining ends of these two runs will be threaded through the ½-inch hole into the bathroom cupboard, and these will be joined with the end of the run from the bathroom push. The three ends are threaded through into the kitchen and coiled up until they are connected to the joint box and indicator.

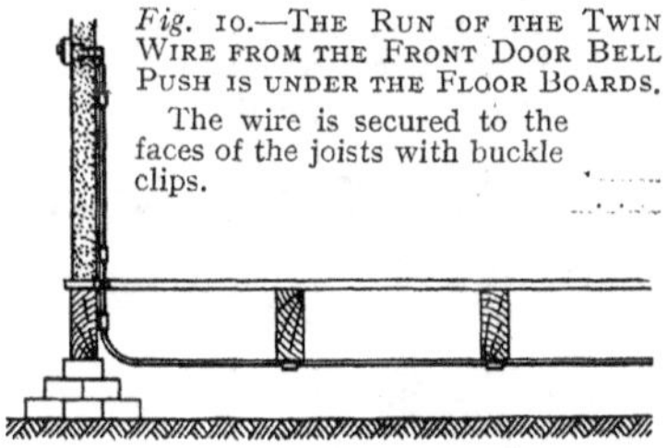

Fixing the Indicator, Bell and Joint Box.

Measure the overall dimensions of the indicator, bell and joint box, and obtain a ¾-inch thick planed deal board large enough to mount the indicator, etc., upon it. Drill and countersink the board in four places for rawlplug fixing screws. The position of these holes in the board is marked off on the wall where it will be fixed, and the wall drilled and fitted with suitable rawlplugs; when drilling be careful not to dislodge any bricks or cause damage to the decorations.

The board is rubbed smooth with glass paper and given a coat of varnish stain and left to dry; when dry, screw the board to the wall

Fig. 9.—Wiring Diagram of the System.

One wire of each pair of the twin wires from the pushes are connected together at the joint box and a single wire is taken from the junction of the wires to the zinc rod of the battery or if a transformer is used to one of the low-tension bell terminals. The remaining wires are run to the terminals of the indicator and there connected to their respective indicator magnet coils. The dotted lines represent the connections if a bell transformer is used instead of a battery.

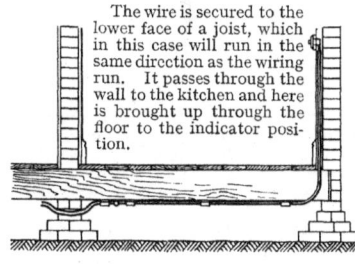

Fig. 10.—The Run of the Twin Wire from the Front Door Bell Push is under the Floor Boards.

The wire is secured to the faces of the joists with buckle clips.

Fig. 11.—The Twin Wire from the Dining-room Bell Push is taken behind the Skirting Board and under the Floor.

The wire is secured to the lower face of a joist, which in this case will run in the same direction as the wiring run. It passes through the wall to the kitchen and here is brought up through the floor to the indicator position.

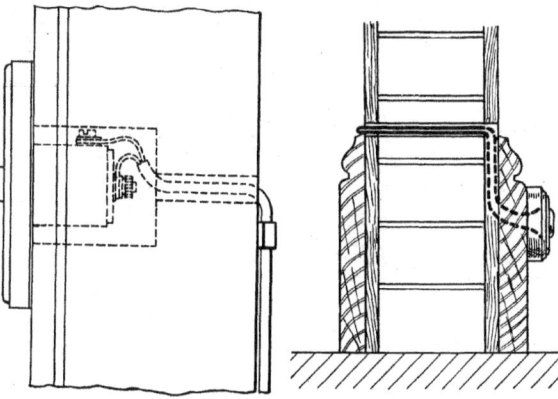

Fig. 12.—Fitting the Front Door Push, showing holes drilled in Door Jamb for Barrel and Wire.

Fig. 13.—Wiring from Bedroom Rosettes, run through Skirting Board and Wall.

and fix the indicator, bell and joint box to the board.

The Battery or Transformer Position and fixing.

In the present example the larder would be a suitable position, and if a battery of cells is used a shelf may be utilised, but if a transformer is used then a 6 × 6-inch polished wooden block is fixed to a suitable place on the wall. The transformer and clock connector fuse-base are mounted on it. If the main switch of the electric light installation is fitted some distance from the larder it would be better to fix the transformer near to the main switch, as only a short run of cab-tyre twin cable would be required to supply the transformer with current. In this case the twin lead-covered bell wire from the kitchen to the larder would be extended to the transformer position.

Connecting the Pushes to the Wiring.

At the front door the twin lead-covered wire is pushed through the hole which has been drilled through the door jamb and the end cut off so as to allow of sufficient length to make the terminal connections. The lead covering is removed from the end for a distance of 1½ inches; this is done by carefully nicking all round the covering with a knife and bending the wire backwards and forwards two or three times when the covering will fracture at this point, and may be drawn off the wires.

The rubber insulation and paraffined cotton winding are removed from the end of each wire for a distance of ⅜ inch. One of the bared ends is connected under the binding screw at the end of the barrel, and the other under the binding screw on the circumferential surface of the barrel.

Make sure the wire is under the washer in each case and is bent round the stem of the screw in the same direction as the screw is tightened.

The push in the bathroom is now connected, adopting a similar method to that used when connecting the front door push with the exception that the wires are brought through their respective holes in the base of the push, making sure that the wiring up to the push will be neat and tight when the push is finally screwed to the wall.

The wall rosettes in each

INSTALLING AN ELECTRIC BELL AND INDICATOR SYSTEM

Fig. 14.—The Wiring from the Bedroom Rosettes is brought through the Walls and taken round the Architraves of the Doors and along the Skirting Boards into the Bathroom Cupboard, and through the Floor into the Kitchen.

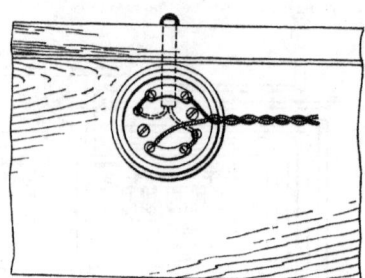

Fig. 15.—Fixing and Wiring the Wall Rosette.

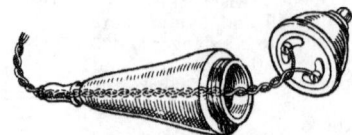

Fig. 16.—Connecting the Flexible to the Pear Pressel Push.

The ends of the flexible are bared, the cover taken off the push and slipped over the flexible. The bared ends are connected to the terminal plates and the cover replaced.

of the bedrooms are now connected, the twin wire being threaded through a hole which has been drilled from the front of the skirting board to the point where the outlet hole in the wall has been drilled; this method makes a neat job of the terminal ends of the wire.

Two lengths of bell wire flexible are now prepared for their connections to the wall rosette terminals and the pear pressel push terminals. When baring the ends of the wires of the terminal connections do not cut away any of the thin copper wires, also whip the braiding back for a distance of ½ inch from the bared ends. When the connections of the flexibles have been made to the wall rosettes their covers should be replaced and the covers of the pear pressel pushes slipped over the free ends, before the connections are made to the terminals of the pushes.

Making the Connections to the Indicator, Bell and Joint Box.

Cut the ends of the five twin wires from the pushes to a suitable length, so as to allow enough to make the connections to the indicator terminals and the joint box terminals, and remove the lead covering from the end of each twin for a distance of about 6 inches, this will allow one of the wires to reach the indicator and the other wire to reach the joint box.

Bare each of the ends for ½ inch. The bared ends of one wire of all the twins are all twisted together along with a single short piece about 2 inches long and the joint soldered. The end of this short piece which has made the common junction is now connected to one terminal of the joint box, and the remaining bared ends of the twins are connected to their respective terminals on the indicator, which connect to the indicator movement to be operated by any desired push.

The twin from the larder is now cut off to a suitable length and the lead sheath removed from the end for a distance of 4 inches. The end of each wire is bared for a distance of ½ inch, one bared end is connected to one terminal of the bell and the other bared end to the other terminal of the joint box. The two terminals of the joint box are connected together with

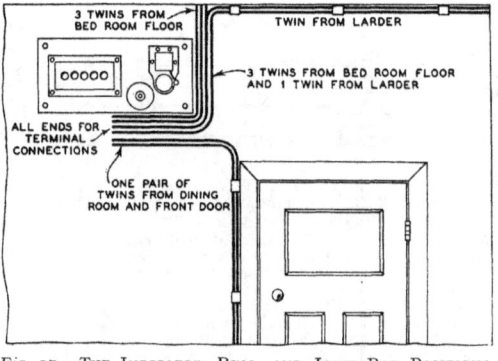

Fig. 17.—The Indicator, Bell, and Joint Box Positions.

The indicator, bell, and joint box are mounted on a board which is fixed on the kitchen wall, and the various twin wires from the pushes and the battery are run to the board.

a short piece of wire and the cover of the box fitted on.

The remaining terminal of the bell is now connected to the common terminal of the indicator with a short piece of wire. All the wires are now

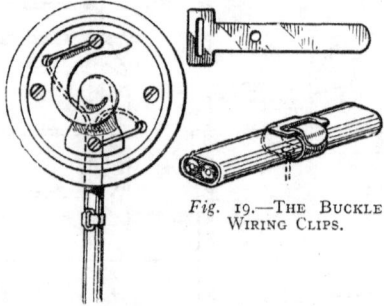

Fig. 18.—The Wiring to the Bathroom Push.

Fig. 19.—The Buckle Wiring Clips.

neatly bunched and bound together with Blackley tape.

Charging and connecting the Battery of Cells.

Fill each of the glass containers of the cells one-third full of warm water and add to each 1½ ozs. of sal-ammoniac; stir the solution until all the sal-ammoniac has dissolved.

Dry the interior and exterior of the upper surface of the container to prevent creeping of the solution and place in each a porous pot and zinc rod. Place the cells in the position they will occupy on the shelf and connect the zinc rods of the second and third cells to the carbon plate terminals of the first and second cells; this leaves the carbon plate terminal of the third cell and the zinc rod of the first cell as the terminals of the battery.

The end of the twin wire in the larder is cut to a suitable length and the lead covering removed from the end for a distance of 6 inches. Remove the insulation from the end of one wire for ½ inch and connect the bared end to the carbon plate terminal of the battery. The insulation is removed for 2 inches from the end of the other wire and a twisted joint is made between the bared end and the terminal wire of the zinc rod; this joint is soldered and covered with a binding of Blackley tape.

The Connections to a Bell Transformer

A complete description of fixing the bell transformer and connecting it to the mains and the bell system is given on p. 248.

Testing the System.

Examine each terminal connection and test with a screwdriver for tightness. Each push is closed in turn and the working of the bell and indicator movement which is connected to the particular push observed.

Separate Bells

It is often preferable to have the back and front door each on a separate circuit with a bell each, and the remaining rooms on a further circuit with a separate bell. All three bells should give a different tone when sounded.

How to Know China Marks
ENGLISH CHINA

   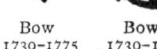

BLOOR 1815-1839	BLOOR 1815-1831	BOW RARE	BOW 1730-1775	BOW 1730-1775	BOW 1730-1775	BOW 1730-1775	BOW 1730-1775

Two examples of marks used by this Derbyshire works. The first, showing a crown and letter B, should not be confused with the Crown Derby mark. | The first example is a rare mark used by the early Bow potters, from a specimen formerly in the Hitchin Manor House Collection. The figures and statuettes produced at the Stratford-le-Bow works were seldom marked. Usual marks are the arrow, bow and arrow, and anchors. The anchor and sword combined is usually found in brown or red on the folds of statuettes. | Two further examples of the anchor marks used at the Bow works. They are akin to the Chelsea marks, but are distinguishable by the nature of the porcelain on which they appear.

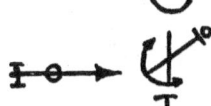  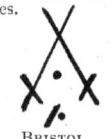 

| BOW 1730-1775 | BOW 1730-1775 | BRISTOL 1768-1770 | BRISTOL 1768-1770 | BRISTOL About 1776 | BRISTOL 1770 | CAUGHLEY 1757-1834 | CAUGHLEY 1757-1834 | CAUGHLEY 1757-1834 |

In these specimens the arrow is treated as a weather vane with the letter E; the anchor is crossed and a simple bow-shaped symbol placed above it. | A plain cross, as here shown, is the customary mark on Bristol porcelain. | This mark, in gold, was followed by a numeral indicative of the individual potter. The numbers range from 1 to 24. | Crossed swords, akin to the Meissen mark, is found on a number of pieces made at the Bristol works. | An early mark probably used by William Cookworthy. | Crescent in outline, usually in blue underglaze. | The initial letter S in blue refers to Shropshire or Salopian ware, often attributed to T. Turner. | Shaded crescent. Another example of the Caughley mark.

| CAUGHLEY 1757-1834 | CAUGHLEY 1757-1834 | CHAMPION BRISTOL 1773-1781 | CHELSEA 1748-1770 | CHELSEA 1748-1770 | CHELSEA 1745 | CHELSEA 1750-1770 | CHELSEA 1750-1770 |

Two examples of disguised numerals, in the Chinese style, associated with the influence of Chinese pottery on British designers. | Mark used on the Bristol porcelain during the time the works were under the control of Richard Champion. | Anchor on an incised background, surrounded by an oval. | The triangle sign was usually incised and was often dated. | A variation of the triangle, with name and date. An early and rare specimen. | The anchor is the most distinctive Chelsea mark, often embossed in gold or colour. | A variation of the anchor design, sometimes dated, usually in red or brown, and found in the drapery of figures or on the stand.

| CHELSEA 1750-1770 | CHELSEA-DERBY circa 1774 | CHELSEA-DERBY About 1778 | DERBY About 1769 | CROWN DERBY 1773-1782 | CROWN DERBY circa 1780 | DERBY 1773-1782 | DERBY 1780-1782 |

Another variation of the anchor design. | The mark of the combined Chelsea and Derby factories. Usually in red or gold. | The Derby crown and Chelsea marks combined. | Initial mark, usually in red. | The Derby marks usually incorporate a crown and the letter D, the crowns becoming more elaborately drawn as time passes. The initial letter in early specimens is separated by batons, while in later examples the initial is surrounded by scroll work, ultimately becoming incorporated in the ornamental scroll work.

| DERBY Late | DERBY 1751-1769 | DERBY MODERN | CROWN DERBY 1780-1815 | DUESBURY & KEAN 1795 | DERBY RARE | LONGTON HALL 1757-1758 | LONGPORT 1773-1835 |

A variation of the early initial letter, with the word Derby in script. | The initial letter D is here shown cleverly duplicated and in the form of a scroll. | Another variant of the crown, batons and initial mark used at the Derby works. | A distinctive mark used when Duesbury was in partnership with Kean. | The crossed swords of Dresden, in early and rare use at Derby. | Initial letters of Longton and Littler. Principally used on table ware. | A place name used as a mark on the products of the Longport works.

| MINTON 1790 | MINTON 1851 | NANTGARW 1813-1820 | PLYMOUTH 1768-1772 | PLYMOUTH 1768-1772 | PLYMOUTH 1768-1772 | PLYMOUTH 1768-1772 |

An imitation of the Sèvres mark, it is one of the earliest Minton marks. | A bold design for a distinctive mark. | The products of this Welsh works are distinguished by the name. | The Plymouth works, in common with those at Bristol, are notable amongst English factories as the only places where true porcelain analogous to the Chinese was produced. The usual mark is the alchemical symbol for tin, the Arabic numerals 2 and 4 conjoined. Rarely used variants are also shown here.

1291

HOW TO KNOW CHINA MARKS

Rockingham Works Brameld
ROCKINGHAM
circa 1840

Royal Rockⁿ Works Brameld
ROCKINGHAM
circa 1850

SALOPIAN
SALOPIAN or CAUGHLEY
1757–1834

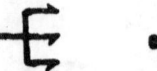
SWANSEA
circa 1810

SWANSEA
circa 1810

Literal marks or place-names, to identify the manufacturer of chinaware, are in very extensive use, including such famous names as Spode, Copeland, Wedgwood, Doulton, and others. Three examples are given. The first two show interesting variations, the third, impressed in the china paste, belongs to the Caughley works and is an exception to the rule.

The characteristic symbol of this Welsh product is the trident, usually impressed and sometimes with the word Swansea in script.

Chamberlain Worcester
CHAMBERLAIN-WORCESTER
1784–1840

WORCESTER
1751

WORCESTER
1751

WORCESTER
1751

WORCESTER
1751

WORCESTER
1751

WORCESTER
1783

Another example of literal marks; in this the maker's name and the place of origin.

Worcester was the third of the great English factories, and was destined to become the most important. The products are distinguished by various marks, several examples of which are reproduced. The solid blue crescent is a rare and early mark, as is the crescent with profile.

WORCESTER
About 1770

WORCESTER
Early Blue

WORCESTER
About 1760

WORCESTER
About 1763

WORCESTER
About 1763

WORCESTER
About 1765

WORCESTER
About 1765

These further examples of Worcester china marks show, from left to right, a mark in the Chinese style; an early mark usually in blue; a variant of the blue W but with a feathered tail. The significance of the next two marks showing crossed swords is unknown, but it is frequently found in underglaze blue on early pieces, details of the swords vary, and the numbers are either 9 or 91. The last two specimens are in the Chinese style, in underglaze blue, usually on early pieces decorated in blue in the manner of Old Nankin china.

CONTINENTAL CHINA

AMSTERDAM

BERLIN, 1830
(KPM stands for Königlichen Porzellan Manufaktur)

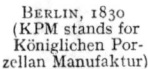
BERLIN
Recent Mark.

BORDEAUX, 1783

BRUSSELS

CAPO DI MONTE, ITALY
Six marks used between 1736 and 1821.

CHANTILLY

CHANTILLY

CHARLOTTENBURG, PRUSSIA, 1760

COPENHAGEN
Usual Mark.

COPENHAGEN
Rare Mark.

FRANKENTHAL, BAVARIA
Mark of Carl Theodor.

FRANKENTHAL

FÜRSTENBERG, GERMANY

GERONA, SAXONY

HAGUE, THE

HAGUE, THE

HEREND, HUNGARY, 1839

HEREND, HUNGARY

HESSE-DARMSTADT, 1758–1772

HILDESHEIM, GERMANY, 1760

LILLE
Mark of Leperre Durot.

LIMOGES
Two marks.

LUNÉVILLE, 1769

MADRID, BUEN RETIRO

MADRID, BUEN RETIRO

MARSEILLES
Mark of Robert Frère.

MARSEILLES
Mark of Joseph Robert.

MEISSEN (DRESDEN)
Mark of Augustus Rex, 1710.

MEISSEN (DRESDEN)
The caduceus of Æsculapius, 1712–1720.

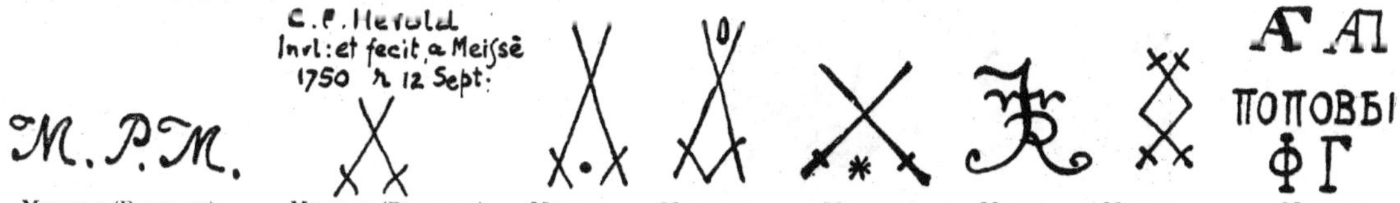

HOW TO KNOW CHINA MARKS

[A chart of porcelain/china maker's marks, organized with illustrations and captions:]

- **Meissen (Dresden)** — M. P. M. stands for Meissner Porzellan Manufaktur.
- **Meissen (Dresden)** — Herold period.
- **Meissen (Dresden)** — King's period.
- **Meissen (Dresden)** — King's period.
- **Meissen (Dresden)** — Marcolini period.
- **Milan**
- **Montreuil, France, 1815.**
- **Moscow** — Three marks.
- **Naples, 1759** 
- **Naples, 1759**
- **Naples** — Fabrica Reale.
- **Niderviller, France** — Four marks.
- **Nyon, Switzerland** — Three marks.
- **Oporto, 1790**
- **Orléans** — Upper mark, soft paste; lower mark, hard paste.
- **Orléans, 1808** 
- **St. Amand-les-Eaux, France**
- **Sceaux, France** — Three marks.
- **Sèvres, 1757** — First Royal period.
- **Sèvres, 1778** — First Royal period.
- **Sèvres, 1792** — First Republican period.
- **Sèvres, 1804.** — First Imperial period.
- **Sèvres, 1821** — Second Royal period. 
- **Sèvres, 1825** — Second Royal period.
- **Sèvres, 1831** — Second Royal period.
- **Sèvres, 1844** — Second Royal period.
- **Sèvres, 1852** — Second Imperial period.
- **Sèvres, 1855** — Second Imperial period.
- **Sèvres, 1871** — Third Republican period. (Second Republican period, 1848–1851, has same mark with appropriate dates.)
- **Sèvres** — Small mark is 1871; larger mark, late Republican period. 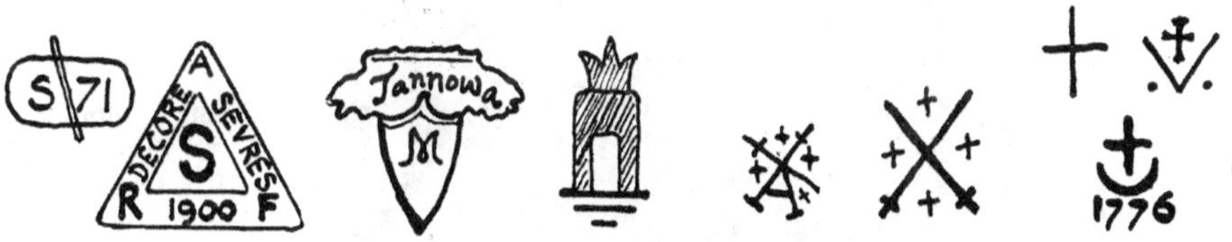 
- **Tannowa, Bohemia**
- **Tournay** — prior to 1755.
- **Tournay** — after 1755.
- **Tournay** — after 1755.
- **Turin** — Three marks.
- **Valenciennes, France, 1785**
- **Vaux, France, 1770.**
- **Venice, 1726.** 
- **Venice** — Cozzi period.
- **Vicenza, Italy**
- **Wallendorf** — Two marks.
- **Würzburg, Bavaria** — Mitre of the Prince Bishop.
- **Zurich** — Three marks.
- **Zweibrucken, Bohemia, 1767.**

MAKING LOOSE SCREWS HOLD

A good method of making a loose screw hold is shown in the sketches. Take a piece of soft copper wire and wind it round the thread of the screw  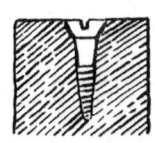 as shown. In this way the diameter of the threaded part of the screw is increased. This simple plan will save plugging or using a larger screw.

Keeping Rabbits for Pleasure and Profit

The keeping of the smaller pets such as rabbits and cavies (guinea-pigs) has received so much attention in the last twenty or more years by men and women who have given the subject as much close study as that given to the rearing of larger animals, that the old sneer that these little animals are "dirty, smelly things" only fit for the fleeting interest of schoolboys, can no longer be sustained. These little animals are not only engaging pets, but can be made profitable hobbies. To-day men and women in all walks of life are breeding for show and profit. Rabbits selling at prices paid for hunters, and cavies for sums ranging from £5 upwards.

Cleanliness and proper housing is the essential basis upon which to start.

An Objection answered.

Neither rabbits nor cavies are, in themselves, dirty, or in any way offensive creatures. Whether it be in the hutches used for rabbits or cavies, a liberal supply of sawdust, mixed with disinfectant, must cover the floors. For those who intend keeping but a few of either of these pets, I suggest obtaining a biscuit tin, filling it with sawdust, pouring into it a teacupful of one of the thick liquid disinfectants and well mixing; then use for the hutch floors. Clean out each hutch at least once a week, and the pleasant odour of pine will be predominant whenever you go near your pets.

HOUSING
The Hutch.

In dealing with the housing and feeding of rabbits and cavies I am bearing in mind that most of my readers will only keep a few. For those who intend to keep a large stud, specially built sheds or an unused stable or garage must be provided.

The hutches should, if at all possible, face south and must be protected from all damp and cold. To fail in this essential precaution is to court illness and failure from the start.

Over the hutches there should be, at least, a slanting roof — easily and cheaply made — of boards covered with tarred felt, and for use in bad weather, a "curtain" should hang down from the roof edge. To throw "something over the hutches" when it rains is to

Fig. 1.—Wrong Way to pick up a Rabbit.

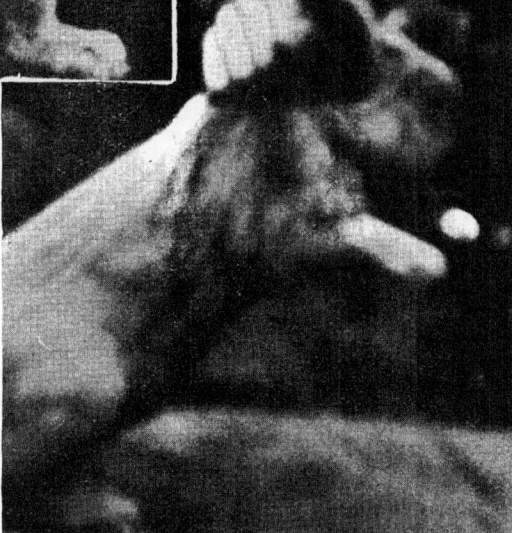

Fig. 2.—Proper Way to pick up Rabbits.
Lift up by the scruff of the neck supporting the body by one hand under the rump.

create an atmosphere of the worst possible kind for the animals. In fact, it is as well to say here that unless such small arrangements as are suggested for the comfort of the animals can be carried out, it is unpardonably cruel to keep pets at all. Pay special attention, too, to the methods of picking up rabbits shown in Figs. 1 and 2.

Size and Details of Hutch.

While, of course, the larger breeds such as Lops, Belgian Hares, Flemish Giants and Angoras require more space, a cube sugar box makes a fine hutch, so long as any cracks are filled up. If completely making a hutch, the following dimensions are suitable for individual animals: 25 inches long, 20 inches high and deep, with a wire front that either takes right away, as illustrated, or is hinged. If hinged so that the whole door opens, it is a good plan to have a strip of wood, about 2 inches wide, running along the front edge, fitted into grooves, so that the sawdust does not fall out at feeding times; it is easily removed when cleaning the hutch. But I prefer the type of front illustrated.

Breeding Hutches.

Breeding hutches for does should be another 12 inches long, the extra length being divided off for a nesting place and with a separate door of wood. Personally, I like this door to be hinged in the centre, as illustrated, so that when there are young ones in the nest only the top half need be opened when it is needful to make a quick inspection of the babies.

Dealing with the Young.

Let me offer a word of warning as to the care necessary when looking at a doe's young. I know full well the anxiety to inspect the new arrivals, lying in the beautiful nest lined with fur that the mother has torn from her breast, but no inspection should be made for twenty-four hours after birth. Then the doe should be removed to another hutch and given a handful of sweet hay to nibble. A quick glance should be made to see if, in the case of marked ones, any are hopelessly mismarked or, if there are more than six, to take out and destroy the puniest. They should then be re-covered with the fur and left to settle down before the mother is returned to the hutch, a carrot or some other tempting morsel being put in to attract her first attention. Many a good doe has killed her young, in fright, on finding that they have been interfered with. At ten days the youngsters will have their eyes open, and be furred, when they can be handled with impunity.

Hutches should be raised at least a foot from the ground, and where they are stacked one upon the other slats of wood should separate them.

A Periodical Overhaul of the Hutch.

It is well to possess at least one spare hutch to every six, so that a regular system of washing, and, say, every three months, whitewashing of the hutches in use can be carried out. In the water used for this purpose, mix an eggcupful of the disinfectant.

KEEPING PETS
How to start.

To start in a small way there are two alternatives. One is to purchase, say, two does and a buck. The other is to purchase does only, and to send them back to the bucks kept by the fancier from whom you purchase. The latter is the best plan, particularly if you purchase from one fancier—a better plan than buying from two or three—for then you reap the benefit of that fancier's years of experience and careful breeding. Any newsagent will get you the weekly paper dealing with the fur fancies (*Fur and Feather*), from which you can obtain names and addresses of fanciers and of club secretaries; in fact, everything that will help you to make a success of your hobby.

FEEDING
Rabbits do drink Water.

In the first place, and most emphatically, rabbits and cavies *do* need water to drink. The fallacy that wild rabbits do not drink water overlooks the fact that they feed at night when the grass is dew laden and they certainly do not fast when there has been a shower of rain. Once a day, when the dry food is given, each rabbit should be given a saucer of clean water, to be taken away some ten minutes later. But in the case of does, either expecting or rearing young ones, fresh water should always be at hand for them to drink. Such a precaution has prevented many a doe from killing her brood.

The Meals.

There is a difference of opinion as to how many meals a day should be given; some fanciers vote for one, but from long years of experience I

Fig. 3.—A Suitable Type of Hutch.
This is suitable for a full-grown rabbit or three or four young, up to three months old. Wire netting front can be taken out completely for cleaning as in Fig. 4. Or it may be opened as in Fig. 5.

consider two. The heaviest meal should be in the evening, the natural time for rabbits to feed. In the

Fig. 4.—Front of Hutch may be taken out.

Fig. 5.—Front of Hutch partially opened.

morning give a supply of green food and a handful of sweet hay; in the evening the corn feed and water; never give the water with the green food.

Fig. 6.—A Breeding Hutch.
This can be made with or without legs. Note the half-hinged wood door leading to the breeding compartment as mentioned in article. This door and the wire one is affixed as explained for the hutch in Fig. 3.

There is little green food that rabbits will not eat but it must always be fresh and wiped free of moisture. While cauliflower leaves, carrot tops, savoy, curly greens and celery tops, all easily procured, are excellent, cabbage leaves should only be given if the others are unobtainable, and lettuce leaves, never. In the winter, roots, of which carrots and swedes are the best, take the place of the summer greens, while anyone who can spare a piece of garden for the growing of chicory will produce at little cost one of the very finest foods.

Bran is Poor Feed.

Another old-fashioned idea which must be exploded is that bran, mixed with oats, is a good feed. Bran is not a good feed, being too heating, except when used in a mash during winter. The staple evening food should be oats and, in the long run, the best are the cheapest. These should be given in earthenware troughs—kept scrupulously clean—and in quantities which the rabbits eat up completely; the amount will soon be ascertained; start with a couple of small handfuls.

As a conditioner for rabbits visiting the show bench, a teaspoonful of soaked linseed, squeezed dry, should be given two or three times a week; it helps to give a gloss to the coat.

For Cold Weather.

In the cold weather a hot mash, and fewer oats, for the evening meal is good and should be made of sharps or oatmeal, a little linseed and stale bread, over which boiling water has been poured. Well mix and then squeeze as dry as possible and give in balls the size of an egg. As a change substitute tea-leaves for the linseed. But again, while differing from some others, I maintain that the very best warm feed is bread and milk for does with young ones; and for the young themselves, when they begin to eat, there is no more valuable food.

The above feeding instructions apply to cavies in the main, though to their hard food can be added beans, peas, lentils, wheat and maize, with plenty of hay. The same size hutches, a little smaller if you like, will also suit.

THE VARIETIES OF RABBITS
Deciding What to take up.

Undoubtedly rabbits are the most popular hobby, due, perhaps, to the fact that there are so many different varieties, and that certain breeds have a marketable value. There are some fifteen different varieties, each with a specialist club working for their betterment, and hundreds of local societies all over the kingdom which run shows and offer valuable prizes for competition.

In an article of this length and nature, it is impossible to do more than just mention the peculiarities and show points of the several distinct varieties. Decide which you will take up and then get the books dealing with that variety; join the special club which looks after its welfare and never miss a chance of studying the winners at local shows. I will divide the breeds into two sections; those whose value depends upon their show points, and those whose value, beside show points, is increased by their marketable value.

English Rabbit.

In the first group we have the English rabbit; black and white, blue and white, and grey and white; its exhibition value lies in the evenly distributed colour spots and chains of spots placed all over the body.

Dutch.

Then the Dutch rabbit, probably the most popular of all show rabbits, a smaller animal, appearing to be cut in half, the hinder part being a colour—black, blue, grey, or tortoiseshell, with white tips to the hind feet, the fore part white, with rounded cheeks and ears of the same colour as the back, a wedge of white running up the nose, its show value lying in the clear-cut lines of demarcation between the coloured and white portions of the body.

Himalayan.

Another small marked variety is the Himalayan. Born white, but the ears, feet and nose-tip of which, at a few weeks old, turn black; it is the density of this black and its even apportioning which is the decisive factor on the show bench.

Polish.

Another small and very beautiful animal is the Polish. Pure white, with pink eyes and the most delicate thin white-pink ears. Purity of colour, texture of coat, size and shape of ears are its show points.

Silvers.

Then there is the family of Silvers, Silver Grey, Silver Fawns and Silver Browns, deservedly popular amongst the small breeds. Born black; at the age of six weeks they begin to "silver" and in another six weeks their coats are an intermixture of silver grey with the darker colour. Chief show points are given for the even intermixing of the grey in the coats.

Tans.

Yet another small-size family are the Tans—black, blue and chocolate, and tan. Judges look for bright tan on the chests and elsewhere.

Belgian Hare.

Of the larger breeds the Belgian Hare is the most popular, a truly beautiful animal with the colouring and "racy" form of the hare, but still a rabbit. Years ago there were those who opined that these rabbits were, in fact, hares, but they overlooked the fundamental difference between the hare and rabbit, namely, that whereas a rabbit is born with closed eyes and furless, leverets (young hares) are born with their eyes open and fully covered with fur. Exhibition value is governed by colour and the "racy" form.

Lop Rabbit.

Next must be mentioned the Lop rabbit, a cumbersome—perhaps one should say sedate—beastie whose show value lies in its abnormally long drooping ears. The record measurements of these freak appendages are, I believe, 28½ inches long and 6 inches in breadth.

Fig. 7.—Clipping Wool from Angora.
The first clipping is done when the rabbit is two months old, followed by clippings three times a year.

Fig. 8.—Keeping Angoras for Profit.
Plucking wool from Angora rabbit: sorting wool and weighing.

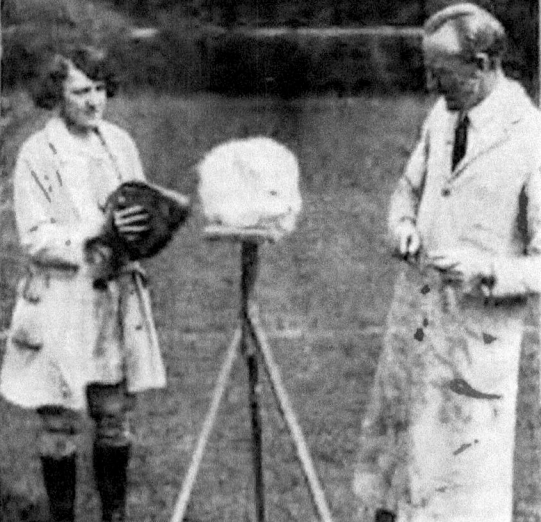

Fig. 9.—Care of Angoras.
Shows type of stand for grooming Angoras and using bellows to separate the wool.

Flemish Giant.

Another elephantine rabbit is the Flemish Giant, steel-grey coloured, the show winners of which have topped the scale at 17 lbs. for a doe and slightly less for a buck.

Angora.

Now we come to the group which have a marketable value for their fur or skins, and the oldest and, in some ways, most beautiful of these is the Angora. Within recent years the enhancement in the value of this rabbit is phenomenal owing to the fact that it has been proved that its beautiful fleecy white—there are some coloured, but these are not much fancied—wool is of exceptional value for the making of soft winter garments. To-day farms containing thousands of these "balls of fluff" are in existence all over Great Britain. While show points are decided on the length and soft texture of the wool, to be completely free from "mats," and for the fluffy tips to the ears, there is an unsatisfied demand for the wool for commercial purposes, where it is divided into three grades, the first grade reaching 30s. a pound.

Sale Prices of Angora Wool.

Recent figures in a year's return from fourteen does showed that the best rabbit's wool sold for £1 7s. 6d., the lowest for 8s. 6d., while the total for the fourteen was just £13. One hundred pounds a year net profit from the sale of wool could be made with two hundred Angoras. Added to this, of course, must be the sale of stock and show prizes, the capture of the latter, of course, increasing the value of stock offered for sale.

How to be successful.

The first clipping of the hair is done at about two months, three clippings to the year.

Two things are essential for the successful breeding of Angoras: first, that the stock should be purchased from a well-known strain; and, secondly, that the rabbits should be regularly groomed from a month old. Start well in these two directions and there is no reason why a novice should not breed specimens fit for the show bench and the production of marketable wool within the first year.

Advertisements from firms asking for the wool are always to be found in the Fancy Press. Young can be bought at 5s., but double or even treble that amount would be necessary if tip-top stock is required. If only a few are kept it will be seen that they are a paying hobby, and on a large scale a business proposition.

Points about keeping Angoras.

Angoras require big roomy hutches. Never attempt to wash them, they keep themselves snow-white if kept in clean surroundings. Remembering that it is quality and quantity of wool that is the chief object, wise breeders do not allow a doe to bring up more than three young at a time. This will mean probably that some have to be destroyed at birth, and it is those with the biggest heads which are likely to turn out the best. There is this great advantage in favour of keeping Angoras over the rest of this second group, namely, that they supply the marketable wool while alive, while the others have to be killed and their skins sold.

Fig. 10.—Grooming Angora with Brush.
The regular grooming of Angoras is one of the essentials of success in breeding these beautifully furred creatures.

Rabbits with Marketable Skins.

In this class are the Chinchilla, Giant Chinchilla—a big rabbit—the Berveren the Argente family of blue, cream and brown, the Havana and the Lilac Pearl rabbit. The latter was first produced by a lady fancier, as a result of a cross between a Berveren and a Havana, and is a typical example of the interesting experiments, ceaselessly carried out by fanciers, which make the hobby of so interesting a character.

The texture and length of the fur of these breeds, while not as long as Angoras, should be longer and silkier than breeds of the first group. Killed at about five months the skins fetch about 15s., and will be bought even when of youngsters of six weeks, these small skins being used for trimmings. With the exception of the Giant Chinchilla, a rabbit more of a size with the Flemish Giant, the rabbits in this group grow to about 5 lbs.

Selling Skins.

There is no difficulty in disposing of the skins outright, or, if preferred, having them properly dressed for making up at home. Several firms advertise each week in the fancy papers; a general price for this work is 9d. a skin. Other firms will buy the carcases for food. Yet other firms will dress and make up the skins into collars, cuffs or gloves.

How to cure Rabbit Skins.

The rabbit should be skinned directly it is killed, its head and feet cut off, and the skin then pinned upon a board, being stretched taut in the process. Use a sharp knife to remove all traces of fat and flesh, and dry with a cloth. An old solution for then treating the skins is saleratus, 1 oz.; alum, ¼ lb.; boiling water, 1½ pints. Put the ingredients into a jug, pour on the boiling water and stir until completely dissolved, then put aside till cold. Sponge the skin, still pinned fur downwards to the board, every day for a week, put it into a warm room or cupboard after each dressing. At the end of the week the skin—or pelt, as it is called—will be stiff and can be removed from the board and packed away until you have a dozen or more to send to a dealer.

When it is stated that it only costs about twopence a week to feed a rabbit, on the lines laid down in this article, it will be easily seen that as just a hobby, keeping only a few, it can be made to pay, while, as in all businesses, if run on a large scale, with a consequent lower cost on the purchase of foods in larger amounts, a livelihood can be secured.

VARIETIES OF GUINEA-PIGS

That which has been written as to the general care of rabbits applies to the keeping of guinea-pigs.

In the trade they are called cavies. The three varieties are Abyssinian, Peruvians and Smooth, which are divided up for show purposes into different colourings.

Characteristics of Each Breed.

Abyssinian cavies have rough coats, the hair being formed into rosettes all over the body; Peruvians have long sleeky coats, and Smooth cavies short glossy coats. Each breed can be had in a definite colour, or with intermixed colours, and show points are largely decided by the purity and density of these colourings or their even intermixing.

Apart from their show value cavies are particularly adapted as pets. They are born with their eyes open and fully covered with fur. In three weeks they are feeding themselves and can be taken from their mother in another ten days. They live four or five years.

How to Cut a Child's Hair

WE all know the old saying that if you want a job done well you must do it yourself. This is excellent advice provided you know how to do the job, and one of the few things we do not suggest readers can do for themselves is haircutting. If some kind member of the family offers to cut your hair we advise you to run away and hide—preferably in a barber's shop!

There is, however, no reason why you should not make a thoroughly successful job of cutting your children's hair, and, incidentally, save quite an appreciable amount of money by doing so. The photographs on this and the following pages have been specially staged to enable you to do the job properly and efficiently. You do not need any special equipment—a pair of scissors and a comb (and a fair amount of patience) are all you require. A pair of clippers for the final operations will be found useful, but are not absolutely essential.

Start at the Base of the Neck.

The first part to tackle is the hair at the base of the neck. Start by combing the hair down straight as shown in Fig. 1, before any attempt is made to start cutting. Then part the top hair to keep it out of the way while cutting the shorter hair at the base of the neck.

The main point to bear in mind when cutting is to work from the bottom of the neck upwards, as shown in Fig. 3. The comb is slid under the hair and the hair trimmed off. This prevents any danger of the scissors cutting the neck.

Tapering the Top Hair.

To make sure of the hair laying down smoothly and to avoid bumps or steps, the top hair should be tapered as shown in Fig. 4. A strand of hair is held in one hand and the open scissors moved downwards towards the head.

Next comb the hair again and then cut the long hair at the back to remove any long ends, as shown in Fig. 5. This completes the hair at the back of the neck, for the moment.

Dealing with the Side of the Head.

The next part to receive attention is the side of the head. Start by parting the top hair away from the underneath to enable the hair over the ear to be cut. Here again the important point is to work in an upward direction.

Shaping behind the Ear.

Note in Fig. 8 the method of holding the ear down with the comb when shaping the hair behind the ear down on to the face. This method ensures that there is no possibility of cutting the ear. Note also that the cutting is done from the back to the front. Balance up the hair nice and evenly on both sides.

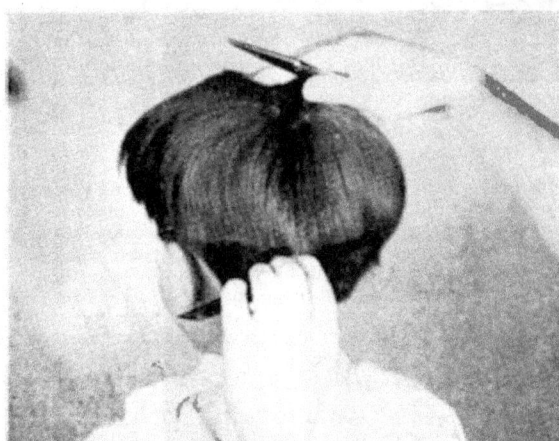

Fig. 1.—First comb the Hair down straight Ready for Cutting.

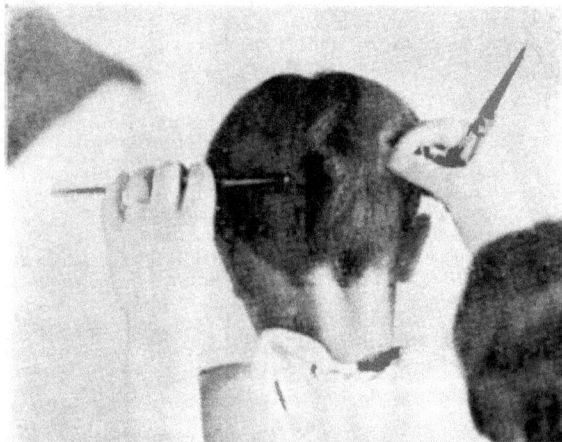

Fig. 2.—Then part the Top Hair to keep it out of the way while cutting the Shorter Hair at the Base of the Neck.

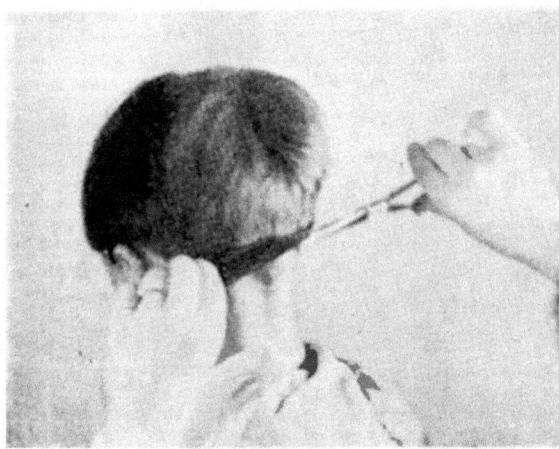

Fig. 3.—Starting the Cutting.
The important point is to work from the bottom of the neck upwards.

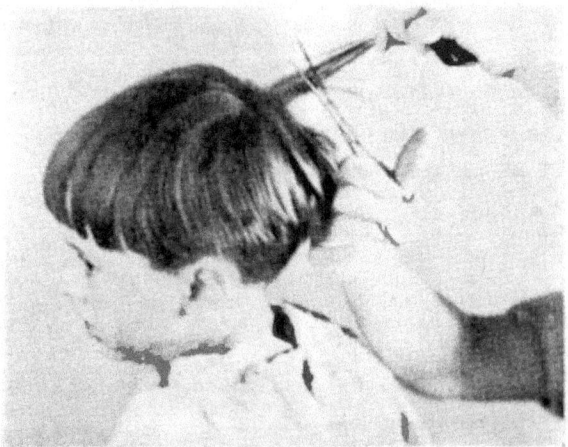

Fig. 4.—Tapering the Top Hair.
This is to ensure the hair laying down smoothly and to avoid bumps or steps.

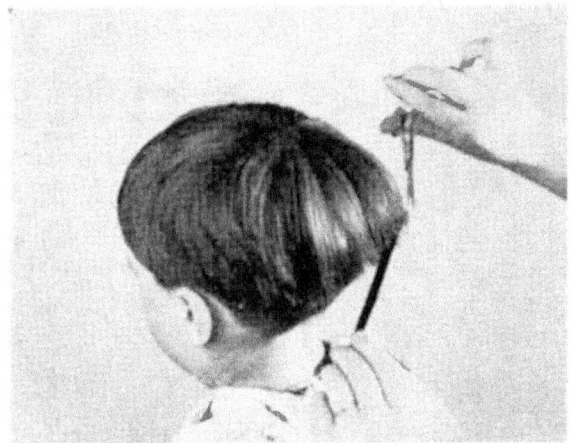

Fig. 5.—Completing the Back of the Head.
Showing method of cutting up the long hair at the back

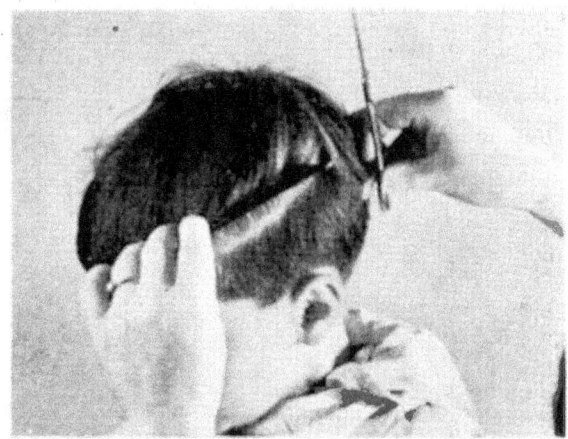

Fig. 6.—Starting the Side of the Head.
Showing top hair parted away from underneath to enable you to cut over the ear.

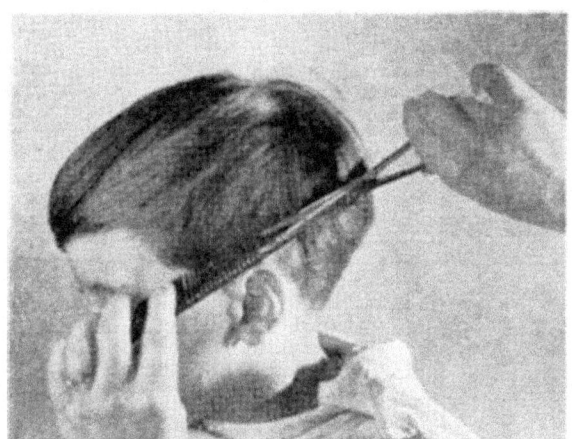

Fig. 7.—Cutting the Hair over the Ear.
Note that this should be done working in an upwards direction.

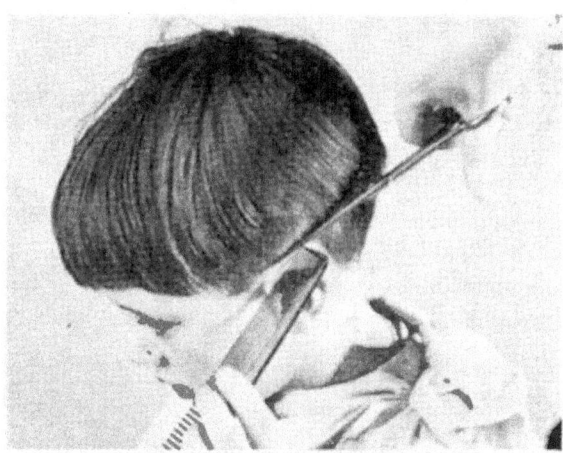

Fig. 8.—Shaping behind the Ear.
Note how the ear is held down with the comb.

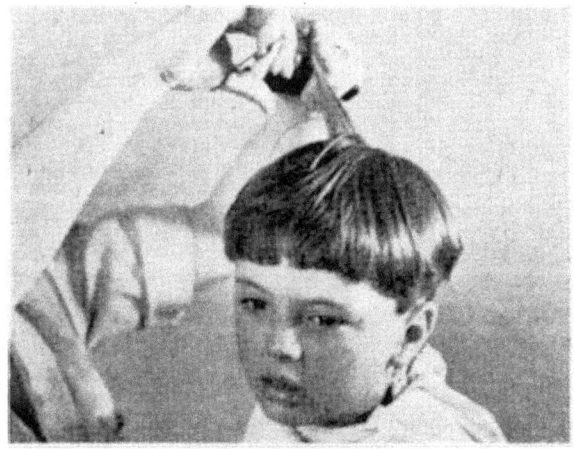

Fig. 9.—The Top of the Head.
Draw the hair on top through the fingers and cut close to the points to prevent fringe being too thick.

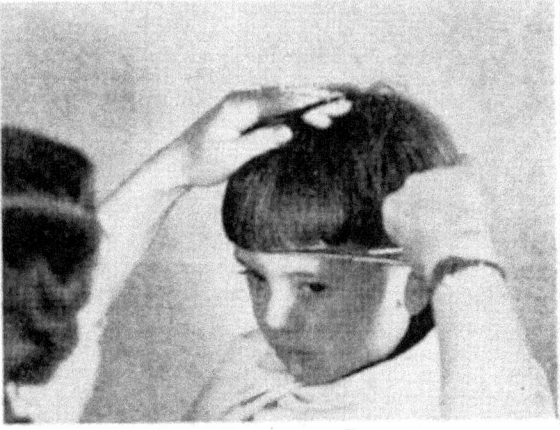

Fig. 10.—Trimming the Fringe.
Note how the child's head is held to prevent it being jerked up suddenly.

HOW TO CUT A CHILD'S HAIR

The Top Hair.

When dealing with the top, draw the hair through the fingers and cut close to the points to prevent the fringe being too thick. Then comb the hair down towards the face so that the fringe can be trimmed. It is a good idea to place one hand on the child's head while the fringe is being trimmed to prevent any danger of the child suddenly jerking his head upwards.

If clippers are available they can be run over the neck to get an absolutely close finish, but quite a clean finish can be obtained by the scissors and comb method already described.

Shampooing.

After the hair has been cut, it is a good plan thoroughly to shampoo the hair with a good liquid shampoo which can be purchased at any good-class hairdresser's. Rinse well and rub briskly with a Turkish towel. While the hair is still slightly damp, massage a small quantity of brilliantine into the scalp with the finger tips. Finally, make a nice straight parting and the job is finished.

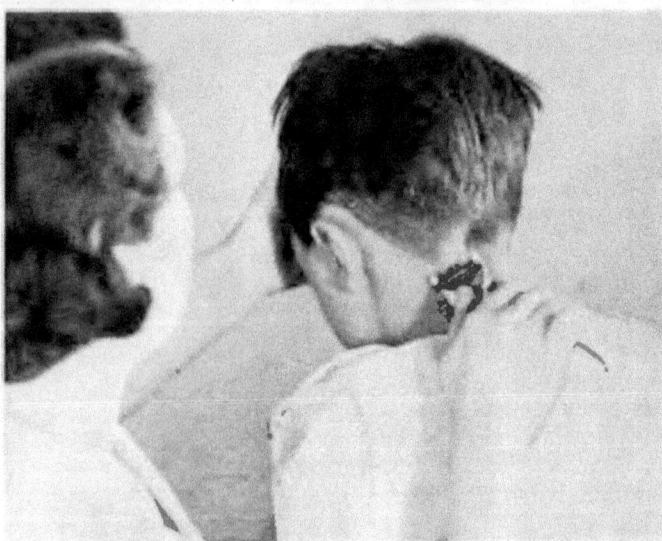

Fig. 11.—A Quick Method of obtaining a Close Finish is to run the Clippers over the Neck.

MAKING A TIE PRESS

THE gift problem is at all times a difficult one, but when the desire is to combine utility and attractiveness, the problem becomes really perplexing. However, the handyman who constructs the tie press described below will find it the solution of his male gift problem which will not only please the recipient but also involve a surprisingly small expenditure.

Dimensions.

When completed the press measures 10 inches by $3\frac{1}{2}$ inches, has a depth of 1 inch, and gives ample room for the average person's requirements. It can be made in oak or mahogany for just under 2s. and, although a personal preference is for oak, an attractive press can be made from either wood.

To ensure Accuracy.

Cut two lengths of the desired wood each measuring $10 \times 3\frac{1}{2} \times \frac{1}{2}$ inch and plane the top and bottom of each piece as flat as is possible. Now, in order to facilitate the job throughout and to ensure accuracy, pin the two pieces of wood together, using four fine $\frac{3}{4}$-inch pins and placing them near the outside edges at the centre. Plane the four sides to make them absolutely even, round off the top edges and corners with a plane and then clean the job well, using first a fine No. 2 glasspaper and finishing with a No. 1 paper.

How to hold the Press while polishing.

The wood should now be stained and the top and sides polished. For this purpose, after staining, a screw should be fixed underneath the press, in the middle and about $2\frac{1}{2}$ inches from one side, as this will enable you to hold the press while polishing it.

The Fittings.

The fittings, two in number, which are obtainable ready for fixing from most woodworkers' and cabinet-makers' supply shops, must now be attached, and for our particular press the size required is No. 0. These fittings have to be screwed to the top and bottom of the press about $2\frac{1}{2}$ inches from each end and, when you place them in position, you will find that it is necessary to cut four grooves for each fitting, two in the bottom for the ends of the fitting and one at each side into which the operating screw will fit. The grooves in the bottom of the press will measure $1\frac{1}{4} \times \frac{3}{8} \times \frac{1}{4}$ inch, and those through the sides about $\frac{3}{8} \times \frac{3}{4}$ inch.

Place each of the bottom sections of the fittings into position, so that the outside edge of each is 2 inches from the sides, and screw on, using $\frac{3}{8}$-inch black round-head screws. Set the top of each fitting in their corresponding positions on the upper part of the press and fix them accurately by tightening the screws which are attached to the bottom section, and to fix them use $\frac{3}{8}$-inch nickel-plated round-head screws.

The two sections of the press can now be parted, the pins withdrawn, rubber feet attached to the under part at each corner, and then, to finish the job, it is necessary only to cut a piece of stout cardboard slightly smaller than the bottom of the press and to insert it between the upper and lower sections.

A less elaborate, but still serviceable, press can be made using only one fitting, which is fixed across the press at the centre.

Fig. 1.—The Finished Tie Press.

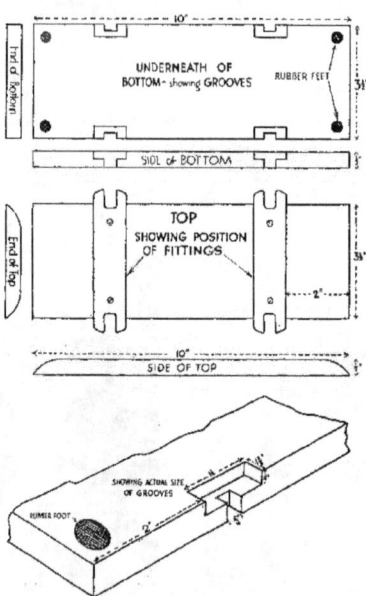

Fig. 2.—Details of Construction and Dimensions.

PRACTICAL METHODS OF BOOKBINDING

BOOKBINDING is one of the most useful and profitable of hobbies; not only does it help us to bind our own periodicals in neat cases, but the experienced worker will soon obtain profitable orders from his friends should he so desire. The tools required need not be elaborate, and many of them can be made at home one at a time until a full equipment has been assembled.

The Bookbinder's Equipment.

Useful work can be done with a thread and needle, a few boards, a small wooden clamp and the paste pot. The ideal equipment will comprise the following tools.

The Press, for applying weight to the books while drying and when finished.

The Lying Press, a most useful tool in which many operations, such as cutting and backing, are performed; details of an excellent home-made article which will do all required of it are given later in the article.

The Sewing Frame—this is not necessary for small case work, but is essential when large leather work is undertaken; here again the amateur can make his own.

The Plough—this is the tool all bookbinders desire to obtain, for it enables the worker to get those clean cut edges which stamp the job as real craftwork. An excellent one can be made, as the reader will see later.

Backing and Cutting Boards are easily constructed from odd pieces of floorboard.

Ornamenting Tools, such as the fillet and roller, are best purchased, but quite useful stick stamping tools which serve the purpose can be made from lenths of brass rod; details of these will be given later.

Fig. 1.—AN IMPORTANT POINT TO REMEMBER BEFORE STARTING TO BIND A BOOK.
Go through the pages and repair the tears, applying a piece of transparent tape to the tear.

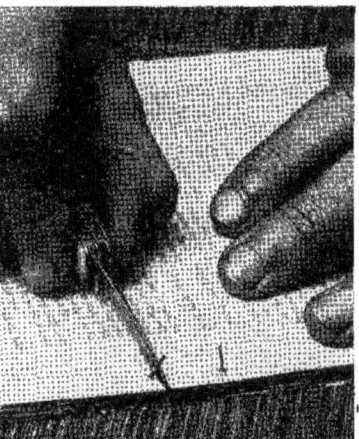

Fig. 2.—HOW TO REMOVE METAL STAPLES WITHOUT DAMAGING THE PAPER.
They should be lifted up with a knife as shown.

The rest of the equipment comprises a bookbinder's hammer, a straight-edge and a cutting knife.

How to make the Lying Press.

Fig. 3 shows a home-made lying press with a plough in position on top of the cheeks. The press is simply two pieces of stout board which can be clamped together by two vice screws. Suitable screws can be obtained in metal for a few shillings, the tubular nut is countersunk and fixed in the face of the rear cheek, while holes to coincide are bored in the front cheek; washers are provided to take the pull on the front cheek. Note the small steps cut out at the ends of the cheeks; these are to facilitate fitting the press across the top of a box of suitable height to lift it 2 feet 6 inches above the ground.

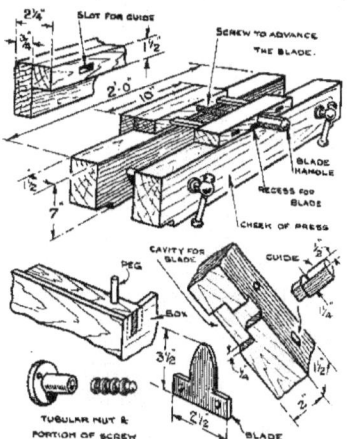

Fig. 3.—DETAILS FOR CONSTRUCTING A SIMPLE LYING PRESS AND PLOUGH.
Although not absolutely essential, this piece of apparatus will considerably facilitate the work.

A box is a very suitable support for the press, since when cutting and ploughing the waste drops within, while the tools can be supported in leather loops arranged round the edge. Note in the small sketch (Fig. 3), that the two edges of the box which support the press are strengthened with 2 × 2-inch bars mortised into the sides, dowel pegs glued into the bars fit into holes at the ends of the front cheek and the rear cheek is, of course, free to move backwards and forwards.

The Plough.

Look at Fig. 3 and you will see that the plough is composed of two runners which slide along the top of the press, the rear one is the guide and is made with two pieces of hardwood screwed together at right angles, the front runner carries the blade. Two thin guide rails are mortised into the front runner, and these are free to slide through square holes in guide runner. The distance between the two runners is regulated by a ⅜-inch screw; incidentally, this also governs the depth of the cut. A nut is sunk into the face of the rear runner, and into this is screwed a length of ⅜-inch rod which has been cut with a Whitworth or square thread.

The handle is a short piece of hexagonal brass with a hole in the end, into which the screwed rod fits; it is secured by soldering or brazing. The blade is shown in the small sketch, Fig. 3; it is ground from a piece of cutting steel, such as an old plane iron, and screwed into a recess in the under side of the runner, as shown. The cutting edge is bevelled and whetted on the oil-stone; it is fixed to the runner with the flat side placed downwards.

Making a Sewing Frame.

Fig. 4 shows a very serviceable sewing frame. The base is a sheet of multi-ply wood stiffened with battens under the ends; into this are mortised two wooden uprights, the tops of which terminate in ¼-inch threaded rod fitted into holes in the end. Across the uprights is a horizontal bar rectangular at the ends and pared

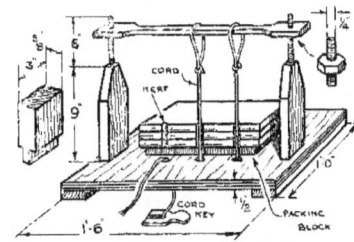

Fig. 4.—DETAILS OF A SEWING FRAME.
This is not required for simple case binding, but is essential when large leather work is dealt with.

down in the middle. The height of the bar is regulated by two nuts placed on the studs under the bar. Three or four holes are bored in the base board directly below the bar; the lower ends of the cords are secured by sheet metal keys, as shown in Fig. 4; these fit over knots and slip into place under the base board.

Backing and Cutting Boards.

Several pairs of these boards are needed, and they can be planed up from lengths of floorboard, but hardwood is better if this is available. Fig. 9 shows one use to which they are put, and the small sketch gives an idea of the tapering edge; the cutting boards do not require so much taper as those shown in the figure.

Making a Press.

A very satisfactory home-made press is shown in Fig. 19. The bed plate is a sheet of ½-inch multi-ply, and fixed above this is a strong wooden yoke. The screw of the press is another vice screw, the tubular nut being mounted in the centre of the horizontal member of the yoke. The moving plate of the press is also a sheet of thick ply; it is fastened to the screw thread by a plate through which projects upwards a screw free to turn in the plate; the screw is sweated into the main vice screw to prevent it turning. Note that slots are cut in the sides of the moving board so that it slides smoothly up and down, the uprights of the yoke acting as guides.

CASE BINDING.

We must now consider the binding of a book; most cheap books are case bound; this means that the sections of the book are sewn to tapes, and it is then fastened into a case which has been made to fit the particular volume; this method is quite strong and serviceable for most work. Leather binding is much more expensive, but more lasting, and is executed in quite a different way, as will be shown later in the article.

Preparing the Parts.

First of all take the book or parts to pieces by removing the cover, taking out all the stitches or wire clips, and cleaning away all glue. Place all the sections together in their correct order face downwards on a flat board; this piece of wood should have a *fence*, that is, a strip of wood 1½ inches high, round two adjacent sides. The sections should be tapped into the corner formed by the fence, with the "head" and "back" of the book against the surrounding wood. Beat the parts with the flat of a bookbinder's hammer until they are tight up in the corner

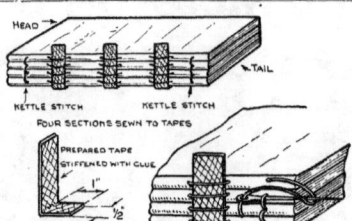

Fig. 5.—Sewing to Tapes for Case Binding.

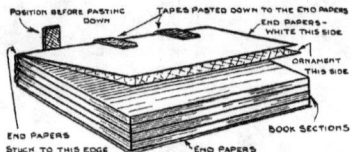

Fig. 6.—Pasting in the End Papers preparatory to fastening in Case.

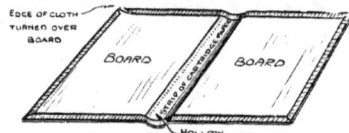

Fig. 7.—Details showing Construction of a Simple Case.

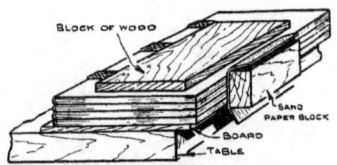

Fig. 8.—Using a Sandpaper Block when a Plough is not available.

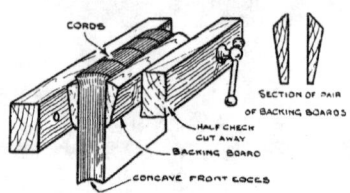

Fig. 9.—A Book without Cover, between Backing Boards in Lying Press ready for Backing, *i.e.*, rounding the Back and making the Front Hollow.

and quite level; this process is called *knocking up*.

Any unevenness in the size of the parts will now show on the front and tail of the book which are not against

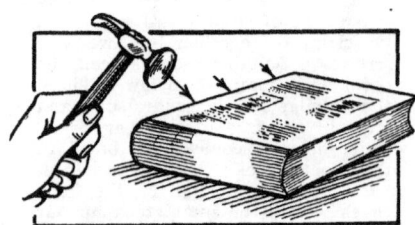

Fig. 10.—Another Method of rounding the Back.
The hammer is used all along the edge marked with arrows. By curving the back edge, a complementary curve is made at the front edge.

the fence. The parts are now trimmed to size with a very sharp knife, the cuts being made on the two open sides, a steel straight-edge being used to guide the knife.

Sewing the Parts.

Take some tape ½ inch wide and soak it in weak glue to stiffen it, and cut off *three* pieces and bend them to the shape shown in Fig. 5. Place the first section face downwards on the table with the *head* to the right, then slip the bent ends of the tape under the section. Hold the section open with the left hand and with a darning needle make holes on each side of the tapes and at the *kettle-stitch* marks. Thread the needle with bookbinder's thread and begin sewing the kettle-stitch at the *head*, leaving a couple of inches of spare thread, and sewing round each tape as shown in Fig. 5. Having finished at the tail kettle-stitch, lay the next section in place face downwards and, commencing with the kettle-stitch, sew back to the *head* again. Pull the thread in the direction of the stitches to make it tight, then tie to the loose end. The remaining sections are added, sewing them in position in the same way as before; when a kettle-stitch is made it must be caught up to the one immediately below, as shown in the small sketch in Fig. 5.

The End Papers.

These are sheets of fancy paper, marbled or printed, with a pattern on one side and white on the other. Choose a colour to tone with the proposed binding, then cut to size and fold in half with the pattern sides facing. Paste a ⅛-inch strip along the folded edge and fix one in each end of the sewn volume, as shown in Fig. 6. The book should then be placed in the press to dry, weights will serve the purpose if a press is not available.

Cleaning the Edges.

If a plough is not to hand place the book on the edge of a table between two boards. With the left hand press the pages together, then take a piece of fine sand paper wrapped round a block of wood and rub the edges perfectly smooth, as shown in Fig. 8.

The method of cutting the edges with a plough is described later.

Final Preparations for the Case.

Place the book in the lying press between two backing boards, as shown in Fig. 9; press on the front edges to make a hollow before tightening up the press. As the press is gradually screwed up tap the back along the edges, the rear of the book will then assume a convex appearance, and the backing boards will make rounded grooves into which the cover boards will

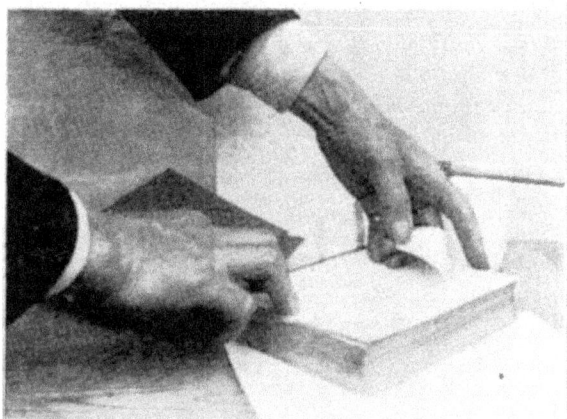

Fig. 11.—Pasting in One of the End Papers.

Fig. 12.—Stitching down the Cartridge Paper which forms the Hollow Back.

readily hinge. Glue the back, working it well into the sections with the fingers, then place a strip of stout paper down the back to cover the tape and stitching. The book is now ready to fit into its case.

Making a Case.

Ready-made cases can be purchased for works published in parts, but excellent ones can be made at home. Cut two pieces of 12-oz. strawboard as wide as the book and ¼ inch longer; also cut a strip of cartridge paper as long as the book and ⅛ inch wider—this is to form the hollow at the back. Then cut a piece of bookbinder's cloth sufficiently large to accommodate the boards and paper strip when set out as in Fig. 7, and leave ⅜ inch spare round the outside. The cloth is usually grained or embossed with a pattern; much of this will be lost if the paste is applied directly to it. Paste the strawboards and paper strip and place in position on the inside surface of the cloth, then apply a weight to prevent bending. When dry, the edges are trimmed and turned in for pasting, the corners being mitred with a slight overlap. Where the cloth is turned in over the paper strip no paste is applied. Leave the work under a weight until dry, it is then ready to receive the sewn and taped book.

Fitting the Book into the Case.

Take the prepared book and paste down the ends of the tapes to the end papers, then spread on an even coat of paste over the whole of the *tail* end paper and place the book in position on one of the boards of the open case. See that it is square, with the board overlapping the head and tail ¼ inch. Now paste the other end paper and lift the remaining board into position until it is directly over the other with ¼ inch projecting round the three sides. Place the book in the press or under weight with the whole of the boards under pressure, but the hollow just projecting beyond the edge of the board, and leave to dry.

The book is now a finished case-bound book; methods of ornamenting and lettering are given later.

LEATHER BINDING.

The most popular type of leather used for covering books is Morocco, although calf and roan are frequently used. Fancy grained leathers made from sheepskins are sold at most leather shops, as is also "skiver," a split hide which looks effective and is not expensive. Skiver forms an ideal medium for the beginner to practice on. Leather work differs from case binding in two respects: firstly, the parts are sewn to cords; secondly, instead of building a case to receive the book, boards are attached to the cords and the leather covering is built on to these.

Preparing for Leather Binding.

The parts to be bound must first of all be taken apart and all stitching

Fig. 13.—Pasting the Tapes down to the End Papers.

Fig. 14.—A Stage in Leather Binding. Cutting the kerfs for the cords.

Fig. 15.—The Next Stage—Lacing on to the Boards.

PRACTICAL METHODS OF BOOKBINDING

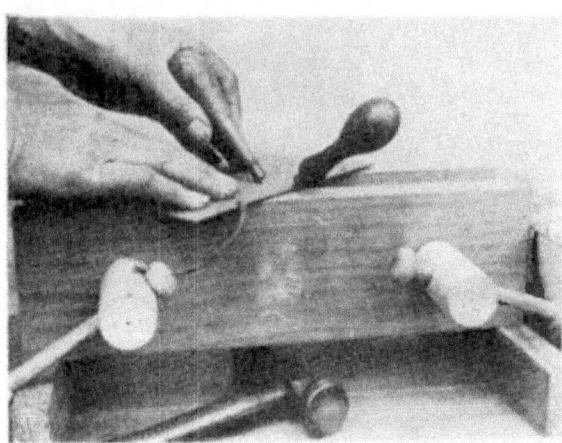

Fig. 16.—Making the Holes in the Strawboard. Note that the two awls are inclined inwards.

and glue removed as for case binding. Place the sections in order face downwards on the board and "knock up" to the *head* and *back;* now trim the two open edges fairly even; the book should then be placed in a vice or lying press and the position of the cords marked; the number of cords will vary from three for small books to five for large volumes. With a fine tenon saw cut "kerfs" or grooves at each point where it is proposed to have a cord; these kerfs should be deep enough to take the cord so that it is flush with the back of the book. Suitable twisted cords can be purchased at shops that sell bookbinding materials. Fig. 14 shows how the kerfs are cut with the tenon saw.

Sewing the Book.

Stretch tightly the correct number of cords in the sewing frame, as shown in Fig. 4. The upper ends are formed into a loop which fits over the bar, while the lower end is knotted and secured with the metal key shown in the figure. Lay the first section in place face downwards with the head to the right and fit the cords into the kerfs. Open the section to the middle with the left hand and proceed to sew round the cords, starting from the head exactly as described above for case binding. Then lay the second section in place and loop up the kettle-stitch, as previously described, and sew back to the head; tie the loose end to the main thread, after first of all pulling the stitches tight. In a similar manner sew on the remaining parts and remove from the sewing frame, leaving about 2 inches spare on the ends of the cords.

The End Papers.

The next step is to cut, fold and stick the end papers as previously described, taking care to choose a design which tones with the colour of the leather selected for covering the boards.

Backing and Rounding.

The next process is backing, that is, obtaining that rounded back and concave front which at once stamps a book as well bound. Holding the book across the back with the left hand, force the centre of the

Fig. 17.—How to use the Hammer when Backing.

back up by pressing on the front edges with the fingers of the right hand. In this way a small hollow will be formed along the front with a corresponding bulge at the back. Now clamp the book in the lying press, as shown in Fig. 9, and tap the back edges with the flat of a bookbinder's hammer, gradually tightening up the press until the back of the book is well rounded.

Lacing on the Boards.

Cut two boards slightly larger than the book from heavy-weight strawboard. Very fine boards can be made by gluing together two thicknesses of card, using a slightly thinner one for the inside; this causes the board to warp a little inwards, a good "fault," as the covers then closely grip the book. Two holes are made through the boards, one near the edge and the other 1¼ inches in, as shown in Fig. 16; note that the holes slope slightly inwards. Untwist the cords, well paste and twirl the end to a point, threading the end first through the hole near the edge and then through the second one (see Fig. 15). Cut off the end within ⅜ inch of the board, spread the ends and paste down, knocking the cords flat with the hammer.

Scratching up and lining.

Place the book in the press with the back protruding and lightly paste the rear, then scratch up the surface with a pointed tool just enough to roughen the paper, but taking care not to damage the stitches. Paste the backs again, this time scratching diagonally from left to right, paste a third time, rubbing the adhesive well into the scratches. Now apply a coating of glue down the back and leave to dry; this operation gives firmness to the back. The back and the outsides of the boards are now lined by sticking on several thicknesses of smooth brown or cartridge paper; this gives stability to the book.

Head-bands should now be stuck in top and bottom with the woven pattern just flush with the edges. These bands are purchased by the yard from the bookbinder's warehouse and are cut up in lengths as long as the thickness of the book, allowing for the curve of the back.

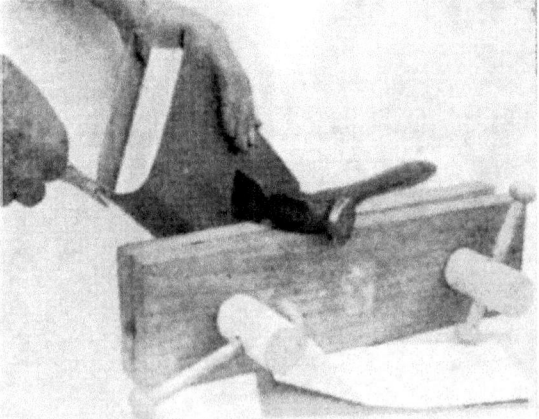

Fig. 18.—Cutting the Nicks at the Head before Turning in the Leather.

PRACTICAL METHODS OF BOOKBINDING

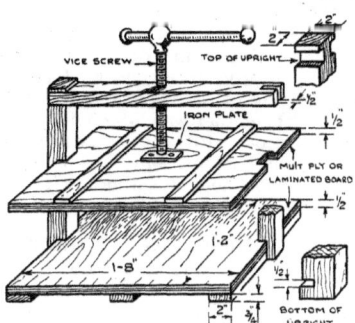

Fig. 19.—Details of an Easily Constructed Book Press.

Cutting the Edges.

Prepare the book as shown in Fig. 20, tieing the pages together and allowing the boards to fall downwards. Press in a couple of "trindles," that is, thin metal wedges; these will temporarily flatten the back and the front edges. Now place the tied book in the lying press between a cutting board (slightly tapered) and a straight runner in the front. The runner should be just level with the cutting mark, while the cutting board wants to be a little higher. Having well "whetted" the blade of the plough, place it on top of the press and adjust the knife so that it will cut through a dozen to fifteen pages. Hold the guide runner down firmly on the rear cheek of the press, and with the right hand across the front runner push the plough across the face of the book. Gradually advancing the blade, proceed to plough through the entire thickness with a series of cutting strokes. Always plough the *head* first, then the tail, and lastly the front. The trindles are knocked out before the book is lowered into the press. When the work is removed from the press, it should regain its rounded back and concave front.

Covering the Boards.

Take a piece of leather that will amply cover the two boards with $\frac{3}{8}$ to $\frac{1}{2}$ inch spare for turning in, and carefully pare the edges down thin. Paste the two boards and lay the book down in its correct position on the flat leather with the back away from the operator. The spare flap is then drawn over the upper pasted board and turned in at the fore-edge. Stand the book on its front, and with the fingers well work the leather over the back. The leather has now to be turned in at the head and tail, small nicks $\frac{1}{4}$ inch long being made on either side of the hollow back, as shown in Fig. 18. The corners are turned in by cutting the leather diagonally to within $\frac{1}{8}$ inch of the board and forming a mitred joint on the inside. The end papers can then be pasted down and the book placed under *light* pressure to dry. When using calf or roan, it is necessary to damp well the leather and smooth out the creases; work with the material still wet.

Case Ornament.

The finished volume should be suitably ornamented with lines or a simple border pattern. For straight lines a *fillet* is used; this is a brass wheel mounted in an iron fork, as shown in Fig. 21. A *roll* is slightly broader than a fillet and has a pattern cut round the edge which it repeats on the leather as it runs over it. To use these tools warm them in a gas flame until a drop of water placed on them evaporates rapidly without hissing, then run the tool over the places it is required to ornament, applying firm pressure and using a straight-edge for a guide.

Hand Tools.

Very good hand tools for "stick" printing or ornamenting can be made as shown in Fig. 22. One is a piece of round brass with two wide cuts at right angles across the face, another a square sectioned piece of brass with a simple cross, while the third is triangular with little flutes filed out of the centre of each side. These stick tools can be mounted in wooden handles and used similarly to the wheels, only stamping the pattern a bit at a time. Fig. 22 shows how the stick tools can be used to make a border design or an ornamental corner, by varying the combination of the sticks a large number of designs can be built up.

Lettering.

Bookbinders letter the covers by impressing the required titles with brass type. These brass letters are rather expensive, but if the amateur can secure some printer's type he can mount these in a holder and obtain as good impressions as with brass type, only he must be careful not to get them too hot or they will melt. The lettering and ornament can be filled in with colour if desired; the best medium for the amateur is poster artists' colours or water colours mixed with isinglass solution and "bodied" up with Chinese white. Before applying to leather, carefully remove any grease or oiliness with methylated spirits, then punch in the colour with a stiff brush, wiping away any surplus before it has time to dry.

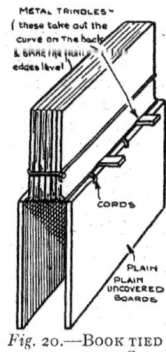

Fig. 20.—Book tied ready for Cutting.

To gild the letters, two methods are available—the letters can be sized in and the gold leaf punched in with a piece of cotton wool, or a section of leaf can be picked up on the gilder's tip and placed over the impressed letters; it is then pressed into place with the type tools while warm; the heat will cause the gold to adhere to the leather. Hints on "gilding" are given in a previous article in an early number of this work.

Finishing the Edges.

These can be coloured to taste with the paints previously described, or they may be gilded. This is done either for ornamental purposes or to hide the discoloration caused by dust. If all three edges of the paper have been trimmed, it is usual to colour the three; but if only the top edge has been trimmed, this alone is coloured. Clamp the book in the lying press so that the colour cannot run between the leaves; spraying the colour on to the edges is an admirable method of applying the medium; an ordinary scent or insect spray will do quite well. When gilding, the edges should be sixed and the gold leaf pressed on with a wad of cotton wool while the size is "tacky."

Dressing the Leather.

Those readers who like a glossy surface to their work can obtain this by applying a thin coat of spirit varnish to the finished cover. Before doing this, however, it will be necessary to apply a coat of "glaire" over the leather; this glaire is made by beating up the pure white of an egg with four times its volume of water. The glaire is rubbed over the leather on a pad of cotton wool and allowed to dry before the spirit varnish is applied.

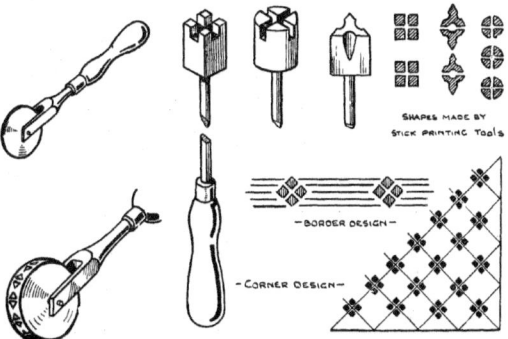

Fig. 21.—Two Types of Rollers for Decoration.

Fig. 22.—Some Typical Stick Ornamenting Tools, showing Variations in Designs.

Making a Dog's Kennel

Dogs, like human beings, vary in size, and it is as well to make the house to fit the dog. The size of the entrance is an important consideration, because not only is it the opening for the dog, but also for climatic conditions.

The Floor.

The floor should be above the ground. If a medium size dog, a kennel 3 feet 6 inches high, 3 feet 6 inches long, and 3 feet wide inside measurements will be sufficient accommodation.

The house can be built so that it comes apart by unscrewing a few screws or bolts, or it can be made a permanent fixture.

The only difference is that a few more pieces of 1½ by 1½ inches of wood will be required for the side sections and the roof. Obtain some 1-inch tongued and grooved boards to form a space 3 feet 6 inches long and 3 feet wide for the floor. Eight 1 by 5½ inch boards will make a width of 3 feet, as, owing to the machining, the tongue and the groove, the boards will not measure more than 5 inches each when they are put together.

Three Methods for Building the House.

Three methods are available for building the kennel. First method, to make up the framework out of 1½ by 1½ inch wood, then to cover it with boards; second method, to make the sides and ends separate units, and to bolt them together, having made arrangements for the fitting of the floor and the roof.

Fig. 1.—A Kennel of the Large Type.

Fig. 2.—A Smaller Type of Kennel.

The other way is to build each section with the boards upon light battens, and then to nail the sections together. This is the simplest and the cheapest.

"PERMANENT" KENNEL

First, cut four pieces of 1½ by 1½ inch 2 feet 4 inches long; put them together, so the ends are level, mark a line 2 inches from the bottom, and another 1½ inches from this for the insertion of the side pieces of 1½ by 1½ inches. From the bottom mark another line 20 inches, then another 1½ inches above this for the other length of 1½ by 1½ inches. These marks are for the housing of the side pieces for the house.

Turn the four pieces and mark them for the front and back of the house.

Fig. 4 shows the distance for the bottom piece, which is 4 inches to the bottom of the cross piece of 1½ by 1½ inches. The housing for the top pieces are 24 inches from the bottom of the uprights. Cut four pieces of 3 feet 1 inch by 1½ by 1½-inch wood, and nail these in the 4- and 24-inch housing of the uprights.

Fig. 5 shows the measurements of the housings, cross piece and the floor-boards.

MATERIALS REQUIRED FOR DIFFERENT TYPES AND SIZES.

FOR LARGE KENNEL

Overall Size about 4′ 0″ wide × 4′ 6″ high × 5′ 0″ long.

Permanent Type.

Framing,	4.	2′ 6″	
,,	4.	3′ 6″	2″ × 2″ wood.
,,	4.	4′ 0″	
,,	4.	5′ 0″	
Flooring,	3.	4′ 0″	1″ × 3″ wood.
,,	10.	5′ 0″	1″ × 5½″
Sides,	12.	7′ 0″	Tongued and
Ends,	10.	9′ 0″	grooved boards.
Roof,	6.	11′ 0″	Weather boards 6″ planed.
,,	2.	5′ 6″	¾″ × 3″ for capping.
,,	2.	3′ 0″	1″ × 3″ for end boards of roof.
Nails .	.	4″ and 2½″ oval brads.	

Sectional Type.

Framing,	8.	2′ 6″	
,,	4.	3′ 8″	
,,	4.	3′ 6″	2″ × 2″ wood.
,,	4.	4′ 0″	
,,	4.	5′ 0″	
Flooring,	3.	4′ 0″	1″ × 3″ wood.
,,	10.	5′ 0″	1″ × 5½″
Sides,	12.	7′ 0″	Tongued and
Ends,	10.	9′ 0″	grooved boards.
Roof,	6.	11′ 0″	Weather boards 6″ planed.
,,	2.	5′ 6″	¾″ × 3″ for capping (fascia).
,,	2.	3′ 0″	1″ × 3″ for end boards of roof.
16 Bolts.			
Nails .	.	4″ and 2½″ oval brads.	

MEDIUM-SIZED KENNEL

Overall Size about 3′ wide × 3′ high × 3½′ long.

Permanent Type.

Framing,	4.	2′ 0″	
,,	4.	2′ 4″	
,,	4.	3′ 1″	1½″ × 1½″ wood.
,,	4.	3′ 7″	
Floor,	2.	3′ 0″	1″ × 3″ wood.
,,	8.	3′ 6″	
Sides,	18.	3′ 0″	1″ × 5½″
Ends,	16.	3′ 6″	⅞″ × 5½″
Tongued and grooved boards.			
Roof,	10.	4′ 4″	Planed 6″ weather boards.
,,	1.	4′ 4″	3″ × ¾″ For capping.
,,	1.	4′ 4″	¾″ × 3½″
,,	2.	2′ 3″	1′ × 3″ for end of roof.
Nails .	.	4″ and 2½″ oval brads.	

Sectional Type

Framing,	8.	2′ 0″	
,,	4.	2′ 4″	
,,	4.	2′ 3″	1½″ × 1½″ wood.
,,	4.	3′ 1″	
,,	4.	3′ 4″	
Floor,	2.	3′ 0″	1″ × 3″ wood.
,,	8.	3′ 6″	1″ × 5½″ Tongued and grooved boards.
Sides,	18.	3′ 0″	⅞″ × 5½″
Ends,	16.	3′ 6″	Tongued and grooved boards.
Roof,	10.	4′ 4″	Planed 6″ weather boards.
,,	1.	4′ 4″	3″ × ¾″ For capping.
,,	1.	4′ 4″	3½″ × ¾″
,,	2.	2′ 3	1″ × 3″ for end of roof (fascia) board.
16 Bolts.			
Nails .	.	4″ and 2½″ oval brads.	

FOR SMALL SIZED KENNEL

Overall Size about 2′ 6″ wide, 3′ 0″ high, 3′ 0″ long.

Constructed Sectionally

Battens	2.	2′ 6″	2″ × 2″ Crosspieces.
	5.	2′ 6″	1″ × 2″ ,,
	4.	3′ 0″	
Floor	2.	2′ 6″	1″ × 3″.
,,	6.	3′ 0″	1″ × 5½″ Tongued and grooved boards.
Sides	16.	2′ 6″	¾″ × 5½″ ,, ,, ,,
Ends	12.	3′ 6″	¾″ × 5½″.
Roof	10.	3′ 6″	6″ Planed weather boards.
,,	1.	3′ 6″	¾″ × 3″ For capping.
,,	1.	3′ 6″	¾″ × 3½″
,,	2.	2′ 6″	¾″ × 3″ for end boards of roof
Nails	.	2″ and 3″ oval brads.	
Screws.			

MAKING A DOG'S KENNEL

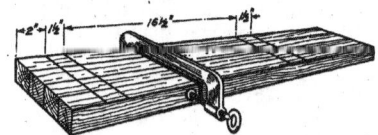

Fig. 3.—How to Mark Off the Side Housings on the Upright Lengths.

Cutting the Roof Struts.

Square up the frame, then tack a strip of wood from the centre of the bottom cross piece to the centre of the top piece. This should extend to 3 feet 1½ inches from the bottom piece (Fig. 4), and will form a gauge for cutting the roof struts. Put a piece of 1½ by 1½-inch wood from A to the top of the upright B at the side and mark off the angles. It is best to cut the outside uprights to the angle of the top bar, and to let these in ½ inch. It strenghtens the framing.

Four pieces will be needed for the struts. The housings for the uprights should be cut out, and the pieces nailed together. The struts should project over the uprights 2½ inches. This gives the house a better appearance and keeps out the wet. The end sections should be joined together by four pieces, 3 feet 7 inches (1½ by 1½ inches), Fig. 6.

Flooring.

Make the floor out of eight pieces of 1 by 5½-inch tongued and grooved board. Cut off the tongue on one board. These boards should be cut the length of the house inside the uprights. Check the boards as they are cut, then nail them together on to two pieces of 1 by 3 inches, 3 feet long.

The floor should fit between the four uprights and should rest on the end pieces of 1 by 3 inches (Figs. 7 and 8).

Covering the Ends.

Cover the ends with ⅞ by 5½-inch tongued and grooved boarding, the boards being vertical and overlapping on each side of the house. Measure for the entrance to the house and bore a ½-inch hole, ½ inch from the edge of the top cross piece, and in the centre of the front. Measure 9 inches from the edges, and mark two lines from the bottom to the top of the section. Nine inches below the hole, make this the radius for the half circle for the top of the entrance to the house. Cut down the lines with a pad saw. The sides can then be covered in.

Boarding up the Sides.

Cut the boards for the sides. Nail them on the framework flush with the back part of the end boards, and level with the front and back strut; when they are nailed on, the top should be

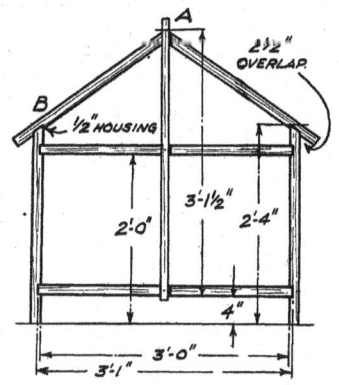

Fig. 4.—Gauging Angles of Roof Struts and Uprights.

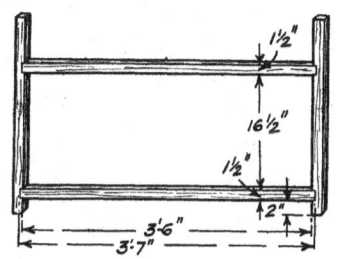

Fig. 6.—Side Frame of "Permanent" Kennel, showing Dimensions.

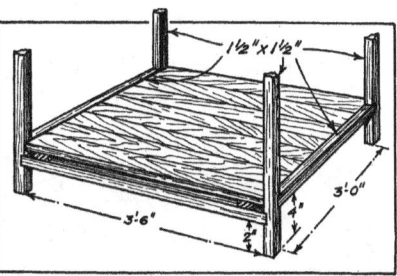

Fig. 7.—How the Floorboards are Fitted.
Flooring laid down within the four uprights on the cross-pieces and level with the front and back rails at bottom of frame.

bevelled with a plane. This makes the kennel a permanent one (see Fig. 9).

The Roof.

The roof for the permanent house consists of planed weather boards, which are cut 5 inches longer than the

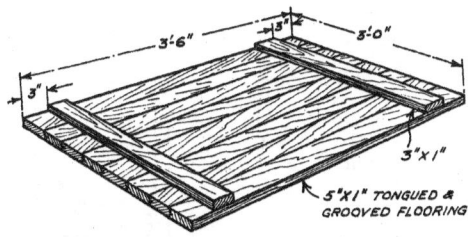

Fig. 8.—Method of Securing Floorboards Together.
Showing them attached to the two 3 in. × 1 in. crosspieces.

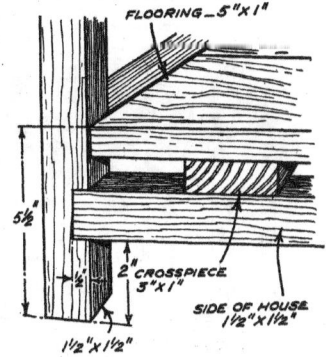

Fig. 5.—Details of Corner of Kennel at Bottom of Upright.
To show sizes of various parts at front and side.

house, and are allowed to overlap 2½ inches at each end. Care should be taken that they are cut square, and they should be nailed on from the bottom. The last two boards at the top should be cut at an angle so that they fit. Six-inch planed weather boards should be used and the rebated part cut off and the edges planed off the two lower bottom boards.

To make capping for the top, nail a piece of ¾ by 3½ inches to a piece of ¾ by 3 inches and attach to the roof as shown in Fig. 10.

SECTIONAL TYPE KENNEL

A kennel of the same or larger dimensions can be easily made in sections. Make the two sides separately (see Fig. 11). Bolt the side framework to the two end sections as shown in Fig. 12. The roof section should be bolted to the front and back roof struts before nailing on the roof boards (see Fig. 12.)

If the house has been made correctly, the floor will fit. It will rest upon the 1½ by 1½-inch stretchers which go into the outside uprights of the front and end sections. Should the house be made in sections, add another 1 inch for the additional uprights for the side sections. The floor should be flush with the top of the 1½ by 1½-inch in the lower part of the front and end sections.

The boards on all sides should extend 1½ inches higher than those of a permanent house. Four pieces of 1½ by 1½ inches are needed to go from front to back. Four 1½ by 1½-inch recesses are cut in the board extension on the front and back of the house. The recesses are cut on an angle, so the 1½ by 1½ inches rests on the top struts at the two ends. The purlins should extend 2½ inches at each end. The best way to cut the recesses is to mark them on a 3-inch board, then to use this for marking out each section. Cut downwards with a rip saw, and across with a pad saw to cut them out.

MAKING A DOG'S KENNEL

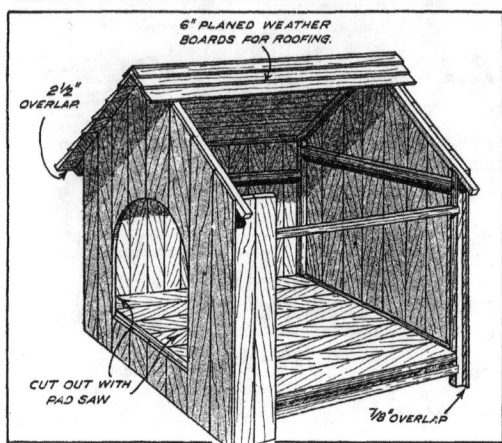

Fig. 9.—Construction of "Permanent" Kennel.

Framework is covered with boards on roof and sides.

The pitch of the roof may be sufficiently steep to allow good tongued and grooved boards to make a weather-proof roof. If not, either cover the boards with roofing felt, nailing this at the edges of the boards every 2 inches, or use weather boards.

For a Large Dog.

If the house is for a large dog, the sizes of the timbers should be increased from 1½ by 1½ inches to 2 by 2 inches.

The tongued and grooved flooring, 1 by 5½ inches, will be stout enough for the large house. It is not necessary to have heavy framing for a small dog's kennel.

A SMALL KENNEL

The Floor.

Cut the floor from ¾-inch tongued and grooved flooring, for a 2 feet 6 inches by 3 feet house, or the size required. Take off the tongue of the outside piece with a plane, then nail them to two pieces of 2 by 2 inches, one at each end. The 2 by 2 inches will act as a support for the house.

Ends.

Make the end sections out of ¾ by 5-inch tongued and grooved flooring. Seven boards are required for each end. Cut these 2 feet by 9 inches, then nail them to three pieces of 1 by 2 inches. One piece at the bottom 3½ inches from the edge, only nail the two outside boards, the next piece 1 foot 10 inches from the bottom, and a short one to cover three boards in the centre at the top (see Fig. 14).

Cut off at the two lower pieces ⅝ inch from each edge. Two sections should be made to this size.

Mark one piece for the opening for the dog, cut the half round at the top with a pad saw, the lower part with the rip saw.

Measure to the eaves from the bottom of the 2-inch piece 1 foot 10 inches, and draw a line to the centre of the section from each side. Cut down the line with a saw.

Side Sections.

Make up the side sections as shown in Fig. 14.

The side sections are put against the floor and a nail driven into the 2 by 2-inch supports at each end. This is stood on end, and the end section is put on

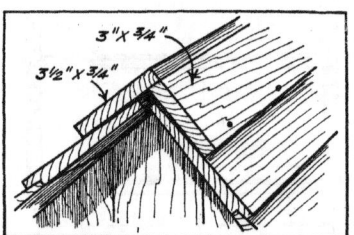

Fig. 10.—Arrangement of Capping for Roof.

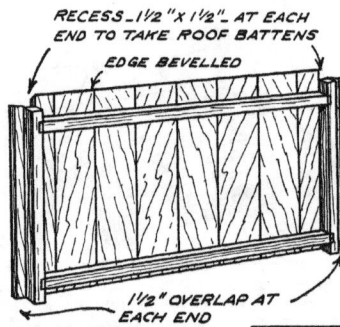

Fig. 11.—Construction of Side Section of Sectional Kennel.

the two side sections and lined up against the 1 by 2 inch pieces at the top and bottom. The end section is nailed to the side sections and the 2 by 2 inch which holds the floor together. The 1 by 2-inch strips should meet inside the house, and can be nailed.

The whole is turned carefully and the end section is nailed to the sides of the 2 by 2-inch support.

Roof.

The house is squared, and planed weather boards are cut to cover the top. Make them 5 inches longer than the house. Nail the two bottom ones so that the boards project 2 inches and make a capping to cover the joint at the top. Fig. 10 illustrates the arrangement of this capping.

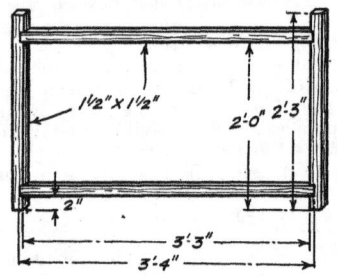

Fig. 13.—Side Section Framework of Sectional Kennel, Showing Dimensions.

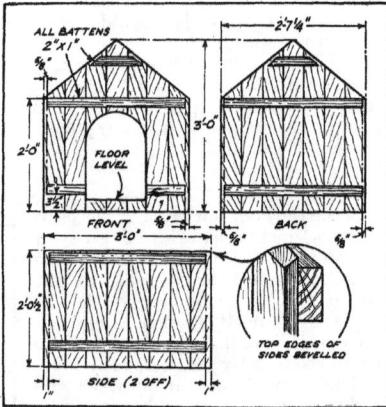

Fig. 14.—End and Side Sections of Small Kennel.

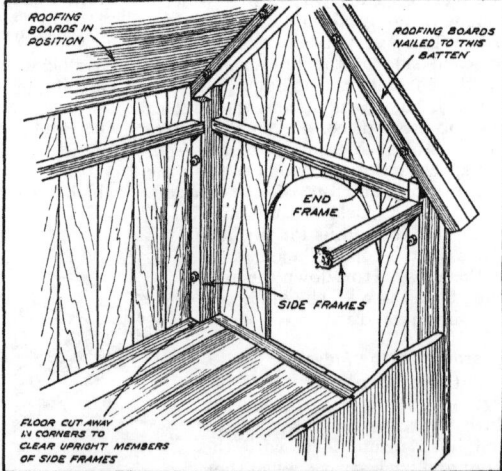

Fig. 12.—Construction of a Large Sectional Kennel.

Inexpensive Nursery Furnishing

If a spare room is available it is very desirable that children should have a playroom of their own, for they are then able to pursue their hobbies and pastimes without inconvenience. Everyone will be happier for this arrangement. The adults will enjoy comparative peace and quietness, and the children themselves will know that, within reason, they are free to express themselves in any way they like without having their precious "work" or amusements tidied up or perhaps even thrown away before it is finished with.

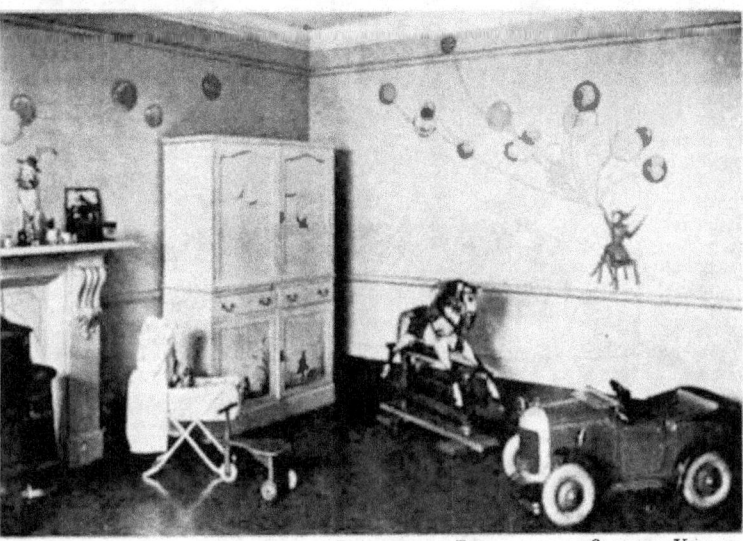

Fig. 1.—Painted in Every Colour of the Rainbow on a Background of Sunshine Yellow, the Walls of this Nursery have a Plain Dado which can be Redecorated at any Time without Touching the Upper Part of the Walls.

Combined Night-and-day Nursery.

If it is not convenient to spare a separate room as a day nursery, it should be possible to equip a combined night-and-day nursery, or one of the children's bedrooms can be furnished as a playroom for daytime use. Supposing, for example, there are two girls and a boy in the family, the boy's bedroom could be used as the playroom, and one of the best ways of doing this would be by installing one of the low modern divan-beds in one corner. The only other essential items of bedroom furniture are a wardrobe cupboard (probably there will be a built-in one beside the chimney-breast), and a chest of drawers and mirror.

Keep Main Floor Space as Clear as Possible.

The rest of the equipment should be quite simple, and it should be so arranged that the main floor space is kept as clear as possible. Open shelves should be fitted in a chimney-breast recess or along one side of the room; there should be a fall table or a workbench against one of the walls, and a capacious toy cupboard. There should also be a small table and small chairs and stools suited to the ages of the children and of a size to enable them to sit with their feet resting firmly on the floor.

No Need for Expensive Articles.

It is a mistake, however, to suppose that nursery equipment need necessarily be expensive or that the children's appreciation of their domain will bear any relation to the amount of money spent on it. Quite the reverse. Instead of an expensive divan-bed with a box mattress, for example, a wire mattress taken from an ordinary enamelled iron bedstead and raised about 9 inches from the floor on wooden blocks placed at each of the four corners will answer just as well. A bed of this kind should be draped with a cretonne bedspread reaching just to the floor, and it will then make an excellent playing couch by day as well as a bed.

Let the Children Furnish the Playroom Themselves.

As a matter of fact, children sometimes get an astonishing amount of satisfaction out of furnishing the playroom for themselves. Nowadays you can get excellent children's carpentry sets costing from 1s. upwards, and children can build their own chairs, stools and tables.

How to set about making Home-made Furniture.

Shallow whitewood boxes can be used for chair seats and table tops, lengths of wood being sawn up and nailed inside the boxes at each of the four corners to form the legs. Strips of wood can be nailed for the chair backs, and a tin of oak stain and a brush complete the work. Although the resulting furniture may be "rough and ready," the children will be extremely proud of it.

If, however, one prefers making some of the nursery furniture oneself, it is an extremely good education for the children if they are allowed to help with the work.

Another decidedly worth-while item is a home-made doll's house. The simplest of these need consist of no more than four or six boxes placed on their sides, each box being a room. Boys as well as girls will take an interest in a doll's house of this kind, for there are painting and staining to be done, the walls have to be papered from a wall-paper pattern book, and there is doll's furniture to be made from match boxes, cream cartons, cotton reels and bits of wood. Also, there is needlework in the shape of cushions, curtains and bedspreads to engross the girls. A home-made doll's house equipped in this way is infinitely more fascinating than a bought one, where everything is perfect to begin with. Full details for making a doll's house are given on p. 304.

Other Equipment for a Nursery.

In addition to the furniture already mentioned, the nursery should include a blackboard and a panel of compo board or compressed cork. The former will be useful if lessons are given at home and can also be used by the children themselves for writing and drawing. It may either stand on an easel or be treated as a wall fixture. The panel of compressed cork or compo board (an ordinary cork bath mat costing a few shillings would be suitable) is to provide a surface on which the children may pin their own drawings, paintings or cut-outs. Children undoubtedly appreciate pictures as a wall decoration, but they prefer their pictures to be frequently changed, and the best course is to let them paint their own and display them on the cork panel.

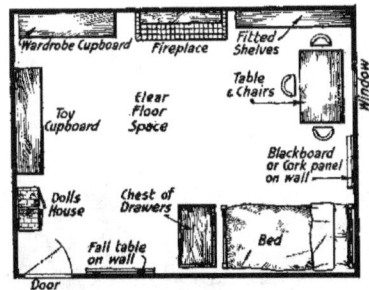

Fig. 2.—Plan of a Well-arranged Combined Night Nursery and Playroom.

INEXPENSIVE NURSERY FURNISHING

How to fix a Blackboard or Cork Panel.

The installation of either a blackboard or a cork panel as a permanent fixture on the wall is a troublesome process, but a similar effect can be obtained quite simply if the panel is fixed immediately above the skirting. First measure the height of the panel and then fix a strip of batten to the wall so that the batten lies along the top of the panel. Then, one has only to screw two wooden catches to the batten and two more to the top of the skirting and the blackboard or cork panel will be held securely in position. Upright battens may be fixed at either side in order to frame the panel all round if desired, but this is not essential.

The advantage of this method, however, is that the panel can be fixed in position or taken down again with the greatest ease, and as cork is liable to crumble after a certain amount of use, this is a rather important point. Also, both sides of the blackboard can be used.

A Good Arrangement.

A plan of a well-equipped combined night nursery and playroom is given in Fig. 2, and it will be seen that the table and chairs stand at the window with built-in shelves for toys, etc., close at hand. The bed is in another corner of the room, the built-in wardrobe occupies a recess, and the chest of drawers and toy cupboards are close against the walls. This leaves the main floor space clear.

Floor Covering.

The ideal floor covering is rubber, for it deadens sound and is warm to the touch, but a good quality linoleum is probably the best alternative. It is important to keep the floor as clear as possible, for it is an instinct with small children to play many of their games and to look at the picture books, etc., prone on the floor, and this is better for them physically and less tiring than sitting in a chair.

Fig. 3.—A Divan Bed in a Corner of the Room is a Suggestion for a Combined Boy's Bedroom and Playroom.

Toy Cupboards.

The toy cupboards, too, are better with doors in the sides, either hinged or sliding to and fro, instead of lift-up lids, for they can then be used as low seats. All the furniture should be as low as possible, including the fitted shelves, for the children should arrange their toys and ornaments themselves, and not expect mother or nurse to keep the room tidy for them.

Decorative Schemes.

As children grow older it will be found that they take a surprising amount of pride and pleasure in their bedrooms if these are decorated and equipped with taste, yet here again very expensive or elaborate treatments are unnecessary. Whether for a boy

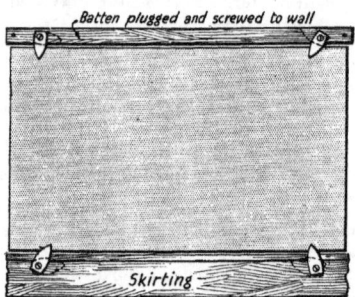

Fig. 4.—Simple Method of mixing Blackboard or Cork Panel to a Wall.

or girl, a bedroom with a very simple scheme is generally the best; and as a guiding principle it may be said that delicate blues and light shades of green and rose are suitable for a girl's room and stronger tones of brown, red and terracotta will definitely appeal to a boy.

Girl's Bedroom.

A bedroom suitable for a girl could have the walls and ceiling done in light apple-green water paint, and the woodwork and furniture in a slightly darker tone of green enamel, with mouldings picked out in delicate blue and pink.

The carpet could be a complementary shade of wine-red, and the curtains and bedspread could be apple green with an all-over printed design in blue and pink. In addition to the ordinary bedroom furniture, a small wall cabinet with glazed doors and shelves for little ornaments and trinkets is a detail which will appeal strongly to almost any girl.

Boy's Bedroom.

A boy's bedroom might have a pale blue ceiling, and the walls papered in grey, terra-cotta, orange and blue. The woodwork and furniture could be painted dove grey with lines of Indian red, and instead of the hanging wall cabinet there should be a simple bookshelf fitment on the wall at the head of the bed. This would make a handsome bedroom without seeming feminine and you will find that brother and sister will both be the happier for this subtle difference. The bookshelves and the wall cabinet are both items which could easily be made at home, and as a general rule it will be found that almost all children will be quick to appreciate taste and attractiveness in their surroundings, and will respond by being surprisingly careful of the furniture and decorations. It is important, however, to plan the children's rooms for practical use, and if the decorations and equipment are on the right lines, you can be quite sure that nothing will go unnoticed, unappreciated or *unused*.

STOPPING A LEAKING CAN

WHEN a watering-can leaks badly at the bottom the following is a very good way of effecting a repair: Cut a piece of sacking, or similar material, which is very slightly larger than the inside of the can. Put this in position, spreading it well out. Now prepare a somewhat liquid solution of cement and water and, after standing the can

on level ground, pour in the mixture to the depth of about a ½ inch or a little more. Leave the can quite still until the cement sets, and it may then be used. In this way a can with a bottom having several holes in it may be made serviceable and the thin layer of cement makes small difference to the weight.

Securing Manhole Covers Against Leakage

Ordinary Covers.

THE ordinary manhole covers of cast iron have a section as shown in Fig. 1. The groove is supposed to be filled with grease or tallow to prevent drain gases escaping, but this detail is often omitted. Another advantage of the grease filling is that it prevents the cover from rusting and becoming so fixed to the frame that it is difficult to remove. When a cover is removed for any purpose, the channel should be recharged with grease. Ordinary stiff motor grease serves the purpose. If the tongue on the cover is a very loose fit to the channel of the frame, or the cover is inclined to kick to traffic over it, a piece of asbestos cord may be buried in the pit of the channel with advantage.

Double Seal Covers.

In positions where the possible escape of drain air would not be quickly diffused, as, for instance, under a porch, in a lobby or covered gateway, a double seal type is recommended. One form has a double channel to the frame and a double tongue around the frame, as shown in Fig. 2.

Condensation Channel.

Another form has what is known as a condensation channel forming the second seal, as indicated in Fig. 3. The warm drain air condenses on the underside cover of this, and trickles down to keep the channel full of water. The top channel is filled with grease and asbestos cord in the ordinary way.

Hollow Sound produced by Traffic.

The hollow sound produced by traffic over a manhole is often objected to. This can be avoided by obtaining an inset cover, as indicated by Fig. 4. The well is filled with paving material to match the surrounding pavement. The one objection to this type is the increased weight of the cover, which makes it somewhat difficult to raise. Inset hinged rings, however, are provided, so that the rings can be lifted up and a bar threaded through them to give power to the lift.

Another Type.

Another form has a light cover close down to the bottom of the manhole provided with a condensation groove to keep it sealed. This is a very good type, as it avoids the large pockets of drain, or sewer-gas the ordinary manhole, with top cover, entails. This type is indicated in Fig. 5. The frame is usually built in during the construction of the manhole, but by obtaining a frame size which would go inside the existing manhole it could be cemented in as indicated. With this form it is not so imperative that the top cover should be air tight unless in a covered gateway, etc.

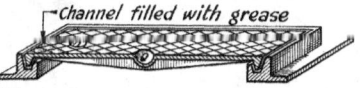

Fig. 1.—Section of Single Seal Manhole Cover.

Fig. 2.—Section of Double Seal Cover.

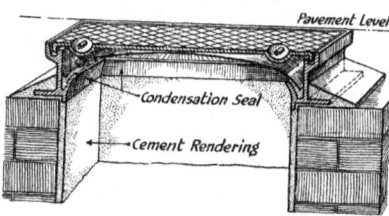

Fig. 3.—Another Form of Cover has a Condensation Channel forming a Second Seal.

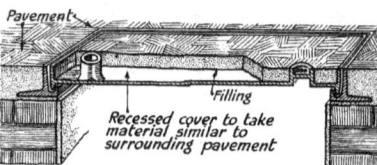

Fig. 4.—Method of preventing the Hollow Sound produced by Traffic.

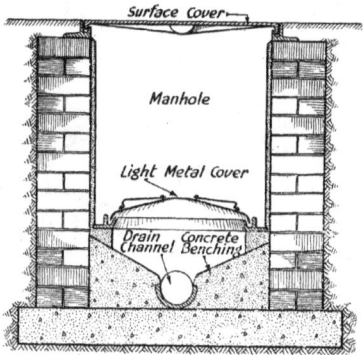

Fig. 5.—Manhole with Light Metal Cover close down to the Bottom.

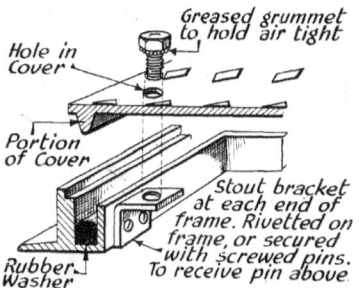

Fig. 6.—How an Ordinary Cover can be converted to the Locking Type.

Manhole over an Indoor Cistern.

Occasionally a manhole cover exists in old buildings over a cistern built within the building. Owing to floor washings the channel can become very offensive. In such cases a pitch filling can be used. The channel must be made perfectly clean and dry and warmed by means of a powerful blow-lamp flame traced round the frame. The cover should also be warmed either with the blow-lamp or by placing it over a garden cresset. When everything is dry and warm, the channel should be filled with molten pitch and the cover gently lowered into place. When cool, the surplus pitch should be chiselled off flush with the cover face.

Locking Type Manhole Cover.

For manholes to which frequent access is required, a locking type cover can be obtained, the bottom of the channel being fitted with a felt pad soaked in grease, or, alternatively, a rubber band can be used. The locking device is so arranged that by means of a key the cover can be screwed down so that the tongue is pressed close on to the packing in the channel to make a perfectly gas- and water-tight joint.

Converting an Ordinary Type to Locking Type Cover.

The ordinary cover can be converted to this type to gain the same effect by improvised means. Figs. 6 and 7 illustrate such a method. Two stout angle brackets from $2 \times \frac{1}{2}$-inch bar iron must be rivetted to the frame or secured each with two stout set pins. To avoid risk of accident, the work should not be attempted overhand. A ladder should be placed in the cistern. The angle brackets must be tapped to take $\frac{1}{2}$-inch screwed set pins. The cover must be drilled exactly over the holes in the brackets at either end.

How to get the Holes correctly placed.

The most sure way of getting the holes correctly placed would be by the aid of an assistant to mark the cover from underneath, scribing through the holes in the brackets. A rubber bed should be fixed in the pit of the channel. The size or section of this will depend upon the amount of play in the channel between the pit and the edge of the tongue on the cover. This varies considerably by different makers. For small channels a piece of $\frac{3}{8}$-inch rubber gas tube may serve, or even a strip of inner tube from an old motor tyre.

Securing Pins.

The securing pins should preferably be of bronze to prevent them "rusting-in." If the hexagonal head is objected to, on account of risk of tripping over, a mushroom head type could be used.

A slot must be sawn in it with a hacksaw, so that it can be screwed down with a large screwdriver. The purpose made type has a recess in the cover, and the pin is turned by means of a special key. If the tongue of the cover is covered with black-lead, it will prevent it from sticking to the rubber and breaking it up when the cover has to be removed.

A warning note may be advisable

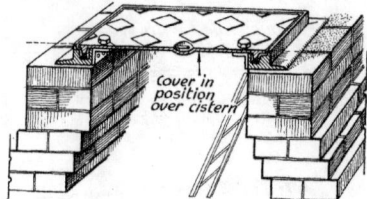

Fig. 7.—Showing the Cover in Position over Cistern.

here against working with a flexible electric lead for lighting purposes when standing in damp places or in water. The same remark applies to working at a storage tank in the roof, as there is risk of the current shorting through the body under such circumstances if there is a fault in the flex or lampholder and it happens to be touched—a situation which may very well end in a fatality.

CUTTING A HOLE THROUGH A WOOD OR METAL ROOF

Soil pipes and round metal chimney pipes have often to be taken through the roofs of wood, corrugated metal or asbestos buildings.

Tools required.

In order to do the work neatly and efficiently, these tools should be at hand : Bevel, chalk line, or a piece of suitable string, jack plane, try square, marking awl, compasses, brace and a small bit, rasp and a piece of three-ply of suitable size on which to set out the template. In the case of metal or asbestos roofs, a pad saw, for metal, wheel brace, morse drill of suitable size and a half-round file of medium size will be required.

How to find the True Shape of the Hole.

The method of finding the true shape of the hole that has to be cut in the roof is as follows :—

First ascertain the pitch of the roof as shown by Fig. 1. Then take the piece of three-ply and plane one edge true and square.

An Example.

Supposing that the pipe being used is 4 inches in diameter, as shown by Fig. 2. First gauge the line AB on the three-ply, then with the try-square and marking awl mark the centre line CD and strike the half-circle with the compasses. Now draw the line AF to the pitch of the roof as obtained by the bevel, then divide the diameter of the circle into eight equal parts, and from the points of the divisions thus obtained strike the vertical lines so that they touch the line AF. From the points where they touch, draw the lines G, H, I, J, K, L, M, at right angles to the line AF.

Now the lengths of these lines should be marked off with the compasses to the lengths of the ordinates in the semi-circle. The line M, for example, should be as long as the line M in the semi-circle, and so on.

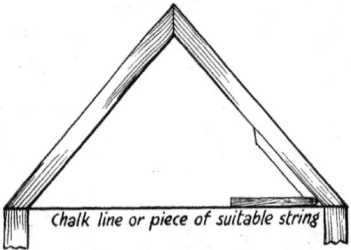

Fig. 1.—Showing how the Pitch of the Roof may be obtained.

The chalk line or a piece of suitable string is stretched tightly across the base of the rafters. Two nails, driven temporarily into position, will secure the line. The bevel is then set to the pitch.

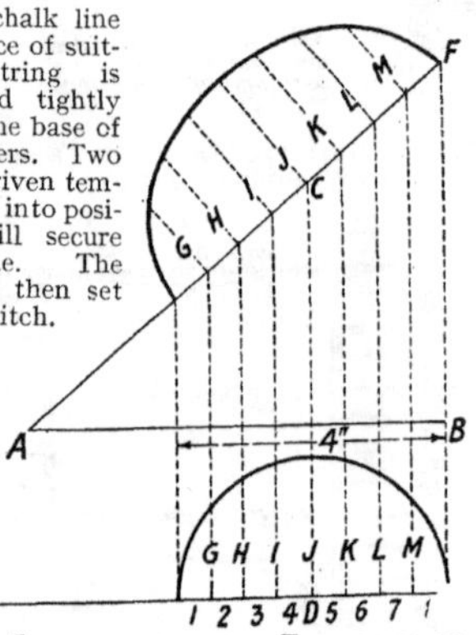

Fig. 2.—Showing how the Ellipse is set out.

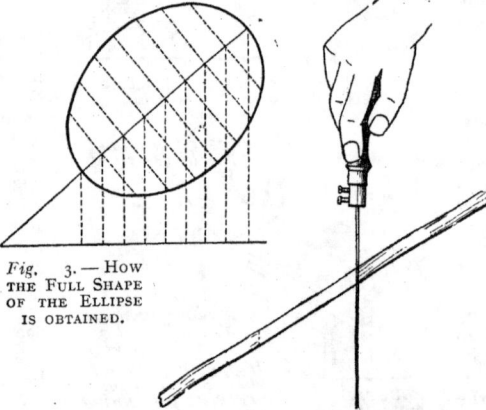

Fig. 3.—How the Full Shape of the Ellipse is obtained.

Fig. 4.—How the Pad Saw should be Held Vertical in Every Position while Sawing out the Hole.

Drawing in the Curve.

When the lines have been marked off in this manner, the points obtained should be joined together by a freehand line to produce the elliptical curve that gives the true shape of one half of the hole to be cut in the roof.

The full shape is, of course, obtained by simply extending the ordinates and marking off the other half, as shown by Fig. 3.

This ellipse should now be cut out with the pad saw and trimmed up to the line with the rasp. Then place it in the required position on the roof and mark off the shape of the hole.

The setting out of this ellipse could be done on the drawing board and a three-ply template marked off from the drawing.

Wooden Roofs.

In the case of wooden roofs, the hole may be cut with the pad saw, a hole being first bored with the brace and bit to make a starting place for the saw. Care should be taken to keep the saw vertical at all positions when sawing out the hole, as shown by Fig. 4. Any adjustments that are found to be necessary to the hole afterwards may be made with the round face of the rasp.

Metal or Asbestos Roofs.

When the roofs are made of metal or asbestos, the pad saw for metal is used and a starting place made with the morse drill fixed in the wheel brace, and any necessary adjustments made with the round face of the file.

Making a Saw for Metal and Asbestos Roofs.

An excellent saw for metal and asbestos roofs may be made from an ordinary hacksaw blade by binding one end with insulation tape to form a handle.

When using this improvised saw, first make a starting place, in the same way as described for the pad saw.

How to Repair a Settee

A SETTEE that has been in use for many years can be renovated quite easily without the use of any special tools. The following article deals with fitting new springs and webbing, and substituting a boxed front in place of a sprung edge. It is often possible to buy a second-hand settee in need of repair, very cheaply, at an auction sale, and a little attention may make it into a first-class piece of furniture.

Fig. 1.—First remove the Old Canvas and Webbing.
Note the method of driving out the tacks by placing an old screwdriver against the head and giving it a sharp blow with a hammer.

Tools and Materials required.

The only tools apart from such things as a hammer, screwdriver, etc., are a "web-strainer" and an upholsterer's needle. A special "web-strainer" can be bought if desired, but a block of hardwood, about 6 × 3 × 1 inches, will serve the purpose quite well. The best type of needle is one known as a "spring needle," but, failing this, an ordinary packing needle will do.

Some webbing will be required and some canvas or hessian, which is usually sold in rolls 6 feet wide, and can be purchased at any large drapery store. Proper upholsterer's twine should be obtained; this has the advantage of being very strong without being too thick. The tacks to use are those known as "improved," and the most suitable lengths are ⅜ inch and ½ inch. Some gimp pins will be required for attaching the gimp, and some nails, known as "covered studs" for "banding."

Obtaining New Springs.

If any springs are found to need replacing, it is best to take one of the old ones to the shop when ordering the new one. It will be necessary to allow for the compression which has taken place in the length of the old springs.

First Remove Old Canvas and Webbing.

The first operation is to remove the old canvas and webbing. As a good deal of dirt, etc., may fall out, it is a good idea to cover the floor with a piece of old sheet, unless the work is being done in a room laid with linoleum. When the settee has been turned upside down, place a chair to support it as shown in Fig. 1.

How to Remove the Tacks.

The tacks holding the canvas and webbing should be driven out by placing an old screwdriver against the head and giving it a sharp blow with a hammer, driving along the grain of the wood and not against it, so as not to split it. The canvas will probably be torn or worn out, but if not, it can, of course, be used again. It is a good idea while removing the webbing to release the outside material of the chair, so that it can be turned back from the wooden frame for easier access to the canvas, and for fixing the new webbing.

Removing Webbing from Springs.

The webbing is detached from the springs by cutting the twine at all points where it is fixed.

Dealing with the Front Edge.

At this stage the settee should be turned back to its normal position for attention to the front. In some cases it will be found that the front edge is already a solid one, in that case all that will be necessary is to remove the canvas roll at the top edge so that the stuffing can be loosened and replaced as evenly as possible.

What to do if Front is Sprung.

If, however, it is found that it has a sprung edge, then the best treatment is to replace it by a wooden framework. The sprung edge will probably have become very slack, and it would be a difficult job to re-spring it.

The old springs should be removed and a framework of wood about 2 × 2 inches erected. Fig. 2 shows the appearance of the finished framework. To lessen the risk of loosening any joints when nailing on the framework, a heavy object, such as a flat-iron, should be held against it so as to take the force of the blows. If any joints should be loosened or be found to be weak, a spot of glue should be applied.

The next thing is to tack on a strip of canvas for the roll on the top of the wooden framing.

How to Cut Canvas Straight.

A useful hint to enable the canvas to be cut in neat, parallel strips, is to nick the edge of the canvas with scissors and pull out a single thread, so that a line is left which will form a guide for cutting.

Putting in the Stuffing.

To help putting in the stuffing, a length of twine should be loosely tacked close to the edge of the canvas. Twist the stuffing material in and around this, working it evenly around and along the string. Then turn the canvas back over the stuffing and tack it as shown in Fig. 4. You will now have the framework completed and a roll of stuffing on top of it.

Removing Old Springs.

Now turn the settee upside down again and remove any faulty springs by cutting the string which holds them in place to the canvas seat.

Replacing Springs.

The main point to bear in mind when replacing a spring is that it must be securely fixed to both the canvas and adjacent springs.

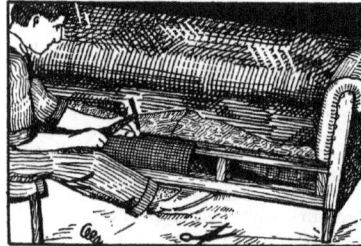

Fig. 2.—Showing the Wooden Framework which takes the Place of a Sprung Edge.
A strip of canvas is being tacked on for the roll on the top of the framing.

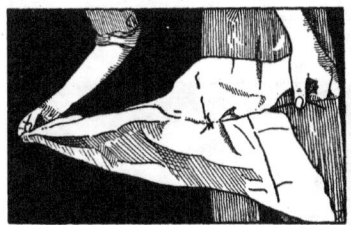

Fig. 3.—How to cut a Straight Strip of Canvas.
Nick the edge of the canvas with scissors and pull out a single thread, thus leaving a line to act as a guide when cutting.

Fig. 4.—Forming the Roll on the Outside Edge.
Note the piece of string tacked alongside the canvas. The stuffing is twisted evenly around it before turning back the canvas.

HOW TO REPAIR A SETTEE

Fix the new springs as closely as possible to the positions occupied by the old ones and stitch securely to the canvas, using the spring needle and twine. Observing the method of stitching employed for fixing the old springs in position, repeat as close as possible. It is absolutely essential that each spring must be lashed as firmly as possible in as upright a position as possible.

Fixing the New Webbing.

The purpose of the webbing is to act as a support for the springs and is strained over the frame exactly over the place where the springs come. It is false economy to use an inferior quality webbing, and allow plenty of surplus for doubling the ends where tacked.

It is not advisable to attempt to fix the webbing in position while pressing on the springs. A simpler plan is to fix the webbing straight and then to slip the springs into position afterwards.

How to Start.

First of all double back one end of the webbing and secure it to one side of the settee with at least four ½-inch tacks, placing it so that when carried across to the other side of the settee it will come over a row of springs.

Next clamp the webbing one turn lengthwise round the wooden block (see Fig. 5) and prise the forward end of the block against the wooden frame. Then press down upon the block so that the webbing is strained as much as possible, and secure it to the frame by three tacks. Remove the wooden block and cut off the webbing, allowing sufficient for 1 inch to be doubled back and secured by two further tacks.

How to tell whether Webbing is Taut enough.

If the webbing has been stretched sufficiently taut, it should give out a comparatively high note when struck and not merely a dull thud.

Continue to fix the remainder of the webbing in place, and do not forget that the cross webbing should be interlaced.

Using the Special Tool for Stretching Webbing.

If the special "web-strainer" is available, the webbing is simply threaded through the tool, and the handle pulled over backwards.

When either of the above methods is used, there is no need to cut off each length of webbing before it is stretched and tacked, so that no webbing is wasted.

What to do if Old Webbing is Used Again.

If it is desired to make use of the old webbing again, the difficulty is

Fig. 5.—Using a Block of Wood to Stretch the Webbing Tight before Tacking.

Fig. 6.—Using the Special Webbing Tool.

Fig. 7.—If the Old Webbing is Used Again, a Pair of Web-pliers will be Needed to Stretch the Webbing.

Fig. 8.—Stitching the Springs in Position.

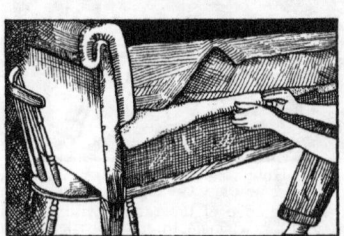

Fig. 9.—Completing the Work.

that the ends are too short to allow it to be strained by the methods described. In this case, the only satisfactory method is to use a special tool called web-pliers.

Stitching the Springs in Position.

Having got all the webbing properly fixed, slip the springs into their correct positions. Each spring must now be fixed to the webbing with twine, and secured the correct distance from adjacent springs.

As far as possible use one long length of twine for the whole job, so as to ensure maximum strength. If it is found necessary to use more than one length, the ends should be tied together. Fig. 8 shows the method of stitching.

Replacing Outside Material.

The settee can now be turned the right way up again and attention given to replacing the outside material. This work is made easier by supporting the settee on chairs placed at each end. Stretch and tack the canvas lining to the framework, and use any surplus stuffing left over when the sprung edge was replaced by a wooden framework by rolling it evenly over the rolled edge as shown in Fig. 9. Then pull down the outside material and tack it underneath the frame, before replacing the under canvas.

How to Hide the Edges of the Cover.

The edges of the cover should be hidden by "banding" or "gimp" which is tacked on. Use "banding" if the settee is of leather, rexine, American cloth or similar material, and "gimp" if of damask, tapestry or similar ornate covering. Brass-headed nails can be used with almost any furniture covering, although it is preferable to use the special gimp pins for fixing the "gimp," and studs for fixing "banding." These studs are tacks covered with similar material to the banding itself and should be obtained at the same time as the banding is obtained so that a perfect match is obtained.

Space the Studs Correctly.

Take care to space the studs an equal distance apart. It is a good idea to use a pair of dividers to prick out the position where each stud should come.

Although only a minor point, attention to details such as the correct spacing of the studs makes all the difference to the job looking really first-class when finished, so that it presents a pleasing appearance as well as being comfortable in use.

For details of repairs to framework of chairs, settees and other pieces of furniture, readers are referred to the article which begins on p. 69.

Screening a Radiator

In addition to open coal fireplaces, one or two hot-water radiators are frequently provided nowadays in the principal living-rooms and bedrooms of new houses. These radiators are a sound economy, in that they help to keep down the coal bill, and if they are placed beneath windows, or as far away from the fireplaces as possible, they enable the house to be warmed much more equably than would otherwise be possible.

Suitable Treatment for a Simply Decorated Interior.

There is frequently a difficulty, however, in deciding whether or not the radiator should be screened from view, and if so, exactly what form the screen should take. In a very simply decorated interior there may be no need to hide the radiator, but it should then be given as smart an appearance as possible. A panel of plywood should be fixed to the wall behind it to form a surround, and both plywood and radiator should then be finished with silver or bronze cellulose lacquer, according to the colour scheme of the room. This very simple treatment will give the radiator a surprisingly handsome appearance, and it has a practical advantage in that the radiator is always accessible, whether for adjusting the regulating valve or for dusting and cleaning.

Treatment in Elaborately Furnished Rooms.

In more elaborately furnished rooms,

Fig. 1.—A Radiator beneath a Window, concealed by a Slatted Fitment in Walnut and Steel, continuous with a Built-in Cabinet and Bookshelves.

however, it is often felt that the radiator is definitely unsightly and that some form of screen or grille which will hide it from view without interfering with its efficiency is desirable. The simplest radiator to conceal is one standing in a recess, or beneath a bay window, and whenever a radiator occupies a position of this kind, an effective and easily arranged form of concealment is a beadwork curtain.

Beadwork Curtain.

The curtain could be hung from the front of a shelf fitted 5 or 6 inches above the top of the radiator, and the shelf itself could be used for ornaments such as choice china figures. The advantage of a beadwork curtain is that it is a form of concealment which does not interfere with circulation of air, and it leaves the radiator thoroughly accessible. Alternatively, the curtain could be of casement cloth or cretonne, but in many respects beadwork would be better.

Wooden Covering.

If, however, a wooden covering is preferred, it is essential that this should be slatted to ensure adequate ventilation, or the heating power of the radiator will be materially reduced. If possible, the regulating valve should be outside the fitment, so that the radiator may be turned on and off with the minimum of trouble, but in any event the casing should be removable, for unless wiped over regularly a surprising amount of dust and dirt will be accumulated on the radiator.

A Simple Type of Screen.

A simple type of screen could be made with 4-inch battens of well-seasoned deal nailed horizontally to a panel constructed to fit the recess occupied by the radiator and held in position with catch fasteners. The screen could be finished in either paint or cellulose, or stained to match the woodwork of the room, and in cases

Fig. 2.—A Bead Curtain is an Effective Screen for a Radiator beneath a Bay Window.

Fig. 3.—A Slatted Casing is a treatment which gives a Radiator the appearance of a Closed Stove.

Fig. 4.—The Screen should be removable so that the Valve can be adjusted and the Radiator cleaned.

where the recess is big enough, one or two built-in bookshelves can also sometimes be included as part of the same fitment.

Giving the Appearance of an Enclosed Stove.

If the radiator stands against a wall and is not set in a recess, a satisfactory effect can be obtained if a screen of deal or plywood is built out from the wall to give the appearance of an enclosed stove. The front may be slatted, or, as an alternative, fitted with an iron or steel grille, and the simplest way of getting at the interior in this instance will be by means of a removable covering for the top. Or the front could be hinged at one side and fitted with a catch fastener.

In elaborate furnishing schemes one often sees highly decorative radiator screens made of wrought iron, stainless steel, or handsomely figured plywood, but a screen on simpler and less expensive lines can be fully as decorative in its way and every bit as efficient.

Fig. 5.—IF THERE IS NO ATTEMPT AT CONCEALMENT A PANEL OF PLYWOOD SHOULD BE FIXED TO THE WALL AS A SURROUND.

The plywood and radiator should be finished in silver or bronze cellulose lacquer.

The main points to bear in mind are that adequate circulation of air must be allowed for and it must be easy to get at the radiator when needed. If dust and dirt are allowed to accumulate on the radiator its heating efficiency will be impaired and the atmosphere of the room will be affected, and this, of course, is quite apart from considerations of general cleanliness or the possible future need of repairs. A well-designed radiator screen can, however, make an enormous difference to the appearance of almost any room, and is therefore well worth the thought, time and trouble spent on it.

The parts of the home where radiators are particularly desirable are the principal bedroom and the entrance hall. The radiator in the entrance hall is, as a rule, most particularly in need of screening. A good position for a radiator is beneath a window, so that it will warm the fresh air as it enters the room.

HOW TO SET PRECIOUS STONES

The Collar Mount.

A SMOOTH stone, as shown at A in Fig. 1, is suitable for setting in a collar mount. It is placed on a piece of paper and an outline made in pencil, as at B. A band of silver, measuring approximately $\frac{3}{16}$ inch wide, is now cut out and bent to fit exactly the outside of the shape, as at C. If necessary, the band should be placed on a length of steel rod or on the end of a small brick iron and tapped with a hammer to enlarge it. The joint is then soldered up, as shown at D. A length of wire is now bent to the inside shape, as indicated at E, and then, with the band bound securely with iron binding wire, the wire should be soldered in position. The stone will now rest on the piece of wire, as indicated in the section at F.

The work is now cleaned up and polished in readiness for fitting in the stone, the latter operation being carried out with a bent steel burnisher or some similar hard surface by gradual pressure (Fig. 2).

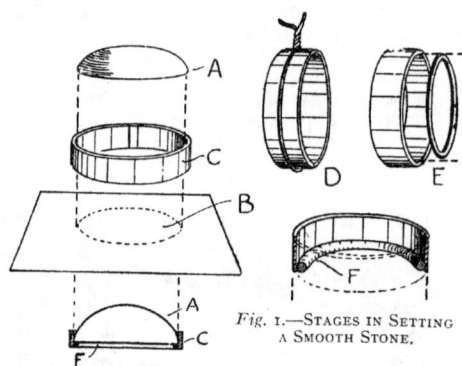

Fig. 1.—STAGES IN SETTING A SMOOTH STONE.

Claw Settings for Stones.

Claw setting for stones can be made similarly to the collet setting shown

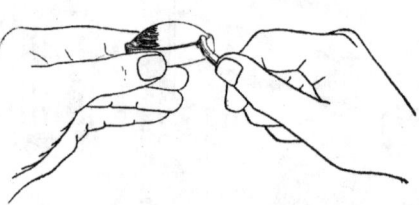

Fig. 2.—FITTING STONE IN ITS SETTING.

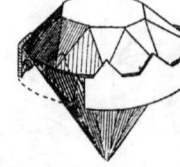

Fig. 3.—A CLAW SETTING FOR FACETED STONE.

here, the claws being formed by filing the upper edges of the band to form projections which are bent over to clip the stone. Fig. 3 illustrates the method, and, if care is taken to make the band to the exact diameter of the cut stone, the claws will hold it quite securely if they are pressed closely to the upper surface.

Many beautiful stones, quite inexpensive, may be obtained; of those suitable to use with silver, the green-blue turquoise, the pale yellow topaz, and the green chrysoprase are admirable, while such effective blue stones as moonstones and Amazon are quite inexpensive. Nearly all the precious stones may be obtained in imitation, but there are so many genuine stones, not usually seen in the jewellers' shops, that there is no need to use substitutes in any form. The faceted stone is usually mounted in a claw setting. Most of the above stones can be obtained cut in various forms.

How to Know Old Prints

PRACTICALLY every print that may be classed as "old" will fall into one of the groups given below. By "old," we mean that it dates back more than fifty years.

If you have a print that you wish to identify, look all over it carefully with a reading-glass and note how the lines or masses of ink are formed. Then study the following headings and see which of them applies to your particular picture.

The value of a print is based on very arbitrary conditions. Some that are 300 years old can be bought for a few pence; others made in our lifetime are worth almost as many pounds. Size hardly counts and no one process makes for rarity more than any other. The subject and the artist are the chief determining factors. Just now, sporting subjects, including hunting and coaching scenes, are perhaps the greatest favourites.

WOOD-ENGRAVINGS
How made.

First, the picture is drawn in a reverse sense on a smooth-faced piece of wood and then the engraver cuts out deep recesses in the wood where he wants the picture to be perfectly plain and white. Next the printer dabs a thick, greasy ink on the face of the block in such a way that the whole of the original surface is covered. After that the paper is brought into contact with the block, and because the paper lies flat on it, and also because the ink does not run into the recesses, the picture is printed. Thus the parts that are not cut away provide the black areas of the picture and the parts that are cut away supply the white areas.

How recognised.

It will be seen from this that a wood block takes a considerable time to cut, as every line adds to the labours of the engraver. Consequently, early prints omitted every portion of the detail that was not absolutely necessary, and it was only when cutting-tools of a very efficient character were produced that wood-engravings, with a multiplicity of lines, were possible. Another clue to identity is the fact that every portion of a picture was black or it was white—there could be no half-tones (Fig. 2).

Allied Process.

Here must be mentioned Chiaroscuro printing. In this case several blocks were cut to provide the same picture. Their mission was to supply wood-engravings that were made up of not only black and white lines but intermediate grey ones as well. This was made possible by using inks of different intensity for different blocks and printing from the blocks under different pressures. A picture printed by this process can usually be detected by carefully examining the corners and edges and noting that the impressions were seldom superimposed exactly one over the other.

Fig. 1.—A LINE-ENGRAVING.
Distinguished from wood-engraving by lines being very close together and much freer.

Fig. 2.—A WOOD-ENGRAVING.
There is no gradation of tone in a wood-engraving. Every portion of the picture is either black or white.

LINE-ENGRAVINGS
How made.

A smooth sheet of metal is taken, and the picture is drawn on it in a reverse sense. Then the engraver digs out the lines with the aid of a pointed tool, known as a graver. In doing this he ploughs up the edges of the channels, and these are removed by means of a scraper. Thus the sheet of metal feels perfectly smooth when a hand is passed over it, but it bears a multitude of fine recessed lines. Following this, the printer smears the plate with ink, then wipes it. All the ink is thus removed except that which is held in the recessed lines. Next he brings a sheet of damped paper in contact with the plate and the picture is printed.

It will be seen that this process is the exact opposite of wood-engraving. In the latter the black areas are produced by the highest levels of the block; while in line-engraving they are caused by the recessed parts.

The metal used for line-engravings was at first copper. Later on steel was employed because it wore out slower, and therefore more impressions could be taken from a plate.

How recognised.

If the lines forming the picture are carefully examined, they will be found to be much freer and less stiff than those seen in wood-engravings. This is because it is easier or quicker to scratch a plate of metal than to cut a block of wood. In addition, it will be found that dark patches of the picture are seldom formed by solid masses of ink because large recesses will not hold the ink. Such areas are suggested by placing the lines very close together. Note also that if the hand is passed over a line-engraving the ink will be felt standing up above the level of the paper.

Allied Process.

Here may be mentioned the Dry Point process, which much resembles ordinary line-engraving. The chief difference is that when the engraver forms the lines the tool is so handled that the edges of the channels are thrown up to a considerable extent. Thus they are provided with a burr on either side. This burr modifies the lines in printing and gives them a characteristic soft appearance.

ETCHINGS
How made.

A smooth plate of copper is given a thin coat of a protecting material, such as a mixture of asphalt, beeswax and pitch. This is put on when hot. As soon as it has become cold and hard, the engraver takes a needle-pointed instrument and with it scratches through the protective covering, thus baring certain portions of the copper. He aims at uncovering the copper wherever he wishes the lines of his picture to be ultimately printed. Then he pours an acid on to the plate and this eats into the copper where it has been bared; but the asphalt mixture protects the other parts.

It will be recognised that by covering up certain of the lines when they have been subjected to the influence of the acid for a considerable while, it is possible to obtain at will fine or heavy lines as well as others of an intermediate strength.

The printing exactly follows the method described for line-engravings.

How recognised.

Etchings may be recognized by the full gradation of lines; they range from soft to hard, with a complete scale between these extremes. The fact that it is easier to scrape a channel in the asphalt covering than in a copper plate makes the lines provided by the former much less rigid than those produced by the latter process.

Fig. 3.—A Lithograph.
If the artist uses wood- or line-engraving forms for the lithograph, it is sometimes difficult to distinguish them.

STIPPLE ENGRAVINGS
How made.

This is a process exactly similar to ordinary etchings; but instead of the picture being suggested by the aid of lines, the etcher produces the required effect by a multitude of dots. These are closely crowded together where the dark parts of the picture occur and are widely separated in the lighter areas.

After the protective coat has been removed, it is usual for the etcher to improve his work by various other means. More often than not, he touches up the plate according to the methods set out for line-engraving. Thus a stipple print that has been considerably worked up by hand may be difficult to tell from a true line-engraving.

How recognised.

The dots form a clue to this process. Note that "stipple" was largely used for portrait work, and Bartolozzi did most of his pictures in it. The reproducers of Reynolds, Romney and Cosway also favoured it. Colour prints were produced in "stipple" by painting different coloured inks on to the block locally.

MEZZOTINT ENGRAVINGS
How made.

In this case a flat sheet of copper is taken and before any pictorial effect is attempted the whole surface is roughened by impressing it uniformly with millions of tiny dots. This is done by running a rocker-tool over the copper, up and down, side to side, and in every conceivable direction. The tool has a head provided with a number of pin-points, and it is these which make the dots on the copper.

When the whole surface has been roughened, the engraver proceeds to smooth down those areas where he wishes his picture to print white, and he partially smoothes the portions that are to give the intermediate tones. Thus he can get any tone required by regulating the amount of hand work. In addition, he may scratch lines after the manner of line-engraving and give his picture a highly finished appearance.

How recognised.

Mezzotints may be recognised by the soft gradation between one tone and the next, which gives the picture what is called a velvety appearance.

AQUATINTS
How made.

A flat plate of copper is given a very thin coating of resin. Then the artist covers those parts, which he wishes to print perfectly white, with a waterproof varnish. When this has dried,

Fig. 4.—An Etching.
Note the gradation of lines from soft to hard.

Fig. 5.—A Stipple Engraving.
A similar process to etching is employed, but the picture is made up of dots instead of lines.

the plate is flooded for a short while with an acid, which eats through the resin and makes an impression on the copper. The next step is to pour off the acid and cover up with waterproof varnish some of the parts that formerly were left uncovered. The plate is again flooded with acid and the process of alternately varnishing and flooding with acid is continued several times.

Thus it will be seen that a whole range of soft tones is obtained by allowing the acid to reach the copper for varying periods of time. When the acid process is finished, it is usual to do a certain amount of handwork on the plate by means of line-engraving.

How recognised.

There can be nothing harsh in the appearance of an aquatint. There are usually masses of soft gradation in the print which make it resemble a delicate water-colour drawing which has been done in various tones of the same colour. On close inspection, the masses are found to consist of very fine dots which are much finer than even those provided by the screen work of a half-tone block.

LITHOGRAPHS

How made.

There are many variations in the way a lithograph can be made; but, briefly, the process is as follows: A smooth stone is drawn on with a specially prepared ink that contains a soapy preparation. Then it is wetted and, while still in this condition, the entire surface is covered with printer's ink. This ink cannot adhere to the wet areas, and flows off; but it can gain a foothold on the parts which have received the lithographic ink and it sticks to them. Therefore when a sheet of paper is brought into contact with the stone, the picture is printed on to it.

A variation of the process is to execute the picture on special paper with lithographic ink and transfer it to the stone. This does away with the need for drawing the original picture in reverse.

Lithographs, it may be said, are readily produced in colour by using special stones, each of which is flooded with a different shade of printer's ink.

How recognised.

It is very difficult to recognise some lithographs with any degree of certainty, because the skill of the artist in drawing the original may take so many different forms. In the simplest cases a lithograph resembles a pen-and-ink sketch; but in a highly finished example the effect may approach that of line-engraving. Many of the coloured pictures which have not been done by the photographic process are lithographs. Those produced by photography can be identified, if examined under a magnifying glass. They are seen to consist of innumerable dots placed in regular formation.

USING UP OLD FELT HATS

Fig. 1.—Using up Old Felt Hats.
The flat portions, when cut to shape, make excellent socks for shoes.

Fig. 2.—Another Use.
Glued to the legs of chairs, pieces of felt will protect the floor.

Two useful hints for using up old felt hats are as follows. From the larger portions forming the brim, cut out pieces sufficiently large for use as socks to be placed inside boots and shoes. Felt is an admirable material for the purpose. Cut to shape with scissors, as indicated in Fig. 1, and fit in the inside of the shoe. After wearing once or twice, the felt will adapt itself to the shape of the shoe and remain in position.

With the smaller portions, one use is shown in Fig. 2. The felt is cut into suitable discs and secured to the bottom of chair and table legs, and will prevent unpleasant scraping on a linoleum floor.

MENDING A WATER TANK

Sometimes in a water tank a hole will appear, and this will render the vessel useless. Often the rest of the tank is in good order and, when this is so, a repair may be effected in the following manner. Cut two pieces of zinc considerably larger than the hole and bore an opening in the centre of each. Now cut two pieces of old rubber, such as might be taken from a disused inner tube, of the same size as the bits of zinc. Put one piece of zinc with the rubber on the outside and the other on the inside of the hole. Now run a nut and bolt through to hold them. Wind up tightly and a splendid repair is the result. The tank will then be good for quite a while longer.

Erecting Outdoor and Indoor Aerials

MODERN wireless receivers are so efficient that they will nearly always give excellent results, regardless of the aerial with which they are used. In spite of this, however, no set can give of its best unless the aerial is of correct design and properly erected. Moreover, a good aerial will always prove a distinct economy, because it is a fact that, say, a three-valve receiver used with an efficient aerial will afford much better reception than a similar type of four-valve set in conjunction with a poor aerial system.

No indoor aerial can ever be as efficient as a properly-erected outside one. A *short* indoor aerial often does prove more selective than a *comparatively long* outside one. But if the outside aerial is made the same length as the indoor one, not only will it prove much more efficient, but also appreciably more selective.

Frame Aerials.

Frame aerials undoubtedly give a greater degree of selectivity than any other type, but only at great expense in the way of efficiency. In other words, at least two more valves are needed in a receiver for use on a frame than in one for a good elevated aerial in order to obtain similar results. Thus, even when an outside aerial is out of the question because of architectural conditions, an indoor one, or even some kind of "makeshift," such as will be dealt with later, is almost invariably to be preferred to a frame. It will be gathered from the latter remarks that a frame aerial has hardly any useful application to present-day wireless, particularly since the extra selectivity which it provides can now be obtained by other and better means. As the writer is so frequently asked about frames by people who have been told of their advantages (although not realising their failings), it is thought fit to mention them and so to avoid any misunderstanding.

Points to consider in erecting an Aerial.

Having dealt in general terms with the principal types of aerials, the most satisfactory method of erecting an outside one can be described. It must be admitted that the question is so much bound up with local conditions and facilities available that it would be impracticable to give any standard design. Therefore, the main items involved will be considered and such information given that it can be applied to any set of circumstances.

Length.

The maximum length of aerial permitted by the Post Office authorities is 100 feet, this including both the horizontal span and the lead-in from

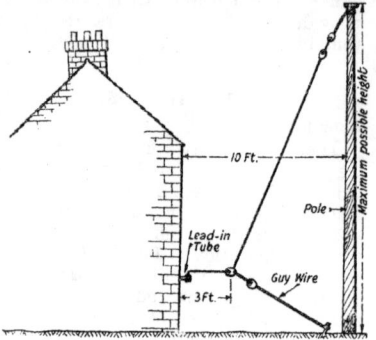

Fig. 1.—Details and Approximate Dimensions for an Excellent Type of Non-directional Aerial.

it. As a matter of fact, however, it is never wise to use much more than half this length, or else the full degree of selectivity of which the receiver is capable will never be realised. Besides this, the additional length

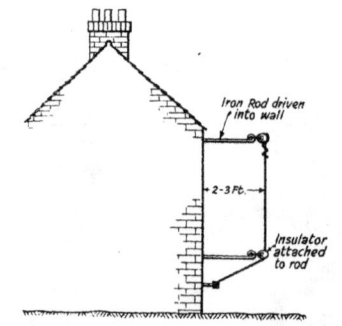

Fig. 2.—A Simple Arrangement for a Vertical Aerial.

will not extend the range of the receiver in the slightest on the medium waves (200 to 600 metres), although it will prove slightly beneficial on long waves. It can be taken as a good rule that the total length of wire used for

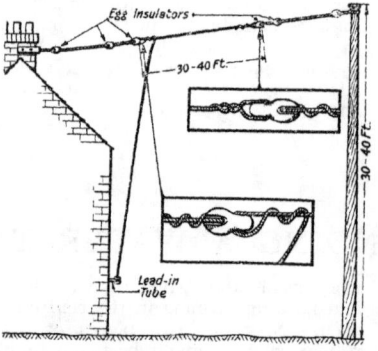

Fig. 3.—Practical Details for an Efficient "Inverted-L" Aerial are given in this Sketch.

the aerial should not greatly exceed 60 feet.

Aerial Position.

The next point is in respect of the position of the aerial. Here, again, local conditions must be deciding factors, but when two or three alternatives are available the wire should be erected in such a position that it is as far away from walls, roofs, trees, etc., as possible. It should also be as high as can conveniently be arranged, although there is little point in exceeding 40 feet or so, provided that at this height the wire is not lower than surrounding objects. The direction in which the aerial points is a factor that is all too often overlooked, and which can influence results to a rather considerable extent, especially when the receiver is of an old type.

As a matter of fact, any "inverted-L" (the most common, and generally best) type of aerial is most sensitive to signals coming from the two diametrically opposite directions in which its ends point. Of these two directions, that corresponding to the end from which the lead-in is taken is responded to in greater measure. It will be clear from this that every attempt should be made to erect the aerial in a direction which is at right angles (or as nearly so as possible) to a line joining the position of the local transmitter to the receiver. If this is done, interference from that station will be minimised.

Another point to consider is that the aerial should be as nearly at right angles as possible to any neighbouring ones in order to prevent mutual interference. Quite often it is found that when two receiving aerials are near together and more or less parallel to each other, one set is incapable of receiving some particular station whilst the other is tuned to it, and *vice versâ*. On the other hand, if one set is of a fairly old type and is allowed to oscillate, serious interference will be caused with the other receiver.

Non-directional Aerials.

In some cases it might be found quite impossible to arrange the aerial so that it is at right angles both to the direction of the local transmitter and also to a near-by aerial, and then it is necessary to modify the above conditions. The best solution is to use an aerial which does not possess any directional properties and which does not consist of both a vertical and a horizontal portion but of the vertical one only; in other words, only the lead-in is used.

This kind of aerial is somewhat unusual, and the sketch at Fig. 1 will make the arrangement quite clear. Approximate suitable dimensions are given for reference, although these

ERECTING OUTDOOR AND INDOOR AERIALS

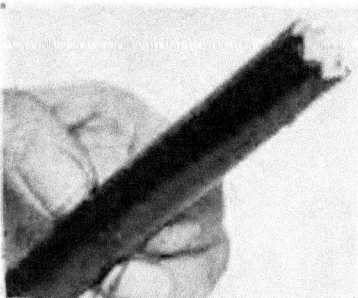

Fig. 4.—How to "Plug" a Wall to hold the Aerial Fixing.

The tool necessary to make a hole suitable for a plug is called a "jumper," and can be made from a piece of gas barrel, at one end of which teeth are filed.

Fig. 5.—How to make the Hole.
Place the "jumper" with the teeth against the wall and tap it with a hammer. Turn the "jumper" and give a few more taps, keeping turning and tapping until a hole of sufficient depth is produced.

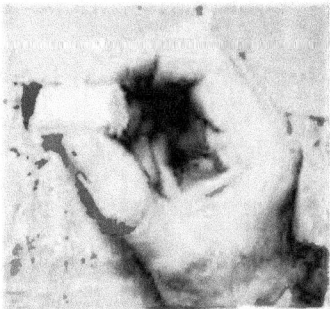

Fig. 6.—Inserting the Plug.
A wooden plug is now inserted in the hole so that it can be pushed in flush to the wall.

will probably require to be modified in many circumstances.

When it is not possible to employ a pole, or even a tree, or chimney of another house, to support the aerial, an arrangement like that shown in Fig. 2 will prove more convenient, although it is not quite so efficient. It will be seen that the vertical wire is held 2 or 3 feet away from the wall of the house by means of iron rods driven into the wall. Each of these has an insulator attached to it, and the wire is fastened to these.

The Most Suitable Kind of Wire.

The best wire to use is that known as 7/22, which consists of seven strands of 22-gauge copper wire. This material can be obtained in two varieties—bare and enamel-covered; and the enamelled is generally to be preferred, due to the fact that the covering protects the copper from oxidation and corrosion. The enamel acts as insulation, but has little value as such, and serves no other purpose than that mentioned.

The Lead-in.

Many engineers, and people who ought to know better, use 7/22 wire for the horizontal span of the aerial and then solder a length of rubber-covered cable to it to act as a lead-in. This latter is quite unnecessary if the aerial is properly erected, so that the lead-in does not touch the wall or any other earthed object, and the method has the serious disadvantage that the soldered joint is always liable to corrode.

The correct procedure is to use a single length of wire and let this extend from the very end of the aerial to the lead-in tube. A suitable method of attaching the wire to the insulators (those of the "egg" type are recommended) is shown in detail in Fig. 3. This drawing also shows the general arrangement of a

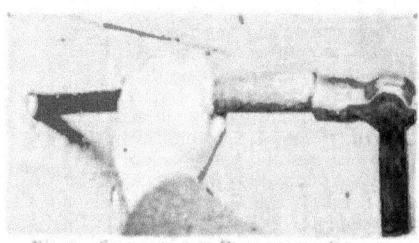

Fig. 7.—Splitting the Plug with a Chisel.
The plug is now split down the centre with a chisel. A wedge is placed in the cut and driven home with a hammer, thus expanding the plug and compressing the wood tightly into the brick.

Fig. 8.—Whipping the Ends of a Rope.
About ½ inch of the end of the rope should be tightly wrapped round with twine in the manner shown.

Fig. 9.—How to join Rope to the Insulator.
The rope should be threaded through the insulator and the end bound in this manner. This is preferable to using knots, which are liable to come undone.

good outdoor aerial, with approximate dimensions. Notice that the wire used to support the aerial at each end is "broken" by means of insulators so that it cannot act as a small aerial on its own and allow useful signal currents to leak away to earth by way of the house walls.

If a pole were used to support the "far" end of the aerial, it would probably be more convenient to fit a pulley to this so that the tension on the wire could suitably be adjusted at any time.

Erecting a Pole.

The principal details for a suitable pole, with pulley, are given in Figs. 10 and 11, where it will be seen that the pole itself is not sunk into the ground, but is supported by two stakes, each measuring 4 × 2 inches. These are driven into the ground for a distance of 3 feet or so, and the pole is held between them by means of three 9 × ⅝ inch bolts. In erecting or lowering the pole, only one bolt is kept in place, and this acts as a pivot. All other details will be clear from the drawing.

In the case of the mast shown in Fig. 11 a strong ground socket should be built of 2-inch timber, sunk into the ground about 2 to 3 feet. The socket consists of three pieces of well-seasoned and creosoted deal or oak, each measuring about 5 to 6 feet in length by 2 inches in thickness; the widths should be slightly greater than the diameter of the lower end of the mast. The three pieces of timber are arranged in the form of three sides of a square above the ground, but are nailed to an internal square-sectioned piece of timber for the portion that is to be below the ground.

For the hinge a ¾-inch Whitworth bolt with nut and washers is employed.

The mast is locked into its vertical position by means of a second bolt

ERECTING OUTDOOR AND INDOOR AERIALS

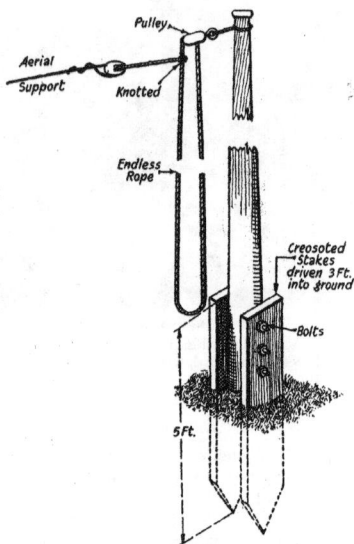

Fig. 10.—This shows what is probably the very best form of construction for an Aerial Pole.

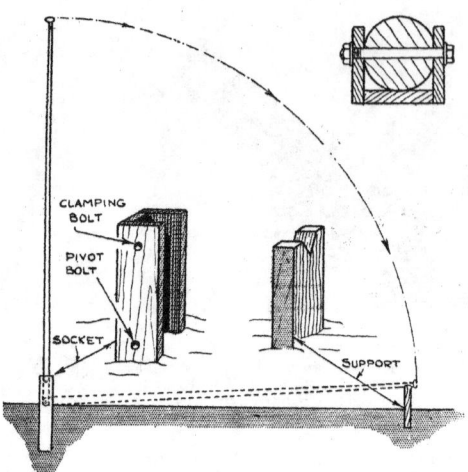

Fig. 11.—Another Design for a Dismountable Mast.

and nut of similar dimensions to the lower one. This bolt should be so arranged as to be about 2 feet above the lower one.

The mast, if a high one, should, in addition, have three or four wire stays going to a ring about half-way up; in the case of small masts, namely, those up to 20 or 25 feet, these stays are unnecessary.

It is a good plan to arrange for a wooden support for the upper end of the pole to rest upon when it is lowered; this support can be readily made out of a piece of 6 × 2 inch or 4 × 4 inch posting sunk into the ground; the upper side can be made with a Vee notch in order to take the rounded portion of the pole.

With the arrangement described it is a very simple matter to paint the pole or to make any adjustments or alterations to the rope or wire fittings at the upper end.

Inside Aerials.

It sometimes happens that permission cannot be obtained to erect an outside aerial, and in that case the best possible use must be made of the space inside the house. The same general rules apply in regard to direction, distance from walls, etc., as for an outside aerial, and therefore the best situation is in an attic, as Fig. 13, where the wire can be carried across an open space well away from the roof and walls.

The lead-in presents rather a different problem, because this wire will no doubt have to run down, and be attached to, a wall; it must therefore consist of well-insulated wire, such as good quality lighting flex or vulcanised-indiarubber cable of the kind sold by garages for use as ignition leads.

It is well to choose the path of the lead-in with some care, because if the wire is allowed to run near and parallel to gas pipes, water pipes, or electric supply conduits there will be an appreciable loss in efficiency. Also, when the wire runs close to electric cables there is a distinct danger of picking up undesirable "mains-hum."

Simple Improvised Arrangements.

Simple improvised aerials are frequently required, either because a set has just been bought or because it is to be removed into another room. Of course, a short length of ordinary bell wire can be strung across the room, but much better results can be obtained by attaching a short wire to a biscuit-tin lid and placing this under the telephone receiver. The tin sheet picks up its signal energy from the telephone wires, due to a condenser effect which is produced. An earth connection also can often be obtained from the telephone leads inside the house, because, it will be found, the telephone engineers earth one wire at some point outside.

Another substitute for a proper aerial consists of using a connection to a gas pipe. If a water pipe also is available, that can be used for an earth connection. When there is only either a gas pipe or a water pipe (it does not matter which) it is always better to use this as an aerial and ignore the earth connection entirely. In the same way, an ordinary "buried" earth can be joined to the aerial terminal when a proper aerial is not available, and this will generally produce quite decent results.

Using the Electricity Mains as an Aerial.

When the house is wired for electricity the supply mains can frequently be used to provide a really good aerial. All that is required is to connect a ·0005 mfd. fixed condenser between one mains lead and the aerial terminal. Provided that the condenser is of good quality, and that the connection from it to the mains is properly insulated, this method is perfectly safe, and is, in fact, made use of in many up-to-date mains receivers. The simplest way to connect the condenser is as shown in Fig. 12, where a short wire is taken from it to one connection on an ordinary power plug. For convenience, the condenser is fastened to the plug with a piece of insulating tape, and its terminal is also covered to prevent its being accidentally touched.

In the case of a mains-operated receiver, whether it is of the A.C. or D.C. type, the simplest method of using the mains as an aerial is to connect a fixed condenser, of the capacity previously mentioned, between one of the mains leads to the on-off switch and the normal aerial terminal provided. It is important that the condenser be of a high-grade type, for otherwise there would be some danger of the insulation breaking down, when the fuse would be "blown" and the operator might possibly receive a shock by touching any exposed metallic parts, such as grub screws in the operating knobs.

Minimising Electrical Interference.

At the present time the question of interference with reception due to electrical apparatus is an important one, and one which can often be influenced by the design of the aerial system. More often than not, the interference is actually "picked-up" by the aerial or its lead-in, and thereby transferred to the receiver. As a matter of fact, it is generally the lead-in which is responsible for the

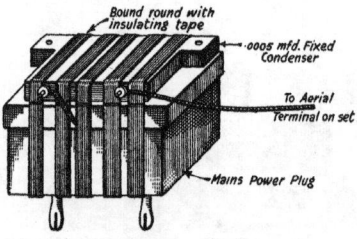

Fig. 12.—A Simple Arrangement for using the Electric Supply Mains as an Aerial.

In the case of mains receivers the ·0005 mfd. fixed condenser would be placed inside the set and joined between a mains connection and the aerial terminal.

ERECTING OUTDOOR AND INDOOR AERIALS

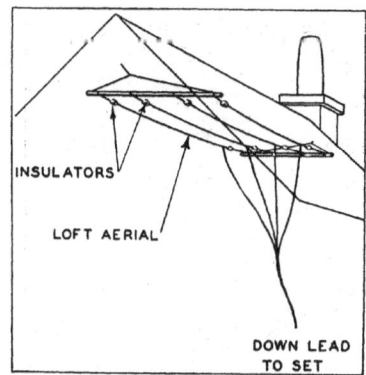

Fig. 13.—An Excellent Indoor Aerial can be erected in the Loft by following the System illustrated.

Three or four strands of wire are stretched out parallel to each other and joined to a common down-lead at one end.

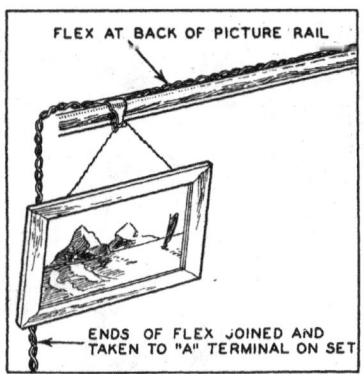

Fig. 14.—A fairly good Makeshift Aerial can be made by running a Length of Insulated Flex around the Picture Rail Moulding, preferably in an Upstairs Room.

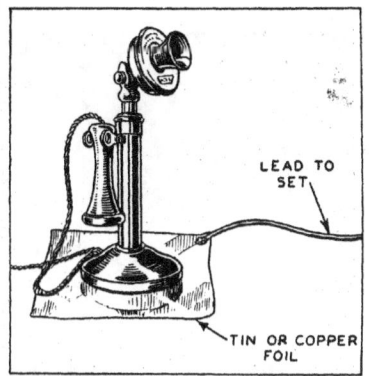

Fig. 15.—A good Substitute Aerial can be obtained by making connection to a Sheet of Metal Foil placed underneath a Telephone.

This functions by reason of its capacity effect with the telephone lines.

"pick-up," and therefore the difficulty can be overcome by screening this with metallic tubing, connecting the screen to earth. There are a number of special screened down-leads on the market, all of which are highly efficient, but a suitable screen can be made at home by using a length of electric conduit tubing of about ½ inch diameter. The lead-in wire is passed through this, and is spaced from the walls of the tube by threading a number of wax-impregnated corks or glass beads over it; the spacers also provide the necessary insulation. For the screen to be effective it is essential that it should be earth-connected. This can be arranged by fixing a terminal at the lower end of the tube and joining a wire from this to the earth lead at the point where it enters the house. The ready-made screens are generally supplied with a length of connecting wire attached to the lower end of the screen, and this is simply joined to any convenient earthing point.

When electrical interference is experienced whilst using an indoor aerial, the trouble can frequently be obviated simply by altering the position of the aerial wire. Sometimes it is only required to take it along two opposite sides of the room, but in other instances it may be better to remove the aerial from, say, the ground floor room to one upstairs. In any case a little experiment will in nearly every case make it a fairly simple matter to cut out the "fizzes" and "bangs" which signify interference caused by electrical machinery.

ADJUSTING IRON PLANES

THE illustrations show two types of adjustable iron planes. The width of the mouth of the plane in Fig. 1 may be made wider or narrower as coarse or fine work may require. First remove the lever and cutter and loosen the two frog screws that fasten the frog to its seat. With a screwdriver turn the centre adjusting screw, as in Fig. 1, to the right

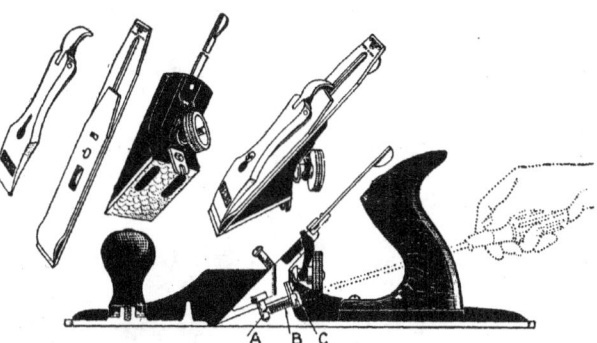

Fig. 2.—Another Type of Adjustable Iron Plane.

Fig. 1.—One Type of Adjustable Iron Plane.

to close the mouth, and to the left to open it. The frog of plane in Fig. 2 may be adjusted either forward or backward without removing the lever and cutter. Just slacken the tension of the two frog clamping screws B, and with a screwdriver adjust the frog as desired by means of screw C in the centre.

Installing a Model Electric Railway

Fig. 1.—A Typical Model Electric Railway Installation erected for Exhibition Purposes.
While full details relating to the erection and operation of the track for an electric railway will be found in this article, readers who are interested in making model houses, sheds, power station, etc., are referred to the article on "Cardboard Modelling" on page 1171.

THE first consideration in the proposal to install a model electric railway is the supply of the current.

Alternating Current for Model Railways.

Where an A.C. supply is available the accumulator is not an essential, as small transformers, costing from about 21s. upwards, are purchasable by which the high voltage mains are reduced to say 20 volts with very little loss. A unit of electricity will run a model railway for 20 to 25 hours under these conditions.

The D.C. Supply.

With the ordinary direct current supply the real difficulty is that the house voltage cannot be reduced in a very satisfactory or simple manner. The use of resistances in any form does not eliminate the risk of danger, especially where children are likely to work the railway, and therefore model makers have to rely on the secondary battery. The cost of these accumulators leads to the adoption of low voltages for the model railway, and the very desirable pressure of 20 or 25 volts cannot be used because of the expense involved. Low voltages such as 6 or 8 volts are, however, quite satisfactory where only one, or at the most two, engines are installed.

The Higher Voltages are to be recommended.

Such low pressures make the presence of dirt on the track and conductor rails troublesome in transmission. The voltage is not high enough to break down the oil and grit that accumulate even on an indoor line. Therefore if the user has a choice in the matter, he is well advised to adopt A.C. Where the line is divided into sections, the separate sections can

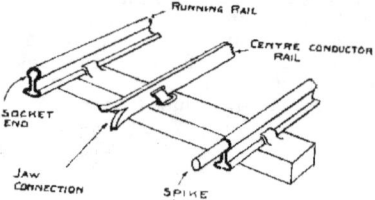

Fig. 2.—Model Electric Railway Track on the "Third Rail" System.

be served by transformers plugged into the nearest electric light socket, a much more convenient method than an arrangement where all leads have to be taken from a central battery.

Fig. 3.—The Driving Section of Electric Locomotive.

With the A.C. transformer scheme, tappings can be taken off at various voltages, say, 20 volts for the power circuit, and 2 or 4 volts for lights and signals.

Briefly, therefore, if the house mains are alternating, then decide on 20 volts for the model railway, using transformers; otherwise employ low voltage D.C. at 6 or 12 volts supplied from an accumulator. The higher voltage is preferable, but it is entirely a matter of how the cells are going to be recharged. Where the house is in the country and is lit by a private power plant, the direct current can be tapped off the main storage battery, and 20 to 25 volts is recommended. The voltage is only a matter of choosing the right number of cells, say 10 for 20 volts and 12 for 25 volts; roughly 2 volts per cell.

The Overhead System not satisfactory.

The next thing is the track. Almost all model electric railways run on the "third rail" system. The overhead scheme is not entirely practical; though it may be easy to fix an insulated conductor over the track and a satisfactory collector on the locomotive, it is found that anything in the nature of overhead wiring gets in the way of the operator in coupling and uncoupling the trains.

Rails: Use the Largest Radius of Curve Possible.

The choice of rails depends on the intentions of the model railway user. If he cannot spare space for a permanent line indoors, then the portable tinplate track, such as made by Hornby's and by Bassett-Lowke Ltd., must be used. Such model

INSTALLING A MODEL ELECTRIC RAILWAY

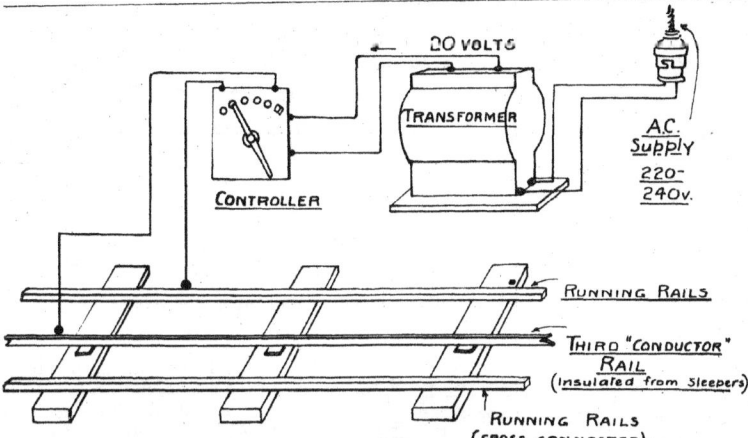

Fig. 4.—Electric Railway Track connected to Alternating Current Supply.

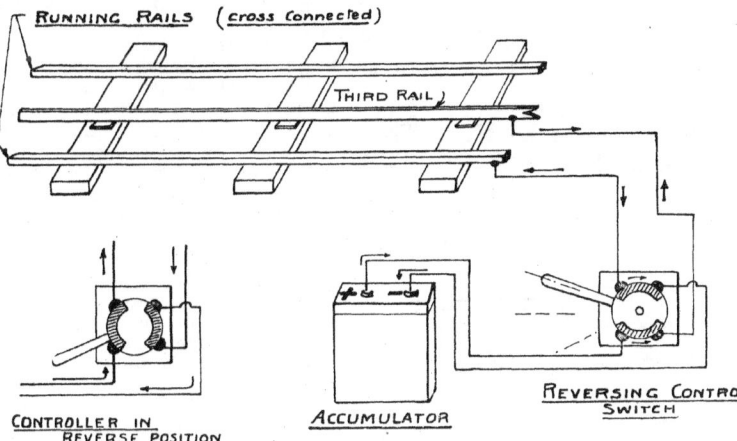

Fig. 5.—Connections to Track using Direct Current Supply.

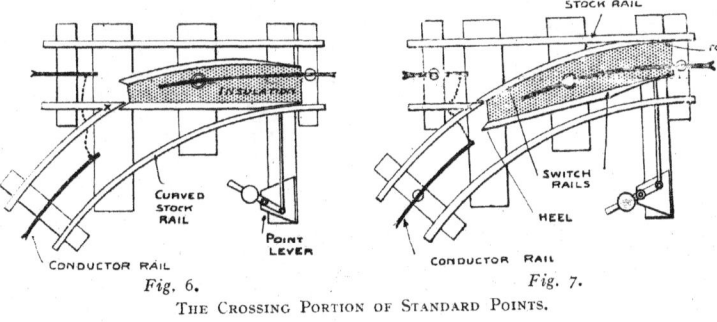

Fig. 6. Fig. 7.
The Crossing Portion of Standard Points.

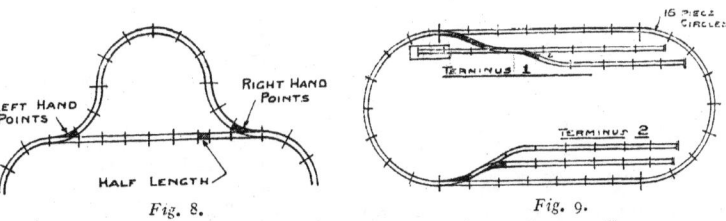

Fig. 8. Fig. 9.
Alternative ways of arranging Points on Simple Oval of Track.

railways are made up in geometric forms from standard lengths of ready-made track, straights, half-straights, curves, crossings and points.

Standard Curvatures.

Omitting the purely child's toy outfits with 1 foot radius curves, there are two curvatures obtainable. The smaller is based on a circle 4 feet diameter, with 12 pieces of rail in each, and the other is 6 feet diameter, made up of 16 pieces. The lengths are therefore different, but the straights are 11 inches long. Straights cost from 6d. each, and small and large radius curves 6½d. per piece. Track costs are therefore easily calculated at round about 9d. a foot, including points.

In deciding between the two curves the larger radius sections are much to be preferred, as these do not limit the model railway operator to small type short wheelbase engines. Once the larger 6 feet radius curves are adopted as a minimum, he knows that the line will accommodate an express engine model, even if he only purchases or makes a small four-wheeled engine at the outset.

Portable Track Construction.

This type of model railway track is made of sheet metal throughout in automatic presses, and for electric traction a brass strip forming the central conductor rail is fixed to the sleepers with insulating material intervening, so arranged that the middle rail is the flow circuit and the running rails the return. Nearly all these model traction motors are arranged with the negative side earthed to the wheels and framing.

Terminal and End Connections.

To ensure continuity of current flow a length of terminal rail is inserted at a convenient point of the track system. To the negative and positive terminals on this section the wires from the switch controller are connected. Where A.C. is used, it does not matter about the polarity of the leads, but as nearly all D.C. models have permanent magnet motors, the particular arrangement of the wires is important. Reversing can be effected by changing over the direction of the current. Although most controllers have a change-over or reversing switch as part of their mechanism, it is best to trace out the wires and fix them up so that on switching on the locomotive goes in the direction required. With the A.C. supply there is no direction, the current is going both ways, and so long as there is no short circuiting, it is immaterial which wire is attached to a particular terminal.

Connections between Adjacent Sections.

Connections between adjacent sections must be perfect. The central

INSTALLING A MODEL ELECTRIC RAILWAY

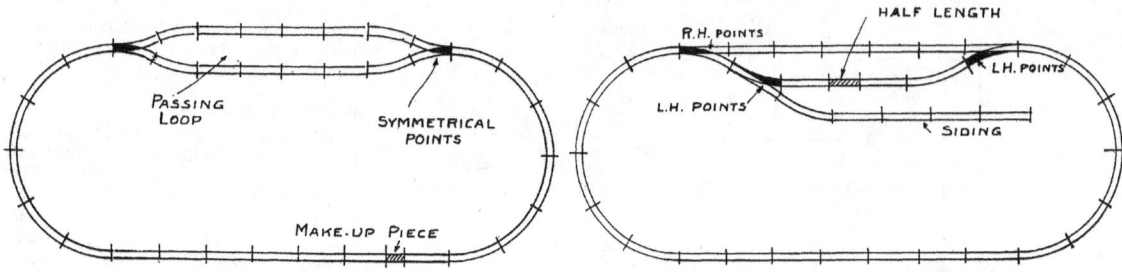

Fig. 10.—SIMPLE LAYOUT INTRODUCING THE USE OF SYMMETRICAL POINTS FOR MAKING A PASSING LOOP.

Fig. 11.—PLAN OF TRACK INCLUDING A PASSING LOOP AND A SIDING.

"conductor" rails are usually joined by a clipping of one rail in another. The return or "running" rails are spiked together. The left-hand rail has a spike or spigot, and the right-hand rail head is hollow, to form a socket. Often there is a clip on the rail ends to keep the sections together, but the design of this depends on the exact make of the rail. Manufacturers' ideas differ in this particular.

Points and Crossings.

Points are made with the curves of the turn-out rails leading either to the right or left hand, and these curves are geometrically the same as the standard. The same applies to the straight arms of the points, therefore, as far as plans and layouts are concerned the parts are interchangeable. The simple oval of track may therefore be arranged with points in any of the formations shown in the diagrams (Figs. 8 and 9).

As the geometry of the circle sometimes creates difficulties in this respect when it comes to a complicated layout, half-lengths and quarter-lengths of both curved and straight are obtainable. An example of the use of a half-length is illustrated in the sketch (Fig. 10), and also in Figs. 11 and 12. The points are shown black, the ordinary straights and curves by open lines, and the half-lengths, which are necessary to make up the connecting straight lengths of line, are shown by the shaded pieces in the drawings.

The Crossing Portion of Standard Points.

Another distinctive feature

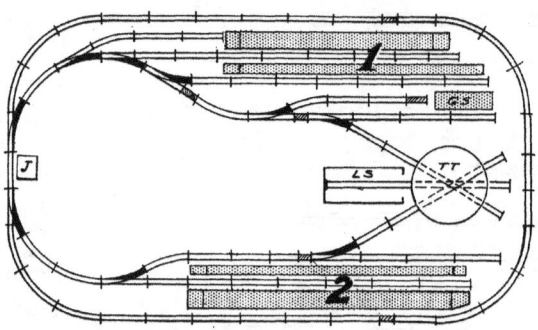

Fig. 12.—A MORE COMPLICATED LINE WHICH PROVIDES FOR RUNNING THE TRAIN BETWEEN THE TWO TERMINALS, 1 AND 2, AND FOR SWITCHING ON TO THE MAIN LINE AT J.

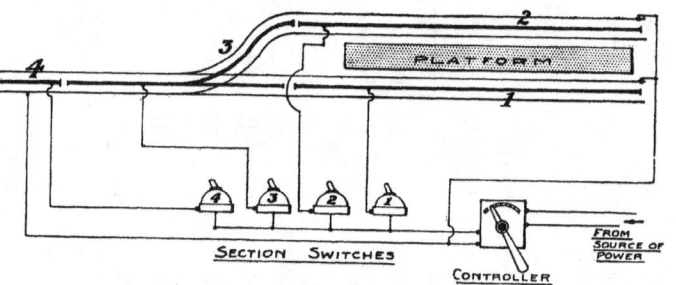

Fig. 13.—SECTIONALISING THE TRACK FOR CONTROL PURPOSES.
Note the section switches for controlling the train at different sections of the track.

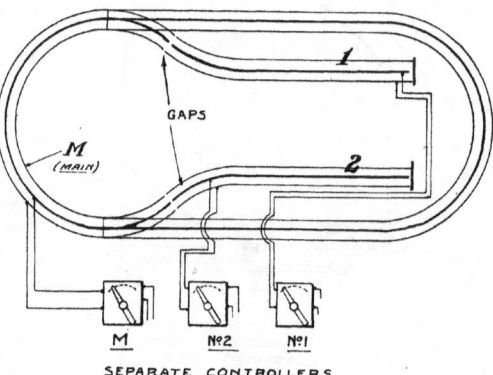

Fig. 14.—AN ALTERNATIVE CONTROL ARRANGEMENT, USING A COMPLETE CONTROL FOR EACH SECTION OF THE TRACK.

of tinplate points is the crossing portion or "frog" as it is termed in full-size permanent-way work. Instead of using wing and check-rails as in the prototype, the two moving switch-tongues are mounted up as a unit and arranged to pivot near the centre of the length.

For electric models the switch is often connected on to a pivoted insulated block, as indicated in the sketch (see Figs. 6 and 7). At the same moment as the tongue of the switch butts alongside the stock rail, the other end, "the heel," as it would be called, joins up with the apex of the crossing at X, and produces a continuous running track for trains moving in that direction. The other line at the same time moves towards the centre of the track, and is out of action. Being insulated it is "dead," and although in its running position it forms part of the return circuit, it may touch the current collector on the locomotive and become virtually a part of the "flow" circuit. This doesn't matter, as it is insulated from positive side.

Planning a Model Line.

The plain circle or oval of track is perhaps the simplest lay-out that can be conceived, but interest in it soon evaporates, and while geometrical arrangements of portable track lengths—round loops, figure eights, and knots—are obvious formations, most model railway enthusiasts demand something more realistic. They must be able to plan a line with stations, goods yards, sidings, placed in a railway-like manner.

INSTALLING A MODEL ELECTRIC RAILWAY

The scheme (Fig. 10) is a simple lay-out introducing, with the aid of a pair of symmetrical points, a passing station and loop, such as is common on single lines of railway. The next arrangement (Fig. 11) is an improvement on this, and includes a siding. The left- and right-hand turn-out, instead of the double curve point, enables a straight main line to be preserved through the station. It will be noted that using the standard track lengths these turn-out points necessitate the fitting of a half-length in the loop-line straight. The siding needs another pair of points, but this is placed on a curve, and the straight track becomes the turn-out. A further development is illustrated in Fig. 9, in which there are two stations, and by placing the siding lines in opposite directions trains can run from one terminal to another.

This plan is still further improved upon in the lay-out, Fig. 12. The main idea of this scheme is to provide for terminal to terminal working, and, at the same time, by switching over the trains on to the continuous main line at the junction J, they may be made to run as many times round the track as may be desired before they are turned into the arriving terminus station.

The Control of Trains (Direct Current Supply).

With D.C. permanent magnet motors the important feature in the control of trains from the side of the line is that reversing can be accomplished by simply changing over the polarity of the current. Control gears therefore comprise a reversing or current commutating switch and a speed regulating resistance, the lever working the last-named having of course an "off" position to stop the trains.

Fig. 15.—A TRACK FITTED WITH GREENLY'S AUTOMATIC COLOUR LIGHT SIGNALS.

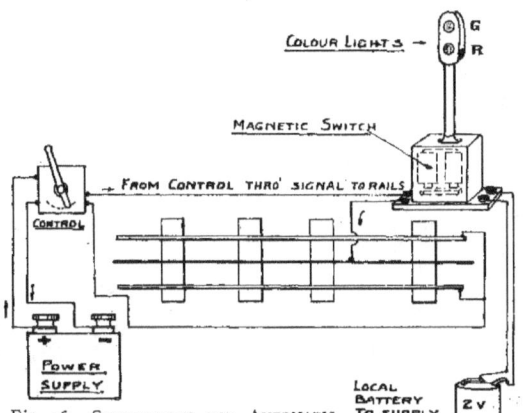

Fig. 16.—CONNECTIONS FOR AUTOMATIC COLOUR LIGHT SIGNALLING.

This control switch can be placed anywhere in the circuit between the accumulator or other source of constant voltage supply and the track. The exact position will depend on the convenience of the user, but all conducting wires should be as short as possible to reduce voltage losses. Further, it is best to arrange the connections near the middle of the track or section of the track, rather than at the ends.

Alternating Current Control.

There are difficulties in the way of a perfect remote control of A.C. models in the matter of reversing, but these are being got over in one way or another, each manufacturer having his own patented device. The hand-switch on the locomotive is positive, but to provide for remote reversing control the sequence system is fitted to some types of model.

The scheme embodies a magnetic-mechanical switch on the engine arranged so that every time the current is shut off, when it *is* re-applied a reversal of direction is obtained. It is quite good, but care must be taken with the perfect maintenance of the track to ensure continuity of current collection. Any momentary interruption will obviously reverse the engine. The rails must be kept clean, likewise the collecting shoe on the model locomotive.

Don't use abrasives, *i.e.*, sandpaper or emery cloth, on the rails unless absolutely necessary; a swab dampened with paraffin is very much better.

Sectionalising Track for Control Purposes—Single Controller Scheme.

Where it is thought desirable to cut up the lay-out into separate sections, for the purpose of better control when two or more engines are employed, the possible schemes are as follows: in the one arrangement (see Fig. 13) there can be a single controller—in the case of a D.C. supply this will govern starting, stopping, speed control and remote reversing, all from one point. From this instrument the "flow" or "positive" wires can go to the centre conductor rail of each section, each wire being controlled by a small tumbler or other simple switch. The conductor rails must, of course, be cut at each section, so that current can only flow by virtue of the section control switch. The running rails form the negative side, and can all be connected up to the return side of the control switch as a common "earth"

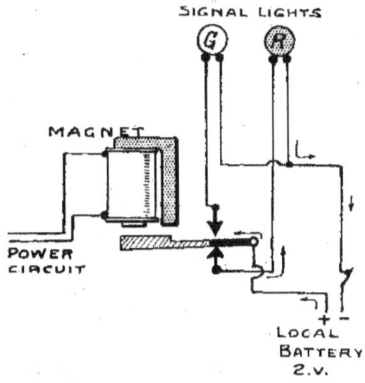

Fig. 17.—AUTOMATIC SIGNALLING SWITCH— RED LIGHT.

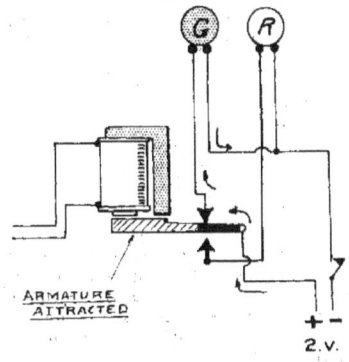

Fig. 18.—AUTOMATIC SIGNALLING SWITCH— GREEN LIGHT.

INSTALLING A MODEL ELECTRIC RAILWAY

INSTALLING A MODEL ELECTRIC RAILWAY 4
TABLE OF MODEL RAILWAY COMPONENTS
LIST OF PARTS REQUIRED FOR PLANS ILLUSTRATED IN FIGS. 9, 10, 11 AND 12

(Rolling Stock not Included)

Plan.	Straights.	Half-straights.	Curves.	Half-curves.	Right-hand Points.	Left-hand Points.	Symmetrical Points.	Terminal Rails.	Buffer Stops.
Fig. 10	15	1	16 or 20	—	—	—	2	1	—
			One Station Platform.						
Fig. 11	18	1	14 or 18	—	1	2	—	1	1
			One Station Platform and One Locomotive Shed.						
Fig. 9	32	—	14 or 18	—	3	1	—	3	4
	Two Station Platforms, One Locomotive Shed and One Goods Shed.								
Fig. 12	52	6	19 or 23	—	4	5	—	3	5
	Four Station Platforms, One Goods Shed, One Locomotive Shed, One Turntable, One Signal Box.								

Costs: Straight and curved rails, 6d. each; half-rails, 4½d. each; right-hand and left-hand points, 6s. to 7s. 6d.; parallel or symmetrical points, 8s. 6d.; terminal rails, 1s. 6d. to 2s. 6d. each; buildings and platforms according to design and size.

circuit. There is no necessity of providing any gap in the running rails at the various sections of the line.

Sections Separately Controlled.

The alternative scheme is to use a complete control switch for each section or group of sections. This is an expensive arrangement if pushed too far, and it is best in a lay-out such as illustrated in the diagram (Fig. 14) to reduce the controllers to three, one for each of the terminus stations, and the other for the junction and main line. As in the case of the single controller idea, the station platform lines and other sidings can be subdivided by plain switches working under the particular controller involved.

Signals.

For an electric railway, colour light signals worked on the Greenly automatic series system are the most satisfactory. The use of the semaphore arm introduces a lot of mechanical complication. The "two-aspect" colour light signals are now made by Messrs. Bassett-Lowke Ltd., London and Northampton, to work with the trains, no connection from signal box or control cabin other than a feed wire, to the particular section involved. These automatic signals are listed at 9s. 6d. each. The lighting of the signals is done by a local dry battery alongside the post, therefore there is no loss in transmission from a central point (see Fig. 16).

The signals contain a small magnetic relay switch, which, when there is no traction current flowing due to a train in the section, is not energised, the contact falls by gravity, and a red light is switched on. When the line is supplied with power and a train enters the section of the line involved, the power circuit energises the relay magnet, and the signal lamp circuit is changed over to the green light circuit. When the train leaves the section the main power current does not flow, and this interruption de-energises the relay magnet, and the signal returns to the "danger" light. The scheme is both up to date and simple. All signal operation wires are eliminated. The cable that feeds the particular section of line operates the signals. This arrangement was first used on the London Transport Board's exhibition model railway at Charing Cross Station, and during the ten days show there were about 54,000 auto-signal light contacts made by the model trains.

Solid Rails on Chairs and Wood Sleepers.

The portable railway made up of ready-made sections does not always fill the bill. The next step is the permanent railway, and for these models a large amount of material is available. The whole of the track laying is accomplished on a boarded table or shelf, according to plan. The usual arrangement is to build up the substructure some 2 feet 11 inches to 3 feet 2 inches above the ground on trestles, brackets or vertical posts, as the case may be.

The track consists of solid drawn rail, either steel or brass, supported in cast white metal chairs on wooden sleepers. Sometimes the chairs are made of pressed-out sheet material. The chairs may be of the "slide on" pattern or the keyed type; the advantage of the latter is an important one—a rail can be removed and replaced without disturbing the rest of the track. Costs of material vary in No. 0 (1¼-inch gauge) from 4d. to 4½d. per foot of plain track, but in this matter everything depends on the number of sleepers per length of track that are used. Electric track is about 25 per cent. above the cost of plain track. The following are average prices :—

Rails (3-foot lengths), 1s. 8d. per dozen lengths.
Chairs, "slide on," 1s. 6d. per 100.
Keyed chairs, 3s. per 100.
Wooden sleepers, 2s. per 100.
Spring fishplates, 5s. per 100.
Spikes, 1d. per 100.
Centre conductor rail (3-foot lengths), 4s. 3d. per dozen lengths.
Centre conductor rail chairs, 3s. 4d. per 100.
Centre conductor rail fishplates, 4s. 3d. per 100.

Reliable makers are Bassett-Lowke Ltd., Northampton; Mills Bros., Sheffield; Leeds Model Co. Ltd., Hunslet, Leeds; Walkers & Holtzapfell Ltd., 61 Baker Street, W. Once a given make of track material is chosen, it should, as far as possible, be continued with throughout the whole system.

GLASS-BLOWING

In glass blowing we have a craft which is little practised outside of laboratories, and yet, contrary to general belief, it is not difficult to acquire a reasonable technique with a little practice. Indeed, as a hobby it becomes very fascinating—one wants to go on making more and more difficult things. However, even in the beginning many useful and ornamental articles can be made quite easily, for example, an ear syringe.

Tools required.

The most essential requirement is a blowpipe. For some reason or other these are rather dear to buy, but very easy to make. Fig. 1 shows clearly how to construct a very efficient model. The tubes are all of brass with soldered joints. The chief point in the construction is to get the air jet central and in alignment with the outer tube. It is advisable to have a tap of some kind in the gas stream to facilitate the manipulation of the flame. The air blast is obtained by any of the methods, as described in the article on Spray Painting on page 1033.

As well as a selection of various sizes in glass rod and tube, the following are required:—

(1) Tweezers—these are made from sheet brass, as Fig. 2A.
(2) Reimer—this is a piece of sheet brass in a wood handle as Fig. 2B.
(3) Charcoal block.
(4) Triangular saw file.
(5) 3 feet of 3/16-inch rubber tubing.
(6) A selection of corks.
(7) Bat's-wing burner.

Glass to use.

As lead glass is too difficult to work, the tubing and rod should all be of soft soda glass, varying in size from 5 mm. to 20 mm. external diameter. In buying coloured glass always try the effect of heat upon it, as many of the poorer varieties change colour badly, leaving only a drab brown.

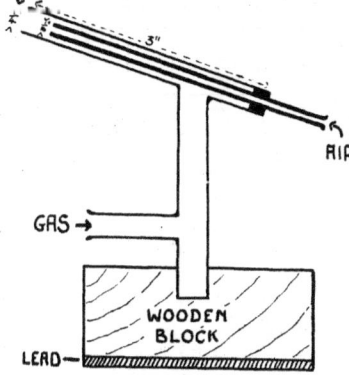

Fig. 1.—Blow-pipe required for Glass-blowing.
This shows how to construct a very efficient blow-pipe. The tubes are all of brass with soldered joints.

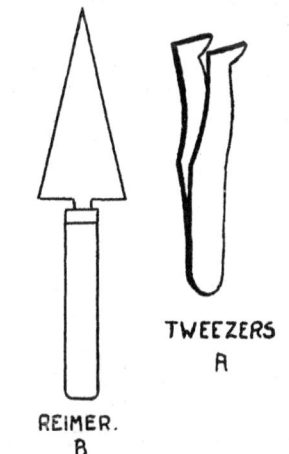

Fig. 2.—Two other Tools required.
Both tools are easily made from sheet brass. A, tweezers; B, a reimer, with a wood handle.

"Stops" for the Tubes.

All the corks should be rolled underneath the foot in order to get them pliable so that they will easily push into the end of a tube. In the case of the smaller tubes, plasticine will be found very useful for the purpose of stopping the ends. Some of the corks should be bored and fitted with a short length of glass tube the ends of which are "fire-polished," that is, they are held in the flame until just soft (Fig. 3B). This takes off the sharp cutting edge.

Prevention of Cracks.

In glass-blowing there are a few very important points to remember, and if these are observed, then a successful piece of work is ensured. Now glass and cracks are almost synonymous, and it is this cracking which must be avoided. The first point to be remembered is always to heat up the work slowly. The duration of this heating depends upon the thickness of the glass. A very thin narrow tube can be put right in the hot flame, whereas a jam jar must be gradually heated up over several days.

When working only on one side of a tube always keep warming up the other, or else a strain will be set up and a crack will appear due to glass being a very bad conductor of heat.

Annealing.

If, when a piece of work is finished, there are any thick parts in it, then it must be annealed. This merely consists in letting it cool down slowly. There are two ways of doing this. One is quickly to wrap the article in cotton or asbestos wool when still hot, and then to leave it undisturbed for about half an hour. The other method is to keep the glass moving about in a smoky flame until it is covered with soot, and then gradually to raise it out but still keeping it in the hot air.

To cut a Tube or Rod.

Hold the file in the hand and press the tube or rod between one edge of it and the thumb. Turn the tube round with the other hand, thus making a complete circle on the surface. Now hold close to the file cut, and lever as one would snap a match.

In the case of wide tubes proceed as above, but instead of snapping apply a small blob of heated glass to the file cut, when a crack will appear and run around the tube. If the crack does not go completely around, assist it to do so by applying another heated blob to the point where the crack finished. Any unevenness in this cutting can be righted by flicking the edge with a piece of stiff iron gauze. If the file is sharpened on an emery wheel so that it has an edge like a steel glass cutter, much cleaner cuts will result.

To reim a Tube.

Cut off a length of tube and heat the end in a large flame. As soon as it begins to soften put the end of the reimer in the tube and turn in opposite directions, thus producing a slight cone

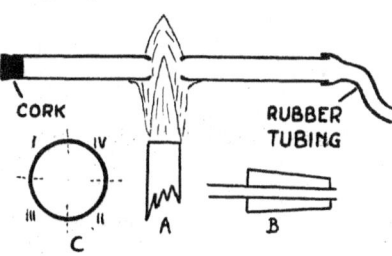

Fig. 3, A and C.—Method of joining Two Similar Tubes.
First heat up the two ends in flame, as at A; when soft, place them together, at same time blowing gently down the rubber tube. The flame is applied to each section of the tube in turn (see C), and, by alternately blowing and sucking, work that part until no sign of the join remains.
Fig. 3, B.—A Cork Stop fitted with Short Length of Tube.

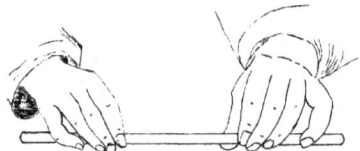

Fig. 4.—Bending a Glass Tube.
Hold tube in bright yellow part of bat's-wing burner flame. As soon as the glass is plastic, bend it to the required angle, applying pressure in the manner shown.

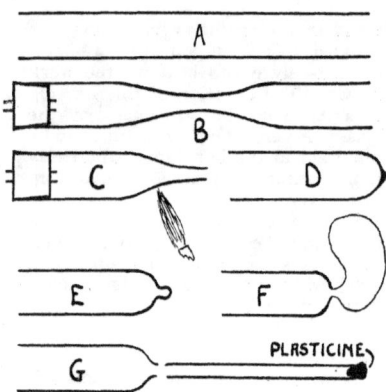

Fig. 5.—Method of joining Two Differently-sized Tubes, shown Step by Step.

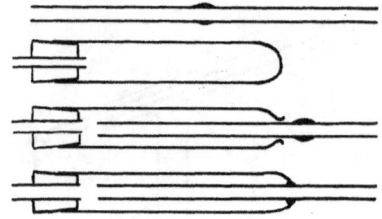

Fig. 6.—How to seal a Tube in a Larger Tube.

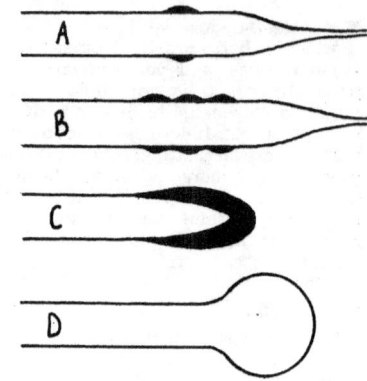

Fig. 7.—Illustrating the Stages of blowing a Bulb on the End of a Tube.

shape at the end. A little practice will soon show the extent of heating and the speed of turning.

To bend a Glass Tube.

Because it is so much easier the amateur is advised to bend all his tubes by means of a bat's-wing burner instead of the blowpipe. The burner consists of one of the old-fashioned household gas jets screwed into a brass tube which is fed with coal gas.

Light the burner and adjust the gas so that the top edge of the flame is more or less straight. Take the tube in the hands as shown in Fig. 4 and hold it in the bright yellow part of the flame. As soon as the glass is plastic bend it to the required angle. Always view the bend from several angles to make sure that it is in one plane, unless, of course, it is required otherwise.

The bending of wide tubes such as are used in the manufacture of Neon signs is very difficult and needs a great deal of practice, so it shall not be described here.

To join Two Similar Tubes.

To begin, select 5-mm. tubing. First stop up one end of one piece and connect the rubber tube to one end of the other, as in Fig. 3A. The free end of the rubber tube is placed in the mouth. Hold the tubes to be joined between the fingers and thumb of each hand, and revolving back and fore heat up the ends in a small flame. When these are soft remove from the flame and quickly place together, blowing slightly. Now heat up one quadrant of the junction (see Fig. 3C), and by alternately blowing and sucking slightly, work that part of the joint until no sign of the join remains. The three remaining quadrants are now similarly worked in the order shown. Between each of these four operations the tube should be revolved in the flame, thus, while the whole joint is kept hot, the side which has just been worked can set. In this way the joint does not get out of control because there is always at least three-quarters of it solid and holding it in alignment.

These operations are being described at length and in detail as they embrace most of the important features of glass-blowing by this method.

To join Two Different Tubes.

The required length of wide tube is pulled off by heating until very soft and then drawing the two pieces apart (see Fig. 5). Fit the tube with a bored cork and, while rotating, heat the shoulder with a small flame, and when soft, pull off the capillary, leaving a rounded shape. Should there be too big a "pip" of glass on the end, it can

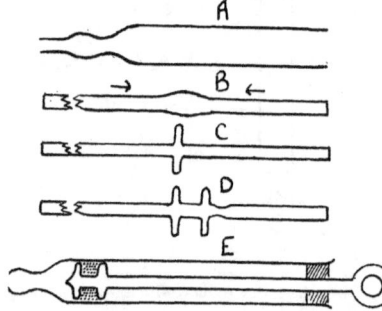

Fig. 8.—Here we see the Different Stages in Making an Ear Syringe.

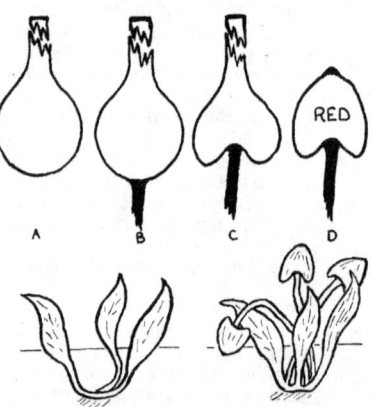

Fig. 9.—Stages in Construction of an Ornament for a Witch's Bowl.

be removed by pulling off with the tweezers when molten. Now connect up the rubber tube and with a small flame heat up a small area in the middle of the rounded surface. Take the glass out of the flame and blow slightly, thus obtaining a protuberance, which should have the same diameter as the tube which is about to be fused on. Heat the end of this swelling until about half of it collapses, then blow strongly, when a large sausage-shaped bulb of very thin glass will be formed. This is brushed off and the other tube, which has its end stopped, is taken up. The two parts to be joined are heated up and fused together as with those of the same diameter.

To make a T-piece.

This consists of joining the end of one tube to the side of another. Proceed as in joining two tubes of unequal diameter, only bore the hole in the side of the tube instead of the end. Do not forget to keep warm the side of the tube away from the join.

To seal a Tube in a Larger Tube.

Cut off a length of the narrower tube and then heat it at the point where the seal is to be made. When it is plastic push the two ends together gently, obtaining a small thick bulb, as in Fig. 6. Place this on one side while the wider tube is rounded off. The secret of a neat and reliable seal depends upon making the hole in the end. It is prepared as previously described, but care must be taken to see that it is as nearly symmetrical as possible. This hole must be just big enough to allow the narrow tube to slip inside comfortably. The beginner will find some difficulty with these operations as the judgments have to be made by the eye, and thus experience is needed before efficiency is obtained.

Get hot the two parts which are to be joined and quickly push the narrow tube into position, remembering that if the cold part of one tube rests on the hot part of another then a crack will ensue. Heat up the part around the joint, keeping the tubes pressed in position. The work is, of course, kept rotating, and when fusion occurs take from the flame and blow into shape. The inside tube will sag during the heating, so when the joint is finished this tube should be kept central by turning to different positions until the glass sets. Now anneal well.

To blow a Bulb.

In all the operations so far described the rubber tube has been employed for the purpose of blowing. This method serves very well, but really perfect work cannot be turned out until the operator has learnt to use his mouth direct. This takes a great deal of practice, still much good work can be done though this skill is never acquired. Thus, while a bulb can be blown by means of the rubber tube, a perfect shape cannot be obtained until the other method is mastered.

The first operation is to collect a sufficiency of glass from which to blow the bulb. Pull off a suitable length of glass, then heat near the end, and when plastic push the ends together, obtaining a thickened part. Repeat this operation, giving a succession of bulges, as in Fig. 7. Heat these up in a flame, and by heating and blowing work them into one. Remove the capillary and get the whole very hot. Now with deliberation blow the bulb into shape with a series of gentle puffs, keeping it steadily rotating all the time.

Should the bulb be required in the middle of the tube adopt the same procedure, only cut off instead of pulling off the length of tube required. The open end is stopped with a cork.

The operations so far described embrace the major part of glass-blowing, and by their variations and combinations a multitude of different objects can be made. A few of these will now be described.

An Ear Syringe.

Pull off a suitable length of about 1½-cm. tubing and blow a small bulb

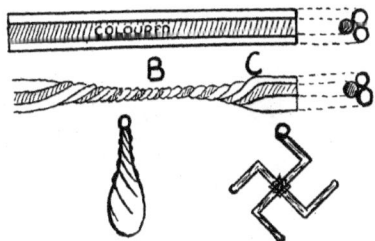

Fig. 10.—Coloured Pendants made from Glass.

as in Fig. 8A, cut off the capillary and fire-polish the end. When this is cold enough to handle slightly ream out the other end. The plunger is made from glass rod. In a medium-sized flame heat up a portion and, by easing the two ends together, collect a mass of glass about the size of a pea. Get this very hot and quickly push the two ends hard together, when the glass will squeeze out as in Fig. 8c. Care must be taken not to get this disc too big to go in the tube. A similar disc is squeezed about ½ cm. behind the first, the spare end of rod being cut off.

At this stage a cork must be bored and fitted on the rod. The other end of the plunger is melted into a small spherical blob or bent round into a ring. Now wrap thread between the two glass discs so that it fits snugly into the jacket as in Fig. 8E.

Many other glass medical appliances can easily be made. Inspection of a chemist's shop window will soon indicate the possibilities.

Glass Ornaments.

The witch's bowl which is in great demand as a table centre-piece can be supplied with ornaments very cheaply. The different designs for these are innumerable, and as a glance in a shop will show the scope, only one will be described here.

Fig. 9 shows clearly the stages of construction. Blow a small bulb in, say, red glass, then fuse a piece of green rod to the end, keeping the bulb in shape by blowing slightly. Heat just round the last join and when plastic push in gently. Now seal off the top. As this seal will suck in, due to the air contracting in the enclosed space, the whole bulb must be kept hot until the seal sets. Make three of these "flowers." No dimensions are given as these depend on the size of the bowl, but Fig. 9 gives the proportions.

A cluster of "leaves" must next be made from green rod. Pull off a piece of this rod and heat half the length by holding it almost in line with the flame. When very hot press flat between an asbestos sheet and the charcoal block. Immediately heat up and bend into a natural-looking shape. In this type of work little faults in shape help to make the work more real. Make three such leaves and join these together so that they will stand firmly, leaving space in the middle to fuse in the "flowers." This last job of assembling is the most difficult. Remember always to keep hot all parts to be worked. Finally, when the correct positions for leaves and flowers are obtained anneal well in asbestos or cotton-wool.

Pendants.

A very pretty effect can be obtained by taking three lengths of rod and placing them together as shown in cross-section in Fig. 10. Heat up as long a length as is possible, and when soft twist quickly and pull slowly. Cut off the piece BC (Fig. 10) and heat the part at C into a neat blob. Now make a tiny ring of rod and fuse on at B, thus producing an attractive "drop." These can be made in a variety of colours. A set of them to match various dresses make a very acceptable present for a lady.

Another easy type is shown in Fig. 10. This simply consists of bent rods. A small piece of different-coloured glass is fused to the junction.

To sum up, the important points in glass-blowing are to keep the work rotating when possible; always anneal when there is any likelihood of cracking; do not work at too high a temperature; think ahead, be patient.

PAINTING OVER ENAMEL

SOMETIMES it is desired to paint the woodwork of a room which has previously been decorated in enamel. Now enamel, particularly if it has been applied a long time ago, is extremely hard and possesses a very smooth glass-like surface.

This is not an ideal surface upon which to apply ordinary oil paint, unless it is first carefully prepared. If the old enamel shows bad signs of cracking, it is best to remove it by means of either the blow lamp or by the use of a chemical paint-removing compound, which can be purchased from any paint merchant's store. If, however, it is in good condition, the old enamel need not be removed, but it will require a thorough rubbing down with either a piece of smooth pumice stone or waterproof sandpaper, using water as a lubricant.

This is the ordinary method of preparing previously painted woodwork or repainting, but, where enamel has previously been used, the rubbing down must be exceptionally thorough, the objects being not merely to render the surface clean and smooth, but to remove the gloss, and thus provide a satisfactory key for the new paint. When, but not until, that has been done, any kind of painting or graining may be executed upon the surface so prepared. Various paint finishes are described in the articles "Painting a Front Door," on p. 65, and "Painting Interior Woodwork," on p. 705, while the article "Graining" on p. 111 is especially informative to those who desire to paint their woodwork to match existing furniture, such as rosewood, walnut, etc.

Simple Garden Tents and Shelters

This article deals with small garden tents suitable for two to four persons, or in the case of tents fitted with extended awnings, from four to six people.

It should here be pointed out that practically all of the tents described are of the portable or easily erected and dismantled types, so that, apart from their specific uses as garden tents, they can also be used for car camping or bathing purposes. They can mostly be packed into a small space suitable for carrying on a car or being dispatched by rail, so that in this way their uses are extended. In all cases these tents can readily be put up in a very short time, usually by one person only.

Types of Small Garden Tents.

There are several alternative types of small garden tent available to the home handyman to construct, and in selecting any particular type consideration must first be given to the accommodation and principal use to which it is to be put. The types selected from the many designs possible to the amateur include the following: (1) the triangular, (2) umbrella, (3) square, and (4) rectangular shelter type.

THE TRIANGULAR TENT

This is the smallest of the available tents for garden use, although by suitably strengthening the construction and adding more guy ropes it can be made in larger sizes, similar in dimensions to the other types described.

Externally, this design of tent has the appearance shown in Fig. 1. It is simple to make and can readily be erected.

The Framework.

The framework, if such it can be termed, consists merely of two vertical tent poles, with a ridge pole connecting them at the top. The lower ends are usually spiked, in order to fix into the ground. If the tent is also required for portability, these three poles can each be made in two or three sections, fitted with brass sockets, as shown in Fig. 2.

Sockets.

The sockets should be made from brass tubing of about 16- to 20-gauge thickness—depending upon the diameter of the poles. They should be a tight fit on the "fixed" side and secured by means of two or three countersunk brass wood screws. The ends of the poles that fit these socket should be a good push fit into the sockets. If the latter be split down with a hack-saw, they will always give a good fit, whereas if left "solid," the wooden members are apt to become loose in time.

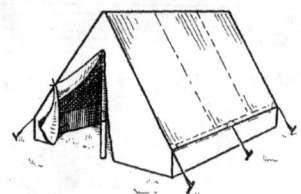

Fig. 1.—The Triangular Tent.

Suitable Dimensions.

Suitable dimensions for the vertical and ridge poles for an average size of tent are as follows:—

Vertical poles: 6 feet 3 inches long by 1½ to 1¾ inches diameter (two).

Ridge pole: 6 feet by 1¾ inches diameter (one).

These poles should be made from ash, although if the tent is of smaller dimensions, pine or silver spruce can be used. The method of fitting the ridge pole, internally, to the vertical poles is indicated in Fig. 3, whilst the external (and simpler) method is that shown in Fig. 4.

The Canvas and Guy Ropes.

The constructor has a choice of coverings for this type of tent. For example, he can use the thinner white fabric similar to that employed for scouts' and hikers' tents, or he can make a much stronger and better job of the tent by using striped tent tick, striped canvas or green rotproof canvas. Where weight is not of primary importance, Willesden green fabric can be employed. The latter has a very long life, but it is apt to bleach to a lighter shade when used in the sun for long periods. The guy ropes can be of hemp or cotton stranded rope, from ½ to ¾ inch diameter, depending upon the size of the tent.

Preparing the Canvas.

The canvas should carefully be measured out and made up into three sections, one for the main ridge and sloping sides and the others for the triangular ends. The latter should be split nearly to the tops, hemmed, and provided with eyelets and ropes. Short lengths of ropes should also be sewn to the edges of the canvas, to enable these sides to be tied in the open position. The dimensions of the canvas for a tent 6 feet high and 6 feet long are shown in Fig. 5.

An addition to the sloping sides that will be found useful to offset their appearance is a rectangular strip of canvas about 6 to 12 inches high, as shown in Fig. 1. This 12 inch strip has been included in the dimensions given in Fig. 5.

In the case of the smaller sizes of triangular tent, the guy ropes can be sewn to the canvas. The rope should, preferably, be looped—or provided with an eye—before sewing, and a double patch of canvas sewn to the main sheet in order to strengthen it where the rope is attached.

For smaller tents, the rope can be sewn along the corners between the vertical sides and the sloping sides, so as to allow the ropes to take the pull directly from the tops of the vertical poles; this method ensures that there is no appreciable pull on the canvas due to the guy ropes.

In some cases, notably with small portable tents, the ridge pole can be replaced by means of a rope stretched between the two verticals. If this method is used for larger tents it will be necessary to provide outside guy ropes similar to those marked "A" in Fig. 6. These take the pull of the ridge rope and thus prevent the two vertical poles from pulling inwards. Even when a ridge pole is used instead of a rope, these additional guy ropes will be found an advantage in holding the tent firm in windy weather. The ropes should be taken from the spikes at the top of the tent poles, at an angle of 45 to 60 degrees, to the ground.

THE UMBRELLA TENT

This is an exceedingly simple form of garden tent that utilises a large "umbrella" or garden sunshade, with

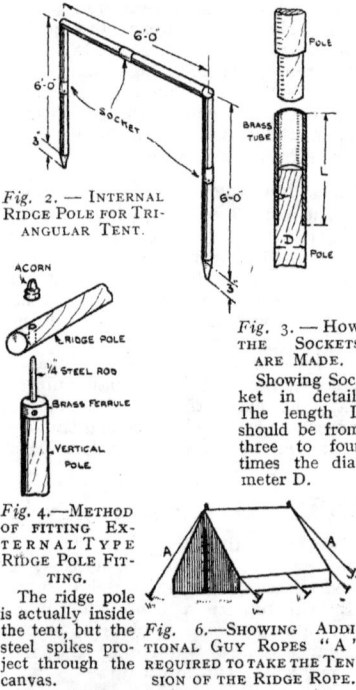

Fig. 2.—Internal Ridge Pole for Triangular Tent.

Fig. 3.—How the Sockets are Made. Showing Socket in detail. The length L should be from three to four times the diameter D.

Fig. 4.—Method of Fitting External Type Ridge Pole Fitting. The ridge pole is actually inside the tent, but the steel spikes project through the canvas.

Fig. 6.—Showing Additional Guy Ropes "A" required to take the Tension of the Ridge Rope.

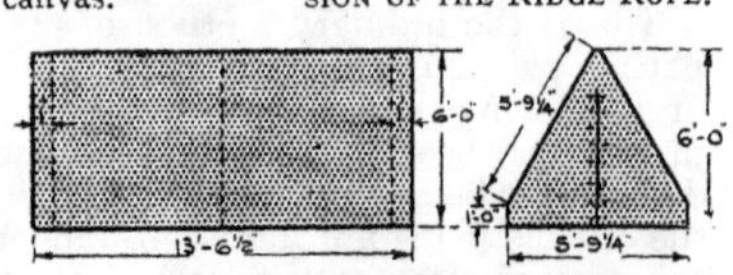

Fig. 5.—Showing Dimensions of Canvases for Triangular Tent.

SIMPLE GARDEN TENTS AND SHELTERS

the addition of side curtains. It is easy to erect, requires no elaborate guy ropes and, if the centre pole is of the jointed type, it is easy to pack up and transport. It has an advantage over the previously described tent of giving more head-room; moreover, it can also be used as a bathing tent.

Dimensions.

Garden or beach umbrellas are from 4 to 7 feet diameter, and are provided with poles of about 6 feet in height. In some cases, also, wire loops are provided near the ends of the ribs for the attachment of the side curtain to form the sides of the tent, as shown in Fig. 7.

If such eyelets are not provided, a simple substitute for these can be made by bending 12- to 14-gauge brass wire into figure-eight shape, attaching one loop of each over the rib end beneath the canvas of the umbrella; if necessary, these loops can be sewn into position with strong thread after bending the wire around the ribs.

The Side Curtains.

The side curtains are made of tent fabric to match the top covering, and are provided with hems at the top and bottom. Small hooks of the type employed for attaching curtains to runner rings are used to connect the top of the side curtains to the rib loops. Although we have used the term "side curtains," actually only a single curtain need be used. This can be made by sewing together several widths of canvas or tent fabric in order to obtain the necessary periphery to suit that of the tent.

If the diameter of the opened umbrella, measured across the loops on the ends of the ribs, is 5 feet, the upper curtain length will be approximately 16 feet. It is advisable to make the lower periphery or curtain length 19 or 20 feet in order to provide greater space inside the tent on the ground.

The canvas will therefore be of a tapered shape. It should have a hemmed and eyeletted slit for ingress and egress, with cotton rope fasteners after the style of proprietary makes of tents. For garden use, some of the upper hooks can be detached in order to form a partially opened tent or shelter, the canvas being allowed to hang open at the sides.

Securing the Lower Edges of Curtain.

Finally, the lower edges of the side curtain should be provided with ropes sewn into position at about 3-feet intervals, for attachment to ground pegs. The object of this is to prevent the wind from blowing the side curtain out of place. If the tent is to be used for bathing purposes, since the ground pegs mentioned cannot effectively be used, strong pockets should be made

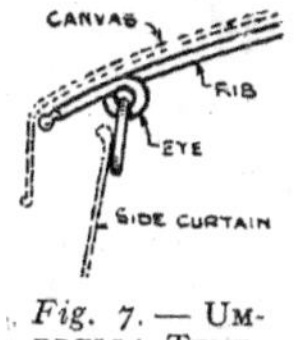

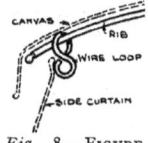

*Fig. 7.—*Umbrella Tent. Showing wire eyelets on umbrella ribs, for attachment of side curtains.

*Fig. 9.—*The Complete Umbrella Garden Tent.

Figs. 7 and 8 show methods of attaching the side curtains to the umbrella.

*Fig. 8.—*Figure Eight Eyelets can be sewn to the Ribs of Ordinary Beach Umbrellas for Holding Side-Curtains.

around the lower edge, so that by filling these with sand or pebbles, the side curtains can be kept in position.

THE SQUARE TENT

The square tent offers certain advantages over the round umbrella type in the matter of giving more space inside and in being somewhat easier to construct.

Although there are several methods of making the square tent, the simplest, from the point of view of portability and ease of erection, is that based upon the four-rib umbrella plan shown in Figs. 10 and 11. As will be seen, later, a square tent can also be

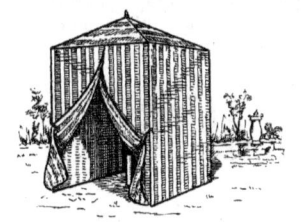

*Fig. 10.—*Appearance of Finished Square Pattern Centre Pole Tent.

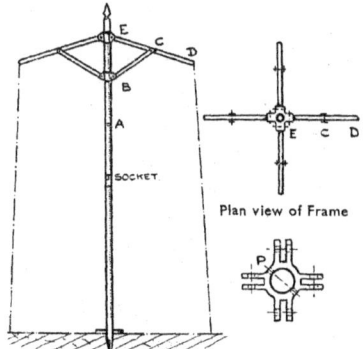

Fig. 11.— Frame for Square Tent.

Fig. 12.— Details of Fixed and Sliding Sockets.

made on the diagonally braced vertical frame method.

Referring to Fig. 10, this shows a centre pole square tent having four symmetrical ribs to hold the corners of the tent fabric. The vertical sides hang down and are secured at the corners of their lower ends by means of short pickets or pegs driven into the ground. Tapes, sewn securely on to the corners of the fabric, are used to secure these corners to the pegs, thus preventing the fabric from blowing out of shape in windy weather. Sand pockets sewn along the lower edges of the fabric can be used as an alternative method of fastening in cases where the tent is used on the beach.

General Arrangement of Framework and Dimensions.

The general arrangement of the framework for this type of tent is illustrated in Fig. 11. Referring to the left-hand illustration, it will be seen that there is a vertical pole A, provided with a spiked end for holding it into the ground. The pole should be about 6 feet to 6 feet 3 inches in height and $1\frac{1}{2}$ to $1\frac{3}{4}$ inches diameter; it should, preferably, be of ash. There are four "ribs" similar to ECD, each attached to a fork end, E, in the ring-socket member shown, in plan view, in Fig. 12; the latter can be cut out of a block of beech or whitewood. It should be secured to the upper end of the pole A, by gluing and pegging, a hole P (Fig. 12) being made for this purpose. The holes for the pins should be from $\frac{1}{8}$ to $\frac{3}{16}$ inch diameter, the pins (which are of brass) being a tight fit in the socket portion and a free fit in the ends of the ribs ECD; brass split pins can be used for this purpose.

The latter should be from 18 to 24 inches in length and about $1\frac{1}{4}$ by $\frac{5}{8}$ inch section, with the longer side vertical. Ash, pine or any other suitable wood can be used. The socket B is similar to that shown in Fig. 12, but is made a sliding fit on the rod so as to enable the ribs to be drawn down nearly flat against the pole when the tent is not in use.

To facilitate easy carrying and storage of the frame, the pole A should be made in two 3-feet lengths, jointed with a brass socket of the bayonet-joint pattern. The end of the upper pole that fits into the brass socket of the lower one should, preferably, have a brass ferrule; otherwise the bare wood will wear slack in time.

The Covering.

The covering of the tent should be made in one piece, i.e., the top and sides sewn so as to form a single unit. It is best to obtain a paper pattern from the framework for the square-pyramidal sides of the fabric, and, after allowing the necessary overlap

SIMPLE GARDEN TENTS AND SHELTERS

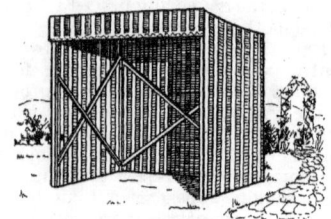

Fig. 13.—A Simple Garden Shelter of the Folding Frame Type.

for the seams, to sew the four sides together.

As the tent is to be used both closed and as a partly open garden shelter, one vertical side should be arranged to be hooked—not sewn—to the pyramidal side. It is also a good plan to make the vertical sides wider at the base (or ground level) than at the top, in order to give greater accommodation.

THE RECTANGULAR GARDEN SHELTER

One of the most popular forms of garden shelter in use to-day is the rectangular type shown in Figs. 13 and 14. The former is a simple tent with a short fringe at the front, whilst the latter has an extending awning, which can, however, be hinged out of the way if not required.

Construction of Framework.

In each of these types the construction of the framework is on the same principle. It consists of four vertical members each of three consecutive pairs being cross-connected by means of bracing struts. The latter are so arranged that the four vertical members can be folded together for transport or storage purposes.

The arrangement of the framework for these shelters is shown in Fig. 15. There are two side frames ABCD and FGHE. These are connected together at the correct distances apart by means of struts S. These two side frames are in their turn connected together by means of the longer struts S, jointed to the back vertical members AB and FG. To complete the framework and to make it absolutely rigid there is a separate framework ADEF, consisting of two longitudinals AF and DE and two sides AD and EF. This top frame drops over pins let into the tops of the four vertical members. There is an alternative top frame arrangement, viz., that shown in Fig. 18, consisting of two longitudinals AF and DE, and two short diagonal struts, made so that the frame can be folded together.

Dimensions of Shelter.

A popular size of garden shelter is one measuring 6 feet in length by 3 feet deep, the front and back heights being 6 feet and 5 feet 6 inches respectively.

Particulars of the side, back and top frames for this size of shelter are given in Figs. 16 to 18. The diagonal stays are pin-jointed with $\frac{3}{16}$-inch rod and washers (or bolts and nuts) to the sides of the verticals, and also to each other at their central parts. In order to enable each side of the framework to fold together, that is to say, for the two verticals to be closed together, one of the diagonals is made in two parts, as shown in Fig. 19. The end of the longer member is at N, whilst MQ is a short member having pin joints at M and at Q.

The overlapping portion MN acts as a guide and a friction surface. When the longer strut is pushed upwards the member MQ hinges as shown by the dotted lines M'N', thus allowing the two struts S to fold flat against the verticals AB and CD (Fig. 16). The same principle is employed for each of the three vertical sides and for the separated top section.

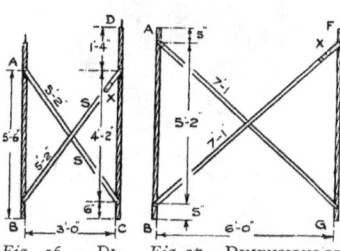

Fig. 16.—Dimensions of the Two Side Frames ABCD and FGHE.
X indicates frame hinging device shown in Fig. 19.

Fig. 17.—Dimensions of the Back Frame.

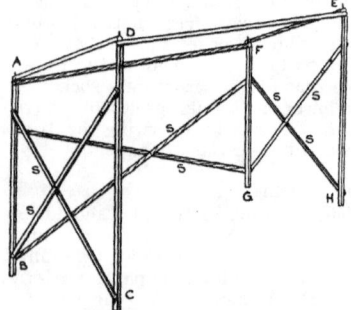

Fig. 15.—The Wooden Framework of Garden Shelter.

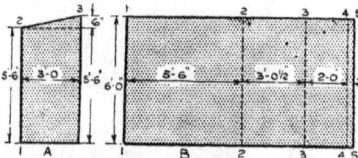

Fig. 22.—Showing Shapes and Dimensions of Two End Pieces A and Back, Top and Canopy Sheet B.

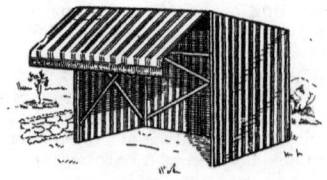

Fig. 14.—Garden Shelter of Folding Frame Type, with Additional Extension Canopy.

In this manner the three sides mentioned will close together, and the top separately.

The principal dimensions of the framework members are given in Figs. 16, 17 and 18, but it should be pointed out that those for the diagonals are approximate only, and should therefore be checked in position; these dimensions are accurate, however, to within about 1 inch.

The sectional dimensions of the verticals are given in Diagram A, Fig. 20, and of the diagonals in Diagram B of the same illustration. These members should be made in well-seasoned straight-grained red pine or silver spruce. Ash can be used for greater strength, but it is, of course, much heavier.

The Covering for Framework.

It will be found more convenient to make the covering in one complete unit by first cutting out the two sides and then sewing these to the common back, top and canopy or awning piece. Allowance should be made when cutting out for the extra widths necessary for the common overlapping portions that are afterwards sewn together.

The dimensions of the two end and centre pieces for the shelter previously described are given in Fig. 22.

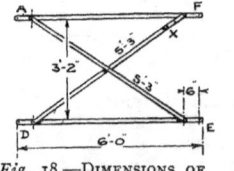
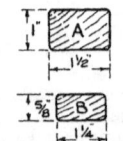

Fig. 18.—Dimensions of Roof Frame.
X indicates frame hinging device shown in Fig. 19.

Fig. 20.—Sections of Main and Cross-members.

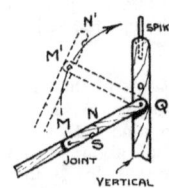
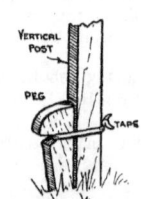

Fig. 19.—Showing one Method of Arranging for the Framework to Fold up Flat

Fig. 21.—The Method of Securing the Feet of the Four Vertical Members to the Ground.

Constructing an Outside W.C.

The all-important consideration when undertaking the construction of an outside water closet is naturally the disposal of the sewage in accordance with local conditions and rules. The result will have to be accomplished to the satisfaction of the sanitary authorities, but the following description will give a general idea as to how to set to work.

Whether there exists main drainage or a cess-pool system will not really concern us in this article so long as the joints connecting up to the main disposal drains are properly constructed.

Foundations.

First of all, the site must be determined and excavations for the foundations must be undertaken.

Assuming that the desired apartment is to be built such as is shown on Fig. 1 and in a position adjacent to the brick wall of a house, and that the ground thereabouts is ordinary earth, first of all measure out the area required, say 3 feet wide by 4 feet 6 inches deep. Mark out the space to be occupied and excavate to about 12 inches deep. Put in about 9 inches of hardcore (broken bricks or tiles, etc.), well ram and then fill in with concrete composed of Portland cement and ballast (hardcore) to about 3 inches above the general level of the ground, then finish off with a coat of cement and sand (one of cement to three of sand) trowelled to a smooth coat after your walls have been built.

We will assume for our purpose that the manhole and main run of drainage is in the position as shown in Fig. 2.

Laying the Drains from the Nearest Manhole.

Now proceed to lay your drain from the nearest manhole up to the W.C. apartment by cutting through the side of the manhole. Cut out the benching (sloping sides on floor of manhole) and build in a channel bend as shown in Fig. 3, and continue to lay your drain in a trench about 9 inches wide from this point in stoneware pipes. (These pipes are 4 inches in diameter, and must be cemented at the junction, Fig. 4, A and B.) They must be laid in a straight line up to the new W.C., and must be finished off with a bend ready to be joined on to the "S" trap (Fig. 5) of your basin (Fig. 5). The fall should not be less than 1¼ inches for every 10-foot run of drain.

Before laying the drain pipes the trench should be concreted.

Covering the Pipes.

Fill in the ground over the pipes. Great care should be exercised to see that you do not ram the earth too hard for fear of disturbing the joints of the pipes.

If the pipes are near the surface,

Fig. 1.—The Outside W.C. built as described in this Article.

they should be entirely encased in concrete before the trench is filled in.

The manhole, if properly constructed, will be of brick, and a part of one side will have to be removed to allow of the new drain being fitted through.

Having laid the drain in position, fix it with cement at the junctions, and replace the brickwork above and around it, thus replacing the side of the manhole as it was before (Fig. 6).

What to do if there is no Manhole nearby.

Supposing there is no manhole nearby and you have to join up your drain pipe to the existing main, you will have to use a bend as shown in Fig. 7. This is done in the country at times, but it is not advisable, by reason of the fact that a stoppage might take place. It is better to build a small manhole with a channel bend connected to the channel drain running through the manhole. Fig. 6 is explanatory as to how a manhole is built. Excavate to a depth of a few inches below the drain and fill in with concrete. Build up the sides with brick. The bottom must be benched as shown in Figs. 3 and 6. The cover and frame should be cast iron, and can be purchased.

Building up the Walls.

Now build up the walls of your apartment upon the concrete foundation described above. The wall of the

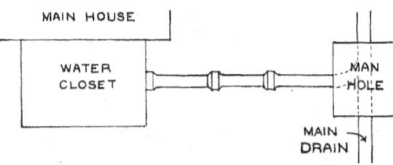

Fig. 2.—Manhole and Main Run of Drainage.

house on to which the apartment butts will form one side, whilst the other three can be built of either brick or 2-inch coke breeze slabs. In both cases cement mortar, Portland cement, and sand must be used, and both walls must have bonded joints. In the case of brick, any bond will do—say Flemish (Fig. 8)—and in the case of the breeze slabs these would be laid as shown in Fig. 9. It will be unnecessary to disturb the main house wall by bonding your new wall into it, but the walls must have footings (Fig. 10).

The walls should be not less than 6 feet 3 inches high from the floor to the lowest side of the apartment.

Damp-course.

It will be necessary to inset a "damp-course" about two bricks up from the ground (Fig. 11).

Damp-courses can be made of slate or of bituminous sheet, which can be purchased cheaply.

If thought advisable, a brick can be left out from one of the outside walls and an iron grating inserted forming a ventilator.

Rendering the Walls.

The walls can be rendered with cement and sand (three parts sand, one of Portland cement, mixed with water), which, whilst still wet, should be scored across in order to give a key to the setting coat of Portland cement, which is trowelled on to a flat and even face. Portland is used as setting coat for outside work in preference to Keene's.

The Floor.

The floor should be raised about 4 inches to prevent rain from beating in under the door, and, furthermore, should be formed to slope outwards towards the door. The floor can be finished in the same way as the walls, the finished face being of Portland cement and sand.

The Door Frame.

Now for the door and frame. The frame can be made of deal, two uprights and a cross-piece or rail. The upright at the side nearest the main wall should be 3 or 4 inches higher than the other, and the other should project above the brickwork about 1 inch in order to line with the wall plate which has to be fixed along the top of the wall for the joist to rest upon: Figs. 12 and 13 are explanatory. The support for the joists on the other side is formed by a piece of deal about 2 × 3 inches morticed and tenoned into the upright and fixed into the main wall. At the other end of the apartment, outside, nail a triangular piece the shape of the front rail to fill up the gap caused by the varied height of the uprights.

All three door-frame pieces should

CONSTRUCTING AN OUTSIDE W.C.

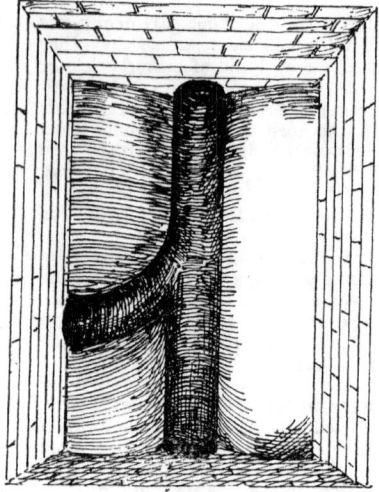

Fig. 3.—Laying Drain from Nearest Manhole.

First cut through the side of the manhole, and then cut the sloping sides on floor of manhole in the form of a channel bend, as shown. Drain pipes are then laid in a trench from this to the new W.C.

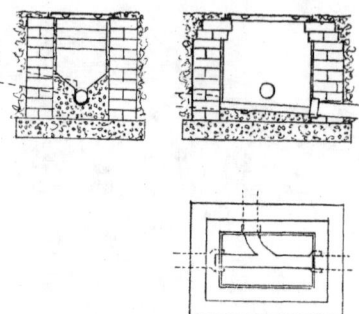

Fig. 6.—The Manhole with the Newly-constructed Outlet to the W.C.

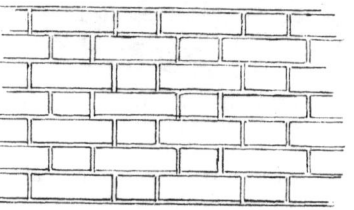

Fig. 8.—Building the Walls of the Apartment with Brick.

A good method of bonding the bricks is the Flemish bond, as above.

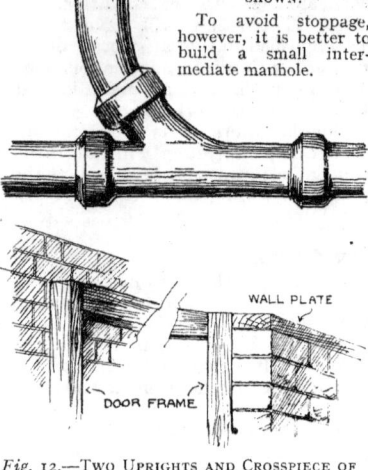

Fig. 7.—Where there is no Manhole nearby, the Drain Pipe can be Joined to the Existing Main, using a Bend as shown.

To avoid stoppage, however, it is better to build a small intermediate manhole.

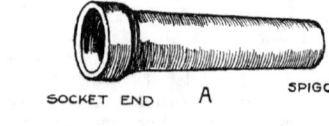

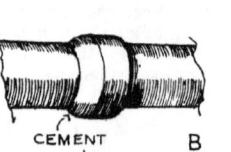

Fig. 4.—Stoneware Pipe for the Drain.

Showing (B) the method of joining the sections of pipe. The pipe must be laid in a straight line up to the new W.C. The fall should not be less than 1¼ inches for every 10-foot run of drain.

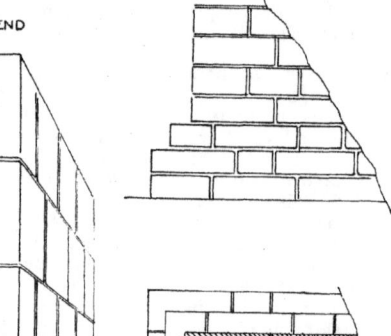

Fig. 9.—Method of Laying Breeze Slabs for Walls.

Fig. 10.—The Walls of the Apartment should have Footings as shown.

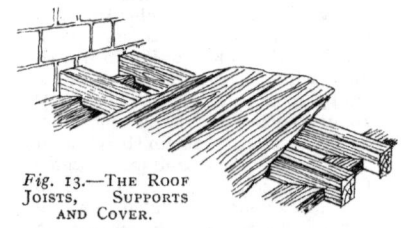

Fig. 12.—Two Uprights and Crosspiece of Door Frame.

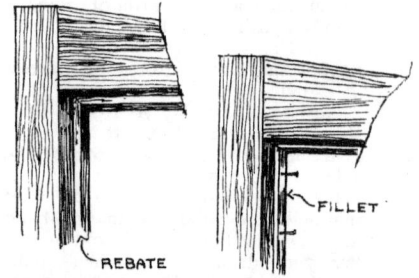

Fig. 13.—The Roof Joists, Supports and Cover.

Figs. 14 and 15.—Two Methods of Rebating Door Frame to form a "Stop" for the Door.

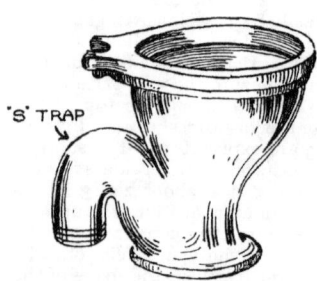

Fig. 5.—The Drain Pipe should be Finished off with a Bend ready to be Joined on to the "S" Trap of the Basin.

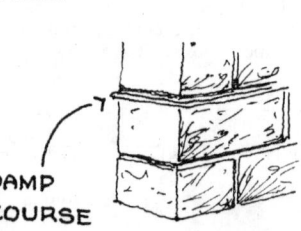

Fig. 11.—Inset a Damp-course in the Walls about Two Bricks up from the Ground.

Fig. 16.—The Door Frame is Fixed into Brickwork by Irons built into Joints of Walls.

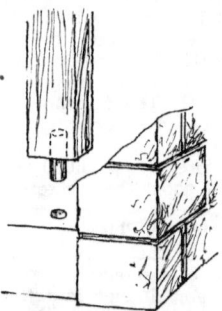

Fig. 17.—How Feet of Door Frame are Fixed into Concrete Floor.

CONSTRUCTING AN OUTSIDE W.C.

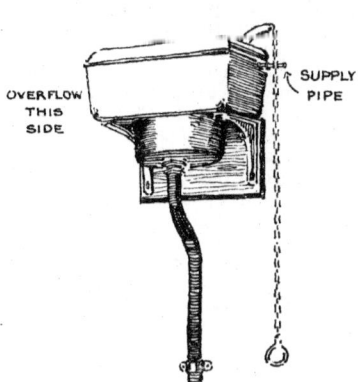

Fig. 18.—Method of fixing Cistern.

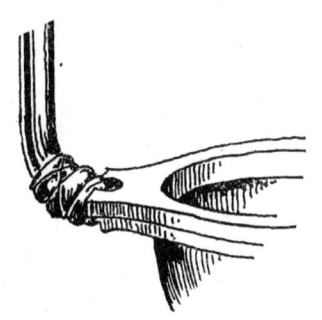

Fig. 19.—The Flush Pipe should be connected to Closet by means of a Putty and Rag Joint.

Fig. 20.—Connect Water Supply Pipe to Closet Cistern to Nearest Supply Point by means of "Wiped" Joint.

Fig. 21.—Don't forget the Overflow Pipe from Closet Cistern.

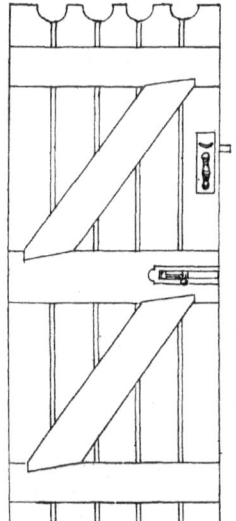

Fig. 22.—Construction of the Door.

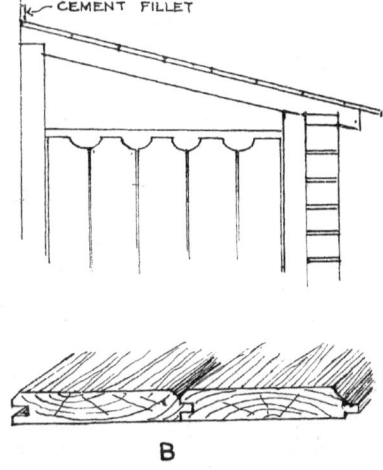

Fig. 23.—Constructional Details of Roof. B shows ½-inch matchboarding for nailing to roof joists.

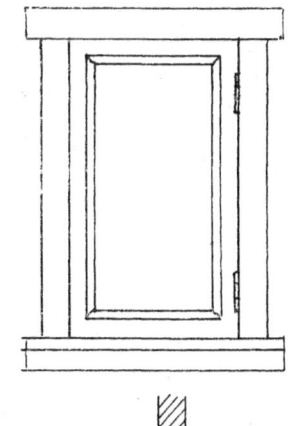

Fig. 24.—Type of Window to fit, if required.

be rebated as shown in Fig. 14 in order to form a "stop" for the door, or a more simple method of forming the "stop" is to nail a narrow piece of wood on to the frame (Fig. 15).

The door frame is generally erected first, and the brickwork built up around it. It should be fixed by means of short lengths of hoop iron nailed to the frames, and built into the joints of the walls (Fig. 16). The feet are fixed by means of small dowels of ½-inch iron barrel or solid iron let into the concrete (Fig. 17).

Fixing the Closet Basin.

Now fix the closet basin (price from 19s.), and connect to bend left in floor and cistern complete with ball valve with a supply pipe connected to the cold water supply from the tank, which, no doubt, will be found in the roof of your house.

Fixing the Cistern.

The cistern—2 gallons—(price 14s.) can be fixed to the wall by means of cast iron cantilever brackets screwed to a flat board fixed to the wall and the flush pipe set as shown (Fig. 18). The pipe should be connected up to the closet by means of a putty and rag joint, shown in Fig. 19.

Connecting up Water Supply to Cistern.

Now the supply. This must be connected up to the cold water supply pipe from the tank, and the joint must be made in the following manner.

First of all turn the water supply off from the cold water tank. There, no doubt, will be a tap somewhere for this purpose. Join on your supply pipe leading into the closet cistern to the nearest convenient point by means of a "wiped" joint (Fig. 20).

Overflow Pipe.

There must be an overflow pipe from the closet cistern. You will find the position for this indicated as shown in Fig. 18. Take the pipe through the wall to project about 6 inches (Fig. 21). This overflow pipe is only put there as a safeguard to prevent the cistern overflowing, and if you see water dripping from it, you will know that there is something wrong with the ball-valve at the cistern which will consequently require attention.

Making the Door.

The door itself can be made of matchboarding nailed on to a frame constructed as shown in Figs. 22 and 23 B. The head of this should be shaped out as shown, forming ventilation.

Hang the door with ordinary butts

or strap hinges as shown, with a stable latch and a bolt on the inside.

The Roof.

Now for the roof. You have made one side of the door frame projecting higher than the other. This is for forming a "fall" for the roof, so as the rainwater will fall away from the main wall of the house (Fig. 12).

Now get some ½-inch matchboarding (Fig. 23B) and nail them on to your joists, allowing them to overlap on the three sides about 1½ inches (Fig. 23). Having done this, cover the whole roof over with tarred felt, nailing it on with broad flat-headed nails specially supplied for the purpose; it should have the edges turned over and up against the wall, and cement fillet to render roof watertight, Fig. 23.

Painting.

The door and frame can be painted two or three coats, and the hinges, bolts, etc., Japan blacked. The cistern

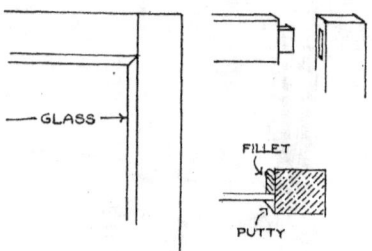

Fig. 25.—Constructional Details of Window.

can also be painted. The walls inside apartment may be twice distempered.

If a Window is required.

No window has been shown on the drawing (Fig. 1) as it may not be deemed necessary, but if it is thought advisable to insert one, it can be made of deal, and is shown in Fig. 24. It can be quite small, and should be set fairly high up. Deal 1½ × 1½ inches will do for the frame, with 4 × 1½ inches for the cill. The cill must slope outwards and should be throated underneath to prevent rain water running down and under and down the face of the wall, Fig. 24A.

The actual casement frame for glazing can be made of deal, 1½ × 1½ inches, and a simple way of making a rebate for the glass is by nailing a fillet on the inside and the glass must be fixed from the outside with putty. Muffled or other opaque glass should be used. Both frames should be morticed and tenoned together to make a good job, Fig. 25.

Hang the casement by means of hinges so as it will open outwards and fit it with a swan-tail catch and casement stay. Paint the wood and other work as you did the door.

It would be well to treat all your timbers, other than that which is painted, with solignum or some other damp-resisting material.

HOW TO CONSTRUCT A SIMPLE BLOW-LAMP

EVERY handy man can, at some time, make use of a blow-lamp.

The design given in detail below offers several advantages—its constructive cost is extremely low—it is foolproof and safe in use and does not require a preliminary warming-up.

It should be borne in mind that this lamp is only intended for short jobs such as soldering and other metal work.

Materials.

One tin 4 inches high × 2¼ inches diameter (*strong* cocoa tin will do).

Three lids to fit the tin.

6 inches thin (metal) tubing—small bore.

1 foot fine rubber tubing (laboratory type).

Two narrow metal bands of length sufficient to overlap diameters of tin and metal tube when soldered together.

One length heat-resisting twine.

Quantity cotton waste.

Methylated spirits.

Solder, etc.

Construction.

Remove bottom of tin at AA.

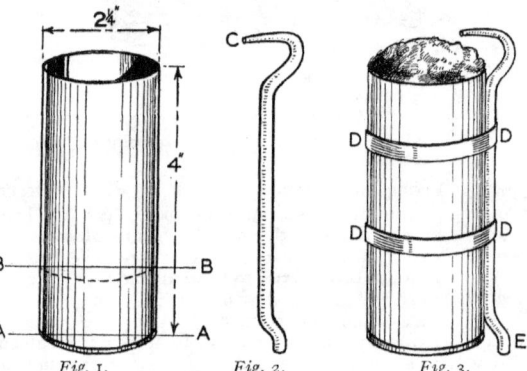

Fig. 1. Fig. 2. Fig. 3.

Perforate one of the lids and insert inside at BB solder, if necessary, for good fit, as in Fig. 1.

Take the metal tube, heat and bend gently to shape as in Fig. 2, taking care to preserve its diameter intact throughout. The orifice of the bent end C should be then tapered to half its normal diameter.

Solder together the tube and the tin and strengthen by soldering the metal bands DD overall.

Bind the twine over to the depth of a handhold.

Fit to bottom of metal tubing the rubber tube, as at E in Fig. 3.

Ram into top of holder sufficient cotton waste to fill to nearly depth of perforated plate.

Sprinkle with sufficient spirits to damp as with a petrol-lighter.

Use.

Light top of waste; flame is then projected on to the work by blowing steadily down the rubber tubing. The resultant heat-power is amazing.

When not in use evaporation of fuel is saved by fixing the two remaining lids on each end of holder.

The rubber end can be made hygienic by fitting thereon a suitable ebonite or bone mouth-piece.

A better quality model can be constructed in brass.

A blow-lamp of this type cannot, of course, be used for burning off paint or other work where continuous and fairly extensive heating is required. In such cases readers would be well advised to purchase one of the excellent commercial types of lamp which are now available at as low a price as 6s. or 7s.

How to Get the Best Service from Your Gas Appliances

There are many simple adjustments which can be made by the average householder in correction of some fault in the house gas supplies.

Some trouble will be beyond home treatment, and recourse to the fitter or supply company will be necessary; but provided common sense is used and these simple directions followed, all the jobs herein specified should be well within the scope of the intelligent handy man.

The Perfect Gas Flame.

To adjust appliances correctly, the principle and general structure of a bunsen flame must be known.

The principle is simply that in passing through the burner tube, gas draws in air through a suitable hole or holes provided for the purpose at the lower end. The two become mixed in their passage up the tube, and the result of burning is as follows:—

It will be noticed that the flame consists of two cones.

The inner cone consists of a partly burned mixture of gas and air of a green colour, whilst the outer cone is almost colourless, but at most slightly purplish, and should result in complete combustion of the mixture, the hottest part being on the outer edge.

There must be no sign of a yellow tip to the flame, otherwise the proportion of gas to air is wrong, and an imperfect mixture is the result.

An ideal burner is one so constructed as to draw in the correct amount of air according to the conditions of the gas supply.

Manipulation of both gas and air regulators on any apparatus so fitted will prove a simple task, the aim being to get a flame as near as possible to that indicated, the inner cone being short and sharp. A slight hiss is desirable.

Care should also be taken to see that the flame is not too long.

Trouble with General Supply.

If not traceable to any particular appliance or pipe, call in the company. It is probably due to service trouble between main and meter, and can only be dealt with by them.

LIGHTING

Pipe stoppages are best dealt with by a competent man, as they require either careful use of a force pump, or relaying.

Fig. 1.—Where Water is Drawn Out of the Gas Supply System.

Condensation of moisture in the gas and its collection inside the gas system causes trouble. In order to collect this free water at one point so that it causes no obstruction and can be drawn off when convenient, what is known as a syphon is inserted. This simply consists of a vertical pipe with a removable bottom end.

Most lighting troubles are traceable to dirt or faulty adjustment of burners. The most probable part is the gas adjuster in an ordinary burner, or the ejector of the Metro burner used by the South Metropolitan and South Suburban Gas Companies.

The adjuster consists of a needle moving up and down within a small hole, and can be clearly seen in Fig. 6. This operation is effected by turning the screw adjustment, the hole being closed when the needle is down.

A stoppage within a burner may often be cured by the sudden turning on of the gas. The obstruction, if very small, like dust, is dislodged by the gas pressure.

If this is not successful, the simplest test for the location of the trouble is as follows:—

See that the burner is clean and free from soot and dust.

Open the gas-way fully by means of the adjusting wheel.

Turn on the gas momentarily, but do not light it.

If the supply is good, there will be a pronounced hiss as the gas passes through the burner.

First examine Burner for Fault and clean.

If the supply is poor, the fault may first be sought within the burner itself.

To trace this:—

Remove mantle, and unscrew the burner from the fitting. Unscrew the adjuster from the body of the burner and clean the needle valve thoroughly with the brush, at the same time turning the adjusting wheel so as to get the gas-way entirely free of dust.

The opportunity should now be taken of dismantling the whole burner for cleaning.

How to adjust Supply of Gas and Air.

With gas on and alight at nozzle, turn the wheel of the gas adjuster until the flame is correct. This is when the inner cone is of a bluish tint and the outer cone pale purplish and not too long—also noiseless (Fig. 5).

If noisy, close air ports slightly, and if tip of flame becomes luminous restrict the flow of gas.

Fix mantle and light up. The flame should just fill the mantle. Further slight adjustment may be made as necessary.

Byepasses.

Accurate resetting is an easy matter. The method is clearly seen in the sketch (Fig. 8). The tip need not usually be more than ⅛ inch in length.

Switches.

If the switch valve operates when switch is opened, but no light results, the byepass must be out.

Should the valve not open it is probably due to stickiness, a condition which is very simple to correct.

Fig. 2.—A Likely Source of Trouble.
Absence of a syphon will mean trouble, such as oscillation of the light owing to the presence of free water in the gas supply system. The picture shows a place in the pipe system where the water would naturally gravitate to and where a syphon should have been inserted.

HOW TO GET THE BEST SERVICE FROM YOUR GAS APPLIANCES

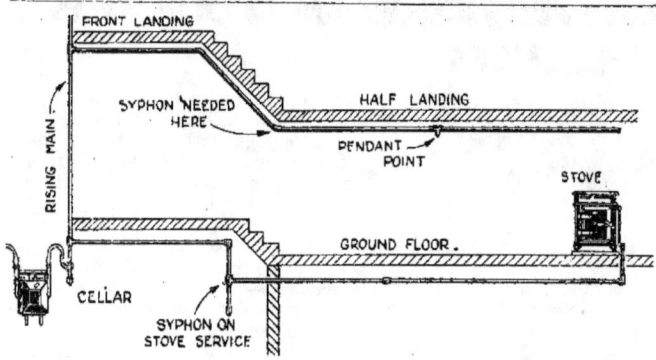

Fig. 3.—A Syphon should be fitted wherever there is a Change in Level of Two Runs of Pipe.

The picture shows a syphon correctly inserted on the ground floor where change of level occurs, but one incorrectly omitted from the first floor.

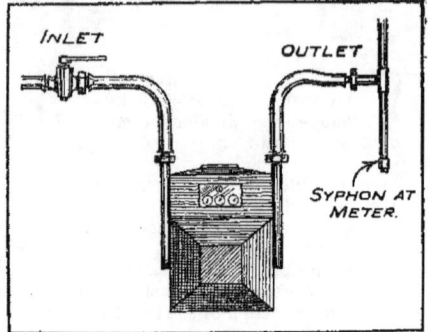

Fig. 4.—Position of the Syphon near the Gas Meter.

This is a short length of pipe with a capped bottom end. Condensed moisture in the system is caught here and should be drained off before it becomes troublesome. It is sometimes desirable to fit a syphon on the inlet also.

Correcting Sticky Valve.

Turn off gas at fitting.

Unscrew knob A shown in Fig. 9 at end of valve and withdraw plunger B.

The inside of the valve and the valve itself can be cleaned out with a piece of chamois leather wrapped round a hatpin or length of wire.

On no account attempt to improve the fit of the valve plunger by filing or by the use of abrasives or metal polishes.

To be always reliable in use, a switch must be operated frequently. It is obviously unfair to decry switches on account of failure due to insufficient use.

Defective Switch Control.

If the valve is not at fault, the trouble is probably within the control itself.

There are two forms of pneumatic switch, one operated by plunger and one by tumbler.

In the plunger switch (see Fig. 11A) the switch knob A is connected to the back of the piston B, which works freely within its airtight chamber. Pulling out the knob sucks the air out of the tube and causes a partial vacuum at the other end, which is attached to the valve piston. Atmospheric pressure then pushes in the knob C until the channel cut in the piston corresponds with the gas-way of the fitting, and allows the gas to flow to the mantle, where it is ignited by the byepass.

Practically the only trouble with this type of switch is loss of vacuum,

Fig. 5.—Method of Adjusting Gas and Air on Inverted Burner.

which is most likely due to a bad fit of the drum within its casing. Or to a slight leak in the air tube, most probably at one or other of the joints where the tubing leaves the switch or enters the valve.

The former is best repaired by fitting a new piston, which is withdrawable after unscrewing the outer casing. Leakage is dealt with later.

Tumbler Switch Trouble.

This may be due to a broken spring.

The tumbler knob is not attached to the piston, as is the plunger, but works on a combination of cam and roller, the latter being on the back of the piston (see Fig. 11B).

Closing the switch compresses the spring which fits on the drum behind the piston. The piston pushes air out of the tube, and the valve at the end is closed.

When the switch is opened the tension of the spring is relaxed, the piston is pushed forward and air sucked out of the tube in the same manner as the plunger type.

Sometimes the tumbler fails to act because the bracket carrying it has come away from the drum.

Reference to Fig. 11B will show that the bracket fits the edge of the

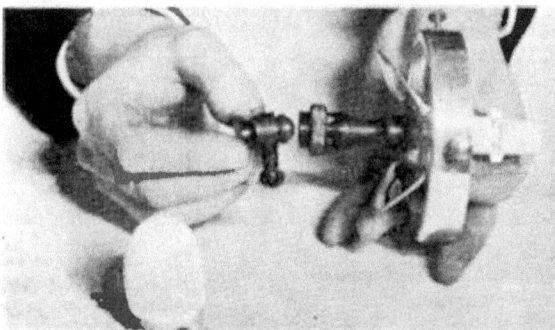

Fig. 6.—The Adjuster consists of a Needle moving up and down within a Small Hole.

Fig. 7.—Clearing a Stoppage within a Burner.

HOW TO GET THE BEST SERVICE FROM YOUR GAS APPLIANCES

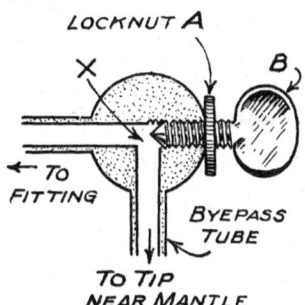

Fig. 8.—How Byepass Flame is Adjusted.
Screw restricts gas supply at X.

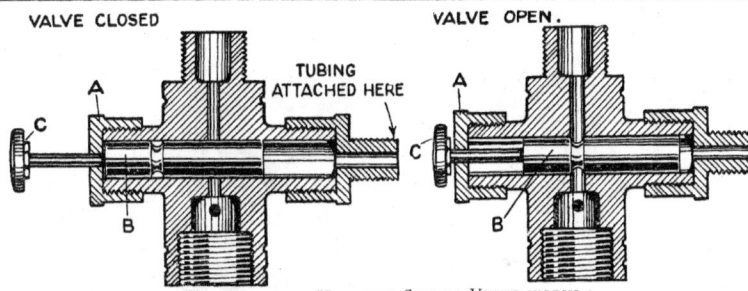

Figs. 9 and 10.—How the Switch Valve works.

Fig. 9 shows the valve closed. It is connected to the switch by air tubing of very small bore. When the switch is opened to switch on the light, the piston B is forced by air pressure into the position shown in Fig. 10. This connects up the gas way and permits the gas to flow to the burner, where it is ignited by the bypass.

drum through the medium of four lugs. Force applied to the switching operation is sufficient sometimes to detach the bracket, which, however, can be replaced with a little trouble.

Dismantling and resetting Tumbler Switch.

Unscrew the outer casing and take completely off.

For the latter trouble—that is, detached bracket—be prepared for dealing with vaseline, as the piston is packed with it, and as soon as the cover is removed the piston will be violently pushed outwards by the spring.

It will be noticed that the two top lugs of the bracket are slightly longer than the bottom ones. This is to allow them to be pushed up sufficiently far to enable the lower ones to be inserted into their own holes at the bottom. When lowered into these there is still some length of lug at the top to hold the bracket upright.

All the time this is being done the spring is pushing against the inside of the piston, so the operation requires patience as well as care.

If the piston is not pushed outward when the cover is removed, the trouble is a broken spring. The bracket will then have to be removed, the piston withdrawn and a new spring inserted.

Keep the piston well greased with vaseline to ensure smooth and easy working.

Defective Tubing.

Kinks and breaks in the tubing can only be repaired by sleeves soldered to the tube.

Particular care must be exercised during this operation, owing to the very small diameter of the brass tubing.

The tubing is joined to the valve and switch by small union connections.

The Newbridge switch control is now widely used. It consists of a wire connecting the switch to the valve on the gas burner or lamp.

It usually works well, but after a long period of use the wire may need tightening by means provided in the device.

HOW TO GET THE BEST OUT OF THE GAS COOKER

Cookers.

Cleanliness is of the utmost import-

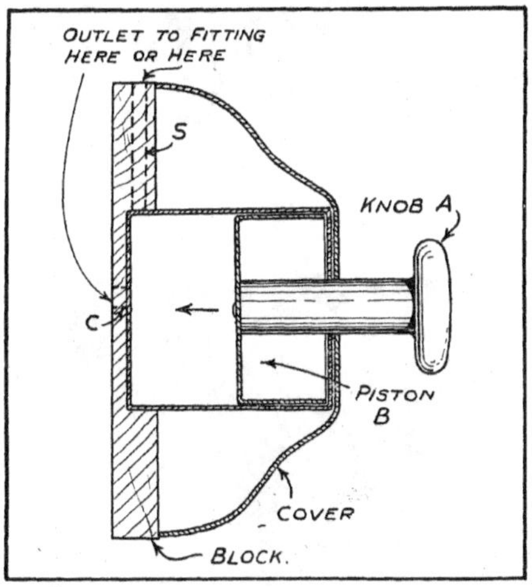

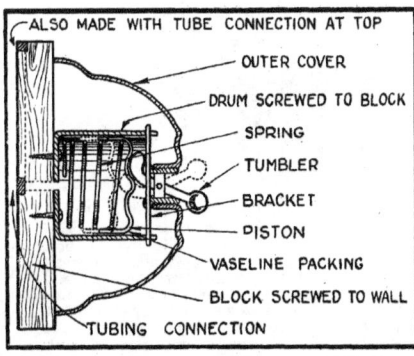

Fig. 11A.—Plunger Switch in Open Position.
C is the outlet for carcassed tubing, S for surface tubing. The only troubles likely to arise with this type of switch are from bad fit of piston and defective tubing.

Fig. 11B.—Tumbler Switch shown Open.

ance in the use of cooking appliances of all kinds.

Burners and feeds must be kept free of dirt and grease.

How to clean Stove Fittings.

Detachable burners may be thoroughly cleaned by immersing in strong soda water and scrubbing with a good hard brush, or boiling in the copper after washing.

Temporary stoppages in odd holes can be cleaned with a brush or piece of wire.

Injectors.—This is another point where grease collects. Dirt too.

Remove burner, turn off gas at stove control cock, clear feed opening of dust, etc., insert soft wire (or pin) into feed, turn on burner tap and clear obstruction with the wire. Replace burner, turn on gas and test. In stubborn cases the gas may be turned on momentarily at the nipple (with great care even lighted), when the flow of gas will probably dislodge any loosened bits of dirt.

Loss of Heat.—If the stove itself is suspected, put a piece of smouldering paper inside the oven and close the door. The smoke will exude from any leaky part.

If the fault occurs at the top of the door, fitting a washer to the hinge will sometimes effect a cure; or the latch can be tightened up.

Oven Gas not burning properly.

Smothering of oven burners is a very dangerous condition to arise in any stove.

It indicates mainly that the products of combustion are being evolved faster than they can be withdrawn from the oven.

Needless to say, it should be guarded against at all costs.

Examining Oven Burners with Hand Mirror.

If oven smells badly when in use, it should be tested for smothering. A small hand mirror will be required. It is obvious that the products will get away as soon as the oven door is opened, whilst the mirror will enable the flames to be inspected with the door closed.

Symptoms of smothering are an unusual roaring noise (somewhat akin to that of the roll of the sea), and in extreme cases a complete breaking away of the flame from the burner jet, followed by its being extinguished altogether.

Some Causes of smothering and the Remedies.

Excessive Consumption. — As incomplete combustion is a matter of adjustment, the burner must be reset.

To adjust oven burner, turn on gas and open air adjuster. Light up and regulate gas flame to suitable length.

Cut down air supply till correct flame is apparent. Flame should be sharp with green inner cone.

Cooker Thermostats.

These seldom go wrong, but if cooking is not perfect, the gas company should be advised.

General Note re Cooker Adjustment.

It should be noted that not all stoves are fitted with variable adjustment, as some gas undertakings have these made and fixed ready for the conditions obtaining in their own areas.

FIRES
Yellow Flames in Gas Fires.

Dust is practically the only cause of yellow flames appearing on a gas fire, barring, of course, a fault in the adjustment. The cure is to clean and readjust.

Cleaning the Burners.

Remove fender from front of fire, take out radiants and burner. Clean out burner tops and feed.

Gas fire burner heads are usually fitted with a gauze, which is fixed at the base of the head.

The simplest test for cleanliness at the gas nipple is to light it at that point. It should burn with a strong steady flame in a direct line towards the centre of the burner orifice. If not directed to the centre exactly, it may be necessary to dismantle the gas injector, but this is a job best done by an experienced fitter.

Adjusting the Flame.

Then adjust gas as for other Bunsen flames, except that a more sluggish flame is required than that for stoves. This fire flame needs to be about 4 inches in length, and should be perfectly silent in use.

Fig. 12.—This Illustration shows the ease with which the Cooker Fittings can be taken out for cleaning.

Fig. 13.—Saving on the Gas Bill.

Much gas will be saved if the gas supply to the cooker is regulated so as to give the best results. Excessive gas supply does not mean more heat. It simply smothers the flame and gives an ineffective yellow flame. The flame should be sharp with a green inner cone. The picture illustrates the adjustment of gas supply. Not all stoves are provided with means of adjustment.

Flue Outlet soon gets choked.

Whilst the fire is disconnected, clean out the flue elbow which fits into the chimney.

Causes and Remedies of Smell.

Insufficient Ventilation.—More pull on the chimney must be provided to correct this fault.

If there is a cowl fitted, it may be damaged, or a brick may be dislodged and block up the flue. If it is necessary to create more updraught, a simple method is to fix sheet iron behind the fire, but to leave a space at the bottom. If the grate opening is entirely covered, there is risk of the chimney pull being too great, lowering the efficiency of the fire by drawing large quantities of cold air through it.

Downdraught.—In this case a chimney cowl fitted outside will in all probability effect a cure.

Sometimes an extra length of flue pipe on the outlet meets the case. This, of course, fits higher up the chimney (Fig. 17).

In obstinate cases a special cowl fixed on the flue outlet may have to be fitted (see Fig. 19).

Noisiness.

This is purely a matter of adjustment.

The gas pressure may be slightly in excess of requirements, and may be cut down at the injector by readjustment.

Lights Back.—Caused by either insufficient gas or excess of air.

Insufficient Heat.

Too Much Updraught.—Usually a case of the fire being fitted too close to the grate, and creating excessive draught.

A typical example is where a gas fire is fixed in front of a tiled surround, completely covering the opening.

Bringing it forward ½ inch will in most cases put things right.

Where sheet iron is fitted, cut a strip off along the bottom at the back of the fire.

Fire Too Small.—This is an obvious fault. There is a tendency in some quarters to judge a fire by the size of the casting, but this is a very dubious method. A surer guide is a chart published by Messrs. Radiation, Ltd. This may be relied on to give complete satisfaction.

Broken Radiants.—Replacement is, of course, easy, and the obvious method. Care must be taken to see that each radiant fits exactly over its burner head; also that the flame is not broken by coming into contact with the edge of the radiant, otherwise only partly burnt gas will be released, causing a smell.

HOW TO GET THE BEST SERVICE FROM YOUR GAS APPLIANCES

Fig. 14.—Adjusting Air to Cooker Gas Ring.
Note the binding screw on the end of the fitting. This is to fix the setting of the air orifice.

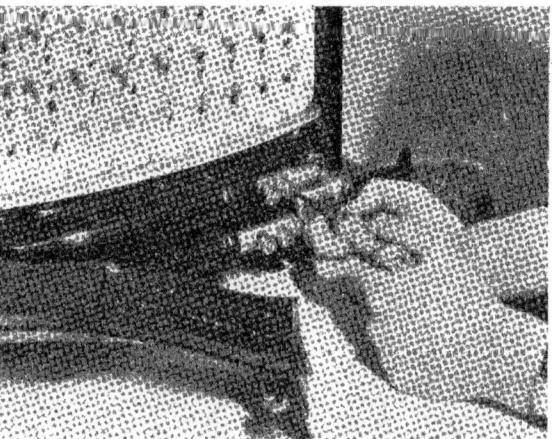

Fig. 15.—Adjusting the Air Supply to a Gas Fire.

Repairing Cracked Firebrick.

Required: Purimachos cement.

In this case, if the crack is a bad one, heat will pass out through the back of the fire instead of being radiated into the room.

Mix a little purimachos cement and fill up the cracks with it. As soon as set (it sets very quickly), replace radiants and test. The brick may also be painted with a very thin solution and will dry white.

Readjust if necessary.

Fig. 23 shows the method of replacing the radiant of a new pattern gas fire now available. The makers call this particular type of radiant a "Unit." It will be noticed that its correct replacement is facilitated by grooved sides corresponding to slanting bars fitted on the casting.

The Welsbach-Kern Radiator.

In time the gauze of this popular little fire gets clogged with dust. This gauze is really a slotted brass sleeve, fitted on to a boss at each end of the burner mixing chamber. It is removable by unscrewing the two screws at the end of the latter. These parts can be clearly seen in Fig. 16 above. The method of reassembly is shown in Fig. 20.

GEYSERS

Water not Hot.

Wrong Sized Burner.—Geysers are usually fitted with luminous burners of the flat flame type, and for every gas supply there is a correct size of burner for geysers. They run from No. 0 upwards, the usual domestic sizes being 0, 1 and 2.

Sooty Burner.—This may also be caused by an incorrectly sized set of burners.

Cleaning and fitting correct burners

Fig. 16.—The Kern Fire Burner.
Shows the gauze sleeve with cap at R.H. end. The boss over which the sleeve fits is clearly seen. This fit must be tight and square, otherwise the burner cannot be properly reassembled.

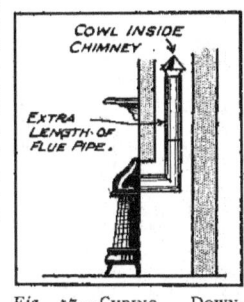

Fig. 17.—Curing Down-draught.
A chimney cowl may be fitted to the flue outlet, with the addition, if necessary, of an extra length of flue pipe.

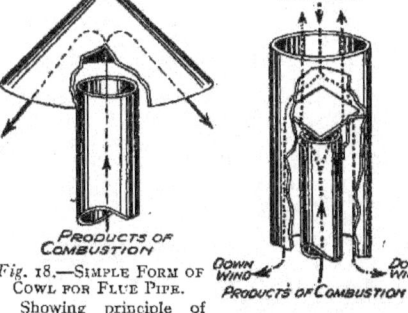

Fig. 18.—Simple Form of Cowl for Flue Pipe.
Showing principle of operation.

Fig. 19.—Cowl incorporating Windguard.

is the only remedy. Your gas company will advise.

Smothering will also cause sooty burners through the flame being forced down upon the burner tips.

Smothering is a very dangerous condition, fully dealt with later.

Feed Water too Heavy.—This is a common complaint.

People expect to get a spout *full* of hot water. With the ordinary domestic geyser this is impossible.

The quantity is more in the region of half a spout full, that is, 2 to 3 gallons per minute.

Too Small Gas Pipe.—Another common fault.

To be sure of complete satisfaction a geyser must have an adequately sized gas supply, at least ¾ inch.

Flues.

Defective Flue.—To be most strongly guarded against. It is almost as bad as no flue at all.

Soot may need cleaning from the geyser. The cowl or baffler may be defective or perforated, or the latter even fitted upside down.

Care should also be taken to see that the baffler or cowl is of efficient type. Cowls are now made incorporating a baffler, but, even so, a baffler should be fitted inside a bathroom whenever there is room for it. See also down-draught.

It cannot be too strongly urged that a geyser should be fitted with a flue

HOW TO GET THE BEST SERVICE FROM YOUR GAS APPLIANCES

outlet to discharge the products of combustion into the open air, or loft.

Importance of Baffler.

Downdraught.—A condition most houses experience at some time or other, and, although difficult to stop, its effect may be considerably lessened.

The function of the baffler is to prevent interference with the flame by wind. It also provides ventilation.

Were the draught allowed to blow directly down the flue into the geyser, the flame would in all probability be smothered and the gas escape.

Baffler Upside Down.—The same effect would be likely to happen if the baffler were fitted the wrong way up. It would be tantamount to its complete absence.

Smothered Flame.

This dangerous condition is due to the absence of a baffler on the flue pipe. It is fully dealt with under downdraught.

A very dirty geyser or a blocked-up flue pipe will create the same effect by preventing the passing of the products of combustion.

Should this occur at any time the geyser must be put out of use immediately and the cleaning put in hand without delay. Delay is dangerous.

Action of Locking Gear Geyser.

In the modern geyser the gas cannot be alight at the burner until water is flowing through, the action being as follows:—

The gas and water supplies are each controlled by a lever tap, the gas tap being locked by the water tap. When off, the latter passes over the former, and not until it has been turned on can the gas tap be fully opened. The moment the water tap is moved, water begins to flow into the geyser.

The gas is first lighted, at the pilot, as it is called. When the water is coming from the spout, not before, the gas tap may be swung round, an action which fully turns on the gas, which is then ignited by the pilot.

Wear may cause the locking taps to be out of gear, but this is a fault easily remedied. Usually the washer on the water tap has failed, and needs replacement. In other cases the head of the tap has worked loose, or worn, allowing the key to pass too far over.

This may be remedied by loosening the screw at the back of the water tap, turning back the lever and tightening up the screw again.

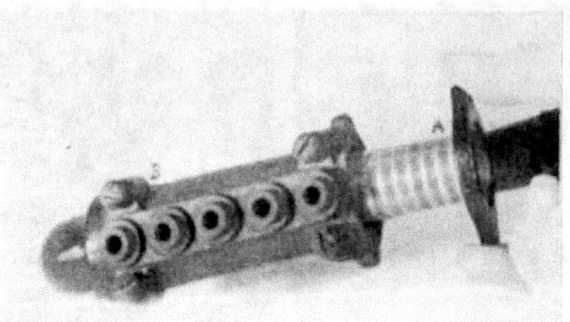

Fig. 20.—The Kern Fire Burner.

Shows method of reassembly. The boss referred to in Fig. 16 is at A, and the other boss at B, at the end of the mixing chamber. The four screws shown are those for securing the burner to the fire casing.

Dual Control Geysers.

Worn Valves.—The above refer only to the locking gear geysers. There are also those fitted with dual valve. These usually have a swing-out burner, in which case all the burner heads act as the pilot.

In spite of the gas being turned on fully, the burners will only light with a tiny tip of flame until the burner is swung in again and the water turned on.

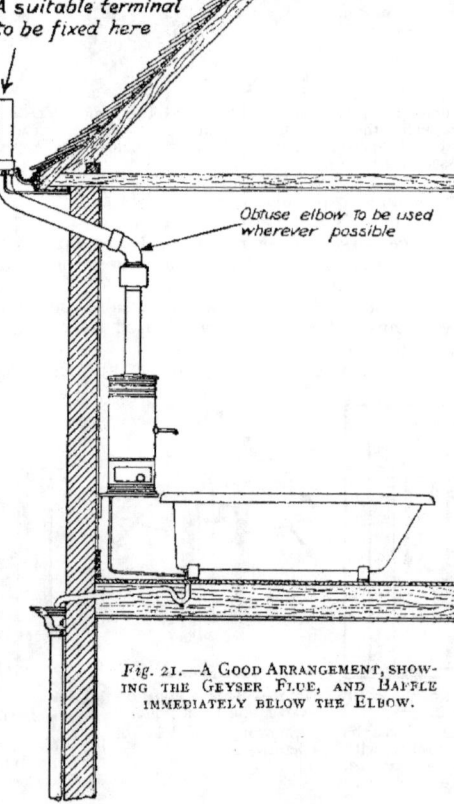

Fig. 21.—A Good Arrangement, showing the Geyser Flue, and Baffle immediately below the Elbow.

The water valve also controls the gas supply, so that if for any reason the water supply fails the gas will be automatically turned down.

The main trouble likely to occur here is wearing of the valves, or perhaps failure to act, but in each case a competent man should be sought.

Some single pilot geysers are also dual fitted.

Slight Noise or "Bump" when Lit.

This is due to the pilot jet being choked and shortening the flame to less than that required to reach the burner when the gas is turned fully on.

It may be rectified by passing a very fine needle through the pilot lighter, momentarily turning on the gas the while. The outside should also be cleaned with a rag or brush.

The noise is due to the accumulation of gas liberated when the burner is turned on, forming an explosive mixture before the pilot has had time to ignite the gas at the burners.

COPPERS

Slow Heating.

Probably caused by a choked burner, which in turn is most likely to occur when the flue outlet runs into a brick chimney which was not swept when the copper was fitted.

There may also be a bad supply of gas.

Precaution when Lighting.

Always apply a light before turning on the gas.

ESCAPES

No article in this section could be considered complete without reference to escapes.

Briefly, the attitude should be "SAFETY FIRST."

Turn off gas at meter and ventilate thoroughly. Never use a naked light near a meter or under a floor. Only on very small points, such as taps or minor joints by stove, etc., may a match be used, AND THEN ONLY AFTER REPEATED ABORTIVE ATTEMPTS BY SNIFFING.

Soap, tallow or even fat will effect a temporary repair.

Advise the gas company at once, but always first turn off the supply at the meter.

How to Pebble-dash a Bungalow

The materials required for carrying out this work are sand, Portland cement, washed pebbles, a sieve, a large builder's trowel and a shovel. You will also require to knock up a tray with three sides in which to mix your cement and sand. This can be made of any old pieces of planks, and should measure about 4 × 4 feet (Fig. 4).

First protect Windows and Doors.

Let us suppose for the purpose of this article that the wall surface to be covered is about 20 × 12 feet. No doubt there will be windows, and also doors, with which to contend. Now, as the pebbles have to be thrown on to the wall, the windows and doors must obviously be protected. This can be done with plywood cut to the shape of the openings and nailed on to the wood door or window frames. The frames may, of course, be of metal, in which case, no doubt, a means of wedging will be found to serve the purpose. As a matter of fact, anything handy would do in place of plywood, such as sacking, or any old pieces of wood or cardboard would serve the purpose just as well.

Rake out Mortar Joints between Bricks.

The mortar joints between the bricks should be raked out with any sharp instrument to about ¾ inch in depth. This must be done in order to afford a key for the cement work. It is also a good procedure to hack the surface of the bricks, which greatly helps to make the key doubly effective.

Brush the Wall to remove Grit and Dirt.

Before proceeding to lay on your cement, well brush the wall with a hard brush in order to remove as much grit and dust as possible.

Now wet the Surface.

Then wet the whole of the surface to assist the adhesion of the cement.

Calculating amount of Material required for the Job.

Having prepared your walls and fixed up your protections to windows, etc., proceed to calculate the amount of material required to do the job.

For the above surface, namely,

Fig. 3.—Applying the Second Coat of Cement.

The second coat should be thinner than the first to make it possible to get a good body of shingle before the second coat sets too hard.

Fig. 2.—The Rendering should be well scored or scratched.

This is to form a key to enable the second coat to grip well. It is essential to score longways so that when damping the undercoat or rendering, the water will lay in the key or scratching.

20 × 12 feet, you will require 1 yard of sand, six bushels of Portland cement and ½ yard of pebbles. Wash the pebbles through the sieve with plenty of water. This process gets rid of all unwanted grit, sand, etc.

Mixing the Cement.

Now proceed to mix your cement. Measure out as much sand as will conveniently go into your tray and form it into a sort of sand basin (Fig. 5). Having done this, pour water into it, thus forming a sand basin full of water. Add the cement gradually and mix up to a creamy substance with the shovel. Then scrape in the sand from the underside of the inside edge, in order that it may mix well with the cement. Gradually mix more sand until the whole is well mixed up with the cement, adding more water if necessary. Great care should be taken to see that the mixture is really well balanced; that is to say, no sand should appear in any way detached and the mixture should be all one colour, indicating a good result. The substance should not be too sloppy, but firm enough for adhering to the surface of the wall.

We have assumed that the wall is composed of brick.

Improvised Scaffolding.

Some sort of scaffold will be required from which to apply your cement. This is easy enough, for an improvised platform can be rigged up with two pairs of steps, or anything else, and a couple of planks.

Fig. 1.—Rendering the Wall.

A coat of cement and sand, gauged three parts of sand and one part of cement, should be applied. In the accompanying photographs the work is shown being done before the woodwork of the bungalow is painted, so that there is no need to protect the windows.

Fig. 4.—Three-sided Tray in which the Cement Rendering can be mixed.

Fig. 5.—When mixing the Cement measure out as much Sand as will conveniently go into the Tray and form it into a sort of Sand Basin, as shown.

HOW TO PEBBLE-DASH A BUNGALOW

Applying the First Coat of Cement.

Now take a pail full of cement and, with a large builder's trowel, spread it over the surface and in the reveals of the windows and doors (Fig. 7) about ¾ inch thick. Care should be taken when spreading it on that an even surface is obtained. To prevent waste, spread sacks along the ground near to the wall. This will catch any cement, for no doubt a great deal will drop.

Making a Key for the Second Coat.

Having covered the surface with the cement mixture, cross hatch it with the point of your trowel or any other instrument whilst still soft. This has to be done in order to obtain a key for the second coat which has to be put on. When the surface of this first coat is nearly dry, prepare another lot of cement in the same way as for the first coat, or rendering, as it is called.

Applying the Second Coat.

The second coat should be laid on in

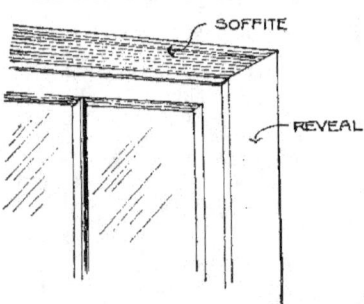

Fig. 6.—Special Care should be taken at the Soffite and Reveal to ensure a Clean Edge is left.

sections, as the pebbles have to be dashed on this coat, and if the whole of the coat were put on at once, the first part might begin to harden before you are ready. Dilution with lime will help to prevent the cement getting hard too quickly. It can be trowelled on in the same manner as for the first rendering, or, better still, use a hand float, if one can be procured, as this will give a smoother surface.

Throwing on the Pebbles.

Having prepared your wall to receive the pebbles, proceed to throw them on with a shovel.

The pebbles should now be pressed in with a large trowel, in order that they shall be properly embedded. It will probably be found possible to do this part of the work from the ground.

The work should be fairly well set in about twenty-four hours, but before leaving it care should be taken to see that clean edges are left up against the windows and doors, etc., before removing the protectors.

Fig. 7.—Throwing on the Shingle.
The shingle and dust are easily brushed off the windows and door frames afterwards.

Fig. 8.—When unable to finish a Wall at One Session, leave the Unfinished Part as an Irregular Shape and not as a Straight Line.
This will make the join not noticeable when the wall is completed. The second coat must be removed from the part which is to be left for completion later.

Fig. 9.—When Restarting after an Interval the Edge of the Join and the Undercoat must be thoroughly damped.
The second coat and shingle can then be applied.

Building a Rockery

It is a sheer delight to the enthusiastic gardener to watch a rockery gradually take shape and become filled with masses of Alpine flowers of many hues. The crannies become veritable rivulets of bloom and the miniature valleys are flooded with enchanting colour in early spring. In rockery building the amateur so often forgets that *form* we have with us always but *colours* fade away; a hurriedly thrown up bank of soil dotted with lumps of stone between which are planted tender creepers does not make a true rock garden. Fig. 4 shows an example of a very badly constructed rock mound while Fig. 2 gives an idea of what should be aimed at.

Making a Start.

Before commencing work, decide upon a definite plan which will be pleasing to the eye even in the dark days of winter when colour is almost absent from the garden. The situation should have a sunny aspect, the rockery must not be tucked away to hide some dark corner, because the best of the Alpines love the sun. The plan should arrange for one or two rising mounds with moraines in the miniature valleys; a path may well meander through to some centre of interest such as a rock pool, and this can with advantage be spanned by a little stone bridge. Clear the site of all weeds and unless the soil is very light cover the ground with stones and small pieces of broken brick to ensure adequate drainage. On this throw up the banks of earth, which should be enriched with a liberal supply of leaf mould.

Types of Rock Stone to use.

The type of stone will depend upon the locality and the amount of money at the reader's command. The most beautiful of all rock stone for the garden is the weathered limestone of Cumberland and Cheddar. Sandstone is popular chiefly because it is cheap, but unfortunately in frosty weather it tends to break and crumble away. Granite is not suitable; it is too hard and affords no grip for the creeping plants. Very attractive prices for limestone F.O.R. are advertised in some papers.

Find out the Cost of Carriage.

Before accepting these the reader is advised to ascertain the cost of carriage, as this often amounts to three or even four times the cost of the stone at the quarry.

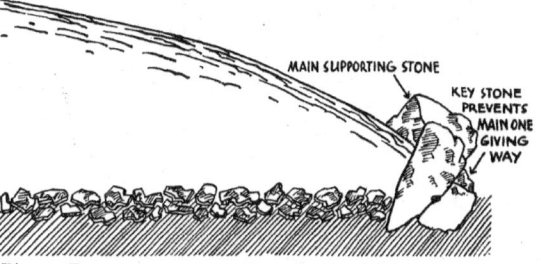

Fig. 1.—The beginning of a Rock Garden—a Bank of Well-drained Soil.

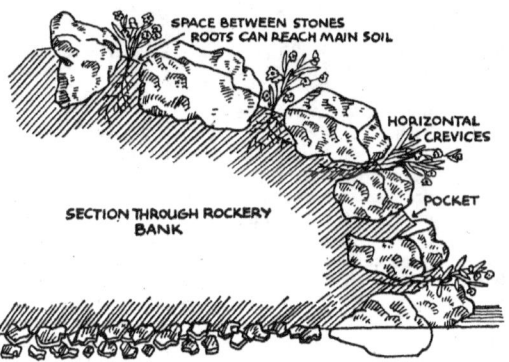

Fig. 2.—Section through Rockery Bank.

Home-made Rocks.

When economy is the order of the day the reader should collect all the odd stones, pieces of broken brick, and lumps of concrete that he can, and then manufacture his rocks in the following manner. Make a two to one mixture of sand and cement and, having thoroughly wetted the rubble, cement several of the broken pieces together so as to form irregular boulders. When these have set, wet again and brush all over the surface with a " runny " mix-

Fig. 3.—The Edges of the Paved Path through the Rockery should be broken up to give it a Natural Appearance.

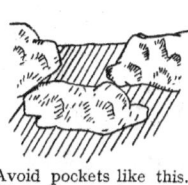

Avoid pockets like this. Roots become starved as they cannot reach the main soil.

How *not* to build—soil will be washed away.

Fig. 4.—Things to avoid.

ture of half sand and cement. While this thick wash is still wet sprinkle on a dusting of sand; when dry the stones will look exactly like real sandstone and be even stronger than the natural material. The reader who likes colour in the rock should make up some coloured sand in the following manner. To three parts of sand add one part of iron oxide (commercial quality), this will give a reddish mixture; a dark brown sand can be made by adding one part of umber in three to the sand, while an orange tinge can be obtained by using one part of ochre in three. The colouring matter should be dry and well mixed in with the sand; the resulting mixture should be sparingly dusted on to the home-made rocks in conjunction with a liberal supply of natural sand. The aim is not to make a red, brown or orange rock, but to obtain a coloured vein here and there; these colours will be found to be quite permanent.

Building up the Terraces.

Having prepared the sloping banks of the mould, around the bottom edge arrange the first ring of boulders securing the main one with a key stone as shown in Fig. 1, to prevent movement in rainy weather. These foot stones should appear like the natural outcrop of rock; at least one-third of each rock should be under ground. Similar irregular rings of stone are arranged at varying heights up the bank so that the mound is thrown into a series of steps or natural terraces. The mould between the rocks should be arranged to form *pockets* in which to plant the Alpines, see Fig. 2. Note that the " pockets " or small crevices are filled with earth which is in direct communication with the main mound, thus there is no danger of excessive dryness or starvation. Fig. 4 shows a very badly constructed pocket in which a small quantity of mould is " trapped " between two rocks. Plants in such a position will suffer from dampness in winter and dryness in summer.

Rockery Paths.

A path which winds through a rockery should be as informal as possible. The sides may be flanked with rockery banks or just broken up by a chain of irregular rocks along the edge. Crazy paving or flat York stone is admirable material for such a path, the slabs being set in sand with small crevices here and there in which

BUILDING A ROCKERY

Fig. 5.—How to build Stone Bridge over Rock Pool.
Part shown in section—note A, the skeleton iron framework, and B, the concrete path. The finished bridge is shown in Fig. 9.

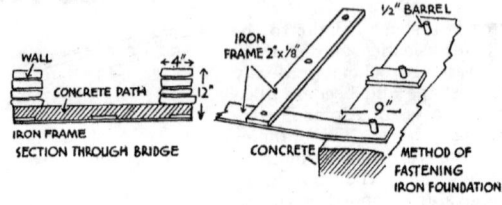

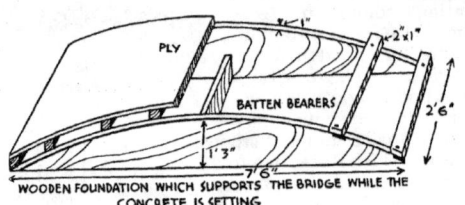

Fig. 6.—Details for building Stone Bridge.

creeping plants such as Stonecrop can be planted. When a path leads down to a moraine or to a rock pool it looks well if the crazy paving gives way to a surface of loose granite. A path through a rockery should never be straight or of uniform width and it always looks better if it is broken with one or two steps.

A Rock Pool.

An informal pool forms an attractive centre of interest to a rockery. It can be placed at the foot of a sloping bank as in Fig. 8, or it may be surrounded by several mounds as in Fig. 9. Fig. 8 shows a small pool at the foot of an imposing precipice of limestone rock; note the small conifers and flowering shrubs planted in the large pockets between the boulders. In the foreground is a stone ornament which forms a shelter and feeding table for the birds. Fig. 9 shows a central pool spanned by a bridge of stone; note the path in the foreground leading down to the edge of the water. To construct such a pond the cavity must be dug out saucer shape to a depth of 18 inches in the centre. The earth is rammed hard and small pieces of stone embedded in the surface to form keys to which the 3 inch cement lining can attach itself. The cement coating should be spread on as described in an article entitled "Garden Ponds."

The Bridge.

The bridge shown in Fig. 5 may at first sight appear rather ambitious, but provided it is not made larger than the sizes given no difficulties should be experienced. Two concrete steps are cast between the rocks on opposite sides of the pool, and while these are still wet short lengths of barrel are embedded in them. These secure the ends of the three strips of iron which form the base of the pathway. The three main iron supports are bent over the pool so that there is a lift of 1 foot 3 inches in the centre and across these at intervals of 12 inches cross members are riveted as shown in Fig. 5. Before casting the path it will be necessary roughly to knock up a wooden arch as in Fig. 6 to support the path while the cement is setting; it also aids in shaping the iron framework. This wooden arch is securely propped up in position and the iron strips bent to it; the metal strips are then covered with a sheet of ½-inch mesh wire netting. The bridge is then covered with a mixture of one part cement to three parts ballast; this is spread to a depth of 4 inches and allowed to stand for five days undisturbed. The cement will be prevented from dropping through by the ply top of the wooden arch, but it will surround the strip iron and wire netting, forming a ferro-concrete structure that will carry any weight to which it is likely to be subjected.

The Bridge Wall.

A miniature stone wall 4 in. wide flanks the path over the bridge. This is built up on both sides, and the best material for this is a supply of 1 in. and 2 in. dwarf walling stone. The low wall is built up to a height of 9 to 12 inches. The stones are arranged as regularly as possible on the inside but left with the rugged edges pointing outwards. They are secured with cement mortar between the stones. The path over the bridge is finally finished by coating the top with a layer of granite chippings. The wooden arch is removed after the work is completed.

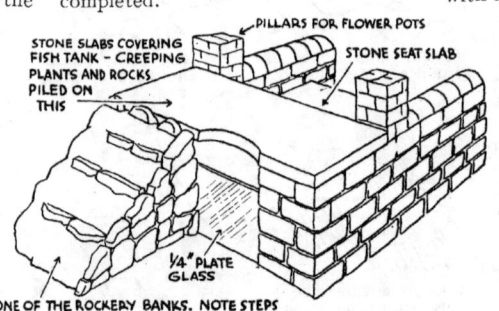

Fig. 7.—Showing Garden Seat, Rockery and Fish Tank combined.
See also Fig. 10. Fig. 14 shows details of construction.

An Original Rockery Seat.

In Figs. 7 and 10, a rather unique stone seat is shown; the wall and armrests are built of weathered bricks; at the back of the seat is a sloping mound of earth forming a terraced rockery, while between the back of the seat and the rockery is a large glass fronted fish tank. This is an ideal position for the fish since they are nicely shaded from the glare of the sun, yet they can be readily seen swimming about from the front and back. Ferns and creepers planted in the sides of the rockery slopes, see Fig. 7, form a natural framing to the glass panel. A stone slab covers the tank forming a platform on which rocks and Alpines can be housed, the central slab being removable for periodical attention to the tank although food can be given through the curved opening in the rear of the slab.

How to build the Seat.

Fig. 14 shows a plan of the rockery seat, showing quite plainly how the walls are set out. A 3 inch concrete foundation is put in for the base of the walls and the bottom of the fish tank, but the ground under the stone seat is turfed. Note the gaps in the bricks which admit the ends of the two sheets of glass. These are later sealed with a grouting of cement. The lower edges of the glass panels are also sealed with a fillet of cement. The brick walls immediately in front of the first glass panel are carried up a couple of courses above the arms; pillars are then formed which will support ornamental flower vases. The main walls are 2 feet 8 inches high and are capped with semicircular bricks; the glass panels are 1 foot 9 inches high, thus a space is left under the slabs which cover the tank sufficiently wide to admit the arm over the top edge. The slabs which cover

BUILDING A ROCKERY

Fig. 8.—A Rock Pool at the Foot of a Precipice of Limestone, as described in the Text.

Fig. 9.—A Miniature Stone Bridge spanning a small Rock Pool.
The method of building the bridge is given in the text.

Fig. 10.—A Unique Garden Seat with a Rockery at the Rear and a Fish Tank under the Rockery, as described in the Text.

Fig. 11.—An Idea for the Rockery.
Dwarf conifers and flowering shrubs on the summits.

Fig. 12.—A Grotto and Pool flanked with Alpines—An Idea for the Rockery.

Fig. 13.—A Rock Border in course of construction showing the Boulders ready for embedding.

BUILDING A ROCKERY

the tank are supported on two lengths of angle iron reaching across the top and cemented into the side walls. The stone slab which forms the seat can be cast in a mould 2½ inches deep, three lengths of ⅜-inch iron rod are embedded in the mixture while wet to prevent fracture should cracks develop. The seat is supported 1 foot 4 inches above the ground by cementing in two iron lugs in the wall on each side. These lugs are pieces of ¼-inch iron 6 inches long and 1 inch wide, half of which is bedded into the brickwork as it is erected, the remainder projecting to support the stone seat.

The Sloping Rockery Beds.

The mould is banked up as shown in Fig. 7, a rock wall being constructed on each side of the path which leads to the fish tank; between these rocks, varieties of finger ferns are planted; they then overhang and form a natural framing to the glass panel. The banks are terraced in two or three steps each supported by a fringe of boulders embedded in the earth to appear as natural outcrop rock.

The Best Time to start.

A rockery is best constructed in the late summer or autumn when it can be left to settle for a couple of months; then it will be ready for planting the bulbs and shrubs. Many of the more tender plants are best left until early spring before planting in their permanent quarters.

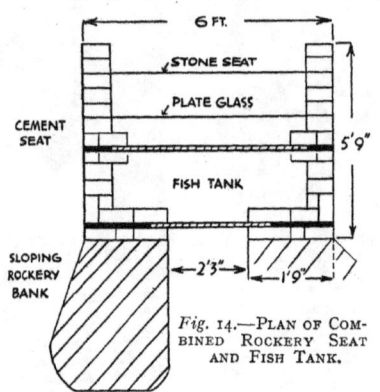

Fig. 14.—Plan of Combined Rockery Seat and Fish Tank.

The Best Rockery Plants to grow.

Alyssum.—Madwort or Golden Alyssum provides a striking splash of colour in early spring. It may be increased by cuttings or raised from seed in the spring.

Aubrietia.—(The Purple Rock Cross) —This is probably the greatest favourite of rock plants; violet, pink, and rose-coloured varieties can be obtained. This looks best when it can drape a rock or bank of soil. It can be increased by division in the autumn.

Campanula.—The rockery bell flower delights in the shade. These can be increased in the autumn by detaching small rooted pieces.

Dianthus.—This is the Alpine pink and gives gaiety to the rock garden in early summer. They love gritty soil enriched with some old mortar, and delight in the sun. They are best grown from seed but can be increased by cuttings or layering.

Primula.—Many forms of rock primroses, violet and rose, can be obtained for the rockery. They like well drained soil in which a little peat has been mixed. They can be grown from seed or increased by division.

The Mossy Saxifrages.—These are cushions of moss like leaves which bear numerous short stalked flowers in white, crimson and rose. They like the shade and sandy soil. These are best propagated by detaching rooted pieces in the autumn.

Sedum.—(Stonecrop). Probably the most easily grown of all rock plants. The common yellow variety grows wild on old walls.

Some useful bulbs for the rockery are, Anemone blanda (blue), Cyclamen ibericum (rose), Grape hyacinth (blue), and Tulipa persica (yellow).

Rockery Shrubs.—Don't forget if space permits to plant some miniature conifers, dwarf rhododendrons, and small Japanese maples near the summits. These add height and give much beauty to the site.

USEFUL PLANTING TABLE FOR ROCKERY PLANTS

For Massed Effects

Sunny Position.	Time of Flowering.
Aubretia, lavender, mauve, rose pink and purple	April to June.
Æthionema Grandiflora, trailing, pink	May.
Gentiana Verna, purplish blue	April to June.
Potentilla, yellow, cerise, scarlet	April to Sept.
Campanula, G. F. Wilson, violet bellflower	June.
Calceolaria Polyrrhiza, leaves form carpet yellow flowers on erect stems	June to July.
Androsaces, choice alpine, rose, yellow, white, rose pink and lilac flowers	May to Oct.
Arenarias, green moss-like growth	April to July.
Aster Alpinus, purplish flowers, 6 inches high	May.
Aster Sub-cœruleus, blue, 1 foot high	June.
Œnothe a Alpine Evening Primrose, yellow and pink	June to Sept.
Iberis Gibraltirica, perennial Candytuft, white flowers	May.
Prunella Webbiana (Selfheal), reddish flowers	July and Aug.
Helianthemums (Rock Roses), evergreen trailing, orange, cerise, yellow	June to July.
Saxifrages, encrusted varieties	May to July.
Sedums, stone crop	June to Oct.
Iceland Poppies, yellow, golden, red, pink, erect flowers	June to Sept.

Shady Position.	
Pulmonaris Augustifolia, blue cowslip	April.
Saxifrages, mossy varieties and dense growth, white, yellow, rose and crimson	April, May, June.
Viola Gracilis, violet blue	May to Sept.
Hutchinsia Alpina, masses of snow-white flowers	May and June.
Primula Denticulata, bright lilac	March to April.
Primula Julieæ, rosy purple	March to May.
Geranium, rock species	June to Sept.
Gentiana Sino-ornata, large deep blue flowers	July to Nov.
Anemone Alpina, wind flower, 1½ feet high	May to June.

For Crevices

Sunny Position.	Time of Flowering.
Sempervivums, succulent rock plants, fleshy leaves in rosettes, flowers red shades and yellow	June to July.
Androsaces, Rock Jasmine, rose pink, rose lilac, yellow, white carmine	May.
Draba species. When planting pack firmly between stones. Shades of yellow and white	March to April.
Sedums, all species are suitable for crevices	June to Oct.

Shady Position.	
Linaria Alpina, purple, prostrate habit	May to Sept.
Saxifraga Aizoides, yellow spotted red	June to July.

For Trailing

Sunny Position.	
Acæna Buchanani, silver foliage, red fruits	June and July.
Dianthus—Alpine Pinks. Good drainage is essential, and sufficient water must be provided during the winter	Summer.
Campanula Muralis, blue flowers	August.
Aubretia. Most varieties do well in crevices	April.
Iberis Sempervirens, evergreen foliage, white flowers	June and Aug.
Saponaria Ocymoides, delicate pale pink	May to Aug.
Alyssum Saxatile, pale yellow	June.
Arabis Albida, beautiful white spring flowering alpine	March to May.
Alpine Thymus. Fragrant plants; in many species the foliage is hidden by sheets of flowers	July to Aug.
Raoulia Australis, carpet of silver for ledge.	

Shady Position.	
Acæna Microphylla, bronze green carpet, ivory stems covered with red fruits	
Waldsteina Trifoliata, an evergreen trailer, yellow flowers	May to July.

A Home-made Chicken Brooder

A PRACTICAL brooder for sixty to eighty chicks can be made by any handy man, at a very small cost for material. The arrangement shown in Fig. 1 is particularly efficient, and consists of two distinct portions, first the covered and sheltered run, and secondly the heated brooder or rearer, the latter raised on legs and provided with carrying handles.

Warmth within the brooder is provided by a hot water tank heated by a simple oil lamp. This is undoubtedly the best all round system. The heated brooder enables newly-fledged chicks to be taken direct from the incubator and reared in the brooder under draughtless and warm conditions.

This brooder can, if required, be brought indoors at night and is easily carried by two persons. The run enables the chicks to take early advantage of every bit of warmth and sunshine.

How the Brooder works.

The sectional view (Fig. 2) shows schematically the internal arrangement of the brooder. The walls are double and built of tongued and grooved boards, the space between being filled with sawdust. A separate compartment is provided for the lamp, which heats a conical "jacket" boiler, from whence the water circulates through the tank situated about 9 inches above the floor. An inspection and cleaning door is provided at the front, while the sloping roof is removable to provide access to the water tank for filling and cleaning purposes.

Materials required.

The following materials will be required for a brooder measuring approximately 3 feet 4 inches long,

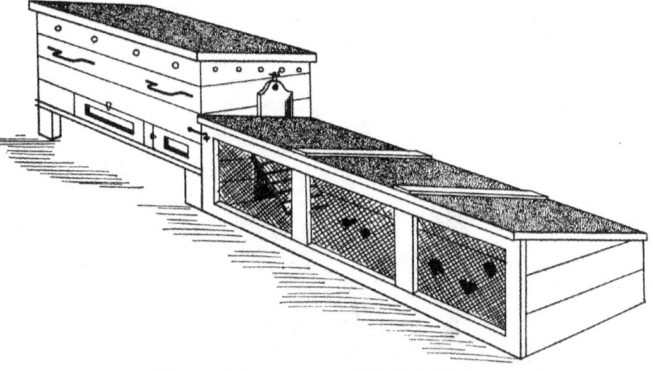

Fig. 1.—Brooder and Run Complete.
The heated brooder provides warm shelter for the chicks. The covered run enables necessary exercise.

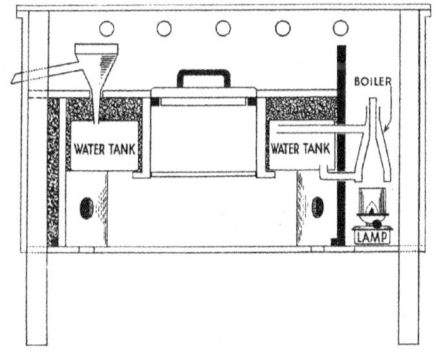

Fig. 2.—Section of Brooder.
The walls are double and packed with sawdust or cork shavings; heating is by lamp and hot-water tank.

2 feet 10 inches wide, and 2 feet 9 inches high from the ground to top, also included is material for a run 7 feet long, 2 feet 10 inches wide and 19 inches high.

Legs.—Four pieces 2 inches by 1½ inches by 2 feet 9 inches.

Casing.—Tongued and grooved boards 6 inches wide by ¾ inch thick.
19 pieces 3 feet 4 inches long.
8 pieces 2 feet 10 inches long.
8 pieces 2 feet 6 inches long.

Fillet.—1 inch square. 8 pieces 3 feet long.

Run.—Frame 2 by 1 inch Deal.
4 pieces 7 feet long.
4 pieces 18 inches long.
4 pieces 12 inches long.
2 pieces 2 feet 10 inches long.
4 pieces 3 feet long.

Roof, Back and Ends of Run.—Tongued and grooved board, 6 inches wide by ¾ inch thick.
6 pieces 7 feet 3 inches long.
2 pieces 7 feet long.
6 pieces 2 feet 10 inches long.

Sundries.—4 butler's handles; 3½ yards "Pluvex" roofing felt; 1 paraffin lamp with ⅝-inch burner; 1 hot water tank and boiler or material for making same, viz., 2 tin funnels, 2 inches diameter; 1 tin funnel, 3 to 3½ inches diameter; 6 feet of ½-inch brass pipe; 2 pieces sheet zinc, 2 feet 9 inches by 2 feet 9 inches.

Building the Brooder.

First prepare the back and the two sides of the outer walls, then glue and nail the end boards to the legs, as in Fig. 3, afterwards saw and plane along the top to attain the desired slope. Next, nail the back boards to the legs thus uniting the two sides, as in Fig. 4, then nail 1-inch square fillets to the inner lower edges to act as a support for the floor.

See that the case is quite square and true, then notch the corners of the first floorboard and glue and nail it in place; add the remaining pieces and finish flush with the face of the legs at the front.

Fitting and Hinging the Front.

Prepare the front boards as shown in Fig. 5 and fix the lower boards in place, but do not hinge either of the doors at this stage. The upper front board also is not fixed at this stage, because its absence enables freer access to the interior.

The next step is to fit the transverse division, shown in Fig. 6, between the

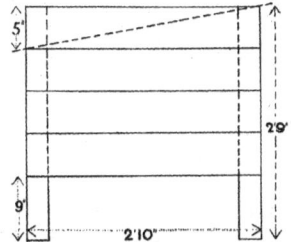

Fig. 3.—Side Boards on Legs.
Four pieces of board are first nailed to the pair of legs, the sloping top is then sawn to shape along the dotted line.

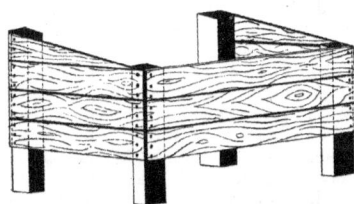

Fig. 4.—Sides and Back assembled.
The two sides are joined by the three pieces of board, forming the back.

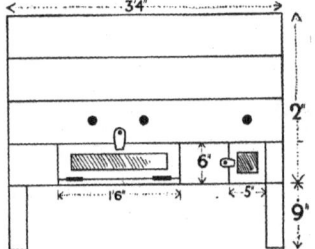

Fig. 5.—Dimensions of Front.
Front view of brooder showing arrangement of inspection and lamp doors and leading dimensions.

A HOME-MADE CHICKEN BROODER

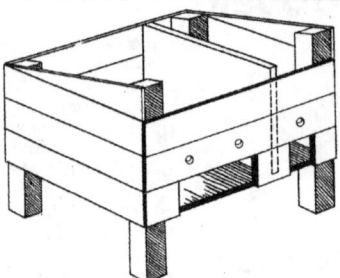

Fig. 6.—Transverse Division.
This separates the lamp space from the warm chamber.

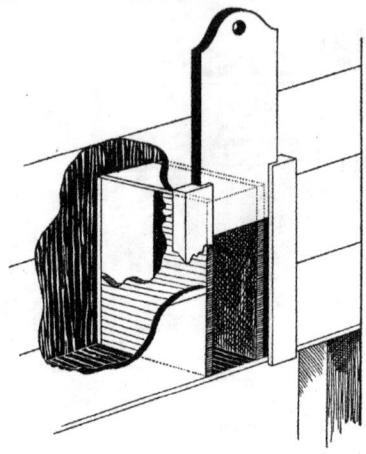

Fig. 7.—Arrangement of Chicks' Door.
The cavity is lined and the door is arranged to slide vertically, and can be held up by a loop of cord and a hook.

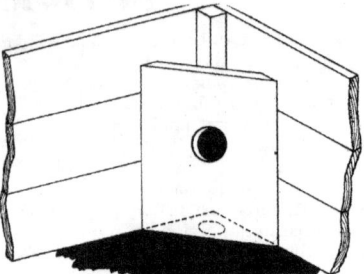

Fig. 8.—Corner Ventilated Supports.
These admit fresh air and also support the hot-water tank—one is fitted to each corner inside the casing.

lamp compartment and the warm chamber. Next cut a small doorway through the outer wall and also through the inner division, then line the space between them with odd pieces of ¾-inch board.

The clear aperture should be about 4½ inches wide and 6 inches high, the outside should be closed by means of a sliding door, as in Fig. 7, and a sloping board, with small fillets on it, fitted below the door to lead down gradually to floor level. This board should be provided with a cleat or with hooks and eyes to hold it in place when required, or it can be fixed permanently in the run, provided the latter fits closely against the brooder.

The Inner Walls.

The next proceeding is to build the inner walls, fastening them at the bottom to fillets and nailing the ends of the front and back boards to the crossway partition. Fillets should also be glued into the inner vertical angles. An opening must be provided opposite the inspection door at the front and it must be lined at the top and sides.

Holes, ½ inch diameter, must next be drilled through the floor in the corners just in front of the fillets, then pieces of 6-inch board, 9 inches long, each with a ¾-inch diameter hole in the centre line, about 6 inches above the bottom, are fixed diagonally across each inner corner, as in Fig. 8, to provide fresh air inlets above the heads of the chicks. Two ¾-inch diameter outlet holes are drilled through the front immediately above the inspection door. These holes must be bushed or lined either with metal or card tubes.

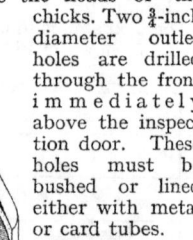

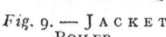

Fig. 9.—Jacket Boiler.
This consists of two conical funnels with the lower end closed by a ring of sheet metal, as here shown in section.

Heating Tank.

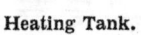

The lamps and heating tank are now required, so that they can be fitted properly into place.

So far as the lamp is concerned, this has only to be placed into the lamp compartment and a few ventilation holes then drilled through the floor of the brooder to ensure an air supply to the lamp.

The jacket boiler can be made with two seamless metal funnels, one placed within the other, as in Fig. 9, and the bottom closed by a ring of sheet metal soldered securely in place to form a watertight joint. The spouts fit one inside the other and must be soldered together to form a watertight joint; the hot air escapes through the spout at the top.

Brass or copper tubes, ½-inch bore, are used for the circulating pipes, one is fitted at the very top of the boiler, that is, adjacent to the spout; the return pipe is fitted into the flat part at the bottom.

Dimensions of the hot water tank are given in Fig. 10, and the sheet metal should next be cut and bent to these sizes. As can be seen in Fig. 11, a square aperture is arranged right through the middle of the tank.

The opening should first be cut out either with a cold chisel and hammer or with a metal fret-saw; the edges of the sheets are then bent down on all sides and the two sheets then placed together and the joints soldered all round, inside and out to ensure a good watertight joint. A strip of zinc is soldered around the inside opening to complete the walls thereof.

Before the final soldering, the pipes from and to the boiler, as in Fig. 12, should be fitted and a filler hole drilled through the top of the tank. A conical filler with open top is soldered into the filler hole and an overflow pipe subsequently fitted to the top part of the filler and taken directly to the outside of the case.

Installing the Boiler.

When the boiler has been completed and tested, or obtained ready made, it should be placed in position on the four diagonal corner pieces and should fit inside the inner casing.

The division between lamp compartment and heater should be cut away to suit the pipes to the boiler, which must come centrally within the lamp compartment.

A mica chimney should be provided for the lamp and should terminate at about the bottom level of the boiler. A top covering over the water tank should next be fitted and the aperture lined, as shown in Fig. 13, the top boards are then removed and the whole of the cavities filled in with sawdust and the linings and top refixed permanently with screws.

A cover or lid with lifting handle should be fixed over the aperture, the ventilation holes drilled at the upper part and the roof or cover then prepared. It is merely a flat board with fillet or battens around the edge and should fit closely but easily on to the case.

The inspection doors should then be hinged in place and preferably provided with glass windows; the inspection door in the brooder must fit closely and should be beaded on the inside to exclude draughts.

Making the Run.

The run shown in Fig. 14, is quite a simple affair, the front is framed up with 2 × 1 inch prepared batten, all joints being halved. The back is similar but is covered by tongued and grooved boards, the ends are made with vertical pieces of board nailed to

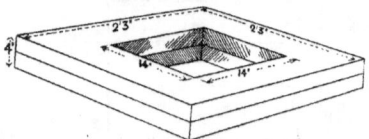

Fig. 10.—Shape and Sizes of Hot-water Tank.
This is made of sheet zinc or copper, or can be purchased ready for use.

A HOME-MADE CHICKEN BROODER

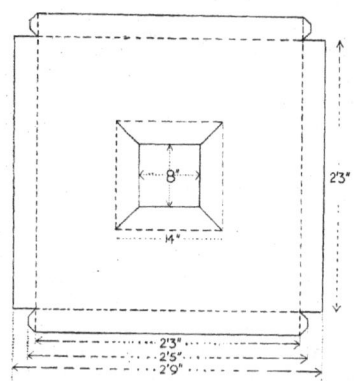

Fig. 11.—Dimensions of Sheet Metal.
Here are given the sizes to which the metal sheet should be cut for the top and outer edges of the water tank.

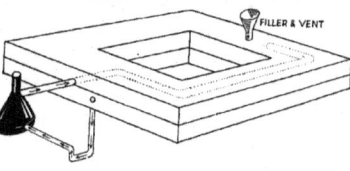

Fig. 12.—Circulating Pipes.
The hot pipe goes from the boiler to the farthermost side of the hot tank, the return pipe goes from nearest part of tank to the boiler.

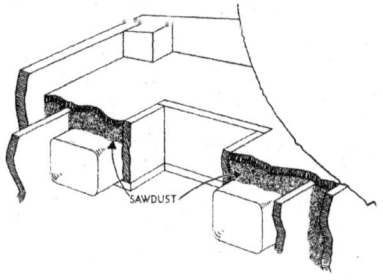

Fig. 13.—Section of Tank and Covering.
The central aperture is lined with wood and provided with a removable cover; the inner cavities are filled with sawdust.

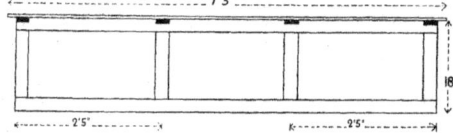

Fig. 14.—Details of Run.

cross pieces of batten and the whole screwed together at all corners.

The rafters—or cross pieces of batten are then fitted into notches cut in the front and back frames, and the roof boards then nailed to them.

The whole is given a coat of wood preservative stain and the roof covered with Pluvex or other good roof covering. The front of the run is covered with fine mesh galvanized iron wire netting, fixed inside the framework with staples and the joint covered with thin strips of wood to prevent accidents to the chicks, which might be possible if the raw edges of the wire netting were left exposed.

Working the Brooder.

The brooder should be tested for a day or two before it is required for the chicks. Warm water can be poured into the tank and the lamp lighted up. A thermometer is placed on the floor near the inspection door and the lamp regulated by raising or lowering the wick so that the water is maintained at a steady temperature of 85 degrees or thereabouts.

When the chicks are introduced their natural warmth will tend to cause a rise in temperature, especially during the day or the early part of the night, consequently the lamp may have to be turned down somewhat at those times.

A little observation and adjustment will soon have the brooder working perfectly, and in any case it is comforting to remember that the hot water tank does not change temperature rapidly, but falls quite slowly and gradually, even if the lamp is accidentally allowed to go out.

SOME MORE RECIPES FOR JAMS AND PRESERVES

Some useful recipes for jams are given on page 1157. Here is a further selection.

Apricots and Apples.

A good preserve containing apricots, is made with the addition of apples, which gives it a very nice flavour. Cut up 1 lb. of dried apricots, and soak in 2 pints of water for twenty-four hours; 4 lbs. of apples and 6 lbs. of sugar will be required. Boil half the apples and strain. Put the juice from the apricots and apples into the pan, add the sugar and bring to the boil; add apricots and rest of the apples cut in small pieces. Boil about twenty or thirty minutes. Test in usual way to see if it is done.

Apricots and Pineapples.

Still another apricot recipe, which is a great favourite with the children. This is made with 1 lb. of dried apricots cut up small and covered with 2 pints of water, which should be previously boiled and allowed to get cold. After standing for about forty-eight hours, put the fruit in the preserving pan and warm through. Then add 3 lbs. of sugar, and when nearly done, add the contents of a small tin of pineapple chunks. After straining off the liquid, finally boil until set, testing it in the usual way.

Marrow Cream.

This is a delightful preserve made with marrow. It is more substantial than lemon curd, and is delicious in tarts, or used with bread and butter will be found a pleasant change. Take 4 lbs. of marrow ready prepared, 4 lbs. of sugar, 6 lemons, ½ lb. of best fresh butter. To prepare the marrow (which should be a perfectly ripe one), cut up as in cooking for the table. Then grate the rinds of the 6 lemons, squeeze and strain the juice, and have in readiness. Now cook the marrow in the ordinary way, but, of course, without salt. It should be cooked well and thoroughly drained, this should be done by straining through a cloth. The easiest method is to place a cloth over the colander, and pour marrow into it. The cloth is then twisted tightly until all water possible is squeezed out. Place the marrow into a bowl, and then beat it up well, add the butter, put in the grated rinds of the lemons and the juice, then add the sugar, and boil all ingredients together for one hour. Test in the usual way.

Marrow Ginger.

This when finished looks very appetising and tastes like preserved ginger: 6 lbs. of marrow, 6 lbs. loaf sugar, 4 ozs. of whole ginger, 4 lemons. Peel the marrow and cut into pieces about 1 inch square. Put the marrow into the preserving pan with the sugar, cover over and leave to stand for twenty-four hours. The ginger should be well bruised, and tied up in a muslin bag, and added with the juice and grated rinds of the lemons. Boil quickly for one hour. The ginger should be removed before placing the preserve in the jars.

How to Make a Pantagraph

A PANTAGRAPH is a piece of apparatus used for enlarging or reducing drawings. There are two forms of the pantagraph, one in the form of a large square divided into two parts and composed of five strips of narrow and thin wood, as indicated in Fig. 1, and the other form, shown in Fig. 2, which is composed of four strips only.

Pantagraph made from Meccano Strips.

The latter form of pantagraph is more commonly used, but the former one is illustrated as it can be made with meccano strips. It will be seen in Fig. 1 that the five strips are joined together with bolts except at two opposite corners of the large square. One of these corners is fitted with a nail for fixing it in position and the other corners should be fitted with a short length of very thin pencil.

How to use for enlarging.

In use the nail is driven into a board or table, the pantagraph should be placed in the position shown and the drawing to be enlarged placed centrally under the centre hole of the middle strip. A piece of drawing paper is now placed centrally under the pencil end, a pointer of hardwood or bone is fitted in the centre hole of the middle strip and guided along the lines of the print. As the pointer is moved along, the pencil will trace to twice the size every movement of the tracing point. Other proportions can be done by altering the position of the points, but for greater convenience in use the second form of apparatus is better.

Pantagraph made from Wood Strips.

It will be seen in Fig. 2 that the middle portion of the pantagraph is fixed together in the form of a square. The strip A has a fixed point at one end so that it can be secured to the board. A short strip B is hinged to the centre point of A and a third strip C is hinged at the far end of A. Joining the end of the strip B, which carries a tracing point, is a strip D hinged to the centre point of C. As set, the pantagraph will enlarge drawings twice the size by guiding the tracing point over the diagram to be enlarged and allowing the pencil at the end of the strip C to move freely on the drawing paper.

How to make the Wood Pantagraph.

The various parts of the pantagraph in Fig. 2 are shown drawn to a larger scale in separate details. A hardwood such as sycamore or pearwood is advised, but special care should be taken to procure straight-grained wood. First plane up three strips to $14\frac{1}{2} \times \frac{9}{16} \times \frac{1}{8}$ inches and one strip to the same width and thickness, but $7\frac{3}{4}$ inches long. Draw a centre line along the whole length of each piece and then mark off the centre of the three long strips. From the centre point of each strip mark off $6\frac{3}{4}$ inches exactly, and from the centre point on each of the long strips and, from one of the end points on the short strip, which is also marked off $6\frac{3}{4}$ inches, set out the distances shown in Fig. 4. First $2\frac{1}{4}$, then follow with $1\frac{1}{8}$, $1\frac{1}{8}$, $\frac{9}{16}$ and $\frac{3}{8}$ inches. The centre point is marked 2, and the next points 3, 4, 6, 8 and 10 in order, as indicated in Fig. 4.

It is now necessary to drill holes as shown in the short strip in Fig. 5, but before this is done it will be necessary to procure some bolts and nuts as shown in Fig. 6. Provide three 1-inch and two $\frac{1}{2}$-inch brass round-head bolts, No. 2 B.A., with nuts and thin washers. Sharpen the end of one of the bolts as at E, file off $\frac{1}{8}$ inch and similarly sharpen the end of another as at F. File off $\frac{1}{8}$ inch from the third 1-inch bolt and slightly round the end as at G. The two $\frac{1}{2}$-inch bolts should be left as they are and shown at H. Instead of the bolt at G, a brass terminal as at K can be used instead.

Find a small metal twist drill that will just take the bolts, and, after making an indentation with a sharp point at each of the marks, drill holes as carefully and accurately as possible at all the marked points, except the one at the end of the strip C furthest from

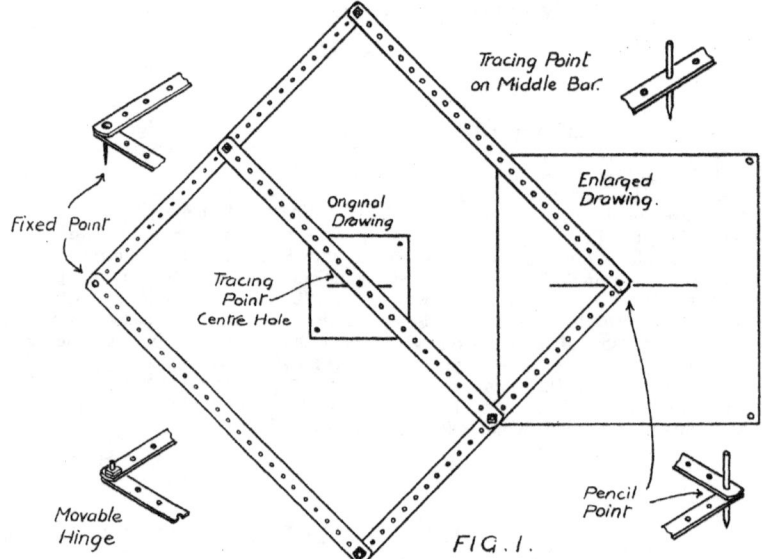

Fig. 1.—Pantagraph made from Meccano Strip, showing also how to use it for making an Enlargement of a Drawing.

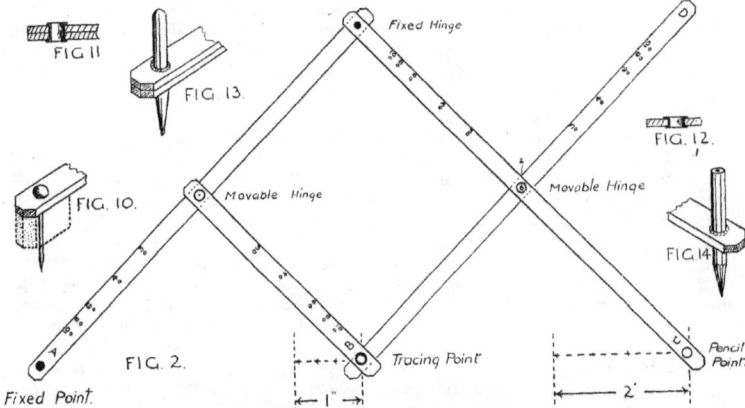

Fig. 2.—Pantagraph made of Stripwood with Simple Fitting. Dimensions and other details are given in Figs. 4 to 9.

Figs. 10 to 14.—These Details illustrate some Improvements that may be added to the Simple Fitting in Fig. 2.

HOW TO MAKE A PANTAGRAPH

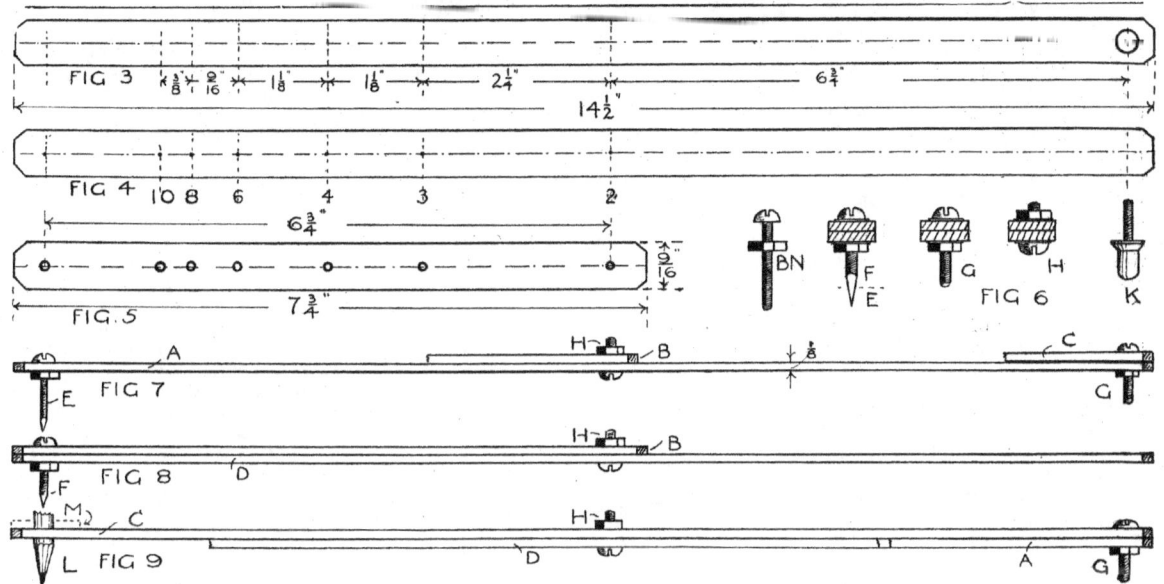

Figs. 3 to 9.—Details for making the Simple Wood Strip Pantagraph, drawn to Half Scale.

the row of holes, this being drilled ¼ inch or large enough for a thin pencil. The corners of all the strips are now trimmed off with a sharp chisel, and to prevent the wood being soiled in use all the strips should be polished, preferably with french polish, but a coating of wax polish will answer.

The parts are now fitted together. First take the strip A, and at the end nearest the row of holes fit in the sharpened bolt E, as indicated in Fig. 7. To the centre hole of this strip fit one of the short bolts H and fit on the end of the strip B, so that the two No. 2 holes coincide. At the far end of A, using the bolt G to join them, fit on the strip C at the hole nearest 10. Join the end of the B strip to the plain end of the D strip, using the sharpened bolt F, as shown in Fig. 8. Finally fit the remaining short bolt H in the No. 2 holes in C and D strips as in Fig. 9.

Adding some Refinements.

It is possible to make small improvements to the above pantagraph by adding a strip of wood to the end of the C strip in order to provide a firmer hold to the pencil. It is also an advantage to have a greater distance than ¾ inch between the tracing point and the wood strips. One way of doing this is to have a longer fixed point, as indicated in Fig. 2; this can be a 1¼-inch nail with a strengthening block of wood underneath, as in Fig. 10. A supporting stud as at G can be made by using a longer bolt to give a distance of about 1 inch below the strips. The tracer point can be made by fitting a short length of thin brass tubing and spreading the top over as indicated in Fig. 11. A similar fitting can be made at the pencil point as in Fig. 12. A length of hardwood or bone can be used as a tracer as in Fig. 13, and the pencil will slide in the socket as in Fig. 14.

How to use for reducing Drawings.

In both Figs. 1 and 2 the pantagraph is set for enlarging a drawing, but, if the apparatus is required for reducing, it will be necessary to reverse the process and place the pencil at the tracer point and trace at the pencil point. In the simple apparatus in Fig. 1 this will be an easy matter, but with the other pantagraph it will be necessary to fit both the tracing and pencil points with brass bushes as in Figs. 13 and 14, so that the two points can be interchanged when required.

A CHEAP PICTURE-FRAMING CLAMP

THE only materials required for the easily constructed and cheap picture-framing clamp shown in the diagram are a length of stout string or light cord, and eight short lengths of deal, off-cuts about 1½ to 2 inches long will do admirably. The thickness and width of these pieces is not very important. A convenient size would be not less than ⅜ inch thick, and not more than 1½ inches wide.

Determining the Length of String.

After cutting and fitting the mitred corners of the frame, tie the string loosely round the frame. The necessary length can be ascertained by trial,

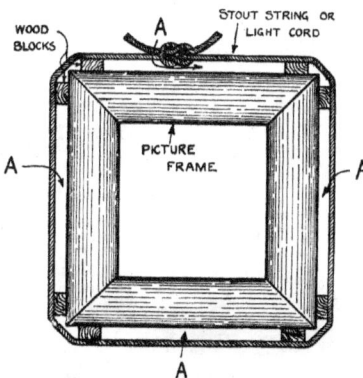

Details of the Picture-framing Clamp.

and should be such that when two of the deal blocks, as prepared above, are inserted between the centre of each side of the frame at A, and slid along to the corners to the position shown in the sketch, the frame should be held taut as in a clamp.

A Point to Watch.

When adjusting the length of the encircling string, be sure that the wood blocks are in such a position that, when the frame is clamped, the string clears the corners of the frame, or they may be damaged by the pressure of the string.

The Cause and Cure of Smoky Chimneys

There are a number of causes that may separately or in conjunction contribute to a smoky chimney, and it is often difficult to determine exactly the seat of the trouble. Although the purpose of a chimney is understood, the conditions that govern the fundamental principle of the flue are not so commonly known. It is generally realised that hot air will rise and the cold air displaced will fall, and in the case of a fire hot air will carry with it, to a certain extent, the lighter products of combustion in the form of smoke formed by particles of carbon known as soot.

Fire will not burn without Good Draught.

A bonfire, for example, composed of materials generating great heat but little smoke, appears to burn without trouble, but when the material is damp or not particularly combustible, a considerable amount of smoke is evolved. Unless there is a strong breeze the fire will not burn, but with a strong wind the fire burns up and the smoke is carried away. The wind creates a draught and provides an essential feature of combustion. The same thing applies to a fireplace, and unless there is a good draught the fire will not burn.

What happens when Fire is first lit.

When a fire is first lit the hot air has to pass through a column of cold air in the chimney and as the heat increases the cold air is forced down. This is the cause of fires burning badly at first and therefore it is an advantage to use plenty of wood to obtain the initial heating. If, after the fire has burnt up it becomes sluggish the probability is that the flue is at fault, but it may be that the flue is still full of cold air. If puffs of smoke enter the room each time the door is opened after the fire has been burning some time it is probable that the flue is choked. If the smoke should fail to pass up the flue there is either a stoppage or severe down draught. The latter trouble is evident when smoke comes into the room during high winds. The flue may be clear, but the pressure of the wind on the chimney top prevents the complete exhaustion of the smoke from the fire.

The Causes of Smoky Chimneys.

The problem of dealing with a smoky chimney resolves itself into discovering the causes of insufficient draught. Generally the fault can be traced to one or more of six conditions. (1) Stoppage or sluggishness caused by excess of soot or by bricks and mortar displaced inside the chimney. (2) Down draught caused by the proximity of surrounding objects such as high walls, roofs higher than the chimney, high trees, etc., forming wind eddies. (3) Insufficient ventilation inside the room thus preventing the air getting to the fireplace in sufficient quantity. (4) The presence of a fire in another room which communicates with the same chimney or which passes through an adjoining flue. (5) Faulty design or construction of the flue. (6) Leakage in the joints of the brickwork, either from the outside or in between two adjoining flues.

Stoppages.

Taking the first condition, it is as

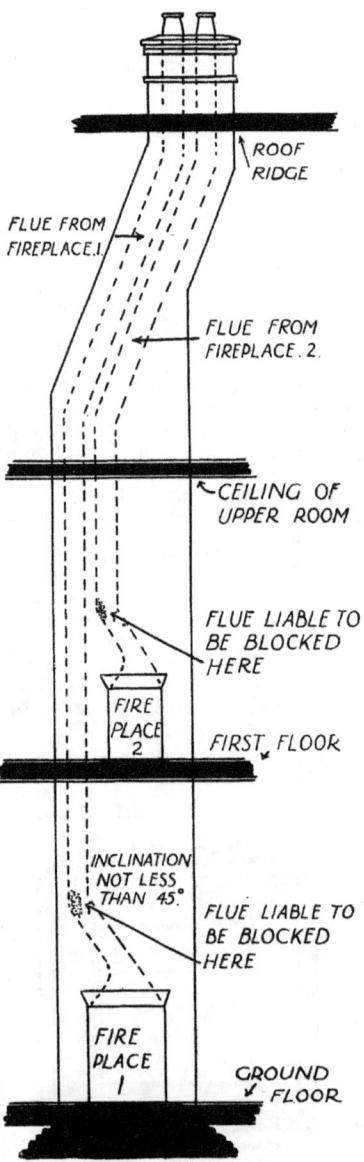

Fig. 1.—Chimney Construction, showing Bends and Parts liable to become blocked.

well to make sure that the chimney has been properly swept before further steps are taken to correct the fault. But if the sweep reports an obstruction which he cannot remove, considerable trouble may be caused before it is cleared. It will be seen in Fig. 1 that chimney construction allows for certain bends; for in no case can a chimney be satisfactory if there is a direct passage to the chimney pot. These bends vary with the particular construction of the house, and in some cases they are very pronounced and tend to form shelves for the deposit of soot and rubbish. Even if the flue is not entirely blocked, the space left may be so restricted that only a small current of air can pass up the flue. In the event of obstruction in a comparatively low bend, there is usually little difficulty in clearing it away by the use of stiff rods, but if the obstruction should be in the middle it may be necessary to open up the brickwork. In any case it is a job for an experienced builder. This may be considered a drastic step but it is the only way of ensuring a satisfactory job. It should be noted that a defective flue not only allows smoke to enter the room, but as well it allows unhealthy fumes to mix with the air in the room and this may cause serious injury to health.

Down Draught—

The second condition, that of down draught, is the most prevalent cause of smoky chimneys, and it may be intermittent or continuous. It is due to the pressure of air in the flue preventing the upward flow of the heated air and smoke from the fire. In the case of new houses it may be caused by the air in the flue remaining damp, but after a time the trouble will disappear. When chimneys are in an exposed position, subject to cold winds, such as those coming from the north or east, or when the brickwork is liable to get very wet as for example on walls facing south-west, the cold air in the flue will take a long time to be displaced. This fault is likely to be temporary only and will improve under better climatic conditions. Down draught is also likely to occur when a flue has not been in use for some time.

—and how to cure it.

It is when the down draught is caused by the pressure of eddying winds that remedial measures will be needed. In this case each chimney must be considered on its merits. It will probably be noticed that the trouble is more evident when the wind blows more in one quarter than another and is deflected by some portion of the roof, or a high wall or perhaps a tree. In the latter case the trouble is more evident in summer than in winter and is easily remedied by suitable lopping. If the top of the chimney should be lower than the roof, as indicated in the diagram at Fig. 2, and many modern houses show this fault, the remedy is either to increase the height of the stack by brickwork or a high pot, known as a tall-boy, or by fitting a down-draught preventer.

It does not follow that all chimneys lower than the surrounding building will cause a down draught; it depends entirely on the effect of the wind pressure. But when the trouble does occur, steps should be taken to fit a suitable pot or cowl, and if this does not prove successful, it will be necessary to increase the height of the chimney to about 2 feet higher than the nearest higher object.

Types of Down-draught Preventers.

As a rule there will be no need for a special form of pot or cowl if the height of the stack is increased sufficiently to clear the nearest high object, but as this remedy is likely to be somewhat expensive, the alternative should be tried first. It is evident that eddying winds directed downwards will have the effect of forcing the air down the chimney and the purpose of the louvre pot is to provide an additional draught at the top of the chimney and force the air in an upright direction. The diagram at A, in Fig. 3, illustrates the simplest form of down-draught preventer. This can be made from zinc or galvanised iron tubing, and the lower portion fitted inside the existing pot. A common form of louvre pot is shown at B, and it is quite effective if the down draught is not very pronounced. The Sankey type shown at C is a popular and efficient form of down-draught preventer and the three-louvre pattern is advised. The tall-boy made of galvanised iron as shown at D is popular, and is made with a square base to fit on the top of the stack, and is also obtainable without it so that it can be fitted inside the existing pot. There are several forms of cowl, one is shown at E; these are provided with a vane which is so turned by the wind pressure that the opening always faces directly away from the wind.

It is difficult to say which of the several types of preventer should be used, but as a general rule it is advisable to fit a louvre pot if the chimney smokes in any high wind and the cowl if the trouble occurs only in certain quarters of the wind. Pots, if fitted, should be bedded in with cement, which should be carried well up the side of the pot.

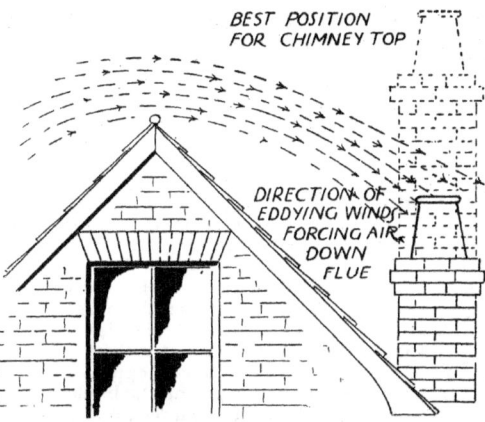

Fig. 2.—How Eddy Wind will cause a Down Draught.
The best position for a chimney top in this situation is shown by dotted lines.

Insufficient Ventilation.

The third condition, that of insufficient ventilation inside the room, is not a common one, but frequently it is considered responsible for smoky chimneys. Although not always the case, when puffs of smoke are expelled from the fire each time the door is opened, the trouble is usually due to faults in the fireplace itself. If the smoking ceases when the window is left open it certainly points to sluggish draught and this is a fault of the chimney to be cured as advised above. As a rule there is generally sufficient ventilation in even a small room to enable the fire to burn properly. But when heavy curtains are placed in front of the windows, and draught excluders to the doors, some means must be provided for the ingress of fresh air.

Tobin's Tube.

It is better for the air to enter the room by means of a Tobin's tube, as shown at Fig. 4, than arrange for extra ventilation close to the fireplace. It is possible to arrange for extra air inlet from the side of the hearth, and although it will provide the necessary increase of draught, it is better to provide more general ventilation.

Although the modern fireplace is adapted to take the mantel register stove, difficulty may be experienced in the case of old houses in which the fireplace was designed for the large open grate. The sectional diagram at Fig. 5 shows how a fireplace should be constructed to obtain the best results. The throat should be as wide as possible from side to side and narrow from front to back. The back should have a considerable forward inclination, and the space behind the firebrick packed with concrete and carried up in a steep slope to the back of the flue. There must be no corners, projections or spaces to form air pockets. The position of the canopy is important, it should be just below the top of the inclined fireback, as indicated in the diagram at Fig. 5.

Two Flues Interconnected.

The fourth condition is not common, but it often occurs in old houses when two flues are interconnected. Apart from the reconstruction of the chimney there is little to be done. The ingress of the smoke into one of the rooms is not caused so much by sluggish draught as by the siphon action of the two portions of flue. Usually when both fires are lit there is no trouble. The best remedy in this case is to close the register when not in use.

Faulty Design.

Faulty design or construction of the flue is another of the causes of smoky chimneys. Referring to the diagram at Fig. 1, it will be seen that bends are essential to a good flue, not so much for the sake of draught but for the purpose of preventing down-draught.

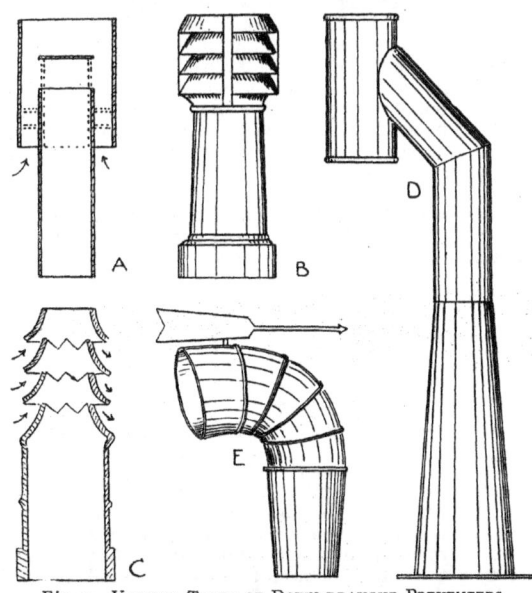

Fig. 3.—Various Types of Down-draught Preventers.
A, a simple cowl in sheet metal. B, a louvre pot. C, a Sankey down-draught preventer. D, a tall-boy. E, a lobster-back cowl.

THE CAUSE AND CURE OF SMOKY CHIMNEYS

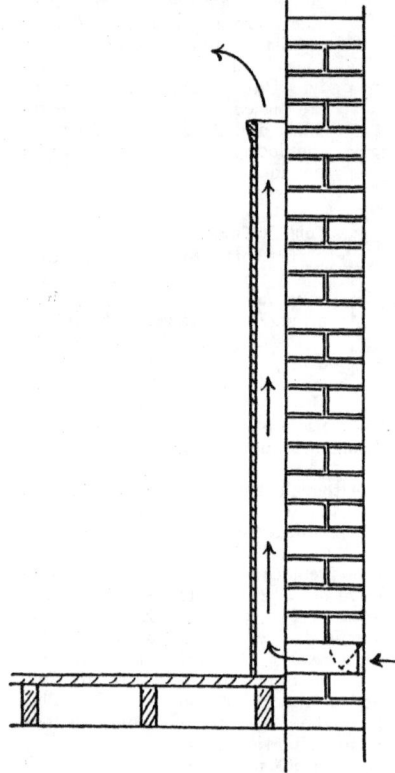

Fig. 4.—A Tobin's Tube, giving Ventilation without Draught.

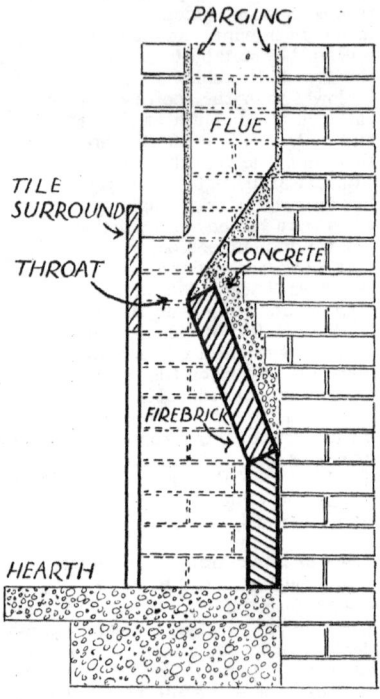

Fig. 5.—The Correct Construction of a Fireplace, showing the Narrow Throat.

traffic and other causes, the same trouble is likely to occur, but, as previously mentioned, the rubbish can usually be removed.

Leaks in Joints of Brickwork.

The sixth condition may occur in new as well as old houses, and is difficult to discover. When the leak shows on the outside, it is not a difficult job to close the opening, but when a single brick partition divides a number of flues and one of the joints is defective, a condition of siphonage is likely to occur. Unless the defective joint can be reached from the top of the flue and the leakage stopped, it will be necessary to open up the brickwork and make a thorough repair.

How to sweep a Chimney.

The most effective form of cleaning a flue is by means of a brush. The chemical cleaner evolves gases which certainly carry off a good deal of the soot in the chimney, but the heavier particles of carbon are left. Generally a fire that is in continual use is the means of depositing a considerable amount of soot and the flue should be swept at least once a year. In a small house with two or three flues, it is hardly worth while investing in a large flue brush, but in a large house it may be worth while. The chimney-sweeper's brush is generally made of whalebone, and the rods of cane in lengths varying from 2 feet 6 inches to 4 feet 6 inches. A cloth with a sliding panel should be secured to the front of the fireplace and the sections of cane added gradually. Before each new section of handle is added the brush should be moved up and down two or three times, and when the top of the flue is reached the brush is pulled down evenly and the sections of the rod unscrewed one by one. A small brush should be used to clear the lower part of the flue immediately above the register.

As a rule a kitchen flue connected with a range does not accumulate a large amount of soot as a considerable proportion of it is deposited on the sides of the range itself. It is therefore necessary to use a small flue brush frequently and to scrape out the bottom very thoroughly.

Chemical Cleaners.

Although a chemical cleaner can be used on an ordinary fire when it is bright, its use is not advised for a range. An effective chemical cleaner can be made by mixing by weight 8 parts of muriate of ammonia, 7 of powdered blue stone, 6 of coarse salt, 5 of saltpetre, 2 each of fine sand and coke dust. Another recommended chemical cleaner is composed of 8 parts, also by weight, of muriate of ammonia, 7 parts each of chloride of sodium, flour of sulphur, and cuprous sulphate, and 4 of potassium nitrate. This is a very poisonous compound and should be used very carefully.

Economy in construction does not allow for superfluous brickwork and therefore the bends in modern small houses are not very pronounced, usually about 50 degrees. The sectional area of the flue should be 100 square inches, but usually it works out at 9 inches square. The parging of mortar, lime and hair should be carried right up the flue which should run with parallel sides. If the parging is carried out with poor materials or is carelessly done, there is likely to be trouble at the bends owing to the parging breaking away, and stoppage will inevitably result. In old houses subject to vibration through heavy

REMOVING MUD STAINS

MUD stains on clothes require special treatment if the marks are to be completely removed. It is most important not to try to remove the mud until it is quite dry. Spread the garment out on a good steady table, or any flat surface, then, with the edge of a coin, scratch the mud spots so that the crust is well broken. You will find that the mud brushes away quite easily. A somewhat soft brush with long bristles is the best for the job. Sometimes after brushing there is still a mark to be seen. When this happens there has been some oil or tar in the mud and you will have to dissolve the substance that makes the mark. In the case of oil, use benzene or petrol, both of which must be kept away from a naked light. Where there is still a mark the presence of tar is indicated, and there is nothing so good to remove this as milk well rubbed. If the rubbing is continued for a while, all traces of milk and tar will vanish.

The Care of Cricket Bats

Most of us who play cricket develop a decided affection for our favourite bat and, when it begins to show signs of wear, are very concerned about its fate. Fortunately, there is much that can be done to restore to its original condition a bat that has seen several seasons of hard usage, and all enthusiasts will agree that this is a much more satisfactory proposition than discarding an old friend in favour of a brand new substitute.

Oiling a Bat.

Take some pure linseed oil and rub it into the blade, taking care not to let it run over the splice. Then take an old stump and rub the face of the bat down; this will work the oil into the blade. Do not allow the oil to cake on the surface of the blade. Oil has a tendency to solidify in the cold weather; if this should happen, sandpaper the face of the blade and lightly rub in some fresh oil. Do not forget to clean the blade before oiling if you have been playing on a "sticky" wicket.

Oiling after Wet Weather.

When the time for oiling arrives and the bat was last used in wet weather, it may be advisable to run over the surfaces of the blade with fine glasspaper and, then, to apply the oil. This should give the bat a new and smart appearance, in addition to keeping it in a fit condition.

Cracked Blades.

When cracks appear on the blade after the bat has been in use for some time, immediate attention should be given. If the cracks are small ones bind over the crack with some adhesive tape, which can be obtained at any sports depot. Slightly warm the adhesive tape before binding round the blade; then when the tape has been applied take the old stump again and rub over the tape; this will make it adhere strongly to the blade.

Repairing a Split Bat.

Should the crack be a deep one, it is necessary to insert a few pegs into the blade where the crack has appeared. Willow pegs are always the best; never use hard wood pegs as they will only cause the crack to go worse, bearing in mind at the same time that the less pegs used the better.

Make about three holes, ¼ inch deep, with a fine awl, on both sides of the cracks. The holes should not run vertically down into the blade but should tilt slightly towards the crack that is to be closed up. Then open the split, run in the glue and close the split, as shown in Figs. 2, 3, 4 and 5.

Next, take the pegs and drive them into the holes as far as they will readily go, but, in doing this, see that the

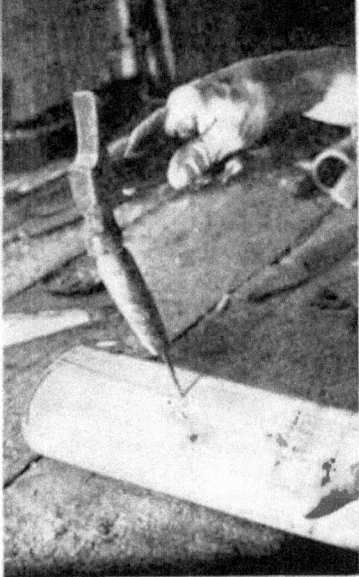

Fig. 1.—Repairing a Split Bat.
First punch the holes for pegs round the break in the bat. It is important that this is done before the split is glued.

hammer does not bruise the blade. Then, when the pegs are standing up in their holes, place a flat piece of wood on top of them and hammer gently on the wood. This will drive in the pegs as far as is required, and it will save the blade from hammer marks.

The next step is to take a very

Fig. 2.—Repairing a Split Bat. Second Operation.
Force open the split at the bottom of blade by means of a wedge, preparatory to gluing.

sharp chisel and shave off the pegs level with the blade. It will be necessary to give a final rub with fine glasspaper.

If done properly, the pegs will close up the cracks; they will prevent further splitting along these lines of weakness and they will in no wise detract from the efficiency of the bat. It is always advisable to bind over the place where the pegs have been inserted, with adhesive tape.

Binding the Blade.

Binding with cord is shown in Fig. 8.

To apply a tape bandage, grip the blade in the jaws of a vice close to but not just where the tape is to be fixed. Arrange the blade so that the grip of the vice presses the blade from edge to edge and not from back to front. Naturally, the jaws must be padded in order that they do not leave an impression in the wood. Then, gradually tighten up the vice so that the cracks are fully closed.

You are now ready to apply the tape. Begin at the back of the blade, bring the tape smoothly round to the front and continue by carrying it to the back again. As the tape is applied, flatten it well down and see that it is quite tight, smooth and straight. Then, go on and place several more turns round the blade, making each turn lap over the previous one to the extent of half its width. When the tape has covered the worst of the offending cracks, it is taken round to the back and the unused part of the strip is cut off.

Such a binding will add considerably to the active life of the bat, and it will not impair the efficiency in the least if the material is not wrapped too thickly around the blade. Naturally, it will not last for ever, but, if renewed when it becomes worn, the bat will continue to be serviceable.

Binding the Handle.

Turning now from the blade to the handle, it may be that the latter needs re-cording. This is a difficult process to carry out well unless the correct manner of starting and finishing-off is understood. It is, then, a straightforward business.

First, obtain a ball of fine cord and wax it from end to end. This is done by holding a piece of beeswax in the palm of a gloved hand and pulling the cord tightly through the wax. Unless gloves are worn, the hands will become very sore before the whole of the ball is finished. As you wax the cord, get someone to wind it up, in order that it may not become tangled.

Arranging the Starting.

Now for the starting. Begin at the tip of the handle and lay 2 inches of the cord straight down it, the end of the cord pointing to the blade.

THE CARE OF CRICKET BATS

Fig. 3.—REPAIRING A SPLIT BAT. THIRD OPERATION.
The split having been forced open, the glue will readily run right into the split.

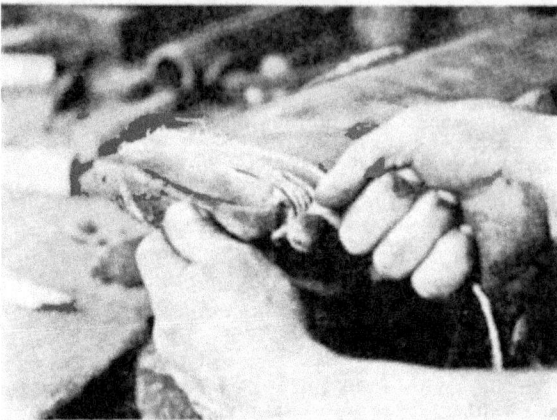

Fig. 4.—REPAIRING A SPLIT BAT. FOURTH OPERATION.
After gluing the split, string is used as a binding to keep the blade together until the glue sets.

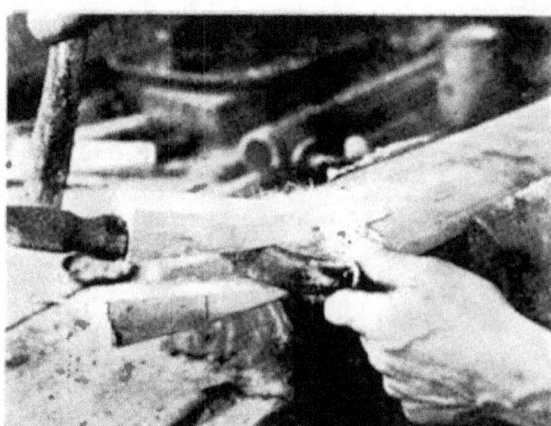

Fig. 5.—REPAIRING A SPLIT BAT. FIFTH OPERATION.
Wedges should now be driven between the blade and the stringing, to make the join as tight as possible.

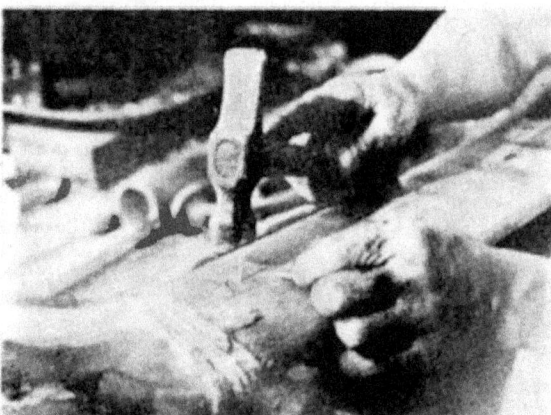

Fig. 6.—REPAIRING A SPLIT BLADE. SIXTH OPERATION.
The pegs are now driven into the holes previously made round the ball-break.

Fig. 7.—FINAL OPERATION PRIOR TO BINDING.
When the glue has set, the stringing is removed and the blade cleaned off with a scraper. The bat is now ready for binding, either with tape or cord. Tape binding is described in the text, while cord binding is shown in Fig. 8.

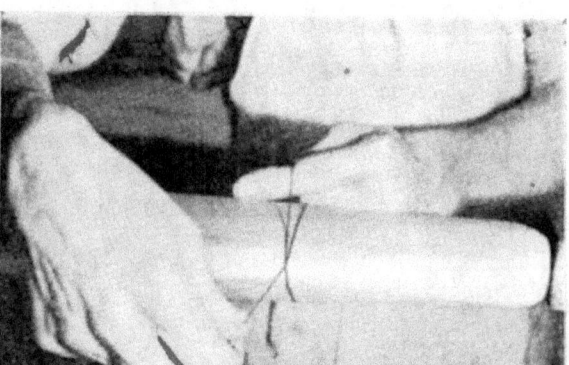

Fig. 8.—HOW TO START CORD BINDING.
Keep one end under the binding for about six turns, then cut off the surplus and continue binding. Make the crossing of the first turn on the edge of the blade as shown. The method of finishing off is similar to that of the handle (see Figs. 9–12).

THE CARE OF CRICKET BATS

Place a finger on this arrangement and then wind the cord evenly round the handle, commencing at the tip. When about a dozen turns have been made, the free commencing end of the cord will be completely hidden and then the cord will be held fast.

The subsequent turns of the cord are merely a matter of winding evenly, each turn being made tight and absolutely touching against the previous turn. The job will be much simplified if an assistant can be persuaded to hold the bat and revolve it slowly while you attend to the winding.

How to Finish Off.

The finishing off is done in the following manner. When the winding has almost reached down to the shoulder of the bat, take a piece of the cord, about 4 to 6 inches long, double it into the shape of a V and place it on the bat so that the angle of the V projects well beyond the position where you imagine the last lap of the cord will come. In addition, the two tips of the V must lie on some part of the cord already wound. This will be made clear by reference to Fig. 10.

Having done this properly, continue with the winding and, when the final lap has been made, cut the cord with several inches to spare. Then, pass the end of the cord through the angle of the V and follow by pulling the two tips of the V. In this way, the loose end of the winding cord can be drawn tightly under the laps and the V-shaped strip of cord is then pulled completely away. It may be necessary to clip off the end of the winding cord

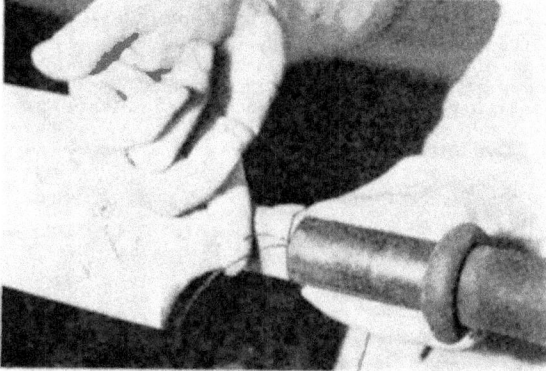

Fig. 9.—REBINDING THE SHOULDER (1).
Start the same as for the blade, but keep the end of the existing binding under the new binding for about six turns. The two ends (one of new and one of old binding) are then cut off flush and the binding continued.

where it emerges. That finishes the job.

Fitting a Rubber Handle Grip.

This requires a special little tool called a handling stick, which is tapered down, so that when the grip is put on the stick you can roll the grip down it and shoot it off the thick end of the stick on to the handle. This is a little job which your local dealer would do for the outside price of 1s., and would save you a lot of trouble, especially if you do not possess a handling stick.

Don't Play with a Damaged Bat.

Do not, under any circumstances, continue to play with a damaged bat; you will probably ruin it completely. "A stitch in time saves nine," and wrapping and gluing will more often than not make the blade sound again. Do not lend your bat to a friend; some people must use bats to drive in the stumps; it is much better to borrow his. Do not use a new ball to "break" in a new bat. An hour or so at the nets with an old ball will help to condition the bat.

A Simple Explanation.

Cricketers are sometimes surprised when the blade of their bat splits or crushes on the edge or the toe if they play a ball hard on the extreme point instead of on the full face of the bat. Yet they will accept a damaged finger as a natural consequence if they fail to field a fast ball with the palm of their hand. Damaged bats, like damaged fingers, should receive immediate attention. Neglect means serious trouble to either.

Choosing a Cricket Bat.

When choosing a cricket bat pay particular attention to the weight, balance and grain. Don't choose a bat that feels too heavy for you.

Hold the bat by the handle with both hands and lift it up and down just as when actually playing. This will enable you to tell whether it comes up well or badly. Using a bat that is too heavy for one's strength soon tires you out and means a continuous physical strain. It causes the fault of playing too late at the ball.

Knots in the blade of a bat are said to strengthen the wood and make it durable. There should, however, be no knots in the lower half of the blade; they form a very hard spot and are liable to produce a jarring feeling.

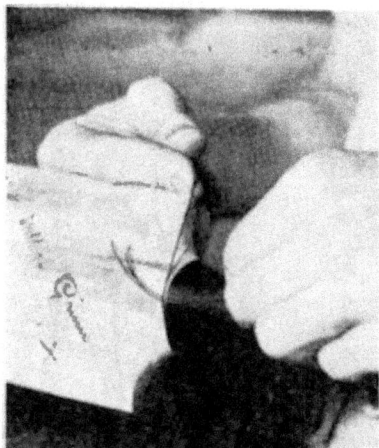

Fig. 10.—REBINDING THE SHOULDER (2).
When ten or twelve turns from the end a loop is inserted and for the remainder of the turns the binding goes over this loop.

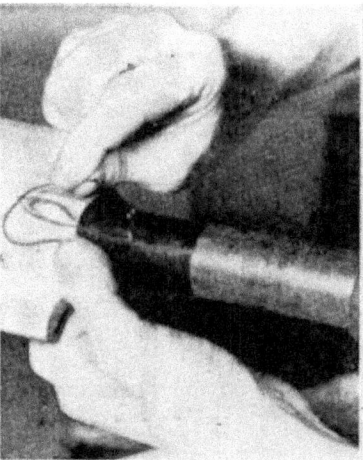

Fig. 11.—REBINDING THE SHOULDER (3).
While keeping the binding tight and firm with the thumb, the end is passed through the projecting end of the loop.

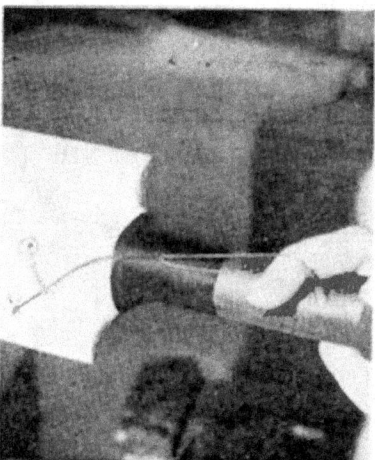

Fig. 12.—THE FINISH-OFF OF THE BINDING.
Pulling the loop which pulls with it the end of the binding, which is then cut off at the point where it emerges from under the binding.

How to Know Period Furniture

CHAIRS have been chosen to exemplify the subject because they above all other kinds of furniture show the progress of style. The general form of the chair cannot be altered fundamentally. It varies in detail in accordance with the skill of the craftsman, the material available and the dictates of fashion, and it is precisely these points that are so useful when dating a piece of furniture.

The following are the approximate dates covered by the periods and styles:—

Tudor Gothic	1485–1558	William and Mary	1689–1702
Elizabethan	1558–1603	Queen Anne	1702–1714
Jacobean	1603–1649	Georgian	1714–1749
Cromwellian	1649–1660	Chippendale	1750–1779
Jacobean	1660–1688	Hepplewhite, Adam, Sheraton	1760–1820

The Oak Period.

OAK CHAIR. ABOUT 1525.
A heavy type of chair panelled throughout. Mortise and tenon joints are used, pegs being used to secure them.

The Walnut Period.

WALNUT CHAIR. ABOUT 1675.
A typical Charles II. chair. Early walnut work followed on similar lines to that of the preceding oak period though it was lighter.

The Mahogany Period.

MAHOGANY CHAIR. MID-EIGHTEENTH CENTURY.
A popular form of Chippendale chair. The shape of the back and the pierced slat are characteristic.

The Satinwood Period.

MAHOGANY CHAIR. SECOND HALF EIGHTEENTH CENTURY.
Although of mahogany, this chair belongs to the satinwood period. It was designed by Adam. It has the wheel back.

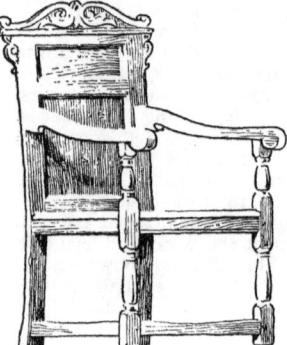

OAK CHAIR. LATE SIXTEENTH CENTURY.
A direct descendant from the chair above. The capping above the back is typical.

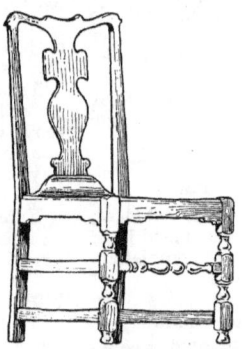

OAK CHAIR. LATE SEVENTEENTH CENTURY.
Although of oak, it shows a definite transitional period in its form. The back foreshadows the coming style.

MAHOGANY CHAIR. SECOND HALF EIGHTEENTH CENTURY.
Note that the cabriole leg has been superseded by the lighter tapered type. The shape of the arms is characteristic.

SATINWOOD CHAIR. LATE EIGHTEENTH CENTURY.
Here we have the work of Sheraton; whereas Chippendale had used carving almost exclusively, Sheraton preferred inlay and painting.

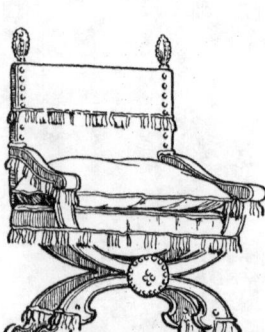

UPHOLSTERED CHAIR. EARLY SEVENTEENTH CENTURY.
This is of special interest as it is the earliest form of upholstered chair in England.

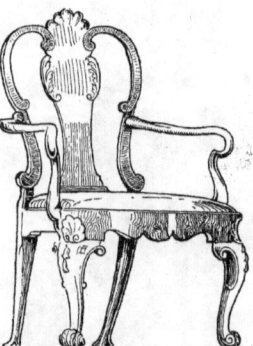

WALNUT CHAIR. EARLY EIGHTEENTH CENTURY.
The stretcher rails have disappeared; the square back is elaborately shaped as foreshadowed above. Note the cabriole legs.

MAHOGANY CHAIR. SECOND HALF EIGHTEENTH CENTURY.
Hepplewhite, who evolved this form, became one of the leading stylists. The shield back was a favourite *motif*. A variation is the oval back.

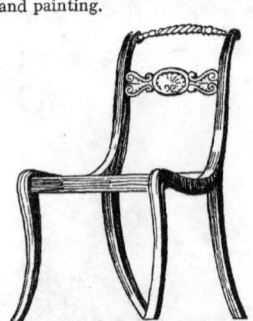

PAINTED CHAIR. EARLY NINETEENTH CENTURY.
Sheraton's last designs were not so happy as his earlier efforts. Many disturbing influences were at work. This chair is of the Trafalgar Period and is at the beginning of the Victorian age.

Making a Combination Wireless Cabinet and Book-Case

THE wireless cabinet illustrated in Fig. 1 is of very modern design and makes a handsome and useful piece of furniture which is in keeping with nearly any form of furnishing scheme. Despite the really modern design, the cabinet could certainly not be termed "futuristic," whilst its appearance will not be found to pall after the cabinet has been in use for a time. In keeping with the present-day trend of high-class radio cabinet design, the one to be described is of the "utility" type, including as it does a useful book-case and good-sized cupboard in addition to the commodious apartment set aside for the receiver itself. Another important feature which should be noted is the special arrangement of the loudspeaker opening and baffle board.

Provision for Dual Balanced Speakers.

It might appear at first sight that the speaker opening is unduly large, but this is explained by the fact that it is arranged to take a pair of dual balanced speakers if desired. Of course, a single speaker unit of the normal type can be used when preferred, but as there is a growing tendency to employ a double speaker, it is well to make provision for this. Besides offering the advantage just mentioned, the large opening is more in keeping with the general design of the cabinet than a smaller one would be.

There is yet another important point in regard to the speaker baffle board, which is that it is not fretted in the more conventional manner, but is simply pierced by two circular holes which are later covered with silk. This method of construction has the advantage of improving reproduction by removing all undesirable restriction to the passage of sound waves from the speaker. A detail which is worthy of mention in respect of the speaker opening is that it can be "flood-lit" by means of a bulb mounted in a holder behind a rectangular hole in the top of the speaker opening, the hole being covered with a piece of thin orange-coloured celluloid or silk. This gives a very effective dim light which is conducive to the maximum enjoyment of many forms of broadcast matter.

Accommodation for practically any Receiver.

In spite of all the modern refinements which have been included in this cabinet, the design has been worked out on strictly practical lines. The dimensions

Fig. 1.—The Finished Combination Wireless Cabinet and Book-case.

have been chosen so that nearly any kind of wireless receiver having overall chassis dimensions not exceeding some 17 × 13 × 9 inches can readily be accommodated; it will be clear from this that the cabinet is ideal for housing such popular kit sets as the Lissen "Skyscraper Four" (A.C. or battery version), the Lissen "Superhet Seven," any of the "Orgola," Cossor "Melody Maker" or G.E.C. "Music Magnet" series, or practically any of the wide range of instruments described in the Wireless Press. When a mains receiver is used,

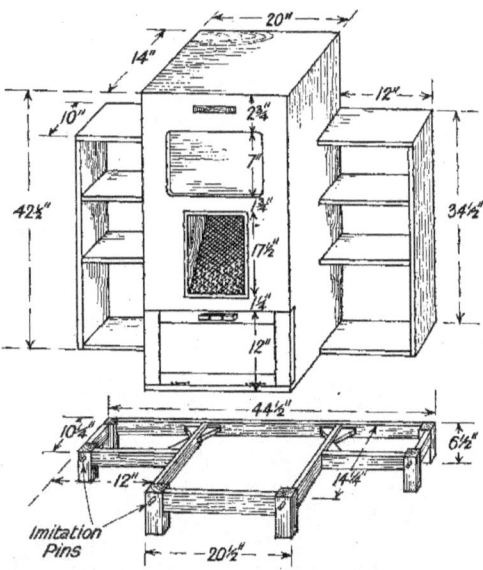

Fig. 2.—Principal Details of the Cabinet.

the cupboard can be employed for storing daily or periodical papers and the like, whilst if the set is battery-operated, the necessary batteries can be stored in the cupboard, where they are particularly accessible. Those who employ a large power amplifier in addition to the ordinary receiver can accommodate this in the compartment provided for the speaker, since there is an ample amount of spare space.

No provision has been made for housing any gramophone equipment, principally because it is considered better to have this as a separate unit, and partly because the design chosen does not readily lend itself to this application.

"Unit" Construction.

Turning to the practical side of things, it should first be explained that the cabinet under consideration is actually composed of two separate parts—the body, and a framework comprising the short legs upon which its stands. The two parts can be made quite separately, as illustrated in Fig. 2. This form of construction not only makes for simplicity, but also ensures a truly rigid assembly, which is essential when the very best results are required from the wireless set.

List of Principal Timber Stock required.

1 sheet oak-faced laminated board (for front), 20 × 28½ inches.
2 sheets oak-faced laminated board (for top and bottom), 14 × 20 inches.
4 sheets oak-faced laminated board (for tops and bottoms of book-case sections), 12 × 10 inches.
4 sheets oak-faced laminated board (for shelves), 11 9/16 × 9¼ inches.
1 sheet ordinary 7-ply (for baffle board) 18¼ × 12 inches.
1 piece oak (for door frame), 58 inches long by 1½ inches wide by ⅜ inch thick.
1 piece oak (for lower framework), 9 feet 9½ inches long by 1¼ inches wide by ¾ inch thick.
1 piece oak (for legs), 39 inches long by 1½ inches square.
2 pieces 3-ply (for backs of book-cases), 40 × 11¾ inches.
1 piece 3-ply (for back of receiver portion), 19 × 41 inches.
1 piece ordinary 7-ply (for receiver shelf), 19 × 13 inches.

The smaller odd pieces of wood required for edging laminated boards, etc., are not given in the above list, since most of these can be obtained from scrap in cutting up the other members.

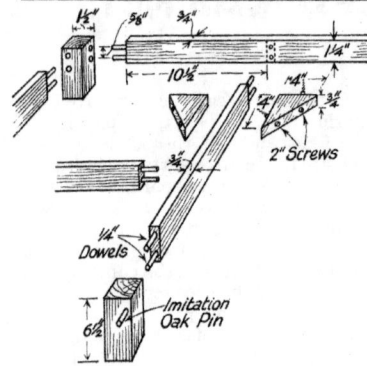

Fig. 3.—Details of the Framework forming the Legs upon which the Cabinet stands.

The Lower Framework.

The framework forming the legs consists of $1\frac{1}{4} \times \frac{3}{4}$-inch material attached to the short $1\frac{1}{2}$-inch square legs by means of short lengths of $\frac{1}{4}$-inch dowel rod. This method of jointing was decided upon due to the fact that the average amateur finds great difficulty in making mortise and tenon joints which will fit sufficiently well to make the perfectly square frame which is required. In order to give the appearance of pinned tenon joints, however, short "dummy" oak pins are fitted, as can be seen from Fig. 2. All frame dimensions, as well as details of the joints, are shown in Fig. 3. It will also be seen from this drawing that a few small triangles of $\frac{3}{4}$-inch wood are fitted in the angles, between four members in order to prevent "racking"; these are simply fixed in position by means of glue and a couple of 2-inch screws. Very little explanation seems to be called for in respect of the method of making the frame, since the drawings are self-explanatory. It might just be pointed out that it is imperative that all the lengths of framing should be cut dead square at the ends, or else difficulty is sure to be experienced in making the joints a perfect fit. Additionally, great care should be taken in boring the holes (with an auger bit) for the dowels, to ensure that they are at right-angles to the end.

Preventing the Frame from Twisting.

After the frame has been glued up and set square, it should be laid on one side until the glue has had time to set perfectly. In doing this, it is a good plan to stand the frame on a flat surface, lay a few large boards over it and stand some heavy article on the boards; this will prevent any possible twisting. Meanwhile, the main part of the cabinet can receive attention. This is built around the central prominent "wireless" section, the latter being made from oak-faced laminated board. This material is not only slightly cheaper than solid wood, but it will not warp, and is more readily obtainable in the wide boards required. Constructional details of the centre section are given in Fig. 4, to which reference should now be made. It will be seen that the joints between the front, sides and top are all "halved." These simple "halving" joints can be made in one of two ways. The first consists of sawing first down the end of the wood to the required depth, and then sawing across the board until the rectangular-shaped strip of wood is removed. The other way is to saw across the board to a depth of $\frac{1}{4}$ inch and then form the rebate by means of a rebate plane. In the latter case the board should be clamped to the bench top whilst planing. Whichever of the two methods is employed, the boards

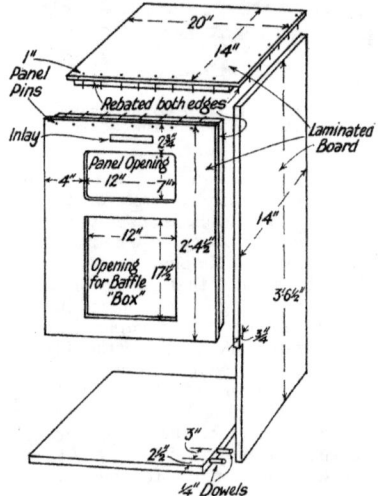

Fig. 4.—Constructional Details of the Central Portion of the Cabinet.

should first be marked out with a marking gauge after they have been cut off to length, and the ends squared up.

The bottom of this section is fixed to the sides by means of $\frac{1}{4}$-inch dowel rod, and consists of laminated board similar to that used for the sides and top. Four pieces of dowelling are used as shown, and these are fixed in position by means of thin Scotch glue. This method of fixing obviates the use of joints which would show in the finished cabinet.

After all the joints for the main (centre) case have been formed, the necessary holes for the panel opening and speaker baffle board assembly should be cut out to the dimensions shown. This can be done quite easily by using a fret-saw, or by making a $\frac{1}{4}$-inch hole in each corner and employing a key-hole or pad-saw. In either case the edges of the openings will require to be cleaned off, and this can be done most easily by using first a rough file and then a strip of glass-paper held flat on a rectangular-section block of soft wood.

Simple Inlay Decoration.

It will be seen from the photograph that a rectangular strip of light-coloured wood is inlaid in the top of the front of the cabinet. The inlay may consist of an odd strip of lighter coloured oak, or may be a strip of beech, birch, or similar wood; alternatively, this may be omitted entirely. If the inlay is to be used, its shape (it will measure about 6 inches wide by 1 inch deep) should first be marked on the front panel, after which a shallow sinking can be made by using a sharp chisel. The inlay should then be cut to the same length and width, but should be somewhat thicker than the depth of the sinking. It will then be fixed in place with glue, and after that has properly set, the inlay can be planed off to the same level as the panel surface.

Assembling the Main Section.

The next step is to assemble the main section of the cabinet, carefully gluing and pinning all the halving joints with $1\frac{1}{2}$-inch panel pins. After that, the door for the lower cupboard can be made. This consists of a framework of $1\frac{1}{2} \times \frac{3}{4}$-inch timber, each frame member being rebated, and the various members being fastened together by means of dowelling. Here, again, mortise and tenon joints would have been more correct, but the difficulty of making these is rather too great for the average amateur. A panel is fitted in the door, that illustrated in Fig. 1, being made of beaten pewter. Those who prefer can fit an ordinary oak-faced plywood panel or a carved one of solid oak. All constructional details for the cupboard door are given in

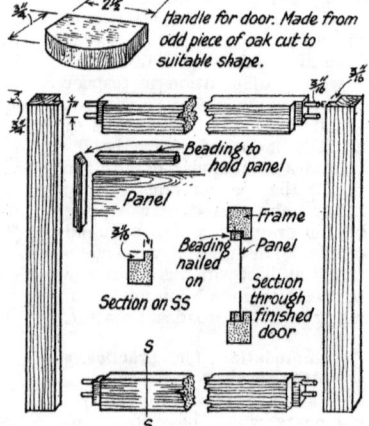

Fig. 5.—Details of the Cupboard Door.
Fig. 6 shows how to remove the notches for the hinges of the door.

Fig. 5. The frame members should first be cut to length, after which the fillets can be formed by means of a tenon-saw, by sawing and chiselling, or by means of a side fillister, according to the tools available. After that it should be assembled, the panel fitted from the back (or inside), and then strips of beading mitred and fitted behind the panel to hold it in place; these are attached simply by means of ¾-inch wire points.

Fitting the Door Hinges.

The 1½-inch butt hinges should next be fitted to the lower edge of the door. The positions for these should first be marked out, lines squared across the edge of the frame and the gauge set to the thickness of the hinges. The depth of the recesses required can then be marked off with the gauge, and the sinkings made with a chisel. First make cuts at each end of the sinkings, across the grain, then make a cut along the grain and finally remove the waste wood as shown in Fig. 6. It will be seen that a "V" notch is first made, after which the wood is removed by means of a 1-inch chisel, working from the surface of the wood to the "V."

The Speaker Baffle "Box."

The speaker baffle calls for attention now, and it will be understood that this is made as a complete assembly which fits into the rectangular opening made in the front panel. Details of the baffle assembly are given in Fig. 7. Half-inch timber is used, and the pieces are mitred at the corners. The front edges of the sides of the baffle "box" are rounded over with a beading plane, and square-section strips are fitted to each edge of the "box" to form a fixing with the front panel without the use of any visible nails or screws. Laminated board is used for the baffle itself, and this has two holes

in it made to correspond with the speaker(s) to be used.

Fitting the Book-cases.

After the main section of the cabinet has been completed, there is no difficulty in adding the book-shelves, details of which are given in Fig. 8. The book-cases are made of oak-faced laminated board, in the same way as is the rest of the cabinet. The top, sides and bottom are fastened together by means of halving joints which are nailed and glued, whilst the top and bottom are fixed to the centre portion by means of 2 inches by 8's screws passed through from the inside. All the shelves are fitted on to ½ × ½-inch runners screwed to the sides, so that they can easily be moved when required in order to accommodate books of different sizes. In order to

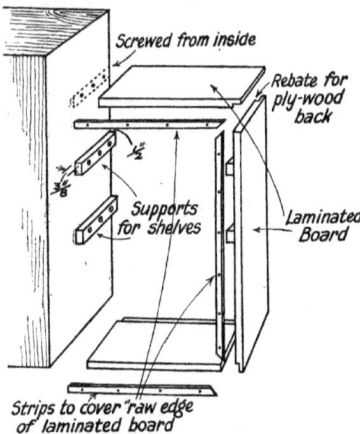

Fig. 8.—Showing how the Book-case Sections are fitted.

hide the "raw" edges of the laminated board forming the book-cases and shelves, strips of solid oak, measuring approximately 3/16 inch thick by 7/16 inch wide, are glued and pinned on to the front edges. These strips are shown in Fig. 8. Such a method of finishing would be unnecessary if solid wood were used throughout, but the advantages of laminated board (provided that it is of the best possible quality) more than justify its use.

No mention has yet been made of the method of fitting the plywood backs to the book-case sections, but it will be seen from Fig. 8 that these are accommodated by rebating the side, top and bottom members, so that the surface of the plywood is flush with the back of the cabinet.

After the complete upper section of the cabinet-book-case has been finished, it can be fixed to the framework comprising the legs by means of 1½-inch nails and glue. Additional strength is given by fitting triangular gluing blocks at intervals around the frame.

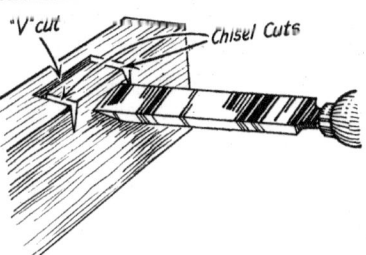

Fig. 6.—Showing the Method of removing the Notches for the Hinges of the Cupboard Door.

Finally, a shelf should be fitted to hold the receiver, and this will consist of a rectangular piece of 7-ply or similar material supported by two 1-inch square side runners screwed to the insides of the cabinet. A back for the receiver portion is desirable, and this should be fretted rather extensively so as not to restrict the sound waves from the speaker and to allow of easy air circulation for cooling purposes when A.C. valves are in use. To prevent the ingress of dust the frets should be covered by stretching and gluing pieces of silk or speaker gauze over them.

Finishing the Cabinet.

It need scarcely be mentioned that, after completing the constructional part of the cabinet, the whole thing should be well rubbed down with fine glasspaper, the nails punched slightly below the surface, and the holes filled with putty or wax coloured with a little of the stain which is to be used. Finally, the whole cabinet may be stained and polished, or otherwise finished by one of the processes described on page 677.

Interesting Modifications.

There are a number of interesting possible alternatives to the exact design described, and a few of these have been tried by the writer with excellent results. For example, instead of using a strip of inlay at the top of the main "receiver" section, a pivoted double tray can be fitted. One side of this can be used as a container for cigarettes, whilst the other side acts as an ash tray. The whole tray can best be made as a U-section piece of oak, and then two small trays about 3 inches long by 2 inches wide should be made to fit. For preference the trays should be slightly tapered along their length so that they will fit tightly into place when pressed from the end; they can then be removed quite easily for refilling or emptying.

The double tray can easily be fitted by using two small pieces of strip brass bent to form angle pieces; these are mounted above and below the tray, two screws forming pivots.

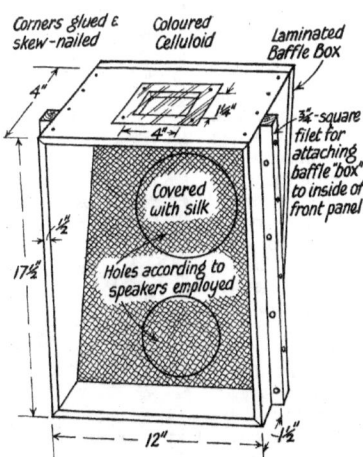

Fig. 7.—Details and Dimensions of the Loudspeaker Baffle "Box."

Cesspools
SOME PRACTICAL METHODS OF DISPOSING OF SEWAGE

IN many localities there is no main drainage, and the sewage from dwelling-houses has to be disposed of by some other method.

The cesspool system is quite efficient if constructed properly, and there is no reason to think that you cannot do it yourself if the directions as set forth here are carefully carried out.

We will assume that there had been only earth closets attached to the house under consideration, and that an outside apartment has subsequently been built with a properly constructed closet, cistern and water waste preventer (ball valve and flush operated by a chain) which has been fully described in a previous article dealing with the subject.

Types of Cesspools. 1. Open Joints.

To start with, a suitable position must be determined upon, and should be as far away as possible from the house.

There are two kinds of cesspools. The first is constructed of brick or stone, with open joints, thus forming a sump or soakaway, and in which case all liquid percolates through the joints and disperses into the ground around.

This class of cesspool should only be constructed where the soil is of gravel or fairly loose soil.

2. Sealed Joints.

The other kind is built in much the same way, but all joints are sealed up. The benefit of the first is that the liquid percolating through does not need to be pumped out, whereas in the latter type the liquid has either to be removed by the local authorities or pumped up and disposed of over a suitable area.

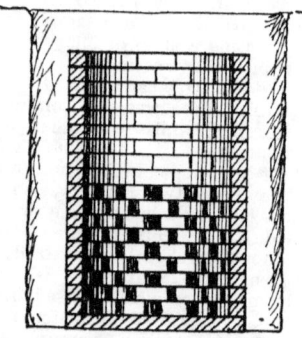

Fig. 3.—How to lay the Bricks round the Hole.

The vertical joints of the brickwork of the lower half should be open, the horizontal ones cemented. The space between the wall and the side of the hole is left only for gaining access for working, and must afterwards be filled in.

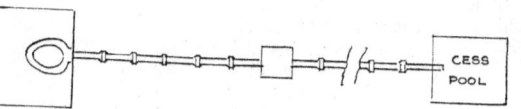

Fig. 1.—General Layout of a Typical Cesspool System.

Precautions.

In the case of the open cesspool or sump, very great care must be taken to see that it is not built in the vicinity of a brook or well, where rainwater is likely to be used, or where cattle graze. Very serious consequences might arise through contamination. Typhoid fever might be caused through neglect in this respect.

General Layout of System.

Fig. 1 illustrates the general layout

Fig. 2.—How the Connecting "Link" of the Drain Pipe is laid.

Showing half a pipe bedded into the concrete bottom, both sides of which should be benched.

of the system. First ascertain the exact position where the outgo of the drain pipe from the closet is situated and dig down to several inches below the point where the underside of the drain pipe will come. Now channel out a trough or ditch in the direction towards the position decided upon for your first receptacle, and form a gradual fall, 1¼ inches in 10 feet, and lay your drain in 4-inch stoneware pipes. This receptacle is termed an intercepting chamber or manhole, and is built as shown in Fig. 2, with bricks and mortar on a concrete and cement foundation.

Manhole Cover.

The cover should be of cast iron, which can be purchased, complete with grooved frame, for £1. The frame is laid on top of the brick sides of the chamber and bedded in with cement. Alternatively, a slab of Portland, York or other stone can be used. This likewise rests on the top of the brick sides. The cast-iron cover, however, is obviously the better of the two.

Laying the Drain Pipe.

The correct way to lay your drain pipe is in such a way as to enter the chamber at floor level. This prevents unnecessary soiling of the brick sides. The connecting "link" of drain pipe is laid as shown in Fig. 2, viz., half a pipe bedded into the concrete bottom, both sides of which should be benched, *i.e.*, sloped away from the brick walls towards the drain pipe.

Intercepting Trap.

At the intercepting chamber end you will have to fit an intercepting trap (Fig. 2). The purpose of this is to prevent any gas travelling back into the house drains. Interceptors may be purchased (£1 5s.). All these outgoes and ingoes can be fixed to the brick sides by means of cement.

Now for your cesspool. We have indicated above the importance of determining the position for this. We will, therefore, assume that a suitable place has been found.

Dig down to a few inches below the position where the outgoing drain from the interceptor chamber will be situated, and then dig a trough, giving a gradual fall of not less than 1¼ inches in every 10 feet to the cesspool site. The drain pipes, if stoneware, can be laid direct on to the ground, if fairly firm, but it is better to form a concrete bed. The laying of these pipes is fully dealt with in the article on outside W.C.'s.

The Question of Size.

The size of the cesspool varies according to what is required of it, and to the number of people occupying the house to which it is connected up, also the various sanitary fittings which discharge into it.

About 25 gallons per person per day is the usual amount to allow for when determining the size of the cesspool.

We will assume for our purpose that a small cesspool only is required, and for this proceed in the following manner:—

We are considering a cesspool with open joints, to allow of the liquid

Fig. 4.—The Drain Pipe must enter into the Cesspool through the Upper Part, where the Construction is firm.

percolating through and dispersing itself into the ground.

Digging the Hole for the Cesspool.

First of all, dig down to about 7 feet a circular hole, slightly larger than your brick hole is to be; well ram and level the bed, and proceed to lay your bricks as shown in Fig. 3, around the side of the hole. The vertical joints of the brickwork of the lower half should be open, the horizontal cemented. The space between the wall and the wall of hole is left only for gaining access for working, and must afterwards be filled in.

The walls of the top half must be also constructed of bricks but laid with properly bonded joints (Fig. 3).

How the Drain Pipe should enter the Cesspool.

The drain pipe must enter into the cesspool through the upper part where the construction is firm, as shown in Fig. 4, which clearly indicates that it is so arranged as to cause all the deposit to be shot clear of the walls in order that they shall in no way be fouled or the joints of the lower half be filled up. Such an arrangement keeps the chamber clean and sanitary.

If this sump, or soakaway, as it is sometimes called, is constructed properly, there is no reason to fear that it should be anything otherwise than completely sanitary.

The drain pipe entering into the chamber must be properly fixed with a cement joint.

Covering the Chamber.

Build up to within about 1 foot from the surface and proceed to cover over the chamber with a reinforced concrete slab.

Cesspools usually have arched roofs, but this may be deemed too complicated a construction for an amateur to undertake, so that the concrete top will be best.

To form this, you will have to lay shuttering, *i.e.*, flat boards, across (Fig. 5), supported on scantling, *i.e.*, thick uprights for the shuttering to rest upon.

This framework is constructed for laying your concrete upon. Mix up cement with gravel and stones to make the concrete and lay it on the shuttering about 6 to 8 inches thick, reinforcing it with iron rods, as indicated in Fig. 6.

The Inspection Hole.

A hole must be left in the centre for building up the access opening. This can be made of brick properly bonded, and must be built upon the concrete and fixed with cement (Fig. 7), and should be about 2 feet square in order to allow of your entering into the chamber to remove the scantling and shuttering when the concrete is thoroughly hard.

Now fill up around this with earth and well ram down.

You have constructed a hole large

Fig. 5.—Showing the Arrangement of Shuttering for forming the Concrete Top.

Fig. 6.—Showing how the Framework is reinforced with Iron Rods.

Fig. 7.—The Inspection Hole.

A hole must be left in the centre for building up the access opening. This can be made of brick properly bonded and must be built upon the concrete and fixed with cement.

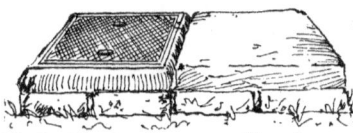

Fig. 8.—How the Inspection Hole Opening is converted to a Suitable Size for the Lid.

enough to form an entrance and exit for the purpose of construction. It remains now to convert the opening into reasonable dimensions for covering so as the lid, which must afterwards be fixed, shall not prove too cumbersome to manipulate when an inspection is desired.

Say the hole is 3 feet by 2 feet or thereabouts, you will have to reduce it to a standard size, about 2 feet by 1 foot 6 inches. Form this in the manner indicated in Fig. 8, which shows the reduction formed by the slab of stone laid across.

The cover and frame, made of cast iron, should be set in as shown in Fig. 8, and bedded down in mastic or cart grease.

The Tight Cesspool.

The construction of what is commonly known as a tight cesspool is similar to that of the open variety, but differs in this respect, that the utmost care should be exercised to see that the construction and ventilation is as near perfect as is possible, inasmuch that as the matter disposed of into it cannot get away, the possibility of sewage gas finding its way back is apparent, and must therefore be counteracted.

A vent pipe of cast iron will have to be constructed, leading out from the side about 12 inches below the roof and carried as high as possible up the side of the nearest tree. A wire balloon grating should be fixed to the top.

The vent pipe is not as necessary in the case of the open cesspool type as in the tight type now being considered.

Construction.

The construction of the cesspool itself is similar to the first as described except that it must have a foundation of bricks and a good layer of cement. Upon this, the brick sides can be constructed, but in this case the bricks must be properly bonded and the joints well and truly cemented.

Having built your chamber, render the sides and ceiling with a good coating of Portland cement and sand. The completion with regard to the cover may be constructed exactly as described for the first type.

Tight cesspools should be thoroughly disinfected every time they are emptied.

The tight cesspool is really more suitable where a considerable amount of sewage matter from water closets has to be disposed of. When the disposal is only confined to sinks and baths, etc., the open type is admirable, but there is always the possibility of the open joint becoming clogged, and also the earth round about.

The benefit, however, of the open type is that it has not to be emptied periodically, as is the case with the other type.

Rain Water.

It is most important to remember that on no account must rain water from roofs and surfaces be allowed to discharge into any cesspool, or it will be quickly flooded in the event of a storm and the whole system thrown out of use.

Periodical Inspection.

Whether the cesspool is of the "open" or "tight" pattern, the manhole should be opened periodically, say about every three months, to ascertain that it is working satisfactorily and does not require attention.

Also at the same time remove the cover of the inspection chamber, and flush out the run of drain and sides of manhole, and leave quite clean—with diluted spirits of salt.

Making Tubular Steel Furniture

TUBULAR steel furniture of modern design offers a fresh outlet for personal endeavour and skill by the handyman—who will soon find by trial that tubular furniture making is a fascinating hobby.

Alternative Constructional Methods.

Essentially, there are two distinct ways of making tubular furniture; the first consists of steel tube of uniform size with all joints "flush" and brazed.

The alternative method consists of steel tube in separate pieces jointed together by "tees" and other fittings, much in the same way that a bicycle is made. At first glance it would seem that the latter method is preferable for the novice, but this is by no means the case, because it is a very difficult matter to get all the separate joints correct and the parts lineable.

It may be pointed out, however, that a number of smaller articles of furniture can be made with some kinds of electrical "conduit," that is, thin steel tube and the stock tee and other joint fittings used with it; the article is built up in stages and an example of this method is given later.

Continuous Tubing.

The first method of construction consisting of what is in effect a continuous tube, is really the best, and is not so difficult to carry out if the job is approached in a common-sense way on the lines to be described. The framework is made entirely with "solid drawn steeltube," such as that used for cycle construction.

The gauge, or thickness, is usually No. 18 to No. 24, the external diameter is about ¾ to 1 inch for average size articles. Supplies of the tubing can always be obtained, either from stock or to order, from any cycle or motor dealer. It is most economically bought in "random lengths" of 6 to 8 feet; it should, however, be quite straight and free from kinks or bruises.

The quantity required depends upon the shape and size of the article—in practice the average is about 16 feet—but an extra amount "in stock" will always be found handy.

Materials required.

Quantities.

The Table Lamp Stand (Fig. 1) requires 18 feet of ¾-inch diameter tube.

Dressing Stool (Fig. 2) requires 13 feet of 1-inch diameter tube.

Small Folding Table (Fig. 3) requires 12 feet of ¾-inch diameter conduit and 4 "tees" and 4 elbows for same.

Armchair (Fig. 4) requires 24 feet of 1-inch diameter tube.

Dining Table (Fig. 5) requires 20 feet of 1¼-inch diameter tube, 4 "flanges" for 1-inch tube, and 8 "tees."

For each article the plywood panels for table tops and trays, also webbing

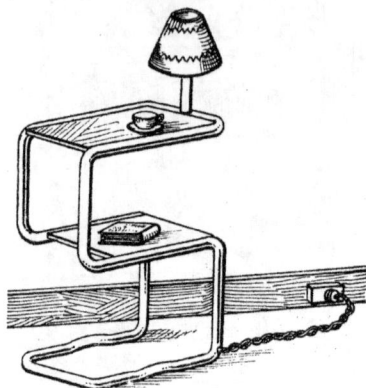

Fig. 1.—COMBINED TABLE AND LAMP STAND.
A novel but very useful article made with four pieces of steel tube.

and upholstery for seats will be needed in accordance with personal taste.

Necessary Tools.

The tools principally required are a fine-toothed hack-saw for cutting the tube. A bench vice with wooden "clams" as in Fig. 6, for gripping the tube. A bench or hand drill with a few twist drills; a blowlamp or gas blowpipe for brass brazing, and a "tube bender" or an extemporised bender as described later.

One or two large rough files for cleaning up the brazed work, plus the usual collection of small hand tools

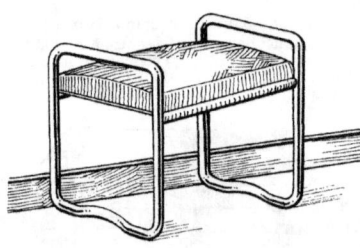

Fig. 2.—DRESSING STOOL.
Chromium-plated steel tube framework and an upholstered seat constitute this neat and attractive stool.

Fig. 3.—SMALL FOLDING TABLE.
The plywood top can be lifted off and the steel frame closed when necessary. The frame is made with conduit and fittings.

possessed by most home craftsman will amply suffice for all ordinary needs.

What to do First.

First of all study the design of the particular article to be made, for example, the combined table and lamp stand, then determine where any necessary joints are to be located. In the stated example there are only five joints, and four separate pieces of tube which are shaped and arranged as shown in Fig. 8 in their proper relationship.

The next step is to prepare a bending table—this can be a strong kitchen table or any sufficiently large surface whereon to lay and complete the bending of the tubes. A large sheet of plywood fitted over the table top is a great asset—it is smooth to draw upon and prevents damage to the surface of the table.

Full Size Drawing.

With a "blue" pencil, draw the full size outline of the main portion, for example, the side piece, shown in Fig. 7, for the table and lamp stand.

Note that only the part of the tube that will be "flat" or will lay in one plane should be drawn, the parts that have subsequently to be bent at right angles should be shown as continuations of the straight parts as at A and B, at the top and bottom. The drawing must be reasonably accurate and should show the thickness of the tube.

Next comes the bending of the tube and the correct sequence in which to make the bends. This is best appreciated by the diagrams (Figs. 9, 10, 11), showing stages in bending. First the middle bend is made, next follows the second or Z bend (Fig. 10), and at this stage it is essential to see that the tube lays perfectly flat on the bench—if not it must be corrected before going further. The top back bend (Fig. 11) then follows, the work is again flattened and lastly the bottom front bend is made. When completed thus far the bent tube must fit exactly within the lines drawn on the board.

The second side is bent in exactly the same way, then the top and bottom pieces are bent over at right angles, cut to length and properly butt-jointed, the middle cross bar being fitted and brazed into place last of all. Methods of doing this work will now be described, as they apply to any article; some specific examples are given later.

Bending the Tube.

Slow, regular, or gradual bends—more properly termed "curves"—such as those on the armchair shown in Fig. 4, can be made "cold," that is, without making the tube red hot.

1368

MAKING TUBULAR STEEL FURNITURE

The best way to curve a tube is to move it backwards and forwards across a slightly curved block of wood clamped to the workbench as in Fig. 12, and while maintaining the too-and-fro motion exert a steady definite downwards pressure, just sufficient to curve the tube. It is most important to curve the tube in one plane only, just as if it had been bent while between two inflexible parallel walls. This is easily tested by laying the tube flat on the table; it must touch the surface for the whole of its length; if it does not, the tube must be bent very carefully between the hands to straighten it.

Straightening a Tube.

As the straightening or flattening of a tube is an important matter, the knack of doing it should be acquired as speedily as possible. Suppose, for example, on looking along the tube that it is curved in three places—as in Fig. 13—of which the first is at A.

The procedure is first to correct one of the errors and thus bring a part of the tube into alignment. When this is done the tube will seem to be worse, because, as sketched in Fig. 14, the two ends point in marked different directions.

Second Stage of straightening.

The next stage is to correct the bend nearest to the opposite end of the tube, as marked B in Fig. 13, and then finish the job by straightening the middle or last bend, which, as shown in Fig. 15, is now very apparent, and is consequently more readily corrected.

Additional Kinks.

Any attempt to straighten the tube piecemeal as by laying it on a flat surface and pressing on it will only result in the formation of additional kinks somewhat as sketched in Fig. 16.

Cold Bending.

Correction of small bends such as those discussed above, can be effected in most cases by resting the kinked

*Fig. 6.—*VICE CLAMS FOR GRIPPING TUBE.
The two blocks are placed between the jaws of the vice and tightened on to the tube.

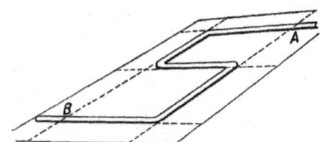

*Fig. 7.—*SETTING OUT THE WORK.
The outline of the piece to be bent is first drawn full size on a flat surface.

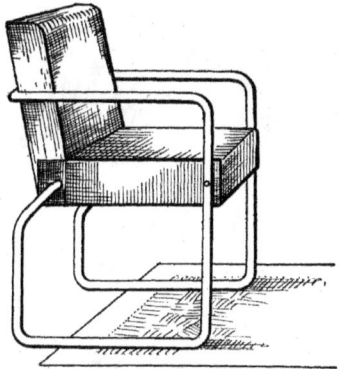

*Fig. 4.—*ARMCHAIR.
Comfortable and enduring, this easy chair can be made by the home craftsman.

*Fig. 5.—*DINING TABLE.
The top is framed up and covered with veneered plywood. The steel tube frame has flanges for fastening to the table top.

part on a block of wood, as in Fig. 17, and pressing the ends of the tube downwards.

The best methods of bending tube without making it red hot are to use an efficient pipe-bending machine, the loan of which can often be arranged through an electrical or hot water fitter. Failing this a hardwood block, shaped as in Fig. 18, will be found quite useful. The cheeks or side pieces should be at least ¾ inch thick, and the thickness of the part between them, which has a half-round groove on its edge, must be exactly equal to the diameter of the tube and be shaped to the radius of the desired curve.

In use, the length of steel tube is held under the clamp bar at the back,

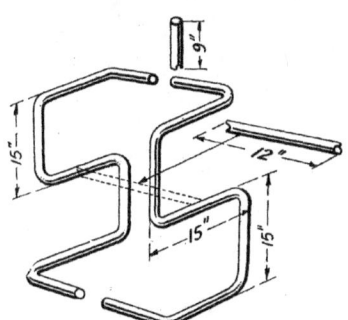

*Fig. 8.—*COMPONENTS OF TABLE AND LAMP STAND.
Here are shown the four pieces of tube in their relative positions.

and the tube is then pressed downwards with a firm decided action, but without sudden jerks.

As the bend takes shape the tube should be hammered down, if necessary, by means of a shaped hardwood block, as in Fig. 19, which must be held firmly on the tube while the hammer blows are administered.

Hot Bending.

Tubes can be bent cold, as already described, or can be bent "hot," that is, while visibly red hot, but must not be bent while in the "black hot" state, otherwise the metal will almost certainly crumble or break. This point should be clearly understood at the start; whenever the metal begins to cool, or turn "black" it must be reheated to a cherry-red colour and in that state it will be found that the tube can be bent as easily as lead pipe.

One important item must be noted, and that is to "load" or fill the tube unless a proper pipe bender is available.

The most convenient method of loading is to use hot bone dry sand. One end of the tube is securely plugged—the hot dry sand is then poured into the tube and well shaken down to exclude all air. The sand is then well rammed down by hammering, as in Fig. 20, on a length of wooden rod that fits easily in the tube. Continue until the sand is rammed absolutely solid, then drive a plug into the end to hold the sand firm. Make sure that the sand and the tube are warm and dry at the start, and that the plugs are very firmly driven home.

Heating the Tube.

The tube is then placed on a metal pan and surrounded with coke or asbestos cubes, as in Fig. 21, and the flame of a blow-lamp directed upon it and continued until the tube is uniformly heated and glows a bright cherry red. Immediately remove the tube and bend it to shape—either with the hands or on a bending block. A pair of leather gloves and a couple of thick pads of linen will be found useful when handling hot metal.

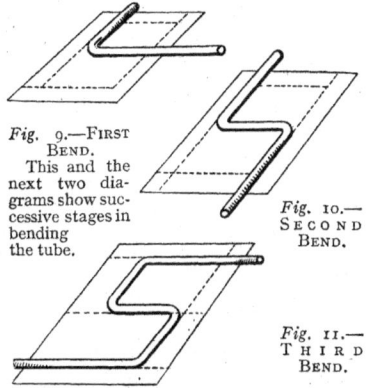

*Fig. 9.—*FIRST BEND.
This and the next two diagrams show successive stages in bending the tube.

*Fig. 10.—*SECOND BEND.

*Fig. 11.—*THIRD BEND.

1369

MAKING TUBULAR STEEL FURNITURE

Fig. 12.—Curving a Tube.
The length of tube is pressed down and drawn backwards and forwards across a block.

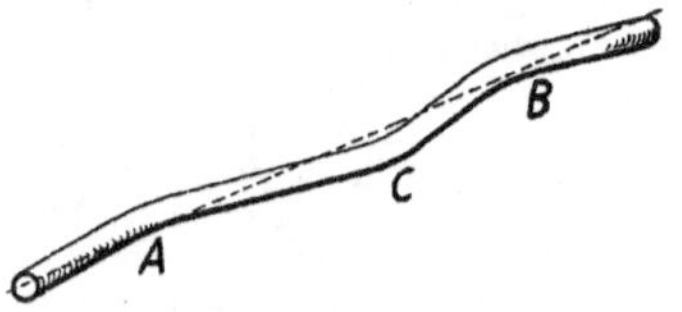

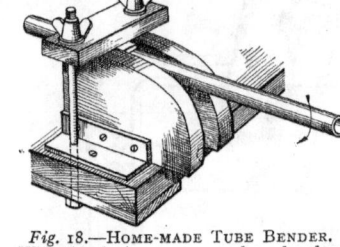

Fig. 18.—Home-made Tube Bender.
With this device numerous sharp bends can readily be made.

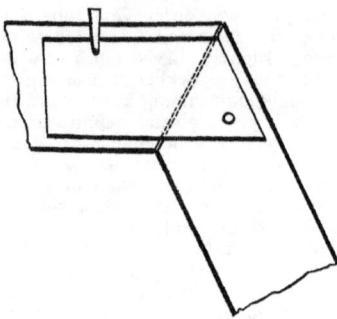

Fig. 23.—Mitre Joint.
Sectional view showing outer tube ends cut and fitted together and the liner in place.

Fig. 13.—Inaccurate Tube.
Bends or kinks are indicated in exaggerated form at A, B, and C. The mode of straightening is explained in the next four illustrations.

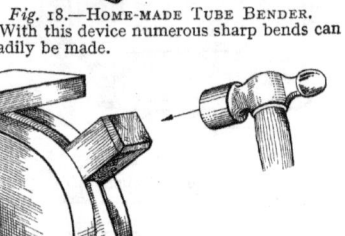

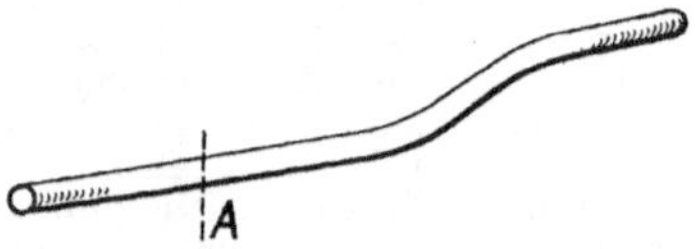

Fig. 19.—Second Stage of Cold Bending.
Close-up showing how a shaped wood block can be used to complete the bend.

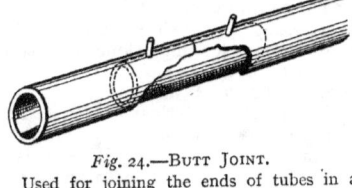

Fig. 24.—Butt Joint.
Used for joining the ends of tubes in a straight line, here shown partly cut away to reveal the liner.

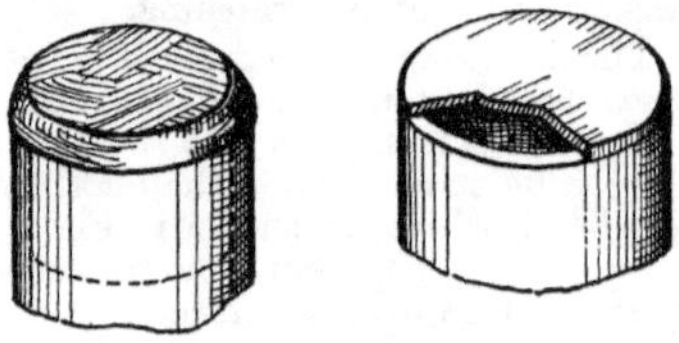

Fig. 14.—First Stage of straightening Tube.
The kink at A is straightened.

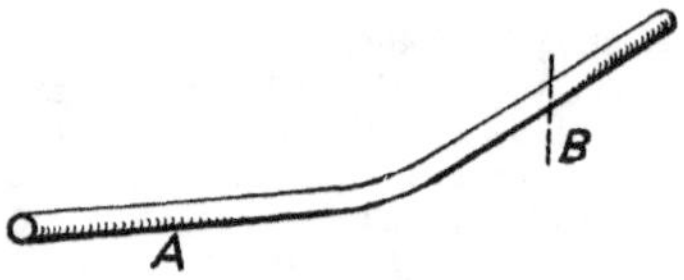

Fig. 25.—Cup and Plug.
Exposed ends of tubes should be plugged with hardwood or have a metal disc brazed on.

Fig. 15.—Final Stage of straightening.
The kink at B has been straightened, leaving only the centre kink to remove.

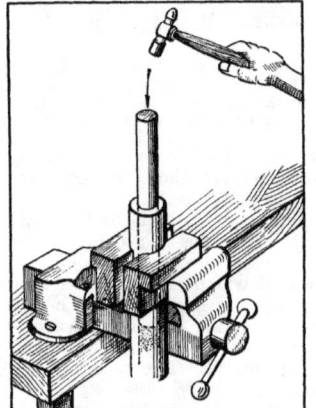

Fig. 20.—Loading Sand into Tube.
Hot dry sand is pressed firmly into thin tube to prevent it buckling when bent while hot.

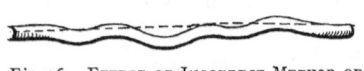

Fig. 16.—Effect of Incorrect Method of straightening.
Any attempt at piecemeal straightening will only result in more kinks, as here shown in very exaggerated form.

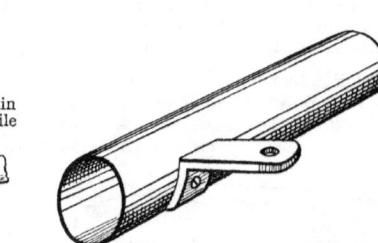

Fig. 26.—Clip Plate for Trays.
These can either be screwed or brazed to the tube.

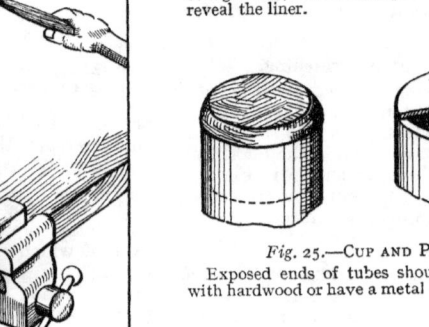

Fig. 21.—Heating the Tube.
Coke or asbestos cubes are built up in a pan and the tube set amongst them so that the heat from the burner can play directly on the tube without loss.

Fig. 17.—Removing Kinks from Tube.
The high part is rested on a hardwood block and the two ends pressed downwards.

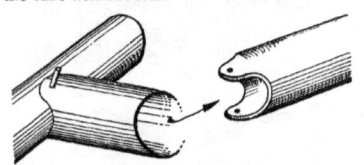

Fig. 22.—Tee Joint.
The end of the tube is shaped to fit exactly to the other tube and is then pegged and brazed.

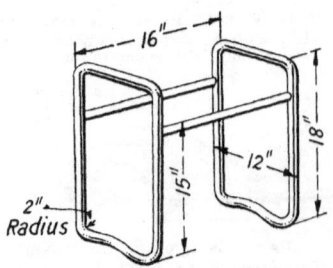

Fig. 27.—Dimensions of Dressing Stool

MAKING TUBULAR STEEL FURNITURE

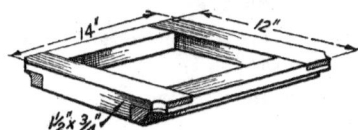

Fig. 28.—Seat Frame for Stool.
Made of hardwood and rebated on the underside to fit on to the steel top rails.

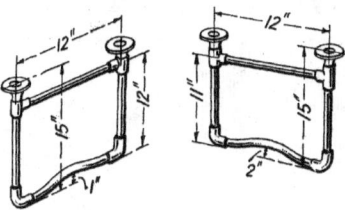

Fig. 29.—Dimensions of Small Folding Table.
This is shown finished in Fig. 3 on p. 1368.

Fig. 31.—Seat Fastening.
The cross bars on the frame fit into slots in the seat frame and are held by cleats.

The danger to guard against is that of the flattening of the walls of the tube at the bend—the metal will try to spread out sideways, hence the need of loading with sand to prevent this deformation.

Making the Joints.

Joints in conduit are generally made by means of screw threads. The tubes are cut to correct length, the ends screw threaded and then screwed into the fittings, but joints in plain steel tube must be properly fitted and brazed.

The tee joint (Fig. 22) is almost universally used for fastening cross members to side frames. The ends of the cross member are very accurately filed to a radius so that it will butt square and true against the main tube. The joint surfaces are then cleaned up bright, the ears of the cross member are drilled through and a soft iron peg driven through each into holes drilled in the main tube. The joint is then brazed in the usual manner.

The mitre joint (Fig. 23) is made by sawing the tube ends to shape, filing them to fit really accurately and then fitting a liner or inner tube and pegging them together as before, after the liner and the inside of the tubes have been filed clean and bright and packed with brazing flux and spelter.

Butt Joint.

This joint, shown in Fig. 24, is used to unite the ends of tubes, it is easily made—the ends are filed square and true, the liner cleaned up, fitted and pegged to one tube and then fitted and pegged to the other, not forgetting to introduce the spelter and flux inside the tube.

Cap ends, as in Fig. 25, can either be brazed on, or the tube can be plugged with hardwood and the cap driven on to it. After the brazing operations the metal must be filed up clean and finished with emery paper.

Finishing the Table and Lamp Stand.

After all the joints have been brazed and cleaned up, the top and bottom trays can be fitted in place. They can either be screwed to flat lugs brazed to the tubular frame or can be held in place by clip plates, as in Fig. 26, fixed to the tube by screws driven into holes suitably drilled and tapped.

A screw-fitting lamp holder is then fixed to the upright and a hole drilled

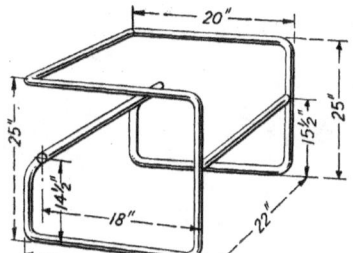

Fig. 30.—Dimensions of Armchair.
The finished chair is shown in Fig. 4 on p. 1369.

and bushed with ebonite for the flexible wire. This hole should be at the bottom part of the side frame.

Dressing Stool.

Dimensions of this simple but attractive piece are given in Fig. 27; it consists of two end frames and two cross bars "tee" jointed to them. The seat has a wooden frame, as in Fig. 28, which is webbed and upholstered as usual.

Folding Table.

Dimensions of this useful article are given in Fig. 29, which also shows how the conduit and the fittings are arranged. The junction of the cross bars is pivoted by a small steel bolt, which enables the legs to be closed together after lifting off the plywood table top.

Armchair.

The dimensions of the armchair are given in Fig. 30, which shows also that it consists of two side frames joined by three cross bars. In this case the best order of bending is first to make the front bend on the arm-rest part, then the lower front bend and finish off at the back where it rises to join the cross bar.

Seat and Back Rest.

The seat and back rest are made with hardwood frames webbed and upholstered in the manner of a box spring mattress. The frames are notched or slotted to drop over the tubes and held on the inside by a clamp plate, as shown in Fig. 31.

Dining Table.

Dimensions are given in Fig. 32, of the table shown finished in Fig. 5, and also illustrates how the "tee" pieces are placed. These are stock fittings as used by cycle makers and others; they are cleaned up inside and out, the tubes also made quite bright and the fittings put into place and pegged.

Assembling the Frame.

It is preferable to assemble the frame complete, stand it on the floor—perfectly level and true—then build up a brazing pan round the joints on one leg, braze them and repeat the operation on the remainder. This ensures accuracy and avoids risk of a distortion of the frame. The table top is framed up and covered with veneered plywood and then screwed to the flanges on the steel frame.

Finishing Processes.

Most modern tubular furniture is chromium-plated, and for this finish it is merely necessary to deliver the metal work to a firm of electro-platers, who will polish and plate it for a reasonable sum.

Painting.

The alternative methods open to the home craftsman is to paint and enamel the framework or to spray it with coloured cellulose finish, the latter being preferable for "conduit" work.

Sprayers or air-brushes for use with cellulose finishes are now obtainable at reasonable prices, and their use will greatly improve the appearance of the finished work.

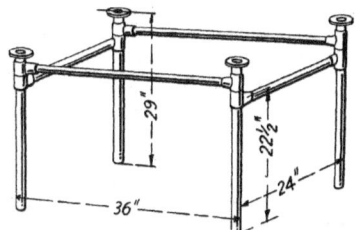

Fig. 32.—Arrangement and Sizes of Dining Table Frame.
The joints are made with steel "tees" brazed in place, the table top screws to the flanges—the finished table is shown in Fig. 5. The legs are continuous through the tee joints.

Rebating, Chamfering, and Moulding

In previous sections reference has been made to the making of rebates, chamfers, etc., in connection with the construction of different woodwork articles. The following section deals with the general principles of rebating, chamfering, and moulding for various purposes.

REBATES

A rebate is a rectangular recess cut out of the edge of framing to receive sashes, doors, glass, etc., and is very often encountered in woodwork. A gauge, chisel, mallet, and a rebate plane are required, and if a plough is available, the work is considerably simplified.

The rebate, as its name implies, is cut so that another part can fit into it, therefore the position must be accurately marked with a gauge. Incidentally the gauge not only provides a guide mark for the tools, but also severs the fibres of the timber to prevent the grain from tearing up. Fig. 2 shows how to set the gauge correctly. The head or stock is moved the required distance and then fixed by a thumb screw; in the case illustrated the gauge is being set to ¼ of an inch.

The head of the gauge is then held firmly against the piece of wood to be rebated and run along for the required distance as shown in Fig. 3. The corner of the stem, as well as the spur, should rest on the timber to obviate any danger of the spur following the grain. Do not press the spur in too much at first, but run the gauge along the wood several times until a good mark is obtained. The rebate should be gauged on both edges and face to the required sizes.

Remove the Waste Wood.

When the size of the rebate has been correctly gauged, the next step is to remove the waste wood. If a plough is available, the work is easy. If not,

Fig. 1.—Cutting away the Waste Wood with a Chisel when forming a Large Rebate.

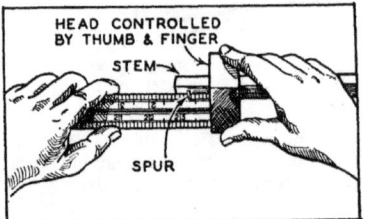

Fig. 2.—How to set the Marking Gauge.

Fig. 3.—The Correct and Incorrect Methods of using Marking Gauge.

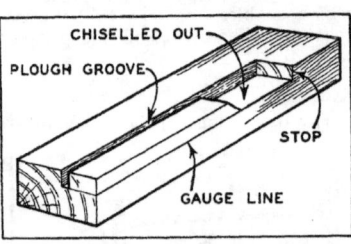

Fig. 4.—Method of forming Stopped Rebate.

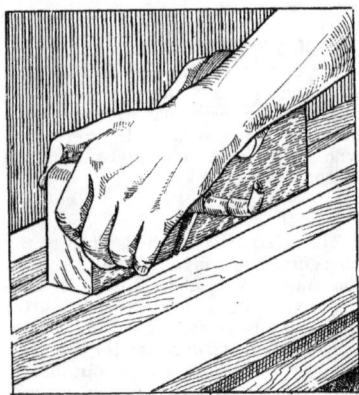

Fig. 5.—Forming a Rebate with Rebate Plane running against Fence.

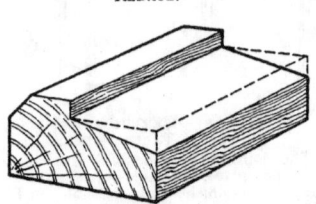

Fig. 6.—Bevelled Rebate.

a rebate plane or chisel and mallet must be used.

Using the Rebate Plane.

The rebate plane is satisfactory for shallow rebates. The first thing to do is to nail a temporary fence on to the wood to act as a guide for the plane. This can be seen in Fig. 5. Begin working at the fore end of the wood and gradually work backwards until the rebate is formed.

Using Chisel and Mallet.

Another method consists of chopping out the waste wood with a chisel and mallet and then finishing off with a rebate plane. This method is probably better if the depth of the rebate exceeds ¼ inch. The method of holding the chisel is important. The cutting edge should not be absolutely square with the wood, but held at an angle so that the inner corner cuts in advance of the outer corner, to help the waste wood break away without going beyond the gauged line.

If Grain of Wood is very uneven.

If a rebate is to be cut in a piece of wood the grain of which is very uneven, it is a good plan to make saw cuts about every 4 or 6 inches across the corner, so that the saw cut just touches the gauged lines. If there are knots, make several saw cuts close together.

Forming Rebates with Cutting Gauge.

When a very shallow rebate is required, i.e., not more than ¼ inch each way, the waste wood can be removed with a cutting gauge. Set the gauge in the same manner as the marking gauge. Keep the knife cutter sharp and make sure it is held firmly in place by the small wedge.

Bevelled Rebates.

In positions such as the bottom rail of outside doors, when panels are formed by tongued and grooved boards flush with the outside face of the door, or for windows to receive the

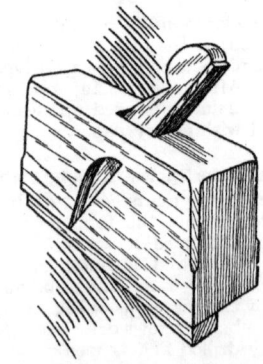

Fig. 7.—Rebate Plane with Fence for Small Rebate.

REBATING, CHAMFERING, AND MOULDING

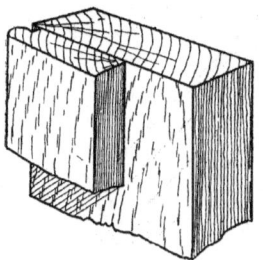

Fig. 8.—Planted Rebate.

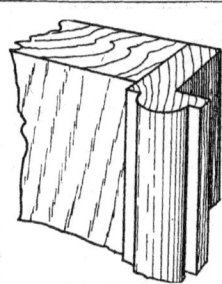

Fig. 9.—Planted Rebate.

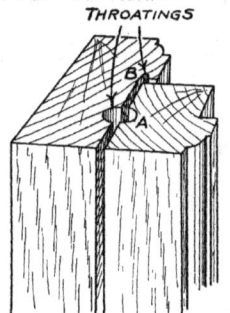

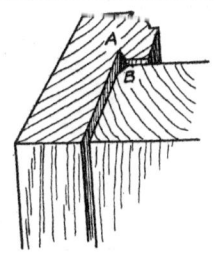

Fig. 11.—Substitute for Throatings.

bottom rails of sashes, a bevelled rebate may be required. The method is shown in Fig. 6, where the dotted lines show how the rebate is first prepared in the ordinary manner. The amount of bevel is then marked with a pencil gauge and the bevel formed with the rebate plane.

Planted Rebates.

Another form of rebate in which no cutting is required is that known as a planted rebate. It is simply formed by planting a thin piece of wood on the face where the rebate is required. This form of rebate is used a good deal for doors, any possibility of the door being hinge-bound being obviated by fixing the rebates when the door is hung. If the edge of the rebate is chamfered or moulded, the corners should be mitred, but if the edge is square the top piece is fixed first and the vertical pieces nailed tightly underneath. A form of planted rebate used largely in cabinet work at the meeting stiles of bookcase doors is shown in Fig. 9. The rebate in this case is glued or screwed to the edge of the door stile.

Stopped Rebates.

When the rebate does not run the full length of the wood, a stopped rebate is required, as shown in Fig. 4. The stop is sawn and a few inches of the rebate removed with the chisel. The remainder of the waste wood can then be removed as for an ordinary rebate.

Throated Rebates.

When dealing with casement windows difficulty is sometimes caused by water working through the joint between the sash and the frame to the inside, due to capillary attraction. This can be prevented by forming throatings to the rebates, as shown at A and B in Fig. 10. Unless special planes are available, these throatings are difficult to make, but a satisfactory substitute consists of forming small Vees to the frame and small chamfers to the sash, as shown in Fig. 11.

CHAMFERS

Chamfering consists of removing the

Fig. 10.—Throating to prevent Capillary Attraction.

Fig. 12.—Setting out a Chamfer with Pencil Gauge.

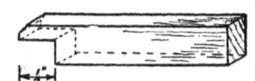

Fig. 13.—Pencil Gauge for marking Chamfers.

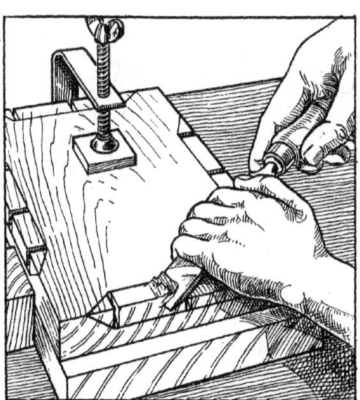

Fig. 14.—How to hold the Chisel to remove Waste when Chamfering.

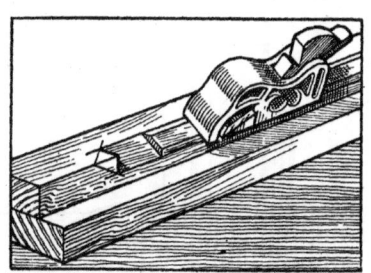

Fig. 15.—Using a Bull-nose Plane for Chamfer.

sharp corners of a piece of wood, the method of doing so depending on the size of the chamfer required. A small chamfer can be dealt with by using a plane, but for a large chamfer it will be found quicker to remove the waste with a chisel and finish off with a plane. The method of holding the chisel is shown in Fig. 14. Note that the back of the chisel is on top; there is less danger of the grain tearing up in front of the cutting edge if this method is adopted. It is necessary to cut with the grain when using the chisel.

For a very large chamfer an axe can be used to remove the waste.

Gauging the Position of the Chamfer.

When gauging the position a marking gauge must not be used as this would destroy the corners of the chamfer. A pencil gauge is used instead, and can easily be made from any scrap of wood. A piece is cut out of the end to the required size of the chamfer; a gauge prepared for a chamfer ½ inch on the face of the wood is shown in Fig. 13. The gauge is then used with a pencil, as shown in Fig. 12.

Chamfering End Grain.

When cutting end grain with either a chisel or plane, the tool should be used at an angle so that it cuts with a shearing action. This will give a much cleaner cut than by holding the cutting edge at right-angles to the direction in which the tool is moving.

To prevent the end of the chamfer from splitting away it is a good plan to fix a piece of waste wood at the end, unless the chamfer can be worked from each side towards the middle.

Nosings.

An extension of chamfering is the forming of a nosing or rounded edge to a piece of wood, as in Fig. 16. The method of doing this is to form small chamfers so that they touch the circular arc forming the nosing, and then finishing with a hollow plane or with rough glasspaper.

MOULDINGS

Unless special moulding tools are available, the shaping, or sticking, of mouldings by hand is rather difficult.

REBATING, CHAMFERING AND MOULDING

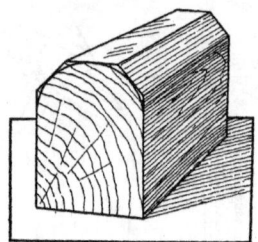

Fig. 16.—Preparing a Nosing by Chamfers.

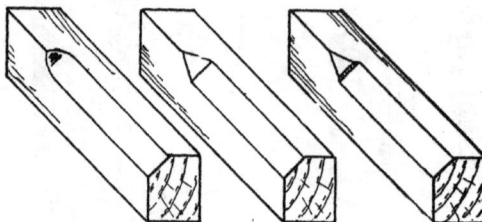

Fig. 17.—Forming Stops to Chamfers.

It is much cheaper to buy mouldings if long lengths are required, but if only short lengths are needed for making repairs, they can be made as described below.

A common type of moulding is shown in Fig. 18, and Fig. 19 shows the method of removing the waste by means of plough grooves. The waste is removed with a chisel and rebate plane when the plough grooves are completed, and the outline completed with hollows and rounds. If these are not available, it is necessary to use gouges to form the outline, and finish off with rough glasspaper.

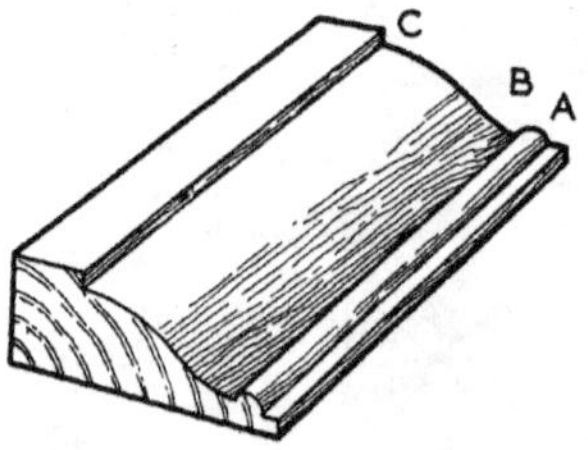

The glasspaper should be wrapped round a rubber specially shaped to the reverse outline of the moulding. It can be made from a piece of waste soft wood about 4 × 2 inches and as thick as required for the moulding. In the example shown in Fig. 18 three rubbers would be required for the parts marked A, B, and C.

Fig. 18.—A Typical Form of Moulding.

Fig. 19.—Method of removing Waste when sticking a Moulding.

A FIRE BLOWER

This blower is simple to construct, and will be found extremely useful in drawing up dull fires. A fire which would otherwise be considered hopeless can be brought to a cheerful blaze in a few minutes. Although designed to suit a modern tiled fireplace, the idea could, with a little ingenuity, be adapted to any type.

Materials Required.

One piece sheet iron, $\frac{1}{32}$ inch thick (22 B.G.).
One iron handle.
Screws and nuts suitable for fixing handle.
One round asbestos baking sheet.

Measure the opening of the fireplace; call the height from the hearth "H," and the width "W." Measure also the height of the grate; call it "G." Obtain a piece of sheet iron W + 2 inches wide and H + 3½ inches long. Cut two slits 2 inches from the sides and G + 3 inches long, measured from one end, as shown in Fig. 2.

As material of the required thickness is difficult to cut with hand shears, it may be desirable to get the ironmonger to cut the slits at the time of buying, and in that case it would be advisable to supply him with a sketch of your requirements.

Mark the vertical centre-line and on it drill holes for the handle in a suitable position fairly near the top. Bend the wide piece between the slits right back till it is flat against the sheet. Bend 2½ inches of the 2-inch strips at right angles in the opposite direction.

Place the handle centrally on the baking sheet and bore holes through corresponding to the screw holes. The baking sheet is fitted to prevent burning the knuckles should the sheet get hot. If the particular handle used provides a wide enough gap the sheet may be omitted.

Fix the handle with the baking sheet underneath on the same side as the feet, and the "blower" is complete.

In using the blower it is, of course, placed flat against the tiles, the front of the grate being left open.

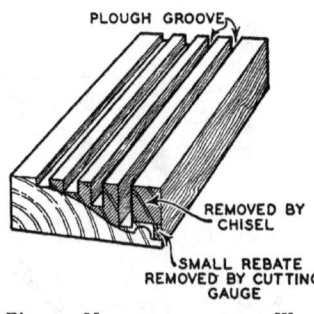

Fig. 1.—The Completed Blower.

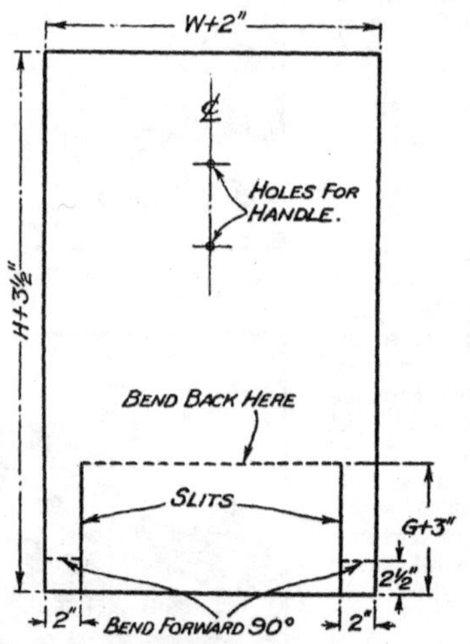

Fig. 2.—Sheet Iron ready for Bending.

Constructing a Toboggan

TOBOGGANS are of various sizes, according to whether they are designed to carry one or more persons. In addition, they are made in a variety of patterns, but the most popular shape in England is a simple platform, supported on two smooth runners. The bull-nosed toboggan, which slides on its under-face and has no actual runners, is much favoured in the United States, but it is doubtful if it would give satisfaction in this country, except in very hard winters.

An Excellent Type of Toboggan.

All things considered, an excellent pattern to construct is the one shown in Fig. 1. It consists of a platform having a length of 2 feet 9 inches and a width of 1 foot 6 inches. The platform is supported on two runners, which are 3 feet 6 inches long and 6 inches high. The wood for both these parts should be 1 inch thick; it may be ordinary deal for the platform, though something more durable is needed for the pair of runners. In their case, elm, pine ash, or even oak may be recommended.

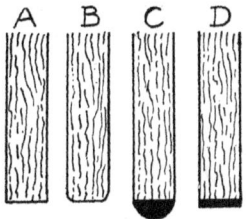

Fig. 2.—Dealing with the Runners.

A is the runner before treatment; B is when the lower edges have been rounded off; C is the runner shod with half-circle iron rod; D is the runner shod with strip iron.

Making the Two Runners.

It is advisable to start the construction by shaping the runners. Naturally, they are both exactly alike. Having trimmed up the two pieces of wood so that they are 3 feet 6 inches long and 6 inches high, the next step is to round off the forward nose in each case. The form of the upward curve, imparted to the nose, may be determined at will as long as it is a fairly sharp curve and both are identical. Its function is to push its way through snow, and almost any curved tip will do this satisfactorily.

Should the Runners be metal-shod?

One thing must be determined at this point. Are the runners to be shod with metal or left plain? It is certainly better to face them with iron of some form, as the wood faces tend to act as a brake when the ice or snow is not hard and the wood becomes wet.

If the running edges are not to be metal-covered, it is necessary to plane off the sharp angular sides which touch the ice, making them no more than slightly curved. Even though the amount of wood shaved off is almost infinitesimal, the difference to the running power is quite noticeable.

When the running edges are to be metal-shod, the best plan is to ask a blacksmith to supply the material. For a few pence, he will shape the two necessary irons to reach from the back end to the curved-up tip. He will find no difficulty in giving the irons the requisite curve, if one of the wooden runners is handed to him as a pattern. These metal runners should be made of

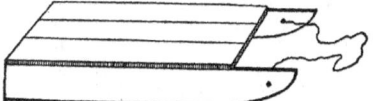

Fig. 1.—The Toboggan described in this Article.

iron rod, the section of which is half a circle, the flat edge being 1 in. long, which is the thickness of the wooden runners. About six countersunk holes should be bored through each iron so that it may be fixed to the edge of the wood by ¾-inch screws. When the screws are put in, they should be gone over with a file to remove any roughness.

A third plan is to face the running edges with strip iron such as is used for strengthening the corners of large packing cases. This iron can be bought for almost nothing and is easily fixed with screws, as before. Naturally, it does not serve so well as the half-circle iron, but it is easier to obtain, it is cheaper and it certainly saves the faces of the runners from wearing and sticking.

Fig. 2 shows a section of one of the runners in all three conditions—unfaced, shod with half-circle iron and covered with strip iron.

Joining the Runners with Cross Bars.

Having attended to all these matters, the next step is to consider how the two runners are to be joined up.

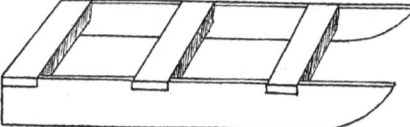

Fig. 3.—How the Three Cross Bars are arranged.

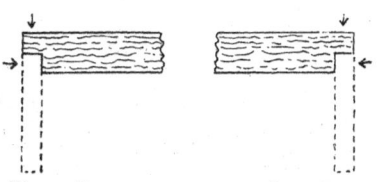

Fig. 4.—This shows one of the Cross Bars. Screws are inserted at the points indicated by arrows.

Fig. 3 suggests the plan to be followed. Three cross bars are cut, 18 inches long. Their width and depth are unimportant, but material 2 inches square in section may be suggested. Each bar is shaped at both ends, as shown in Fig. 4, and spaces are cut to correspond in the upper edges of the wooden runners. When screws are inserted at the positions indicated by arrows in Fig. 4, the whole framework should be braced together firmly and the toboggan will be strong enough to stand a great deal of rough usage.

Constructing the Platform.

The platform is the next item for consideration. It should be composed of three strips of wood, each 2 feet 9 inches long and 6 inches wide. It is best to fix the strips with 1½-inch screws, but long nails are almost as good. In either case, the screws or nails should be driven into the cross bars, so that the whole of the construction is drawn firmly together.

At this stage, it will be advisable to go over all the surfaces and smooth them, since there must be no screw heads nor splinters to tear or scratch the hands. This is, perhaps, more important than may be imagined, and it is a piece of work that should be done thoroughly.

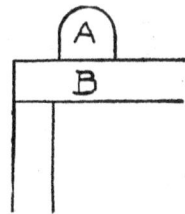

Fig. 5.—The Part marked A shows a Curved Strip of Wood which serves as a Hand Rail; B is the Platform.

Fitting a Hand Rail.

Anyone who has enjoyed the thrill of careering madly down a hill on a toboggan knows the helpless feeling that is experienced if there is nothing for the hands to grip. For this reason some sort of a hand rail is advisable. A useful pattern is made of wood 1 inch square in section. All that is necessary is to take two strips of this wood, each 2 feet 9 inches long, and to turn three of the flat sides of each piece into a curve. The strips are then screwed one to each side of the platform, an inch inwards from the long edges (see Fig. 5). Such a rail affords all the grip that is necessary, and as it is not placed actually on the edge of the platform there is no fear of a hand being damaged by passing obstacles.

A Foot Rest.

All of us have our own ideas as to how a toboggan should be used. Some of us prefer to lie flat on the platform, but the majority of users favour a sitting attitude with feet forward.

CONSTRUCTING A TOBOGGAN

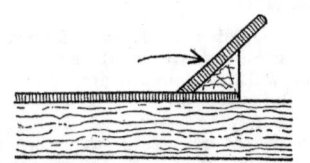

Fig. 6.—Foot Rest Erected at the Forward End of the Platform.

of dark oak varnish, or it may be preferred to apply a covering of some bright-coloured enamel. Either will help to preserve the wood. Finally, why not christen the toboggan and give it some name to suggest speed, swiftness or celerity?

A Steering Device.

As a rule, toboggans have no steering device—the foot of the rider being used for the purpose. Perhaps this is as well, since any form of mechanical steering may prove dangerous in the hands of an inexperienced user.

Nevertheless, some enthusiasts will feel the need for a device, other than their feet, which will enable them to slow up or turn corners. In such cases the arrangement shown in Fig. 7 may be suggested. It consists of a stick 15 inches long and 1 inch square in section, made of ash, elm, etc. Five inches from one end, a hole is bored centrally through the wood; a bolt is passed through the hole and, also, through the iron bracket shown at the side of the runner. The bracket is fixed in the centre of the length of the runner and 2 inches from the top

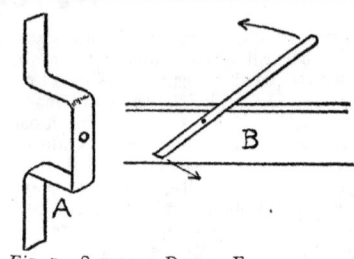

Fig. 7.—Steering Device Fitted to both of the Runners.
A shows the iron bracket to which the stick is bolted. B shows the stick in position.

edge. The stick is rounded at the upper end to form a handle and cut slightly slanting at the lower end, to provide a " shoe " effect when pressed into the snow.

One such stick is fitted to either side of the toboggan and, in both cases, the nuts should be fully tightened on the bolts. A slight pull on one stick steers the toboggan out of its forward course and a pull on both slows down the forward rush. The user should fully understand that any violent jerk on the sticks may lead to trouble.

When this is considered the ideal position, it will be advisable to screw a strip of wood across the front edge of the platform. The feet may be pressed against it, and then there will be no opportunity for them to slide off. Fig. 6 shows how this rail may be shaped. The exact dimensions are unimportant.

Attaching a Draw-rope.

So that the toboggan may be dragged uphill or along the level, it is necessary to fix a rope. For this, make a hole in each runner, near to the forward tip, and tie on from 2 to 3 yards of rope.

Finishing Details.

The last operation is to give the whole of the woodwork two good coats

FURTHER NOTES ON USING VEGETABLE DYES

ON page 1251 are given some notes on the use of vegetable dyes, with recipes for madder red, orange red, yellow, and a range of reds from pink to crimson. Some recipes for other colours are given below.

Green.

A beautiful shade of green can be made by first dyeing the wool in the above yellow dye. The material is removed, and sufficient indigo extract is added to give the required colour, and thoroughly mixed. Do not put the material in until the dye has cooled down, and then it must be stirred carefully for about half an hour or until the depth of the colour is sufficient.

Indigo extract can usually be purchased at the chemist's, but it is prepared by stirring 1 oz. of finely ground indigo into 4 oz. of sulphuric acid and allowing it to remain with an occasional stir for several days, when a quarter of a teaspoonful of carbonate of soda should be added. Owing to the powerful nature of the acid, the utmost care should be taken in using it, and on no account should it be allowed to touch the skin or the clothes. It will keep well if the bottle containing it is securely corked, and to avoid accident it should be labelled poison.

A good green dye for cotton and linen goods can be made by using fustic powder with the logwood dye. By varying the quantity of logwood and fustic almost any shade of green can be obtained.

Black.

A black dye requires a mordant of copperas, 2 oz. to 1 gallon of water, and boiling the wool for about half an hour. The dye bath is prepared by boiling 1 oz. of logwood chips in 2 gallons of water, or, better still, use 3 oz. of logwood extract instead, and then add the material, boiling for about three-quarters of an hour, removing and draining, and then boiling again for the same length of time.

Brown.

A very pleasant brown dye may be obtained from the peels of green walnuts, but, as this is obtainable only in the summer (although the extract can be obtained), a more accessible dye, and a fast one, can be made by mixing 6 oz. of madder, 1 oz. of fustic powder and ½ oz. of logwood extract. Boiling them together with sufficient water to cover them, fill up to 2 gallons with cold water and place the material in the bath, boiling slowly for about three-quarters of an hour. It is not necessary to dip the wool in a preliminary mordant with this dye, but as a fixing agent, 1 oz. of sulphate of iron previously dissolved in hot water should be added to the boiling liquid and the material thoroughly stirred about, so that the added mordant is well mixed with the liquid. The wool is boiled again for about half an hour, when it is removed and washed in the usual way.

All the dyes mentioned above can be obtained at most chemists, and are quite inexpensive. It is possible as well to obtain extracts of many of the dyes; the use of extracts saves a lot of preliminary boiling, and, although they are more expensive than the raw material, the saving of time may be a greater consideration.

How to Remove Colour from Fabrics.

It should be remembered that it is not possible to dye everything the exact colour desired. Some people think that dark colours can be dyed lighter, but, of course, this is impossible. However, one can get the colours out of many fabrics, cotton in particular, by thoroughly washing and afterwards boiling in fairly strong soda water; this usually moves the colour. If this does not it can be bleached with a solution of chloride of lime (a tablespoonful to ½ gallon of water), and then boiled in soda water, rinsed and thoroughly dried. Chloride of lime should not be used for silks or the more delicate fabrics. For these a solution of hydrosulphite of soda is best (a tablespoonful to ½ gallon of water). Thoroughly wash and then dry before dyeing it. There are several preparations on the market which remove colour that are quite simple to use.

Giving a Plain Wall a Half-timbered Appearance

THE method adopted for this treatment is much the same as for pebble-dash, described on p. 1345, with regard to the wall surface, except that the pebbles here are mixed with the cement before application, for producing what is termed "rough-cast."

Let us suppose that the space to be covered is the same as for the pebble-dash, namely, 20 × 12 feet. Mix the cement and sand in the same way as before, but this time mix the pebbles with it and also add some lime.

For an area this size, the following quantities will be required for the rough-cast:—

    Cement   .   .   4 bushels
    Sand   .   .   12   ”
    Pebbles   .   .   5   ”

For the groundwork, approximately 3 bushels of cement and 9 bushels of sand will be required.

Marking out the Wall.

First of all determine how you want your wall to look when finished, and mark it out accordingly. Take, for instance, the arrangement shown in Fig. 1. Decide on the width and thickness of your oak battens. These should be about 5 inches wide by 1 or 1½ inches thick, and for carrying out the design here illustrated various lengths, from about 4 feet upwards, will be required. They should be bevelled on the inside so that they will lap over the rough-cast.

Fig. 1.—An Attractive Half-timbered Wall.

It will be easier to carry out the work in sections.

First fix Temporary Framework.

First procure some rough deal boards the same width and thickness of your oak, and bevelled on the inside. These will serve as frames to fix on temporarily as gauges for your rough-cast, and also because they are bound to get messy, and you do not want the oak to suffer. The pieces of deal should be fixed with brads on to the wall as in Fig. 2.

Applying the Rough-cast.

Next apply two coats of cement and sand as ground work. These are made in exactly the same way as for pebble-dash, after which apply the rough-cast with a trowel.

Now remove the Rough Wood.

Now remove the rough wood, which will serve for the remaining sections until the whole wall is covered. You will then have a wall with rectangular spaces covered with rough-cast, the parts which were covered with the wood battens will be bare brick with neat and clean edges (Fig. 3).

Fixing the Oak.

Now for the oak pieces. These will fit in exactly the same spaces from which the deal pieces have been removed. They should be given a coat of solignum on the back. Then fix with brads on the wall. The brads should be driven in slanting downwards slightly.

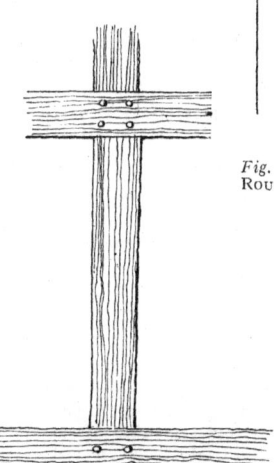
Fig. 4.—Oak Pegs placed as shown improve the Appearance.

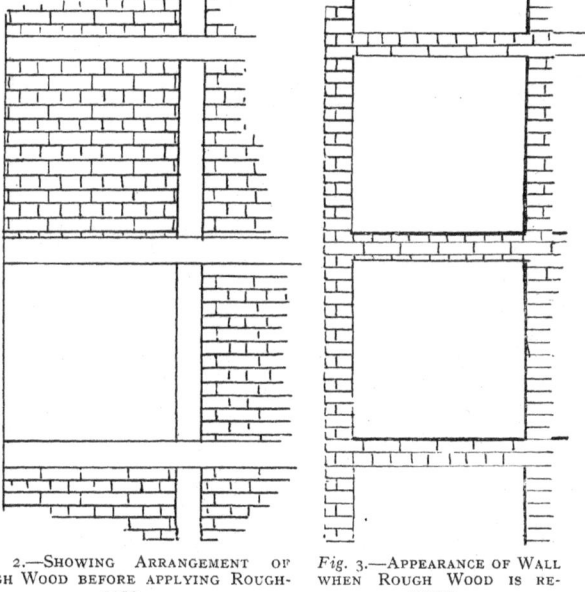
Fig. 2.—Showing Arrangement of Rough Wood before applying Rough-cast.

Fig. 3.—Appearance of Wall when Rough Wood is removed.

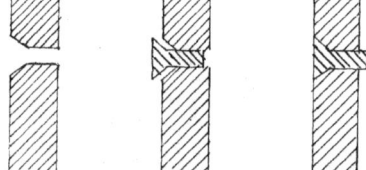

A   B   C
Fig. 5.—How the Pegs are fixed.

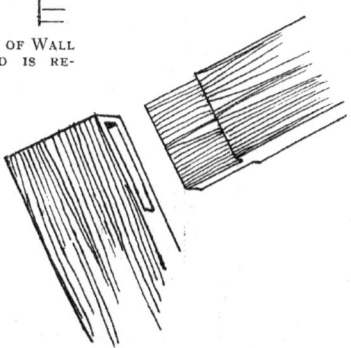
Fig. 6.—Another Method of fixing the Woodwork is to mortise and tenon the Battens together.

GIVING A PLAIN WALL A HALF-TIMBERED APPEARANCE

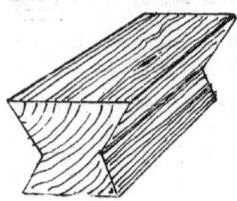

Fig. 7.—Showing Shape of Wooden Bricks for fixing into Wall.

Oak Pegs.

To give a more realistic appearance to the work, fit in oak pegs just below the brads, which are above the eye-line, and above where they are below the eye-line. They will serve to hide the brad-holes. These pegs are only fitted in at positions where the battens meet, and serve to represent wood fixings, and should be driven in as shown on Fig. 4. First punch the brads in below the surface, or you can use rawlplugs and screws if you like.

How the Pegs are put in.

The pegs must be put in before fixing the battens up, and can be done as follows: With a centre bit and brace make holes about $\frac{3}{4}$ inch in diameter. At the back of the battens enlarge the hole and bevel the sides of it (Fig. 5A). Now cut some oak pegs longer than the thickness of the battens (Figs. 5B and 5C). Glue the holes and drive the pegs in from the back, allowing them to project about $\frac{1}{8}$ inch or so on the right side, the back side being flush.

After your rough-cast is dry, lime-wash it.

An Alternative Filling.

Another filling in place of rough-cast can be made of cement and sand, with a setting coat of finer stuff smeared on to represent old plaster—or marb-le-cote can be used—and then lime-washed.

It will be better not to fix your lowest rail at ground level, but render about a foot of brickwork with cement below the lowest rail (Figs. 1 and 8).

Another Method of fixing the Woodwork.

A longer and more laborious method of fixing your woodwork would be to mortise and tenon the battens together (Fig. 6), and still further you can for your fixing remove bricks at different points, for the long battens, and insert wooden bricks in their place. These can be fixed in with mortar, but it will be better to cut them as shown on Fig. 7, which will serve as a key for the mortar.

The battens are then fixed into the wooden blocks. The woodwork can now be treated with solignum or any other weather-resisting preparation, the holes made by screws or brads first having been made good with stopping.

Fig. 8.—A More Elaborate Form of Half-timbering.

Woodwork can be painted Brown.

You can paint the woodwork brown if thought more advisable.

Fig. 8 shows a more elaborate form of half-timbering.

A NEAT NAIL AND SCREW BOX

THE following will be found to be a neat method of keeping small nails, pins, screws, etc., tidy, and one that will not easily allow of their being upset.

It consists essentially of a number of Oxo or Beefex tins built into a wooden container, the whole making a strong solid job.

It will be necessary to collect from friends or the local grocer, a number of Oxo or Beefex tins, which have contained six cubes. Remove the lids by withdrawing the hinge pin and then hammer flat the projection in which this pin fitted.

The size of the wooden case will be determined by the number of tins used and their arrangement. The one illustrated is a convenient size and measures $7\frac{1}{2} \times 5\frac{3}{4}$ inches inside. The inside dimensions must be the exact size of the tins. Half inch material is a good thickness for the bottom and $\frac{1}{4}$ inch for the sides. The base should be the size of the inside dimensions and the sides should have a width equal to the depth of the tin plus the thickness of the base. The ends of the side pieces should be mitred to form the corners.

When this has been done, well coat the sides and bottoms of the tins, one side of the baseboard and the insides of the side-pieces with glue and bed the whole lot together. Cramp up and allow to set. When dry glasspaper smooth and fill the spaces between the corners of the tins with plastic wood or putty.

A lid can be hinged on if required, and if covered with baize or felt will prevent the pins, etc., from mixing.

A further refinement is to make the lid slide, and further still a nest of these boxes could be made to slide into one another, the top one having a lid and the others having for a lid the box above. A neat method of doing this is indicated in section. All that is required is a piece of $\frac{1}{8} \times \frac{1}{4}$-inch stripwood glued to three sides of the lid or upper box, and a piece of $\frac{1}{2} \times \frac{1}{4}$-inch stripwood with an $\frac{1}{8} \times \frac{1}{8}$-inch groove in it glued to the three sides of the lower boxes. The strips should run the length of the three sides and mitred at the corners.

With one of these boxes there need be no more spilt screws or nails.

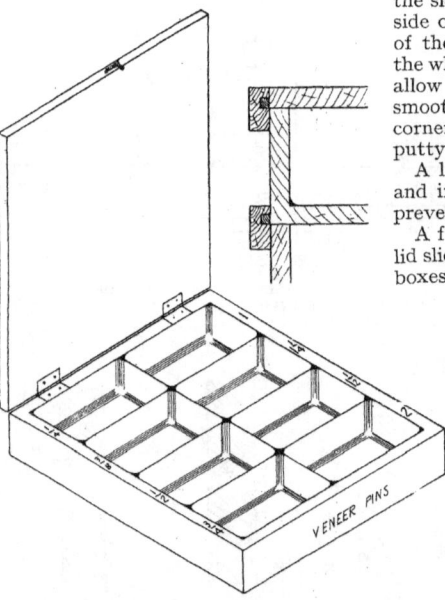

The Nail and Screw Box.
Inset, method of making a nest of boxes.

Decorative Treatments for Wall Boards and Asbestos Sheeting

ONE of the many developments in the construction of houses during recent years has been the displacement of the older materials and methods by new substances, and by the use of the older materials in new forms.

Formerly, almost all ceilings were of plaster, and interior division walls were generally of either brick with a plaster face or of partitions consisting of a wood and lath framework with plaster superimposed. But, nowadays, many division walls are composed of hollow breeze blocks which are plastered in the traditional way, or of wall boards or asbestos sheets which need no facing of plaster. These wall boards and asbestos sheets call for special methods of decorative treatment.

WALL BOARDS

Turning our attention first to the wall boards, of which there are many varieties, we need not concern ourselves here with the details of their assembly or construction into ceilings and walls, for these matters are fully covered in the article "How to Erect Wall Boards" on p. 653.

Although wall boards vary considerably in composition, most of them contain wood, either in the form of laminated layers, wood pulp or compressed paper, or a combination of two or all three of these materials.

They all possess a smooth surface very tempting to decorative experiments, but some of them are stamped with the inscription, "Not suitable for papering upon."

The reason for this is that they are generally somewhat absorbent and the water contained in the paste with which wallpaper is hung is apt to cause a swelling and buckling of the board, which is followed, as the moisture dries out, by a shrinkage which may cause an unsightly gap between the edge of the paper and the wood fillets used to hide the joints.

This same defect of swelling and shrinking may occur in a modified form even when other forms of decoration are used, unless certain precautions are taken.

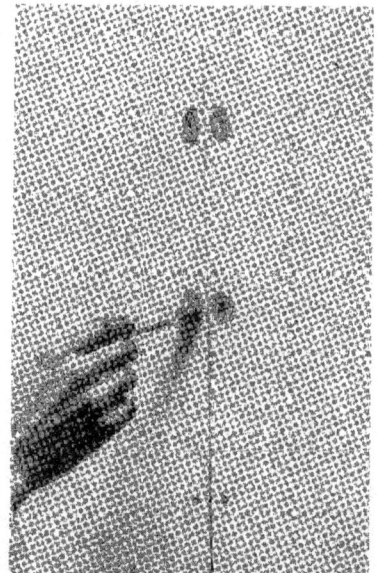

Fig. 1.—If the Joints of the Boards are not to be covered with Fillets, the Nail Heads should be coated with Shellac Knotting to prevent Rust Stains.

Fig. 2.—After the Nail Heads have been knotted the Holes and the Joints between the Boards should be filled with a Stopping composed of Water Paint and Plaster of Paris.

Preparing Wall Boards for Decorative Treatment.

The only sure way in which this tendency of the boards to expand and contract after fixing can be corrected is to coat both the face side and the back of each sheet with some substance that will render it impervious to moisture.

If, before fixing and while the boards are perfectly dry, the boards are given a coat of oil paint on both their fronts and backs, this object will be achieved, and they can afterwards be finished with oil paint (glossy or dull), water paint, washable distemper or even wallpaper, without fear of undue expansion or contraction.

The whole object of this preliminary

Fig. 3.—When the Joints have been filled they should be covered by gluing Strips of Canvas or Coarse Scrim over them in the manner shown.

coating of oil paint is to correct the porosity of the board and prevent any absorption of moisture either from the air, any material afterwards applied, or any other source. In this way the present writer has successfully carried out all kinds of decorative schemes on wall boards and has even covered with wallpaper those varieties which could otherwise not be so treated.

What to do if Back of Wall Boards cannot be reached.

Where the wall boards are already fixed it may not be practicable to get at their backs to give them this protective priming of oil paint. In such a case, the front should be so treated, and any practicable means should be adopted to see that the backs are protected from moisture.

If they are fixed against a perfectly dry wall, well and good. Or if they are used to form a ceiling underneath, and some distance from, a quite sound roof no trouble may be anticipated. But sometimes wall boards are used to cover a faulty or uneven, or even a damp, wall surface, and there may be, behind them, either a percolation of dampness, condensation or other forms of moisture. In such cases some means of ventilating the space behind the board should be contrived.

Joints between Sheets of Boarding.

Another point to be noted is the treatment of the joints between the various sheets of boarding. It is, in practice, not possible to make per-

DECORATIVE TREATMENTS FOR WALL BOARDS AND ASBESTOS SHEETING

Fig. 4.—Plastic Paint should be applied liberally to the Surface of the Boards by means of a Full Bristled Brush.

fectly smooth and permanent joints between the boards, and it is, therefore, almost the invariable rule to cover these joints with a fillet of wood as described in the article on p. 653.

This need not be a disadvantage from the decorative point of view. If the sheets are chosen in suitable sizes so that the fillets, when fixed over the joints, form panels of sizes suitable to the size and proportions of the room, these panels become an integral part of the decorative scheme.

Using Plastic Wall Paints.

The only exception to this general rule that the joints should be covered with wood fillets is where it is intended to finish the surface in plastic wall paints, which produce a rough surface granulated or otherwise made purposely uneven.

In such a case the joints are covered by gluing strips of rough scrim or canvas over them. The slight irregularities produced by these strips are hidden in the general thickness of the applied plastic material.

The boards when fixed, and having received the priming coat of oil paint previously mentioned, will take any of the usual forms of wall and ceiling treatment.

Distempering.

They can be distempered with ordinary distemper according to the general instructions given in the article " Practical Methods of Distempering " on p. 9, although such a method of treatment would only be adopted where economy was imperative and where the work would not be subject to much wear and tear.

Washable Distemper.

A better method with large surfaces would be to give two coats of a good waterpaint or washable distemper. For instructions as to the application of these materials also, reference should be made to the article on p. 9.

Painting.

The boards can be treated with two coats of paint, finished either glossy or dull as may be desired. The necessary formulas for mixing the paints for this kind of finish will be found in the article, "How to Mix White Lead Paints" on p. 432. For a glossy finish, formulas Nos. 2 and 3 will be suitable for the two coats, and, for a flat dead finish, formulas 2 and 6 would serve admirably.

Finally, the panels of wall-boarding may be covered with wallpaper, but

Fig. 5.—A Texture Effect produced in Plastic Paint by the use of a Steel Comb which is worked with a Circular Motion as shown.

only if the boards have been coated with the priming paint mentioned earlier.

Dealing with the Wood Fillets.

The wood fillets which are an integral part of the decorative scheme may be treated either like the rest of the work or they may be done in a distinctive colour, this latter being the more usual method.

Like the sheets themselves, the wood fillets should first receive a priming coat of oil paint, all knots being first coated with shellac knotting to prevent the sap contained in the knots from eating into and staining the paint. After the priming coat has been applied and has become dry, all nail holes and open angle joints need to be faced up with "hard stopping," which is a kind of putty composed of stiff white lead paste and dry whiting in equal parts, with a little gold size to reduce it to a stiff but workable consistency.

If the boards themselves are to be hung with wallpaper the fillets should be finished (before the paper is applied) with oil paint.

Contrasts in Colour and Gloss.

If the boards are being finished in a water paint, either water paint or oil paint of a different colour may be used on the fillets. If the panels are being oil painted, then the fillets should certainly be done in oil paint, preferably of a contrasting colour.

In addition to the various schemes made possible by the use of contrasting colours on the panels and fillets, there may be a contrast of gloss. The panels themselves may be left flat, as water paint naturally dries, or as oil paint may be made to dry by using paint mixed according to formula 6 mentioned above. The fillets could be made glossy either by finishing them in a paint mixed according to formula 3 or by varnishing them with a pale copal varnish over a finishing coat of paint mixed to formula 6.

Decoration in Pastel Shades.

If a scheme of decoration in delicate pastel shades is being carried out, variety and interest can be imparted by finishing the whole of surfaces, both wall boards and fillets, with one colour of either water paint or flat oil paint, and then varnishing the fillets only with a pale copal varnish. The quali-

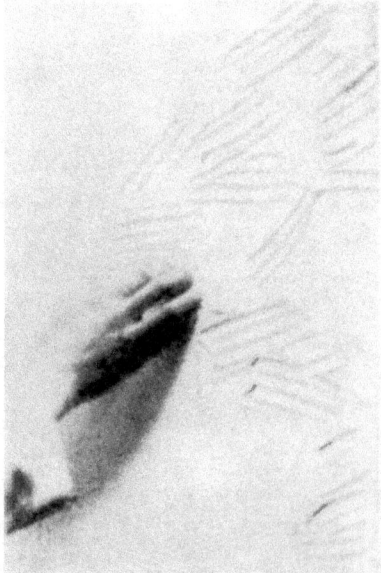

Fig. 6.—Another Effect is produced by drawing the Tips of the Fingers in Short Strokes across the Moist Surface in various Directions.

ties known as Copal Paper Varnish or White Decorative Varnish would be suitable.

The effect of this treatment would be twofold. In the first place there would be the contrast between the dull boards and the glossy fillets. In the second place there would be a slight colour contrast, for, as no varnish is perfectly water white, its application to the fillets would turn them a slightly deeper shade than the panels.

In some cases, a very marked difference of colour between the fillets and the boards is desired, and this can be achieved by treating the field of the panels in a pale colour as described above, and then painting, brush graining and varnishing the fillets to give them the appearance of real wood. The various methods of brush graining are to be found in the article on "Graining" on p. 111.

Stencil Ornamentation.

Generally, the breaking up of the surface of a wall-boarded room by its fillets, particularly if these are coloured differently to the rest of the work, is considered sufficient ornamentation, but occasionally further variety is given by the judicious addition of a little stencil ornament. For information regarding the making and application of stencils, see p. 470.

If stencils are used, however, the ornament should be designed so as to envisage separate panels as complete units. Where stencilling is adopted, it should be done with restraint, and, if ornament is used on certain panels which alternate with others left severely plain, it would be much more effective than a too crowded scheme in which every panel is elaborated.

Plastic Painting.

Reference has been made to the process called plastic painting. This may be applied either to wall boards which have had their joints covered with canvas as already described, or to the plain surface of boards separated from each other by wood fillets.

It consists in applying to the primed boards a thick plastic substance, and, while this is still soft, working it into various grains or patterns by means of

Fig. 7.—WHATEVER TEXTURE EFFECT IS BEING PRODUCED, IT IS ALWAYS ADVISABLE TO CONCLUDE THE PROCESS BY LIGHTLY DRAWING THE STRAIGHT EDGE OF A PIECE OF CELLULOID ACROSS THE SURFACE TO SOFTEN THE SHARP EDGES OF THE RELIEF.

tools such as stiff brushes, steel combs, sponges, rolling pins, etc. It is then allowed to set, and, when it is quite hard and dry, it may be finished with either water or oil paints in any colour.

Recipe for Plastic Paint.

There are a number of proprietary plastic paints upon the market, but a very satisfactory one can be made by mixing equal parts of White Walpamur Water Paint and Plaster of Paris and thinning the mixture to a stiff working consistency with Walpamur Petrifying Liquid.

This is floated on with a stiff wall brush and worked upon immediately after. The number of different textures that can be produced by the use of suitable tools and a little ingenuity is remarkable.

How the Patterns are produced.

One or two instances may be given. Square or angular patterns may be produced by dragging the surface with a sponge or brush, manipulating it with a painter's scraper, or stippling it with a coarse brush, such as a scrubbing brush, which is given a half or quarter twist as impact is made with the wet surface.

One quite simply produced texture is obtained in the following way. Take a brush of any kind so long as the bristle part is 5 or 6 inches wide. Beginning at the top left-hand corner, drag the brush down the wet surface for, say, 6 inches. Immediately below this, execute the same motion horizontally. Below this, again use the perpendicular motion. Thus, by dragging the whole surface in alternate squares downwards and across a complete weave pattern is produced. One or two other textures are shown in our illustrations, but endless variety is possible, and this kind of surface decoration is not only in great vogue to-day but it is not difficult of execution, and is extremely fascinating.

ASBESTOS SHEETING

Finally, we come to the matter of asbestos sheeting. This material has come into increasing vogue during recent years for the surfacing of ceilings and walls instead of plaster.

It possesses certain advantages, one of which is that it is not affected by conditions of heat and cold. But it has one manifest disadvantage, especially when new, in that it contains a considerable quantity of alkali which is very harmful to paint, as it attacks the oil and causes it to saponify, with very objectionable results. No form of ordinary oil paint can be safely applied to asbestos sheeting unless the sheets are at least twelve months old, by which time the alkali will have "weathered" out.

If, for any reason, some immediate decorative treatment is imperative, a first-class water paint is the best material to use, as it contains very little oil to be affected by the alkali, and, even if it does not stand perfectly, the damage it receives will be comparatively slight. Moreover, the water paint will be a satisfactory basis upon which to apply either further coatings of a similar material or oil paint at a later date when chemical reaction has ceased and a more permanent result can be expected.

PAINTING A LINING BAND ON A WALL

IF the walls of a scullery are whitened so far down and painted, say, green below, a surprising improvement can be made by painting a black line about an inch wide all round to "break" the two colours. But to paint a nice "clean" line on a wall is not so easy as it sounds. Here, however, is a simple way out of the difficulty.

Obtain a roll of brown, gummed paper, usually about an inch wide. Cut off two pieces, each piece the length of one of the walls. You can wet it best by drawing the gummed side across a wet sponge. Now stick the two pieces to the wall (dabbing firmly with a cloth pad) straight and quite parallel, leaving a space between the two strips an inch wide, with the "meeting" of the two colours in the middle. You can then paint your black strip without the slightest care regarding the edges, as you will only run your brush on to the paper-strips.

Do all the walls the same, and when the paint is dry, just peel off the gummed paper.

Making a Cabinet Bedstead

The advantage of the cabinet bedstead shown open in Fig. 1 and closed in Fig. 2 over the collapsible or settee bed is that it is always ready for use by opening the doors and pulling the bed down. The mattress and bedclothes are kept in position by a running cord, which is quickly removed. In addition, owing to the space which is available inside the doors when the bed is pushed back, the cabinet can be used as a wardrobe.

The construction provides for panelled sides and doors, but laminated wood can be used instead; although the cost would be more, a considerable amount of time would be saved in cutting joints and fitting the panels. In the main, the same construction is followed, but thinner material could be used.

Materials required.

The cabinet can be made in oak or any hardwood to match existing furniture, but oregon pine or whitewood is suitable if stained.

The following material will be required:—

Sides.—Four styles A, 7 feet 1 inch × 3½ × 1 inches. Two rails B, 14 × 4½ × 1 inches. Two rails C, 14 × 10 × 1 inches. Two rails D, 14 × 3½ × 1 inches. Two plywood panels E, 15½ × 8½ × ¼ inches; and two F, 48½ × 8½ × ¼ inches.

Top.—Two lengths G, 3 feet 7½ inches × 3½ × 1 inches. Two H, 14 × 3½ × 1 inches. One piece plywood, 40 × 13 × ¼ inches. One length, 42 × 3 × 1 inches. Two lengths, 14 × 1 × 1 inches. One length, 3 feet 6 inches × 1 × ¼ inches.

Bottom.—One rail J, 3 feet 8 inches × 3 × 1 inches. One board (two pieces) K, 3 feet 8 inches × 14¾ × 1 inches. Two lengths L, 14¾ × 3 × 3 inches. Two lengths M, 12 × 3 × 3 inches. One length N, 36 × 4 × 1 inches. Two lengths O, 4 × 3 × 1½ inches. One length P, 3 feet 10 inches × 10 × 1 inches. Two lengths, 1 foot 4 inches × 10 × 1 inches.

Back.—One piece plywood, 6 feet 10 inches × 3 feet 6 inches × ¼ inches. Two lengths, 6 feet 8 inches × ¾ × ¾ inch.

Doors.—Three styles, 6 feet 3 inches × 3½ × 1 inches. One style, 6 feet 3 inches × 4 × 1 inches. Four rails, 20 × 4 × 1 inches. Two rails, 20 × 4 × 1 inches. Two lengths, 6 × 1 × 1 inches. Two plywood panels, 15½ × 14½ × ¼ inches and two 48½ × 14½ × ¼ inches.

Foot of Bed.—Two pieces, 16 × 2½ × 1½ inches. One piece, 36 × 2½ × 1½ inches. One piece S, 36 × 2 × 2 inches.

Two bolts and nuts approximately 6 × ⅜ inches, and two approximately 4 × ¼ inches.

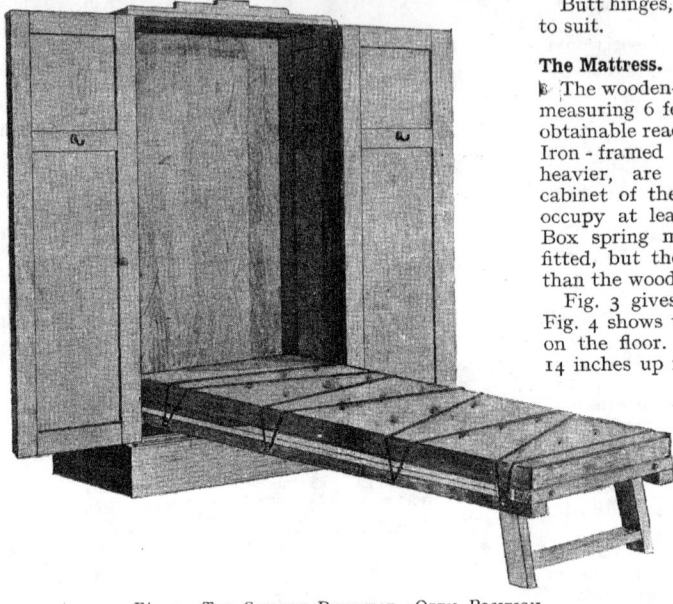

Fig. 1.—The Cabinet Bedstead—Open Position.

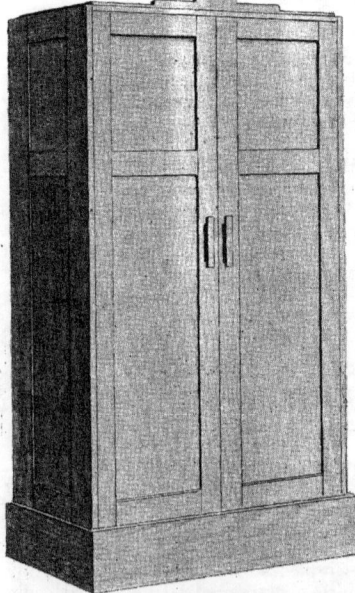

Fig. 2.—The Cabinet Bedstead—Closed Position.

Butt hinges, knobs, lock and screws to suit.

The Mattress.

The wooden-framed spring mattress, measuring 6 feet 2 inches × 3 feet, is obtainable ready for fixing in position. Iron-framed mattresses, although heavier, are thinner and, with a cabinet of the same dimensions, will occupy at least 3 inches less space. Box spring mattresses may also be fitted, but the depth will be greater than the wooden-frame mattress.

Fig. 3 gives the all-over sizes, and Fig. 4 shows the bedstead in position on the floor. The pivoting point is 14 inches up from the floor level and 5 inches from the front of the cabinet. If an iron-frame mattress is used, the point can be nearer the inside, but the exact position should be obtained by measurement; due allowance must be made for the thickness of the mattress, etc., to give sufficient clearance at the top as well as at the back.

Making the Cabinet—the Side Pieces.

The parts of one of the side pieces are shown at Fig. 5 and consist of two styles A, each finished to 7 feet 1 inch × 3½ × 1 inches; one top rail B, 14 × 4½ × 1 inches; one bottom rail C, 14 × 10 × 1 inches; and one inner rail D, 14 × 3½ × 1 inches. The top panel E should be 15½ × 8½ × ¼ inches, and the lower one F, 48½ × 8½ × ¼ inches. Begin by marking out the position of the mortises on the uprights A, placing them side by side as shown at Fig. 6. First set off a line from one end 4¼ inches along, then follow with others 3, 3½ and 3 inches; these provide for the two mortises for the bottom rail C. Next measure along 48½ and 3 inches; this is for the inner rail D, and then 15½ and 3 inches gives the position of the top rail B and will leave 1¼ inches.

The Three Rails.

The three rails should be placed together as indicated at Fig. 7, and first 3 and then 8 inches marked off. The lines are now in each case marked completely round the four sides with cut lines made with a sharp marking knife, and, using the try square, they should be extra deeply marked on the sides. The gauge lines should be made with a mortise gauge if possible; if not, a mark should be made with the ¼-inch mortise chisel to leave ⅜ inch each side and the gauge set to the extreme edges of the cut. Rather more space is left each side of the tenon than usual, but

MAKING A CABINET BEDSTEAD

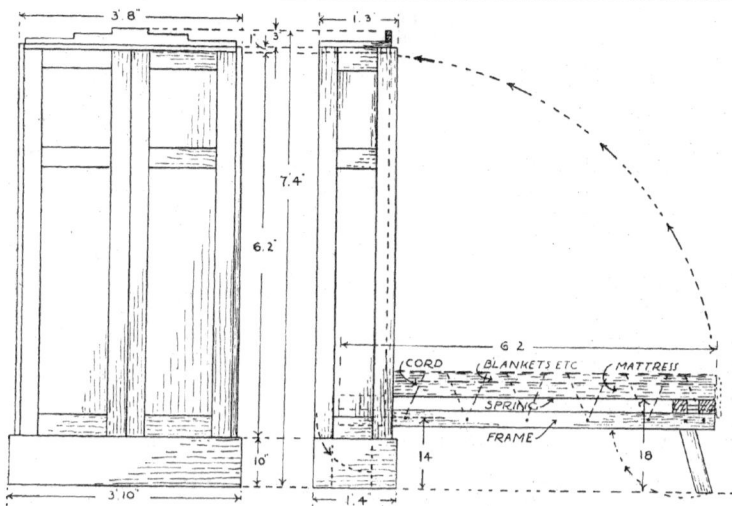

Fig. 3.—Diagram showing Overall Sizes.

Fig. 4.—Dimensions with Bed Open.

the thickness of the panelling has to be taken into consideration. If thicker panelling is used, the thickness of the tenons can be correspondingly increased, but with careful workmanship the suggested increase can be avoided.

The Shoulders.

The shoulders are now sawn down on the waste side of the lines, but the greatest care must be taken to prevent the saw going past the gauge lines, or the tenon will be seriously weakened. The beginner will find it better to cut the mortises first to a depth of 3 inches, considerable care being taken to keep the mortise chisel quite upright. If the mortises are not exactly square, it is very difficult to keep the framework true. It is a good plan to fit a strip of $\frac{1}{4}$-inch thick wood in the mortise and then test with the square. If the strip inclines to one side, the side of the mortise at fault can be trimmed up. This is poor workmanship, but it is a method by which the frame can be kept true in gluing up.

The whole of the grooving or ploughing is now carried out, and for this job a plough plane will be found most convenient. It is however possible to plough a groove with a 1-inch rebate plane by screwing a fence on one side and using a $\frac{1}{4}$-inch iron. It is not recommended and is only a makeshift. The home woodworker who is fond of cabinet making will find a plough very useful and the old wooden form can often be bought second-hand very cheaply. When the grooving is done on sides and rails, the shoulders of the tenons can be cut, as the extra length will aid the beginner if left on for ploughing.

Assembling the Frames.

The two frames should now be glued together, and while the glue is heating the cramps should be prepared. If a pair of joiner's cramps are not available, a pair of makeshift cramps should be made, as it is of the utmost importance that the cramping should be done immediately the gluing is finished. Place all the parts in the proper position with the panels preferably rubbed down smooth. Place one style on the bench, glue the tenons on one end of each of the rails in turn and tap them in position. Fit in the panels (there is no special need to glue them), then coat the remaining tenons with hot glue as rapidly as possible, place the style in position, tap down with a mallet and then proceed to cramp the frame and draw the joints quite close.

Forming Top of Cabinet.

The top of the cabinet is formed by a framework, shown at Fig. 8, and is composed of two 3 feet 7$\frac{1}{2}$-inch and two 14-inch lengths of 3$\frac{1}{2}$ × 1-inch wood. Place the two lengths G together and mark off first $\frac{3}{4}$, then $\frac{3}{4}$ inch, and follow with 1$\frac{1}{4}$ and 2$\frac{1}{4}$ inches. Mark these lines on all sides and place the two short pieces H together, set off 3 and 8 inches from one end. Set a mortise gauge to a $\frac{3}{8}$-inch chisel and gauge lines on each of the pieces to give the thickness of the tenons and mortises. Gauge 2$\frac{1}{4}$

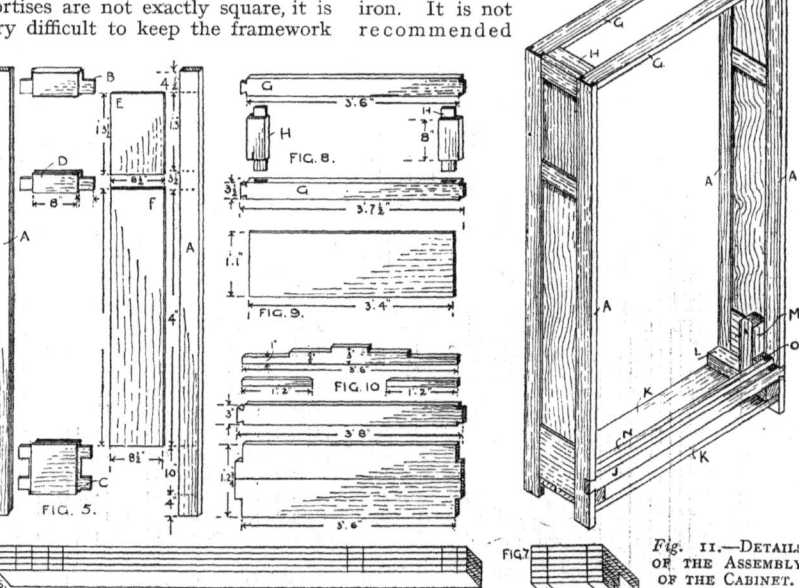

Figs. 5–10.—Constructional Details and Dimensions of Various Parts of the Cabinet.

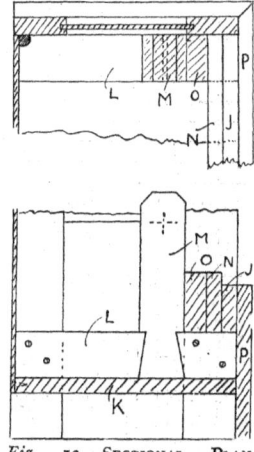

Fig. 11.—Details of the Assembly of the Cabinet.

Fig. 12.—Sectional Plan and Elevation of the Lower Portion of Cabinet.

MAKING A CABINET BEDSTEAD

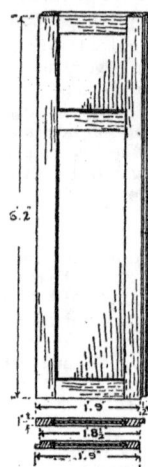

Fig. 13.—SECTION OF ONE OF THE DOORS. Note specially the rebates.

inches from the inner edges of the two short lengths and proceed to cut the mortises and tenons. Next mark off and cut the dovetails on the ends of the long pieces, the thickness being ½ inch; care should be taken that the shoulders of the dovetail halving are quite square.

The top framework is now glued together and the back edge planed down ¼ inch to allow for the back. The dovetails are then placed on top of the side frames, marked off and the sockets cut out to fit. Although the top can be left at this stage for the present, it will be necessary to prepare a length of plywood as at Fig. 9; this should measure 40 × 13 inches, and is screwed to the top of the framework flush with the back edges to leave 2 inches in front and at each end. In addition, the three pieces shown in Fig. 10 are shaped from wood 1 inch thick. The front piece is 42 × 3 inches and the end pieces 14 × 1 inches. The front corners are mitred and they are screwed on.

Fixing Bottom Board and Back.

The sides are held together at the bottom by a rail as at J, Fig. 11, and a board as at K. The rail is 3 feet 8 inches × 3 × 1 inches, the ends are dovetailed the whole thickness. The board is 3 feet 8 inches × 14¾ × 1 inches, with notches 3½ × 1 inches and 3¼ × 1 inches as shown. The bottom board is screwed to the under side of the two lower rails and the rail J is fitted in slots cut in the sides 7 inches from the bottom of the sides as indicated in the view of the carcase in Fig. 11. It will help to keep the work true if the back is fitted in position at this stage. For this purpose a 6 feet 10 inches × 3 feet 6 inches piece of ¼-inch plywood will be required. Allowance has been made for screwing the back to the top rail and the bottom board, but it will be necessary to provide two 6 feet 8-inch lengths of beading ¾ inch square in section with the inner corner chamferred or rounded as indicated in the sectional plan and elevation of the lower portion of the cabinet at Fig. 12. Screws should be driven at intervals on the sides as well as at the top and bottom to keep the back in position.

Hinging the Bed Frame.

Figs. 11 and 12 show the provision for hinging the bed frame. Some 3 × 3-inch wood will be needed and for each side of the cabinet a 14¾-inch length as at L should be prepared. An upright M, cut to a length of 12 inches, is now dovetailed to it as shown, at a distance of 3½ inches from the front edge; the dovetail need not be more than 1 inch thick. At a height of 10 inches mark off a centre for the bolt, which should be at least ⅜ inch diameter. The hole should be bored and the top corners cut off as indicated. These two parts are now screwed to the inside, two screws into each upright style will be sufficient. A 36 × 4 × 1 inches length N is now prepared and screwed to the inside of the piece J, it will project 1 inch above and form a stop for the door at the bottom of the cabinet. A 4 × 3 × 1½ inches length O is now fitted in the space between the upright M and the strip N; this piece can be glued in position, there is no need for screwing or nailing.

Adding the Plinth.

The cabinet may now be completed by the addition of a plinth, as at P; the front piece should be cut to 3 feet 10 inches and the side pieces to 1 foot 4 inches from material 10 × 1 inches. The front corners are mitred to a neat fit and the three parts screwed from the inside with glue at the mitred corners. The two doors are framed up similarly to the sides of the cabinet.

Preparing the Doors.

One of the doors is made with one style finished to 6 feet 2 inches × 3½ × 1 inches and the other to 4 × 1 inches. The other door has both styles 3½ × 1 inches. In preparing the material, cut the lengths for the styles to 6 feet 3 inches to allow for ½ inch waste at each end. This should be cut off after the framing is finished. Two of the rails are each prepared to 20 × 3½ × 1 inches and the upper rail to 20 × 4 × 1 inches. Place the four uprights together and set out the position of the mortises, measuring off first ½ inch and following with ¾ inch and 3 inches for the bottom rail, 48½ and 3 inches for the upper rail, and 15½ and 2½ inches for the top rail.

Place the three rails together and mark off 3 and 14 inches. Cut the lines deeply on the sides of the rails and then gauge as in the framing of the side frames. Plough the grooves to a depth just over ¼ inch, and remember that the inner edges only of the top and bottom rails, but both edges of the inner rail, are grooved.

Cut the shoulders of the tenons and then prepare the panels, the top ones are 15½ × 14½ inches and the lower ones 48½ × 14½ inches. Glue up the frames as before, and when the glue has set the ends of the styles are sawn off and trimmed up smooth with a plane. The rebating on the two meeting styles, ½ inch along and ½ inch deep, can be done with a rebate plane; sections of the doors showing the rebates are given at Fig. 13.

Fixing the Doors.

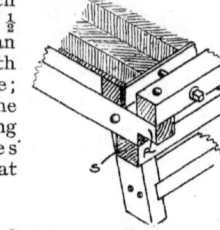

Fig. 14.—DETAILS OF METHOD OF FIXING LEG AT END OF THE BED.

The doors should be hung with three butt hinges for preference, and a suitable lock fitted. The handles shown should be shaped from material shaped to 1-inch square section and cut to 6 inches long. To provide a stop at the top of the door, screw on a strip of 1 × ¼-inch wood cut to 3 feet 6 inches long. The particular form of finish depends on the material used in the construction, but for simplicity of treatment a wax polish or wax polish stain is best. For those who require a high polish, it is possible to obtain easily worked French polishes which are satisfactory, although they do not last with the same brilliancy as the heavily bodied polishes.

Fixing the Bed Frame.

It will not be difficult to fix on the bed frame. First of all the projections to carry the cord should be fitted in position; large round-headed screws can be used, but small brass knobs will be found very convenient in use—from four to six should be used on each side. The foot at the end of the bed frame should be made from fairly stout material, approximately 2½ × 1½ inches. Taking the centre line along the side member of the bed frame at 14 inches, the length of the two lengths for the foot should be about 16 inches. As most of the frames have a recess R at the ends for the bolts, sufficient distance must be allowed for the stop shown at S in Fig. 14. The cross piece should be let in the two leg pieces about ½ inch and must be screwed in firmly. The legs will fit inside the frame when the bed is in its upright position.

Holes for Hinging Bolts.

The holes for the hinging bolts at the head of the bed should be bored along a centre line about 6 inches from the end. This distance will allow for approximately 5 inches of thickness above the spring for the mattress and bedclothes. The bolts should be about 6 inches long, but the exact length depends on the width of the side member of the frame. Owing to the weight of the portion above the pivoting point, there will be no need for fastening the bed in position when upright.

How to Fit a Simple Shower Attachment to the Bath

A SIMPLE shower bath attachment that can be fitted to any bath which has the usual hot and cold taps can be made very cheaply. It will supply water of any temperature from cold to hot, provided the hot water for the bath is obtained from a storage tank system. If the hot water supply is obtained from a geyser, then the attachment can only be arranged to provide a cold shower.

Fittings required.

The following fittings, which can be obtained at any ironmonger's, will be required:—

Four ¾-inch elbows.
One ¾-inch tee-piece.
Two ¾- to ½-inch reducing bushes.
Two connecting nipples for ¾-inch pipe.
Two pieces of ½-inch pipe, each 3 inches long.
One piece ¾-inch iron pipe about 3 feet long.
One piece ¾-inch iron pipe about 2 feet long.
Two pieces rubber hose about 2 feet long to fit on the bath taps (probably about ⅝-inch bore).
One rose head about 6 inches in diameter.
Three or four pieces of 2-inch square deal.

Ordinary "gas" fittings will be suitable, but a better quality known as "steam" or "hot-water" fittings are preferable. The exact length of the iron pipes will be determined by the space available in the bathroom.

For fixing the curtain round the shower, a piece of ⅜-inch or ½-inch diameter brass or aluminium rod about 7 feet long will be required, and about 8 feet of flat strip brass or aluminium, measuring ¾ inch wide, and a bare ⅛ inch thick.

How the Attachment works.

The principle of the shower bath attachment is quite simple, and is shown in Fig. 1. It will be seen that the hot and cold water supplies are connected to a mixing element consisting of two elbows and a tee-piece. The mixed water then flows along the pipe and comes out of the rose head, which is placed at a convenient position to allow the user to stand under it in the bath. If only the hot tap is turned on, the shower will naturally be hot, but if both hot and cold taps are turned on an equal amount, the resulting shower will be nicely warm. The exact temperature can be varied to suit individual requirements by turning one or other of the taps on more than the other.

Fig. 1.—The Completed Shower Bath Attachment.

Curtains.

In order to prevent the water from the shower being splashed over the walls and floor, waterproof curtains should be suspended on rings from a rod fixed either to the upper part of the pipe system or to the wall and ceiling if more convenient.

Constructional Details.

The first thing to do is to assemble the mixing element. Prepare a mixture of red lead and gold size, or obtain some thick paint. This is for smearing on the screw threads before fixing the various parts together, so as to ensure a water-tight joint. Take the tee-piece and screw into it the two connecting nipples as shown in Fig. 2. Then screw two of the elbows on to them to complete the fitting shown in Fig. 2.

Now screw in the reducing bushes marked R in Fig. 2, and into these screw in the short pieces of pipe, P.

Next take the longer of the two pieces of iron pipe and screw it into the upper leg of the tee. At the other end of the pipe fix an elbow, so that the parts now assembled appear as shown in Fig. 2 (bottom left), with the elbow at right angles to the tee-piece.

The second piece of pipe is now screwed into the elbow, and the remaining elbow screwed into the other end. Finally screw the rose head into the elbow and the pipe part is completed as in Fig. 2. Paint the whole with aluminium paint and set aside to dry.

Fixing the Pipes.

The next consideration is fixing the piping in position on the wall. At least two brackets should be used, one at the top and the other at the bottom. The brackets are bent to shape from the strip metal.

Bending the Metal for the Bracket.

Cut off a piece about 15 inches long, bend it at the middle of its length around a 1¼-inch wooden or metal bar, as shown in Fig. 3, and press the ends together so that they are parallel. Place them in a vice as in Fig. 4, so that the two ends can be bent out at right angles. The length of these two ends should be about 2 inches, and the ends can be neatly rounded off with a file after any surplus has been cut off with a hacksaw.

Holes for Fixing Screws.

Drill the holes for the fixing screws and for the ¼-inch diameter brass bolt and nut. When one bracket has been completed a second one, exactly the same, should be made.

The brackets are fixed to two pieces of hard wood screwed to the wall with rawlplugs.

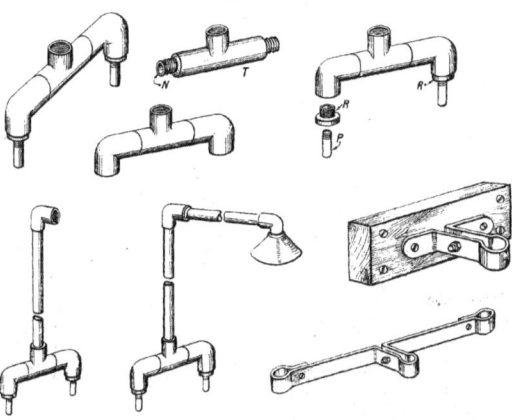

Fig. 2.—Details of the Various Fittings required.

HOW TO FIT A SIMPLE SHOWER ATTACHMENT TO THE BATH

Fig. 3.—Bending the Strip Metal for the Supports.

The Curtain Rod Fixing.

Now bend the curtain rod to shape. It rests upon the upper bracket, and is held to the upper pipe of the shower by a wide clip; it should be made as wide as the bath. Details of the clip are shown in Fig. 2. The centre part fits round the pipe and the outer parts go round the rod.

Rubber or rubberised fabric will make suitable curtains, and they are hung from the rod by curtain rings.

Attaching the Piping to the Taps.

The two pieces of hose pipe should be attached permanently to the elbow fittings by means of copper wire bindings or clips. The free ends are slipped over the taps whenever the shower is required.

Fig. 4.—Forming the Ends of the Brackets.

SOME USEFUL SALADS

BELOW we give recipes for several salads, salad dressings, etc., which can be easily prepared.

French Dressing.

    4 tablespoonfuls of olive oil.
    2 tablespoonfuls of vinegar.
    1 small teaspoonful of salt.
    ¼ teaspoonful of pepper.

Stir the salt and pepper into the olive oil, using a wooden spoon for the purpose and, when thoroughly mixed, add the vinegar gradually, stirring all the time. Continue to mix well until a smooth, thick cream is obtained.

More vinegar may be added, if a sharper flavour is desired.

Mayonnaise Dressing.

    2 egg yolks.
    A little pepper and salt.
    ½ teaspoonful of mustard, moistened with a little vinegar.
    1 gill of olive oil.
    ½ gill of vinegar.
    1 teaspoonful of brown sugar.

Put the egg yolks into a basin, add the pepper and salt, and stir in the made mustard; mix well. Then add the olive oil very slowly, stirring all the time, until the mixture becomes quite smooth. When all the olive oil has been added and well blended with the rest, stir in the sugar and vinegar, and continue mixing lightly until a smooth cream results.

Green Salad.

    2-hard boiled eggs.
    Cooked beetroot.
    Lettuces.
    A small onion.
    Tomato sauce.
    French dressing.

Wash, drain and shred the lettuces, and mix lightly with a little tomato sauce. Turn this into a salad bowl, and cover the surface with a sprinkling of grated onion. Slice thinly the hard-boiled eggs and the beetroot, and arrange them in rings round the edge of the bowl. Pour French dressing over the surface just before serving.

Egg Salad.

    Sliced hard-boiled eggs.
    Sliced cucumber.
    Sliced beetroot.
    French dressing.
    Watercress.
    Chopped parsley.

Arrange the sliced eggs, beetroot and cucumber in alternate straight rows on a flat dish. Decorate with small bunches of watercress, pour over all some French dressing, and sprinkle the surface with finely chopped parsley and powdered yolk of egg.

Endive Salad.

    Endives.
    French dressing.
    Beetroot.
    Celery.
    Hard-boiled eggs.
    Mustard and cress.

Soak the endives in salted water, wash, drain and break them into small tufts.

Pour a little French dressing into a salad bowl, mix it lightly with the tufts of endive. Add a layer of sliced beetroot, and cover this with a sprinkling of finely chopped celery. Decorate with an edging of sliced hard-boiled eggs and chopped mustard and cress.

Cabbage and Apple Salad.

    1 cabbage.
    French dressing.
    Cabbage lettuce.
    Beetroot.
    1 apple.
    Celery.
    Hard-boiled eggs.
    Mayonnaise dressing.

Wash, drain and shred the heart of a raw cabbage, and pour over it some French dressing; mix lightly.

Wash, drain and shred the heart of a cabbage lettuce, and with it mix some finely chopped beetroot, apple and celery. Add the prepared cabbage, mix well and turn all into a large salad bowl.

Decorate the edge of the salad with slices of hard-boiled egg, and cover the surface, at the centre, with some thick mayonnaise dressing.

The inclusion of some substantial ingredients will transform a mere salad into a dish which may be a meal in itself. This is also a useful method of using up cold remains, such as chicken, fish, etc.

Chicken Salad.

    Remains of cold chicken.
    Lettuces.
    Celery.
    Apples.
    Walnuts.
    Mayonnaise dressing.

Remove all skin and bone from the chicken, and chop the meat very finely. Peel and chop one or two apples, add some celery cut into dice and mix these with the chicken.

Prepare and shred a lettuce, and arrange it on a flat dish. In the centre pile the chicken, apple and celery mixture, pour over all some mayonnaise dressing, and lastly sprinkle the surface with finely chopped nuts.

A Quick Salad Dressing.

This may be made with a small tin of condensed milk, add pepper, salt, vinegar and mustard, which thins it, and at the last moment put in ordinary milk, which softens it and thickens it up again. It curdles and at the same time thickens to the right consistency.

Building a Brick Fireplace

To undertake the converting of a Victorian fireplace into a brick fireplace suitable for a modern house and decoration is not really a difficult job.

We will assume that there is in existence in your house a mantelpiece of either marble or wood, such as in Fig. 1, and you want to turn it into a much more respectable chimneypiece and one of pleasing appearance, such as is shown in Fig. 2.

Removing the Old Mantelpiece.

If it is marble, with the help of a hammer and a cold chisel lever out the shelf. You will find it set into the wall about ¾ inch or so. The whole chimneypiece will have been put together in separate pieces, viz., the shelf, frieze, jambs, plinth, etc., and they will all have been fixed together with plaster, and, furthermore, with cramps fitted into the wall. Wrench these out. There will be a mess, but that can soon be cleared up.

If the chimneypiece be of wood, it will come out in one piece.

Removing the Grate.

Now, having taken it down, proceed to remove the grate. This will also be an easy, but a somewhat messy, job. If it is an old one, it will probably break. It will be of no value.

The fireplace itself will have a firebrick back, which will in all probability fall to bits when moved.

You will find an opening such as is shown in Fig. 3.

Clear out all the mess and rubbish.

Fig. 1.—An Old-fashioned Victorian Fireplace such as this is Particularly Suitable for conversion into a Modern Type Brick Built Fireplace, such as that shown in Fig. 2.

Fig. 2.—A Modern Type Brick Fireplace.

A Word of Warning.

There is one thing that must be remembered. On no account tamper with the party wall, especially in such cases as this one under consideration, namely, behind a fireplace.

Consult the District Surveyor.

If you find the bricks worn away you will naturally want to make a good job of it and hack down the old worn bricks and insert new. This you must on no account do without first advising the district surveyor. Now, district surveyors are not at all formidable; in fact, in nearly every case they are most amenable and are nearly always ready to help.

If the surveyor for your district agrees that what you propose to do is quite in order, then you are covered, and you can go ahead; but if by chance the house next door catches fire and the origin is traced to some spot in the neighbourhood of the back of your fireplace, then, whether you are quite innocent or no, and it transpires that you had in some way tampered with the party wall without first informing the district surveyor, you may get into serious trouble. This is only a hint, but one of very *great* value.

Of course, different rules and regulations obtain in different districts, and this warning may not be applicable to the district in which you reside, but it is a general covering hint which should not be ignored.

Building the Fireplace.

We will suppose, then, that the wall at the back is quite sound, needing no repairs.

The fireplace shown in Fig. 2 is composed, in the main, of right angles, and therefore easy to fix.

The Bricks.

The most artistic-looking bricks for this job are "multi-coloured," but they are rather on the expensive side, so you could use ordinary red bricks, but it would be better to have them 2 inches or less in thickness, or if you can vary the thickness, all the better.

There are many different kinds of bricks which could be used for the work in addition to the red bricks referred to above. You could vary

Fig. 3.—An Opening similar to that shown above will be found when the Old Mantelpiece and Grate have been removed.

Fig. 4.—The Wooden Frame upon which the Voussoirs or Tapering Bricks are built.

Fig. 5.—A Tapering Appearance can be obtained by making the Mortar Joints wider at the Top than the Bottom.

BUILDING A BRICK FIREPLACE

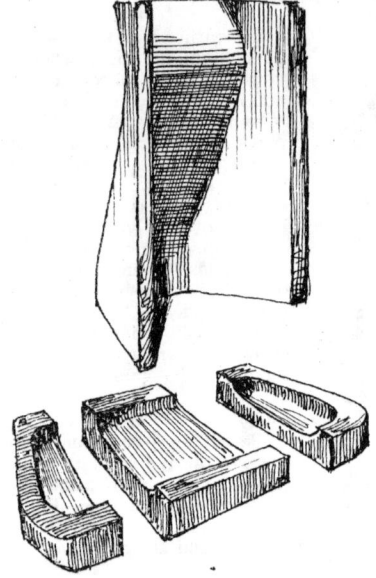

Fig. 6.—The Four Pieces of Firebrick which make up the "Devon" Fireplace.

Fig. 7.—How the Four Pieces of Firebrick are assembled.

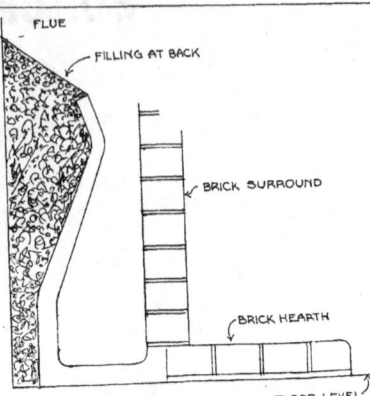

Fig. 8.—The Devon Fireplace in position. Showing how rubble is used to fill up the spaces on both sides and at the back.

Fig. 12.—Showing Brick inserted into the Space to form a Bond with the Old Wall.

Fig. 9.—Showing how the Wooden Frame is used for building the Arch.

Fig. 10.—Several Bricks should be knocked out as shown to form a Key for the New Bricks.

Fig. 13.—The Front Hearth.

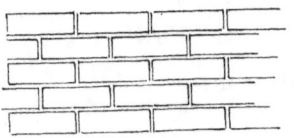

STRETCHING BOND

Fig. 11C.—How to lay the Bricks—Stretching Bond.

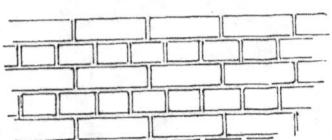

ENGLISH BOND

Fig. 11A.—How to lay the Bricks—English Bond.

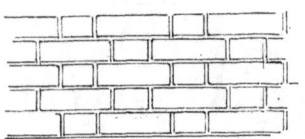

FLEMISH BOND

Fig. 11B.—How to lay the Bricks—Flemish Bond.

ENGLISH GARDEN BOND

Fig. 11D.—How to lay the Bricks—English Garden Bond.

Fig. 14.—An Alternative Design. Showing tiles laid alternately with bricks.

your design with tiles for laying alternately with the bricks, and make up your voussoirs with tiles also (Fig. 14).

Here is a list of bricks which could be employed, and which, if thought advisable, could be mixed. Multi-coloured. Red bricks. Stock bricks. Stock bricks with black in them. Red sand-faced. Wire-cut red. Sand-faced tiles. Roof tiles. Flooring tiles.

You will also require Portland cement, sand, and a little lime to make your mortar.

The Arches.

In Fig. 2 two arches are indicated, and to form these you will have to make wooden frames (termed " centering ") (Fig. 4), upon which to build up your voussoirs. Voussoirs are tapering bricks, but you need not go to the expense and trouble to get them. The bricks you have will do, and you can rely on your mortar joints to form the tapering appearance (Fig. 5), or you can chip off the sides of the bricks.

FIXING A " DEVON " FIREPLACE

Supposing you decide to fix an interior such as a " Devon," the procedure would be as follows : There may be a very good bed of concrete existing, but the surface may be somewhat uneven and worn, so make it up a bit and run a coat of cement and sand over evenly to form a foundation for your new fireplace.

The " Devon " fireplace is composed of four pieces of firebrick (Fig. 6), which must be placed upon the concrete bed (Fig. 7).

Now cement the base together (three parts sand to one of cement) and set the top part upon it. The top will be set to reach the flue. Having done this, place your wooden centering in position and build up your bricks on either side, and your voussoirs on top.

When the bricks are set, fill up the spaces on both sides with rubble (broken bricks, etc) to the top, then cover over with cement (Fig. 8).

Having completed your small arch, proceed to build up your large one.

Hack off some of the Plaster.

First of all hack off some of the plaster from each side and disclose the brickwork. Now knock out several bricks in selected positions, as shown in Fig. 10.

The bricks can be laid in a position as shown in Fig. 11, A, B, C or D.

Place the large centering as you did the small for the voussoirs.

The spaces formed by removing some of the bricks at the side are made in order to form a key for building the brickwork, some of the bricks being inserted into the spaces, thus forming a " bond " with the old wall, as in Fig. 12.

The small course of bricks on the shelf speaks for itself.

The Hearth.

The front hearth will have to be on a higher level than the lower part of the firebrick grate, namely, on a level with the top of the base of the grate (Fig. 13). There, no doubt, will be a stone hearth in existence which will serve as a good bed for your new brick hearth.

Chip the surface in order to give a key for the cement and sand, which must be laid on for your bricks.

If you cannot get " bull-nosed " bricks (Fig. 13) you can rub down the front and side edges with another brick.

To give a better effect, you can scrape out the joints of the upright courses somewhat, but the joints on the hearth, however, must be left flush.

TWO USEFUL WOODWORK ARTICLES

FIG. 1 shows a device that will be found useful when paperhanging. It consists of two pieces of 11-inch shelving hinged together to form a papering board that can be packed away in some corner when not in use.

The construction is quite straightforward, the main point to watch being the method of fitting the hinges ; they are let in on one side only and the other flap is screwed direct to the wood. The trestles are, of course, quite simple to construct from the details given on the drawing, but it should be noted that a cord should be inserted through the two cross pieces when a suitable height for working from has been found.

Portable Workbasket.

The portable workbasket shown in Fig. 2 can also be constructed quite easily. The 3 feet 6 inch lengths are swung on bevel screws before the cross members are put on, and requires accurate measurement to make them fold flush. Do not screw them up too tight. Note that the two frames have different sized cross members so as to enable one frame to fit inside the other.

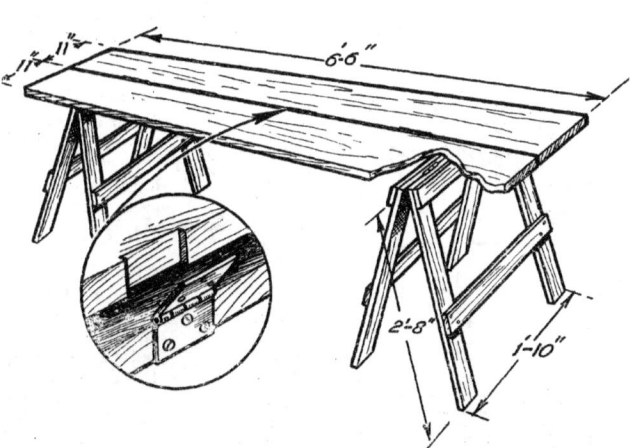

Fig. 1.—A useful Paperhanging Board.

Fig. 2.—A Portable Workbasket.

Making a Private Loudspeaking Telephone Installation

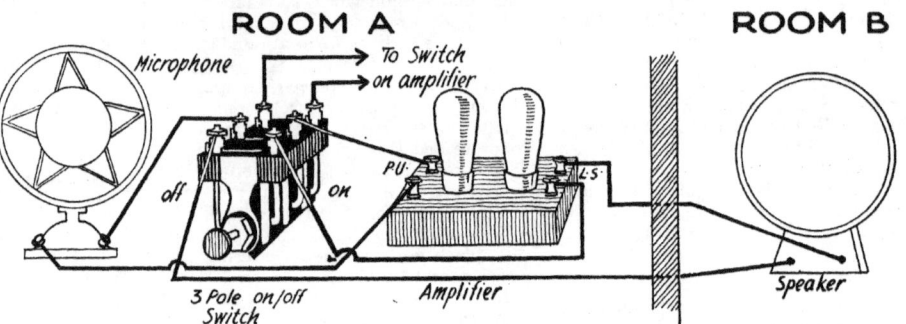

Fig. 1.—The Circuit Arrangement for a Simple "One-way" Loudspeaking Telephone System.

There are many situations in which a private telephone line proves very useful, and in this respect one might mention a line running between, say, the garage and the house, or between an outside workshop and the house. Quite apart from the actual utility of the system, an arrangement of this kind has many points of interest for those home mechanics who are interested in electrical and wireless experiments.

There are few homes to-day in which a wireless set is not installed, and the normal receiver can be made use of as an excellent form of telephone amplifier. The idea is that a microphone, either of a standard type or of an improvised nature, is connected to the input, or pick-up, terminals, a loud speaker being used and connected in the conventional manner.

A Suitable Microphone.

The choice of a microphone is to-day extremely wide, since a large number of manufacturers have lately introduced a variety of special models particularly designed for home recording, home broadcasting and similar purposes. Most of these instruments are already fitted with the necessary microphone transformer, small dry battery and on-off switch, so that they may be connected directly to a valve amplifier of any type. To aid readers in the choice of a suitable microphone of the pattern referred to one might mention the General Electric Company's "Home Broadcaster," a range of microphones made by the Scientific Supply Stores and a number of instruments of various types which are distributed by Messrs. Electradix Radios. A unit made by any of these firms should be obtainable, if desired, through the local electrician or wireless dealer.

In many cases the microphone will be all that is required, with the exception of a switch for bringing it into circuit, and the connections will be as shown in Fig. 1. Here it will be seen that a three-point on-off switch is

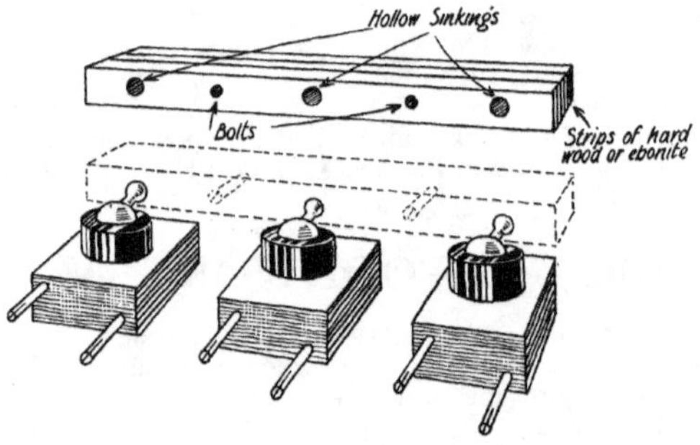

Fig. 2.—The Operating Levers of Three Toggle Switches may be Joined Together, as shown in the above Sketch.

employed, this being of the rotary type for preference. The switch is so connected that when it is in the "off" position, the amplifier (this will generally be a wireless set), microphone and loud speaker are all disconnected. Turning the switch to the "on" position, however, switches on the amplifier, connects the microphone to the input or pick-up terminals, and connects the speaker to the appropriate terminals simultaneously.

A "One-way" Arrangement.

The method of wiring up the switch will readily be followed by referring to Fig. 1, and it should be explained that the two leads marked "To switch on amplifier" should simply be connected to the two terminals which are to be found on the switch fitted to the wireless receiver. In the illustration in question it is assumed that the microphone will simply be used to speak from the house "end" to the person in, say, the garage or out-building. The speaker is therefore in the room remote from that in which the receiver is installed. When the telephone system is not in use—the telephone switch being "off"—the receiver can be used in the ordinary manner without any alteration whatever being called for, provided that the set is fitted with the customary "radio-gram" switch; the latter will, of course, be turned to the "radio" position.

The connections given are rather on the assumption that the receiver is of the battery-operated type, since if it is a mains-driven instrument the rotary microphone-speaker on-off switch will be unsuitable. In that case it would be better to employ three of the quick-make-break toggle switches which are designed for switching mains appara-

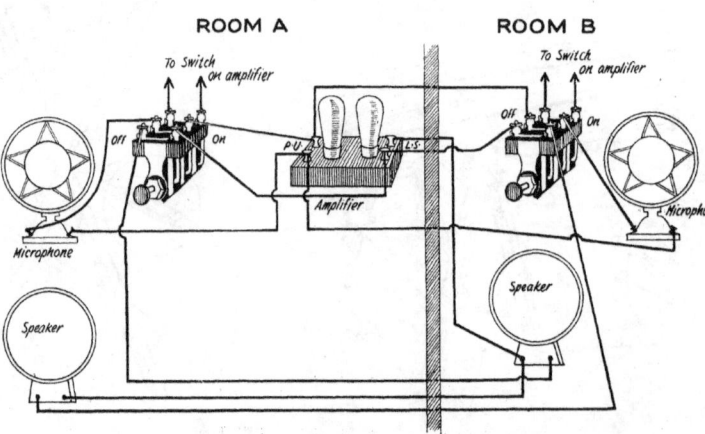

Fig. 3.—Complete Connection for an Efficient Two-way Circuit.

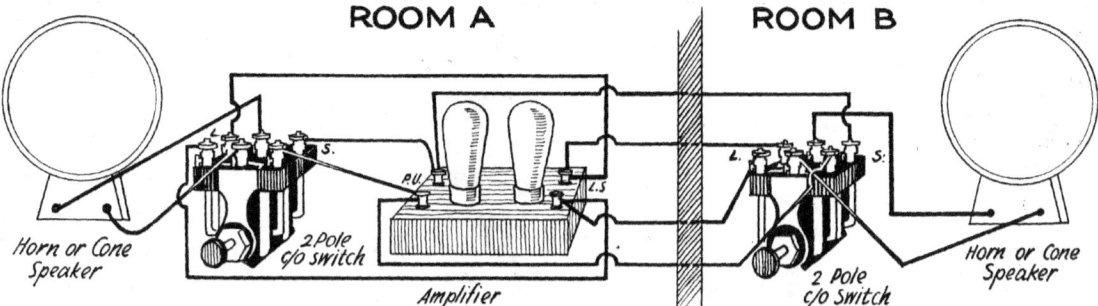

Fig. 4.—A Simplified Two-way System in which Speakers are used for both "Transmission" and "Reception."

tus, and join the three toggles together by means of a couple of wooden strips arranged as shown in Fig. 2. Alternatively, of course, use could be made of three electric light switches whose toggles were joined together; such a combination of switches can be bought ready assembled.

There is another very important point which should be mentioned. This is that, in the case of a battery set, the two leads to the on-off switch should be of heavy-gauge or multi-strand wire so that the voltage drop along them will be reduced to the absolute minimum. Cotton-covered bell wire of about 16-gauge is quite suitable, although if the length of the wires does not exceed some few yards it is quite in order to employ ordinary lighting flex, this latter also being suitable for use with a mains set, even if the length is several yards.

Use Screened Leads for the Microphone.

It is also rather important that the leads from the microphone to the switch and from the switch to the pick-up terminals should be screened. In other words, the insulated wires should be passed through lengths of metal braiding which is sold especially for this purpose. The braiding must not be allowed to make contact with either of the wires which pass through it, but it should be connected to the earth terminal on the receiver by means of a short length of thin wire. As a matter of fact, a number of the microphones on the market are sold complete with a long, twin-screened lead, so that the braiding mentioned need not be bought. In connection with the leads to the loud speaker, it should be mentioned that it is wise to keep these fairly well apart, and for that reason they may consist of two lengths of single-bell wiring carried overhead and spaced about 6 inches apart. Indeed, they may be identical with ordinary telephone wires, being supported by means of brackets fitted with porcelain insulators.

A Two-way Circuit.

The system referred to is of the simplest type and has the disadvantage that it is only "one-way." In other words, it is only possible to speak and call up from one end of the line, although the microphone may be either in the house or in the outbuilding as desired. It is, however, a perfectly simple matter to duplicate the arrangement by connecting a second microphone, switch and loud speaker as shown in Fig. 3. In this case a call can be made from either end of the line, and a conversation can be carried on between two persons, one at each end. Unfortunately it is not a very simple matter to design the circuit so that "cross-talk" can be maintained without using the switches. That is, each person must turn the appropriate switch to the "on" position when speaking, and then turn the switch "off" in order to listen. This slight disadvantage can undoubtedly be overcome, but the complications so involved would not normally be considered worth while.

In installing the two-way system described the methods to be employed are identical with those dealt with in connection with the Fig. 1 arrangement and no further explanation is called for.

Dispensing with the Microphone.

A simpler version of the two-way telephone system shown in Fig. 3 is illustrated in Fig. 4, and in this case microphones are dispensed with. Loud speakers, which must be of the older "horn" or "cone" type, are used both for "transmission" and "reception" by connecting them to the set through two-pole change-over switches. When the switch in "Room A" is in the "L" (listen) position the corresponding speaker is connected to the loud-speaker terminals of the amplifier, whilst when the switch is in the "S" (speak) position the speaker is joined to the pick-up terminals; exactly the same thing applies at the other end of the line.

The only real disadvantage of this simplified arrangement is that the speakers do not function as efficient microphones, with a result that speech sounds a little unnatural and is not reproduced so loudly as in the previous system. Even so, the idea is quite workable and can be used with complete success for most ordinary purposes. All connecting wires should be placed a few inches apart. Up to 20 feet or so they should be separated by 2 inches or so, but for greater distances it is better to keep them about 6 inches apart.

Two-way Switching.

No switch is shown for the amplifier, but this can be easily arranged for by making the simple connections given in Fig. 5. Here two single-pole change-over switches are used, and they are wired in exactly the same manner as similar switches are in the case of lights which can be controlled from two different points. The switches may be separate ones, as shown, or they might be incorporated in the other change-over switches shown. In the latter instance it would be necessary to replace the two-pole components by others having three poles; the amplifier would then be switched on from either end of the line by turning the switch to the "speak" position, and the amplifier would remain in circuit when a change-over from "speak" to "listen" (and *vice versâ*) was made at both ends.

One use of the loud-speaking telephone systems described, although it might seem rather complicated, is to put the ordinary G.P.O. telephone in the house "through" to the outbuilding or similar remote point. All that is necessary to do this is to place the microphone (or speaker used as such) near to the ear-piece of the 'phone and the speaker (when used) near to the mouth-piece. Obviously this would be rather an awkward procedure, since the switches at both ends of the line would have to be made use of, but the method might be considered for occasional use.

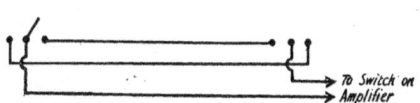

Fig. 5.—Showing how Two-way Switching can easily be provided in the Case of a Circuit like that given in Fig. 4.

The switches may be separate or combined with the two-pole ones.

How to Know Sheffield Plate

IN the year 1743 a Sheffield cutler, named Thomas Bolsover, was placing a thin layer of silver on the copper handle of a knife, when the idea of making what is now known as Sheffield plate occurred to him.

For centuries previous to Bolsover's time, it had been possible to coat articles made of base metals with a covering of silver and even gold; but the covering was always laid on after the articles had been finally shaped.

How the Plating was done.

Bolsover's idea was entirely different. With his process, the first step was to make an ingot of copper of approximately the same shape and size as an ordinary brick and then to place a layer of silver, about ⅛ inch thick, on one of the largest faces of the ingot. A certain amount of flux and solder was sandwiched between the two metals, and after that they were heated until the solder fused and the copper and silver became intimately attached.

The next step was to take the silvered ingot of copper to the rolling mills, where it was rolled out into sheets of any desired thickness; but always with one surface showing a covering of silver.

At this stage the sheets were cut up into convenient pieces, and each piece was used for making an article in Sheffield plate.

From this brief account it will be seen that, with the Bolsover process, the silvering was done *before* the article was shaped, and that in earlier processes it was done *after*. It may be added that, in electro-plating, it is also performed *after*. Thus, Sheffield plate alone required the silvering to be undertaken before the article was fashioned. This fact is an important one to remember, because it offers a very helpful clue when deciding whether this or that heirloom is really Sheffield plate or not.

Fig. 1.—A Sheffield Plate Candlestick.
Dating from the early years of the nineteenth century.

Double-coated Plate.

Bolsover's idea was quickly taken up by other silversmiths, who improved on his process in several ways. Probably the greatest step forward was to cover the two largest faces of the copper ingot with silver. Articles made from such sheets were silvered, not only on the outside, but on the inside as well. Naturally, the demand for double-coated pieces injured the sale of those that were single-coated, and their manufacture almost ceased. Here, then, is another point for collectors to note. If a piece of Sheffield plate has two skins of silver it was made between 1753, roughly, and 1850, when electro-plating completely ousted the Sheffield process. But if it has only one skin, it is fairly safe to say that it was made between 1743 and about 1753. An exception must be allowed in the case of such things as teapots, since to be silvered on the inside is no advantage to them.

Discriminating between Sheffield and Electro-plate.

While reading these lines many people will probably think of some piece which is in their possession, and they will wonder whether it is an example of Sheffield plate or not. The chief difficulty lies in discriminating between electro-plate and Sheffield plate. Solid silver articles will appear outwardly the same; but there is no trouble in recognising them, as they bear the Assay marks, which are fairly widely understood.

An Important Clue to Sheffield Plate.

It is with the Bolsover wares and the electros, then, that we must deal somewhat fully. In the first place, it is well to recognise that all the articles made of Sheffield plate were shaped out of copper sheets, covered with silver. Accordingly, wherever there was an edge, the copper showed or, if it did not show, it was because it had been hidden in some way.

This is a very useful clue, since it proves conclusively that if a streak of copper is visible in the thickness of the metal, it is good evidence of Sheffield plate; but, let it be understood, few crafts

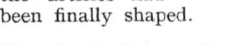

Fig. 2.—Marks of the most Noted Workers in Sheffield Plate.
The names given in brackets are not part of the mark, neither are the dates.

Fig. 3.—A Plain Bowl in Sheffield Plate.
Note the turned-over edge to hide the streak of copper.

Fig. 4.—How the Pattern is evolved.
Two good examples. The outer ring, in both cases, is provided by silver wire to hide the copper. The inner rings are added to give a decorative meaning to the wire.

men left the edge raw, because this was a sign of unfinished work. What we shall be more likely to find are devices for obscuring such edges. Sometimes the metal was neatly folded over. On other occasions an ornamental banding of filigree or pierced metal was soldered on to hide the streak of copper; but the most frequent way of getting over the difficulty was to solder an edging of silver wire to obscure the copper. If an article, treated in this way, is carefully examined, it will be seen, without much trouble, that the wire is something added to the article itself. With other processes, the edging may be thickened, gadrooned, or otherwise finished; but close inspection will usually show that it is an integral part of the thing and not an addition.

Another Clue.

Since Sheffield plate was a process which made use of sheet metal, it will be recognised that this form of material had serious limitations, unless means to overcome them were devised. For instance, the fashionable teapots, sugar-basins, cream-jugs and other things of those days stood on dainty and decorative legs; but the earliest specimens in Sheffield plate stood flat, without any legs at all. Naturally, this did not serve the purpose of the makers, who wished their wares to look as attractive as those made of solid silver. Accordingly, legs were cast in silver and soldered on to the bodies. This is clearly another useful point to remember.

Fig. 5.—A Sugar Basin.
Showing a pattern much favoured by makers of Sheffield plate.

Characteristics of Sheffield Plate Decoration.

In the case of large and ornate articles, it was a custom for silver pieces to be inscribed with the owner's monogram or crest. What held good for silver had to be followed by Sheffield plate, and it, too, had to be suitably engraved. But here a difficulty arose. To scratch lines on Sheffield plate sufficiently deep to form letters meant that the silver would be pierced and the copper bared. Obviously this would not do; so a way out was devised. To carry the owner's sign, a small shield made of solid silver was sweated on to the Sheffield plate, and it was on this that the monogram or crest was designed. Therefore, whenever the owner's symbol is found on a shield that is an addition to the body of the article, we may very reasonably suspect Sheffield plate. It must not be inferred from this that pieces made by the process could not be decorated with a pattern; but merely that, when they were ornamented, the pattern could only be impressed very lightly.

Distinguishing Electro-plate.

Now, perhaps, it will be well to speak of the characteristics of electro-plate. The silver in this case can be deposited as thickly or thinly as the manufacturer likes. Very often the deposit is remarkably thin, much thinner than was ever the case with Sheffield plate. The thin electric deposit often perishes, when it

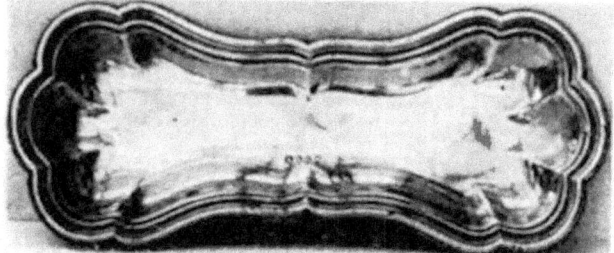

Fig. 6.—A Snuffer Tray in Sheffield Plate.
The edges are masked with a thread of silver wire to hide the streak of copper.

Fig. 7.—Another Snuffer Tray in Sheffield Plate.
The edges are masked with a heavy mounting.

flakes away from the base metal and resembles a piece of silver foil.

Another clue for electro-plate is offered by the feet on which the article stands. If the silver has worn away and the base metal shows through, it is practically certain that the article is an electro; because, as we have already said, the feet for Sheffield ware were nearly always made of solid silver, certainly not a plated silver. Sometimes, it is true, they were composed of silver, loaded with a base metal, but the silver was usually too thick to wear away.

Is the Piece Cast?

The general survey of an article often provides something in the nature of another helpful clue. The patterns, it is true, will not tell us much, because these were copied. When one factory evolved a pleasing design, others imitated it. But we may gain a very good impression by noting whether the article is cast or not. If it is cast, it will probably be thicker in some parts than others, and the thickness will increase or diminish gradually. Casting is, of course, a possible process with electro-plated wares, but not with Sheffield plate. Pieces made on the latter principle are of more or less the same thickness throughout, except for the added bandings, feet, handles and other mounts.

The Factory Marks.

In trying to distinguish between Sheffield plate and electro-plate, it is not advisable to attach too much importance to the factory marks, since some makers have used the same mark on both Sheffield and electro-plate. In addition, many valuable pieces bear no mark at all; in fact, it was an offence at law to mark Sheffield plate in any way between the years 1773 and 1784, because silversmiths complained that the Sheffield ware was being stamped with various devices purposely to imitate real silver.

Value of Sheffield Plate.

Lastly, a word or two about the value of Sheffield plate. If it is really good and in fine condition, it will sell for very nearly as much as a silver article of the same character and age.

Collecting Silver Plate.

In many ways it is more satisfactory to become a collector of Sheffield plate than of articles made of solid silver. The latter is a costly pastime if a representative collection is to be made, since the available articles offer a very extensive range and the period of time concerned is a long one. On the other hand, Sheffield plate was used for a comparatively short while only, and was reserved for a limited class of articles.

As a rule, it is unwise to buy pieces that are in poor condition, and in these days of small houses it is a good plan to collect only those things which are both useful and ornamental.

Pieces should be cleaned no more than is necessary to keep them attractive and in good preservation, while the use of a cheap metal polish must be avoided. The correct method is to rub them occasionally with a good plate powder similar to that intended for silver, and to shine them with a soft chamois leather.

Perhaps it should be said that a piece of Sheffield plate should never be electro-plated when it has become worn in parts. The fresh plating may give the article a more presentable appearance, but its value as a piece of genuine Sheffield plate is lost entirely.

PICKLE AND CHUTNEY RECIPES

PICKLES and chutneys form a welcome addition to the cold meat menu and, given the necessary materials in good condition, a number of appetising recipes can be made up for use when required.

It is essential, in preparing the vegetables and fruits mentioned in the following recipes, that everything be of the best quality and thoroughly clean, if success is to be assured.

CHUTNEYS

Ripe Tomato.

3 lbs of tomatoes.
¼ lb. of Demerara sugar.
1 lb. of sultanas.
1 quart of vinegar.
12 small onions.
1 oz. of mustard seed.
4 teaspoonfuls of salt.
2 teaspoonfuls of pepper.
1 teaspoonful of cayenne.
1 teaspoonful of ground sugar.
2 tablespoonfuls of cornflour.

Boil the tomatoes in the quart of vinegar until quite tender, then strain. Chop the sultanas and onions very fine and add the other ingredients, and boil all together for twenty minutes. Then thicken with the cornflour and boil for ten minutes, stirring all the time to avoid burning. Put into warm jars and tie down.

Another Good Chutney.

3 lbs. of tomatoes.
3 lbs. of apples.
2 lbs. of sultanas.
½ lb. of onions.
2 lbs. of raw sugar.
¼ lb. of salt.
1½ oz. crushed mustard seed.
1 oz. ground ginger.
½ oz. crushed chillies.
2 quarts of best vinegar.

Method of Making.—Peel the tomatoes, peel and slice the apples. (Which should be good, reliable cookers.) Clean and chop the sultanas, and chop the onions.

Boil the tomatoes, apples and onions in one quart of vinegar until soft, then add the other ingredients together with the other quart of vinegar. Bring to the boil and continue boiling until the ingredients thicken to about the consistency of jam.

Or Try This.

Another very appetising chutney is as follows:—

2 lbs. of marrow.
¾ lb of Demerara sugar.
¼ lb. onions.
¼ lb. sultanas.
1 lb. of green apples.
1½ oz. of crushed ginger.
3 or 4 chillies.
¾ oz. of turmeric powder.
1½ oz. of mustard.
3½ pints of vinegar.

Method.—Cut up the marrows and onions quite small and boil in the vinegar for about three hours. Mix the turmeric powder and mustard with cold vinegar, and add to the above when nearly done. If rather thicker chutney is liked, add a little cornflour with the turmeric powder and mustard. Boil up just long enough to thicken.

PICKLES

Mustard Pickle.

This is a delicious recipe for those fond of mustard pickle.

Take equal quantities of onions, cauliflower, beans, or any other vegetables liked, and cover with brine. (The latter is prepared by adding a teacupful of salt to two quarts of water.) Leave the vegetables in soak until the next day. Pour off the brine into a saucepan and bring it to the boil, then pour it over the vegetables again, leave to get quite cold, and then strain.

Boil enough vinegar to cover the vegetables, adding a teacupful of Demerara sugar to each quart; also mix to a smooth paste half a teacupful of cornflour, 2 ozs. of dry mustard, and one dessertspoonful of turmeric powder. These quantities are also required in respect of each quart of vinegar used. When the vinegar boils pour it very slowly into the paste, stirring well all the time; now pour it over the already prepared vegetables while hot, and bottle when quite cold.

This is ready to eat in a week or two.

How to Use Boring Tools
DEALING WITH THE BRADAWL, GIMLET, BRACE AND DRILL

THE tools most used for boring and drilling holes in wood are the bradawl, gimlet, brace and drill. In this article details are given of the best methods of using and taking care of these tools.

THE BRADAWL

As the bradawl is probably the simplest of all boring tools we will deal with this first. Its chief use is for boring holes for screws, and it can only be used for comparatively small holes. The hole made by the bradawl is that in which the actual screw part of the screw engages and not the hole through which the shank passes.

It resembles a very small screwdriver and the edge is sharpened on an oilstone in a similar manner to a chisel, except that both sides are sharpened equally. When the edge has been sharpened several times, it will probably be found that the bevel has become rather steep, giving it a thick edge. The correct treatment then is to file a long bevel and finish the edge on the oilstone.

One of the great advantages of the bradawl is that it is intended for use with one hand only. Therefore it is particularly useful when a door has to be hung single-handed; the door being supported with one hand while the holes for the screws are bored with the other.

Using the Bradawl.

When using the bradawl the edge should be held at right angles to the grain as shown in Fig. 1, so that it cuts its way through the wood and does not split the grain as it might if the edge were parallel to the grain. Do not rock the bradawl about, but turn it back and forth without leaning to one side or the other. This is specially important if the bradawl is a thin one.

THE GIMLET

The gimlet is another tool used for boring small holes for screws. Its main advantage lies in the fact that as it has a screw end very little force is required to use it; the small screw at its end pulls it down into the wood.

One drawback to the gimlet is the risk of splitting the wood when this tool is used. On this account it should not be used near the end of a piece of wood. This is particularly the case with soft woods such as deal. The gimlet is not very suitable for boring into end grain as the screw at its end cannot obtain a good grip.

Using the Gimlet.

Always start the gimlet absolutely upright. It will be difficult to correct any inaccuracy in the direction of the hole being bored once it is well into the wood.

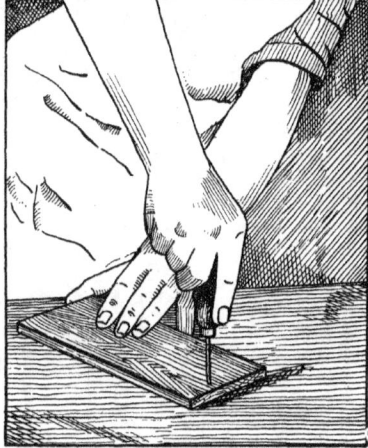

Fig. 1.—How to use the Bradawl.
Note that the edge should be held at right angles to the grain, so that it cuts its way through the wood and does not split the grain, as it might if the edge were parallel to the grain.

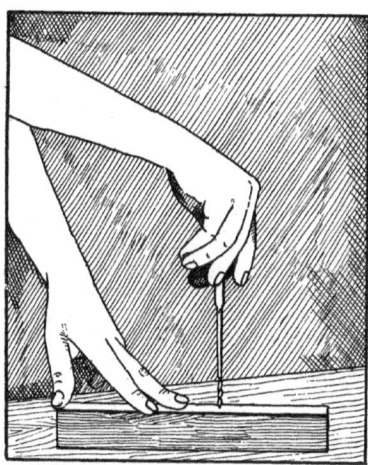

Fig. 2.—How to use the Gimlet.
Always start the gimlet absolutely upright. The gimlet should not be used near the end of a piece of wood because of the risk of splitting the wood.

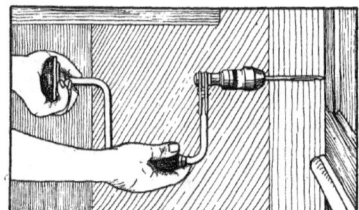

Fig. 3.—Using a Ratchet Brace.
The ratchet brace is particularly suitable in circumstances such as shown above, when a hole is to be drilled near a corner, and the wall would prevent the crank of a plain brace from being turned through a complete revolution.

Sharpening the Gimlet.

After a considerable period of use, the gimlet loses its edge. A small round file, known as a rat-tail file, is needed to sharpen it again. Hold the file flat in the hollow spiral and gradually revolve the gimlet whilst the file is working, so that the latter gradually travels towards the end. The method of holding the file on the gimlet is clearly shown in Fig. 8. Remember to keep the file in alignment with the spiral of the bit. The screw part near and at the actual tip can be touched up with a three-cornered file.

THE BRACE

The brace is a more complicated and efficient boring tool than the bradawl and gimlet. Large holes can be cut with ease because of the leverage given by the sweep of the crank. Bits for use with the brace are obtainable in a wide variety of sizes.

There are two types—the plain brace and the ratchet brace, the latter being specially useful for working in awkward corners when the full sweep of the crank cannot be made. It can also be adjusted to turn in either direction while a locking device enables it to be used as a plain brace when required.

How to use a Brace.

Generally it will be found most convenient to hold the brace upright when boring. Allow the forehead to rest on the left hand, unless quite a small bit is being used. This helps to steady the tool and enables a heavier pressure to be applied.

Fig. 3 shows a typical instance where the ratchet brace has a definite advantage over the plain type. The latter could not be used because the wall would prevent the crank from being turned through a complete revolution. With the ratchet brace, however, it is taken through half a stroke and then reversed. The crank moves backwards, but the bit remains stationary until the crank is brought downwards again.

Auger or Twist Bit.

The auger or twist bit bores a perfectly straight hole. It has a small screw end which pulls it into the wood so that it is not necessary to maintain heavy pressure. The spiral body of the bit fills up the hole as it is made, so that the point cannot move out of the straight, thus ensuring a perfectly true hole.

A typical example of the use of the twist bit is for making a dowel hole as shown in Fig. 5. The piece of wood is gripped in a vice and the worker stands at one end so that he looks down the edge and not across it. The

HOW TO USE BORING TOOLS

Fig. 4.—Boring with the Centre Bit.

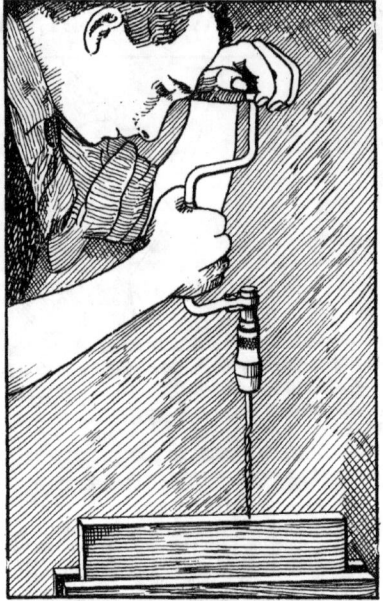

Fig. 5.—Boring at Edge of Wood for Dowelling.

Fig. 6.—How to use a Tee Square to gauge the Verticality of a Brace.

reason for this is that although the hole should be as dead upright as possible it is better for it to lean in a direction parallel with the wood than in one at right angles with it, if any error is to occur at all. It is a simple matter to tell whether the brace should lean more to the left or right, but it is more difficult to gauge whether one is leaning too far forward or not.

When boring a Number of Holes of Equal Depth.

If it is required to bore a number of holes all of equal depth a useful hint is to stick a piece of paper on to the bit at the desired distance from the end and to bore in as far as this each time.

Using Twist Bit in mortising.

Another use for the twist bit is when a mortise has to be cut. As much of the waste wood as possible should be removed by boring as shown in Fig. 6. Use a bit that is about $\frac{1}{16}$ inch smaller than the width of the required mortise.

Testing Verticality of the Brace.

A good method of testing the verticality of a brace when it is especially important that the hole being drilled should be exactly at right angles, is by placing an ordinary bench square near the work as a guide, as shown in Fig. 6. Any inaccuracy will then be immediately noticeable.

Centre Bit.

The centre bit is generally used for boring large holes in thin woods. As the point is liable to run in the grain of the wood its use is not advised for deep holes in thick wood when it is important that the hole is straight. For this reason it is not used for dowelling where a straight hole is imperative. It is especially liable to run out of truth in end grain.

Using the Centre Bit.

The method of using the centre bit for thin woods is first to mark out the centre of the hole required, then place the centre of the bit on it and start boring. The pointed cutter will reach the wood first and will cut in the circumference of the circle. Then the knife-edge cutter follows, and shavings are gradually taken off until the hole gets deeper and deeper.

As soon as the centre point of the bit projects through the wood at the underside, the wood should be reversed and the boring finished from this side, placing the point of the bit in the hole.

Special attention should be paid to finishing off when using the centre bit, as there is danger of the bit being forced right through before the cutting is properly finished.

Should this happen, the bit will be locked and the core will have to be removed with a gouge or some other tool.

It is advisable to cramp the wood firmly to the bench with a handscrew, as shown in Fig. 4 when boring holes with the centre bit. The method of sharpening this bit is described on p. 589.

Gimlet Bit.

The gimlet bit should never be used for thin wood or near the edge of a board owing to its tendency to split the grain. It is similar in this and other respects to the ordinary gimlet. The method of sharpening is the same as for the gimlet.

Fig. 7.—Using the Brace in a Horizontal Position.

Fig. 8.—Sharpening the Gimlet Bit.

HOW TO USE BORING TOOLS

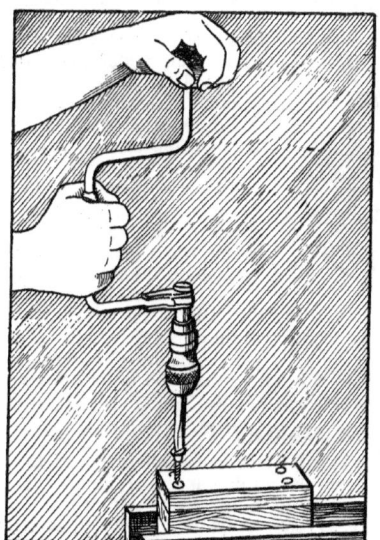

Fig. 9.—Putting in a Screw with a Turnscrew Bit.

The Countersink.

This is a tool used to cut a depression in the end of a hole to allow a screw to sink in flush with the surface of the wood. There are two types generally used—the snail countersink and the rose countersink. The former has a hollowed-out depression which forms the cutting edge and which is kept sharp by running a rat-tail file along the depression. The latter has several cutting edges and is somewhat similar to a bevelled cogwheel in appearance. Brass as well as wood can be dealt with with a rose countersink.

Turnscrew Bit.

The turnscrew, as its name suggests, is used for driving home screws, and is particularly useful and labour-saving when a large number of screws have to be driven in as in the case of screwing on the back of a large cabinet. All the screws can be started and then driven in with the brace and turnscrew bit. Far more leverage can, of course, be obtained than is the case with a screwdriver, while it can also often be used to advantage for removing an old screw that has become rusted in.

DRILLS

When very small holes are required, it will be found more convenient to use a drill. The bits used with the brace are too large for very small holes, but drill bits are obtainable in small sizes. As a rule they have a V point, and can be sharpened on the oilstone.

Archimedean Drill.

The archimedean drill is one of the most handy types, and the method of using it is shown in Fig. 10. When drilling thin wood the work should be fixed down on a flat bench or board to

Shell Bit.

The shell bit is also used for boring holes for screws, and can be used for all the purposes for which the gimlet bit is used without any danger of splitting.

As it has no screw point rather more pressure is required than is the case with the gimlet bit.

Sharpening the Shell Bit.

The shell bit is sharpened on an oilstone in a similar manner to a gouge. A file can be used to restore the bevel when it becomes too acute as the result of several sharpenings.

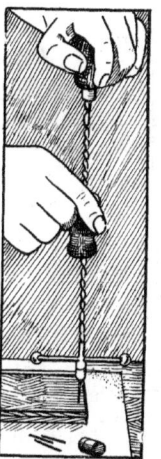

Fig. 10.—The Archimedean Drill.

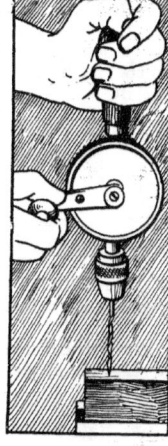

Fig. 11.—The Metal Hand Drill.

prevent the drill splintering the underside as it comes through.

A typical example of the use of the archimedean drill is when two small thin pieces of wood are to be pinned together. If the nails were driven straight into them there would be danger of splitting unless the holes were first made with the drill.

Metal Hand Drill.

Another useful type of drill is the metal hand drill shown in Fig. 11. It will be seen that the handle is fitted to a geared wheel which makes the bit revolve as the handle is turned.

As a rule metal working drill bits are used with this tool; they are, however, quite suitable for drilling in wood and have, in fact, the advantage that they are very unlikely to cause the wood to split.

THREE INEXPENSIVE COOKERY RECIPES

Savoury Rissoles.

Mix together 2 breakfastcupfuls of cold potatoes, which should be mashed with milk and a good knob of butter, one breakfastcupful of breadcrumbs, the remains of any cold meat finely minced, ½ lb. fresh minced beef, 1 small teaspoonful of sweet herbs, and salt to taste; 1 egg should be mixed with the ingredients to bind them together. Minced onion can be added if liked.

Make into firm shapes, roll in flour, and fry to a nice deep brown colour in boiling fat.

If there is plenty of cold meat, the minced beef can be omitted. Should the meat be ham or pork, sage should be used to season instead of mixed herbs.

Lentil Cutlets.

These are very nice and a most inexpensive dish. Take 1 pint of lentils, ½ lb. of breadcrumbs, 2 large onions, 1 dessertspoonful of butter, 1 tablespoonful of O.K. or similar sauce, 1 egg, pepper and salt to taste.

Boil the lentils until soft enough to mash, strain and mix with the onions (which should be very finely chopped) and the breadcrumbs. Add the butter and seasonings, mix in the egg, make into cakes, roll in flour, and fry to a nice golden brown.

Risotto.

Put a finely chopped onion into a stewpan with 2 ozs. of butter, and fry to a pale brown. Add ½ lb. of well-washed rice, stirring constantly for a few minutes with a wooden spoon; then add ½ pint of good stock gradually, and simmer gently until rice is just soft, stirring frequently.

Before quite finished, add about 3 ozs. of grated cheese (Parmesan is best), but odd pieces of cheese can be used up quite well in this way. Boil up for a minute, and serve in a hot dish. A little more butter added to the final boiling up is an improvement.

Making a Child's Pedal or Electric Motor Car

CHILDREN love any kind of car on wheels, much more so a really smart machine, such as that illustrated in Fig. 1, and capable of propulsion by foot power or, if preferred, by means of an electric motor and accumulator.

Despite the imposing appearance of this toy motor car, it is not by any means difficult to make, if the work is carried out in due order.

There is considerable scope for the exercise of individual ideas in the construction of this model, but the main dimensions here given should be fairly closely followed.

Fig. 1.—The Finished Motor Car.
Based on a modern type of open sports car.

Materials Required.

The following comprise the principal items for the pedal-driven toy motor car.

Chassis.—One complete set comprising wheels, axles, steering gear, pedal gear and chain. Wheel track, 16 inches; wheel diameter, 10 inches.

Frame and Body. — Hardwood "stripwood," $\frac{7}{8}$ inch thick, $1\frac{1}{2}$ inches wide, 3 pieces 4 feet long, 4 pieces 15 inches long; 1 sheet "Venesta" plywood, $\frac{3}{16}$ inch thick, 50 × 24 inches; 1 sheet plywood, $\frac{1}{8}$ inch thick, 48 × 48 inches; 1 piece plywood, $\frac{3}{8}$ inch thick, about 24 inches wide, 36 inches long; deal, 2 pieces, $1\frac{1}{2}$ × 2 × 20 inches.

Batten.—One inch wide, $\frac{1}{2}$ inch thick, 3 pieces 4 feet long. These quantities allow for cutting and shaping.

Fittings.

These are optional, but are inexpensive and add enormously to the appearance of the finished machine. Plated radiator front, windscreen, one pair dummy headlights, one tail light, dummy starting handle and click, one pair number plates, and dummy speedometer, clock and licence holder fronts, for dash-board mounting. Hooter and spare wheel.

Electric Motor Equipment.

For driving the model a regulation motor-car starting motor and a 6- or 12-volt accumulator are admirable and can generally be purchased second-hand at small cost, together with a "pedal" starter switch. The latter is very useful because the young driver has to keep it depressed as long as the machine is running; immediately the pressure is released the current is cut off and the motor stops. Most of these have "lugs" or metal straps with which they are fastened to the engine and the same fittings can be used again.

The power required to drive the toy motor car will depend partly on the weight of the passenger and the nature of the road, but as a basis an output of about 60 watts would normally be ample—in other words, the current consumption would be about 12 amperes at 6 volts or 5 amperes at 12 volts as a maximum.

Commencing the Work.

The general design of this toy motor (Fig. 2) is based on an up-to-date sports model two-seater—a fine, appealing type—that is reasonably simple to make and is very strong, because each side is formed in one piece without a doorway opening.

First make the frame, which, as is shown in Fig. 3, consists of two outer members, three principal cross members and a central bar on which the pedal gear is mounted.

Dimensions are given in the drawing (Fig. 3), and are suitable for the usual stock size "chassis" or underworks, but before actually starting the work measure the distance between the centres of the springs on the axles of the chassis and make the distance between the centres of the outer members of the wooden frame the same, so that the springs can be bolted direct to the woodwork.

Cross Members.

The various cross members of the frame should be jointed to the sides by a simple form of housing joint shown in Fig. 4, the depth of the housing being not more than $\frac{1}{4}$ inch.

Fasten the cross members with glue and a single long screw to each joint.

Central Bar.

The central bar is notched to fit on to the cross members, for which purpose a diagonal notch is cut in each cross bar, as shown in Fig. 5, the wedge-shaped parts serving to locate and hold the pieces in position, but a firm joint must be made with glue and a screw as before.

Take care to keep the frame perfectly flat while making the joints, then strengthen them with triangular blocks of wood, glued and pinned in to all internal angles.

A piece of $\frac{3}{8}$-inch plywood (shown in Fig. 6) should be prepared and fitted on to the back of the frame; it is merely glued and screwed to the bottom faces of the frame at the back. A plain round bar $\frac{3}{4}$ inch diameter made of hardwood dowelling is fitted across the front end of the frame, and the top and bottom edges of the frame tapered towards it.

Building up the Body.

The front of the body consists of a piece of $\frac{3}{8}$-inch plywood, cut to shape as in Fig. 7, and intended as the foundation of the dummy radiator front. This board is screwed to the front of the first cross member on

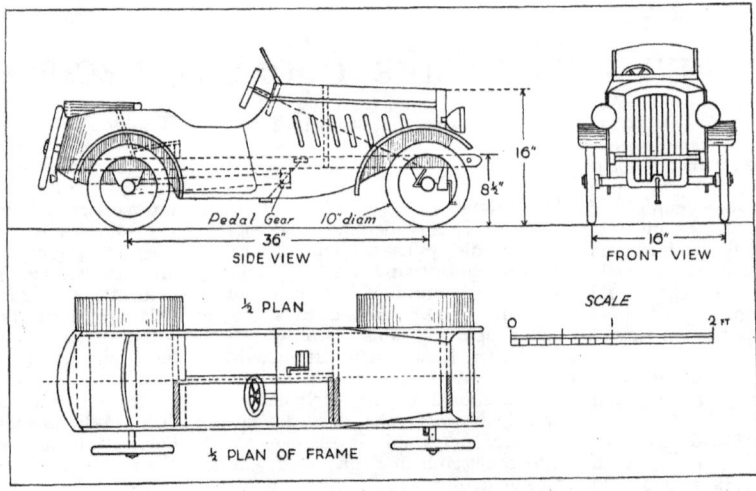

Fig. 2.—Working Drawings for the Motor Car.

MAKING A CHILD'S PEDAL OR ELECTRIC MOTOR CAR

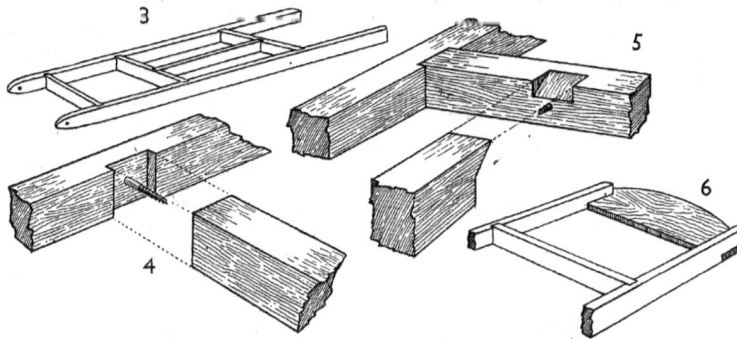

Figs. 3–6.—Details of Frame and Joints.
3. The two side members of the main frame are connected by cross-pieces and a central member. 4. Simple housed joints are used at the sides. 5. The centre joints. 6. The backboard in place.

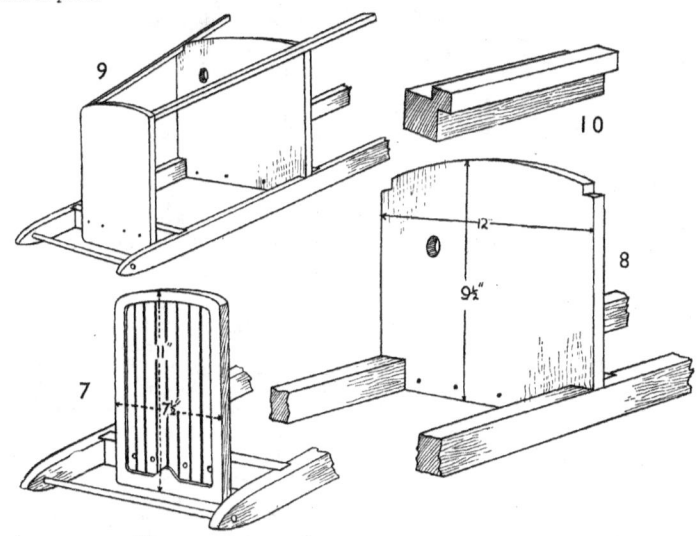

Figs. 7–10.—Details of Radiator, Dashboard, etc.
7. The front is painted black and can be faced with a dummy plated radiator or with vertical strips of wood and an edging to represent the radiator. 8. A strong plywood member supports the bonnet top and steering column. 9. Details of the front. 10. Section of side rail.

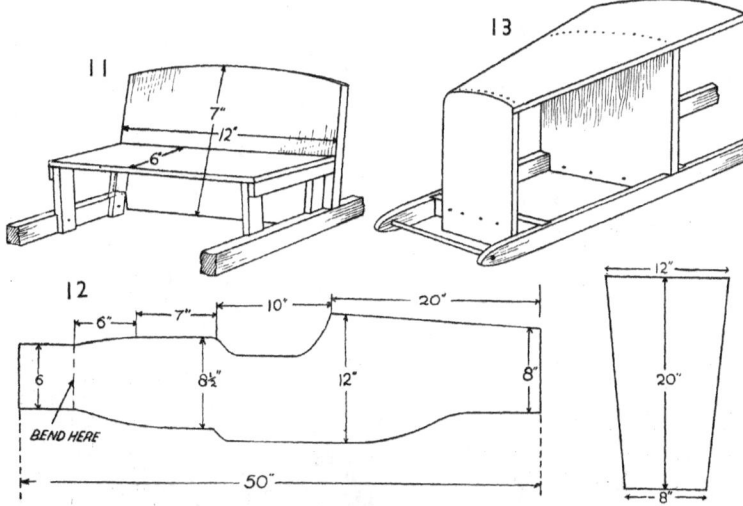

Figs. 11–13.—Arrangement of Seat Frames (11); Shape of Side Pieces (12); and Top of Bonnet (13).

the frame and projects below it slightly. Next cut out the dashboard (shown in Fig. 8), and screw this to the second cross member of the frame.

If making a motor-driven machine a large rectangular piece should be sawn from the centre of it and be hinged to provide access to the front part of the frame, where the motor and accumulator will later be fitted.

Next take two pieces of deal about $1\frac{1}{2}$ inches square and 20 inches long, and fix the front ends to the top corners of the radiator, as in Fig. 9, and glue them into notches in the corners of the dashboard.

Next work a rebate on the side and another on the top, leaving a solid part at the corner, as seen clearly in the sectional sketch Fig. 10, the rebates being $\frac{3}{16}$ inch deep; their purpose is to take the top and side pieces of plywood that compose the body.

The Seat Framing.

This is composed of batten about 1 inch wide, $\frac{1}{2}$ inch thick, glued and screwed to the frame and connected by the seat and backboard, both of which should be cut from $\frac{3}{8}$-inch plywood and glued and screwed together, as shown in Fig. 11, and also in Fig. 2, the general arrangement working drawing.

The next step is to prepare the two side pieces (shown in Fig. 12) by cutting to shape with a fretsaw. Plywood $\frac{3}{16}$ inch thick will suffice for these pieces, and when cut they should be glued and nailed to the edges of the radiator, dash-board and seat framing.

Note that at the front the sides fit above the frame, at the centre they drop below the bottom line of the frame, but sweep upwards at the back.

The sides should be fitted carefully into the rebate on the rail between the radiator and dash-board, for which purpose a sharp chisel or a small plane will be needed to remove any surplus from the edges and ensure a close fit.

The side pieces have to be sent around the back to fit closely to the curbed board, but this bending is best done by easy stages, for which purpose the ends of the wood can be drawn into place with cords and left for an hour or so to enable the wood to acquire a certain amount of curvature.

Finishing the Bonnet.

Next fit the bonnet top (shown in Fig. 13); it merely fits into the rebates on the rails and on top of the curved tops of the radiator and dash-board.

When fixed with glue and fine cabinet pins, round off the outer corners of the two rails, thus blending the curve of the bonnet top with the side pieces.

The instrument board (Fig. 14) should now be sawn to shape, then fitted nicely to the inner end of the bonnet top and to the sides. The edges of the board will have to be bevelled and shaped to fit nicely into place, and should then be fixed with glue and pins.

The back of the body can now be finished off by cutting the top board to the shape shown in Fig. 15, and then gluing and screwing it to the seat framing and to the edges of the side pieces, which by now should have acquired a reasonable amount of permanent curvature and be easily forced into place and held there with glue and screws driven into the bottom board and with very fine screws or nails into the edge of the top piece. The sides may project above the top board, but any such happening can be corrected after the glue has set by planing away the surplus and finishing by sandpapering.

This completes the main part of the bodywork except for the triangular filling pieces at the front, which have to be glued and pinned to the top of the frame at the front.

Mounting the Body.

The body and frame should now be turned upside-down and the wheels and axles screwed very securely to the frame, using stout wood screws with round heads. Take care to fix the axles exactly at right angles to the centre of the frame and be sure they are absolutely parallel. This can be tested by measuring the distance between the axle caps on each side; the distance should of course be the same on both sides.

Steering Gear.

The steering gear is quite simple—it is a plain bar with the steering wheel on the inner end; a short arm at the front connects to the steering arms or "track rod" on the front axle. The steering bar or "column" should be fitted through holes drilled for that purpose in the dash-board and the instrument board.

Fixing the Pedal Gear.

In the case of the pedal-driven car it only remains to screw the complete pedal gear to the centre bar on the frame, placing it at such a position that the child when seated in the car can rotate the pedals with ease. The driving chain is then fitted.

Fitting up the Electric Motor.

The electric motor must first be provided with two bearers of hardwood about $1\frac{1}{2} \times 1\frac{1}{4}$ inches, which must be securely screwed to the frame between the two front members, and so placed that the motor

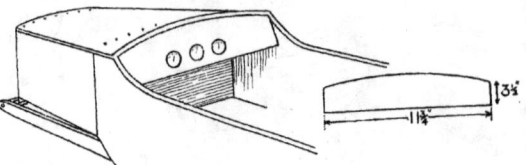

Fig. 14.—The Instrument Board in Place.
This fits under the end of the bonnet top and to the sides.

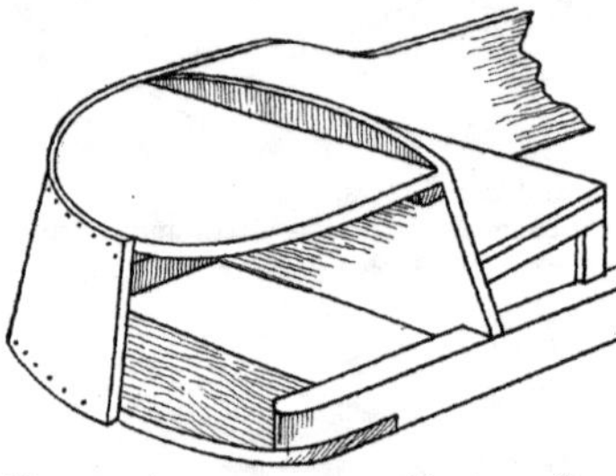

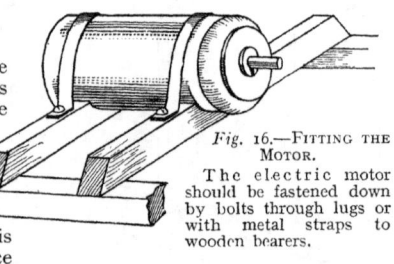

Fig. 15.—Arrangement of Back of Car.
The plywood backboard and one side are shown fixed.

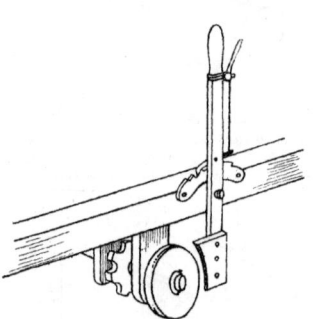

Fig. 16.—Fitting the Motor.
The electric motor should be fastened down by bolts through lugs or with metal straps to wooden bearers.

Fig. 17.—Brake Gear.
A pulley is fixed on the pedal gear spindle and a fibre block in the end of the lever is used as a brake pad. The quadrant and latch is optional.

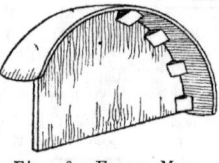

Fig. 18.—Front Mudguards.
This shows the scheme for making plywood "wings" or mudguards; shape and sizes should be as shown in Fig. 2.

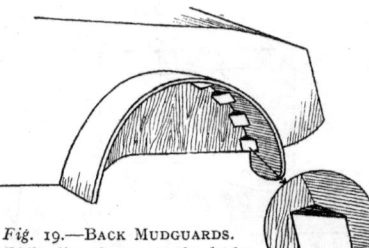

Fig. 19.—Back Mudguards.
Built directly on to the body side and secured with angle glue blocks.

spindle will be parallel to the back axle and the driving end of the motor be in line with the side of the pedal gear.

The sketch, Fig. 16, shows what is really required better than it can be expressed in words. Exact dimensions cannot be given because of the wide variation of types of electric motor that can be used for the purpose.

The motor should be fixed by screws through holding-down lugs, when same are provided on the motor, otherwise metal straps about $\frac{3}{4}$ inch wide and $\frac{1}{16}$ inch thick can be fitted bodily over the motor and screwed to the wood frame.

Transmission Gear.

Some form of speed reduction gear must be provided in the transmission between the motor spindle and the pedal gear. Some starter motors have a self-contained reduction gear, and when this type is used could be connected directly by a belt or chain drive, but in other cases a reduction will have to be used.

The method of determining the correct ratio is to settle upon the maximum speed of the car, say about 4 m.p.h. or 450 feet per minute. Divide this by the periphery of the road wheel in feet—which for practical purposes can be taken as 3 feet. The answer—in this example 150—is the number of turns per minute of the road wheels to drive the car at a speed of about 4 m.p.h.

The next step is to ascertain the speed of the motor—that is, its number of revolutions per minute—or in the case of a motor with a reduction gear, the number of turns per minute of the driving spindle.

Assuming a motor speed of 1,000 r.p.m., it follows that the reduction gear must have a ratio of 1,000 to 150, or, say, 7 to 1. This means that a small pulley, say 1 inch diameter, must be fixed on the motor spindle and a large wheel 7 inches diameter fixed on the spindle of the pedal gear.

Ordinary commercial V pulleys can be used and connected by a twisted rawhide belt, as used for driving small machines. Alternatively, chains could be used or a pair of spur gears, but the belt drive is generally the best. The pedals can be removed from the pedal spindle and the large wheel fixed direct to it on one side, and on the other should be fixed a similar wheel to be used as a brake drum.

Brake Gear.

The brake gear can be quite simple (as

MAKING A CHILD'S PEDAL OR ELECTRIC MOTOR CAR

Fig. 20.—The Windscreen.

The fitting is purchased ready-made and fixed to a cross member curved on the lower edge to fit on to the bonnet end.

shown in Fig. 17), and consist of an oak, or preferably metal lever pivoted on a stout bolt to the centre frame member. The lower end of the lever has a block of red fibre screwed to it and shaped to fit in the V groove on the brake drum.

If a second-hand motor-car brake lever of a small size can be obtained, it can be used very successfully in this way, and the ratchet and quadrant gear be used to hold the brake in the " on " position.

Connecting up the Motor.

The accumulator should be a regular " starter " battery, and be housed in a simple wooden framework built on to the frame at the opposite side to the motor.

Connections are normally from the negative or black terminal direct to one terminal on the motor. The red or positive terminal on the battery is connected to the pedal starter switch, which should be fixed on a footboard fastened across the frame in a comfortable position for the young driver's foot.

From the second terminal of the starter switch a wire is taken to the second terminal on the motor. Use very good quality, well-insulated cable for the connections. Cab tyre sheathed cable known in the trade as C.T.S. will be found most serviceable for this purpose. Fit a switch in the negative lead so that the current can be switched off and the starter switch rendered inoperative when necessary.

It is, of course, possible to omit the starter pedal switch and use only a simple " on-off " switch, but it is far safer for the young driver to have always to hold the switch down with his foot, since if an accident should happen the foot will almost certainly come off the switch and the motor at once be stopped, whereas with only an " on-off " switch the motor car will continue to travel until deliberately switched off.

Finishing the Toy Motor Car.

After a preliminary road trial the motor can be completed and finished. The mudguards can be made from ⅜-inch plywood or be purchased, ready to fasten in place. The plywood guards are quite serviceable, and Fig. 18 shows how the front guards are made. They consist of a flat piece, screwed to the side of the frame, and the projecting part then bent round and secured with glue and pins. The inner angle should be strengthened by triangular-shaped blocks of wood glued in place.

The back mudguards (Fig. 19) are plain strips of plywood bent to a semi-circular shape and fastened by glue blocks direct to the sides of the body.

The windscreen (Fig. 20) is supplied with a wooden piece at the bottom, which has merely to be curved to fit on the top of the bonnet and secured there with glue and screws. Lamps, a spare wheel, and other details already mentioned can be fitted to personal choice.

The appearance of the car is greatly enhanced by narrow half-round moulding glued and pinned to the top edge

Fig. 21.—Dummy Hood.
A lath is bent to a U-shape and covered with brown waterproof material.

of the body and to outline the low dummy doorway.

Short pieces of the same moulding can be glued at regular intervals to the sides of the bonnet to represent the louvres on a real car. The seat and back rest can also be padded with Kapok and covered with Rexine and a dummy hood made from brown waterproof material stretched over a frame, as sketched in Fig. 21, and the whole screwed to the sides of the body at the back of the seat.

The best finish is to apply several coats of good under-coating paint of the chosen colour and finish with " Brushing Belco," or one of the special motor-car enamels sold in convenient size tins for car renovation purposes. The instrument board should be stained brown and varnished, and dummy speedometer and fittings added afterwards.

Suggested colour schemes are red body, black wings, cream wheels. Green body, black wings and wheels. Grey body, blue lining, cream wheels, black wings or mudguards.

All the smaller fittings should be removed while the painting is in progress.

When an electric motor is used the transmission gear must be entirely enclosed in a simple plywood or metal cover screwed to the centre frame member, and all so arranged that neither fingers nor feet could get entangled in the gear.

REMEDYING LOOSE AND WORN DOOR KNOBS

THE somewhat older types of door knob, of which many are still in use and giving good service as far as latch and lock portion are concerned, are, however, often found badly worn and loose in the recess where the metal part of the knob fits into the outer guide plates on the outside of the door. They make the door unnecessarily noisy.

A fairly thick washer is usually required to take up this worn space, one which will just go over the square bolt rod and snugly fit down into the plate recess. A considerable number

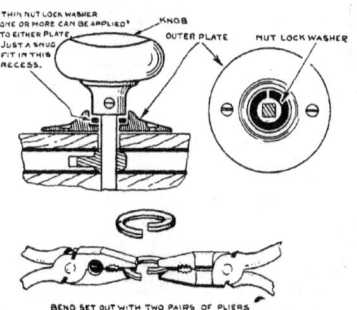

of ⅜-inch thin nut lock washers can be bought for a few pence. These measure a trifle over ⅝ inch on the outside and drop snugly down into the outer plate recess. The inside diameter is just sufficient to go nicely over the square latch or handle rod. The set or spring is easily taken or bent out of the washers with pliers so they will lie flat in the plate recess.

A considerable number of old locks can be quickly and easily given snug handling and noiseless knobs in this simple inexpensive manner.

Repairing a Conservatory Roof

The roof of a conservatory probably receives less attention than any other part of the house, and is often left unrepaired until it is in a dangerous state. Apart from the annoyance of large patches of wet on the floor after a shower of rain, the fact that the woodwork is allowed to become rotted makes the danger from falling glass quite a considerable one.

One of the main reasons why a conservatory roof is neglected is due to its inaccessibility, especially in the case of lean-to buildings, but this is not a very serious objection if the methods outlined in this article are followed.

Locating the Leaks.

The first thing to do, however, is to locate the position of any weak and leaky spots.

For obvious reasons, the best time to do this is on a rainy day when the water is coming in. Do not assume that the leaks are necessarily above the spots where the puddles form. It is quite likely that they will be located somewhere higher up, the water finding its way through the wooden stays and running along before it drops. The method of determining the exact spot is to run a finger along the woodwork towards the highest part of the roof, until the point where the woodwork is dry is reached. Make a mark with a pencil at this spot; do not rely on your memory, especially if several spots are found.

As it is useless to attempt any repair from inside the roof, it will now be necessary to wait until the rain ceases and the woodwork has become dry. Temporary measures to keep the rain out from inside will probably do more harm than good, and will only encourage the decaying of the wood.

Obtaining access to the Roof.

Unless you are quite certain that the framework of the conservatory is in a perfectly sound condition, as, for example, if simply replacing a pane that has become accidentally broken in a newly erected building, it is unwise to attempt to get on the roof by using a board fixed to the horizontal rows of metal projections that are provided for this purpose on most roofs. It is safer to do the work by some other means, even if it entails a certain amount of extra trouble. The lowest panes of glass can, of course, be quite easily reached by standing on the top rung of a step ladder placed close to the side of the conservatory. But make sure the ladder is placed quite firmly, so that you do not have to make any sudden wild movements to regain your balance.

Access to other panes can be obtained by opening the skylight and standing on a ladder placed immediately below it, while others can probably be reached by leaning out of a window in the house.

Even when all these possibilities have been explored, it will probably be found that there are some parts of the roof that still seem inaccessible. To reach these parts it will be necessary to obtain a piece of wood 1 inch square and about 2 or 3 yards long. To the end of this a putty knife or paint brush can be fixed quite firmly with string. It is, in fact, advisable to prepare two of these implements, one for the putty knife or brush and another with a piece of rag attached to the end for wiping off any paint that may drop on to the glass.

First remove the Putty.

The first thing to do is to scrape away all the old and cracked putty and then remove all the loose powdery material by sweeping the crevices with a long-handled broom. The new putty can then be applied. It should be soft and plastic, and the best method of bringing it to this condition is to work it about in the hands for a few minutes. It is applied with the putty knife, and Fig. 3 shows how the improvised tool is used for this purpose. Allow the putty to overlap the glass for at least a ¼ inch; it should also rise up to the uppermost edge of the wooden beading.

When all the faulty places have been treated with new putty, two coats of a good white lead paint should be applied. It is advisable to paint the whole of the wooden ribs while one is about it, and not just the parts that have been filled in with putty. When using the brush tied to the pole, the paint should not be used too lavishly, although if any drops of paint should fall on the glass they can easily be wiped away with the second pole.

Refitting the Panes.

In the case of a roof where there are several panes broken and all the putty has more or less perished, it is best to remove all the panes and refit them.

Start removing the panes at the lowest edge of the roof and work upwards. Do not forget that one pane is arranged to overlap another, so that before a lower pane is dislodged the one above it must be loosened.

When all the panes have been removed, all old putty must be scraped away from the wooden ribs.

Replacing the Panes.

A start can now be made with replacing the panes, sufficient new ones having been obtained to take the place of the broken ones. The panes are relaid from the top so that the work can be carried out by standing on a pair of steps placed inside the conservatory.

Run a thin strip of putty along the

Fig. 1.—A Typical Example of Trouble due to a Defective Joint.

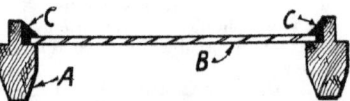

Fig. 2.—Sectional View showing Wooden Stays (A), Pane of Glass (B) and Fillet of Putty (C).

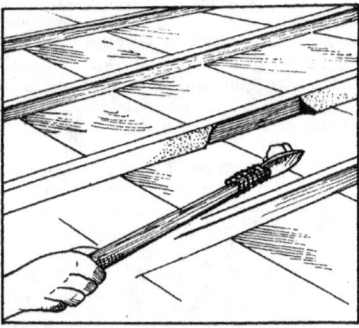

Fig. 3.—Showing how a Putty Knife can be Attached to a Long Pole for Dealing with Spots that are Out of Ordinary Reach.

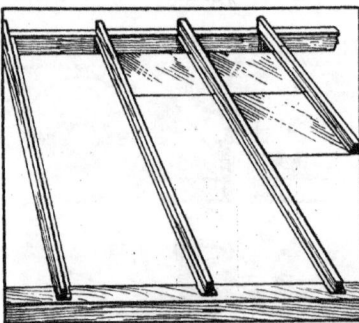

Fig. 4.—When refitting the Panes, start at the Top and Work downwards.

wooden bed on which the glass rests and place the top pane in position.

Now take another pane and slide it under the first one for at least an inch. Now take some more putty and put a bevelled fillet along the two sloping edges, allowing it to lap over the glass at least a ¼ inch.

After two or three panes have been fixed in this manner and before the first pane fitted is out of reach, the wooden strips should be painted. By doing it at this stage there is no need to use the long-handled brush.

Faulty Lead or Zinc Edging.

Lean-to roofs generally have a strip of sheet lead or zinc fixed where the conservatory roof meets the brickwork of the house. If this sheeting becomes loose or twisted, rain will work its way underneath and into the conservatory. Examination of the sheeting will show that one edge is tucked into the pointing between two rows of bricks.

The first thing to do is to rake out the old pointing and press the edge of the metal firmly into the lines that have been opened out. Then make up some cement, gauged one part of Portland cement to two of sharp sand, into a wettish paste and repoint the brickwork. Wet the bricks thoroughly before applying the cement with the tip of a trowel.

Now examine the part of the sheeting which overlaps the glass panes. This may have cockled up and become twisted due to the heat of the sun. If so, press it down again and run a fillet of putty under the edge to make it perfectly watertight.

Dealing with a Sagging Roof.

Another fault that is likely to occur after a conservatory has been erected for some time is a sagging roof, *i.e.*, the wooden fillets carrying the glass have become curved and bowed, as shown at A in Fig. 7. Prompt treatment is advisable, for there is danger of the roof crashing.

The best treatment is, of course, to remove all the glass and fit new fillets of wood, making sure that they are supported at both ends on sound horizontal beams, but, as this is rather a costly and laborious business, a simpler treatment will be described.

It consists of supporting the old roof on a purlin or beam which passes under the roof from side to side about midway across the sagging part, as shown at B and C in Fig. 7.

A suitable beam for this purpose is one about 3 inches square in section, and it must be supported at either end on a stout piece of woodwork.

No attempt should be made to force the roof back to its original position before fitting the purlin, or the whole structure may be loosened and damaged.

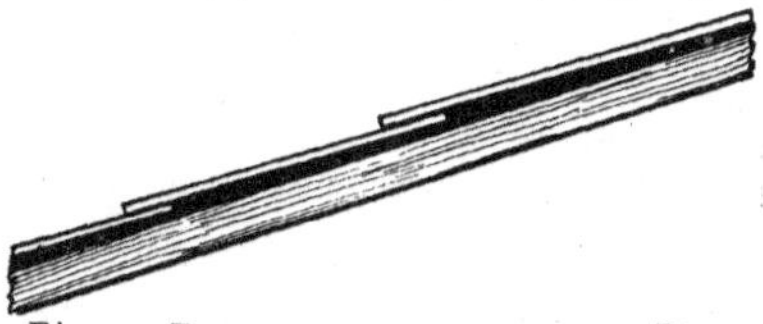

Fig. 5.—Diagram showing how one pane is lapped under another. The black space below the panes indicates the bed of putty.

Fig. 6.—Details of Metal Edging along the Side of Glass Roofs. A is the piece of metal sheeting; B the edge of the glass pane; C the wooden beam; and D the window.

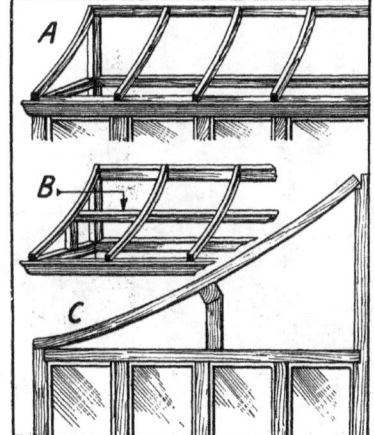

Fig. 7.—How to deal with a Sagging Roof. A shows a roof in bad condition; B and C show how a purlin is fitted to support the sagging part.

Fig. 8.—The Cornice of Brickwork between Two Conservatories is often found in a Porous and Permanently Damp Condition.

The beam should be placed so that the roof just rests on it.

Porous Brick Wall.

Not all conservatories are built up against the side of a house. In some cases the conservatories of two adjoining houses are built together with a brickwork wall separating them, as shown in Fig. 8. The bricks are generally built up about a foot higher than the glass. A frequent fault with conservatories built in this fashion is that the wall is always stained through dampness, as the bricks at the top become very friable, soak up the water and allow it to percolate through to the partition wall.

The simplest treatment is to wet the whole of the exposed brickwork and give it a thin coating of cement.

Another treatment is to cover the bricks with a bituminous preparation such as Farotex, in which case the bricks must be quite dry before the material is applied. It is spread over the surface with an old flexible knife. It will work on smoothly if the blade is constantly dipped in creosote.

How to clean a Glass Roof.

The panes of a conservatory roof naturally get very dirty after a time, and ordinary washing has little effect. A good method of cleaning away the dirt is to prepare a rag at the end of a long pole, dip it in spirits of salts, and rub it up and down the glass until the dirt is removed. Then rinse the roof with the hose before the spirits of salts has time to do any damage to the paintwork.

Cutting Curves in Glass.

It may happen that the shape of a piece of glass that requires replacing is not rectangular but oval or round. It may be also that you wish to use up an odd piece of glass that you have by you and that you do not wish to buy a new piece cut specially to the shape required.

Curved shapes of glass are more difficult to cut than straight lines, but provided the diamond (or other glass cutter) is held at the correct angle and even pressure is given during the scratching process, there should be no difficulty in cutting various shapes.

It is a good plan when cutting out a circular or oval shape to make a number of scratches to the edges, so that the unrequired outer sections may be removed progressively until only the central piece that is required remains.

It sometimes happens, when cutting out discs of glass, that a small angular projection is left in one place. If the glass is scratched on both faces at this part the unrequired projection can usually be removed by means of a pair of flat pliers.

Making a Pair of Ladies' Gloves

It is a very surprising fact that of the numerous persons who admire hand-made gloves, few have attempted to make them, although glove-making, besides being a very useful hobby, is one of the most interesting and fascinating pastimes. Even a beginner's first pair of gloves, if carefully cut out and evenly and securely sewn, can be quite a success. Simple and straightforward patterns in all sizes may be obtained at small cost from most of the suppliers of gloving leathers, and with a well-cut pattern, a suitable leather, and a little common sense and patience, a good pair of gloves cannot fail to be the result.

On page 458 details were given for making a pair of lined gauntlet gloves; this article describes how to make a pair of ladies' slip-on gloves.

The Leather Used.

Most of the leather used in glove-making is obtained from the sheep or lamb, dressed and finished to various styles, but the most usual for the beginner are the chamois and the Cape Tan. Chamois is specially dressed by a process which renders it soft and pliable to work, while at the same time being hardwearing and washable. This is excellent for ladies' gloves. Cape Tan is used more for men's gloves, and a stout Cape Tan is very serviceable when used for motoring and other gauntlet gloves. Prices of leather vary, of course, with quality, but a good average washable chamois costs about 8s. 6d., and will cut two pairs of ladies' gloves.

A Simple Slip-on Pair of Gloves.

It is well for the beginner to choose a simple slip-on pattern, as illustrated in Fig. 1. Later, as more experience is gained, buttonholes and other fastenings may be attempted. This slip-on pattern is very suitable for a chamois leather, and when sewn with a contrasting colour can be made to look quite effective.

The Pattern.

The pattern itself is usually cut out of very stiff paper and consists of three pieces, namely, the main part of the hand or "trank," the thumb, and the "fourchette"—the little strip which goes between the fingers. There are two or three different types of fourchettes and often two types (the single and the double) are supplied with the pattern. The single fourchette is generally considered the most simple, and twelve of these are required for one pair of gloves. Of the double fourchette only six are required, but it is necessary to insert a tiny extra piece called a "quirk"; this is not a favourite, however, by reason of its smallness. The choice of the fourchette is a matter of taste, and whichever style is used the same result is obtained.

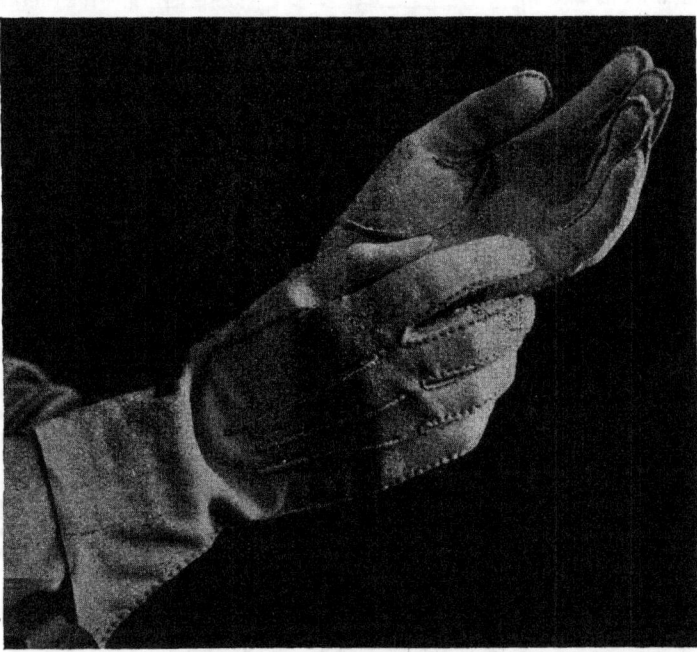

Fig. 1.—Hand-made Ladies' Gloves.

These gloves, of washable chamois leather, were made by a beginner at a total cost of 4s. 4d.

Stitching Thread required.

Strong cotton is necessary for the sewing, and a good buttonhole thread used double is easy to work with, and gives good results. Lister's Buttonhole Thread No. 12 may be obtained on small reels of 1 dozen yards. Two such reels are sufficient for the average pair of ladies' gloves.

Needle required.

For the needle, an ordinary No. 7 or No. 8 is usual. There is a special gloving needle—three-sided, with each edge very sharp—but this is only used by experts, and is not advised except for very stout leathers. Without special care it will cut through the edge of the leather.

Stretch of Leather should be round the Hand.

Greatest possible attention should be paid to the cutting out, as it is largely upon this that the ultimate result depends. It is important to remember that the stretch of the leather must always be across the glove, or *round* the hand. Therefore care must be taken when cutting out to ascertain which way the skin gives, for although in most cases it will be found to go across the animal, this is not a general rule, as no two skins are alike. A gentle tug each way will soon convince the worker of the importance of this point.

Avoid Poor Patches of Leather.

Before cutting out it is usual to hold the leather up to the light and mark—on the wrong side, of course — any poor patches or holes, so that these may be avoided when marking out the patterns.

Marking out the Patterns on Leather.

The skin is then laid upon a table (right side downwards), the patterns are placed to the best advantage upon it, and, with a sharp-pointed pencil, the whole of the outline is traced on the leather. Two tranks must be cut, two thumbs, and twelve single fourchettes (or, if preferred, six double ones and six quirks). As only one pattern for each is supplied, it is necessary to reverse the pattern for the second glove, thus making the right and left hands. Fig. 2 shows a pair of ladies' size 6½ slip-on shape gloves marked to the best advantage on a very small, rather poor leather. In this instance the stretch was across the leather, consequently *all* the pieces have been placed so that the finished glove will have the stretch going round the hand. Certain parts of the neck of this skin were too thin to be used.

The pencil markings are taken right round the trank and the curves at the tops of the fingers, but not between the fingers. Instead, a dot is placed at the base of each finger, and when the pattern has been lifted from the leather a straight line is drawn, with the aid of a ruler, from the dot to the top of the finger. This is to ensure a perfectly straight finger. Dots are also marked to show the base of the "points" or tucks at the back of the hand. If the pencil is very sharp it can be pricked right through the pattern and will mark these dots sufficiently for guidance.

Cutting Out.

Having marked all the pieces required for a pair of gloves, the worker proceeds to cut them out, using a pair of sharp long-bladed scissors. Care is taken to make long, clean cuts, where possible, taking the full length of the blade and thus avoiding those little awkward jags which cannot afterwards be straightened. At this stage the separate fingers are not cut, but the trank is rounded over the tips of the fingers, as shown in Fig. 3. The object of this is to avoid unduly stretching the leather. Often the shape of a pair of gloves has been ruined because the weight of the leather has been allowed to hang from the fingers when cutting out. It is well to bear in mind, also, when sewing the fingers, that the weight of the leather is liable to spoil the shape, so the trank should either be resting on a table or caught up in the little finger. When cutting the hole for the thumb the trank should be folded and a small piece of leather snipped out in order to insert the scissors. The outline can then be carefully followed. To jab the point of the scissors through the trank badly strains the leather.

How to Stitch the Pieces together.

There are many styles of stitching, but the most usual is the "prix" seam or stab-stitch. This is done by holding the two edges of the leather between the thumb and forefinger, and stabbing the needle through, as shown in Fig. 4, making even stitches about $\frac{1}{16}$ inch in length on either side. The leather must not be taken round the finger, as in general sewing, as this would cause the stitches to be irregular and the seam uneven.

First Sew the Tucks at the Back of the Glove.

Care should be taken to avoid joining the thread. Therefore it is necessary to take a sufficient length each time a needle is threaded. It is general to commence with the points at the back of the hand. The thread is used double; the needle is pricked through the first dot marking the base of the point, then another needle or pin can be pricked through the leather immediately below the cut between the first two fingers and about $\frac{1}{4}-\frac{3}{8}$ inch down. This acts as a guide to keep the point straight. The leather is then folded quite straight from needle to needle, and the first stitch is taken over the tuck. This is for strength. The sewing is then continued to the top of the point where another stitch is taken over to strengthen the top. The other two points are worked in exactly the same way, each time great care being taken to keep them straight, as upon this much of the smartness of the finished glove depends.

Thumb.

The thumb is then folded and sewn

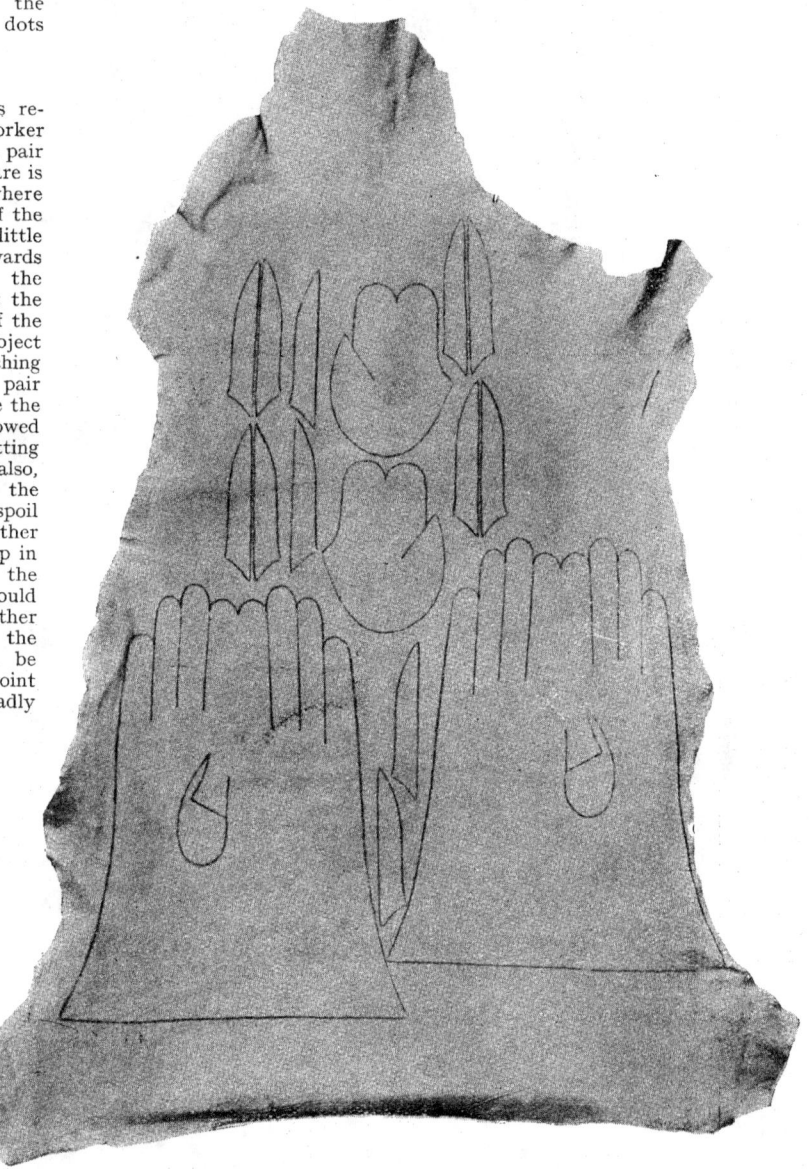

*Fig. 2.—*Leather marked ready for Cutting.
Note the pattern is placed so that the stretch of the leather goes round the hand. Suitable patterns may be purchased from suppliers of gloving leathers.

from the tip, the first stitch being taken round the seam (Fig. 5). The sewing is continued down to the slit; then, with the needle on the inside of the thumb, point A (Fig. 3) of the tongue of the trank is joined, as indicated in Fig. 7. The sewing is then taken along the

MAKING A PAIR OF LADIES' GLOVES

bottom of the tongue to B (Fig. 3), and if the cutting out has been accurately done, the tongue will be found to fit exactly into the slit of the thumb. At point B the sewing is continued up to C (Fig. 3), care being taken to securely fasten each corner. This will be quite easy, providing the thread is drawn sufficiently t i g h t, though the work must not be puckered. From C the sewing continues to about half-way down the palm, where the thread is drawn through to the inside of the trank and left, as indicated in Fig. 6. A fresh thread is then taken from the inside of the trank at point A, and sewn to D, then down the side and right round the bottom of the thumb until the hanging thread on the palm side is met. It may be found necessary to measure it occasionally while sewing round the bottom of the thumb, but on no account may either the trank or the thumb be cut.

Here again the worker will be reminded how important it is to start right by marking and cutting out the glove correctly. Where the two ends meet, the threads are carefully drawn to the wrong side, the stitches being arranged so that the join is not apparent on the right side and the two threads are securely tied.

Sewing on the Fourchettes.

Now the fourchettes are taken in pairs, the right sides facing each other, and with a single thread are joined at the bottom with an oversewing stitch. This gives six pairs, three pairs being

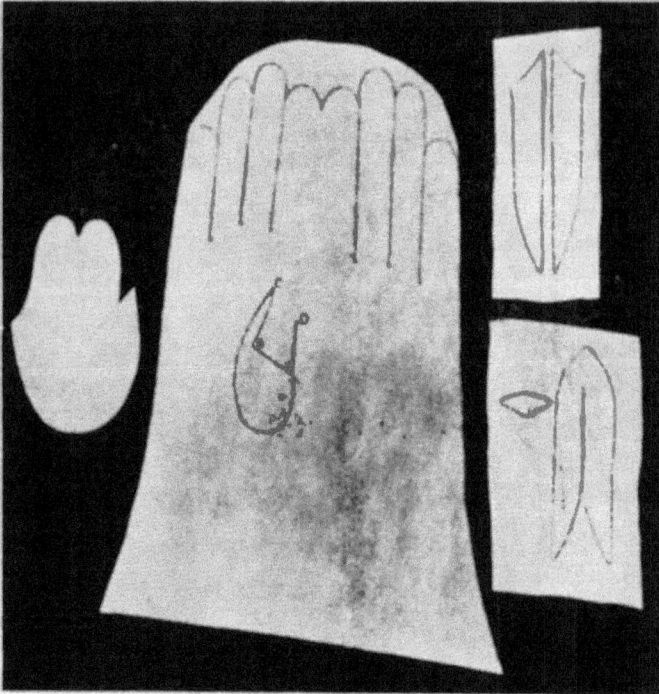

Fig. 3.—Parts of a Glove.
When cutting out the trank, first round over the tops of the fingers to avoid undue stretching. On the top right is shown a pair of single fourchettes, and bottom right a double fourchette and quirk.

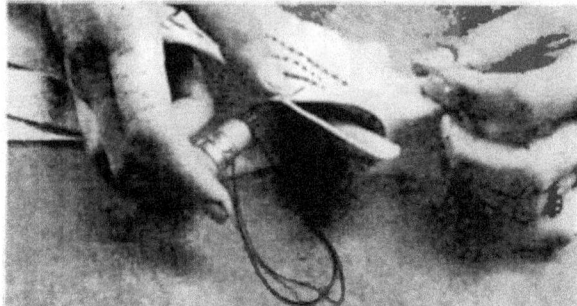

Fig. 4.—How to Stitch the Pieces together.
Notice that the leather is not taken round the finger as in general sewing, because this would tend to stretch the leather. Instead the needle is stabbed through. The stitches should be spaced regularly.

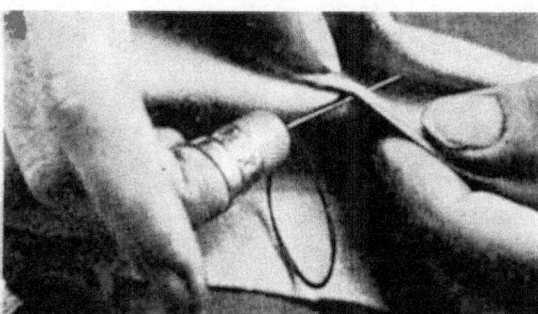

Fig. 5.—Joining the Thumb to the Trank.
The sewing with the first needle is continued to about half-way down the palm.

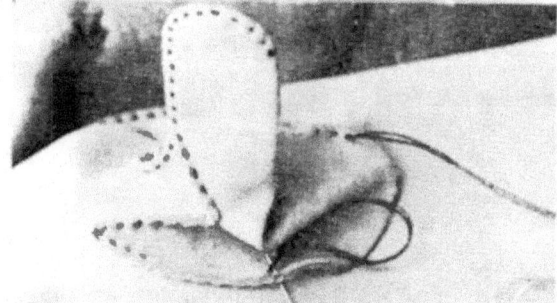

Fig. 6.—Inserting the Thumb.
The slit of the thumb is joined to the lowest point of the "tongue" of the trank.

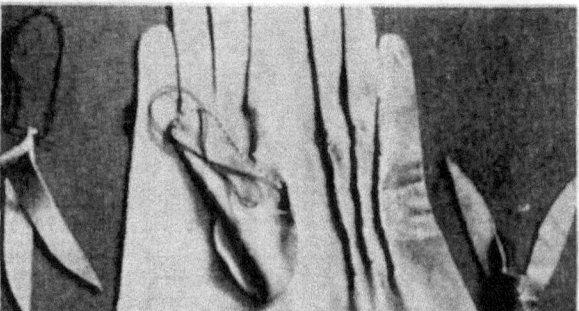

Fig. 7.—Stitching on the Thumb.
The second needle is started from point A (Fig. 3) and continues round the base of the thumb until the first thread is met. Here are two types of fourchettes ready for insertion.

MAKING A PAIR OF LADIES' GLOVES

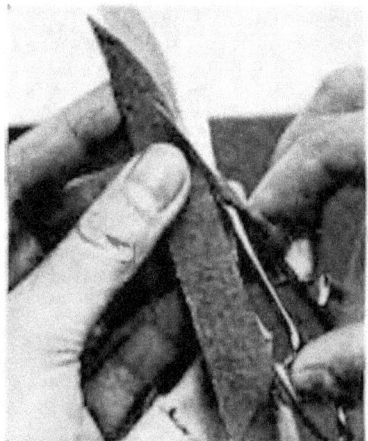

Fig. 8.—Sewing the Fourchettes.
When about half of the fourchette has been sewn to the finger, the length should be measured and the surplus point cut away, using the pattern as a guide.

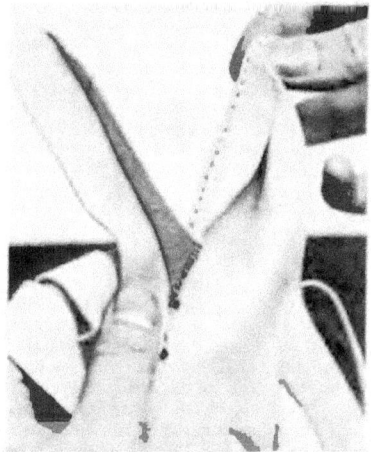

Fig. 9.—The Finger-tip.
The point of the fourchette should be long enough to go round the curve of the finger, leaving the space of about two stitches at the tip.

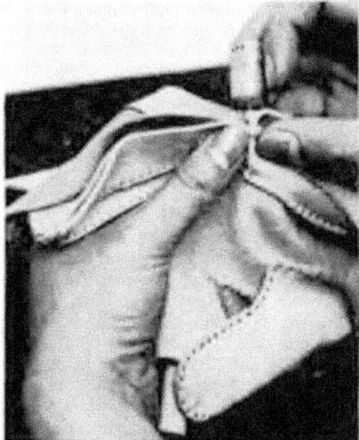

Fig. 10.—Joining the Fingers.
The thread should be tightly drawn at these points.

required for each glove. It will be noticed in Fig. 3 that the backs of the fingers are cut lower into the trank than the fronts. Correspondingly the lower point at the base of a pair of fourchettes is fitted into the *back* of the glove. A double thread is now taken, and the needle having been pricked through the lowest point of a pair of fourchettes, it is drawn through to the right side of the trank between the first and second fingers. If this is done carefully the end of the thread will be on the inside of the glove, and the point of the fourchette will fit exactly between the fingers. The stitching is now continued to about half-way up the first finger, the two edges of the leather being kept evenly together. Before proceeding farther the fouchette must be measured and cut to the required length. That is, the point at the top should be level with the tip of the finger to which it is being sewn, so that when the stitching is taken to the extreme end of each fourchette there will be left the space of about the length of two stitches at the finger-tip.

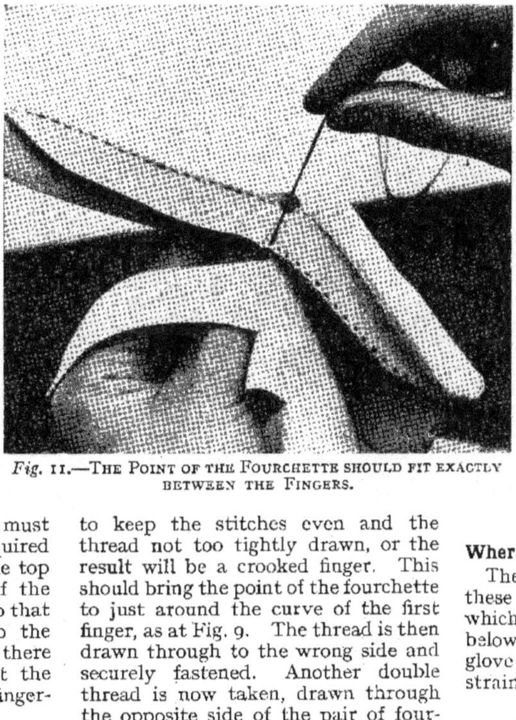

Cutting to fit Finger Lengths.

It follows that as all the fourchettes have been cut to the one pattern they must naturally be adjusted to the length of each individual finger. To do this the pattern itself is placed in the half-sewn fourchette, and the surplus point is neatly cut away (as shown in Fig. 8).

The sewing is now continued to the end of the fourchette, care being taken to keep the stitches even and the thread not too tightly drawn, or the result will be a crooked finger. This should bring the point of the fourchette to just around the curve of the first finger, as at Fig. 9. The thread is then drawn through to the wrong side and securely fastened. Another double thread is now taken, drawn through the opposite side of the pair of fourchettes, as in Figs. 10 and 11, and to the base of the second finger. The stitching continues half-way up the finger, then the pattern is placed on it, the fourchette adjusted to size, and the stitching continued to the finger-tip. Each pair of fourchettes is inserted in this manner, but to ensure a straight finger it is essential that the same length of thread be used for each side. To be sure of this it is well to leave the first thread hanging while the second thread is being used.

Fig. 11.—The Point of the Fourchette should fit exactly between the Fingers.

"Closing Up."

When all the fourchettes have been inserted there remains only the "closing up" of the glove. To do this a double thread is taken and the trank folded from the tip of the first finger. The first stitch is taken round the seam for strength; the sewing is then continued over the tip and down the first finger, picking up the fourchette where it joins the back of the finger and making sure that the extreme point is neatly tucked between the front and back fingers. If the pattern has been correctly cut, and the sewing evenly done, it should be simple now to proceed to sew up and down each finger, and finally down the side of the glove, but here again the point of each pair of fourchettes must fit exactly between the fingers.

Where the strain is greatest.

The sewing is pulled rather tighter at these points to ensure no slack threads which may pull into holes, for it is below the fingers on the palm of a glove that there is always the greatest strain.

Pressing.

The finishing touch of a pair of gloves is the pressing. The fourchettes are neatly tucked into the fingers, and the thumbs folded into their correct places and light tacking stitches are taken between the fingers to keep them all in position. The gloves are then placed under a substantial weight for a few days, after which the tacking is carefully removed and a thoroughly serviceable and attractive pair of gloves are ready to wear.

Making Briquettes from Coal Dust

Coal dust, which otherwise may be wasted, can be turned to useful account by making it into briquettes that can be burnt in exactly the same manner as ordinary pieces of coal. They usually burn at a slower rate, however, and are therefore more economical. The best coal dust to employ for making briquettes is the finely pulverised variety, as this will bind more readily and uniformly than a dust containing coal particles of appreciable size. The principle of the various available methods of making briquettes with coal dust is to employ some binding agent to hold the dust together and to keep it so during the combustion process. Obviously it would not be satisfactory to have a binding agent that merely held the dust together until the briquette commenced to burn, and then allowed the briquette to collapse into powdered form again.

It is proposed to describe various practical methods of utilising coal in the form of small blocks, or briquettes, commencing with the simplest ones.

The Bag Method.

A simple but thoroughly practical scheme for utilising coal dust is to first dampen it and then place it into brown paper bags, or bags of thick paper similar to those used for holding lump sugar. The moistened coal dust should be packed down as tightly as possible without, however, bursting the bag. The bag should be tied with a piece of thin wire in two directions. It is then ready for use, and is placed on the open fire in the same way as a piece of coal. The contents will not break up into coal dust again, but, owing to the fusing of the outer surface of the briquette, the latter will burn in a similar manner to a lump of coal.

Using Clay for binding.

If ordinary clay be employed for binding the dust, it should be moistened until it becomes a wet, thick, pasty mass. The well-pulverised coal dust is then added and mixed thoroughly with the clay. Commence with small

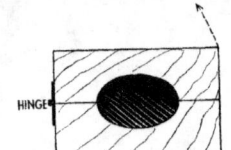

Fig. 1.—Wooden Mould for making Coal Dust Briquettes.

quantities of the dust and mix this with the clay. Then add further small amounts and mix thoroughly, until the mixture becomes of a stiff consistency with as much coal dust as possible in it.

The more coal dust that the clay can be induced to take up, the greater will be the heating value of the briquette. Care should be exercised, however, to avoid making the briquette with too little clay, otherwise it will break up in the fire.

Having made the coal dust and clay mixture, quantities of the latter are made into balls, blocks or ovoids, either by hand or in an improvised machine made on the same lines as the metal-moulding machines used in foundries.

A suitable mould, in two halves, can be made out of hard wood, such as oak, or in concrete. If the mould is arranged to have several cavities for the briquettes, a corresponding number

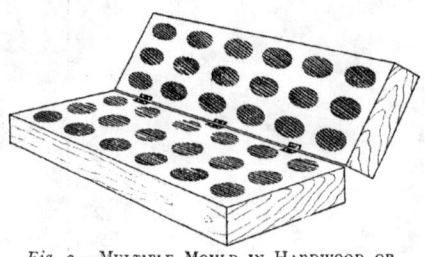

Fig. 2.—Multiple Mould in Hardwood or Concrete for Quantity Production of Briquettes.

of the latter can be made at one operation.

After making the briquettes, they should be placed in a warm dry place on a board in order to dry and harden. They should not be used in the moist condition.

Using Cement as a Binder.

Another method that is often employed for making briquettes is to mix one part of coal dust with six to nine parts of Portland cement, taking care that the mixture is uniform, and then to add water until the mixture becomes a stiff paste of mortar-like consistency. The mixture should be well stirred, so as to obtain a perfectly uniform distribution of the coal dust. Afterwards mould it into the required shapes, e.g., balls, ovoids or blocks, and allow it to set or dry for about twenty-four hours. These briquettes are used in the same manner as pieces of coal. In place of cement ordinary *garden mud* can be used, but it should not contain any sand or stones.

Other Methods.

The preceding methods give briquettes containing, besides the coal dust, a certain proportion of non-combustible material which forms ash. These briquettes burn more slowly than those using a combustible substance for binding the coal dust, and they do not give the same amount of heat as the latter type.

In order to obviate these drawbacks, briquettes are often made by using ordinary *coal tar* as a binder, but in this case they burn with a more smoky flame and more quickly.

One satisfactory method is to mix the coal dust with melted pitch, adding as much of the dust as the pitch will take up. Allow the mixture to cool, and then press it into slabs, afterwards cutting the latter into rectangular blocks with bench shears. The plastic mixture can be rolled out into slabs, and the latter pressed out into briquette shapes before they cool right down if a large number of briquettes are required.

Another method is to mix three parts of coal dust to one part of sawdust and add liquid tar, stirring well until the mixture has become fairly stiff, when it can be moulded into briquettes and the latter allowed to harden. Coal tar is now used to a considerable extent as a binding medium for coal dust briquettes.

Effervescent Bath Tablets

When tired, there are few things more refreshing than a bath in which effervescent tablets have been placed. These are easily made, and may be perfumed according to fancy. The mixture for the bath tablets is prepared in the following proportions: Tartaric acid, 10 parts; carbonate of soda, 9 parts; rice flour, 6 parts.

Any amount can be mixed providing the proportions are observed. A few spoonfuls of this powder added to the bath water will lead to a copious liberation of carbon dioxide, a gas which has a most refreshing effect on a tired body. It is more handy to have the powder in the form of tablets. Of course, in doing this, water cannot be used, as it would start the effervescence. For moistening the powder, employ a little spirits of wine. When a stiff paste has been secured, press it into the form of tablets. The perfume should be added just before the making of the tablets. A few drops of pure oil of lavender sprinkled on the powder and well mixed in will give a delightful fragrance. Any other perfume may be used. Spread the moistened powder in a layer on a board and then punch out the tablets with the lid of a small round tin. The bath tablets are used two or three at a time according to the amount of water. Keep them in a closed container, as the moisture from the air will harm them in course of time.

Choosing the Right Paint for the Job

Very often when planning to do some painting work the handyman experiences some difficulty in deciding what kind of paint to use for the job. Before paint manufacturers developed ready for use products to the present high standard of efficiency, it was the practice of decorators to make their own paints from white lead and other pigments (which were ground to a stiff paste in linseed oil) by adding turpentine, raw or boiled linseed oil and driers in various proportions according to the type of surface to be painted. Whilst this procedure was satisfactory for the craftsmen who were trained in the proper formulation and mixing of paints, the handyman was unable to obtain suitable paints for the many small jobs about the house.

With the enormous increase in the number of house owners, and the necessity for large quantities of paints of uniform quality, a demand has been created for ready-mixed paints for both decorator and amateur use.

This article will be confined to an explanation of the several different types of paint that are available in a ready mixed form, and the most suitable type of paint for a particular surface.

The object of painting a surface is threefold, namely, preservation, decoration, and hygiene. In most cases all three are required, and many paints are available which combine these qualities. In other cases it may be necessary to use two or more paints to attain the desired object, for example, in painting ironwork, such as railings, gutter pipes, etc., protection is required to prevent corrosion, and the most suitable paint for this purpose is red lead ; red lead, however, is not a decorative paint, so that a second material such as a green or brown oil paint must be used for the decorative effect. An example of combined preservation and decoration is aluminium paint, regarding which more details will be given later.

Oil Paints.

These consist of a mixture of pigments, oils, driers and turpentine in carefully balanced proportions. The type of pigment and oil that is used depends upon the purpose for which the paint is intended, and whilst, strictly speaking, most paints are oil paints, there are several different types which will be explained under their respective headings. Painting must be considered as a process consisting of primer, undercoat and finishing paints. Each material has a particular function to perform and is so formulated that it has an affinity for the coat previously applied. It is important, therefore, that paints made by the same maker should be used for all coats of any job, and not one maker's primer and another maker's finishing paint.

Fig. 1.—The Correct Preparation of the Surface to be Treated is Almost as Important as Choosing the Right Paint.

Remove all the fitments that are likely to be in the way when rubbing down the old paintwork and during repainting.

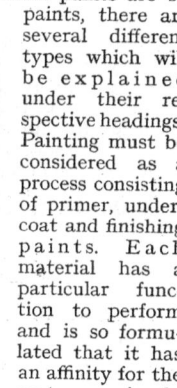

Fig. 2.—Preparing Old Paintwork for Repainting.

Rub down the surface with special waterproof glasspaper and liberal applications of water. The paper will work into mouldings. Clean up the work with sponge and water as you proceed.

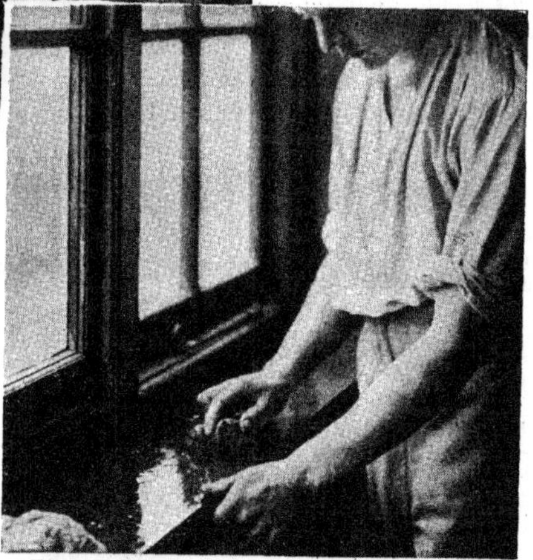

Fig. 3.—Rubbing Down before Repainting.

It is desirable to smooth the surface of the old work both to ensure a good finish and give a bite for the new paint. Rub flat surfaces with pumice stone or waterproof glasspaper and use plenty of water applied with brush or sponge.

Primers for Wood and Metal.

The use of a primer is not generally understood, but this is one of the most important operations in building up a finish, as upon this coat depends the success of all subsequent coats. Primers for wood are usually composed of red and white lead, raw linseed oil, turpentine and driers; they are of thin consistency, as they must penetrate the pores of the wood and so stop the suction. The minute particles of lead pigment are of rough texture, and this forms a "key" which aids the adhesion of subsequent coats of paint.

Primers for wood contain a large proportion of raw linseed oil to ensure penetration, and lead pigments assist in the drying of this.

Primers for metal contain less oil and the pigment may be either red or white lead, oxide of iron, or aluminium powder ; gums and resins are sometimes incorporated to confer elasticity and adhesive properties.

A primer in which aluminium powder is incorporated has excellent anti-corrosive properties on metal, and is also suitable for wood, as it forms in effect a thin sheet of aluminium which is absolutely waterproof.

Primers other than aluminium are supplied in white, grey, pink, and some metal primers are transparent like varnish ; they are supplied either by weight or measure. The spreading properties of the ready-for-use primers are approximately 40 square yards per 14 lbs. and 100 square yards per gallon respectively.

Primers have very little weather resistance, and must be subsequently coated with finishing paints. Primer is only necessary on bare surfaces; for repaint work, undercoat can be applied over the old finish when same has been properly prepared. Primers require from twenty-four to thirty-six hours to dry.

Undercoats.

The object of an undercoat paint is to build up film thickness and provide an obliterative coating. For this reason extra pigment is incorporated in paints made specially as undercoats. Special undercoats are not necessary in all cases, and two or more coats of the finishing paint—when properly adjusted—are satisfactory. A rule on the matter of paint undercoats is that when gloss paints or enamels are to be used for the finishing coat, a special undercoat is required; it is also recommended when dark-coloured surfaces are to be painted with light shades.

Due to the relatively large proportion of pigment in undercoat paints, and the fact that pigments are chosen primarily for their obliteration rather than protective properties, undercoat paints have little or no weather-resisting qualities.

Undercoats dry with a matt or dull finish, and should thinning be necessary, use only pure turpentine; on no account add linseed oil unless recommended by the manufacturer, as this would cause the paint to dry with a gloss and the film would be softer than it should be, and may cause the finishing coats to crack or shrivel. The covering capacity of undercoats varies considerably, but on an average 1 gallon covers 80 square yards.

Covering Capacity.

It might at this stage be advisable to include a brief explanation of what is meant by covering capacity. This term, when applied to paint, is often misunderstood, even amongst tradesmen. In the general sense, it is used to indicate how far a paint will *spread*, but a surface can be spread or covered with a paint without the original surface being obliterated or hidden, as when varnishing. To many people the term covering capacity indicates the power to hide the original surface, but the correct term for this is "*hiding power*," or obliterating properties. The liquid part of a paint determines its spreading properties, and upon the pigments depends how well it obliterates the old surface. The covering capacity stated for the paints described in this article are based on the proper obliteration of the surface when the paint is spread over the area mentioned.

Finishing Paints.

The number of different paints that can be classed under this heading is so large that subdivision is necessary according to the type of work on which they are to be used. Finishing paints are made in two grades—inside and outside quality; the weather resistance depends upon the quantity of oil and the kind of pigment. It is not necessary to discuss the relative merits of the different kinds of pigment because, as previously mentioned, paints can be purchased in a ready-mixed form, and if a reputable brand of paint is labelled as suitable for outside use, it can be taken for granted that it will be satisfactory.

Outside Quality Paint.

An outside quality paint is made on what is known as a long oil base; that is, a large proportion of oil is incorporated to confer weather resistance, waterproofness and elasticity, which is necessary to enable the film to withstand expansion and contraction as occurs under changes of temperature, such as hot sunshine and frost. The oil may be either raw linseed oil, boiled linseed oil, tung oil (obtained from a bean grown in China), a specially treated mixture of oils known as stand oil, or a mixture of several of these. Pigments which have the maximum protective value, fastness to light and durability, are used for outside quality paints; some of the pigments such as red lead, graphite and oxide, do not produce a beautiful appearance, but afford excellent protection.

Inside Quality Paint.

Inside quality paints are made on a short oil base, and this permits them to dry to the harder finish which is required for surfaces which must resist constant handling, cleaning, friction and abrasion. As they are not subject to direct sunlight or weather, inside quality paints can have incorporated in them pigments which have good appearance rather than protective properties. Whilst an outside quality paint can be used for inside work subject to certain exceptions, if an inside quality paint is used where it will be subject to weathering it will quickly disintegrate, lose its colour, crack and become powdery; "chalking" is the technical term.

Enamel Paints.

These paints are also referred to as High Gloss Paints, Varnish Paints, Hard Gloss Paints, etc., and as their name implies, they dry with a glossy enamel-like finish. They should not be confused with real enamels, however, which are different materials. Enamel paints can be used for finishing doors, window frames, cupboards, kitchen cabinets, garden tools and furniture, and any surface, wood or metal, which may be constantly handled and on which a smooth glossy hard-wearing finish is desired. An outside quality should be used for any work subject to exposure.

Undercoats suitable for enamel paints are supplied in shades approximating the finishing colour and one coat of undercoating (two if repainting a dark-coloured surface), and one of finishing are sufficient in most cases, but should it be desired to apply an extra coat of finishing, the gloss on the first coat must be removed, either by rubbing with pumice and water, or with fine sandpaper. This is called "flatting" or "mossing down," and is very necessary because if a glossy drying paint is applied over a previous gloss finish it is liable to "ciss," *i.e.*, run off like water from glass, or if this does not happen it will lack adhesion and may peel off or chip after a short time, as the hard glossy undersurface does not permit the finishing coat to key properly.

Enamel paints dry dust free in six to eight hours and are hard in eighteen to twenty-four hours. One gallon covers approximately 70 square yards. Do not thin these paints with turpentine or the gloss will be impaired. Avoid gloss paints which dry in a few hours, as these are usually very brittle and are not durable.

Flat Paints.

For walls, ceilings, and general interior decorations. Flat paints contain a large proportion of pigment, and only a small quantity of oil. They are supplied in a variety of soft pastel shades and are of heavy consistency to be thinned as required with oil and/or turpentine according to the work being done. Flat paints dry with a velvet smooth matt finish which is washable. Two coats are usually required, using the same material but thinning differently for each coat.

On bare plaster surfaces a special sealer is mixed with the first coat to act as a primer and seal the suction. When the special sealer material is not used the first coat must be thinned to brushing consistency with half raw linseed oil and half turpentine. This makes it dry with a slight sheen. The finishing coat, however, must be thinned with turpentine only, as the addition of oil would destroy the matt appearance.

Flat paints appear to dry in an hour or two, but this is only surface drying, and an interval of at least twelve hours should be allowed between coats.

One gallon of flat paint, when

Fig. 4.—Coating Knots in New Wood with "Knotting" before Painting.

If a small brush is not available, knotting can be applied with a bunch of rag or sponge.

CHOOSING THE RIGHT PAINT FOR THE JOB

TABLE SHOWING COMPARATIVE SPREADING POWER, APPROXIMATE COST AND TIME TO DRY OF VARIOUS PAINTS

Type of Paint.	Approximate Spreading Power.	Approximate Cost.	Time Required to Dry. Dust Free.	Hard or Ready to Recoat.
Primers, Wood	20 sq. yds. per 7 lbs.	2/6 to 3/- per 7 lbs.	6 to 8 hours	24 to 36 hours
Primers, Metal	25 sq. yds. per ¼ gall.	3/9 to 4/- per ¼ gall.	6 to 8 hours	24 to 36 hours
Undercoats	25 sq. yds. per 7 lbs. 20 sq. yds. per ¼ gall.	Lead 4/6 per 7 lbs. Spec. U/C. 4/- to 5/- per ¼ gall.	4 to 6 hours	18 to 24 hours
Varnish Gloss or Enamel Paints	17 to 20 sq. yds. per ¼ gall., according to nature of U/C.	3/6 to 4/6 per ¼ gall.	6 to 8 hours	18 to 24 hours
Flat Paints	Average for all coats, 65 to 70 sq. yds. per ½ gall.	7/- to 8/- per ½ gall.	1 to 2 hours	18 to 24 hours
Oil Paints	Average on all type surfaces. 20 sq. yds. per 7 lbs. 25 sq. yds. per ¼ gall.	Lead 4/6 to 5/- per 7 lbs. Mixt. 4/- to 5/- per ¼ gall.	8 to 10 hours	Thinned with Turps 12 hours. Thinned with Linseed Oil 24 hours. Thinned with half Oil and half Turps 18 hours.
Enamels	17 yds. per ¼ gall.	6/- to 7/6 per ¼ gall.	12 to 18 hours	30 to 40 hours
Bath Enamel	½ pt. is sufficient for two coats on ordinary size bath	2/- to 2/6 per ½ pt.	12 to 18 hours	48 to 60 hours
Radiator Enamel	8 sq. yds. per pt.	3/- to 3/6 per pt.	12 to 18 hours	24 to 36 hours
Distemper (Oil Bound Type)	50 sq. yds. per 7 lbs.	3/3 to 3/6 per 7 lbs.	½ to 1 hour	8 to 12 hours
Distemper (Powder Type)	40 to 60 sq. yds. per 7 lbs., according to how thinned	2/6 to 3/- per 7 lbs.	½ to 1 hour	8 to 12 hours
Structural and Barn Paints	80 sq. yds. per gall.	8/- to 10/- per gall.	8 to 10 hours	18 to 24 hours
Metallic Paints	9 to 10 sq. yds. per pt.	3/6 to 3/9 per pt.	4 to 6 hours	10 to 12 hours
Brushing Cellulose Paint	6 to 7 sq. yds. per pt.	4/6 to 5/- per pt.	10 to 15 minutes	2 to 3 hours
Oak Varnish	8 sq. yds. per pt.	2/6 to 3/- per pt.	6 to 8 hours	18 to 24 hours
Copal Varnish	8 sq. yds. per pt.	3/- to 3/6 per pt.	8 to 10 hours	24 to 36 hours
Pale Decorative Varnish	8 sq. yds. per pt.	3/6 to 4/3 per pt.	8 to 10 hours	24 to 36 hours
Flat Varnishes	8 sq. yds. per pt.	2/6 to 3/- per pt.	4 to 6 hours	10 to 12 hours
Floor Varnish	8 sq. yds. per pt.	2/3 to 2/9 per pt.	8 to 10 hours	24 to 48 hours
Paper Varnish	8 sq. yds. per pt.	2/6 to 3/6 per pt.	3 to 4 hours	8 to 10 hours

thinned ready for use, will cover about 120 square yards, slightly less for the first coat on porous surfaces. Flat paints should not be used for outside work as they are not resistant to weather, and are not to be recommended for surfaces which will be constantly handled, such as doors, etc., for such surfaces use a flat enamel finish.

Oil Paints.

This is probably the most used and best known of all paints. It dries with a slight gloss and is suitable for practically any type of surface. Inside and outside qualities are available. Quite a number of oil paints have white lead as a pigment either alone or combined with zinc or other pigments; for outside use a genuine all-lead pigment is best. Any paint containing more than 4 per cent. of lead pigment must under a Government regulation have a label on the container to this effect, but an "all-lead" paint is described as "Genuine Lead Paint," and contains only genuine lead, linseed oil, pure turpentine and driers. Oil paints give a good finish in one coat on previously painted surfaces unless a light finish is required over a dark-coloured surface.

For inside work they should be thinned with half raw linseed oil and half turpentine, and when more than one coat is to be applied increase the linseed oil in the second coat.

For outside work one coat, thin with raw linseed oil or if a higher gloss is required, boiled linseed oil. Do not use turpentine only for thinning outside finishing coats, as this detracts from the durability; turpentine only can be used for thinning oil paint for inside use when only a semi-gloss finish is desired.

When oil paints are used on brick, stone, plaster or concrete surfaces a special primer is required to stop the suction and seal the alkali which is present in such surfaces. One gallon of oil paint, when thinned ready for use, will cover from 80 to 100 square yards, according to the type of surface.

Drying times depend upon what the paint is thinned with; when turpentine only is used, allow twelve hours between coats; raw linseed oil-thinned paint requires about twenty-four hours to dry; half and half about eighteen hours, and, when boiled linseed oil is added, the film remains somewhat soft for about two days. Genuine lead oil paints are usually sold by weight, and 14 lbs., when thinned, will cover about 40 square yards.

Enamels.

Two separate qualities are supplied, inside and outside; these dry with either a high gloss, semi-gloss or matt finish. Whilst enamel *paints* are made by the addition of varnish, real enamels contain specially-treated oils which make them resistant to repeated washing, abrasion, and permit them to flow out well so that no brushmarks occur.

Enamels are of thick consistency, and must be brushed out well; they have very little obliterating properties, and the work must be brought up to a uniform shade with a suitable quality undercoating, or a patchy finish will result.

On no account should enamels be thinned; if too thick to brush out well the tin should be placed in warm water for a short time before using. Dust-free surroundings are essential to good results when applying enamels, and should a second coat be necessary, the first coat, when thoroughly dry, must be "flatted" with pumice dust and water. At least two days should be allowed for the first coat to harden before flatting.

Enamels dry dust free in twelve to eighteen hours, and hard enough to handle in about thirty hours. One gallon will cover about 70 square yards. Use good quality enamels; a cheap enamel will rapidly lose its gloss and may crack in a short time; whilst relatively expensive in first cost, a good enamel will repay the extra expense by permitting a finish to be obtained that will last for years.

Bath Enamel.

The conditions of sharply contrasting temperatures, moist heat, abrasion from cleaning, and body pressure to which baths are subjected, impose a severe test which no ordinary enamel is fitted to stand. Specially treated stand oils are used for bath enamels that produce a hard yet elastic film under the severe conditions. Like other enamels, bath enamels have not good obliterative properties, and special undercoats, which must also be hard and heat resisting, are necessary to build up an even coloured and smooth surface. Bath enamels dry to the touch in twelve to eighteen hours, but are not hard enough for use before forty-eight to sixty hours. A half pint of bath enamel is sufficient for two coats on an ordinary sized bath. These enamels are also available in pale pastel shades as well as white.

Radiator Enamels.

These enamels are also formulated to withstand conditions of constant heat and moisture. They can be obtained in a glossy or semi-gloss finish; this latter looks the most effective. An undercoat is required unless the enamel being used is of the same shade as the present colour. The undercoats dry in eight to twelve hours, and the finishing enamels in twelve to eighteen hours. Covering capacity is about 70 square yards per gallon for both undercoat and finishing. Aluminium paint is quite suitable for painting radiators provided a heat-resisting medium is used.

Distempers.

These are also known as Waterpaints, Colourwash, etc. There are several different types of distemper, but all of them consist essentially of pigment such as whiting, lithopone, blanc fixe, etc., with a binder or fixative such as glue, casein, linseed oil or varnish. They are thinned with plain water or a special liquid sold as petrifying solution to make them ready for use. Correctly speaking, the term "distemper" should be applied only to those materials which have glue or gums as a binder, and whilst these are bound sufficiently not to rub off on the clothes, they are readily attacked by damp, and can be washed off with water.

Water paints or washable distemper is the correct name for those materials which have a binder such as linseed

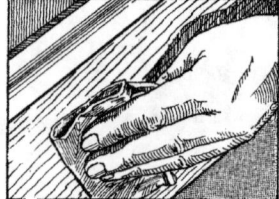

Fig. 5.—Each Coat should be Sandpapered to remove Brushmarks and Local Thickening.

Use the special waterproof glasspaper.

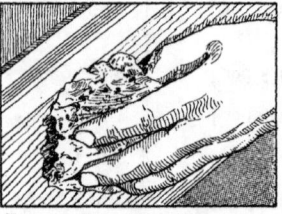

Fig. 6.—The Next Step is to Sponge off after Sandpapering to remove Sludge.

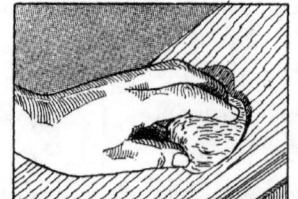

Fig. 7.—Pumice Stone is as Effective as Sandpaper for dealing with Flat Surfaces.

Take care not to scratch the surface.

Fig. 8.—The Surface should then be Dried by Wiping with a Washleather.

oil, casein or varnish, and as these binders are waterproof the finish can be washed when dirty. This does not mean, however, that they can be scrubbed like paint or enamel; only gentle rubbing with a sponge or soft cloth lightly moistened with water is required. Vigorous rubbing or excessive water will soften the film and spoil the surface.

Distempers can be purchased in two forms—dry powder and heavy paste form; the latter is a water/oil emulsion and consequently must be protected from freezing when stored or the emulsion will be broken and the material spoiled. A common mistake when mixing up distempers is to make them too thin; best results are obtained if the distemper is used in a "round" consistency, and with good brands no difficulty will be experienced in brushing out.

Two coats are usually required to make a solid finish, and from eight to twelve hours should be allowed between coats.

On absorbent surfaces, such as new plaster and brickwork, it is necessary to thin oil-bound distempers with a special solution known as petrifying liquid. This should be of the same brand as the distemper. Petrifying liquid should also be used for thinning when the distemper is employed on surfaces subject to weather, such as gable ends, brick walls, stucco, roughcast, etc.

An oil-bound distemper can, when thoroughly dry, be varnished over, and this is an excellent way to finish dados and other surfaces subject to conditions that would quickly dirty unprotected distemper.

Special ceiling distempers are offered by almost all paint manufacturers, and these, when correctly thinned and applied, make an excellent job. They are so cheap that it is not worth the trouble for the handyman to make up whitewash according to the recipes given in the older reference books.

The covering capacity of powder distempers varies so much that no figures can be given; for paste distempers of the oil-bound type, 14 lbs., when thinned, covers about 100 square yards. As distempers are largely used for interior wall decoration, a few words relative to the influence of colour will not be out of place.

A small room that is badly lighted appears lighter and larger when light yellow, cream or light buff is used. In small rooms bright strong colours make the room appear smaller, while light pastel shades make it look larger.

For north or sunless rooms use colours such as cream, yellow, tan, buff, or pale fawn; never use shades such as blue, green, grey or white.

For south or sunny rooms these

Fig. 9.—BEFORE APPLYING A SECOND COAT MAKE QUITE SURE NO DUST HAS GOT ON TO THE SURFACE.

latter colours are ideal, and whilst the shades recommended for sunless rooms can be used if desired, if they are of strong tint they will add to the effect of heat and sunshine.

The ceilings in most rooms can with advantage be finished in the same colour as the walls, but in a very much lighter shade; this can be obtained by adding white distemper to that used for the walls.

Structural and Barn Paints.

These are relatively cheap ready mixed paints suitable for barns, outbuildings, fences, rough timber, ironwork, corrugated iron, etc., where resistance to weather is the main requirement. They are for the most part made from iron oxide or other protective pigments and boiled linseed oil which gives a tough, waterproof,

Fig. 10.—APPLYING THE FIRST UNDERCOATING ON OLD PAINT WHICH HAS BEEN RUBBED DOWN AND DRIED.

Note that the mouldings and panels of a door are done first.

and weather-resisting film. One coat is sufficient for most surfaces, and this covers solid and dries with a moderate gloss. One gallon will cover about 80 square yards.

Metallic Paints.

In this class there are only the aluminium and gold paints which are of interest to the householder. Aluminium paint provides a protective as well as decorative finish, which is excellent for rain pipes, gutters, railings, and all exposed metal or woodwork; it also makes an ideal primer for wood or metal.

This paint is sold in two forms, ready mixed, and as a clear varnish-like medium and powder; the latter is the best as it permits sufficient material to be mixed as required. Ready mixed aluminium paints lose their brightness with storage and take on a dull lead-like appearance; sometimes they thicken up to a stiff gel which cannot be made workable again by the addition of thinners. This does not occur if the medium and aluminium powder are stored separately and mixed up to a paint as required.

From $1\frac{1}{2}$ to 2 lbs. of aluminium powder is required per gallon of medium, and 1 gallon of such paint will cover about 90 square yards if the medium is on an oil base.

Gold paints are mainly used for finishing small household articles, and the same remarks with regard to mixing medium and powder apply as for aluminium; the covering capacity is also about the same. When a cellulose medium is used the covering capacity is about 70 to 80 square yards per gallon.

Cellulose Paints.

The composition of these paints is quite different from that of oil paints, and their use is generally confined to small surfaces except when applied with a spray gun. Cellulose paints dry by the evaporation of the solvents, and this makes it impractical to coat large areas by brushing methods as the solvents evaporate so quickly that the paint begins to dry before it is properly brushed out and the brush drags, leaving an uneven coating. The solvents used in these paints also dissolve old coatings of oil paint so that discrimination is necessary when using them to repaint surfaces previously finished in oil paint or varnish.

As a general rule, the older, *i.e.*, more oxidised, the old paint the less likely is the cellulose paint to disrupt it, but before commencing any work a small area should be coated as a test.

To prevent or minimise the solvent action of cellulose paints, special undercoats are sold; these form an isolating coat between the old paint and the cellulose film. Undercoats are also necessary when starting from bare wood and other absorbent surfaces as they overcome the suction, fill the grain, and provide a good groundwork for the cellulose which permits it to dry with a good full glossy film.

Cellulose undercoats are made on a special oil base and require from eight to twelve hours to dry, after which they are sandpapered smooth. The usual colours for undercoats are white, grey and buff colour, and any of the cellulose enamels will cover solid in one coat over them.

Undercoats cover from 8 to 10 square yards per pint on bare wood, slightly more on metal and non-absorbent surfaces.

The cellulose enamels are supplied in small tins of no definite measure at 6d. to 9d. per tin, and also in ¼, ½ and 1 pint tins, which is the best way to buy them. A large range of colours is available, and with most brands these can be intermixed to form additional shades. Clear lacquer for finishing wood in place of french polish is also available, as well as stain lacquers. With the colours it is most important that the contents of the tins be thoroughly stirred before use, as, with storage, the pigments settle to the bottom and insufficient stirring will not produce the correct shade, nor will the enamel cover solid.

Brushing cellulose lacquers and enamels are not suitable for surfaces that will be exposed to the weather. Special thinners are necessary for cellulose paints, and whilst it is seldom necessary to thin the paint, some thinners should always be available for washing out brushes, cleaning the hands, etc., as turpentine and linseed oil will not dissolve the paint. Cellulose paints and enamels are highly inflammable, and the same care should be taken with regard to their use and storage as is accorded to petrol and benzine.

Varnishes.

This article would not be complete without some reference to the above, and whilst space does not permit a description of all types of varnishes, those mostly used by the handyman are dealt with. Varnishes, like paints, are made on a long oil base for outside use, and short oil base for interior work.

Oak Varnish.

This is a hard drying varnish suitable for inside work on natural or grained woods or over any dark-coloured paints where a hard glossy surface is required. As it is rather dark in colour it should not be used over light-coloured surfaces as it will turn them a pale yellowish brown. This varnish is fairly quick drying, being dust free in six to eight hours and hard overnight. For outside use a special grade is made. In 1 gallon tins this varnish costs from 18s. to 20s. per gallon.

Copal Varnish.

This type is suitable for inside or outside use; it is fairly pale in colour, and is suitable for use over all but the palest colours. It dries dust free in eight to ten hours and is fairly hard after drying for twenty-four hours, but will be damaged if the surface is handled before thirty-six to forty-eight hours. This is a good all-round varnish for the handyman to use. In 1-gallon tins it costs from 20s. to 25s. per gallon.

Pale Decorative Varnish.

This is similar in character to Copal varnish, but is very pale in colour, so that it is quite suitable for use over white or pale colours. Pale varnishes are more expensive than others, and this type costs from 25s. to 30s. a gallon in 1-gallon tins.

Flat Varnishes.

Most people think of a lustrous glossy finish in relation to varnish,

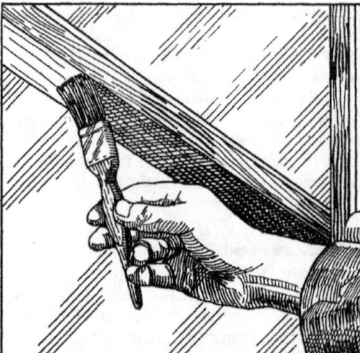

Fig. 11.—Painting a Window Sash with a Sash Tool.
This method of holding the brush is particularly convenient when the underneath side of a horizontal surface has to be painted.

but for certain types of decoration a "matt" or "semi-gloss" varnish provides a more pleasing effect. Natural wood panelling in halls, or furniture and woodwork in studies, bedrooms, etc., where the trend of decoration is restful, if finished with a flat varnish, look much better than a high gloss which is too glaring against the softness of the other decoration and furnishings. Flat varnishes are applied in exactly the same way as the other types, but dry with a soft matt or semi-gloss appearance. Drying time is from ten to twelve hours. They cost in 1-gallon tins from 18s. to 20s. per gallon.

Floor Varnish.

This is a specially formulated material which dries with a very hard and wear-resisting film. It can be applied to wood, lino, or painted floors, and if allowed to harden thoroughly before being walked on, will wear for a very long time and retain its gloss. Varnish dries dust free in eight to ten hours, but should be allowed to harden for two to three days or longer before the floor is walked on. Floor varnish costs from 16s. to 18s. per gallon in 1-gallon tins.

Paper Varnishes.

These are the palest varnishes made and are formulated specially for coating wallpapers such as in bathrooms, kitchens, halls, etc. They dry very quickly, being dust free in three to four hours and hard in eight to ten hours. Before these varnishes are applied to paper, the paper must be coated with two coats of glue size—this prevents the varnish from sinking into the paper and giving it a dark patchy appearance. As paper varnishes are made in a different way to ordinary varnishes they are not suitable for surfaces other than paper.

Paper varnishes cost from 18s. to 25s. per gallon in 1-gallon tins according to quality. The usual packings for varnishes are 1-gallon tins, ½-gallon, ¼-gallon, 1-pint and ½-pint tins. Due to the cost of the tins and extra labour in filling them, the smaller sizes are more expensive in proportion to the quantity of contents and the price per gallon is increased on an average by 1s. for ½-gallon, 2s. for ¼-gallon, 3s. 6d. for pints, and 6s. for ½-pint tins.

On no account must thinners of any kind be added to varnish or the gloss and drying properties will be upset and the varnish may curdle. In cold and damp weather varnish thickens up a little and is harder to spread; if possible varnishing should be avoided under these conditions.

Varnish should be stored in a warm, dry cupboard when not in use, and an hour or so before it is required it should be placed in the room where it will be used; this will make it spread and flow well.

The covering or spreading properties of a varnish are difficult to state as this varies with each user; as a guide, however, a ½ pint of varnish should be sufficient for an average front door and door pillars. Although small tins of varnish are more expensive than gallon tins, it will be found expedient to buy ½- or 1-pint size tins, as it is seldom that more than this quantity is required at a time and a large tin only partly full, no matter how well corked, will skin over during storage.

The success of any painting work largely depends upon using the correct type of paint for the job. Other articles in PRACTICAL ENQUIRE WITHIN deal with the method of application and coat sequence for specific surfaces, so that, by studying the information given here in conjunction with other articles, there is no reason why the handyman should not obtain a really professional finish on all his painting jobs.

Dealing with an Insanitary Gully Trap

Nine out of ten gully traps receiving the waste pipe from baths, sinks, etc., on domestic property are in an insanitary condition from the fact that the waste pipe discharges over the top of an iron grating. This leads to splashing and fouling of the adjoining area, the solids drying and beating up as dust to be breathed by passers-by, or by children playing in the vicinity. Further, the grating breaks the flushing force of the discharge so that the interior of the gully trap is in a filthy state and has to be periodically cleared and cleaned by hand.

Crevice between Stoneware Fitting and Wall.

The waste water is splashed on the wall rendering it damp, and usually there is a crevice at the back, between the stoneware fitting and the wall which allows the wet filth to creep in to foul the earth surrounding the gully trap (see Fig. 1).

Gully Traps with Back or Side Inlets.

Special gully traps with back or side inlets to receive the waste pipe can be obtained, but in domestic buildings they are seldom used because of the extra cost. Fig. 2 shows this type of gully trap which avoids the evils mentioned and provides a good scouring effect to the attached drains.

Where, however, the ordinary gully exists (as it does in nearly all domestic property), it is a troublesome and expensive matter to have it replaced with the "purpose-made" fitting, and the evils referred to can be avoided in a simple manner.

Using a Special Grating.

Firstly, a special grating can be obtained from some builders' merchants which has a U-piece cast in the grating (see Fig. 3). The waste pipe discharges over this space, thus avoiding the unfavourable conditions produced by the ordinary grating.

Fig. 1.—Waste Pipe fouling Yard and Wall; ponding in Earth and Damp Wall; Flushing effect to Gully and Drain Loss.

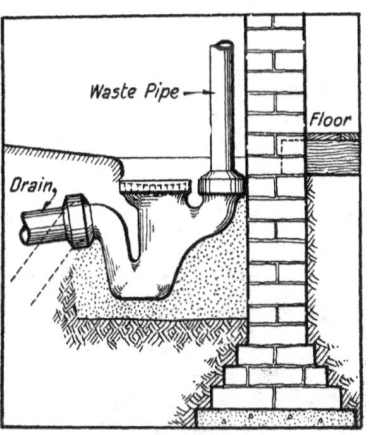

Fig. 2.—Back Inlet Gully Trap.

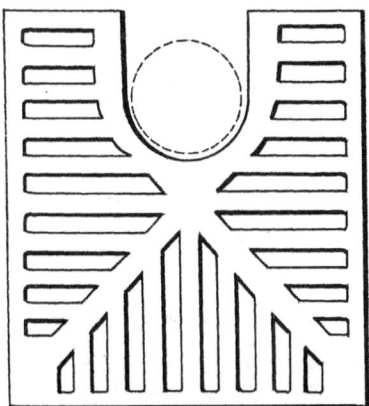

Fig. 3.—Plan of Special Grating.

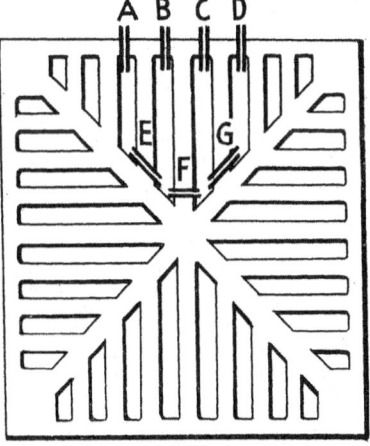

Fig. 4.—Ordinary Cast-iron Grating cut to receive Discharging End of Waste Pipe.

Cut at points A, B, C, D, E, F and G.

Converting an Existing Grating.

Failing this special grating, the existing grating can be cut with a hacksaw to produce the same result (see Fig. 4). Place the grating in a vice and with a hacksaw cut through the webs of frame as at A, B, C and D respectively. Then the webs E, F and G must be cut. The ordinary hacksaw will not reach these points, but they can be partly cut with a three-cornered file, and cast iron, being brittle, may be broken. Alternatively, the broken blade of a hacksaw can be used by riveting or bolting it in between two strips of wood to form a handle.

How to break the Bars.

To break the bars out after cutting the frame and nicking the bars as indicated, place the grating on the solid jaws of the vice and strike the bars one at a time with a small hammer, when they will snick out.

To prevent Grating breaking in the Wrong Place.

Care must be taken to see that the bar to be broken is perfectly solid on the vice when struck with the hammer or the grating may break in some other place. Time in filing a deep nick is well spent to reduce risk of fracture in the wrong place. If the bars are sawn through by blade the risk is avoided. The end of the waste pipe should be secured so that it discharges over the space cut in the grating.

Cast-iron Shoe.

Occasionally the end of the waste pipe is fitted with a cast iron shoe (see Fig. 5) when the conditions may be worse than those indicated in Fig. 1. In this case the shoe should be taken off by drawing the nails with a hammer and chisel, using the chisel as a wedge behind the head of the nail, and the projecting piece cut off.

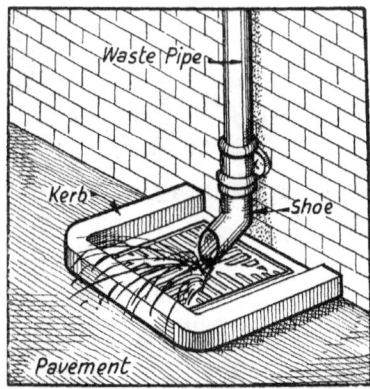

Fig. 5.—The Shoe for Waste Pipes is worse in effect than the Plain Pipe End. Such a shoe is intended for rainwater only.

DEALING WITH AN INSANITARY GULLY TRAP

Cutting a Piece off a Cast-iron Shoe.

To do this cut a nick all round with the corner of a sharp file. Then get an assistant to hold it over a piece of deal quartering placed on the earth or other solid position, and slowly revolve the shoe.

Do not Hit too Heavily.

With a small sharp chisel and a little hammer, chase round the filed nick with light blows on the chisel, when the piece will snick off. Do not be tempted to hit heavily if this does not happen on the first revolution, but continue in the same manner. The iron below the chisel edge becomes what is known as "stunned," and it will soon break off at the correct line.

A Hacksaw can be used.

To hit heavily will probably produce a longitudinal slit or crack in the shoe. It can, of course, be cut off with a hacksaw, but this is a somewhat tedious process.

Slip a Piece of Tube over the Pipe.

The piece can now be lengthened by slipping a piece of tube over made from sheet metal, zinc or copper, just to enter the slot made in the grating.

Refixing the Shoe.

In refixing the shoe a timber pad will probably be needed behind the ears to give the pipe a little more projection from the wall to clear the thickness of the stoneware edge of the gully trap (see Fig. 6). The tube should not be made to dip in the water seal, as the air must be allowed to blow in at the grating to ventilate the stack of waste pipe.

A little attention to the gully trap, on the lines indicated in this article, will go a long way towards reducing and preventing any objectionable smells that may arise from the traps.

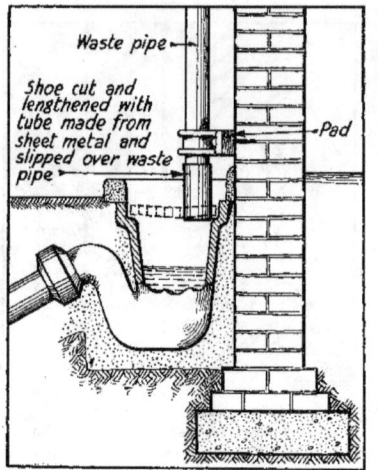

Fig. 6.—GRATING CUT AND PIPE SLIPPED THROUGH TO OBTAIN SELF-CLEANSING RESULT.

AN EMERGENCY TABLE FOR THE SMALL FLAT OR KITCHEN

A stout piece of plywood is cut slightly larger than the top of the gas stove. A batten ½ × 1½ inches is hinged to this which is fixed to the wall at the back of the stove. Then a batten and button are added to hold the table flat against the wall when not in use. It now acts as a splasher. It should be painted both sides with three coats of heat-resisting enamel (6d. tin at a big 6d. store). It can then be kept clean and fresh with soap and water. An enamel plate can be fixed underneath as shown.

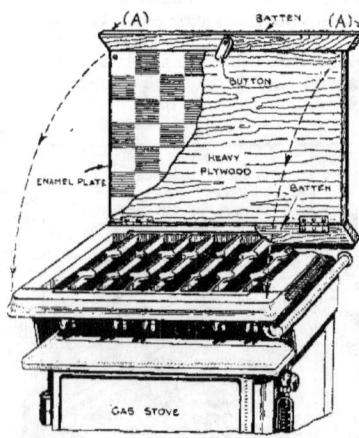

DETAILS OF THE EMERGENCY TABLE FOR A SMALL FLAT OR KITCHEN.

The same idea is most useful over the bath.

A shelf may be added as indicated at A, if desired.

TAKING FINE DENTS OUT OF THIN METAL

It is very difficult indeed to get small nicks and dents absolutely out of thin sheet brass or other metal

USING AN OLD FURNITURE CASTOR TO REMOVE DENTS IN METAL.

pieces. They must, of course, be carefully rolled out with a perfectly smooth hard wheel, rounded on the edges. It is a good idea to make use of a new or even old furniture castor as shown. Force the pin or stem of the castor frame up into a file handle. Lay the thin damaged sheet metal on a piece of heavy glass or other smooth hard surface. Run the improvised affair over it as shown. The small nicks and imperfections will smooth out easily and completely. The rounded edges of the castor wheel prevent it from leaving a mark of any kind. Enamel or other coatings will run on as smoothly as if there had been no spots on the surface, the real test of such a job of smoothing.

BENCH GRIPS, WHERE NO VICE IS AVAILABLE

A piece of hardwood measuring 9 × 6 × ⅞ inch sawn down the centre and cut to shape (as sketch) can be used effectively for planing the edge of thin boards. The pieces are fastened to the bench by screws which are placed half-way in each piece, these acting as pivots. When the board to be planed is pushed between, it will come into contact with the wedge-shaped pieces, A, which automatically closes the ends, B, and so secures the board rigidly for planing. These grips can

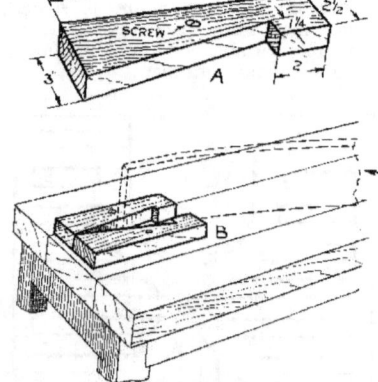

DETAILS OF THE IMPROVED BENCH GRIP. Showing also how the wood is gripped.

be used for the ordinary bench stop if the wood is too thick to go between the grips, as the wood will come up against the ends, B.

The Care of Oil Stoves

The following article deals with the care of oil stoves used for cooking purposes. To simplify the descriptions of the various operations, the article has been confined to the care of the "Florence" stove.

In the "Florence" stove there is no wick is usually applied. The oil is converted to gas, and having been mixed with a large volume of air, is completely consumed without smoke or smell. A "Florence" stove is shown in Fig. 1, and consists of four burners, with an oil tank on the left side. This oil tank is fitted with a window to allow the level of oil to be seen, and works on the chicken fountain principle, the filler being turned down into a trough which communicates with the burners by the oil pipe seen below them in Fig. 1. The burner (Fig. 2) consists of two parts, the base, which contains the kindler, a ring of asbestos millboard, and the flame ring. Oil is fed to the channel in which the kindler fits by a small pipe (Fig. 3). The oil level is maintained at a constant height in the oil pipe (Fig. 4), and the base of the burner in its "out" position is above this level. To bring the burner into action it is lowered by the quadrant and handle shown in Fig. 1.

Lighting Position.

The lowest position of the burner is called the lighting position, and as soon as the kindler has been ignited the burner is raised to the full position. The flame ring (Fig. 5b) is not attached to the base, but fits in the narrow channel provided (Fig. 6).

Flame Ring.

The flame ring consists of three parts, the outer guard ring, which is enamelled the colour of the stove, and the two inner rings, EE (Fig. 5c), the innermost of which resembles an inverted cup. Both of these rings are perforated with large numbers of very small holes. The ring is lifted to one side to allow the kindler to be ignited, and then replaced, giving it a rotary motion by the handle provided (Fig. 5c) to see that it is truly in its groove. The heat from the kindler is soon imparted to the base of the burner, and the incoming oil is gasified and rises between the two perforated rings, where it is mixed with large volumes of air, burning at the top with a pure bunsen flame. To extinguish the burner it is only necessary to raise it to its highest position, when the oil can no longer enter the base, and the flame dies out. If given a reasonable amount of attention, these stoves will give very satisfactory service, and are very economical in oil and upkeep. The first point for proper working is that the stove must stand perfectly level.

Fig. 1.—Florence Stove with Four Burners, Three being Standard, One a "Giant" under the Oven, on Right.

Note oil pipe from tank on left. The small projection in the centre is a spirit-level.

Fig. 2.—A Florence Burner with Outer Jacket cut away to show Flame.

Note the first perforated flame tube and base or cup in which the kindler is fitted.

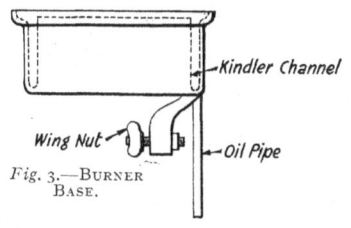

Fig. 3.—Burner Base.

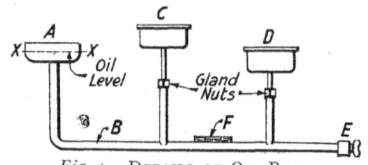

Fig. 4.—Details of Oil Pipe.

A, Oil trough in which tank fits. B, Oil pipe (see Fig. 1). C, Burner raised in "out" position. D, Burner lowered in "light" position. E, Cleaning plug. F, Spirit-level.

Importance of Correct Level.

A spirit-level is attached to the oil pipe at about its centre (Figs. 1 and 4), and levelling screws are provided in the legs (Fig. 7). This only gives the level in a longitudinal direction, but it is equally important that the stove should be level transversely, and it is a good plan to remove one of the flame rings and place a spirit-level across it (Fig. 8).

The oil must be an equal distance from the top of the base at all points. If the flame is unequal or inclined to smoke at one side, look to the level of the burners. The kindlers should be placed in the channels in the base with the corrugated edge of the asbestos upwards, the edge level with the tin ring (Fig. 9) must be at the bottom. See that the kindler is pressed equally down all round, so that it is quite level on its top edge. Once a week at least the kindler should be withdrawn, and with the tool provided the grooves should be scraped out, the burner being at its highest or out position.

Scrape any carbon off the kindler, and before replacing push a wire down the oil pipe (Fig. 6) to see that it is clear. It does not pay to use a kindler too long; they cost only a few pence each, and should be replaced every month or six weeks if the stove is in constant daily use.

Removing Burner from Stove.

Neglect of the kindlers is the chief cause of trouble with these stoves, and after many weeks' use without removing the kindlers for cleaning they become firmly embedded in their channels. Attempts are then made to cut them out with a table knife or other sharp implement, and in doing this the burner base is frequently bent (Fig. 10), so that it will not work properly. If a kindler through neglect has become fixed in its place the best thing to do is to remove the burner from the stove. To do this take off the oil tank and undo the plug at the end of the oil pipe (Fig. 4). Draw off the oil, which will be found to be dirty and probably mixed with water, and throw it away.

Undo the small wing nut (Figs. 3 and 6) and turn the handle of the burner to the start position. The burner base can now be lifted out of its place. The gland nut (Fig. 11) should not be unscrewed, though it can be slackened if tight. The kindler can now be picked out with a tool such as a bradawl or small screwdriver, and if the tin ring can be got hold of with a pair of pliers, it can be pulled out, and will usually bring the remains of the kindler with it.

Clean the channel thoroughly and replace the burner, fitting a new kindler in the ordinary way. It is a good investment to purchase a spare

THE CARE OF OIL STOVES

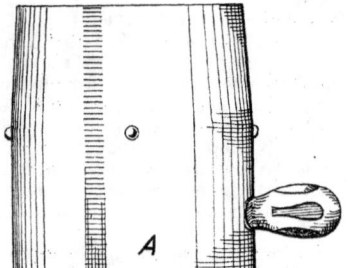

Fig. 5A.—Elevation of Flame Ring.

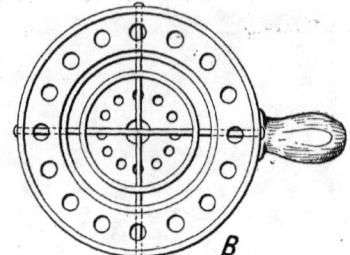

Fig. 5B.—View of Flame Ring from Below.

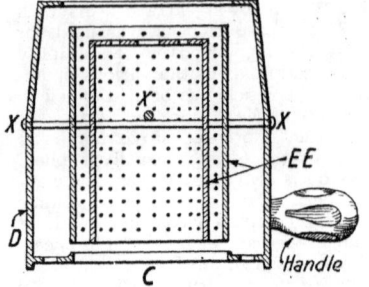

Fig. 5C.—Section of Flame Ring.
D, outer guard; EE, inner flame rings; XX, Supporting wires for flame rings.

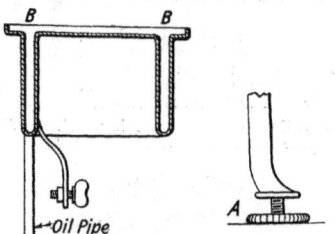

Fig. 6.—Section of Base. *Fig. 7.*—Leg of Stove, showing Levelling Screw A.
The flame ring fits in the channel marked BB.

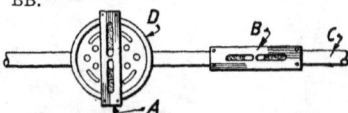

Fig. 8.—Flame Ring removed and a Spirit Level A placed across the Burner Base or Cup. B, Spirit-level on Oil Pipe C. D, Burner Base.

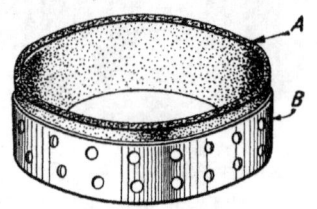

Fig. 9.—Kindler.
A, Asbestos. B, Tin ring. The kindler must always be fitted with the tin ring downwards.

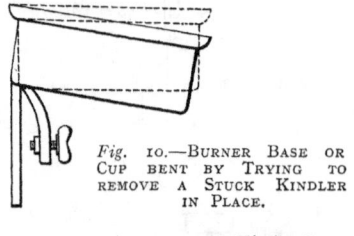

Fig. 10.—Burner Base or Cup bent by Trying to remove a Stuck Kindler in Place.

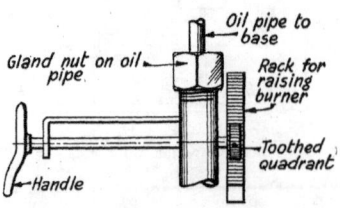

Fig. 11.—The Gland Nut.

burner base (Fig. 3), and this can be put in and the other cleaned out at leisure. A kindler which has had long service may be quite free in its channel if it has had periodical attention, and appears in order, but the flame will take a long time to run up the flame ring, so it does not pay to retain an old kindler. When replacing a burner base test for level both ways in case the oil pipe has been bent in removing it.

Water in Kindler Channel.

If kettles, etc., are allowed to boil over on the burners and put them out, the water, etc., will sometimes invade the kindler channel and the burner cannot be relighted. In such a case replace the kindler and dry the wet one off, when it can be again used. Water from this cause and water in the oil will in time accumulate in the oil pipe (Fig. 4), and periodically, say once in three or four months, the plug E (Fig. 4) should be unscrewed and the oil pipe drained. At the same time the oil trough A (Fig. 4) should be cleaned out with a cloth, and it is a good plan to push a length of thin wire cord right through the oil pipe. Cases have been known where through neglect the oil pipe has become choked and no oil could get to the burners.

Air Holes on Flame Ring stopped up.

Allowing food, etc., to boil over on the burners will stop up the air holes on the flame ring. If the space between the rings is observed while the burner is alight, a patch of holes may be noticed covered with a red-hot deposit, and the flame will be unequal. The flame ring should be removed and the rings cleaned by a blunt knife or a wire brush. In bad cases it may be necessary to take the flame ring apart and open out the holes with a sharp-pointed implement, such as a fine awl or a scriber. To take the flame rings apart the two long pins XX (Fig. 5C) must be removed. On one end of these will be seen thin washers fitting in grooves in the ends of the pins. These washers should be forced up with a knife or screwdriver, and the pins can then be withdrawn, and the flame ring will come apart into its three sections (Fig. 5C). Clean all the holes care-

fully and reassemble. No harm is done if the stove is allowed to go out through lack of oil, as the kindlers do not consume like wicks and never require trimming. On no account should the burners be left in the start position unlighted. If this is done the oil will creep up the sides of the flame rings, and when the burner is lighted it will vaporise off and make an unpleasant smell and smoke.

When the burner is finished with, turn it to the "out" position, and do not lower it again until it is required for lighting. There are two sizes of burner, the standard and the giant. One of the latter is usually fitted to stoves to heat the oven, and in no way differs apart from size from the standard burner.

A stock of kindlers of each size should be kept on hand in case of damage during cleaning or working with water due to boiling over. Kindlers can be made at home by cutting strips of $\frac{1}{16}$-inch asbestos millboard and clipping them in the tin bands of the old kindlers, but it is really not worth the trouble as the kindlers cost only a few pence each to buy.

The Oil.

With regard to the oil used as fuel, it is not necessary to use such good-quality oil as with wick stoves, and the cheaper grades as used for oil-engines and tractors can be used quite successfully with a considerable saving. These fuels are known as vaporising oils, and are supplied by the large oil companies in lots of not less than 50 gallons at a time. Such oils must not be used in wick stoves, however.

Gland Nuts.

The gland nuts (Figs. 4 and 11) on the burner pipes should be kept only just tight enough to prevent leakage; if done up too tightly the burner will move jerkily, and it will tend to strain the quadrant and handle. If the packing in the gland nut ever needs renewal—a very unlikely thing—it can be replaced with graphited asbestos string packing.

Keeping an Electric Vacuum Cleaner in Good Order

AN electric vacuum cleaner should run for many years without giving any serious trouble. There are two types in general use. One type has the bag suspended from the handle and with the fan between the mouth of the machine and the bag, thus permitting the use of a wide bag with a wide filtering surface and little or no " back pressure " to spoil the suction. The other type has the bag enclosed in a metal container and the fan is fitted behind the bag. A current of air is drawn through the material being cleaned and up the hose into the enclosed bag which permits the air to filter through and pass on round the motor, eventually escaping at the rear of the machine. This arrangement is neat, and the air currents cool the motor.

Fig. 1.—A Sudden Rattle in a Vacuum Cleaner is a Sign of something Hard in the Fan.
Switch off at once before it becomes wedged in and stops the motor.

FAULTS

The following are some of the most likely faults; the methods of dealing with the faults are described later in the article.

Total Failure of Motor.

Generally due to burnt-out armature, but do not omit to make sure that the electric supply is turned on. There will probably be signs of charring on the insulation of the armature winding. This fault is usually the result of using the machine on too high a voltage. The remedy is, of course, to have the armature rewound by a competent electrician.

Loss of Motor Speed and Erratic Running.

Generally due to a worn or broken brush. Undue sparking will be observed when the cover is removed, and there will be an excess of black dust on the commutator. The method of replacing a brush is described later.

Drop in Motor Speed.

This is due to a dirty commutator, and is not a fault that makes itself apparent immediately. The remedy is to clean the commutator.

Weak Suction.

May be due to a leaking bag or hose. The air passage between the nozzle of the dusting tool and the bag should be as air-tight as possible. Make sure that all joints between tubes are tight and avoid dents at the ends of metal tube extensions.

If the bag is accidentally torn it should be repaired with self-vulcanising patches.

Shock Felt on Touching Instrument.

May be caused by worn or broken flex. The most likely places for the cable to wear are near the two ends, and if the insulation appears worn the cable should be replaced.

Machine refuses to Start.

A defective switch may be the cause. Most switches are of the tumbler pattern, and the spring breaks in time. If the switch is old, replace with a new one. If the switch does not incorporate a device to take the "pull" on the cable, the ends of the flex may have come away from the switch terminals.

Rattle.

A sudden rattle denotes the presence of something hard in the fan which is too large or too heavy to pass through into the bag. The cleaner should immediately be stopped and a search made for the offending object.

REPAIRS
To obtain Access to the Motor.

Access to the motor can, in the case of bag type machines, be obtained by removing the aluminium cover which

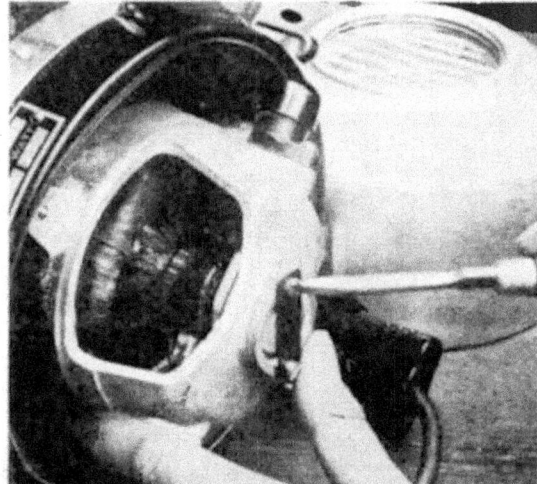

Fig. 2.—To remove the Cover over the Ball Bearings in an Enclosed Bag Machine, unscrew the Strap which secures the Dust Cap

Fig. 3.—Withdrawing the Carbon Brush from an Outside Bag Machine.
The brush is attached to the end of the spiral spring.

Fig. 4.—CLEANING THE SEGMENTS OF THE COMMUTATOR—OUTSIDE BAG MACHINE.

Rotate the armature with one hand while holding a rag moistened with petrol against the commutator.

Fig. 5.—CLEANING THE SEGMENTS OF THE COMMUTATOR—ENCLOSED BAG MACHINE.

The slight movement of the motor housing will not be felt on this machine, due to a semi-floating suspension which reduces vibration and noise to minimum.

Fig. 6.—REPLACING A FRAYED FLEX.

Showing switch removed from handle. Note the sheet insulation being held back by the thumb and the clamping collar on the right.

encases the upper end of the unit. In the case of the other type, the guard or shield which covers the air exit at the rear of the machine should be withdrawn.

Oiling.

The central portion of the motor, the armature, revolves between the field magnets surrounding it and is mounted on ball bearings. These bearings are packed with a high melting-point grease which must be replenished from time to time. Never use oil unless specially instructed by the makers of the machine. A special oil hole is provided in some of the older types of models having plain bearings. Care must be taken to see that no oil or grease reaches the windings, commutator, or brushes.

The Commutator and Brushes.

At the end of the armature spindle will be seen the commutator. This is composed of a number of small copper segments mounted on a cylinder of fibre or some suitable insulating material.

The brushes, consisting of small rectangular "carbon" blocks, rub on these segments, and should slide freely in their housing. The brushes can be removed by unscrewing the plug at the end of the brush guide. A spiral spring will emerge, and by pulling this the brush will slide out for examination.

Examining the Brushes.

Examine the brush and make sure it is free from cracks. The

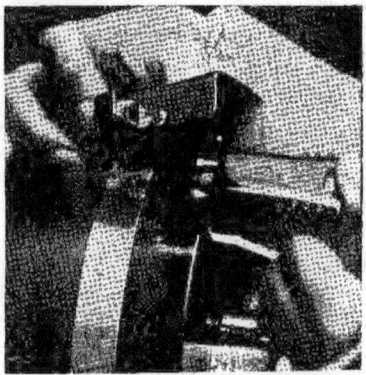

Fig. 7.—THE SWITCH ON AN ENCLOSED BAG MACHINE.

The cover carries the push rod which operates the switch. Note the adaptor on the right which contains the flexible cable.

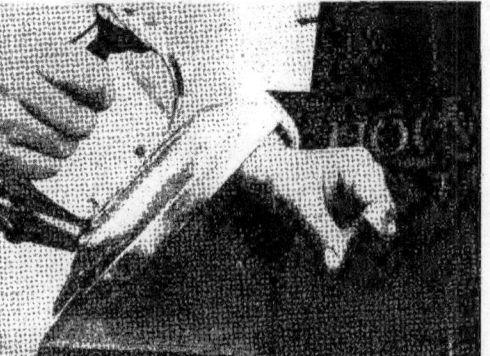

Fig. 8.—A SLIT IN A BAG CAN BE REPAIRED WITH A SELF-VULCANISING PATCH.

The patch is placed in position and a hot iron held on it for a few moments.

contact end should be concave with a polished surface. If damaged, replace with a new one.

The Brush Housing.

Examine the brush housing for carbon dust, which should be carefully wiped away.

Cleaning the Commutator.

To clean the commutator slightly dampen a piece of white rag with petrol and wipe the commutator clean by revolving the armature with one hand while the rag is held against it with the other. The object is to remove any fine carbon powder which may be clogging the gaps between the commutator segments.

The brushes can now be replaced in their housings and the plug replaced in position.

Renewing a Frayed Cable.

Cab-tyre cable, which is very strong and tough, should be used when replacing a cable. The first thing to do is to remove the switch (in the case of machines having the switch in the handle). This is generally held in place by two screws, and when these are released the switch can be pulled away, as shown in Fig. 6.

Thin "paper" ebonite or fibre will probably be found wrapped round the switch to prevent accidental contact with the metal handle. A contracting collar which grips the outer casing clamps the cable to the switch to prevent any "pull" being transmitted to the terminals.

It will be seen that there are two wires coming up the handle from the motor. One of these is attached to a terminal of the switch and the other is spliced or soldered to one end of the cable. The remaining end of the flex is joined to the second terminal of the switch.

When connecting up the new length of cable do not forget to tighten the contracting clip which grips the cable, and wrap the joint or splice with rubber tape.

Another Type of Switch.

With another type of switch fitted to some enclosed bag models, it is not necessary to touch the connections to the switch for the purpose of renewing a cable. The switch is inside the body of the machine and has two wires from it leading to insulated contact pegs which fit into a bakelite adaptor.

This adaptor is in two halves, which can be released by undoing a bolt through the centre, enabling the old cable to be removed from the contact pegs or terminals and the new cable fitted in its place.

Dealing with a Broken Switch.

The small coil spring which actuates the switch may break after it has seen a considerable period of use. If the switch is worn it will probably be more satisfactory to fit a new switch altogether. A new spring can, however, be fitted by placing one end on the fixed locating pin, compressing the spring with a knife blade and releasing it so that the free end beds down on to the locating pin in the tumbler.

Fig. 9.—Replacing a Flexible Belt.
It must be looped correctly on the pulley so that the motor causes the brush to revolve towards, and not away from, the mouth of the machine.

Air Leaks.

If the ends of any of the lengths of metal hose are dented, thus causing air leaks, they can be hammered out after placing a round mandrel inside the tube. Air leaks due to small punctures in the hose can be cured by bandaging the defective parts with rubber tape.

If a bag is torn on some sharp object it need not be scrapped. It can be repaired with one of the self-vulcanising outfits in the following manner.

Remove the bag and carefully clean the material around the hole, both on the outside and inside. Next cut two patches of the self vulcanising material large enough to cover the hole and extend well all round. Place one of the patches on the inside and the other on the outside, with the adhesive side placed against the material. Then hold a hot iron over the patches for a few moments. In some cases where the inside of the bag has a fluffy nap, it will not be possible to place a patch on the inside, but, wherever possible, this should be done.

Rotary Brushes or Agitators.

Some of the more expensive of the outside bag machines have an added improvement in the form of revolving brushes and beaters which agitate the surface of the material being cleaned, thus bringing deeply seated dirt and cottons into the air stream. The rotary brush is driven by a flexible endless rubber belt which encircles the brush spindle and is attached to a small pulley on an extension of the fan shaft.

The tension on this rubber belt must be considerable to avoid " slip," which will cause the belt to wear and decrease the brushing efficiency.

Replacing the Belt

When replacing the belt, it must be looped correctly on the pulley so that the motor causes the brush to revolve towards, and not away from, the mouth of the machine. Attention must also be given to the lubrication of the bearings in the end of the rotary brush.

DOGS AND TAR

DURING hot weather the tar on roads often becomes very sticky. If possible a dog should be prevented from walking over the soft surface, but this is difficult to avoid. If you find your dog has any tar on its feet, it is most important to remove the stuff at once, otherwise serious foot trouble will be likely to arise; in addition considerable damage can be done to carpets and other floor coverings if the tar is not removed at once. The tar does no harm to the hard pads, but it works its way in between the dog's toes to the soft skin, and, if it remains, it is likely to set up a serious inflammation, and in the end the dog may be hardly able to walk at all.

Use Fresh Butter.

If after a walk you find a dog is fidgeting over his feet, examine them for tar. Water will not dissolve the tar, and it is useless to apply this. The only handy thing to do what you wish is butter, which must be fresh and not salt. Apply the butter to the dog's feet, working it very gently between the toes with the finger. Leave the butter on for a few minutes, and then use a soft rag to clear it away when, to your delight, the tar will come too. Finally, bathe the dog's feet in warm water.

If there are many tarred roads in your district it pays to take some precautions. In hot weather when the tar is likely to be soft, rub lard or vaseline well between the toes of each foot. This will prevent the tar from doing any harm.

A Good Treatment.

Where a dog's feet have already been affected by tar, the following is a good treatment. Make a solution of 1 part of methylated spirits, the plain not the coloured kind, to 3 parts of water, which is just off the chill, and soak or freely bathe the dog's feet with this. Do this each night and morning, and in a few days the dog will probably be as well and happy as ever.

How to Make Inexpensive Saw Clamps

WHEN a saw of any description is being sharpened, the most essential point is that the saw should be held firmly in a good saw clamp to prevent chattering or vibration as the teeth are being filed.

An expensive metal clamp is quite unnecessary. Inexpensive and effective clamps are easily made out of wood by the handyman.

Fig. 1 shows a saw clamp that may be used either in the workshop or on outside jobs. The chief use of this saw clamp is to enable the saw to be sharpened as required on rough outside work where a bench is not available, as the clamp may be used by holding it firmly in position, with the knee or foot, against a low wall or trestle. The dimensions given in Fig. 1 may be varied a little according to the wood at one's disposal.

The Jaws.

The jaws of the clamp are made as shown in Fig. 2. The most important point to watch, when making these jaws, is that the notched-out portions marked X are cut on the taper as shown, so that they tighten when they are gently tapped into position with the mallet.

The Tops of the Legs.

Fig. 3 shows how the top of each leg of the clamp is cut to fit the jaws. Note the saw cut marked A. This should be deep enough to allow the saw to drop to the required depth. The shape of the dotted outline marked B has to be cut away when the clamp is intended for tenon saws as well as for hand and rip saws. This slot is easily made by boring a series of holes with the brace and a small twist bit, and then paring out the slot as required.

Saw Clamp for use in Vice.

A saw clamp that is made for use in the vice is shown in Fig. 4. The clamp is placed in the vice so that it rests on the battens marked X, and in use the action of the vice tightens the jaws of the clamp. The chief dimensions on the drawing are A and B. If these dimensions were altered to any extent the handle of the average saw would not slide in between the sides of the clamp. The bottom edges of this clamp should be hinged, as shown by Fig. 5.

Another type of saw clamp is shown in Fig. 7. The leg marked X may be either gripped in the bench vice or fastened to the edge of the bench by two screws. This clamp has the advantage of being adjustable to various heights when used in the vice, according to how long the leg marked X is made, and thus enables the operator to avoid continually stooping while saw sharpening.

The wing nut tightens the jaws of the clamp, and care should be taken, when making this clamp, to fix the bolt, on which the wing tightens, to the given dimensions in order to avoid fouling the back edges of the saws as they are placed in position. Fig. 6

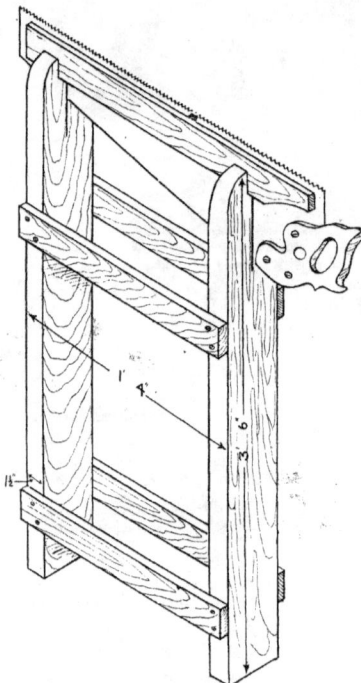

Fig. 1.—Showing the Saw Clamp with a Hand Saw fixed in position ready for sharpening.

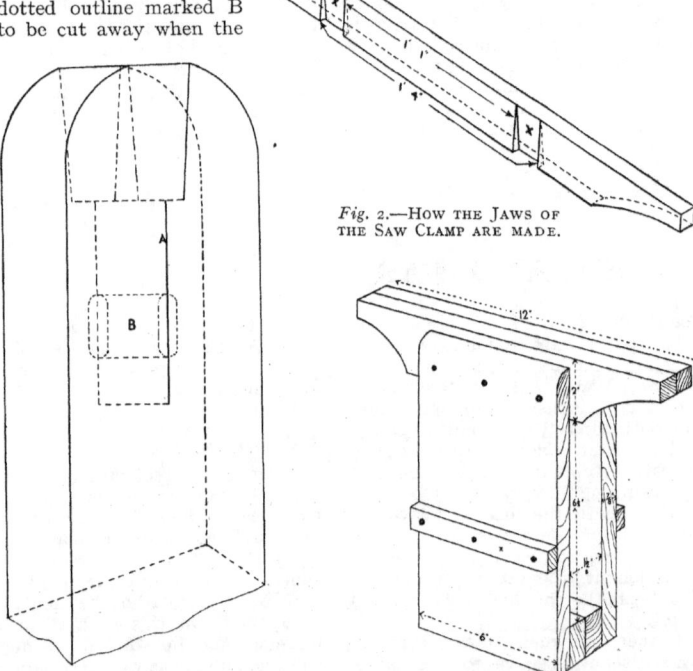

Fig. 2.—How the Jaws of the Saw Clamp are made.

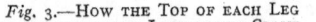

Fig. 3.—How the Top of each Leg is cut to fit the Jaws of the Clamp.

Fig. 4.—Saw Clamp made for use in a Vice.

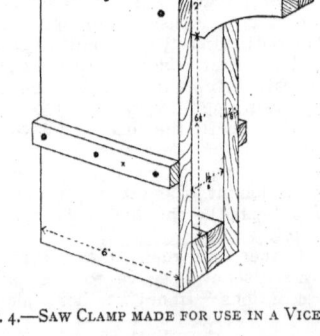

Fig. 5.—Showing the Clamp opened and fitted with a Hinge.

HOW TO MAKE INEXPENSIVE SAW CLAMPS

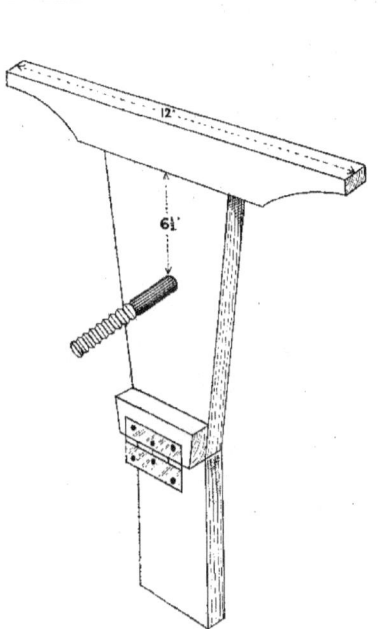

Fig. 6.—The Back Half of the Clamp with the Bolt in Position and a Hinge Fitted.

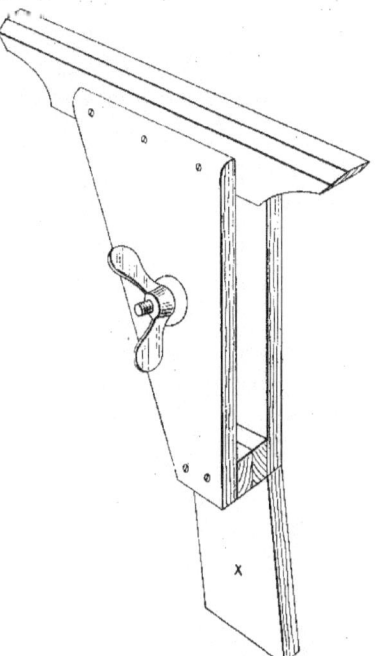

Fig. 7.—Note the Washer Against which the Wing Nut Tightens.

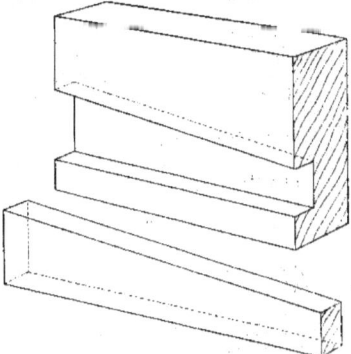

Fig. 8.—Simple Device for holding File used for Topping the Saw Teeth.

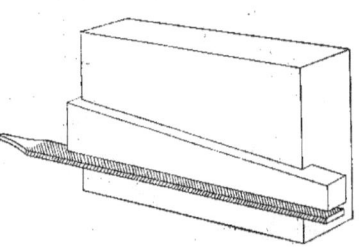

Fig. 9.—The File Wedged in Position.

shows the back half of this clamp with the bolt in position and a hinge fitted.

These clamps should be fitted together by screws and may be made of deal. For the jaws, however, hardwood, preferably beech, would be more suitable.

EASY GLASS CUTTING

Now and again it is wished to cut a piece of glass, and if a diamond or proper cutter is not available, it is useful to know that the process can be done with a pair of scissors under water. When doing the work, the glass, hands and scissors must be entirely plunged in a tub or pail of water. It will then be found that the glass can be cut in any desired manner almost as easily as if it was a piece of cardboard. This is due to the fact that the water kills the vibrations which would otherwise be present in scissors and glass. It is most important that everything must be under water as, if only a corner of the scissors was above the surface, the cutting could not be carried out in a satisfactory way. As a guide to the line along which one has to cut, it is a good plan to tie a piece of string round the sheet in the correct position.

If wished, the glass can be cut in curves without the least risk of fracture. In cutting out a circular piece of glass it is best to use a round card of the right size. This is held down on to the glass with one hand, meanwhile one works round the edge with the scissors.

Holding a File.

Fig. 8 shows a simple device for holding the file that is used for topping the saw teeth before the actual sharpening is commenced. The block and the wedge are made out of pieces

USING AN OLD SHOVEL HANDLE

Accident and mishap often overtake the common all-wood shovel handle. If the upper end is not broken, it can easily be converted into an excellent tool for countless home gardening and building purposes. Cut off the broken shank, and trim and smooth it to the curve of the lower part of the handle. This portion will be found very handy and convenient to use in easily breaking small clods of dirt, tamping earth in close places, setting brick for decorative purposes, knocking dirt from roots, and countless other purposes.

of suitable deal. Fig. 9 shows the file wedged in position. By means of the file held securely in the block the tops of the teeth may be filed perfectly true and straight, while cuts and scratches are avoided.

CURING SQUEAKY BED SPRING

Before one can suggest a satisfactory cure it will be necessary to examine the bed, with the mattress removed, testing it by pressing heavily on various parts.

Usually it will be found that the cause of such squeaks is a general slackness of the wire springs. If the latter are tightened, this trouble can generally be cured.

Tensioning the Spring.

In the ordinary design of wire mattress, two or more screws and nuts are provided for the purpose of tensioning the spring.

A close examination of the mattress will show by the polished surfaces where parts of the spring have been rubbing together. If these parts are separated and a piece of insulated adhesive tape placed between them, the squeaks due to the rubbing action will disappear. In the case of separated upholsterer's spiral springs these will often squeak if their fixings become loose, or the springs are allowed to deflect sideways. In these circumstances the cure consists in centralising and securely fastening the top and bottom ends of the springs.

HORTICULTURAL PREPARATIONS, FERTILISERS & MANURES

It is quite an easy matter for the amateur to decide which fertilisers to use on his crops if he bears in mind the following few simple facts.

Every crop needs certain chemicals which play a definite part in its growth to maturity. The principal ones and their functions are given below, and a reference to this, bearing in mind what the particular crop in question lacks in the way of growth, will decide what fertiliser to use.

It is then only necessary to look through the tabulated list to find the one most easily obtained.

Nitrogen. The function of nitrogen is to promote the vegetable growth of the plant, that is the leaf and stem, without which no plant can be completely developed. Lack of nitrogen produces stunted growth with poor colour foliage. Even though a soil is rich in the other necessary chemicals it will not produce good crops unless there is sufficient nitrogen present to produce strong healthy growth.

Phosphoric Acid. Whereas nitrogen is concerned with the stem and leaf of the plants, phosphoric acid affects the reproductive parts. It has a very definite effect on the production of flowers, fruit and seeds. The comparison can be easily illustrated by a plant such as lettuce. If this is given only nitrogen, large tender leaves will be produced, but if it be given phosphoric acid only, then small tough leaves will be obtained and the plants will early go to seed.

Potash. The function of the potash is to enable the plant to assimilate the other substances necessary for its growth. Potash is definitely necessary for this, especially in plants producing tubers in which starch, sugar, etc., are stored.

Lime. This is particularly useful in preventing an acid soil, for breaking up clay soil, and by combining with other substances in acting as a carrier.

Ammonium Carbonate. Substitute for nitrate of soda as a liquid fertiliser. Strength must not exceed ½ oz. per gallon of water.

Ammonia, Liquid. This is another source of nitrogen, but it can only be used with great caution, as ammonia fumes will destroy the foliage of plants. It should be used on the soil only, the solution being not stronger than a liquid ounce to a gallon of water.

Ammonium Nitrate. This is one of the strongest nitrogen fertilisers. Yellow foliage is easily changed to a deep green in a few days if the plant is watered with a solution of ½ oz. of this salt in a gallon of water.

A good all-round fertiliser is made by mixing ammonium nitrate with potassium phosphate in equal proportions. Greenhouse plants requiring extra nourishment should be watered once in ten days with a solution of this mixture of the same strength as given above.

Ammonium Phosphate. Gives results similar to those obtained from the mixture described in the last paragraph.

Ammonia, Sulphate of. A very useful fertiliser which can be applied to the land before the crops are sown. Do not, however, use it on soils of a chalky nature, as the lime will cause the liberation of the ammonia, which will therefore be lost. The quantity to be applied before planting is 2 oz. per square yard, or alternatively the same quantity can be given in two or three applications when the crops are growing.

Basic Slag. A product from the manufacture of steel, containing phosphoric acid, lime, sand, magnesia, and iron. Apply well before the crops are sown at the rate of 3 ozs. per square yard. Do not use with sulphate of ammonia.

Basic Superphosphate. Useful for acid soils. Generally contain about 25 per cent. of phosphate of lime. Apply at any time of the year at the rate of 4 ozs. per square yard.

Blood. Quite a useful fertiliser which contains nitrogen, phosphates, and lime. When decomposing, its odour can be very objectionable however, and it is therefore better either to dry it before use, or else to mix it to a compost with earth, etc. The dried blood can be used at the rate of 2 ozs. per square yard.

Bone Ash. A valuable phosphate fertiliser containing as its chief ingredient phosphate of lime. Useful for fruit trees and flowering plants. Use at the rate of 4 or 5 ozs. per square yard.

Bone Charcoal. Another source of phosphate of lime. Use as for bone ash.

Bone Meal. This consists of bones ground to a powder and contains about 45 per cent. of phosphate of lime together with nitrogen and magnesia. For vegetables, use when the ground is being dug in the spring, while for other purposes it should be used as a winter dressing. The rate of application is 3 ozs. per square yard.

Bordeaux Mixture. One of the best-known preventatives of disease among plants, *e.g.*, potato disease, bean canker, beet rust, etc., etc. Dissolve in 2½ gallons of cold water ¼ lb. of copper sulphate. In a similar lot of water dissolve 1 lb. of quicklime. In a wooden vessel add the dissolved lime to the dissolved copper sulphate. Do not reverse this part of the process.

Burgundy Mixture. Mix as for Bordeaux mixture, for which it is a substitute. Materials are copper sulphate 1 lb., washing soda 1¼ lbs., water 7½ gallons.

Chalk, Carbonate of Lime, or Limestone. Either of these is valuable as an autumn dressing for loamy or sandy soils. It is also good for growing pot plants, and is helpful for tomatoes. Use at the rate of 2 lbs. per square yard.

Charcoal. Chiefly valuable as a means of preventing soils becoming waterlogged.

Coal Ashes. Of great use on clay soils. Splits up the clay and keeps it open. Anthracite ashes are particularly useful.

Dung—Farmyard Manure. This is one of the oldest and most used of the manures. It consists of litter, water, nitrogen, potash, phosphoric acid, lime and small quantities of other salts. Farmyard manure is not of much use, except as an " opener " for clay soils, until it has been fermented. This is done by placing it in heaps when fermentation takes place, changing the complex salts into simpler ones more suited to absorption by the soil.

Parsnips and carrots do not as a rule benefit by an application of farmyard manure, but it is extremely useful for all other crops. Use at the rate of up to 2 tons per 10 square rods. Strawberry beds require it at the rate of 1 cwt. per 10 square yards.

For potting, use the very best well-decomposed manure.

Liquid manure, made by dissolving out the soluble contents of farmyard manure with water (a good way is to suspend a small sack of the manure in the water supply tank) is a very useful stimulant. As an all-round manure its usefulness is increased by adding to the liquid superphosphates at the rate of 1 oz. per gallon. The liquid manure should never be used stronger than when of a light brown colour.

Feathers. A source of nitrogen. When available they can be dug into the vegetable garden or into the fruit beds.

Flue Dust. Its composition varies very considerably. Can be used on light soils at the rate of about 4–5 cwts. per square rod.

Fowl and Rabbit Manure. This is one of the most valuable of the easily obtained farmyard excrements. It also is best used when it has been matured and when it will be found to be in a dry state ready for easy application. To mature it, store for two or three months in a box between alternate layers of dry fine soil. Apply as a top dressing at the rate of 4–5 ozs. per square yard.

A liquid manure can also be made from the poultry manure.

Garden Refuse. Store all waste materials such as lawn cuttings, cabbage stumps and leaves, foliage of plants, etc., etc., in a heap sprinkled from time to time with lime. When decomposed use in the autumn by digging into the soil.

If there is no room to store them they can either be buried direct in the soil, or preferably, be burnt and the ashes sprinkled on the soil.

Guano. The excrements of sea birds. Contains nitrogen, potash and phosphates and is usually bought on analysis on this basis. Should be used on growing crops at the rate of 2 ozs. per square yard. It is preferably watered in either by rain or artificially.

Gypsum (Sulphate of Lime). Will liberate the potash from the silicate of potash when it is applied to the soil. When sprinkled on manure heaps it will fix the ammonia. For soil, use at the rate of 1 lb. per square yard.

Hops, Spent. Useful only for mixing with heavy land to keep it open.

Iron Sulphate. Only needed on land which is definitely short of iron. This is often shown by pale green foliage instead of dark, but the addition of nitrogen should be tried first.

Kainit. A natural source of potash. Is cheap and is very useful for farm and vegetable crops, but is not recommended for fine crops. Apply in the autumn so that the winter rains will wash it into the soil. Rate of application is 4 ozs. per square yard.

Lime, Quick. That from ordinary limestone is good for crops, but that made from a magnesium limestone should not be used. Used for peaty soils and also for those rich in humus. Sometimes used for clay soils in order to make them more easily worked.

Lime, Slaked. Use for same purposes as quick lime. Rate of application approximately 1–1½ lbs. per square yard.

Lime, Superphosphate of (Superphosphates). This material is sold at varying prices which differ according to the amount of soluble phosphates which it contains. Use the cheapest grade for all farm, etc., work, and the medium one for special fertilising. The superphosphates are applied at the rate of 3 ozs. per square yard.

Lime, Nitrate of. Another source of nitrogen. Produces firm growth Used for growing plants at the rate of 1 oz. per yard super.

Naphthalene. One of the cheapest and most effective insecticides and fumigants for soils. It is harmless to all vegetable life, but will destroy all insects, etc. The rate of application is 2 ozs. per square yard. It is spread on the soil either just before digging is commenced, or just after, in which latter case it is raked into the soil.

Potash, Carbonate of. Rather expensive, but a good source of potash. Use in the autumn at the rate of 2 ozs. per square yard. Will kill most soil pests.

Potash, Chloride of (Muriate). Can be used in place of sulphate of potash, but never for potatoes. Rate of application is 2 ozs. per square yard.

Potash, Nitrate of. This fertiliser has the advantage of containing both nitrate and potash. It is a concentrated one used only for specialised work. Dissolve 1–2 ozs. in a gallon of water and use not more frequent than once a fortnight.

Potash, Phosphate of. This contains both phosphoric acid and potash, and is also a concentrated fertiliser for special work. Use as for nitrate of potash.

Potash, Sulphate of. An excellent form of potash fertiliser. Used at the rate of 1–2 ozs. per square yard. It can be applied at any time of the year, but is preferably used before the winter rains so that the latter can wash it into the soil.

Pyrethrum Wash. Dissolve one tablespoonful of soft soap in a gallon of water and add to it one teaspoonful of pyrethrum powder dissolved in a little boiling water. This insecticide is admirable for killing greenfly, and it has the added advantage that it is not poisonous.

Quassia Solution. Soak in water for three days 1 lb. of quassia chips and then allow them to simmer for three hours. Dissolve 1 lb. of soft soap in water and mix with the strained quassia extract, making up to the total of 8 gallons.

The solution is used to prevent attacks of aphis.

Salt. Does promote the growth of asparagus, beet, potatoes, etc. Should be used sparingly at a rate not exceeding 1 oz. per yard super.

Salt Solution. Five ounces per gallon of water. Used for spraying cabbages, etc., in order to drive out caterpillars.

Sulphur, Liver of. This solution is used by spraying as a remedy for mildew, etc. Take 2 ozs. of sulphide of potassium and 8 ozs. of soft soap and dissolve them in 8–10 gallons of water. Use while fresh.

Tobacco Powder. Used for black-fly attacks. Sprinkle on the affected foliage and then spray with clean water about an hour later.

REMEDIES AGAINST GARDEN PESTS

Cuckoo Spit, or Frog-hopper. The presence of this pest is detected by blobs of froth on roses, chrysanthemums and other plants. An effective spraying fluid is pyrethrum wash. Before applying the spray blow off a little of the froth with the empty syringe.

Earwigs. Chrysanthemums, dahlias, violas and similar flowers are liable to have their petals eaten by earwigs. To get rid of the pests use flower-pot traps or hang a partly opened matchbox or little rolls of corrugated cardboard among the plants. The traps should be looked at daily and the catch destroyed by dropping into boiling water.

Leather-jackets. These destroy the roots of crops, particularly greens. To protect plants sprinkle naphthalene around the roots. Another treatment is to mix 1 lb. of bran with 2 ozs. of Paris green and lay in little heaps between the plants. The mixture is, of course, poisonous.

Red Spider. A tiny orange-red mite which attacks rambler roses, gladioli, stocks, etc. The remedy is to syringe vigorously with water, carrying out the syringing on three successive evenings.

Slugs. Slugs do a great deal of damage in the garden. A slug-infested bed can be cleared by mixing 1 lb. of builder's lime with 10 gallons of water, allowing it to stand for two hours, then drawing off 5 gallons without any sediment and mixing with it 1 lb. of commercial aluminium sulphate. The mixture is then sprayed over the bed or border.

Another treatment is to get 14 to 21 lbs. of kainit, a potash fertiliser, and mix with it 1 lb. of bluestone, a cheap commercial sulphate of copper. Keep in a tin and dust lightly over the ground.

Thrips. Small black, brown or yellow feathery-winged insects which eat tiny holes in flowers and tender foliage. Treat as for red spiders.

Wireworms. Wireworms in small areas can be dealt with by skewering potatoes, turnips, carrots, etc., on wires and burying them in various places with the wire protruding from the soil. Pull up once a week and kill the wireworms. Another scheme is to pierce an old tin with holes, fill with potato peelings and bury just below the soil. Pull up once a week and shake the contents into hot water containing insecticide.

Lime added to soil from time to time counteracts wireworms. When applying the lime mix with every 14 lbs. of it, 2 lbs. of naphthalene.

Practical Notes on Using a Lathe

The lathe is without doubt an essential tool for anyone who does a considerable amount of woodworking and metalworking. Although primarily intended for turning, the lathe can also be used for drilling, boring and cutting screw threads, while special attachments make it possible to use it as a milling machine. Metal bars can be sawn through and slots cut by mounting a circular saw on the lathe spindle.

The Parts of a Lathe.

Fig. 1 shows a typical 4½-inch screw-cutting treadle lathe, together with the names of the various parts. A lathe consists essentially of a flat bed of any desired length, a head-stock which carries a spindle exactly parallel with the bed, and a slide rest for feeding the tool on the work. Some lathes are designed for hand turning only, in which case the compound slide rest is replaced by a T-rest which can be fixed in position anywhere along the bed. The variety of work that can be done by hand turning is necessarily limited, and the advantage of the compound slide rest is that it enables a cut to be taken parallel with the work for reducing the diameter, and at right angles to the spindle for facing cuts.

Fig. 1.—The Parts of a Lathe.
General view of a 4½-inch screw-cutting treadle lathe showing the names of the various parts.

The Tail-stock.

The tail-stock has a spindle in line with the mandrel or head-stock spindle, which can be fed forwards or backwards to enable drills to be fed up to the work.

The bed of the lathe sometimes has a gap which permits narrow work of large diameter, such as wheels, to be worked.

A screw-cutting lathe has a long threaded spindle called the lead screw which, when revolved, moves the slide rest bodily along the bed in a definite relation to the revolving of the mandrel by means of gearing between the mandrel and the lead screw.

The most important dimensions of any lathe are: the length that can be carried between the lathe centres, the height of the centre above the top face of the lathe, and the maximum diameter that can be revolved over the tool holder and slide rest.

To find Speed at which Work should revolve.

To find the speed a piece of work should revolve a minute, knowing the diameter of the work and the cutting speed in feet per minute, multiply the cutting speed by 12 and divide by the circumference of the work, or

$$\frac{\text{Cutting speed} \times 12}{3\tfrac{1}{7} \times \text{diameter of work}} = \text{revs. per minute.}$$

Cutting Speeds for Bench and Foot Lathes.

Tool steel annealed	45 ft. per min.
Malleable cast iron	60 ,, ,,
Mild steel	70 ,, ,,
Wrought iron	75 ,, ,,
Medium cast iron	50 ,, ,,
Rough-cast steel	30 ,, ,,
Cast iron	50 ,, ,,
Brass	120 ,, ,,
Copper	160 ,, ,,
Aluminium	180 ,, ,,

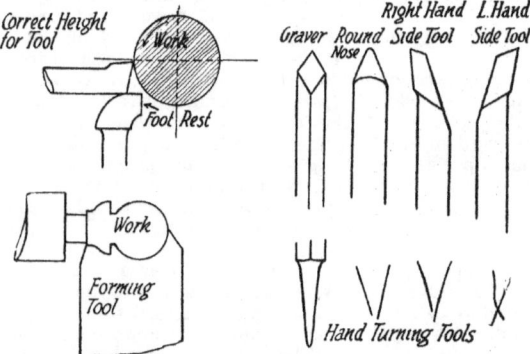

Fig. 2.—Hand Turning Tools in general use.

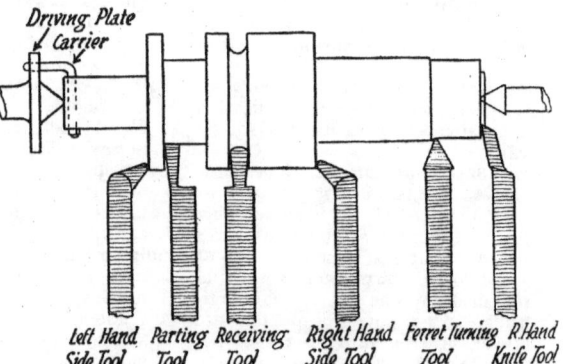

Fig. 3.—Lathe Turning Tools.

Fig. 4.—Turning the Base of a Table Lamp Standard
The corners have been cut off and the piece of wood screwed on to the faceplate with the planed side towards the plate.

Fig. 5.—Here we see how the Hand Rest of the Lathe is brought up with the "T" of the Rest parallel with the Face of the Work.

HAND TOOLS

The hand turning tools in general use are shown in Fig. 2; they consist of a front turning tool or graver, a round-nose tool, and side tools for left-handed or right-handed turning. In all cases when using hand tools the tool rest should be arranged so that the cutting edge of the tool is level with the axis of the work, as shown.

Soft metals, such as brass alloys, can be formed into shape by making a forming tool out of a piece of flat cast steel or an old flat file; the method is clearly shown in the illustration.

TURNING TOOLS

When work has to be turned between centres, it is first drilled and countersunk to the same angle as the lathe centre, usually 60 degrees. A carrier is then placed on the work, a little oil in the centres, and it is ready for mounting. The tail-stock centre is adjusted so that the work can be moved freely by hand without end play.

Lathe tools are frequently ground to shape from the solid bar; they are made in a great variety of forms, each tool having its own particular use. The tools illustrated at Fig. 3 would be quite sufficient for the great majority of jobs. All tools should be held firmly, with the base of the tool quite level, and the cutting edge in line with the axis

Fig. 6.—A Stage in Finishing the Base.
Showing the upper side of the base being shaped. This is done with a gouge, using the centre of the rounded cutting edge. The convexed portion towards the centre is finished with the chisel.

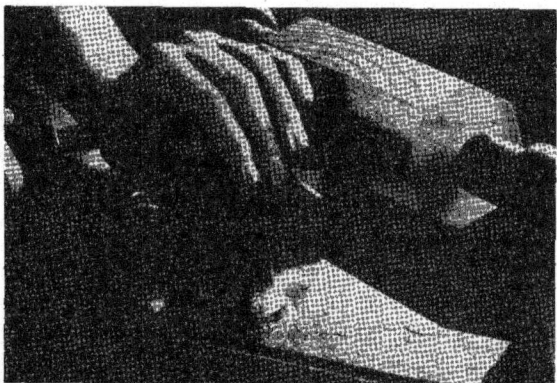
Fig. 7.—Turning the Shaft for a Table Lamp Standard.
Showing wood mounted between centres of the lathe, and the tool on the rest ready to begin cutting. Note not only the upward angle of the gouge, but also the horizontal angle which it makes with the centre line of the work.

of the work. The secret of turning is to keep the edge of the tool sharp, at the correct height, and as close to the tool holder as possible.

TURNING A SIMPLE TABLE LAMP STANDARD

Before dealing with the use of chucks, etc., we will describe in detail the process of turning a simple table lamp standard, as this is probably the sort of work to which the lathe is most likely to be put.

Turning the Base.

The first part to be dealt with is the base. Plane one side true and determine the centre by drawing diagonal lines from corner to corner. Next scribe the circle representing the diameter of the base, cut off the corners of the square to within ¼ inch of this scribed line, and screw on to the faceplate of the lathe with the planed side towards the plate. This is clearly shown in Fig. 4. Place the screws as far away from the centre as possible, so that the holes they leave will be turned away when the base is finished on the reverse side.

Trueing up the Face.

Now true up the face across its whole diameter in order to make it quite flat. This is done by bringing the hand rest of the lathe up with the T of the rest parallel with the face of the work, as shown

PRACTICAL NOTES ON USING A LATHE

Fig. 8.—FINISHING OFF THE ROUND CURVES WITH A CHISEL.

Turn the whole width of the groove at one time, reversing the tool constantly and working inwards until the full depth is obtained.

Finish off by glass-papering the outside of the work and then reverse it upon the faceplate, screwing it on as before.

Dealing with the Upper Side of the Base.

The gouge is used for shaping the upper side of the base as shown in Fig. 6. Use the centre of the rounded cutting edge. Finish the convexed portion towards the centre with a chisel. The hollow, however, will have to be completed with the gouge, taking light cuts and letting the tool travel in a fine spiral direction from where the convex finishes towards the periphery. Scraping will be best at the very last stage.

Next cut in the little break on the outside of the ogee curve with a chisel, using the point side of the cutting edge. Then complete the bead, one-half of which is already formed, and bore the socket to take the dowel or spigot on the shaft. Finish all over with glasspaper. This completes the base.

Turning the Shaft.

The next operation is to turn the shaft, starting with the lowest section. Mount the wood between the centres of the lathe, as in Fig. 7. The gouge is held on the rest as shown. Note the upward angle of the tool and the horizontal angle which it makes with the centre line of the work. Whilst making this angle and pointing in the direction shown, the tool must be moved to the right, otherwise it would dig in and possibly tear the work from the lathe.

For cutting from right to left the tool should point in the opposite direction, that is, towards the headstock.

Obtaining the Moulded Shape.

Having made the wood cylindrical, the next step is to mark with a pencil the principal members of the moulded shape. This can be done while it is still revolving. Now take a flat, round-nosed tool (not a gouge) and proceed to cut into and form the hollows. Complete the round curves with a drill, as shown in Fig. 8.

Lastly, shoulder down at the ends to form spigots.

Turning the Cup.

The cup is turned on a

Fig. 9.—AFTER TURNING THE WOOD SHOULD BE GLASS-PAPERED.

in Fig. 5. Use the gouge for the first roughing cut, holding it in a similar manner to that shown in Fig. 6, but inclined somewhat more steeply. Start cutting at the outside and work towards the centre. Only a light cut will be required if the wood is fairly uniform in thickness. Next test the surface for flatness by laying a straightedge across it.

Turn the edge of the work with the gouge in the same way as the face and continue cutting until the wood becomes cylindrical and of the correct diameter. To remove the marks of the gouge, finish with the chisel, taking very light cuts with the heel of the cutting edge. Take care not to let the edge towards the point touch the wood or it will probably dig in.

The sharp angle where the cylindrical parts meet the flat must be rounded off, thus forming one-half of the beaded edge of the base.

Turning the Groove.

The next operation consists of turning the groove for the lead groove, and this is shown completed in Fig. 5. It is done with the point of the chisel. As the angle of the tool on the rest cannot be very steeply inclined, scraping instead of direct cutting will have to be resorted to.

As the groove is to be dovetail shaped in section to form a "key" for the lead, the tool is used with the point towards the periphery of the disc when shaping the large diameter of the groove, and turned over towards the centre when shaping the smaller diameter.

Fig. 10.—A FINISHED STANDARD IN THE LATHE AFTER BEING ASSEMBLED AND GLASS-PAPERED.

PRACTICAL NOTES ON USING A LATHE

Fig. 11.—USING THE LATHE AS A DRILLING MACHINE.
Block of wood placed under the work prevents damage to the top slide.

Fig. 12.—DRILLING A HOLE IN A ROUND BAR.
A V-back centre holds the work in the correct position.

Fig. 13.—DRILLING IN THE LATHE WITH THE WORK REVOLVING IN THE SELF-CENTRING CHUCK.

smaller faceplate and is held by the central screw of the screwed chuck. It is dealt with in the same manner as the base, *i.e.*, first turned on one side, then reversed on the faceplate and turned on the other side. Before it is removed from the faceplate it should be bored to the diameter of the dowel, which will be formed at the top piece, to within $\frac{1}{64}$ inch from the other side.

Then glass-paper the surface as shown in Fig. 9, unscrew it from the faceplate, and remove the centre piece left in boring by a circular cut with knife or gouge.

The Top Piece.

Finally, turn the top piece between centres with the dowel portion nearest the prong centre of the lathe; the other end, which will be the extreme top, of the standard can then be recessed.

The small projecting piece of wood left by which the work is carried by the back centre can be reduced to about $\frac{1}{8}$ inch with either the smallest side chisel or a left-hand pointed chisel. The top is then removed from the lathe and the central projection cut away with an ordinary chisel, holding the job in the hands.

The pieces can then be drilled and assembled, and the standard is complete.

TURNING WITH SELF-CENTRING CHUCK

A self-centring, three-jaw chuck can be used to hold any jobs which are circular with sufficient accuracy for most purposes. It has two sets of jaws, one set for holding work on the outside and the other set for holding work on the inside, as in the case of tubes or rings when the outside is being turned.

How to change the Jaws.

When changing the jaws, the other set must be inserted in the correct order or else the chuck will not centre properly. The jaws are changed by winding out the set in the chuck by means of the key until they are free of the scroll, and then pulling them out of their grooves.

Now place the other set of jaws in their correct order (they are usually numbered 1, 2 and 3) and turn the chuck round to No. 1 groove. Next wind the scroll backwards with the chuck key until the end of the thread is just past this groove and push the jaw in as far as it will go. The key is now given half a turn in the other direction to hold No. 1 jaw. Turn the key until the thread is just in front of No. 2 groove and insert No. 2 jaw. Repeat the process for the third jaw and the chuck is ready for use.

Turning Long Bars.

Long bars can be turned with the

self-centring chuck if the free end is supported by a centre placed in the tail-stock spindle, although it is better to do such jobs between centres.

Setting up between Centres.

The self-centring chuck is usually not accurate enough for jobs such as axles which have to run perfectly true and have necessarily to be turned on each end; they are therefore turned between centres.

The first operation in setting up a bar between centres is to face up the rod with a round-nosed tool and centre drill it with a Slocomb centring drill to give a conical recess in each end of the bar into which the points of the lathe centres fit exactly.

Next put the front and back centres in the head-stock and tail-stock respectively and screw the driver-plate on the mandrel thread. Then screw a carrier on to one end of the bar, which engages with the stud on the driving-plate and so revolves the work. Now place the bar between the centres and tighten up the tail-stock spindle so that the spindle revolves fairly freely on the centres without any shake.

The back centre should then be oiled. It must also be readjusted after taking several cuts, because the centre wears loose. When one end has been shouldered down, the bar and carrier are reversed so that the other end can be dealt with.

Supporting the Work.

In the case of a long thin rod, such as an armature spindle, the work must be supported behind the tool as it travels along, and for this purpose a travelling steady is used. This is clamped on the saddle of the slide rest and follows the tool. It has to be reset after each cut.

Spindles turned between Centres.

One advantage of turning spindles between centres is that they can be set up again at any time for re-turning, and will still run truly if the centres are undamaged. Also, the work can be removed from the lathe while unfinished and replaced without disturbing the accuracy of the work.

Split Chucks.

Another method of holding the work in addition to self-centring chucks and turning between centres is by means of split chucks. As these are only suitable for holding one particular diameter of rod, it is necessary to have several different-sized chucks available. They are chiefly used for holding small diameters when self-centring chucks would either mark the work badly or not hold it, owing to the flats on the jaws.

Another use for split chucks is for holding threads without damage when

Fig. 14.—Facing up the Ends of a Bar preparatory to turning between Centres.

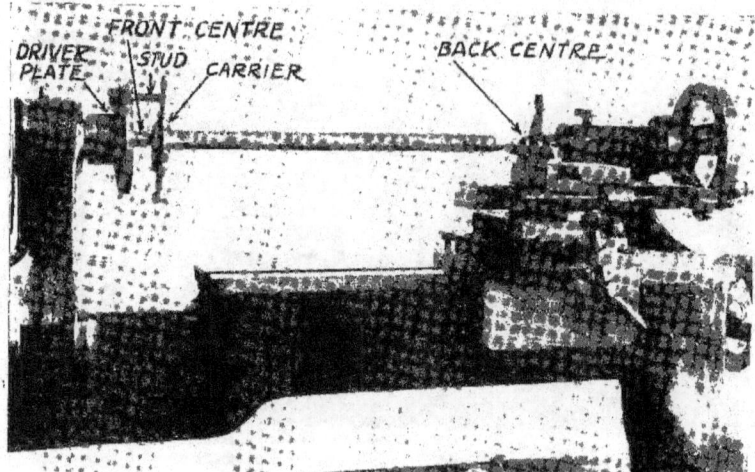

Fig. 15.—Turning an Axle between Centres.
If a long cut is to be taken, the change gears are set up to move the slide rest automatically.

Fig. 16.—Using the Travelling Steady when turning Slender Bars or Rods.

finishing off the heads of screws or turning down the head of a bolt.

Faceplate.

As already mentioned, a faceplate is used when an independent chuck is not available. It is simply a circular plate which screws on the mandrel thread. It should be noted that when a heavy job is set up on the faceplate out of centre, a counterbalance weight must be clamped to the faceplate or the machine will vibrate badly when rotated.

NOTES ON TURNING METALS

The tools most generally used for turning metals are the side tool or knife tool (see Fig. 21) used for turning a square shoulder, and the round-nosed tool, shown in Fig. 14, used for turning on an outside diameter for facing cuts and for roughing out.

When using the side tool, set its cutting point exactly centre height and at such an angle that the front and side faces are clear of the work. When taking facing cuts the tool should be at centre height, so as not to leave a pip in the centre of the work.

A lubricant is required for turning most metals.

Turning Steel.

Mild steel can be lubricated with soapsuds or lard oil, the latter being preferable, as the suds are liable to make the parts of the lathe rusty. Cast steel or silver steel can be worked dry or with lard oil. Run the lathe at a low speed or the tool will overheat and lose its cutting edge very quickly.

Turning Brass.

No lubricant is needed when turning hard brass, and the lathe can be run at a good speed. Soft brass is best worked with oil for all operations, especially drilling. Hard brass can be distinguished from soft brass by the fact that it screams when being turned and does not form shavings, while soft brass forms large shavings

Fig. 17.—Boring a Crank Bearing.
Using the 4-jaw independent chuck. A small round-nosed tool is clamped in the hole at the end of the boring bar.

Fig. 18.—Boring an Engine Crank Bearing.
Using the faceplate with an angle plate. Two of the lathe change wheels are used as a counterbalance weight.

easily and throws a burr in front of the tool.

Turning Aluminium and Copper.

Turpentine should be used to lubricate the turning tools and drills when dealing with aluminium and copper. The former tears badly if turned dry. When drilling long holes in these soft metals, the drill should be frequently released and the cutting edge cleared.

DRILLING

There are two methods of using a lathe for drilling. In one the work is held stationary, in the other the work rotates.

Drilling with Work stationary

The method of using a lathe as a drilling machine is shown in Fig. 11. A three-jaw self-centring chuck is used to hold the drill if it is one of the larger sizes, and the work is fed on to the drill by the tail-stock. The smaller sizes of drills are held in a drill chuck, as shown in Fig. 12.

A block of wood placed under the work prevents the top slide from being damaged.

Firmer support for the work is given by inserting a drilling pad in the hollow spindle of the tail-stock.

Keep Thrust Bearing well oiled.

The thrust bearing should be kept well oiled when drilling is being done. It will minimise the friction caused by the drill pressure; also lubricate the cutting edge of the drill.

Drilling with Work rotating.

This method is adopted when the work cannot conveniently be held in the manner described above, as, for example, when a hole is to be drilled in the centre of a round disc or in the end of a long bar.

The work is revolved in the chuck and the drill kept stationary in a drill chuck, the shank of which is inserted in the hollow spindle of the tail-stock.

The work must be set

PRACTICAL NOTES ON USING A LATHE

Fig. 19.—Facing Bar preparatory to making a Bush.

Fig. 20.—Centring the Bar shown in Fig. 19 with a Slocomb Centring Drill before drilling the Hole for the Bush.

Fig. 21.—Turning the Shoulder of the Bush with a Side Tool after Drilling.

Fig. 22.—Making a Bush.
Cutting the bush off the bar with a parting tool after drilling and turning.

Fig. 23.—Boring a Large Bush with a Round-nosed Boring Tool.

Fig. 24.—Cutting a ½-inch Whitworth Thread.
It is important to set the tool at exactly centre height when cutting threads.

PRACTICAL NOTES ON USING A LATHE

running truly in a self-centring chuck and the Slocomb centring drill used to make a small starting hole. If this is not done, the twist drill being comparatively flimsy runs out of centre, causing the hole to be eccentric with the periphery of the work.

MAKING A BUSH

An operation that is frequently carried out on a lathe is making a bush when rebushing a worn hole in a bearing.

The first thing to do is to place the rod in the self-centring chuck and face off the end square. Then mark off the centre with the Slocomb drill and drill the hole, reamering it to size if necessary.

Next turn the shoulder so that it fits tightly in the bearing. The outside diameter of the bush can be trued up at the same time.

The bush is then cut off the bar with a parting tool, after which it is rechucked and the large end faced up.

A large bush should be bored on the inside so as to get the hole perfectly true with the shoulder. A round-nosed boring tool is used for this purpose after drilling a hole slightly smaller than the required size.

SCREW CUTTING IN THE LATHE

In order to be able to cut threads in a lathe, it is necessary for the lathe to be provided with a lead screw or guide screw. This screw usually has a pitch of $\frac{1}{4}$ inch or $\frac{1}{2}$ inch; the pitch being the distance from the centre of one thread to the centre of an adjacent thread (see Fig. 25). The pitch determines the movement of the saddle of the lathe per revolution of the screw, and for every revolution of the lead screw the tool will move a distance equal to the pitch; it follows that should the lead screw only make a fraction of a turn, then the tool will only move that fraction of the pitch; thus if the pitch of the lead screw is $\frac{1}{4}$ inch and it makes a quarter of a revolution while the work is making one complete turn, then the tool will move $\frac{1}{4} \times \frac{1}{4}$ or $\frac{1}{16}$ inch.

Change Gears.

In addition to the lead screw, the lathe must be equipped with a set of change gears; these usually number 22, the smallest wheel making 20 teeth and the largest 120. The principle of screw cutting is ratio, that is, the proportion of the pitch of the lead screw to

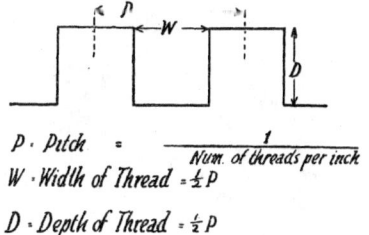

$P \cdot Pitch = \dfrac{1}{Num. \ of \ threads \ per \ inch}$

$W \cdot Width \ of \ Thread = \frac{1}{2} P$

$D \cdot Depth \ of \ Thread = \frac{1}{2} P$

Fig. 25.—Screw Cutting.

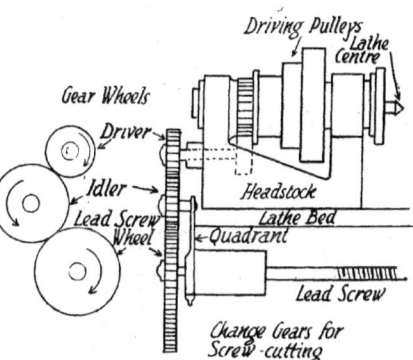

Fig. 26.—Change Gears for Screw Cutting.

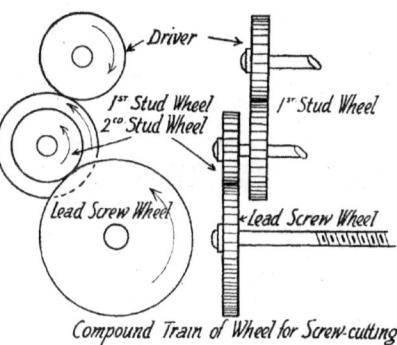

Fig. 27.—Compound Train of Gears.

the pitch of the screw to be cut. As an example, let the lead screw have a pitch of $\frac{1}{4}$ inch and the screw to be cut $\frac{1}{10}$ inch, then the ratio is as 4 is to 10 or as 2 is to 5, and gears in that ratio must be used.

How Work is held.

When a thread is cut in the lathe, the work is either held between the lathe centres or by means of a chuck; in either case the work revolves at the same speed as the lathe spindle. A little consideration of the gear wheels will show that the job is really geared by means of a number of wheels to the lead screw. It will also be seen that in order to cut one complete turn or helix of a thread, the work must make one complete revolution, and also that the distance the screw-cutting tool moves while the work is making one revolution will be equal to the pitch of the thread being cut.

Change Gear Calculations.

A simple train of wheels is shown at Fig. 26, and the only wheels that have to be considered for calculation are the driver and the lead screw wheel. If the driver has 20 teeth and the lead screw wheel 40 teeth, then for every complete revolution of the driver the lead screw wheel will move half a turn, and if the pitch of the lead screw is $\frac{1}{4}$ inch, the tool will move $\frac{1}{4} \times \frac{1}{2}$ or $\frac{1}{8}$ inch. Should the driver have 40 teeth and the lead screw wheel 20, then the tool will move $\frac{1}{4} \times \dfrac{2}{1}$, or $\frac{1}{2}$ inch.

In all cases of simple trains, the ratio of the number of teeth in the driver to the number of teeth in the lead screw wheel must be exactly the same as the ratio of the pitch of the lead screw to the pitch of the thread to be cut. Or

$$\dfrac{\text{Number of threads per inch on lead screw}}{\text{Number of threads per inch to be cut}} = \dfrac{\text{number of teeth in driver}}{\text{number of teeth in lead screw wheel}}$$

To cut nine threads per inch on a lathe with a lead screw of $\frac{1}{4}$ inch pitch: threads per inch on lead screw, 4; threads to be cut, 9; then ratio of 4 to 9; thus a wheel with 40 teeth as driver, a wheel with 90 teeth as lead screw wheel and any suitable wheel as an idler, or 20 driver and 45 lead screw wheel.

Compound Trains.

A compound train of gears is shown at Fig. 27, and is used in cases when the required ratio cannot be obtained with a simple train, for example, if it is necessary to cut a thread having a pitch of $\frac{1}{28}$ inch, on a lathe with a lead screw of 4 threads per inch, the ratio of 1 to 7 cannot be obtained with a simple train, and therefore a compound train must be used. To find suitable gears, make the number of threads per inch on the lead screw the numerator, and the number of threads to be cut the denominator of a fraction, thus $\frac{4}{28}$, resolve the numerator and denominator into factors $\dfrac{2 \times 2}{4 \times 7}$, and multiply by any convenient number in order to obtain the desired change gears, thus:

$$\dfrac{(2 \times 10) \times (2 \times 10)}{(4 \times 10) \times (7 \times 10)}$$

then 20 teeth in driver, 40 in first stud wheel, 20 teeth in second stud wheel, and 70 teeth in lead screw wheel.

Making a Wall Desk

THE attractive writing desk seen in Fig. 1 is a very useful piece of furniture, admirably suited to small rooms and capable of being finished in a manner to harmonise with any style of furnishing.

Furthermore, it has the added attractions of ease of construction and low cost for material.

Materials required.

Selection of the wood most suited to the purpose should be governed by the intended style of finish; for example, if a "cabinet" wood is desired—that is, mahogany, oak or walnut—then choose veneered plywood; but for a stained finish order American white-wood, or for an enamelled or cellulosed finish use deal for the framework, and birch plywood for the fall front and interior parts. In all cases the same quantities of wood are necessary as set out hereunder.

Framework.—Two pieces, $6 \times \frac{1}{2} \times 14$ inches; two pieces $6 \times \frac{1}{2} \times 24$ inches.

Back.—Birch plywood, $24 \times 14 \times \frac{1}{8}$ inches.

Fall Front.—Plywood, one piece, $24 \times 14 \times \frac{1}{2}$ inches.

Interior Fittings.—One piece, $19 \times 5 \times \frac{1}{4}$ inches; two pieces, $14 \times 5 \times \frac{1}{4}$ inches; one piece, $19 \times 6 \times \frac{1}{4}$ inches; two pieces, $6 \times 4\frac{1}{2} \times \frac{1}{4}$ inches; two pieces, $5 \times 1\frac{1}{2} \times \frac{1}{4}$ inches.

Sundries.—One pair combined hinge and stay for fall fronts (Type C505), one gripper spring catch (Type F48), one handle or knob to choice (Frank Romany Ltd.).

First build the Framework.

The framework or carcase (Fig. 2) should be made first; it measures 24 inches wide, 14 inches high and 6 inches deep from front to back; the joints at all corners should be made with a simple rebate, as shown in Fig. 3. To make this, first cut the side pieces to exact length, square them up and then cut the rebates on the inner faces.

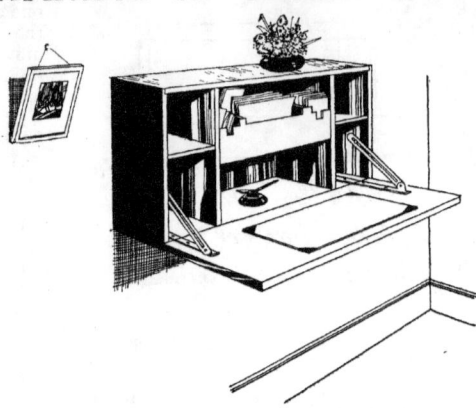

Fig. 1.—The Finished Desk—open for Writing.
The hinged surface folds flat when not required for writing.

Cut Top and Bottom Members to Length.

The top and bottom members are then cut to length, squared up and then glued and pinned to the rebates.

Take care to have everything square and true, also make the length of the

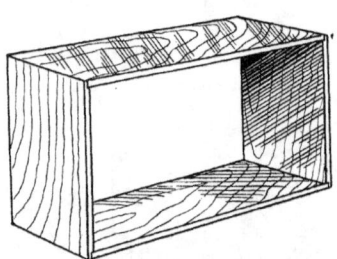

Fig. 2.—Framework of Wall Desk.
The rectangular frame is first made and the plywood backboard then added.

top and bottom pieces such that when in place the overall width is 24 inches.

Backing Piece.

Fix the backing piece of plywood with glue and fine cabinet pins; when dry, plane off the surplus edges so that everything finishes flush.

Making and hingeing the Fall Front.

The writing flap or fall front is a plain rectangle of plywood and can best be fitted by planing the bottom edge square and true and placing it against the lower front edge of the frame.

Fitting the Hinges.

Next take the pair of combined hinges and stays, place them in position as shown in Fig. 4, mark the whereabouts of the hinges and fit them into shallow recesses, which should be cut out with a chisel. This is not absolutely essential, but makes a workmanlike job.

The Stay Plates.

When the hinges have been fixed, the stay plates can then be screwed in position to the inside of the uprights on the frame, taking care to set the studs at the top of the slot in the stay, and both in the same relative position so that each does its share of the work of holding the flap in a horizontal position. Next close the flap and carefully plane the edges so that they finish flush with the outside of the frame. Fix the spring clip as shown in Fig. 5, also fix the selected knob or handle.

Interior Work.

The interior can be fitted out in any way to suit individual ideas, but the arrangement shown in Fig. 6 is generally convenient. The whole should be made up with simple butted joints, glued and pinned together, all surfaces then sand-papered clean and the whole inserted into place. It is held in position by glue and a few pins driven through the backboard.

Finishing the Exterior and Interior.

The whole of the interior can be lightly stained and either varnished or polished. The exterior can be finished off in any desired manner; limed oak finished with a white wax polish is

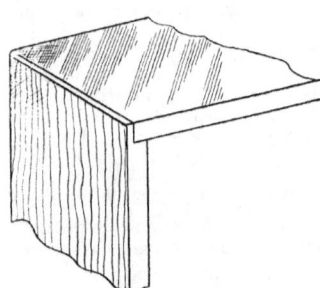

Fig. 3.—Corner Joint of Framework.
The upright side pieces are rebated to take the top and bottom boards.

Fig. 4.—Fitting Combined Hinge and Stay.
This fitment simplifies the work of fixing the hinges and stays in correct alignment.

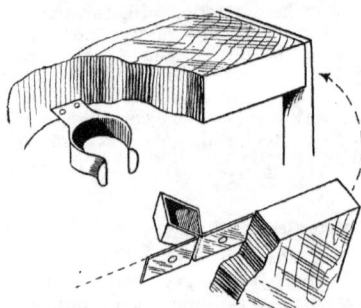

Fig. 5.—How to fix the Spring Clip.
One part screws inside the framework, the other part to the flap.

MAKING A WALL DESK

very effective, while a particularly rich effect is obtained by using walnut veneered plywood, enriched with warm brown stain and finished by French polishing.

In all cases the surface of the wood should be prepared in a suitable way, first by cleaning down with fine sandpaper, then applying a coat of grain filler and when dry again rubbing it down with sandpaper to produce a perfectly flat, even surface. This is especially necessary when a cellulose or enamel finish is intended, because either has a tendency to enhance any surface blemishes. Full instructions for this kind of work are given on other pages of " Practical Enquire Within."

Fixing Desk to Wall.

The finished article should be fixed to the wall with screws driven through the backboard into rawl plugs in the wall.

It is important to set the desk

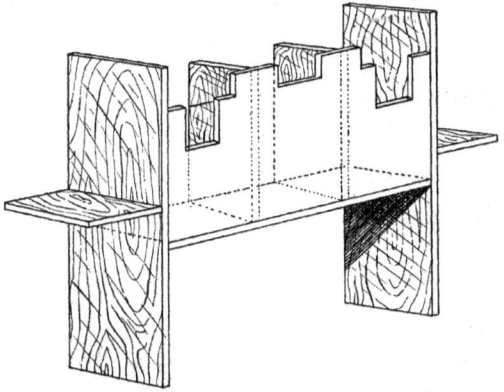

Fig. 6.—Interior Divisions.
This arrangement allows ample space for letters, notepaper, inks and other items. The fitment is here shown ready to insert into the case.

with its top edge horizontal—which can be done by testing with a spirit-level, or if that is not available, a line can be drawn on the wall—parallel to the floor—and the desk set against the line. Another point to watch when fixing the desk is that the fixture must be rigid, for which purpose at least four separate screws should be used; two can be driven through the top corners of the backing and the other two screws through the lower corners.

Should the wall surface not be quite true and flat, the desk will necessarily only touch at a few places, and when this is the case, a few slips of thin wood or card should be inserted between the desk and the wall so that the desk is quite firm. It is a good plan to fasten the packing slips to the backboard with seccotine, to prevent their falling out of place. Round-head screws are the best to use, especially if a washer is placed under the head before driving the screw home.

AN INEXPENSIVE BAR BENDER

THE bar bender here described can be made up for a few pence from pieces of tubing and bolts usually associated with the junk box. If the whole lot has to be bought the cost only amounts to 2s. 9d.

With its aid it is possible to bend steel or brass bars up to ¾ inch diameter or 1½ × ¼-inch flat bars into almost any shape.

Materials required.

The materials required are as follows : 5 feet of 2 × ¼-inch black mild steel slat ; short length of 9/16 or ⅝-inch diameter gas barrel ; three ½-inch diameter bolts, 2 inches long, with nuts.

First cut a piece 7 inches long off the 2 × ¼-inch strip. In this, drill two ½ inch diameter and two ¼ inch diameter with holes in the positions shown in the sketch. One end of this piece will have to be filed to a curve struck from one of the ½-inch diameter holes as indicated. This is to allow the nut on the other piece to pass freely.

One end of the remaining piece of flat will also have to be filed to a curve struck from the end ¾-inch diameter hole. In this piece will have to be drilled one ¾-inch diameter and one ½-inch diameter hole.

The Pieces of Barrel.

Now for the pieces of barrel. Cut off two pieces a full 1¾ inches long and one piece a full 1½ inches long. The ends of all

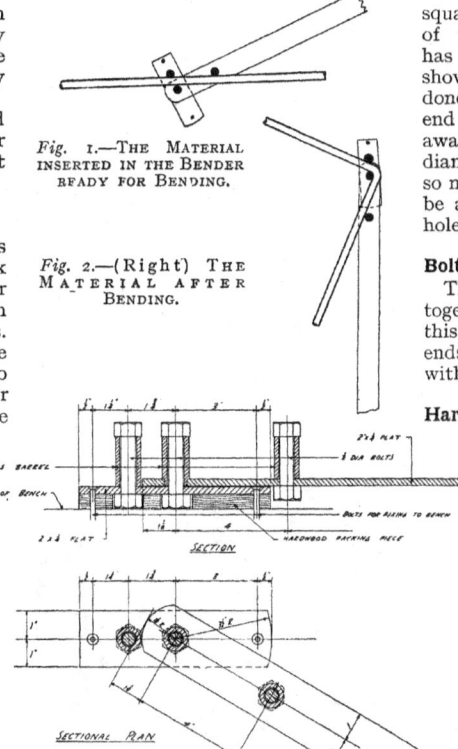

Fig. 1.—The Material Inserted in the Bender Ready for Bending.

Fig. 2.—(Right) The Material After Bending.

Fig. 3.—Constructional Details of the Bender.

these pieces must be filed dead square and flat. On the end of one of the 1¾-inch lengths a shoulder has to be formed a ¼ inch wide, as shown on section. This can easily be done by cutting a line ¼ inch from one end with a hacksaw, and then filing away the shoulder, until it is ¾ inch diameter. If this can be turned down, so much the better. This should now be a loose fit in the ¾-inch diameter hole.

Bolting Pieces together.

The pieces must now be bolted together. The section should make this quite clear. After assembly, the ends of the bolts can be sawn off flush with the nuts.

Hardwood Packing Piece.

It will also be necessary to make a hardwood packing piece, the same size as the small strip and ½ inch thick. In this must be drilled two 1¼-inch diameter holes to receive the two nuts and two ¼-inch diameter holes to correspond with those in the strip.

Now all that has to be done is to screw or bolt the short strip and packing piece to the bench and the bender is ready for use.

It will be found extremely useful for bending brackets, etc., and other intricate shapes, and will save a lot of time and trouble.

The Painting and Preservative Treatment of Garages

THE enormous increase in the number of motor cars has been accompanied by a need for places in which to house them, and whereas twenty years ago few houses possessed a garage, the reverse is now the case.

They all call for some kind of protective treatment either on part or the whole of their structures.

Brick-built Garages.

The more substantially built garages often have outer walls of brick or stone, and such walls need no further external coating to protect them from the weather. The inside faces of such walls, however, are often of inferior material and surface, and therefore they are often coated with

Fig. 1.—When dealing with a Brick-built Garage the Doors and Windows should be painted to conform with the Adjacent House.

some material, if only for the sake of appearance.

In some cases these interior walls are limewashed, and, where economy is requisite, this is by no means a bad method provided that the limewash is properly made and applied.

Recipe for Limewash.

A useful recipe for limewash for this purpose is to get a quantity of lump lime, slake it with boiling water, and then thin it with skimmed milk. A further improvement is to add 1 oz. of alum, which has been dissolved in water, to each gallon of the mixture.

Coloured Limewash.

If some other colour than white is required, this can be obtained by adding one of the common dry colours which are resistant to lime, such as ochre, venetian red, umber, lime blue, or lime green.

Cement or Asbestos Sheet Garages.

A type of building fairly common for the housing of cars is that where the walls are constructed of slabs or sheets made from cement, asbestos, or a compound of these substances held together by a framework of wood. In such cases the door and window are also of wood.

Here we are confronted with two kinds of material, one of which, the timber, requires paint or other protection on erection, while the other, the sheeting, does not.

The Priming Coat.

If a new building is being erected, the woodwork, if it is to be finished in paint, should have its first coat (known as "priming") before it leaves the workshop where it is prepared, if this is at all possible. The back side of the rails, which will cover the joints between the sheets and will afterwards be inaccessible, should receive at least this one coat of priming as a protection against any moisture which may find its way between the sheets and the bars. The same consideration applies if the wood is to be treated with a wood preservative instead of paint. But more of this subject later.

On the other hand, the composition sheets do not require, nor is it desirable to give them, any protective treatment while new. They contain a considerable amount of alkaline matter, and this will attack any kind of oil paint,

Fig. 2.—If Tools and Garden Implements are to be hung on the Walls inside the Garage, the Dado should be carried out in Oil Paint with a Glossy Finish which is easy to keep clean.

saponifying the oil therein, and causing unsightly patches and streaks.

This kind of material is best left in its natural state for twelve months or so, by which time its alkali content will have become exhausted.

If, however, for any reason some decorative treatment is required, one or two coats of a reliable water paint (outside quality) is the most suitable material to use, as it will be less affected by the alkali, and it can be oil-painted over at a later date if necessary.

The Finishing Coats.

The wood parts of the building should receive their second and third coats of paint, or second coat of wood preservative, after the building has been erected.

By far the most common form of garage, particularly in the rural and suburban districts, is that which is entirely made of wood, with a wood roof which is perhaps covered with a kind of felt sheeting.

The usual treatment for these covered roofs is to coat them with liquid tar, either while the felt is new or within a month or two after fixing. No special skill is called for in the application of tar. It can be purchased cheaply from any gasworks, in thick liquid form; it generally requires warming before use, and it can be applied with any kind of brush, such as an old whitewash brush, either of the flat or turk's-head type.

Tar Splashes.

Great care should be taken to prevent any splashes of tar getting on to the wood sides of the building, particularly if those sides are to be painted. One of the disadvantages of tar is that any mark made by it upon woodwork will show through any number of later coats of paint as a very ugly brown smear.

Should it happen that, despite every care taken, a splash of tar gets on to the woodwork, as much of it as possible should be removed with the blade of a knife or a rag soaked in paraffin. The patch of wood affected should then be given a coat of shellac knotting, which will isolate the remains of the tar splash and prevent it bleeding through subsequent coats of paint.

The wood walls may be treated in any one of several ways.

The Untreated Garage.

Sometimes, when the erection of the building is complete, the owner's

Fig. 3.—IF THE SIDES OF THE GARAGE CONSIST OF CEMENT OR ASBESTOS SHEETING, NO PROTECTIVE TREATMENT IS REQUIRED WHILE NEW.

If, however, it is desired to give it a decorative treatment, a water paint should be used, as it can be oil-painted over at a later date.

Fig. 4.—THE ALL-WOOD TYPE OF GARAGE SHOULD BE PROTECTED FROM THE WEATHER BY ONE OR TWO COATS OF TAR, A PROPRIETARY WOOD PRESERVATIVE, OR BY PAINTING, THE LATTER TREATMENT ALLOWING AN INFINITE VARIETY OF COLOUR TREATMENTS.

enthusiasm evaporates and the exterior woodwork is left, as it were, in the raw. This is unfair to the structure itself, to the neighbours to whom the building may be an eyesore, and, ultimately, to the owner, who will have a repair bill to pay in due course.

The woodwork gradually changes its first clean whiteness for a dirty grey or brown, as the impurities from the atmosphere fall upon it and are partly absorbed by it. And as all kinds of soft wood require protection if exposed to the weather, the structure itself begins, after a time, to rot and decay.

It may be accepted as an axiom that the ordinary woods, such as spruce and deal, used in the construction of such buildings as garages, require complete protection from the weather.

The cheapest form of protection is probably one or two coats of tar. This is a fairly good method in some respects, but it has manifest disadvantages. One is that, in hot weather, the tar is apt to soften and run down in streaks. Also it is, while soft, detrimental to anything, such as the clothes of a passer-by, which comes into contact with it. Moreover, black, and a glossy black at that, is not the most pleasing colour æsthetically.

An Alternative.

There are, however, certain proprietary wood preservatives on the market at a reasonable price. These are in the form of a thin antiseptic liquid stain, and they have excellent preservative and germicide qualities, but the range of colour is small (brown and green being the usual colours), and therefore the variety of possible decorative effects is limited.

They have the disadvantage, too, that as they are generally made from some derivative of tar; paint cannot be successfully applied immediately over them.

All things considered, and particularly if a little additional expense is no bar, paint is probably the best external treatment. It allows of an infinite variety of colour treatments, and the choice of two or more tasteful colours will enable the owner to make his garage, which is seldom a beautiful thing in itself, harmonise with its surroundings and become not unpleasing to the eye.

Colour Schemes.

Differing shades of green, two tones of brown, dark brown and cream, brown and blue, and buff and maroon, are but a few of the many possible combinations of colour which, with due regard to its surroundings, may be adopted to make a garage a quite inoffensive feature of the landscape.

On new external wood walls three coats of paint is the minimum for proper preservation of the timber. First, all the knots should be coated with shellac knotting; otherwise they will show through the finished work, spoiling its appearance.

Then the priming coat should be applied while the timber is perfectly dry. This priming coat should be mixed according to formula No. 1 in the article "How to Mix Lead Paints" on page 432. The formulas for the second and third coats are those numbered 2 and 3 in the article just mentioned.

Stopping-up.

After the priming coat, all nail holes and other voids should be filled with a suitable stopping. A good putty for this purpose is made by mixing equal parts of stiff paste, white lead and ordinary glazier's putty, stiffening the compound to a real putty consistency with a little dry whitening.

Obviously, the painting of a garage is not a job calling for great technical efficiency, but care should be taken in the choice of materials and in the conditions when they are applied. As with all other outside work, no paint should be applied in wet, damp, or foggy weather; and it improves the work if the surface is lightly sandpapered over between the application of the first and second, and second and third, coats.

One other point may be mentioned here. If it is desired to purchase the paint mixed ready for use, genuine white lead should be demanded as the basic pigment, as no other basic substance is quite so resistant to wind and weather.

The Interior.

So far, we have been largely concerned with exteriors. A note or two on garage interiors may be useful. We have already dealt with the limewashing of the interior walls of a brick or stone building.

A more pleasing and somewhat more durable treatment would be to make good the larger inequalities of the walls with plaster of paris, and then coat them twice with one of the well-known water paints, such as "Walpamur," "Hall's Distemper," etc.

If variety is desired, two colours could be used, a pale one for the upper parts of the walls and a darker shade, in contrast, as a dado.

In some cases, water paint is used for the upper parts, and the dado is carried out in oil paint which, if it has a glossy finish, is more easily kept clean.

The Wood Parts.

In all such brick and stone buildings there will naturally be certain wood fittings such as doors and windows. These will require painting, not less than three coats if new, and two coats if previously painted.

For the treatment of such woodwork the reader is referred to the article, "Painting the Outside of a House," on page 847, partly because the conditions in painting the outside of a permanent garage are likely to be similar to those of the house to which it belongs, and partly because the interior has to endure a greater amount of wear and tear than other kinds of interiors. Therefore the painting of the interior woodwork may well be done by the methods usually applicable to exteriors.

The Ceiling.

Some of these better-class garages have flat lath and plaster ceilings. In such cases they are best treated with a good water paint. If there is no flat ceiling and the wood principals and rafters are therefore visible, this timber may be either left untouched, or, if a comelier appearance is desired, they can be given a coat of one of the preservative wood stains previously mentioned.

Limewash is sometimes applied to such roof timbers, but this is not to be recommended, for, sooner or later, the lime may begin to disintegrate and flake off, to the manifest detriment of the car standing beneath.

In the case of the second class of building mentioned, where the major portion of the structure is cement or asbestos, no coating of any kind should be applied to the interior surfaces for at least a year, after which a suitable water paint can be used, if some kind of finish is desired for appearance' sake. The inside wood framework may well be coated with one of the preservative wood stains, always provided that, if the interior is painted, none of the wood preservative is allowed to pass through any joint to the outside where it would stain the paint there.

Another alternative would be to paint the internal woodwork in the same manner as the outside. But this, the more expensive protective method, is not so necessary as in the case of external surfaces.

The All-wood Building.

To come to the class of garage buildings made entirely of wood, it may be said that while painting the internal walls affords the greatest choice of colour treatment, the cost may be a deterrent.

In many cases these interiors are left in the bare wood, and, as such buildings are generally dry enough inside, no great harm will come to the timber if the walls are left bare.

Alternatively, one coat of one of the wood stains mentioned above would be quite a suitable treatment, would have sufficient preservative effect, and would make the interior less crude in appearance.

The doors, particularly if they open outward, should in such cases have two coats of preservative or not less than two, and preferably three coats of paint.

The Iron Building.

There remains one type of building not yet mentioned, and that is the garage constructed of sheets of corrugated iron fixed over a framework of wood.

The right treatment for corrugated iron is described in the article "Painting Ironwork" on page 167, while the treatment of the wood framework and fittings has already been covered in the earlier part of these notes.

HOW TO SOLDER ALUMINIUM

THE successful soldering of aluminium depends upon the effective removal of the extremely thin film of aluminium oxide that always forms during the preliminary heating up of the metal.

It is for this reason that the amateur who uses the ordinary methods applicable to brass and copper fails to obtain a satisfactory joint, even though he employs the proprietary makes of aluminium solders and fluxes.

Bearing in mind the presence of this oxide film, the operator must take suitable steps for its removal, when the soldering of aluminium will present little difficulty.

How to soft-solder Aluminium.

In the process of soft-soldering a solder is used which melts at a comparatively low temperature, and it is this type of soldering that has given rise to the fairly general opinion that aluminium is difficult to solder.

A mechanical process must be used to get rid of the oxide film. The method now employed is first to clean the surfaces to be soldered, before they are heated, using either a scraper or emery cloth.

The metal is next heated slowly until the solder begins to melt on it. This solder, it will be found, will not adhere to the aluminium owing to the troublesome oxide film preventing contact. If, however, this film is broken up by scraping the aluminium surface under the molten solder with a hack-saw blade, file or similar scratching device, the oxide will be dispersed and cannot reform under the solder; the latter will then be free to alloy with the aluminium. The solder will therefore spread over the surface in a somewhat similar manner to ordinary plumber's solder on a brass surface. Once the surface of the aluminium is covered with molten solder the adhesion can still further be improved by using a wire scratch brush (similar to a file card) on the surface; this breaks up any remaining traces of oxide. After "tinning" the surfaces to be joined in the manner described they can be sweated together in the ordinary way.

Various proprietary makes of aluminium solder are now available and, if the above precautions are taken, will mostly give satisfactory results. On the other hand, the compositions of these solders is not of great importance. They consist, usually, of zinc and tin with or without the additions of small amounts of other substances.

Hard-soldering Aluminium.

In this process a stronger joint is obtained in virtue of the fact that a higher melting-point and stronger solder are employed. The solder used has a melting-point between 500° and 600° C., and usually contains from 10 to 13 per cent. of silicon; the best results are obtained from this solder.

The oxide film is removed in this case by means of an alkaline halide flux similar to that used for aluminium welding. At the temperature at which the soldering is carried out the flux is melted and rapidly attacks the oxide, thus permitting the molten solder to come into intimate contact with the aluminium surface and to alloy with it.

In carrying out this process it is best to use a gas blow-pipe for heating the solder and aluminium, in a similar manner to that of hard-soldering brass.

The flux is applied on the end of the stick of solder, which readily melts and flows freely, sweating the parts together. Certain manufacturers supply silicon alloy solder in the form of a hollow rod, the flux being contained in the interior.

Wherever a strong aluminium joint is required hard-soldering should be used in preference to soft-soldering, for the joint—apart from being stronger—is capable of withstanding the action of steam or boiling water without protection.

Reaction Soldering.

This is a fairly recently developed method utilising a solder in the form of a chemical mixture which is spread on the parts to be joined, and then the latter are heated by means of a blow-pipe flame to about 200° C. A chemical reaction then takes place resulting in the deposition of pure zinc in a molten condition on the aluminium surfaces to be joined. The zinc flows readily between the edges and alloys freely with the aluminium, thus making a very satisfactory joint; the latter is stronger and more permanent than that obtained by the soft-soldering process. Materials for reaction soldering can be obtained from Messrs. Grant & West Ltd., 17 South Street, London, E.C.2.

MAKING A SILVER-MOUNTED CLARET JUG
A TYPICAL EXAMPLE OF SIMPLE SILVERWORK

SILVER is so cheap at the present time that it is quite practicable as a material for use by home craftsmen, although, if preferred, such materials as sheet copper, pewter or aluminium can be substituted and can be worked in a similar way, the copper, of course, being finished by silver-plating.

Materials and Tools.

Necessary materials and tools for making a claret jug, such as that shown in Fig. 1, and described in this article, are as follows:—

Sheet Silver.—One piece, 4 inches wide, 12 inches long. This should be quite thin, something about the thickness of ordinary note-paper will suffice.

Silver Strip.—One piece, $\frac{1}{4}$ inch wide, $\frac{1}{16}$ inch thick and 12 inches long for the handle.

Glassware.—One glass jug or bottle; the one here described had originally contained liqueur. One good cork to fit the neck of the bottle.

Solder.—$\frac{1}{4}$ oz. soft silver solder.

The tools chiefly needed are a pair of strong scissors or tinman's snips, a few "jeweller's files" of various shapes—they can be bought at any tool shop for a few pence and are generally sold on cards of six assorted shapes.

A blowpipe—a plain bent tube costing only a few pence—a lump of borax, some fine "blue back" emery paper—not emery cloth—and some rottenstone or rouge for polishing.

A piece of smooth fine-grained wood or some thick cardboard is needed when cutting out the silver, also a strong penknife, or the like, with a short stout blade and an oilstone whereon to sharpen it.

Commencing the Work.

Commence by making a paper pattern to fit closely around all four sides of the selected bottle, then lay it flat on a smooth surface and outline upon it the design which has to be pierced in the metal. Only one panel need be outlined in detail, as the design has to be traced on to the silver. This is the next proceeding, and is effected by pasting the paper pattern to the flat sheet of silver, then cutting the metal to the outline with the scissors or snips. The design is then traced on to the silver by placing a piece of carbon paper under the paper pattern or by scratching the outline on to the silver by cutting through the paper pattern with the point of a knife.

Repeat the pattern on all four panels, then proceed to cut out the design. The cutting can be done with a fretsaw—using a fine "metal-cutting" blade instead of the usual coarse-toothed wood saw, but otherwise proceeding as when cutting fretwork wood.

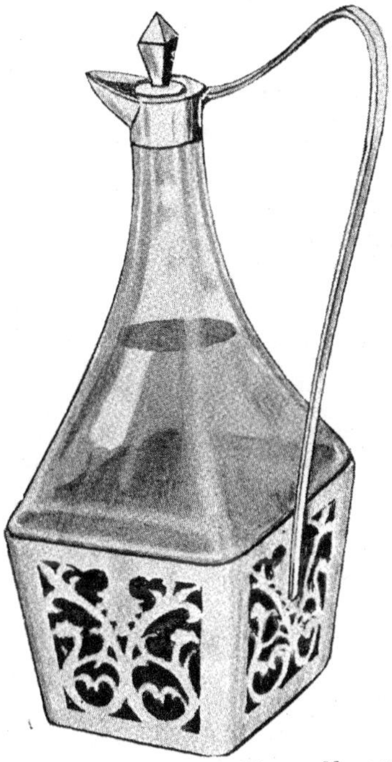

Piercing the Design.

Quite a good way of piercing the metal is to lay it flat on a piece of wood or cardboard and then drill or punch small holes at all angles and corners—keeping just on the waste side of the lines, as indicated in Fig. 2, and then cutting out between them with the cutting knife.

Next file the edges of the openings with the jeweller's files, holding the work during this process in a hand-made vice, sketched in use in Fig. 3. This vice consists merely of two pieces of wood, shaped somewhat like a small butter pat, and held together with a couple of wood screws or with bolts and flynuts. A hole an inch or so in diameter is drilled through the pieces of wood, so that the metal is grasped between them, so that a portion shows through the hole; and is thus held firmly while the filing operation is in progress.

When the whole design has been filed to shape and all roughness removed from the edges, bend the metal so that it assumes a box-like form and will fit snugly around the bottom of the bottle. See that the joint at the corner just fits, that is, touches along the whole of its length, then remove it and solder up this joint.

Silver Soldering.

To solder the joint, first scrape both sides of the metal on each joint part, then fasten the silver together with wire or thread so that the joint keeps closed. Next rub the borax on a piece of clean stone or slate with some water, until a white paste is formed.

Apply some of this paste with a clean brush to each side of the joint, then cut a narrow strip of the silver solder as long as the joint, and scrape it clean and bright, then lay it on the wet

Fig. 1.—Claret Jug with Silver Mounts.
The ease with which this can be made at home is clearly explained in the text.

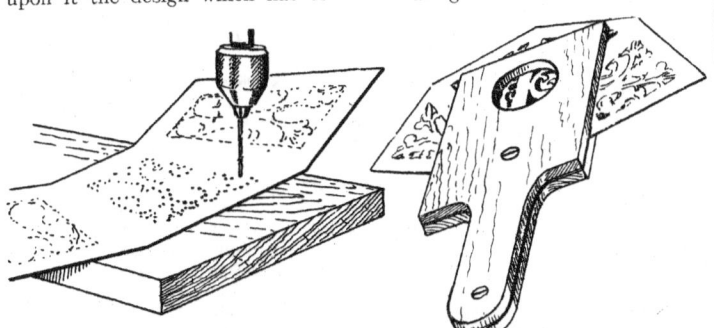

Fig. 2.—Piercing the Plate.
Small holes are drilled preparatory to cutting out the metal.

Fig. 3.—Wooden Hand-Vice.
The metal is held between two pieces of wood and the file worked through the hole.

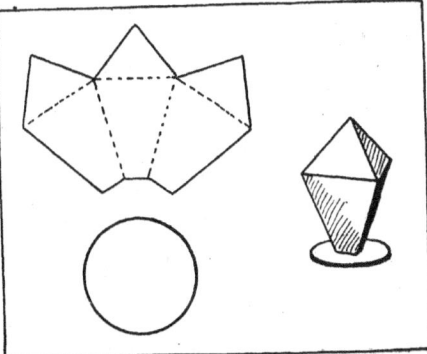

Fig. 4.—The Stopper.
Shapes to cut the metal; also sketch of the completed stopper.

MAKING A SILVER-MOUNTED CLARET JUG

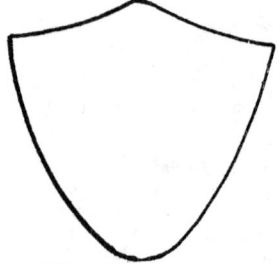

*Fig. 5.—*Shape of Lip.
After cutting to this shape the lip is formed by bending. (Actual size.)

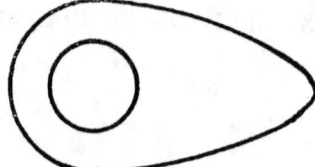

*Fig. 6.—*Cover Piece for Lip.
This part fits on the top of the bottle. (Actual size.)

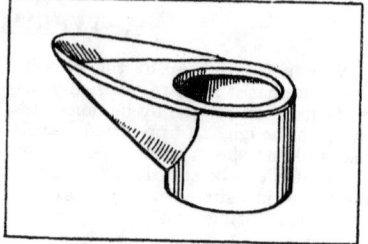

*Fig. 7.—*The Complete Lip.
Appearance of the fitting for the neck of the bottle.

borax paste exactly over the seam.

Arrange for a gas jet or provide a small methylated spirit lamp, then with the blowpipe blow a stream of air and burning gas on to the solder.

Commence with gentle heat and watch the borax; it will gradually bubble up and turn white, and at this stage increase the heat until the solder melts and runs into the joint. Immediately remove the heat or the silver work will be melted; allow it to cool, then clean the surfaces with a file or emery paper, and if there are any places where the solder has not run, repeat the operation.

Clean the silver by rubbing with the "blue back" until it is bright, then try it in place on the bottle; press it firmly into position so that it fits closely.

Making the Lip and Knob.

The neck of the bottle has now to be covered with a plain band of silver about ¾ inch wide, wrapped around the neck, the seam soldered as before described. Next prepare the lip or spout, which is cut from sheet silver to the shape in Fig. 5, and then doubled over on the outside edges and bent to shape with the fingers. Fit it closely to the neck band, then solder it in the manner before described; finally cut out the cover piece, shown in Fig. 6, and shape it by bending and filing until it fits into the lip and on to the neck band, as shown in Fig. 7, then solder it to both those parts, and afterwards work the edge of the circular hole downwards so that it fits closely into the neck of the bottle. This can be done by pressure applied with the pointed end of a round piece of wood a trifle smaller than the hole in the neck of the bottle.

The stopper is a plain cork cut off flush so that it finishes about ¼ inch above the neck. The knob is a triangular pyramid, cut, bent and soldered to the shape shown in Fig. 4, and soldered to a circular piece of silver which is flanged downwards and fitted tightly to the top of the cork. Additional security is attained by rolling a piece of silver to form a tube and soldering it to the underside of the knob. A hole is then pierced through the cork, the tube passed through it, and a silver washer soldered to the

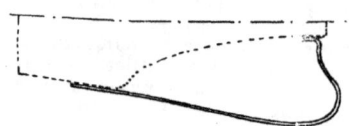

*Fig. 8.—*The Handle.
The handle is a plain strip of silver bent to the shape shown.

outer end while the cork is in place. If the cork is wetted and the soldering is quickly done the cork will not be burned.

Fitting the Handle.

The handle, shown in Fig. 8, has only to be bent to shape with pliers, the jaws of which should be covered with leather to prevent marking the silver. The parts are then removed from the bottle and the handle soldered to the lower part. The neck fitting is then wired in place and the joint soldered, after which both joints are cleaned up with file and "blue back," and the neck fitting pressed firmly on to the bottle. The bottom fitting is pressed firmly into place. A paste made of whiting and white of egg can be applied to the neck fitting and will make everything secure.

Finish the work by carefully rubbing the silver with the finest "blue back" emery paper until it has a uniformly matted or grained appearance, then polish it by rubbing with rottenstone and water applied with a piece of linen rag, finish off by polishing with rouge in the usual way.

The result will be a lasting valuable and pleasing addition to the stock of family plate.

REMOVING STAINS FROM ENAMELLED BATH

If the stains are due to rust, they can usually be removed by rubbing the surface with pumice powder, using a damp flannel to apply the latter.

Ordinary "Vim" domestic cleaning powder will also be found to give satisfactory results if the stains are not too deep.

Chemical stains can often be removed by rubbing the affected areas with a piece of flannel soaked in a concentrated solution of potassium bichromate; the latter is sold in the form of red crystals for photography purposes.

Ordinary grease stains can be removed with paraffin or petrol, but it is advisable to wash the surface afterwards with a hot concentrated solution of common washing soda and water.

WAX CRAYONS

The following recipe for making *red* wax crayons may possibly be used as a basis for making others. The pigment (red lead) might be substituted by other coloured pigments such as yellow ochre, vandyke brown, ultramarine blue, bone black, etc.

The recipe is as follows:—

Spermacetti	4 ozs.
Tallow	3 „
Beeswax	2 „
Finely powdered red lead	6 „

Melt slowly and well mix by stirring. Whilst hot add the following: One fluid ounce of (heated) saturated solution of caustic potash. Keep warm for half an hour, stirring occasionally. Then pour into moulds, which may consist of pieces of glass tubing, or can be made by drilling holes through hard wood blocks. Plaster of paris moulds, made in two halves, can also be used.

TRUING THE OILSTONE

After long periods of constant use oilstones become worn and uneven, so that flat tools such as chisels and plane irons can no longer be trued up accurately. To recondition a worn oilstone of this type, wet a sheet of No. 1½ sandpaper and lay it with the sand face upwards on a flat block of hard wood, or, better still, of metal. Then rub the worn face of the oilstone on the sandpaper, giving it a kind of oval motion. When the surface, as tested with a straightedge (or steel rule) is found to be quite true, the oilstone can be finished off by rubbing it upon another sheet of finer grade sandpaper, or on another oilstone, if available. If a grindstone is available the oilstone can be finished off by holding it against *the side* of the former, using plenty of water.

Making and Fitting Sun Blinds

Sun blinds to yield the maximum satisfaction should be specially planned to suit each individual window or other place to be protected. This article deals with a diversity of methods suitable for various characteristic sites, and the special points calling for particular attention are fully dealt with; in most cases one or other of these methods can be adopted completely or readily adapted to special conditions.

Materials for Sun Blinds.

For most domestic purposes the best material to use is the striped awning canvas obtainable in many attractive colours from most house furnishers.

Quantities of Material.

Owing to the variations of size of windows and doors, it is impossible to give exact quantities of material required, but the following table shows the approximate number of yards of material needed for single windows

Length of Material of Given Width for One Sun Blind.

Window Opening.		Width of Material.							
High	Wide	21	24	27	30	36	48	54	Ins.
Ins.	Ins.								
30	24	—	1	1	1	—	—	—	Yards
36	24	—	1¼	1¼	1¼	—	—	—	,,
42	24	—	1¼	1¼	1¼	—	—	—	,,
48	24	—	1½	1½	1½	—	—	—	,,
36	36	—	—	—	—	1⅛	1⅛	—	,,
42	36	—	—	—	—	1¼	1¼	—	,,
42	48	2½	—	2½	2½	—	1½	1¼	,,
42	54	—	—	—	2½	2½	—	1¼	,,
60	24	—	2	2	2	—	—	—	,,
60	36	4	—	—	—	2	—	—	,,
60	48	—	4	—	—	—	2	2	,,
72	36	4¼	—	—	—	2½	2½	—	,,
72	48	—	4½	4½	—	—	2½	2½	,,
78	48	—	5	5	—	—	2½	2½	,,

of different size. Various widths of material are given; hence, to ascertain the required amount of material, select the size nearest to the actual window, then select the nearest width of material and under it read off the number of yards required for one window. Multiply by the number of windows to ascertain the total material required.

Durability of Material.

As regards durability, sailcloth and awning canvas take pride of place, but much depends upon the conditions of usage and the care with which they are stored when out of use, particularly after a shower of rain. Awnings or blinds of any kind should never be closed while wet or damp unless absolutely necessary, and even then should be opened and dried at the earliest opportunity.

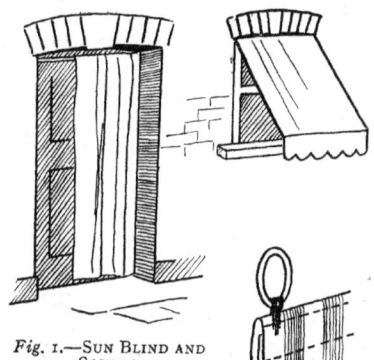

Fig. 1.—Sun Blind and Screen.

The door is protected by a simple hanging screen, the window by a strutted blind.

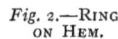

Fig. 2.—Rings on Hem.

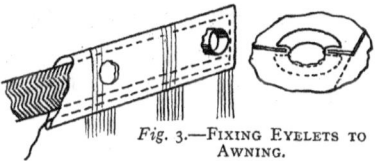

Fig. 3.—Fixing Eyelets to Awning.

The hem is strengthened by an inner band of webbing, a hole punched and the eyelet inserted and turned over as shown in inset.

Fig. 4.—Awning fixed to Screw Hooks.

Screw hooks are fixed to Rawlplugs driven into the wall the usual way

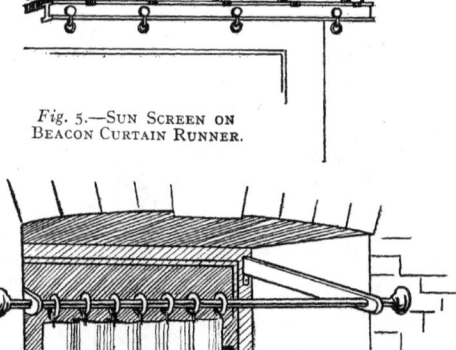

Fig. 5.—Sun Screen on Beacon Curtain Runner.

Fig. 6.—Porch Screen on Extended Rail.

The side strips are hinged to the door frame, the front rod rests on the outer wall face.

Simple Screening Blinds.

Two simple sun screens are sketched in Fig. 1; the first is a simple drawscreen over an entrance door and is suspended by rings from a rod fixed to the upper part of the door frame. The window is shielded by a simple hook-on screen extended by rods at the bottom, as explained in detail later.

Draw screens for porch doors can be made of any durable material; something fairly thin, which allows some light to pass, is most desirable when the door is glazed.

The screen is made preferably with single-width material double-hemmed at the top (as in Fig. 2) and furnished with rustless steel or chromium-plated rings, which should be strongly sewn through the hem, the stitches coming just below the top stitching.

A fairly long loop should be left between the hem and the ring, and then nicely bound round with the sewing thread. The bottom of the screen should hang about 2 inches above the ground level and be securely hemmed.

Detachable Awning Screens.

Removable sun screens can usefully be made with eyelets and arranged to hang from screw hooks. Brass eyelets similar to those used on boots but considerably larger are used for this work, and should be fixed to a reinforced hem, as shown in Fig. 3, where the strengthening band of webbing about 1½ inches wide is shown in place. After this has been securely stitched into the hem, a series of holes have to be punched in the middle of hem and through the webbing band. The hole should be punched with a "wad" punch and be a shade smaller than the shank of the eyelet. The eyelets are then put through the holes and the shank part turned over with an eyelet punch.

Both punches can be had at small cost from most tool shops and house furnishers. The wad punch is driven home by a sharp blow with a moderately heavy hammer while the webbing is resting on a piece of soft lead or a smooth piece of wood. The eyelet punch has rounded end and is forced down with a fairly sharp blow of a hammer, which has the effect of turning the tubular shank over and spreading it outwards, as shown in Fig. 3 in the insert.

The screw hooks by which the awning is suspended should be of the type shown in Fig. 4, and can be driven directly into small holes bored with a bradawl into the wooden framework, or screwed into rawl-plugs driven in the usual way into brick or concrete walls.

The lower end of such awnings

MAKING AND FITTING SUN BLINDS

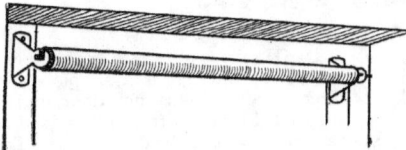

Fig. 7.—Spring Roller Fittings for Window Sun Blind.
The brackets are screwed to the window frame. The roller has an internal spring and works automatically.

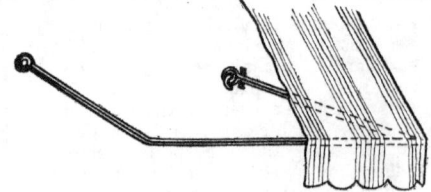

Fig. 8.—Bottom Fittings for Sun Awning.
A light metal rod, bent as shown, is used to extend the bottom of the sun blind.

can hang freely or be supported by suitable rods or by guy ropes.

Sun Screen on Runners.

Sun blinds over doors are often inconvenient unless capable of easy movement, and one of the best methods to adopt to secure this result is to fit a solid brass or rustless metal curtain rail and runners, such as that shown in Fig. 5. One that can be recommended is the Beacon 456 curtain rail, which, although more frequently used for indoor curtains, serves the purpose admirably. No tugging and pulling is required—the curtains answer to a mere touch. The rail can be fixed direct to woodwork, but when it is to be fixed to stone, brick or concrete work, it is best to fasten a strip of wood about 2 inches wide and ¾ inch thick directly to the wall, using rawlplugs and screws in the usual way. The rail is then screwed to the wooden strips, the sun screen or blind attached by rings or hooks to the runners.

This arrangement is especially handy when it is intended to leave the sun blind in place throughout the summer.

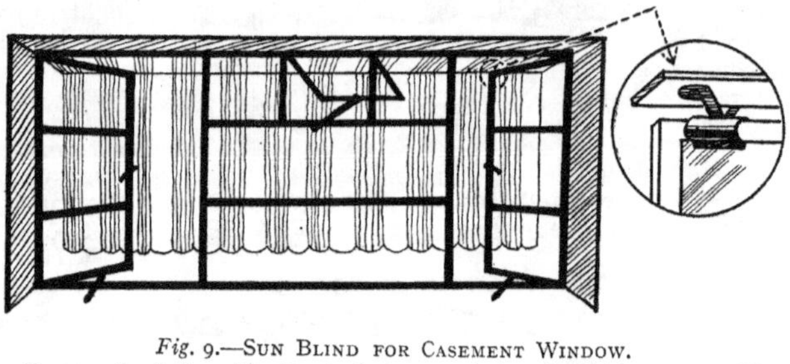

Sun Blind for Porch.

The sun blind over an entrance door having a recessed porch should be fixed as near to the front wall as possible, and should leave open spaces at the top and bottom to enable the air to circulate.

One simple way of doing this, shown in Fig. 6, avoids the need for fixing to the brickwork whether plain or roughcast. A strip of hardwood about 1¼ inches deep and ¾ inch thick is hinged to the door post—one on each side—as in Fig. 6, as near the top of the frame as possible and close to the porch side walls or "reveals." These strips must be about 3 inches longer than the distance from door frame to face of porch. Holes about ½ inch diameter are then drilled through the strips and a brass- or chromium-plated rod put through the holes and held in place by wooden or metal knobs. The side strips will then fall slightly until the knobs rest on the walls, and thus hold the rod very securely. The sun blind is fitted with rings so that it can slide easily when required. A number of lead weights can be sewn into the bottom hem to help in preventing the curtain blowing about on a windy day, or, if divided sun

Fig. 9.—Sun Blind for Casement Window.
Two wooden laths with clips to fasten to window itself when open. Here shown from inside the room.

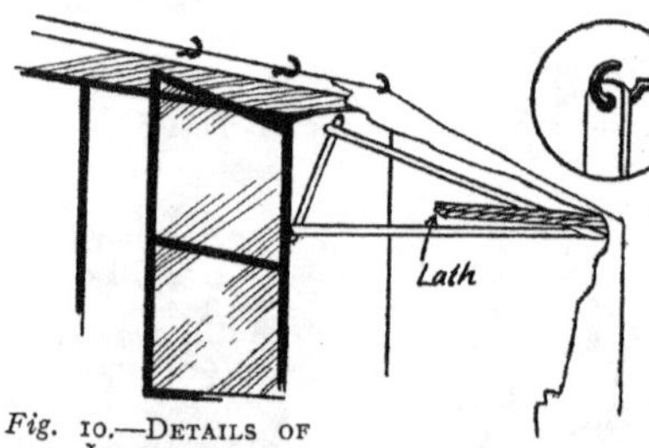

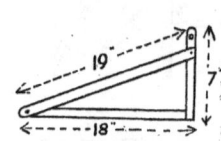

Fig. 10.—Details of Ironwork.
Casement sun blind providing ventilation and shade. The irons, shown separately, hook on to a screw hook beside the window and extend the sun blind at the top.

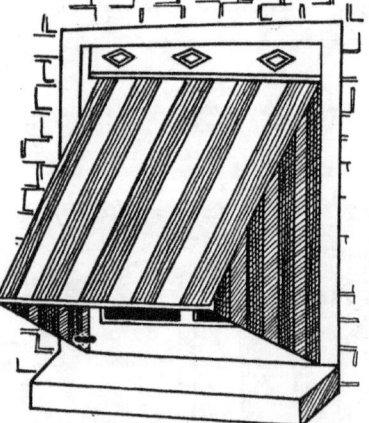

Fig. 11.—Boxed Sun Blind.
The roller is concealed with a boxing, built at the top of the window.

screens are used, the lower corners can be fastened by a hook and eye to the sides of the porch wall.

Spring Roller Sun Blinds.

The arrangement shown in Fig. 7 makes a very practical sun blind when it can be fitted to a wooden frame over the top of a window. A spring roller of substantial pattern is obtained of a suitable length for the window, and the end fittings then screwed to the window frame, or to a wooden strip screwed to brickwork.

The sun blind is attached as usual to the roller, and is made long enough to reach nearly to the bottom of the window. The sun blind is extended at the bottom, as shown in Fig. 8, by means of a rod—preferably of rustless metal—about ¼ inch diameter for windows about 2 feet wide, 5/16 inch diameter for 3-foot windows, and ⅜ inch diameter for wider windows. The rod is turned inwards and the ends finished in the form of either a hook or an eye, which can generally be done by bending and hammering the rod while held in a vice. Hooks or eyes are then screwed to the window frame to hold the ends of the rods.

When not required, the rods are unhooked and the blind allowed to roll up. The rod is fixed to the curtain material by tabs at each side arranged to fasten with a patent grip buckle or with strong spring fasteners, as used on gloves.

Sun Blinds for Casement Windows.

Metal-framed and other casement windows present additional problems because it is generally necessary to arrange the blind to stand forward sufficiently to clear the opened window. A very simple method of meeting the difficulty is shown in Fig. 9, and consists of two hardwood strips the full width of the windows, and provided with simple spring clips of the "Bull Dog" variety, as sold by stationers. The awning material is tacked to the strips, and the latter placed on the tops of the opened windows and held there by the clips. This device is suit-

MAKING AND FITTING SUN BLINDS

able for the usual form of window with two casements that open, but can only be used when both are open.

Another pattern, rather more elaborate, but suitable for all types of metal-framed windows, is shown in Fig. 10, and consists of two sets of light ironwork made of strip metal about $\frac{5}{8}$ inch wide and $\frac{1}{8}$ inch thick, all joints being made with $\frac{3}{16}$-inch diameter stove screws or bolts and nuts.

To make this ironwork it is merely necessary to cut the strips to length, drill holes through them at the points indicated, and fasten together by the bolts and nuts. The sun blind is fixed by hooks and eyes to the upper part of the window opening.

A wooden lath about $1\frac{1}{4}$ inches wide and $\frac{3}{8}$ inch thick is slipped into a pocket formed in the sun blind about 18 inches from the top, and the irons then fixed to it either with hooks and eyes or by a bolt and small thumb nut. The side-irons are held in place by means of round-headed screws driven into a rawl-plug on each side of the window opening. A hole is drilled in each iron large enough to slip over the head of the screw.

Boxed Sun Blinds.

These are generally similar to the foregoing except that the blind and roller are concealed by a neat boxing—as in Fig. 11—which is permanently fitted to the window opening.

The method of construction is shown in Fig. 12, and comprises two end-pieces of wood which are screwed to the walls and an ornamental front-board, which should be screwed in place with brass screws after the end-pieces have been fixed. The front face of the boxing can be finished with a moulding or may have a scolloped or

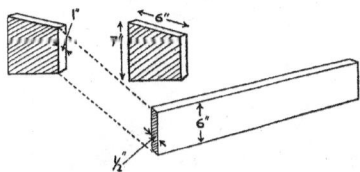

Fig. 12.—Construction of Top Box.
The parts of a simple box shown separately but in relative positions.

curved edge, as personal fancy dictates. Suitable woods to use are good clean deal 1 inch thick for the side-pieces; the front should be a clean piece of deal or preferably mahogany or plywood at least $\frac{1}{2}$ inch thick; a usual and convenient depth is 6 inches for windows of nominal size.

Fig. 13.—Awning Blind.
Covers several windows, has box-spring roller at top, side rods and a front board.

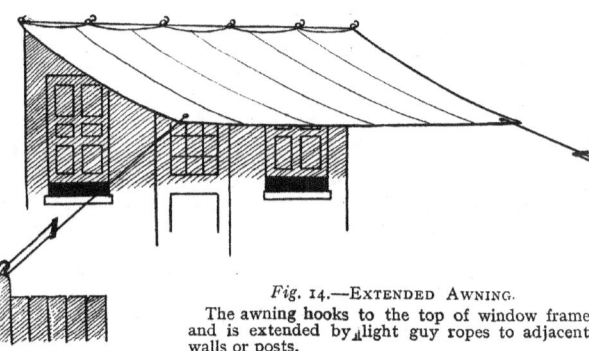

Fig. 14.—Extended Awning.
The awning hooks to the top of window frame and is extended by light guy ropes to adjacent walls or posts.

Awning Sun Blinds.

A large sun blind capable of covering several windows at once is shown in Fig. 13, and consists of a boxed-spring roller—as before described—but the outer end of the awning is fixed to a board about 4 inches wide and 1 inch thick, which is hinged to two side arms of metal or hardwood, about 2 inches deep and 1 inch thick, the inner ends of which are hinged to the sides of the window or to wood blocks in the wall. The latter hinges must be so placed that when closed the awning board shuts up against the spring roller box.

A more simple method of attaining a similar protection consists of using a sun blind with eyelets at the top and at the lower corners. The upper part is hooked above the window as in Fig. 14, and the lower corners extended by means of light guy ropes and runners fixed to hooks on any adjacent wall or post within about 10 feet of the blind.

Conservatory Sun Blind.

This consists of a plain roller blind, but in the case shown in Fig. 15 the upper end of the blind is fixed by clout nails or a wooden fillet to the ridge or top piece of wood on the conservatory roof. Two cords—such as strong "sash-line"—are fixed under the blind, as in Fig. 16, and pass around the roller, which should be from 3 to 4 inches diameter, the cord then passes up to pulleys fixed above the blind and the ends are brought down through guide pulleys to a convenient point.

The blind is raised by pulling on the cords, which causes the roller to wind itself upwards. When raised sufficiently the cords are fastened securely to a cleat. This simple device is quite trouble-free, and enables the blind to be set at any desired depth and is held there by fastening the cords to the cleats.

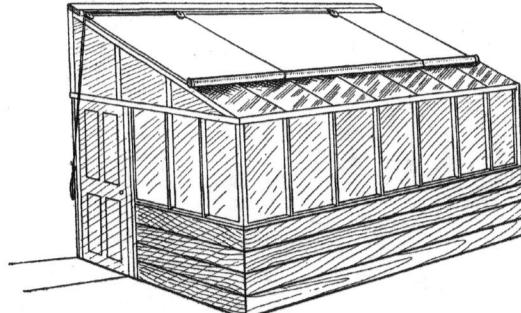

Fig. 15.—Conservatory Sun Blind.
The blind is fastened at the top and has a roller at bottom; it is rolled up by hauling on the cords.

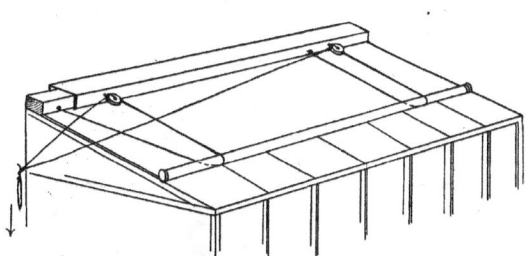

Fig. 16.—Arrangement of Rollers and Pulleys.
Side view, showing arrangement of boxing, pulleys, roller and cords.

MOSAIC WORK

MOSAIC is a decorative process for floors and walls in which small pieces of coloured marble, stone, pottery, glass and other materials, known as tesseræ, are embedded in cement to form a pattern. It is one of the oldest forms of floor decoration and attained a high standard of perfection in Roman times. As a method of decoration in the home in place of tiles for walls or floors, it offers considerable scope for the home handyman. The materials are easily procured, the actual process is simple, the opportunities for design in pattern and colour practically unlimited, and the effects may be highly decorative.

Two Varieties.

Of the two varieties—Roman and Terrazzo—the former offers greater possibilities for decorative work in pattern, the latter being more suitable for colour effects only, but both varieties may be adapted for application in the home, both inside and outside. For example, hearths offer opportunities for decorative work, and instead of tile replacements on the bathroom walls, excellent colour effects can be produced by mosaic. In wall mosaic it is possible to use a number of different materials in working out a coloured pattern. Hard stone and marble may be used in conjunction with pottery, cement and glass, but for use on floors, as far as possible the materials used should be of the same hardness; for example, marble and pottery tesseræ should not be used together, as the floor would wear unevenly.

The Materials required.

The tesseræ used in Roman mosaic should be about ½ inch square, and although it is possible to obtain various coloured marble chips, the labour involved in sorting out and shaping is considerable. This material, if it should be easily procurable, is more suitable for use in the terrazzo method. For amateur use, coloured cement offers such a variety of colour, combined with simplicity of preparation, that it is strongly recommended. It

Fig. 1.—A Floor decorated with Mosaic.

should be noted that broken glazed tiles provide excellent material for certain forms of mosaic, and as it is often possible to obtain a variety of colours, full advantage should be taken of any opportunity of obtaining a

Fig. 2.—Preparing the Board for making the Tesseræ.

Fig. 3.—How the Notched Pieces are fitted on the Sides.

supply of what would otherwise be waste material.

Colours available for Cement.

As colour enters largely into the pattern design, it is as well to know the colours that are available for cement. Generally, any powder colour can be used, but as many are fugitive the following colours recommended by the Concrete Utilities Bureau should be used. In each case the colour should be thoroughly mixed with best finely ground Portland cement, and it is essential that both the cement and the powder colour should be quite dry. Wide-necked bottles or clean tins should be used for storing the material until it is used.

Blue: Cement 86 parts and 14 parts azure blue or ultramarine; Green: 90 parts cement, 10 parts oxide of chromium; Yellow: Cement 88 parts, yellow ochre 12 parts, also cement 90 parts, barium chromate 10 parts; Green: Cement 90 parts, oxide of chromium 10 parts; Red: Cement 86 parts, red oxide of iron 14 parts; Pink: Cement 97 parts; Crimson lake (alumina base), 3 parts; Brown (chocolate): Cement 88 parts, black oxide of manganese 6 parts, red oxide of iron 4 parts, black oxide of iron or copper 2 parts; Black: Cement 90 parts, black oxide of manganese or any carbon black 10 parts; White: Cement 67 parts, powdered chalk or common barytes 33 parts.

In addition to these colours, the following may be obtained in powder form: Purple brown, Vandyke brown, vermilionette, signal red, emerald green, brunswick green, prussian blue, chrome in three tones, including orange. The proportion is approximately 1 part of colour to 9 parts of cement, but as the colours are liable to differ in intensity, it is advisable to mix up a small quantity, say a teaspoonful of the colour to nine teaspoonfuls of cement, add an equal quantity of fine sand with sufficient water to form a thick cream. Leave the cement to dry and note the result. The amount of colour can be varied to give the required tone.

Mould for making the Tesseræ.

As the tesseræ should be about ½-inch cube, a mould large enough to make a number at once should be made. A board measuring 8 inches wide and about 1 inch thick will be found a convenient size, and with a length of 2 feet will allow for three lots. The board should be stiffened at the ends with strips

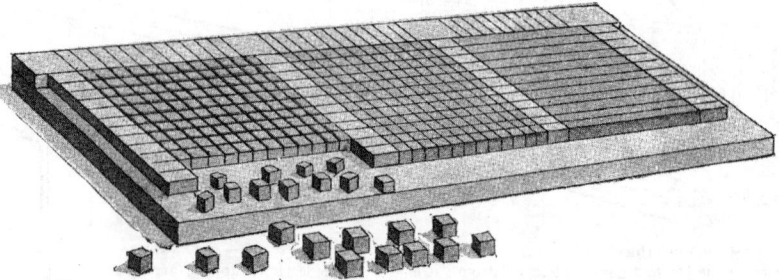

Fig. 4.—The Moulds after the Slabs have been divided into ½-inch Pieces.

Figs. 5–8.—Some Suggestions for Patterns for Mosaic Work.

5, An effective design in blue and red with a white background ; 6, How green can be added to increase the size ; 7, Another method of increasing the length of the pattern ; 8, Formation based on Roman mosaic.

of 2 × 1-inch wood screwed on, and then four 6 × 1 × ½-inch strips should be screwed on as indicated in Fig. 2. Now provide two 24 × 1 × ½-inch strips and six pieces of 2 × 1-inch wood cut to about 7 inches long, having 1½-inch notches, as shown in Fig. 2. The notched pieces are fitted on the sides, as shown in Fig. 3. Lines ½ inch apart should be cut into the top of all pieces as a guide to subsequent cutting.

These moulds will produce a slab 6 × 6 × ½ inch, which when divided will produce 144 cubes.

A small mixing box should now be made measuring 3 × 3 × 2 inches. Pour enough sand to half fill the box, and then add enough of the coloured cement to fill it completely. Pour into a bowl, mix together very thoroughly, and add sufficient water to form a creamy paste and pour into the mould. Fill the bowl with water immediately to prevent the clinging cement setting hard, and then tamp the cement in the mould with a strip of wood or a trowel and leave it to set. Do the same thing with the other colours and leave for a period of from four to six hours.

Dividing the Slabs.

The slabs will now be sufficiently set to allow of division, and this can be done with a trowel or an old knife and a length of wood as a ruler. Make quite sure that the trowel cuts through the slab, and then leave again for about twenty-four hours. The mould may now be taken apart, the slabs slipped off, and the small cubes will fall apart. If any of them should still be attached at the bottom, they will not be difficult to break apart. Fig. 4 shows the moulds after the slabs have been divided into ½-inch pieces.

Preparing a Pattern.

Having some knowledge of the colour possibilities in the tesseræ, it will now be possible to work out a pattern which can be done on squared paper. An effective design in blue and red with a white background is shown at Fig. 5 ; this pattern can be adapted to almost any rectangle. It will be seen that the rectangle measures, using ½-inch squares, 18½ × 12½ inches. By adding green as indicated at Fig. 6

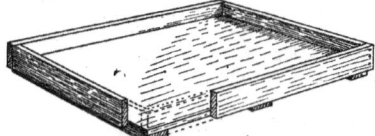

Fig. 9.—The Baseboard on which the Pattern is built up.

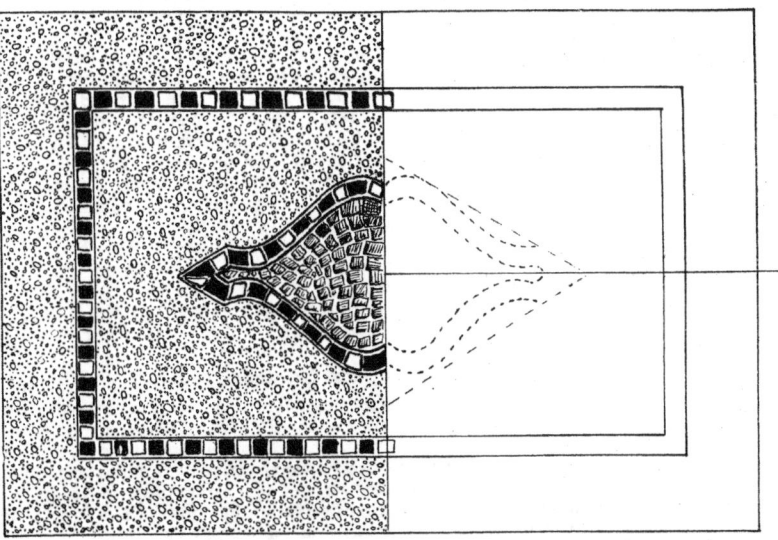

Fig. 10.—A Suggestion for a Decorative Pattern.

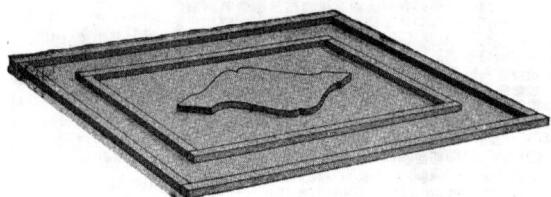

Fig. 11.—The Wooden Strips are first glued in position on a carefully prepared Foundation.

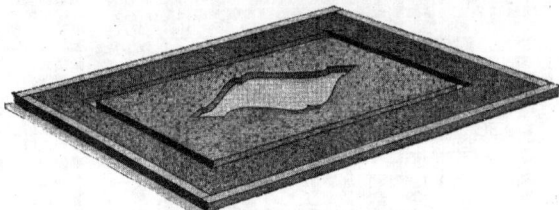

Fig. 12.—Showing Spaces left when Wooden Strips are removed.

the rectangle can be increased to $25\frac{1}{2} \times 19\frac{1}{2}$ inches. Another method of increasing the length of the pattern is shown at Fig. 7. Another pattern formation based on Roman mosaic is shown at Fig. 8; this arrangement of shapes can be adjusted to fill almost any space.

Draw the Pattern out Full Size.

Having decided on a pattern, the next thing is to draw it out full size to the exact size required, make a baseboard somewhat larger than the paper and attach strips about $1\frac{1}{2}$ inches thick on the edges, as shown in Fig. 9.

Gluing on the Tesseræ.

The tesseræ are now placed conveniently and some glue prepared. The various colours are now arranged on the pattern, each cube being coated with glue before being placed in position, care being taken to leave a space between each one on all sides. The whole of the pattern should be completed before the white or other background pieces are fitted in. The back of the pattern is now covered with thin, dark-coloured cement to a depth of $\frac{1}{4}$ inch or so, and the remainder of the space filled in with a mixture of coarse sand and cement in the proportion of 4 parts to 1 of cement. The slab is left for at least twenty-four hours, when the wooden rim can be removed, and after being trimmed where necessary and left to harden for a day or so longer, the completed mosaic slab can be placed in position and the paper covering removed with a stiff brush after soaking it with hot water.

The joints or divisions between the tesseræ should be raked over with a pointed steel tool, an old round file sharpened to a square point is suitable, and a coating of dark-coloured cement washed over the whole of the work. After the cement has been worked into the joints, the surface is wiped over to clean it as far as possible. Leaving it for a day or so, the whole of the surface should be rubbed over with a flat piece of stone, using water as a lubricant. This will remove any unevenness and complete the work. It should be noted that the interstices between the tesseræ should form a prominent part of the design, and should be sufficiently wide to form a definite separation between the colours.

In cases where it is impossible or inconvenient to use a slab of the thickness suggested, the mosaic pattern can be prepared on a large board or piece of plywood to which the pattern paper can be glued with glue thinned down and mixed with a little nitric acid to keep it moist. The pattern is preceded with in the manner described above, and, when finished, wiped over very thoroughly with a dark-coloured or black cement so that the joints are completely filled in. The surface on which the mosaic slab is to be placed should be rough and coated over with a film of cement. Allow the surface to harden slightly, and then turn the slab over in position. Press it down carefully, twist the board about, and slide it off, and then allow the slab time to set. Proceed with the raking and joint filling as before, and finally rub down with a stone.

Using Coloured Marble, Pottery or Glass.

Another form of mosaic which may be used as a decorative feature itself or in combination with a tesseræ pattern is made by using coloured marble, pottery or glass. The chosen material is mixed with cement and sand and forms a kind of concrete, but before the mixture has set the surface of it is scrubbed over with a stiff brush with a liberal application of water. This has the effect of removing the covering film of cement and exposing the coloured material. The surface is finally smoothed by rubbing. Excellent border effects in various colours are obtainable by this means, and a good imitation of the terrazzo mosaic can be produced.

A Typical Decorative Pattern.

A suggestion for a decorative pattern is shown in Fig. 10. This can be carried out to any convenient size by the use of wood strips and a pattern formed by clay. First prepare the wooden strips and glue them in position on a carefully prepared foundation, as in Fig. 11, allowing a depth of at least $\frac{1}{8}$ inch. The ground should not be smooth, and, if necessary, it should be roughened with a steel tool. The pattern is now prepared from a slab of ordinary modelling clay, allowed to dry, and placed in position with glue. If more than one of the shaped patterns is required, time may be saved by making a mould in plaster and then making the actual patterns in plaster.

The coloured filling is made by breaking up coloured marbles, coloured pottery or glass small enough to pass through a $\frac{1}{4}$-inch or smaller mesh, all dust should be removed, and a small quantity of sand added or not as desired. The filling is now prepared by adding 1 part of cement to every 4 of the coloured material with water to a creamy consistency. It is now poured over the empty spaces in the pattern and carefully tamped down to ensure thorough uniformity. Leave alone for at least twenty-four hours, and then remove the wood strips and pattern. The spaces so provided, as shown at Fig. 12, are now filled in with a similar mixture of another colour or with tesseræ as desired. Leave again for an hour or so, and then rub the surface over with a block of wood with a little water. The main point in this portion of the treatment is to rub the surface down before the cement has set hard, and as weather and other conditions have to be considered, the exact time cannot be estimated other than approximately. Finally the work is rubbed with a stone to give the final finish.

The $\frac{1}{2}$-inch unit of measurement for the tesseræ, while suitable for ordinary purposes, need not be retained; but anything more than $\frac{3}{4}$ inch square is not usually effective unless used for large floors with broad pattern effects. But it is usual to use thin tesseræ for wall mosaic. The method of making the tesseræ is the same, but greater care is required in building up the pattern and making the slab. Usually the dull surface of the coloured cement will be found attractive, but some little brilliancy can be imparted to wall mosaic made from cement by applications of linseed oil. When glass forms the basis of the foundation, the brilliancy is effected very slightly by the final rubbing with stone.

A Sand Tray for the Children

PLAYING with the sand is probably the one feature of the seaside holiday that appeals most to small children. It satisfies an instinct allied to the making of "mud-pies." There seems no reason why children should not be able to play with sand all the year round, excepting for the way it gets distributed around into places where it becomes a nuisance.

This sand tray is designed for the purpose of holding a sufficient quantity of sand in such a manner that it affords endless joy and amusement to a child, while avoiding those objectionable tendencies, even indoors by the fireside. This "fireside seaside" will be found a solution of many problems.

The Most Suitable Sand.

When buying the sand make sure it is quite clean and does not contain anything that might stain the hands. Silver sand is quite satisfactory, but it must be remembered that if used near a fireplace it tends to become very dry, and should be dampened occasionally by pouring some water on it, so that "pies" and moulds can be made. The quantity required will depend on the size of the tray.

The Tray.

It consists of a very simple shallow, but strong, wooden tray (see Fig. 2), the sides being of ordinary floor-board and the bottom of a sheet of five-ply. Owing to the weight of a quantity of sand it is best to glue and screw this together. The dimensions can be what the constructor pleases, the example illustrated measuring about 30 × 20 inches, and nearly 6 inches deep. It will be noted that the top edges are rounded to prevent discomfort which sharp edges might cause to the child.

The Lid.

On the open front of the tray is screwed another piece of plywood, shaped as in Fig. 4. Again the actual dimension as regards the narrow way matters not greatly, excepting for the following remark: If the narrowest part of this lid is one-third of the length of the tray, the latter can be filled with sand to one-third of its depth and other sizes *pro rata*. For instance, in the present example this ply lid covers about 10 inches of the 30 inches of the tray, and permits of a 2-inch depth of sand when spread flat.

If a greater depth of sand is desired, the lid must be larger, leaving a smaller open area available for playing in.

Of course the tray can be slid under the table, for which purpose castors are fitted at the corners, as shown in Fig. 3, and a handle is also a convenient feature. A coat of spirit stain is quite a sufficient finish for an article of this description.

Fig. 1.—On Dull Days Indoors this is an Amusement that Never Palls.

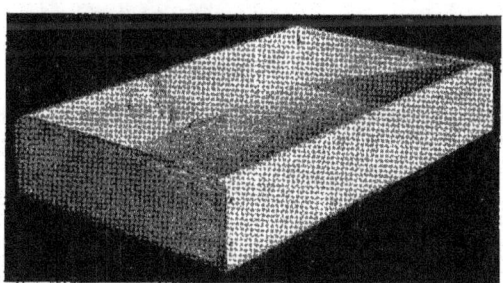

Fig. 2.—A Simple Wooden Tray forms the Basis. The Actual Size is Immaterial.

Fig. 3.—As Sand is very Heavy, a Set of Casters fixed under the Tray, and a Handle at one End, will be found convenient for moving the Tray.

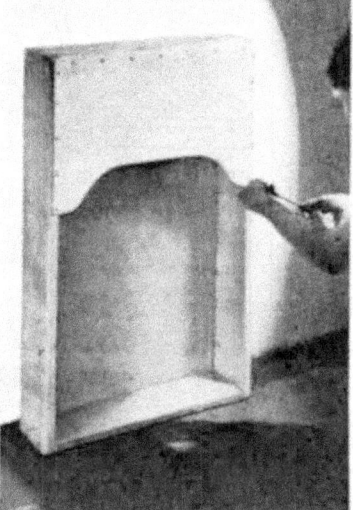

Fig. 4.—A piece of Plywood cut to this Shape forms the Part-lid.
The holes should be countersunk, so that the heads will not project and scratch small hands.

Fig. 5.—The Tray occupies very small Space when out of use.

A Small Monk's Bench

ONE of the reasons for the present popularity of the monk's bench is the excellent accommodation it provides. It can be used either as a table or a seat, and it has a most useful chest space enclosed by a lid. It makes an attractive item for the hall. The name, "monk's bench," adds somewhat of a glamour to it, though it is doubtful whether it had any particular connection with monks in its origin. In all probability it was just an early attempt at economy in furniture.

The bench shown in Fig. 1 has a top some 3 feet 6 inches by 2 feet 1 inch, a handy size for the modern small hall. Its length could be increased if desired. The conventional methods of construction are followed to an extent, though certain simplifications have been introduced to make the whole thing as straightforward as possible. The movement can be followed from the accompanying illustrations. There is a main chest-like structure, with the corner posts continued upwards in the form of turnings. They are joined at the top by shaped pieces which form the arms when the bench is used as a seat, and provide a support for the top when the table is required. These

Fig. 1.—THE MONK'S BENCH IN OAK.
This attractive piece of furniture is 3 feet 6 inches long by 2 feet 1 inch deep. The table height is 2 feet 10 inches.

arms have grooves extending from the centre backwards.

The top or back is provided with shaped cross-bearers screwed to the underside, and dowels are inserted in them to project into the grooves. When the top lies flat to form the table top, the dowel is in the centre. To convert it into a seat the top is pushed backwards, the dowels sliding in the grooves. When the back is reached, the whole thing pivots over and takes up the position shown in Fig. 2. The top partly turned and with the dowel withdrawn is shown in Fig. 3.

The Main Structure.

The corner posts of this are prepared first. The reader can either plane up some 2-inch squares and have them turned or he can buy them ready made. In the latter case, it may be necessary slightly to adapt the general sizes. In the old-time benches the panels fitted in grooves. This is a somewhat awkward job as the grooves have to be stopped. To get over the difficulty we suggest the addition of fillets glued and nailed to the posts. These provide a rebate in which the panels fit, and a moulding fixed at the front makes the whole secure. This is shown clearly in Fig. 5.

In this way only the joints for the rails need be cut, and these are given in Fig. 6. Mortises are cut for the seat and lower rails, and at the top tenons are formed to fit into the arms.

The rails are grooved to hold the panels. There is no difficulty about this, since grooved moulding for the purpose can be obtained. All one has to do is to cut tenons at the ends to fit into the mortises in the posts. A point to remember is that the groove

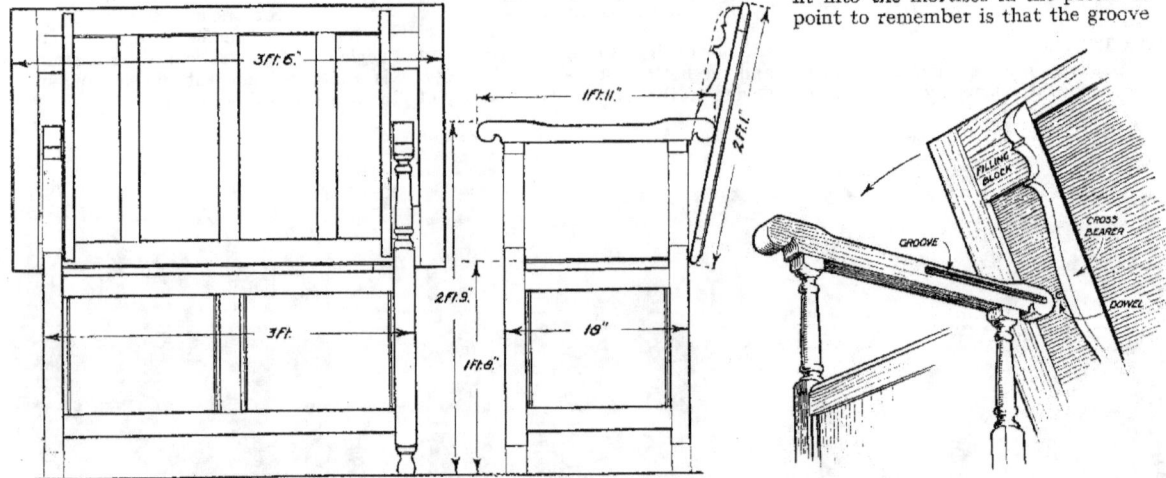

Fig. 2.—FRONT AND SIDE ELEVATIONS WITH SIZES.   *Fig.* 3.—HOW THE MOVABLE TOP WORKS.

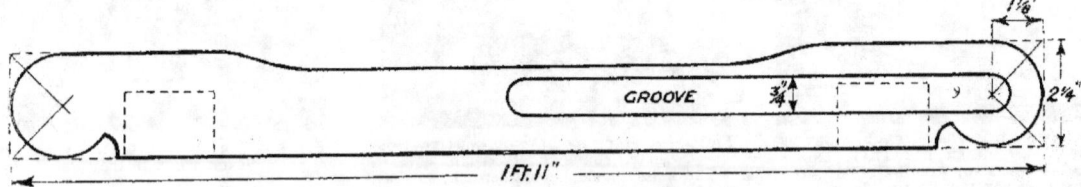

Fig. 4.—SIZES AND MARKING-OUT OF ARMS.

necessarily cuts away a portion of the tenon, and this means that the length of the mortise must be cut down correspondingly. This is shown in Fig. 7.

When marking out the posts, it is an advantage to fix them together temporarily and square the marks across them all. This ensures all being marked alike. Afterwards, the marks can be squared round on to the adjacent faces. The width of the mortises is best marked with the mortise gauge, though, failing this, an ordinary marking gauge can be used if set twice.

A great deal of the wood in the mortises can be removed by boring with a bit slightly smaller than the finished width. These are finished off by chopping with the chisel. When the mortise gauge is available, it is, of course, set to the width of the chisel. To give the tenons their maximum length, the mortises on the adjacent faces can meet in the thickness of the wood.

The rails can be fixed together in the same way as the posts when marking. It is a good plan to square in the shoulder marks with the chisel. This provides a definite shoulder, and enables a small sloping groove to be cut on the *waste* side, this forming a channel in which the saw can run. Cut the sides of the tenon first, and the shoulders afterwards. The centre upright in the front and back is grooved on both edges.

The Arms.

At this stage the arms should be taken in hand. They measure 1 foot 11 inches long by 2¼ × 2 inches, and the first step is to mark and cut the mortises to take the tenons at the top of the posts. The shape is then marked out and the position of the grooves plotted in, as in Fig. 4. The grooves are ¾ inch wide and ¼ inch deep. They extend from the centre to the centre of the rounded portion at the rear. Fig. 4 shows how the marking out is done. Note that the rounded end is struck with compasses from the same point as the centre of the rounded end of the groove. The shape is cut by sawing and chopping away the waste, and finishing off with the spokeshave.

Assembling.

The main carcase is now glued up. Put the two ends together independently first, and add the front and back rails after the glue has set. Insert the two rails into one post, put

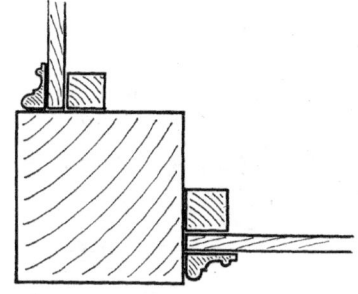

Fig. 5.—Plan Section through Corner Post.

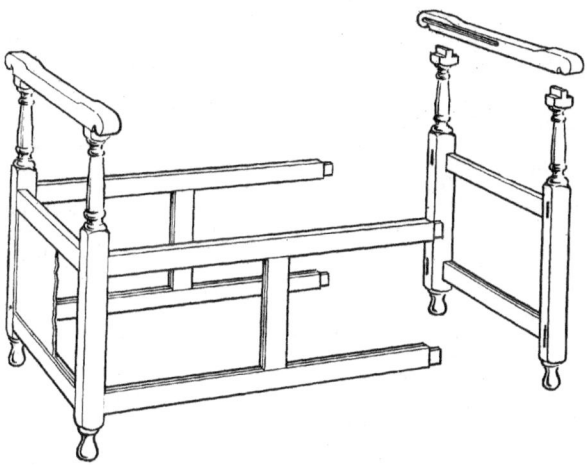

Fig. 6.—View showing General Construction.

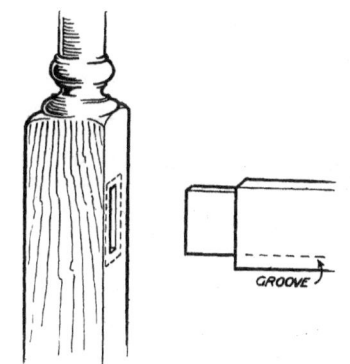

Fig. 7.—Detail of Mortise and Tenon Joint between Corner Post and Rail.

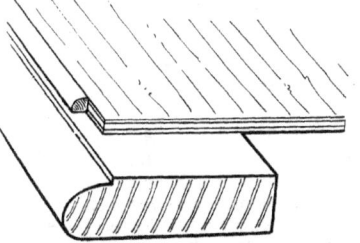

Fig. 8.—How the Top is made

on the other post and glue on the arm. A cramp is an advantage to secure tight joints.

Front and back rails are added in a similar way. It is essential that the panels are added during the assembling, because they have to fit into the grooves. If solid wood is used for them they must not be glued, because, in the event of shrinkage, they would be liable to split. There is no danger of this when plywood is used.

It has been already mentioned that strips of wood are fixed to the posts to form rebates in which the panels can fit. These can now be added, and the mouldings fixed at the front (Fig. 5). The bottom rests upon ¾-inch square strips glued and nailed all round to the bottom rails.

The seat can be a solid piece of ¾-inch stuff either clamped at the ends, or fitted with battens screwed to the underside. To enable it to clear the posts when opened, pieces of ¾-inch wood 2 inches wide are fixed between the front and back posts and between the back posts. The back piece forms a convenient surface to which to hinge the seat.

The Top.

A simple way of making this is to make a framework consisting of a front and back rail joined by five cross rails, as in Fig. 2. These are mortised and tenoned together. Over the top is laid a sheet of plywood. This stands in a trifle all round, so that a quarter-round moulding can be fixed, so concealing the edges, as in Fig. 8. The moulding of the framework can be applied if desired.

To the underside of the top are screwed the two cross-bearers, as in Fig. 3. They are positioned so that they fall just inside the arms. They can be shaped as shown, or can be just rounded over, as given by the dotted lines in Fig. 2. A ¾-inch dowel is let into the centre of each to fit into the grooves in the arms. The position is ascertained by placing the top in position and marking. Notice the filling blocks glued beneath the plywood in Fig. 3. These serve to make a firm surface on which the top can rest. The dowels are glued in their holes and the cross-bearers screwed on after the top is laid in position.

The whole thing can be stained a dark oak shade and given a coat of french polish. It is afterwards waxed. A good lubricant for the grooves is candle grease, but this should not be applied until after the whole has been stained.

CONDENSATION ON EXPOSED PIPES

The drip of water from the outside of a cold-water service pipe can be a distinct nuisance. The cause is produced by a warm moist air, striking, or coming in contact with, the chilled surfaces of the pipe. With thin-walled smooth pipes of good conducting material, such as mild steel or copper, the effect is somewhat pronounced over that of the ordinary lead pipe.

Thorough ventilation of the room is a reducing factor of the nuisance, but may not entirely eliminate it. The effect of condensation is increased if the service is directly off the town main instead of from a storage tank, as the cold water comes directly from the comparatively cool earth in which the mains are buried.

Water stored in a tank on the premises gradually takes on the temperature of the rooms below, hence the reduction of condensation effect because of the even temperature of the water in the pipes from the tank and the air of the rooms which is in contact with it.

On the other hand, however, from a sanitary standpoint, at least the service to the kitchen sink is best taken direct from the town main, and of course the supply to the ball-valve supplying the storage tank must be so.

Covering Pipes with non-conducting Material.

Apart from the suggestions already conveyed, the trouble may be entirely eliminated by covering the pipes with some good non-conducting material. The ordinary insulating materials, however, are unsightly for domestic work and many of them insanitary.

Boxed-in Skirting.

The pipes running on skirtings, etc., may be boxed in with boards. One way is to form a "boxed-in skirting," as illustrated in Fig. 1, but the typical light-gauge copper tubes cause a rather large projection owing to the method of fixing out from the walls entailed by the large nuts of the compression joints on the fittings.

For these pipes and for pipes running in a vertical direction or

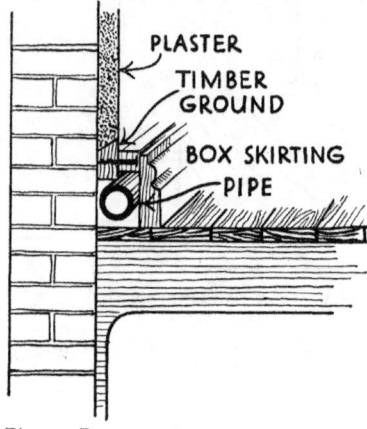

Fig. 1.—Boxed-in Skirting to prevent Condensation from exposed Water Pipes.

across a ceiling, a special insulating material can be obtained which is fairly neat in appearance. This consists of strip cork cut to form a spiral. It is on a linen backing to keep it from tearing, and when bound round the pipe has a spiral effect as indicated in Fig. 2. Naturally it increases the diameter of the pipe to make it more prominent, but in cases where the condensation is considerable the advantages gained may outweigh that disadvantage.

Using "Gesso."

If the stretch of exposed piping which causes condensation is short and the condensation not excessive, even a thick coat of smudge paint will reduce it. Alternatively a coat of "gesso" applied to the surfaces of the pipe may form a cure.

The pipes should be drained and

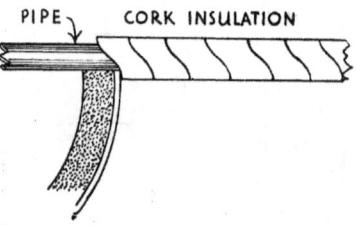

Fig. 2.—In some cases it may be more satisfactory to cover the Pipes with special Insulating Material.

the applied coating allowed to dry thoroughly before turning the water on. The surface is best painted to prevent moisture disintegrating the coating. This forms a thin insulating jacket between the cold metal pipe and the moist warm air, which causes the condensation. "Gesso" is a paste used for raised ornamentation either by squeezing it from a tube like toothpaste or applying it with a brush.

For the large quantity indicated it may easily be mixed at home. A quick-drying form is to boil together one part of powdered resin to six parts melted glue and four parts of linseed oil. When thoroughly mixed, whiting which has been water-soaked should be added to form a consistency of thick cream. It may be applied with a soft brush, and before it sets it should be smoothed off with a piece of gelatine rubber as cut from the inner tube of a motor tyre. The coating should completely encircle the pipe.

If the pipe is of smooth copper and it is difficult to make the "gesso" hold to the under surface, a thin coat may be applied and left with a rough surface. When dry, a second coat can then be applied and smoothed off as indicated. The "gesso" must be kept hot during application in a glue-pot or in a jam jar immersed in a basin of boiling water.

TO PREVENT BLACKENED WALLS AND CEILINGS

In many modern dining-rooms the boiler is behind the fire and the pipes pass up the side of the wall by the fireplace and are encased in wood. The heat causes the wood to shrink slightly from the wall and allows hot air to pass out which blackens the walls and ceilings. To overcome this, soak some newspaper, torn to shreds, in boiling water until pulpy. After squeezing dry, mix this with flour paste and carefully plaster it into the crevice between the wall and wood. This can be done without marking the walls.

If cement is used instead of the papier-maché and paste, it is liable to crack away in time, also it is necessary to damp the walls, etc., to make it adhere, and this often spoils the decorations.

DEALING WITH A SPLIT CHISEL HANDLE

It is often difficult to know what to do when the handle of a chisel, hammer shaft, etc., splits.

A good repair can be effected with a suitable length of copper wire (bell wire will do after stripping and cleaning). Drive a small tack into the handle at the top of the split and another at the base of the split. Twist one end of the wire round the top tack to hold it in place and bind the wire tightly round the handle, keeping the turns close together. When sufficient wire has been wound on fasten the end round the bottom tack.

Now apply flux to the whole of the wire on the handle, and using a medium hot iron run solder over the wire. When cold, pull out tacks, break off the wire close, and finish with sand-paper. This will make a strong ferrule which should last for years.

Painting with Sealing-Wax

In an earlier article on the first steps of sealing-wax craft, the method of forming flowers, fruit, leaves and stems was outlined (pages 361 to 363), and the beginner has, by this time, doubtless worked on the imagination and learnt to form and group many interesting designs of varied shapes and colour, with, it is to be hoped, such success that a desire to obtain further knowledge of the possibilities of this art has resulted.

Painting with wax is an exceedingly fascinating addition to one's work, as will be observed from the illustration herein given of the Victorian lady and the garden scene, both of which are examples of the combined work with wax and wax paint. As may be imagined, the originals are naturally much more effective in colour than it is possible to produce in a plainly reprinted copy, but at the same time, it serves to show the immense possibilities of the craft.

Preparing the Paint.

To prepare the paint, various coloured sticks of wax are procured and for each colour a small screwed top jar is necessary; these can b provided from used face cream pomade, vaseline or any like jars no expense being therefore necessary in this connexion.

Break the wax into very small pieces (if crushed, it obviously dissolves much quicker), place it in the jars and pour over it just sufficient methylated spirit to cover the wax, which should become dissolved in a few hours. A good thing to remember is that, should the resultant liquid be required the following day, it may be prepared either the previous afternoon or evening. If when required for use it is found to be too thin, all that has to be done is to remove the lid and allow the air to get at it until the mixture is of a workable consistency; care must be exercised, however, as it very quickly thickens. On the other hand, if the paint appears too thick, a careful addition of methylated spirit will soon rectify.

For working purposes it is used in precisely the same manner as with ordinary paint and brush, and in conjunction with sealing-wax outlines the effect is really astonishing.

In the previous article it was shown how coloured wax can be blended, and with paint it is equally possible. There are many ways of using it, and the worker will, with experience, do so with advantage to his or her own desires and designs.

Outlining the Design.

It is a good method to outline on a parchment-covered article, such as a bridge box, calendar or blotter, a preferred design, and then to proceed with the painting with the melted wax in any chosen colour or colours. One needs but little imagination in the grouping and toning of colours to obtain the most novel combination of shades.

How to make a Calendar.

Calendars similar to that shown in Fig. 1 can be purchased at many of the art stores, and this applies also to most of the other articles previously enumerated. They are available at a very reasonable price, with parchment already affixed and ready for immediate work; in some instances they can be purchased plain, but it is considered inadvisable to obtain these; firstly, because of the very slight difference in the original price; secondly, the cost of the parchment, time taken in cutting to shape, and trouble in pasting is more than compensated by the advantage of being able to obtain them in completed workable form.

It is not, of course, necessary to confine oneself to any particular design; imagination plays a big part in work of this nature, and many original ideas can be incorporated according to the size of the article and the wishes of the worker.

Beginning the Design.

Begin by outlining the design in sealing-wax, for which purpose either the wax container (the working of which is explained on page 363) or spatula may be used; either is equally effective, and it is rather a matter of choice as to which is the more convenient to work with. The container is undoubtedly the quicker method, but for the beginner it will perhaps be wiser to use the spatula, as a more even outline is likely to result.

Selecting the Colours.

We now come to the colours of wax paint to be used for the final decoration, and here one's own choice can be given full play. In the completed example shown in Fig. 1 various colours were utilised and they are now given as a guide.

For the hat, cerise paint was chosen, the ribbon band being azure blue. The flesh-coloured tints for the neck and arms were obtained by blending white and pale pink paint, while the dress was coloured with the rich tones of cerise, magenta and azure blue, the latter giving the "shot" effect. To obtain the appearance of frills and folds on the skirt an outlining with gold wax was done, the pencilled impressions being carefully followed to ensure an even and corresponding design. The protruding curls from under the brim of the hat are of gold wax dropped, as explained in the article dealing with the first steps in this art, and shaped with the moulder to form ringlets.

Completing the Figure.

The figure is completed by the apparent holding of a posy of flowers, all of which are formed by carefully placed and arranged "blobs" of wax in various colours. These are worked into shape with the moulder. The foreground of crazy paving was first of all painted over with a mixture of white, yellow, and a little blue paint, giving the greyish effect required; this was then indiscriminately picked out with a much darker-toned mixture consisting of blue and black paint, which gives the appearance of a crazy path, at the interstices of which varied coloured green wax was utilised, and with

Fig. 1.—Calendar painted with dissolved sealing-wax.

Sealing-wax paint can be put on almost any kind of article, with brilliant and colourful effect.

the spatula, used pencil-like, shaped to represent grasses. The addition of a few flowers dotted about on the top of each tuft of grass completes a very beautiful and pleasing picture.

The Final Touch.

As an additional and final adornment, a few birds on the wing made with gold sealing-wax were added. These latter are formed by scraping a little of the wax on to the spatula, and, as previously mentioned, using it in the manner of a pencil to shape and form the birds.

The completed article is now ready for the calendar, which can be either pasted in the position shown in Fig. 1 or hung from the base of the card according to choice. The ribbon or cord from which the calendar is suspended can be of any chosen shade, but naturally a contrasting colour is more effective; in the example given it was a narrow ribbon of nigger brown.

Sealing-wax paint can be utilised for painting on almost any kind of article, viz., glass, china, wood, parchment, lamp shades, and even silks, but before any additional decoration is attempted, the first applied paint must be thoroughly dry.

DESIGNING WITH CUT-OUTS

This particular branch of sealing-wax craft is perhaps a little more difficult than that already described, but it is closely allied with the latter work, though in a more advanced stage.

Obtaining the Cut-out.

First, with regard to the designs. These are obtainable from Dennison's, of Kingsway, Holborn. This firm have innumerable crinkled paper patterns in various forms and sizes, and an inspection by those interested will prove profitable and enlightening. There are patterns of figures in national dress of almost every country, scenes, birds, flowers, fruit, etc., so that the wish of each individual worker can be met.

Having chosen a suitable scene, the first thing to do is very carefully to cut out the design.

In the case of a smaller article, viz., match box, card box or bridge-scorer cover, an obviously smaller print would be obtained. A very effective design, for instance, on a card box is made by cutting out from crinkled paper the aces of each suit of a pack of cards, which are pasted on each corner of the box, while in the centre a cut-out of the figure of either of the Court cards completes a very effective piece of work; these latter patterns are also available from the firm above mentioned.

Cutting the Shape.

The object of these patterns is merely to serve as a guide, and much

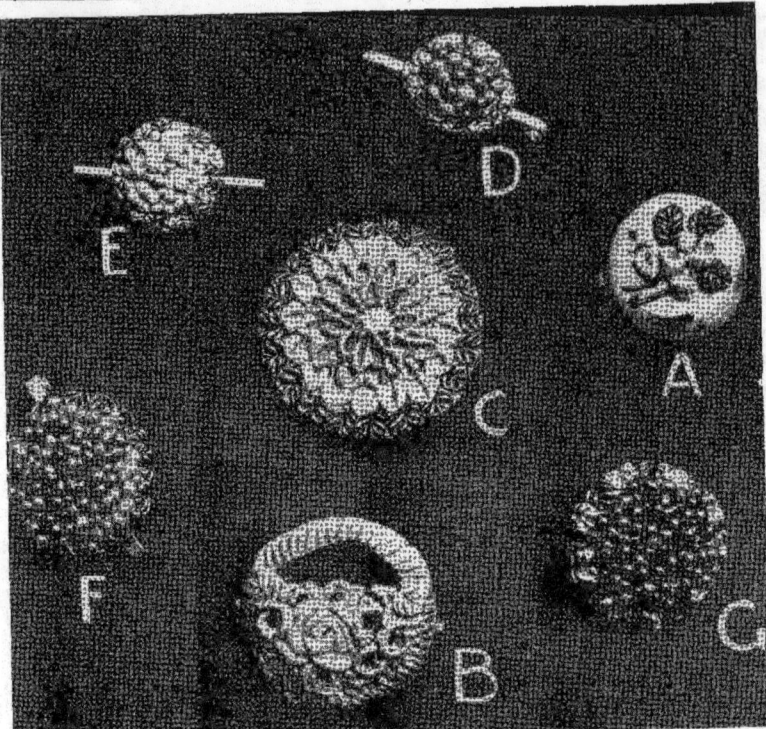

Fig. 2.—BROOCHES WORKED IN SEALING-WAX.
Practice in sealing-wax craft on the lines laid down in the previous article (pages 361-363) will enable the reader to produce more advanced work, seen above.

must be left to the imagination of the worker.

The Best Adhesive.

The pasting of the cut-out is the next step, for which purpose an efficient adhesive is necessary, and the writer has found that a mixture of paste and glue answers the purpose very effectively. It appears strange, but experi-

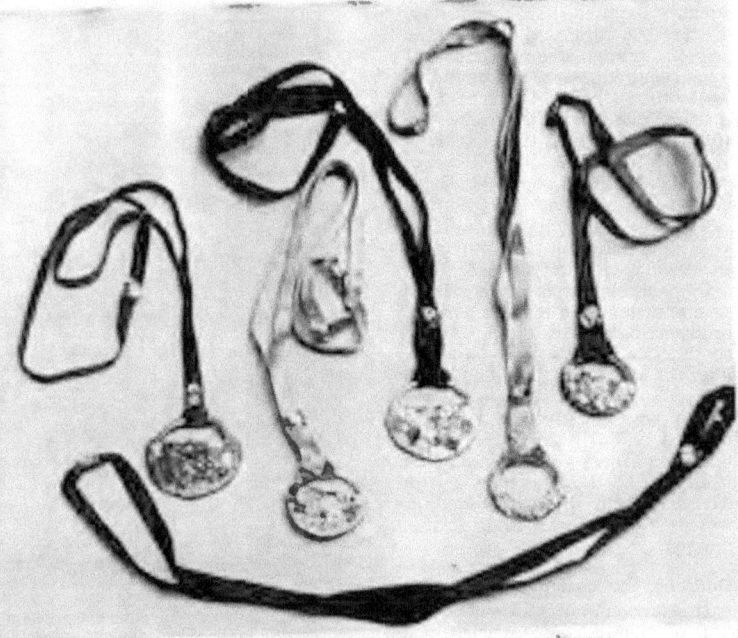

Fig. 3.—PENDANTS DECORATED WITH SEALING-WAX FORMS.

PAINTING WITH SEALING-WAX

ence has shown that ordinary paste does not adhere as it should, although when "wet" it is as satisfactory. After the period allowed for drying, the design has in many instances curled up and occasionally been found completely separated from the parchment. With the mixture above mentioned these difficulties are non-existent.

Sticking Down the Cut-out.

An equal quantity of each is taken and thoroughly mixed together with the brush provided in the box of paste. The design is now laid face down on a clean sheet of plain paper (this is to retain the fresh appearance on the printed side), and with the brush a thin but even quantity of the adhesive is applied over the whole of the paper design. Care must be used in this operation, as the thin paper is inclined to "curl" and, being of such a flimsy nature, will tear with anything but careful handling.

Applying the Pasted Paper.

The pasted paper is now ready for transfer to the article, and here again extreme caution must be observed to prevent tearing. It is advisable to lay one end down first, then, holding the paper in the left hand and taking a pad of some soft material in the right hand, gently dab down a little at a time until the whole design is affixed. It is important to see that this is perfectly accomplished; there must be no ridges, creases, or air pockets, as the presence of either of these imperfections would mar the finished work.

Another important feature is that, prior to pasting down, spacing must have been considered, as symmetry is obviously necessary; before pasting the paper, therefore, lay it on the article and place it in the exact position it is required; mark lightly with a pencil a few prominent points which can be subsequently used as a guide when fixing the pattern.

Preparing the Varnish.

Having successfully arranged the spacing and fixing, it is now left to completely dry before any further attempt is made to work on it. When ready, the design is varnished with a mixture previously made from a stick of amber transparent wax dissolved in methylated spirit. When this in turn is dry, the picture assumes an oil-painting effect and is now ready for outlining.

Begin outlining tree trunks (assuming the design is one of a country scene) with wax and decorating with leaves and grasses, the major portion of which work is done with the spatula, the moulder being brought into use to accentuate the foliage and give it a "full" appearance.

Outlining the Trees.

The copper-bronze wax is heated and a small portion at a time is scraped on to the spatula, which is applied carefully to the side of the tree trunks, keeping to the printed outlines as much as possible, although it is not entirely necessary to strictly observe a straight contour, as this would appear unnatural. After the stems have been completed the more pronounced branches are proceeded with. Minor details such as window frames, roofing patches, chimneys, door frame, paths, etc., are then outlined, which completes this part of the work. The final preparation is that of the leafed branches, for which green bronze and ordinary green wax of varied tones is used.

Using the Moulder.

The method employed is to drop wax at frequent intervals, and with the moulder, work into formation to give the idea of leafy boughs. It is unnecessary to fully cover the whole of the design, as the beauty of light and shade would be lost thereby. Tree in the distance, for instance, should have very little wax decoration—only a few strokes of dark blue and dark green wax put on with the spatula, the result giving a distant and rather darker effect.

A DOG EXERCISING TRACK

ONE of the difficulties when a large dog such as an Alsatian or Airedale is kept in a more or less confined area is giving it sufficient exercise. Often there is a path by the side of the house which extends for perhaps 10 yards or more, but the dog cannot be allowed to run loose on account of the danger to tradesmen.

The arrangement shown in the accompanying diagram enables full advantage to be taken of the space beside a house for the purpose of allowing a dog plenty of exercise. It consists of a length of wire stretched from end to end of the path and fixed a short distance above the ground. The dog's chain is attached to the wire by a pulley, enabling the dog to run from end to end.

Materials Required.

Stout piece of floor joist or half a railway sleeper (A).
U-bolt about 2 feet long (B).

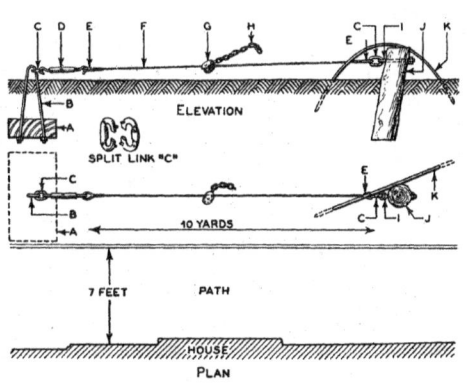

DETAILS OF THE DOG TRACK.

Two split links (harness) (C).
Straining bolt (D).
Two thimbles, 1½ inch diameter (E).
Length of single-strand wire, ¼ inch diameter (F).
Stout pulley (G).
Chain (H).
Ring bolt (I).
Oak stump (J).

Piece of old iron rail (K).

Constructional Details.

Place the split link through the U-bolt, which is then fitted to the piece of joist, which is next buried in the ground, leaving the end of the U-bolt projecting about 3 inches above the ground. Fix one end of the wire to the straining bolt, which should be hooked on to the split link. Thread the other end of the wire through the pulley, fix the thimble on. Insert the ring bolt through one end of the oak stump, which is then driven into the ground until only about 6 inches is showing. Connect up the thimble to the ring bolt by means of a split link and tighten the wire up taut by adjusting the straining bolt.

Bend the piece of old iron rail to the shape shown in the sketch and push it well into the ground. The object of this rail is to prevent the chain from wrapping round the end of the bolt or round the stump; the chain just rides over it when the dog pulls and turns.

Constructing an Electric Fan

THE fan described in this article is of original design, the motor is an induction type of machine with a rotor in place of the usual armature; thus no commutator or brushes are necessary, and all sparking is eliminated. This is a very useful factor when using the fan in a room near a wireless set, as this motor cannot possibly cause any disturbance. It is easy to construct as there is no armature to wind, and no commutator to make. This motor will, of course, only work on A.C. mains; its consumption is about 30 watts.

Materials required.

Sheet iron (soft), gauge 18 to 20, 5 square feet.
Strip iron, $\tfrac{3}{4}$ inch wide, $\tfrac{3}{32}$ inch thick, 1 foot.
Strip iron, 1 inch wide, $\tfrac{3}{32}$ inch thick, 6 inches.
Steel bolts, $\tfrac{3}{16}$-inch diameter, 1$\tfrac{1}{4}$ inch long, 4.
Steel rod, $\tfrac{1}{4}$-inch diameter, 1 foot.
Sheet brass, gauge 22, 1 foot by 1 foot 3 inches.
Sheet brass, $\tfrac{3}{16}$ inch thick, 2 × 2 inches.
Brass rod, $\tfrac{7}{8}$-inch diameter, 6 inches.
Brass tube, $\tfrac{3}{4}$-inch bore, 6 inches.
Brass wire, gauge 14, 5 yards.
Sheet copper, $\tfrac{1}{16}$ inch thick, 4 × 4 inches.
Copper wire (tinned), gauge 24, 2 ozs.
Copper wire (D.S.C.), gauge 34, 8 ozs.
Insulating tape, 1 roll.
Rivets, $\tfrac{1}{8}$ × $\tfrac{3}{8}$ inch, 2.
Bolt and butterfly nut, $\tfrac{3}{16}$-inch diameter, 1.

The Field Laminations.

Fig. 4 shows how the field magnet is built up from laminations, while Fig. 2 gives the size and shape of a single "stamping." The amateur can cut these laminations out of a piece of sheet metal with a fret-saw fitted with a metal cutting blade. Set out one of the laminations and cut this to shape as a pattern for all the remaining ones. Now rough out a number of sheet-iron squares with 3$\tfrac{1}{4}$-inch side and bolt six or eight together with two bolts through the waste material in the centre. Having scribed out the pattern on the front and back of the batch of squares, proceed to cut them out with the fret-saw. Those readers who possess a washer-cutter will find this tool very useful for roughing out the outside and the centre circle. About thirty-six to forty laminations will be required; these are bolted together by the four bolts shown in Fig. 4, and then the edges are trued up, special attention being shown to the pole pieces (see Fig. 4). When the edges have been trued the tunnel formed by the poles should be a perfect cylinder,

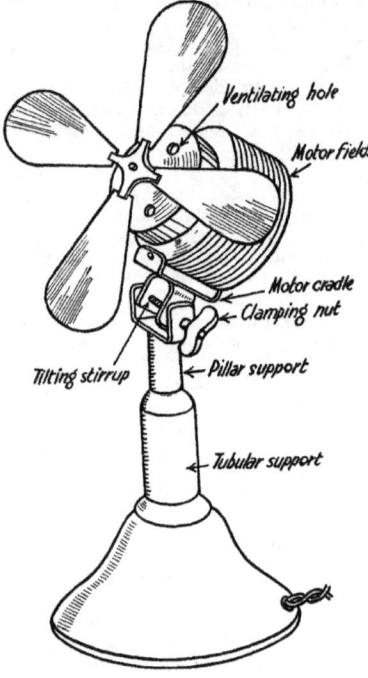

Fig. 1.—The Complete Electric Fan and Stand.

of which the poles form part of the circumference. The laminations must be taken apart again, coated with shellac, and reassembled. Observe the eight saw cuts across the sides of the poles (see Fig. 4), these are made after the laminations are bolted together; a brass band slides between these slots as shown, to hold the field winding in place.

The Rotor.

Details of this are given in Fig. 3; it consists of a number of circular iron laminations assembled on a spindle like an armature. Round the edge of the rotor are sixteen holes opened up from the outer edge with a saw cut to form slots; in these are carried the copper conductors which take the place of the armature winding. The rotor laminations are not assembled with the holes in line with the shaft; note that the saw cuts which open up the holes slope slightly towards the right hand when viewed from the side; this is because the tunnel formed by a row of rotor holes slopes a little to the right. The extreme right-hand lamination is turned one hole further round than the corresponding left-hand lamination, and the remaining "stampings" are so placed that a continuous sloping tunnel is formed. The holes round the edge of the rotor are best drilled $\tfrac{1}{16}$ inch under size; the laminations are then assembled as described above, and sweated to the shaft; a $\tfrac{3}{16}$-inch drill can then be run through each tunnel to clear the sharp edges. The saw cuts are made after the rotor is assembled.

Loading the Rotor.

Lengths of 24-gauge tinned copper wire are introduced through the saw cuts in the rotor until each tunnel is full. Solder is then run into each slot to secure each bundle of wires. The tinned copper wires must be long enough to project $\tfrac{3}{16}$ inch beyond the ends of the rotor. True up the projecting ends, and then slip on the tinned copper rings as shown in Fig. 3; these are then securely sweated to the bundles of wire in the rotor slots; thus all the copper conductors are bonded together by the rings.

The End Plates.

In Fig. 5 the rear end of the motor is shown; notice that a circular dished cover is bolted over the end of the field tunnel. The amateur can best make this by cutting out a circular disc 2$\tfrac{1}{2}$ inches diameter, and around this solder a ring of sheet brass $\tfrac{3}{4}$ inch wide; the outer flange is then cut out like a washer and soldered to the edge of the ring. Note that slots are filed in the flange to accommodate the securing bolts; these permit the end-plate being turned so that the rotor can be centred in the field tunnel. Three holes are bored in the end-plate for purposes of ventilation. The small sketch (Fig. 5) shows the brass bush which forms the bearing; this is sweated into the end of the end-plate. Two such plates will be required, one for the front and the other for the rear end of the field tunnel.

The Field Windings.

These are wound with fine wire on a wooden former similar to the one in Fig. 4. The upper block is slightly larger than the pole piece A in the figure, and around this two layers of waxed paper are wound; a piece of card can be tacked on to the block D to prevent the wire slipping off. Now proceed to wind on the gauge 34 wire, placing a layer of tissue between each layer; each coil will take a little over 3 ozs. Both coils should be wound in the same direction and joined together

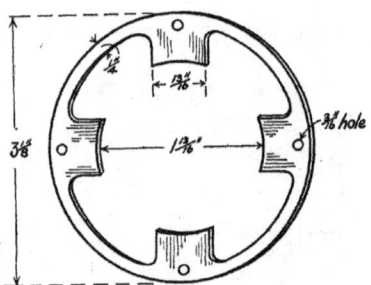

Fig. 2.—One of the Field Laminations.

CONSTRUCTING AN ELECTRIC FAN

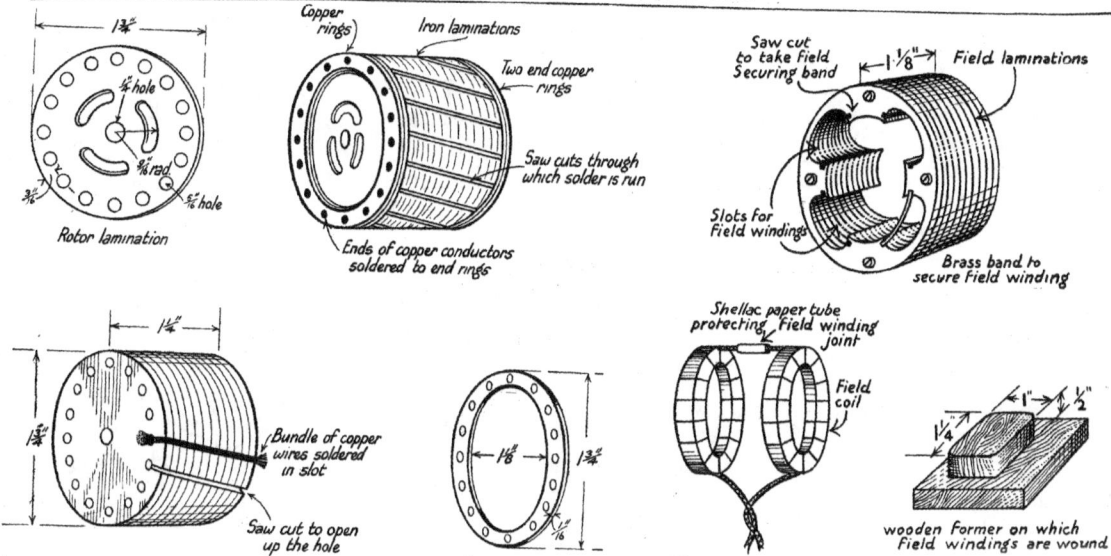

Fig. 3.—DETAILS OF THE ROTOR WHICH TAKES THE PLACE OF THE ARMATURE.

Fig. 4.—HOW THE FIELD MAGNET IS BUILT UP FROM LAMINATIONS.

as shown; a small tube of shellac paper surrounds the soldered joint between the coils, this prevents fine wire from fracturing. Each coil is taped as shown, and then placed on the poles; it is held in place by the brass bands which slide into the saw cuts in the side of the poles (see Fig. 4).

The Fan.

Fig. 6 shows the details of the fan; four blades are cut out of brass as shown, and these are mounted in a centre piece which is like a four-pointed star. Saw cuts are made in each point of the centre piece, and the blades are soldered into these and secured with a small rivet. Notice that a bush is soldered to the back of the centre piece and a grub screw in this fastens the fan to the spindle. The blades are twisted to give them "pitch," the right-hand edge (viewed from the front) of each blade is slightly bent backwards towards the motor; thus when they revolve the current of air is pushed forwards.

The Complete Rotor Assembly.

In Fig. 6 may be seen the spindle with its parts assembled. The rotor itself is fastened to the shaft ⅜ inch from the end; in front of this is the bearing bush which is soldered to the front end-plate, and immediately after this the fan centre (shown in section) is attached to the spindle. A small thrust collar is fastened to the axle inside the end-plate immediately after the bearing bush; this collar is simply a ring of brass ⅝-inch diameter with a grub screw in the side so that the washer can be locked in position to limit the end "float" to 1/16 inch. Note that small oil holes are provided

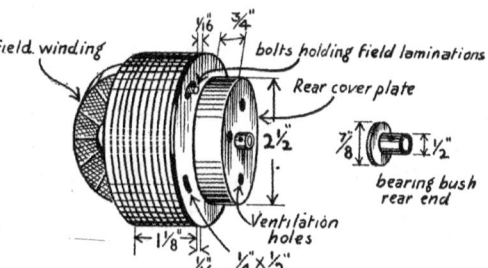

Fig. 5.—REAR VIEW OF MOTOR SHOWING REAR COVER PLATE AND BEARING.

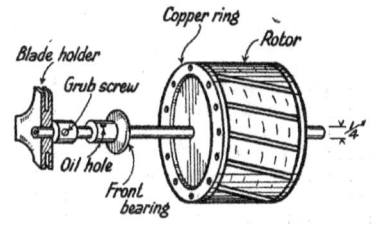

Fig. 6.—ROTOR ASSEMBLED WITH FRONT BEARING AND BLADE HOLDER (IN SECTION) IN POSITION.

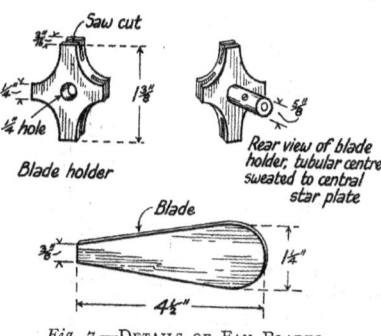

Fig. 7.—DETAILS OF FAN BLADES.

in each bush, and these must be well furnished with high-grade thin oil.

The Motor Tilting Support.

From Fig. 8 it will be seen that the motor is supported in a strip-iron cradle, which is secured by one of the bolts passing through the field laminations; sideways movement can be prevented by soldering on a small curved lip to the uprights of the cradle so that the edges of the motor rest on the lip. Riveted at right angles to the cradle is a tilting stirrup (see Fig. 8), this is pivoted across the uprights of the bracket fixed to the pillar; this is also shown in the figure. The fixed bracket is screwed and sweated to the ¾-inch rod which forms the main supporting column. A hole is bored down the centre of the pillar, and through this is carried the flex; a hole in the side near the top allows the cable tube to be brought through, so that it may be connected to the field windings of the motor. The brass rod fits at the lower end into a length of brass tube to which it is sweated; the complete pillar is then mounted in a weighted base filled with lead (see Fig. 1).

The Wire Guard.

It is necessary to surround the blades with a guard to prevent accidents—a suitable wire cover is shown in Fig. 9. It is constructed of brass wire and takes the form of two rings held apart by six short lengths at right angles, while across the front are three wires radiating like the radii of a circle. The joints are twisted and soldered. It is held in position by two arms at right angles at the back, which are bolted to

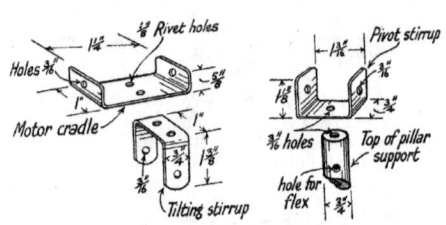

Fig. 8.—Details of Motor Support and Tilting Device.

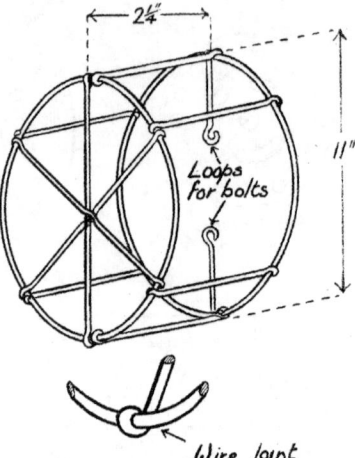

Fig. 9.—Wire Guard for Fan Blades.

the front of the end-plate with two B.A. screws.

The Finish.

The stampings which form the shell of the motor should be enamelled a colour to taste. The four blades are best cleaned and lacquered and the base also looks well lacquered, but some readers may prefer to paint it the same colour as the body of the motor.

The Brass Brushes should be left bright.

The brass bushes should not on any account be enamelled; these are best left bright. The wire guard looks well if it is coloured to match the body of the motor.

Final Hints.

The No. 34 winding will suit A.C. circuits from 200 to 220 volts, but for pressures higher than this, such as 230 to 250 volts, the field windings must be filled with No. 36, using $4\frac{1}{2}$ ozs. on each bobbin. When working with No. 36 wire it is best to use enamelled in place of the silk-covered.

Use only on A.C. Mains.

Finally, do not on any account try to run this motor on D.C. mains.

CLEANING EXTERIOR SURFACES OF BUILDINGS

THE following are a few typical methods of cleaning materials such as marble, stone, brick, plaster and cement in the case of building exteriors.

Marble.

The usual cause of the dirty appearance of marble is that of grime from smoky chimneys, dust and dirt from the roads. In most cases the deposits can be effectively removed by scrubbing well with a soapy water solution or with warm soda water made by dissolving a liberal quantity of ordinary washing soda in hot water. A scrubbing brush should be employed to loosen the deposits. Afterwards wash down with plenty of clean cold water.

If the surface of the marble has *grease stains* rub well with Fuller's earth and benzine, or petrol. Common clay mixed with benzine will generally remove any oil stains, but it may be necessary, afterwards, to restore the lustre of the surface by polishing with putty powder.

Ink stains on marble can be removed by rubbing them with a cloth saturated with a strong solution of oxalic acid. Other kinds of stains that do not come under the previously mentioned headings are generally removable with a weak solution of oxalic acid. Afterwards, the surface should be well rubbed with a damp cloth dipped into powdered chalk.

Coloured marbles should be cleaned, not with soapy solutions, but with a moistened mixture consisting of 2 parts of sodium carbonate (or common washing soda) and 1 part of chloride of lime. This mixture should be rubbed over the surface with a piece of flannel until the surface becomes dry.

Stone.

The method of cleaning stone depends largely upon the nature of the stone, *i.e.*, whether sand stone, Portland stone or a cement composition. The alkaline solution method, in which soapy water, soda water or ammonia solution is used in conjunction with a scrubbing brush will invariably be found to give satisfactory results. If a steam jet is available this will be found a quick and convenient method of cleaning the stone surfaces of buildings. In most cases it is necessary, after using alkaline solutions to wash the surfaces down with clean water.

Brick.

Brick walls that have become stained can usually be restored to their original appearance by wiping over with a dilute solution of spirits of salt (hydrochloric acid), afterwards washing them well with clean water.

If the red colour of the bricks has faded it is a good plan to make up a solution of 1 oz. of glue to 1 gallon of water, adding while hot 2 ozs. of alum and a sufficient quantity of pigment to give the desired shade. Venetian red, red ochre and vandyke brown pigments should be used for this purpose.

Plaster Mouldings.

These are best cleaned by wiping or scrubbing with a soda-water solution, or with a solution of lump ammonia and water. Most of the deposits due to grime from smoky chimneys can be removed in this manner.

If the mouldings are of the cement composition cast variety it will save a good deal of time and trouble if they are lightly brushed over with a suitably tinted cement wash or grout. For cement coloured mouldings a mixture of Portland cement and water, or cement and fine sand in equal proportions and water, made to a thin pasty consistency will be found to give satisfactory results.

Cement and Concrete.

Exterior surfaces of cement or concrete can usually be cleaned effectively by scrubbing with hot soapy water, but if they are seriously stained it will probably be quicker to brush over with a cement wash as in the preceding case.

Tiles.

Discoloured or faded tiles can be reconditioned by brushing over with a suitably coloured cement wash. There are now proprietary makes of tinted cements, such as Cementone, to match practically every shade required. These give a practically permanent and weather-proof surface to tiles, bricks, concrete, etc.

How to Make a Model Glider

THIS makes a most interesting toy for the youngsters. It is easily made, and has the great advantage of being a working model. It is capable of long flights, and, by adjusting the wings, can be made to loop and perform other evolutions.

Materials required.

Thin plywood (about $\frac{1}{16}$ inch) is used for almost the entire construction. This is extremely strong and, being thin, is light. Another point in its favour is that it can be cut easily with ordinary scissors. The wings are covered with silvered or gilt paper, which has the effect of stiffening them. Rubber bands are used to attach the main wing to the body or fuselage. This has two advantages. It enables the wing to be adjusted to various positions, and it enables it to "give" in the event of a crash. If the wing were fixed rigidly it would probably smash.

A piece of deal wood is required for the nose; also a screw-in dresser hook.

Cutting out the Parts.

The completed glider is shown in Fig. 1. Fig. 2 shows the parts to be cut out. Full-size patterns of the various parts are given in Figs. 3, 4, 5 and 6. Half the main wing only is shown. Obtain a piece of $\frac{1}{16}$-inch plywood (thicker stuff is unsuitable, as it

Fig. 1.—Easily-made Model Glider.

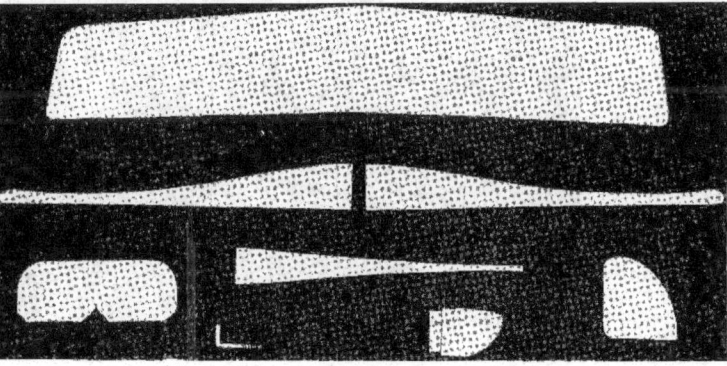

Fig. 2.—Parts cut out ready for assembling.

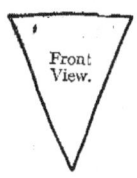

Front View.

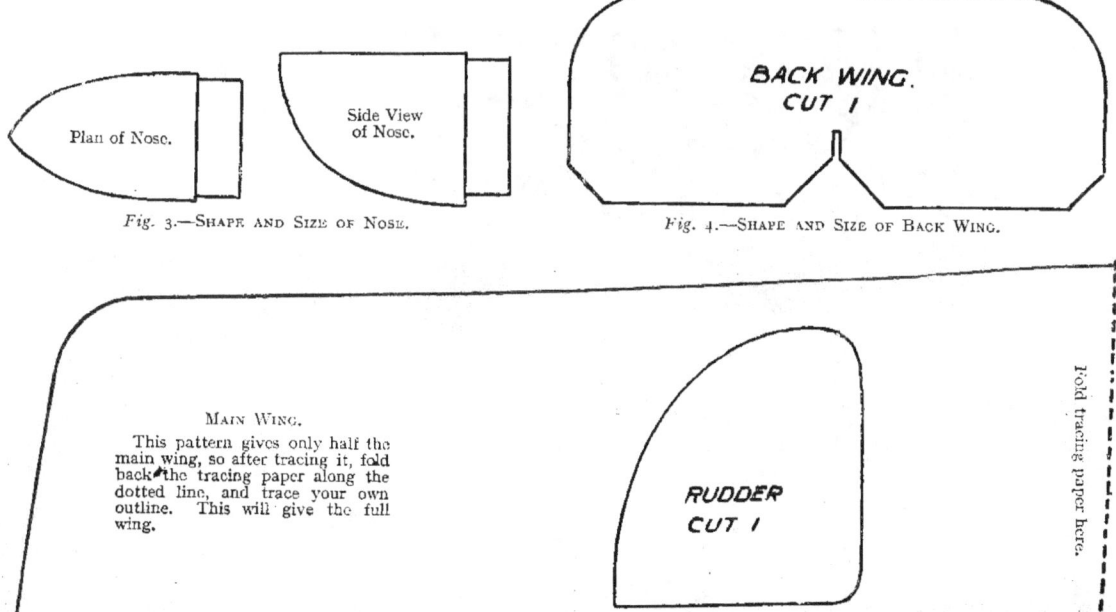

Fig. 3.—Shape and Size of Nose.

Fig. 4.—Shape and Size of Back Wing.

Main Wing.

This pattern gives only half the main wing, so after tracing it, fold back the tracing paper along the dotted line, and trace your own outline. This will give the full wing.

Fig. 5.—Shape and Size of Main Wing and Rudder.

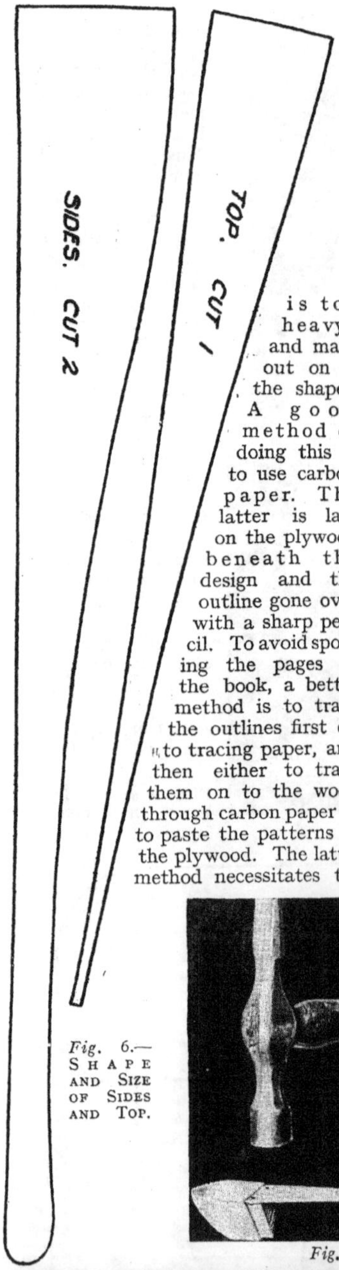

HOW TO MAKE A MODEL GLIDER

paper being afterwards soaked off.

Fig. 7 shows the design being cut out. Follow the outline as closely as possible. The nose or front of the fuselage is cut from a piece of deal measuring 1⅜ × ⅞ × ¾ inch. Full-size patterns of the shape are given in the diagram. First cut a plain block to the sizes given and mark out on the top the curved shape, and on the front the wedge shape.

Cut the wedge shape first with either a chisel

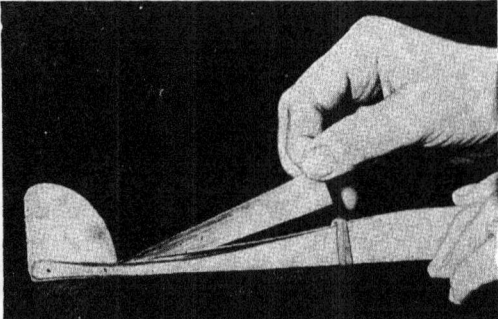

Fig. 10.—Use of Gummed Paper to Fix Sides and Top.

is too heavy), and mark out on it the shapes. A good method of doing this is to use carbon paper. The latter is laid on the plywood beneath the design and the outline gone over with a sharp pencil. To avoid spoiling the pages of the book, a better method is to trace the outlines first on to tracing paper, and then either to trace them on to the wood through carbon paper or to paste the patterns to the plywood. The latter method necessitates the

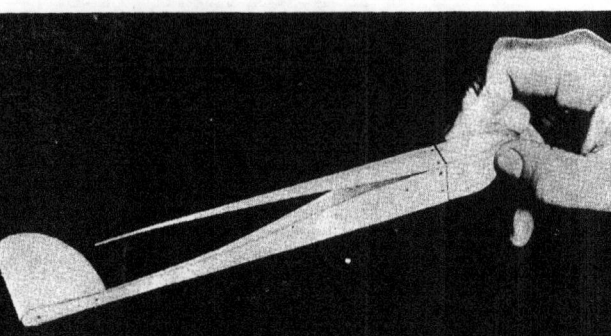

Fig. 9.—The Sides fixed to the Rudder.

away the waste wood.

Assembling the Fuselage.

Fig. 8 shows the first step. Put a little glue on the rebate of the nose, and with fine nails fix the top in position. If a vice is handy, the nose can be placed in it so that the sides are supported whilst the nails are being driven in.

The sides follow. These are secured in the same way. At the back the rudder is fixed between them, as given in Fig. 9. Put a little glue on the joining surfaces, and drive small nails through them. The nails can pass right through, be cut off short, and clenched.

To fix the top to the sides and the last-named to each other, gummed paper is used. The ordinary brown gummed paper is the most convenient in use, as it dries rapidly. To hold the parts together, a rubber band can be passed over the whole as in Fig. 10. This can be removed afterwards. Gummed paper is also used to secure the back wing to the sides. It is simply folded into the angle.

The Main Wing—Giving a Silvered Finish.

Having cut out this to the pattern given, it should be covered with silvered paper. Ordinary note-paper can be used, but the silvered or gilt paper has a more attractive appearance. The paper can be in one piece if cuts are made at the centre and at the ends, to enable it to be folded. The front edge should have the paper folded over it. Place the whole thing beneath a flat board, with a weight above, so that the paper beds down flat.

For the wing to have the maximum lifting power, it must be bent slightly across its section. This is shown clearly

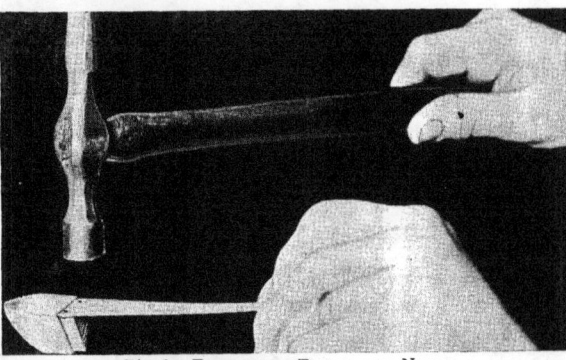

Fig. 8.—Fitting the Top to the Nose.

or a penknife. The sides are then chiselled to form the pointed front, and lastly, the sides are rounded to make the bottom curve upwards to the top at the front. It is necessary to cut the notch or rebate at the back to provide a fixing for the plywood sides. This is easily done by cutting across the grain and afterwards chiselling

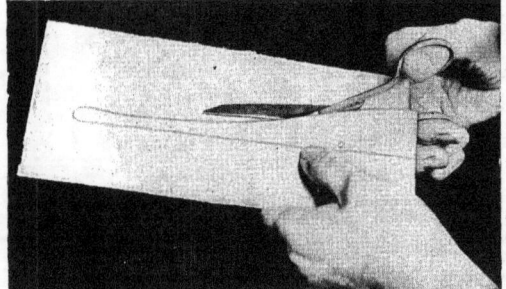

Fig. 7.—Cutting out the Parts in 1/64-inch Plywood.

Fig. 6.—Shape and Size of Sides and Top.

in Fig. 1. This is easily done with the fingers. An ordinary screw-in hook should be driven into the bottom edge of the nose. The purpose of this is to enable the glider to be launched with a catapult.

It is impossible to give the exact position of the main wing on the fuselage, as the weight is bound to vary. Experience soon shows the best position. In the same way the corners of the wings can be bent to make the plane rise or fly level, according to the flight desired.

A Catapult.

A catapult is easily made from a piece of stout plywood. It should be in the form of a letter Y. Notches are cut at the ends of the upper arms, and rubber bands fixed to them with thread.

A glance at Fig. 1 will show how the hook is screwed into the bottom edge of the nose. To send off the glider into flight, hold it by the lower part of the rudder, connect the hook with the rubber bands of the catapult, which is held in the left hand, draw the bands taut and let the glider go in the direction required.

MAKING A CHEMICAL WEATHER FORECASTER

Most persons are familiar with the old-fashioned type of weather-glass, consisting of a vertical glass tube filled with a cloudy crystalline solution that behaves in a definite manner according to the kind of weather immediately expected.

These weather-glasses are not difficult to make, and, when suitably mounted on a polished mahogany or oak stand, provide an attractive and useful addition to the hall or conservatory.

How the Weather-glass indicates.

Before describing the method of making a weather-glass it will, no doubt, be of interest to those who are not familiar with its changes of appearance to describe the accompanying weather indications to these changes. They are as follows:—

Solution in Tube Soft and Powdery, almost Filling Tube.—Rain will occur in the near future, accompanied by southerly or south-westerly winds.

Solution in Tube becomes Crystalline, almost Filling Tube.—Fine weather will follow, with winds from the north-east, north or north-west.

Portion of Solution Crystallises on one Side of Tube.—Wind may be expected from that direction (the tube being in the open air in this case).

Crystalline at Bottom, Clear Solution above.—If the solution is perfectly clear above the crystals at the bottom, fine weather is to be expected.

Crystals Rise gradually into Clear Solution above.—Approaching rain.

Substance partly at Top, Leaflike in form, agitated appearance.—Approaching storm or gale will occur.

In Winter.—The substance usually lies higher in the tube. *Snow or white frost* is shown by whiter appearance with small star-like crystals in motion in the liquid.

In Summer.—The substance generally lies quite low.

How to make the Weather-glass.

First procure from a chemist's or firm of chemical apparatus manufacturers * a length of glass tubing or a large test-tube. The best form is a flat-bottom glass tube of about 1 inch internal diameter and about 10 to 12 inches long.

This should be cleaned with warm (not hot) soda water solution made by dissolving washing soda in water. If there are any persistent stains inside the tube, clean with dilute hydrochloric acid. Afterwards rinse out well with clean water and dry.

A soft cloth should be used to polish the inside of the tube when the latter has dried.

The Weather-glass Solution.

The solution employed for filling the weather-glass must be carefully apportioned and made up as follows:—

Camphor . . 2½ drachms
Alcohol . . 11 ,,
Water . . 9 ,,
Saltpetre (Nitre) . 38 grains.
Sal ammoniac . 38 ,,

All of the chemicals can be obtained from the local chemist, or, alternatively, the latter will make up a sufficient quantity of solution to this recipe.

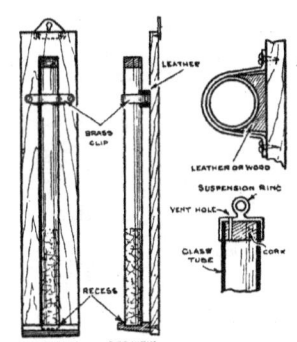

Figs. 1–3.—Front and Side Views of Chemical Weather Glass, with Details of Method of clamping Tube to Board.

Finishing the Weather-glass.

Having mixed the above chemicals thoroughly, pour into the cleaned glass tube right up to the top; the tube should, of course, be supported in the vertical position for this purpose.

Next, take a suitable size of cork and coat it with melted paraffin (or candle) wax. Pierce a hole through the cork, using a red-hot darning needle or piece of wire of similar diameter. Press the cork firmly into the top of glass tube, and then seal the edges with more melted paraffin wax. The tube should then be mounted on a piece of polished oak or mahogany board, so that it will be in a vertical position when the board is fixed on to the wall, using a brass picture-plate type of mounting.

The tube can either be clamped to the wall-board, as shown in Fig. 2, or suspended by means of a metal ring and brass cap from a hook arranged near the top of the board, as shown in Fig. 3.

The brass cap should be just a loose fit on the top of the glass tube. It can be firmly attached to the latter by means of cellulose cement; Durofix liquid cement will do admirably for this purpose. A $\frac{1}{16}$-inch hole should be drilled through the top of the brass cap so as to come opposite the hole in the cork, previously mentioned.

The advantage of the suspension method of mounting the weather-glass is that it ensures the latter always remaining in a vertical position.

To complete the apparatus, a neat card, upon which the corresponding weather predictions and solution appearances are printed, should be mounted on the side, or sides, of the weather-glass. The latter, it may be mentioned, in concluding this description, is sometimes known as a *Chemical Barometer*.

* Messrs. Griffin & Co., Kemble Street, Kingsway, London, W.C.2, and Messrs. Townson and Mercer, Camomile Street, London.

Making a Simple Pair of Steps

This article deals with the construction of a simple pair of steps the height of which is 5 feet 6 inches. The following timber, machine planed, will be required:—

- 2 side members, 1 × 4 inches × 6 feet long.
- 2 back stay sides, 1 × 4 inches × 6 feet long, which is ripped to form 1 × 2 inches.
- 2 horizontal braces for sides, 1 × 4 inches × 3 feet long.
- 8 steps, total length approx. 9 feet of 1 × 4 inches.
- 1 piece for back, 1 × 9 inches × 1 foot long.

In addition the following materials will be required:—

- 36 2 × 10 inch steel screws.
- 12 1¼ × 7 inch steel screws.
- 2 2½ × ¼ inch bolts with washers.
- 1 piece of cord 8 feet long ¼ inch diameter.
- Putty and nails of various lengths.

Method of Construction.

First take the two side pieces and rip sufficient off them so that when the steps are placed in the housing at an angle of 68 degrees the two edges just come flush with the sides of the side-pieces, as shown in Fig. 3. Then plane the edges smooth and square and make a face mark on the two pieces so that they pair. Now set the bevel at an angle of 68 degrees and proceed to mark out the sides. Note that when the position for the housing of the step has been marked the next mark is made 7¾ inches up the side, an extra ¼ inch being allowed for the sides to fit into the top.

Fig. 1.—The Completed Steps, showing Overall Dimensions.

Fig. 2.—Alternative Method of fitting Back Legs.

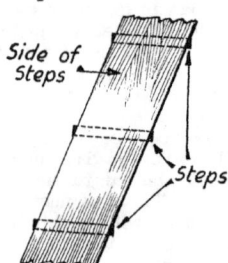

Fig. 3.—The Steps are placed at an Angle of 68 degrees.
The two edges come just flush with the sides of the side pieces.

Fig. 5.—How the Housings are cut.

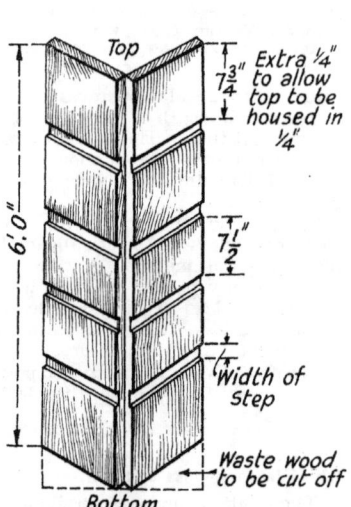

Fig. 4.—Details of the Two Side Pieces.

Fig. 6.—Sawing out Housings with Tenon Saw.

When one side piece has been carefully marked out, place the other side piece against it and mark off the corresponding positions so that when the housings are cut the two side pieces will form a perfect pair.

Cutting the Housings for the Steps.

The next operation is to set a gauge to ¼ inch and run it along the wood where the housings are to be cut out. Then square down the bevelled lines to meet the gauge line. Now cramp down the side piece to the bench and cut down with a tenon saw just inside the bevel lines to the ¼-inch gauge lines. Pare away all waste wood and finish off with a routing plane if one is available. Then cut the top and bottom bevels. This completes the side pieces.

Preparing the Steps.

Set the bevel to 88 degrees and proceed to cut the steps from the 9-foot lengths of 1 × 4 inches. The length of the various steps is as follows:—

1st step	1′ 4″
2nd ,,	1′ 3″
3rd ,,	1′ 2″
4th ,,	1′ 1″
5th ,,	1′ 0″
6th ,,	11″
7th ,,	10″

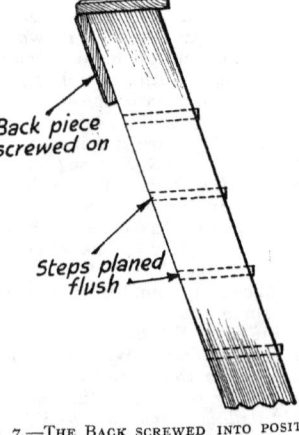

Fig. 7.—The Back screwed into position and Back of Stops planed off.

Fig. 8.—How the Front of the Steps is finished off.

The 8th or top step is housed out to allow the sides to go in and overlaps about 1 inch each side.

Fixing the Steps to the Side Pieces.

Now place the 7th and bottom steps in position with the bevel sloping away from the front. Then try the other steps, and if the bevels fit take to pieces and clean up with a smoothing plane. If any of the steps do not fit ease them with the smoothing plane by planing from each edge towards the middle. When they have all been made a nice fit bore holes with a $\frac{1}{4}$-inch shell bit in the side for the 2×10 inch screws. Cramp up each step as you go and drive home the screws, first countersinking the holes.

Fitting the Top.

The next operation is to fit the top. Place it in the position it is to occupy and run a pencil along each side of the side pieces and square the lines over. Then run the gauge along the front edge. The housing should not reach right to the back, so that the back end of the housing should be cut out with a chisel. Chamfer the edges and fix in position with nails.

Now take the remaining piece of 1×9 inch and place it under the top which projects on the back and mark the bevel on each side so that it fits flush with the top. Cut and plane the end grain edges and put a chamfer on the sides and bottom edges before screwing into position.

Now plane off the projecting pieces of the steps at the back, put a small chamfer on the front and finish by chiselling the corners off as in Fig. 8.

The Back Legs.

Now rip the 6-foot lengths of 1×4 inch down the middle and plane the sawn edges. Then take the 3-foot length and cut off the top and bottom horizontal braces which are approximately $13\frac{1}{2}$ and $19\frac{1}{2}$ inches long. Screw the braces in position so that there is $\frac{1}{8}$ inch clearance between back legs and side pieces. The top of the bottom brace should come flush with the top of the bottom step, and the top brace should be about $1\frac{1}{2}$ inches below the 7th step.

Place two 2-inch screws in each side in each brace, then place the frame on the back and mark and bore the holes for the bolts about $5\frac{1}{2}$ inches above the top of the brace.

Next cut the cord into two 4-foot lengths and bore two $\frac{1}{4}$-inch holes in the bottom step about $1\frac{1}{2}$ inches from each side and 1 inch in from the back; also bore two holes midway in the width of the bottom brace and about $1\frac{1}{2}$ inches in from each side. Pass the cord through the holes and tie a knot in each end, making sure the legs are equidistant. All screw-holes should then be stopped and the steps given a coat or two of good lead paint. Fig. 2 shows an alternative method of fitting the back legs, using hinges instead of bolts.

NOTES ON INFRA-RED PHOTOGRAPHY

INFRA-RED photography consists in using only the infra-red rays which are present in the light reflected from almost every object. This is done by means of an "infra-red" filter on the lens, that is, a filter which allows infra-red rays to pass and cuts out all other rays. The exposure is made on a plate specially sensitive to infra-red.

Cameras for Infra-red Pictures

As the best examples of infra-red photography are subjects at a great distance, a camera of long extension for use of a long-focus lens is needed. It is impossible to see the image on the focussing screen once the filter has been placed in position, so that the subject must be arranged and focussed beforehand. However, a good hand camera for plates with finder and focussing scale can serve equally well when used on a tripod, or even, on occasion, in the hand.

Filters.

There are many filters which may be used, and these may be classified under two headings: the red filters and the infra-red filters. The red filters allow orange, red and infra-red rays through them; the infra-red filters allow only a very little of the deep red to pass through them in addition to the infra-red.

If one of the extreme red sensitive materials is used, a red filter must be used. If, however, true infra-red sensitive films or plates are to be used an infra-red filter may be employed, but for all ordinary work a red filter will act just as well.

Exposure.

All the available infra-red materials are rather slow in their infra-red sensitivity, although it is impossible to give an exact estimate for any particular exposure it can be taken as a general guide that the speed of an Ilford infra-red plate with filter in position is roughly H. and D. 20, which will give approximately forty to fifty times the exposure that would be required if a very rapid plate or film were being used. This, of course, sounds very slow until it is remembered that it is usual to give exposures of from $\frac{1}{50}$ to $\frac{1}{100}$ second for open landscapes during the summer months, so that it only means a range of from $\frac{1}{8}$ to 2 seconds, even if a moderately small lens stop is used.

Dash Slides.

It should be mentioned that infra-red rays are able to pass through some kinds of wood of some thickness, and for this reason it is best to employ metal dark slides whenever possible. Mahogany is an offender in this respect, while pine woods are very much worse. Some woods, such as walnut, teak and ebony, are fairly safe, but a test should be made.

Development.

The development of infra-red plates presents no especial difficulties. Any standard developer can be employed in the usual way, and if the work is done in the light of a suitable bright green safelight, ample illumination can be available to watch each stage of the process.

Application of Infra-red Photography.

Broadly speaking, infra-red photography has two types of application in common use at the present time. One is haze penetration, the other recording differences in objects which to the eye are indistinguishable.

The obscuring action of haze, mist and fog is mainly due to the scattering of light by the countless millions of tiny particles suspended in the atmosphere between the observer and the object which he wishes to see. There is a second effect, viz., the absorption of light by the particles themselves. Infra-red photography sometimes succeeds in overcoming these difficulties, because infra-red radiation is generally scattered much less than visible light. Thus by using an infra-red plate with suitable filter much of the scattered light is ignored.

There is no doubt that in days of summer when the distance is lost in bluish haze and ordinary photographic materials fail, the infra-red yields marvellous results. Cloud forms are often recorded in extremely beautiful manner.

Photographing Ancient Documents.

A use to which infra-red photography has been put is that of photographing ancient documents, the original dark characters being thrown into contrast and becoming legible. In another instance, when the original writing in old censored books was photographed, the censor's ink was transparent to infra-red and so the original writing which had been blotted out 300 or 400 years ago was rediscovered.

Constructing an Aviary

In aviary construction there are at least seven important points to be borne in mind. They are: aspect, natural lighting, ventilation, warmth, prevention against damp, draught and vermin. All these points are covered in the structural details which follow.

Size.

A useful size, and one which can be accommodated in most gardens, is 8 × 6 feet in area, with an open wire flight 8 feet wide and of any length available; the longer the better. A plan adaptable to most positions is given in Fig. 1A.

Concrete Floor.

Wherever possible the whole of the floor should be of concrete laid on earth. It affords precaution against rats and mice entering, and can be kept clean. The ground surface must be levelled off and rammed solid.

Concrete should consist of 1 part Portland cement, 2 parts sand and 4 parts broken brick, granite chippings or small pebbles in volume.

The materials should be mixed together dry, and then sufficient water added to moisten thoroughly the whole, when it is ready for laying in position. As the concrete is to stand above ground level some 2 or 3 inches, it will be necessary to provide some support at the outer edges, and this is formed by a wooden frame made to the size required in which the concrete is laid.

The drying-out of concrete should be as gradual as possible, and therefore in very dry weather it is necessary to moisten the ground upon which the concrete is going to be laid, and in the case of extreme heat, the concrete should, as soon as it has hardened sufficiently, be covered with sand to a depth of about ½ inch to keep the sun's rays from the concrete. On the other hand, during winter it is not usually necessary to moisten the ground, but precautions should be taken against frost attacking the concrete before it sets, otherwise, due to the expansion of freezing, the concrete would burst up and be useless. If possible, concrete should not be laid during frosty weather, but if it is absolutely necessary that the work should be carried out under such conditions, the concrete should be preserved by laying sacking over it during the frosty period; even this is not absolutely safe, but it is a precaution. It will be found that the concrete will take from some four to six days to set, and after this it will be found quite safe to remove the supporting woodwork from around the edges. It is advisable to set bolts in the concrete for holding down the building (see Fig. 2).

Wooden Floor.

If a wooden floor is preferred, it should as far as possible be made proof against rats and mice. This can be accomplished in two ways, although the first is not to be recommended.

In the first case, the floor joists of 5 × 2 inches are supported on brick piers sufficiently high from the ground to allow a cat to enter. Floor boards are nailed across the joists and the floor is formed. Shrinkage of timber in time makes this type of floor draughty.

An improvement on the foregoing is a double-boarded floor reinforced by light-gauge mild-steel sheets laid between the boards. This makes a draught-proof and rat-proof floor. In this case there should be no access for cats under the floor, but small cross-ventilation holes must be made to prevent dry rot (see Fig. 3).

Framework of Building.

One and a half or 1¼-inch square section deal should be used for all the framework, and all joints should be made so that the faces of each timber are flush with one another to receive the covering boards referred to later. In Fig. 4 are given the details of the framework erection, and Fig. 5 gives details of the principal joints. In the case of a concrete floor, holes are drilled in the bottom rails of the framework to suit the holding-down bolts already set in the concrete.

It is generally agreed that this class of building should always be sectional in character, and if this be adopted, it is necessary to construct each wall frame with corner posts to each and bolt the frames together, as shown also in Fig. 5.

The Roof.

The cross-members supporting the

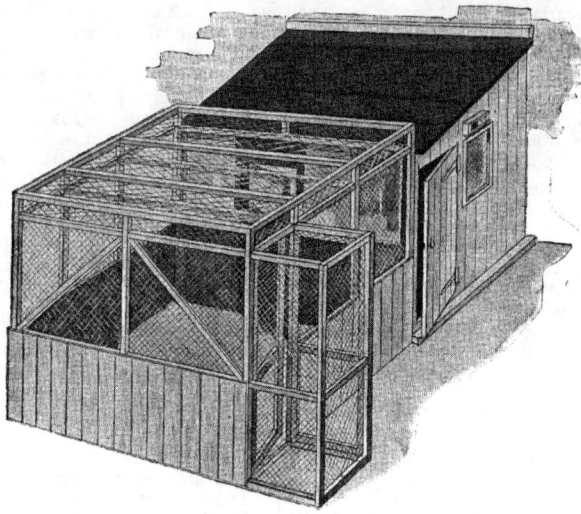

Fig. 1.—The Completed Aviary.

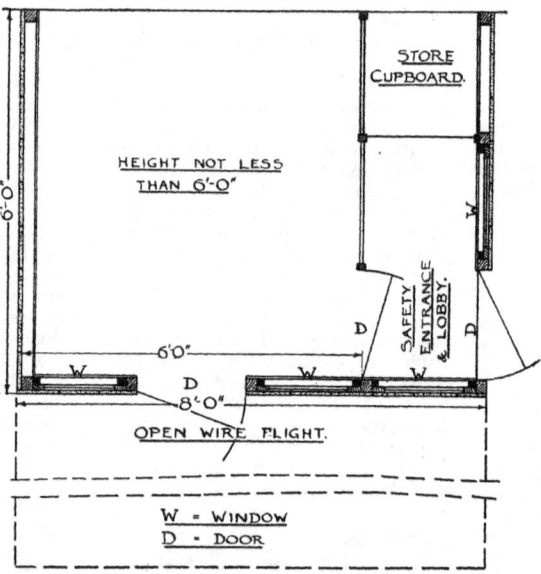

Fig. 1A.—Plan of Aviary.

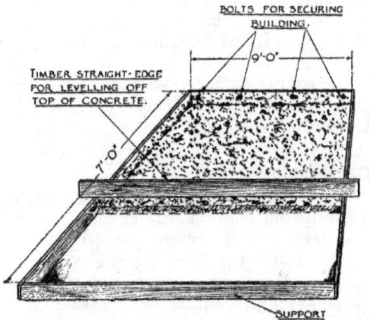

Fig. 2.—Concrete Floor in course of Construction.

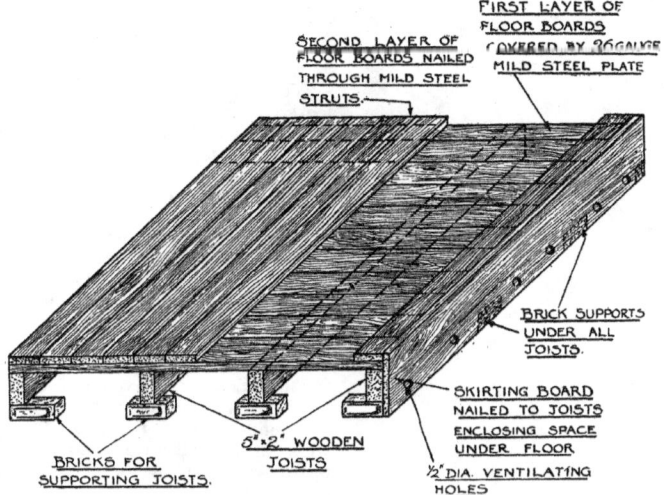

Fig. 3.—THE DOUBLE WOODEN FLOOR.

roof boards should be 2 × 1 inch fixed on edge to afford greater strength. Roof boards, ⅝ or ¾ inch thick, should be nailed across these timbers, and should extend 4 inches beyond the end and front walls of the building.

For a sectional building the cross-members should be laid loosely in slots cut in the end walls of the building, but these can be nailed in position in a non-sectional building.

Waterproof roofing felt, which is usually 36 inches wide, should be secured in position by flat-headed rustless nails, and should be laid with the length of the building, starting fixing from the bottom edge of the roof. An overlap of 1 inch should be allowed at the roof edge. After fixing the first length, each subsequent piece should be allowed to overlap the former by 3 to 4 inches.

At the point where the roof adjoins any adjacent building, the roofing felt should be turned up for a distance of 4 inches and an apron flashing of wood fixed to seal the joint (see Fig. 6).

Outer Covering.

Two kinds of boarding are suitable for this class of building, viz., "matchboarding" and "weatherboarding," but if a fire-resisting material is desired, "Asbestos-cement" sheeting 3/16 inch thick should be used.

Matchboarding is always fixed with the joints vertically, so that rain is conveyed to the ground line. The joints should be tightly wedged up, so that the tongue of one board is driven well home into the groove of the preceding board before nailing in position.

Whilst weatherboarding is the cheaper, there is a disadvantage in using it, inasmuch as it is almost impossible to make it draught-proof.

If, however, weatherboarding is used, an overlap of at least 1 inch should be allowed. Care should be taken in nailing this type of boarding to avoid splitting (see Fig. 7).

In either case the boarding should be fixed to finish flush with door and window openings.

Asbestos-cement sheeting should be cut to size and nailed direct on to the outside of the wooden framework. All nail-holes should be drilled to prevent cracking, but only sufficient nails should be used to hold the sheet in position temporarily. All joints should be made on the wooden framework and a space of ⅛ inch left between the edges of the sheeting. Over all joints should be nailed 1¼ × ⅜-inch planed wooden strips, the nails passing through the space between the sheets, thus holding them in position permanently.

Doors.

The door to the enclosed quarters should be constructed entirely of wood, but the door between the quarters and the "flight" should be of wood and wire netting. Fig. 8 shows the construction of wholly wooden doors of matchboarding and a door of wood and wire netting.

Windows.

The windows between the quarters and the flight should be removable, and should in any case be fitted with ⅜- or ½-inch mesh wire netting on the inside.

The window frames should also be grooved to receive glass for the winter period.

Special attention must be paid to the corner joints to ensure perfectly square and flat corners being formed. If the frames are twisted, there is a liability of splitting the glass when fitted.

Windows thus made, and in accordance with Fig. 9, can be held in position by turn buttons.

In order to prevent the window frames from falling into the quarters, ½-inch square section strips of wood should be cut to the correct length and nailed inside the framework with the face flush with the inside of the 1½-inch square section framework (see Fig. 1A).

The window to the safety porch should be constructed in a similar manner, fitted with wire netting and glass and nailed in position to the framework of the building.

Ventilators.

Small ventilators should be provided in each end of the building. These should be fitted with the sliding type of door and the framework covered with ⅜-inch wire netting on the inside.

The groove in which the door is to slide is formed by mounting 1½ × ½-inch planed timber on to 1-inch square section planed timber, and the door consists of a flat plain piece of board.

The ventilators are fixed on to the

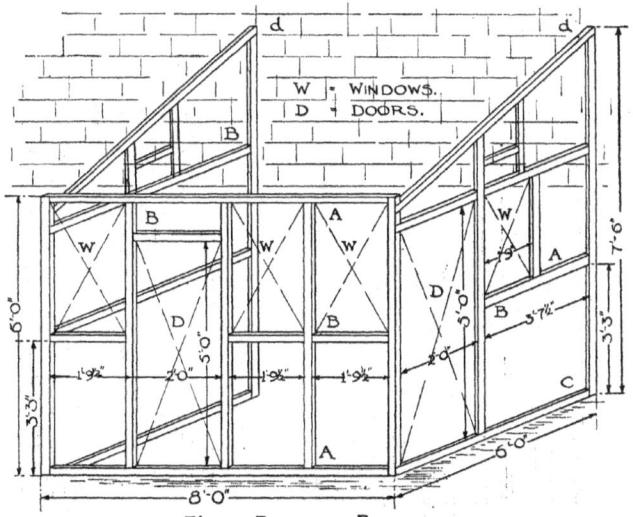

Fig. 4.—DETAILS OF FRAMEWORK.
Using 1½-inch square timber, to be built upon concrete or wooden floor

CONSTRUCTING AN AVIARY

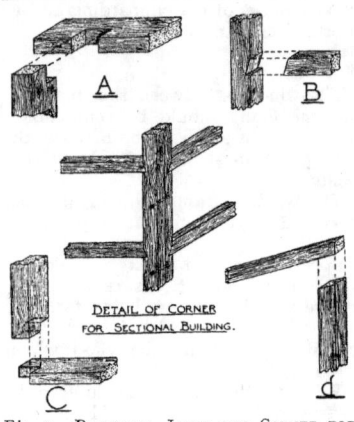

Fig. 5.—Principal Joint and Corner for Sentinel Building.

The letters refer to the parts shown on Fig. 4.

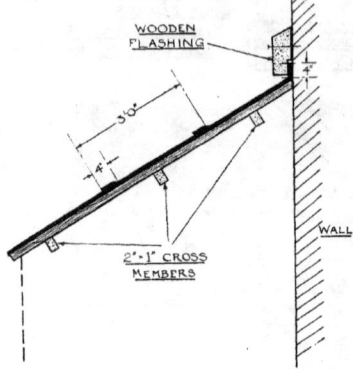

Fig. 6.—Waterproofing the Roof.

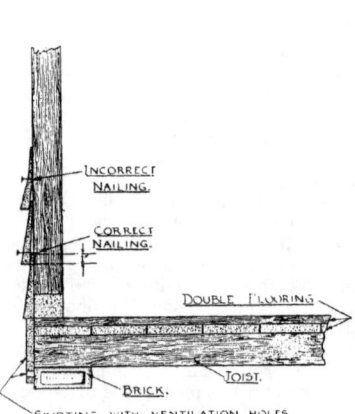

Fig. 7.—Fixing the Weatherboarding.

Showing the correct and incorrect methods of nailing.

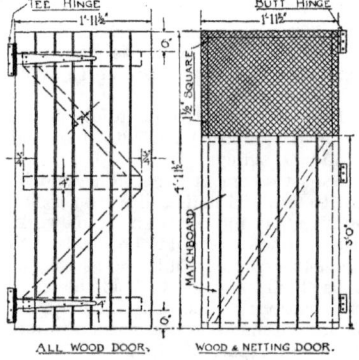

Fig. 8.—Details of the Doors.

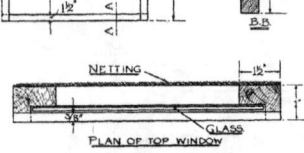

Fig. 9.—Details of Windows.

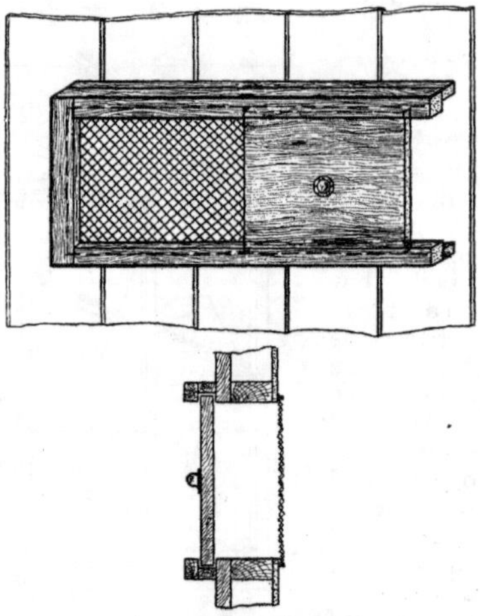

Fig. 10.—How the Ventilators are Arranged.

outside of the finished covering to the building, all as shown in Fig. 10.

Safety Entrance.

Whether the aviary is to house birds loosely or in cages, a partition should be fixed as shown in Fig. 1. This affords a safety porch to enter, and thus assures the safety of a bird which may otherwise be lost.

The partition should be of wire netting with a wire-netting door, all fixed to the $1\frac{1}{4}$-inch square timber fixed to suit. The portion forming the side of the cupboard, however, should be of light wood to complete this enclosure.

Covering for Inside of Quarters.

The most easily fixed covering for the inside of the quarters is plywood. The underside of the roof and the whole of the wall surfaces not occupied by doors, windows and ventilators should be covered. As a preventative against rats, metallic-faced plyboard should be used near the floor and should extend up for a distance of 2 to 3 feet from the floor. The metallised face should be placed against the framework of the building.

Asbestos-cement sheeting about $\frac{1}{8}$ inch thick is also very suitable, and has the advantage of being fireproof. A special hand-saw should be kept for cutting this material, and all nail holes should be drilled. Great care must be taken in handling this class of sheet, as it is very brittle and cracks easily.

A combination of these two coverings can be made by using asbestos-cement for the lower portions of wall surfaces and plyboard for the remainder of the walls and roof.

Painting and finishing.

In all cases, the whole of the inside should be limewashed. If available, a sprayer should be used, as with such a tool an even surface can be obtained and the limewash can be forced into all crevices.

Limewash is made from Buxton lime. Three pennyworth of lime placed in a bucket and just covered with cold water will form a stiff putty. When breaking down the lime water will boil, and care should be taken to avoid splashing. After it has cooled down, water is added until a thick cream is obtained. It is then ready for use with a common whitewash brush, but if it is to be used through a sprayer a thinner mixture is necessary, and the whole must be strained through a fine sieve or muslin to extract the small particles of limestone, which would otherwise clog the sprayer jet.

If matchboarding is used for the external covering, it should be painted at least two coats of oil paint of any colour to suit the surroundings. Before applying the first coat of paint, patent knotting should be applied to every knot in the wood with a stiff paint brush to prevent the resin working through the paint.

As weatherboarding is not usually planed, it is somewhat difficult and expensive to paint with oil paint. Creosote or solignum should therefore be used, and can be obtained in various shades of brown and green. At least two coats should be applied.

When asbestos-cement sheeting is used, oil paint should again be applied, and a pleasing effect can be produced by using a darker shade of paint for the wooden strips used for holding the sheets in position. The result is a panelled effect.

The Wire Flight (Fig. 11).

The flight should be at least 6 feet 6 inches in height, the width of the quarters and as long as possible.

A framework of 1¼-inch square timber is formed, and match-boarding or weatherboarding fixed from the floor to a height of 3 feet. Above this and over the roof, ⅜- or ½-inch mesh wire netting is attached to the framework, enclosing the whole of the flight. All wire should be secured by means of staples every 3 inch distance.

To ensure perfect safety, every flight should be fitted with a safety porch formed at the most convenient point. Many valuable birds are lost per annum by escaping when the owner is entering the flight.

Asbestos-cement is not to be recommended for the flight on account of the ease with which it can be broken.

With flat top flights, cats are sometimes a nuisance and cause annoyance to the birds by sitting on the top wire. This can be prevented to a certain extent by fixing large mesh netting over

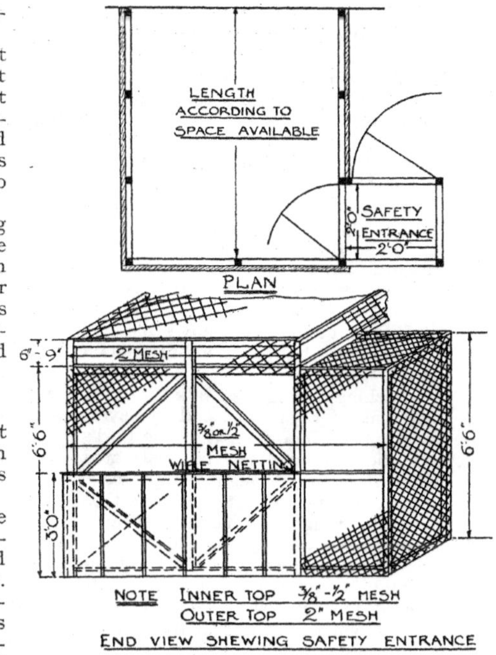

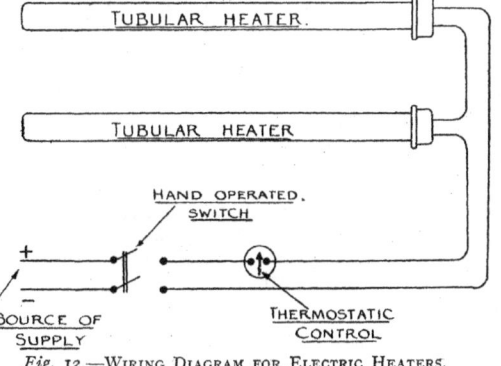

Fig. 11.—Details of the Flight.

Fig. 12.—Wiring Diagram for Electric Heaters.

the whole surface at a distance of 6 to 9 inches from the fine-mesh netting.

Heating the Quarters.

The system adopted should be designed to maintain an even temperature within the building during the winter months, no matter how the external temperature varies. This can only be ensured by installing a system which is capable of maintaining the desired temperature when the outside temperature is, say, 25° F., and incorporating in the system a thermostatic control which will cut in and out as required, and thus maintaining the required temperature.

Electric heating is therefore the most convenient type to adopt, as thermostatic control can so easily be introduced.

The heating surface should consist of two or three elements conveniently placed to give a good distribution of heat, and the elements, switches and controls should all be guarded by wire netting.

All heating elements should be of the enclosed type, such as the "Tubular Heater."

A simple wiring diagram is given in Fig. 12.

Internal Equipment of Quarters.

The internal equipment must of necessity depend entirely upon the type of birds to be housed, but perches should be made from natural tree branches with stems and twigs of varying sizes from 1 inch diameter down.

The aviary described will be found suitable for keeping practically any birds, such as budgerigars, canaries, etc., and some practical notes on the care of birds are given below.

NOTES ON THE CARE OF BIRDS

THE best time to stock an aviary is probably in the late spring just as the breeding season is in full swing. The choice of birds for the aviary is a fairly wide one. In the following notes birds suitable for cage life and aviaries are dealt with.

Budgerigar.

The budgerigar is probably better known as the "Love Bird," and is generally kept in pairs. No difficulty should be experienced in keeping these successfully. A budgerigar is actually a small parakeet and is obtainable in blue, silvery, mauve and other hues of plumage in addition to the familar green.

It does best in a sunny aviary, although also suitable for cage life. Food should consist chiefly of millet seed with suitable greenstuff in season.

Budgerigars breed very freely during the late spring and early summer, and as there is quite a demand for them in most districts it is often worth while to breed them for profit. When this is being done a start should be made about Easter with an unrelated pair, and by August quite a small flock should be possessed. Naturally the price varies in different parts of the country, but roughly speaking from 10s. 6d. to 12s. 6d. a pair is the price asked by dealers.

Canary.

Its cheerful song and ready companionship make the canary probably the most popular of all cage birds.

Points to watch when buying a canary are the brightness of the eyes, active manner, clean, smooth feet and legs, and compact plumage.

The food for canaries should consist chiefly of seed mixtures, with a little hemp three or four times weekly, this latter depending on the condition of the bird. In season, give greenstuff, such as groundsel, dandelion and sprigs of watercress, if perfectly fresh.

Sand is essential in keeping the birds in good condition and the drinking water should always be kept perfectly fresh and clean. A bath should also be provided almost daily throughout the summer, but less frequently in winter.

For breeding purposes an oblong cage at least 24 inches in length will be required. The best plan will be to keep the male and female birds in separate cages or separate apartments all through the winter and then to bring them together in the breeding cage sometime about the end of March.

Specially made nests or suitable nesting materials can be purchased at most animal stores. Five eggs usually form a "clutch" and the period of incubation is fourteen days.

Feed in the usual way at the commencement of the sitting period, but about three days before hatching time it is a good idea to give the birds some finely chopped up hard-boiled egg mixed with small crumbs from stale bread. This food will be used by the parents to feed the offspring.

Probably two or three weeks will elapse after hatching before the babies leave the nest, and the food mentioned above should be given during this time.

When the young birds can feed for themselves and take small seeds, the parents should be separated, as they should not be allowed to go on breeding continuously. About three broods should be hatched and reared in the course of the late spring and summer.

Provide a little fresh greenstuff, such as young dandelion leaves, tender lettuce, groundsel and watercress during the setting period to prevent the birds' blood becoming disordered.

Blackbird.

With proper care and attention a blackbird will become a very attractive songster and an intelligent pet. They are most likely to do well in a roomy wicker cage, but when tamed can be allowed to have the run of the house at suitable times. It is, generally speaking, too active a bird for a small aviary.

In the way of food, it will usually take a few seeds, particularly hemp, and is partial to garden worms and an occasional snail. Variety in feeding can be introduced by giving soaked bread, a little cooked potato and even minced meat at times. Ripe fruit is generally appreciated.

Parrot.

Apart from their talking propensities, parrots are also home favourites on account of the great age to which they live. Parrots are generally quite contented in a roomy cage, although the most healthful way of keeping them is on a T-shaped stand with a light chain. If the bird is normally kept in a cage it should be allowed on a stand for at least a part of the day, preferably out in the garden in a sheltered spot during summer weather.

Fresh drinking water must be provided regularly, also means for taking a daily bath, while it is important to have gravelly sand or earth at the bottom of the cage.

Parrots are decided vegetarians. Keep rigorously to seeds, such as oats and sunflower seeds for the staple food. This can be supplemented with nuts of all kinds and pieces of ripe fruit, such as apple, orange, banana, and pear. Biscuits and crusts of stale bread are also sometimes appreciated. Never give meat in any form. Even the picking of a bone is not advisable, nor should bread that has been buttered be given.

Teaching a parrot to talk is a task that calls for patience and perseverance. It is important that the bird's attention should not be distracted while it is being taught, so the cage should be covered. The sentence that is to be taught should be repeated over and over again, slowly and deliberately, stressing at first only one word at a time. Do not forget to reward the bird with some piece of food to which it is particularly partial, on making good progress.

Parrakeet.

This is a small member of the parrot family and usually has a long tail. Like the budgerigar it thrives better in an aviary than in cages. It should be treated much the same as a parrot.

Cockatoo.

Another bird similar to a parrot. It is best kept chained to a T-shaped stand, which it prefers to a cage. It should, however, be kept in a cage at night. The method of treatment is the same as for parrots.

Jackdaw.

This is a bird whose home is best made in a spacious wickerwork cage and which should be allowed the run of the house at convenient times of the day. It is nearly always easily tamed. The flight feathers are usually clipped away from one wing by fanciers so that the bird cannot fly away.

For food, give minced meat, garden insects, oats, soaked bread and suchlike foods.

Tit.

Tits are very suitable occupants for an aviary, the great tit probably being the most popular. Being of a rather pugnacious nature they are generally kept in a compartment to themselves. They will sometimes breed in captivity if conditions are favourable.

Insects are their favourite food, and a bone should be provided for them to pick, in addition, of course, to half-coconuts, which should be suspended by strings.

Pigeons.

Although hardly coming under the designation of cage or aviary birds, pigeons are frequently kept in a small way for garden decoration or profit. Pigeons should either be kept in a suitable cote or in a lofty roomy shed, care being taken to see that the floor is efficiently drained and covered with a layer of sandy shingle. Keeping the quarters scrupulously clean is very important. Provide plenty of clean drinking water, placing it in a fountain in which they cannot tread. Bath water should also be provided in a suitable receptacle, daily in summer and on mild days in winter.

Some varieties of pigeons roost on the floor of their cote; others require special roosting brackets or perches.

Feeding Pigeons.

Special care should be taken with the feeding of pigeons. Overfeeding must be avoided, and as appetites vary with the weather the safest plan is probably only to go on giving the food as long as the birds pick it up eagerly and hungrily. The food should consist of seed and grain mixtures, the ingredients of which vary according to the time of year. A special mixture should also be obtained during the breeding season.

Mating Pigeons.

It is not advisable to mate related male and female birds. The breeding season usually starts about the middle of March, when a pair should be put in a large wooden box with a temporary front of wire netting until they have properly paired off. When mating is assured put some perfectly clean sawdust in a pigeon's nesting pan and place in the box, also sprinkling a small quantity of straw, cut into short lengths, on the floor.

Only two eggs are laid by pigeons, and the period of incubation is eighteen days. Male and female birds sit on the nest in turn.

When the "squabs," as the young birds are termed, hatch out, they are at first fed on a pap-like fluid which the parents bring up from their crops.

The youngsters are generally able to look after themselves after about four weeks. During the nursing period the material at the bottom of the nest should be renewed every few days.

Do not allow one pair of pigeons to nest more than three or four times during one breeding season.

Disposing of Pigeons.

When considering the question of obtaining profit from pigeon breeding, one method is to raise youngsters of good strain with a view to selling them alive. Another method—and this is only applicable to certain districts—is to sell the plump young pigeons to a poulterer for table purposes.

Constructing an Air Pump Suitable for Aerating an Aquarium

ANYONE who is keenly interested in keeping fish in aquariums is confronted sooner or later with the problem of providing artificial aeration. As mentioned on page 1030, the most satisfactory method is by the use of a small electrically driven air pump. In the following article will be found details for the construction of a suitable pump.

Materials.
All the metal parts can conveniently be constructed of brass, with the exception of the shaft carrying the pulley, etc., and the connecting rod, which too should be of steel.

The pulley itself can be constructed of hard-wood or, alternatively, of fibre.

For the base (which can be extended as necessary to carry an electric motor, etc.) use either hard wood or, preferably, mild steel $\tfrac{3}{8}$ inch thick.

Framework.
All holes must be very carefully drilled in the exact positions given on the drawing.

The bushes to carry the shaft are to be soldered into the holes provided in the top of the frame. They must be true.

Piston.
The rings marked on the drawing are just slight depressions cut with a tool while the piston is still in the lathe. These serve as oil seals when the air pump is working.

Cylinder.
This is a piece of brass tube having an internal diameter of $\tfrac{1}{2}$ inch. To it is soldered, as shown in the drawing, a face plate carrying a $\tfrac{3}{4}$-inch bolt. The face of this plate must be machined true.

Plate carrying Air Ports.
The face of this also must be machined true. Also the holes in it must be accurately drilled.

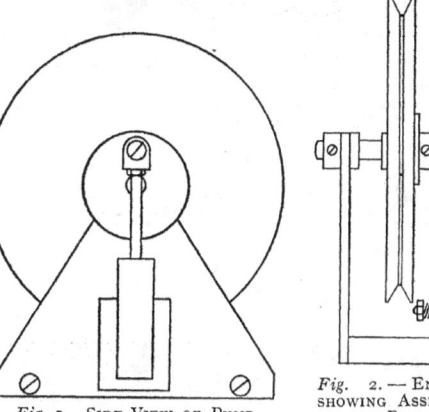

Fig. 1.—Side View of Pump.

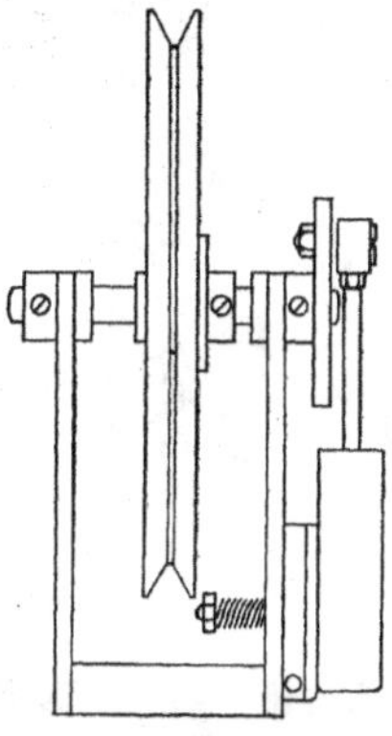

Fig. 2.— End View showing Assembly of Pulley.

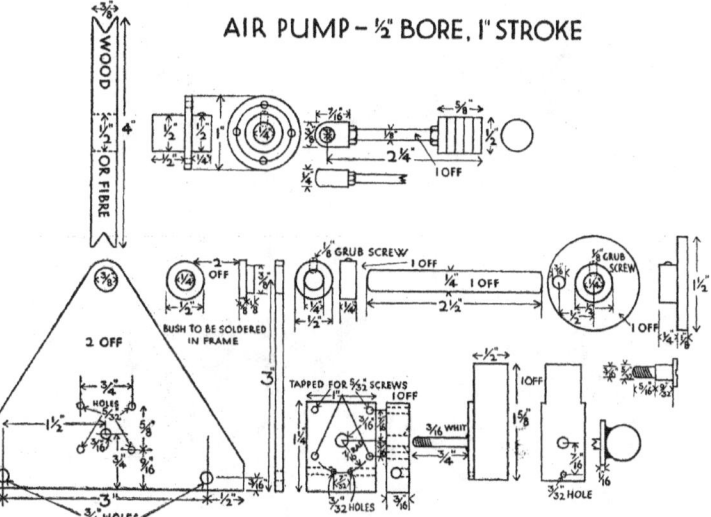

Fig. 3.—Constructional Details of Air Pump.

Assembling.
This is perfectly straightforward provided that the individual parts have been accurately made. Too much stress cannot, however, be laid on the importance of having a perfect joint between the face plate attached to the cylinder and that fixed to the frame. It has already been pointed out that the face of each of these must be machined true, and in order to ensure perfect contact at all points it is preferable to also grind them together with a little ordinary grinding paste. The spring at the back of the frame will then keep them in contact.

Drive.
The pulley shown in the drawing is for a belt-type drive, but by varying the type of pulley the air pump will run equally well with a friction or a geared drive.

Speed.
The best speed is about 75 r.p.m., but it can if necessary be run up to 100 r.p.m. So long as this speed is not exceeded, it will run satisfactorily for years without attention except for occasional oiling.

Input and Output.
Suitable connections can be made to these. Which is which will depend on the way the pulley is run.

Double Pump.
If desired, it is a simple matter to fix a similar pump on the other side of the frame. By making this one suck while the other one is delivering, a constant stream of air is obtained.

WORN LEATHER

When the surface of leather wears in patches such as may happen in the case of upholstered chairs, etc., there are rough areas where the surface has gone. A very good way of restoring the surface may be carried out with the help of white of egg. The white of egg should be painted on the roughened part rather freely and given time so that it may soak in. When this has happened make another application, and this is followed by further treatment on the same lines. The whole process may be spread over several days, and in the end it will be found that the leather has been given quite a good new surface. Finish the process by polishing with a soft cloth.

BARBOLA WORK

BARBOLA is one of the most beautiful of the many artistic crafts suitable as a home occupation. It is extremely popular as a decorative craft, and one which, when properly learnt, can be made very profitable.

Barbola itself is a decoration, or a decorative craft. It can be done on pulpware, wood or glass. The process is a form of modelling, comparatively simple in character, applied to the surface of some useful or ornamental object. It is usual to use either flower or fruit forms as decoration. The objects to which the decoration is applied can be obtained ready made.

Barbola, or barbolette, is a modelling paste, easily worked by hand, is adhesive and dries hard quickly without cracking. It is supplied ready for use in a tin, which should always be kept closed.

Lacquering the Surface of Articles.

Although barbola can be applied directly to glassware when the method is known, other objects made of pulpware or whitewood must be enamelled or lacquered.

At least two coats should be applied, the first one being rubbed down with fine glasspaper before the second coat is applied. The lacquer should be put on with light, even strokes and will then cover the surface without brush marks. An hour or so should elapse before the decoration is done, in order that the surface can harden sufficiently to prevent fingermarks showing.

Decorating a Powder Bowl — Lacquering.

The small pulp powder bowl shown in Fig. 1A will be found a simple piece of work for the first stages in modelling the barbola paste. First give the bowl, which when purchased is grey and known as "blank ware," a coat of lacquer, preferably in white newinlac, and after stirring it up with a thin piece of wood, dip a large brush into it, and spread it evenly on the inside of the lid.

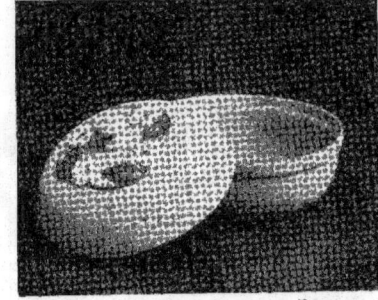

Fig. 1A.—Barbola-decorated Powder Bowl.

A full-size design or the powder bowl is given in Fig. 4.

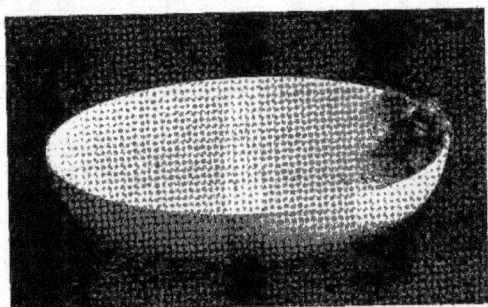

Fig. 1B.—Barbola-decorated Tray.

Fig. 2.—Moulding Barbola Petals for Powder Bowl.
The various stages are shown in detail in Fig. 5.

Fig. 3.—Easily Modelled Dragon.

When covered, place the lid level somewhere out of the reach of dust, and then proceed with the inside of the bowl, taking care to make even brush strokes and to cover the whole of the surface. Leave the work now, not forgetting to clean the brush in methylated spirit, and allow the lacquer to harden; this will take about twenty-four hours to be on the safe side. The outside is now coated with blue lacquer, special care being taken to prevent the blue from encroaching on the white lacquer on the inside of the bowl. If the lacquer has been applied carefully, the surface will be quite even in colour; but if not, it will be necessary to apply a second coat, the first one being rubbed over very lightly with the finest glasspaper. The finest surfaces in lacquer are obtained in this way, but considerable care is required in the way the glasspaper is used.

Transferring the Design.

The next stage of the work is to apply the barbola decoration, but it is important this should not be done until the lacquer is perfectly hard. The wild rose design shown in the illustration is drawn in a circle, as in Fig. 4, and in order to obtain a symmetrical arrangement, the drawing should be traced over with thin tracing paper and transferred to the top of the lid. If the centre is cut away, the tracing will lie flat on the lid, the lines being lined in with a hard pencil or steel style so as to slightly indent the surface of the lacquer. Another method is to place a piece of carbon paper under the tracing paper and go over the lines with a sharp hard pencil. When the outline is sufficiently plain, take a sharp penknife and scratch the surface to leave the pulp showing; it need not be perfectly clean as long as sufficient of the lacquer is cleaned off to allow of the decoration to be attached to the pulp.

Moulding and applying the Barbola Petals.

The next stage is to take a small portion

of the modelling paste from the tin, and roll up a ball slightly larger than a pea, as shown at *a* in Fig. 5. Now press the ball with the finger on a plate; the effect of this pressure is to spread the paste, as at *b*. Continue as at *c* until the paste is quite thin, as indicated at *d*, and forms a petal, as shown at *e*. The thin layer of paste is now taken between the fingers and pressed carefully, as indicated in Fig. 2, and laid down on one of the spaces, which should be very lightly coated with a little glue from the tube. Another petal is formed in the same way and placed alongside the first, with the edge slightly overlapping. Continue in this way until the five petals are complete. The centre is formed by a very small round, marked with lines formed by a knife blade pressed into it. The shape of the petals will be found easy enough, the only difficulty being in placing the last petal under the edge of the first, which is raised up and then pressed down again.

Leaves and Stalks.

The leaves are formed by first spreading out a small ball of the paste, working as near to the shape as possible, and then, with the modelling tool, cutting out the serrations on the edges. Place the leaves in position with a little glue underneath, and then roll out some small pieces of paste between the fingers to round threads and lay them down in position to form the stalks. After the modelling paste has been used for a few of the petals and leaves, the pliability of the material will be realised, and it will be found that it can be spread out quite thin between the fingers just as well as on the plate; but it is better to work on a flat

Fig. 4.—Wild Rose Design for Powder Bowl.
This drawing should be traced over with thin tracing paper and transferred to lid of powder bowl, as described in text.

glazed surface, as it is so much easier to get the petals to lie flat. When all the petals, leaves and stalks are in position and the design looks regular, final shaping and touching up can be done with the point of the modelling tool. If it should be found that the paste sticks to the fingers, just dip them in a little "gesso" powder, but this should be avoided as much as possible.

Painting the Modelled Decoration.

The modelled decoration is now left for about twenty-four hours in order to give it time to set hard. When this time has elapsed, the petals, leaves and stalks are coated with paint; pink, green and brown water-colours or poster-colours are suitable. The paint should be pressed out of the tubes as they are required on to the underneath of a small saucer, a portion taken up with a small brush and applied direct to the paste. For the centre of the rose, apply some yellow to the rounded centre after filling in the knife cuts with brown. If the flower were larger, separate stamens could be added, but they are not necessary in small work. If some of the paint should go on the lacquered surface, it can be wiped off with a clean rag. Poster-colours should not be diluted with water—they are of the correct consistency for the work.

Varnishing.

The paint should be allowed to dry thoroughly, and then it is coated with the transparent spirit varnish. The effect of the varnish is to brighten up and preserve the colours. Special care should be taken not to touch the work after varnishing, and to place it in a position free from dust until the varnish has set dry.

The powder bowl is now finished, and should be a most artistic production if

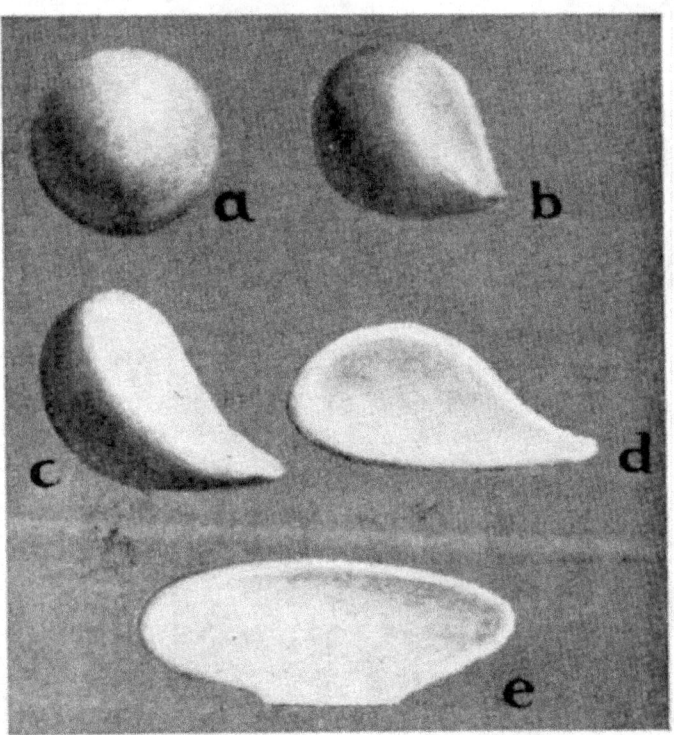

Fig. 5.—Stages in Moulding a Petal in Barbola.

BARBOLA WORK

Fig. 6.—Articles decorated with Fruit in Modelled Barbola.

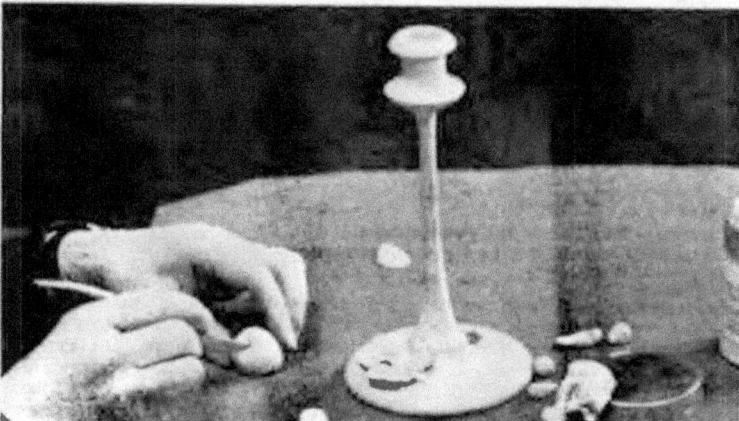

Fig. 7.—Moulding Fruit Decoration.

Fig. 8.—Four Powder Bowls with Simple Barbola Work.

Fig. 9.—Folding Bookstand, showing Fruit-Spray Decoration.

the instructions have been carried out carefully. It will be realised that although a beginning has been made, only the fringe of the actual possibilities of barbola has been touched.

Modelling Fruit in Barbola.

Having had some experience of handling the paste, it will be possible to carry the modelling a stage further and attempt some fruit, as shown in the illustration in Fig. 6. Apart from the greater freedom in the modelling of the leaves, there is nothing difficult in the work shown. The apple is quite easily modelled from a slightly flattened ball, the markings at the top being made with a small boxwood tool, as shown in Fig. 7.

A Modelled Dragon.

The modelled dragon shown in Fig. 3, although it appears very difficult, is really a simple piece of work. The body, tail and legs are modelled on a foundation of cottonwool in order to economise material; the head and two sets of wings are made from fish bones, and the claws from fish teeth. The head and wings are prepared from cod bones by first boiling them and selecting the suitable portions and leaving them to dry. It will be found that the barbola paste will hold the bones in position, and when thoroughly hard will be immovable. It is an advantage to have an illustration of a dragon when modelling, but with the fish-bone head and wings the most difficult part of figure-modelling is avoided. The scale-marking should be done with a tool, and when the whole is painted red the effect is quite realistic.

A MIRROR WITH BARBOLA DECORATION

Mirrors ornamented with barbola work, of the kind illustrated in Fig. 10, are expensive to buy because of the time expended by the artists who make them, but any home worker possessed of reasonable ability can make something equally effective for an outlay of well under half a sovereign.

Materials and Tools.

Necessary materials for a frame of the kind here described can be purchased separately or as a set of parts. The following are necessary:—

Mirror.—Oval, bevelled edge, 10¾ inches by 8 inches.

Backing and Strut.—Plywood or soft yellow pine, ⅜ inch thick; 1 piece 12 inches by 8 inches; 1 piece 8 inches by 4 inches; 1 piece 2½ inches by 1½ inches.

Sundries.—Three small plated clips and screws; 1 brass butt hinge, 1½ inches long with screws; 2 wooden balls, ¾-inch diameter; 1 tin barbola; 1 tin gold paint.

Apart from simple woodworking tools the only special requirements are a few wooden "modelling tools" similar to those sketched in Fig. 11, and may be purchased or be shaped with penknife and sandpaper from slips of smooth wood.

Backing and Strut.

Commence by making the backing and strut. Lay the mirror on the wood and draw the outline upon it, then draw a curve above the oval, as in Fig. 12, to form a base for the decorative work.

Saw the wood to shape, plane, file or sandpaper the edge to a perfect curve, then make the strut and back block to dimensions, as in Fig. 14. Carve out of the oval backing a recess for one part of the hinge, as shown in section in Fig. 13, and recess the other part of the hinge into the top end of the strut. Screw the hinge in place, file off the projecting ends of the screws, and bevel the top edge of the strut so that when extended the bottom is about 4 inches from the back; the hinge is thus covered by the small back block, as shown in Fig. 15; then fix the mirror temporarily with the slips, fit the two ball-feet at the bottom and remove the mirror and clips.

Filling the Grain.

Sandpaper the woodwork, give it a coat of wood filler, or make a paste of whiting and water and rub this well into the wood. Sandpaper it quite smooth when dry, especially the gap between the strut and back block, which should be cleared out, as shown in Fig. 16, with a piece of sandpaper doubled to a wedge shape.

Modelling the Flowers.

Cover the top half of the mirror with tissue paper and fix the whole to the backing with the metal clips, then commence the barbola work. A simple floral design is given in Fig. 17 as a guide to the novice, but the best work is generally attained when the modelling is a spontaneous expression of originality.

Begin at the top centre by modelling the rose, which is built up piece by piece, commencing with a central conical-shaped lump formed by rolling the barbola between the fingers and thumb. Press this firmly on to the backing, then take a small piece of barbola and flatten and squeeze it between the fingers and thumb, as shown in Fig. 18, until it assumes a leaf-like form.

Placing the Petals in Position.

Place it against the central mass, and similarly prepare and place several other petals, pushing them into position with a modelling tool, as shown in Fig. 19, and curving them gracefully by manipulation of two modelling tools, one in each hand, as shown in Fig. 20, so that the barbola is twisted or curled over gracefully.

To prevent Barbola adhering to the Fingers.

To prevent the barbola adhering to the fingers, dust them frequently with french chalk, and for the same reason dip the modelling tools in water from time to time.

Continue in a similar way, but model the veins and other delicate details by pressing lightly with a knife-like modelling tool or one with a pointed end.

Painting the Flowers.

Work some of the leaves over the edges of the backing to impart a graceful and finished appearance.

Leave the barbola for a time to set or harden, then remove the mirror and the tissue paper, and proceed to paint the flowers with water-colour paints or poster colours, applied with a small sable hair brush.

Finally give Two Coats of Crystal Varnish.

When the painting is completed, give it two coats of crystal varnish.

Fig. 10.—The Finished Mirror.
The subtle fascination of a mirror is enhanced by a posy of flowers modelled in barbola and gaily coloured.

Fig. 11.—Modelling Tools.
These can be purchased or be made at home from smooth wood about 6 inches long and ¼ inch square, shaped with a penknife and made smooth by sandpapering.

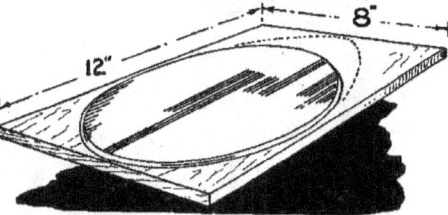

Fig. 12.—Marking out the Wooden Backing.
Draw the outline of the mirror and then add a curved part at the top whereon to model the barbola.

Fig. 13.—Section of Hinged Joint.
This sectional sketch shows the hinge recessed into the backing and to the strut.

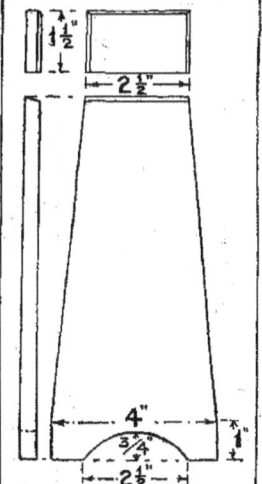

Fig. 14.—Dimensions of Strut and Back Block.
The strut and block should be made to the sizes given.

BARBOLA CIGARETTE BOX DECORATION

A very simple barbola decoration is that shown in Fig. 21. First obtain a small wooden cigarette box such as that shown in the illustration. Only a very small portion of the barbola paste is needed, and it should be rolled with the fingers on a piece of clean paper until it is the same diameter and length as a cigarette.

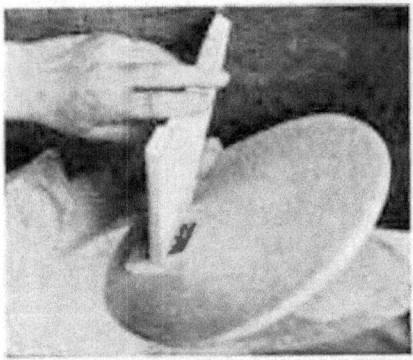

Fig. 15.—Backing and Strut Assembled.
The relative positions of the before-mentioned parts are here shown and the manner in which the strut is prevented from opening too far.

Fig. 16.—Sandpapering the Back.
Efficient sandpapering is essential if a good surface is to be attained by the subsequent coats of gold paint. Be particular to clear out the hinge joint, as here shown.

and finally a little grey to represent the ash should be applied at the end.

The other end of the "cigaretto" is coated with water colour gold and left to dry.

Fixing on the Box.

The modelled cigarette is now placed in position and a little of the lacquer shaped away from the box to expose the wood. Fix the cigarette in position with glue which is run along the mark on the box and underneath the cigarette, and the latter pressed down in position.

Fig. 17.—Simple Floral Design.
This outline design can be used as a guide by the novice, but good craftsmen should aim at originality in their own work.

Fig. 21.—Simple Barbola Decoration on a Cigarette Box.

Roll the Shape to make it round.

The next stage is to place the shape between the paper and a flat piece of wood and give it a roll or two to make it quite true. The whole of the length is now coated with water-colour chinese white.

A little red is stippled at one end

When the glue has had time to set the box and modelled ornament should be coated with transparent spirit varnish to complete the work

This simple form of decoration really illustrates the essentials of the craft and forms useful practice before more serious and advanced work is undertaken.

Fig. 18.—Placing a Petal.
The flowers are built up by adding leaf to leaf and working them into shape with a modelling tool.

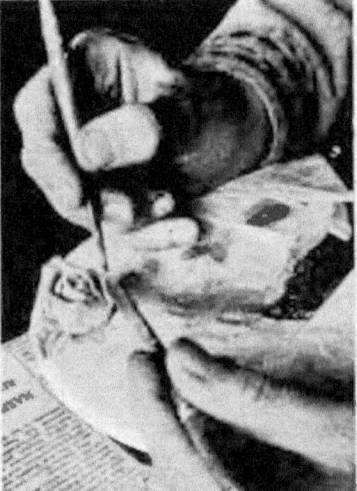

Fig. 19.—Modelling the Rose.
Individual leaves are modelled by curling them between the ends of the modelling tools.

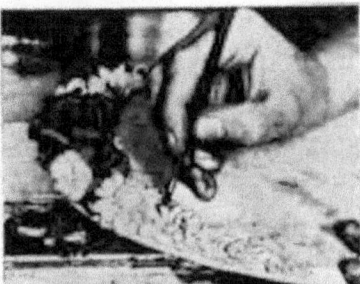

Fig. 20.—Painting the Flowers.
Commence by painting the lowest and most difficultly placed places, working the brush well down into the hollows.

Practical Hints on the Insurance of Private Dwelling Houses and their Contents

Every house-owner and every tenant has at some time or another to consider the question of insuring either the building and/or the contents of his house, but very few, after having decided on the amount for which they wish to be covered, take the trouble to study details of the policy when they receive it, with the result that when a claim arises they often find that the insurance company are not liable for a particular loss. Unfortunately, this situation is very largely due to the name given to this class of policy, as the name "All In or Comprehensive" is undoubtedly misleading and tends to give the impression that every conceivable loss is covered.

INSURING THE STRUCTURE OF A HOUSE

This article deals in detail with the cover given by the abovementioned policies, and starts by considering cover given in respect of a policy covering the building, i.e., structure of a private dwelling-house.

The Simplest Form of Cover.

Generally speaking, there are three ranges of cover, the cheapest being obtainable at a rate varying between 1s. 6d. per £100 with the larger insurance companies to 1s. 3d. per £100 with Lloyd's and the non-tariff companies. For an annual outlay therefore of 12s. 6d. to 15s. it is possible to cover the building of a house value £1,000 against the risks of fire, explosion, lightning, and thunderbolt, provided always that the house is constructed of brick, stone or concrete, and roofed with slates, tiles or metal. The insurance would apply to any domestic offices communicating with the main building and constructed of any of the aforementioned materials.

Additional Cover provided for an Extra 3d. per £100 Value.

This form of policy has in recent years been improved upon, and for an extra 3d. per £100 value it is possible to add damage by burglary or housebreaking, damage by aircraft or any articles dropped therefrom, riots and civil commotion, military or usurped power and labour disturbances. Property owners' liability is also included for this additional premium, and this forms a very important section of the insurance, for the owner of a house is liable at law for any damage caused to persons and their property through any defect in his premises, and many claims have been paid as the result of falling chimney stacks, tiles, gutters, etc.

Tenants and Property Owners' Liability Act.

Where the occupier is only a tenant he is not liable under the Property Owners' Liability Act, but should he detect any default in the construction of the house he should at once make complaint in writing to the owner, as he can then make the landlord responsible for any trouble caused in this way. For instance, a serious crack in the ceiling should be reported immediately, otherwise he may find that when the ceiling falls, the landlord will not be responsible for any damage done.

Loss of Rent due to Premises being rendered Uninhabitable.

Where the occupier is only a tenant, and is therefore paying rent to some other person, he can recover loss of rent due to the premises being rendered uninhabitable by any of the abovementioned perils, such recovery not to exceed 10 per cent. of the amount for which the house is insured, and this again provides a very important cover for the tenant.

Damage by Storm, Tempest, etc.

For an additional annual premium of another 6d. per cent., making 2s. 3d. per cent. in all, it is possible to add damage to the building by storm, tempest, bursting or overflowing of water apparatus or pipes, earthquake, and impact by any road vehicle, horses or cattle not belonging to or under the control of the assured person.

Risks not covered by an Ordinary Policy.

Flood, subsidence and landslip are definitely excluded from the cover, and the insured is made to bear the first £5 of each and every loss arising from damage to the building from storm, tempest, bursting or overflowing of water apparatus or pipes. Damage by storm and tempest to gates and fences is also excluded from the policy, but it is possible even to include these risks for an additional premium amounting to approximately £2 per annum for each house.

Risks that are covered only while Owner is in Occupation.

Another point to be remembered is that damage from burglary and housebreaking, overflowing of water apparatus or pipes is not covered while the building is unfurnished, and only applies, therefore, whilst the owner is in occupation.

Loss from Impact.

The section of the policy abovementioned, which includes loss from impact, does not at first appear to be very advantageous until one realises the large amount of damage caused by collision or accidents by motor vehicles. Here again large claims have been paid, particularly in respect of damaged property situated on main roads, where perhaps a lorry has smashed fences and walls of a house, but has itself been able to proceed on its journey. Unless the householder was in at the time of the occurrence he would probably have no knowledge or possible means of finding out the owners of the vehicle, and would not, therefore, be in a position to claim compensation. Again, where the occupier is the tenant, he is covered for damage from any of the abovementioned perils to the landlord's fixtures and fittings for which he is responsible, and therefore, should a domestic boiler belonging to the landlord be damaged by explosion, he could claim under his policy.

INSURING THE CONTENTS OF A HOUSE

The question of insuring the contents should also be a matter of great care, and before advising how best to arrive at the values to be covered, we again deal with the general cover given by the companies and Lloyd's Underwriters in return for an annual premium of 5s. per £100.

Firstly, the policy covers the loss or damage to the whole contents of the building, provided such contents be the property of the insured or for which he is responsible, or the property of any permanent members of his household or of his servants, including (where applicable) tenant's fixtures and fittings, telephone installation, and gas or electric apparatus for which he legally is responsible, but excluding all motor vehicles and accessories, live stock, deeds, bonds, bills of exchange, promissory notes, securities for money, stamps, documents, cash currency or bank notes. The policy also excludes any part of the structure or landlord's fixtures, which includes boilers, water pipes, water tanks, central-heating apparatus, ceilings, or wallpapers.

The Risks covered

The risks covered are:—
(1) Fire, lightning, explosion (including explosion of boilers), thunderbolt, earthquake or subterranean fire.
(2) Bursting and overflowing of water tanks, pipes or apparatus (excluding damage done to the tanks, pipes or apparatus themselves).
(3) Burglary, housebreaking, theft or larceny, or any attempt thereat.

It may be interesting at this point to study the difference between the four last-mentioned perils, as it is not generally known that in making a claim for burglary and housebreaking, proof must be forthcoming that forcible entry or some attempt thereat occurred.

An example of loss by theft would be where an article was stolen by some person putting his hand through an open window or entering through an open door and taking anything on which he could lay his hands. Again, larceny would be a loss arising from anyone authorised to be in the house, such as domestic servants or anyone calling on business. The risks of theft and larceny automatically become void should the house be sub-let and do not apply to loss of cash, treasury notes or bank notes. Further, no such loss would be recoverable should anything be stolen from one's person.

(4) Loss of cash currency and/or bank notes is covered by any of the insured perils for a sum not exceeding £25 provided that they are contained in the private dwelling-house itself and not in any outbuildings. It must here be remembered that loss from larceny or theft is not covered in respect of this item.

(5) Aircraft and any articles dropped therefrom, and an illustration of the advantage of this cover, may be forthcoming if the reader will remember the recent accident close to Croydon Aerodrome, when an aeroplane failed to rise and crashed into some houses, doing a large amount of damage, but, fortunately, without setting fire to the premises.

(6) Riots, civil commotion, military or usurped power, strikes or labour disturbances or malicious persons acting on behalf of, or in connection with any political organisations; and here again one has only to remember the damage done in the General Strike in 1926 to appreciate that this risk is not so remote as it at first appears.

(7) Storm, tempest or flood damage to the contents; and it should be noted that the full loss is payable by the company in this section.

(8) Impact by any road vehicle, horses or cattle not belonging to or under the control of the insured person or any member of his family.

(9) Accidental breakage of mirror glass other than hand mirrors.

(10) Domestic servants' effects are also covered against any of the above-mentioned risks.

(11) Accidents to domestic servants including chauffeurs. Claims under the Workmen's Compensation Act, comprising full wages for one month, with an allowance for board and lodging and medical expenses not exceeding £5. Under this section the insured person is covered for any claim made by any domestic servant for injury caused during employment, but care should be taken not to confuse this with the National Health Insurance scheme operating as the result of incapacity through illness or disease.

(12) Liability to the public in respect of claims, including costs, for accidents happening in or about the insured's dwelling-house, causing either bodily injury or damage to property, with a limit of £500 in respect of any one accident or series of accidents, inclusive of costs. Thus the tenant is covered should a guest bring a successful claim for injury caused as the result of falling electric-light fittings, provided such fittings were his property.

(13) The insured is covered for a sum of £1,000 should death occur in the house as the result of fire or attack by burglars or housebreakers.

(14) Loss of rent limit of 10 per cent. of the sum insured, including reasonable hotel expenses incurred in consequence of the dwelling being rendered uninhabitable by any of the perils specified from Nos. (1) to (7), this section would apply only where the occupier was a tenant and therefore paying rent.

(15) Should the occupier be a tenant, he is covered against damage to the building for which he is responsible, caused by storm, tempests, bursting or overflowing of water apparatus or pipes (excluding the first £5 of each and every loss) and burglary or housebreaking. The total liability being limited to 10 per cent. of the sum insured.

Cover during Holidays.

It is a condition of every policy that the house may be left without an inhabitant for ninety days in any one year, so that the occupier is fully covered whilst away on his annual holidays or for occasional week-ends. Should it be desired, the cover can be extended beyond the ninety days, provided the company or underwriters be notified and small additional premium paid.

A person's property is also covered in transit and whilst on the person against fire, explosion and lightning, so that it is possible to recover for damage done to suits, etc., through a box of matches becoming ignited in the pocket.

Property taken away by Insured Person.

We have dealt with the question of uninhabited dwellings, and have shown that within certain limits the insurance companies are liable, but no mention has been made of cover in respect of property taken away by the assured person. Here again the insurers have added cover to meet these demands, and the policy extends to insure contents whilst temporarily removed (but not for sale or exhibition or in depositories) against any of the risks from Nos. (1) to (7) (with the exception of larceny and theft) whilst at any bank, safe deposit or occupied dwelling-house or in any building where the insured or member of his family is residing; also, in course of removal to or from any bank or safe deposit whilst in charge of the insured, member of his family or authorised servants. The total amount recoverable in this extension is limited to 15 per cent. of the total sum insured, and it is unnecessary to notify the company at the time of removal provided that such removal is only temporary.

Destruction or Damage due to short-circuiting of Electrical Appliances, etc.

Destruction of or damage to any dynamo, transformer motor, wiring main or other electrical appliance which is directly caused by short-circuiting, overrunning, excessive pressure or leakage of electricity is not covered by the policy, but any damage caused by fire as the result of short-circuiting, etc., originating outside the dynamo, transformer, motor, wiring, main or other electrical appliance is covered. (It will be seen that as far as possible the policy has been drawn up to meet present-day demands, but any reasonable additions to the cover can be arranged at a slight additional charge varying with the nature of the risk; as, for instance, anyone owning valuable china or glass can include the risk of breakage).

The Full Value of the Contents must be insured.

It should be understood that the full value of the contents must be insured, for, should a loss arise and the company find that there is an under-insurance, they will pay only a loss in the proportion which the insured value bears to the actual value of the contents. Thus, if the amount of the property is worth £1,000 and is insured for a sum of only £500 he will be deemed to have taken one half of the insurance himself, and in the event of a claim would be paid only one half of his loss.

Insurance of Jewellery, etc.

Another point of interest arises when it is realised that jewellery, watches, gold and silver articles and furs are covered only up to a sum not exceeding one third of the amount of the contents, and should such property be more than that portion, an additional premium would be required.

It is generally advisable to have a separate policy in respect of jewellery, watches, gold and silver articles and furs, as this constitutes property which is generally worn, and is easily lost outside the house. For an annual premium of approximately 12s. 6d. per £100 it is possible to cover these articles against loss from any cause anywhere within the limits of the United Kingdom.

For such a policy it would be necessary to make a list and description of each different article to be covered and to place a value against each one. A well-known company are willing to pay for a valuation to be made by a licensed valuer and to agree to settle the definite sum as shown against each item should loss occur, and this form of insurance is really a very necessary one, as practically everybody owns jewellery, furs, etc., which are of considerable value. Where the insured travels beyond the limits of the United Kingdom the cover can be extended for the period of such journeys, provided details are given to the company and an additional premium paid.

Valuing the Contents of a House.

It is of the greatest importance that correct values should be arrived at when effecting the insurance, as a policy merely gives the insured the right to make a claim up to the total amount insured and to recover his loss provided he can establish his rights in accordance with the conditions of the policy. In the event of a fire the owner of the property must produce, either to the insurance company or underwriters or his assessors, evidence of the value of each item claimed for, and it will be realised how impossible this would be in many cases, especially where the property was purchased many years ago, in addition to the fact that one could not remember a large number of the articles destroyed.

However liberal the insurance company may be, it is generally found that the insured is the loser as the result of a fire, unless he has a valuation made at the time of effecting the policy, a copy of such a valuation to be lodged with the company and the values stated therein taken as a basis of settlement.

How to obtain a Correct Valuation.

To obtain a correct valuation of the contents of the house is not the costly item which it at first appears, as several firms specialise in this class of business and are able to quote very reduced terms as compared with the usual charge in accordance with the Surveyors' and Valuers' Institute. It is necessary to state only the position of the property for a representative to be sent, free of charge in the first place, in order to look at the property to be valued and quote the required fee. It is impossible to give details of the fees charged, as they must necessarily vary according to the position of the property and the amount of travelling expenses incurred, but the reader can rest assured that the cost is really small as compared with the great assistance resulting from a proper valuation, and represents approximately a payment of five or six years' annual premiums for the policy plus reasonable out-of-pocket expenses.

Experts are called in whenever it is necessary to value such items as pictures, antique furniture, china, glass and books, and it has often been found that a person possesses treasures of which he had no knowledge.

It is as well to remember that sooner or later a valuation will be required by almost every householder or by his executors in the event of his death, and it will be seen, therefore, that the valuation will serve a double purpose. One firm gives considerable service in addition to the preparation of the valuation, for they are willing to act on behalf of the insured should a claim arise.

When the valuation is completed, a rough copy is sent to the client for his perusal, and assuming that he is satisfied, he is supplied with a bound copy complete with index and summary, and a similar copy is lodged with his insurers. The result is that the company will be willing to endorse the policy to the effect that the valuation is accepted as the basis of settlement in the event of a claim, and the production of invoices and other evidence of cost is therefore dispensed with. Should it be necessary to revise the valuation, the valuers must be informed and they will bring it up to date at little or no cost in accordance with the terms mentioned in their usual form of quotation.

HOW TO CUT BORDERING PAPER

DIFFICULTY is sometimes experienced in cutting bordering paper unless the correct method is known. We will assume that you wish to cut a piece of paper which is the full width of the roll and about 10 feet long.

Fold Paper Paste to Paste.

The first thing is to paste the paper and fold it paste to paste, as in Fig. 1. Now cut down the paper with scissors, and at the point marked X separate a pair of border strips from the four remaining on the folded sheet.

Now bring the pair of strips to the edge of the table, and holding in the right hand a piece of wood to act as a guide for the centre of the strip, score down the strip with the point of a pair of

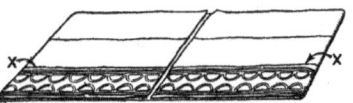

Fig. 1.—Paper Folded Paste to Paste.

Fig. 2.—Scoring down Centre of Strip.

scissors as in Fig. 2. The little finger of the right hand acts as a guide against the edge of the table.

The paper, still folded, is cut down this strip, and thus two strips are cut with one cut. The remaining paper comes to no harm whilst it is waiting to be used.

To avoid Paste Marks on Wallpaper.

When wallpapering, annoying marks are sometimes caused by the pasted side of a piece of paper touching that already placed on the wall. This can be avoided by stirring in a teaspoonful of powdered alum when mixing the paste. Any paste which does touch the paper should, of course, be carefully wiped off while wet; the alum will prevent a stain being left.

REMOVING IODINE STAINS

OCCASIONALLY when treating hand abrasions or other superficial injuries, some iodine is accidentally spilled on the clothes.

Although iodine, which is a very penetrating substance, is apparently very difficult to remove, actually this can be done very readily, and a badly soiled article of clothing can be restored to its former condition in a few minutes.

It is only necessary to rub the soiled parts with a piece of cotton-wool soaked in a diluted solution of ammonia.

Wiring a Bungalow for Electric Light and Domestic Power

The wiring of a bungalow for electric light and domestic power can be successfully accomplished by anyone having normal intelligence and ability to use the tools which are to be found in a domestic tool chest.

The work is best done whilst the building is in the course of erection, but in the event of the building being completed, more time will be required to do the work, and special precautions taken when making the wiring runs so as to prevent undue weakening to the structure and unnecessary damage to the plaster work and decorations.

Planning the Light and Plug Points and Switch Controls.

The light and plug points and their switch controls in each room should be so fixed as to give the maximum of convenience and efficiency; two-way switch control of light points arranged for in all cases where it would be of advantage, as the extra cost involved is not heavy. Staircase and hall lighting are particularly suitable for two-way switch control, and bedroom lighting, where drop pendants are fitted, should also have two-way switch control.

In living-rooms a central light point will give a good light distribution, but the artistic effect obtained by using wall fittings, standard lamps and bracket fittings should be considered, although the light distribution is not so efficient.

A study should be fitted with a flexible table or standard fitting to enable the light to be projected in any desired direction.

Hall and landing lights may be made artistic by using Newel post fittings of suitable design.

Bedroom furniture is often fitted with suitable bracket fittings, which may be supplied from plugs fixed on the skirting boards of the room; this method allows of the furniture being moved about, without impairing the efficiency of the lighting.

The kitchen light point should be fixed in a position so that the sink will be well illuminated, and the larder lighting to give good illumination of the shelves.

Bathroom fittings call for special consideration. They should be fixed in a position so that no shadows will be produced when the wash bowl is used, and in the event of a fault on the fitting it should be impossible to obtain an electric shock from them.

Domestic power plugs are fitted in the various rooms where the appliances will be used. When it is desired to limit the number of plugs, one or two central positions should be decided upon, although this method will mean that the flexible wire connections in some cases will pass under doors, and this practice is not recommended.

If electrical heating of the bathroom water cylinder is to be used, a plug will be required for this purpose.

A separate circuit to an electric cooker will be required, as the loading

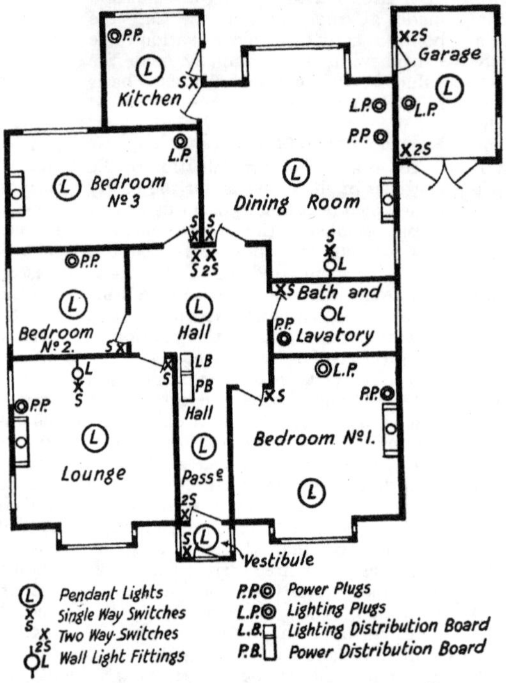

Fig. 1.—Plan of Typical Bungalow showing the Positions of the Lighting and Power Points and the Switches.

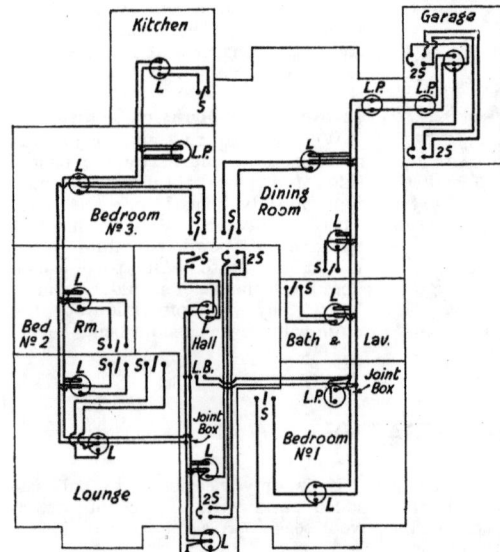

Fig. 2.—Wiring Diagram for the Lighting Circuits.

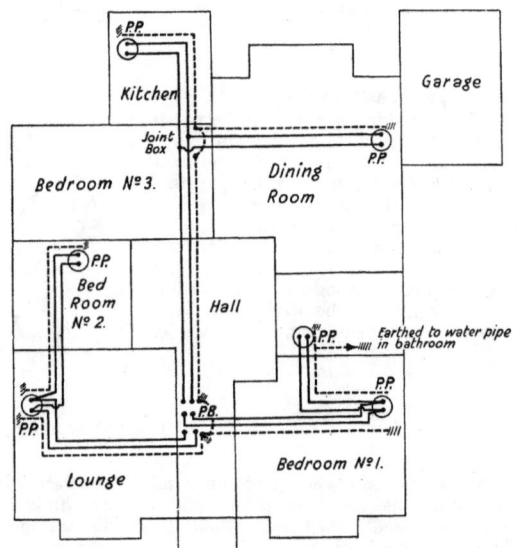

Fig. 3.—Wiring Diagram for the Domestic Power Circuits.

WIRING A BUNGALOW FOR ELECTRIC LIGHT AND DOMESTIC POWER

is heavy, and a separate main switch and fuses are used to control it.

The Wiring System.

There are various systems of wiring which may be used, each of them having special merits.

Ease of erection and low initial cost is a consideration which will help in making a choice, provided that the system when installed will be safe and free from faults.

In the present circumstances the C.T.S. system will make a good and efficient job, the initial cost of the cable and cable accessories is not high, and the system is not difficult to erect.

Special precautions must be taken to protect it from damage, where it may be subjected to rough treatment or the possibility of having a nail driven into the cable where it is sunk in plaster.

In the garage it is advisable to run the wiring in steel conduit in order that it may be fireproof, and thus avoiding a possible difficulty with the insurance company.

The amount of wiring to be run in the garage will not be great, and the extra work and cost involved in enclosing the wiring in steel conduit will not be excessive. Grip continuity fittings may be used at the conduit junctions and joints, thus avoiding the necessity of obtaining screwing tackle to do the job.

The Approximate Cost of Material and Accessories.

C.T.S. cable, 3/·036″ twin, £2 per 100 yards.

C.T.S. cable, 1/·044″ single-core, 15s. per 100 yards, for lighting and power circuits 600 megohm grade.

C.T.S. cable, 1/·044″ twin, £1 3s. per 100 yards, for lighting and power circuits 600 megohm grade.

C.T.S. cable, 7/·029″ three-core, £3 12s. per 100 yards, for lighting and power circuits 600 megohm grade.

C.T.S. cable, 7/·064″ twin, £5 17s. 6d. per 100 yards, for power mains.

Bakelite junction boxes, 1s. each.

Metal channelling for C.T.S. cable, 12s. per 72 feet.

Wood capping for C.T.S. cable, 10s. per 100 feet.

⅝-inch welded galvanised conduit, £1 per 100 feet.

Buckle wiring clips, 1s. per gross.

14/·0076″ double vulcanised flexible wire, £1 1s. per gross yards.

Crabtree sunk switches, oxidised copper finish, 15s. doz.

Crabtree sunk switches (two-way), oxidised copper finish, 2s. 3d. each.

Wooden switch fixing boxes, 1s. 9d. doz. (for one switch), 2s. 6d. doz. (for two switches).

Switch plates, oxidised copper finish, 5s. doz. (one-hole), 10s. doz. (two-hole).

Switch plates, plate glass, 10s. doz. (one-hole), 23s. doz. (two-hole).

China ceiling roses (three-plate), 8s. 8d. doz.

SCHEDULE.

Position of Point.	Type of Fitting.	Position of Switch.	Type of Switch.	Power Consumption.	Circuit.
Lounge ceiling.	Ornamental bowl.	Door.	Single-way.	100 watts.	Lighting No. 1.
Lounge wall.	Wall Bracket.	Below fitting.	Single-way.	60 watts.	Lighting No. 1.
Lounge skirting board.	10-15 ampere Wylex plug.	—	—	Appliance not exceeding 3 kilowatts.	Power No. 1.
Dining-room ceiling.	Ornamental Bowl.	Door.	Single-way.	150 watts.	Lighting No. 2.
Dining-room wall.	Wall bracket	Below fitting.	Single-way.	60 watts.	Lighting No. 2.
Dining-room skirting board.	5 ampere Wylex plug.	—	—	Wireless set, 40 watts.	Lighting No. 2.
Dining-room skirting board.	10-15 ampere Wylex plug.	—	—	Appliance not exceeding 3 kilowatts.	Power No. 3.
Kitchen ceiling.	Pendant with reflector.	Door.	Single-way.	40 watts.	Lighting No. 1.
Kitchen skirting board.	10-15 ampere Wylex plug.	—	—	Appliance not exceeding 3 kilowatts.	Power No. 3.
Bath and lavatory ceiling.	Ceiling fitting.	Door.	Single-way.	60 watts.	Lighting No. 2.
Bath and lavatory skirting board.	10-15 ampere Wylex plug.	—	—	Appliance not exceeding 3 kilowatts.	Power No. 2.
No. 1 bedroom ceiling.	Pendant with shade.	Door.	Single-way.	60 watts.	Lighting No. 2.
No. 1 bedroom skirting board.	10-15 ampere Wylex plug.	—	—	Appliance not exceeding 3 kilowatts.	Power No. 2.
No. 1 bedroom skirting board.	5 ampere Wylex plug.	—	—	Bed light fitting, 60 watts	Lighting No. 2.
No. 2 bedroom ceiling.	Pendant with shade.	Door.	Single-way.	60 watts.	Lighting No. 1.
No. 2 bedroom skirting board.	10-15 ampere Wylex plug.	—	—	Appliance not exceeding 3 kilowatts.	Power No. 1.
No. 3 bedroom ceiling.	Pendant with shade.	Door.	Single-way.	60 watts.	Lighting No. 1.
No. 3 bedroom skirting board.	5 ampere Wylex plug.	—	—	Bed light fitting, 60 watts.	Lighting No. 1.
Hall ceiling.	Ornamental bowl.	Dining-room door.	Single-way.	60 watts.	Lighting No. 1.
Hall passage ceiling.	Lantern fitting.	Front door dining-room door.	Two-way.	60 watts.	Lighting No. 1.
Garage ceiling.	Pendant with shade.	Front doors, outlet door to back of house.	Two-way.	60 watts.	Lighting No. 2.
Garage wall.	5 ampere Wylex plug.	—	—	Inspection lamp, 40 watts.	Lighting No. 2.
Porch.	Watertight fitting.	Porch.	Single-way.	40 watts.	Lighting No. 1.

WIRING A BUNGALOW FOR ELECTRIC LIGHT AND DOMESTIC POWER

Ceiling connectors (three-plate), 14s. 6d. doz.
Ceiling plates, 18s. doz.
Bakelite cord-grip lampholders (metal lined), 6s. doz.
Wylex plugs, 3-pin, 5 ampere ; 3-pin, 10–15 ampere.
Lighting distribution board, two-ways, 7s. 6d.
Power distribution board, 10s.
Main lighting switch and fuses (15-ampere), 5s.
Main power switch and fuses (50-ampere), 15s.
Small meter board for main switches, 1s. 6d.

The exact amount of material required will be obtained by measuring up the length of the various runs, and referring to the schedule. The price of the cable and accessories given in the list is an average for good-class material; inferior material should not be used, as it would increase the cost of maintenance and may be the cause of "faults" occurring.

The cost of the reflectors and fittings will depend upon choice of types, and is seldom regarded as part of the cost of the installation.

General Scheme of Wiring for Lighting.

Twin cable is used throughout the job, although more wire will be required than if single-core cables were used. The extra cost is compensated for by having straightforward wiring runs and simple connections at the various terminal points, also a saving in time for fixing. At each light point a three-plate ceiling rose or connector is fixed, the third terminal of the rose or connector in each case being used as a looping-in connection for the feed to the switch.

Preparing for the Wiring Runs.

Mark off on the ceilings the positions of the various pendant lights, and at each of these positions make a hole through the plaster and laths into the false roof above. The positions of the switches and the wall bracket lights are marked off on the walls, and if it is decided to sink the cables in the plaster, a channel is cut in the plaster from the switch or bracket position so as to give

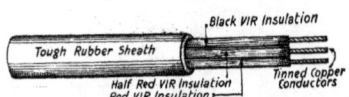

Fig. 4.—A 7/·029" C.T.S. Three-core Cable.

The wires are separately insulated, one with black V.I.R. insulation, the second with half-red and half-black V.I.R. insulation, and the third with red V.I.R. insulation. The sheath is removed by cutting round at the place where it is to come away and then cut longitudinally to the end of the cable.

Fig. 5.—A 1/·044" C.T.S. Twin-core Cable.

access to the wiring from the false roof to the marked position.

In some cases one channel may be used to accommodate the cables, which run down to the switches in adjacent rooms and which will be fixed on opposite sides of the same wall, a hole being cut through the wall at this

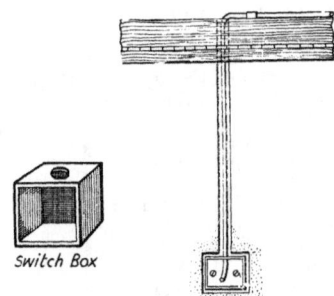

Fig. 6.—The Twin Cable run from the False Roof to the Switch Position.

The plaster is channelled out for the run and cut away for the switch box, which is secured to the face of the brickwork with rawlplugs.

point so as to give communication from the channel to each side of the wall. Where lighting plugs are fixed on the walls, channels are cut in the plaster to give access for the wiring to them.

The wiring for the power plugs is run below the floors and brought up behind the skirting boards to the various positions. These positions may conveniently be on the skirting boards so as to give an easy and secure fixing for the sockets.

Access to below the floors is obtained through the "trap," and when the various plug positions are located from below the floors, the plaster is channelled out from behind the skirting board at each position. A hole is then drilled through the skirting board to the channel which has been made behind each position, so that access is obtained for the cable from the floor below to the plug position on the skirting board. A "fish" wire should be threaded from below the floor through the channel, and the upper end of it pulled through the hole in the skirting board at each position. This will facilitate the passage of the cables to the various plug positions.

The positions for the lighting and power distributing boards are fixed on the wall in the passage from the front door to the hall.

A channel is cut in the plaster from the lighting board position vertically upwards into the false roof and another is cut vertically downwards to below the floor. This second channel must be wide enough to accommodate the lighting and power mains, in addition to the cables for the power circuits. The main switches will in all probability be fixed in a cupboard situated in the vestibule, and the cables from them to the lighting and power boards will be run below floors.

The Wiring for the Lighting Circuits.

Access to the false roof is gained through the manhole, the cover is removed, and then take into the roof some safe means of illumination (a storm lamp will be quite suitable, and is easily moved about from place to place). When moving about inside the roof, always obtain a footing on the wooden rafters; a false step on the plaster laths will probably make a *hole through the plaster ceiling.* Fix the positions of the two joint boxes in the roof, one over the hall passage for No. 1 circuit, and the other over the No. 1 bedroom for No. 2 circuits. Taking No. 1 circuit, measure up the

TABLE OF CABLES AND THEIR CURRENT-CARRYING CAPACITY REQUIRED FOR THE INSTALLATION

Circuit.	Size and Type of Cable.	Carrying Capacity in Amperes.
Power mains	7/·064" twin.	38·5
Power plug circuits	7/·029" three-core	17·5
Lighting mains	3/·036" twin.	12·0
Lighting circuits	1/·044" twin.	6·1

TABLES OF FUSES AND THEIR MELTING CURRENTS REQUIRED FOR THE INSTALLATION

Position of Fuse.	Size and Type of Fuse.	Melting Current in Amperes.
Power main switch.	20s S.W.G. copper.	62
Lighting main switch.	28s S.W.G. copper.	17
Power distributing board.	26s S.W.G. copper.	22
Lighting distributing board.	20s S.W.G. lead tin alloy.	7

TABLE OF FLEXIBLE CORDS REQUIRED FOR INSTALLATION

Purpose.	Size and Type.	Current-carrying Capacity.
Lighting pendants	14/·0076" twin twisted.	1·8
Reading lamps	14/·0076" twin circular section.	1·8
Power plugs for iron, kettle, vacuum cleaner.	40/·0076" three-core circular section.	5·0
Power plugs for radiators.	110/·0076" three-core circular section.	13·0

WIRING A BUNGALOW FOR ELECTRIC LIGHT AND DOMESTIC POWER

lengths of the three twin cables, which will be run from the joint box to the lighting board, hall passage light and the central light position of the lounge, respectively. These lengths are cut off the coil of 1/·044-inch twin cable and laid in approximately the position they will be fixed in the roof, the end of the cables which feed the light positions being pushed through the ceiling for about 6 inches and the end of the cable which will be connected to lighting board passed down the channel towards the lighting board position. Another length of twin cable is measured off and run between the joint box for No. 2 circuit and the lighting board position, this length being laid in approximately the position it will occupy in the roof.

The Wiring between the Light Positions of No. 1 Circuit.

Measure the lengths of the twin cables which will be run between the following light positions:—

(1) Hall passage light to vestibule light.
(2) Central lounge light to lounge bracket light.
(3) Lounge bracket light to No. 2 bedroom light.
(4) No. 2 bedroom light to No. 3 bedroom light.
(5) No. 3 bedroom light to No. 3 lighting plug.
(6) No. 3 bedroom lighting plug to kitchen light.

These cables are cut off to length from the coil of cable and fixed in approximately the positions they will occupy in the roof, the ends being pushed through the holes in the ceilings for a length of about 6 inches at their respective positions.

The lengths of the twin cables which will be run from the light positions to their respective switch positions are now measured up and cut off. These lengths are placed in their approximate positions which they will occupy when fixed. In most cases they will run alongside the twin cables which connect the various light positions together until they branch off to run down the channels, which lead to the

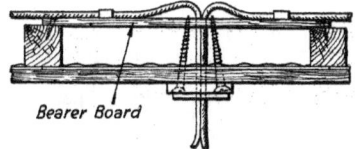

Fig. 7.—Fixing the Ceiling Connector Block.

A bearer board is fixed across adjacent joists and the block secured to the board with countersunk head wood screws.

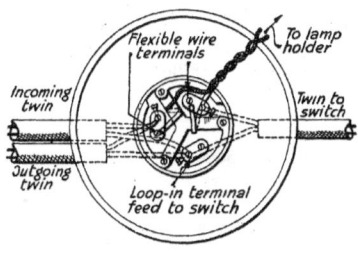

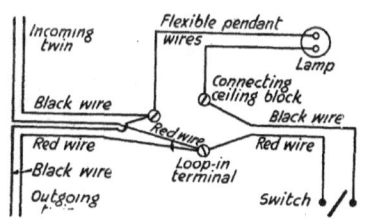

Fig. 8.—The Wiring to a Ceiling Connector Block and the Switch controlling the Light fed from the Connector.

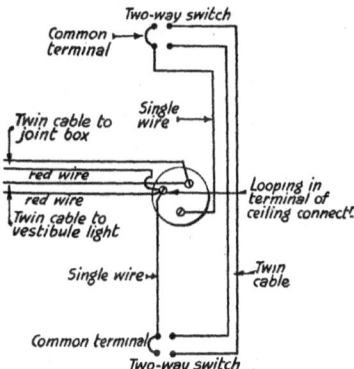

Fig. 9.—The Wiring of the Hall Passage Light, which is controlled by Two-way Switches.

switch positions. In the case of the hall passage light, a twin cable is run between the two two-way switch positions, and a single-core cable from the light position to each of the two-way switches.

The Wiring between the Light Positions of No. 2 Circuit.

Twin cables between the joint box and the light positions in No. 1 bedroom and the bathroom are placed in their approximate positions in the same manner as employed when wiring No. 1 circuit. From the bathroom light position, the twin cables are run between the various successive positions until they terminate at the garage light.

The twin cables which connect the light positions to their respective switch positions are now measured up, cut off from the coil of cable, and placed in their approximate positions.

Where the cables pass from the lighting plug in the dining-room into the garage, a hole will be drilled through the wall behind the plug position, and the cables which emerge into the garage will feed the lighting plug in the garage and then rise up the wall to the garage light. This last run of cable may be run in a piece of steel conduit, if so desired, which has been previously fixed in position. The run of conduit should extend to the two-way switch positions and be fitted with inspection fittings where any bends or T-branches occur.

Fixing the Wiring in Position.

Buckle wiring clips are fixed on the ceiling joists along the lines of run of all the cables run in the false roof with brass pins and in the various channels down to the switch and plug positions. Rawl-plugs will be fitted into the joints of the brickwork in the channels about every 2 feet, and the buckle clips fixed in position with rawl-plug screws. In some cases it may be desirable to cover the cables in the channels with a metal protective covering, which may be obtained in suitable lengths; this precaution will prevent the possibility of a nail being driven into the cables

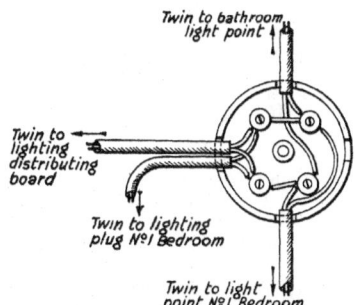

Fig. 10.—Joint Box Connections on No. 1 Lighting Circuit.

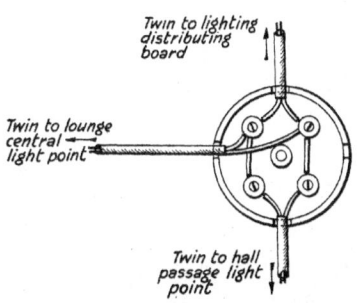

Fig. 11.—Joint Box Connections on No. 2 Lighting Circuit.

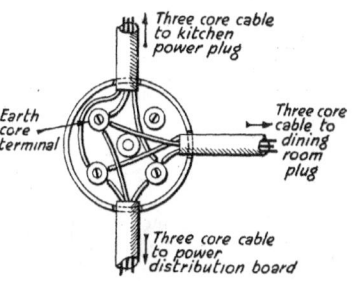

Fig. 12.—Joint Box Connections for Power Plug Circuit.

1479

WIRING A BUNGALOW FOR ELECTRIC LIGHT AND DOMESTIC POWER

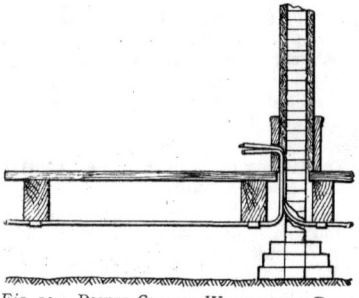

Fig. 13.—Power Circuit Wiring to a Plug Position.
The wiring is run below the floor and brought up behind the skirting board to the plug position.

Boxes are sunk in the plaster and fixed in position for sunk-lighting plugs, the cables passing into the boxes from the channels through holes which have been drilled in their upper sides.

If the plugs are to be fixed on the surface of the skirting boards, holes are drilled through the skirting boards and the plaster cut away behind the boards to communicate with the channels carrying the cables to the plug positions. A fish wire is placed through each hole and the end of it pulled up into the channel, so that the cables may be pulled through to the front of the skirting board at each plug position.

Wiring the Power Circuits.

The three-core 7/·029-inch cable is used for wiring the power circuits, the third wire in the cable being used for earthing purposes, because all the portable power appliances and those whose metal casings are exposed should be efficiently earthed.

For power circuit No. 1 two lengths of cable are required, one from the power-distributing board to the power plug in the lounge, and the other from the power plug in the lounge to the power plug in No. 2 bedroom.

These lengths should be measured up and cut off from the coil of three-core cable. They are laid approximately in the positions they will occupy when fixed, the ends at the plug positions being pulled up from below the floors to the outlet holes in the skirting boards, with the "fish" wires. The end which comes up to the power board

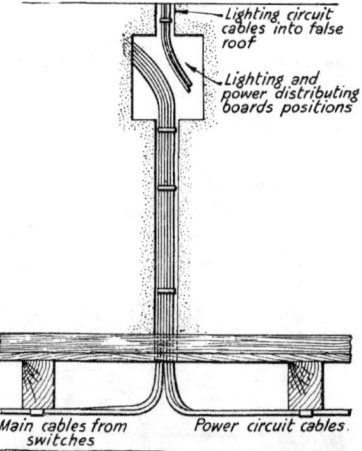

Fig. 15.—The Cable Runs to the Lighting and Power-Distributing Boards.
The lighting and power boards are fixed in the hall passage. A channel is made between the false roof and the floor, and the plaster is cut away for the lighting and power-distributing boards positions. The boards are fixed by screwing the battens to the surface of the brickwork.

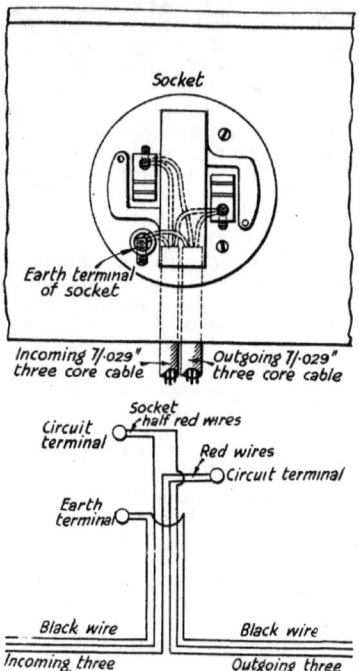

Fig. 14.—The Wiring to a Domestic Power 3-Pin Plug Socket.

should be coiled up neatly and hung up to prevent the cable being damaged until it is fixed in the channel leading to the board.

Power circuit No. 2 is run in a similar manner. In power circuit No. 3 the position of the joint box is fixed in a dry place under the floor, and a length of cable run from the power board to this position; two lengths of cable are run from the joint box position to the dining-room and kitchen power plugs respectively.

Fixing the Wiring Runs in Position.

Buckle clips are fixed with brass pins to the lower faces of the floor joists along the lines of run and the cables stretched taut before the clips are bent over to secure them in position.

The Wiring Runs for the Lighting and Power Mains.

These will be run under the floors between the main switches in the vestibule and the distributing boards in the hall passage.

A twin 3/·036-inch cable will be used for the lighting main, and a twin 7/·064-inch cable for the power mains. The lengths of the runs are measured up, and the cables cut off from their respective coils. They are then laid under the floors and the ends to the distributing boards brought up to them in the channel which accommodates the power plug circuit cables. The cables are secured to the lower

when the plaster is finally made good.

The cables are now placed in position and the buckle clips bent over to secure them; any slack wire should be pulled towards the light or switch position, so that a neat job is made.

Fixing the Switch Boxes, Ceiling connecting Blocks and Patresses.

At each light position a short piece of board should be fixed across adjacent joists. These are called "bearer boards," and will give a secure fixing to the ceiling connecting blocks which will be screwed to them. A hole about ¾ inch diameter is drilled through each of these boards, and this hole will be immediately above the hole in the ceiling when the board is fixed in position. The cables to the light position will pass through this hole and so on through the ceiling to the connecting block.

Each of the connecting blocks are drilled in two places and temporarily fixed in position on the ceiling with screws, which are screwed into the bearer boards. The cables at the light outlet positions are pulled up into the roof, until the connections to the connecting block are made.

The switch boxes are placed on the walls in the positions where they will be fixed, and their outlines marked off on the plaster; the plaster is now cut away so that the boxes will be sunk to the surface of the brickwork and their edges flush with the surface of the plaster.

The boxes are now drilled on their upper sides for entry of the cables, and on their bases for two fixing screws. The walls are drilled in two places at each switch position and fitted with rawl-plugs, and the boxes screwed down with rawl-plug screws into their positions. The cables are brought through the holes which have been drilled on their upper sides and pulled out to the front of the boxes.

At the wall bracket positions the walls are drilled and fitted with rawl-plugs for the bracket fixing screws.

faces of the floor joists with buckle clips.

Fixing the Distributing Boards.

Place the lighting board in the position it will occupy centrally over the channel which carries the cables and about 1 foot from the ceiling, mark the outline of the case on the plaster. Take the board away and place the power board directly under the marked outline of the lighting board, and mark the outline of the power board case on the plaster. The plaster is cut away to the surface of the wall inside the marked lines for each of the boards.

The battens of each of the boards are drilled for the fixing screws and the positions of these holes marked on the surface of the wall by placing the boards in position again. The wall is drilled and rawl-plugs fitted at these marked positions, and the boards are secured in their respective places on the walls with rawl-plug screws.

MAKING THE TERMINAL CONNECTIONS AT LIGHT, SWITCH AND PLUG POSITIONS

Light Positions.

Unscrew the porcelain interior from the ceiling connection block, and pull the cables to be connected through the hole in the ceiling from the false roof. Cut the ends of the cables so that there is a length of about 4 inches below the surface of the ceiling for each cable. Carefully remove the rubber sheath from each cable for a distance of 2 inches. In most cases there will be three twin cables to have their rubber sheaths removed. The rubber insulation is now stripped from the ends of all the six wires for a distance of $\frac{3}{4}$ inch, and the bared ends of the three red wires carefully twisted together and connected into one of the terminals of the porcelain interior; this terminal is the looping-in terminal. The bared ends of the black wires of the incoming and outgoing twin cables to other light positions are twisted together and connected into another terminal of the porcelain interior. The remaining bared end, which will be the black wire of the twin cable from the switch, is bent over double to ensure firm connection and connected into the remaining terminal of the porcelain connector.

Examine all connections for being tight, and note there are no bare wires projecting beyond the back of the terminal holes of the porcelain interior. The porcelain interior is replaced into the recess in the ceiling block and screwed up, also finally tighten the fixing screws for the ceiling block.

Switch Positions.

The twin cable is cut so that a length of about 1 inch projects beyond the front of the switch box and the rubber sheath is removed for a length of $1\frac{1}{2}$ inches.

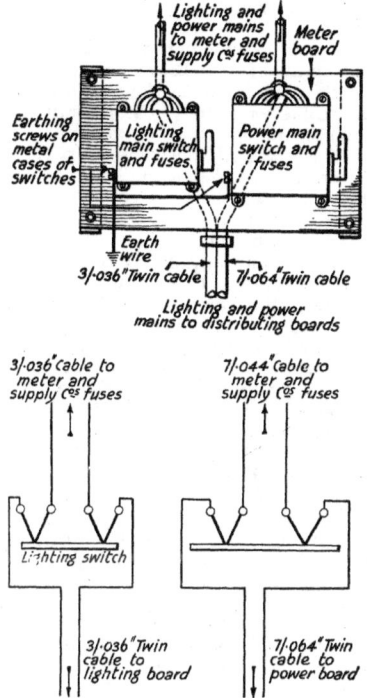

Fig. 16.—The Wiring to the Main Switches.

Strip the rubber insulation from the end of each wire for $\frac{3}{8}$ inch, bend the bared ends double in each case, and connect them into their respective terminals of the switch. The switch is now placed in position inside the

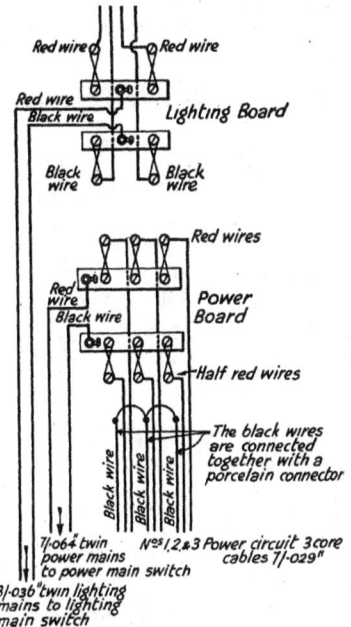

Fig. 17.—The Wiring to the Lighting and Domestic Power Distributing Boards.

box, so that the "dolly" is centrally placed and the switch secured with the fixing screws. Any slack wire should be carefully spaced inside the box, and the switch plate placed over the "dolly" and secured in place with the "dolly" locking ring.

Plug Positions (Lighting).

The twin cables, incoming and outgoing, are cut off to a suitable length to allow of ample wire for connections to the terminals, and the rubber sheaths are carefully removed for a distance of 2 inches. Strip the rubber insulation from the four wires for a distance of $\frac{3}{4}$ inch and twist the bared ends of the two red wires together, and also the bared ends of the two black wires together. These are now connected into the two outer terminals of the socket, leaving the centre earth terminal free. This terminal should be earthed if the portable fitting supplied from the plug has any exposed metal work from which it would be possible to receive an electric shock.

The socket is now fixed in position on the skirting board, or, if of the sunk type, in the wooden box, and secured with the fixing screws.

Plug Positions (Power).

The incoming and outgoing three-core cables are cut off to a suitable length and their rubber sheaths removed for a distance of 2 inches. Strip the rubber insulation from the ends of the six wires for a distance of $\frac{3}{4}$ inch and twist together the bared ends of the black wires, then the half-red wires, and lastly the red wires. The twisted ends of the black wires are connected to the earth terminal of the socket, and the ends of the red and half-red wires connected to the two circuit terminals of the socket respectively.

The black wire of the power circuit cables is earthed in the bathroom by connecting the earth terminal of the socket in that position to the cold-water pipe. The earthing wire should be not less than a 7/·029-inch, bare preferably, and be secured to the water pipe with an earthing clip. Clean the surface of the pipe before screwing up the clip on the pipe.

CONNECTING THE CIRCUIT AND MAIN CABLES TO THE DISTRIBUTING BOARDS

The Lighting Board.

The cover of the board is opened and the fuse-holders removed. Cut the two twin 1/·044-inch circuit cables, and the twin 3/·036-inch main cables to a suitable length so as to allow of sufficient slack to enable the connections to be made. Remove the rubber sheath from the circuit cables for a distance of 3 inches, and from the main cable for a distance of 2 inches.

Strip the rubber insulation from the ends of all the six wires for 1 inch, and double back the bared ends in each case so that a good connection to the terminals will be made.

The bared end of the main red wire is now connected into the upper bus-bar terminal, and the bared end of the main black wire connected to the lower bus-bar terminal.

The circuit cables are connected to their respective terminals at the fuse clips, the red wires to the upper terminals and the black wires to the lower terminals. Make sure that the circuits are not crossed, that is, the red and black wires of any one circuit are connected to the fuse clips which are in line with each other.

The slack wire is carefully packed at the back of the board, and the fuse holders replaced.

The Power Board.

The red and black wires of the main and circuit cables are prepared in a similar manner to those connected to the lighting board, and then connected to their respective terminals on the board, taking care that the circuits are not crossed.

The ends of the black wires of the three-core circuit cables, which are used as earth wires, are all connected together; a porcelain connector will serve to make the connection, and when the connection is made, the connector can be packed away with the slack wire at the back of the board.

Fixing the Main Switches and connecting the Cables to them.

The wall in the vestibule is plugged and the meter board fixed in position.

The main switches are spaced symmetrically on the board and screwed to it. Holes to admit the cables to the front of the board above the switches are drilled in the board, and the cables for the lighting switch brought through the hole above the lighting switch, and those for the power switch through the hole above the power switch.

The ends of the cables are cut off to length and the ends of the wires bared for connection to the switch terminals.

The red wires of the twin from the meter and the twin from the distributing board are connected to one pole of the switch, whilst the black wires are connected to the other pole of the switch. This is repeated for the cables connected to the power switch. Test the connections for being tight.

The Flexible Pendants, etc.

All the permanent wiring is now completed and the flexible pendants for the various lights are made up and connected to the terminals of the ceiling connector blocks in the various places.

Remember to slip the ceiling plates over the ends of the flexibles before making the connections to the ceiling connectors. The ends of the flexibles should be placed under the binding-screw washers to ensure good connections, and all stray ends of copper wires of the flexibles gathered under the washers so as to prevent "short circuits." When the connections are made, the ceiling plates are screwed to the blocks so as to completely cover the porcelain interiors.

The connections to wall bracket lights are made by stripping and preparing the ends of the twin cable, and making the connections to the terminals of the lampholder in the bracket, the twin cables having been threaded through the stem previously.

Inspecting the Work.

When all the wiring is completed and all connections made, the work should be carefully inspected. Loose connections tightened up, switch contacts adjusted, and all fixings made secure.

Test out each circuit for continuity by connecting a battery and bell across the bus-bars of the distributing board; short circuiting the lampholder of the light circuit to be tested. When the switch is closed the bell should ring to indicate continuity.

Making Good the Plaster Work.

If the plaster has been channelled for the wiring runs and the various fittings which have been fitted, it should be made good with plaster of paris, which is filled in the channels until flush with the walls. If the wall runs are to be protected against the possibility of driving a nail through the cables, a length of metal channelling should be fitted over the cables before the plaster of paris is filled in.

Notify the Supply Authority.

When all the consuming appliances are fitted, the supply authority should be notified that connection to their supply mains is required. They will make an inspection of the work and test the insulation resistance to earth of the installation. This test will have to conform to the value given by the rules of the I.E.E. before the connection is made.

HANDY DEVICE FOR UNDOING KNOTS

KNOTS which are difficult to loosen are a continual source of annoyance. A simple device can be made from a common medium-sized pocket comb, one of those which broken teeth have rendered otherwise useless. Cut out the remainder of the teeth, and also break off the heavy or guard tooth on one end. Round it on the stone or with a file to a neat handle-like end.

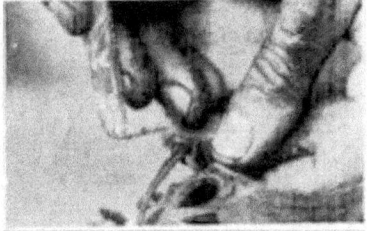

Smooth off the inside of the comb along where the teeth have been removed. The large tooth left on the other end will be found an excellent point with which to attack any small knot. The smooth celluloid will not cut any fine cord or string fabric, yet pulled with the handle-like portion above it, a knot can be easily entered and spread apart.

A BICYCLE TIP

OCCASIONALLY when riding a bicycle which has seen considerable service, the free-wheel suddenly ceases to function, and the sprocket remains permanently "free" and no result follows rotation of the pedals. This is extremely annoying when it occurs out of doors far from home, and it is not practicable to dismantle the free-wheel by the roadside. Sometimes the trouble is due to the pawls in the free-wheel having worn badly, but often it is simply due to the pawls sticking because of dirt. In this case a temporary cure can usually be effected by lifting the back wheel and banging it down rather sharply on the road. This sounds rather drastic, but in an emergency such methods are pardonable. If paraffin is at hand, the back wheel should be placed horizontal and some paraffin placed on the free-wheel in such a manner that it gets inside and cleans the pawls and springs.

How to Make a Roll-top Desk

Although the constructional details of a roll-top desk are not difficult, considerable care will be needed in marking out the parts and cutting the various joints and in assembling the several members of the carcase to insure a workmanlike job. The design shown at Fig. 1 reduces the constructional work to a minimum and provides for a desk of the average dimensions. It includes the usual conveniences, together with an automatic locking device for the drawers.

The main dimensions are shown in the front elevation and the sectional elevation at Figs. 2 and 3. The material suggested is oak, and the following cutting list shows the total amount of wood required.

Fig. 1.—The Completed Roll-top Desk.
This design reduces the constructional work to a minimum and provides for a desk of the average dimensions.

Materials required.

Pedestals.—Eight uprights, A and B, $29\frac{1}{2} \times 3 \times 1$ inches; four top rails, C, $23 \times 2\frac{3}{4} \times 1$ inches; four bottom rails, D, $23 \times 2\frac{3}{4} \times 1$ inches; eight muntins, E, $21\frac{3}{4} \times 2 \times \frac{3}{4}$ inches; twelve panels, oak-faced plywood, $20\frac{1}{4} \times 5\frac{1}{2} \times \frac{1}{4}$ inches.

Runners.—Twenty pieces, F, $22 \times 1\frac{1}{2} \times \frac{3}{4}$ inches; ten pieces, G, $11 \times 2 \times \frac{3}{4}$ inches; ten pieces, H, $9\frac{1}{2} \times 2\frac{1}{2} \times \frac{3}{4}$ inches; sixteen pieces, W, $6 \times 1 \times \frac{1}{4}$ inches; sixteen pieces, Y, $19 \times \frac{1}{2} \times \frac{1}{4}$ inches; plinth, 11-foot run, $4\frac{1}{4} \times \frac{1}{2}$ inches.

Extension Tops.—Two pieces, I, $10 \times 1\frac{1}{2} \times \frac{3}{4}$ inches; four pieces, J, $21\frac{1}{2} \times 1\frac{1}{2} \times \frac{3}{4}$ inches; two pieces, K, $10 \times 2 \times \frac{3}{4}$ inches; two oak-faced panels, $19\frac{1}{2} \times 8 \times \frac{1}{4}$ inches.

Desk Top.—Two lengths, L, $42 \times 3 \times 1$ inches; two ends, M, $20 \times 3 \times 1$ inches; two rails, N, $19 \times 3 \times \frac{3}{4}$ inches; one oak-faced panel, $37 \times 18 \times \frac{1}{4}$ inches.

Upper Part.—Top, O, $42 \times 11 \times 1$ inches; rail, P, $39\frac{1}{2} \times 1\frac{1}{4} \times 1$ inches; sides, two pieces, Q, $12\frac{1}{2} \times 3 \times 1$ inches; two pieces, R, $23\frac{1}{2} \times 2\frac{1}{2} \times 1$ inches; two pieces, S, $26 \times 6 \times 1$ inches; two panels, from $30 \times 6\frac{1}{2} \times \frac{1}{4}$ inches.

Locking Attachment.—Eight pieces bar iron, $3 \times \frac{1}{2} \times \frac{1}{4}$ inches; two pieces, U, approx. $15 \times \frac{1}{2} \times \frac{1}{2}$ inches; two pieces, V, $24 \times \frac{1}{2} \times 1$ inches.

Roll Top.—80-foot run, $\frac{3}{4} \times \frac{1}{2}$ inches; two pieces $40 \times 2 \times \frac{1}{4}$ inches; two pieces $40 \times 1 \times \frac{1}{4}$ inches.

Back.—14-foot run, $3 \times \frac{3}{4}$ inches, plywood, $35\frac{1}{2} \times 34\frac{1}{2}$ inches.

Inside Fitment.—One piece $35\frac{1}{2} \times 7\frac{1}{4} \times \frac{1}{2}$ inches, approx. 15-foot run $7\frac{1}{4} \times \frac{1}{4}$ inches; for drawer fronts, $18 \times 2 \times \frac{1}{2}$ inches.

For Pedestal Drawers.—5 feet $\times 4 \times 1$ inches; 27 feet $\times 4 \times \frac{1}{2}$ inches; 15 feet $\times 9\frac{1}{2} \times \frac{1}{4}$ inches; 20 $\times 8\frac{1}{2} \times 1$ inches; 9 feet $\times 8\frac{1}{2} \times \frac{1}{2}$ inches; $16\frac{1}{2} \times 4 \times 1$ inches; $24 \times 16 \times \frac{1}{4}$ inches; 5 feet 6 inches $\times 2 \times \frac{1}{2}$ inches; 33 feet $\times \frac{1}{2} \times \frac{1}{2}$ inches.

Handles.—5 feet $\times 1 \times 1$ inch.

First make the Two Pedestals.

The two pedestals should be made first; they are identical, and the instructions given below for one should be carried out for both. The sides, as shown in elevation and section at Fig. 4, are composed of two uprights, A and B, finished to $29\frac{1}{2} \times 3 \times 1$ inches; a top rail, C, $23 \times 2\frac{3}{4} \times 1$ inches; a bottom rail, D, $23 \times 2\frac{3}{4} \times 1$ inches; two muntins, E, $21\frac{3}{4} \times 2 \times \frac{3}{4}$ inches; and three panels, $20\frac{1}{4} \times 5\frac{1}{2} \times \frac{1}{4}$ inches. The shoulders of the two rails are marked off to leave 19 inches between; in the top rail the tenon is $1\frac{3}{4}$ inches wide, in the bottom rail it is $2\frac{1}{2}$ inches wide, and on one side of each rail the tenon is set back $\frac{1}{4}$ inch to allow for the ploughed groove. The mortises for the muntins are $1\frac{1}{2}$ inches wide, the lines being $5\frac{1}{4}$, $1\frac{3}{4}$, $5\frac{1}{2}$, $1\frac{3}{4}$ and $5\frac{1}{4}$ inches. The mortises on the rails are marked off 1, $1\frac{3}{4}$, $20\frac{1}{4}$ and $2\frac{1}{2}$ inches, leaving 4 inches.

The plough grooves on the inner edges of the uprights and rails and both edges of the muntins are $\frac{1}{4}$ inch from the face side, $\frac{1}{4}$ inch wide and deep, the thickness of the tenons being cut to correspond.

The sides are glued up complete with panels and, of course, should be cramped up tightly after gluing.

Drawer Runners.

The five drawer runners are now made, as shown at Fig. 5. In each case the two side pieces, F, are $22 \times 1\frac{1}{2} \times \frac{3}{4}$ inches; the front pieces, G, are $11 \times 2 \times \frac{3}{4}$ inches, and the back pieces, H, are $9\frac{1}{2} \times 2\frac{1}{2} \times \frac{3}{4}$ inches. Both joints required are indicated, the framework being made up to 22×11 inches, with front notches $\frac{1}{2}$ inch wide and 1 inch deep as shown.

Grooves on Framing.

Grooves are now cut on the inside of each pair of the framing as shown at Fig. 4. Measurements for the grooves from the top are as follows: $1\frac{1}{4}$, $\frac{3}{4}$, 4, $\frac{3}{4}$, 4, $\frac{3}{4}$, 4, $\frac{3}{4}$, $8\frac{1}{2}$, $\frac{3}{4}$ inches, leaving 4 inches. It will be seen that the grooves are stopped 1 inch from the front edges, those at the top and bottom are $\frac{1}{2}$ inch deep on the front uprights and $\frac{1}{4}$ inch deep on the rails, the others being $\frac{1}{2}$ inch deep on the

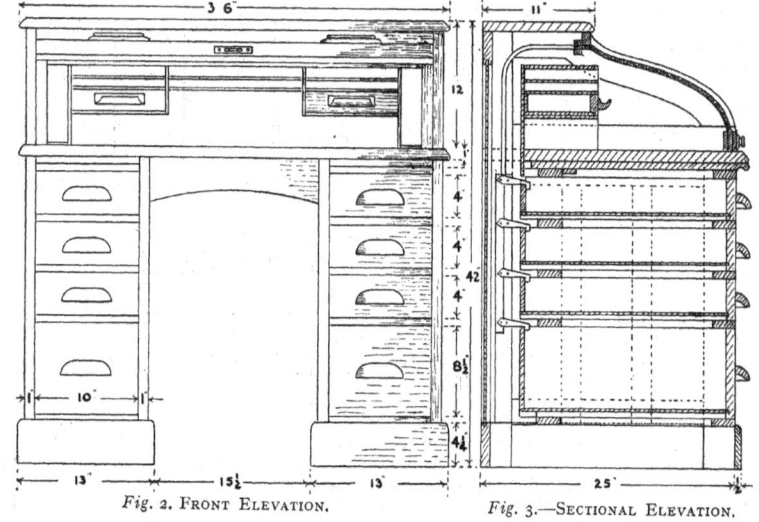

Fig. 2. Front Elevation. *Fig. 3.—Sectional Elevation.*

HOW TO MAKE A ROLL-TOP DESK

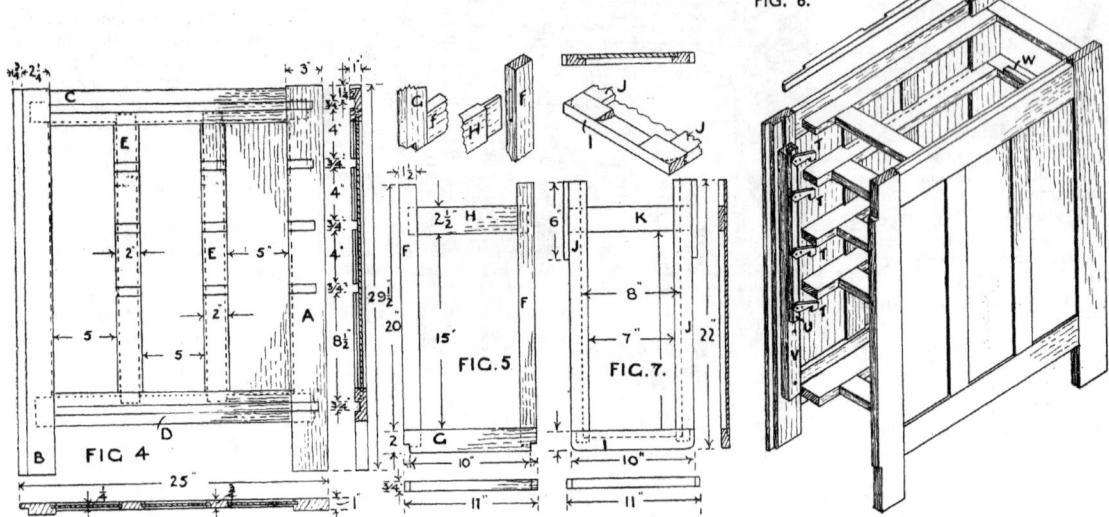

Figs. 4 to 7.—Details of Pedestals, Drawer Runners and Frame Assembly.
4. Elevation and section of sides, showing also grooves cut on the inside of each pair of the framing. 5. The five drawer runners. 6. Showing the frames glued in position. 7. The two side extensions shown in two sections.

front uprights and ¼ inch deep on the muntins only.

Make sure all Grooves are correctly marked out.

It is important to make quite sure that the marking for the grooves corresponds exactly on each side, and it is preferable to set out the distances in pencil on the front edges of all four front pieces placed together. A ¾ × ⅜-inch rebate is cut on the outer uprights at the back on the inside as shown in the section at Fig. 4, and the inner uprights are planed down ½ inch to allow for the back, and, in addition, two 3 × ¼-inch notches are cut to allow for the top and bottom frame of the back panelling.

Next glue Five Frames in Position.

The five frames are now glued in position, as indicated at Fig. 6, which shows one of the pedestals without the bottom plinth and minus the drawers. Guides are now fitted on the four lower runners as indicated by the dotted lines shown on the second runner in Fig. 6 and shown separately at the top. These strips can be of deal, ½ inch square, in section, with slots 2 × ¼ inches to allow for the muntins. The two side extensions, shown with two sections at Fig. 7, are made with a front piece, I, 10 × 1½ × ¾ inches; two side pieces, J, 21½ × 1½ × ¾ inches; and two 6 × ½ × ¾ inches; one back piece, K, 10 × 2 × ½ inches, and a panel, 19½ × 8 × ¼ inches. The side pieces are rebated on the top inside edges ¼ inch down and ½ inch wide and are tenoned into the front piece. The back piece is tenoned into the side pieces 1½ inches from the ends, and a rebate is then cut on the front piece 8 × ½ inches to a depth of ¼ inch.

The underside of the front piece is notched underneath, as indicated above the plan of the framework, and, in addition, the upper portion with panel in position is shown in section. When fitted on the top runner the extension will project 15 inches when pulled out beyond the front of the desk.

The Top of the Desk.

The top of the desk is framed up as shown at Fig. 8, two lengths, L, 42 × 3 × 1 inches; two ends, M, 20 × 3 × 1 inches; and two inner lengths, N, 19 × 3 × ¾ inches. These lengths are framed up to allow for the rebate on the top, ½ inch inside and ¼ inch deep, to take the top panel, 37 × 18 × ¼ inches.

An alternative method of making the frame is to use 2½-inch wide wood for the outside members and glue and brad ¾ × ½-inch fillets to form the rebates. In order that the finished surface of the oak-faced plywood need not be touched, special care should be taken with the rebates.

How Top is fitted to Pedestals.

The top is fitted on the pedestals by slots cut to allow for the projections left on the top of the uprights, but if

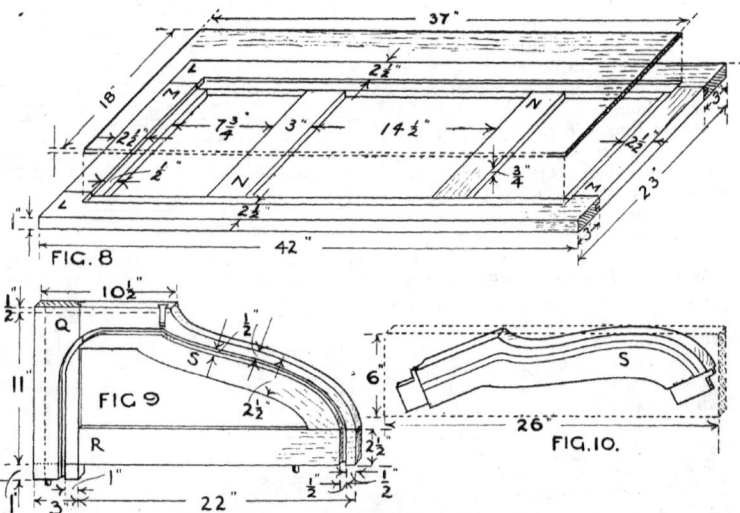

Figs. 8-10.—Details of Upper Portion of Desk.
8. Showing how the top of the desk is framed up. 9. Showing how upper portion of desk is formed by two shaped frames, a top piece and a rail. 10. Details of shaped member.

desired the projections on the inner frames can be planed down and the tops left flush with the bottom surface of the two inner rails, N.

Upper Portion of Desk.

The upper portion of the desk is formed by two shaped frames, as shown at Fig. 9, and a top piece, O, 42 × 11 × 1 inches, and a rail, P, $39\frac{1}{2}$ × $1\frac{1}{4}$ × 1 inches, dovetailed into the sides. The frame is built up with one back piece, Q, $12\frac{1}{2}$ × 3 × 1 inches; one bottom piece, R, $23\frac{1}{2}$ × $2\frac{1}{2}$ × 1 inches; and one shaped member, S, cut as indicated at Fig. 10 from a piece 26 × 6 × 1 inches. The frame when jointed up should measure, with the exception of the bottom projection of 1 inch in height, $11\frac{1}{2}$ inches, which allows of $\frac{1}{2}$ inch for the depth of the groove in the top board, and 25 inches long. The exact shape of the curve is not important, but to enable the curved member to be marked out accurately the whole of this portion of the construction should be marked out full size so that measurements can be taken off. The panelling should correspond with that in the lower part of the desk, grooves being made $\frac{1}{4}$ inch wide and deep and the same distance from the outside.

Grooves for Roll Top.

The grooves for the roll top should be cut after the framing is finished. Beginning $\frac{1}{2}$ inch away from the front end of the frame, the line of the grooves should follow the curve and then follow a straight line $1\frac{3}{4}$ inches from the top. Next mark off a line $1\frac{1}{2}$ inches from the inner edge of the upright, Q, and join the two lines with a curve of 3 inches radius. Draw a line $\frac{1}{2}$ inch away and parallel to give the width of the groove, which is taken to a depth of $\frac{3}{8}$ inch. The whole of this grooving should be done with a chisel and must be most carefully done as the running of the roll top depends on the grooves. The two frames should be placed in position with two $\frac{3}{8}$-inch dowel pins, as shown, on the desk top, so that the groove can be marked off on the lower portions and carried to a depth approximately 4 inches.

Making and fitting Roll Top.

The roll top should be made and fitted at this stage; it is made by strips glued to a stout canvas back as indicated at Fig. 11. The strips, as shown in section at Fig. 12 to a large scale, are each $39\frac{1}{4}$ × $\frac{3}{4}$ × $\frac{1}{2}$ inches and planed down each side to $\frac{3}{8}$ inch at the top. Allowing for a 2-inch wide piece at the bottom and a 1-inch wide length at the back, approximately twenty-three strips will be needed, but this will depend on the exact length of the groove, measured from the desk top level to the back of the strip, P.

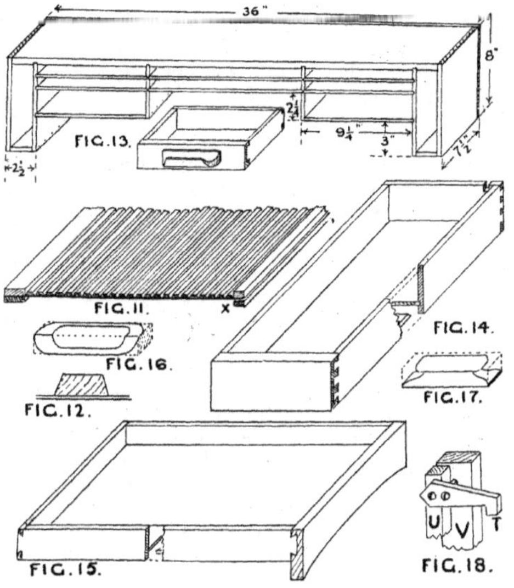

Figs. 11–18.—DETAILS OF ROLL-TOP, DRAWER, AUTOMATIC LOCKING DEVICE, ETC.

11. How the wooden strips for the roll top are glued to canvas. 12. Strip shown in section. 13. Details of inside fitment. 14. The pedestal drawers. 15. The drawer between the pedestals. 16. Handles for the drawer fronts. 17. Handles for the roll top. 18. Enlarged detail of top catch of automatic locking device.

It is a good plan to measure off the length of a piece of tape run along the bottom of the groove and to cut the width of the canvas to this length. The 2-inch strip is now placed at one end and the 1-inch strip at the other and the distance between measured off. It will be seen if twenty-three strips will fit in or if it will be necessary to vary the width of the strips. It is not advisable to have them more than $\frac{3}{4}$ inch wide.

Glue Strips on to Canvas.

Having prepared the strips, glue them down to the canvas, making quite sure that there is perfect contact by turning the whole over and rubbing each strip before the glue sets hard. The end strips are doubled in thickness as shown by gluing on similar pieces on the other side of the canvas backing. The additional strip at the back should be glued on afterwards. The roll top should be placed in position and any adjustment made before final assembling.

Preparing the Fitments.

The various fitments should now be prepared. The inside fitment shown at Fig. 13 is made of $\frac{1}{4}$-inch thick material with the exception of the top, which is $\frac{1}{2}$ inch thick. The measurements shown will be found sufficient to make this portion. The two drawers are made with dovetail sides and a bottom grooved in. The ends of the fitment leave a space between them and the end framing, which should be filled up with suitable lengths as indicated.

The pedestal drawers, as shown at Fig. 14, follow ordinary drawer construction, with 1-inch thick fronts and from $\frac{5}{8}$ to $\frac{1}{2}$-inch thick sides, and ends with $\frac{1}{4}$-inch plywood bottoms. In each case the front of the drawer should be fitted before the rest of the work is carried out. The drawer between the pedestals, shown at Fig. 15, has a shaped front cut from a length approximately $16\frac{1}{2}$ × 4 × 1 inches, the sides of the drawer being $2\frac{1}{2}$ inches wide, runners of $\frac{1}{2}$-inch square section wood being screwed on underneath.

The handles for the drawer fronts should be shaped as indicated at Fig. 16 from pieces measuring 1 inch square in section and 6 inches long. The under edges should be slightly rounded. The two handles for the roll top, as shown at Fig. 17, are shaped from similar pieces; the size felt on top should be about $5\frac{1}{2}$ by $\frac{3}{4}$ inches. The handles for the two small drawers in the desk fitment are shaped from pieces 5 × $1\frac{1}{4}$ × $\frac{7}{8}$ inches and form penholders as well. The handles should be glued on, but it is advisable to screw them from the inside in addition.

Automatic locking Device.

The automatic locking device, shown in the sectional view at Fig. 3 and in the pedestal at Fig. 6, is an interesting part of the construction. The catches, T, are attached to a $\frac{1}{2}$-inch square section length, U, and also to an upright, V, which is fixed to the side of the pedestal. The catches should be about 3 inches long and cut from $\frac{1}{2}$ × $\frac{1}{4}$ inch iron bar. Holes are drilled $\frac{1}{4}$ and $\frac{5}{8}$ inch from the ends, which are filed off as shown. The under portions are filed to leave a notch which catches over the top of the drawers at the back. It will be seen that when the catches are pivoted to the piece V, the extra length in front will cause them to fall, notwithstanding the connecting strip, U. The height of the top of the strip, U, is adjusted so that the back of the roll top will press on it when it is pushed back. It may be necessary to cut a slot in the back of the top drawer as shown at Fig. 14, but the necessary adjustments can be made when fitting. An enlarged detail of the top catch is shown at Fig. 18.

Finishing off Outside Surfaces.

It is suggested that the final adjustments of the various parts are carried out after the work is assembled, but it will be as well to finish off all outside surfaces and apply a coating of glaze or wax polish to the separate parts beforehand. The pedestals have to be completed with a plinth of 4¼ × ½-inch wood, with the top outer corners rounded. The desk top should be bevelled off on the outside edges and slightly rounded on the corners as also the top board, O. The corners of the shaped pieces, S, may also be slightly rounded. The upper part rests on the desk top, but is prevented from movement by dowel pins as shown. This allows of the whole of the top being easily removed in case of necessity and is the easiest method of construction.

When fitting the Drawers.

When fitting in the drawers a strip of thin wood is bradded on the front of the pieces, G, as indicated at W in Fig. 6; the strips need not be longer than 6 inches and are set back 1 inch from the front to prevent the drawers being pushed back too far. When all adjustments are completed, and the locking device acts properly when the roll top is moved, the back can be framed up with 3 × ¾-inch framing fitted with plywood panelling. It will also be necessary to provide strips on each side to continue the outside projection of the desk top on the bottom of the pieces Q.

TIME, LABOUR AND MONEY SAVING IDEAS

WHEN HANGING PICTURES OR MIRRORS

Very often when changing the position of pictures or medium-sized wall mirrors, it may be difficult to get the picture to hang at the right angle. With the nail or hook generally farther away from the screw-eyes in the frame, a longer wire or cord, and a different wall angle of the frame desirable, it is frequently necessary to change the eyes, which procedure would require a bit of doubtful experiment. Simply

slip a small cork between the wire and frame back, close to the eye. Move it until the frame hangs on the wire at the desired angle. The cork is never visible, and will stay there securely. A nick can be cut or made in the small end of the cork for the wire.

TIP FOR REMOVING VARNISHED WALLPAPER

When removing varnished wallpaper, it will be found that by wetting the surface with water, then rubbing it with a file card, the surface will be scratched sufficiently to allow the paper to be soaked off.

It is essential that the paper be wetted before using the file card, otherwise you will inhale the particles of varnish. Hot water is best to use on the paper after it has been scratched with the file card.

PLATE CLOTHS

Plate cloths are easy to make and are excellent for imparting a brilliant polish to silver and plated articles. Select a piece of very soft material and boil it for five minutes in a pint of milk to which has been added 1 oz. of powdered ammonia. Place it for a moment in cold water. Then wring out and dry rapidly before a fire. A cloth of this kind can be used to rub up plated articles and will do good service until it is very much soiled. Then it may be thoroughly washed and retreated.

GARDEN HOE FROM AN OLD HOUSE SHOVEL

An old house shovel that has worn away at the end need not be thrown away. It can be brought into use as a garden hoe by cutting a half moon shape, as shown in the diagram, and putting on a longer handle.

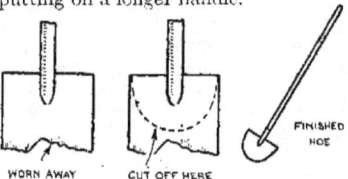

TOUGHENING CHINA AND GLASS

To lessen the damage of breakages it is a good plan to toughen china and glass, and this may be done in the following manner: When the article is new, put it into a pan of cold water placed over a fire. Then bring the water slowly to the boil and keep it boiling for about three hours. Do not remove the article until the water is quite cold. China and glass toughened in this manner will never crack when in contact with hot water.

CAR POLISH

A very good car polish that will throw off the rain is made as follows: Melt 25 ozs. of yellow wax and 25 ozs. of ceracin using gentle heat. When melted, stir in 1 oz. of boiled linseed oil and about 30 ozs. of turpentine, the mass on cooling being a thick cream. It is applied with a soft flannel and well polished with a dry soft cloth.

HANDY HOME-MADE SEAT

Comfortable seats properly padded and cushioned for picnicking, etc., are not only a luxury, but a necessity, due to damp ground. One is often needed when such an affair is not readily obtainable. The illustration shows a neat and comfortable seat, made at a moment's notice. One end of an empty orange crate is used for the base or bottom. The top is a piece of rubber cut from an old motor-car inner tube, while the padding consists of several old sugar sacks. The rubber is securely tacked to the edges of the crate end, and the overlapping portions again tacked to the bottom.

A BOOT-MENDING TIP

When fixing a rubber heel (fixed pattern) which is too large for the leather heel of the boot or shoe, do not attempt to shave off the overhanging piece as the knife cuts will show, it being impossible to cut rubber and leave as fine a surface as is obtained by the "moulding" practice followed by manufacturers. Instead, cut a V-shape out from centre of heel and squeeze sides together before fixing to the heel.

WHEN TAKING DELIVERY OF SAND OR BALLAST

When sand or ballast is to be tipped, say into one's garden or un-made-up road, do not allow it to be tipped direct on to the earth, subsoil, gravel or other loose surface, as if this is done the sand, etc., will become mixed and spoiled, and the underlying surface will also suffer. Instead, first roughly level the site and then spread a square of disused linoleum. This, with care, will give an excellent working surface when the time comes for material to be shovelled up.

HOME-MADE WINES

Home-made wines are, roughly speaking, those prepared from fruit, etc., other than grapes. There are very many recipes which have been handed down from family to family and which make excellent wine. We give in this article a useful selection of recipes that are fairly easy to prepare.

Sloe Wine.

Sloe wine to be really satisfactory should be made with the addition of spirits, although this can be dispensed with if preferred. One good recipe requires the following ingredients:—

1 gallon of sound ripe sloes.
1 gallon of water.
4 lbs. of preserving sugar.
½ pint of brandy.
½ oz. of isinglass.

When the sloes have been picked they should be thoroughly washed and put in a tub. One gallon of boiling water is then poured over them, after which they should be covered and left for about a week, stirring once or twice daily. At the end of the week add the 4 lbs. of preserving sugar and when dissolved pour the mixture into a clean cask or jar. When fermentation has ceased add the ½ pint of brandy to give body. The ½ oz. of isinglass is then placed in a muslin bag and tied to the bung, and the cask closed tightly. It is best kept for a year before bottling.

If it is preferred to dispense with the brandy, then the procedure is slightly different. Damsons or elderberries should be mixed with the sloes in the proportion of one to four. The fruit should be washed, placed in a strong vessel and bruised. Allow 1 gallon of boiling water to each 8 lbs. of fruit. Strain off the liquor in two days' time and add 2½ lbs. of fine sugar to each gallon. Place in a cask, which must be close-stopped, and keep in a cool cellar for a year before bottling, when a lump of sugar should be added to each bottle. The wine is ready for use in about another two months.

Another Sloe Wine Recipe.

Another simple and inexpensive sloe wine recipe is to gather the ripe sloes, remove all stalks and leaves and then place alternate layers of sloes and sugar in a whisky bottle. First put in a good layer of sloes, then two tablespoonfuls of sugar and continue until the bottle is full. Cork down and place on one side for about a month until the sloes have shrivelled and sunk to the bottom.

The wine is then drawn off and corked down and left for an indefinite period—the longer the better.

Elderberry Wine.

Elderberry wine is another very popular home-made variety and there are several good recipes. The berries should be gathered on a dry day and should be ripe and fresh. Remove all stalks and measure in a tub or earthenware pan.

Next pour boiling water on them to the proportion of 2 gallons of water to 3 of berries, press the berries down in the liquor, cover closely and leave until the following day.

The juice should then be strained through a sieve or cloth, after which squeeze from the berries any remaining liquid. Measure the whole and for every gallon add 3 lbs. of sugar, ¾ oz. of cloves and 1 oz. of ginger. Boil for twenty minutes, keeping the liquid thoroughly skimmed.

When it has cooled down to just above milk-warm pour into a dry, sweet cask, which should be absolutely filled, when a large spoonful of new yeast mixed with a very small quantity of the wine is finally added. If only a small quantity of wine is being made, large stone bottles can be used instead of casks.

Another Elderberry Wine Recipe.

Obtain the following ingredients:—

7 lbs. of elderberries.
3 gallons of water.

For each gallon of liquid obtain:—

3 lbs. of loaf sugar.
1 lb. of raisins.
½ oz. of ground ginger.
6 cloves.
¼ pint of brandy.
½ teaspoonful of yeast.

The berries should be carefully stripped from the stalks, the boiling water poured over them and then left to stand for twenty-four hours. They should then be bruised and drained through a jelly bag or hair sieve.

The liquid obtained should be measured and the ingredients mentioned above, except the brandy and yeast, added to each gallon, in a preserving pan. Boil gently for one hour, skimming as necessary. Before stirring in the yeast allow the liquid to become milk-warm, then pour into a clean, dry cask. The bung hole should be covered with a folded cloth and the cask left undisturbed for a fortnight, when the brandy should be stirred in, the cask bunged tightly and left for six months before bottling.

And Another.

Add 2 quarts of cold water to every quart of elderberries and boil very gently for three quarters of an hour, bruising the fruit with a wooden spoon. Drain the liquid through a jelly bag, add ¾ lb. of lump sugar to every quart of juice obtained and bring to the boil again, this time for an hour. Some Jamaica peppers, root ginger and cloves should be tied in a cloth and put in the liquid while it is boiling.

At the end of the hour remove the spices, allow the liquid to cool to blood-heat, then add yeast on a piece of toast. When the liquid ceases to work or hiss the wine can be put into bottles, which should not be tightly corked for a few days. The longer this wine is kept before using, the better it is.

Rhubarb Beer.

A simple rhubarb beer which is ready for use in about twelve hours is as follows:—

Obtain about a dozen thick stalks of rhubarb, wash them and cut into short pieces. Next cut a medium-sized lemon into slices, and bruise 2 ozs. of ginger. Add these to the rhubarb together with 1 oz. of cream of tartar and 2 lbs. of brown sugar. Two gallons of boiling water should then be poured over the ingredients, which should then be covered over. Leave until lukewarm when ½ oz. of yeast dissolved in a little of the liquid should be added, allowing it to ferment for eight hours before skimming and bottling.

Rhubarb Wine.

Obtain the following ingredients:—

10 lbs. of rhubarb.
6 lbs. of best white sugar.
2 gallons of cold filtered water.
2 lemons.
Powdered ginger.
1 oz. of isinglass.
Glassful of brandy.

To prepare the rhubarb, wipe each stick with a damp cloth, then cut into pieces about 2 inches long and place in a deep, wooden tub. The rhubarb should now be crushed to a pulp and the water poured over it. Next roll 6 lbs. of white sugar and sift it into the tub with the grated rind and juice of the lemons and as much powdered ginger as will cover a shilling.

The isinglass should now be dissolved in the glassful of brandy and added to the mixture.

Leave the mixture in the tub for three days, stirring it well three or four times a day. It should then be pressed through a sieve and replaced in the tub. Fermentation should have begun by this time and it should start to stop in from five to six days, when the film or crust that has risen to the surface should be removed, the liquor drained off and poured into a wooden cask. The cask should be bunged in about a fortnight's time—more sugar can be added before this is done if the liquor tastes too sour. A nice colour can be obtained by adding the strained juice of black currants. It is essential that the cask should be brim full before bunging. Bottling off should be carried out in about six months' time, and the wine left in the bottles for a further six months before use.

Dandelion Wine.

A simple wine that has many beneficial properties in the spring is that prepared from dandelions. The dandelion is a blood cleanser and acts as an aperient. To prepare the wine, gather 1 quart of dandelion flowers and lay them out to dry. Boil for half an hour with ½ gallon of water, then strain and add 1 lb. of sugar to each gallon of juice and boil again. As soon as the sugar is dissolved pour the liquor into an earthenware pan, add a little yeast on a piece of toast, let it stand for about three days until it has worked sufficiently, then add ½ pint of brandy to each gallon of juice. Put in a stone jar, leaving it to stand for two months before bottling.

Cowslip Wine.

For an effective cowslip wine obtain the following ingredients :—

4 quarts of cowslip flowers.
6 lbs. of powdered sugar.
2 gallons of water.
Lemons.

First put the sugar in the water and boil for forty minutes, removing any scum as it rises. Then pour into a tub to cool and add the rinds of the lemons. When cold add the cowslip flowers, with the juice of the lemons. Allow to stand in the tub for two days, stirring every two or three hours. Then put in a barrel for about a month before bottling, when a lump of sugar should also be added to each bottle. If brandy is added it will be an improvement.

Another Cowslip Wine Recipe.

Another cowslip wine requires the following ingredients :—

Cowslip pips.
Water.
Lump sugar.
Seville orange.
Lemon.
Yeast.
Brandy.

First add 3 lbs. of lump sugar to every gallon of water, and boil for half hour, removing any scum as it rises. When the liquid has cooled down add a crust of bread dipped in thick yeast and allow to ferment in a tub for thirty-six hours.

Next into the cask put, for every gallon, the peel of 2 and the rind of 1 lemon, and the peel and rind of 1 Seville orange, and 1 gallon of cowslip pips, finally pouring the liquid on to them. Stir carefully at intervals every day for a week, then add a bottle of brandy to every 5 gallons of liquor. Closely stop the cask and stand for six weeks before bottling.

Bilberry Wine.

Obtain the following ingredients :—
4 gallons of bilberries.
6 gallons of cold water or 3 gallons of water and 3 gallons of cider.
10 lbs. of good, moist sugar.
½ gallon of brandy.
2 ozs. of powdered ginger.
2 ozs. of powdered tartar.
Handful of lavender and rosemary leaves.

The berries should be picked when they are quite ripe and on a very dry day. Weigh the fruit after removing leaves and stalks. To the 4 gallons of fruit add either 6 gallons of cold water, or 3 gallons of water and 3 gallons of cider. Add also the 10 lbs. of moist sugar and allow to ferment in an open tub until all working has ceased. The remaining ingredients can now be added after which the liquor should be left for a further forty-eight hours before straining carefully through a hair sieve into a clean cask. Lay the bung lightly over the bung-hole until the working has ceased altogether and no hissing sound can be heard. The cask can then be tightly bunged and the liquid bottled off after three months. The wine is best kept in the bottle for six or eight months before use.

Bullace Wine.

A good recipe for bullace wine is as follows :—

Put 8 gallons of ripe bullaces in a wooden tub and pour on 8 gallons of boiling water, and allow to soak for five days, stirring frequently with a wooden rod. Then add 3 lbs. of preserving sugar for every gallon of liquid. When this has dissolved strain the liquid and pour into a cask, adding 1 quart of brandy or gin to every 3 gallons. The wine should be left for a year in the cask before bottling.

A rather simpler recipe for bullace wine is to place 4 lbs. of bullaces in a stone vessel, pour on 1 gallon of water that has been boiled and allowed to become cold, and leave for ten days, stirring at frequent intervals. After straining add 4 lbs. of sugar to every gallon of juice, leave for a further ten days, then remove any scum which may appear. Finally bottle, leaving the corks loose for six months before corking down tightly.

Apple Wine.

A simple recipe for apple wine for immediate use is to cut up 1 lb. of apples into quarters, add ½ lb. of sugar and then pour on ½ gallon of boiling water. Leave the mixture to get cold, then pulp the apples, pour the fluid over the pulp, let it stand for an hour and strain before bottling.

Another apple wine recipe is as follows :—

Add 2 gallons of cold water to 10 lbs. of apples which have been bruised and allow to stand until all the goodness is out of the apples and it begins to ferment. After straining through a bag or sieve add 6 lbs. of candy-sugar to each gallon of liquid. Then add a little bruised ginger and some cloves. The liquid should now be left to stand for nine or ten days, stirring three times a day. The next step is to pour it into a barrel, and when fermentation has ceased add 1 lb. of lump sugar in the barrel and fasten up. Bottling should be undertaken when the wine has cleared.

Parsnip Wine.

Only good, sound parsnips should be used, and they should be cut into strips about the size of a middle finger before being weighed. For every 4 lbs. of parsnips add 1 gallon of water and boil until tender in a large pan or kettle. Next strain carefully through a large-holed sieve, care being taken to ensure that none of the fibrous vegetable passes through the sieve. Now measure the liquid again and to every gallon add ½ oz. of cream of tar, stir for several minutes and mix in 3 lb. of loaf sugar.

For every 3 gallons add a teaspoonful of fresh yeast spread on a piece of toast. This should be added when the liquid has cooled to 85° F. The pan should now be covered with a cloth and left for about a fortnight until fermentation has ceased. Stir every day, and keep in a warm, even temperature, removing the yeast crust as it rises.

The wine can be poured into a dry cask when all the yeast has risen and the wine is thoroughly skimmed. Do not fill the cask but leave the level about 3 inches from the bung-hole. As the froth appears the wine should be stirred, the cask being bunged down when all is still. Bottling should not be carried out for a year.

Primrose Wine.

To 6 quarts of fresh primrose blossoms (without stalks) add 2 quarts of cowslip pips. Then in a pan put 7½ lbs. of loaf sugar, ½ oz. of powdered ginger, and 2½ gallons of soft water. Boil for three-quarters of an hour, skimming frequently, then add the well-beaten whites of three eggs to clarify the liquid and continue boiling and skimming until perfectly clear. While the liquid is still boiling pour it over the flowers. Stir well and add 1½ lbs. of stoned and chopped raisins and the juice of three lemons. Then cover the jar and allow to infuse for three and a half days, after which it should be strained and filtered into a cask, which should be completely filled. Put only a slight covering over the bung-hole and leave until fermentation has ceased. Finally pour in ¾ pint of brandy in which has been dissolved ⅛ oz. of isinglass. Leave the cask bunged for a year before bottling, and leave for a further six months before using.

Carrot Wine.

A wine that is best made up in the autumn months is carrot wine. Boil 7 lbs. of carrots in 4 gallons of water until soft (not mushy), then strain off the liquor and add 10 or 12 lbs. of lump sugar. Now boil the liquid for an hour, stirring as required, and when it has cooled down to 85° F. add two tablespoonfuls of yeast spread on toast. The wine should then be allowed to stand for ten days, stirring and skimming every day before being put into a vessel, which should be closed up for six to twelve months.

Colt's-foot Wine.

Put 20 quarts of colt's-foot flowers into a wooden tub. Then pour on to them a boiling liquor consisting of 5 gallons of water, 15 lbs. of sugar, the juice of five lemons, the juice of five sweet oranges, a handful of raisins and the thin rind of three lemons and three oranges. Stir well and leave until nearly cold, when fermentation should be started by adding some yeast spread upon a small piece of toast. The wine can be casked in four days' time, but should not be bunged until fermentation has ceased.

Turnip Wine.

To every 3 quarts of turnips, washed and sliced, add 4 quarts of water and boil. Add the pulp of as many Seville oranges as there are gallons of water. To every 9 gallons add ¼ lb. of hops. Boil all gradually for half an hour, then take out the turnips, add the orange peel and put in 3 lbs. of sugar to every gallon of wine. Put in a cask with the peel, and cork. The wine will be ready to drink in a year's time.

Bramble Blossom Wine.

The following ingredients are required :—
- ½ peck of bramble blossoms.
- 1 gallon of water.
- 1 gill brandy or gin.
- Yeast.
- Sugar according to quantity of liquor.

Boil the water and leave until luke-warm and pour over the blossoms which have been placed in a tub. Add the yeast, stir well and cover over. Leave for a week, stirring several times a day, then strain. To each gallon of strained liquid add from 1 to 2 lbs. of sugar and put into a cask. Do not bung until fermentation has ceased, then leave for a week before adding the brandy. Leave the wine for five or six months before drawing off into another vessel and bottle in two or three days.

Black Cherry Wine.

To each gallon of liquid obtain the following ingredients :—
- 24 lbs. of small black cherries.
- 2 lbs. of sugar.

The cherries should first be bruised (without breaking the stones), then stir well in the water and leave to stand for twenty-four hours, before straining through a sieve. The sugar can next be added, the liquid stirred again and left for another twenty-four hours. The clear liquor should then be poured into a cask and closely bunged when fermentation has ceased. The wine is ready for bottling in six months' time and will keep for about a year.

Black Currant Wine.

To 3 quarts of black currant juice put the same quantity of unboiled water. Add 3 lbs. of pure moist sugar to every 3 quarts of the liquor and put into a cask, keeping a small quantity back for filling up. The cask should be placed in a warm, dry room and the liquor allowed to ferment. When fermentation has ceased, skim off the refuse and fill up the cask with the liquid that was put on one side for the purpose. To every 40 quarts of liquor add 3 quarts of brandy, when working has ceased. Bung the cask tightly for nine months before bottling the wine. Drain the thick part through a jelly bag until it is clear and bottle that. The wine is best kept for about a year before use.

Damson Wine.

The fruit should be picked when ripe and dry, only sound fruit being used. The stalks should be removed, the fruit wiped clean and placed in a wooden tub and gently bruised. Do not crack the damson stones, but two or three bitter almonds, blanched and shredded, should be added. To 8 lbs. of fruit pour over 1 gallon of boiling water and cover closely to keep in the steam. Leave to stand for four days, stirring at frequent intervals, before straining off the liquor and adding 3 lbs. or more of sugar to each gallon of juice.

Pour all into a dry, clean cask when the sugar is dissolved and add brandy in the proportion of from 1 to 2 gills to the gallon. The bunghole should only be lightly covered until fermentation has ceased, after which it can be closed up tightly and left undisturbed for about a year. A little isinglass can be used to clear the wine when fermentation is over, if this is considered necessary. The wine can then be bottled, a raisin being placed in each bottle.

Orange Wine.

Peel twelve sweet oranges and put the peel into 1 gallon of water. Simmer until tender, then cut up the twelve oranges and pour the boiling liquid, after straining, over the oranges. Leave to stand for two weeks, stirring several times a day. After straining again add 4 lbs. of lump sugar and leave for four days, stirring each day, before bottling. When fermentation has ceased in about three months' time a little brandy may be added.

Raisin Wine.

Put 8 lbs. of fresh raisins in a tub to every gallon of spring water and leave for a month, stirring thoroughly every day, then press the raisins in a horse-hair bag until as much liquid as possible has been squeezed out. Put the liquor into a cask and when hissing has ceased pour in a bottle of the best brandy. Close stop the cask for a year. The liquid should now be racked, i.e., the contents drawn off into a tub, where it is exposed to the air for a while if possible before being put back into a fresh, clean cask. It should be racked off without the dregs, which should be filtered through a bag of flannel of three or four folds and the clear added to the remainder, and pour in 1 or 2 quarts of brandy according to the size of the vessel. Stop up the cask and leave for three years, when it can be either bottled or drunk fresh from the cask.

Ginger Wine.

Boil together for half an hour the following ingredients :—
- ¼ lb. of best ginger (bruised).
- 12 lbs. of sugar.
- Thin rinds of six large lemons.
- 14 quarts of water.

When the liquor has cooled to milk-warm pour into a clean, dry cask with the juice of the lemons and ½ lb. of sun raisins. Add one large spoonful of thick yeast and stir the wine every day for ten days. When fermentation has ceased add 1 oz. of isinglass and 1 pint of brandy. Leave closely bunged for two months before bottling; if too sweet at the end of two months leave longer in the cask. If cider fresh from the press is substituted for the water a very superior wine will be the result.

How to Make a Small Transformer

The Essentials of a Transformer.

A TRANSFORMER consists essentially of a primary winding, and a secondary or output winding wound on an iron core which forms part of a closed magnetic circuit. The primary winding is connected to the supply mains and the secondary or output winding to the apparatus for which it is designed.

Power is transmitted from the primary winding to the secondary winding whenever a current is drawn from the secondary. When there is no current in the secondary winding, the power taken from the supply mains by the primary winding is negligible in small transformers. Therefore a transformer primary may be permanently connected to the supply mains without any appreciable power consumption.

The principles of construction of all small transformers is the same, but they differ in such details as the size of stampings, number of turns and arrangement of windings. Where there are several secondary windings and the size of the stampings permits, the different windings are divided into two or more sections on separate bobbins so as to obtain the best linkage between the windings.

Fig. 1.—The Finished Transformer provided with Flexible Leads in place of Terminals.

This method is adopted when the transformer is to be permanently wired to other apparatus.

Fig. 2.—The Essential Components used for the Construction of a Transformer.

Material for Bell Transformers.

The materials for small transformers are obtainable in several standard sizes. The different sizes of stampings and bobbins are known by numbers, but as different manufacturers use different notation for the same thing, the actual sizes are given in the schedules. For a transformer, with an output of 4-6 or 8 volts at 1 ampere, the following material is used:—

40 pairs of No. 15 " Stalloy" stampings, ·014 inch thick (window $1\frac{1}{2} \times \frac{3}{4}$ inch, middle limb $\frac{5}{8}$ inch wide).

1 bakelite bobbin No. 15 with $\frac{5}{8}$ inch square hole.

8 ozs. of 20 S.W.G. enamel covered copper wire for secondary.

6 ozs. of enamel-covered copper wire for primary, the size depending on the mains voltage (see table on p. 1492).

1 pair of cast clamps or 16 inches of $\frac{1}{2} \times \frac{1}{2}$-inch angle iron.

4 steel 2 B.A. screws 1 inch long for clamps.

Short lengths of ·75 mm. systoflex, and empire cloth $1\frac{1}{2}$ inches wide.

6 terminals and ebonite or bakelite terminal block.

The Primary Winding.

The size of wire and the number of turns put on the primary winding depends on the voltage and frequency of the supply. The table on page 1492 gives the necessary data for 50-cycle supplies (the standard frequency), also the maximum primary current which it is necessary to know when a fuse is included in the primary circuit.

Where the voltage of the supply is different from any of the values given in the table, the number of turns may be estimated by multiplying the voltage by twenty. If the frequency is higher than 50, less turns are necessary. Thus, if the frequency is 100, half the number of turns are required, because the reactance is

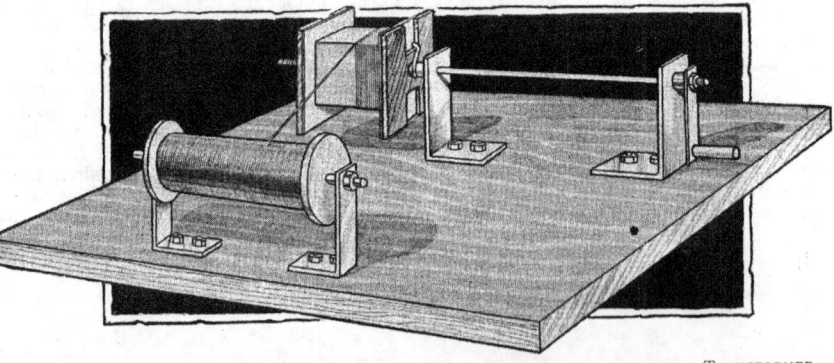

Fig. 3.—A Simple Winding Machine and Reel Carrier rigged up for winding a Transformer.

HOW TO MAKE A SMALL TRANSFORMER

Fig. 4.—PREPARING THE WIRE FOR WINDING.
Before the wire is started on the fine wire coils, a four-strand lead is formed on the end of the wire.

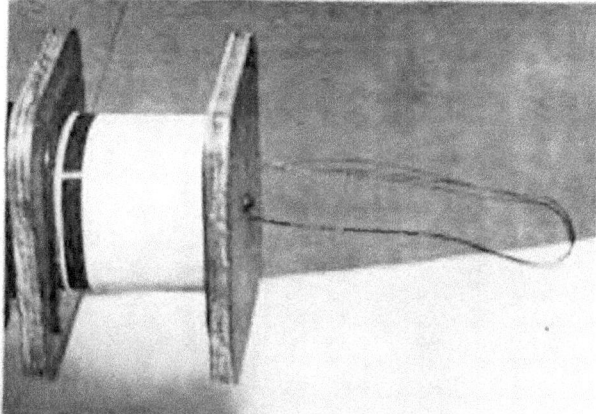

Fig. 5.—FINISHING OFF THE PRIMARY WINDING (1).
The last few turns of the primary winding frequently only partly fill a layer, but this does not matter. Note the use of a sheet of white paper underneath the bobbin to provide a contrast with the black wire and make it easy to follow.

Fig. 6.—FINISHING OFF THE PRIMARY WINDING (2).
This is done with a four-strand lead. Note how the empire cloth, which is used to cover the soldered joint, is tied down with silk thread.

Fig. 7.—MAKING A TAPPING ON THE SECONDARY WINDING OF THE TRANSFORMER.
This is done by soldering a lead on to the wire without cutting the winding.

Fig. 8.—HOW THE JOINT OF THE SECOND TAPPING IS INSULATED WITH EMPIRE CLOTH.
Note how the first tapping has been wound in.

Fig. 9.—THE FINISHED BOBBIN.
Taped up with the leads covered with ·75 mm. systoflex sleeving, ready to receive the stampings.

1491

HOW TO MAKE A SMALL TRANSFORMER

directly proportional to the frequency. For a lower frequency, such as 25 cycles, a larger iron core must be used or the number of turns becomes excessive with consequent high copper losses.

Supply Volts.	Max. Primary Current (Amps.).	No. of Turns.	S.W.G.
100	·1	2,000	32
110	·091	2,200	33
120	·083	2,400	33
200	·050	4,000	36
210	·048	4,200	36
220	·045	4,400	36
230	·043	4,600	37
240	·042	4,800	37
250	·040	5,000	37

Winding Jig.

Before commencing the winding a wooden jig is made to support the bakelite bobbin. These bobbins are made necessarily very thin to accommodate the maximum amount of wire on a given core, and they must be provided with some extra support during winding or the cheeks will bulge out and prevent the stampings from being properly assembled. The jig shown in Fig. 13 consists of a square piece of wood ⅝ inch square and 2½ inches long with two plywood cheeks ¼ inch thick. The cheeks of the jig may be larger than those of the bobbin so that the same jig may be used for other sizes of bobbins. One cheek of the jig is screwed to the wooden core and the other has a square hole made to fit tightly on the wooden core. The excess length of the core is utilised to hold the jig in a lathe chuck or other winding arrangement. The wooden cheeks are provided with slots and holes to enable the ends of the different windings to be brought out where necessary. When the winding has been made the removable cheek is taken off and the bakelite bobbin pushed into position and the cheek replaced and firmly pressed home. If the removable cheek is not a tight fit on the core, two screws are put in to hold the cheek firmly against the bobbin.

Winding the Primary.

The primary winding is put on first, because as it is a fine wire coil the length of the turns must be kept as short as possible to minimise the losses due to the higher resistance of the wire. The primary is also wound close to the core to obtain the maximum choking effect when the transformer is unloaded. Before starting the actual winding a flexible lead is formed on the end of the wire. This is done by doubling a length of the wire twice and soldering the ends together, as shown in Fig. 4. It is essential to do this to provide a strong flexible lead which

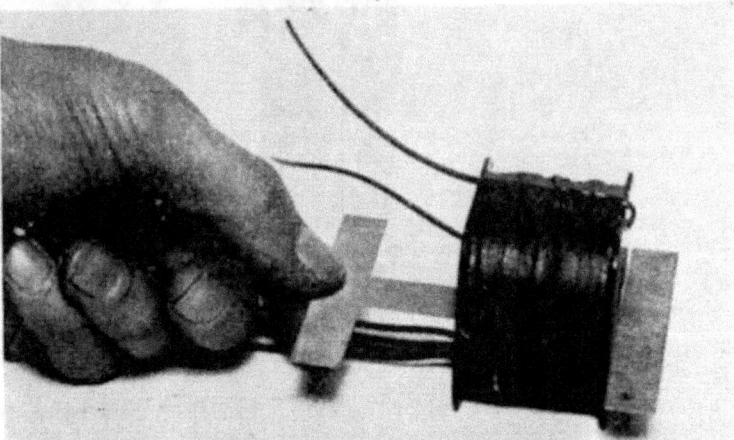

Fig. 10.—Assembling the Stampings. First Stage.
Take care to keep the paper-covered sides of the stampings all the same way up.

Fig. 11.—Assembling the Stampings. Second Stage.

Fig. 12.—Assembling the Stampings. Third Stage.

will not easily break off at the entrance to the hole in the cheek of the bobbin. The next step is to draw the flexible end of the wire through the hole in the bobbin shown in Fig. 13 so as to leave just less than one turn of the four-strand wire inside the bobbin. The soldered joint is then insulated with a small channel of empire cloth and the winding commenced.

Some difficulty may be experienced at first in keeping the turns even on the square core when the winding is done by hand, but after the first few layers and paper insulation have been put on, the winding becomes more rounded and easier to handle. Once the knack has been accomplished it will be found easier to keep the winding even if the bobbin is revolved at a good speed, although when the wire does run back there is more to unwind. It is essential to keep the turns side by side and to put thin (1½ mils) paper between each layer for high voltage coils. Pay particular attention to the ends of the layers. Much space is wasted if the paper is cut too long, and the end turns will slip down to preceding layers if the paper is cut too short.

HOW TO MAKE A SMALL TRANSFORMER

Finishing the Primary.

It almost invariably happens that when the correct number of turns is reached the final layer of wire is only partly wound, as shown in Fig. 5. This does not matter. When this stage is reached the last turn is unwound and a stranded lead is formed on the end of the wire and one turn of the lead is put back on the winding after insulating the soldered joint, as shown in Fig. 6. The finishing end of the primary is brought out through a hole in the cheek of the bobbin. The two ends of the primary are brought through the opposite cheeks, but on the same side of the coil. When the primary has been finished off two layers of empire cloth are put on to insulate it from the secondary, which is now wound on.

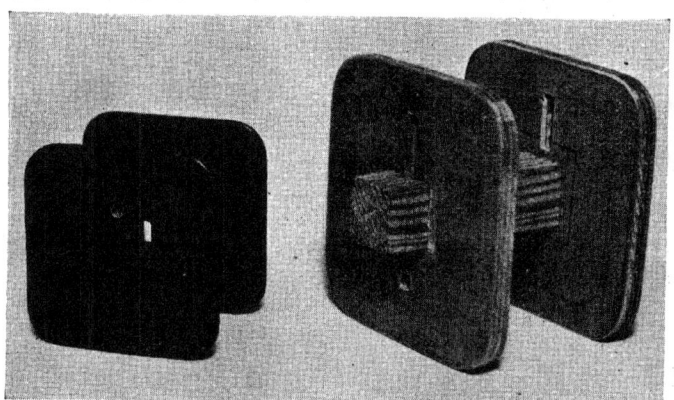

Fig. 13.—The Black Bakelite Bobbin of the Transformer.
Showing the wooden winding jig used to support the bobbin during winding. Note the hole in the bobbin for the start of the primary winding. The size of the holes in the bobbin cheeks should be such that the systoflex sleeving fits in them.

Winding the Secondary.

The secondary winding is started through a hole in the bobbin cheek, but there is no need to provide multistrand leads with this thick gauge. The total number of turns for 8 volts is 170. When 85 turns have been put on, a lead is soldered on, as shown in Fig. 7. After insulating the joint the winding is carried on, winding on either side of the lead. Fig. 8 shows the second tapping, at the 127th turn, being insulated. A piece of ·75 mm. systoflex is put on the lead as far down as it will go and the joint is then lapped with empire cloth. This method of making the tappings on a winding of few thick turns is more economical of space than when each tapping is brought through the bobbin cheek.

Finishing the Coil.

After threading systoflex sleeving on the remaining leads, the secondary leads are bent back over the winding and the coil taped up with empire cloth or black tape, as shown in Fig. 9. The bobbin is now ready to receive the stampings.

Assembling the Stampings.

Figs. 10, 11 and 12 show the order of assembling the stampings. Two of the T-shaped stampings are threaded through the core first, one from each side, as shown in Fig. 11. A U-shaped stamping is laid on next from the opposite side to the second T-stamping and then a U-stamping from the other side (see Fig. 12). The process is then repeated until the bobbin is tightly packed with stampings. It will be noticed that one side of the stampings is covered with very thin paper, and it is important to keep the papered side the same way up throughout so that each stamping is insulated from the next. The purpose of laminating would be nullified if there were no insulation at all between the leaves.

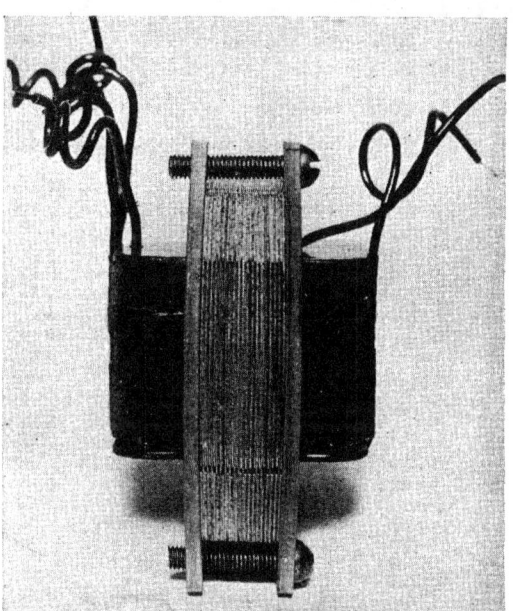

Fig. 14.—How not to clamp the Stampings.
The use of flat strips should be avoided. When tightened up the flat strips bend and produce an unsightly job. This illustration also shows the result of using a bobbin too big for the stampings or allowing the winding to spread the cheeks of the bobbin. The stampings do not close up properly.

For most uses the black oxidised surface of the metal provides sufficient insulation between the laminations.

The object of laminating the iron core is to minimise the eddy currents which would otherwise be set up in the core by the rapidly alternating flux.

Clamps.

When the stampings have been assembled and carefully tapped square and level, a pair of clamps are screwed on to hold the stampings rigid. Fig. 1 shows the transformer finished off with clamps made from $\frac{1}{2} \times \frac{1}{2}$-inch angle-iron $\frac{1}{8}$ inch thick. Nuts may be used instead of tapping a thread in the clamps. One pair of the clamps is provided with fixing holes, and the terminal block, if required, is screwed to the top pair of clamps or fixed between the ends of the clamp.

When the transformer is mounted with the longest side horizontal with angle clamps, as shown in Fig. 1, the limbs of the outside U-stampings are not clamped, so that about two-thirds of the length is cut off. Rectangular clamps, which clamp all four sides of the stampings, are preferable because they prevent the stampings from bulging and so producing an unsightly job.

What to avoid.

Do not use flat strips of metal to clamp the stampings. Fig. 14 shows the result of so doing. Although the strips shown are steel $\frac{1}{8}$ inch thick and $\frac{1}{2}$ inch wide, they bend quite easily when tightened up and produce a very unsightly job. Fig. 14 also shows another defect caused by the cheeks of the bobbin not being properly supported when winding. They have bulged and prevent the stampings from being assembled properly, leaving a small air gap between each, which lowers the efficiency of the iron circuit.

Finishing Touches.

The clamps of the transformer should be enamelled, especially if they are made from angle iron; green and black are suitable colours. The exposed edges of the stampings are given a coat of insulating varnish. Clear brushing cellulose is very suitable for this.

Greenhouses on Dwarf Brick Walls

Fig. 1.—Span-roof Greenhouse, with the Lower Part of the Sides and Ends of Brick. The upper part is of unit construction, bolted together at the corners.

The span-roof greenhouse shown in Fig. 1 has the lower part of the sides and ends of brick. The wooden framework of the upper part is of unit construction, that is, there are separate side, end and roof frames which are bolted and screwed together. Each side and roof frame has two ventilators, or eight in all. One end has a door opening inwards. Dimensions will vary according to requirements or area of the site available. A greenhouse 8 feet wide and 12 feet 4½ inches long, as shown in Figs. 2 and 3, has been selected as one which will meet a popular demand.

All-Brick Sides.

Another style of span-roof house is illustrated in Fig. 21. In this instance the roof rises directly from the top of the brick wall. Plants may be grown in pots standing on shelves, or the building is designed as a forcing house, that is, there is a pair of inside dwarf walls between which and the outer walls are placed the beds. Brick-wall construction may also be adapted to the three-quarter and lean-to roof patterns (see pp. 868 to 872).

Half-Brick Wall.

The brick wall and its footings are shown in Fig. 6. It is a half-brick wall, that is, 4½ inches thick with 9-inch footings, or row of headers which is continued across the door opening. The wall is to be approximately 3 feet high above its concrete foundation, so that, in addition to the footings, eleven courses of bricks are required. Each side course is made up of sixteen bricks and each side-footing thirty-two bricks, or a total of 416 for the two side walls. The two door-end walls consist of eleven courses each, of three and a half bricks, and a footing of twenty-one bricks, or a total of ninety-eight, ignoring the corner bricks which are common to both sides and ends. For the other end-wall ten and a half bricks are allowed for each course, or a total, with footings, of 137 to the nearest whole number. The grand total for the walls is, therefore, 651 bricks, or, say, 675, to allow for wastage.

Preparing the Site.

The method of preparing the foundation and building a wall is described and illustrated in detail on pp. 993 to 996. With the greenhouse shown in Fig. 1 the whole of the site is dug to a depth of 1 foot. The floor may be finished in cement or paved with bricks or stone. When the cement has hardened, the header course of footings is laid to an overall dimension 4½ inches wider and longer than the overall dimensions of the walls, or 8 feet 7½ inches and 13 feet respectively.

Door Frame.

Before proceeding further with the bricklaying, the door posts with their sill and head are erected (Fig. 4) in the middle where the door-end walls are to be built, so as to form a guide for the correct size of door-opening. All timber is of red deal. The door posts are of 4 × 2 inch material and are tenoned at the foot into the open mortises of the sill (Figs. 18 and 19), which is 4 × 3 inches. The door head is tenoned into the posts. This framework

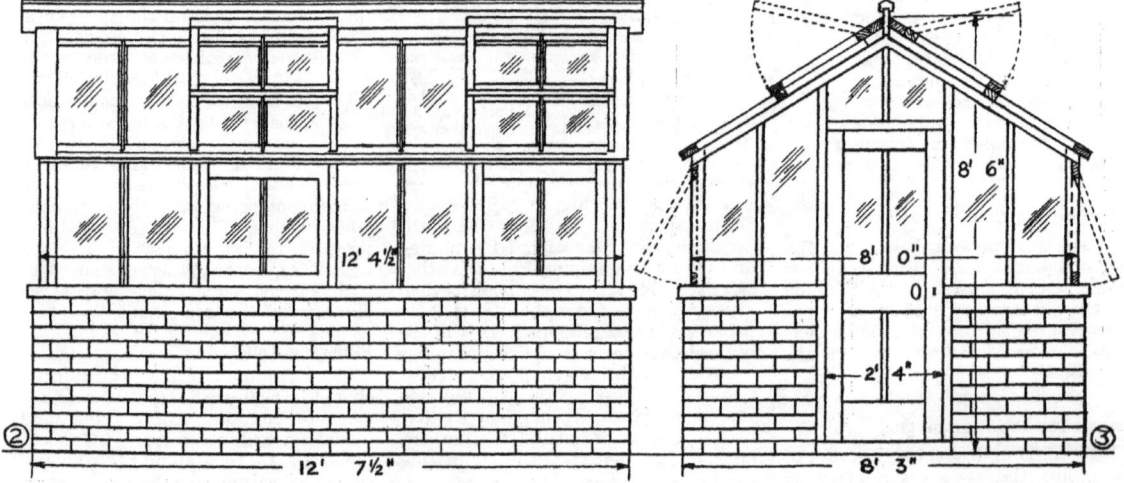

Fig. 2.—Side View of the Greenhouse shown in Fig. 1.   *Fig. 3.*—Leading Dimensions of the Door-end Elevation.

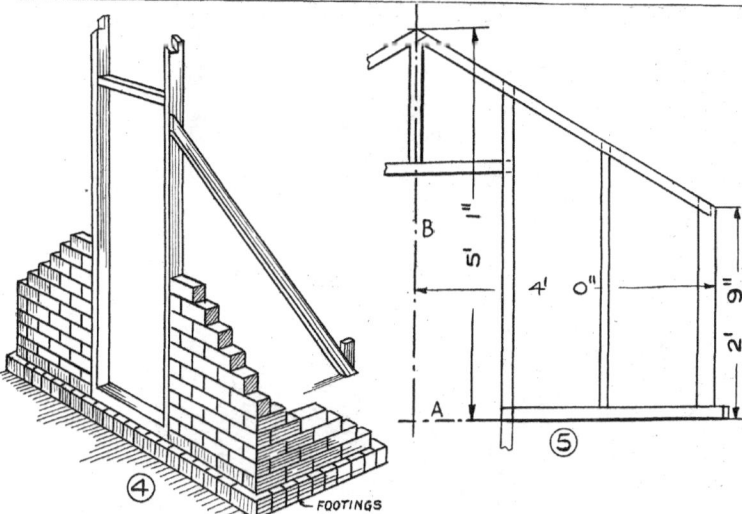

Fig. 4.—After the Brick Footings are laid, the Door-end Frame is erected in position as a Guide for the building of the Wall.

Fig. 5.—Roof-frame Diagram from which the Lengths of the Wooden Framework, also the Bevels of the Joints are obtained.

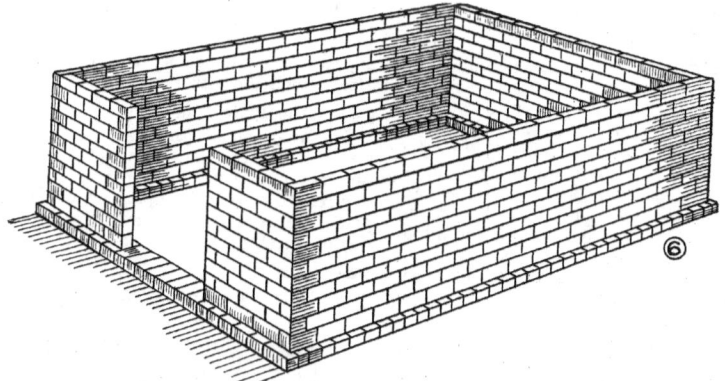

Fig. 6.—The Complete Dwarf Wall with its Footings.

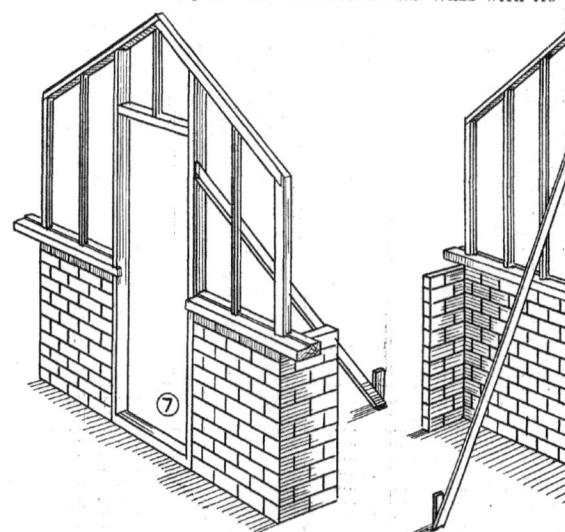

Fig. 7.—Door-end Frame supported on its Wall. Sufficient Length of Wall Plate is left for cutting the End Mitres.

Fig. 8.—Plain-end Frame ready for plugging to the Wall.

is designed to accommodate a ready-made door 6 feet × 2 feet 4 inches.

Roof Frame Diagram.

In order to complete the door frame, a diagram (Fig. 5) is prepared from which the exact length of the door posts, wall plates and rafters are obtained, also the bevels of all tenons and other joints. For a full-size diagram, a piece of paper or boarding, 5 feet × 5 feet 6 inches, is necessary. If this is not available, a half-size diagram is a good compromise. Draw the base line A and erect the perpendicular B. Set out half the width of the door-opening from the framework already assembled, then a half-width of the greenhouse of 4 feet and a height of 2 feet 9 inches from the base of the wall plate to the outer corner of the door post. The height of line B is 5 feet 1 inch, thus giving a roof slope of about 30 degrees. The sash bars are 2 × 1½ inches, the corner post 3 × 2 inches, with the larger dimension showing. The rafter is 3 × 2 inches, with the smaller dimension showing.

Finishing the Door Frame.

The door frame is completed by cutting the top laps of the door posts (Fig. 4). The bevel of the shoulders is taken from the roof frame diagram. The door frame is provided with a strut so that it may be held upright while building the wall.

Building the Wall.

The brick end of the greenhouse is 8 feet 3 inches long, or 3 inches wider than the wood framework above, measuring over the corner posts. Assuming that the door opening is 2 feet 4 inches wide and the thickness of the posts is 2 inches each, then the width over the door posts is 2 feet 8 inches. This dimension, deducted from 8 feet 3 inches and the result halved, gives the length of the wall on each side of the door, or 2 feet 9½ inches. With a little extra allowance beyond the usual ⅜ inch for the mortar joints, there should be no difficulty in working to this dimension when laying the bottom course of three stretchers and a header. In order to accommodate sixteen stretchers in the side wall this is 12 feet 7½ inches long. The other end-wall, which is 8 feet 3 inches long, is built with courses each of ten and a half bricks. The brickwork then appears as shown in Fig. 6.

Door-End Frame.

While the brickwork is setting, the door and other end-frame are put together (Figs. 7 and 8). The wall plate is 5½ × 3 inches and is flush with the back of the brickwork (Fig. 11). It is tenoned into and lapped round the door post as shown in Figs. 14 and 15. The tenon is marked out so that it clears the screws on the door-hinge side, while the end grain of the tenon is covered by the door fillet (Fig. 10A). Cut sufficient length of wall plate to allow for the end mitres with the side wall-plates (Figs. 7, 9 and 10C). Mark out the mortises for the sash bars (Fig. 11) and corner posts (Figs. 9 and 10C) and arrange that the rebate for the glass comes in the same straight line parallel with the edge of the wall plate. The ends of the rafters are lapped to the corner posts.

The door-end frame is knocked apart because it is more conveniently assembled finally after the door frame is fixed to the brickwork.

Plain-End Frame.

The rafters and corner posts for the plain-end frame (Fig. 8) are marked out at the same time as those for the door-end frame. The wall plate and rafters are set out for five equally spaced 2 × 1½-inch sash bars. In order to obtain the correct lengths of the sash bars and the bevel of the tenon shoulders, the appropriate lines are added to the roof-slope diagram (Fig. 5). This end-frame is put together ready for fixing to the brickwork in one unit and held in position by a strut, as shown in Fig. 8.

Fixing the Door Frame.

The door frame is released from its strut in order to prepare the brickwork fixings. These consist of three wood plugs each side (Fig. 16). Mark the centre line of the door post on the brickwork, and with a plugging chisel rake out a slot in the mortar joints about 2 inches wide and 3 inches deep. Prepare deal wedges as shown in Fig. 17, at least an inch longer than required for the depth of slot, drive home the wedges and saw off flush. Chisel a pair of slots in the footings for a pair of wedges for the door sill. Replace the door frame, test with a plumb line and mark on the inside centre line of the plugs. Drill the posts and sill and secure with nails or screws.

Patent Plugs.

A neat job is made of the door frame and other fixings if patent plugs are used, such as the Rawlplug or Metlex, particularly in those positions where it is necessary to drill the brickwork because a mortar joint is not available.

Priming Coat.

Before fixing, all woodwork should be given a coat of priming or other paint so that surfaces concealed by the brickwork have some protection from the weather. Plugs may be painted or creosoted before being driven into position.

Completing the Door-End Frame.

The two short wall-plates are tenoned into the door posts temporarily and the top brick course is examined for suitable mortar joints between the sash bar and corner post, also between the sash bar and door post (Fig. 20). Two plugs having been inserted in the brickwork on each side of the door opening, the wall-plate tenons are inserted finally in the door-post mortises. The centre lines of the plug positions are transferred to the wall plates, which are now nailed or screwed to the brickwork. Next, the sash bars and corner posts are erected (Fig. 12), after which the rafters are added.

Fixing the Plain-End Frame.

The plain-end frame having been given a coat of paint, including the underside of the wall plate, it is secured to four wall plugs, which are placed close to the centre of the first, third, fourth and sixth openings.

Side Frame.

The side frame is built between the

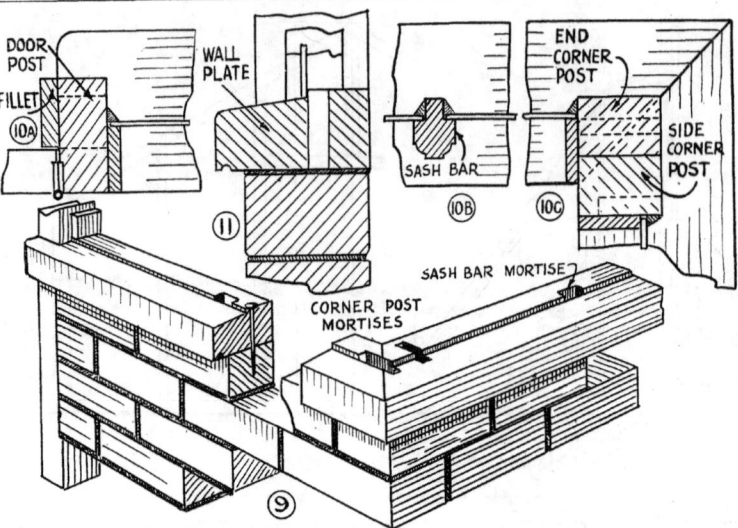

Figs. 9–11.—DETAILS OF CORNER POST, WALL PLATE, ETC.

9. Corner view showing position of corner post and sash-bar mortises, also section through wall plate and top brick course. 10A. Plan of wall plate at door post. 10B. Plan of wall plate at sash bar. 10C. Plan of wall plate at corner posts. 11. Section through wall plate.

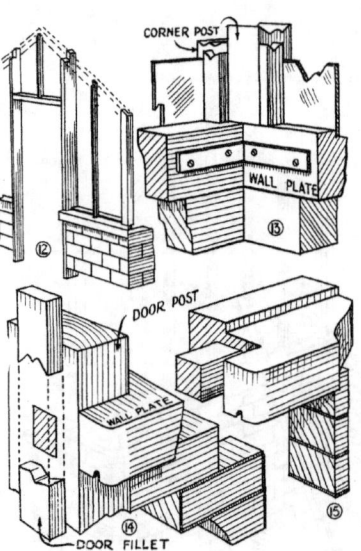

Figs. 12–15.—DETAILS OF DOOR-END FRAME ASSEMBLY.

12. Assembly of door-end frame. 13. Inside view showing wall plate with inside corner plate, also base of corner posts. 14. Outside lap of wall plate with corner post. 15. Wall plate showing tenon for door post mortise.

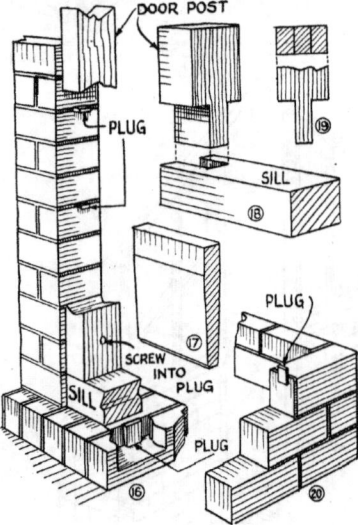

Figs. 16–20.—DETAILS OF WALL PLUGS.

16. Position of wall plugs for door post and sill. 17. Tapered wall plug. 18. Mortise and tenon joint of door post and sill. 19. End view of door post tenon. 20. Corner of wall showing a plug for wall plate of end frame.

GREENHOUSES ON DWARF BRICK WALLS

Figs. 21-24.—Roof Built on Side Walls.
21. Door-end of greenhouse, with roof rising from a 9-inch wall. 22. Joint of end rafter and wall plate. 23. Lap at wall-plate corner. 24. Assembled joint of rafter and wall plate.

end-frames (Figs. 2 and 10C) so that its overall length is obtained by measuring between the corner posts of the two end-frames which have now been erected. The length of side wall-plate required is equal to the distance apart of the two end wall plates. The side frame consists of two corner posts 3×2 inches (with the smaller dimension showing), wall plate $3 \times 5\frac{1}{2}$ inches, top plate 3×2 inches, four sash bars $2 \times 1\frac{1}{2}$-inches (including those for the ventilators), three sash bars $2\frac{1}{2} \times 1\frac{1}{2}$ inches, four ventilator stiles $2 \times 1\frac{1}{2}$ inches, and four ventilator rails $3 \times 1\frac{1}{2}$ inches.

Set out on a length of batten the position of the corner posts, divide it into eight equal parts and mark the positions of the sash bars. With this batten, or marking-rod, set out the mortises in the top plate. Assemble the side frame and hold it in position with a strut, so that it may rest on top of the end wall-plates for the marking of the mitres. Cut the mitres. The side wall plate is then marked for three plugs. Remove the side frame, insert the plugs and replace the side frame in its correct position. Drill two holes through the combined side and end corner posts and secure with $\frac{1}{4}$-inch bolts, and fasten the wall plate at the plug positions. The mitre joint of the wall plate is strengthened with an inside corner plate (Fig. 13).

Roof Frame.

The roof-frame stiles overhang 1 inch each end and the bottom rail projects 2 inches at the eaves (Figs. 2 and 3). It rests on top of the end rafters, and the two roof frames are divided by the ridge board, which runs the full length of the greenhouse and overhangs 3 inches at each end. To facilitate marking-out, add these items to the roof-frame diagram (Fig. 5): (1) A roof-frame stile $1\frac{3}{4}$ inches thick and projecting 2 inches beyond the outer line of the corner post; (2) A ridge board $6 \times 1\frac{1}{2}$ inches projecting 2 inches above the apex of the rafters; (3) A top-rail butting against the ridge board and 4 inches wide, with the outer edge at right angles to the roof slope; (4) A bottom rail 4 inches wide and $1\frac{1}{4}$ inches thick. This rail is $\frac{1}{2}$ inch thinner than the top rail next to the ridge board, because the glass continues over its top surface.

Roof Rails.

The marking-out rod, made for setting-out the wall plate and top rail of the side frames, is used for setting out the positions of the sash bars and ventilator bearers on the top and bottom rails of the roof frame. Keeping the sash bar positions the same as for the side frames, set out on the marking-out rod an overall length 2 inches greater than the length over the end frames. Inside these limits mark the 5-inch width of the roof stiles. At the ventilator positions, allow for a bearer each side 2 inches wide.

Assembling the Roof Frame.

The top and bottom rails are tenoned into the stiles. The top rail is grooved for the glass, or a fillet is added at the same level as the sash bar rebate. With the bottom rail the sash bar is notched in position, so that its rebate is flush with the top surface of the rail. Prepare the two sets of roof framework at the same time. The roof frame is conveniently put together by placing the top rail on the ground against the side of the greenhouse. The ventilator bearers are then framed into this rail. The frame is stood upright and the bottom rail added, after which the stiles are driven on to the tenons of the top and bottom rails.

Ridge and Capping.

The ridge board is marked to notch over the ends of the roof frame, and two parallel lines are marked on it to represent the position of the top rail. Nail on the capping and attach the ridge board to one roof frame with three screws, placed obliquely, one at each end and one in the centre. Lift the roof frame on to the end frames, adjust it to its correct position and hold it with cramps at each end. The stiles of the roof frame are then screwed to the end rafters, after which a similarly assembled roof frame is screwed to the rafters of the other side. The fixing of the two top rails to the ridge board is now completed by standing on steps inside the house. The intermediate sash bars are added last so as to provide a large enough opening for working at the ridge.

Lean-to Greenhouse.

For a lean-to greenhouse, as shown in Fig. 14 on p. 869, the wall plate is fixed to the dwarf wall, as already described for the span-roof pattern. If the back wall is not perpendicular, it is fitted with a packing-piece the full height of the house and tapered as necessary. The adjacent posts of the house are then screwed to this packing-piece.

Three-quarter Span Roof.

This type of greenhouse, illustrated on p. 869 may require a similar packing-piece for the wall posts. Before fixing the top wall-plate it may be desirable to point the brickwork of the upper courses in order to ensure a firm foundation. A packing-piece will also be required if the top line of the wall is not parallel with the horizontal lines of the greenhouse framework.

All-Brick Sides.

If the house is more than 10 feet wide and the head-room exceeds 8 feet 6 inches, it is desirable to build a 9-inch wall instead of a $4\frac{1}{2}$-inch one. In Fig. 21 a 9-inch wall is shown. The wall plate (Figs. 22 to 24) is 6×3 inches, and it is flush with the outer edge of the brickwork. In this position the attachment of an iron gutter is facilitated. The side wall-plate is notched for the lap of the rafter (Fig. 22) and the end wall-plate is lapped to the side plate (Fig. 23). This lap is on the underside and it is flush with the inside edge of the wall plate, also 4 inches long and wide, so that, when framed to the other wall plate, its end is concealed.

How to make a Pair of Finely Balanced Scales

A REALLY accurate pair of scales for weighing in grains and ounces is a refinement that the home handyman seldom possesses, although there are many occasions when such an instrument would be of very great value.

In this article details are given for the construction of a pair of scales which will weigh correctly anything from half a grain upwards, and which can be dismantled when not required for use. The total cost should not exceed 1s.

Uses for the Scales.

A typical use for the scales is when articles of furniture are being finished by means of home-made stains and polishes, and they will be greatly appreciated if aniline dyes (spirit soluble) are used, as, owing to their great penetrating power, only very small quantities are needed at any one time.

A great many photographers prefer to make up their own developers, bleaching solution for bromoil work, intensifiers, reducers and restrainers, and all these call for accurate weighing in grains and ounces.

The garden lover, too, will appreciate the use of a pair of scales such as these, when artificial plant foods are being used, as, to get the best results from these artificial foods, accuracy in weighing is essential.

The Materials required.

The following materials are required, the letters in brackets referring to the lettered parts in Fig. 1.

(A) Wooden base, measuring approximately 9 × 3 × 2 inches.
(B) Upright, a length of old broom handle or dowelling measuring 12 × 1 inch diameter.
(C) Fulcrum, piece of sheet steel measuring 2 × 1 × 1/8 inch.
(D) Cross-bar, old length of conduit measuring 9 inches.
(E) Two pans—two cocoa-tin lids.
(F) Stays, length of copper wire.
(G) Sundries—two small bolts and nuts.

Most of the above will be found in the average amateur's junk box, but even if all the materials had to be purchased, the cost would be trifling compared to the bought article.

First plane the Base.

First of all the base should be planed and sandpapered, and if desired, a bevel can be worked round the edge; then bore a hole in the centre to take the upright. This hole should be of slightly smaller diameter than the upright, so that when the latter is sandpapered it will be a nice fit in the base; this is to enable the scales to be dismantled whenever desired.

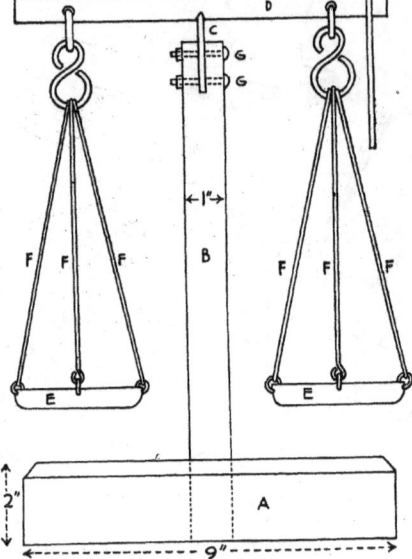

Fig. 1.—Front View of the Scales.

Saw-cut for the Fulcrum.

A saw-cut is next made in the top of the upright to take the fulcrum. When the metal has been trimmed to size, one end should be filed to a knife edge and two holes drilled to take the bolts which hold it in position, after which it can be bolted in place.

Dealing with the Length of Conduit.

The length of conduit is the next to receive attention, and this should have a V-shaped piece cut from the centre with a hacksaw, as shown in the sketch. Two holes must next be drilled right through, one at each end. To obtain the correct position for these holes, measure the radius of the tin lids and drill the holes the same distance from each end of the cross-bar.

Give all Joints a touch of Solder.

After the wires have been bent to shape and fitted, the job will be greatly improved if all joints are given a touch of solder.

What to do if one Side is heavier than the other.

After the various parts are assembled it will, in all probability, be found that one side of the scales is slightly biased or heavier than the other. This can easily be overcome by twisting a loop of copper wire as shown, which is placed over the lightest end of the scale and rests in the shallow groove on the cross-bar filed for the purpose. The wire is shortened very gradually, first with pliers, and then, as the difference becomes negligible, with a file. By this method a perfect balance is secured.

Improvements that can be made.

If expense is no object, various improvements can be made, such as an iron base filled with lead and a metal upright, and chain instead of wire for the stays.

The Weights.

Discs or squares of tin can be used for weights down to 12 grains, but below this weight thin galvanised wire cut to the lengths required will answer for the purpose. For extreme accuracy it will probably be found more satisfactory to obtain the weights ready made from one of the following firms.

Messrs. Sneade & Webber, 520 Lodge Lane, Liverpool 8, who can supply a set from 1/2 gr. to 1 oz. at 3s. 6d. per set, carriage paid. Messrs Derry & Warmington Ltd., 37 Byrom Street, Liverpool 3, who can supply a set from 1/2 gr. to 1 oz. at 2s. 6d. per set, carriage paid. Messrs. W. T. Avery Ltd., Soho Foundry, Birmingham, who can supply the weights in metric down to 1 mg., in grains down to ·01 gr., in troy down to ·001 oz., in avoirdupois down to 1/2 dram, and in apothecary weight down to 1/2 gr.

Dismantle the Scales when not in use.

As already mentioned, the scales can be dismantled when not in use, so that there is no likelihood of them being accidentally damaged or getting dirty, which might have an effect on their accuracy.

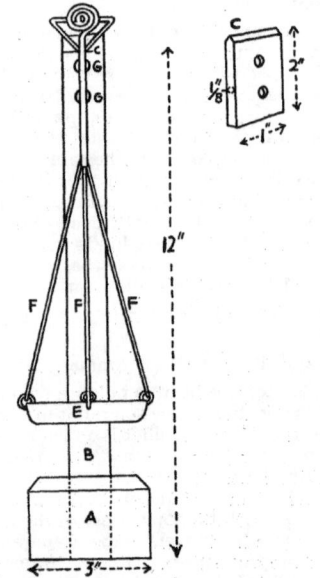

Fig. 2.—Side View of Scales.
Showing also details of the construction of the fulcrum.

POKER WORK ON VELVET

The art of burning a pattern on any material, known as Pyrography, is so generally associated with wood and leather that its possibilities with fabrics, such as velvet, have not been sufficiently realised. With the crude tools used in the early days of burnt decoration, it was impossible to use any other material than bone and wood. But with modern appliances it is now possible to ornament many attractive and useful articles, of which a selection is shown in Fig. 1.

Possibilities of the Craft.

As a fascinating craft, poker work will appeal to many readers who are looking for a useful occupation. Among the suggestions given in this article will be found many useful ideas for profitable work, especially in the making of such small articles as comb cases, ties, hatbands and small bags. These things, however, do not exhaust the possibilities of the craft, for delightful table-runners, cushions, table centres, and other useful decorations are quite easily made.

Tools required.

The cost depends on the kind of tools used. A simple piece of apparatus fitted with a lamp burning benzoline, bellows and the necessary tubing, together with a platinum point can be purchased for under 30s. A wood stand costs only a few shillings; it converts the hand bellows into a foot machine and its use allows both hands to be free.

Electrical Tools.

For use where electricity is available, a really soundly constructed model, encased in bronze, to take any voltage for alternating current, can be obtained for £2 10s. This includes two points, cork handle, flex and light plug. There is no doubt that the electric apparatus is the more convenient, but for occasional use, the spirit-heated point will be found quite satisfactory.

Fig. 1.—Some Articles with Burnt Decoration.

The Burning Point.

There are several forms of platinum point. For general use, the ordinary small flat point is best. Outlining can be done with the edge. Wider lines can be burnt with the side. The shading point is useful for fine work. The cost of the point, which is made of platinum, varies from 7s. 6d. to 19s. 6d. A small flat point suitable for most of the work illustrated in Fig. 1 is obtainable at the lower price.

Material Suitable for Poker Work.

Poker work can be done on felt and heavy cloth, velveteen and velvet, but millinery velvet gives the best results. The pile being deeper, the work stands out in greater relief. Shades of gold, green, pink, fawn and light grey are good, as the delicate soft tones of the burning show to best advantage on these colours.

How to work.

It is more convenient to work on an easel or an inclined board and advisable to practice on some odd pieces of velvet or felt before undertaking a good piece of work. A quick, light touch with the heated point is to be aimed at (see Fig. 3). For a beginning, it is advisable to burn a few straight lines, then some curves and finally to achieve a simple pattern.

Working with a Spirit-heated Appliance.

To commence work with the spirit-heated apparatus, first half fill the bottle with benzoline and the lamp with methylated spirit. Next fit the connecting cork in the bottle, attach the bellows to one connection and the cork handle of the point to the other side, using the rubber tubing. Now light the spirit lamp, place the platinum point in the flame and keep on pressing the bulb until the point is red-hot.

A little practice will soon enable the worker to keep the point hot. The supply of air from the bulb container must be kept going, or the point will cool off at once. Beginners are liable, in thinking about the actual burning, to forget to keep the bulb container fully pumped up.

Fig. 2.—Calendars and Book Markers Decorated and Lettered with Poker Work.

POKER WORK ON VELVET

Fig. 3.—Poker Work with Spirit-heated Apparatus.

The better quality outfits are provided with a pyro top to the bottle of benzoline. This allows the benzolene vapour to be lit up and heat the point. When first heating the point, turn the tap on the pyro top vertical, press the bulb slightly and light the jet. Hold the point in the flame until it is red-hot, then turn the tap horizontally and continue pumping with the bulb as before to keep the point red-hot.

Working the Electrical Appliance.

The electrical appliance is much easier to use. One length of flex is plugged into the nearest electric light point; the other being attached to the platinum point. Immediately the switch on the apparatus is turned on, the point becomes hot and is ready to use.

Only scorch the Fabric.

The main thing to look to in using the poker point on velvet or other fabric is to scorch the surface and not burn it. A light touch is all that is needed, but care must be taken not to have the point too hot or to linger on any portion of the line. The outlining should be done quite quickly, otherwise the fabric will burn.

Decorating a Comb Case.

Having mastered the elementary technique, a beginning should be made with a simple comb case. Half a yard of ribbon velvet, 1½ inches wide, and a suitable comb can be purchased for 6d. Cut one end to a slope, as indicated in Fig. 7, which shows the stages of work, place the ribbon on the easel or board and then burn a line along both ends.

Transferring Design to Material.

The design, shown full size in Fig. 8, may be drawn on direct with a soft crayon or a stick of charcoal, but a convenient method of transferring the design is to make a tracing with pencil on ordinary tracing paper. Turn the tracing over on a piece of white paper and go over all the lines with a stick of charcoal sharpened to a point. Now place the charcoal side down on the velvet, hold it down firmly at one end and then rub the fingers lightly over the paper and it will be found that

Fig. 4.—Working with the Hot Point.
Hold handle lightly and keep point moving. Edge of point is being used for outlines of flowers and leaves.

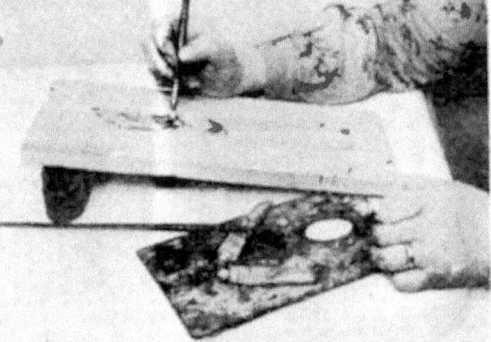

Fig. 5.—Colouring the Scorched Design.

an impression of the pattern has been transferred to the velvet. Care must be taken to avoid touching the charcoal with the fingers in the subsequent burning, otherwise the delicate colouring will be soiled. Another way of transferring the design is by pouncing. There is no reason why the design should be copied exactly, provided that the spray contains leaves and flowers and occupies about the same area.

Burning the Pattern.

The velvet is again placed on the inclined easel and the point heated up. Hold the handle lightly, as shown in Fig. 4, and then just touch the lines, keeping the hot point moving all the time. The edge of the point is used, as shown in the illustration, when working on the outlines of the flowers and leaves; the broad side is used when working on the wide stalks. The effect of the outlining will make the pattern larger (see C in Fig. 7).

Painting the Pattern.

The work is now ready for painting, the following materials being required: One tube each of student's oil colour, in chrome yellow, deep sap-green, prussian blue, and flake white. Two or three flat hog-hair brushes will also be needed. A Winsor and Newton series F, Nos. 1, 2 and 3, will be found useful. A palette may be used, but it is more economical to press the paint direct from the tube on to the brush.

Begin by touching the tips of the leaves with yellow. The brush is just laid on the velvet with a light touch, as in Fig. 5, so that a little of the colour is left. Now take the green and begin at the stalk end of the leaf and work up to the tip, blending the two colours where they meet.

The bottom flower is filled in entirely with blue; the next one and the bud should be filled in with a lighter blue, made by mixing a little white with the blue as it is worked over the surface. Delicate blending is possible with a little care. For the centre of each flower, spread a little yellow on the end of a match stick and leave a thick spot of the paint, as in Fig. 6.

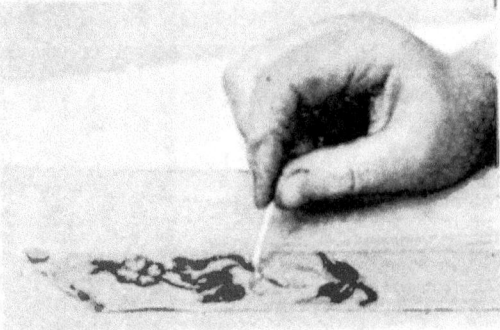

Fig. 6.—Painting a Thick Spot.
Using a match stick to dab a blob of paint in centre of flower.

POKER WORK ON VELVET

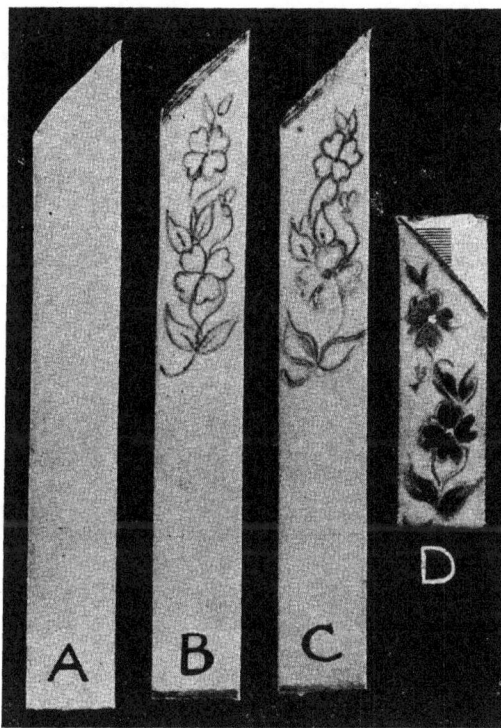

Fig. 7.—Making and decorating Comb Case. Work shown in stages. See Fig. 8 for full-size design for copying.

Fig. 8.—Full-size Design for Poker Work on Comb Case. Methods of transferring design are described in text.

Completing the Comb Case.

The work should be left until the paint is quite dry and then the sides of the velvet are sewn up with mercerised silk, close in colour to the velvet.

Book-Match Case.

Another piece of work on similar lines is a book-match case. First provide a 7½-inch length of ribbon velvet, 2½ inches wide, a 2¾-inch length of narrow ribbon, ⅜ inch wide, and a packet of book matches. A simple flower decoration is then transferred to the bottom of the strip. The top and bottom edges and lines of the pattern are now outlined with the point, and the flower and leaf forms filled in as before with oil paint. When dry, the bottom is rounded off to the burnt line and the piece of narrow ribbon folded over at each end and sewn to the edges, the bottom edge being 3½ inches from the straight end. Finally, fold the straight end over 2¼ inches and then make a stitch ⅛ inch up each side.

Hatband.

Further practice in the use of the point can be obtained by using the same flower and leaf form in a continuous pattern for a hatband. In this case, the ribbon is 1½ inches wide and ¾ yard long. The pattern is traced off with pencil on a strip of tracing paper, lined in on the other side with charcoal and then transferred to the velvet. The pattern is repeated to fill the length, outlining again with charcoal if required, from the ends of the ribbon to the pattern.

Begin the burning at one end and gradually work to the other, so that the traced lines are not likely to be touched until they are being outlined with the paint.

Colouring the Band.

When this part of the work is complete, use the same colours as before, but use the pure blue for every fourth or fifth flower, the other being filled in with either a light blue—cobalt, for example—or with the dark blue and white mixed. In no case should the flowers be entirely a pure colour or a tint. With the light blue, mix a spot of white and work it in lightly and touch it here and there with a spot of the light blue, merging it in with the surrounding tint. Little spots of white can be mingled with the dark blue in the same way.

Letter work and Calendars.

Excellent practice in the use of the point is obtained with lettering, as shown in Fig. 2. For this piece of work the following materials will be needed: A piece of ribbon velvet, 12 inches by 31 inches, about 21 inches of narrow ribbon to match, a wooden skewer and a small calendar.

It is an advantage to do the burning direct on the velvet, but a fair amount of skill in spacing and forming the letters is needed. The pattern is easily transferred with tracing paper and charcoal, as mentioned above.

One of the advantages of poker-work decoration is that it is possible to burn in the words of the motto in one's own handwriting; this gives the work a more personal touch.

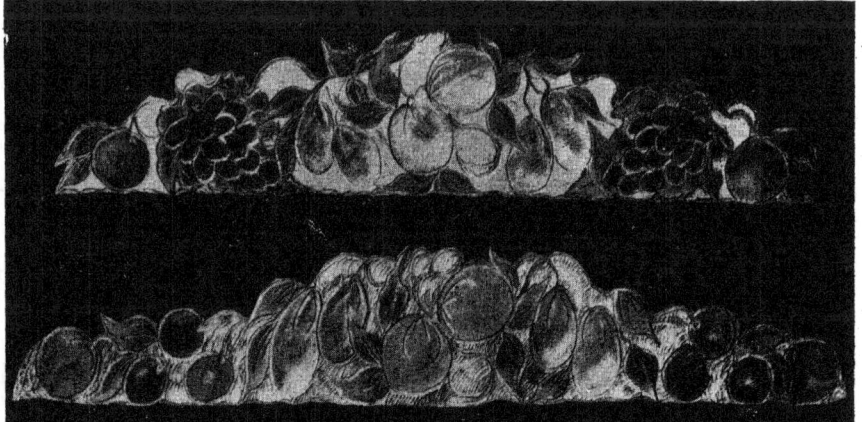

Fig. 9.—Poker Work for applying to other Materials.

Constructing a Cupboard with Flap Fronts

A FIXTURE such as you see in shops nowadays (Fig. 1) is a most useful contrivance, in that so much space is saved by utilising the lift-up sliding fronts in place of doors. This naturally economises space, for it is not always convenient to give sufficient room for the opening of doors.

We will consider for the purpose of this article two eventualities. Firstly, the making of a complete bookcase such as is shown in Fig. 2, and the second the conversion of a cupboard which already exists.

Fig. 1.—A Complete Bookcase with Sliding Flap Fronts.

We will assume that the chimney-breast in a room projects and leaves recesses either side, and that it is desired to fill the recesses with a cupboard as shown in Fig. 2, say a three-tier one with the top forming a shelf.

Materials required.

For the sake of economy it need have no back, and for constructing a cupboard such as is shown in the illustration, 4 feet 4 inches high by 3 feet wide, the following materials will have to be obtained. It can be made in oak as being a suitable wood, or, if still further economy is desired, deal can be used. The prices of both woods are given below.

The dimensions are given "full" to allow for "scribing" and cutting.

Whether the cupboard is to stand "free" or has no back and has to be fixed into a recess, the parts will have to be fixed together first, because to make a neat job the shelves and flaps should be fitted in from the back. Also, all the parts should be stained and polished before fixing to allow any shrinkage to take place. The method of staining is described later in the article.

Preparing the Wood.

First of all procure your wood (which you should be able to get from your local builder) to the dimensions given in the accompanying table, and plane them to a smooth surface. See that all the edges are right angles. This may be accomplished with the help of a square.

Fig. 2.—A Three-tier Cupboard built into a Recess.

Next cut the Grooves for the Shelves.

Look at Fig. 3, showing one of the sides. The grooves for the shelves, and also for the flaps, are indicated, and it will be seen that they stop short of the front face edge. This is in order to present a neat appearance from the front. The grooves in the sides of the cupboard can be made with a sharp chisel, and to do this lay the sides flat on a table or a bench if you have one, and hold them down with two thumbscrews. You will now have a firm basis to work upon.

Measure out the distance as shown in Fig. 3, and with the help of a T-square draw with a pencil the grooves to be cut. These should be about $\frac{1}{2}$ inch deep, and should be finished with glasspaper. To obtain a neat finish, fold a piece of No. 0 glasspaper round a piece of flat wood slightly thinner than the groove and work up and down the grooves.

The Hollow underneath the Shelf.

Now look at Fig. 4 showing a section of shelf and indicating a hollow underneath in the front. This is in order that the top edge of the flap may be cut as square as possible, the hollow allowing for the radius when the flap is lifted and slid into place when open.

To make the hollow, fix the shelves down as you did the sides. First rule a line about $1\frac{1}{2}$ inches from the front edge, which indicates the back line of the groove. The hollow can be made with a large gouge if you can procure one, and should be finished with glasspaper. As before, fold a piece of glasspaper round a piece of wood, but in this instance the edge of the wood must be rounded the exact shape of the hollow, work up and down until a smooth surface is obtained. Fig. 4 shows this. Fig. 5 shows an alternative method of dealing with the flaps, viz., when the shelf has no hollow and the front of the flap has to be rounded off to allow of it passing the underside of the shelf.

The first method described eliminates the possibility of causing a dust ledge.

Constructing the Flaps.

The front of the flaps should have chamfered edges on the inside, made with a chisel, and mitred at the corners.

CUTTING LIST AND PRICES OF MATERIALS REQUIRED

No.	For	Length.	Width.	Thickness.	Oak Price.	Deal Price.
2	Sides	4' 4"	1' 2"	1"	10 0	
1	Top	3' 0"	1' 2"	1"	3 6	
3	2 shelves, floor	3' 0"	1' 2"	1"	10 6	50 per cent. less than oak.
1	Skirting	3' 0"	0' 3"	$1\frac{1}{2}$"	1 3	
6	Frames for flaps	3' 0"	0' 2"	$\frac{3}{4}$"	3 0	
6	Ditto	1' 3"	0' 2"	$\frac{3}{4}$"	1 6	
2	Frames for floor	2' 10"	0' 3"	1"	—	9d.
2	Ditto	1' 0$\frac{1}{2}$"	0' 3"	1"	—	3d.
3	Panels for flaps, or	2' 6$\frac{1}{2}$"	0' 10$\frac{1}{2}$"	21 oz. sheet glass	—	—
3	Wood panels	2' 6$\frac{1}{2}$"	0' 10$\frac{1}{2}$"	$\frac{1}{2}$"	2 3	—
6	Brass pins	0' 1"	—	$\frac{1}{4}$"	—	—
3	Knobs	—	—	—	—	—
1	Top backrail	3' 0"	0' 3"	1"	0 9	—

CONSTRUCTING A CUPBOARD WITH FLAP FRONTS

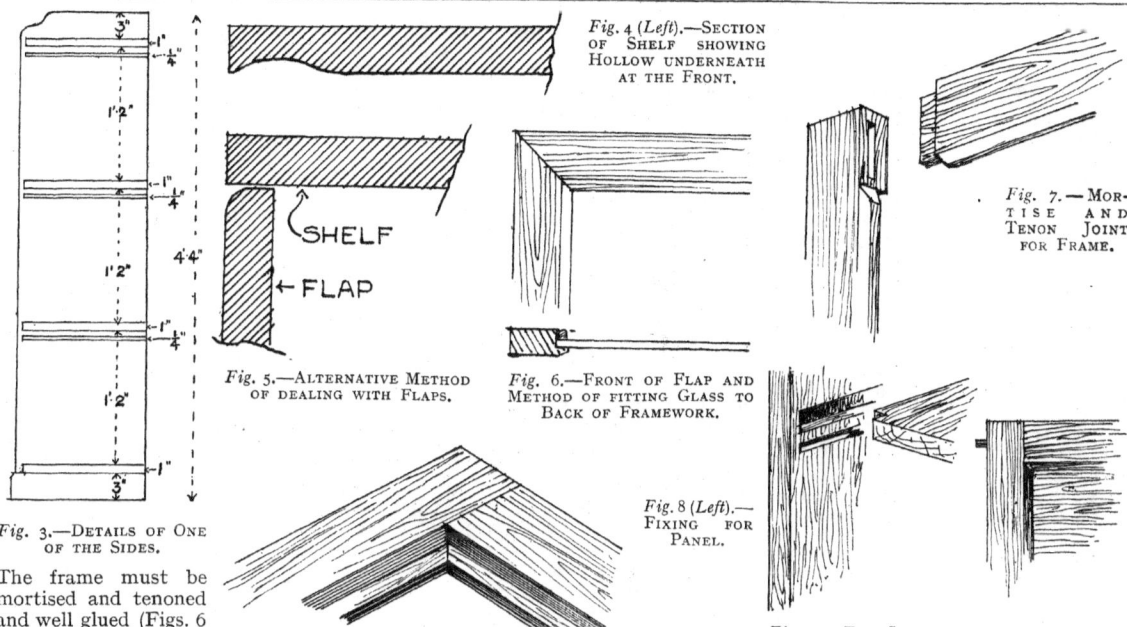

Fig. 3.—Details of One of the Sides.

Fig. 4 (Left).—Section of Shelf showing Hollow underneath at the Front.

Fig. 5.—Alternative Method of dealing with Flaps.

Fig. 6.—Front of Flap and Method of fitting Glass to Back of Framework.

Fig. 7.—Mortise and Tenon Joint for Frame.

Fig. 8 (Left).—Fixing for Panel.

Fig. 9.—The Shelves are let in their whole Thickness.

The frame must be mortised and tenoned and well glued (Figs. 6 and 7).

The Panels.

Either glass or wood can be used for the panels. If glass this must be fixed into the rebate formed in the back of the framework with a chisel (Figs. 6 and 8) and held in place by means of a bead fixed in with pins.

If a wood panel is required, a similar method of fixing can be adopted. The panels could be ½ inch thick.

The shelves can be let in their whole thickness, as shown in Fig. 9. The grooves for the flaps should be about ¼ inch full, to take ¼-inch metal

Fig. 10.—Assembly of Sides and Back.

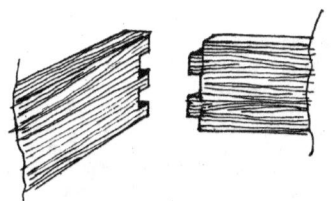

Fig. 11.—Fixing for Back Rail.

"dowels," which are driven into the flap each side, and project about ¼ inch, and which cannot come out by reason of the fact that the frame will fit fairly tight up against the side (Figs. 9 and 10).

The Dowels.

The "dowels" can be fitted in by making a hole with a centre bit and brace, just a fraction smaller than the dowel. Then drive the dowel home with a hammer.

The Sides and Back.

It will be seen that the sides project above the top shelf, and with the piece at the back finishing at the same level a gallery is formed round. This back rail can be fixed, as shown in Fig. 11, box-pinned into the sides.

Assembling the Cupboard.

Having grooved the sides for the shelves and flaps, proceed to fit the cupboard together, first sliding the shelves in from the back. They should be well glued in order to make a firmer fixing.

Now slide your flaps in also from the back. Screw a small knob into the front of the bottom rail of each flap.

The Bottom Frame.

Now you have your cupboard complete. Put it into the recess and fix to the wall by means of rawl-plugs.

The Bottom Frame.

The next operation is to construct the bottom deal frame, details of which are given in Fig. 12. It is set back somewhat, sufficiently to allow of the polished top of the skirting to show about 1 inch, i.e., the thickness of the bottom flap.

The back rail can be box-pin jointed into the sides, and the sides tenoned into the front and the front rail into the bookcase sides. Fig. 12 shows this construction.

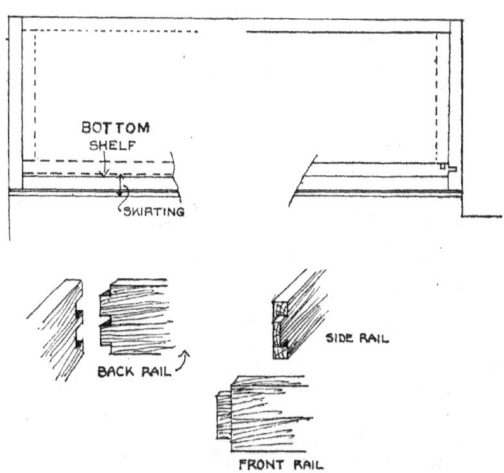

Fig. 12.—Details of Bottom Deal Frame.

CONSTRUCTING A CUPBOARD WITH FLAP FRONTS

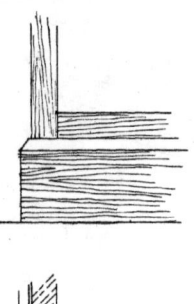

Fig. 13.—Arrangement for Cupboard to Stand "Free."

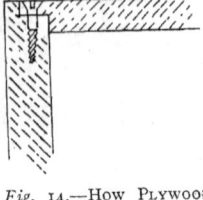

Fig. 14.—How Plywood is Fixed.

The deal frame should then be screwed into the bookcase sides and also to the floor. The bottom shelf or floor of bookcase of oak is then screwed to the deal frame. This bottom shelf must project over the deal frame about $\frac{1}{8}$ inch to $\frac{3}{16}$ inch to cover the deal, but care must be taken to see that a clear inch is left for the bottom flap to fit into when closed.

Finishing the Surface.

Now a word about the finishing. Before fitting the several parts together, well glasspaper them, using No. 0 for the finish. As already mentioned, the staining and polishing of the wood should be done before fixing the parts together for two reasons: Firstly, that all timber, if alive, however well seasoned, is liable to be affected by atmospheric conditions, and therefore, supposing a slight shrinkage takes place, say in the panels of the flaps which would be the most noticeable place, a nasty white line would appear, whereas, if the panels are stained and polished beforehand, any slight shrinkage would not show. Secondly, a much neater job can be made of the corners if the wood is polished first.

A final rub-over with polish afterwards will be necessary, but the main polishing must be done first.

Dark Oak Finish.

If you want a dark oak finish, a stain can be made of potash bichromate dissolved in water applied with a rag or brush, or another method is to use liquid ammonia.

Light Shade.

If a light shade is required, various tones can be produced with powdered ochre or umber mixed with size. Before staining the wood, you will have to glasspaper the work well.

The Polish.

Beeswax dissolved in turpentine put on with a rag, and when dry rubbed hard with a cloth or brush, produces a very satisfactory result.

If the Cupboard is to stand "free."

If it is not desired to fit the cupboard into a recess but to make it to stand "free," the deal floor frame must, of course, not be screwed to the floor, but it can be screwed to the sides of the cupboard to hold them together, and the skirting will have to be carried round the sides (Fig. 13).

There will also have to be a back. This would have to be constructed as shown on Fig. 14, and in which case the sides should be made to project at the back about 1 inch and the back board, which may be composed of $\frac{3}{4}$-inch plywood (because it can be procured in wide widths), should be fixed as shown in Fig. 14 and secured with screws.

Converting an Existing Cupboard.

If you have a cupboard enclosed by two doors, and with, say, two shelves inside, and you want to convert it into a similar kind as described above, all you will have to do is to remove the two doors and fit flaps in between the shelves.

It is not supposed that you will want to undertake the laborious business of taking the cupboard to pieces, so you will have to do your work from the front. If you can remove the back temporarily, it would help matters somewhat, in which case you can slide the flaps in from the back, as described above.

If you are unable to remove the back, you will have to slide them in from the front, in which case you will have to make a cut in the sides, which afterwards will have to be filled up with wood, and painted and stained, as the case may be.

The flaps in this instance will have to be rounded on the top edge, as it is unlikely that you will be able to groove the undersides of the shelves without taking them out, which you would not want to do.

MENDING DROP-IN SEATS

THE most usual fault with drop-in seats, such as are fitted to many dining-room chairs, is failure of the webbing. A drop-in seat consists essentially of a wooden frame, separate from the chair itself, across which is a lattice-work arrangement of webbing over which is a layer of padding and finally a covering of leather, damask, cretonne or other ornamental material. This seat rests on ledges in the chair itself.

Fitting New Webbing.

The first thing to do when fitting a new webbing is to remove the ornamental material and padding and strip away the old webbing, so that the wooden frame is left bare. Next go over the frame very carefully and pull out any tacks, and glue the corner joints if any should be loose; in which case string should be tied from side to side and from back to front to keep the frame firm while the glue is drying.

Fixing the New Webbing.

The new webbing should now be fixed across the frame; it is nailed across the upper face of the frame and not below, as is usual with most other re-webbing repairs. Measure the frame to see how many yards of webbing are required and obtain it all in one piece. Then take the free end of the webbing and arrange it so that the edge overhangs the frame of the chair by about an inch. Then drive in two nails with fairly big heads, turn back the overhanging edge on to the nails and drive in three more nails all in the same line.

Next take the coil of webbing over to the opposite side of the frame and pull it downwards. Then, when it is as tight as possible, put in two nails, after which the webbing can be cut about an inch beyond the nails. Turn back the spare inch and put in three more nails.

Repeat this process for the remaining strips of webbing, not forgetting to lace the crossing pieces one over another.

The Padding.

When the webbing has been properly laced and fixed it should be covered with a sheet of canvas which should be tacked down at several points. Next arrange the stuffing so as to give the seat a comfortable domed shape, to soften down the harsh edges of the frame. It will probably be necessary to freshen up the old stuffing by spreading it on a newspaper in the open and beating it and fluffing it up.

Pack the edges first, then fill in the centre by first giving an even layer all over and then adding to the centre parts until the actual middle is the highest spot of all. When the padding has been suitably arranged, a covering of thin pliant canvas or calico is spread over it and the edges of the material are neatly carried round the frame to the under side, where they are tacked down.

The Ornamental Covering.

Finally put on the covering which serves to ornament the seat.

Make sure that sufficient allowance is made for turning it under, and in arranging it take care that the material is neatly folded at the corners. If it is merely bunched at these points the work will have an amateurish appearance.

REPAIRING ELECTRIC IRONS, FIRES AND OTHER APPLIANCES

In the following article will be found some practical notes regarding the repair of domestic electrical appliances.

ELECTRIC IRONS

The most common faults arising from the use of electric irons are:—

(1) Broken or short-circuited flex.
(2) Burnt out element.
(3) Burnt or corroded terminals.

The Parts of an Electric Iron.

With one or two exceptions all electric irons are manufactured on the same principle, and the various parts are shown in Fig. 1. It will be seen that they consist of A, a flat suitably-shaped metal surface; B, an electric heating element; C, a cast-iron weight; D, a cover with insulated terminals; E, a handle; F, a tilting stand; G, a suitable socket; and H, a flexible cord by means of which the source of supply is brought to the cover terminals.

Dealing with a Broken or Short-circuited Flex.

Breakage of the flex is generally caused by pulling out the plug or socket, at the iron end, by means of the cable, instead of by gripping the insulated plug body.

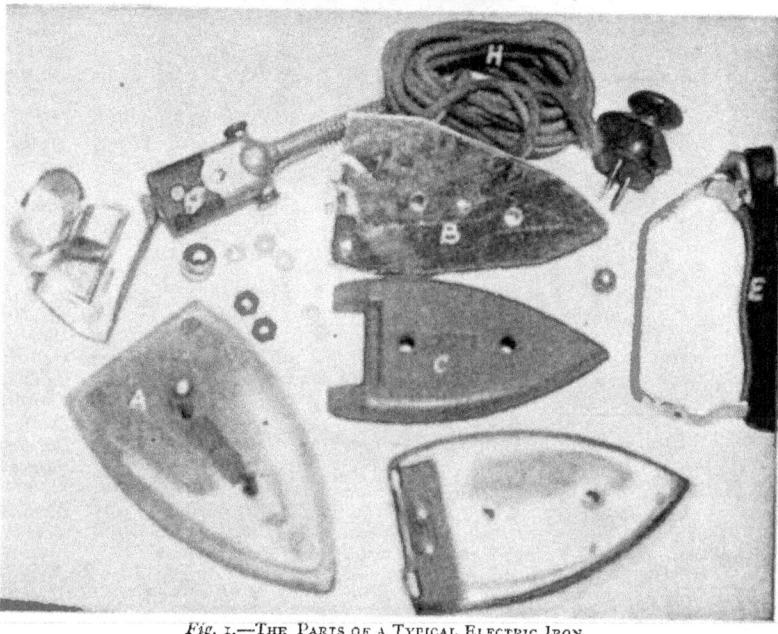

Fig. 1.—The Parts of a Typical Electric Iron.

Removing the Old Flex.

The flex is fixed in a bakelite holder or socket which fits on to two pegs projecting from the iron. This holder is in two halves which are held together by two or more bolts. Unscrew the nuts from the bolts so that the two halves can be separated to reveal the internal connections. It will be seen that the wires are fixed by screws to the contact pieces. These screws should be slackened so that the wires can be withdrawn.

If it is only the very end of the flex that is damaged there is no need to replace it with an entirely new length of flex. Cut off the last inch or two of the flex, then carefully unfasten the braiding and expose the inner rubber covering the wires. Scrape off the insulation for a distance of about 1 inch, then replace the wires in the bakelite holder and tighten up the screws. Now make sure that the outer braiding is well inside the holder. A small piece of black insulating tape should be wound round the end of the braiding. The outer cover can then be replaced.

Another Type of Bakelite Holder.

Not all types of holders are quite the same. In one type the two halves are held in place by five small bolts, the heads of three of them being on one side, the other two being on the other side. Loosen the three first, then remove the two from the other side that fit into a rectangular piece of fibre countersunk into the face of the bakelite, forming a clamp to hold the cable securely in the adapter. When the two halves have been separated it will be seen that the ends of the flex are attached to two helical coils of spring brass which can be removed from the ends of the wire by slackening two small clamping bolts.

Reassembling.

To reassemble, prepare the ends of the wire, thread through the armoured covering which fits into the upper end of the adapter and fasten to the brass

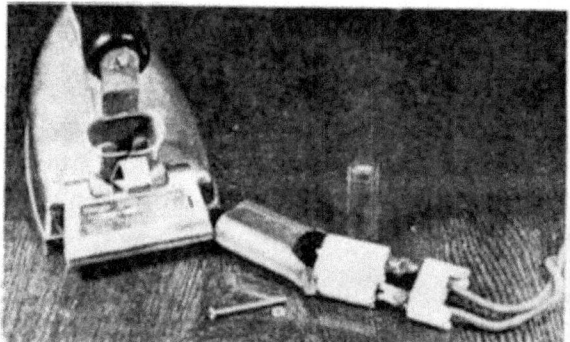

Fig. 2.—Dismantling the Holder
In this type of iron, a small nut and screw secure the holder in a metal casing. This fits into the back of the iron.

Fig. 3.—Removing the Upper Case of the Iron.
Note the iron weight held by two nuts. The heating element is under this weight.

coils, which are then replaced into the grooves of one-half of the bakelite holder. Then lay the top section in position and bolt together with the three screws. Next put back the two bolts which grip the main cable and adjust these to hold it firmly without unduly crushing the outside cover.

If New Flex is Required.

If new flex altogether is required it should be of first class quality (2,500 megohm grade), preferably of the round asbestos braided type and of ample carrying capacity.

A three-core flex should be used whenever possible as a safeguard against shocks due to short-circuiting in the iron itself. One end of the extra core should be connected to the iron cover and the other end to the third (or thick) pin of a three-pin plug. If the iron is being used off the lighting circuit by means of the usual adapter this is not, of course, practicable.

Fitting a New Element.

Before a new element can be fitted the iron will have to be dismantled. Undo the two nuts or set-screws which hold down the handle and remove the handle. It will now be possible to lift up the cover at the tip of the iron to expose the back of the terminals.

Next unscrew the nuts which hold the strips from the element on to the terminals and remove the cover.

In some types of irons the terminals are mounted on a separate block which is held on to the cover by two screws which pass through the tilting stand. If such is the case, when these two screws are undone the cover can be lifted off, leaving the terminals still attached to the element.

Removing the Weight.

The cast-iron weight should now be removed by undoing the two nuts marked A in Fig. 4, which will leave the element exposed.

The Element.

The element consists of a coil of high resistance wire embedded in

Fig. 4.—How to Fit a New Element to an Electric Iron.
The cover can be removed by unscrewing the nuts holding the strips from the element on to the terminals. The two nuts A are removed so that the top weight can be lifted away, leaving the element exposed.

a packing of asbestos compound or sandwiched between sheets of mica. It is rather fragile and should be removed carefully for examination in case a new element is not needed.

It is sometimes found that the two broken ends can be joined up again to effect a temporary repair by twisting them tightly together. It would, of course, be useless to solder them. In all probability, however, a new element will be required, and this should be obtained from the manufacturers of the iron. In order to obtain one of the correct voltage and shape, the serial number which is generally found on the nameplate fixed to the handle should be quoted.

It is worth pointing out here that should you move to a new district where the supply voltage is different to that of the old premises there is no need to scrap your iron or other appliance. It is only necessary to obtain a new element suitable for the new voltage and fit it to the appliance.

Reassembling the Iron.

Having obtained the new element it should be carefully placed in position and the top weight placed over it and screwed down tight. If it is not screwed down absolutely tight the element will burn out very quickly.

The small strips from the element should now be fastened to the terminal block or cover, as the case may be, and the cover replaced. Make sure the strips are bent into such a position that they will not touch any part of the iron when the cover is fitted.

Corroded or Burnt Terminals.

Corroded or burnt terminals are caused by the socket fitting too loosely. If the burning has not been allowed to become too extensive the metal should be scraped clean or filed. If badly damaged new terminals should be purchased from the manufacturer. When they are fitted in position the spring contacts in the socket should be adjusted with a pair of pliers until a firm contact with the terminals is obtained.

The Donaldson Wireless Iron.

This is a special type of iron which does away with the chief cause of trouble, i.e., the flexible cord. The incoming cable from the supply is taken to an insulated block in the interior of the stand and thence through two brass springs to two carbon contacts which are pressing on another slotted insulating block. The terminals of the iron are placed at the extreme end and project horizontally instead of vertically.

When the iron is placed on the stand it slides down the sloping portion and the terminals pass through the slotted insulated block and make electrical contact

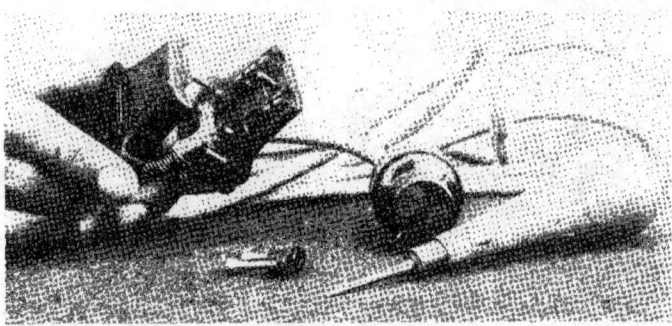

Fig. 5.—Separating the Two Halves of a Bakelite Adapter.
Note the brass coils fitting snugly into the lower half.

with the carbons, so that the iron is heated in the ordinary way. The main advantages of such an iron are that there is no danger due to shorting or breaking of the flex, and a saving in current is effected as no current is used while the iron is off the stand.

ELECTRIC FIRES
Bowl Fires.

Bowl fires are fitted with a central "element" (see Fig. 7) which consists of a coil of resistance wire wound spirally round a fire-clay core of cylindrical shape. This heater is surrounded by a semi-spherical copper reflector.

Broken Element.

The most frequent fault with this type of fire is breakage of the element by an accidental blow, in which case it is best to fit a new element. The element can easily be removed by giving it a sharp pull (after removing the guard which fits over the front of the bowl), as it is only plugged into two sockets. In most cases the new element will be supplied with two split pegs so that it can be pushed straight away into place.

If, however, it is supplied without pegs all that need be done is to undo the two nuts holding the pegs to the broken filament and then fix them on to the new element.

Make sure, of course, that the new element is suitable for the voltage of your supply.

Cleaning a Tarnished Reflector.

It is, of course, essential that the burnished copper reflector should be bright. When new the surface is lacquered, and it should not be cleaned with metal polish. The correct treatment is to put a little wax polish on a very soft rag and rub it over the surface. This will keep the reflector bright in damp weather.

When the reflector has become badly tarnished it is best to clean off the old lacquer with methylated spirits and reburnish the metal with rouge applied on a chamois leather. A coat of cold lacquer should then be applied with a camel-hair brush.

Electric Radiators.

In a full-size electric radiator the "element" of the bowl fire is replaced with a fire bar. The body of the bar is moulded in fire-clay and asbestos and has a long coil of resistance wire embedded in a channel running down the centre of it. These bars are held in position by a screw at each end and are insulated from the body of the radiator by means of mica washers on

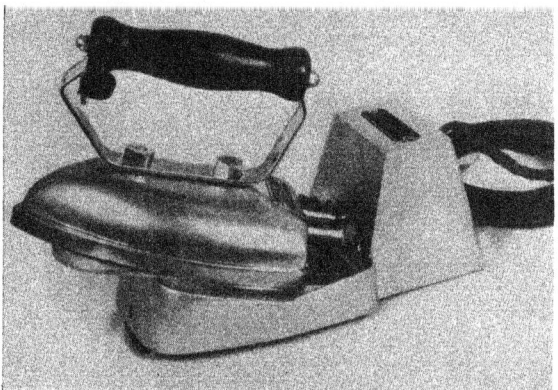

Fig. 6.—The Donaldson Wireless Iron.
This iron does away with the use of flexible cord.

the securing screws. New bars can be purchased complete with wire or without.

How the Bars are Connected Up.

Fig. 8 shows a typical method of wiring a three-bar radiator. It will be seen that it is so arranged that one or more bars can be used at will. To examine the wiring remove either the back or base of the radiator, which is usually bolted in place with small 2 B.A. bolts. One end of each bar will be found connected to a common terminal, shown at A in Fig. 8. The other end of each bar is also connected to a second common terminal, B, but first passes through a switch. The terminals marked A and B project through the base and are fitted with nuts to which the ends of the flex leading to the power supply are connected. These terminals are usually protected by a cover box.

Connections to Supply.

All electric fires should be connected to the supply by means of a three-wire flexible asbestos-covered cable through a three-pin plug. Two of the wires serve to supply the electrical energy to the elements and are connected to A and B; the third wire connects the metal framework of the fire to "earth," which is, in most cases, the steel tubing in which the electric wires are run. The earth wire is connected to the longest pin on the plug, which ensures that the earth connection is the first to be made when the plug is inserted in the socket.

Replacing a Flexible Wire.

If it is desired to replace a flexible wire which has become frayed or damaged,

disconnect the wires from the plug terminals, taking careful note which is the earth wire and how the wires are arranged inside the plug to prevent a direct tug or pull from being applied to the connections.

Next cut completely through the cable about an inch below the frayed portion, push back the braiding for about 3 inches and remove the insulation from the three exposed wires for about ¾ inch.

Then bend each bared end over on itself and twist solid. Insert and screw each bared end into its appropriate terminal so that the insulation is flush with the terminal. Make sure no stray strands of wire are left. Finally, arrange the wires in the plug base as they were originally, pull down the braiding and replace the cover.

On no account should the plug be pulled from the socket by pulling on the flexible wire.

Dealing with a Broken Element.

When an element has burnt out or broken it should be carefully examined to see where the break has occurred before a new element is bought. It may be found that the break has occurred where the wire has been bent to make connection to the terminals, or near the end coil of a spiral. If this is the case a repair can very quickly be effected by removing the broken bit of wire and carefully stretching out the end coil until connection can be made with the terminal when it is clamped between the washers in the usual way.

If the break has occurred in some other part a temporary repair may perhaps be possible by twisting the broken ends of the wires together very tightly. It is more probable, however, that a new element will be required, in which case the old element should be removed bodily from the case, after unscrewing the screws which secure it, and returned to the makers so as to ensure the new element being of the correct size.

ELECTRIC KETTLES

Many of the commonest troubles associated with electrical kettles are due to the split terminal pins. These may have become pressed together by careless fixing and

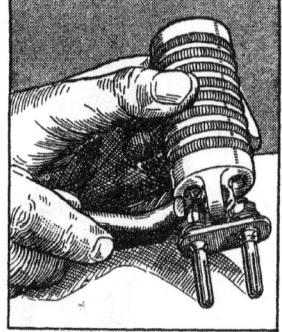

Fig. 7.—A Bowl Fire Filament.
Tightening up the nuts after fitting the contact pegs to a new element.

removal of the connector, resulting in loose contact, the pins may have been damaged mechanically, or they may be loose due to the fixing nuts having slacked back. The method of dealing with any of these faults is obvious. Other faults requiring rather more attention are element wire broken or burnt out, or breakdown of the insulation—either broken beads or faulty mica—resulting in the body of the appliance becoming "alive." The details given below are applicable to almost any make of kettle, although different makes vary in certain details of construction.

First Remove Bottom Cover Plate.

The first thing to do is to undo the screw or screws which hold the bottom cover plate in position. This will reveal the element.

The split pin terminals are insulated from the side of the kettle by mica washers and are clamped in position by nuts (*a* and *b*, Fig. 10). Two more nuts connect the element tails (or end connections) to the terminal pins (A and B. Fig. 10). These tails are commonly bead insulated.

Removing Terminal Pin.

The first step in removing a terminal pin is to disconnect the element tails by slacking back or removing the units A and B. As the nuts may have become tightly fixed owing to the heat to which they are exposed in use, a spanner of the correct size should be used, and not pliers. The nuts *a* and *b* should also be held with a second spanner before applying pressure to the first nuts. If this is not done there is a danger of the terminal pin screwing round in its seating, with resultant damage to the mica insulation washers.

Similarly, when slacking back the terminal pin holding nuts the terminal pin itself should be rigidly gripped with pliers. The pins should not be gripped in such a way that the two halves are pressed together, but with the slit at right angles to the jaws of the pliers. Similar precautions should be taken when reassembling the pins, as the main point to watch is to avoid damaging the electrical insulation materials.

The Bead-insulated Element Tails.

If the element tails are insulated by beads, care must be taken that none of the beads is lost. A useful tip in this connection is to twist a loop in the end of the tail as soon as the wire has been disconnected from the terminal pin, then no beads can drop off accidentally. Any beads that are broken or lost should, of course, be replaced by new ones before connecting up the tails again.

Replacing Damaged Heating Element.

The first thing to do when replacing a damaged heating element is to dis-

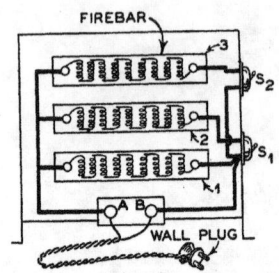

Fig. 8.—How a Three-bar Electric Radiator is Wired.
A and B are common terminals in the base of the fire to which the flex is attached. S₁ is the switch controlling bar 2. S₂ controls bar 3. Bar 1 is operated from the wall-plug switch.

connect the tails from the terminal pins as already described. Next slack back the nuts holding the clamping plate in position. The proper tool to use is a box spanner of the correct size. All the nuts should be slacked back for about a quarter of a turn at first and should be dealt with in such an order that opposite points of the clamp plate are relieved of stress alternately. If the plate shows any tendency to stick when all the nuts have been removed, lever it up slightly at the four corners in succession until it is free. Similarly, if the mica encased element sticks, prise it off carefully, and when lifting it away see that the mica does not catch in the threads of the studs and pieces flake off. Care is advisable in case it is found that the old element can be used again.

Re-assembling.

When replacing the element fit it in position very carefully to avoid damaging the mica insulation. Then fit on the clamping plate and screw up one nut near the centre just sufficiently tight to hold the plate in position. Now screw on the remainder of the nuts but not sufficiently tight to apply pressure. Now tighten up all the nuts a quarter or half turn at a time in the reverse order to that in which they were removed.

Fig. 9.—Connecting New Flex to Electric Radiator.
Note the cover box which prevents pull on flex reaching the terminals.

The element must be gripped between the kettle bottom and the clamping plate with uniform pressure over the whole area. The tightness and uniformity of the pressure by which a mica-wound element is clamped in is one of the main factors in ensuing a long life.

Finally the element tails should be connected up to the terminal pins.

"Safety" and "Automatic" Kettles.

In many modern kettles a protective device is incorporated which automatically cuts off current if the kettle should accidentally boil dry or if it should be plugged on to the supply current when empty. Most of these devices require a rather delicate adjustment, and if anything goes wrong with them it is best to let the manufacturers handle the repair job.

ELECTRIC COOKERS

Modern electric cookers are almost foolproof, and it is very unlikely that any fault will develop. There are various types of cookers. Some have fixed terminals in the elements with a removable oven, others have a fixed oven interior but plug-in elements. For the purpose of this article we will confine our remarks to one of the latter type, a good example of which is the "Dolphin" cooker.

In this cooker the oven interior or inner lining is fitted to the outer lining and the intervening space is packed tightly with a form of asbestos wool and then cemented round the front edges.

Switches and Fuses.

The switches are all on one side and are dust proof; space for a kettle plug is provided on the switch plate immediately under the hob, while the fuses are found immediately under the switches in the same order.

The Hot Plates.

The hot plates are easily removable, as shown in Fig. 11. In the event of failure of an element the complete unit, *i.e.*, hot plate and undercover, or, in the case of oven elements, the sheet metal cover and undertray, should be returned to the makers.

Renewing a Fuse Wire.

As the fuses are easily accessible no difficulty should be experienced in renewing a fuse. Remove the white enamel fuse plate, take out the fuse and renew the fuse wire. The fuses are of knife contact pattern and simply "pull out" and "push in."

What to do if a Fuse "Blows" Continually.

Should a fuse "blow" again as soon as it has been replaced the following should be examined :—

See if the element pins are clear of the casing. A porcelain may be broken, or more likely a small piece of bone or fat may possibly have got across the pins and carbonised.

If it is an oven fuse that is "blowing," take off the sheet metal cover as the element may have failed or be touching the cover through being carelessly "banged" down when removed for cleaning.

If the element is found to be in order or a new one has been fitted and the fuse still "blows," then a further search for a possible cause must be made. Remove the side cover to expose the wiring and trace back the connections of the faulty circuit. It may be found that there is a loose contact or switch or fuse line which requires tightening. If everything is in order, examine the switch; the spring may have gone, and set up an arcing, although this is very unlikely.

If the cooker is wired in bare copper strip see if any of the strips have got bent out and are touching the case.

Repairing Broken Element Wire.

If a spiral on the element, and this applies, too, to the grill, has broken any distance up to ½ inch from the terminal, it is safe to stretch the element wire and reconnect to the terminal as a temporary measure. Also, if the element has failed in the middle a temporary repair can be made by twisting the broken ends together. Take care to nip off any projecting ends and put the wire back securely in the fireclay former. Solid hot plates cannot, of course, be dealt with, the reason being that the element wire is laid in a special cement in a cast-iron tray.

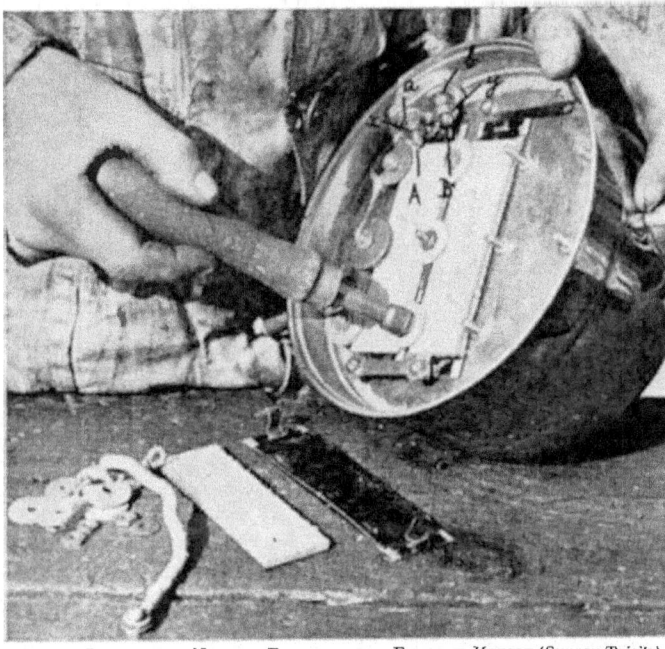

Fig. 10.—REPLACING A HEATING ELEMENT IN AN ELECTRIC KETTLE (*Sunray Tricity*).
Showing how a box spanner is used to unscrew the nuts holding clamping plate. A and B are the split terminal pins; *a* and *b* the nuts holding the pins; *x* and *y* the nuts holding the element tails. Note the bead insulated tail in the foreground at the left.

ELECTRIC BELL REPAIRS.

Two common types of cell are in use for electric bells, the dry cell and the Leclanché wet cell. Dry cells have the appearance of cylindrical

Fig. 11.—METHOD OF REMOVING FOUR-PIN BOILING PLATE FROM DOLPHIN ELECTRIC COOKER.
This illustration also shows the adjusting screws, one on the extreme left, just under the right-hand little finger, and the other two on the extreme right. These screws enable the height of the boiling plate, when fitted, to be adjusted, so that it is dead level with the hob, ensuring perfect contact for the utensils.

pots with two terminals on top; they require no charging or attention, but must be renewed at intervals of about eighteen months. Leclanché cells have a glass container full of a solution of sal-ammoniac with a porous pot and a zinc rod standing partly submerged in the fluid.

Preparing Sal-ammoniac Solution.

To make up a solution of sal-ammoniac, 4 ozs. should be dissolved in each pint of warm water. The solution is best made up in a jug and allowed to cool before pouring into the glass containers. The level of the fluid should not be above the lower edge of the black pitch mark on the porous pots, otherwise it has a tendency to creep up the conductors and cause corrosion.

When adding water to compensate for the loss due to evaporation it is not necessary to add more sal-ammoniac. When the cells have been in use for about two years, a tablespoonful of sal-ammoniac can, however, be added to each cell.

If the solution develops a "milky" appearance it is a sign that more sal-ammoniac is needed. A deposit of undissolved sal-ammoniac crystals at the bottom of the cells indicates that too much has been used and the solution is too strong.

The chief faults in an electric bell may be summarised as follows:—

(1) Dirty or badly adjusted bell contact.

(2) Battery failure.

(3) Bell push defective through a broken C spring or tarnished contacts.

(4) Broken or corroded wire: examine near the battery and at all sharp bends.

(5) Short circuit caused by a staple cutting through the covering of the lead wires.

Passe-Partout Picture Framing

PASSE-PARTOUT framing for pictures consists briefly of securing the picture between a piece of cardboard and a sheet of glass by means of paper strips pasted around the edges. It is a very neat and inexpensive method of dealing with pictures, and as the paper binding is not confined to a plain strip of one pattern or colour, there is plenty of scope for the exercise of individual tastes.

Materials required.

Ready-gummed paper strips for passe-partout can be bought in rolls in a fairly extensive range of colours, but it is also equally satisfactory to use strips of wallpaper for the purpose. In the latter case, the fact that the strips can be cut much wider than the ready-gummed rolls is sometimes an advantage. An adhesive consisting of ordinary flour paste rather on the thick side, or thin glue, will be required if wallpaper is used, and a generous amount of ordinary sugar should be dissolved in the adhesive (either flour or glue). This will prevent the paper coming away from the glass during extremes of weather.

In addition, a knife, ruler, supply of old newspapers, stiff brush for the paste, glass and cardboard mount will be required, and these should all be gathered together before the work is begun.

The Glass.

As the edge produced with a glazier's diamond is much cleaner and squarer than that resulting from a wheel glass cutter, it is advisable to obtain the sheet of glass cut to the exact size you require. Much of the workmanlike finish of the final result depends on the smoothness of the edges.

First mount the Picture.

The first operation is to mount the picture. The size of the cardboard will, of course, depend on whether it is desired to show a surround of the card itself between the picture and the paper binding. When dealing with a

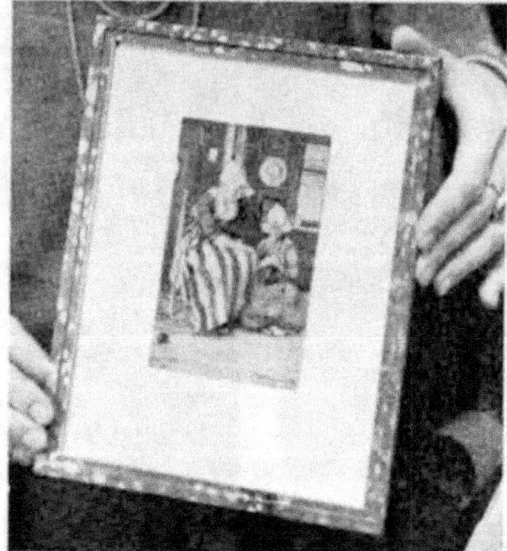

Fig. 1.—A Finished Picture Frame in Passe-Partout Framing.
This is an example of deep framing.

Fig. 2.—Many Varieties of Wallpaper make Excellent and Inexpensive Passe-Partout Binding Materials.
The wallpaper should be cut into strips.

Fig. 3.—How to Flatten out the Mount.
The picture is mounted on a card a little larger than finally required. Damp the back of the card, then lay it between the sash-board and the glass under a heavy weight.

picture that is already fairly stiff it will probably be found unnecessary to mount it; a thin picture should, however, be pasted down on the card and allowed to dry.

Cut the card mount slightly larger than the glass for the front and make two tiny pencil dots where the top corners of the picture are to come. Now lay the print face down on some old newspapers and damp it all over on its back with a sponge. Leave it for a few moments until it has become evenly limp, then spread the paste over it. It can then be lowered so that the two top corners come on the two dots. Place a clean sheet of paper over the whole job and rub down with the hand. There will then be no danger of the surface being damaged or the picture moving on the mount.

To prevent the Picture buckling.

It is now necessary to take steps to prevent the picture buckling, as is often the case when pasting a picture upon cardboard. As soon as the mounted picture is dry, or nearly dry, lightly sponge the back of the mount with water. The amount of water to use depends, of course, on the thickness of the mount; the thicker the cardboard the more it should be damped.

Now place the damped mount upon the backing board, which should be resting on a perfectly flat surface. Then place the glass on the mount and on top of it place a heavy weight, such as a pile of books. If possible leave like this overnight, at any rate for several hours.

This simple preliminary treatment will make all the difference in obtaining a neat result when the job is finished.

Centralising the Picture.

The next step is to get the picture absolutely central with the glass cover. The method of doing so is shown in Fig. 4. Measure the distance from the edge of the picture to that of the cover glass, first on one side and then at the other. If the measurement at one side is found to be greater than at the other

Fig. 4.—Centralising the Position of the Picture under the Glass.

Fig. 5.—Trimming Mount and Backboard together.

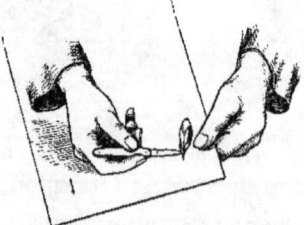
Fig. 6.—Making Picture Hangers with a Piece of Tape.

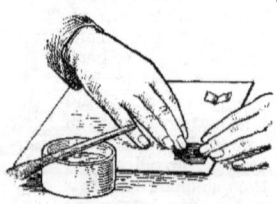
Fig. 7.—Fixing the Picture Hangers with Pieces of Paper.

PASSE-PARTOUT PICTURE FRAMING

*Fig. 8.—*How to make the Binding Strips Limp enough for Use.
Damp the front side with a sponge.

*Fig. 9.—*Attaching the Binding Strip.
Clip the pack together. The paper patch on the glass acts as a guide for correct alignment of the binding strip.

*Fig. 10.—*Binding the Edges.
In order to secure a clean edge press the edge of the pack on to the table.

*Fig. 11.—*Securing a Clean Edge (Second Stage).
Pressing the pack upright, smooth the rest of the binder on to the backboard.

*Fig. 12.—*Mitreing the Corner.
It is better to mark the corner with a knife edge than by means of a pencil, because no rubbing out is required which might spoil the damp surface.

*Fig. 13.—*The Shape of the Ends when the Mitre has been Cut.

*Fig. 14.—*Two Examples of Passe-Partout Fancy Binding.

side, just slide the glass over to that side for half the distance of the difference between the two measurements. It will be seen by Fig. 4 that it is usual to allow a little more of the mount to show below the picture than at the top and sides.

Next trim the Mount and Backboard.

Having now got the picture in the centre, the surplus edges of the mount and backboard should be trimmed off with a sharp knife as shown in Fig. 5, cutting through the two pieces of cardboard flush with the edges of the glass.

The Hangers.

At this stage the loops for hanging up the picture should be fixed to the backboard. This loop consists of ordinary tape pushed through two slits cut in the backboard as shown in Fig. 6. The slits can be made with the point of the knife near the top of the backboard and the tape pushed through with the point of the knife. The ends of the loops should be pasted or glued to the reverse side of the backboard and a small square of paper stuck down over them as shown in Fig. 7.

Reassemble the glass, mount and backboard and clip them together with bulldog clips or spring clothes pegs.

How to make sure the Margins are Equal.

The two sides should be bound first, and it is necessary to ensure that the margins are equal all the way round. There are two quite simple methods of ensuring this.

One is to cut out a piece of paper the size of the cover glass, *less* the width of the margin required. This is then stuck on to the centre of the surface of the glass. The passe-partout strips are then laid so that the edge just comes to the paper guide, which is removed when the job is finished.

Another method is to draw on the mount with a pencil a line all round slightly narrower than the width of the required margin. When laying the strip, the pencil mark seen through the glass should be just covered by the edge of the binder.

Preparing the Binding.

Unless the ready-bought binding is used, the binding material will probably require a little attention if the best results are to be obtained. If the paper is on the stiff side, then the face side should be damped with a sponge so as to make it limp enough to be bent round from the face of the glass to the back of the backboard, without tending to spring away before the paste has secured a hold.

A difficulty may, however, be experienced. It may be found that the paper is spoilt if moisture is applied to the surface. In such a case the limpness can be obtained by placing the paper face down upon a towel, damping the back with a sponge, leaving it for a few minutes and then giving it another damping. As soon as the water has dried in, the paper will be found limp enough for use.

Paste the first two binding strips by laying them face downwards upon a newspaper and applying the paste with a stiff brush. Place each strip in position, lay a piece of dry, clean paper over it and rub it down. The binding should then be bent over the edge and rubbed down upon the back.

To secure a clean edge, press the edge of the pack on to the table. While pressing it upright, smooth the rest of the binder on to the backboard. There should be no need to do any rubbing upon the outside edge, since, on drying, the previously damped paper will contract, and in so doing cling closely to the cut edges of the card and glass.

The ends of the first two strips can be trimmed off flush with the mount and glass with a knife or scissors.

If time permits, it is a good plan to allow those first pair of strips to dry before the remaining pair of strips is put on, because to do so it would be necessary to remove the clips. If, however, it is desired to get the work through quickly, then the clips should be moved one at a time to the sides which have been bound, leaving the ends free without having allowed the parts to slip.

A closer resemblance to wooden picture frames will be obtained if the corners of the second pair of strips are mitred. This effect is quite easy to obtain. Lay the pasted strip in position and then mark the line of the mitre from where it crosses the first strip to the corner of the glass, then cut this portion off with the scissors. The strip is then rubbed down and treated exactly as before. Do not

1511

PASSE-PARTOUT PICTURE FRAMING

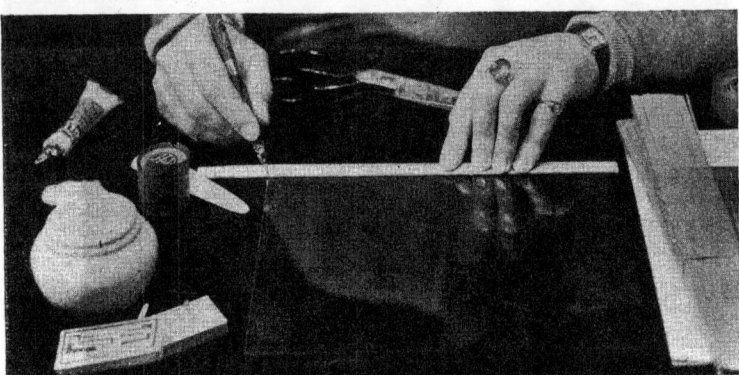

*Fig. 15.—*Deep Framing—First Operation.
Take cardboard strips ½ inch wide, and, starting with the long sides of the picture, measure and cut off two strips to fit both sides of the glass. Always cut strips separately for each side of the glass, owing to slight variation of size.

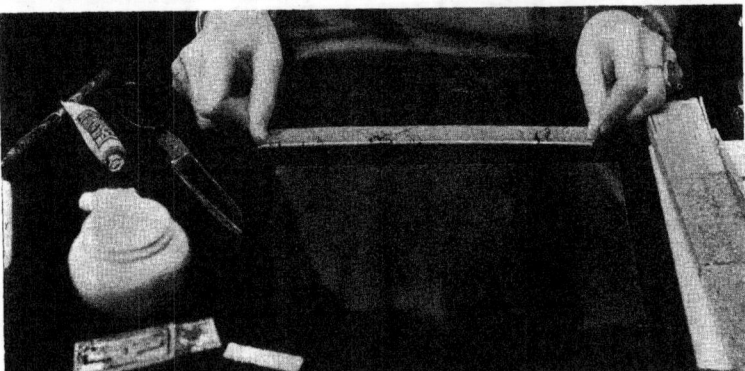

*Fig. 16.—*Deep Framing—Second Operation.
Cut binding about an inch longer than the strips. Now moisten the binding and lay it on the cardboard strip, the edge of the binding being almost level with edge of the strip (as illustrated).

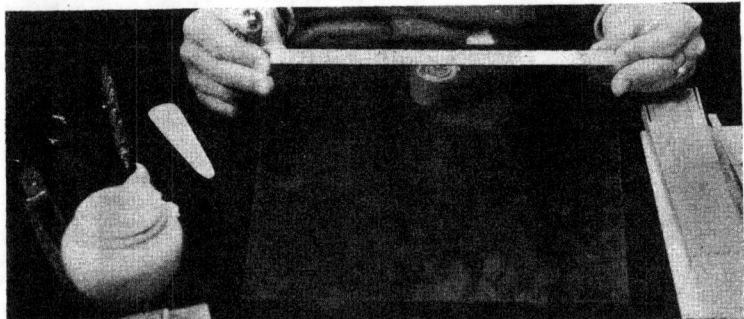

*Fig. 17.—*Deep Framing—Third Operation.
Lightly apply glue to the covered strip and fasten it to the glass, level with the edge.

remove the clips until all the strips are dry.

Fancy Bindings.

There is practically no limit to the effects that can be obtained by using different shades and patterns of paper. An attractive result can be obtained by fixing on the outer surface of the glass before binding, a frame consisting of strips of different paper from that used for the binding. A narrow edge of the different paper is arranged to project from underneath the binding strip.

DEEP FRAMING

A very attractive treatment with passe-partout consists of making it into frames which give the appearance of wooden mouldings by the means of cardboard strips covered with the binding.

Materials required.

These strips can be bought in two sizes—¼ inch and ½ inch, and cost 6*d.* and 8*d.* a bundle of twenty-four respectively. They can be cut and added to, so that a small or large picture can be obtained as the worker wishes. Not only that; very deep framing with a sunken picture can be made with the aid of several layers of strips built one on top of the other.

Further, as passe-partout binding is made in such lovely colours and designs, as well as wood and leather finish, frames to suit every kind of room can be fashioned.

For a deep frame, the only additions to ordinary passe-partout requirements are the cardboard strips and a pot of good liquid glue or gum.

Take the cardboard back and pierce holes in it for the hangers. It is better always to use metal hangers for deep framing work, as the picture will be much heavier than one bound with flush passe-partout binding. Struts for standing the picture up can also be used, as, in this case, the weight will be evenly distributed on to the front of the picture and the strut. Place the hangers in position. It is needless to say that the picture, backing sheet and glass must be *absolutely* of the same size.

Glue round the edge of the picture to the backing sheet. This is not a necessity, but keeps the picture firm.

Cutting Cardboard Strips.

Take the ½-inch cardboard strips and cut to the long length of the glass. There is no special reason for cutting the long length first, except that it is usual to do so. The two strips should be cut separately, as it might happen that the glass should be a fraction out one side (Fig. 15).

Attaching the Binding.

Cut the binding about 1 inch longer than the strips. Moisten and carefully lay it on the cardboard strip, so that the edge of the binding and the edge of the strip are practically level. Press all over very firmly with a clean cloth to remove any air bubbles, and cut surplus binding to level with strip (Fig. 16).

Lightly apply glue or gum to the covered strip and fasten it to the glass, level with the edge (Fig. 17).

Mitreing.

Next cut the two sections of cardboard strips to fit *exactly* between the two strips glued on to the glass (Fig. 18). Be careful to make a clean cut and to see that they fit exactly.

Cover with the binding as you did the long lengths, but leave the surplus binding for mitreing the corners, as in Fig. 19. To mitre, cut the binding in half down the fold and turn back until level with the strip, as in Fig. 20. Next

PASSE-PARTOUT PICTURE FRAMING

Fig. 18.—Fourth Operation.
Cut two sections of cardboard strips to fit exactly between the two strips now glued on the glass.

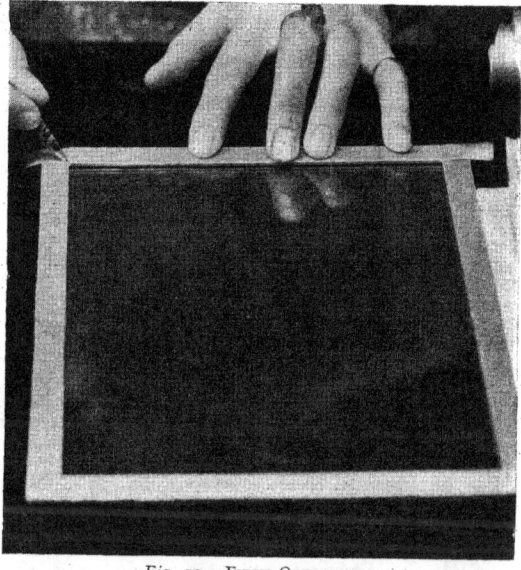

Fig. 19.—Fifth Operation.
Bind the strips as before, but leave extensions at the ends. Cut away the back of the extensions, and place strip between those on the glass, as shown. Now pencil off exact angle before cutting binding for mitre.

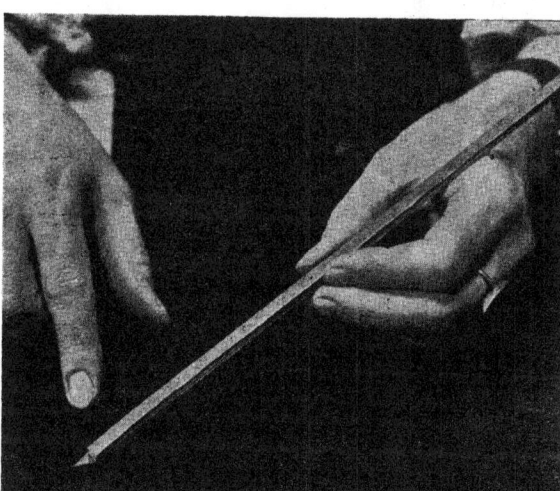

Fig. 20.—Sixth Operation.
Cut the mitres on binding at the ends of the strips. Finally glue strips to glass, as previously shown.

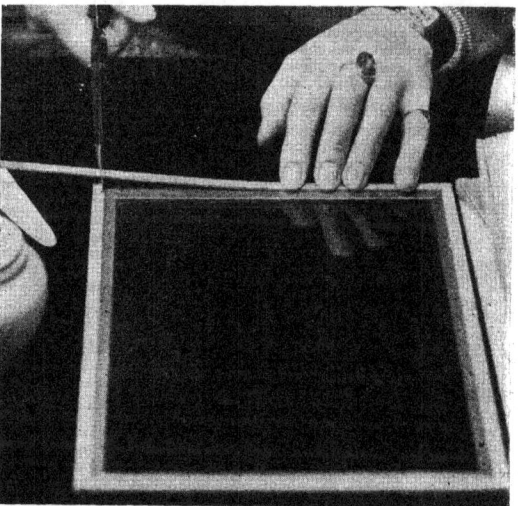

Fig. 21.—Second Layer of Framing Strips.
Commencing with the long sides as before, measure, cut and glue strips to those already on the glass, level with the outer edge.

put the strip between the glued ones on the glass and pencil off the angle for mitreing before doing so. Lastly glue these strips to the glass, as before.

Take four ¼-inch strips of cardboard, measure and cut as you did the ½-inch ones, and glue them over the strips already stuck on the glass, *level with the outer edge*. (Fig. 10)

Binding Frame to Glass and Picture.

These strips have now to be covered with the binding, but before this is done, place the backing sheet, the picture and the glass together. (An ordinary "limpet" paper clip is quite a good implement to keep them from slipping.) Cut the binding to the longer sides first—about 1 inch longer than the glass on either side. Moisten the binding and fasten firmly to the underneath strip, allowing a beading of it to show. This must be pressed well in, carried over the ¼-inch strip, and, by turning the picture over quickly, pressed well down over the backing sheet. It is essential that this work should be done quickly, so that the binding does not dry. A good method is to moisten half the width of the binding first of all, and then, when the picture is turned over, to moisten the other half. The fixing of the binding over the two end strips is similar to that already done for the ½-inch strips, taking care to mitre the corners very neatly.

The picture is now completed.

Very deep Framing.

Very deep framing is made in a similar manner, building up layer after layer of strips. Where the outer edge becomes too deep to take the other half of the binding, a full width of the binding is placed along the edge.

Joining Strips End to End.

Strips can be placed side by side or end to end as required. After binding, they should be allowed to dry before placing on the glass.

How Assessments and Rates are Made

In order to meet the financial calls of public works, service and administration within a district, a rate (or rates) is levied by the Local Authority upon the owner or occupier of every rateable hereditament therein; but the English law of rating is of so complex a nature that, notwithstanding the introduction of new legislation through the 1925 and subsequent Rating and Valuation Acts, there still exists a great amount of doubt among numerous ratepayers as to how their assessments are made and rates levied. Actually, the basic principles of valuation have been little affected by the 1925 legislation (the history of rating goes back to the year 1601), which, putting an end *inter alia* to all the old anomalies, incidentally created a new era for rating law, ratepayers and administration.

The two terms around which the whole controversy rages are:—

(1) Gross value, indicative of annual rent.

(2) Rateable value, upon which rates are paid.

What is Gross Value?

Gross value (G.V.) is essentially the key figure, the rateable value (R.V.) the lower figure, being governed by the former's variations. As every rateable house must possess a gross value, the legal definition is interesting as

"the rent which might reasonably be expected from a year to year letting if the tenant undertook to pay all usual tenants rates and taxes (not Sched. A, income tax) and the landlord undertook to bear the cost of repairs, insurance, etc., necessary to maintain the hereditament in a state to command that rent."

What is Rateable Value?

To arrive at R.V. a deduction known as the "statutory deduction" is made from G.V., the difference representing that portion of the rent which should be set aside for repairs, etc. The scale is as follows:—

From G.V. not exceeding £15: 40 per cent.

Exceeding £15 and not exceeding £20: £6, together with an amount equal to 30 per cent. of the amount which the G.V. exceeds £15.

Exceeding £20 and not exceeding £28: £7.

Exceeding £28 and not exceeding £40: 25 per cent.

Exceeding £40 and not exceeding £100: £10 or 20 per cent., whichever is the greater.

As the *reasonable and present-day* rental value is the basis of assessments, it must be carefully noted that that figure may be different from the *rent actually paid*.

How Gross Value is arrived at.

To arrive at G.V., it is necessary to classify the houses under one of the following heads:—

(1) Short-term tenures (weekly, etc., lettings).

(2) Leaseholds.

(3) Owner-occupiers.

And whilst not being influenced by the known rent, using same as a guide. To ascertain the fair letting value a method of comparative survey is applied to

situation, facilities, relationship to other and similar property in the *immediate district*, elevation (external appearance), area: (a) internal, (b) site and land: amenities (bathroom, garage, etc.), structural alterations, and the standard rent in the district.

An Example of G.V. in the Case of Short-term Tenures.

In the first case the problem is fairly simple. Normally, the landlord maintains the property, the tenant pays rates and, therefore, the known rent is multiplied to yield its annual return; the resultant figure, influenced by the comparative survey, giving G.V. Where the landlord pays rates, the rent is naturally increased and must be stripped of its rate. For example:

Rent of house 14s. 9d. per week *inclusive*, landlord responsible for repairs. Values in force £26 G.V., £19 R.V. Rate in £ = 6s. 6d. per half year.

∴ £(6s. 6d. × 2) × 19 = annual cost of rates.
= £12 7s.

∴ £12 7s. ÷ 52 = weekly cost of rates.
= 4s. 9d.

∴ 14s. 9d. − 4s. 9d. = rent stripped of rates.
= 10s.

∴ 10s. × 52 = Gross value
= £26.

An Example of G.V. in the Case of Leaseholds.

In leaseholds the tenant usually pays the cost of both rates and repairs, insurance, etc., external, internal or both. The owner's liability for maintenance having decreased, a lower rent can be expected. By law 5 per cent. is added to the annual rent for inside repairs, etc., and 10 per cent. for full cover if they are tenant's liabilities. The length of tenure and any special clauses in the leasehold must be examined and, if necessary, adjusted with the rent, after which the comparative survey is applied. The example given below is of a new house let on a three years' inside-repairing lease at £52 per annum *exclusive*. The method of rate calculation (which may be used for any class of property dealt with in this article) is also illustrated, assuming general rate at 4s. 6d. in the £ per half year and water rate 5 per cent. of G.V. per half year.

Assessment Calculation.

Assuming rent charged to be a fair one.

∴ Rent = £52 0 0
Plus 5 per cent. for internal repairs = 2 12 0
Gross value = £54 12 0
Less 20 per cent. statutory deduction approx. 10 18 5
approx. 43 13 7
Rateable value = £44 0 0

Rate Calculation.

General Rate.
£(4s. 6d. × 2) × R.V. = annual cost
9s. × 44 = £19 16 0

Water Rate.
£(5 per cent. of G.V.) × 2 = annual cost
£1($\frac{1}{20}$ of £54 10s.) × 2
£2 14s. 6d. × 2 = £5 9 0

Total cost = £25 5 0

Weekly cost = £25 5s. ÷ 52
= approx. 9s. 8½d.

Gross Value and the Owner-Occupier.

The owner-occupier buys his house as an investment, and the return therefrom stripped of all burdens represents R.V., just as payment of taxes on a capital outlay in stock produces net income. The percentage fixed to attain this varies considerably with the condition, etc., of the property. To achieve uniformity, the method of comparison and rent factors provide the only sound basis. The owner-occupier must consider himself as the hypothetical landlord demanding rent from himself as the tenant.

Additions or Deletions to Property.

Additions or deletions to property must be settled by the question: "Is the present-day value or letting capacity affected?" Naturally, a landlord seeks gain from an investment, and only the rent can give him that. Likewise, a tenant owning a garage must be prepared to pay rates on it. Small huts and tool sheds with little productive value are not generally assessed. The important question of controlled and decontrolled rents must be investigated, and so on until every channel has been exhausted.

Re-valuations.

New valuation lists are prepared quinquennially (every five years) and a re-valuation made. A ratepayer has the right of proposing his own figures

PASSE-PARTOUT PICTURE FRAMING

Fig. 18.—Fourth Operation.
Cut two sections of cardboard strips to fit exactly between the two strips now glued on the glass.

Fig. 19.—Fifth Operation.
Bind the strips as before, but leave extensions at the ends. Cut away the back of the extensions, and place strip between those on the glass, as shown. Now pencil off exact angle before cutting binding for mitre.

put the strip between the glued ones on the glass and pencil off the angle for mitreing before doing so. Lastly glue these strips to the glass, as before.

Take four ¼-inch strips of cardboard, measure and cut as you did the ½-inch ones, and glue them over the strips already stuck on the glass, *level with the outer edge*. (Fig. 10)

Binding Frame to Glass and Picture.

These strips have now to be covered with the binding, but before this is done, place the backing sheet, the picture and the glass together. (An ordinary "limpet" paper clip is quite a good implement to keep them from slipping.) Cut the binding to the longer sides first—about 1 inch longer than the glass on either side. Moisten the binding and fasten firmly to the underneath strip, allowing a beading of it to show. This must be pressed well in, carried over the ¼-inch strip, and, by turning the picture over quickly, pressed well down over the backing sheet. It is essential that this work should be done quickly, so that the binding does not dry. A good method is to moisten half the width of the binding first of all, and then, when the picture is turned over, to moisten the other half. The fixing of the binding over the two end strips is similar to that already done for the ½-inch strips, taking care to mitre the corners very neatly.

The picture is now completed.

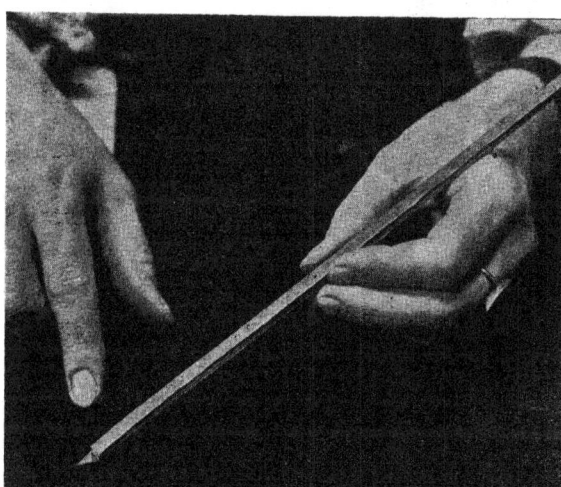

Fig. 20.—Sixth Operation.
Cut the mitres on binding at the ends of the strips. Finally glue strips to glass, as previously shown.

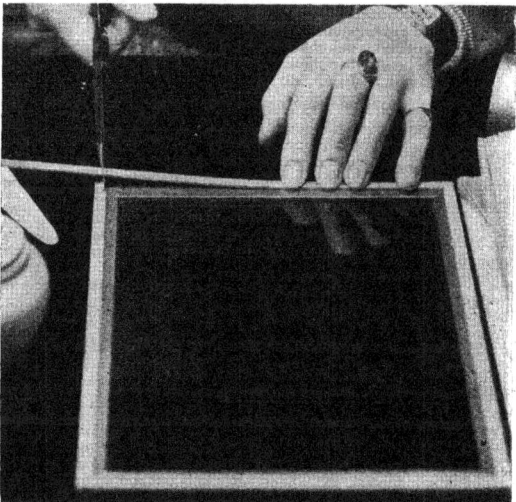

Fig. 21.—Second Layer of Framing Strips.
Commencing with the long sides as before, measure, cut and glue strips to those already on the glass, level with the outer edge.

Very deep Framing.

Very deep framing is made in a similar manner, building up layer after layer of strips. Where the outer edge becomes too deep to take the other half of the binding, a full width of the binding is placed along the edge.

Joining Strips End to End.

Strips can be placed side by side or end to end as required. After binding, they should be allowed to dry before placing on the glass.

How Assessments and Rates are Made

In order to meet the financial calls of public works, service and administration within a district, a rate (or rates) is levied by the Local Authority upon the owner or occupier of every rateable hereditament therein; but the English law of rating is of so complex a nature that, notwithstanding the introduction of new legislation through the 1925 and subsequent Rating and Valuation Acts, there still exists a great amount of doubt among numerous ratepayers as to how their assessments are made and rates levied. Actually, the basic principles of valuation have been little affected by the 1925 legislation (the history of rating goes back to the year 1601), which, putting an end *inter alia* to all the old anomalies, incidentally created a new era for rating law, ratepayers and administration.

The two terms around which the whole controversy rages are :—
(1) Gross value, indicative of annual rent.
(2) Rateable value, upon which rates are paid.

What is Gross Value ?

Gross value (G.V.) is essentially the key figure, the rateable value (R.V.) the lower figure, being governed by the former's variations. As every rateable house must possess a gross value, the legal definition is interesting as

"the rent which might reasonably be expected from a year to year letting if the tenant undertook to pay all usual tenants rates and taxes (not Sched. A, income tax) and the landlord undertook to bear the cost of repairs, insurance, etc., necessary to maintain the hereditament in a state to command that rent."

What is Rateable Value ?

To arrive at R.V. a deduction known as the "statutory deduction" is made from G.V., the difference representing that portion of the rent which should be set aside for repairs, etc. The scale is as follows :—

From G.V. not exceeding £15 : 40 per cent.
Exceeding £15 and not exceeding £20 : £6, together with an amount equal to 30 per cent. of the amount which the G.V. exceeds £15.
Exceeding £20 and not exceeding £28 : £7.
Exceeding £28 and not exceeding £40 : 25 per cent.
Exceeding £40 and not exceeding £100 : £10 or 20 per cent., whichever is the greater.

As the *reasonable and present-day* rental value is the basis of assessments, it must be carefully noted that that figure may be different from the *rent actually paid*.

How Gross Value is arrived at.

To arrive at G.V., it is necessary to classify the houses under one of the following heads :—
(1) Short-term tenures (weekly, etc., lettings).
(2) Leaseholds.
(3) Owner-occupiers.

And whilst not being influenced by the known rent, using same as a guide. To ascertain the fair letting value a method of comparative survey is applied to

situation, facilities, relationship to other and similar property in the *immediate district*, elevation (external appearance), area : (*a*) internal, (*b*) site and land : amenities (bathroom, garage, etc.), structural alterations, and the standard rent in the district.

An Example of G.V. in the Case of Short-term Tenures.

In the first case the problem is fairly simple. Normally, the landlord maintains the property, the tenant pays rates and, therefore, the known rent is multiplied to yield its annual return ; the resultant figure, influenced by the comparative survey, giving G.V. Where the landlord pays rates, the rent is naturally increased and must be stripped of its rate. For example :

Rent of house 14s. 9d. per week *inclusive*, landlord responsible for repairs. Values in force £26 G.V., £19 R.V. Rate in £ = 6s. 6d. per half year.

∴ £(6s. 6d. × 2) × 19 = annual cost of rates.
= £12 7s.
∴ £12 7s. ÷ 52 = weekly cost of rates.
= 4s. 9d.
∴ 14s. 9d. − 4s. 9d. = rent stripped of rates.
= 10s.
∴ 10s. × 52 = Gross value
= £26.

An Example of G.V. in the Case of Leaseholds.

In leaseholds the tenant usually pays the cost of both rates and repairs, insurance, etc., external, internal or both. The owner's liability for maintenance having decreased, a lower rent can be expected. By law 5 per cent. is added to the annual rent for inside repairs, etc., and 10 per cent. for full cover if they are tenant's liabilities. The length of tenure and any special clauses in the leasehold must be examined and, if necessary, adjusted with the rent, after which the comparative survey is applied. The example given below is of a new house let on a three years' inside-repairing lease at £52 per annum *exclusive*. The method of rate calculation (which may be used for any class of property dealt with in this article) is also illustrated, assuming general rate at 4s. 6d. in the £ per half year and water rate 5 per cent. of G.V. per half year.

Assessment Calculation.

Assuming rent charged to be a fair one.

∴ Rent = £52 0 0
Plus 5 per cent. for internal repairs = 2 12 0
Gross value = £54 12 0
Less 20 per cent. statutory deduction
approx. 10 18 5
approx. 43 13 7
Rateable value = £44 0 0

Rate Calculation.

General Rate.
£(4s. 6d. × 2) × R.V. = annual cost
9s. × 44 = £19 16 0
Water Rate.
£(5 per cent. of G.V.)
× 2 = annual cost
£1(1/20 of £54 10s.)
× 2
£2 14s. 6d. × 2 = £5 9 0

Total cost = £25 5 0

Weekly cost = £25 5s. ÷ 52
= approx. 9s. 8¼d.

Gross Value and the Owner-Occupier.

The owner-occupier buys his house as an investment, and the return therefrom stripped of all burdens represents R.V., just as payment of taxes on a capital outlay in stock produces net income. The percentage fixed to attain this varies considerably with the condition, etc., of the property. To achieve uniformity, the method of comparison and rent factors provide the only sound basis. The owner-occupier must consider himself as the hypothetical landlord demanding rent from himself as the tenant.

Additions or Deletions to Property.

Additions or deletions to property must be settled by the question : "Is the present-day value or letting capacity affected ?" Naturally, a landlord seeks gain from an investment, and only the rent can give him that. Likewise, a tenant owning a garage must be prepared to pay rates on it. Small huts and tool sheds with little productive value are not generally assessed. The important question of controlled and decontrolled rents must be investigated, and so on until every channel has been exhausted.

Re-valuations.

New valuation lists are prepared quinquennially (every five years) and a re-valuation made. A ratepayer has the right of proposing his own figures before the list is made law. He may also object to his assessment within the period of any rate. If rates have been paid before an objection is filed, and which objection secures a reduction, then a refund may be claimed for the amount involved. An objection involves attendance before an Assessment Committee (not compulsory), and a clear, concise statement supporting the claim, unhampered either by sentiment or politics, is necessary. In an extremity an objection may be listed with a court of summary jurisdiction, or even the higher judicial benches. The ratepayer has the right of access to the valuation list at all reasonable times.

Levying the Rate.

As rates are actually paid on R.V., it is seen that to produce money for public expenditure the local authority must have funds for future works, and therefore a budget is compiled at the financial year-end. By taking the total rateable value of the district and estimating what a $1d.$ rate will yield in conjunction with the proposed expenditure, the local authority fix the rate in the £ in proportion to cover their liability. The ultimate demand note is, by law, actually payable *on demand*. Before the annual audit of accounts the ratepayer is given the opportunity of examining same and taking extracts.

X-RAY PHOTOGRAPHY

PERFECTLY good X-ray photographs can be taken with comparatively simple apparatus. The following is a list of the necessary requirements :—

Spark coil, giving a $1\frac{1}{4}$-inch or 2-inch spark.

X-ray tube, size 6 cm., with regenerator (*Griffen & Tatlock Ltd.*).

X-ray film or paper, $6\frac{1}{2} \times 4\frac{3}{4}$ inches.

One or more exposure holders, $6\frac{1}{2} \times 4\frac{3}{4}$ inches.

Retort stand and clamp, or, alternatively, a wooden box $15 \times 7 \times 8$ inches, two Terry clips to hold a $\frac{3}{4}$-inch diameter tube, sheet lead and wood for base and uprights.

Six-volt accumulator.

Usual developing and printing apparatus.

An X-ray tube of the type mentioned can be obtained for about £2, while a coil to give a $1\frac{1}{4}$-inch spark can be obtained for just under £5; a coil to give a 2-inch spark would cost about £8. Often, however, a coil can be obtained for less than £1 at wireless shops selling ex-Government disposal stock.

The X-ray films give better photographs with greater contrast and require less exposure than paper, but they cost about twice as much and, of course, give a reversed print. The film, paper and exposure holders can be obtained from either Ilford Ltd. or Kodak Ltd., at the following prices: Paper, $3s.$ $5d.$ per dozen sheets; films, ordinary wrapping, $6s.$ $8d.$ per dozen, double-wrapped, $7s.$ $6d.$

Holding and shielding the Tube.

The simplest way of holding the X-ray tube is to use an ordinary retort stand and clamp. The tube must be enclosed in a lead shield. It is advisable to use a wood box, covered on the *outside* with sheet lead, which should be $\frac{1}{16}$ inch thick. The tube will then be completely shielded and safe in operation.

Adjusting the Spark Coil.

Into the two secondary terminals at the top of the coil clamp two pieces of stiff wire, so that their ends form a spark gap about 1 inch long. Connect the coil to the accumulator and turn the hammer adjusting screw anti-clockwise until it just clears the contact on the vibrating arm. Switch on the current by turning the handle of the commutator switch and slowly screw the adjusting screw clockwise; the hammer will begin to vibrate.

Adjust this screw until a hot, fat spark streams across the spark gap. A thin straggly spark is no good. When the coil is working properly, switch it off and remove the sparking wires. Whenever the apparatus is in use never touch the high-tension terminals or wires or a nasty shock will be experienced.

Adjusting the X-ray Tube.

When the X-ray tube is received, a small packet will be found containing one long and one short wire with loop ends. These wires should be clamped to the two metal terminals at the ends of the regenerator tube, and at first should be pushed up so that the gaps are each about 1 inch long. Place the tube either in the shielded box or hold it in the retort clamp, taking care that the jaws are only clamped just tight enough to hold the tube securely. Connect the cathode terminal and the anti-cathode terminal of the X-ray tube to the secondary terminals of the induction coil by means of pieces of high-tension magneto cable, keeping these leads as short as possible. Now switch on the coil; the tube will be filled with a bluish-green glow; *do not look at the tube closely when running*, but from a distance of about 2 feet observe the nature of this glow carefully. Now reverse the commutator of the coil, or, if one is not fitted, change over the accumulator wires to the coil. It will be noted that this glow, or *fluorescence*, is more intense with the accumulator connected one way round, and the tube is more filled with light. The tube is connected the correct way round *when the glow is faintest, and the glass opposite the anti-cathode fluoresces*. If there is any strong fluorescence of the tube behind the anti-cathode, the tube is connected the wrong way round, and will not give X-rays. Make a note of the correct connections of the accumulator and commutator.

Making an Exposure.

Having adjusted the coil and tube, we can now make a trial exposure. If *double-wrapped* films have been purchased, all that is necessary is to open the box and take out one of the black envelopes containing a film. This envelope must not be opened. When single or *ordinary wrapped* films or paper are used, the box must be opened in a dark-room. Undo the outer wrappings, and remove a film in its black folder; place the film (still in its folder) in the exposure holder. The method of doing this and closing the holder will be sufficiently obvious, but see that the film is well secured before taking it out of the dark-room. Be sure to close the film box.

Choose some simple objects, such as keys, coins, etc., for the first exposure. The X-ray tube should be arranged so that the film is supported about 6 inches from its centre. A double-wrapped film should be placed below the tube with the plain side towards the tube; if an ordinary wrapped film or paper in an exposure holder is used, it should be placed with the face marked "Tube Side" towards the tube.

Place the objects to be photographed flat upon the film, and see that everything is directly below the X-ray tube. Switch on the coil, making sure (by observing the fluorescence) that the tube is the correct way round; leave the coil running for one and a half minutes for film, or two and a half minutes for paper. Switch off, and take the film into the dark-room for development.

Developing and printing.

The X-ray film or paper is developed in just the same manner as an ordinary negative, except that slightly more care should be taken.

An Electric Stirrer

THE stirrer described in this article shows one application of the small electric motor recently shown in these pages; any available motor can, however, be utilised in a similar manner, the only deviation from the design will be a modification in the bearers which support the power unit. The main upright is a right-angled bracket of Tee-sectioned iron, this is hinged to a broad G clamp, which is fastened to the table or bench; when removing the stirring vessel the apparatus is lifted by swinging it sideways on the hinge. The motor drives a horizontal shaft by means of two pulleys and a belt; this axle drives through a reducing worm gear a vertical shaft carrying the stirring paddles. Gears are not used throughout the transmission, as the pulleys and belt allow a certain amount of flexibility in the drive and so protect the worm drive from damage. Some readers may prefer to mount the standard and motor on a revolving base so that the machine turns instead of tips when removing the paddles from the stirring vessel.

Material required.

Iron, Tee-sectioned : 2 inches × 2 feet.
Iron, sheet, $\tfrac{3}{32}$ inch thick : 6 inches × 1 foot.
Iron, sheet, $\tfrac{1}{8}$ inch thick : 8 inches × 1 foot.
Brass strip : $\tfrac{3}{4} \times \tfrac{3}{4} \times 3$ inches.
Brass rod : $\tfrac{7}{8}$ inches diameter, 4 inches.
Brass rod : $\tfrac{3}{8}$ inches diameter, 2 inches.
Brass rod : $1\tfrac{1}{8}$ inches diameter, 2 inches.

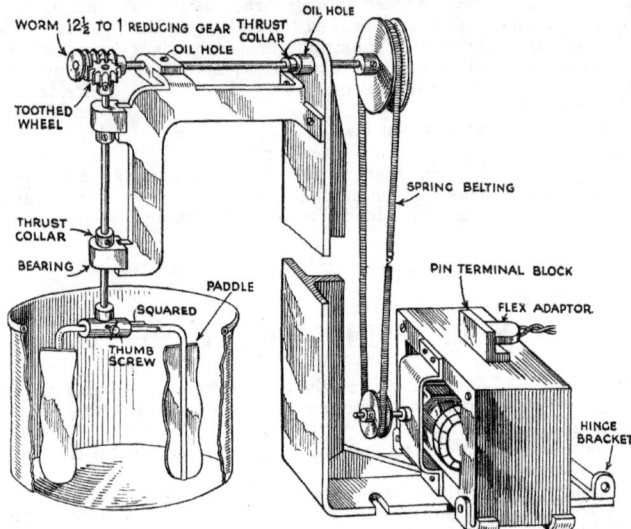

Fig. 1.—The Completed Stirrer.

Steel rod : $\tfrac{3}{16}$ inch diameter, 3 feet.
Worm gear : $12\tfrac{1}{2}$ to 1 reduction (obtainable from Messrs. Bond's, of Euston Road, N.W.1).
Two pulleys, say, $1\tfrac{1}{4}$ and $2\tfrac{1}{4}$ inches.
Spring or leather belting : 2 feet.
Six screws, 4BA.
Six bolts, 2BA.
Sheet tin, gauge 22 : 6 inches × 1 foot.

Making the Shaft Bracket.

The first step is to cut out the shaft bracket as shown in Fig. 3, and bend to shape. The horizontal shaft is supported in one bearing at the top of the main vertical standard and another attached to the small tongue A in Fig. 3. The piece A, which is bent at right-angles to the horizontal arm, should be as near the end as possible so that the shaft is supported close up to the worm, thus preventing unwanted side "play."

The bracket is attached to the vertical standard by two flat feet, these are obtained by cutting the horizontal arm down the middle for a distance of $\tfrac{3}{4}$ inch and then bending the two free ends sideways, one to the left and the other to the right. The feet are secured to the standard with bolts, or rivets if preferred.

The Shaft Bearings.

The small sketch, Fig. 3, shows one of the two bushes for the vertical shaft; these are filed up to shape from square brass strip. The slot is filed out so that the bush fits on to the projecting tongue of the bracket to which it is soldered. The horizontal shaft is carried on one bearing attached to the tongue A and another bush in the main upright (see Fig. 6). Before fixing the horizontal bushes it will be necessary to fit the vertical one with the toothed wheel in position, then engage the worm and carefully set out the centres for the bushes.

If you carefully examine Figs. 1 and 4 you will see that each shaft is fitted with two thrust collars, which prevent "end float." These are simply drilled sections of $\tfrac{3}{8}$-inch brass rod, carefully faced up and firmly secured to the shaft. Before finally fixing these it will be necessary to adjust them until the worm and toothed wheel mesh correctly; they must then be firmly secured, using a touch of solder if necessary.

How the Gears are fixed.

Fig. 4 shows how the worm and toothed wheel are attached to the ends of the journals. Small flats are cut near the ends of the shafts to form a hold for the grub screws. It is essential that the shaft should be a tight fit in the collars which are part of the gear wheels; any slackness can be remedied by "tinning" the end of the journal.

The Standard.

Fig. 6 shows details of the standard

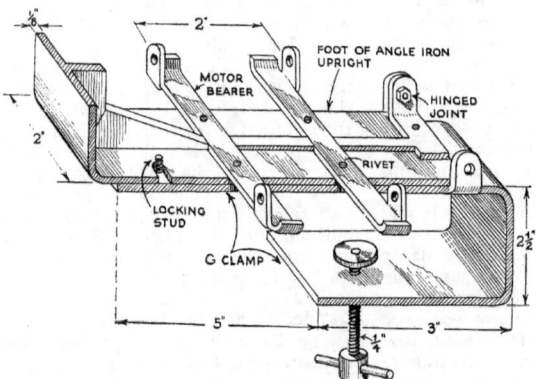

Fig. 2.—Details of Motor Support and Hinged G Clamp.

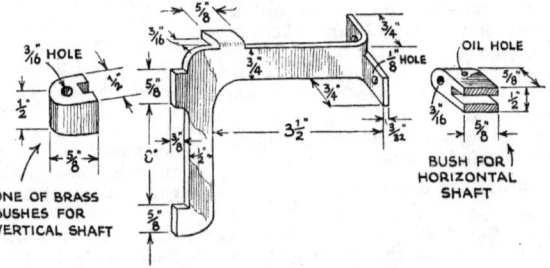

Fig. 3.—Details of Shaft and Bearings.

AN ELECTRIC STIRRER

and base bracket. The bush which supports the pulley end of the horizontal shaft is sweated into the upright; note that this is not centrally placed, its position being governed by the mesh of the worm; its centre will be approximately $\frac{3}{8}$ inch out of centre. Observe in Fig. 6 how the iron is bent at right-angles, the rear web being cut away and mitred; on the horizontal part of the standard most of the web is cut away, small grooves being made to accommodate the bearers which hold the motor in place.

The Motor Bed.

In Fig. 2 details are given of the motor support and the G clamp. Three strips of metal are riveted at right-angles across the foot of the standard; these have the ends turned up as shown. Two of them form bearers for the motor, while the third on the extreme end forms the hinge bar between the G clamp and the foot of the standard. The clamp is made from stout-gauge sheet iron; note the two "horns" which are bent up at right-angles—these form the fulcrum upon which the hinge turns. Look at Fig. 2 and observe the locking stud; this is screwed into the G clamp and locates itself in a slot in the foot of the standard and is fastened with a winged nut. Usually the locking nut will not be required, as the weight of the motor will hold the stirrer quite steady; it may, however, be necessary when the machine is under heavy load.

The Pulleys.

Assuming that the motor will run at a speed of 1,500 revolutions per minute, it will be necessary to greatly reduce this, as it is much too high for stirring or mixing. The introduction of the worm gear gives a reduction ratio of $12\frac{1}{2}$ to 1; thus, if both pulleys are the same size, the speed of the vertical shaft will be 120 revolutions per minute. This is a little fast for the work of stirring, so a further reduction is obtained by fitting a pulley one and a half times as large in diameter as the driving pulley on the motor spindle; in this way we obtain a speed of approximately 80 revolutions per minute. Some readers may like to have a series of two or three pulleys in line so that the speed can be varied to suit the medium being mixed. The belting can be a length of spiral spring cable or a piece of round leather as sold for the purpose.

The Stirring Paddles.

Fig. 5 shows one of the paddles and the Tee to which it is fixed. The sheet tin paddle blade is soldered to a length of flattened $\frac{3}{16}$-inch rod, which is bent at right-angles at the top so that it can be passed through the Tee at the lower end of the vertical staff. The bent ends of the paddle rods are

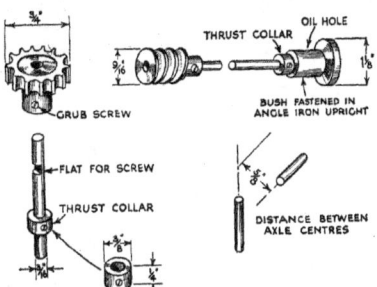

Fig. 4.—Details relating to the Two Shafts carrying the Worm Gear.

rectangular in section so that they can fit side by side in the Tee, as shown in Fig. 1. It should also be noted in Fig. 1 that one paddle is adjusted much nearer the centre than the other. This creates a much better mixing action than if the paddles are equidistant from the centre; this is especially useful when working with thick liquids or powders.

The Tee bracket at the end of the vertical shaft is made from $\frac{7}{8}$-inch

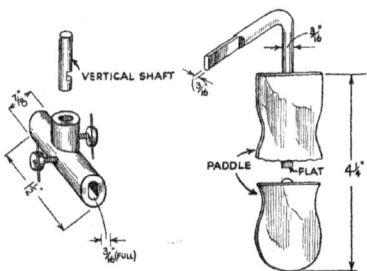

Fig. 5.—Details of Stirring Paddles

brass rod. Two thumb screws (2BA) are needed, one to fasten the paddles and the other to grip the shaft. Note that the horizontal hole in the Tee has flat sides to accommodate the ends of the paddle rods. The stirring blades shown in Fig. 5 are $\frac{7}{8}$ inch wide. A graduated set ranging from $\frac{3}{8}$ to 1 inch should be made so that they may be changed to suit the density of the medium or powder to be mixed. The efficiency of the apparatus is greatly

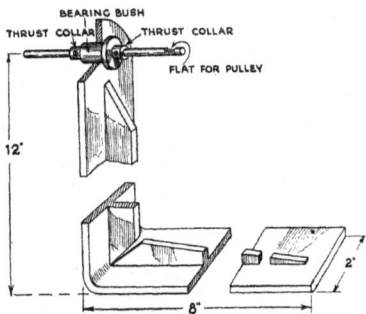

Fig. 6.—Details of Standard and Base Support.

increased if a special mixing vessel is constructed, with a small fixed paddle attached to the bottom around which the two revolve. Another useful aid when dealing with thin liquids is to have two narrow blades soldered vertically to the inside wall of the vessel; these greatly increase the agitation of the liquid.

Final Hints.

The four shaft bearings must be well oiled with thin lubricant, while the worm must be supplied with a thick grease, preferably one impregnated with fine graphite. It is a wise plan to have a variable resistance in the circuit supplying the current so that the power may be gradually increased as the motor takes up the load; this is especially necessary if the apparatus is used to mix thick fluids or heavy powders.

LENGTHENING A POLE

Often it is advantageous to lengthen a pole—as for wireless aerials, etc.—and the simple method shown will be found very effective.

The bottom end of the upper pole, A, is laid alongside the upper end of the bottom pole B, and may be nailed together by a couple of wire nails clinched over to keep them in position while making the fastening. Then a sheet of thin iron about a foot wide is bent round the two poles and securely nailed to them with clout nails. To make this fastening tight, two wedges shaped as shown in the sectional view are driven in between the overlapping sheet iron and the poles — one each side.

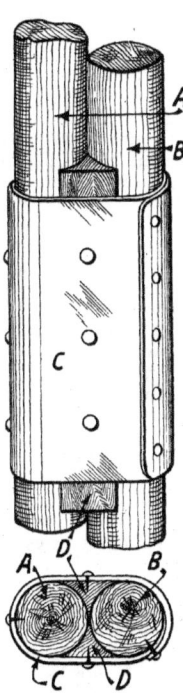

Details for Lengthening a Pole.

The wedges should be very long with a very gradual taper, and should be finally driven up tight when the poles are in position.

A long nail projecting $\frac{3}{4}$ inch may be driven into pole B, at the bottom of pole A, to act as a further support.

Galvanised iron can be used, and so as to ensure against weakening by rust, the nails should also be galvanised.

The Rudiments of Painting in Water-colour, Oil and Pastel

The object of the following instructions is to provide the beginner in the art of painting a picture with the essentials that are required to transfer to paper or canvas the impressions of a subject. Like every other craft, success comes only by practice and knowledge of the principles involved in the particular process. An appreciation of colour, a knowledge of the elements of perspective and a keen observation will go far in the production of a picture.

Colour-sketching.

One of the difficulties experienced by the beginner in colour sketching is to be able to appreciate the effect of changing intensity of light and the effect of distance on individual colours. For example, green, in various lights, may range from yellow to blue, and a green tree in the immediate foreground will seem blue in the middle distance and purple in the far distance. But the blue and purple is greyed and is effected by surrounding colour as well.

A Simply made Colour Scale.

If any great difficulty is experienced in determining the colour in distance, it is a good plan to make a colour scale, with green and red as a basis. First cut out an opening about ¾ inch wide in a post card, with two smaller openings below to take a strip of paper, as shown at Fig. 1. Next prepare a few strips of cartridge paper and paint some green, gradually add blue, then pure blue, and add violet and finish with violet. Make another strip, but add grey to each colour. Red, brown and violet can be treated in the same way. Slip the strips in the card, as at Fig. 2, and when looking at a landscape, move the strips along until the colours in the middle and far distances correspond approximately.

Aerial Perspective.

This alteration of appearance by the changing of tones or relative values of light and dark is known as aerial perspective, and is an essential feature of a landscape sketch. It is not experienced to any great extent in flower-painting or in a collection of still-life objects.

Another aspect of the same subject can be seen when looking at a tree close at hand, in which the roundness of the trunk is noticeable, the leaves are defined and the branches are marked. A few hundred yards away the leaves cannot be defined, but the tree becomes masses of light and shade distinctly outlined in defined shapes. The colour, compared with the near tree, is different, although it may be exactly the same kind.

But when the same tree is seen a mile or two away, the masses of light and shade become less defined, and it appears light on one side and dark on the other and is probably blue-grey. When seen on the horizon, the mass only, although very small, is seen; light and shade is not discernible and the colour is approximately a greyish purple. As a rule, these things are not really observed until it is necessary to translate them in paint.

The Law of Converging Lines.

There is another aspect of perspective that forms a feature in landscape sketching as well as in the drawing of still-life objects. It is the law of converging lines. It is not essential that the beginner should make a thorough study of the principles of perspective. Perspective was understood by the old painters before the scientific principles were evolved, and the accompanying sketches will help in making them plain. In the first place it must be realised that the eye line, or horizon, is really the starting position. All horizontal lines, for all practical purposes, will converge somewhere to the horizon or a line on the level of the spectator's eye, as in Fig. 3.

For example, a wide road immediately in front will appear to converge, as shown in Fig. 4. A similar road lined with trees and telegraph poles will appear, as in Fig. 5. A pencil held horizontally will help to indicate the amount of the inclination, and if the pencil is inclined, the exact direction of the line can be transferred to the paper.

Useful Appliance for View finding.

A very useful appliance for view-finding and for help in judging the directions of lines can be made quite easily with a piece of cardboard, 11 × 9 inches, and some black cotton or thread, as shown at Fig. 6. The opening should be about 4½ × 3 inches and the thread laid across ¾ inch apart; it can be kept in position by gummed-paper tape. When held at arm's length it is a simple matter to note points of perspective; also the opening acts as a view finder.

As the observation becomes more acute, it will be a simple matter to deal with such perspective problems as are shown in the illustrations Figs. 7, 8 and 9. The first one shows a church outline facing the spectator, the next two diagrams show how the lines of the building would converge from different points of view. Before leaving the subject of perspective it will be as well to note the appearance of the circle in various positions, as at Fig. 10. Fig. 11 shows the appearance of a semi-circular arch in a perspective rendering.

Draw Preliminary Lines with Charcoal.

It will be seen that some ability to draw is necessary before a picture can be painted, but a high degree of pencil technique is not required. In either of the three mediums to be dealt with it is not necessary that the pencil should be used at all; what preliminary lines are required can be done with a piece of charcoal. The main thing is to be able to fix the approximate position of any prominent features of the view on the paper. But it should be noted that very considerable help is derived from pencil sketching, and a would-be artist should most certainly invest in a sketch book and a BB pencil and make as many sketches as possible. Effects of light and shade should also be noted whenever possible, and instead of always drawing in outline, shapes should be formed by masses of dark against light.

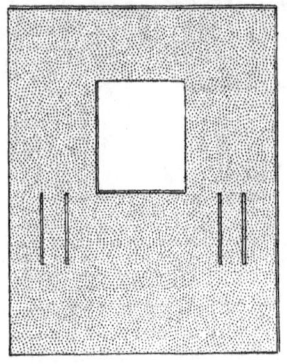

Fig. 1.—A Simply-made Colour Scale.
Cut an opening about ¾ inch wide in a post-card and make two smaller openings below to take a strip of paper.

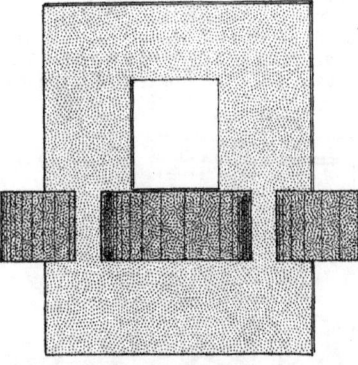

Fig. 2.—Using the Simply-made Colour Scale.
Strips of cartridge paper painted in various tones of different colours are placed through the smaller openings and moved along until the required tones are obtained.

THE RUDIMENTS OF PAINTING IN WATER-COLOUR, OIL AND PASTEL

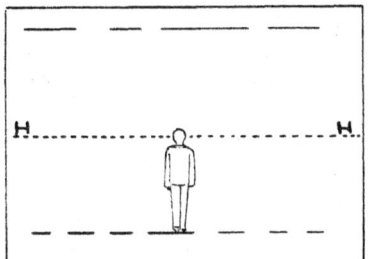

Fig. 3.—All Horizontal Lines will converge somewhere to the Horizon or a Line on the level of the Spectator's Eye.

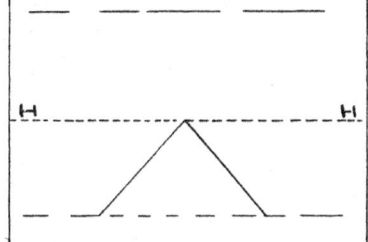

Fig. 4.—A Wide Road immediately in Front will appear to converge as shown.

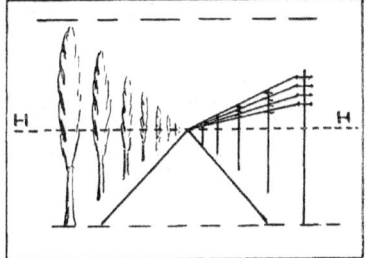

Fig. 5.—How a Road lined with Trees and Telegraph Poles should appear.

THE USE OF WATER COLOURS

Before water colours are used in an attempt to make a picture, it is advisable to begin with a few colours and get to know what happens when they are applied to the paper. The first thing is to know how to apply a wash of colour evenly over the paper, and then to experiment with graduations or mixing with several colours. It must be understood that the medium known as water colour is more or less transparent and that the colour of the paper will affect the colour of the paint when applied. Usually white paper is used, but excellent effects can be obtained by the use of tinted papers.

The Paper to use.

The paper should be of good quality and as thick as possible. For preliminary work thick cartridge should be used if possible, but for any good work, use a hand-made paper such as Whatman or "A.C.M." A little more expensive but ideal for sketching purposes, as it need not be stretched and will not cockle when damp, is Green's Pasteless Board.

Making the Paper Damp.

As it is necessary in the preliminary stages of picture-making to have the paper damp, it is more convenient to stretch ordinary paper on a board. This is done by taking a sheet of paper and folding about ½ inch all around. The tray thus formed is covered with water and left for a few minutes until it is quite wet right through. The water is poured off and the turned-up edges are covered with a layer of strong paste or glue and turned down on a drawing-board. When the paper is dry it will be stretched and will not cockle when damped. By using Cox's sketching-frames, costing from 3s. according to size, pasting is avoided. Whatman and "A.C.M." paper can be obtained mounted on boards and is not expensive.

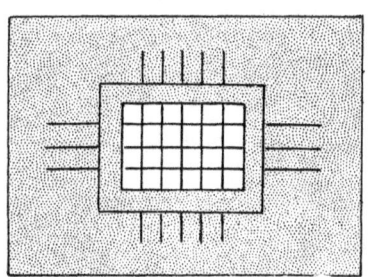

Fig. 6.—A useful Appliance for View-finding and Judging the Direction of Lines.

The Choice of Colours.

The choice of colours is important, and for all ordinary work there is no need to use more than twelve colours, but they should be of the best possible quality. The colours known as students' quality will serve for practice, but for purity and transparency the best colours should be obtained; they cost more, but they last a long time. A suitable selection to begin with is yellow ochre, gamboge, light red, cobalt blue, ultramarine, alizarin crimson, Hooker's green 1 and 2, raw umber, raw sienna, vermilion and lamp black. Permanent and antwerp blue can be substituted, and emerald green stocked instead of raw sienna. If additional colours are desired, they should be cadmium, vandyke brown or sepia, rose madder and neutral tint.

Brushes.

The best possible brushes should be used, the ordinary so-called camel-hair brush should be avoided. At least two sable brushes, Nos. 5 and 8, and one fine hog-hair, No. 4. If one brush only is used, a No. 6 will do. Always wash out the brushes after use and stroke them to a point. When brushes are carried about, special care should be taken to prevent the hair being disturbed. A good quality sable brush, size No. 8, costs about 3s. 6d., and No. 5 about 1s. 6d.

A Simple Picture to begin with.

It is a good plan to begin with a simple sky picture on paper about 7 × 5 inches. Use some thick cartridge and rub a damp but perfectly clean sponge over it. Now, using the well of the paint box or a saucer, fill up with about a dessert-spoonful of water, dip the brush into it, pick up some yellow ochre and just colour the water. On no account make the colour full strength. Now tilt the paper slightly, preferably using a board, begin at the top with a brushful of colour and carry it from one side to the other. Dip the brush in with a stir, and quickly take the brush across the paper again a little lower down

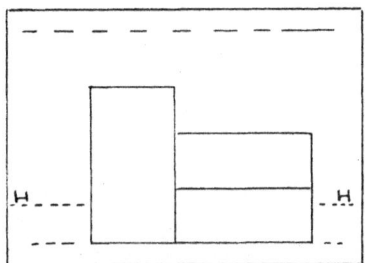

Fig. 7.—A Church Outline facing the Spectator.

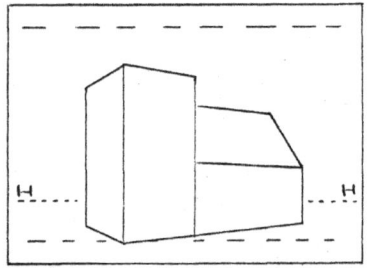

Fig. 8.—How the Lines would converge from a Different Viewpoint.

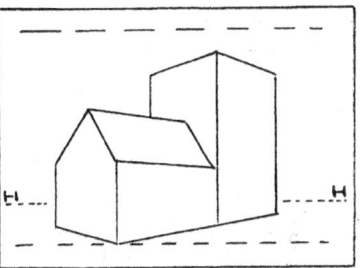

Fig. 9.—A Third Viewpoint showing how the Lines converge.

and so on to the bottom of the paper. The result should be a perfectly even coating of yellow over the paper. Let the paper dry and then rub a damp sponge over and leave it again.

Now mix up some cobalt blue in the same way and begin at the top of the paper again with blue; but when about a quarter of the way down, dip the brush into clean water before taking up more colour—this will lighten the wash. Do the same with the next line and stop about one-third of the way down the paper. Now add a little crimson to the blue to give a purple, and run a line across the paper; run this along for a few strokes and then add brown and continue to the bottom. Before the paper dries, rub out some of the sky to form clouds and add green and dark brown to the foreground. The idea is shown at Fig. 12. Skies in yellow and red, merging into purple, can be done in the same way and will provide a wonderful insight into the possibilities of picture-making.

Some useful practice can be obtained by studying tree forms and working out simple sketches as at Fig. 13. For the first stage, use yellow for the whole of the shape, then while still damp add blue, as indicated in the second stage, allowing the blue to run into the yellow. Now run a little red into the blue to give the dark shadows, as in the third stage. More yellow, blue or red can be added while the surface is still damp. Last of all, mix the yellow, blue and red together to put in the branches and trunk.

Choose Subjects having Strong Contrasts.

The beginner is advised to begin with subjects having strong contrasts, a country cottage or church in a strong light giving a distinct shadow. If the colours appear too strong, the sketch should be allowed to dry and then be sponged over with a fine sponge or even placed under the tap. Many an artist has retrieved what would have been a spoilt picture by the use of a sponge and water. There are many books on water-colour painting and sketching, but they are apt to be somewhat confusing to the beginner. A very suitable series is that entitled "Art for All," by J. Littlejohns, R.I., R.B.A. Another useful little book is "Sketching and Painting for Beginners, Young and Old," by D. D. Sawer.

PAINTING WITH OIL COLOURS

In many respects oil painting is easier for the beginner than water colour—the technique is simpler. The equipment is however more expensive, and for outdoor work is heavy to carry, and special care has to be taken to prevent damage to the painting before it is dry. As a rule, a water-colour sketch must be completed in one sitting, but with oil colour the sketch can be carried on periodically, although the palette containing the paint should be cleaned after each time it is used. This applies particularly to the brushes.

Oil painting is done on canvas or wood panels, and for the beginner pasteboard covered with canvas is the most convenient surface to use. A 12 × 10-inch canvas board prepared for painting costs 8d. A sketching-board slightly smaller can be obtained for 3d. A stretched canvas on a frame would cost about 2s., and a prepared wood panel about 3s. 6d. It will be found that a student's quality canvas board will be found quite satisfactory.

The Brushes.

Oil painting is done mainly with bristle brushes known as hog hair. A variety of shapes and sizes are available, but for use at first about four will be enough. These should be flat and numbered 1, 4, 6 and 8. Others can be added later, as it is an advantage to use several brushes, as it saves cleaning each time a new colour is required. A quality suitable for the beginner can be obtained at prices 6d. for No. 1, 7d. for No. 3, 8d. for No. 6, and 1s. 1d. for No. 8, in the flat shape. A tin should be provided for cleaning purposes, and a bottle of turps at hand, not only for cleaning the brushes, but for thinning the paint when required.

Colours.

A useful range of colours arranged in the order that is most convenient for use on the palette is flake white, cobalt, french blue, alizarin crimson, light red, yellow ochre, raw sienna, light cadmium, deep cadmium, viridian, burnt sienna and raw umber. These colours, in tube form, are obtainable in student's as well as in artist's quality, and for the beginner the former will be quite good enough. Much more of the pigment is used in painting in oils than in water colour and the difference in cost is appreciable. The 2-inch tubes in the student's quality range from 3d. each, but a large tube of white will be required. In the artist's quality the cost ranges from 5d for a 4-inch tube of the cheaper pigments to over a 1s. for a 2-inch tube of the more expensive ones.

Palettes.

Palettes vary in size and quality and are oblong and elliptical in shape. A fitted box containing a good selection of colours, brushes, palette, dipper, turpentine and linseed oil can be obtained for approximately 12s. 6d., but for indoor use, the materials can be bought separately and kept in a suitable box. A palette knife, though not essential, is useful for cleaning the palette. One or two pieces of clean rag will be needed for wiping the brushes and palette.

In working out of doors, an easel of some kind is almost essential, but a special form of sketching box can be used. It rests on the knees, with the colours in the bottom of the box; the lid is held by a tape or hinge at a convenient angle and the canvas supported against it.

Starting an Oil Painting.

In beginning a painting it is advisable to paint in the broad effects with as few simple large strokes, using the large brush or brushes. The principal colours for the sky are yellow ochre, cobalt and alizarin crimson mixed with white. The top of the sky is usually cobalt, then either yellow ochre or crimson are added according to the requirements. The grey of the distance is mixed with cobalt yellow and crimson, but considerable care will be needed in adding the yellow—it should be done after the blue and crimson are mixed. Yellow ochre and cobalt are the best colours for the middle and far distance, and with raw sienna most of the general effect can be obtained. For trees light cadmium, viridian, french blue and burnt sienna are useful colours, and for grass, deep cadmium is a basis, with yellow ochre and cobalt.

How to apply the Paint.

As a general rule the paint is applied to the canvas by touches rather than daubs. The strokes of the brush should not run in any one direction, but be varied. The character of the subject will often suggest the stroke of the brush. It is generally found convenient to hold the brush about half way along the handle so that the paint can be applied in any required direction with little trouble. All colours should as far as possible be mixed on the palette and not on the canvas—this is one of the differences between water and oil techinque. Much can be learnt from the study of several oil paintings, and notes should be made when examining a painting as to combinations of colours and of the use of contrasting colours, particularly noting the methods of indicating shadow.

Mixing and thinning the Colours.

Mediums are often suggested for use in mixing and thinning colours, but generally a little turpentine with a spot of linseed oil will be all that is necessary. As a rule, the paints will be found of the right consistency and will need no thinning. It should be noted that when it is necessary to place a second colour on the top of one previously painted on the canvas the first colour should be dry.

PAINTING IN PASTEL

By far the most convenient medium for making colour studies is by means

THE RUDIMENTS OF PAINTING IN WATER-COLOUR, OIL AND PASTEL

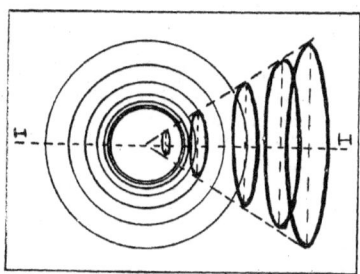

Fig. 10.—EXAMPLES OF A CIRCLE IN PERSPECTIVE IN VARIOUS POSITIONS.

Fig. 11.—THE APPEARANCE OF SEMI-CIRCULAR ARCHES IN A PERSPECTIVE RENDERING.

of pastels. The pigments can be applied with great rapidity, and there is not the difficulty experienced in using water-colour of quick drying, or in oil colour of slow drying. Pastels are really coloured chalks, and they are made in a great variety of tints, hues and shades. There are three varieties, hard, medium and soft—it is the latter that is most useful. For ordinary landscape sketching, about 150 pastels will form a useful collection, but some care is needed to select the correct proportions of colours.

Use Paper with a slightly Rough Surface.

Paper with a slightly rough surface is used, but ordinary brown paper is quite suitable for the beginner. Pastel paper is, however, quite inexpensive, not more than ordinary good cartridge. It is made in a variety of tints, and several should be obtained, as much of the paper can be left untouched when it is suitable in colour. Michallet paper is a little more expensive, but has a most suitable surface. Any necessary drawing can be done with charcoal—when dusted off the lines are hardly noticeable and will not affect the lightest tints. It is always advisable to use folded sheets for pastel drawings. When completed, the paper is folded with the picture inside, and it will not rub off. Pastel paintings, when finished, should be mounted on cardboard and framed up behind a fairly thick mount. Pastels are less likely to fade than any other medium even when hung in a strong light.

Choice of Colours.

The selection of pastels for general use should be arranged in order with a few only of the deeper shades and a larger number of light tints. Begin with a range of violet leading to the palest violet greys, blue to palest, green to palest, light yellows and orange tints, and red from deep to very lightest. It will be found that the grey tints will be required much more than pure hues, and therefore more of the light tints than the dark shades should be stocked.

In distinct difference to water-colour or oil technique, pastel colours are not mixed or merged together except under special circumstances. As a rule, the side of the pastel is applied with a firm pressure directly to the paper in the exact place where it is required. The end or point of the pastel should be used when clearly defined edges are needed. In cases where broad effects are needed, such as expanses of sky, distant hills, grass, etc., the pastel can be lightly rubbed into the paper with the finger.

It should be noted in connection with the use of pastel that one colour should not be applied on top of another, but that as far as possible the original layer of colour should remain untouched. A firm pressure is required to the pastel being rubbed off, and considerable care is needed when working to avoid touching the finished portions of the picture. It is advisable to work from the top downwards. After the sketch is completed, the paper should be shaken lightly and then turned over. Bright lights can always be added after the paper is mounted.

Fig. 12.—A SIMPLE WATER-COLOUR PICTURE.

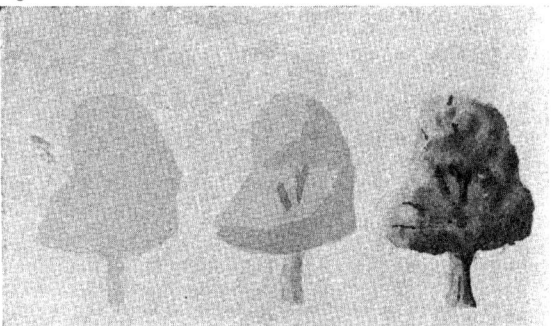

Fig. 13.—USEFUL PRACTICE CAN BE OBTAINED BY STUDYING TREE FORMS

MAKING LANTERN SLIDES

A LANTERN slide is simply a transparent print on glass made for viewing upon a white surface, usually a screen, by means of a projection lantern. The only materials required are a packet of lantern plates, a plain glass plate the same size, edging material, a gaslight paper developer, hypo, etc.

For contact printing any ordinary printing frame can be used. The negative from which the slide is to be made is placed film side up in the frame, and the lantern plate, film side down, is placed on it. The emulsion of lantern plates is so thin that it is difficult to recognise it. In case of doubt breathe on the side believed to be glass. A film of moisture will be seen on the glass side but not on the film side. It is advisable to make a test exposure before printing all the plates. When testing exposures it is unnecessary and costly to use an entire plate each time. You can cut a plate into three 1-inch strips with a diamond or wheel glass-cutter. You will be able to gauge the correct exposure by exposing a strip so that it will include both sky and foreground, developing it, and dipping it in the fixing bath until the creamy emulsion has disappeared.

With a standard gaslight developer, development is usually complete in thirty seconds. The lantern plate can be masked with strips of black paper, or black paper masks of any shape can be cut with a sharp knife and placed between the slide and cover glass. As a guide to projection it is a good idea to leave two white spots in the black paper at the top.

Passe-partout binding is very satisfactory for holding the slide and cover glass together.

How to Make a Xylophone

THE xylophone is a percussion instrument of small size used in a band or orchestra to mark the rhythm, or as a solo instrument; it consists of a series of small wooden staves or laths, progressively varied in size and resting upon wooden bars, and is played by striking the staves with two small wooden hammers.

A practicable instrument can be made without much trouble by any handy man—the result will give a good deal of pleasure and amusement; furthermore, if pains are taken to tune the staves carefully, a tolerably good musical scale can be obtained.

Before dealing with the actual construction it will be found helpful to consider briefly the fundamental principles on which the xylophone and kindred instruments are based to enable an understanding of what has to be done.

Fig. 1.—A Simple Xylophone.

Fundamental Principles.

The sound so created by a xylophone is caused by the vibration of the bar or "stave" and is largely determined by the natural vibration period of the material. The volume of sound is enhanced by arranging matters so that each stave is isolated and rests separately upon a kind of sounding board or resonator, which by sympathetic vibration adds to the loudness of the note.

It is important to realise that the sound emitted when the stave is struck is largely—if not wholly—governed by the frequency of vibration of the stave. In general, if the staves are all of equal density and cross-sectional area—the notes will vary in accordance with the physical lengths of the stave. The shorter the stave, the higher will be the frequency of vibration; that is, a short stave will vibrate many more times per second than a long stave; hence the short stave emits a high note, the long staves emit low notes, while intermediate notes are given out by intermediate lengths.

If the material used for the staves varies in density or in physical properties, this grading by length may not hold good. From the foregoing it should be realised that to make a really good xylophone with musical pretensions calls for considerable specialised skill and ability; furthermore, it is impracticable to give exact sizes for staves because it would be impossible in practice to be sure that the material used by the reader was exactly alike in physical and resonant qualities to that described.

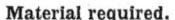

Fig. 2.—Arrangement of Framework.

Simple Practicable Instruments.

A very simple xylophone or glockenspiel can be made with metal staves and a simple wooden framework (as shown in Fig. 1). It can be of any reasonable size—the one illustrated has a pleasant musical tone and will make an admirable plaything for a youngster; it also serves as an excellent introduction to a more ambitious production.

Material required.

Staves.—Eight feet of hard-drawn brass strip, $\frac{3}{8}$ inch wide, $\frac{1}{16}$ inch thick.

Frame.—Two pieces deal, $1\frac{1}{2} \times \frac{1}{2} \times 20$ inches long; 1 piece deal, 7 inches long; 1 piece, 1 inch long.

Hammers.—Two pieces $\frac{3}{16}$ inch dowel rod, 15 inches long; 2 pieces deal, $\frac{1}{2}$ inch diameter, $\frac{3}{4}$ inch long.

Commence by making the frame, as shown in Fig. 2, the two cross-pieces being slightly bevelled at the ends and then glued and nailed in place with panel pins.

Next fit the resonator strings, as shown in Fig. 3; drill a small hole near each end of the frame, then take a piece of smooth, soft but thick string, stretch it thoroughly, then insert one end in the hole at the narrow end of the frame and secure it with a hardwood peg. Draw the string fairly tight so that it rests along the middle of the edge of the frame, then cut to length and peg the end into the hole. Treat the other side in the same way, then prepare the metal staves.

Making the Staves.

The bass stave measures $9\frac{5}{8}$ inches long, the treble is $2\frac{3}{8}$ inches long. Prepare these two first by cutting the metal to length and then drilling holes $\frac{1}{8}$ inch diameter, and $\frac{3}{4}$ inch from each end of the metal (as in Fig. 4), and slightly countersink the holes on each side.

Next fasten these staves one at each end of the frame by driving small brass or iron nails through the holes, but leaving about $\frac{1}{8}$ inch of space between the stave and the nail head to allow the stave to vibrate freely. The nails must not pinch or grip the staves and must be quite slack in the holes.

The intermediate staves vary their length as follows: 9-inch, 8-inch, $7\frac{1}{2}$-inch, $6\frac{9}{16}$-inch, 6-inch, $5\frac{3}{8}$-inch, $4\frac{3}{4}$-inch, $4\frac{1}{2}$-inch, 4-inch, $3\frac{3}{4}$-inch, $3\frac{1}{2}$-inch, 3-inch, $2\frac{7}{10}$-inch.

Next lay the staves in place on the frame—spacing them so that an equal amount overhangs at each end; mark the positions for the nail holes, then drill and fix them as before.

Making the Hammer.

The hammers are easily made (as shown in Fig. 5), by drilling a $\frac{3}{16}$-inch diameter hole through the hammer head, then gluing the $\frac{3}{16}$-inch diameter shaft into place—finish off by rounding off the corners of the hammer heads with coarse sandpaper.

On striking the staves, each should give out a distinct note and the whole should cover practically two octaves. Probably several staves will be out of tune, but this can be remedied by filing the metal.

Tuning the Staves.

If a stave is "flat" it can be raised in pitch by reducing its length or by filing away the metal at the ends so as to reduce its thickness. To lower the pitch the metal is filed away from the middle part of the stave—or a longer one should be fitted and then be reduced until the note is in tune.

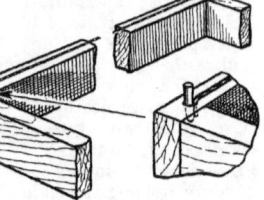

Fig. 3.—Fixing Resonator Strings.

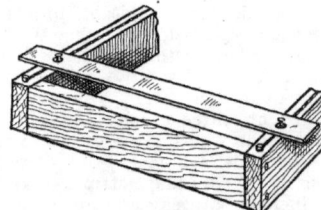

Fig. 4.—Fixing the Metal Staves.

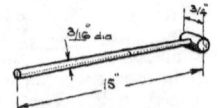

Fig. 5.—Detail of Hammer.

Making the "E.W. 3" Receivers
FOR A.C., BATTERY AND D.C. OPERATION

This article deals with the construction of three types of practical wireless receiving sets; the first is for use with A.C. mains, the second is a battery receiver, and the third a general-purpose set for use with D.C. mains.

THE "E.W. 3" FOR A.C. MAINS

Quality of reproduction is the outstanding feature of this set, which has been specially designed to ensure the utmost purity and tonal fidelity from local and powerful Continental transmissions.

A high-frequency stage is not employed, and for the purpose in view is not necessary; its omission is a step towards securing the "silent background" so necessary for purity of reproduction.

Another unusual but practical feature is the disposing of the "mains" part of the set behind a vertical and shielded division, thus cutting out any chance of interference from the mains transformers.

Intervalve coupling is entirely effected by means of resistances and suitable condensers, thus assuring linearity of amplification. The volume is more than ample for any domestic purpose, while interference from adjacent stations is non-existent, nor is there any trace of mains hum or mush, thanks to the foregoing features of design and the incorporation of an efficient mains interference eliminator.

Components required.

Coil.—One dual range K5 ("Colvern Ltd.").

Variable Condensers.—One differential reaction, 0·0002 mf. ("Utility"); one 0·0005 mf. with straight line dial ("Utility"); one 0·0003 mf. "Mite," all with knobs ("Utility").

Switch.—One "on-off" Toggle ("Bulgin").

Sockets.—One pair "L.S." ("Belling-Lee"); one pair "A.E." ("Belling Lee"); one pair "Mains" ("Belling Lee").

Fuse.—One baseboard, Type 150 ma. ("Belling Lee").

Loading Light.—One baseboard lampholder ("Bulgin"); one 6-volt 1-amp. lamp ("Bulgin"); one 4-volt 1-amp. dial lamp ("Bulgin").

Rectifier.—Type "HT8" ("Westinghouse").

Transformer.—Type W16 ("Heayberd").

Choke.—Type 753 ("Heayberd").

Condensers.—Three 4-mf., six 2-mf. 800 V.D.C. ("T.C.C."); one each 0·0001 mf., 0·0005 mf., flat M Type ("T.C.C."); two tubular 0·01 mf., one 0·05 mf. ("T.C.C.").

Resistances.—Dubilier Metallised.— One 500 ohms, one 750 ohms, two

Fig. 1.—The "E.W. 3" Receiver for A.C. Mains.

The set is self-contained in an oak table cabinet and has remarkably fine tonal quality.

Fig. 2.—Back View of A.C. Set before the Mains Unit is fitted.

Fig. 3.—Plan View of Completed Set.

Showing clearly the vertical division and the arrangement of the components.

50,000 ohms, one 75,000 ohms, three ¼ megohm, one 10,000 ohms, one 25,000 ohms.

L.F. Choke.—Type L.F. ("Lewcos").

H.F. Choke.—Type HFP ("Wearite").

Wiring.—Twin 5-amp. flex rubber covered ("Ward & Goldstone"); Quickstrip sleeving, metal braided ("Ward & Goldstone").

Panel.—15¼ × 8 × ¼ inch.
Base.—15¼ × 10 × ⅜ inch.
Division.—15¾ × 7⅝ × ¼ inch.
Sides.—Two, 8 × 3½ × ¼ inch.

Valve Holders.—Three 5-pin ("Benjamin").

Loud Speaker.—P.M. Type M3T ("Ferranti"), or Mains Energised Type 154 ("Magnavox").

Valves.—One each 41/MHL metallised ("Cossor"); AC/HL metallised ("Mazda"); "A.C. PEN" ("Mazda").

Interference Suppressor.—One mains interference unit ("T.C.C.").

Cabinet.—One kit of prepared parts, No. 257 in Oak ("C. A. Osborn Ltd.").

Metallised Paper.—One sheet "Konductite" ("C. A. C. Ltd.").

What to do first.

First of all obtain the components, then study the diagrams (Fig. 3A) showing the circuit of the receiver proper and the mains unit circuit. Compare these with Fig. 2, showing the receiver components in place before the mains unit is assembled, and study the diagrams showing the whereabouts of the components on the baseboard, the panel, and the components on the "mains" panel.

The whereabouts of all the parts can well be realised from Fig. 3, which is a plan view of the completed receiver and mains unit.

Preparing the Baseboard.

Having thus obtained a grasp of the location of the various parts, then prepare the baseboard by squaring up the edges and covering the upper surface with "Konductite" metallised paper, which should be fixed by means of thin glue or thick paste.

Then make the front panel, cut out the slot for the straight line tuning dial, as in Fig. 3A, and drill the various holes for components and fixing screws. Mount on the panel the reaction condenser, aerial series condenser—which acts as a volume control—also the "on-off" switch and the aerial and earth connector strips and the loud speaker connector strips, or these last two items may be fixed at any convenient place on the cabinet.

The panel is used to keep the components in place and simplify the wiring—it fits closely against the cabinet front and could be omitted entirely and the components be fixed to the cabinet, but when this is done the wiring becomes a very awkward job.

Mounting the Components.

Screw the various components to the baseboard—as in Fig. 3A—and fit the tuning dial in accordance with the template and instructions supplied with it; then wire up the receiver part, taking care to use high-grade well-insulated wires as specified.

The filament heater circuit should be wired with heavy lighting flexible, and the two leads twisted together. See that all connections are firmly screwed or properly soldered; good tight joints are essential on a mains set.

Next prepare the mains unit panel by gluing and screwing on the two side pieces, noting that they extend below the bottom of the panel so that they can be screwed to the baseboard later on.

Mount the components on this panel after the rear surfaces have been covered with "Konductite"; then proceed to wire them up, as shown in Fig. 3A.

This having been done, screw the panel sides to the base and complete the wiring by adding the various wires which connect between the two parts, passing them through the holes drilled for that purpose and taking especial care to see that the wires do not come into contact with the metallised surfaces. Add a bridging wire to connect together the metallised surface of the mains unit to the metallised baseboard, and connect both to the "earth" terminal or main earth wire.

Testing the Set.

If a simple continuity test meter is available, all the circuits can be checked with it; if not, carefully compare the actual wiring with the circuit diagrams, and, if all is in order, connect the loud speaker temporarily, insert the valves and connect up the aerial and earth.

Insert the mains plug in the house supply, then switch on, and in twenty to thirty seconds' time the heaters should have warmed up sufficiently and the local station can then be tuned in without difficulty and the volume regulated by the combined action of the series aerial condenser and reaction condensers.

Note that at the start the series aerial condensers should be all "in"—that is, the moving blades turned in between the fixed blades.

Reaction should be about half-way "on" until the station is picked up, it can then be turned back and the volume adjusted by moving the series aerial condenser, which will be found to be a very smooth-acting volume control.

Note should be made of the small 6-volt loading light on the baseboard; this is introduced to absorb surplus current in the filament heater circuit and prevent undue voltage rise which would, of course, reduce the valve life. The light could be placed anywhere on or adjacent to the set should an extra light be required.

Sensitivity.

At first this set may not seem to be particularly sensitive, but after a little experience it will be found that by suitably adjusting the volume control and by critical adjustment of the reaction condenser and fine adjustment of the tuning condenser a good selection of stations can be tuned in and be brought up to adequate loud speaker strength.

Mains Energised Speaker.

The permanent magnet type of loud speaker gives very good results, but the greatest volume is obtained by the use of a mains energised speaker, such as the No. 154 "Magnavox," which should be connected somewhat differently, the transformer primary being connected in place of the P.M. speaker and the field winding connected in the H.T. plus lead and decoupled by an extra 4-mf. 800 V.D.C. condenser. The extra smoothing due to the inclusion of the speaker field and condenser will obviate any chance of mains hum.

Interference Unit.

This can be connected as shown in the circuit diagram and be placed within the cabinet, but better results are obtained by connecting it across the mains switch—on the "house" side. In all cases, when working on the electric supply or service wire, *always* switch off and disconnect the plug contacts before making any alterations or adjustments to the set or unit.

Making the Cabinet.

The cabinet can be made by any handyman if the specified kit of parts is used. The leading dimensions are 20 × 16 × 10⅜ inches, and the mode of making the four corner joints is shown in Fig. 3A; the top and bottom pieces have only to be glued and pinned to the rebated sides. The front is then glued and pinned on, the edges planed or sandpapered smooth, and the whole given a coat of stain to enrich the colour. The feet are made—as shown in Fig. 3A—by superposed blocks, stained black and screwed to the bottom of the case.

Drill the holes for control knobs as for the panel, cut out the dial slot and fit the escutcheon; glue the gauze over the speaker fret and screw the loud speaker in place. Polish the case, insert the set, and fix the backboard with two turn buttons or screws and the set is complete.

THE "E.W. 3" BATTERY MODEL

This up-to-date receiver (Fig. 4) incorporates all the latest devices that are advisable for a general purpose receiver. A "Colpak" tuning unit with "Ferrocart" coils, a band pass input filter and three tuned circuits—as in Fig. 3B—ensure remarkable selectivity, while an efficient H.F. stage with variable-mu valve provides both range and volume.

The output stage incorporates a pentode valve with a 1,000 milli-watt output, but despite this, the demands on the H.T. battery are very small, thanks to the inclusion of a "Westector" economy circuit that operates in such a way that the current consumption is strictly proportional to sound output.

An efficient tone control circuit is another good feature, it enables correction of high note loss; it compensates for loss of bass, by the simple turning of a single knob, thus affording good tonal quality under all conditions, as well as reducing "mush" and unwanted background noises.

Arrangements are also made for the electrical reproduction of gramophone records, the tone control being operative both when playing records and receiving radio transmission.

The advantage of using a unit such as the "Colpak" is that all the coils and tuning condensers are perfectly ganged and matched, thus ensuring the maximum efficiency; in fact, this straightforward little set will receive practically all worth-while transmissions on the medium- and long-wavelengths in a manner only surpassed by expensive "superhets."

Recommended Components.

Tuning Unit.—One "Colpak" Ferrocart Tuning Unit, Type H ("Colvern Ltd.").

Dial.—One straight line "Utility" No. W330 ("Wilkins & Wright Ltd.").

Valve Holders.—One Triple I.F. Base, No. 48 ("Lewcos").

Transformer.—One Type TOCO 4/1 ("Multitone Ltd.").

Tone Control.—One graded potentiometer, 4 megohms ("Multitone Ltd.").

H.F. Chokes.—One "Astatic" LN987 ("Lissen"); one Type HFPA ("Wearite").

Condensers.—Five 1-mf. Type 50 ("T.C.C."); one 0·5-mf. Type 50 ("T.C.C."); two 0·0002-mf. tubular ("T.C.C."); one 0·0003-mf. tubular ("T.C.C."); one 0·1-mf. tubular ("T.C.C."); one 0·01-mf. tubular ("T.C.C.").

Fixed Resistances.—Metallised 1-watt type. One 500 ohms, one 10,000 ohms, one 15,000 ohms ("Dubilier"); one 200,000 ohms, one 50,000 ohms ("Dubilier"); one 5,000 ohms, one 100,000 ohms, one 1 megohm, one 2 megohm ("Dubilier").

Volume Control.—One 25,000-ohm potentiometer ("Lewcos").

Reaction Condenser.—One Bakelite 0·0002 mf. ("Telsen").

MAKING THE "E.W.3" RECEIVERS

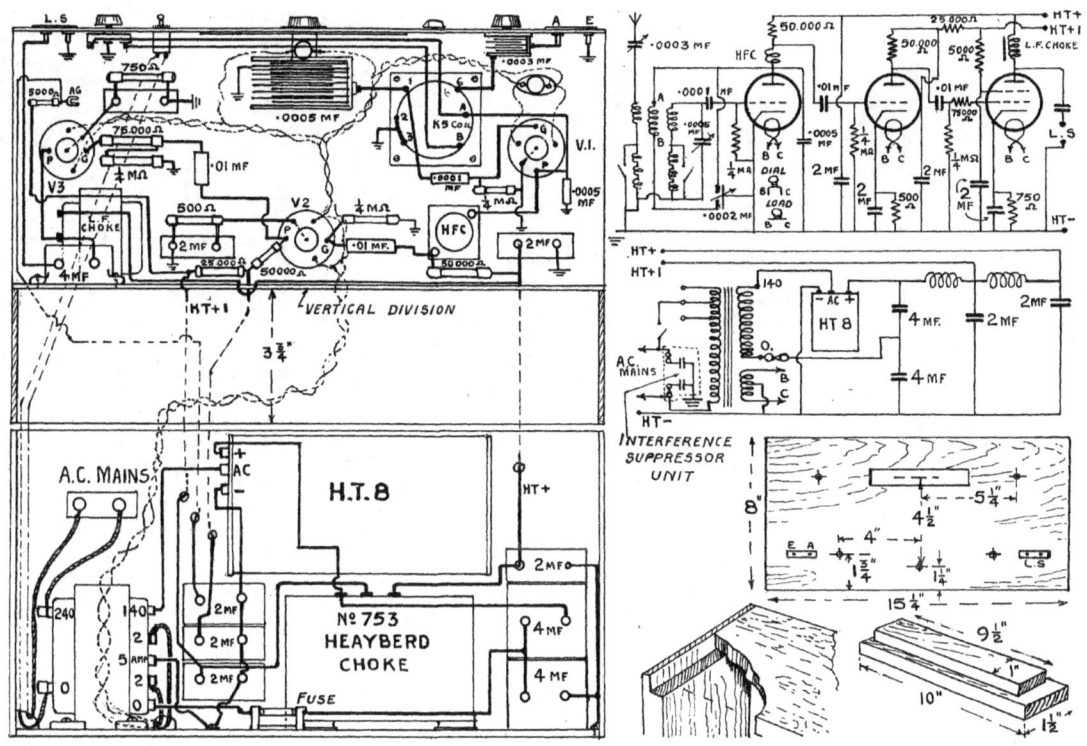

Fig. 3A.—Details of the A.C. Mains Set.
Top left, components and wiring on baseboard; bottom left, components and wiring of mains unit on vertical division; top right, theoretical circuit of set with circuit of mains unit below; centre, panel sizes; bottom right, joint at top of cabinet and detail of foot.

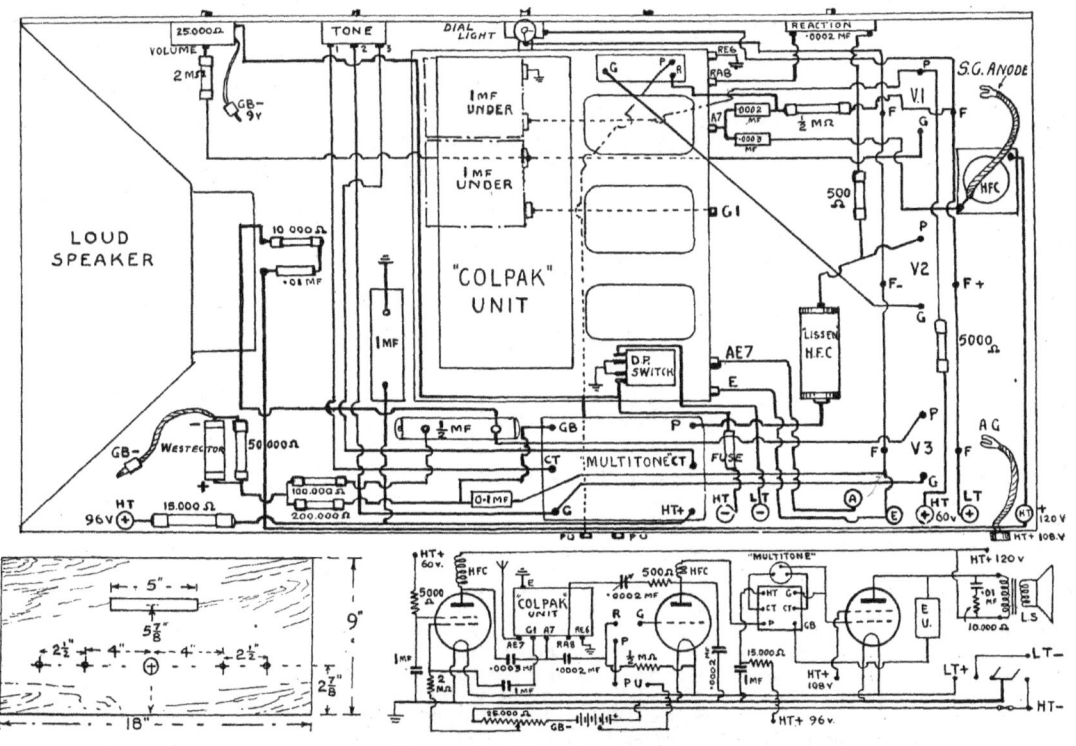

Fig. 3B.—Details of Battery Set.
Top, components on baseboard, showing all connections; bottom left, details of panel; bottom right, theoretical circuit.

MAKING THE "E.W. 3" RECEIVERS

*Fig. 4.—*The Complete Battery Receiver withdrawn from Cabinet.
Note loud speaker at left and external L.T. and H.T. batteries. The bias and economy batteries are in their place on the baseboard.

*Fig. 5.—*Fitting the Blocking Condensers.
Underside of Colpak showing one condenser fixed and one prepared for fixing. These are only required when the earth leads have to be isolated.

Terminals.—One each marked A, E, PU +, PU −, HT +, HT + 1, HT + 2, HT −, LT −, LT +, LS +, LS −, or one 7-way battery cord ("Belling-Lee Ltd.").

Accumulator Connector.—One pair ("Belling-Lee Ltd.").

Fuse.—One single open baseboard type with 250 m/a. fuse ("Belling-Lee Ltd.").

Wander Plugs.—One each marked GB +, GB + 2, GB − 1, GB − 2, HT +, HT + 1, HT + 2, HT + 3, HT − ("Belling-Lee Ltd.").

Dial Light.—One high-efficiency type 2-volt ("Bulgin Ltd.").

Baseboard.—⅜-inch plywood, 18 × 9 inches ("Frank Romany Ltd.").

Wiring.— Two coils "Glazite" ("Lewcos"); 3 yards twin flex ("Ward & Goldstone Ltd."); 2 yards twin-shielded pick-up flex ("Ward & Goldstone Ltd.").

Loud Speaker.—One "Multex" ("R. & A. Ltd.").

Batteries.—One L.T. 2-volt Type HZ4 ("Exide"); one H.T. 120-volt Type 1012 ("Drydex"); one G.B. 16½-volt Type H1008 ("Drydex"); one G.B. 9-volt ("Drydex").

Valves.—One 220VS metallised ("Cossor"); one PM 1HL metallised ("Mullard"); one Pen 220A with side terminal ("Mazda").

Economy Circuit.—One Westector Type W4 ("Westinghouse Brake & Saxby Signal Co.").

Panel and Baseboard.

This set has been designed to be housed in a small cabinet together with the grid bias batteries and loud speaker, with external L.T. and H.T. batteries; but, if it is desired, the whole outfit, including batteries, can be accommodated in a cabinet such as that described for the A.C. Mains set, and, if this is done, the panel and baseboard must be reduced in length to suit and the loud speaker placed at the top. However, the arrangement shown in Fig. 4 is neat and effective, and is here described.

Prepare the baseboard and panel as before. Fig. 3B gives the details of the holes for the components which are mounted on the panel.

Next cover the baseboard with "Konductite," and then fix the panel to it. Note that two battens are screwed beneath the base to stiffen it.

The "Colpak" Unit.

The next step is to disconnect the two "earth" leads on the underside of the "Colpak" unit and interpose a 1-mf. condenser between each earth lead and the metal frame, as shown in Fig. 3B, where one condenser is fixed and the second ready to be bolted in place.

Next fix up the "Utility" slow-motion dial, which is readily done by following the maker's leaflet, and noting that the footpiece on the dial support has to be bolted to a prong already screwed to the "Colpak" case. The prong must be accurately bent upwards to fit nicely under the dial foot.

Solder the flexible leads to the dial light holder and fit a length of "Glazite" to the tag on the wave-change switch, which is visible through an opening at the end, as in Fig. 5, and is immediately under the terminal marked "G" on the switch. Pass this wire out through the third opening in the side casing, where it will be conveniently ready to connect to the detector grid terminal.

This done, screw the "Colpak" to the baseboard and fix the other components in place as shown in Fig. 3B, then proceed with the wiring.

Wiring the Battery Set.

Wiring on this set is a very simple matter—much of it is already done in the "Colpak" unit. The filament circuit can be completed first and the dial light flexibles then connected up. Next connect the resistance between detector plate terminal and reaction condenser, join one terminal of the latter to terminal marked RA8 on the "Colpak"; the next terminal—marked RE6—is connected to earth.

The next step is to connect the grid leak from terminal R on "Colpak" switch to L.T. plus; then connect from terminal R a 0·0002-mf. tubular condenser to the detector grid. Connect a 0·0002-mf. tubular condenser between detector plate terminal and L.T. minus. Connect terminal G1 to one terminal of a 1-mf. condenser. Connect the second terminal on condenser to one end of 2-megohm leak, and also to grid terminal of H.F. valve.

The remainder of the wiring of the valve holders can then be completed, as shown on the wiring diagram, Fig. 3B. At this stage the reader should decide if all battery leads are to be connected to terminals or if a battery cord will be used, the latter is the neatest, and, when used, the variously coloured wires should be connected up according to the designations. Alternatively, short leads can be taken from the various points on the set to the terminal strip at the back.

In the photographs of the set the battery cord system is used, but on the wiring diagrams short leads to a terminal strip are shown; the wiring is the same in both cases, it is merely a question of interposing a number of separate terminals on the insulating strip.

Tone Control Circuit.

The tone control circuit comprises the "Multitone" L.F. transformer and the specially graded "Multitone" potentiometer mounted on the panel. Connections are shown clearly on wiring diagram. The leads from the potentiometer can best be made with rubber-covered flexible wires passed through the space under the "Colpak" unit. The outer pair of terminals on the potentiometer connect to the terminals CT on the transformer. The centre terminal of the potentiometer connects to terminal G on the transformer and to the grid of the output valve.

Volume Control Circuit.

This comprises the 25,000-ohm potentiometer also mounted on the panel, and a 9-volt grid bias battery,

Fig. 6.—THE D.C. VERSION OF THE "E.W. 3."

Fig. 7.—VALVE SIDE OF THE D.C. SET.

connected as shown on wiring diagram and as follows.

Outer terminal on "Lewcos" potentiometer to 2-megohm leak already fixed on 1-mf. condenser in the H.F. grid lead on the "Colpak." One end terminal of potentiometer to G.B. minus 9 volt, the remaining potentiometer terminal is connected to the metallised base.

The plus terminal on the G.B. battery is then connected to H.T. minus wire on the D.P. switch on the "Colpak." The L.T. minus wire is soldered to second contact on same side of D.P. switch, the remaining two switch contacts are connected together and to the metallised base; in this way the G.B. battery circuit is broken when the switch is in the "off" position.

Economy Circuit.

The current economiser circuit comprises the "Westector," one 0·5-mf. condenser, one 0·1-mf. condenser, three resistances and a separate grid bias battery.

One side of the 0·5-mf. condenser is connected to plate of output valve, the other side is connected to a 100,000-ohm resistance which is connected to the red plus end of the "Westector" and to one end of a 200,000-ohm resistance.

The free end of the 200,000-ohm resistance is connected to terminal marked G.B. on "Multitone" transformer. The 50,000-ohm resistance is connected to each end of the "Westector," the negative (black) end of the "Westector" is connected to G.B. minus, and the plus terminal on the G.B. battery is connected to earth. The 0·1-mf. condenser is connected to G.B. terminal on transformer and to earth. To adjust the economy circuit to the best value insert a milliammeter in the plate circuit of output valve and adjust the grid bias so that anode current reads about 1 m/a. when signals are not being received. A grid bias value of about 13½ volts negative will be about right for the specified valve. In use, a negligibly small part of the L.F. output from the output valve is rectified, and after suitable filtering is fed back as a D.C. component to the grid circuit of the output valve, thus reducing the high negative bias applied by the G.B. battery. The valve therefore works in such a manner that it takes just sufficient anode current to suit the grid swing at any instant and thereby achieves maximum output with minimum anode current consumption.

The grid bias battery used for this purpose must be entirely separate and not used for any other purpose.

Completing and testing.

The few remaining wires can now be added and the loud speaker connected up; note that the "R and A Multex" recommended for use with this set has a multi-ratio transformer which can be adjusted by trial to give the best results. Switch off the set each time before making an adjustment; on test the best combination was terminals Nos. 3 and 5 on the primary and Nos. 8 and 9 on the secondary.

Check over the circuit and wiring, insert the dial lamp and switch on, when the lighting of the dial lamp will show that the L.T. circuit is in order. Switch off, insert the valves and connect to aerial and earth. Set the reaction condenser about half-way in, volume control to "full on"—that is, turned two-thirds towards the right—and set the tone control knob about midway of its movement. Switch on by rotating knob on "Colpak" unit to M—indicating medium wave band. Tune in a station and bring it to full strength by adjustment of volume and tone controls and by aid of reaction. Rotate switch knob to "L," indicating long waves, and again tune in a few stations—if all is well, the set is correct, but, if not, then slightly readjust the trimming condensers on top of the "Colpak." Rotate them only a trifle at a time, using an insulated screwdriver and preferably on a fairly weak station at about 25 to 30 degrees on the dial on the medium wave-band. Once adjusted in this position, the set will remain correctly gauged over the whole of the medium and long wavebands.

To operate the set for gramophone record playing, rotate switch knob to "G" and connect the pick-up terminal P on switch to one side of a pick-up on the gramophone, connect the other side of pick-up to 1½-volt negative and connect the positive side of the 1½-volt battery to earth. Alternatively, the bias battery used for the variable-mu valve can be employed—in which case one lead goes from a wander plug in the 1½-volt negative socket to the pick-up on the gramophone, the other pick-up lead goes to "P" on the "Colpak" switch.

THE "E.W. 3" FOR D.C. MAINS

This receiver (Fig. 6) embodies latest practice in D.C. mains sets and includes an H.F. pentode with variable-mu characteristics, an efficient detector and a powerful output pentode valve. It will receive all worth-while European stations at good loud speaker strength.

Several important points must be carefully watched when making and operating a D.C. set. Firstly, a voltage of 200 to 240 is necessary, and it is imperative to isolate the receiver from "earth"—for which purpose a small mica insulated fixed condenser is included in the aerial lead, and a 800-volt D.C. working 4-mf. condenser in the earth lead. These are essential in order to avoid all risk of earthing the D.C. mains supply, as should this happen a "dead short" would follow, the main fuses be blown and the house supply be cut off thereby.

When building the set always remember that the expression "earth" means the negative side of the set, which is isolated from the earth proper by means of the 4-mf. condenser.

Recommended Components.

Tuning Unit.—"Colpak" Type H ("Colvern Ltd.").

Reaction Condenser.—J.B. Bakelite, 0·0002 mf. ("Jackson Bros. Ltd.").

Aerial Condenser.—One J.B. Baseboard Trimmer ("Jackson Bros. Ltd.").

H.F. Chokes.—One Type 751 ("Heayberd"); one Type HT13 ("Wearite").

Mains Chokes.—Two Type HF9 ("Wearite").

Output Choke.—One Type HT13 ("Wearite").

L.F. Transformer. — "Hypernik" ("Lissen Ltd.").

MAKING THE "E.W. 3" RECEIVERS

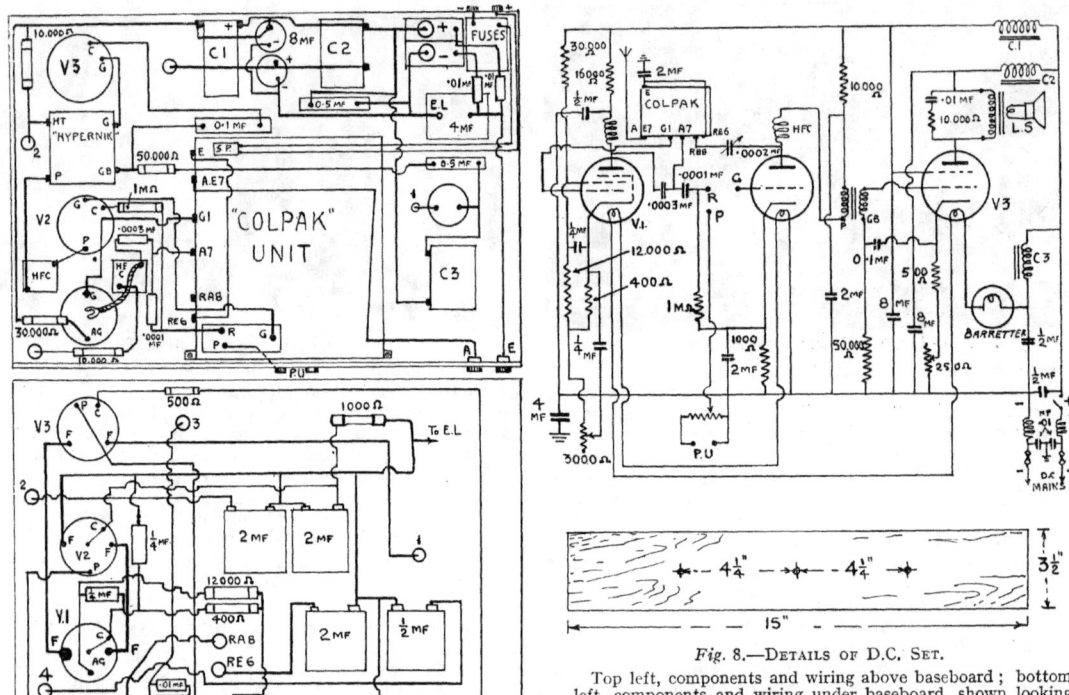

Fig. 8.—DETAILS OF D.C. SET.
Top left, components and wiring above baseboard; bottom left, components and wiring under baseboard, shown looking downwards as if baseboard were made of glass; top right, theoretical circuit; bottom right, panel.

H.F. Chokes.—One HFP; one HFPA ("Wearite").

Valve Holders.—Three 5-pin, one 7-pin ("Benjamin Electric Co.").

Fixed Condensers.—Two 4-mf. Type 80, two 8-mf. dry electrolytic Type 902, two 0·25-mf. Type 80, one 0·05-mf. Type 80, one 1-mf. Type 80, two 2-mf. Type 80; one each 0·0005-mf., 0·0003-mf. flat M Type; one each 0·0001-mf. tubular, 0·0003-mf. tubular ("T.C.C.").

Fixed Resistances.—One 30,000 ohms, one 16,000 ohms, one 12,000 ohms, one 400 ohms, one 50,000 ohms, one 1,000 ohms, one 500 ohms, two 10,000 ohms, one 1 megohm ("Dubilier").

Dial.—Slow-motion straight line, Type 330 ("Utility").

Potentiometers.—One 3,000-ohm Type Q.V.C., one 250-ohm Type Q ("Wearite").

Baseboard.—Plywood, 15 × 12 × 3/8 inches ("Frank Romany Ltd.").

Panel and Strip.—Two pieces plywood, 15 × 3½ × ¼ inches ("Frank Romany Ltd.").

Loud Speaker.—"Multex" ("R. & A. Ltd.").

Valves.—One each VP20 metallised, HL20, Pen 20 ("Mullard").

Barretter.—One Type 1927 ("Phillips Lamps Ltd.").

Terminals.—One pair "mains" insulated, one each marked A, E, PU +, PU −, LS +, LS − ("Belling-Lee Ltd.").

Fuse.—One D.P. Safety Type with 1-amp fuses ("Belling-Lee Ltd.").

Plug and Socket.—One "mains" shrouded type ("Belling-Lee Ltd.").

First Stages of Assembly.

Prepare the baseboard as before, then drill and shape the panel as in Fig. 8, screw the components into position on baseboard, as shown in Fig. 8, noting that a strip of wood 3 inches deep and ½ inch thick is screwed at the back to support the baseboard and leave room for condensers beneath it.

Four valve-holders are used, the fourth being required for the barretter, which regulates automatically the current supplied to the valve filament heaters which are wired in series, *not* in parallel.

H.F. smoothing chokes, one in each mains lead, are in series with a D.P. safety type mains fuse. Separate smoothing chokes are used for the earlier stages of the receiver, that for the high-frequency valve and detector should carry 10 m/a. without saturation and that for the output valve should carry 30 m/a., each with an inductance value of 30 to 40 henrys.

Wiring the Receiver.

This should preferably be done in distinct stages—first the mains input through the H.F. chokes and fuses, noting carefully the polarity of the mains, which must always be ascertained by testing, for example, with "pole-finding" paper.

Next connect up the filament choke, barretter and filaments, using high-grade insulated wire in every case.

The radio-gramophone switch is connected up as before, but in this case the grid leak goes from "R" to the cathode terminal of detector valve.

Connect up the L.F. "Lissen" "Hypernik" transformer and the pentode output circuits, noting the 250-ohm potentiometer in the pentode cathode circuit to enable critical adjustment of bias.

Finally, check over the entire circuit, look out especially for any casual "earth" connection, and when all is in order connect up the aerial and earth leads and the loud speaker. Insert the valves, connect up to the mains supply, and then switch on. When the filament heaters have warmed up, the set will come to life, and can be tuned and adjusted as described for the battery set.

Housing the Set.

This set can be fitted in a cabinet on similar lines to the "E.W. 3 for A.C. Mains," or can be fitted in the radio-gramophone cabinet as described on page 1253.

Simple Stonework in the Garden

WELL considered decorative schemes for the garden frequently incorporate some feature that is built of stone, apart from the obvious use of stone for paving and paths.

The variety of structural work that can be carried out in the garden, using inexpensive stone, is limited only by the skill and ingenuity of the designer. Simple analysis of all such structures reveals the fact that they are all carried out by very simple processes, which any handyman can follow.

Take, for example, the terraced pergola sketched in Fig. 1; this may at first glance seem a formidable task for the amateur, but in reality it is merely a repetition of a few simple operations, each of which is adaptable to numerous other garden features.

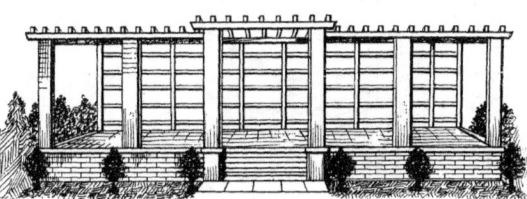

Fig. 1.—Terraced Pergola.

This design is particularly adaptable for the smaller gardens, and can easily be made because the operations involved are few and simple.

Simple Processes.

Examination of the pergola shown in Fig. 1 reveals the fact that it consists of paved areas, shallow steps, a low stone wall and the columns. A knowledge of the methods of making these elements enables the amateur to construct practically anything in stonework suitable for the garden. To emphasise this point, each process will here be described separately, with an example of a simple feature, and the mode of combining the processes then dealt with.

Choice of Material.

There are two groups of material for garden use; first the natural stone, which is sold in various sizes and thicknesses, as well as "crazy" or random size, and second the artificial stone.

The cheapest natural stone is the thin random paving stone, generally known as "crazy"; the most useful sort is about 1 inch thick, and may range in size from small triangular pieces 2 or 3 inches long upwards to a piece about 30 × 20 inches, but there are no standard sizes.

"Walling" stone is roughly shaped and is about 2 inches thick, generally of the order of 9 to 12 inches long, and about 4 to 5 inches wide.

"Rockery" stone is simply a natural lump of rough stone, and is used to pile up in heaps to form a rock garden. In each case there are many different kinds of stone, varying in hardness, colour and texture; in most cases "Yorkshire" stone is suitable for paving, because it is hard and durable. In practice, a visit should be paid to the nearest stone merchant's yard and the material selected on the spot.

Quantities required.

Rough stone varies so greatly in weight and shape that it is impossible to specify quantities required, an amount that would be ample for a given job using one kind of stone would most likely be insufficient if some other stone were used; but, as a rough average guide, a ton of hard thin crazy paving stone will cover about 18 square yards, or if used for walling would be sufficient to make about 27-foot run of wall 2 feet high and 9 inches thick.

The mortar used to bed the stone can either be ready mixed "pan" mortar, obtainable ready for use at a builders' merchant's store, or Portland cement and sand can be used; the former is the cheapest when a ton or more of stone is to be used, the cement mortar is the strongest and is the most convenient when small quantities are needed.

Synthetic Stone.

There is a growing tendency to use artificial or synthetic stone for garden buildings; there are various kinds and a good selection of stock sizes, for example, "Noelite," which is obtainable in soft shades of brown-bluish-grey and other tones. It is nominally $1\frac{1}{4}$ inches thick and can be reckoned as $1\frac{1}{2}$ inches thick when bedded in mortar. Convenient stock sizes measure 9 × 9 inches, 9 × 12 inches, 6 × 12 inches, 12 × 12 inches, 12 × 18 inches, 18 × 18 inches.

Quantities required for any purpose can be reckoned up to a nicety; it is merely a simple matter of addition, so many of each size according to the pattern required. For example, a plain wall 2 feet high, 9 inches thick, and 10 feet long, using 9 × 12-inch stones, would require 160 in all.

Foundations.

In every case the top soil must first be cleared away to a sufficient depth to reach solid ground, then the surface should be covered with flints, large pebbles, broken pieces of stone or brick and well rammed down. A bed of concrete composed of cement 1 part, sand 1 part, and small broken brick or other hard material should be laid over the site and the top levelled off with mortar. The surface of this mortar should be approximately flush with the normal surface of the garden, and upon it the stonework will be laid, bedded in mortar and levelled off as described in the article on building brick walls.

Small Paved Area.

Paved areas on which to erect a sun-

Fig. 2.—Stone Paved Area.
South is shown cut away.

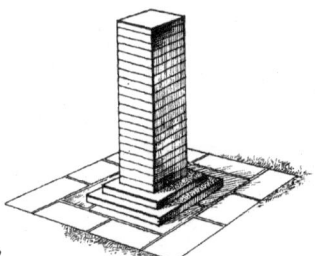

Fig. 4.—Sundial Column.

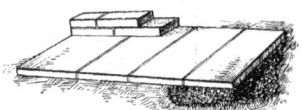

Fig. 6.—Foundations and First Step.

Fig. 3.—First Stage of Building Sundial.

Fig. 5.—Shallow Steps Built of Synthetic Stone.

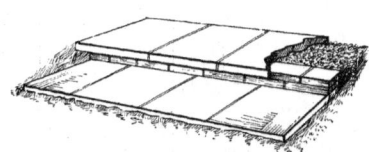

Fig. 7.—Second Step in Place.

SIMPLE STONEWORK IN THE GARDEN

Fig. 8.—Rough Stone Wall.

dial, bird bath or the like can be constructed with artificial stone, as shown in Fig. 2; the border is first defined with straight wooden battens, about 2 × 1 inch, pegged to the ground, the inner surfaces being the exact shape and size of the desired paving. Note that when using synthetic stone it is best to make all dimensions some regular multiple of the same size, for example, 36 or 48 inches when using 12-inch stone, as this avoids the necessity of cutting. If the top edges of the surrounding battens are set perfectly level, it will greatly facilitate the work, as it only remains to spread some mortar over the surface, place the stone upon it and press it down until the top of the stone is flush with the woodwork. Commence at one corner and work outwards along each adjacent side until the whole is complete.

Simple Sundial.

A simple sundial pedestal can be developed on the foregoing foundation, as sketched in Fig. 3, which shows the arrangement of the first few stones, while in Fig. 4 the column is completed. Synthetic stone is best for this purpose and should be laid and "plumbed" as described in the article on brick wall building.

Briefly stated, each stone is laid flat or horizontal and adjusted by means of a spirit level, the column is kept true in a vertical position by setting the outside face against a plumb rule, which must read "vertical" on each face. It will now be appreciated that the pergola columns are built in exactly the same way by laying sufficient stones.

Shallow Steps.

To build a short flight of shallow steps, as in Fig. 5, prepare foundations as before, then lay the stone for the bottom step. Next lay on the back part of the bottom step two or three courses of stones, as in Fig. 6, to form the "riser" of the step. Fill in the space behind it with hard core and level off with mortar. Lay the second step (Fig. 7) as before, except that the front stones should overhang about 1½ to 2 inches at the front.

Repeat these operations as necessary until sufficient steps have been built. On sloping sites, the soil should be excavated in the form of steps and each surface prepared as for plain foundations, the "riser" stones being set against the front of the stepped foundation and any gaps filled in with mortar.

Stone Walls.

Rubble stone walls can be laid without mortar, but the novice is advised to use pan mortar or cement mortar, as this somewhat simplifies the work and ensures adequate stability.

Fig. 9.—Garden Wall.

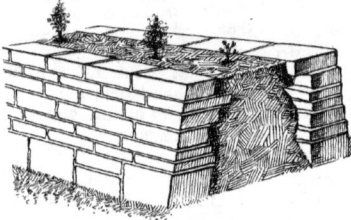

Fig. 10.—Double-faced Wall.

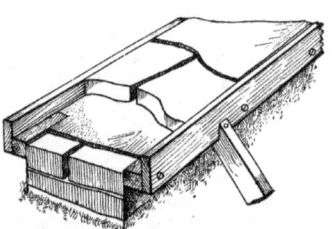

Fig. 12.—Coping Rig-up.

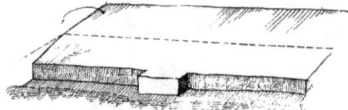

Fig. 13.—Preparing Ground for Terrace Pergola.

Fig. 14.—Terrace Wall in Early Stages.

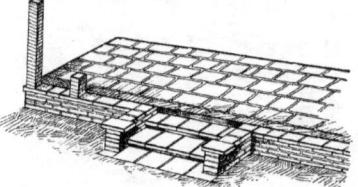

Fig. 15.—Concluding Stages of Terrace Building.

Walling stone generally is reasonably uniform in thickness and has one smooth face, which should always be brought to

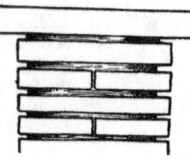

Fig. 11.—Coping Stone.

the front or visible side of the wall if the latter is used, as sketched in Fig. 8, as a retaining wall. The stones are merely bedded in mortar and should be laid with a "batter" or slight backward inclination towards the earth.

Double-faced rubble stone walls, as in Fig. 9, are laid with the face sides outwards and any deficiencies within the fall filled in with mortar.

A useful alternative is to lay the two faces of such a wall about 18 to 24 inches apart, as in Fig. 10, and fill in the gap with mould, in which suitable plants can be grown.

Coping Stones.

Rubble stone walls or those built with synthetic stone look best when finished with a capping of regular width stone, laid to overhang an inch or so on each side, as in Fig. 11, such stones being nicely bedded in mortar and levelled off. The joints should later on be pointed with cement mortar to ensure a durable weatherproof surface.

A "rig-up" that facilitates the use of "crazy" stone as a wall coping is shown in Fig. 12, and consists of two strips of wood about 1½ inches square placed against the wall sides and held fast by temporary struts. Side pieces of wood about 3 inches high and 1 inch thick are nailed to these strips and the top edges set horizontal. Mortar can now be spread on the wall between this wooden trough and the most suitable pieces of stone laid thereon. Set the straightest edge against the woodwork and avoid sharp-pointed pieces as far as possible.

Building the Terraced Pergola.

It should now be clear that the terraced pergola of Fig. 1 can readily be built by an extension of the foregoing methods. If the site slopes upwards, as in Fig. 13, it is excavated at the front for the low walls, and the foundations laid for them and the steps. Next, the walls are built as before described, and as shown partly completed in Fig. 14, after which the surplus earth at the back is shovelled into the space behind the wall and the whole area then covered with hard core, cemented over as before.

The next operation is to build the steps, as in Fig. 15, after which the terrace is paved and the columns and walls built up and finally the wooden purlins and rafters are set upon the columns.

How to Make a Helter-skelter

A CHILD's outdoor slide or helter-skelter, such as that in Fig. 1, can be made at relatively small cost and will prove a never ending source of amusement.

Outstanding features of the work must be rigidity, durability and freedom from splintering or roughening of the wood, all of which have received special attention in the design here described.

Materials required.

The following comprises a list of materials needed for a helter-skelter measuring 6 feet high, 10 feet long and suitable for use by several youngsters.

Frame.—Deal 4″ × 2″, 2 pieces 7′ 6″ long.

Deal 3″ × 2″, 2 pieces 9′ long, 2 pieces 2′ long, 2 pieces 18″ long.

Struts.—Deal, 3″ × 1½″, 2 pieces 5′ long.

Treads.—Deal, 2″ × 1″, 3 pieces 6′ long.

Cross Bars.—Deal, 3″ × 1½″, 2 pieces 5′ long.

Deal, 6″ × 1″, 2 pieces 18″ long.

Platform.—Deal, 9″ × 1½″, 1 piece 18″ long.

Slide.—Deal, 8″ × 1″, 2 pieces 13′ long.

Sides.—Deal, 6″ × 1″, 2 pieces 13′ long.

All timber should be first grade, clean, straight and nicely planed.

Handrail.—Wrought iron bar, 1″ wide, ¼″ thick, 3′ long.

Bolts.—8 galvanised iron bolts, nuts and washers, 5″ long, ⅜″ diameter.

Sundries.—1 cwt. bag of cement, 2 bushels sand, 1 pint linseed oil, 2-lb. tin garden paint.

What to do first.

Fix on the best site, allowing sufficient room at the landing or bottom end for the children to land on the grass or on to a suitable mat.

Next excavate two holes about 12 inches square and 18 inches deep to receive the ends of the back frame uprights. Obtain a bucketful of clean stones or broken brick and mix with them half a bucket of cement and 1½ buckets of sand. Moisten with water and thoroughly mix together, then put some in the bottom of each hole.

Next saw off the top end of each of the two back uprights to the shape and size given in Fig. 3, and drill a ⅜-inch diameter hole through each. Then cut off the top ends and drill ⅜-inch holes through the two front frame members, as shown in Figs. 2 and 3.

Fig. 1.—The Helter-skelter completed.
This inexpensive garden slide will prove a delight to all children.

Next cut the set of nine treads from 2 × 1-inch deal, and screw them firmly to the pair of back frames, as shown in Fig. 4, taking care that the screw shanks pass easily through the treads but bite firmly into the frames. Two screws about 2½ inches long, No. 8 gauge, should be used at each end of each tread and the holes for them must be drilled and countersunk. Brass screws are preferable, as they do not rust and discolour the work.

Erecting the Frame.

The next step is to set up the back frame by resting it on the concrete in the bottom of the holes already prepared for that purpose. Take particular care that the back frame is vertical when viewed from the back; the side members splay outwards, but a plumb line dropped from the centre of the top tread should be in line with the centre of the bottom tread. If it is not, then insert a packing piece of slate or hardwood under the bottom of the "low" side.

Next bolt the two front frame members in place and draw them forwards on the ground, as in Fig. 5, until the back frame inclines at the correct angle, as seen from the side. To check this, a plumb line can be dropped from the top tread and should be about 15 inches in front of the back edge of the back frame. Press the front or slide frames into the ground temporarily, to hold the back frame steady while the holes are filled in with some more concrete, which ought to be well rammed around the frames to hold them fast.

Posts and Slide Frame.

Next set up the two front posts in holes excavated in the soil, as shown in Fig. 6, bolt the front or slide frames to them and see that they are parallel. This can be tested by nailing a batten across them, at right angles to one side, and then testing with a spirit level; if all is correct, the bubble in the spirit level should be central—that is—should give a horizontal reading.

The object in taking these precautions at this stage is to guard against subsequent "winding" or twisting of the slide, which if very pronounced might upset an incautious slider.

All being correct, fill in the holes with concrete or cement mortar mixed as before, then leave this part of the work for a day or so to allow the concrete to set and harden.

Fixing the Struts.

The next operation is to fix the two struts between the slide frame and the back frame, as shown in the working drawings (Fig. 2). These have simply to be cut to length and bolted in place, thus completing the main framework, which by now should be quite firm and rigid.

Clear away any grass where the landing end of the slide is to come, then well ram down the soil, and, if it is at all loose or soft, make a little platform of concrete by pouring the latter into a light batten framework fixed on the ground with small stakes.

Embed the two front cross bars in the concrete, or in the ground, as the case may be, and fix them to stakes driven down into the ground.

A cross piece of 6 × 1-inch deal must next be curved on its upper edge as in Fig. 7 and then be screwed to the front of the front uprights; a similar

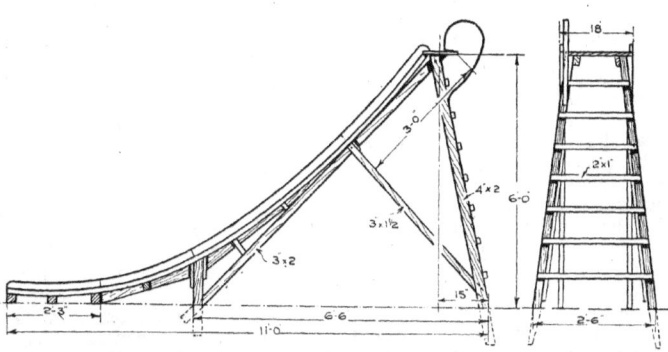

Fig. 2.—Constructional Drawing of Helter-skelter.
The arrangement of framework and leading dimensions of parts are here given.

HOW TO MAKE A HELTER-SKELTER

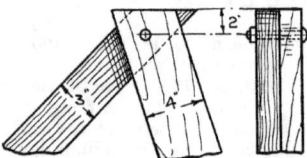

Fig. 3.—Top Ends of Frames.

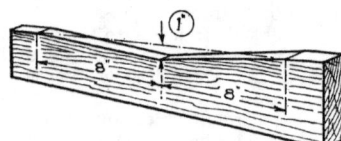

Fig. 7.—Detail of Cross Bar.

Fig. 8.—Detail of Slide.
The two frames and struts, upper cross bar and the slide boards and side pieces are here shown in part section.

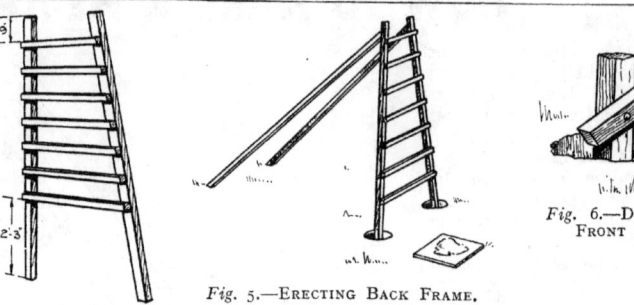

Fig. 4.—Back Frame with Treads.

Fig. 5.—Erecting Back Frame.

Fig. 6.—Detail of Front Post.

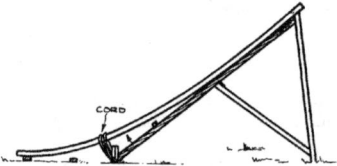

Fig. 9.—Fitting the Slide Boards.

Fig. 10.—Detail of Platform.
The slide boards are fixed to front edge of platform, which in turn is screwed to the top of frames.

Fig. 11.—Section Showing Cross Bars.

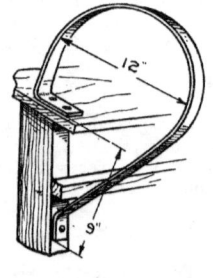

Fig. 12.—Detail of Handrail.
Strip iron is bent as here shown and then screwed or bolted to the platform.

cross piece should be fitted to the upper face of the struts, as in Fig. 8, which also shows the slide boards and the side rails in place, forming a shallow trough with slightly curved bottom.

Cut the top faces of the two fixed cross bars at the landing end in a similar way, then proceed to fit up the two slide boards.

Fitting the Slide Boards.

The slide boards should be tongue and groove jointed, and when in place should slope down a little towards the middle. Set them with the "way of the grain" downwards, as this minimises the risk of splintering. To fix the boards, lay them in place on the frame and then take several turns of cord around them and under the bottom of the foot of the slide frames, as in Fig. 9, and draw the cord tightly enough to pull the boards down into place and force them to take a suitably curved shape. Should the boards be rather stiff, they could be left under pressure for a few hours, but in most cases the cord will suffice to pull them into position. Then fasten the lower ends of the boards, with carefully countersunk brass screws, to the lower cross members, working upwards to the cross bar on the struts.

Next fit the platform at the top, as in Fig. 10, bevel the front edge to fit snugly under the slide boards and screw them in place. Cut off any surplus from the ends of the boards and round off the edges. The platform should be screwed to the ends of the frame members.

Side Pieces.

The slide boards can now be screwed or nailed to the frames at all available places, from the top to about 6 inches below the strut cross bar.

Next take the 6 × 1-inch boards and cut off a piece from each long enough to reach from the top to the struts. Round off the top edge, fit the upper parts neatly around the platform and then screw them with 2-inch No. 6 screws to the edges of the slide boards, but see that the rounded edge is 2 inches above the surface of the slide. Cut short pieces of 3 × 1½-inch deal to fit closely between the sides and the frames and nail or screw them in place, as in Fig. 11, spacing them about 12 inches apart.

Fit similar cross pieces, but sloped on the upper edge to fit closely.

Below the strut cross bar the slide boards will curve away from the straight frame members, consequently the cross bars of 3 × 1½-inch deal must be left full length to fit between the side pieces, and must be notched to fit on to the frames. The cross bars that come nearer the front upright can be supported by blocks or short struts of 2 × 1-inch deal to the frames.

A piece of 6-inch board should next be cut to a length of about 4 feet, or sufficient to reach from the end of the side piece already fitted to the cross piece on the back face of the front posts. Fix it temporarily with a couple of rails, then mark on the face the actual curvature of the top surface of the slide boards. Parallel to this line, but 2 inches away from it, draw another line to show the curvature to which the top edge must be shaped.

Shape the edge either with a pad-saw, spokeshave or chisel and round it off as before, mark off and similarly shape a board for the opposite side, then screw them in place as before and finish off the sides by fitting the remaining pieces in the same way.

The slide and side pieces should be thoroughly sand-papered. Apply a generous coat of linseed oil to the slide surface and to the inner and top faces of the side pieces.

METHODS OF RAISING MONEY

WHEN the average individual is faced with the necessity of raising money or negotiating a loan the first thing to remember is that loans can be arranged readily if there is good security, but it is very difficult—and often impossible to borrow money safely without security.

Importance of Security.

Good security for a loan really means the possession of something of real worth, that does not readily change in value, and is not liable to premature destruction.

The owner of a freehold house or land, that is fully paid for and is "unencumbered"—that is, has not already been pledged—has an excellent security for a loan up to about two-thirds of the market value of the said house or land. The evidence of possession is the owner's title deeds, which, after certain formalities, are deposited with the person lending the money.

Next in order comes leasehold property that is unencumbered, and has a sufficiently long "unexpired" time. For example, the usual period for a lease is ninety-nine years, hence a property purchased ten years ago would have an "unexpired" term of eighty-nine years and would be a good security for a long-term loan. On the other hand, if the house were, say, eighty years old, the unexpired term would only be nineteen years, which would be poor security for anything but a very short-term loan.

Other first-class securities include "gilt edge" stocks, government and municipal bonds, and stocks, "Trustee" stocks and shares, as well as those in substantial and well-established industrial enterprises, railway companies and the like.

In the case of stocks and shares it is the readiness with which they can be sold on the open market that determines their value as securities, hence it is not the face value of the security, but its market value that determines its worth as a security. For this reason shares in small companies or in "private" companies are seldom of value as a security.

Stock in trade, jewellery, motor cars and so forth, although things of worth are not much use as securities because their value is ephemeral—they can be readily removed without the knowledge of the lender. For this reason they are mostly employed as security for an advance by a pawnbroker who takes physical possession of them and retains them in his custody during the period of the loan. Should the borrower default and not redeem his pledges, that is, repay the loan with the agreed interest within the specified time, the pawnbroker is entitled to dispose of or sell the goods to recoup his losses.

First Steps in arranging a Loan.

The first step when contemplating any loan is therefore to seek for some adequate security, judging the value on the basis outlined above. The course to be followed will thus be determined by the possession or absence of "good" security.

In the absence of any adequate security it may yet be practicable to arrange a loan, because it is often possible to create sufficient security for the purpose as is explained later, but much depends upon the amount to be borrowed, the duration of the loan, and in some cases the purpose for which the money is required.

It is obviously impossible in a general article to deal specifically with every contingency of borrowing, but a number of characteristic examples will now be considered and will in many cases be directly applicable, or may be adapted to personal needs by substituting the appropriate amounts and terms.

Bank Overdraft.

This form of borrowing from a bank is mainly applicable to traders and others with an "active" account, that is, one into which money is paid and withdrawn in a continuous and consistent manner. The regularity of turnover and the way in which the business is conducted—also the length of time the customer has used the same bank, affect the ease or otherwise with which an overdraft can be arranged. The procedure is for the borrower to approach the bank manager, state the amount required and the period, also to answer his questions concerning the loan.

If the advance is granted the borrower will in most cases have to sign a form embodying the terms or conditions and also deposit with the bank securities for two or three times the amount of the loan.

An overdraft is, or should be, a short-term loan; it is not the function of a bank to provide "long term" loans.

It is important to remember that, in general, the bank can "call in," that is, require the liquidation of the loan, at very short notice. The interest payable on an overdraft is governed by the "bank rate" and is generally 1 per cent. or more above the current rate; it is therefore one of the cheapest ways of borrowing for a short term.

Bank Advance.

A bank may in some suitable case when sufficient security is deposited arrange an advance or loan—not strictly an overdraft—which may be in force over a period of years, and be repayable in one lump sum, or more often it is progressively liquefied, by the creation of a reserve account—or otherwise—to which an agreed amount of the borrower's funds in the custody of the bank is transferred at agreed intervals, for example, weekly. Interest is charged at an agreed rate; such loans are cheap and in appropriate cases are very useful as the rate of repayment is fixed.

Straight Mortgage.

Owners of house property or land can borrow money generally for long terms on the security of those properties by means of a mortgage. In law the mortgage creates in the property an interest in favour of the person or firm loaning the money which is to cease when the loan with interest is repaid by the specified date.

A mortgage is generally arranged through a solicitor, or a financial firm dealing with this class of business. In the ordinary way it is best to approach a solicitor, who will act for the borrower in preparation of the requisite deeds.

In all cases a mortgage should only be arranged under the advice of a qualified solicitor—the transaction is a serious one—which, stated in general terms, is as follows.

Mortgagor.

The borrower, called the mortgagor, executes a deed conveying the house or land to the lender, called the mortgagee, and agrees to pay back the money with interest in six months. At common law, therefore, if the money was not repaid in six months, the mortgagee would become the absolute owner of the property. But the Court of Equity would interfere in such a case, and in practice the mortgagee does not assume possession of the property provided the principal and interest are repaid on an agreed basis. Furthermore, a mortgagee who requires repayment must give three months' notice, and thereafter—if the whole of the money and interest are not repaid the mortgagee can either (a) sell the property and repay himself the principal, interest and costs of sale, or (b) can "foreclose."

Foreclosure.

To foreclose means that the mortgagee must obtain an Order of the Court that unless the mortgagor repays in full within a specified time he will lose his equity rights to redeem and the property will become the absolute property of the mortgagee.

If the mortgagee sells the property and it realises more than the amount of the loan interest and costs of sale, the balance must be handed to the mortgagor; on the other hand, if the sale does not realise sufficient the mortgagor can be sued for the balance, including all costs.

Points for and against a straight mortgage include (a) the mortgagee holds all the assets; (b) the mortgagor must be very careful to pay the interest promptly; (c) the money can only be called in on three months' notice; (d) in the event of failure a valuable asset may be lost; (e) the loan may remain outstanding for a lengthy period if the interest is paid regularly.

In practice, however, if a mortgage is arranged between responsible persons, it affords a convenient and inexpensive method of borrowing, usually for a lengthy period. In the event of the mortgage being called in it is nearly always possible to find a new mortgagee who will arrange a fresh mortgage.

The law relating to mortgages is far more intricate than that outlined above, hence every case should be treated on its merits and be the subject of a solicitor's advice.

Finally, it may be mentioned that when property is mortgaged, the deeds are handed to the mortgagee (who becomes responsible for their safe custody) and the mortgage deed is registered. Consequently when a mortgage is redeemed, the registration of the mortgage should be cancelled to show that the property is again "unencumbered" and that the mortgage has been discharged.

First and Second Mortgages.

Sometimes a mortgage is raised on a property for only a part of its mortgageable value, and later on the borrower desires to raise further moneys on the remaining security of the property. Practically speaking, the foregoing procedure is followed and the existence of the second mortgage is duly registered. The position of the mortgagor is now more difficult because there are two mortgagees each with well defined powers. Stated in general terms, however, the mortgagor is as safe as before, provided the interest to both mortgagees is paid promptly.

It is generally wise in cases of dual mortgagees to liquidate the second mortgage at as an early a period as possible, because the position of the second mortgagee is not so sound as the first mortgagee's, hence he is more likely to call in the second mortgage or to take active steps to protect his security.

Costs of a Mortgage.

The initial cost of arranging a private mortgage is somewhat difficult to generalise. Exact figures are a matter for individual arrangement, but assuming a mortgage of £1,000 the costs would probably work out as follows :—

	£	s.	d.
Surveyor's fee and expenses	5	5	0
Mortgagee's solicitor's fees and costs, say	20	0	0
Mortgagor's solicitor's fees and costs, say	15	0	0
	£40	5	0

These fees cover the cost of an independent, qualified and mutually agreed surveyor to assess the present value of the property, and it is upon his report that the value of the security is determined. The amount advanced upon it is nominally not in excess of two-thirds. Thus a house valued at £1,000 is normally good security for a total advance of about £675.

The various solicitors' fees and costs include their time and expenses in examining and verifying the title deeds, preparing and agreeing the terms of the mortgage, and the payment of statutory fees and stamp duties. The figures given are only approximate, they may be exceeded, or may be considerably reduced by agreement, especially if a solicitor is willing to "act between parties," that is, to act simultaneously for both the mortgagee and the mortgagor, and is then willing, voluntarily, to reduce his personal fees, hence the wisdom of agreeing the fees beforehand.

The rate of interest on a mortgage is a matter for individual settlement, but a fair average is 5 per cent. per annum on first mortgages and 7 per cent. or more on second mortgages, thus if a mortgage of £1,000 is outstanding for ten years the total cost to the borrower would work out as follows :—

	£
Initial expenses, say	40
Interest at 5 per cent. per annum	500
Redemption of loan	1,000
Solicitor's fees, say	20
	£1,560

The last item is a variable factor but something must be allowed to cover the costs of the re-conveyance of the deeds and the extinguishing of the mortgage deed.

It will be seen, however, that the entire cost of interest and fees works out at only £5 12s. per cent. per annum.

Should the money have been needed for only a short time, say, three months, and a Bank overdraft had been arranged, based on the security of the title deeds, the cost would work out at about 4¾ per cent. per annum.

Alternatively, should the same amount of money have been needed during, say, three years and been arranged as a Bank advance on a diminishing scale the cost would work out roughly as follows :—

	£
Initial fees, say	10
Interest at 5 per cent. per annum on outstanding balances	80 (approx.)
	£90

Which averages only £30 per annum over the three years. The principal is in this case assumed to be repaid in twelve equal quarterly amounts and the interest is only charged on the outstanding balance, hence the cost is exceptionally low when such a transaction can be arranged.

Borrowing for House Purchase.

When a person wishes to buy a house and to borrow the money to do it, there are several courses open. The best, when it can be arranged, is a Municipal or Local Council Loan. The terms and fees vary somewhat, but a typical example is a house valued at £750, on which the council will advance, say, £600 repayable over fifteen years at a rate of interest at 5 per cent. per annum on the outstanding balance.

Stated in general terms, it is a form of mortgage with the council in the position of mortgagee, but there is a bargain to accept repayment of principal in equal quarterly, half-yearly or yearly sums, and interest is only charged on the unpaid principal, thus in the above-mentioned case the annual repayment is £40. Interest for the first year is payable on the whole amount, but decreases year by year because the amount of the loan decreases by £40 each year.

Thus on this basis the total cost over fifteen years would work out as follows :—

	£
Initial fees and expenses, say	10
Interest	240
	£250

Which is equivalent to an average interest rate of £16 13s. 4d. per annum, or roughly 2¾ per cent. Adding the amount of the loan, makes the total repayment £850 over fifteen years or an average of £56 13s. 4d. per annum.

Building Societies Loan.

Building societies advance money against the security of house property, but in most cases the loan is granted solely for the purposes of purchasing the house. The rates and terms vary a little in different districts and by various societies, but characteristic rates are given as examples.

Ordinarily, a building society will advance to a private borrower from 70 to 85 per cent. of the purchase price on their surveyor's valuation, whichever is the lower, but in some approved cases 90, or even 95 per cent. will be

METHODS OF RAISING MONEY

advanced provided some "collateral" security is forthcoming.

Collateral Security.

Collateral security may take the form of the deposit with the society of approved investments, National Saving Certificates, or a Life Assurance Policy with a sufficient surrender value. Alternatively, the borrower can deposit cash equal to the sum borrowed in excess of the normal advance.

Thirdly, an assurance company's guarantee policy can be taken out by the borrower which indemnifies the society against loss. A single premium is charged by the assurance company, and in most cases the amount will be advanced by the building society and is repayable over a period of years.

Another way of giving the required collateral security is to obtain the guarantee of a local authority under the powers of the Housing Acts. The borrower then proceeds as for ordinary mortgage and upon completion the loan becomes repayable over a period of years varying from five to twenty-two years.

The scale of fees payable to the surveyor and to the solicitor are usually stated in the Society's prospectus, and are generally very moderate.

Costs of Deeds of Conveyance.

A borrower who already owns the property has no legal costs to pay except the solicitor's charges for preparing and completing the mortgage to the society, but when the borrower is purchasing the house, a Deed of Conveyance from the vendor to the purchaser is necessary and the cost of this and any search fees and stamp duties must be borne by the purchaser.

The following gives an idea of the ordinary charges involved in negotiating a purchase and mortgage.

Legal Costs when Borrower owns the Property offered as Security.

	Loan £500			Not Exceeding. £1,000	
	£ s.	d.		£	s.
Investigating title	1 1	0		1	1
Mortgage Deed	2 12	6		3	3
Inland Revenue Stamps on Mortgage Deed	0 12	6		1	5
Survey Fees	1 1	0		2	2
Solicitor's charges	5 0	0		7	10
Registration (Land Transfer Act)	1 1	0		1	1
Registration Fee	1 10	0		3	0
Search Fee	0 13	0		0	13
	£13 11	0		£19	15

Additional Costs when purchasing the Property.

In addition to the foregoing there will be additional charges to cover the expenses of investigating the vendor's title, preparing the Deed of Conveyance and the cost of the Inland Revenue Stamps on the Deed of Conveyance. There is no fixed rate for this service—it varies according to the amount of work and the time taken in the search and so forth. There is usually a fee of £1 1s. or £1 11s. 6d. to the vendor's solicitor for producing the deeds for inspection; the Inland Revenue Stamps on Deed of Conveyance up to £500 is £2 10s., and over £500 up to £1,000 is £10.

It will thus be seen that legal costs incident to the purchase of a house and the arranging of a mortgage thereon is an expensive matter. As a rough guide the solicitor's fees for the Deed of Conveyance may be reckoned as about the same as those for a mortgage.

Repayments of Advances.

The normal method of repayment to a building society is by regular monthly payments which include interest and repayment of principal.

The amount to be repaid is determined by the number of years during which the repayments have to be made. The rates vary a little with different societies but a characteristic scale is given below. The figures given in the column of monthly repayments is the amount charged for each £100 advanced.

Scale of Repayments for each £100 Advanced.

Period. (Number of years)	Monthly Instalment (12 per year)		
	£	s.	d.
22	0	12	8
20	0	13	4
18	0	14	3
15	0	16	1
12	0	18	10
10	1	1	7
7	1	8	10
5	1	18	6

Inspection of the table shows that the most favourable terms for the borrower are those for the lower periods of repayment. In other words, if a borrower feels capable of repaying on the ten-year rate at £1 1s. 7d. it will be cheaper than taking, say, the twenty-year rate of 13s. 4d., because £1 1s. 7d. is less than double 13s. 4d., hence there is relatively between the two a saving of 5s. 1d. per month.

An example will make this clear.

Cost of an Advance of £500 on the Ten-year Scale.

	£	s.	d.
Monthly repayments	5	7	11
Annual repayments	64	15	0
Total repayments	647	10	0

Thus in ten years the loan of £500 has cost £147 10s. in interest.

Advance of £500 on Twenty-year Scale.

	£	s.	d.
Monthly repayments	3	6	8
Annual repayments	40	0	0
Total repayments	800	0	0

Thus in twenty years the loan of £500 has cost £300 in interest. The cost of any advance up to about £1,000 can be worked out in the same way—any fractional parts of a £100 being charged proportionately.

All-in Payments.

In recent times the purchase of a new house is greatly simplified by many house builders, who manage to provide the requisite collateral security with a building society, and also undertake responsibility for all legal costs and stamp duties. The purchaser, who is really the borrower of money to the value of the purchase price of the house has then only to pay an agreed inclusive monthly repayment to the building society, this sum including repayment of principal and interest, the interest on the collateral security and the other incidental and legal costs. All this service only adds a few pence to the amount of the monthly repayments.

House Purchase and Life Assurance Combined.

It is possible to secure a loan on a building and to combine with it a special life insurance. The scheme is quite simple, and briefly is as follows. An insurance on the borrower's life sufficient to cover the amount owing at any time upon the mortgage is underwritten with a reliable insurance company on payment of a single premium, which in approved cases may be lent by the building society in addition to the normal loan, the borrower repaying this to the society by a slight addition to the monthly repayments. In the event of the death of the borrower during the period of the society's mortgage the amount outstanding will be paid by the insurance company; the building society will thereupon release the property to the deceased's representative free of debt. Figures for this class of business cannot usefully be given, they vary with the age of the borrower, the term of repayment and so forth.

Raising Money on Life Insurance Policy.

In most cases it is possible to raise money on a "Whole of Life" or on an "Endowment" policy that has been in force for more than two or three years. The surrender value is arrived at by an actuarial calculation, or a guaranteed surrender value may be stated on the policy. Normally, it is a minimum of one-third of the premiums paid. A loan up to about 95 per cent. of the surrender value can generally be obtained from the insurance company on the security of the policy at a very modest rate of interest. The cost of effecting the loan is usually limited to the stamp duty on the mortgage. The loan may be repaid at any time, but if the policy is to remain in force the premiums and interest must be paid as usual.

Surrender Value.

Some idea of the possible surrender value of a policy can be obtained by dividing by three the total premiums paid since the commencement of the policy; the best and proper course, however, is to write direct to the insurance company concerned and ascertain the true value.

When the surrender value of an insurance policy is sufficient it is possible to utilise it as collateral security for a short-term bank overdraft, or as building society "collateral."

The relative value of an insurance policy as security for a loan can be judged by the following figures. Suppose the borrower to be aged thirty-five years and to have taken out at age twenty a simple whole of life policy for £1,000. The annual premiums would be about £10 9s. 2d., hence the total premium paid would be £96 8s. 4d., hence the minimum surrender value would be about £32 and would be worth a loan of at least £30.

Had the same borrower taken out at age twenty an endowment policy maturing at age forty the premium would be about £50 17s. 6d. per annum, and at age thirty-five there would have been paid over £700 or about enough to justify a loan of £250 or more. In each case the sum assured is £1,000. The difference in borrowing power is due to the amount paid in premiums.

Loans on Personal Security.

Responsible persons of good character but not personally in possession of adequate negotiable security can negotiate a substantial loan of, say, £500 or upwards through some of the big assurance companies.

Briefly, the procedure is as follows. The borrower approaches the company, fills up a form of application and undergoes a medical examination; this being satisfactory the business proceeds. The borrower takes out an insurance policy with the company for an amount equal to at least one and a half times the amount of the loan, and also names at least two persons of good financial standing who will join with him in signing an Assignment and Deed of Covenant to secure the repayment of the principal with interest, and the premiums on the insurance.

Assuming therefore that the borrower can obtain two responsible guarantors who are willing to guarantee him and are accepted by the company, a loan repayable over a period of years can be obtained at a reasonable rate.

Exact rates cannot be quoted as they vary with age and each individual case is the subject of a special quotation. One actual example is as follows:—

Age of Borrower, Thirty-seven Years.

	£
Amount of loan	500
Repayable by 10 half-yearly amounts of	50
Amount of life insurance	750
Interest 6 per cent. per annum	30
Insurance premium	22 p.a.
Total of first annual repayment	152
Cost during five years to extinguish loan, pay interest and insurance premiums	700

The cost of this particular loan in interest and insurance therefore averages £40 per annum or about 15s. 5d. per week, which is extremely modest in view of the borrower's lack of negotiable securities.

Furthermore, at the end of the period there would be a surrender value of about £38 on the life policy if surrendered—or it could be carried on—or converted to a fully paid policy, thus gaining some further return and reducing the actual cost.

Another advantage of this method of borrowing is that in the event of the premature death of the borrower the loan is extinguished, the guarantors are relieved of their responsibility and any surplus is paid to the deceased's relatives or assigns.

Temporary Loans.

Short-term loans can be arranged between acquaintances willing to lend the money, either on terms set out in an agreement, or by way of I.O.U. or otherwise. An I.O.U. is merely a written acknowledgement of a debt; it is neither a promise nor an agreement to pay, but as it is evidence of a debt it can be sued upon and the borrower made to pay.

Promissory Note.

A promissory note is an unconditional promise in writing, between one person and another to pay on demand or at some stated time a certain sum in money. It is a negotiable instrument and can be sued upon. As a general rule, it is unwise to give a Promissory Note as security for a loan.

Bill of Exchange.

A bill of exchange is a document by which debts are discharged; it is an unconditional order in writing to pay a stated sum of money at a fixed date. It is also in effect a convenient means of borrowing money by the person who takes the bill, because—provided the person who gives it is financially sound—the bill can be discounted through a bank or by a bill broker. A common form of bill may be for, say, £100 payable in three months' time and the cost of discounting it—or borrowing the money on the security of the bill—would be about 5 per cent. per annum or 25s. for the period of three months. A bill is primarily intended as a means of facilitating trade, and the person who gives the bill must only do so for "value received." The bill must carry a revenue stamp of appropriate value—a 1s. for a bill not exceeding £100. The person to whom the money is owing "draws" the bill thus.

£100   London, *January 1st*, 1934.

Three months after date pay to me or to my order the sum of £100 for value received.

JOHN JONES.

S. SMITH, 5000 High Road, London, N.1.

To

The person who has to pay the bill, and who agrees to do so, then "accepts" it and writes across the face of the bill the words: "*Accepted payable at Blank's Bank, London Street, E.C.*—S. SMITH."

Jones can discount the bill and draw the money, but if he does so, and S. Smith does not pay on the date due, Jones can be sued by the person who discounted the bill or by anyone into whose hands it may lawfully come before maturity.

Bill of Sale.

In case of dire necessity and as a last resort, money can be raised on a mortgage Bill of Sale. It is a very risky procedure unless the party accepting the bill and lending the money is a known and reputable person, who is willing to accept the bill as security for the money lent.

Bills of Sale are regulated by Acts of Parliament, must be properly stamped and attested and must be registered within seven days of execution, in the High Court of Justice, and particulars of it must appear in the *London Gazette*.

In practice, anyone who executes a Bill of Sale seriously jeopardises his credit.

The general effect of a Bill of Sale is to transfer the ownership of personal chattels—furniture, trade machinery, growing crops and so forth—from one person to another either absolutely or as security for a debt which must exceed £30. Bills of Sale given as security for money must be in the legally specified form. The goods conveyed by the bill are usually left in the possession of the original owner, but the lender has the right either with or without notice to forthwith or at a stated future time to take possession of the goods.

Ways of Saving and Investing Money

DEALING WITH POST OFFICE SAVINGS, NATIONAL SAVINGS' CERTIFICATES, GOVERNMENT STOCKS, POST OFFICE ANNUITIES, BUILDING SOCIETIES AND FIXED INVESTMENT TRUSTS.

THE Post Office offers several different means of saving money and gives absolute security, as the British Government guarantees the return of all moneys invested through this medium.

It is possible to open an account at any branch of the Post Office, and it is only necessary to fill in a form and make a small initial deposit in exchange for which the depositor receives a book with the amount saved entered therein.

Interest at the rate of 2½ per cent., i.e., ¼d. per £1 per month is added from the first day of each month following the deposit. Deposits may be made at any of the 15,000 branches and not necessarily at the original branch used. In the same way it is possible to withdraw up to £3 on demand at any Post Office, and up to £10 by return of post or within an hour or two by telegram.

Savings may be made in cash, cheque, postal order or money order and the strictest secrecy is guaranteed with regard to each individual account.

Home Safes.

Alternatively, it is possible to obtain a Home Safe for the sum of 2s., which sum is refunded when the safe is given up, and the Post Office takes charge of the key, the safe only being opened when presented by the depositor and the amount credited in the savings' book. To obviate inconvenience in the event of illness, etc., it is possible to authorise anyone to make deposits or to make withdrawals. It will be seen, therefore, that the Post Office offers every facility to the small investor, and reference to the table of comparisons shown later in this article will give some idea of the growth of money put aside in this manner.

To enable people who may be travelling either on holiday or for business to have access to their money Travellers' Warrants may be obtained, each to the value of £3, and provided that the necessary balance is there, as many as six of these warrants may be demanded.

Cruising Credits enabling depositors who are cruising on British ships to have access to their money are also issued on demand.

Deposits up to £500 in any one year may be made in this way, but there is no limit to the total deposits over a term of years.

Accounts may be opened in the name or names of a child or children under the age of seven years, and the child can make withdrawals after attaining that age, and this form of saving should prove a good means of instilling thrift into the young.

Clubs and societies may also take advantage of the Post Office provided that a copy of their rules is forwarded to the Controller at the time of opening the account.

NATIONAL SAVINGS CERTIFICATES

Another form of investment and saving is through the medium of National Savings Certificates, which may be purchased at any Post Office at a cost of 16s. each. At the end of the first year 4d. interest is added; during the second year 1d. is added at the end of each completed three months; during the third, fourth, fifth and sixth years 2d. is added at the end of each completed four months, and thereafter 2d. is added at the end of each completed period of three months to the end of the twelfth year, when a bonus of 4d. is added, bringing the total value of the certificate up to 23s. This means a rate of interest equal to £3 1s. 5d. per cent. per annum over the whole period.

No Income Tax is payable on interest on these certificates, and there is no need to include them in any return of Income Tax.

Certificates may be cashed together with accrued interest at any time provided short notice be given to the Post Office authorities.

Once again, no one individual may hold more than 500 of these certificates, but there is nothing to prevent each member of a family from holding the maximum number.

Table showing Growth in Value of National Savings Certificates

Value After.	Number of Certificates.		
	One. Original Cost 16s.	Five. Original Cost £4.	Ten. Original Cost £8.
	£ s. d.	£ s. d.	£ s. d.
1 year	0 16 4	4 1 8	8 3 4
1 do. 3 months	0 16 5	4 2 1	8 4 2
1 do. 6 do.	0 16 6	4 2 6	8 5 0
1 do. 9 do.	0 16 7	4 2 11	8 5 10
2 years	0 16 8	4 3 4	8 6 8
2 do. 4 months	0 16 10	4 4 2	8 8 4
2 do. 8 do.	0 17 0	4 5 0	8 10 0
3 years	0 17 2	4 5 10	8 11 8
4 years	0 17 8	4 8 4	8 16 8
5 years	0 18 2	4 10 10	9 1 8
6 years	0 18 8	4 13 4	9 6 8
7 years	0 19 4	4 16 8	9 13 4
8 years	1 0 0	5 0 0	10 0 0
9 years	1 0 8	5 3 4	10 6 8
10 years	1 1 4	5 6 8	10 13 4
11 years	1 2 0	5 10 0	11 0 0
12 years	1 3 0	5 15 0	11 10 0

Provided that the Certificates are left untouched as regards both principal and interest for the full period of twelve years, the rate of interest works out at £3 1s. 5d. per cent. per annum.

INVESTMENT IN GOVERNMENT STOCKS

It is possible to buy and sell through the Post Office any of the Government securities shown in the following list whether you have a Savings Bank Account or not.

On application to the Controller, to be made on a form which may be obtained from any Post Office, you may send your Savings Bank book, or a remittance for the required amount, and obtain in return any of the Government stocks up to the value applied for.

Up to £1,000 stock may be purchased at a time and there is no limit to the total amount you may hold. You will receive an acknowledgment of your application and money and the certificate of your investment, with a statement of costs as to charges for commission, etc.

The values of the stocks vary according to the current price as quoted by the Stock Exchange, and it should be noted that any transaction of this kind done through the Post Office is made at the price certified as the current figure at that time, and an order to buy or sell at any given figure cannot be accepted.

Commission

The commission charged for this service is very small, as will be seen from the following table:—

On stock not exceeding—
  £10 the commission is 1s. 0d.
  £25   ,,   ,,   1s. 6d.
  £50   ,,   ,,   2s. 6d.
  £75   ,,   ,,   3s. 6d.
  £100   ,,   ,,   4s. 6d.
and 1s. on every additional £50 of stock over the last amount.

Payment of Dividends

Dividends may be paid either by credit to a Savings Bank Account or by warrant payable at a Post Office or through a Bank. No Income Tax is payable on these dividends, but they must be included in any return of Income Tax.

An investment can be made in the name of a child if desired, but the holdings cannot be sold or transferred until attainment of the age of seven, and all dividends must be credited to the account until that time is reached.

Securities in which Investment can be made.

The following list shows the various securities in which it is possible to invest, together with the dates on which the dividends become payable.

It must be realised that the stocks mentioned, if bought at their present-day market price, do not necessarily yield the investor the rate of interest shown as the original yield, and in fact it will be found that prac-

Description.	Dividends Payable.
2½ per cent. Consols	5th January and 5th April.
2½ per cent. Annuities	5th July and 5th October.
2¾ per cent. Annuities	5th January, April, July and October.
2¾ per cent. Guaranteed Stock.	1st January and 1st July.
3 per cent. Local Loans	5th January, July, April and October.
3 per cent. Guaranteed Stock	1st January and 1st July.
3 per cent. Conversion Stock, 1948–1953	1st March and 1st September.
3½ per cent. War Stock	1st June and 1st December.
3½ per cent. Conversion Stock	1st April and 1st October.
4 per cent. Funding Stock, 1960–1990	1st May and 1st November.
4 per cent. Consols	1st February and 1st August.
4 per cent. Victory Bonds	1st March and 1st September.
4½ per cent. Conversion Stock, 1940–1944	1st January and 1st July.
4½ per cent. Treasury Bonds	1st February and 1st August.
5 per cent. Conversion Stock, 1944–1964	1st May and 1st November.

tically all of them are priced to produce the same return of approximately 3 per cent. per annum.

POST OFFICE ANNUITIES

Another form of investment for people who have reached their old age and are desirous of obtaining as large an income as is possible may be found in the purchase of an annuity from the Post Office.

It must be fully realised that the money so utilised becomes the property of the Government and is not returnable in any circumstance, and consequently the yield given is much larger than would be got from an ordinary investment.

The charge for an annuity depends upon the age and sex of the person concerned, and depends also on the current price of 2½ per cent. Consols, but an idea may be obtained from the rates given later on.

It is possible to purchase an annuity of £1 per annum, payable quarterly on the 5th days of January, April, July and October, and continuing during the lifetime of the purchaser, and the amount of £1 may be increased up to as large a sum as £300 per annum for a proportionately larger original outlay. Obviously an annuity is somewhat a matter of chance from the purchaser's point of view, for should he or she live many years after the purchase there is the possibility of receiving back considerably more than the amount of the original outlay. On the other hand, should death occur within a few years of the purchase the Government would gain, as there is no return of the capital beyond a single payment of one quarter of one year's income if claimed within two years from the date of death. No charge is made on this class of transaction.

How the Annuities are paid.

Annuities may be paid in cash at any specified Savings Bank Post Office, or may be credited to the annuitant's Savings Bank account if preferred.

It can also be arranged for the annuity to be paid during the joint lifetime of two persons, with continuance in full to the survivor, and it is only necessary to complete the small form of proposal to arrange a contract of this kind, as no medical examination is required.

Anyone contemplating the purchase of an annuity should not only obtain a quotation from the Post Office, but also from one or two of the first-class insurance companies, as, owing to the fluctuations in the price of Consols, it is sometimes possible to obtain a better result from an insurance office.

The following table shows the cost of an annuity of £1 per annum payable every quarter, and I have taken the price of Consols to be between £80 and £83, and the amounts therefore would

Table showing the Sum for which an Annuity of £1 per annum will be Granted. The Price of 2½ per cent. Consols is taken at between £80 and £83.

At the time of Purchase.	Cost of the Annuity of £1 per annum.	
	Male Lives.	Female Lives
	£ s. d.	£ s. d.
If 45 or over	18 9 8	20 3 6
,, 46 ,,	18 2 6	19 17 2
,, 47 ,,	17 15 3	19 10 8
,, 48 ,,	17 7 9	19 4 0
,, 49 ,,	17 0 2	18 17 2
,, 50 ,,	16 12 5	18 10 2
,, 51 ,,	16 4 6	18 3 0
,, 52 ,,	15 16 6	17 15 8
,, 53 ,,	15 8 5	17 8 2
,, 54 ,,	15 0 3	17 0 6
,, 55 ,,	14 11 11	16 12 9
,, 56 ,,	14 3 7	16 4 10
,, 57 ,,	13 15 2	15 16 9
,, 58 ,,	13 6 8	15 8 6
,, 59 ,,	12 18 2	15 0 1
,, 60 ,,	12 9 8	14 11 7
,, 61 ,,	12 7 1	14 3 4
,, 62 ,,	11 13 5	13 14 10
,, 63 ,,	11 5 3	13 6 2
,, 64 ,,	10 17 3	12 17 5
,, 65 ,,	10 9 4	12 8 7
,, 66 ,,	10 1 6	11 19 8
,, 67 ,,	9 13 2	11 10 8
,, 68 ,,	9 6 2	11 1 10
,, 69 ,,	8 18 9	10 13 0
,, 70 ,,	8 11 6	10 4 3

be slightly larger should the price of Consols recede or smaller should their price advance, for all moneys received by the Government as purchase price for an annuity is invested in 2½ per cent. Consols.

LIFE ASSURANCE AS AN INVESTMENT

The possibility of Life Assurance as an investment should not be overlooked, for there are many advantages in putting one's savings into the purchase of an Endowment Policy. Full details are given in the article on "Practical Notes on Life Assurance."

INVESTING WITH A BUILDING SOCIETY

There must be many people who are confronted with the difficulty of investing comparatively small sums of money of about £200 or £300 to obtain a reasonable rate of interest coupled with absolute security. There are two schemes worthy of special attention:—

(1) Investment with a Building Society;
(2) Fixed Investment Trusts.

We will deal first with a Building Society Investment.

One of the largest societies in the world offer facilities for saving on investment in a most simple and straightforward manner. They welcome the smallest sums, and no expenses are incurred in the purchase of their shares and no deduction is made on withdrawal.

For a monthly payment of 10s. it is possible to purchase one share bearing interest at the rate of 3½ per cent., together with the right to participate in any distribution of annual profits.

Investing 10s. a Month.

The following table shows the growth of a 10s. monthly investment share calculated at the rate of interest mentioned, and it is as well to point out that the interest is payable free of tax.

Year.	Amount Saved by Investor.	Interest Added.	Total at End of Year.
	£ s. d.	£ s. d.	£ s. d.
1	6 10 0	0 1 11	6 11 11
2	13 0 0	0 8 6	13 8 6
3	19 10 0	0 19 7	20 9 7
4	26 0 0	1 15 7	27 15 7
5	32 10 0	2 16 10	35 6 10
6	39 0 0	4 3 5	43 3 5
7	45 10 0	5 15 7	51 5 7
8	52 0 0	7 13 4	59 13 4
9	58 10 0	9 17 2	68 7 2
10	65 0 0	12 6 11	77 6 11
11	71 10 0	15 2 11	86 12 11
12	78 0 0	18 5 7	96 5 7
13	84 10 0	21 15 0	106 5 0
14	91 0 0	25 11 5	116 11 5

The value of each share is £120 inclusive of interest and any distribution of annual profits, and the advantage of purchasing a share or number of shares by means of monthly instalments will be obvious to the reader.

The accumulated savings, together with accrued interest and profits, can be withdrawn at any time without deduction or expense of any kind, and it will be seen therefore that not only is the purchaser obtaining a very good rate of interest on his money, but he is also to all intents and purposes a shareholder in the building society and entitled to participate in the profits made.

The assets of the society whose figures I have quoted are in the region of £92,500,000, whilst there is also a reserve fund, after providing for all interest and bonuses allotted, of over £3,250,000. One has only to realise the tremendous number of mortgages arranged in the last few years and to notice the enormous expansion in house building to appreciate that the building societies of to-day are in an unrivalled position, and should be able to easily maintain their profits for many years to come.

In addition to the above-mentioned form of investment, the same society is willing to accept investments up to £1,000 for their paid-up shares bearing interest at the rate of 3½ per cent. per annum, and up to £4,500 bearing interest at the rate of 3 per cent.

FIXED INVESTMENT TRUSTS

For the investor who prefers a slight gamble with his investment the following scheme will probably be of great interest. It is a fact that many people would very much like to purchase shares in a well-known industrial concern but are prevented from so doing on account of the high price of such shares. Obviously the small man cannot offer to purchase a £1 share whose present value is in the neighbourhood of £3 or £4, as owing to his limited amount of capital he is only able to buy a very small number.

To overcome this difficulty certain Fixed Investment Trusts have been formed, and it is possible to purchase certificates representing a holding in twenty-seven British industrial concerns. In this way it is possible to distribute funds over a well-balanced selection of investments in companies with world-wide interest in different forms of industry, and for as small an initial payment of approximately £20 it is possible to have a certificate which will give a share of the profits received from the concerns in question.

A Fixed Trust is one in which the investments are determined at the time of formation and remain unalterable (except for very special reasons) for the period of the Trust. The investor who buys sub-units in a Fixed Trust is in precisely the same position as if he had bought a small holding in every one of the securities which constitute the Trust unit.

The interest and dividends paid on the securities are collected by the Bank trustees and distributed half-yearly by warrants to registered certificate holders.

The Advantage of Fixed Trust Investment.

Small investors have realised that a purchase of "Fixed Trust Certificates" enabled them to obtain the security of capital with stability of income previously only enjoyed by the large investor, who was able to distribute his funds over a well-balanced selection of investments in companies with world-wide operations in different forms of industry and public utility. The large denominational values of many companies' shares, and the high market prices of others, precluded hitherto the average investor from enjoying the protection of this diversified distribution, which is now available by the purchase of Fixed Trust Certificates for as small an initial investment as approximately £20.

Each company included in the unit has been selected after careful consideration of its past record, its present financial resources, and the possibilities of its growth and continuing success in varying operations and interests in British industry and trade.

Under Trust Deeds the Fixed Investment Trusts purchase according to demand, and transfer to the trustees the various securities, the aggregate cost of a unit fluctuating only with the Stock Exchange prices of its component securities at the date of purchase, and each unit is divided into 4,000 sub-units acquired in the unit chosen. Sub-units may be purchased in any multiple of ten at any time, the minimum purchase in the first instance being ten sub-units.

Purchase and Sale of Sub-Units.

The inclusive purchase and sale prices of sub-units of most Fixed Trust Certificates are published daily in the public press. These sub-unit prices are calculated upon the daily market value of the securities, and include the usual Stock Exchange charges, settlement duty and a service charge for providing the facilities for the purchase and sale of sub-units in any amount, including the remuneration of the trustees for collecting and distributing dividends, bonuses, rights, etc., during the trust period of twenty years. The service charge, if distributed over the period of the Trust, approximates to one-quarter of 1 per cent. per annum on the capital invested in the purchase of sub-units. There is no other charge to certificate holders throughout the period for this service.

At the termination of the trust period of twenty years, the Fixed Investment Trust will provide certificate holders with an opportunity of continuing their investments in Fixed Trust certificates in other units, or, as provided by the Trust Deed, of realising their holdings through the trustees.

A purchaser increasing his holding to a complete unit, or to 1,600 sub-units or any multiple thereof, has the right at any time to have this proportion of the actual securities forming the unit transferred into his own name upon payment of the usual stamp duties, transfer fees, etc.

Collection of Dividends, Bonuses, etc.

All the securities forming the unit are registered in the name of the trustees, who receive all dividends, bonuses rights, etc., direct from the companies and distribute the proceeds half-yearly without any deduction whatsoever to certificate holders upon the following dates in each year:—

15th May and 15th November, thereby distributing to an investor in all of the units an income payable on fixed dates.

The net amount of all accrued dividends on the underlying securities is included in the price payable by the purchaser of sub-units, but is returned to the purchaser in full in his first half-yearly dividend distribution. Income Tax will only therefore be deducted on dividends paid after the date of the purchase of sub-units, and the certificate of Income Tax deduction will be in accordance therewith.

Income Tax.

Income Tax having been deducted from the dividends before receipt by the trustees, no further tax other than sur-tax is personally payable by the certificate holder upon the net income distributed by the trustees. Vouchers are issued by the trustees certifying that Income Tax has been deducted in order to enable certificate holder to claim repayment in appropriate cases.

The opportunity provided by the Trust in this particular form of fixed unit investment has appealed to a large section of investors, who prefer to receive their incomes upon fixed dates and to be spared the continuous management and supervision of their funds, while, at the same time, enjoying the security of a very complete distribution of their investments in well-known securities held on their behalf by the trustees.

Method of Purchase or Sale.

All the investments forming the units are securities freely marketable on the Stock Exchange. Fixed Trust Certificates can be purchased or sold daily against cash settlement directly through any bank or stockbroker.

For the purpose of deposit as Collateral security or Lien, Fixed Trust Certificates are regarded by bankers as being proportionately of the same value as the various securities forming each unit.

Converting a Sash Window to a Casement Window

It is not a difficult job to replace a sash window with casement frames, as shown at Fig. 1. The material required for the frames can be purchased ready moulded from a timber merchant. A typical sash window is shown in elevation and two sections at Fig. 2. AA are the stiles of the sliding sashes; B the bottom; C the top, and D the meeting rails. They are separated by parting beads P attached to the jambs, which have an outside lining E, an inside lining F, a head H and a sill S; to the inside edges of the inner lining F are attached the guard or staff beads G, which are removable.

The New Frames.

The new frames are shown in elevation and four sections at Fig. 3, and consist of two casements and a fanlight separated by a transom K, which is fitted to the jambs of the outside frame. The casements are made with two stiles L and M, and two rails N and O. The fanlight has two stiles R and two rails T and U. There are two methods of fitting the casements, as shown in the sections; in one they open inwards and in the other outwards, but in this case they will be narrower unless a considerable amount of trouble is taken to remove a portion of the outside lining of the frame, a job hardly worth the time involved.

Measurements required.

As it is advisable to make the new frames before the old sashes are removed, the first job will be to decide which way the casements are to open and then to measure up accordingly. For inside opening casements the total width should be the same as the width of the old sashes, and the height should be the distance between the head and the level of the sill under the guard bead G; these positions are indicated by italic letters "a" and "b" in Fig. 2. It will be realised that the frames will fit against the projecting portions of the outside lining E. For casements opening outwards, the measurements required are indicated by "c" and "d," and it will be necessary to fill in the jamb to bring it level with the inside edges of the outside lining E.

Next decide position of Transom.

The next job is to decide on the position of the transom K which divides the fanlight from the casements; this may be one-quarter of the height down from the top, but a more pleasing proportion is to have the centre line of the transom two-sevenths, leaving five-sevenths below for the casements. The measurements should be drawn out to a suitable scale

Fig. 1.—These Casement Windows have been fitted in Place of the Existing Sash Window.

so that the casements and fanlight can be prepared ready for fixing in position directly the frame is adapted. It would probably be inconvenient to remove the old sashes and face up the framing before the casements are ready, but in order that the method of adapting the outer framework is thoroughly understood, two stages in the work are indicated for each form of casement opening.

Inside Opening Casements.

In preparing for the inside opening casements, it will be seen at Fig. 4 that the parting and guard beads have been removed and that notches have been made in the outside and inner linings to receive the transom. The latter should be prepared from material 2 inches thick and a width equal to the jamb, somewhere about 5 inches, with an additional ¾ inch or so outside the lining. The rebate should be in keeping with the inside of the lining E and about ¾ inch deep. The bead underneath should correspond. It will be seen that the transom is in position at Fig. 5 and that the sill is made up to the level at S and a bead is fixed in front to correspond with the projecting lining at E. One or two holes should be drilled from the front to allow for driving rain to run down the sill outside.

Outside Opening Casements.

The necessary preparations for the outside opening casements are shown at Fig. 6. The transom is prepared first to 1 inch thick and the same width as before, but the beads can be left until later; they should be about ¾ inch thick. It will be seen that a notch is cut in the edge of the outside lining E to take the transom, and that the guard beading G is replaced after the sashes have been removed.

In Fig. 7 the transom is shown in position and is supported underneath and above with lining strips W, which bring the surface flush with the edge of the outside lining E. The beading at X corresponds with that on the transom, and similar lengths of beading are fixed on the sill and underneath the head, as indicated at X and Y in the sections given in Fig. 3.

Frames for Casements.

The frames for the casements are

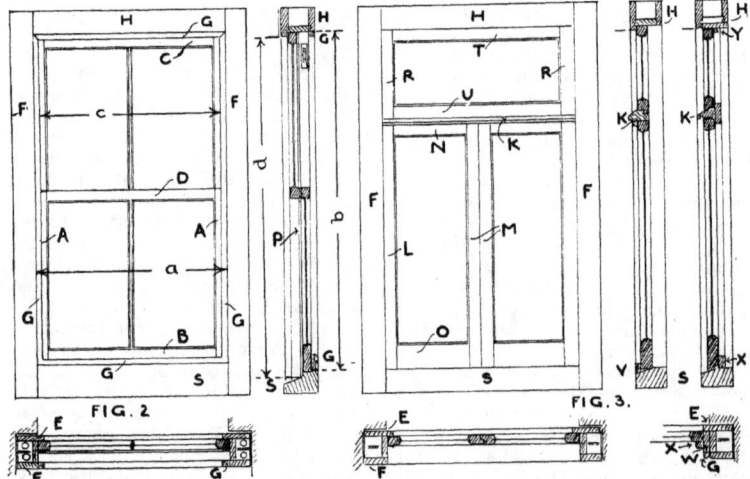

Fig. 2.—Elevation and Section of a Typical Sash Window.

Fig. 3.—Elevation and Section of Frames for Casement Windows.

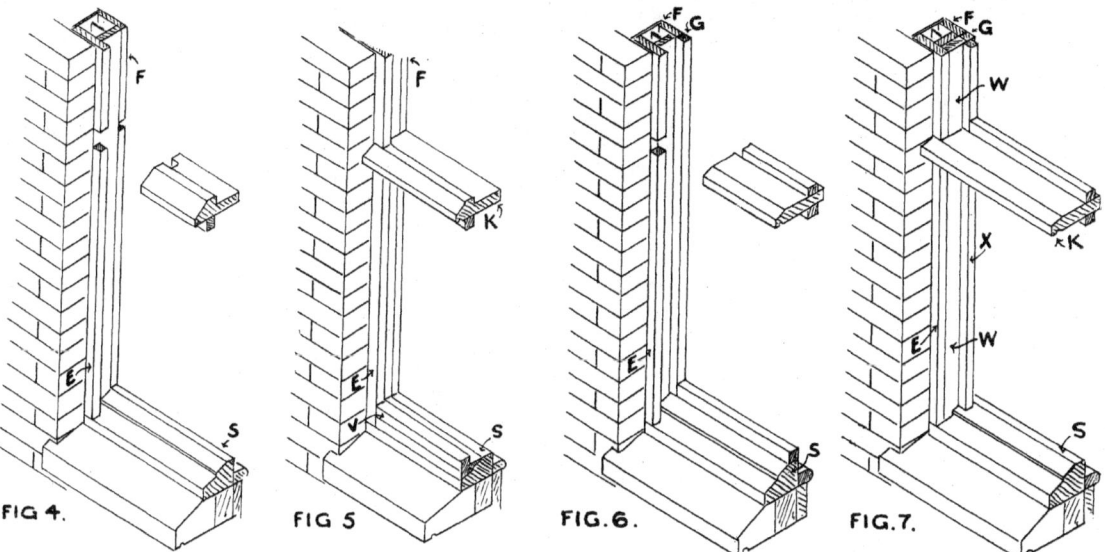

Figs. 4 and 5.—Details for Inside Opening Casements. *Figs. 6 and 7.*—Details for Outside Opening Casements.

shown at Fig. 8, the wood used for the stiles and top rails being approximately $1\frac{7}{8} \times 1\frac{7}{8}$ inches in section, while the bottom rail is about 4 inches wide. The fanlight is made entirely with the $1\frac{7}{8} \times 1\frac{7}{8}$-inch prepared moulding, as at Fig. 9. The joints are haunched mortise and tenon. Fig. 10 shows one of the joints from the outside, and Fig. 11 the same joint from the inside with a section below showing the method of fitting the round of the moulding.

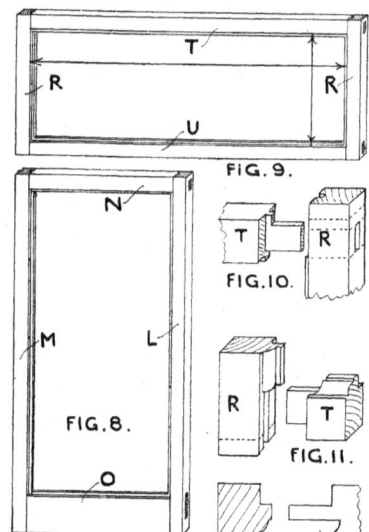

Figs. 8–11.—Details of Frames.

8, Frames for casements; 9, Fanlight frame; 10, The haunched mortise and tenon joint from outside; 11, Joint from inside.

Marking out and cutting Tenons and Mortises.

The method of marking out and cutting the tenons and mortises is given in stages at Figs. 12 and 13 because of the care that must be taken in allowing for rebates and moulding. The framework is measured up to fit the openings, but it is always advisable to make them larger to allow for close fitting. The joint measurements are taken from the rebate level, as indicated by the lines in Fig. 9. The tenons should be approximately the same thickness as the top of the moulding and be about half the total width of the wood. The hauncheon should be about $\frac{1}{2}$ inch each way.

First mark off the length of the tenons to give the correct distance between the shoulders which butt on the rebate level, and set off the width to allow for the hauncheon, as in stage 1 in Fig. 12. Gauge to the required thickness and then saw off, as indicated in stage 2. Leave the tenons at this stage and proceed with the mortises, as shown at Fig. 13. It will be seen that the dotted lines on the side and on top indicate the actual width of the mortise and allow for the length of the hauncheon with some waste at the end; the latter is important and should be carefully noted.

In stage 2 the moulding has been cut off to the rebate level and the lines for the mortise have been gauged on the flat surface, they are also carried across the end and underneath. It will be noted that the mortise is on a level with the rebate line in Fig. 9. When the mortises have been cut, as shown in stage 3, the joint can be fitted together, so that the scribing of the edge of the moulding on the tenoned rails can be marked; the cutting should be done with a scribing gouge to an exact fit.

Glue and clamp up Frames.

Although not essential, the tenons can be wedged, but if the work has been done accurately there is no need to do more than glue and clamp up the frames. It is quite usual to paint the tenons and drive them home without glue, but the latter makes a better job. On one of the casement stiles it will be necessary to run a rebate; this should be $\frac{1}{2}$ inch down and half-way along. On the corresponding stile, known as the meeting stile, on the other basement, glue and brad on a bead to correspond with the space formed by the rebate in the other meeting stile. This could have been worked on the original

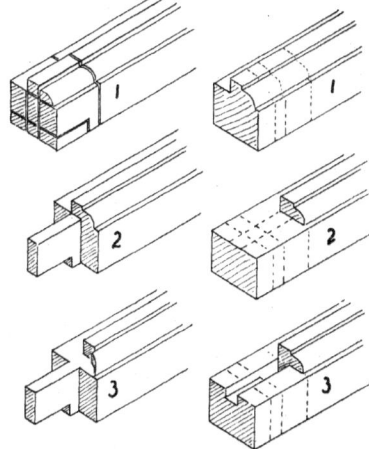

Figs. 12 and 13.—Method of marking out and cutting the Tenons and Mortises.

framing, but this is the easiest method and prevents confusion in marking out. The fanlight is made similarly as regards joints. The projections on the stiles should be left until the three frames are fitted in position.

Owing to the variety of sizes in sash windows, it is impossible to give actual dimensions for making the frames, but if accurate measurements are taken in the first place and a large scale drawing prepared, no great difficulty should be experienced. In large casement windows it is usual to fit a vertical division, known as a mullion, between the casements, but with the comparatively narrow frames usual with sash windows the mullion can be omitted, as it would take up at least 3 inches of the opening.

Removing the Old Sashes.

The actual work of removing the old sashes is not difficult. First remove the inside guard beads at G; a wide chisel should be driven in and the bead prized open and gradually pulled out. The sash cords should be cut on the lower sash and the sash pulled out. Lower the top sash and cut the cords, then pull out the parting beads and remove the sash.

Removing the Weights.

The weights can be pulled out by opening the two pocket pieces, but unless they are required this need not be done. Proceed with the work of preparing the framing, as shown in Figs. 4 to 7, and then proceed to fit the casements and fanlight. They are hung with ordinary butt hinges and should fit easily, but not loosely.

Casement Stays.

Casement stays are fitted to both casements and the fanlight, and a suitable fastener provided for the casements. The ordinary fastener is made with a plate to fix on a mullion, but it will not be a difficult job to obtain a small gate or other suitable catch in place of the usual plate. It will be necessary to fit two small flush bolts on the meeting stile having the rebate on the outside; this is the opposite one to that on which the fastener is fixed. The glass from the old sashes will probably be sufficient to glaze the casements and fanlight.

REMOVING STAINS FROM PAPER

ACCIDENTS happen in every home, and one of the most disconcerting results is the disfigurement of documents and other papers by staining. Many of the common domestic stains are capable of removal, and the technical methods adopted for some of these are as follows:—

Blood Stains

Immerse in cold water and move the paper gently until the stain is washed away. On no account should hot water be used, as the heat will fix the albumen, and consequently render the stain ineradicable.

Coffee Stains

Immerse in a solution of glycerine and ammonia.

Fox Marks

These are stains which have been brought about by a combination of moisture and age. Two methods are available: (1) Immerse in a very weak solution of hydrochloric acid; (2) immerse in a solution of permanganate of potash and, when the whole sheet has turned a deep brown, wash for some seconds in running water. The sheet should finally be placed in a dish of bleaching solution, usually sulphurous acid. Special care should be taken not to confuse the latter with sulphuric acid.

Fat Stains (including tallow and sealing-wax).

To begin with, iron the stain with a hot iron through blotting paper, and as soon as the stain has loosened dip a piece of cotton-wool into boiling essence of turpentine and dab each side of the stain. The paper will now appear to be transparent at the stain, and the white opacity may be restored by a touch of warm spirits of wine. This is most suitably applied on a piece of fine linen.

Finger Marks.

In addition to the common application of breadcrumbs or indiarubber, finger marks may be removed by coating the portion with soap-jelly, and, after leaving for a short time, washing off in running water.

Ink (Writing)

Wash the sheet, first in a solution of oxalic acid and then—after allowing to dry—in a solution of chloride of lime. It is interesting to note that writing ink which has faded may be restored by the following combination: soak in a solution of tincture of iodine and then steam over a dish of hot muriatic acid.

Ink (Marking)

These difficult stains can usually be removed by immersion in two solutions: (1) Tincture of iodine, and (2) cyanide of potassium.

Jam Stains

These may be removed with ammonia.

Mud Stains

The paper should be washed in order to clean away the dirt deposit, and then the remaining stain should be treated (1) with a solution of muriatic acid, and (2) a solution of chloride of lime.

Oil Stains

The spreading of the oil should be checked by applying ether in a circle round the stain and gradually working inwards. The grease should then be shifted with a hot iron and blotting paper.

Water Stains (*i.e.*, **Damp, but with a sharp edge**).

Dissolve a little powdered alum in hot water and, when cold, immerse the stained sheet.

It should be noted that any of these washing processes will tend to weaken the paper, and, if desired, the strength may be restored by re-sizing. Dissolve an ounce of isinglass in a quart of water and immerse the sheet which is to be strengthened, while the liquid is at 150° F.

As several of the liquids used in the washing processes are bleachers, it is not advisable to attempt to clean coloured papers. A cream or light buff shade, however, may be restored with cold tea, coffee or permanganate of potash. This is best done by adding to the sizing solution.

Making a Domestic Refrigerator

DEALING WITH ICE AND ELECTRIC EVAPORATIVE TYPES

THERE is little doubt that a refrigerator or cold-storage chamber is an extremely useful and practically essential adjunct to the domestic equipment of the ordinary house. The only way to store certain types of perishable foods such as meat, fish, poultry, milk, etc., is in a refrigerator.

The bacteria causing the deterioration of such foods cannot multiply at temperatures below about 50° F., so that if one can keep these foods below the temperature in question they will retain their freshness practically indefinitely. Apart from this, one can keep salads fresh, drinks cold and in certain types of refrigerator can actually freeze water and make ice-cream.

Three Principal Types.

There are three principal types of refrigerator or cold-storage chambers now in general use, viz., as follows:—

(1) The automatic self-contained type, using a liquefied gas such as carbon monoxide, or ammonia, which is alternately compressed and expanded.

(2) The ice or freezing-salt type, in which regular replenishment of the refrigerant is necessary.

(3) The evaporatively cooled type, where no external source of power or replenishment are necessary.

The first type is necessarily a fairly complicated one, involving the use of a liquefied gas, an intricate circulating system, condenser, expansion valve and necessitating either an electrically driven compressor or electric or gas-heating.

Apart from the fact that the present successful commercial types are the subject of special patents, their construction is considered to be beyond the capabilities of most of our readers; in any case, the construction of such a refrigerator would hardly be a profitable proposition in view of the materials required and the work involved.

It is not proposed, therefore, to describe the construction of this type, but to confine the present article to a descriptive account of the second and third types.

The Ice Refrigerator.

This type of cold-storage chamber has been the most popular one for a very long period. A very simple form of Ice Chest is described on page 1183. It is cheap to construct, and requires only an occasional re-charging with ice or a mixture of ice and freezing salt. In

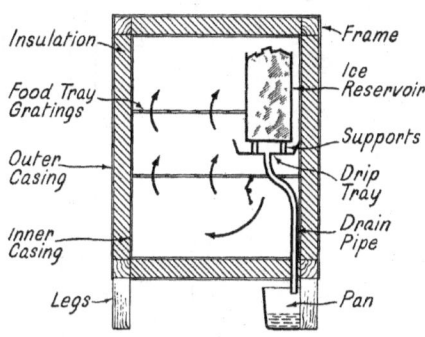

Fig. 1.—Front Sectional View showing General Arrangement of Ice Refrigerator.

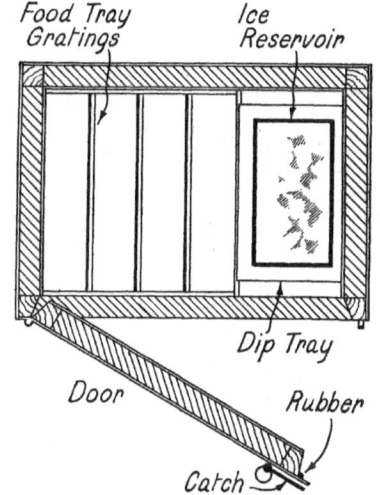

Fig. 2.—Plan Sectional View, showing General Arrangement.

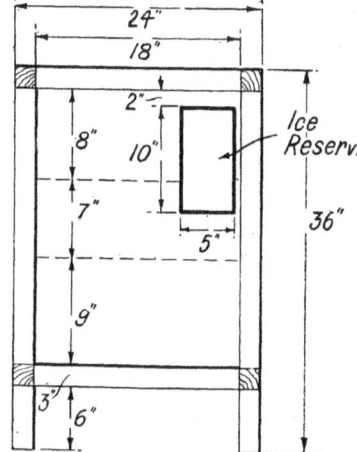

Fig. 3.—Front Elevation, showing Dimensions.

the latter case a much lower temperature can be obtained, comparable with that of the more expensive automatic refrigerator previously mentioned. In practically all towns and villages it is now possible to obtain regular supplies of ice, for a few pence weekly, so that one of the earlier disadvantages of this type, viz., the difficulty of obtaining ice, has practically disappeared. The local butcher or fishmonger will generally supply the small quantities of ice required, if more direct arrangements cannot be made.

The principle of the ice refrigerator is that of providing an insulated food safe, in which an ice container is placed near the top. Instead of having the usual solid shelves, wire or rod frames (similar to those used for the shelves of gas ovens) are provided for placing the food items.

The object of this is to *promote the free circulation of cold air* inside the refrigerator so that the whole of the interior will tend to be at an even temperature. This is an important point to remember, for unless there is a free circulation of the air inside, parts of the chamber will be at a higher temperature than others. *The heat insulation of the chamber* is another important matter, as it is essential to insulate the inside of the refrigerator from the much warmer outside air. This is done by providing a covering all around the chamber, consisting of a material that is a poor conductor of heat.

General Arrangement of Refrigerator.

The general arrangement of a modern design of ice-charged refrigerator is shown in Figs. 1 and 2. Referring to Fig. 1, it will be seen that there is an outer and an inner chamber separated by means of a heat-insulating material. The ice reservoir is arranged near the top of the right-hand part of the inner chamber. It consists of a metal box of rectangular section, having a perforated metal base. This box stands on convenient supports, which take the form of two strips of wood, or metal. The supports are attached to a sheet metal tray, having a central hole, at which is attached a length of metal tubing leading down and through the base of the cabinet.

The object of this arrangement is to allow the water which drips from the ice reservoir to be caught in the metal tray below and then led through the pipe to a bowl or pan placed underneath the cabinet. The idea of the supports for the ice reservoir is to enable the latter to be slid out, for replenishment, without having to lift

1543

MAKING A DOMESTIC REFRIGERATOR

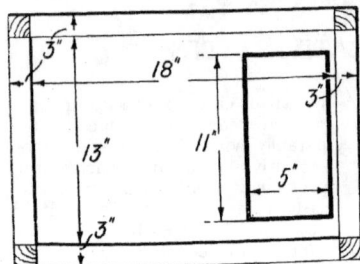

Fig. 4.—Plan View, showing Dimensions.

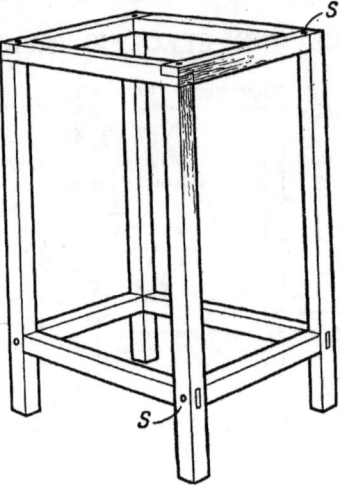

Fig. 5.—The Framework of Refrigerator.

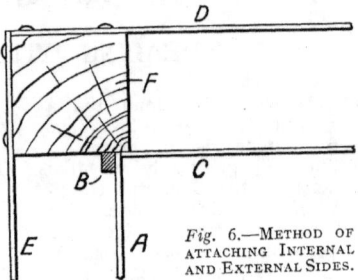

Fig. 6.—Method of Attaching Internal and External Sides.

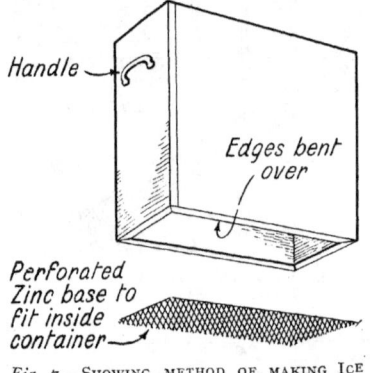

Fig. 7.—Showing Method of Making Ice Reservoir.

The perforated zinc base fits inside against the bent over edges shown above. It is secured by soldering.

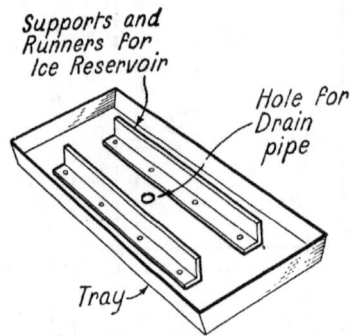

Fig. 8.—The Drip Tray and Supports for Ice Reservoir.

it up and over the edges of the drip tray. As will be noticed from Figs. 1 and 2, the cabinet is provided with a door on the front side—as in the case of the commercial automatic type refrigerator—as this is considered a much more convenient arrangement than that of the old-fashioned ice chest type, with its lid on top. A further advantage of the present over the latter type is that the top, being fixed, can be used as a table or for any similar domestic purpose.

The cabinet is provided with an insulated door of wedge shape and with a rubber pipe edge, for the purpose of ensuring that no air can leak through the joint.

Finally, the cabinet is provided with four corner supports, or legs, to raise its base above the floor, for the purpose of allowing room for the catch pan that collects the drip water, and for general convenience in using the refrigerator.

Construction and Dimensions.

The construction of this type of refrigerator is quite a straightforward matter, and it can be made in any convenient size to the particular requirements of the person making it. The only really important points to observe are the correct proportions of the ice reservoir (to suit the size of the cabinet) and the proper heat insulation of the cabinet.

Figs. 3 and 4 show the leading dimensions of an ice refrigerator suitable for the average domestic requirements. It has an internal capacity, including the space taken up by the ice reservoir, of about 3¼ cubic feet. The ice-reservoir capacity is about one-third of a cubic foot. It can therefore be reckoned, in making any other size of refrigerator, that one should allow 1 cubic foot of ice reservoir to each 9 to 10 cubic feet of cabinet. The internal dimensions of the cabinet part are 2 feet high, 18 inches wide and 13 inches deep. Provision is made for two wire-frame shelves at the heights shown by the dotted lines. The top of the ice reservoir should be about 2 inches below that of the cabinet. It will be observed that there is an air space all around the sides of the ice reservoir.

The Framework.

Fig. 5 illustrates a convenient method of making the framework. The woodworker will need no specific instructions on the best method of making such a simple structure, but for the benefit of those who are not so well versed in these matters it is suggested that the top frame be made first, using half-lapped joints. The four verticals are cut to length (3 feet) and are joined, 6 inches from their lower ends by the four connecting members, either by mortise and tenon joints, screws or brackets. The two opposite horizontal members can be jointed and the other two screwed through the mortise and tenon joints as shown.

The top frame is shown screwed down to the tops of the four verticals by means of the screws.

The timber used for the framework should be 2½ to 3 inches square-section deal. This enables a 2½ to 3 inches insulating thickness to be obtained. Whilst this width certainly gives the best as insulation for the inside of the cabinet, in cases where final weight is an important consideration, 2-inch square-section timber can be used with satisfaction.

The Sides.

The most convenient material for the exterior is ¼ inch thick 3-ply (birch or maple) nailed or screwed to the framework. Similar material can be used for the interior, and in this case a convenient method of attaching it so as to give a neat interior appearance is indicated in Fig. 6. There the vertical is shown at F and the two external sides at E and D. A strip of wood B is nailed to the vertical, and the internal side A is nailed to this strip. The other side C is nailed to the vertical member F. When fixing the side A, care should be taken not to reduce the insulation space more than can be avoided.

A Zinc Lining.

Those who are familiar with sheet metal work will not find it difficult to make a zinc lining in place of three-ply. The edges should be turned over where the adjacent sides meet, in order to avoid leaving air spaces.

Alternatively, the complete inside lining can be made in the form of a box, which can be slid into the framework and there secured by a few screws. The overlapping seams in this case can be soft-soldered so as to make airtight joints.

The Insulation.

The space between the internal and external sides must be fitted with a

1544

good heat-insulating material. Cork slab is generally used in commercial refrigerators. This material can be obtained in sheets of different thicknesses. For the present purpose one can use two 1-inch thick slabs screwed, respectively, to the internal and external sides; an air space is left between the slabs in this case. When fixing the sides due allowance must be made for inserting the insulation before finally screwing or nailing down these sides.

As an alternative to cork slab any of the following materials may be used, viz.: granulated cork, sawdust, slag-wool, kapok or magnesite. The only drawback of such loose materials is the difficulty of inserting them between the walls of the chamber.

The Ice Reservoir and Drip Tray.

The ice box can be made by bending a sheet of zinc of 20 to 24 gauge, as shown in Fig. 7, leaving turned-over portions at the base. A rectangular piece of perforated zinc, measuring 5 × 11 inches, is then dropped down inside the "open-ended" box and secured by soldering to the base rim portion.

The drip tray can be made by bending up a sheet of zinc and soldering the edges. It should measure 12 × 6 × 1 inches. A piece of ⅜-inch copper pipe is used to drain away the water.

Fittings.

The hinges and toggle-action handle for holding the door tightly when closed can be purchased from Messrs. F. Romany Ltd., 52 High Street, Camden Town, London, N.W.1. This firm will also supply the cork slab and plywood.

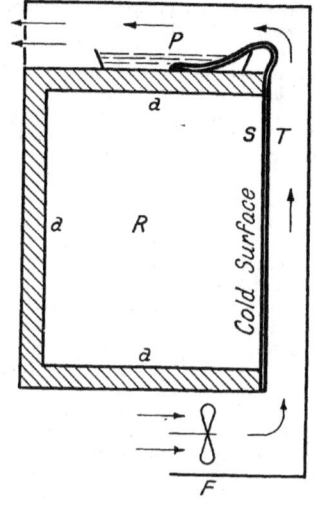

Fig. 9.—Illustrating principle of Evaporation-type Refrigerator.

An Important Reminder.

It is important to remember that before fixing the plywood, or zinc, to the framework, the contact surfaces should be brushed over with bitumastic paint. The surfaces can then be screwed or nailed together. Further, the nails or screws used for the interior should be of copper or brass—*not* steel.

Finish.

The whole of the interior and exterior, *with the exception of all zinc surfaces*, should be given a priming coat of matt white cellulose or enamel and then finished off with two coats of a good hard-drying white enamel or cellulose.

Making an Electric Evaporative Refrigerator.

The third type of cold-storage chamber, previously mentioned, depends upon the well-known principle that a liquid in evaporating absorbs heat from the medium with which it is in contact. This fact can readily be illustrated by pouring a little ether, petrol, or even water, on the back of one's hand, when the cold produced by the evaporation will at once be evident.

This principle is made use of in the construction of the refrigerator in question by utilising the cold produced by the evaporation of water. In order to obtain the greatest cooling effect, it is necessary to employ *as large a cooling surface as possible*, so that in the design of this type of refrigerator—known as the evaporative cooling one—the maximum evaporation area should be employed. Another important item is to use *a good conducting material for the side* of the chamber that is to be evaporatively cooled. One of the best materials for this purpose is sheet zinc, as, unlike aluminium (which is a much better heat conductor), it does not corrode when in contact with water and air. The thinner the gauge of zinc that can be used, the better will be the transmission of the "cold" through it.

Referring to Fig. 9, this illustrates the application of the previously mentioned principle to a domestic refrigerator. In this case, in order to maintain a constant supply of water to the evaporating surface T, a reservoir P is arranged on top of the chamber R that is to be cooled. Leading from this reservoir there is a piece of moisture-absorbent material such as linen, cotton fabric or towelling, one end of which dips into the water contained in P, whilst the rest hangs down against the thin metal back S of the chamber R. The other sides (including the door) of the chamber R are heat-insulated in order to preserve the cold atmosphere produced by the evaporative cooling of the side S. The absorbent material T becomes soaked with water and the latter then evaporates, thus producing a marked lowering of temperature.

Now, it is a well-known fact that the quicker one can make a wetted surface evaporate, the lower will be the cooling effect produced. It is for this reason that we have employed an electric-motor-driven fan, similar to that used for ventilating rooms in the hot weather. This fan F provides a current of air which carries away the water

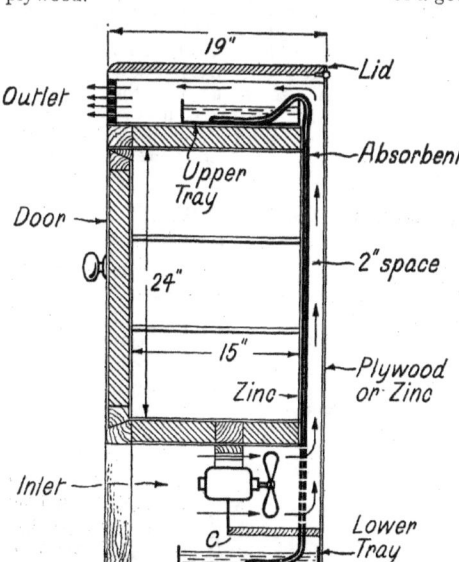

Fig. 10.—Side Sectional View of Electric Evaporative Refrigerator.

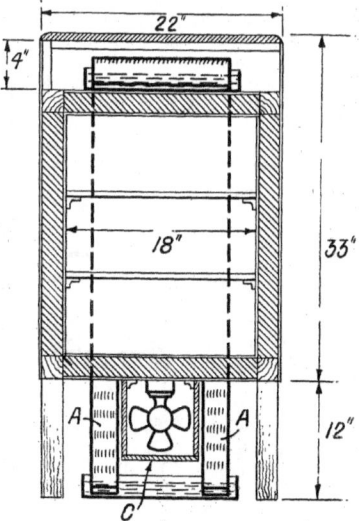

Fig. 11.—Front Sectional View of Electric Evaporative Refrigerator.

MAKING A DOMESTIC REFRIGERATOR

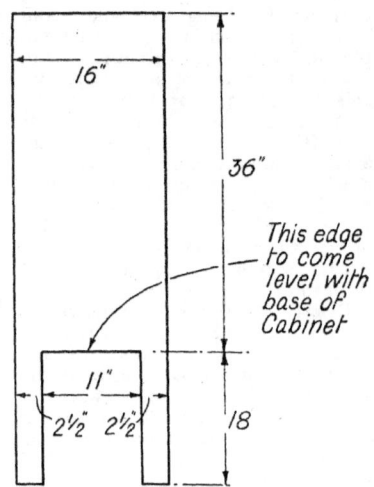

Fig. 12.—Showing Dimensions of Absorbent Material.

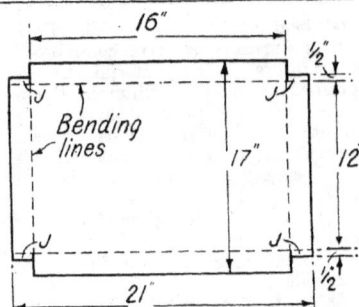

Fig. 13.—Illustrating Method of Making the Water Trays.

The zinc sheets are cut to the dimensions shown, bent along the dotted lines, and the parts marked J lapped and soldered.

vapour and thus produces an increased cooling effect.

Direction of Air Flow.

There are two alternative directions for the air flow over the absorbent material, viz., the one shown in Fig. 9 and that in which the direction is reversed. Each has its advantages. Thus, the one given in Fig. 9 gives a greater cooling effect near the base of the chamber and ejects the air well above ground level. The other draws air in well above ground level, but causes a draught at ground level.

Description of Typical Refrigerator.

A design, with leading dimensions, is given in Figs. 10 and 11. Fig. 10 shows a section taken right through the centre of the refrigerator as seen from the side, whilst Fig. 11 gives a central section as seen from the front.

The general arrangement resembles that of the ice-charged refrigerator illustrated in Figs. 1 to 4. It is of approximately the same dimensions and has the same type of door, general framework and insulation.

In this case, however, as the cooling effect obtained by the evaporative principle is not so much, it is only necessary to have a 2 inch insulation space all round, so that 2 × 2-inch deal can be used for the framing.

The back of the interior cold chamber is made from a flat sheet of zinc of about 22 to 24 gauge, nailed on to the frame with copper nails. The back of the cabinet is arranged 2 inches beyond, thus allowing a 2-inch air space for the absorbent material and also for the air current. Plywood or sheet zinc can be used for this panel, the former being preferable if it is of the waterproof type.

A lid, made of 1-inch tongued and grooved timber, is provided in order to give access to the upper water reservoir. The lower reservoir is placed on the ground underneath the refrigerator, as shown in Fig. 10.

The Electric Fan.

The electric fan can very conveniently be an ordinary 10-inch model as used for domestic ventilation purposes. It should be mounted on a block of wood affixed to the base of the cabinet. In order to guide the air stream, the fan should be surrounded with a round or square channel (marked C in Figs. 10 and 11). This should have about ¼-inch clearance from the tips of the fan blades. This channel fits into the base of the vertical air column members, care being taken that no air can escape except up through the 2-inch space. When mounting the fan make sure that it is placed the correct way round, viz., to give a draught in the desired direction.

On the top of the cabinet a number of holes are provided (Fig. 10) for the air-stream outlet; alternatively, a piece of perforated zinc can be fitted for this purpose.

Absorbent Materials.

In regard to the absorbent material, the constructor of this type of cold chamber has a fairly wide choice. Thus, he can use ordinary smooth-surface towelling, which is sold by the yard in various widths. The smooth variety has an advantage over the rougher types, such as Turkey towelling, in giving better contact with the zinc. Linen or cotton fabric can also be used. Any material that absorbs water readily can be employed for this purpose.

There is one important point regarding the absorbent material, viz., that only the outside 2½-inch widths dip into the lower tank; this is to allow clearance for the fan chamber in the centre.

Fig. 12 shows the dimensions of the absorbent material, due allowance having been made for sufficient material to rest in both tanks.

Suggested dimensions of the latter are 16 × 12 × (2 to 3 inches). These tanks can readily be made out of sheet zinc by cutting out the shape shown in Fig. 13, bending them along the dotted lines and then soldering the lapped joints, marked J in the diagram.

There is one final injunction regarding the use of this cold-storage chamber, viz., that it is necessary to replenish the upper tank every three or four days, and the lower one about once a week.

WHEN DECORATING A BORDER

A useful gadget to assist home decorators, particularly when painting or treating in some way the border of a room above the picture rail is shown in the accompanying sketch, in which all constructional details are given.

This device prevents the splashes of paint getting on to the wall below the picture rail.

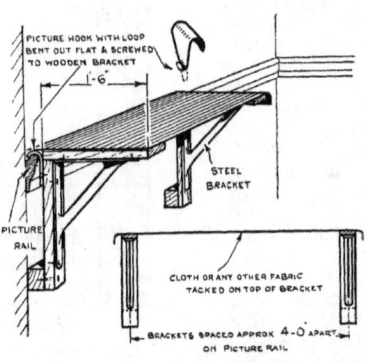

Fig. 1.—A Handy Device.

TO MAKE A HOLE IN SPRING STEEL

A simple but effective method of making a hole in spring steel which *is too hard to drill* is to place the steel on a piece of lead or copper and make an impression with a centre punch (Fig. 1). Then grind away the protruding metal so as to leave a hole right through the metal. Block springs may be perforated in this manner.

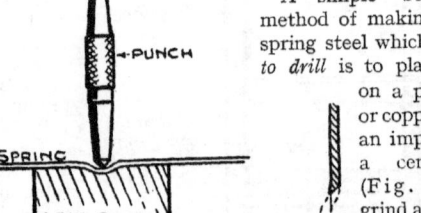

Fig. 1.—Showing how a Hole can be Made in Spring Steel.

How to Make a Sculling Exerciser

The inexpensive sculling exerciser shown in Fig. 1 is a splendid thing for the rowing enthusiast, but is equally valuable as a home trainer or exerciser for every member of the family. With its aid the general health and poise can vastly be improved if only a few minutes' exercise is taken on it every day.

The essentials of the machine are a fixed frame, a sliding seat and foot-rest, outriggers and dummy oars, the whole suitably connected by springs that the motions of rowing can be simulated and the muscles agreeably developed by the exertion necessary to expand the springs. The tension of the springs can readily be adjusted to meet the needs of various members of the family and for the same reason the foot-rest is adjustable.

Materials required.

Frame.—Two pieces 4 feet 3 inches long, 4 inches wide × 1 inch thick.

Cross-bars.—Three pieces 3 × 1 × 14 inches long.

Bottom.—Three pieces 6 × ½ × 14 inches long.

Oars.—Two pieces 1½ inches square, 16 inches long.

Foot-rest.—One piece deal 12 × 6 × 1 inch thick.

Fillets.—One piece deal 1 inch square, 36 inches long.

Outriggers.—Two pieces iron 36 inches long, 1 inch wide, ¼ inch thick.

Oar Irons.—Two pieces iron 15 inches long, 1 inch wide, ¼ inch thick.

Wheels.—Four brass, or iron, 2 inches diameter, ⅜ inch wide, with axles and washers.

Bearing Plates.—Two pieces brass ¾ inch wide, ⅛ inch thick, 24 inches long.

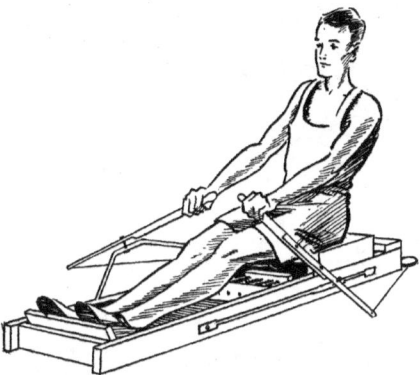

Fig. 1.—Machine in use.
This home-made exerciser is a great aid to the development of physical fitness.

Springs.—Four extension springs 10 inches long, gymnasium type.

Spring Bar.—Oak, 1 piece 8 × 2 × 1 inch.

Pulleys.—Three guide pulleys, 2 inches diameter, with screw shanks.

Seat.—

1 piece deal 14 inches long, 11 inches wide, 1 inch thick.

2 pieces deal 11 inches long, 3 inches wide, 1 inch thick.

2 pieces deal 5 inches long, 2 inches wide, ½ inch thick.

2 pieces deal 11 inches long, 2 inches wide, ½ inch thick.

Cord.—One piece strong sashline about 4 yards long.

Eyebolts.—Four, ¼ inch diameter, 3 to 4 inches long, with nuts.

The wood for the frame and other parts is preferably a hard wood such as oak or ash, but good, sound, clean sitka pine or white deal can be used; in all cases it should be bought ready "prepared," that is, planed up smooth on all sides.

The total cost of all the above-mentioned parts should not amount to more than a few shillings, as none of the items is expensive.

What to do First.

The frame is the first part to have attention. It is shown complete in Fig. 2, and consists of two side members, three cross-bars and the floor or bottom boards.

The side members have to be grooved across the grain, as shown in Fig. 3—which can be done in the usual way by making two cross-cuts with a fine tenon saw and then chiselling away the unwanted wood between the saw-cuts. A recess ½ inch deep and 18 inches long is cut from the underside of each side member to take the bottom boards. The front and middle cross-bars should be cut to such a length—approximately 13 inches—that when fitted snugly into the cross grooves, the outside width of the frames measures exactly 14 inches. These two cross-bars and the back-bar are then glued and screwed into place and the bottom boards similarly fixed.

A piece of felt or linoleum should be glued to the outside of the bottom boards and a shallow rubber stud fitted near the front ends of the side members.

Bearing Strips.

The next step is to screw the two brass bearer strips to the top edges of the side members starting from the front edge of the back cross-bar.

These strips are provided to take the wear of the wheels on which the sliding seat is mounted, and although not absolutely essential, are very desirable additions that add greatly to the

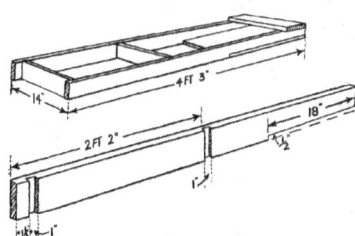

Figs. 2 and 3.—Arrangement and Dimensions of Frame, and Side Member prepared.

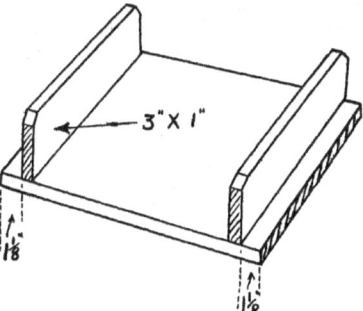

Fig. 5.—Underside View of Seat Board and Bearing Blocks.

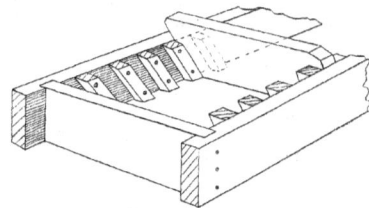

Fig. 7.—Arrangement of Footboard.

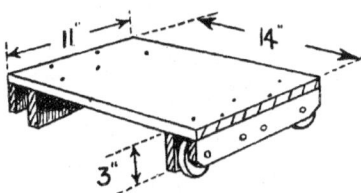

Fig. 4.—The Sliding Seat

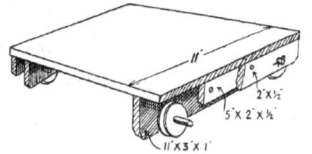

Fig. 6.—Seat Wheels and Guards.

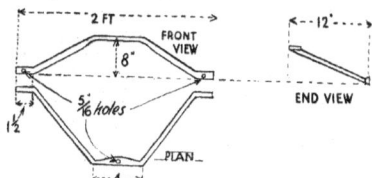

Fig. 8.—Shape and Dimensions of Outrigger.

HOW TO MAKE A SCULLING EXERCISER

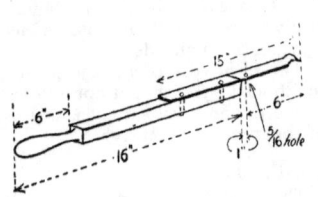

Fig. 9.—Oar Handle and Iron Work.
The wooden handle is bolted to the strip of iron.

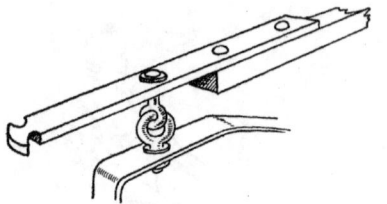

Fig. 10.—Oar Pivots.
Eyes are fitted to each part to form a universal joint.

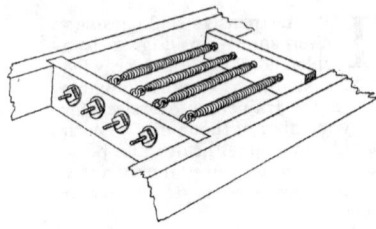

Fig. 11.—Tension Springs.
The four springs are anchored to the middle cross-bar and connected to the movable spring bar by screw eyes.

durability of the machine. The strips are simply screwed centrally in the frame members.

The Sliding Seat.

The sliding seat is shown complete in Fig. 4, and consists of the seat board, the inner and outer bearing strips and two spacer pieces. The two inner bearing blocks, measuring 11 inches long, 3 inches deep and 1 inch thick, should be glued and screwed to the underside of the seat, leaving a space of 1⅛ inch from each end, as shown in Fig. 5; then the spacer blocks of 5 × 2 × ½ inch deal are glued to the face of each inner bearer, the outer bearing pieces, measuring 11 × 2 × ½ inch, are then glued to the face of the spacer blocks and glued and screwed to the seat board.

Holes are then drilled through the bearing blocks to take the wheel axles—as in Fig. 6—the wheels are put in place and the axles, after being oiled, are slipped through the holes and secured with nuts and washers or with washers and split pins.

The top of the seat can be padded with cotton wool and covered with leather or an odd piece of tapestry, or the wood can be left plain, the corner edges rounded off and narrow strip of wood fastened to the front and back edges.

When completed, the seat should roll easily up and down on the bearer strips.

Adjustable Footboard.

The footboard is a plain piece of board slightly under 12 inches long and rounded on the top edge; it is arranged to slide into any one of a series of grooves formed by gluing and screwing strips of 1-inch square fillet to the inner faces of the side members—at the front end—as shown in Fig. 7. Each fillet is spaced 1 inch apart, thus leaving the requisite grooves for the footboard to slide into.

These fillets must be fixed very securely, as they have to withstand a considerable pressure.

The Outriggers.

These should be made of strip iron bent to the shape shown in Fig. 8, and then bolted to the sides of the main frame. Note that the centre part of the outrigger stands about 4½ to 5 inches above the level of the top of the frame. The centre of the outrigger comes exactly 2 feet 2 inches from the front end of the frame.

The iron can easily be bent to shape while cold if a strong vice is available—alternatively, any ironmonger would bend them for a few pence and also drill the three holes in each.

The two dummy oars should next be made, as shown in Fig. 9. The square wood should be rounded off to form a handle and be well linseed-oiled. The iron bars should be fastened on with ¼-inch "stove screws."

The next step is to mount the oars on the outriggers, which can be done by riveting a large metal screw eye to each outrigger, as in Fig. 10, noting that the screw eye is free to turn in the outrigger, but is securely held therein by the two washers and the riveted end of its shank.

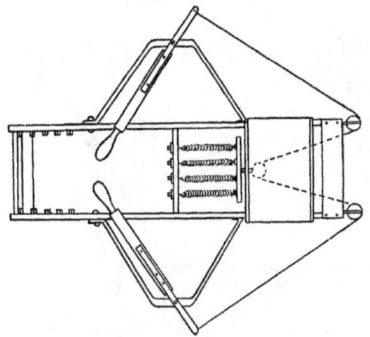

Fig. 12.—Plan of Machine showing Arrangement of Tension Cords.

A similar eye is fitted in like manner to the oar, the eye being opened enough to allow it to slip over the one on the outrigger and then closed up again.

Tension Springs.

The arrangement of the four tension springs is clearly shown in Fig. 11. The springs are spaced about 2 inches apart and are attached to the adjustable eyebolts, which pass through holes in the middle cross-bar. The opposite ends of the four springs are fixed to screw eyes in the spring bar, which rests freely on the bottom boards.

A pulley wheel with screw shank is screwed into the middle of the spring bar; another similar pulley is fixed to the back end of each side member, as shown in Fig. 12, and the oars then connected to the spring bar by the sashline.

One end of the line is fastened securely around the notch in the outer end of the oar iron, then the line is passed over the side pulley, then around the pulley on the spring bar, out and over the second side pulley and then to the other oar iron, to which it is securely fixed.

The length of the cord should be so adjusted that when both oars are fully forward the cord is just taut.

The woodwork should be painted or varnished and the metal blacked, after which the machine is ready for use. No special instructions are needed for working the exerciser. The "rower" simply sits on the seat, presses his feet firmly on the footboard, takes up the oars, slides the seat forwards and pulls on them. This action extends the springs, and the rower is thereby caused to put out some energy to pull the oars home, and in so doing, to complete the stroke, straightens his legs and propels the seat and himself backwards, an exercise that develops the arms, legs and the muscles of the abdomen and back.

Practical Notes on Life Assurance

Generally speaking, Life Assurance may be divided into two categories. When the first assurance companies were formed it was only possible to obtain a policy which provided a capital payment on the death of the policy holder, and it was necessary to keep up payments of the annual premium until death occurred, the result being that in many cases the total premiums paid were in excess of the benefit ultimately derived. These early policies were for a flat sum only and did not participate in any of the companies' profits, and were thus merely a means of protecting one's dependants in the event of death.

Eventually, when the offices became more widely known and had collected considerable data from some years of business experience, a form of policy was offered which gave the right to share in the surplus or profit made, and naturally the annual premium required for this contract was more than for a non-sharing policy, although it should be noted that premiums were still payable throughout the life of the insured person. These two forms of contract are still in existence to-day and are largely taken up, chiefly on account of their cheapness as compared with later types and schemes.

Whole of Life Policies.

The name given to the above-mentioned policies was "Whole of Life Policies either With or Without Profits," as the case may be, and we propose first to show the advantages and uses of this type of policy.

Firstly, we must examine the reason for wishing to effect a policy of this description, and it is usually found that people leave the question of insurance until they have reached an age when they find it too expensive, as they rarely consider the matter until they either become engaged or married or even later, when a family arrives. They then find that they require a large cover according to their circumstances, and as a Whole of Life Policy offers the greatest cover for the smallest annual outlay they effect a policy of this class more from necessity than desire.

Actually they have done a very wise thing, for, should their financial position improve as time goes on, they can always change their policy into an Endowment, payable on attaining a certain age, by paying the difference in premium as and from the date of such substitution, and they will have enjoyed the larger insurance at a small premium for the hard years.

As stated, a Whole of Life Policy may be effected either without the right to share in any surplus or with the added benefit of obtaining this right in return for a small additional premium, and it will be found that a With Profit Policy proves to be the better proposition provided that the insured lives a reasonable number of years, for the longer he lives the greater the amount added to the face value of his policy in the form of bonus, although it should be remembered that he can obtain a larger original cover under the Non Profit scheme, than under the With Profit scheme, and it must therefore take a number of years' bonuses to bring the latter cover up to the same amount.

Whole of Life Policy without Bonus.

Table I., on p. 1550, shows the cost of a Whole of Life Policy for £100 without the right to share in bonuses, and also the result should death occur at age sixty. The figures given are definitely guaranteed, and although the surrender values appear to be rather on the low side, it must be remembered that the annual premium payable is also small, and obviously the company must try and re-coup themselves for the risk that they carry and for the expenses incurred in obtaining the business, commission payable on the introduction, and the cost of the policy, stamp duty, etc.

Whole of Life Policy with Bonus.

The next table (Table II.) shows the cost and result of a similar policy to that quoted above, with the difference that in this case bonuses are added to the policy from time to time, and it will be noticed that should death occur at age sixty, as in the above figures, a very much larger return is obtained. It must be remembered that the bonuses shown are not in any way guaranteed, and must always depend on the profits earned by the company, and, consequently, may be larger or smaller, according to general conditions over the period taken. Actually the bonus figures shown have been calculated on the actual amounts paid by the company concerned, and are not estimated on any fictitious figures or abnormal bonus declaration.

The surrender values attaching to this policy are inclusive of any bonus additions that may have been made at the time of surrender and are not therefore guaranteed, for, as pointed out above, the bonuses are liable to fluctuation.

Policy Conditions.

Policy conditions of to-day are free from the irksome restrictions which were in force some years ago, and almost all policies now issued are free of travel conditions from the very outset, provided of course that the insured person is not proceeding to some unhealthy climate or engaging in some dangerous occupation at the time of effecting the insurance. In the latter instances an extra premium is usually required for the period of such residence or occupation.

Non-Forfeiture.

A policy cannot now lapse through non-payment of the premium provided that its surrender value is sufficient to enable the company to advance the amount due, and thus a policy is kept in force so long as the surrender value will meet the outstanding premiums. Naturally, the policy must lapse when the surrender value is no longer large enough, but it is possible to revive it in its original form on payment of the arrears of premium together with interest at a rate of approximately 5 per cent. per annum. However, the point I wish to make is that a policy will not lapse through oversight to meet the premium when due.

Surrender Values.

All policies now contain a clause stating that the policy has a surrender value after the first two or three years, and although the amount of such surrender must of necessity vary with the amount of the premium, the term of the policy and the type of contract, it is usually found that the company guarantees to return not less than 40 per cent. of the premiums paid, together with the surrender value of any bonuses in the case of a With Profit Policy. Some companies actually include a schedule of guaranteed values in their document, so that it is possible to see the exact worth of the policy at any given time.

Paid-up Policies.

To explain a Paid-up Policy it will be best to assume that a policy holder finds that he cannot conveniently continue the payments required, although he is not in need of actual cash, and therefore does not want to surrender his policy and so forfeit his cover. Upon application to the company he can obtain a Fully Paid-up Policy for a reduced amount and free from any further payments, and the reduced amount would be payable by the company either on the death of the person or upon his attaining a specified age should the policy be an endowment. Here, again, bonuses would be taken into consideration in the case of a With Profit Policy, and some companies' policies would still continue to participate in the profits earned, but on the basis of the reduced amount.

Loans.

A company is always willing to advance money on the security of its policies nearly to the extent of the surrender value. The rate of interest charged is moderate, approximately 5 per cent. per annum, and the cost of effecting the loan is usually limited to the amount of the stamp duty on the

TABLE I.—Whole Life Assurance of £100 Payable at Death, No Bonus Additions

Age next Birthday	25	30	35	40	45
	£ s. d.	£ s. d.	£ s. d.	£ s. d.	£ s. d.
Annual Premium	1 9 8	1 13 9	1 19 1	2 6 1	2 15 1
Income Tax Rebate	0 3 0	0 3 9	0 4 5	0 5 1	0 6 2
Net Annual Cost	1 6 8	1 10 0	1 14 8	2 1 0	2 8 11
Value of the Policy	100 0 0	100 0 0	100 0 0	100 0 0	100 0 0
Outlay at 60	46 13 4	45 0 0	43 6 8	41 0 0	36 13 9
Difference	53 6 8	55 0 0	56 13 4	59 0 0	63 6 3

Guaranteed Surrender Values for Above Policies

Age at Entry	25	30	35	40	45
	£ s. d.	£ s. d.	£ s. d.	£ s. d.	£ s. d.
Years in force— 5	1 18 0	2 14 0	3 14 0	5 2 0	6 12 0
,, ,, 10	6 10 0	8 2 0	10 8 0	13 4 0	16 4 0
,, ,, 15	11 4 0	14 12 0	18 0 0	22 2 0	26 12 0
,, ,, 20	17 18 0	21 16 0	26 10 0	31 4 0	37 2 0
,, ,, 25	24 16 0	29 16 0	35 10 0	41 10 0	47 14 0

TABLE II.—A Whole Life Assurance of £100, Payable at Death, with Bonus Additions.

Age next Birthday	25	30	35	40	45
	£ s. d.	£ s. d.	£ s. d.	£ s. d.	£ s. d.
Annual Premium	2 4 7	2 10 1	2 17 0	3 5 9	3 16 8
Income Tax Abatement	0 5 0	0 5 7	0 6 4	0 7 4	0 8 7
Net Annual Cost	1 19 7	2 4 6	2 10 8	2 18 5	3 8 1

Estimated Value Assuming Death to occur at Age 60

	25	30	35	40	45
Sum Assured	100 0 0	100 0 0	100 0 0	100 0 0	100 0 0
Bonuses	103 0 0	83 0 0	66 0 0	50 0 0	35 0 0
Total	203 0 0	183 0 0	166 0 0	150 0 0	135 0 0
Less Net Cost	69 0 0	67 0 0	64 0 0	59 0 0	51 0 0
Difference	134 0 0	116 0 0	102 0 0	91 0 0	84 0 0

Surrender Values

Age Next Birthday at Outset.

Number of Annual Premiums Paid	25	30	35	40	45
	£ s. d.	£ s. d.	£ s. d.	£ s. d.	£ s. d.
5	7 0 0	8 0 0	9 0 0	10 0 0	12 0 0
10	16 0 0	18 0 0	21 0 0	24 0 0	28 0 0
15	27 0 0	31 0 0	36 0 0	42 0 0	48 0 0
20	41 0 0	47 0 0	54 0 0	62 0 0	70 0 0
25	57 0 0	66 0 0	76 0 0	85 0 0	96 0 0

mortgage. Alternatively, a Bank is also willing to advance money against the security of a Life Policy, so that it forms a very good means of providing collateral security against the time when money is urgently required.

Medical Examination.

Most offices issue their policies subject to a satisfactory medical examination by their own appointed doctor, and no expense is incurred by the person effecting the policy, as the fee is paid by the company. In the case of unfit lives, the office either charges an extra premium over and above their normal rate of premium, or, in very bad cases, declines the business outright. To-day it is possible to effect certain classes of policies without a medical examination, provided that the amount required is not too large and subject to a satisfactory proposal form which does not disclose any serious illness or bad family history.

Participation in Profits.

A person effecting a With Profit Policy really becomes a shareholder in the insurance company, and as such is entitled to participate in any or part of the profits earned, and in effecting a policy of this type it is very necessary to examine such details as the expense ratio, the reserve funds and the past records of the company in question.

Payment of a good bonus over a period of years can only be maintained provided there is a careful selection of fit persons in the first place, a small expense ratio in obtaining and running the business and a careful investment of the funds available. Different companies have varying ways of paying their profits, for in some instances the distribution is made every year, in others every three or five years. Probably the company who makes an annual distribution is the most satisfactory to the public.

Again, some offices pay a bonus calculated on the value of the policy, whilst others calculate theirs on the amount of the premium payable; the higher the premium, the higher the bonus.

As already pointed out, some offices pay their bonus at a flat rate on the face value of the policy, and it is advisable to find out whether they are calculated on a simple or compound interest basis. In the case of a compound bonus, the face value of the policy is increased by the amount of the bonus and any future bonuses are added on the basis of the increase. Over a period of years this system makes a very considerable difference to the amount eventually received either at death or on the maturity of the policy. In the illustrations which follow later, we have taken the figures of a company who pay their bonuses on the compound system calculated on the face value of the policy, and the record over a period of thirty years is beyond reproach.

Income Tax Rebate.

To encourage thrift by means of Life Assurance the Government allows a rebate of Income Tax at one-half the standard rate at present in force, and thus it is possible to obtain a reduction of 2s. 3d. in the pound on all premiums paid, provided that the total amount expended in premiums does not exceed one-sixth of a person's total income, and provided also that the rate of premium charged by the company is not over 7 per cent. of the sum insured by the policy. Naturally this rebate fluctuates with the rate of Income Tax levied for any one year, and in the tables which follow it has been assumed that the present rate of

TABLE III.—Endowment Assurance of £100 without Profits Payable at Age 60 or at Previous Death.

Age next Birthday	25	30	35	40	45
	£ s. d.	£ s. d.	£ s. d.	£ s. d.	£ s. d.
Annual Premium	2 1 5	2 10 8	3 3 8	4 3 7	5 17 9
Income Tax Rebate	0 4 8	0 5 8	0 7 2	0 9 4	0 12 3
Net Annual Cost	1 16 9	2 5 0	2 16 6	3 14 3	5 5 6
Value of Policy at Age 60	100 0 0	100 0 0	100 0 0	100 0 0	100 0 0
Less Total Net Cost at 60	64 6 3	67 10 0	70 12 6	74 5 0	79 2 6
Difference	35 13 9	32 10 0	29 7 6	25 15 0	20 17 6

Guaranteed Surrender Values for the Above Policies

Age at Entry	25	30	35	40	45
	£ s. d.	£ s. d.	£ s. d.	£ s. d.	£ s. d.
Years in force— 5	4 14 0	6 14 0	9 14 0	14 12 0	22 18 0
,, ,, 10	12 16 0	17 8 0	24 8 0	35 8 0	54 18 0
,, ,, 15	22 16 0	30 16 0	42 14 0	62 2 0	Matures.
,, ,, 20	35 6 0	47 12 0	66 6 0	Matures.	
,, ,, 25	51 0 0	69 2 0	Matures.		

TABLE IV.—Endowment Assurance of £100, Payable at Age 60 or at Previous Death, with Bonus Additions.

Age next Birthday	25	30	35	40	45
	£ s. d.	£ s. d.	£ s. d.	£ s. d.	£ s. d.
Annual Premium	2 18 3	3 9 0	4 4 3	5 6 3	7 3 9
Income Tax Abatement	0 6 6	0 7 9	0 9 5	0 11 11	0 15 9
Net Annual Cost	2 11 9	3 1 3	3 14 10	4 14 4	6 8 0

Estimated Value at Age 60

	25	30	35	40	45
Sum Assured	100 0 0	100 0 0	100 0 0	100 0 0	100 0 0
Bonuses	103 0 0	83 0 0	66 0 0	50 0 0	35 0 0
Total	203 0 0	183 0 0	166 0 0	150 0 0	135 0 0
Less Net Total Cost	91 0 0	92 0 0	94 0 0	95 0 0	96 0 0
Difference	112 0 0	91 0 0	72 0 0	55 0 0	39 0 0

Surrender Values

Age Next Birthday at Outset.

Number of Annual Premiums Paid	25	30	35	40	45
	£ s. d.	£ s. d.	£ s. d.	£ s. d.	£ s. d.
5	9 0 0	12 0 0	15 0 0	21 0 0	30 0 0
10	22 0 0	28 0 0	37 0 0	50 0 0	73 0 0
15	39 0 0	50 0 0	66 0 0	91 0 0	
20	63 0 0	81 0 0	107 0 0		
25	95 0 0	123 0 0			

4s. 6d. in the pound remains in force during the term of the various policies shown. Obviously this rebate can only be claimed by anyone whose earnings are sufficiently large to bring them within the Income Tax paying scale.

ENDOWMENT ASSURANCE

Endowment Policies, which provide for the payment of a certain sum on the attainment of a specified age or at previous death, were a much later development, and rank as much as an investment as for Life Assurance Cover against death. Here again it is possible to effect a policy of this description either with or without the right to share in the bonus distributions of the company.

Policy Conditions.

Policy Conditions are in every way similar to those governing Whole of Life Policies, although Surrender Values, Loan Values and Paid-up Values are considerably higher than those allowed on Whole of Life Policies, by reason of the fact that a larger annual premium is payable and that the policy has a definite maturing date.

Uses of Endowment Policies.

Endowment Policies provide a very good way of saving money for retirement, or, alternatively, they can be taken out for a period of years, say, fifteen, to accumulate a fund for the purpose of paying educational expenses for the children.

Yield.

I have shown in a previous article that it is possible to invest money through the Post Office to obtain interest at a rate of approximately 3 to 3½ per cent. A With Profit Endowment Policy, always assuming the continuation of good bonus payments, will show a yield of between 4 and 4½ per cent. free of tax in addition to the protection against death from the outset of the policy, so that readers will realise why Endowment Policies are so favourably considered to-day, even by people in very good positions.

Income Tax Rebate.

The same rules apply to the annual premiums payable on an Endowment Policy as to those in respect of Whole of Life Assurances.

Payment of Premiums.

These may be payable either yearly, half-yearly or quarterly, and, provided that payment is made by means of a banker's order, by monthly instalments of not less than £1. If this last method is adopted the company will deduct any outstanding monthly payments due in any one year should the policy become a claim by the death of the insured person.

Tables III. and IV. show the cost and return of an Endowment Policy of £100 payable at age sixty or at previous death at ages varying from twenty-five to forty-five, together with surrender values at certain times. Bonuses are shown in the case of the With Profit Policy, and the same remarks apply as regards the bonus estimates and surrender values as were made in the Whole of Life tables.

The advantage of effecting policies when one is young will be obvious if a comparison is made between the annual premium charged for a life age twenty-five as against that required for a life aged forty-five.

Fitting a Modern Grate in Place of a Kitchen Range

To remove an old kitchen stove with a boiler at the back and replace it with an ordinary grate and still obtain hot water, sounds rather a formidable undertaking, but it need not be if systematically taken in hand.

In these days of smaller accommodation and limited households the idea seems a very good one and need not cost much; in fact, the only outlay would be the new fireplace itself and the incidentals, such as cement, sand, a few tiles and a few bricks, etc.

We will assume that the old stove to be removed is something after the design of that which is shown on Fig. 1 and the fireplace to be fitted in its stead like that shown on Fig. 2.

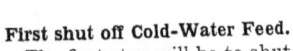

Fig. 1.—The Original Kitchen Range.   Fig. 2.—The New Grate.

First shut off Cold-Water Feed.

The first step will be to shut off the cold-water feed to the boiler. The cold-water tank, which, no doubt, will be in the roof, must be emptied and the supply from the main turned off. The hot water must then be drawn off at the lowest tap.

Removing the Range.

The next thing will be to remove the range. On p. 1089 a full description of how to remove a range is given, and after having removed the range, the boiler must be disconnected from the pipes. These can be cut with a pipe-cutter, hacksaw or cold chisel and hammer.

Removing Surplus Water in Boiler.

There will be a certain amount of water left in the boiler, but this can be removed by taking off the cleaning cover on top of the boiler with the help of a screw hammer.

The boiler may or may not be set higher than the position in which you will want to fix your new boiler, and for the sake of example we will assume that the position is as shown in Fig. 3, which is more or less what you will see when the recess is laid bare.

Cut the Pipes.

The pipes, flow and return, as shown on Fig. 3, must be cut and fitted to the new boiler at the tapping holes in the sides. Bends will have to be fixed if the new boiler is at a different level to the old.

When you have disconnected the old boiler, clear out the opening of rubbish, of which, no doubt, there will be a good deal. It will be easy enough to clear out the mess, and if it is rubble (broken bricks, etc.), set it aside for use when fitting the new fireplace.

Fig. 4 indicates the type of fireplace shown in section which can be fitted in, complete with boiler at the back.

The opening having now been laid bare, be sure that the sides and floor are sound.

When you have laid bare the opening, you may find that it is too high or too wide to accommodate your new fireplace without alteration. This eventuality can be overcome by inserting a chimney bar, (a piece of iron) for reducing the height and filling up the space at the top with bricks. If too wide, build up bricks at the sides, see Fig. 5.

On p. 1387 special stress is brought to bear upon the importance of not tampering with the party wall. Now in all probability the back of the opening will be a party wall, and if, in your opinion, the brickwork requires repairing, it will be well to read the comments made in the article above mentioned concerning the necessity of first consulting the district surveyor. Bricks may have to be renewed on the joints repointed with cement. Anyway, see that the recess is quite sound before starting to set out your new fireplace.

Put the grate temporarily in place first in order to ascertain correct position for boiler, and the height of the brickwork required from the floor to the level of the boiler flue. To form the flue place a firebrick at each corner of the boiler as Fig. 6.

Fix the Boiler First.

The boiler to be fixed will in all probability be detachable from the other parts of the grate. This being so, it can be fixed first. It should be supported on brick piers properly cemented. These will work out at approximately two bricks high. Fig. 6 shows this.

Boiler Flue.

The fire is drawn under and through to

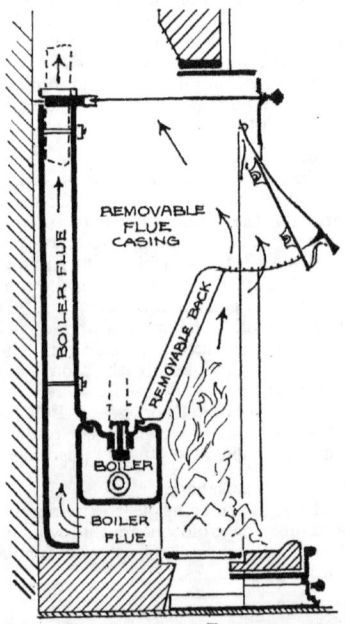

Fig. 3.—The Flow and Return Pipes.

Fig. 4.—Section of the Fireplace which can be fitted in Complete with Boiler at the Back.

FITTING A MODERN GRATE IN PLACE OF A KITCHEN RANGE

Fig. 5.—Showing how Sides can be built up with Bricks if Opening is too wide.

Fig. 9.—The Method to be adopted for Tiled Sides.

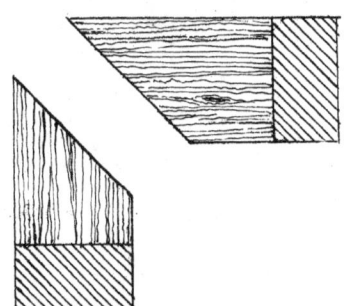

Fig. 10.—The Mitres at Ends of Jambs and Crosspieces.

Fig. 6.—The Boiler in Position.

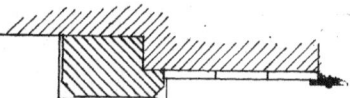

Fig. 7.—Section of Wood Surround.

Fig. 8.—The Fixing Ring.

the flue at the back. The flue from the boiler (see Figs. 4 and 6) is a three-sided iron shaft about 9 inches wide, which rests on the top of the boiler. It need not have a fourth side, this being formed by the brickwork at the back of the opening, but in connection with this it is imperative to make sure that the existing brickwork is not less than 9 inches thick. The reason for leaving out the fourth side is that it has been found that the heat is inclined to warp the iron and choke up the flue; therefore the brickwork is better.

Securing the Top of the Shaft.

The top of the shaft is secured to the brick back by means of the damper, which runs through from the front of the grate, fixed to the back wall and operated by means of a knob in the front.

Now build up the Sides.

Having fixed your boiler, proceed to brick up the sides to form a foundation for the tiles, which have to be fitted in later on. The front only need be brick; the space at the back can be filled with the rubble you have set aside to use again.

It will be well to screed over the floor of the recess with cement and sand before building the brickwork, in order to give a good foundation upon which to work.

The brickwork at the sides must be built up to the top of the opening and finished off with cement and sand in a neat manner to meet the existing flue, but before entirely finishing off at the top, the grate must be placed in position.

The Wood Surround.

The wood surround suggested in the illustration is about 3½ inches thick, and therefore the bricks which you build up at the side of the grate should project about 2 inches (see section, Fig. 7).

On the top of the ledge thus formed by the projecting bricks, build up another few courses in order to form a foundation for the frieze of tiles of the same width as the sides.

You will note by looking at the illustration (Fig. 4) that the flue from the grate joins the flue at the back.

The Grate.

At each side of the grate you will observe a ring. This is for fixing, and the method is by means of wire $\frac{3}{16}$ inch thick passed through the ring and bedded into the cement between two courses of brickwork at the top. This is why you must not finish off the brickwork until you have set your grate in position (Fig. 8).

The firebrick sides are detachable and can be fixed after the grate.

The Tiled Sides.

Tiles suitable in colour for your decorative scheme can be purchased at about 15s. per yd.—3-inch tiles look best. First mix up cement and sand and lay it on with a trowel to the brick sides. Whilst still wet proceed to fit your tiles from the bottom and build upwards; Fig. 9 shows the method to be adopted.

You will find that the outer rim of the grate is rebated. This is for assistance in holding in the tiles.

Materials required for Mantel

	Width.	Thickness.	Length.	Price. Pine.	Price. Oak.
Two uprights	6″	3½″	4′ 0″	15s. 6d.	£1 10s.
One crosspiece	6″	3½″	4′ 0″		
Two plinth blocks	6½″	6″	0′ 6″		
Four sockets and screws for fixing mantel to wall	—	—	—	Few shillings.	
— yds.: hearth and side panels	—	—	—	15s. per yd.	

FITTING A MODERN GRATE IN PLACE OF A KITCHEN RANGE

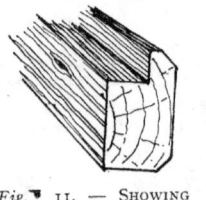

Fig. 11.—Showing Rebate and Chamfering.

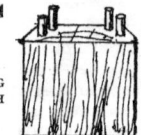

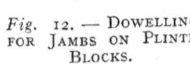

Fig. 12.—Dowelling for Jambs on Plinth Blocks.

Fig. 2 shows an illustration of a complete grate and mantelpiece. There are many kinds which may be purchased, but it would be much more interesting and, moreover, less costly, to make the mantel or surround as shown yourself.

A moulded surround is neater and easier to keep clean than the orthodox and more elaborate chimney piece.

Wood for the Mantel.

It can be made of any wood you like, but the most suitable wood seems to be either deal or oak, and the table on p. 1553 gives the prices of both woods, together with the necessary dimensions for your requirements:—

The sizes in the table are approximate, as it depends on the size of the grate, but are given "full" for cutting to the dimensions as shown on the illustration.

The method of making and fixing is as follows:—

Cut the jambs and top crosspiece out of solid wood, 6 × 3½ inches. This will be easier than framing it up.

With a 45-degree set square cut off the ends in order to form mitres (Fig. 10).

With a sharp chisel rebate the inside edge (Fig. 11).

Chamfer the inside and outside edges (Fig. 11).

The mitres should be tongued and glued.

The jambs should stand on plinth blocks and should be dowelled and glued (Figs. 2 and 12).

Now get slots and screws (Fig. 13) (these may be purchased very cheaply) and fix the slots into the back of your wood surround. They should be let in and finished flush.

Now plug the walls with wooden plugs and insert the screws, allowing them to project about ¾ inch. Upon these "hang" your surround. This will give an excellent fixing.

Laying the Hearth.

Having fixed your surround, the hearth must be laid, which can be of tiles to match the others.

First see that the foundation upon which to lay the tiles is level. For this mix up 3 parts sand and 1 of Portland cement and trowel it over the surface. Use a spirit level for accuracy. While still wet, score it across to give a key to your second layer, which must be laid on when the first is hard. Upon this lay your tiles. The tiles should finish flush with the floor. The wood uprights should therefore be raised up ½ inch off the cement hearth level.

The wood surround, if of deal, can be painted or stained and wax-polished.

Painting.

If you decide to paint it, rub it well down first with coarse glasspaper and finish with No. 0 to obtain a smooth surface upon which to work.

Three coats of paint should be sufficient, but between each coat well smooth down the surface with glasspaper.

Fig. 13.—Slots and Screws for fixing Mantelpiece.

You may like to finish it with a glossy enamel, or you may want a matt finish, in which case add more turpentine to your paint.

Staining.

If you want to stain and polish the wood you can make up stain in several ways, but to get a good mellow tone to the deal use permanganate of potash dissolved in water.

When quite dry, well glasspaper the surface and rub hard with wax diluted in turpentine. Elbow-grease is the best way to obtain a good result.

Oak can be treated in the same way. Stain first with powdered ochre or umber mixed with size, then wax-polish and rub hard.

If a dark finish is required apply liquid ammonia with a brush, or potash bichromate.

TWO USEFUL ARTICLES

THE drawings below show constructional details of two useful woodwork articles. One is a combined pair of steps, seat and waste container; the other a simple-shaped soiled-linen basket.

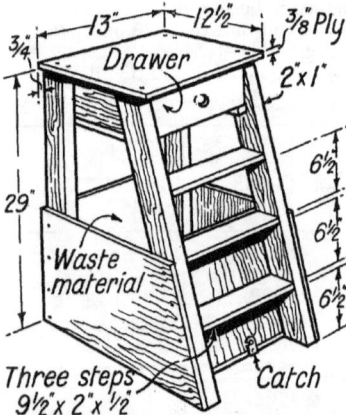

Fig. 1.—Constructional Details for Combined Steps and Waste Container.

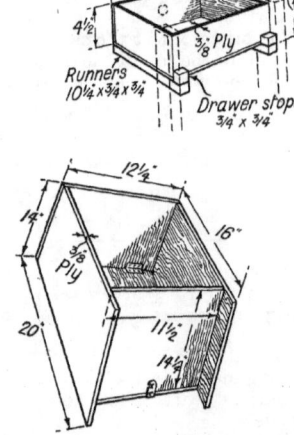

Fig. 2.—Details of Top and Bottom.

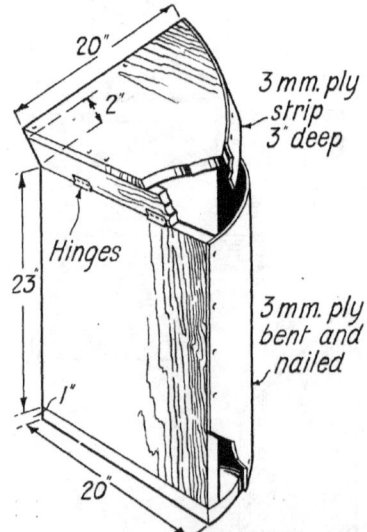

Fig. 3.—Details of Simple Soiled-Linen Container.

The Camera Lucida and Obscura

Both these pieces of apparatus are used for drawing landscapes and copying drawings; the camera lucida is an expensive optical instrument, but the camera obscura is a comparatively simple and inexpensive aid to drawing and sketching; it can be made without difficulty, and will be found quite effective for all ordinary purposes.

Principle of the Camera Lucida.

The principle of the camera lucida is shown at Fig. 1, and consists of a prism which so refracts the rays of light proceeding from the image observed that the observer is enabled to see, on the paper below, the exact shape of the image in front. In the example, the prism is a right angle on one corner, the opposite corner being 135 degrees. Actually the camera lucida is a valuable addition to the microscope and enables microscopic enlargements to be drawn with ease. Owing to the need for a rigid support and the high cost of the specially ground prisms and silvered surfaces, its manufacture is a specialised job.

Principle of the Camera Obscura.

The camera obscura, as shown in the diagram at Fig. 2, consists of a lens, a mirror and a sheet of ground glass. The view is focussed on to the mirror and is reflected on to the ground glass in which it can be traced with a pencil. The principle is similar to that of the viewfinder attached to a hand camera. Another form of the camera obscura is still to be seen in many seaside resorts, in this case a large lens is placed at the top of a round chamber in which is a round table. The surrounding view is reflected by a mirror on to the table.

A Simple Form of Camera Obscura.

A portable form of the camera obscura suitable for sketching is shown

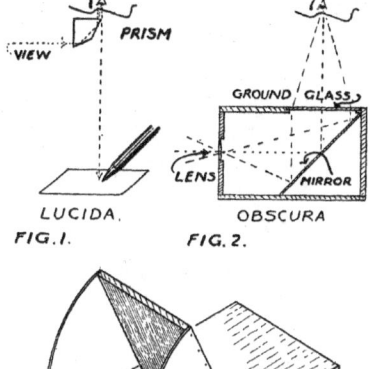

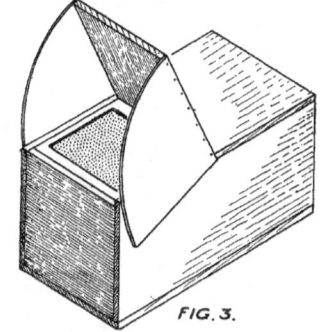

Figs. 1–3.—The Principle of the Camera Lucida and Obscura and a Simple Form of Obscura.

at Fig. 3, and consists of a box made of wood, ¼ in. thick and measuring 9 × 6 × 6 inches. A hood, with sides of tinned sheet, is necessary to shield the ground glass from direct rays of light. The dimensions given are those suitable for a lens having a focal length of 9 inches. Any variation in the focal length of the lens will affect the length of the box. An ordinary double convex lens enclosed in a tube will do; in fact, such a lens fitted in a short length of cardboard postal tube will be found quite as effective as a lens mounted in a brass tube. It is quite possible to pick up a suitable lens in a second-hand shop for a shilling or two, or failing that, a small magnifying glass will answer the purpose when mounted.

How to find the Focal Length.

The focal length may be found quite easily by focussing the view through the window on to a piece of paper and measuring the distance between the lens and the paper. It is advisable, in order to obtain accurate focussing, for the lens to be adjustable, and for this reason it should be enclosed in a tube.

Constructional Details.

The positions of the various parts with measurements for a lens of 9-inch focal length, are indicated in the elevations and plan at Figs. 4, 5, 6 and 7, the latter being a front elevation of the closed box, the others show the hood open. Plywood, ¼ inch thick, will do quite well for the box, the joints being glued and bradded. Before the box is made it will be advisable to obtain the lens and make quite sure of the focal length. If the lens is purchased from an optician the exact length can be ascertained at the time.

Having the necessary measurements, the box can be made, as shown at Fig. 8, which indicates the first stage in the construction. The two side pieces, A, are 9 × 5½ inches, glued and nailed to a base B, which is 9 × 6 inches. The back piece, C, is 5½ inches square approximately; it should fit exactly inside. The next job is to prepare two right-angled triangles from ¼-inch thick wood, and with allowance for the thickness of the mirrored plate, the height should be about 5 inches. Glue these two pieces in position as shown to complete the stage.

The holder for the ground glass is cut off to about 7 × 5½ inches and a hole cut about 4½ inches square, measured ½ inch from both sides and one end.

The Mirror.

The mirror, a piece of silvered glass, should measure 5½ inches wide and be just under 8 inches long, but it would do if it were 5½ inches square providing that it is mounted in the centre. It can be kept in position by an angle of glued tape each side or by narrow wooden fillets. The piece of ground glass should fit exactly in the rebates of the top piece, E, the measurements being approximately 4¾ inches square. The surface should be finely ground and similar to that used for the focussing screen of a camera.

The lens should be able to be moved backwards and forwards, but it is important that the fit should be a close one so that no light enters the box other than that going through the lens. The side shields should be painted, the inside being painted with dead black.

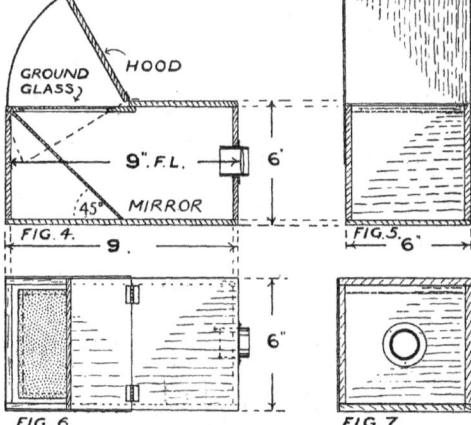

Figs. 4–7.—Details of Lens Arrangement in Simple Camera Obscura.

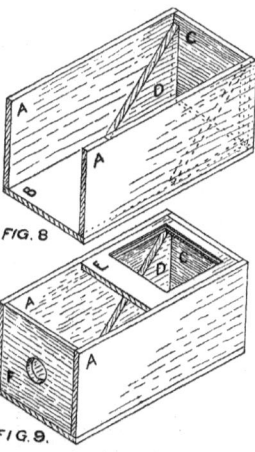

Figs. 8 and 9.—Constructional Details.

Domestic Slow Combustion Boilers
PRACTICAL NOTES ON THEIR CARE AND OPERATION

THE boilers used for the hot-water supply of private houses are generally termed independent boilers, that is to say, they have no connection with the boiler usually fitted in the cooking range, but the hot-water storage cylinder is often common to both and will allow either boiler to be used separately or both together, as desired.

There is usually little choice in the type of boiler, as it is generally fitted in the house when it is taken over; so, unless a new boiler has to be fitted, the best must be made of the boiler in use. A great deal of efficiency in domestic boilers is lost by the attempt to combine a boiler with limited cooking facilities, or to show an "open fire."

The fault of the old kitchen-range boiler was that it was sacrificed to the main use of the range—cooking purposes—so it is inadvisable to sacrifice the water-heating capacity, which is what the boiler is required for, in order that cooking can be done on the boiler fire if ever required, while the open-fire feature is seldom required and is dearly bought in the loss of efficiency it causes.

Three Types of Heating Surfaces.

There are three types of heating surfaces — vertical, horizontal above the flame, and horizontal below the flame. The efficiencies are: horizontal, 100 per cent.; vertical, 50 per cent.; horizontal below the flame, nil. It will be seen, therefore, that boilers having horizontal heating surface are, other things being equal, more efficient than boilers with all-vertical heating surface.

Some boilers are sold with water passages below the firebars, and this is described as heating surface, while in fact it is valueless and merely acts as a harbour for sludge and scale. Many of the boilers with all-vertical heating surface have this so much reduced in providing an open fire that the efficiency—by which is meant the amount of fuel which has to be burned to heat a given quantity of water—is greatly reduced.

Fig. 1 shows a boiler with all-vertical heating surface, and it will be seen what a large proportion of this is lost owing to provision being made for an open fire and cooking facilities. Figs. 2 & 2A show a boiler with all-vertical heating surface but no open fire. Fig. 3 shows a boiler with both horizontal and vertical surfaces but with an open fire. The majority of boilers fitted, in order to save initial expense are too small for their work.

A small boiler, which has to be forced, is far more extravagant in fuel than a boiler too large for the work, run easily. A very small fire is also more difficult to keep in for long periods; the amount of fuel in proportion to the heating surface is not enough to maintain the heat necessary for slow combustion when the draught is cut down, and has the annoying habit of going out during the night.

There are very many types of boilers, so it is only possible to deal in general terms with the correct management, the main points of which, however, will apply to all types.

Draught.

The first point is that of draught. Unless the flues are clear and there is a good draught, no hot water can be obtained. The flues of the boiler should be swept regularly, using a proper flue brush. On the flue elbows cast-iron doors are arranged (Fig. 4). If the nuts at each end are slackened, the door can be swung off and the pipe swept. Owing to the heat, these doors often warp (Fig. 5) and air can leak into the flue and spoil the draught.

Asbestos Joint.

In such cases an asbestos joint should be cut out of $\frac{1}{8}$-inch asbestos millboard, obtainable at any ironmongers, and bolted up under the door to make a tight joint. The flue of the boiler is often run into the same flue which serves the range (Fig. 6), and if the range fire dampers (AAA, Fig. 6) are open, there may not be enough draught for the boiler. Unless the range is in use, the dampers should be closed, but if this is not possible a separate flue should be run for the boiler (Fig. 7).

Where sheet metal stove piping is used for the boiler flue, this often rusts or burns through, and while no smoke or fumes may leak out, air can

Fig. 1.—Boiler with All-vertical Heating Surface.

Showing open fire feature. Note that there is no heating surface on the whole front.

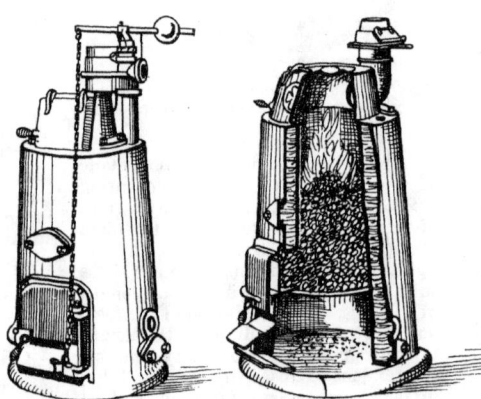

Fig. 2.—Boiler with All-vertical Heating Surface but no Open Fire or Cooking Feature.
Note automatic damper control.

Fig. 2A.—Section of Boiler. Note cleaning doors, or mudholes.

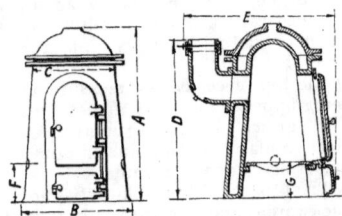

Fig. 3 and 3A.—Boiler with both Vertical and Horizontal Heating Surfaces and with Open Fire.

Note that whole top of boiler can be removed for cleaning. In the section 3A it will be seen that there is a water space round the flue outlet.

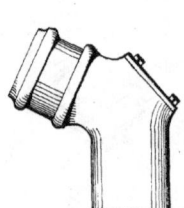

Fig. 4.—Cast-iron Flue Pipe Elbow.

Showing cleaning or soot door on back. This must make an airtight joint.

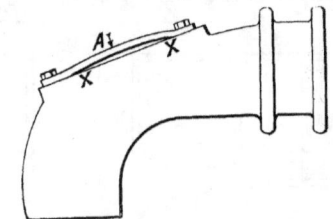

Fig. 5.—Door A warped by Heat at X X allowing Air to leak in.

DOMESTIC SLOW COMBUSTION BOILERS

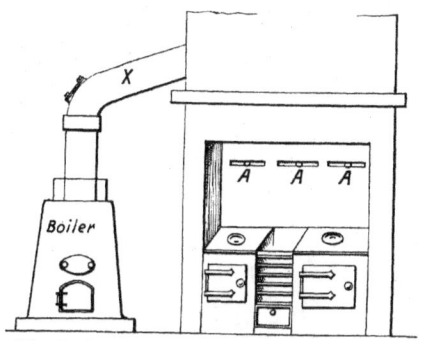

*Fig. 6.—*Kitchen Range with Boiler Flue, X, using same Chimney.

If the dampers of range, A A A, are open the draught of boiler may be interfered with.

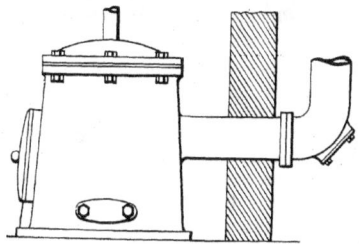

*Fig. 7.—*Flue of Boiler taken through Wall and run up outside of House.

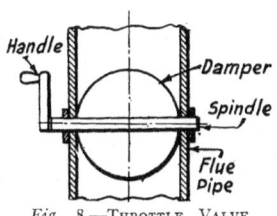

*Fig. 8.—*Throttle Valve Type of Damper.

leak in and spoil the draught. Where the flue pipe joins the brickwork, there is often air leakage owing to the mortar falling out. In such cases the joint should be made good with Pyruma, Purimachos or other fire cement, obtainable at most hardware merchants. In boilers like Fig. 1 the top plate often warps with heat, and air can leak in over the top of the boiler.

A good way to test this is to close the damper and light a piece of brown paper in the firebox and see if smoke leaks out under the top plate. If it does, make good all round the top plate with fire cement.

Flue Dampers.

Flue dampers, especially of the throttle-valve type (Fig. 8), are liable to get stuck through the spindles rusting. Unless the damper can be easily adjusted, it is not possible to get the fire to keep in during the night or to control the fire. It is of no use to oil the damper spindle—the heat will carbonise the oil and the damper will again be fixed. A little powdered graphite should be mixed up with paraffin and worked well into the bearings of the damper spindle, and will prevent it sticking up for a very long period.

Sliding Dampers.

Sliding dampers should have the slots in which they work cleaned out with a stiff wire, and the edges of the damper where it fits into the slots should be well coated with the graphite paste already mentioned

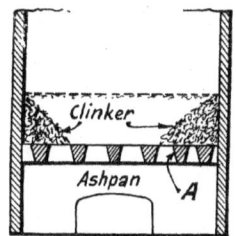

*Fig. 10.—*Section of Firebox showing how Clinker tends to grow from Edges to Centre of Fire and Choke the Bars, A.

(Fig. 9). The fronts or doors of open-fire type boilers tend to warp and admit air which will allow the fire to burn out when made up for the night.

In such cases new doors should be fitted; they are generally very cheap and the saving in fuel and worry will soon pay for them. The only air admitted to any boiler when closed

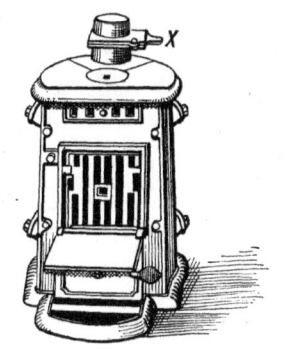

*Fig. 9.—*Boiler with Sliding Door Type Damper, X.

The damper should be removed periodically and the slot in which it works cleaned out with a stiff wire.

should be through the ashpan damper, otherwise the fire cannot be controlled. There is next the question of fuel. Use the fuel recommended by the makers if it is known and obtainable, and especially adhere to the size of fuel advised.

The Fuel.

Much trouble is met with in small boilers by using too large fuel. The best all-round fuel is gas coke broken into pieces not more than 1 inch cube or round. Furnace coke can be used, but requires more draught and is much more liable to clinker, while the ash content is greater.

Anthracite is advised by many boiler manufacturers, and here again the size and quality is important; the quality known as horticultural anthracite is not suitable for these small boilers, being liable to break up in use and fall through the bars and burn in the ashpan.

Clean out the Firebox once a Week.

Many boiler users try to consume household rubbish in the boiler. This will prevent the boiler working properly. The small fireboxes of these boilers need the best clean fuel to do their work properly, and if paper, potato peelings, etc., are burned, little hot water will be obtained and the fire will go dead and clinker up. At least once a week the fire should be allowed to burn out and then the firebox should be thoroughly cleaned out and the fire relighted. Clinker tends to form round the sides of the firebox and cannot be removed by poking with the fire alight. It grows inwards and gradually reduces the area of the grate until it is insufficient to maintain the heat (Fig. 10).

Clean the Ashpan Daily.

The ashpan should be cleaned out daily, as, if allowed to get full of ash, the fire would go out. When stoking up for the night, the firebox should be filled with fuel as high as the charging door will allow. The ashpan damper should be closed entirely and the flue damper almost closed. Enough air will leak into the ashpan to keep the fire alight.

In the morning the flue and ashpan dampers should be opened, the firedoor opened and the fire given a good rake to remove the ash (Fig. 11). The

*Fig. 11.—*Raking out the Ashes in the Morning to Revive Fire.

DOMESTIC SLOW COMBUSTION BOILERS

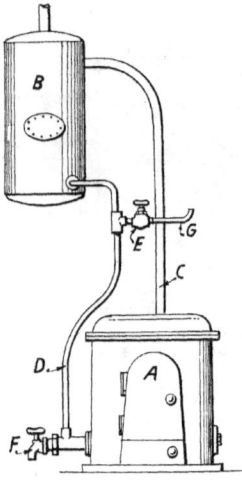

Fig. 12.—Details for Drawing the Boiler.

A, Boiler; B, Hot-water cylinder; C, Flow pipe; D, Return pipe; E, Cold-water stop valve; F, Drain tap; G, Cold-water pipe.

ash should be cleared from the ashpan, and after giving the fire a few minutes to draw up, it should be made up and the dampers regulated to give the heat desired.

If the boiler is of ample size, attention at morning and night only should be required, the closed position of the dampers will give water of the required heat and the maximum economy of fuel. A small boiler will require the fuel replenishing several times during the day and careful attention to the dampers, or it may burn out.

Hard-water Trouble.

In districts where the water is "hard," trouble will be met with due to the furring up of the boiler, the lime, etc., in the water depositing on the boiler plates. A very thin layer of deposit will greatly affect the efficiency of the boiler, and if the deposit is allowed to get to a considerable thickness, the plates of the boiler may burn through.

In installing a boiler in a hard-water district, particular attention should be paid to the cleaning facilities provided. These, in some types of boiler, are very poor, and it is almost impossible to clean the boilers out properly. Not only should a sufficient number of mud- or man-holes be provided, but they should be in positions which enable every part of the water spaces to be reached.

The boiler shown in Fig. 3 possesses unusual advantages from this point of view, as the whole top of the boiler can be removed, giving easy access to the entire water space. The period which should elapse between cleaning will depend on the hardness of the water and the amount the boiler is used. If the water is known to be hard, the boiler should be opened up after the first three months' use and the condition ascertained.

Draining the Hot-water System.

If it is good, then six months might be allowed to elapse before the next cleaning, and a fixed period could be arrived at in this manner. To clean the boiler out, it is first of all necessary to drain the hot-water system. The cold supply must first be shut off. This is generally arranged to enter the return pipe between the hot-water cylinder and the boiler (Fig. 12), but sometimes it enters the bottom of the cylinder (Fig. 13). Close the cold-water valve and then open the hot tap on the lowest point and allow the system to empty.

This will not drain the boiler, and to do this a tap is generally fitted on the return pipe just where it enters the boiler (Fig. 12), or sometimes a tap is fitted on the bottom of the boiler itself. When all water has been drained off, the mudhole covers can be removed. These are generally held on by two studs and nuts (Fig. 14), and care must be taken that the studs are not twisted off on removing the nuts if very tight. If considerable effort is required, the nuts should be well anointed with lubricating oil, thinned down with paraffin and allowed time to soak into the threads. When the nuts are off, the doors can be removed; a chisel or other tool, such as a screwdriver, forced between the door and the boiler face may be required to shift them.

Cleaning the Boiler.

All mud, sludge and scale should be removed as far as possible and the boiler washed out. Before replacing the doors, see that the faces on the boiler are quite clean, any fragments of the old joint can be scraped off with a putty knife or paint scraper. The joints may come off clean and whole, and if so can be used again, a little graphite mixed with oil being smeared

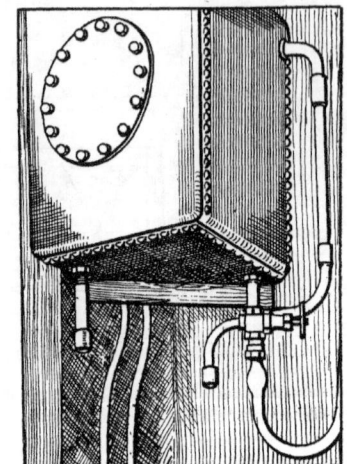

Fig. 13.—Showing Alternative Method of Cold-water Supply.

on the face of the joint before replacing and also on the threads of the studs, which will enable the doors to be removed easily next time.

Remaking the Joints.

If the joints are broken or defective, new joints must be cut. These can be made from $\frac{1}{8}$-inch thick asbestos millboard, sold at most ironmongers, or, better still, from one of the many jointing materials, the names of which end in "ite"—Klingerite, Hallite, Walkerite, etc. This need not be so thick as asbestos; $\frac{1}{16}$ inch is plenty. The jointing is held on the cover and struck lightly all round the edge with a hammer, which will cut through the material. The bolt holes can be punched through with a piece of rod, using the cover as a guide.

Clean the face of the cover, coat the joint on both sides with graphite mixed with oil, and bolt up. Undue force should not be used, as, if one of the studs is broken off in the boiler, a very awkward job will result.

Removing a Screwed-in Cleaning Plug.

On some boilers screwed-in cleaning plugs are provided, and these may be very difficult to remove.

If the plugs are of brass they may be got out easily, but if of iron, as is often the case, great force may be required to remove them. In such cases, before the plug is damaged by spanners slipping on the hexagons or squares, proceed as follows.

Blow the plug hot with a blowlamp and then paint all round it with a mixture of oil and paraffin. Tap the plug gently with a hammer to break

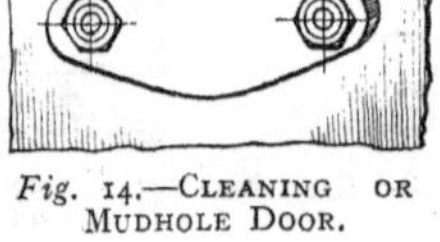

Fig. 14.—Cleaning or Mudhole Door.

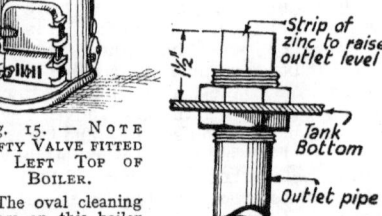

Fig. 15.—Note Safety Valve fitted to Left Top of Boiler.

The oval cleaning doors on this boiler are of very ample size to give easy access.

Fig. 16.—Zinc Sheet used to raise Outlet Level.

1558

DOMESTIC SLOW COMBUSTION BOILERS

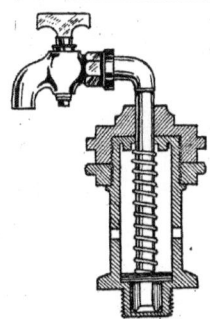

Fig. 17.—A GOOD TYPE OF SAFETY VALVE.
This is fitted with hollow spindle and tap to test freedom of passage under seating. If no water issues, especially in frosty weather, the fire should not be lighted.

down the rust and adhesions. When cool, try to remove. If still tight, repeat the operation, giving the oil plenty of time to soak in.

When the plugs are being replaced, coat the threads well with graphite mixed up to a paste with oil, and the plug will be able to be unscrewed easily next time. After replacing the covers or plugs, the cistern should be refilled by turning on the cold supply, seeing that all draw-off taps are closed.

For a short time after cleaning out the boiler the water may be discoloured, but this will pass off. In districts where the water is soft or is derived from peaty soils there will be no incrustation of the boiler, but mud and sludge will be deposited and have to be cleaned out.

Preventing Discoloration of the Water.

One trouble often met with in such cases is discoloration of the water due to it attacking the iron of the boiler. In such districts the boilers fitted should be specially treated to resist rust or corrosion. In bad cases the boiler and pipes are sometimes made of copper, but this is an expensive matter.

The Lime Method.

In one district the discoloration of the water was prevented by making the water "hard" for a time until a coating of scale was deposited in the boiler. The cold-water tank from which the supply for the boiler was taken had all other supplies shut off, and a quantity of lime mixed to cream consistency with water was added to the tank daily.

At the time of adding the lime solution the water in the tank was well stirred to prevent any large accumulation of lime on the tank. In the case in question, 2 lbs. of lime was fed each day for fourteen days, and the water had by then lost its rusty colour, showing that the boiler surfaces were coated. A muslin bag holding about 7 lbs. of lime was kept immersed in the tank for some days after. The water outlet in this tank was about 1½ inches from the bottom, but to avoid any chance of chokage, should the tank outlet be in the bottom, a strip of sheet zinc about 1½ inches wide should be bent round to form a short tube and inserted in the mouth of the outlet pipe on the tank (Fig. 16).

The Cement Method.

If the boiler is of a type in which the interior is readily accessible, such as Fig. 3, a thin wash of Portland cement can be given to it, forming a scale about the thickness of a sixpence. This will stop all discoloration of the water; but very soft water will soon attack the hot-water tank, even though it is galvanised, and a coating of cement inside the tank will be an advantage. Copper hot-water tanks are often fitted in such cases and are good investments, as the labour cost

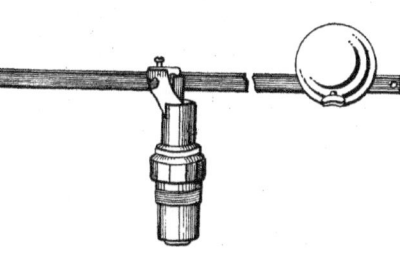

Fig. 18.—THE AUTOMATIC REGULATOR SHOWN FITTED IN FIG. 2.
Note adjusting weight on right which slides along the lever. The stem below the hexagon screws into the boiler.

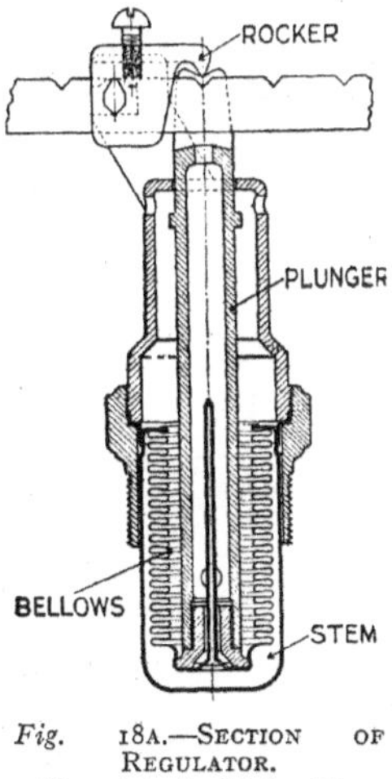

of removing old and fitting new tanks is generally greater than the cost of the tank.

In the case of hard water, prevention is better than cure, and if the water can be softened, all the trouble due to incrustation will be prevented. Preparations are now sold in block form, one of which dropped in the cold-water tank at given periods will soften all water used and save a large proportion of the soap, tea, etc., used in the house. One of these preparations is marketed by Clensol Ltd., and is entirely harmless in water used for human consumption.

Safety Valves.

During every spell of cold weather a number of

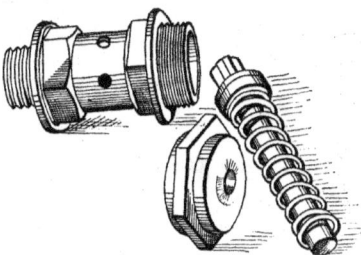

Fig. 17A.—VALVE SHOWN TAKEN APART FOR CLEANING.

explosions of domestic hot-water boilers are reported, often with fatal results. The cause is generally the freezing of the pipes while the boiler is not in action. When the boiler is lighted up, there is no outlet from it and an explosion follows. No domestic boiler should be installed without a safety valve being fitted. This should be fitted as close to the boiler as possible, so that in the event of pipes near the boiler being frozen the safety valve will be able to act.

Cases have been known where the safety valve, situated some distance from the boiler, has itself been frozen and therefore inoperative. Even the fitting of a safety valve is of little use unless the valve is inspected periodically to ensure that it is in working order. Each time the boiler is cleaned out, the safety valve should be taken apart and examined.

In use, deposit tends to form under the seat (Fig. 17) and sets into a hard mass, rendering the valve useless, so that it would not lift at any pressure. This is the more encouraged, as the valve is generally fitted on a tee or branch on the flow pipe, so that it is on a dead end through which there is no flow to clear the deposit.

Automatic Regulators.

One of these is shown in Fig. 2, and its action is to control the damper door of the ashpan, closing it as the temperature of the water rises and maintaining the heat at any desired degree. Actually, on small domestic hot-water boilers these devices have little value. The drawback is that if the fuel level is low and the temperature drops, the regulator will open the damper and allow the fire to burn right out in the vain attempt to maintain the set temperature. In a large boiler receiving attention at periodical intervals, regulators give valuable service.

A small boiler will keep the water hot for many hours on a low fire, such as through the night, when the fire would be burned out in a very short time if a regulator was in use and the damper would remain open and the boiler cooled down. Figs. 18 and 18A show the construction of one of the best types of regulators.

Fig. 18A.—SECTION OF REGULATOR.
The stem is filled with a volatile fluid which, expanding with heat, compresses the copper bellows and lifts the plunger, actuating the lever.

How to Make Kites

Box kites can be made of any desired size, but for general utility a kite about 42 inches long and 18½ inches on each face can be recommended.

Materials for Box Kite.

The following materials are required for a box kite 42 inches long, 18½ inches square:—

Corner Spines.—4 pieces ⅜ inch square, 42 inches long.

Struts.—4 pieces ½ × ¼ inch × 26 inches long.

Fabric.—2 pieces Nainsook, 14 inches wide, 76 inches long.

Suitable woods for the spines and struts are spruce, basswood or white deal, but in any case must be free from knots and should be as straight-grained as possible.

First clean up the sticks with sandpaper to remove all roughness, then apply a coat of varnish and put them aside to dry and harden.

Making the Bands.

The bands are preferably made of nainsook, but fine cambric or a very light "doped" aeroplane fabric could be used instead. First hem each long edge to make a band 12 inches wide, then overlap the ends of one band and double-sew them together, as in Fig. 2, thus making an endless band, which when laid flat should measure 37 inches long.

Prepare the other band and make it exactly the same size as the first. Set the joint at one end and then fold over the band on to itself as in Fig. 3, thus dividing it roughly into four, as will be indicated by the creases.

The first corner spine should now be inserted under the band—at the sewn joint, and be fixed with small tacks. One band is fixed at each end of the spine, and when the latter is placed horizontally, as in Fig. 4, the bands should hang straight down and be quite parallel. The second spine is then laid in the loops of the bands and fixed with tacks as before. This procedure ensures that these spines are equally spaced.

To determine the position of the third spine, place the first two against each other, as in Fig. 5, and allow the loops of the bands to hang straight down; slip the spine into them and fix as before, then similarly fix the fourth spine.

Diagonal Struts.

The next proceeding is to prepare the diagonal struts, as in Fig. 6, by laying one over the other and binding the joint with strong twine. Next bind twine around the ends of all the struts as in Fig. 7, but leave sufficient material to allow of notching the ends. The struts must be cut to such a length that when notched to fit over the spines they are just long enough to extend the bands and hold the material taut. To prevent endways movement, small blocks of wood should be glued to the spines to come on each side of the struts, as in Fig. 8. Arranged in this way, the struts can easily be sprung out of place and removed, thus allowing the kite to be rolled up for transport.

Fig. 1.—Box Kite in Flight.

Fig. 2.—Band, Hemmed and Joined.
The band of fabric is first hemmed on each side and the ends then double-sewn together.

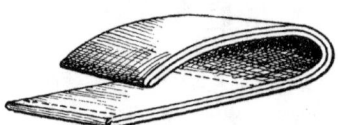

Fig. 3.—Dividing Band into Four.
The band is doubled over with the joint at one end and the opposite end then turned over to the joint end to divide it into four.

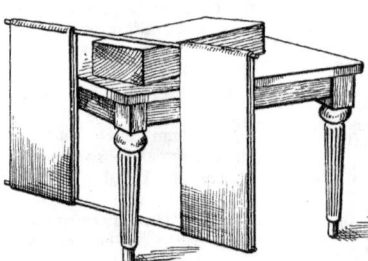

Fig. 4.—First Spine Fixed.
The spine is fixed with tacks to the bands at the sewn joint; placed horizontally and the bands allowed to hang down and the second spine laid in the bottom loops.

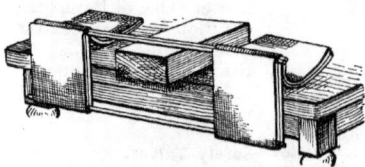

Fig. 5.—Determining Position for Third Spine.

Flying the Kite.

Before the kite can be flown it is necessary to fix the bridle, as in Fig. 9, which should be a piece of strong string each end. The kite line should be fixed to the bridle and must be adjustable for position. This is best done by tying a simple square knot in the bridle, and fasten the kite line to it with a bowline knot. Full details for tying these knots are given on pp. 793 to 795.

The position of the bridle knot must be adjusted according to the strength of the wind; in a light wind bring the knot nearer to the front or "windward" side, in a strong wind bring the bridle knot more to the back, but in a very strong wind fasten the kite line directly to the corner spine just behind the front band.

Simple Chinese Kite.

A very simple tailless kite (Fig. 10) can be made with a sheet of tough light tissue paper about 20 inches square and two thin slips of bamboo cane.

To make this kite, lay the square piece of tissue paper flat on the table, then place on it a strip of cane about ¼ inch wide and 3/23 inch thick. Cut the ends to length and then apply some gum or other adhesive to the cane and press it on to the tissue paper so that it reaches from top to bottom corners, as in Fig. 11. Then take a piece of the tissue paper, about 2 inches wide and 4 inches long, and paste it over the corner to strengthen it and form a pocket for the stick; fasten one of these strengtheners to each corner.

The bow is made of similar size cane to the backbone, but has first to be bent to such a shape that the upper part of the arch comes about a quarter of the distance from the top of the backbone, while the ends of the bow come to the free corners of the tissue.

Smear some adhesive on the cane, and when it has become "tacky" spring the bow to shape, lay it in place and hold it there for a minute or so while the adhesive sets. The springiness of the cane bow draws the paper taut at the lower edges, and after the strengthening corners have been fixed the kite is ready for flying. The bridle is fixed at its upper end to the junction between the two canes, the lower end is fixed at a corresponding distance from the bottom. The kite line is attached and the kite balanced for flying by adding little pieces of

Fig. 6.—Arrangement of Struts.

HOW TO MAKE KITES

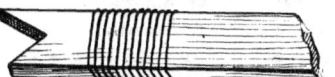

*Fig. 7.—*BINDING AT ENDS OF STRUTS.
To prevent the wood splitting it is bound tightly with waxed thread.

*Fig. 8.—*STRUT AND STEADY BLOCKS IN PLACE.

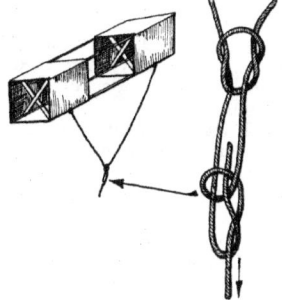

*Fig. 9.—*BRIDLE, LINE AND KNOTS.

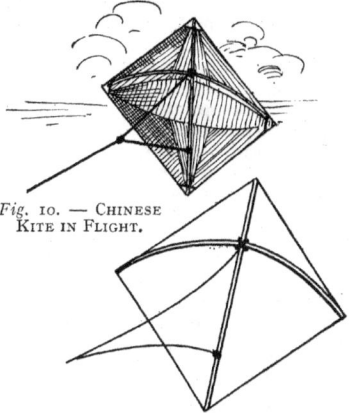

*Fig. 10.—*CHINESE KITE IN FLIGHT.

*Fig. 11.—*ARRANGEMENT OF STICKS AND BRIDLE.

paper until the kite hangs horizontally when suspended by the kite line.

Tailless Kite.

Another type of tailless kite, shown in Fig. 12, is rather stronger than the foregoing, but is almost as easy to make and fly.

Materials for Tailless Kite.

Sticks.—2 pieces pine, $\frac{3}{8}$ inch square, 36 inches long.

Cover.—3 sheets tissue paper, size 30 inches × 20 inches.

To make this kite, first tie the cross-stick to the backbone at a distance of $5\frac{1}{2}$ inches from the top. Then notch the ends of the cross-stick and stretch a string tightly across it to cause the stick to bend into a bow shape. When correctly bent, the middle part of the bow should be $4\frac{1}{2}$ inches above the ends.

Next take a length of smooth strong string and tie it from corner to corner, thus outlining the shape of the kite.

To make the cover, cut one sheet of tissue paper into two and then paste together this piece and two full sheets, as shown in Fig. 13, and cut them to the sizes and shape shown. Lay the tissue over the strings on the frame, apply paste to the edges and fold them over around the strings. Reinforce the corners as before, and fasten the bridle to the junction of the two sticks and to the bottom corner. The kite can be decorated with a pattern or the outline of a bird in coloured tissue paper.

Festooned combined Kite.

When more than one kite is formed on the same framework the result is generally known as a combined kite, as, for example, that in

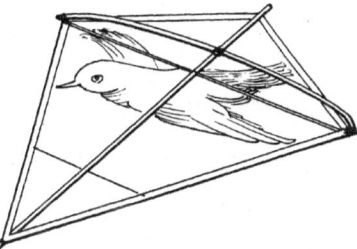

*Fig. 12.—*TAILLESS KITE.
Another easy-to-make kite that flies well.

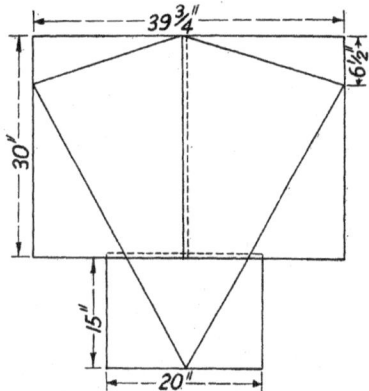

*Fig. 13.—*ARRANGEMENT OF TISSUE SHEETS.

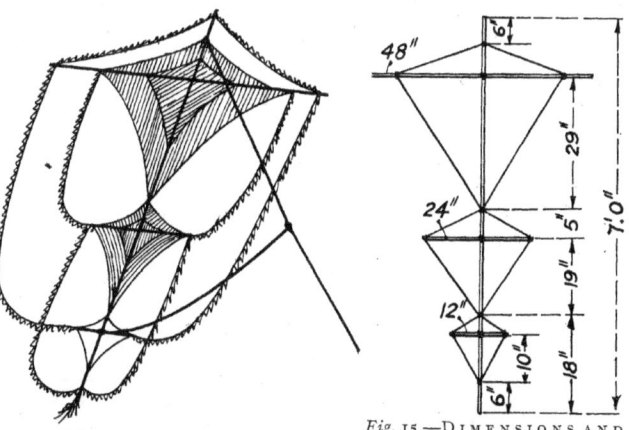

*Fig. 14.—*FESTOONED KITE.

*Fig. 15.—*DIMENSIONS AND ARRANGEMENT OF FRAMEWORK.

Fig. 14, which really consists of three superposed kites with additional festoons.

Material for Festoon Kite.

Sticks.—Backbone: 1 piece spruce or pine $\frac{1}{4} \times \frac{1}{2}$ inch × 7 feet long.

Bowsticks: 1 piece spruce or pine $\frac{1}{4} \times \frac{1}{2}$ inch × 4 feet long; 1 piece spruce or pine $\frac{1}{4} \times \frac{3}{8}$ inch × 2 feet long; 1 piece spruce or pine $\frac{1}{4} \times \frac{1}{4}$ inch × 1 foot long.

Covering.—5 sheets tissue paper, 30 × 20 inches.

To make this kite, lay the backbone flat on the table, place the bowsticks on it (in the positions shown in Fig. 15), and fasten them with glue and a thread binding.

The most important things are that the three bow sticks must be parallel and that all three are in the same plane, as if one is out of line the kite will be unsteady in flight.

The next step is to string the kite, which is done by tying the string first to the backbone, at a distance of 6 inches from the top, then taking it down to the first bowstick and so on until the kite is completely outlined. Tie the string firmly at each junction and take care to keep each section taut, but be equally careful not to distort the frame.

Covering.

Then cover the kites with brightly coloured tissue paper—as before —then apply the fringe festoons, which can be made from strips of tissue paper about $2\frac{1}{2}$ inches wide—one edge pasted around a very thin string and the free edge cut with scissors to form the fringe.

Starting in Business with Small Capital

The most profitable and stable businesses are, in general, those which cater for the needs of the largest number of people in the vicinity; more particularly all businesses connected with foodstuffs, simple luxuries and clothing. Under this general heading are grouped many kinds of businesses, some calling for specialised knowledge, others that anyone with ordinary common sense can carry on successfully.

Grocery.

A small grocery business is eminently suitable for, say, a married couple with a son or daughter to assist—or with the aid of a lad to call for orders or deliver goods.

No particular specialised knowledge is required, travellers from wholesale firms call for orders at regular periods, most of the stock is boxed or put up in packets or cartons, the cost of fixtures and fittings is small, desirable machines such as automatically reading scales, bacon slicer and refrigerator can be had on easy deferred terms.

Greengrocery.

Another sound business that does not call for specialised knowledge, although ability to judge and buy the best types of vegetable is a distinct asset; it can be acquired by experience, more especially if samples of the stock are tested personally. The cost of fixtures and fittings is small, trade can be done entirely on a cash basis with personal shoppers only, or a door-to-door sales service can be run in conjunction with the shop. The greatest difficulty for the beginner is to judge the stocks required to have enough for the trade, but to leave none, or the absolute minimum of stock on hand at the end of the day. Supplies should be fresh in daily, preferably purchased direct from the central market. This entails early rising—somewhere about four o'clock in the morning; the cost of going to market and bringing back the goods must be added to the purchase price. For all but the very smallest businesses the use of a motor van—conforming with the new transport regulations as to fitness for purpose—is essential.

Fruiterer.

This is somewhat akin to the greengrocery business, but, being restricted to fruits, is more flexible as regards stocks, which keep better, but needs more specialised knowledge and buying ability. Much stock is obtained through agents and merchants, and is delivered by rail in crates or boxes which are generally charged for, but credited in whole or in part on their return.

Florist.

A business that is peculiarly adapted to women and is mostly patronised by them. A wide knowledge of flowers, their habits, "keeping" properties, also some artistic ability in display and colour grouping are essential. By their nature, cut flowers are a very perishable stock, and buying must needs be done with skill and judgment. The associated work of making wreaths, wedding bouquets and floral tributes calls for specialised knowledge and skill. Early rising is often necessary to ensure fresh market supplies.

Fancy Cakes.

In some localities a small shop specialising in biscuits, cakes and the like is a profitable venture. The stock is mostly obtained from manufacturers and delivered daily. No special knowledge is necessary, only about half the stock is perishable, business is customarily on a cash basis, fixtures and fittings are, however, an expense to be reckoned with at the start. Hours of opening are regulated by the district authorities.

Café or Tea Rooms.

Ability to cook well and to serve food in a clean attractive manner are outstanding requirements for any small catering business. The chief capital expense is in the equipment; tables, chairs and particularly cutlery, china and linen. Consumable stocks need not be large, the cooking equipment can be expanded with the trade. Business is entirely for cash; one assistant will be sufficient at the start. One disadvantage is that hours are long and often entail Sunday work.

Newsagent and Tobacconist.

A straightforward business easily mastered by anyone, but entailing long hours, commencing between four and five o'clock in the morning to collect the newspapers, sort and mark them for the lads to deliver at the doors of regular customers. There is usually no respite on Sundays, the shop is often open till nine o'clock or later and then comes the "booking up" of accounts and the daily preparation and dispatch of the special orders to the wholesale distributors. Varied stocks of tobacco and cigarettes are—in many cases—purchased for cash daily from visiting wholesalers.

Gowns and Millinery.

A specialised business calling for shrewd buying and exceptionally good selling ability. Chief capital outlay is associated with an attractive shop window, adequate lighting and some simple wardrobes and fitting-rooms. Working hours are normal.

Ironmongery and Domestic Stores.

Essentially a masculine business, calling for wide knowledge of the trade and preferably backed with practical knowledge and a good general repairs department. Once it has become established, however, it can be developed into a miniature gold mine. A considerable standing stock is essential to real success and implies substantial capital resources or the capitalisation of profits for several years.

Coffee Stall.

In the right locality a coffee stall is often a very desirable small business, yielding a steady income. A cheerful ability to work all night and to sleep by day is generally necessary. Capital invested is small, the business is mobile and a fresh pitch can be sought if necessary.

Fried Fish.

An excellent and profitable business for a married couple. The chief capital outlay is the special frying stove, the trade is for cash over the counter. Ability to choose good frying fish and to cook it well are essential. Late hours are customarily worked—with a correspondingly late start in the morning.

Boot and Shoe Repairs.

An example of a specialised business, depending largely for success upon good material, excellent workmanship and moderate charges. The initial capital outlay on machinery can usually be spread over a period.

Landscape Gardener.

A specialised business, but one that is ideal for a man with the requisite knowledge. A journeyman landscape gardener could very well expect to succeed in any newly developed district. The capital involved is small, the work is done for cash on the customer's premises, and the client can always be persuaded to purchase direct the plants and materials needed.

During the first year the landscape gardener will improve his assets by planting seeds and raising plants for sale later on and gradually build up a valuable connection.

Private Library.

A private library—loaning volumes at about 2d. per book—is another profitable small business that can be worked up with a little capital, especially in newly developed districts where library facilities are limited.

Motor Car Repair and Maintenance.

This is another possible outlet for anyone with the requisite ability; this can be operated either from a small garage or as a door-to-door service.

Photography.

Photography—when done really well—or in a novel and artistic way is a useful line for the man or woman with the requisite ability, but it needs a good deal of advertising and personal recommendation to build up a sufficiently large practice to be a permanent success.

Numerous other examples could be given. For instance, piano tuning, house repairs, hairdressing, dressmaking and renovation; but in general the best and safest course is to take up a "bread and butter" business, and sell simple things that everyone wants, things that are bought day after day, all the year round.

HOW TO ACQUIRE A BUSINESS

There are several ways of starting a business; chief interest, however, centres around a shop. Small shop businesses can be started in two ways, first by purchasing a "going concern," that is, an existing business; secondly by starting an entirely new one. Lastly there are several door-to-door businesses that can profitably be developed.

Whatever the nature and size of a business there is a certain relationship between the turnover, profits and costs which must be observed if success is to be assured.

Relation between Turnover, Profit and Cost.

From the viewpoint of the small shopkeeper the best way to approach this vital matter is to look upon the business as a regular means of livelihood for himself and family. The item "Profits" must, therefore, be big enough to meet all his normal wants. On this basis "profit" is the difference between the entire cost of the business and the total cash receipts during any given period. Suppose for example, the shopkeeper needs say £6 per week for living expenses, then it follows that during a year the cash sales must be £312 more than the entire cost of the business.

Gross Profit.

On the average the gross profit is about 33⅓ per cent., that is to say an article sold for 1s. costs 8d.; consequently, to realise the required £312 the turnover—or sales—would have to be £936. But this is not all the story, because the shop itself costs something in rent, rates, taxes, light and heat, and there are incidental or "overhead" expenses for wrapping paper, string and other items.

These of course vary with every business, but taking an average figure of £200 for rents, light and other overhead costs, the relation between

Outgoings.	£ s. d.	Income.	£ s. d.
Rent, rates, etc.	100 0 0	Turnover	1,536 0 0
Overheads	100 0 0	Less cost of goods	1,024 0 0
Personal expenses or "Drawings"	312 0 0		
	£512 0 0		£512 0 0

Turnover, Cost and Profit can be set out and compared in tabular form as shown above.

Analysing a Business.

Any contemplated business—or business offer—can be analysed in this simple way to arrive at a clear idea of its possibilities. All that has to be done is to fill in the fixed items, for example, the actual rent, rates and so forth, the minimum safe amount for personal drawings and then ascertain the average gross profit, that is, the difference between cost of buying the goods and the price obtained for them. From this the absolute minimum turnover—on a cash basis—can be calculated.

The following table shows the turnover needed—at different rates of profit—to ensure a nominal "profit" of £300 per annum, reckoned as before, that is, with rent and overheads at £200, making the outgoings £500.

small turnover at a high profit, but in practice the reverse is generally the best, a large turnover with a small profit is preferable—the volume of trade is bigger, the number of customers is larger, and the risk is smaller because the loss of a few customers is more easily offset by new clients.

Practical Examples.

The foregoing is a simple way of judging a business, but it should be noted that an Accountant's methods of reckoning profits would be arrived at by different methods. Actual figures of various small businesses recently in the market are set out at foot of the page and will serve to give an idea of what can be expected in the way of capital outlay, cost and returns.

ACQUIRING A GOING CONCERN.

Existing businesses are generally acquired through a business transfer

	Gross Profit.				
	50 per cent.	40 per cent.	33 per cent.	25 per cent.	10 per cent.
Turnover	£1,000	£1,250	£1,500	£2,000	£5,000
Cost of goods	£500	£750	£1,000	£1,500	£4,500
Gross profit	£500	£500	£500	£500	£500

Examination of these figures shows that the turnover varies inversely as the profit rate to yield a given "profit" or net return.

The cost of goods also varies inversely with the profit rate but at a different ratio. For example, at 25 per cent. turnover has to be double that necessary at 50 per cent., but the cost of goods at 25 per cent. is three times the amount of corresponding goods at 50 per cent. profit.

At first glance it would seem that the best business would be one with a

agency (fees are charged) and the first thing to do on approaching any such agency is to ascertain the nature and amount of their fees, if any. If a deposit, "booking fee" or preliminary payment is demanded it would be wise to "think it over" before doing anything more.

Small businesses are sometimes advertised in the Press and direct negotiations are possible. Never buy any business no matter how tempting the offer without seeing the premises, the stock in hand, and finding out all

Business.	Purchase Price.	Rent P.A.	Turnover P.A.	Total Cost P.A.	Profit.
Confectionery	£50	£65	£520	£430	£90
Café (roadside)	£55	£52	£728	£643	£85
Confectionery and Tobacco	£165	£104	£1,300	£1,100	£200
" "	£150	£65	£860	£710	£150
Boot repairs	£50	£70	£520	£440	£80
Patent medicines	£175	£40	£624	£506	£118
Fish and chips	£160	£104	£1,560	£1,240	£320
Cooked foods	£260	£78	£3,640	£2,960	£680
Grocery	£200	£80	£2,080	£1,890	£190
Fancy cakes	£300	£110	£1,660	£1,310	£350
Ironmongery	£200	£125	£1,500	£1,250	£250
Coffee stall	£100	£6	£900	£600	£300
Greengrocery	£175	£80	£1,650	£1,420	£230

about the lease or agreement for letting.

Evidence of Turnover.

Do not set too much store on stated figures of sales or turnover—it is not here suggested that they are wrong, but a qualified accountant's report, after going over the books of the business, is the only safe guide. Failing other evidence, inspection of the invoices and receipts for goods purchased during a period is the best evidence of turnover.

Another point is that the letters S.A.V. mean "stock at valuation" and implies that the price asked does *not* include the stock, but that it will be valued and the purchaser will have to pay the amount assessed by the valuer, and also—in most cases—the valuer's fees!

One test of the worth of a business is to judge the reason for the vendor wanting to sell it; if the business is good, it needs a good reason on the part of the vendor to part with it; if in fact it is a bad business, it is folly to buy it.

Goodwill.

Much is often made of the advantage of a going concern and its "goodwill." In practice, however, one has to remember that with the good part of the business one has to buy also the bad, for example, soiled or out-of-date stock, unknown and bad debts and other things.

Another point to bear in mind is that some charges, such for example as rates, gas and electricity, are often levied on the occupier; hence when purchasing an existing business see the receipts for the payment of these items; do not accept a verbal assurance that they are or will be paid. There is little chance of redress if these items have not been paid by the outgoing tenant; they will in most cases have to be met by the newcomer.

Books of the Business.

By far the most satisfactory way of buying a going concern is to take it clear of all encumbrances as at an agreed date.

By this is meant that the outgoing owner pays everything due and outstanding up to the date of purchase. He also collects any moneys owing to the business up to the date of purchase. From that date, therefore, the new owner possesses the stock in hand, fixtures and fittings and so forth, all free of debt. Similarly, he is not owed anything by any of the customers; whatever they may in fact owe to the business before the date of purchase must be paid to the outgoing owner. Generally an arrangement is made between the parties to work together for a week or two and make the needful adjustments between them.

Who has the Books?

In such cases the outgoing owner is obviously entitled to retain his books, but the new owner should be handed receipts for the payments of such things as rent, rates, lighting and so forth up to date, or a proportionate amount can be deducted from the purchase price and the new owner then pays the said accounts.

Buying the Debts.

If a business is bought with all its debts and credits, some care should be taken to verify the accounts, first to see that there are no hidden claims—accounts not entered in the ledger and so forth. Also, on the other side, that the sums stated as owing are accepted and agreed by the persons liable to pay them.

If the amounts owing are at all considerable in amount, it may be well to ascertain from the debtors that they are willing to pay the new owner. It has been known in such cases that the debtor repudiates liability on the ground that his bargain was to pay the original owner, and that he is not liable, and cannot be made liable, to pay anyone else.

Purchase Money in Trust.

In some such cases the best solution of the difficulty would be for both the vendor and the purchaser of the business to conclude the transaction by leaving a part of the purchase money in trust for a limited period, pending settlement of outstanding debts.

It must also be remembered that the vendor is equally concerned so far as to see that the purchaser pays all liabilities of the business, otherwise he—the vendor—might have to pay them himself for the reasons given above.

When a business is bought with its debts, it is usual for an account to be taken between the parties as at date of purchase, and the original books—covering the period in question—should be retained by the purchaser.

Choice of Locality.

With so small a capital as £200 it is out of the question to expect to get a shop in the best "market" street, therefore seek out a location surrounded by dwellings occupied by a class likely to patronise the shop; or one that is easily reached by the largest number of people. Do not forget that all streets have a "good" and a "bad" side. Shops succeed on the good side and fail or hardly exist on the bad side. Find out all about this and the general neighbourhood before coming to any decision.

Another point to remember is that when a shop is taken, a certain outgoing commences at once and continues week by week as a permanent drain on the business.

The most practical way of starting is to acquire an inexpensive "lock-up" shop if one already owns or rents a residence not too far away and at a reasonable rental.

Shop and Residence.

If a shop with living quarters is obtained, there is the added risk that if the business fails badly the whole of one's possessions might be lost, and in any case there would be the expense of removal to a fresh residence.

This question of living on the shop premises is a very difficult matter to decide; there are many points for and against, with some businesses and some individuals the fact of always being at hand is an asset of considerable importance.

This being decided, the next point to consider is how long will the capital last? In other words, for how many weeks can the shop be open until all the capital has been absorbed?

Capital required to start a Business.

Obviously, to succeed, the business must make enough profit to be self-supporting before all the capital is exhausted, otherwise fresh capital will have to be found, which is generally a risky thing to do, or the business must be closed and the whole transaction will be almost or completely a dead loss. One example may suffice to make this point clear.

Assume a lock-up shop at an inclusive rental of 35s. per week, and that the owner has to draw £4 per week for personal expenses. Before a start can be made there will be preliminary expenses which must be paid in cash, and other liabilities incurred payable over a period. Taking the preliminary expenses at £20, the outgoings for three months should work out roughly as follows:—

Preliminary expenses	£20	0 0
Rent (inclusive)	21	0 0
Lighting and heating	2	0 0
Insurance	1	10 0
Advertising	15	0 0
Personal drawings	48	0 0
Miscellaneous	5	0 0
	£112	10 0

This leaves £88 available for some necessary expenditure on shop fittings, say, £18, leaving a net balance of £70 with which to buy stock during the three months.

Margin of Profit.

If the margin of profit were 50 per cent., that is, an article sold for 1s. costs 8d. to buy, it follows that if all the £70 worth of goods were sold during the three months the gross sales could not exceed £105, which would show a loss of £7, and it would appear that such a business could not run for three months on an initial capital of £200.

In practice, however, the position could be improved, thanks to the existence of credit trading. Provided the shopkeeper has a clean record and is a reasonably responsible person, most wholesalers will allow time in which to pay for goods, varying in different trades, but averaging about one month from time of delivery.

On this basis, therefore, if £70 worth of goods were ordered during the three months, it would only be necessary to pay for two-thirds of them during that time. Consequently, there would remain of the capital a sum of practically £22 less the loss of £7 10s., leaving £14 10s. net remaining.

Therefore, under the assumed figures, it would appear that retail sales of £8 15s. per week are not sufficient to turn the scale and make the business successful.

Increasing the Sales.

If, however, the sales can be pulled up to £15 per week steadily after the first three months, the business should become profitable, the second quarter working out as follows :—

Rent	. . .	£21 0 0
Lighting, etc.	. . .	2 0 0
Insurance	. . .	1 10 0
Advertising	. . .	15 0 0
Personal	. . .	48 0 0
Miscellaneous	. . .	5 0 0
		£92 10 0
Sales	. . .	£180 0 0
Less cost	. . .	102 0 0
Gross profit	. . .	£78 0 0

Therefore the drain on capital is now reduced to £14 10s., which is just covered by the balance of £14 10s. carried forward from the previous three months' trading.

Having thus arrived at a figure of £15 per week as the absolute minimum sales—or, say, £2 10s. per day—it is next necessary to get an idea of the average amount likely to be spent by each customer.

For example, if ladies' dresses at, say, an average of 10s. each were sold, it would be necessary to make sales to at least five customers every day of the week, and to attend to probably three to four times that number, because several people will call for each one that buys.

On the other hand, if, say, dry goods—confectionery or other low-priced articles were chiefly stocked, the average per customer might not exceed 2d. per head, and then it would be needful to serve 300 people per day. This might be far more likely of achievement than the former example, and certainly the risk would be lower : after all, this only works out at thirty per hour, or one customer every two minutes.

It is only by setting out the facts in this way—of course, inserting the actual figures where they are known—that it is possible to arrive at any sort of conclusion as to the wisdom or otherwise of going in for a particular business.

HOW TO START A NEW BUSINESS

The best way to start a new business is to decide the class of trade to be done, then select a suitable locality. Next find out from all the estate agents what premises are in the market, the rent and other charges to be met, and if there are any restrictions.

Pros and Cons.

In general, a novice is not advised to start a new business unless with the co-operation of someone with experience, both of business—as a going concern—and with the problems peculiar to any new business. All that has been explained previously must be carefully considered and borne in mind.

If, however, a person has reasonable knowledge of the selected business, the points in favour of starting a new business instead of purchasing a going concern are that the shop is fresh and clean, there is no dead or dirty stock to pay for, there are no previous traditions to follow, no " special " customers to study nor bad reputations to live down, which may or may not be the case with a " going concern."

Increased Initial Costs.

Against a new shop is the relatively heavy initial cost, the greater difficulty of acquiring credit, the necessity of finding suitable sources of supply, and generally getting the machinery of shopkeeping in going order.

No Bad or Concealed Debts.

One point stands out pre-eminently in favour of a new shop, and that is the complete absence of bad or concealed debts. One starts with a clean sheet, neither owing nor owed. When buying a " going concern " one buys a certain amount of assets, but one also buys a generally unknown liability for unpaid bills or doubtful book debts.

Probably the best course when it can be followed is to rent a shop already fitted up in a way that will be suitable ; this saves the heavy cost of shop front, fixtures and fittings, not to mention the cost of installing electric light, heating and other requirements.

Comparison between Costs of starting New Shop and acquiring a similar Going Concern.

	Going Concern.	New Business.
Purchase price .	£90 0 0	—
Stock at valuation	£85 0 0	£100 0 0
Rent per week .	£1 5 0	£16 0 0
Expenses per week	£6 5 0	£6 5 0
Turnover per week	£10 0 0	£10 0 0
Shop fittings .	—	£35 0 0
Light and heat per week . .	£0 15 0	£25 0 0
Advertising .	—	£15 0 0
Miscellaneous .	£0 5 0	£3 10 0
Total (purchase price and first week's outgoings . .	£193 10 0	£210 15 0

There does not appear to be much difference between the two propositions, but in practice the new shop would have to be rented for a week or so while being fitted up and equipped, which would increase the outgoings to probably £250.

FINANCE

If the capital is readily available in the form of cash, all is well. The best course is to open a local bank account and conserve the cash to the utmost.

Should more cash be required than is available, a loan in some form or other must be arranged. Banks will not offer much, or any, help unless valuable securities are deposited for three or four times the amount desired. Moneylenders should not in any circumstances be approached ; their rates of interest are far too high to allow of earning enough to pay off the loan.

If a good life insurance policy is available, the assurance company may be willing to advance a certain amount if the policy is lodged with them. The loan is repayable over an agreed period at a fixed rate of interest.

Another method of arranging for financial aid is possible if two or three friends of sufficient substance are prepared to stand as guarantors. Stated briefly, an assurance company provides the capital against the security of a life insurance—backed by the guarantors. Repayments are at a fixed rate or over a fixed period—all subject to individual arrangement. This is a very practical plan if the needful guarantors can be found. The question of raising money is fully dealt with on page 1533.

Partnerships.

Two or more persons can agree between themselves to start a business, but if they do so this becomes a partnership, and, amongst other things, implies that each individual is responsible for the acts and the debts of his partners. Partnerships should not be entertained unless the parties are well known to one another, and even then only under the advice of a good solicitor, who should be instructed to draw up a partnership deed, which must be agreed to and signed by all parties.

Limited Companies.

The formation and registration of companies are regulated by various Acts of Parliament, but from the point of view of the small trader a company has the advantage that it limits the liability of its members to the amount of his share-holding or the amount of shares he contracts to acquire. The cost of registering a small company varies, but is of the order of £20 to £25 and upwards.

Very often the registration of a small company has an adverse effect on the small trader's credit, because by the creation of the company he has limited his liability to the amount of his share-holding, which may be a purely nominal sum. When, therefore, the said company wants to place an order, either with a firm or an individual, the only asset possessed by the company may be the cash subscribed for shares; hence it offers little or no security for credit. This does not always apply, because the company as such may own something of value other than shares which would justify the desired credit.

Advertising.

Some amount of advertising is most desirable. The difficulty is to advise on the best media; the national Press is excellent, for example, if a postal sales business is being developed, but not for the small shopkeeper; a regular insertion in the local paper, and a display in the vestibule or on the screen of a popular local cinema are perhaps the best. Circulars are of very doubtful value; in many cases it will pay to consult a firm of advertising agents who specialise in the needs of the small trader.

Licences and Restrictions.

Before finally deciding on any business, it is well to ascertain the nature and effect of any licences that may have to be acquired, or restrictions that are imposed by Government or local Acts.

For example, excise licences are required to carry on such trades as that of an auctioneer, or to sell patent medicines, playing cards, tobacco, wines and spirits, to kill game, to act as a pedlar and to carry on numerous other avocations.

For instance, a dealer in game needs an excise licence and another issued by the Justices of the Peace. Particulars can be had from the local Customs and Excise Officer, or in many places from the Income Tax office. Particulars of justices' licences can usually be had from the clerk at the local town hall or county court.

There are numerous restrictions on traders: those imposed by the Shops Acts largely regulate hours of opening, the provision of holidays for assistants, and so forth. If any kind of manufacturing work is carried on, the provisions of the Factory Acts must be complied with, while if anyone is employed—either for part or whole time—the employer becomes liable to make provision for the said employee if an accident occurs. This risk is best covered by insurance, the premium for which is often based on a sliding scale, governed by the amount paid in wages during a year or other agreed period. This is fair and equitable to all concerned, but in any case some adequate insurance should be taken up by all employers.

Despite the apparent irksomeness of these licences and restrictions, it will in most cases be found that there is good reason for them, and in any case it is necessary to comply with all their requirements.

Income Tax.

The amounts payable under this heading are regulated by the provisions of the Finance Acts, and vary from time to time. A return will have to be made whether there is anything to be paid or not, but in all probability the profits of a small business, after deduction of all statutory allowances, will not be sufficient to make any payment necessary. The trader is strongly urged to engage a fully qualified chartered accountant to prepare the returns; the fee for this service is very modest and will ensure the preparation of a correct—but the most favourable—return.

BOOK-KEEPING

Even in the smallest business it is necessary to keep proper books and to record systematically every transaction in money or money's worth. The system known as "double entry" is the most satisfactory, and is in universal use; it records each transaction in at least two accounts, one the debtor and the other the creditor. The fundamental rule is "credit the account which receives and debit the account which gives."

For example, the trader A. buys goods valued at £5 from B. & Co. and debits the goods account with £5. This debtor entry is counteracted by crediting B. & Co.'s account with the same amount, viz., £5. Suppose the trader pays the whole or part of the sum due to B. & Co., say, one-half the amount, the trader then debits B. & Co.'s account with £2 10s., and credits his own cash account with £2 10s.

Debit and Credit.

Treating all transactions in the same way, the result is that at the end of the week or other period the total of all the "debits" will equal the total of all the "credits," and is a proof of the correctness of the entries. An individual account does not necessarily have the same total on each side, but it is "balanced" when required by inserting an item to "balance" it on the debit or credit side as may be necessary to bring both sides to the same total.

For example, in the case of B. & Co.'s account in the trader's book, the debit side will show £5, the credit side £2 10s., therefore to balance the account a further amount of £2 10s. must be entered on the credit side. This makes a total of £5 on each side, but as the "balance" item is on the credit side, it infers that B. & Co. is a creditor for £2 10s., because B. & Co. have given more than they have received; hence the trader is a debtor to that firm for the amount of the unpaid balance.

Hence, by adding together all the credit balances, the trader can see at a glance just how much he owes. Accounts for the supply of gas, electricity, the rates, or anything else the trader has to pay for, should be treated in the same way.

Creditors.

In the same way the amounts (if any) due to the trader will appear as debit balances, and the sum of all such items represents the total amount due to the trader from his debtors.

In most cases it is inconvenient to make direct entries into the ledger, consequently it is usual to record all the transactions in a book of first entry and post from it to the book of final entry—that is, the ledger.

The following books are customarily kept, and should be used as requisite by every small trader who wishes to have an accurate record of all his business transactions.

Cash Book.

In this one enters all cash and bank transactions. A convenient ruling has three cash columns on the right-hand side used for items paid into the bank, office cash or petty cash, and for discounts, which, being a concession in lieu of cash, are treated as cash.

The three columns on the left-hand side are for the debtor or receipts items.

Amounts received are entered in the bank or petty cash columns as requisite, while payments are entered on the opposite side.

Purchases Book.

This should contain particulars of all goods purchased on credit. The total is the amount of goods received and has to be debited in the ledger, consequently each personal account is credited.

Sales Book.

This should contain a record of all goods sold on credit. The total is the amount of goods given out, or credited in the ledger, consequently each of these personal accounts is debited.

The Journal.

This book is used for miscellaneous transactions and adjustments. In some businesses other books of first entry may be needed, but the principle is the same; that is, transactions are entered in them as they occur, under date order; these items are then sorted out at monthly or other convenient and regular periods, and posted in the ledger under their respective accounts. In many cases a journal alone will suffice for all first entry items.

Balancing the Books.

To balance the books, first see that everything has been correctly posted in the ledger, then take a trial balance to ascertain that debits equal credits. If not, seek and remedy the fault, which may, for example, be a wrong entry, incorrect extension of an item, or an error in casting or adding up the columns of figures. The ledger is then balanced.

Trading Account.

At the end of the year or other convenient period the ledger is balanced. The stock on hand is posted to a trading account on the credit side, and the various other items will all be brought into the reckoning to show the true financial state of the business. This aspect of book-keeping is seldom fully understood by the small trader, and it will be found well worth while to secure the services of a professional chartered accountant, who for a modest fee will check the books and prepare the trading accounts and balance sheet.

The procedure is, unfortunately, considered an unnecessary expense by the trader, who, however, will find it is a case of "penny wise, pound foolish," because an accountant's fees are generally more than counterbalanced by savings on the Income Tax returns, which, as everyone knows, are awkward things to deal with by the uninitiated, whereas the professional accountant is fully acquainted with all the allowances and off-sets that the law allows to the trader; hence the saving secured by employing an auditor for the annual statement of affairs.

Purchases Book.

Page 1										Page 2				
	1934		s.	d.	£	s.	d.					s.	d.	£	s.	d.
Folio	August 1st									Brought fwd.				3	7	4
101	Summit		1	8						August 5th						
	do.		3	4					106	Wisbey		14	2			
	do.		2	9	0	7	9									
106	Wisbey				1	2	6									
	August 2nd															
108	Clements		2	9												
	do.		1	5												
	August 3rd															
	J. Jones				1	7	4									
101	Summit		3	4												
	do.		1	8												
	do.		4	9	0	9	9									
	Forward				£3	7	4									

Choice of Books.

Simple, inexpensive books will suffice for the needs of most small businesses, but, if preferred, a loose-leaf ledger and journal could be used, especially if there are likely to be a large number of separate entries. The advantage of such books is that new leaves can be added at any time and the full ones removed and stored in a binding case or box. Whatever books are kept, the primary requirements are accuracy, completeness and regularity. Accounts (if any) payable by customers should always be rendered in detail and sent out with great regularity, accompanied when needful by a courteous but firm request for payment.

Practical Book-keeping.

The foregoing remarks cover the general principles of book-keeping. It would obviously be impossible to give details applicable to every business, but the following specimens of an actual small business, dealing in tobacco, cigarettes, newspapers, magazines and a small lending library, may be taken as a sound representative guide.

PURCHASES BOOK

In this book are recorded all purchases, either for cash or credit. A convenient ruling is shown at the top of the page.

Entries are made daily in the purchases book. Small items from the same firm of less than £1 are entered separately, and the total entered in the cash column. Every week or month the purchase items are carried to a *ledger*, conveniently ruled as shown at foot of this page.

When the purchase items are entered in the ledger, the page number of the purchases book is entered in the column marked "folio." Similarly, in the purchases book the page number of the ledger containing the account is entered in the folio column in the purchases book.

At the end of the month the total of goods purchased is entered up, and the record of payment by cheque (or cash) entered on the opposite side, together with any discount that may be allowed.

Cash Book.

This is a simple book, ruled as under:—

				£	s.	d.
Aug.	3	Sales, cash		3	2	6
		,, cheque		1	3	4
		J. Jones				
	4	Cash sales		2	14	3
		Postal order			2	6
		(Robertson)				

In this book are recorded all moneys received by the business.

Petty Cash Book.

This is similarly ruled to the cash

Ledger.

Page 101										Page 101				
	The Summit Co. Ltd., 4000 Fare Street, London, E.1.													
1934		Folio	£	s.	d.	1934					Folio	£	s.	d.
Sept. 1	By cheque	2	2	8	6	Aug.	1	To goods			1		7	9
	,, discount			1	4	,,	3	,,			1	9	9	
						,,	10	,,			3	10	7	
						,,	17	,,			3	7	6	
						,,	21	,,			6	14	3	
			£2	9	10			Total (at end of month)				£2	9	10

book. In it are recorded all small disbursements in cash.

Sales Book.

This is exactly the same in appearance as the purchases book, but it is used to record all goods sold on credit to customers, and later on the totals are entered on a billhead and sent out to the customer.

A sales ledger, similar to the bought ledger, is used to record the totals and the payments received. The following show specimen entries.

Sales Ledger.

Page 21   R Robertson, Esq.,   The Mill, Sitcombe Road.   Page 21

	1934			£	s.	d.					£	s.	d.
Aug.	1	To goods	16	–	3	4	Sept.	1st	By cash	.	–	19	1
,,	2	,,	16	–	3	6							
,,	4	,,	16	–	3	9							
,,	19	,,	23	–	5	4							
,,	27	,,	30	–	3	2							
				–	19	1					–	19	1

Sales Book.

Page 16

	1934			s.	d.		£	s.	d.
21	Aug. 1st	Robertson		1	3				
27	,, 2	,,		2	1		–	19	2
21	,, 2	Phillips		3	6		–	3	6
21	,, 4	Robertson		1	3				
		Do.		2	6		–	3	9

Details of the individual items sold are generally entered at the time the goods are ordered or taken away—in a day book; that is, a simple notebook ruled like the cash book.

Comprehensive Booking.

A very convenient and practical method of keeping books, especially for the small trader, is known as the " Kwik-an-Eeze " business account book, published by Jas. McQueen Ltd., Moat Road, Leicester. It costs 4s. 6d., and comprises a complete weekly analysis of receipts and payments entered under convenient headings; for example, " Rent," " Rates," " Petty Cash," " Payments for other than Stock," etc. One sheet is used for each week; then at the end of a period these items are posted to a second part of the same book, called the private ledger, which contains a concise summary of the weekly analysis. A third section of the same book, called the profit and loss account, is provided, ruled in convenient form and printed in readiness to receive the separate items—in total—derived from the previous pages.

Finally, there is a balance sheet, all ready printed and only requiring the appropriate totals to be filled in. This book, in conjunction with a purchases and sales books and a ledger, would comprise a most efficient, easy to keep set of books suitable for practically any business.

BOOKBINDING IN LEATHER

THE following notes relating to bookbinding in leather are intended to amplify and simplify the instructions given in the article on page 1301

The book should be sewn in the manner outlined, but if obtainable hemp should be used in place of cord as it frays out more softly. A stronger method of fixing the endpapers is to paste a folded coloured sheet on to a folded white, and, when dry, sew it on to the book; the thread in this case passing through the fold of the white paper leaving the coloured fold, which must be outside, as the ultimate board paper.

The back of the book should now be treated to a thin coating of glue, which should be well rubbed in between the sections and as soon as this is dry, but before it has had time to become brittle, the concave in the front edge should be formed. This is best done by tapping the back gently with a hammer first on one side and then on the other.

Correct Method of backing a Book.

The correct method of backing a book, which is the next and perhaps the most important operation, is as follows. Place a backing board on either side of the book, the space between the clean edge of the board and the joint being the same as the thickness of the board which is to be used for the cover. Now lower gently into the press, and only when it is screwed up tightly should the book be hammered lightly into shape. If the book is not gripped firmly the hammer blows will cause ugly dents to appear—an undesirable disfigurement when the book is open—and may even split the paper.

The cover boards should now be selected from good hard millboard, lined on one side with a thin paper—using paste—and, when dry, cut to the length of the book and the width from the inside of the joint to the front edge of the book. They may now be attached in the manner described, taking care that the lining is towards the book. This lining plays an important part, as the warping it creates compensates for the pull of the leather covering which must contract as it dries.

Cutting must, of necessity, be the next process and may be performed in the manner described. It is important to remember, however, that when cutting the head and tail the actual cutting should only take place on the forward movement. As a precaution it is advisable to raise the plough slightly on the return for, if the knife should cut towards the back, it will tear pieces of paper away from the fold of the sections.

Lining up.

Headbands should now be glued into position and the book will be ready for " lining up."

Glue a layer of brown paper on to the back of the book, trimming it neatly to the joint but allowing a little to project at each end. Again glue the back—now lined—this time more thickly, and quickly place another piece of paper—usually about 12 inches wide—into position as if to " line up " again. Fold it back to the joint and, lifting it from the back, fold a second time in the same direction, thus bringing the section, which has collected a layer of glue from the back, inwards. This action gives a hollow with two thicknesses of paper on one side and one on the other. Now lightly glue the back and place the hollow—single thickness downward—into position on the back. It now only remains to rub the whole lining down, trim the projecting paper level with the headbands, slit the hollow up about ½ inch at each end, nick the corner of the back of the boards and the book is ready for covering.

Covering.

When covering, in the manner already outlined, several points should be remembered. The leather should be pasted twice, on the first occasion allowing it to soak until it has become pliable. When mitreing the turned-in corners an overlap should be allowed for the contraction of the leather when drying and, for the same reason a fullness of leather should be worked over the joint.

BUILDING YOUR OWN BUNGALOW

AMONG the many readers of PRACTICAL ENQUIRE WITHIN who have been able to make improvements in their homes themselves, there are without doubt some who have the greater ambition to build their own house from start to finish, on their own plot of ground, to suit their own needs.

In this article we give a design for a small bungalow suitable for the usual building plot, describe how it is built, and discuss the materials to be used.

Such a design should not be used indiscriminately. It should be adapted to the site, particularly considering the aspect and also noting adjoining buildings. Perhaps, for instance, the site has a wide frontage, windows might then be suitably placed in the side walls.

It will be noticed that the plan and all the building forms are quite simple. This is a most desirable quality in any case, but it is of the utmost importance if one is actually to build the house by one's own labour. Space is not wasted in passages; at the same time the comfort of the living room is not destroyed by doors on several sides, as too often is the case with bungalows. Here a screen would shut off any draught there might be in cold weather from the front door.

Before leaving the subject of plans, it should be pointed out that the local Council—the Borough Council, the Urban or the Rural District Councils, as the case may be—will require a plan, block plan, section and elevations to be submitted before the work is started, from which the surveyor can see if the building bye-laws will be complied with. In particular, the drainage will have to be shown in detail. This plan should be sent to the council's surveyor. When the plans are passed, forms will be sent which must be returned to the council when various stages of the building are reached. Eventually, when the house is finished, a habitation certificate must be applied for saying the house is fit for occupation.

SELECTION OF SITE

It would be of little value to enumerate the qualities possessed by the ideal site, because the choice is generally limited either by what land is available in the locality in which one must live, by the amount one can spend or by some other over-riding consideration.

Perhaps a more useful method of treating the subject would be to point out the possible drawbacks so that a plot of land is not purchased and then later on found to offer such difficulties

Fig. 1.—THE FINISHED BUNGALOW.

that either a building of the type wanted cannot be put up upon it at all, or that the cost of building would be increased beyond what was anticipated.

POINTS TO LOOK FOR ON THE SITE
Levels.

A level site is generally the least costly to build upon. On the other hand, varying levels in a garden, particularly if a large one, are very attractive. A site with moderate slopes, and having a fairly level piece where the house can suitably be built, will be the best of all. The levels have an important bearing on the drainage. If the site falls rapidly from the road and the sewers under the road are not deep, it may be difficult, or even impossible, to drain the house.

Again, the levels of the ground may make it necessary to place the house some distance back from the road—possibly an advantage in these days of noise and dust from the traffic, but extra cost is entailed not only in paths but in extra lengths of all the service pipes—gas, water, electric cable and drains.

Nature of the Soil.

The depth of the foundations and the consequent expense of excavation will depend to some extent upon the nature of the soil. There may be in unusual cases some hidden trouble such as an old gravel pit or pond filled in largely with rubbish, perhaps many years ago, and foundations of buildings would have to be carried right down to the natural earth. Especial caution should be taken when the plot is one of a few unbuilt on and there seems no apparent reason for its having been left.

Other points to look at on the site itself are whether there are any expenses to be incurred in cutting down trees, or otherwise clearing the site, whether the garden would be too large or too small, what fencing would be required. On the latter point, it should be ascertained which fences must be put up by the purchaser and which by the adjoining owners.

Drainage.

The value of a building site for a small house is largely affected by the provision made for drainage, and so it is important to find out if there is main drainage and whether the sewer is of reasonable depth, that is, deep enough to give a sufficient fall for the house drains and not so deep as to need especially deep digging for the drains.

If there is no main drainage, careful enquiries should be made of the methods adopted in the neighbourhood and considered satisfactory by the sanitary authority. It might be necessary to put in a small sewage-disposal plant, and this would mean a substantial increase in the money to be expended.

Water and Other Supplies.

It should be ascertained whether water, gas and electric supplies are available.

Restrictions on the Site.

It is quite a mistake to think you can do what you like with a piece of land even if it is your own freehold. There are often restrictions running with the land as to the sort of house that can be built, its cost, and even the chief materials of which it may be built. Particulars of these restrictions can be ascertained from the owner or the estate agent.

Then there will probably be a town-planning scheme of the local council which will limit the number of houses to the acre and the area of the site that can be built on in relation to the area to be left as open space. Road widening may also be contemplated, which may involve the acquisition by the council of some of the land. Information about these points can be obtained at the council offices.

Road Charges.

If the building estate is a new one and the roads have not been taken over by the highway authority, there may be road charges to pay. If the frontage is large, and particularly if the site is at the corner of two roads, the cost to the frontager of making up the roads may be a substantial sum of money. It is becoming a frequent practice for estate developers to include the road charges in the purchase price of the land.

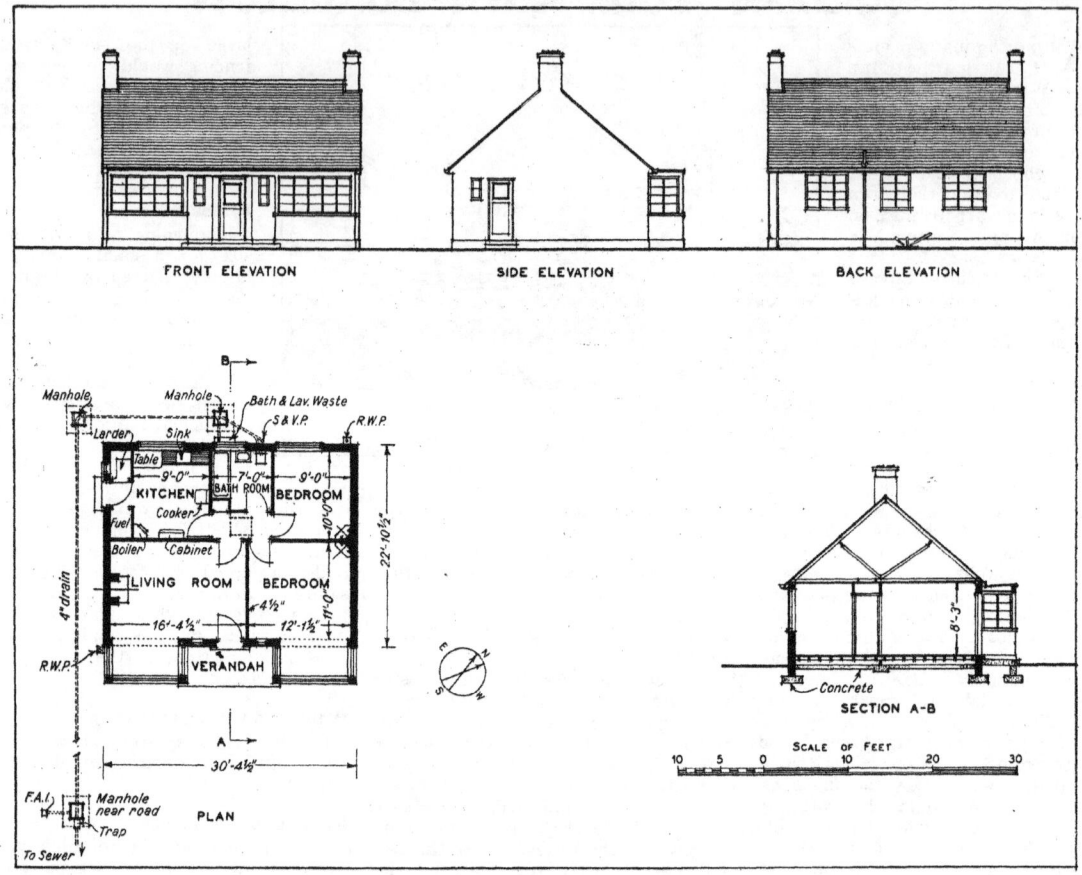

Fig. 2.—Design for a Small Bungalow.

Having decided that the land is suitable and of sufficient size for the desired house, and having agreed the price, the next question is

How to purchase the Land.

The important point at this stage is to make sure that the title of the vendor to the land is a good one. A solicitor should be instructed to investigate the title. If a building society or an insurance company is advancing money on the security of the land, they will engage a solicitor to examine the title, and this should be sufficient for a purchaser. The point to be remembered is that if there is a flaw in the title it may be exceedingly difficult to sell the property later on, apart from the risk of a rightful owner turning up.

A contract to purchase should not be signed before a solicitor is consulted, unless the words are inserted "subject to the approval of title by purchaser's solicitor."

The solicitor will advise on the steps to be taken in completing the purchase.

GENERAL NOTES ON PROCESSES AND MATERIALS

In the following notes the processes and materials relating to house or bungalow building are dealt with in approximately the order in which the work would be carried out. A later section describes the actual constructional work in connection with the bungalow shown in Fig. 1.

Foundations.

When the main lines of the building have been set out on the site, excavation for the foundations is commenced. Arrange beforehand where surplus earth is to be carted to, double handling is a waste of labour. Keep the top vegetable soil separate from the rest, it will be valuable for the garden later on.

The depth of the foundation will depend on the nature of the soil. Generally 2 feet deep from the surface will suffice, but if the ground is a clay liable to dry up in hot weather, a depth of about 3 feet is desirable.

Brickwork.

The bricks used for the walling will depend upon the price in the district in which the building is to be built. Cost of cartage is an important item in building costs, and it will generally be found cheaper to use local material. Over a large part of England, Fletton bricks from the Peterborough neighbourhood are principally used for general walling, but if it is a brick district, the local brick, if hard, well burnt and good shape, would probably compete favourably in price.

If a brick facing is desired, there is a wide range of choice; the best are the hand-made sand-faced bricks, but these are expensive. Stock bricks, obtainable in various colours, are cheaper, or if Flettons are to be used, the rustic Fletton is specially made for facings, and is a much more attractive brick in appearance than the ordinary Fletton.

If the wall is to be cemented or rough cast on the outside, facing bricks will not be required. The joints should be left rough, to give a good hold for the cement work.

Site Concrete.

When the brickwork is built up to

the ground level the site within the walls should be cleared and the ground dug down to the required level for laying the bed of concrete over the whole of the site. This concrete is usually 5 inches thick, smoothed on the surface. It is well to lay it at an early stage, as it forms a dry platform on which the other parts of the building can be set out.

The Main Internal Walls.

These should be built of brickwork, half brick (that is 4½ inches) thick. They can be built on the site concrete. If they have to carry an upper floor or any great weight, it is usual to increase the thickness of the concrete under them.

Other partitions may be in breeze concrete blocks, 2 inches thick for short lengths of partitions, and 3 inches thick for the longer ones. The partitions should be bonded into the outside walls. Wood-framed partitions covered with wall board may be preferred.

Damp Courses.

The best damp course for a small building is slate laid in two courses in Portland cement mortar, the courses " breaking joint." It is a mistake to economise and use a tarred felt. It will not last, and trouble from damp will be well-nigh impossible to correct later on. There are several types of bituminous damp courses on the market which are suitable for the purpose.

The damp course should be laid at a level of 6 inches above the ground outside, and beneath the lowest timbers of the ground floor. If a part of the floor is solid, such as for tiles, care must be taken to see that the damp course is so arranged that no timber comes against the walling in contact with the soil, or rot is bound to occur.

Ventilation.

Air bricks must be inserted in the walls to give a through current of air under every part of the floor. The sleeper walls (those carrying the ground floor) must be built honeycombed.

Windows.

These can be obtained ready made. Windows in steel of standard sizes, already fitted to wood frames, may be purchased. Those shown on the drawings are of standard size. A variety of opening parts is offered from which a suitable selection for all requirements can be made. The bay windows shown are made up of standard steel windows in wood frames fixed to 4 × 4-inch wood posts at the angles. The sills of these standard windows are made sufficiently wide not to require any stone or tile sills as well.

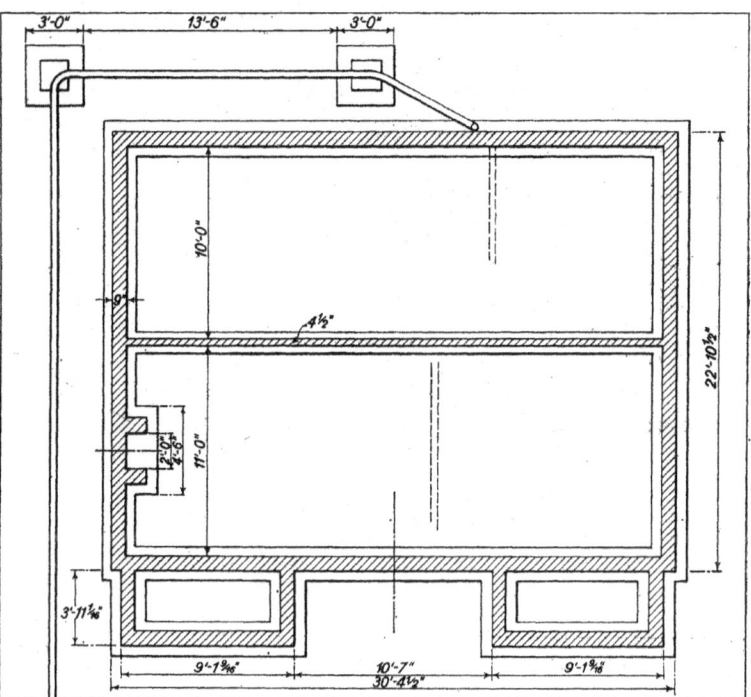

*Fig. 3.—*Foundation and Drainage Plan.

Wooden Window Boards or Tile Sills.

Window boards of wood are fitted on the inside, or, if preferred, tile sills may be used instead, they are more difficult to form, but they are easily kept clean and, unlike wood, require no painting. Plaster can be carried right back to the window frame on the two sides and head.

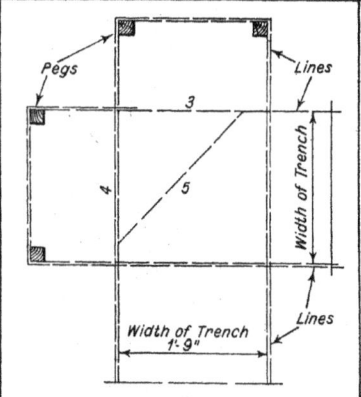

*Figs. 4 and 5.—*Showing Pegs at Corner for Setting out Site and the 3 : 4 : 5 Method of Checking for Right Angles.

The dimensions should be taken to the outside face of the peg and the line stretched along these faces to avoid confusion.

Doors.

There is a big selection of ready-made doors offered by builders' merchants, some already fitted to frames. Choose the simple patterns and keep the same character throughout the house, not vertical panels in one room and horizontal in another. Do not be tempted to get thin doors, the extra few shillings for a 1¾-inch door are well worth it. Doors that twist and will not shut properly are exasperating. If mortise locks are required, the doors must be thick enough to receive them.

The doors themselves will not be hung until a later stage of the building, but the frames will be required.

Roof.

When the walls are built up to the top of the rooms a wall plate is bedded on the walls to receive the rafters. The roof will have been carefully set out on the ground and the rafters cut to the proper sizes with the suitable forms to fit to the wall plates and ridge. The two end pairs of rafters will be erected and carefully trued up, not forgetting to " tie " them in at the feet to prevent them spreading outwards. The remainder of the rafters can then be put up at 12-inch or 13-inch intervals. The joists for the ceiling should be laid by the sides of the rafters, and on the same wall plate, and rafters and joists

BUILDING YOUR OWN BUNGALOW

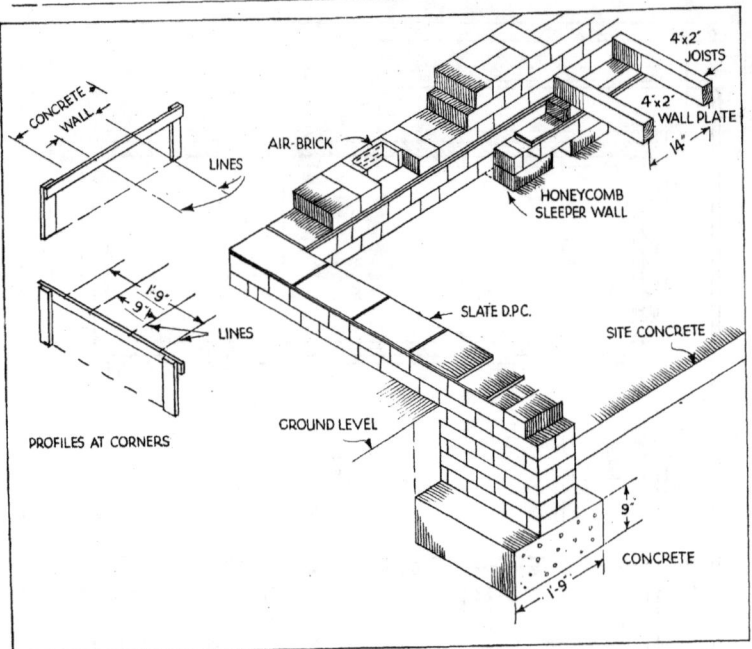

Fig. 6.—Isometric Sketch of Profiles, Concrete Wall, Site of Concrete, Slate Damp-proof Course and Joists.

should be nailed together and both of them to the plate.

Purlins should be fitted to the underside of the rafters, half-way up their length, built into the walls at each end and strutted up from the main internal walls—not from the ceiling joists—every 6 feet of their length.

Tiling.

There are several kinds of material for covering the roof—slates, tiles, concrete tiles and asbestos are the chief of them. Slates are out of favour for house roofs now, their general use a few years ago was on account of their relative cheapness as compared with tiles. This does not apply in the same degree now, and tiles give the brightness of colour so much favoured to-day.

Tiles may be obtained of several forms and many colours. The simplest are known as plain tiles, about 10½ × 6 inches. They are hung by nibs, formed on the underside, to wood battens nailed to the backs of the rafters, or to the ledges of feather-edge boarding. One course in five should also be nailed. For plain tiles the pitch of the roof should not be less than 40 degrees with the horizon. Pantiles have a curved surface, they are larger than plain tiles. They give an attractive appearance, but they are difficult to keep watertight in exposed situations. The pitch of the roof is often less than for plain tiles, but it is inadvisable to reduce it much, or there may be trouble in keeping water out. Many old pantiled roofs are pointed in cement. An improved pattern of pantile is now on the market that is quite sound, but these tiles are expensive.

There are also several good types of interlocking tiles obtainable at moderate cost.

Glazed tiles in various colours of each of the types mentioned are becoming increasingly popular.

Concrete Tiles.

These are now much used both in the

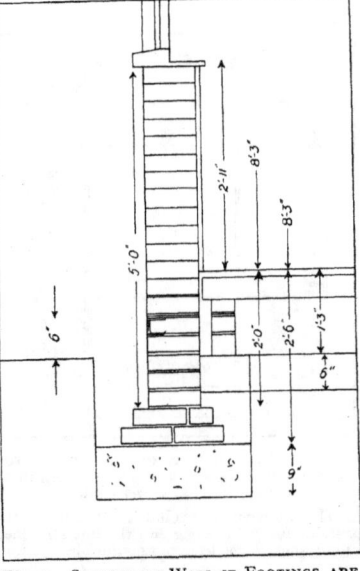

Fig. 7.—Section of Wall if Footings are Required.

ordinary reds and in greens and browns. They are hung just like the burnt clay tiles.

Asbestos Cement.

A cheap and light form of roof covering. It does not possess the good reputation of tiles, largely because of the terrible colour of the early product and from the thinness of the material and its large scale, upsetting the general scale of the building. The russet-brown asbestos pantiles have overcome these drawbacks, but they do not readily acquire the "weathered" appearance of either clay or concrete tiles.

The flat roof should be formed with joists laid level, with firring pieces to give a fall, covered with 1-inch unplaned boarding and completed with lead or zinc or one of the asphalte types of roof, of which there are several kinds available. Asphalte itself forms one of the best coverings for a flat roof, but for a single small roof it would hardly prove economical unless other work was in hand close by.

Loft and Skylight.

There would be useful storage space in the loft, it would be of much greater value if a skylight was placed in the rear slope of the roof. The simplest and best form of skylight is a cast-iron one made especially for fixing in roof slopes. It would be screwed to the rafters trimmed to receive it, and only a strip of lead would be needed at the top and at the bottom of the skylight, not at the sides.

A lifting trap-door should be formed in the ceiling or, if light is desired in the small passage, the trap-door could be glazed. A certain area, according to one's needs, should be boarded in the loft. The boarding should be nailed down before the plastering of the ceiling is carried out, or it will be jarred and may fall.

Alternatives to the skylight are windows in the gable walls, but with chimneys in the centre they could not easily be provided, or, if only a little light is wanted, a few glass tiles could be fitted in with the ordinary tiles.

Chimneys.

After the timbering of the roof has been put up, and before the tiling is laid, the gable ends would be built up. As there are chimney stacks in the gable, it would be best to build them in brickwork, otherwise timber framing covered outside with tiles or weather boarding would be sufficient for the purpose. The chimney stacks would be built in with the walling, the foundation being widened out to receive the extra brickwork. The opening for the fireplace would be covered over with a concrete lintel. The flues should be built with easy bends and rendered smoothly on the inside in cement.

1572

The stack should be carried up 3 feet above the ridge of the roof.

The flues for the gas fires in the bedrooms need not be in brickwork, special precast concrete blocks with small flues sufficient to take away the fumes from the fires can be bought. The stack is shown in brickwork on the drawing to match the stack at the other end of the roof. It would spoil the appearance if one stack were larger than the other. There will be no necessity to form a hearth for the gas fires, they are now made as panels let in flush with the wall and fixed a few inches above the floor.

The flue from the hot-water boiler should be carried in an upward slope to the outer wall and then bent upward to combine with the living-room flue in one chimney stack. If the bend is a quick one, a soot door should be built in the outer wall for cleaning purposes where the fire takes an upward direction.

The type of fire for the living-room is a question of taste, a simple design in brickwork with a firebrick back and an iron bottom and fret and a brick hearth will be economical and will look homely.

The joint between the chimney stacks and the roof may be formed in lead, but a simple and satisfactory method is to form the angle in cement and bed narrow strips of tiles in the cement placed at an angle.

Services.

When the building has been covered in, the services—water, gas and electric installations—are put in.

Several articles on these subjects have appeared previously, to which the reader is referred. It is, of course, advisable wherever possible to group the sanitary fittings of the house together to reduce the plumbing work. This will be noticed in the plan, Fig. 2, where sink, bath, lavatory basin and water closet are grouped, needing only short connections for hot and cold water and only one gulley to the drains.

Drains.

While the walls and roof are being finished off, the drains will be laid. See the article on drainage, p. 833.

Floors.

The floors will then be laid. The boarding should be protected by sawdust laid down, or in some other suitable way, to save permanent damage.

Plastering.

The next stage will be the plastering, or alternatively one of the many kinds of wall boards would be used instead. If the house is being built by non-professional labour, the use of a wall board would be preferable. Walls

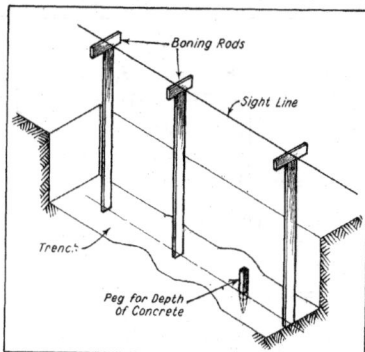

Fig. 8.—Levelling Trench with Boning Rods.

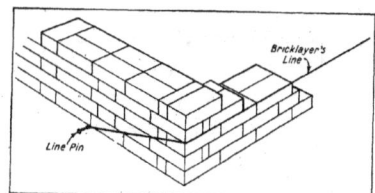

Fig. 9.—Garden Wall Bond.

must be battened first, the battens being arranged to suit the sizes of the boards, as no edge must be without its backing of wood. Edges should be covered with wood strips, because the wall boards expand or contract and the joints will open and close, cracking any paper covering put on the boards, and appearing very unsightly.

Joinery will now be proceeded with, cupboards fitted, doors hung, architraves, skirtings and picture rails fixed. All the other trades will complete their work, and finally the painter will hold the field with the decoration. Such

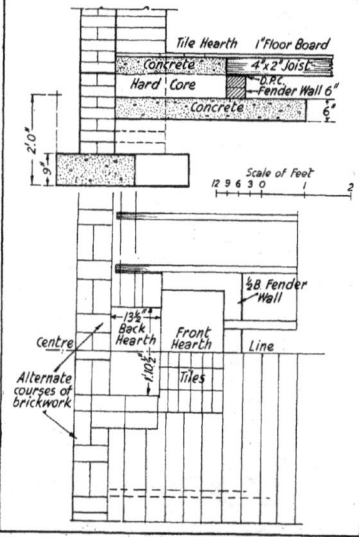

Fig. 10.—Detail of Fireplace Opening and Arrangement of Joists.

good colours may now be had that it will be worth while to choose an attractive scheme for each of the rooms.

THE CONSTRUCTION OF A BUNGALOW

The quantities, etc., given here are for the construction of the bungalow shown in Fig. 1. This should be built for £480 to £540, according to district.

Setting out the Foundations.

Setting out the foundations for a small bungalow or other small building will be found to be a simple matter.

Before commencing any operation, the eighth-scale drawings should be carefully examined and their dimensions checked. The dimensions running across the width should be added up to find if they agree with the overall dimensions, as sometimes a discrepancy occurs. This also applies to the dimensions running from back to front.

The first thing to do is correctly to peg out the corners of the building. It is usual to assume a base line, which is taken as the building line, or the main front wall, and to set out all the other walls from this line. Fig. 3 is the foundation plan.

In setting out, dimensions should be taken to the outside face of the peg and the line stretched along those faces to avoid confusion. Right angles are obtained by the use of a square and checked by measurement; a right angle or square given by the ratio of sides being 3 : 4 : 5, known as the 3-4-5 method (see Fig. 4).

Levelling the Surface.

Levelling for the surface excavation is obtained by fixing a series of pegs over the site at convenient intervals with their tops all level or alternatively with the levels marked on their sides. These are fixed at the required depth of the excavation, or the excavation may be taken below or kept above the top of the pegs a certain amount.

The turf is taken off in strips 3 feet by 1 foot, rolled and stacked, and used afterwards in making lawns, etc.

The vegetable soil is next removed to a depth of one "spit," or spade depth, about 9 inches.

Surface Excavation.

The area of the surface excavation is taken to the outside edge of the trenches, and measures 32 feet 10½ inches by 25 feet 4½ inches, giving a superficial area of 93 super yards. Adding the area of the bays and verandah, the total area is 106 super yards, approximately.

Trench Work.

The trenches for the foundations are next set out by erecting profiles at the corners of the building at a safe

BUILDING YOUR OWN BUNGALOW

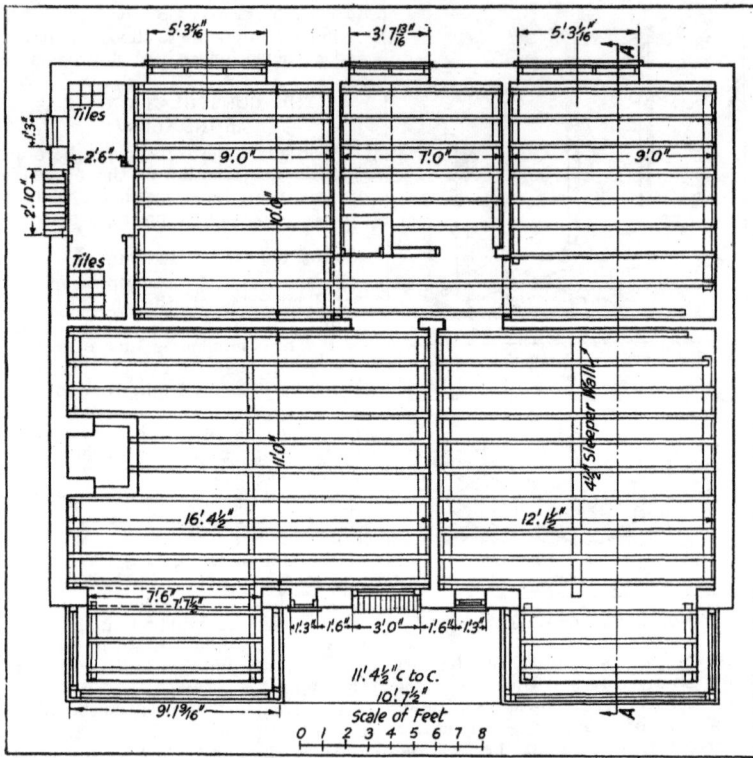

Fig. 11.—Ground Floor Plan.

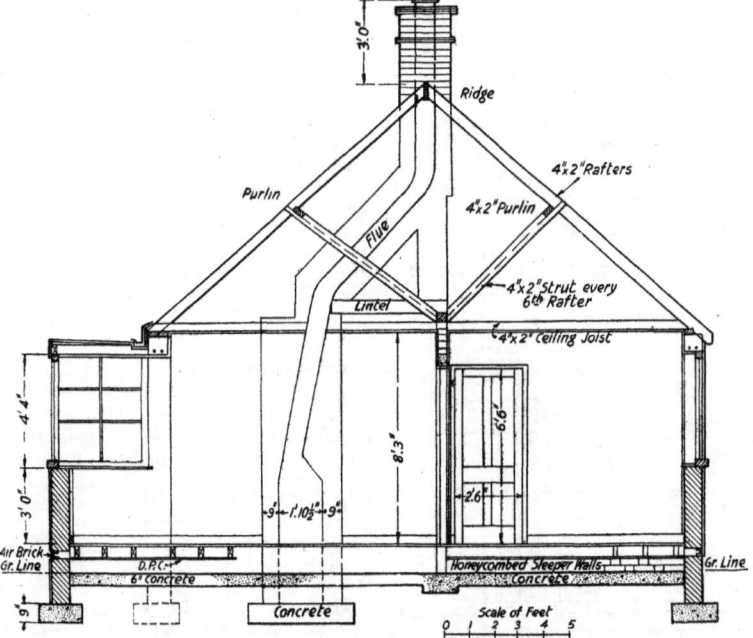

Fig. 12.—Section at AA of Ground Floor Plan.

distance from the side of the trenches (see Fig. 6). The width of the wall, footings (if any) and concrete is marked on the profiles by a saw cut at the distances required. From these points lines are stretched and plumbed down for working purposes.

The depth of the trench is 2 feet, and width, if no footings are required, 1 foot 9 inches. Where the bye-laws require footings, then the width of the trench will be 2 feet 3 inches (see Fig. 7).

For levelling the bottoms of trenches for foundations, the simplest method is to use boning rods (see Fig. 8). These are T-shaped, and three used as a set, two being placed 8 feet or 10 feet apart and levelled with a spirit level and straight-edge. The third rod is placed at a similar distance and levelled. Other levels can now be obtained by sighting over the first and third rods. When these are level the proper depth has been found.

The amount of excavated material for a wall without footings is $8\frac{1}{2}$ cubic yards, and for a wall requiring footings 11 yards.

Before placing the concrete in position, the bottoms of the trenches are well rammed to consolidate them and prepare them for the concrete. Pegs are next driven into the centre of the trench with their tops levelled as a guide for the level and thickness of the concrete, in this case 9 inches.

Concrete Foundations.

The concrete is mixed in the proportions of one part of Portland cement to eight parts of aggregate, *i.e.*, the coarse material, gauged by bulk. The aggregate may be ballast or broken brick, with sufficient sand to fill all the interstices.

Quantity of Concrete required.

It will be understood that one part of cement, four parts of sand and eight parts of shingle or gravel do not make thirteen parts of concrete, as these materials contain a large percentage of voids. One cubic foot of cement plus 30 per cent. of water equal $\frac{9}{10}$ cubic foot when solid. Sand will contain from 25 to 33 per cent. of voids, and gravel about 40 per cent. Therefore, to make 1 cubic yard of concrete of a 1 : 4 : 8 mixture requires 290 lb. of cement, 13 cubic feet sand, and 26 cubic feet broken brick or stone. The amount required for the trenches will be $3\frac{3}{4}$ cubic yards, approximately. The strength of this mixture is about 14 tons per square foot.

Mixing the Concrete.

The materials should be thoroughly mixed on a clean platform, being turned over twice in a dry state and twice in a wet state, the sand and cement being mixed first and the gravel added afterwards. Great care should be exercised in the use of water in the mixing, as little as possible should be used, as too much considerably reduces the strength of the concrete. It is important that all materials are clean.

Test for Amount of Water.

A simple test for determining the correct amount of water to be used is

known as the "slump test." A truncated cone, 12 inches high, 8 inches diameter at the bottom, and 4 inches diameter at the top, provided with handles at the side, is placed on an impervious slab. The concrete, when newly mixed, is filled into the mould in 4-inch layers and lightly tamped with a rod. When filled, the mould is immediately removed and the settlement of the concrete noted. This should not exceed 2 inches.

Brickwork.

When the concrete has set, the brickwork is commenced by setting out with lines from the widths marked on the profiles at each end, and a number of courses at the angles being laid and plumbed.

Footings.

Where the bye-laws require footings, the trench will be 2 feet 3 inches wide. The bottom course of footings should be twice the thickness of the wall, and diminished in regular offsets (see Fig. 7). Footings are built as far as possible all headers—the end of the brick—in elevation. To keep the courses level, lines are stretched from end to end of the wall and brought over the quoin, or angle brick, on the return face of the wall a few courses below the one being laid (see Fig. 6).

Brick Bonding.

There are many types of bond used in brickwork, but double Flemish or Garden Wall bond will be found suitable. Double Flemish is shown in Fig. 6, and Garden Wall bond in Fig. 9. The latter makes a good sound job if the bricks are properly laid in good mortar.

Fig. 10 shows the construction of the fireplace opening and arrangement of joists, and Fig. 11 the arrangement of the ground-floor joists. The number of bricks required for the external and partition walls is 20,000 approximately. The quantity of cement mortar, one part Portland cement to four parts of sand, is 15 yards cube. Fletton bricks can be used throughout.

Damp-proof Course.

To insure the building against dampness rising from the earth, a damp-proof course of durable material, impervious to moisture, is inserted for the full thickness of the wall at least 6 inches above the outside ground line and below the lowest wall plate. Two courses of second-quality thick slates, special sizes, 14 × 9 inches and 14 × 4½ inches, laid in two layers, breaking joint, and bedded in cement mortar 1 to 3. The number required for all walls will be 240 14 × 9-inch slates and 380 14 × 4½-inch slates.

Air Bricks.

Air bricks are next inserted in the walls above or below the damp-proof course to provide ventilation to the underside of the floor. Three or four bricks on each face would be employed.

The brickwork is taken up to the sill level and the windows placed in position and propped up temporarily until built in. The doors would be put in position at an earlier stage.

Site Concrete.

The concrete over the site could be put down at the same time as the trench concrete or when the wall is only a few courses high. The bye-laws demand that the whole ground surface within the external walls shall be covered with a layer of cement concrete at least 6 inches thick, or 4 inches if properly grouted, to prevent damp rising from the ground below.

This layer of concrete, if made 6 inches thick, will require for a 1 : 2½ : 5 mix 5,840 lbs. of cement, 160 cubic feet of sand and 320 cubic feet of coarse material.

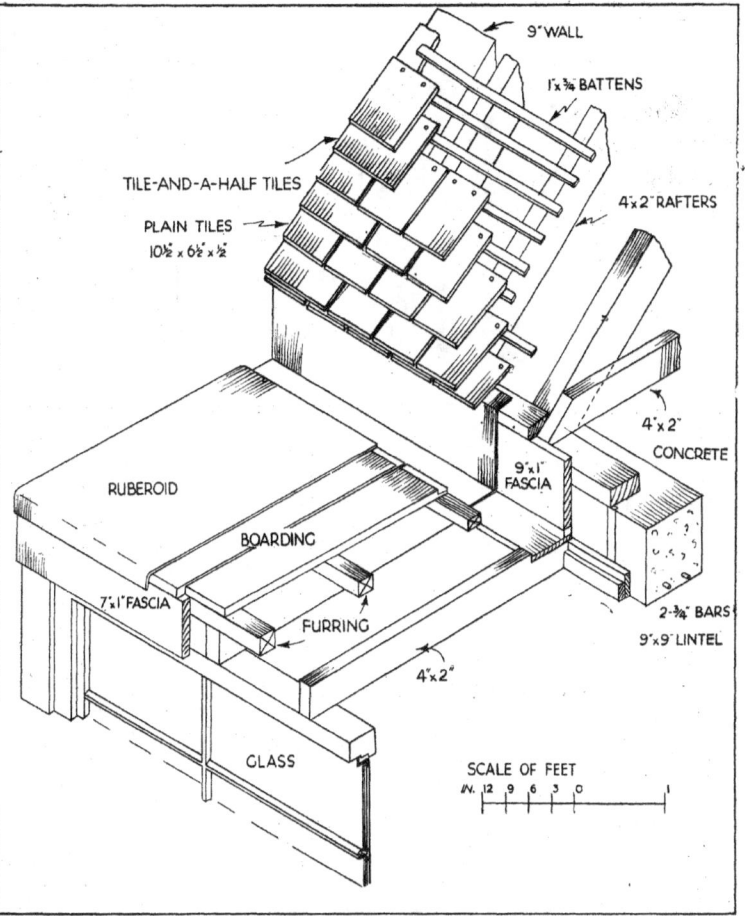

Fig. 13.—Sketch of Tiling and Flat Roof over Windows.

Sleeper Walls.

The sleeper walls are placed upon the site concrete and built honeycombed, to allow for thorough ventilation to the underside of the floor. About 450 bricks for the sleeper walls (see Fig. 21). The damp-proof course is included in the quantity given before for the slates for this purpose.

Windows.

The windows required are given below. The sizes are taken from a well-known maker's catalogue :—

No. 2. Square bays, 9 feet 1 $\frac{9}{16}$ inches × 3 feet 11 $\frac{1}{16}$ inches × 4 feet 4 inches.

No. 2. 5 feet 3 $\frac{1}{16}$ inches × 4 feet 4 $\frac{9}{16}$ inches.

No. 1. 3 feet 7 $\frac{13}{16}$ inches × 4 feet 4 $\frac{9}{16}$ inches.

No. 2. 1 foot 3 $\frac{9}{16}$ inches × 3 feet 7 $\frac{11}{16}$ inches.

No. 1. 1 foot 3 $\frac{9}{16}$ inches × 2 feet 5 $\frac{5}{8}$ inches.

These windows have a wood surround, which is grooved on the inside for plaster or a wood lining. The heads

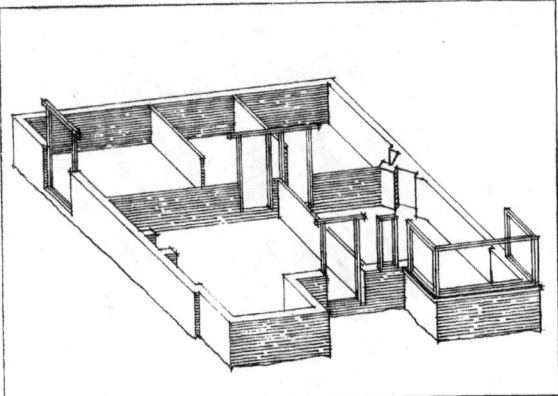

Fig. 14.—Walls up to Window Sill. Frames being fixed.

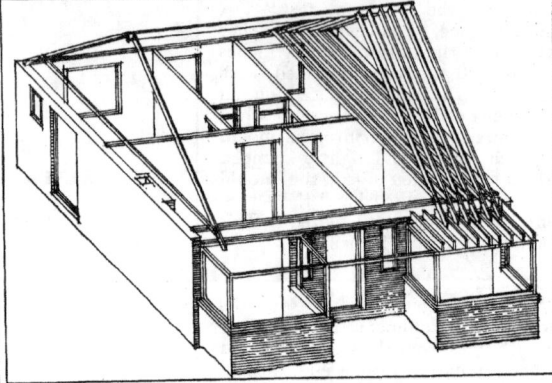

Fig. 15.—Roof being formed. Note Gables are built afterwards to Lines of the Roof Slopes.

and jambs are left projecting 3 inches beyond the joint of the frame, to form horns for building in.

Window boards, 1¼ inch thick, form the inner sill. These are tongued to the back of the window sill and project about 1 inch beyond the plaster.

Reinforced Concrete Lintels.

Reinforced concrete lintels are now placed over all door and window openings. Their depths vary according to the span. As a general rule they are made 6 inches deep for spans up to 3 feet; from 3 to 6 feet, 9 inches deep, and from 6 to 10 feet, 12 inches deep. The reinforcement also varies according to span and width of wall. One ½-inch diameter bar is allowed for each half brick thickness of wall up to 6-feet span. Above 6-feet span, ¾-inch diameter rods are used. The concrete should be 1 part cement, 2 parts sand and 4 parts aggregate. The aggregate should not be larger than ½-inch gauge.

The number and sizes of lintels required are as follows :—
No. 2. 8 feet 6 inches × 9 × 12 inches.
No. 2. 6 feet × 9 × 9 inches.
No. 1. 4 feet 6 inches × 9 × 9 inches.
No. 2. 3 feet 9 inches × 9 × 9 inches.
No. 3. 2 feet × 9 × 4½ inches.
No. 6. 3 feet 6 inches × 9 × 4½ inches.

An additional one to carry stack, 4 feet 9 inches × 14 × 9 inches (see Fig. 13).

Material required for Lintels.

The amount of material required for the lintels is 35 cubic feet net, or 626 lbs. of cement, 5·6 cubic yards of sand and 11·2 cubic yards shingle. There will be about 70 feet run of ½-inch diameter bars and 32 feet run of ¾-inch bars. These lintels are usually precast on the site some time before they are required, to allow them to mature.

The next proposition is the construction of the roof (see Fig. 13).

Roof.

The roof timbers consist of rafters spaced at 15-inch centres to carry the roof boarding or battens. The rafters are notched and nailed to the wall plates at the bottom and butted and spiked to a ridge board at the top. The rafters are further secured against spreading by a tie which, being attached to each pair of rafters, becomes a ceiling joist to carry the ceiling. To give longitudinal stability, and to prevent the rafters sagging, horizontal members, termed purlins, span from wall to wall, placed at the middle of the length of the rafters. These purlins are in turn supported by struts, which take a bearing on the top of the partition wall. With the exception of the ridge board, which is 7 × 1¼ inches, all these members can be 4 × 2 inches in section.

The material required is 90 feet run of wall plate, 29 feet 6 inches run of ridge board, 745 feet run of rafters, 553 feet run of ceiling joist; struts, 60 feet run for the front and 6 feet 6 inches for the back of the roof; 59 feet run of purlins. The flat roof over bays and verandah will require 100 feet run of 3½ × 2-inch timber. The front end of these rafters is supported by the head of the frame, and the inside end by a small fillet piece fixed to the concrete lintel; small fixing strips, 1 × ¾ inch, being fixed in the lintel during the casting (see Fig. 13). The top of the flat roof is furred to fall towards the gutter, arranged along the eaves of the sloping

Fig. 17.—Roof Construction (2).
Rafters spiked to wall plate. Ceiling joists being fixed.

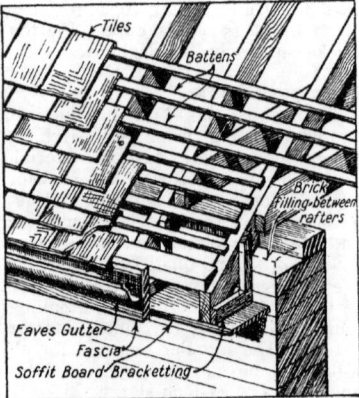

Fig. 18.—Roof Construction (3).
Battens fixed, tiling being laid, fascia and soffit boarding fixed, also ogee gutter.

BUILDING YOUR OWN BUNGALOW

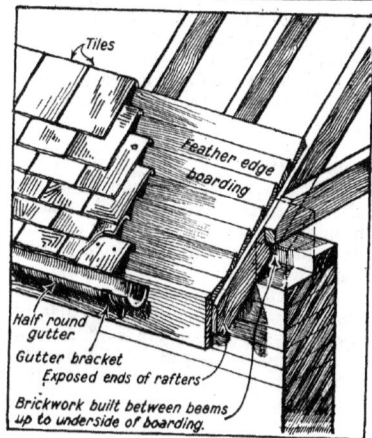

Fig. 19.—Roof Construction (4).
Alternative to Fig. 18, with feather edge boarding, exposed rafters and half round gutter.

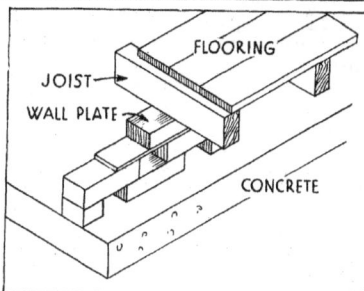

Fig. 21.—Sketch of Honeycombed Sleeper Wall.

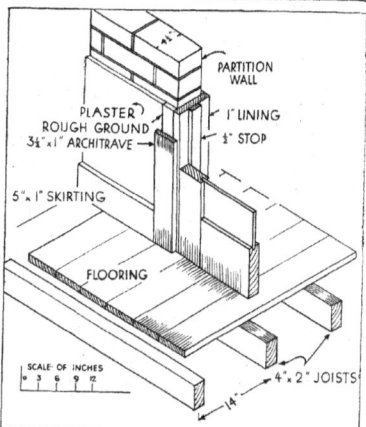

Fig. 23.—Sketch of Internal Door.

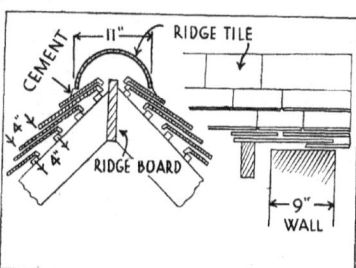

Fig. 20.—Section through Ridge of Roof.

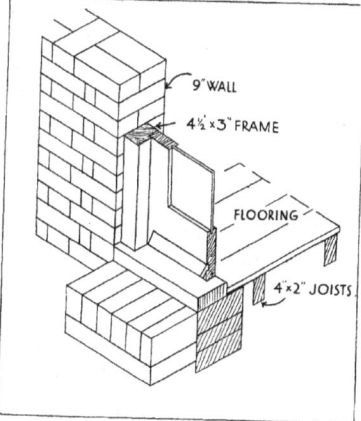

Fig. 22.—Sketch of External Door.

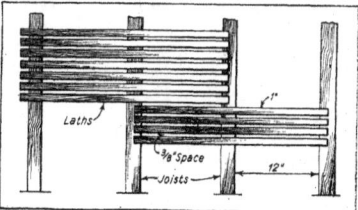

Fig. 24.—Lathing.
Showing joints broken.

roof. If Ruberoid or Rok is used as a covering, a fall of 1 inch will be ample. This material is laid on ¾-inch boarding in the direction of the fall. Each length should overlap the adjoining length 2 inches, and should be well painted with Ruberoid cement between the laps, and nailed 2 inches apart. It is sold in rolls containing 24 square yards. The gutter should be laid first, in two layers, and bedded in Ruberoid mastic. It should be laid in long lengths to avoid joints, and the top layer nailed only at the joints. One side of the gutter is formed by the 9-inch fascia board, the other by the furring piece, and the bottom of the gutter by a ¾-inch board.

One 30 feet 6-inch length of fascia board and two 30 feet 6-inch lengths of 7 × 1-inch fascia boards are required.

Tiling to Roof.

The roof is to be covered with plain tiles laid to a 4-inch gauge, fixed to 1½ × ¾-inch battens, and every fifth course nailed (see Fig. 13).

A tilting fillet is placed along the eaves to make the first two courses bed tight, to prevent the wind stripping off the tiles. The first course is a short one, termed the under-eaves course, the length of these tiles being 7 inches.

Plain tiles measure 10½ × 6½ × ½ inch. To obtain the bond between the courses, every alternate course is commenced with a half tile or a tile-and-a-half tile (see Fig. 13). The laying is commenced at the left-hand verge of the roof, the outer tiles projecting over the wall 1½ inches and their edges pointed in cement. The ridge is covered with half round tiles and their lower edges pointed in cement.

The roof area is 936 feet, requiring 5,340 tiles, 2,750 feet run of 1 × ¾-inch battens, 27 ridge tiles and 27 eaves tiles. Fig. 20 is a section through the ridge.

When the Roofing is finished.

When the roof is covered in and there is protection from the rain, work may proceed in the interior, which would be liable to damage if exposed. Electric conduits, for instance, must be kept free from water.

So it is at this stage that several other "trades" are introduced, principally those connected with piping, so that hidden pipes and wiring may be put in before the plasterers come, or the floor boards are laid.

Laying the Floors.

The next operation is to lay the floor boards.

Ground Floor Joists.

The joists are spaced at 14-inch centres and are supported at intervals by the sleeper walls. The length of wall plate required is 140 feet, and the run of joists 550 feet, 4 × 2-inch section.

Flooring.

The floor boards are 5 × 1 inch butt-jointed, and laid to break joint every 3 feet. Flooring required will be 6½ squares (a square being 100 square feet). The flooring is usually left until the building is almost completed.

The floor to the larder, fuel store and lobby can be finished in cement or tiles, as desired. To bring the floor up to the same level as the wooden floor, a 9-inch layer of hardcore should be filled in before the concrete is placed.

The steps to the doors can be formed with bricks on edge in cement mortar. Also the step to verandah, and the remainder of verandah floor tiled using '4 × 4-inch or 6 × 6-inch tiles.

Doors.

The next operation will be the fixing of the door frames. External door frames are usually solid, and made 4½ × 3 inches in section (see Fig. 22). The frame consists of the jambs, which are tenoned into the head at the top and into a sill at the bottom, or secured to a stone step with a dowel.

The internal doors are hung to linings. These linings are made the width of the wall plus the thickness of the plaster on both sides, and 1 inch thick. A small fillet piece, 2 × ½ inch, is nailed to the lining to form a door stop. Rough wooden grounds or battens are fixed to the wall behind the lining to serve as a guide to the plasterer and also to secure the architrave. The architrave is made sufficiently wide to cover the joint between the ground and the edge of the plaster (see Fig. 23). The skirting is 5 × 1 inch, and is fixed to wooden plugs driven into the wall about 4 feet apart (see Fig. 23).

The usual type of door for entrances and internal work is the machine-made framed door.

Doors are generally made to well-known proportions and sizes.

Plastering.

The ceilings are prepared for plastering by nailing laths to the underside of the joists. Double laths are used for ceilings. They are butt jointed at their ends and nailed where they cross the joists (see Fig. 24). Owing to the tendency of plastering to crack along the joint of the laths, it is important to break the joints. This should be done in bays of from 3 to 4 feet, or by using 3 and 4 feet laths alternately. Laths are fixed about ⅜ inch apart. A bundle of laths containing about 300 to 400 feet run, when nailed with butt joints, will cover approximately 4 yards super. Each bundle of laths, when properly nailed, will require 1¾ lbs.

Plastering is applied in one, two or three coats. Two-coat work will be suitable in the present case. When applied to walls it is termed *render* and *set*, and when applied to laths, lath plaster and set.

The first coat of *coarse stuff* consists of 1 part lime, 2 parts sand and 1 lb. of hair to every 3 cubic feet of stuff. The *setting* or *finishing* coat is composed of lime putty and fine washed sand. The thickness of this coat is about ⅛ inch. Plaster slabs sometimes take the place of the coarse stuff, and if preferred the smooth side of the slab can be turned outwards, giving a finished ceiling.

Rendering and setting on walls require 34 cubic feet of unslaked lime, 54 cubic feet of sand, 22 lbs. of hair and 200 gallons of water for every 100 yards super. To obtain a good level surface when plastering, it is necessary to place guides, termed *screeds*, both horizontally and vertically. These screeds are formed with plaster, about 2 inches wide and the thickness of the coat of plaster, and placed about 6 to 8 feet apart. These screeds are plumbed, and when set the plaster is applied and ruled off with a straight edge, termed a floating rule. For ceilings, the treatment is somewhat similar.

Rough Cast.

The external walls should be rough cast. This is a mixture of grit, gravel, chippings and cement thrown on while in a semi-fluid state, the wall being first rendered or floated in cement and sand in the proportion of 1 part Portland cement to 2½ parts of sand. For a clean gravel finish, a cement and sand coat is laid on the wall and the gravel, after being washed, is thrown on lightly while the cement is soft

The material could be put on order as described, or, as the job is a small one, the whole of the materials could be ordered at the one time and delivery taken at short intervals in the following order: concrete, bricks, window and door frames, roof timbers and floor joists, tiles, 31 feet 4-inch half round eaves guttering, two 8 feet 6 inches run 3½-inch diameter rain-water pipes with ears cast on, No. 2 rain-water shoes, 9-inch fascia board, tarred plinth.

GARAGE DOOR OPENER AND ELECTRIC LOCK

THE accompanying diagrams show a method of converting garage doors to automatic operation.

The gear comprises a plain steel bar, called a track bar, which is pivoted externally to a bracket on the right-hand door, and pivoted to an internal bracket on the left-hand door.

The only other mechanism is a simple pull cord and a guide pulley, by means of which the doors are opened simultaneously from a distance. The track bar is so arranged that once the doors have been pulled open they can only be closed by pulling the left-hand door; consequently, both doors are automatically kept open and will not move about with the wind.

A handle is fixed to the end of the pull rod and placed in a convenient position.

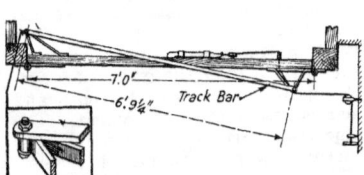
Fig. 1.—The Doors Closed.

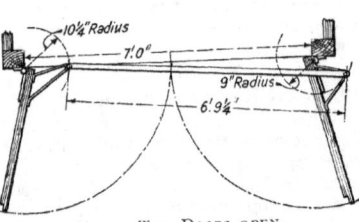
Fig. 2.—The Doors Open.

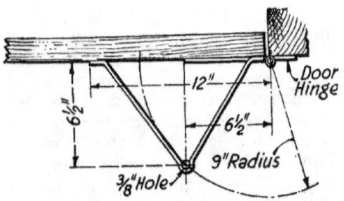
Fig. 3.—Detail of Right-hand Bracket.

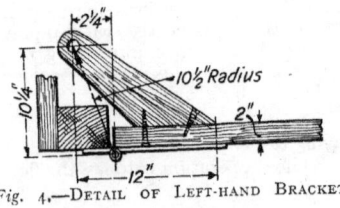
Fig. 4.—Detail of Left-hand Bracket.

By fixing sash weights to the cord an electric lock can be made to operate the doors. A simple type consists of a solenoid or magnetic plunger arranged as shown in Fig. 5. The wooden bobbin of the solenoid is about 3¼ inches in diameter and 1¼ inches long, and is wound with 3,000 turns of No. 26 D.S.C. wire (about 1½ lbs.). Current can be obtained from a few dry cells in series to give about 12 volts.

Fig. 5.—The Solenoid.

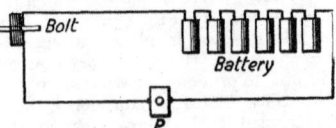
Fig. 6.—Circuit for Solenoid.

GLOSSARY OF TOOLS, MATERIALS AND METHODS USED IN HOUSE CONSTRUCTION AND MAINTENANCE

A

Adze.—A hand-cutting tool, having its blade at right-angles with its handle and usually curved. It is used for dressing and chipping timber, etc.

Air Bricks.—When a ground floor is laid with boards or joists it is necessary to provide thorough ventilation beneath it. Air bricks of cast iron, equal in size to an ordinary brick, are therefore built into the wall above the damp course and below the floor level.

Air Lock.—A fault in a water pipe due to an air pad being trapped between two columns of water and preventing the water from issuing when the tap is turned on.

Air Space.—The area in front and in the rear of dwelling-houses on which building is not allowed. This area in the rear of a building must not be less than 150 square feet, but the depth, i.e., the distance from the building to the nearest erection, varies according to the height of the house.

Angle Bracket.—A form of support commonly used for a shelf.

Architrave.—The term applied to the surround, usually moulded, which forms the frame of a door, window or any other opening or recess.

Arris Rail.—A length of wood, triangular-shaped in section, used in the construction of fencing and gates.

Auger.—A tool that bores well in the direction of the grain of the wood, and used to bore holes of considerable size and depth. It consists of a steel rod, having a round eye at one end, through which a round wooden handle fits at right-angles. On the other end is a spiral twist of larger diameter, terminating in a conical screw with a sharp point. The edge of the spiral is a nicker which cuts the grain of the wood around the edge of the hole.

Awl.—A pointed steel instrument used for making small holes.

B

Back-flap Hinge.—A hinge in which the plates are wide and short instead of long and narrow, as with a butt hinge. It is used to connect two flat surfaces which are desired to be hinged in such a way that they may be level when the hinge is opened out.

Back Iron.—A part of the cutting arrangement of a plane which is fixed to the cutter with a screw, its object being to break the shavings and prevent the grain from tearing out.

Badger Plane.—A plane useful for making wide rebates. Its shape is similar to a jack plane, but the cutter at one edge is exposed.

Balance Weights.—The weights used for sash windows.

Ballast.—The name given to any heavy substance, such as sand, stone, gravel.

Baluster.—A piece of wood, generally square in section, supporting a staircase handrail from the stairing.

Ball-pane Hammer.—A hammer which has one flat and one rounded striking surface. Specially suitable for such work as riveting.

Ball Valve or Ball Cock.—Device employed in a water cistern to regulate the flow of the water. It consists of a copper ball of very thin-gauge metal attached by a lever to the body of the valve by a pivot pin. In the body of the valve there is a plug which is moved by the floating ball according to the level of the water in the cistern. When the level reaches a predetermined limit the plug, at one end of which is a rubber washer, is forced against the seating and shuts off the water. In the Croydon-type ball valve the plunger works vertically; in the Portsmouth type the plunger works horizontally.

Barefaced Tenon.—A tenon flush with one side of the rail, with a shoulder on the other side. It is used where the rail is thinner than the stile and where it is desirable to have the mortise near the centre.

Barrel.—The name given to pipes used for gas installations.

Batten.—A narrow piece of wood running across the backs of boards that have been jointed to strengthen them. They should be fixed by nails and screws.

Batten Flooring.—This flooring is generally laid over deal joists of 2 × 4 inches upwards, although occasionally put down on to a composition of coke breeze. Batten floorings are available in thicknesses of $\frac{7}{8}$ inch nominal up to about $1\frac{1}{2}$ inches in widths of from 3 inches up to 5 inches, and in lengths running from 4 to 20 feet. They are prepared either square-edged or in a variety of secret nailed joints, or they are grooved and jointed up with a loose tongue.

Bay Window.—A projecting window structure of angular plan reaching to the ground.

Beam.—A long member which spans between two points, at each of which it is supported. The following are all beams: floor joists, trimmer joists, bressummers, lintels, purlins, rafters and ceiling joists.

Bedding Putty.—A small quantity of soft putty placed evenly round the rebate of woodwork, to provide a bed for the glass to rest upon.

Bed Joint.—The mortar joint between horizontal bricks.

Bell.—In a flushing cistern, the bell is the part that is operated by the chain. When the chain is pulled the bell rises, and when released it traps the water within the well so that it rises up inside the bell and starts a syphonic action, which continues until the cistern has emptied.

Bench Hook.—A device used when cutting off short lengths of wood or for shouldering tenons. It allows the work to be cut through without damaging the bench.

Benching.—When levelling a sloping site, the trenches for the foundations would be unnecessarily deep at one end if the bottom of the trench were made level. The trench bottom is therefore stepped or benched.

Bench Stop.—A small peg inserted in the top of a bench against which or between which work is held for planing.

Bibcock.—A tap having the nozzle bent downward.

Binder.—An ingredient of paint consisting of a vegetable oil, that most generally used being linseed oil. This oil possesses the quality of absorbing oxygen from the atmosphere, causing it to solidify gradually into an elastic substance, which is of great value in the drying of paint.

Bird's-mouth Joint.—The joint used at the foot or bottom of a rafter where abutting against the wall-plate.

Bit.—A wood-boring tool adapted to be used with a stock or brace.

Black Japan.—A pigmented oil varnish which provides a jet-black glossy finish. It is used for stoves, grates, etc.

Block Flooring.—This type of flooring is laid in mastic direct on a concrete foundation. Block floorings are manufactured either tongued and grooved on both sides and at the edges, or just grooved on both sides. The most generally used sizes are 12 × 3 inches and 9 × 3 inches; thicknesses, 1, $1\frac{1}{4}$ and $1\frac{1}{2}$ inches nominal.

Block Plane.—A small metal plane used for any small work. As it has no back iron it is unsuitable for fine work and for wood having an awkward grain.

"Blooming."—The formation on the dried surface of varnish, of a dull film something like the "bloom" often observable on black grapes.

Boards.—Wood less than 2 inches thick and over 6 inches wide.

Bodying.—A process in French polishing which consists of building up a full, flat surface of polish by continuing the "skimming-in" process. It is done by rubbing a small amount of linseed oil over the surface with a specially-prepared rubber.

Bonding.—The name given to the method of laying bricks, i.e., garden-wall bond, Flemish bond, herring-bone bond, etc. The garden-wall bond is used in what are known as half bricks or those which are $4\frac{1}{2}$ inches thick. The Flemish bond is the usual bond for ordinary brick walls of 9 inches thickness. The arrangement consists of two stretchers and a header in regular sequence. Quarter bricks, or closers, are used at all quoins and stopped ends. The herring-bone bond is used mostly for decorative effects.

Boning Rods.—Rods used for levelling a site. They are posts about $1\frac{1}{2}$ inches square, pointed at one end, and having a cross-bar about 18 inches long nailed to the upper end.

Bossing-out.—The term used for the process of enlarging the end of a lead pipe. It is done by driving a tapered boxwood pin, called a tan pin, in the end, or inserting a round bar of iron a short distance down the pipe, pulling it sideways with considerable pressure and then revolving it round in the pipe.

Boundary Gutter.—A rectangular gutter $4\frac{1}{2}$ to 5 inches wide. It lies on the outer $4\frac{1}{2}$ inches of a 9 inch wall, the outer face flush with the boundary of the wall.

Bow-saw.—Sometimes called a turning saw, and is used for cutting all types of open curved work. The blade is thin and narrow and is held in tension by being fitted in a frame and tightened by the action of a twisted string or bolts.

Bow Window.—A projecting window built up from the ground-level, properly one of curved ground-plan.

Box Tenon.—Joint used on angle posts in lantern lights, bay windows, and work of a similar nature.

Brace—A crank-like handle which can be fitted with a great variety of bits, enabling holes of all sizes and kinds to be made.

Bradawl.—Tool used for boring small holes in wood for screws.

Brazing.—A form of soldering in which a higher temperature than that used for ordinary hard soldering is required. Brazing spelter is used instead of silver solder. The process is particularly suitable for jointing steelwork.

Breeze Block.—The name applied colloquially to rectangular slabs of concrete composed of Portland cement and coke breeze or other appropriate aggregate, the usual proportions being 4 of coke to 1 of cement. Breeze concrete slabs from 2 to 4 inches in thickness to 12 inches wide, or up to 6 feet in length can be purchased ready prepared. They are light in weight, hygienic and fire-resisting and form an attractive walling material. Owing to the porosity of the material it must be faced with an impervious material.

Bressummer.—The name given to the lower horizontal members in floor construction.

Brick.—A prepared block of moulded and burnt clay, averaging 7 lb. in weight, 9 inches long, $4\frac{1}{2}$ inches wide and 3 inches thick.

Building Line.—An imaginary line joining the front main walls of dwelling-houses, beyond which bay windows and porches only are allowed to project.

Bull-nose Plane.—Similar to a shoulder plane, but has the mouth near the front, making it useful for working in awkward edges.

Bunsen Burner.—A burner giving a powerful gas flame, used for heating up soldering bits, and for hardening small tools, etc.

Burnishing.—The process of rubbing a copper surface vigorously with a chamois leather pad coated with rouge and moistened with methylated spirit.

Butt Hinge.—The simplest form of hinge used for hanging doors, etc. It consists of two flaps moving on a wire pivot.

Butt Joint.—The most common joint met with in home carpentry, where one member is fastened securely at right-angles to another.

C

Camel-hair Mop.—Brush used for applying stains, French polish, cellulose lacquers and enamels. The mop is a bunch of hair mounted into a quill which is bound with wire. Sometimes a handle is fitted into the quill. They are sold in sizes which are numbered according to the quantity of hair in the quill. The flat brushes are from $\frac{3}{8}$ to 3 inches wide and the thickness of hair is from $\frac{1}{8}$ to $\frac{1}{4}$ inch.

Capping.—Specially shaped lengths of timber for placing along the top of posts, etc., to protect from the weather. Saddle-back cappings are obtainable in sizes 2 × $1\frac{1}{4}$ inches, 2 × $1\frac{1}{2}$ inches, $2\frac{1}{2}$ × $1\frac{1}{2}$ inches, 3 × $1\frac{1}{2}$ inches.

Capping Brick.—A brick used as a protection for the tops of exposed walls.

Casement Window.—The term "casement" in connection with domestic architecture refers to the cottage type of window where the opening light or casement is hinged like a door. The frame can be either of metal or wood; both types of frames are built into the wall as in the case of an outside door.

Cavity Wall.—A form of wall construction used in many small houses. It consists of an inner and outer wall with an air space between, the purpose being to ensure a warm, dry building. The usual width is 11 inches, each wall being $4\frac{1}{2}$ inches thick and laid in garden-wall bond. The two walls are united by galvanised iron ties or bars about 10 inches long.

Ceiling Joists.—These members tie in the feet of rafters and prevent the roof spreading. They also carry the plastered or other ceilings.

Cement.—Any substance, such as a preparation of glue, red lead or lime, which, by hardening, causes objects between which it is applied to adhere firmly. In building, cement is any compound or substance applied in the form of a mortar and used for producing a hard and stony or smooth, or a waterproof surface.

Cement Mortar.—Mortar prepared with Portland cement and sand, in the proportion of 1 to 3.

Centre Bit.—A useful tool for boring large holes. It consists of a piece of steel shaped to fulfil three requirements: (a) a centre, (b) a circle-cutter, and (c) a chisel to remove the core of the hole.

Cesspool.—A method of disposing of sewage from dwelling-houses in localities where there is no main drainage. There are two types, the open joint or the sealed joint. The former is constructed of brick or stone, with open joints, thus forming a sump or soakaway, the liquid percolating through the joints and dispersing into the ground around. This type should only be constructed where the soil is of gravel or fairly loose soil. With the sealed joint type the liquid has either to be removed by the local authorities or pumped up and disposed of over a suitable area.

Chamfer.—To cut a channel or bevel. Chamfering

consists of removing the sharp corner of a piece of wood, either with a plane, or by chiselling.

Chalk Line.—A line made against a wall by means of "flicking" a piece of string which has been chalked, so that it hits against the wall and leaves a line of chalk on the wall. The chalk line is used for ensuring that shelves, etc., are fixed horizontally.

Chimney Breast.—That portion of the walls of a room that usually projects into the room and into which is built the range or grate. It is formed by two 9-inch pillars built up straight from the footings, and standing out far enough to cope with the range to be fitted.

Chisel.—A hand tool for removing wood in thin layers. The action is a paring one, consequently the edge is bevelled so that the paring is bent aside as the chisel advances. The firmer chisel is most generally used, as it is strong enough to withstand fairly hard usage. A convenient size is 1 inch. A mortise chisel is made specially strong to withstand the blows of a mallet, and a convenient size for all-round purposes in $\frac{5}{16}$ inch.

"Cissing."—A defect in varnishing when the varnish runs together in globules, such as water does on a greasy surface.

Claw Hammer.—The most useful type of hammer for household work. One end of the head is shaped like a claw and is used for extracting nails from timber.

Cleat.—A strengthening device consisting of a strip of wood or iron fastened across another material or nailed against a wall, etc.

Closers.—Sometimes called bats. They are small pieces of bricks nominally one-fourth the length of a brick, and used to preserve the bond or proper arrangement of the bricks.

Clout.—A special large-headed galvanised nail for fixing roofing felt.

Cogged Joint.—A joint occasionally employed to connect the tie-beam and wall plate.

Cold Lacquer.—A cellulose mixture which can be applied to all classes of metal without warming.

Collar-tie Roof.—Form of roof construction used when the eaves are so low that if the ties were fixed at the wall-plate level there would not be sufficient head room.

Compass Plane.—A plane that can be adjusted to practically any curve, as the sole is a piece of steel which, by adjustment of the screw, bends to the desired curve. The metal type has now practically ousted the wooden type. It is used for shaped work generally and, being provided with a back iron, it can tackle the finest work.

Concrete.—A hardened mass such as gravel or broken stone united by cement. The following proportions make good concrete: Hardstone, 4 parts; Builder's sand, 2 parts; Portland cement, 1 part.

Conduit.—A thin steel tube used for protecting electric wires.

Connecting Socket.—A screwed socket used for connecting together two pieces of metal piping.

Connector.—A piece of pipe of any length up to 24 inches with a special British standard thread.

Consolidate.—To make firm or solid.

Coping Brick. See Capping Brick.

Coping Saw.—Similar to a fretsaw, and has a very fine blade. Used for cutting to all kinds of small curved outlines, and, by threading the blade through a hole, can be used for closed curves where conditions allow.

Copper Plating.—The process of depositing copper electrically upon various metals, including iron and steel, tinned iron, lead and its alloys, brass, bronze, zinc, etc.

Corbel.—A bracket projecting from the face of a wall, or a short piece of timber placed lengthwise upon a wall, etc., under a girder or joist to increase its bearing. Also formed by stepping two or three courses of bricks to provide a support for a wall plate.

Cornice.—The horizontal moulded projection at the top of a building or of a component part of a building, usually under the eaves. An ornamental moulding running round the walls of a room close to the ceiling. Also a slight wooden moulding running round the walls of a room at a convenient height for the support of pictures by hooks. Also a frame of moulding, often gilded, covering the rods and hooks used for hanging curtains.

Corrugated Iron.—Wrinkled metal sheets, used chiefly for covering the roofs of sheds, etc. The normal width of a sheet is 2 feet 3 inches.

Countersink.—Tool used to cut a depression in the end of a hole to allow a screw to sink in flush with the surface of the wood. There are two types generally used, the snail and the rose. The former has a hollowed-out depression which forms the cutting edge, the latter has several cutting edges and is somewhat similar in appearance to a bevelled cogwheel.

Couple-close Roof.—Differs from a couple roof (*q.v.*) in that ties are introduced across the walls of the building, which are fastened to the rafters and the wall plate, so taking the outward thrust off the walls.

Couple Roof.—A roof formed with two slopes pitched up from the opposite walls of a building, each rafter resting on the wall plate at its foot, whilst the heads are fastened on either side of the ridge plate.

Course.—The name given to a row of bricks.

Cramp.—A tool used to hold work on the bench, to hold together work in course of construction, to facilitate the making of articles in which tight and accurate joints are essential, and to hold together glued joints until the glue is dry.

"Crazing."—Fine hair-like lines running all over the surface of rubber.

Crazy Paving.—A form of path construction consisting of random pieces of flat stone laid on cement to form a more or less attractive pattern.

Cripple Rafter.—A rafter which has no foot resting on the wall plate.

Crossbanding.—An effective form of decoration that can be carried out in veneer.

Cross-cut Saw.—Used for cutting across the grain of timber. Each tooth is pointed so that it cuts in a manner similar to the point of a knife when held at an angle. Obtainable in lengths of 26, 24, 22, 20 and 18 inches, with five to eleven tooth points to 1 inch.

Cutting-in.—The process of finishing off the edges in painting or distempering. For example, when a wall has been distempered, the edge that adjoins the fixed woodwork is "cut-in" with a small brush, so as to avoid any distemper going on the woodwork.

D

Dado.—The term used to describe the part of the wall from the skirting up to a height of about 2 feet 9 inches to 3 feet. This space, if covered with panelling, fulfils the double purpose of protecting the lower part of the wall and adding to the decorative effect of a room.

Damp Course.—A layer of slates or other damp-resisting material inserted in a brick wall to prevent the dampness of the earth from ascending through the walls.

Deadlock.—A lock worked from the outside by a key and from the inside by a handle or knob. A lock in which the bolt has to be turned in each direction by a key.

Deals.—Wood over 2 inches thick and less than 10 inches wide.

Die.—A hardened block of steel having teeth by which to cut male screw threads on a metal object, such as a bolt.

Die-stock.—A double-handled holder for screw-cutting dies.

Distemper.—A substance used for the decoration of walls and ceilings. It consists of a pigment such as whiting, lithophone, blanc fixe, etc., with a binder or fixative such as glue, casein, linseed oil or varnish.

Distemper Brush.—Brush used for applying distemper. There are two types, the flat and the two- or three-knot round head. The flat is easier and lighter to use, and is less liable to splash.

Distempering.—The process of applying distemper to a wall or ceiling. It is probably the easiest and cheapest form of decoration.

Dormer Window.—A vertical window in a small gable rising from a sloping roof.

Double Tenons.—These are tenons used when the framing is very thick, also on the end of a middle rail of a door where a mortise lock is to be fixed. There are two tenons, sometimes referred to as twin tenons, side by side in the thickness of the timber.

Dovetails.—A dovetail joint may be defined as a joint made with tenons shaped like a dove's spread tail. It is the strongest and one of the best methods of joining two pieces of timber, end to end, at right angles to each other. There are three chief types of dovetail joint: the plain through joint, as used for boxes, etc.; the stopped joint, as used for drawer fronts; and the secret or mitre joint.

Dovetail Saw.—Similar to tenon saw, but the blade is shorter and thinner and has smaller teeth. Used for cutting small dovetails, mouldings and other delicate work.

Dowel.—A small round wooden pin used in dowelling. Dowels are seldom used in wood under $\frac{3}{4}$ inch thick. They must be the same in diameter as that of the bit with which the dowel holes are bored. Almost any straight-grained strong wood can be used for dowels.

Dowelling.—A quick method of jointing woodwork. A hole is drilled in one of the pieces of wood to be joined and a dowel glued in the hole. Another hole is drilled in the second piece, which is then placed over the protruding dowel. Accurate measurement of the position of the holes for the dowels is, of course, essential.

Dowelling Gauge.—A gauge made from a piece of deal, 2 inches or 3 inches long, notched out at one end and having a steel point driven in at a given distance and sharpened up as a marking gauge.

Down Draught.—A prevalent cause of smoky chimneys, due to the pressure of air in the flue preventing the upward flow of the heated air and smoke from the fire. In the case of new houses, it may be caused by the air in the flue remaining damp.

Drain Rods.—Rods used for removing an obstruction in outside drain pipes. The rods themselves consist of a number of malacca canes with screwed joints.

Drier.—An ingredient of paint added to help the paint to dry in a reasonable time. There are two forms of drier, the liquid and the paste, the former being more powerful in action.

Dry Cell.—A form of battery used for operating electric bells. Dry cells cannot be recharged, and must be renewed at intervals of about 18 months.

Dry Rot.—A fungoid growth which flourishes in damp stagnant air. It thrives principally on wood, and will soon destroy its strength. It is easily distinguished because it is accompanied by a thick blanket-like fungus and a pungent and very unpleasant smell. The timber is discoloured with red and black stripes. Dry rot will not thrive in a dry and ventilated atmosphere, but in damp and stagnant, and it spreads rapidly.

Duster Brush.—A brush used for dusting off a painted surface after sandpapering, or removing dust from the moulding, picture rail, etc. The bristles are about 4 inches long.

E

Eaves.—The lowest part of the sloping surface of the roof, where the gutter is usually supported.

Elbow.—A metal pipe fitting for joining lengths of pipe at right angles.

Electro-plating.—The name given to the process in which a metal held in solution in the form of a metallic salt dissolved in water is deposited on a metal surface when electric current is caused to flow through the solution.

Elevation.—A drawing of the front view of a building, etc.

Enamel Brush.—A flat type of brush similar to a flat paint brush, but having shorter and stiffer bristles, the tips of the bristles being bevelled.

Excavating.—The process of digging out sufficient soil from a site to enable a concrete, brick or other form of foundation to be inserted.

Expansion Pipe.—A pipe leading from a hot-water cistern and either taken right through the roof of a house and curved over at the end, or curved over the cold tank. Its object is to prevent the hot-water system becoming a "closed" one if the cold-water supply were turned off.

F

Fadding-in.—A process in french polishing which consists of applying the polish by means of a specially prepared rubber. Fadding-in is the first process to be carried out after the grain of the wood has been filled and smoothed off.

Fascia.—The jutting of the bricks beyond the windows.

Fascia Board.—A piece of wood nailed to the ends of rafters and on which is fixed the supports for guttering.

Female Thread.—A thread cut on an interior surface, such as the thread of a nut.

Fence.—A wall, hedge or line of posts and rails to protect or enclose land. English oak is without doubt the best fencing timber, although fir, larch and sweet chestnut are also satisfactory. For a 6-foot high fence, the posts should be set at least 3 feet in the ground; for 5 feet high, $2\frac{1}{2}$ feet; for 4 feet high, 2 feet. The distance from centre to centre of posts should not be greater than 9 feet.

Fence.—The guard of a plane.

File.—A tool, the face of which is formed by grooves. It is intended chiefly for metal work, but is used sometimes as a substitute for glasspaper.

Firebrick.—A special heat-resisting brick used as a backing to all parts exposed to the direct flames of a fire.

Fitch.—A brush used for painting. It is the smallest size of sash tool.

Flashing.—Before the tiles or other roof covering can be completed around a chimney stack, a sound water-tight joint is provided by means of a strip of lead "flashing," which is turned over on to the roof surface and also turned upwards and fixed into the brickwork of the stack.

Fletton.—A variety of brick.

Flight.—A set of steps that goes from one level to another, without an intermediate landing.

Flooring.—(See under Batten, Block, Parquet, etc.)

Floor Sander.—A simple device for obtaining a smooth, clean surface to a floor. It is briefly a box on the bottom of which is fixed a sheet of glasspaper. The box is weighted with stone, etc., and pulled over the floor.

Flue.—A channel or passage for smoke, air or gases of combustion; a chimney.

Flushing Cistern.—The type of cistern used to flush the w.c.

Flushing-up.—A process in bricklaying. When the second brick is laid against the first, the joint between them must be completely filled up with mortar. This process is called flushing.

Flux.—A preparation used to assist the flowing of solder and to prevent the surface of the clean metal from oxidising when it is heated by the soldering bit. The three fluxes required for most soldering jobs are zinc chloride, resin and tallow.

Footings.—These are courses of ordinary bricks laid directly on the foundation, and bedded in cement mortar. Each course is one half-brick wider across than the course above, and projects equally on each side of the wall.

Fox Marks.—Rusty-coloured marks ranging in size from pin-points to long streaks, which disfigure prints which have been attacked by damp.

Fox-wedged Joint.—This is a mortise-and-stub tenon joint used in hardwood, and is secretly nailed. The mortise is undercut at its ends to make it longer at the bottom than on the edge of the stile. The tenon, with slightly tapered wedges loosely inserted in saw kerfs, is pushed into the mortise, the joint is cramped up and the wedges are forced into the kerfs to spread the tenon and make it fit the mortise.

French Polish.—The name given to a wide range of material used in french polishing, either in the polish rubber or by brush. The following is a list of various french polishes as applied to several kinds of timber. *French polish* is the cheapest grade sold and is chiefly used on floors or cheap grades of furniture of all classes. *Button polish* is used on mahogany where it is required to obtain a medium to a light colour; on oak which is required to be light, such as light oak, and where a lighter yellow colour is required and for medium to dark walnut. *White polish* is used on natural oak, light walnut and on all work where natural or very pale colours are required. *Garnet polish* should be used on oak, mahogany, walnut, etc., where dark shades are required. *Red and black polish* are used where depth of colour is required, and *brush polish* on all kinds of timber with colour as required by mixing.

French Polishing.—The process of applying a thin film of shellac over a properly prepared surface of wood with the object of beautifying the grain and producing dull, semi-dull and bright finishes. It can be applied to any of the chief woods used for furniture, such as walnut, mahogany and oak.

Frog.—A depression formed in the broad, flat face of a brick, reducing the weight of the brick and affording a grip, or " hey," for the mortar.

Front Door Lock.—A front door lock has no wards, but has three or four levers instead of only one. In the centre of each pivoted lever there is an irregular slot, and when the bolt moves in unlocking the door, the peg, which is part of the bolt, slides through the slot in the lever. The peg, however, cannot slide freely unless the levers are lifted sufficiently to give a clear passage. Hence it will be noticed that in this kind of lock the key is cut into a series of steps.

Frieze.—An ornamental horizontal band or strip on a wall.

Fuming.—An unusual and attractive method of finishing oak. The process consists of placing the article to be fumed in a box or chest in which are placed one or two saucers containing strong ammonia. The oak contains gallic acid, which is chemically acted upon by ammonia fumes, the result of the action being the forming of a greyish-brown substance.

"Fur."—The name given to a lime deposit that forms on the inside of boilers in districts where the water is hard.

Fuse.—A protective device inserted in an electric wiring installation. It consists of a special piece of metal wire held in a porcelain holder. Should the current suddenly rise to limits of danger, the fuse wire immediately melts and automatically breaks the circuit.

G

Gable.—The part of the roof formed by continuing the roof straight to the end wall, which is then built up to the slopes of the roof and the ridge plate. The upper part of an end wall above the level of the eaves, beneath the end of a ridge-roof that is hot hipped or returned on itself. Generally triangular.

Gable Window.—A window in a gable or one having a gable top.

Gauge Box.—A strong wooden box about 18 × 12 × 12 inches, used as a measure when gauging the quantities of materials for making cement, etc.

Gauge Rod.—A straight batten of convenient length with brick courses clearly marked. It is used like a rule, the lower end being rested on a piece of slate or iron projecting from the bed joint of the starting course.

Gesso Work.—A simple craft consisting of modelling or painting with a brush, using a thick liquid instead of a paint.

Gilding.—A form of decoration applied to picture frames, lead lights, name boards, etc.

Glasspaper.—Paper glued and sprinkled with powdered glass. Glasspapering is the final operation when preparing the surface of wood, and is necessary to remove the plane marks. It must be kept dry, as dampness softens the glue. Waterproof paper may be obtained for outside work. Grade " 0 " is used for very fine work, and grade " 2 " for rough work.

Glazing.—The process of fitting a piece of glass into a wooden frame.

Glue.—A sticky substance extracted from the hides, hoofs, etc., of animals boiled to a jelly. Scotch glue is generally considered to be the best. It is sold dry in cakes, the strongest being of an amber colour, and is used hot. Glues are also obtainable for use cold.

Glue Block.—Small blocks of wood, square in section, glued in the angle of the joint formed by two pieces of wood, to strengthen the joint. The blocks are prepared in a long length and cut off to suit the particular position in which they are required.

Glue Pot.—A special pot for heating glue. The vessel holding the glue is placed in an outer container partly filled with water, so that the heat reaches the glue through the medium of water.

Going.—The going of stairs is the horizontal distance between the faces of two adjacent risers. It does not include the nosing of a tread.

Gouge.—A gouge is similar to a chisel, but is curved in shape for circular work. There are two kinds, known as " outside ground " and " inside ground "; the former is used for forming a hollow depression, the latter in cases where the shape is curved in one direction only.

Graining.—The process of imitating in paint the colours and markings of oak, mahogany, walnut, maple or other wood. It possesses many advantages over plainer treatments; it lasts for a long time, can be re-varnished from time to time, and any knocks or abrasions can be easily touched up. A groundwork of plain paint in the lightest colour of the real wood is required. Graining colours, or scumbles, as they are called, are generally oil colours mixed at such a consistency as to be semi-transparent. Brush graining is done by simply coating the ground colour with the approximate scumble colour laid on very sparingly. Various effects can be obtained by combing while wet with a grainer's comb, by stippling or by rolling.

Graining Papers.—Transfer papers used for a useful form of decoration for walls, doors, etc. The principle of the transfer graining method is the printing of the grain pattern with a mixture of colouring matter and glue or other binder, which is soluble in water, so that when the graining paper is moistened with water the glue is softened and allows the colouring matter to be transferred to a prepared surface.

Granolithic Floor.—A floor with a top surface consisting of stone or marble chippings.

Grating.—(See Airbrick.)

Gravel Planks.—Boards ranging in sizes from 1 × 6 inches to 1½ × 9 inches, used at the bottom of fencing to resist earth pressure.

Grindstone.—A circular stone so hung that it can be rotated upon an axis, as for sharpening tools. It is not used for producing a cutting edge, but one for removing a superfluous thickness of metal.

Grouting.—A process of finishing the surface of a brick path. It is accomplished by pouring liquid cement over the surface and brushing it vigorously into the joints. The grouts on the surface must not be allowed to harden, but should be washed off with clean water and the bricks scrubbed to cleanse them.

Grummet.—A washer made of tow.

Gudgeon Bolt.—Similar to a Lewis bolt, but has a gudgeon instead of a bolt and nut.

H

Half-lap Joint.—A form of halved joint, the difference being in the projecting ends.

Half-round Gutter.—A gutter, semi-circular in shape, carried on wrought-iron stays.

Half-timbered.—Built of heavy-timbers with the spaces between filled with plaster.

Hammer.—A tool used for driving in nails. The shaft is held at the end and not near the head to obtain the best results. The driving face must be kept clean by rubbing it on emery cloth, and the head must be securely wedged to the shaft.

Hard Soldering.—A convenient method of joining or repairing metal surfaces when a stronger join than that given by soft soldering is required. Hard soldering cannot be applied to metals with a low melting point, such as aluminium, lead or pewter, but silver, copper, steel, nickel-silver, gunmetal, etc., can all be worked with successfully. The solder used is known as silver solder.

Hardwood Overlay Strip Flooring.—This consists of thin boards, prepared all round with square edges to sizes such as ¼ × 3 inches, ¼ × 3½ inches, 5/16 × 3 inches, 5/16 × 3½ inches, etc., in random lengths running from 4 feet to 14 feet. The strips are laid over a deal sub-floor with warm glue and nailed through the top with panel pins.

Hasp.—The fixed portion of a lock into which the bolt slides.

Haunch.—A short piece of a tenon left where the tenon has been reduced in width. The haunching is the recess cut to receive the haunch. The purpose of the haunch is to prevent a rail from warping or twisting out of position, and also to permit a tenon to be wedged when at the end of a stile.

Haunched Tenon.—A type of mortise-and-tenon joint used in the construction of panelled doors and other similar framing. A joint cut on the door rail which finishes flush with the end of the stile.

Hawk.—A flat piece of wood about 9 inches square, used for holding small supplies of mortar.

Headers.—The name given to bricks laid across a wall.

Hearth.—The floor of a fireplace.

Heel.—That part of a tool that is nearest to the handle.

Hip.—The junction of the two adjacent slopes of a hipped roof.

Hipped Roof.—A roof which, instead of having a gable, has the eaves continued across the end of the building, and the roof is sloped up from these eaves, so that a triangular surface of roof is formed, terminating at the ridge and with the sides of the triangle meeting the two main slopes of the roof.

Hip Rafter.—A rafter which has its foot on the wall plate at the corner of a building and its head fitting up to the end of the ridge plate.

Hod.—A box-shaped device for carrying bricks. About 1 cwt. of bricks are generally carried in the hod.

Holdfast.—A staple mostly used for inserting between the joints of brickwork.

Hot Lacquer.—A methylated spirit and shellac solution coloured with a natural colouring matter such as turmeric, dragon's blood, etc. The lacquer is applied to the heated article.

Housed Joint.—A joint made by sinking the end of one piece of wood into another piece without reducing its thickness.

Housing.—When the end of one timber is resting in another piece it is said to be housed. Where strength is of first importance, it is usual to house about ½ inch of the rail in addition to the tenon. Housing joints are often used for rails when they are thinner than the post.

Hydrometer.—A device used for testing the specific gravity of acid.

I

Inlay Banding.—A branch of woodwork similar to marquetry. It consists of making a recess in the wood to be inlaid, fitting the banding to it and gluing it in. The recess may be at the edge or a little way in.

Iron Screws.—These screws are stronger and cheaper than other metal screws, but corrode quickly, especially in oak or outside work. They should be greased before insertion, to prevent corrosion. They may be obtained up to 6 inches long.

J

Jack Plane.—The most useful general-purpose plane. It is used for rougher work and for reducing wood approximately to size. A useful average size is a length of 16 inches or so, with a cutter 2¼ inches wide.

Jack Rafter.—The shorter rafters carried between the hip rafter and the wall plate. Also the rafters extending from the valley rafter to the ridge.

Jamb.—A side post or side of a doorway, window, etc.

Joist.—A horizontal timber in a floor or ceiling. Different kinds of timber are used, according to the size of joist and class of work. For joists of small section, such as for dwelling-houses, northern pine, more commonly referred to as Scotch fir, red or yellow deal, is used.

Jumper.—The portion of a tap to which the washer is fixed. Its object is to prevent the rotation of the washer when the tap is turned. If the washer were to rotate with the tap it would soon wear out on the seating. In most taps, when the spindle of the tap is unscrewed, the jumper will remain in the cavity, and must be lifted out. Some taps, however, are made with the jumper fixed.

K

Keene's Cement.—A very pale-pink coloured substance, which when mixed with water is used for repairing cracks in plaster ceilings, walls, etc. It dries fairly rapidly, and only sufficient quantity for the immediate job in hand should be mixed.

Kerf.—The channel made by a saw, or the width of such a channel.

Keyhole Saw.—(See Pad Saw.)

Knot.—A defect in a piece of wood, which weakens the timber from a constructional point of view and is bad when in a tenon or mortise.

Knotting.—The process of treating each knot and woodwork immediately surrounding it with a special " knotting " compound to prevent resin exuding from the knot and staining the finish. Knotting can be purchased already prepared or can be made by dissolving 4 ounces of shellac in 1 pint of methylated spirit.

L

Lap.—The horizontal distance between vertical joints of brickwork. It should be one-fourth the length of a brick.

Lap Joint.—One in which the two pieces of timber or other material slightly overlap each other.

Lapped Dovetail.—A joint used in the construction of drawers and fittings of a similar nature where the end grain is not to be seen on one side.

Latch.—A cheap mechanism for holding a door closed.

Lath.—A thin strip of wood, such as one of a number nailed to studs or beams and serving to support a coat of plaster, or on rafters to support shingles or slates.

Lath-and-plaster Wall.—A comparatively light form of wall capable of being supported by the standard floor joists and used when support for a brick wall cannot be arranged. It is constructed by nailing a piece of timber, 3 × 1½ inches, on the top of the floor boards and fixing a similar one under the ceiling joists. Upright studs are then erected between these two rails, being evenly spaced, about 14 inches apart (except where the doorway occurs). Laths are then nailed horizontally to this framework on either side, about ¼ inch apart and these are then covered by hair plaster.

Leaded Window.—A window in which the glass is fixed in by strips of lead of H section instead of putty.

Lean-to Roof.—A roof with only one slope. The rafters are supported at their head and foot on wall plates. Specially suitable for small outhouses, etc.

Leclanché Cell.—A small primary battery used for operating electric bells. Leclanché cells have a glass container full of a solution of sal-ammoniac with a porous pot and a 3-inch rod standing partly submerged in the fluid.

Lewis Bolt.—Sometimes called a rag bolt, this bolt is used for heavy fixings. The body of the bolt is larger than the threaded portion and the surface is roughened. It is inserted in the wall and cemented in.

Lift and Force Pump.—A pump used for cleaning out the waste pipes from bath, lavatory basin and sink.

Lime Mortar.—Mortar prepared with lime and sand in the proportions of 1 to 2. There are two kinds of lime generally used, the ready-ground limes, used in much the same way as Portland cement, and the blue bias, or semi-hydraulic lime.

Limed Oak.—An attractive method of finishing oak which leaves the wood very light.

Limewash.—A substance used as a cheap form of decoration for walls. A useful recipe for limewash is to set a quantity of lump lime, shake it with boiling water and then thin it with skimmed milk. One ounce of alum, dissolved in water, should be added to each gallon of the mixture.

Lining.—The word "lining," as used in relation to carpentry and joinery, is the term applied to the more or less decorative woodwork which covers the jamb and undersides of lintels in door and window openings, protecting the angles and, in the case of doorways, forming the framework to which the door is hung.

Lino Brads.—Small headless nails used for fixing linoleum.

Lintel.—A beam placed across the top opening of a window or door and of sufficient strength to carry the weight of the wall above and that portion of the roof which bears upon it. A common plan is to set a pre-cast concrete beam on the slabs at each side of the opening and to build it into the wall. Another plan is to use a piece of stout angle iron bedded on the jambs.

M

Male Thread.—A thread cut on an exterior surface, such as the thread of a bolt or screw.

Mallet.—A tool used for driving wood chisels, for knocking light framing together, and for other purposes where the use of a steel-faced hammer would leave unsightly marks.

Manhole.—A chamber built of bricks set in cement mortar on concrete foundations and provided with a removable cast-iron airtight cover, enabling the condition of the drains to be inspected.

Mantel.—The wooden framing to a fireplace, used primarily to provide an architectural finish to the more unsightly fixing of the fireplace interior to the brickwork, and secondly to enhance the beauty of the room.

Mantel Register.—A type of combined surround and mantel, usually made of cast iron.

Marquetry.—A form of inlay in veneer, just as ordinary inlay is carried out in solid wood. It is laid either on solid grounds or else inlayed into a solid piece of wood, as in the case of a finger plate with a piece of marquetry let in.

Matchboard.—A board that has a tongue on one side and a corresponding groove on the other.

Maul.—A heavy wooden hammer.

Metal-faced Plywood.—Plywood faced with metal on one or both sides. It is used for panelling outbuildings or for purposes where it will be exposed to severe conditions. It can be obtained in all such sizes in which ordinary sheet metal is sold. The standard thicknesses are $\frac{3}{16}$, ¼, ⅜ and ½ inch.

Mitre.—The angle between any two pieces of wood or moulding where they join or intersect.

Mitre Block.—A simple device for cutting a mitre, and consists of two pieces of wood planed up true and screwed or nailed together, the top piece being smaller to leave a platform on which to place the work. Saw cuts are made in the top piece at an angle of 45°, one left-handed, the other right.

Mixing Board.—A large wooden board placed flat on the ground and surrounded on three sides with vertical pieces held in place with pegs and nails, used for mixing cement, etc.

Mortar.—A prepared substance used to bed and joint brickwork. It has several functions. It distributes the pressure evenly throughout the brickwork, it holds the bricks in place, and prevents the transmission of moisture, sound and heat from one face of the wall to another. Mortar is composed of two ingredients, one called the aggregate and the other the matrix, the strength of the mortar depending on the proportion of these ingredients. Portland cement or lime is usually the matrix, sand the aggregate.

Mortise.—A hole, generally rectangular, cut in a piece of wood.

Mortise-and-tenon Joint.—A joint in which a hole is cut in one piece of wood into which fits a projecting piece cut in the end of the second piece.

Mortise Lock.—A lock that is fixed in a special slot, cut out from the edge of the door.

Mosaic Work.—A decorative process for floors and walls in which small pieces of coloured stone, marble, pottery, glass and other materials, known as tesseræ, are embedded in cement to form a pattern.

Mullion.—A division piece between window lights or panels.

N

Nail.—A pin or slender piece of metal used for driving through or into wood or other material to hold separate pieces together. It may be of iron, steel, etc., and may be wrought cast or cut. The oval wire nail is the best where appearance is important, as it can be punched below the surface without leaving an unsightly hole, because of the small head. These nails can be obtained up to 6 inches long. The round wire nail does not bend so easily as the oval wire, and the larger head is an advantage when appearance does not matter. Sizes are the same as for the oval wire. Cut nails are seldom used except for flooring, and sometimes fencing. They are stamped from a sheet of metal, and are therefore parallel in thickness but tapered in width. Usual sizes are 2½ inches and 3 inches long. Wrought nails are chiefly used where strength is a consideration. The spiral nail revolves when driven with the hammer, so that it acts like a screw and does not work loose easily.

Newels.—The upright members into which the ends of the strings, steps and handrails of stairs are fitted.

Night Latch.—A form of lock that can be opened with a key only from the outside, a knob being provided on the inside for pulling back the catch.

Nose.—The part of a stair tread which projects beyond the face of the riser, and is often moulded.

Nut.—A small block of metal having an internal screw-thread so that it may be fitted upon a bolt or screw.

O

Ogee Moulded Gutter.—A form of guttering usually screwed on to the wall plate or fascia board, wrought-iron stays being sometimes used in addition.

Oilstone.—Stone used for sharpening tools. Sweet oil and neat's-foot oil in equal parts may be used for oiling the stone.

Oriel Window.—A window built out from a wall and resting on a bracket or like support.

Ovolo.—A convex moulding ; a quarter round.

P

Pad Saw.—Saw used for cutting to curved outlines, the blade being very narrow. The blade is fixed in a wooden handle, and to start a cut a hole is bored through the material close to the line large enough to allow the saw to pass through.

Paint Brush.—The name generally given to a flat brush sold in sizes from ½ inch up to 4 inches. Best-quality brushes have the bristle set into rubber mastic, which is then vulcanised.

Paint Remover.—A chemical compound used for removing paint. There are two types, caustic and spirituous, the latter being the safest although also the dearest. A half-pint tin costs, usually, about 1s. or 1s. 6d. The compound is applied in a fairly thick film and left for a short time, after which the softened paint is removed.

Panel Gauge.—A gauge used to mark a line parallel to the true edge of a panel, or of any piece of wood too wide for the ordinary gauge to take in.

Panel Plane.—A metal plane used for cleaning smaller work in which a perfectly true surface is essential, or for trueing the surface of a board. A convenient size is 15½ inches long with a 2½-inch cutter.

Pantile.—A tile with a curved cross-section, making laps on each side with ad acent tiles of reverse form.

Pantograph.—A piece of apparatus used for enlarging or reducing drawings.

Paperhanger's Paste.—Paste used for fixing wallpaper to the wall. A suitable paste can be made by placing some flour in a bucket and adding cold water to it, stirring all the while until it becomes a paste of thick consistency. Beat it up thoroughly with a stout wooden stick and then, continuing to stir, add boiling water until it becomes a thin paste. Allow to cool before use.

Parliament Hinge.—A window hinge with very long flaps, which swing the window when open away from the frame, leaving sufficient space to admit the passage of the arm for cleaning the exterior.

Parquet Flooring.—This flooring may be laid direct on a sub-floor or on a base of plywood, and its main feature is the wide variety of decorative designs possible by the fitting together and gluing of pieces of hardwood of geometrical shape.

Party Fence Wall.—Walls separating the lands of different owners, when built partly on the land of one owner and partly on the land of the other are called party fence walls. They are the mutual property of the two adjoining owners and are maintainable at the joint expense of the two owners.

Party Wall.—Where two buildings adjoin it is customary, on the score of economy to build one wall instead of two to divide them. Such a wall would be built in part of the lands of each owner and becomes a party wall. The whole wall must be considered as the joint property of each owner. Nothing must be done to the party wall without notice having been given to the adjoining owner. Both have power to raise upon it, thicken it, and generally to carry out any necessary work provided the adjoining owner is not unduly inconvenienced thereby.

Pebbledash.—A method of finishing the outside walls of a house. It consists of throwing small washed pebbles on to a coat of cement.

Pent Roof.—(See Lean-to Roof.)

Perpends.—The vertical joints on the face of a wall.

Pigment.—The main ingredient of paint of which there are many of varying quality and characteristics. One of the best known is white lead.

Pincers.—Tool used for extracting and beheading nails and for other purposes where a form of hand vice is wanted for momentary use.

Pitch.—The pitch of a screw thread is the distance between the adjacent threads.

Plan.—A drawing showing the proportion and relation of parts.

Plane. A tool used to true a piece of wood, smooth it or reduce its thickness. In a sense the action of a plane is similar to the ordinary wedge-cutting action of a chisel, but differs in that the thickness of shaving it removes is controlled by the projection of the cutter from the sole ; also the angle of the cutter with the wood. An angle of 45 degrees gives the best compromise for all-round purposes.

Planks.—Wood above 9 × 1½ inches for hardwoods and 10 × 2 inches for soft woods.

Planted Rebate.—A rebate formed by planting a thin piece of wood on the face where the rebate is required. It is a form used a good deal for doors, any possibility of the door being hingebound being obviated by fixing the rebates when the door is hung.

Plaster Filling.—A method of filling in the grain when French polishing. Fine plaster of Paris is used, with which is mixed a little rose-pink.

Plinth.—The slab, block or stone on which a column, pedestal or statue rests. The uppermost projecting part of a wall or cornice.

Plumb Line.—A device for ensuring that uprights are not sloping at an angle. One can easily be constructed by attaching a weight to a piece of string and attaching to the upright to be tested.

Plywood.—From three to twenty-five layers of wood, glued or cemented together. Thickness for thickness, plywood is stiffer than ordinary wood.

Pointing.—The art of neatly finishing off the faces of the mortar joints of a brick wall.

Priming.—The first coating of paint applied to a new or bared surface.

Punch.—A tool used for driving the head of a nail below the surface of wood, so that the nail hole can afterwards be stopped.

Purlins.—The wooden beams supporting the rafters. They must be of sufficient strength to perform their duty to prevent sagging in themselves. They are supported by struts, and probably by walls also. Their size depends on the distance apart of their supports and the area of roofing carried by them.

Put Logs.—The cross-bars used in scaffolding.

Putty.—Whiting mixed with linseed oil to the consistency of dough. Used for filling holes or cracks in carpentry work, securing panes of glass in the sash, etc.

Putty-and-rag Joint.—A joint used for connecting flush pipes. Putty is passed into the cavity between the pipe and the pan and plastered around the outside in egg-shaped form. A piece of linen, painted, is then bound spirally round the putty.

Q

Quartering.—The name given to small timber approximately square in section.

Quirk.—A small groove in, beside, or between mouldings or beads; also a moulding or bead having a groove on one or both edges.

Quoin.—The external corner of brickwork.

R

Rafters.—The members that support the roofing material. They are usually supported at their ends by walls, ridges, hips, etc., and intermediately by purlins and other members. Rafters should not, as a general rule, be more than 15 inches apart, centre to centre, or 13 inches in the clear if 2-inch thick rafters are used.

Rainwater Drain.—The drain into which the water from gutters flows.

Rasp.—A tool used chiefly for shaping wood, especially prominent corners, shaping across the grain and for circular work. It is coarser than a file as the surface consists of projecting teeth, and is used as a substitute for the spokeshave and the gouge.

Rebate.—A rectangular recess cut out of the edge of framing to receive sashes, doors, glass, etc. It is cut so that another part can fit into it, therefor the position must be accurately marked with a gauge.

Rebate Plane.—A plane used for making rebates. A convenient size of cutter is $1\frac{1}{4}$ inches. The cutter is exposed at one edge.

Reducing Socket.—A socket reduced at one end and having threads to fit two different-sized pipes.

Relief Decorations.—Wall or ceiling coverings which depend for their decorative effect upon pattern and ornament which is embossed. The best-known and most widely used are Lincrusta, Tynecastle, Maglypta, Lignomur and Leatherettes.

Rendering.—The process of covering the surface of a wall with a thick layer of mortar. Two, or sometimes three, coats are applied separately and the mortar is spread with a rectangular trowel.

Resin Flux.—Flux used when soldering electrical connections.

Ridge.—The highest point of a roof where the two opposite slopes meet.

Ridge Plate.—The plate or member which runs along the ridge between the heads of the rafters.

Rim Lock.—A lock screwed against the inside surface of a door, with the bolt shooting in a box arrangement on the door stile.

Rip Saw.—As its name suggests a rip saw is used for ripping large work, i.e., cutting parallel with the grain. Each tooth is designed to act as a chisel when used for chipping out small grooves. The length of blade is either 26 or 28 inches, with three to seven teeth points to 1 inch. Generally there are from one to one and a half more tooth points to the inch at the point of the blade than at the handle.

Riser.—The vertical piece of wood between the treads of a stairway.

Rising Main.—The main supply pipe of a water system. It is usual to provide at least one draw-off tap for a supply of drinking water.

Rising-butt Hinge.—A form of hinge which raises a door slightly as it is opened, to enable it to clear a carpet or floor covering. In one type the lifting movement is obtained from a pin in the form of a square-cut spiral thread and the loose flap of the hinge which has a similar thread formed in the inside of the joint. In another type the rise is obtained by means of the flap being cut in a semi-spiral fashion at the joint.

Roller Blind.—A blind that is wound round a roller by means of a spring, when a cord is pulled.

Roof.—That part of a house which gives protection against wet weather, and binds in the walls that support it and enclose the building.

Roof Slope.—To prevent rain being driven so far under the tiles or slates as to cause water to enter the interior. The roof must slope at a certain degree of inclination.

Roughing Plane.—A plane used only for very rough work. It has no back iron, as the nature of its work demands a coarse shaving. A useful size is $9\frac{1}{2}$ inches long with a $1\frac{1}{2}$-inch cutter.

Rubber Flooring.—A floor covering consisting of specially manufactured rubber strips or tiles.

Rubber-set.—The name given to paint brushes with bristles set into a rubber mastic which is then vulcanised.

Rubbing-down.—A preparatory process before painting, after the wood has been washed down. The rubbing down is done with either pumice stone and water or waterproof glasspaper and water.

"Ruberoid."—A trade name for a roofing material made in several forms.

Rule Joint.—A device used by cabinet makers and joiners to hide the hinges which connect various parts of table tops, shutter flaps, etc., where a neat appearance is desired. It resembles the joint of an ordinary rule.

S

Sandpaper.—(See Glasspaper.)

Sanitary System.—The internal fittings, such as the w.c., bath and sink waste pipes, various traps and manholes out-of-doors, the drain pipes, the intercepting trap and connections to the public sewer.

Sash Fastener.—The name given to the small fitting usually placed on the top bar of a bottom sliding sash and on the top of the bottom bar of the top sliding sash, so fitted that one piece engages in the other, thereby preventing the window from being opened from the outside.

Sash Tool.—A brush used for painting, in which the bristle is in a round bunch. They are sold in sizes from $\frac{1}{4}$ inch diameter of bristle, rising in $\frac{1}{4}$-inch sizes up to a bunch of bristle 2 inches in diameter.

Sash Window.—A sash window is one which has two lights or sashes which slide up or down in separate channels. The top sash slides in the outside channel for the sake of weathering. The sliding sash type of window is much more easily made weatherproof, and on this account is to be preferred to the casement motion. The sashes require balancing, and this is achieved by attaching cords to each side of the sash, the cords running over pulleys fitted in the framework, weights being tied to the ends of the cords.

Saw.—A cutting instrument with pointed teeth arranged continuously along the edge of the blade. It is essentially a tool for use across or at right angles to the fibre of wood. For the purpose of separating a bundle of fibres an edge drawn across will cut the surface fibres only. A saw is required to separate fibres below the surface and this separation must be a cutting and not a tearing action. In an ordinary cross-cutting saw the forward thrust is intended to separate the fibres by removing a small piece by two parallel cuts. Each tooth is pointed so that it cuts in a manner similar to the point of a knife when held at an angle and drawn across the timber to sever the fibres. The points of the teeth are bent outwards alternately to ensure that the saw kerf is wider than the thickness of the blade.

Scaffolding.—An arrangement of wooden poles lashed together with strong cords and placed round a building to facilitate the construction. Metal tubular scaffolding, connected by patent clamps and bolts, is now used to a great extent.

Scantling.—Miscellaneous pieces of wood left after sawing large timber. Generally a timber less than 5 inches in breadth and thickness.

Scarf Joint.—A lapped joint made as by notching two timbers at the ends and bolting them together so as to form one continuous piece without increased thickness.

Screeding.—The name given to the cement coating on which tiles are fixed.

Screen Hinge.—A screen hinge is in principle several hinges connected together so as to allow the leaves to fold into each other. By their use, three or four leaves can be hinged to fold in one of four directions at any one time.

Scribing.—A method of ensuring a good joint between two surfaces such as the foot of skirting board and floor. The skirting board is temporarily fixed in position with the top edge level and the bottom about $\frac{1}{2}$ inch clear of the floor. A pair of compasses are then set to the deepest point, and starting at one end, are drawn along the floor so that one point rests on the floor and the other point marks the skirting as the compasses are drawn along. Thus any irregularities in the surface on the floor are marked on the skirting board which can be cut to the scribed mark with a panel saw.

Scroll Saw.—(See Coping Saw.)

Scumble.—(See Graining.)

Section.—A view of an object as it would appear if it were cut down the centre. A longitudinal section is a view representing an object as cut lengthwise through the centre; a horizontal section, one cut horizontally and usually through the centre.

Sectional Building.—The term applied to small houses built in parts or sections capable of being bolted or otherwise fastened together.

Secret Nailing.—A method of inserting a nail so that the head is not visible. It is done by lifting up a thin strip of the wood, about $\frac{1}{8}$ inch deep, with a small chisel. The nail is driven under the strip, which is then glued and pressed back into position. When nailing tongued boards it is usual to nail in the edges for secret nailing. The nails are driven on the skew through the tongue.

Secret Tenon.—When it is not desirable to show the tenons on the edge of framing a stub tenon is used; that is, the mortise is only made part way into the stile. To fix this kind of tenon, saw cuts are made in the tenon and their wedges inserted and glued before the tenon is driven into the dovetail mortise.

Set (on a Saw).—This is obtained by bending (springing) the points of the teeth outwards alternately in opposite directions, to ensure that the saw kerf is wider than the thickness of the blade.

Shavehook.—A small heart-shaped tool used for removing old paint from curved and hollow mouldings and the fine recesses.

Shell Bit.—A bit used for boring holes for screws. It has no screw point, but enables holes to be drilled without danger of splitting the wood.

Shingle.—A thin tapering piece of wood about 18 × 4 inches, used in courses to cover roofs.

Shooting Board.—A board used for trueing up the edge of square stuff. It is made of two pieces of plank, the lower one wider than the other, to support the plane, and the upper to form a base on which to hold the wood.

Shoring.—A method of temporarily supportin walls. The wall is supported by a stout beam.

Short Graft.—A tool used for digging post holes. It has a long narrow blade and is suitable for most soils.

Shoulder Plane.—A metal plane for fine work and when cutting end grain. It can be set to take extra fine shavings. Its pitch is low and the mouth is fine.

Shuttering.—An arrangement of wooden boards or framework to keep concrete in position while it is setting.

Sill.—A horizontal member forming the foundation or part of the foundation of a structure of any kind. It is specifically a horizontal piece of wood or stone at the bottom of a casing in a building, especially in the case of doors and windows.

Silver Solder.—A form of solder sold in thin sheets used for hard soldering.

Size.—A solution of gelatinous material as, for example, preparations of flour or glue, used to glaze a surface.

Skirting Boards.—A wooden board, the face of which is generally moulded or shaped at the top, and placed at the bottom of a wall, resting on the floorboards. Its object is to protect the bottom of the wall from knocks and also to provide a decorative finish.

Skylight.—A small window or light let into a roof.

Sleeper Walls.—Walls built parallel to the main wall and at distances of about 5 feet. They are built with bricks in a honeycomb form to allow the air to circulate, and a damp course is necessary. Sleepers are laid along the top of the sleeper walls.

Sliding Bevel.—A tool used for setting off angles in duplicate, a set-screw enabling the blade to be placed at any required angle with the stock.

Slot-screwed Joint.—A joint made by fixing screws into the edge of one board and cutting slots in the edge of the other. The slots are made about 1 inch in length, $\frac{3}{4}$ to 1 inch in depth, and of a width to fit the stem of the screw.

Slump Test.—Method of testing whether enough water has been added when mixing concrete. A funnel-shaped cone 12 inches high, 8 inches diameter at the bottom and 4 inches diameter at the top provided with handles is placed on an impervious slab. The concrete, when newly mixed, is filled into the mould in 4-inch layers and lightly tamped with a rod. When filled the mould is immediately removed and the settlement of the concrete noted. It should not exceed 2 inches.

Smoothing Plane.—A plane used for giving a smooth finish after trueing. The sizes vary considerably, but a cutter width of not less than $2\frac{1}{2}$ inches is desirable.

Socket.—A short cylinder provided with a female thread similar in size and pitch to the outside thread of the barrel it is intended to fit. It is used to join together two lengths of barrel.

Soffit Board.—A board covering the underside of eaves.

Soft Soldering.—A method of uniting metals by means of an alloy composed of tin and lead. The process is suitable only when the joint area is large or where a joint of low mechanical strength is sufficient. The following metals are all readily united with ordinary tinman's solder: copper, brass, gunmetal, bronze, nickel silver, lead, zinc, tinplate, wrought iron and mild steel. Cast iron cannot be soft soldered with any degree of success.

Soil Drain.—The drain into which the discharge from w.c., sinks, bath, etc., flows.

Soil Pipes.—The pipe taking the discharge from the w.c. and delivering it into a manhole. Usually made of cast iron and of 4 inches diameter.

Soldering.—The process of joining two pieces of metal together by means of solder.

Spar.—A rafter.

Spirit Level.—A device used for determining whether a piece of wood is perfectly horizontal. A frame firmly holds a closed glass tube nearly filled with anhydrous ether or with a mixture of ether and alcohol. When the level is lying on a flat and horizontal surface a bubble will be seen in the centre of the tube.

Spokeshave.—This tool is really a form of small plane and is used to trim off the rough surface of curved work.

Spray Painting.—A process of painting carried out with a suitable gun and air compressing device to feed the gun. In the smaller guns the paint container forms part of the gun and usually holds about a pint of spraying medium. The use of a relatively high air pressure, something in the neighbourhood of 50 to 60 lbs. per square inch is desirable. The paint is sprayed on the surface to be coated, the superior speed of application and finish offering many advantages over brush painting.

Stencilling.—A method enabling a design to be

duplicated with ease and rapidity. Briefly, the process consists in obtaining a plate having the design cut out of it. The plate is placed on the material to be ornamented and the colour brushed over the plate and only where there are areas cut away can the colour reach the material. The process can be applied to the decoration of walls, etc., and for embellishing small articles such as blotting pads, Christmas cards, etc.

Stile.—The horizontal member of a door or window into which the top and bottom rails are fitted.

Stippling.—A process of obtaining broken colour effects on a painted surface. A special stippling brush is used, consisting of a square or rectangular stock with a large number of bristles or strands of rubber fixed in at right angles, and a handle attached to the back. The stippler is simply dabbed against the wet paint.

Stock. — The block or body of a plane. The "handle" in which a die is fixed.

Stopcock.—A tap for turning off the main water supply, generally where it enters the house, or in a small brick or iron box in the ground just outside the house.

Stopping.—The process of filling small holes in wood such as the holes left when a nail has been punched below the surface. For painted work, glazier's putty is generally used, or, for inside work, whiting and glue. Litharge is used for pitch pine that has to be polished. Hardwoods to be polished require filler of the same colour. These are made by melting beeswax and mixing it with a suitable stain. Stoppers usually contract on hardening, hence the holes should be filled above the surface.

Stretchers.—The name given to bricks laid lengthways.

Strings.—The members that support the ends of the treads and risers of stairs. They are in effect beams that assist in carrying the stairs.

Struck Joint.—A joint between bricks formed by pressing the mortar with a small trowel along the upper edge of the joint, slightly below the surface of the brickwork so that the mortar joint slopes from just under the upper course of bricks to the face of the lower course. This joint presents a neat appearance and the slope throws the rain to the face of the wall.

Strut.—A piece of wood placed between two others to strengthen them.

Strut Plate.—A piece of timber against which the bottom end of a strut is supported.

Struts.—The members that support the purlins in a roof. They are compressional members, and a load applied on them tends to buckle them. Struts should be square, or thereabouts, in section.

Strutting.—When joists have a span of 8 feet or upwards they must be connected together by one or two rows of herring-bone strutting consisting of short pieces of 1½-inch square timber nailed diagonally.

Stub Nipple.—A short connection with a male thread cut from each end towards the centre, but not quite continuous. It is of just sufficient length to provide jointure between two fittings, each having only female threads.

Stucco.—A method of facing external walls. Stucco is generally composed of Portland cement and sand.

Stud.—A short intermediate post, as in a building-frame; a post to which laths are nailed.

Sweating.—A method of soft soldering without using a soldering iron. The parts to be jointed are fluxed and wired or screwed together. They are then heated and the solder is fed into the joint.

T

Tallow.—Used as a flux for soldering lead pipes or sheet.

Tan Pin.—A tapered boxwood pin used for bossing out the end of a lead pipe.

Temper.—The degree of hardness or softness of a piece of metal.

Tenon.—A projection cut on the end of a piece of wood (rail) to fit a mortise. The thickness of a tenon should not exceed one-third the thickness of the material in which the mortise is cut. The width of a tenon if the joint is to be secured with wedges should not exceed five times its thickness.

Tenon Saw.—This saw has a thinner blade than the rip or cross-cut saws, and is stiffened by inserting its upper edge in a solid steel or brass back. The blade is from 10 to 16 inches in length, with from 10 to 14 teeth to 1 inch. It is used for cutting shoulders, mitres to mouldings, and other small material.

Tessellated Path.—A path paved with blocks of alternating colours.

Tesseræ.—The name given to the small pieces of coloured stone, marble, pottery, glass and other materials used for mosaic work.

Thinner.—An ingredient of paint added to make the paint more fluid and easy of application. Also, in the case of previously bare surfaces, it helps the paint to penetrate the woodwork. White spirit or turpentine are generally used as thinners.

Three-wheel Cutter.—A cutter with three wheels, one of which is adjustable, used for cutting through metal pipes.

Throating.—A groove formed along the underside of a projecting sill and a little way from the outer edge, the purpose being to prevent rain-water finding its way under the sill and so into the wall.

Tie.—A wooden beam introduced across the walls of a building and fastened to the rafters and wall plate. A tie usually takes the form of a ceiling joist.

Tie-irons.—Pieces of metal used to tie the two walls of a cavity wall together.

Tinning.—The operation of covering the bit of a soldering iron with a thin layer of solder.

Toe.—The front part of the underneath of a plane.

Tongued and Grooved.—The name given to a form of floorboarding where one board has a projecting tongue which fits in a corresponding groove of an adjacent board.

Toothing.—When a partition wall has to be built into an outer wall a series of gaps are left in the outer walls so that the partition wall can be bonded into it. This arrangement is known as toothing.

Toothing Plane.—A plane with a scraping action rather than a cutting action, used mostly for veneering. The cutter is vertical and has a series of fine grooves parallel with the sides, so that when sharpened its edge is a series of fine points. Its object is partly to roughen the groundwork to give the glue a suitable surface to which to grip.

Transfer Graining Paper.—See Graining Paper.

Transom.—A horizontal piece framed across an opening, such as a window above a transom bar.

Transom Bar.—A horizontal construction dividing a window into stages.

Trap.—The U-shaped pipe leading away from the vent in a sink or wash basin. Normally it contains water in the two upright arms, forming a gas-tight seal to the pipe leading from the drain.

Tread.—The part of a stair on which one treads.

Trellis Work.—An arrangement of thin wooden laths arranged in meshes of various size and of square or diamond pattern, used for fencing, garden arches, etc.

Trimmer.—A short joist, spanning the joists which run on each side of the chimney breast and used because floor joists are not allowed to run into the breast owing to the risk of fire. The trimmer supports the joists which would otherwise be supported in the chimney breast. Two very short joists are then let into the trimmer at the limits of the hearth and are supported about 1 inch in the breast.

Trimming.—The framing of joists to form an opening in the floor or ceiling, as the case may be, such as a manhole, well-hole for stairs, etc., and also to avoid running the ends of the joists into the chimney breast.

Trying Plane.—A plane similar to a jack plane, but longer. It is specially used for shooting extra long joints. The length varies from 20 to 24 inches, with cutters either 2¼ or 2½ inches. As it is a somewhat heavy tool, the handle is usually closed.

Try Square.—A tool used for setting out and testing work. It consists of a stock of rosewood or ebony with a metal blade set in at right angles at one end.

Turnscrew Bit.—A bit used for driving home screws.

Twist Bit.—A tool that bores a perfectly straight hole. It has a screw end which pulls it into the wood. The spiral body of the bit fills up the hole as it is made so that the point cannot move out of the straight.

U

Undercoat.—The object of an undercoat of paint is to build up film thickness and provide an obliterative coating. Extra pigment is incorporated in undercoat paints.

Undercutting.—Before repairing a crack in a plaster ceiling the edge should be undercut so as to form a dovetail-shaped ridge for the new plaster, so that it is keyed in the crack and cannot fall out.

V

Vacuum Pump.—A pump used for removing an obstruction in a drain. It has a rubber cone which is larger than the trap, and which is fitted to a handle.

Varnish Brush.—A flat type of brush with white, stiff, springy bristles. The bristles are bevelled.

Veneer.—A thin piece of wood of which two types are obtainable, knife-cut and saw-cut, the difference being in thickness. Knife-cut veneers are obtainable in thicknesses varying from that of brown paper up to about $\frac{1}{32}$ of an inch, and have a smooth surface. Saw-cut veneers are often $\frac{1}{16}$ of an inch or even more in thickness, and the saw marks can be clearly seen on the surface.

Veneering.—The process of applying a veneer to a suitable groundwork. There are two processes, hammer veneering and caul veneering. Hammer veneering consists of gluing the veneer, laying it in position, heating the glue with a flat iron and pressing out with a veneering hammer. In caul veneering the caul consists of a flat piece of wood slightly larger than the groundwork. In use it is heated and cramped down tightly over the veneer.

Veneering Hammer.—A small hammer having a thin brass strip set into a wooden head. It is used for veneering.

Venetian Blinds.—A venetian blind is a blind composed of a number of wooden slats or laths fixed together by means of tapes and operated by a cord.

Verge.—That part of the roof covering which terminates over the gable wall.

W

Wall Board.—The name given to a variety of boards used for walls. Most of them contain wood, either in the form of laminated layers, wood pulp or compressed paper, or a combination of two or all three of these materials.

Wallpaper.—The covering used on walls. Wallpapers are usually 21 inches wide and are supplied in rolls of 12 yards.

Wall Plate.—Beam of timber placed along a wall on which the joists rest. It can be carried on a set-back or on wrought-iron corbels or supported on brick corbelling.

Wall Plug.—A wooden plug inserted in a hole made in the vertical seam of mortar in brickwork and used for fixing skirting boards, etc. The plugs should be cleft, and not sawn and should be bevelled off diagonally on each side so that the plug twists itself as it enters the hole.

Warding Files.—Files used for cutting keys.

Weatherboard.—A board prepared for the outside covering of wooden buildings, nailed on so as to overlap and shed the rain. Also a board running under the gable or eaves of a building.

Web Strainer.—A special tool used for straining the webbing across the frame of a chair or settee.

Wet Rot.—Wet rot is due to chemical decomposition of the wood, due to alternate wet and dry conditions. The condition of a house is very bad if wet rot takes place anywhere except in the outside timbers, such as the feet of door posts, window sills, etc. Soft timbers are easily attacked, and the decay is easily recognisable as the timber turns brown and crumbles away.

Wing Nut.—A nut having two projections or wings enabling it to be tightened up by hand.

Wiped Joint.—A joint used by plumbers for repairing a crack in a burst lead pipe, etc. Special coarse wiping solder is used, which can be "wiped" round the pipe while in a plastic state with a felt pad soaked in tallow and held in the hand.

Wire Coil Plug.—A plug consisting of coils of wire made on the same size screw that is to be used for fixing so that when the screw is turned into it the threads of the screw will correspond to the threads of the plug. The plug is cemented in.

Woodfiller Filling.—Woodfiller can be obtained in all shades in a stiff paste condition, and it is used for filling the grain of wood prior to french polishing. It can be thinned with genuine American turpentine.

Wormholes.—Small round holes frequently found in old furniture and oak beams and caused by the boring activities of a small grub or worm known as the Xestobium, which is the larva of the death-watch beetle.

CLASSIFIED KEY

THE HOUSE

FINANCIAL AND LEGAL

	PAGE
Buying a House	740
Having a House Built	737
Building a Bungalow	1569
Raising Money for Hire-purchase	743
Hire-purchase and Credit Trading	1273
Practical Notes on Income Tax	345
Law Concerning Purchase, Leaseholds and Rent	750
Legal Aspect of Erecting Outbuildings	756
Height Permitted for Outhouse Buildings	97
Law Regarding Fireguards	235
How to Make a Will	1276
How Assessments and Rates are Made	1514
Methods of Raising Money	1533
Ways of Saving and Investing Money	1537
Starting a Business	1562
Practical Notes on Life Assurance	1549

DECORATION AND MAINTENANCE
General.

Periodical Examination of a House	161
Leaving a House	337
Cracks in Buildings	490
Cleaning Exterior Surfaces on Buildings	1456
Planning the Redecoration of a House	198
Decorative Schemes for Rooms	624
Choosing and Furnishing a Flat	1217
Simple Rules for Colour Harmony	225
Simple Colour Schemes	974
After Decorating a Room	1266
Furnishing Nursery	1309
How to Pebble-dash a Bungalow	1345
Arranging and Equipping Small House	600
Decorating a Bathroom	673
Modernising a Bathroom	371
Fixing Wood Mantelpieces	1129
Modernising Dining-room Fireplace	1158
Name Plates	105
Fumigating a Room	334
Use of Mirrors	1262
Screening a Radiator	1315
Use of Cellulose Brushing Lacquers	455
Varnishing	141, 966
Graining	110

Painting.

Choosing the Right Paint for the Job	1409
Cellulose Painting	1153
When and How to Use Enamel	1249
Spray Painting Outfit	1033
Blow Lamps	563
Painting over Enamel	1331
Painting a Kitchen	208
Enamelling a Bath	27
Repainting Perambulator	629
Painting over Tiles	781
Removing Paint from Oak Woodwork	612
Painting Outside of House	847
Painting Interior Woodwork	705
Painting Brasswork	623
Painting Corrugated Iron	15
Painting Ironwork	167
Aluminium and Gold Paints	234
Mixing White Lead Paints	432
Paint Table	807, 1411
Tinting Paint	1115
Selection and Care of Paint Brushes	905
Preserving Brushes	26, 700
Removing Smell of Paint	827
Paint Brush Scrapers	630

Floors.

Construction of Floors and Floorings	908
Dealing with Floors	45
Waterproofing Concrete Floors	14
Plywood for Floors	158, 932
Raising Tongued and Grooved Floorboards	360
Warped Skirting Board	1072
Scribing and Fixing Skirting Boards	395
Dry Rot	808
Laying Strip Oak over Deal	873
Sinking Well for Doormat	664
How to Lay Rubber Flooring	1057
Laying Linoleum	16, 291, 366
Renovating Linoleum	15, 297
Care of Carpets	389
Rejuvenating Carpets	165
Removing Tacks	381
Laying a Parquet Floor	449
Laying Coloured Concrete Floor	190
Mosaic Work	1444
Selection of Carpets	389

Walls.

Cracks and their Causes	490
Repairing Plaster Cracks	7
Pointing Brickwork	1001
Damp Walls	24, 592
Driving Nail in Plaster Wall	271
Plugging Walls for Fixings	696
Erecting Wallboards	653
Hiding Defects in Wallpaper	118
Cleaning Wallpaper	408, 832
Making Paperhanging Board	1389
Paperhanging	53, 272, 1161
Wallpapers for Period Furniture	137
New Ways of Using Wallpaper	885
Varnishing Wallpaper	344
Painting Lining Band on Wall	1381
Using Transfer for Graining Paper	1207
Distempering	9
How to Fix Tiles	810
Imitation Tiles	983
Relief Decorations	513
Panelling in Plywood	560, 653, 933
Giving Plain Wall Half-timbered Appearance	1377
Decorative Treatments for Wall Boards and Asbestos Sheeting	1379

Ceilings.

Repairing Plaster Ceiling	7, 1219
Removing Marks	366
Distempering	9
Paperhanging	272
Decoration	292
Relief Decorations	513
Opal Ceiling	638

Windows.

Window Cleaning Preparations	907
Preventing Rain Leaking Through	1025
Stopping Rattles	894
Replacing Broken Window Panes	107
Repolishing Plate Glass	15
Frosting Glass Windows	44
Dealing with Rusty Frames	411
Fitting and Repairing Roller Blinds	184, 562
Fitting Sun Blinds	1441
Venetian Blinds	227
Draught Excluding Curtains	884
Stretching Curtains	775
Curtains	79
Curtains and Pelmets	786
"Swinging" Curtains	717
Window Painting Hint	1280
Imitation Leaded Lights	1040
Converting Sash to Casement Window	1540

Doors.

Painting a Front Door	65
How to Cure Draughts	159
If Door Shuts Badly	246
Shrunk Door Panels	487
Sliding Doors	728
Fixing Rising Butt Hinges	125
Fitting Parliament Hinges	526
Fitting a Coiled Spring	137
Spring Door Stop	809
Preventing Latch Noise	366, 718
Hints on Cylinder Locks	534
Yale and Mortise Locks	193
Loose and Worn Door Knobs	1401
Cleaning Door and Knocker Plates	492
Safeguards against Burglars	491
Wrong-handed Doors	341

Stairs.

Curing Creaks	934
Laying Carpet	1281
Avoiding Dusty Corners	15
Flexible Stair Tread Nosing	695
Stair Carpet Holders	992
Strengthening Stair Post	969
Repairing Cement Step	718
Installing Loft Ladder	769
Fitting Light on Newel Post	1267

Roofs and Chimneys.

Roof Faults and Remedies	779
Plywood	931
Repairing Gutter	1109
Coverings for Small Buildings	941
How to Cut a Hole	1312
Roof Fanlight Adjustment	566

	PAGE
Making Skylight Waterproof	1076
Repairing Conservatory Roof	1402
Smoky Chimneys	1357
Cleaning Chimney	271

Utensils.
	PAGE
Repairs to Knives, Forks and Spoons	191
Repairing and Sharpening Scissors	174
Sharpening Domestic Tools	577
Care of Razors	937
Cleaning Inside of Glass Vessels	1263
Cleaning Greasy Bottles	249
Repairing Enamelware Dish	965
Repairing Cracked Glass Vessels	214
Repairing Stoneware Jars	1237
Washing Chamois Leather	1274
Brooms	465
Sewing Machine Maintenance	348

THE WATER SYSTEM
Systems.
	PAGE
Installing Hot Water System	682
Fitting Modern Hot Water Boiler	1089
Installing Electric Immersion Heater	902
House Drainage Systems	833
Operation and Repair	545
Fitting Modern Grate in Place of Kitchen Range	1552
Slow Combustion Boilers	1556

Pipes.
	PAGE
Condensation on Exposed Pipes	1450
Burst Pipes	143, 609
Protecting Pipes from Frost	289
Preventing Drain Pipes from Splashing	700

GENERAL
	PAGE
Modern Upholstered Furniture	1264
Making Easy Chairs Comfortable	566
Making Loose Chair Covers	257
Modernising Chest of Drawers	107
Identifying Period Furniture	1362
How to Know China Marks	1291
Identifying Sheffield Plate	1392
Identifying Old Prints	1317
Identifying Marks on Silver	1275
Converting Victorian Wardrobe into Two Modern Fitments	1264
Uses for Cushions	1144
Lining Cupboard Shelves	102

UPKEEP
	PAGE
Renovating Old Furniture	63, 446
Renovating Picture Frames	182
Wormholes in Furniture	146
Dents in Furniture	446
Repolishing Old Furniture	215
Preserving Furniture	92
Polishing Leather	576
Furniture Revivers	219

	PAGE
Renovating Clothes	147
Dry Cleaning	701
Making Chair Trouser Press	1116
Keeping Shoes in Good Condition	351
Re-heeling High-heel Shoes	68
Repairing Wellington Boots	1010

	PAGE
Cleaning Choked Sink Pipe	557
Cleaning a Sink Trap	12
Curing an Air Lock	618
Leaky Flush-pipe Joint	640

Bathroom.
	PAGE
Fitting Shower Attachment to Bath	1385
Preventing Condensation	214
Fitting Bath Panels	75
Enamelling a Bath	27
Removing Bath Stains	1440
Remaking Joints on Bath Taps	785

General.
	PAGE
Cleaning Storage System	284
Mending a Tank	247, 1319
Repairing Leaky Ball Cock	19
Refitting Tap Washers	77
Dealing with Insanitary Gully Trap	1415
Cleaning Dirty Drains	298
Gutter Grating Idea	630
Securing Manhole Cover against Leakage	1311
Cesspools	1366
Water Softener	877
Water Filter	1055

THE GAS SUPPLY
	PAGE
Gas and the Therm	468
How to Obtain the Best Service from your Gas Appliances	1339
Keeping a Gas Cooker Clean	229
Detecting Gas Leakage	44
Levelling a Gas Stove	461

ELECTRICITY IN THE HOUSE
Wiring.
	PAGE
Extending the House Wiring	120

FURNITURE AND FITTINGS
	PAGE
Furniture Polishes	164
French Polishing	33, 488
Faults in Polished Surfaces	340
Restoring Cracked French Polish	124
Polishing Stained Wood	347
Polishing Inlay Work	992
Varnishing	140, 966
Darkening Solid Walnut Bookcase	1034
Enamelling Whitewood Furniture	117
Care of Billiards Table	39
Curing Tight Drawers	226
Cleaning Chairs	702
Reupholstering Chairs	155, 1284
Worn Leather	1467

FIXING
	PAGE
Bedstead Knobs	279
Castors	288, 952, 469
Drawer Knobs	197
Drawer Stops	894
Plate on Drawer Runner	652
Secret Drawer Lock	699
Clockwork Door Bell	103

CLOTHING
	PAGE
Boot Repairing Hint	143
Sewing on Buttons	1241
Mending Stockings	1248
Renovating Old Furs	264
Storing and Care of Furs	889
Removing Ironmould	1203

	PAGE
Fitting Additional Lighting and Power Points	801
Fitting Lighting and Power Points in a Garage or Outhouse	922
Fitting an Additional Switch	613
Remedying Defective Wires	507
Wiring a Doll's House	240
Saving Bell Wire	672

Lighting.
	PAGE
Best Way of Using Electric Light	853
How to Colour Electric Light Bulbs	222
Electric Christmas Tree Illumination	295

General.
	PAGE
Repairing Electric Irons, Fires and Other Appliances	1505
The £ s. d. of Electricity	356
Rigging Up Door Bell Switch	687
Fitting Electric Burglar Alarm	309
Installing Electric Bell and Indicator System	1287
Sluggish Electric Bells	637
Installing Several Loud Speakers	49
Installing Electric Immersion Heater	902
Private Telephone Installation	1390
House Telephones	435
Use of Small Power Transformer	205
Converting Bell from Battery to "Mains"	248
Care of Electric Vacuum Cleaner	1419
Electric Lock	1578

OIL STOVES
	PAGE
Care of Oil Stoves	1417
Reconditioning Oil Lamp Burners	1115

	PAGE
Furniture Steadiment	87
Glass Shelves	93
French Catch	342

REPAIRS
	PAGE
Repairing Furniture	69
Repairing Furniture Legs	116
Upholstering Chairs	155, 1284
Mending Broken Chair Frames	109
Repairing a Broken Deck Chair	142
How to Repair a Settee	1313
Cleaning and Repairing Clocks	129
Repairing Piano	1077
Repairing China and Pottery	38, 134
Resilvering Mirror	133
Remaking a Mattress	474
Curing Squeaky Bedspring	1423
Restoring Old Copper Articles	827
Removing Stains from Polished Surfaces	896
(See also "Things to Make," "Woodwork" and "Recipes")	

	PAGE
Removing Mud Stains	1358
Straw Hat Cleaner	190
Use for Old Felt Hats	1319
(See also "Things to Make.")	

CLASSIFIED KEY

RECIPES

CLEANERS

	PAGE
Window Cleaners	907
Silk Cleaner	701
Tar Remover	1421
Rust Remover	136, 1168
Paint Remover	29, 44
Varnish Remover	652
Silver Tarnish Remover	136
Furniture Revivers	219
Alabaster Cleaner	781
Household Metalwork Cleaners	135
Marble Cleaners	755
Cement Cleaners	1181
Straw Hat Cleaner	190
Removing Stains from Paper	1542

PAINTS

Undercoatings	850, 1249
Paints	234
Stucco	850
Paint for Kitchen Decoration	208
Paint for Roofs	190
Anti-rust Paints	139
White Lead Paint	66, 236, 237, 434
Red Lead Paint	411
Luminous Paint	264
Flexible Paint	214
Waterproof Paint	180
Bitumastic Paint	284

STAINS

Walnut	143
Mahogany	33
Hardwood	141
Whitewood	508
Floor	46
Shellac Solution	64
Ground Colours for Graining	534

POLISHES

French Polishes	488
Furniture	164
Floor	492

CEMENTS

	PAGE
Linoleum	15
Marble	755
Glass	15
Metal	181
Leather	576
Inlay Work	992
Grate Polish	340
Boot Dubbin	952

Pipe Joints	405, 469
Bricks	995
Mortar	95
Slates	366
Red	469
Aquarium	271, 1028
Waterproof	190, 1028
Earthenware and Stone	901
Marble	446
Glass	732, 901
Felt to Marble	901
China	38
Lead Strips	901
Window Putty	87
Coloured Floor	190
Crazy Paving	278
Rapid Hardening Concrete	816
Concrete	953
Celluloid	213
Ivory	960
Leather	901
Meerschaum	901

MISCELLANEOUS

Electrolytes for Plating	670
Etching Compounds	331
Distemper	9
Indelible Ink	1118
Invisible Ink	718
Wax Stopping	72
Wax Crayons	1440
Wax for Paper Flowers	1054
Cobbler's Wax	718

WOODWORK

	PAGE
Glue Size	32
Fly-papers	1108
Insecticide Spraying Fluid	1108
Glue for Fixing Letters on Glass	732
Insoluble Glue	44
Paper Hanging Paste	274
Hard Stopping	674
Vegetable Dyes	1251, 1376
Printing Dyes	1210
Waterproof Paper	405
Sailcloth Waterproofing	15
Fabric Waterproofs	1047
Waterproofing for Walls	596–597
Waterproofing for Stone	815
Gesso	619
Bronzing Preparation	1130, 1268
Oxidising Preparation	480
Silver Solution	133
Silver Plating Solution	379
Silver Anti-tarnish Solution	210
Lacquer	441
Solid Methylated Spirit	599
Oil Stone Lubricants	214
Raising Paste	442
Weather-glass Solution	1459
Tennis Net Preservative	446, 1163
Weed-killers	846
Wormhole Preventative	146
Bee Syrup	822
Bath Tablets	1408

FOODSTUFFS

Rissoles	1397
Cooked Meats	1237
Cutlets	1397
Pickle and Chutney	1394
Risolto	1397
Sandwiches	1198
Meringues	1257
Pot Pourri	1212
Jams	1157, 1353
Salads	1386
Drinks	1184

METHODS OF WORKING

Choosing Timber for Indoor and Outdoor Work	893
Methods of Preserving Wood	88
Plastic Wood	676
Plywood	929
Planes and Planing	481
Saws and Sawing	520
A Saw Hint	298
Using Gauges, Spokeshaves, Chisels, etc.	724
How to Use Boring Tools	1395
Drilling Soft Woods	151
Making Dowelled Joints	84
A Strong Framework Joint	1139
Tightening a Joint	468
How to Use Glue	385
Separating Glued Work	621
Simple Woodwork Joints	31
Setting Out Dovetails	1133

Knots and Splices	793
Watch Cleaning and Repair	1192
Sewing on Buttons to Hold	1241

Scoring Wood for Gluing	87
Rebating, and Chamfering	1372
Fixing Wood Screws in End Grain	534
Fixing Screws in Hard Woods	1175
Veneering	1100
Woodcarving	412
Picture Framing	1140

FINISHING

Giving a Professional Finish	677
Sandpapering Curved Surfaces	143
Wood Fillers	87
Graining	110
French Polishing	33
Polishing Stained Wood	347
Polishing Inlay Work	992
Varnishing	140, 966
Stains for Light Woods	1123
Staining American Whitewood	508

USEFUL CRAFTS

Hair Cutting (Child's)	1298
Keeping Shoes in Good Condition	351
Repairs to Wellington Boots	1010

Staining Oak	35
Staining Wood Grey	508
Colouring Oak and Mahogany	1032
When and How to Use Enamel	1249
Cellulose Painting	115
Preserving Wood	88
Creosoted Wood Treatment	64

GENERAL

Cleaning off Distemper	77
Fixing Door Lining and Architraves	975
Weatherboard Fixing Hints	30
Fitting Small Butt Hinge	733
Hinges for Screens	87
Tools for the Workshop	572
Protecting Edge Tools	536, 894
(*See also* "Things to Make," "Recipes" and "The Amateur's Workshop.")	

Mending Umbrellas	448
Renovating Pictures	183
How to Frame Pictures	1140

CLASSIFIED KEY

	PAGE
Passe-Partout	1501
Restringing Tennis Rackets	1162
Bookbinding	1301
Duplicating	981
Repairs to Eyeglass Frames	428
Repairs to Attaché Cases	203
Mosaic Work	1444
Woodcarving	412
Wood Engraving	688
Veneering	1100
Attractive Pictures for Framing	343
Gilding with Gold Leaf	232
Decoration with Transfers	1064
Marquetry	1035
Gesso Work	619
Barbola Work	1468
Working with Cellophane	567

MUSIC (WIRELESS INCLUDED)
Gramophones.

Storing Gramophone Records	265
Making a Record Filing Cabinet	887
Making Records	1169
Cleaning a Gramophone Motor	115
Replacing a Gramophone Spring	61
Mounting Gramophone Pick-up	797

Radio-Gramophones.

Making Radio-Gramophone Cabinet	1253

Wireless.

Fault Finding Chart	144-145
Eliminating Distortion	106
Care of Accumulators	710
Small Leclanché Cells	727
Reconditioning Old H.T. Batteries	431
Making Battery Charger	840
Erecting Aerials	1320
Protecting Earth Connection	110
How to Build Combination Wireless Cabinet and Bookcase	1363
Making a Modern Type Portable Receiver	1013
Building Clock Case Wireless Set	917
Constructing Radio Lounge Chair	1083
Making the E.W.3 Receivers	1523

Miscellaneous.

Repairing Piano	1077
Making a One-string Violin	921
Making a Xylophone	1522

PHOTOGRAPHY

Developing and Printing Films	397
Home-made Enlarger	1073

FOR THE PORCH

Glass Canopy	1181
Copper Step	704
House Name Plates in Wood	105
Illuminated Name Sign	524

FOR THE HALL

Hall Light	114
Copper Lantern	447
Umbrella Stand	956

	PAGE
Repairs to Handbags	569
Waterproofing Fabrics	1047
Rug Making	21
Glove Making	458, 1404
Weaving	503
Basket Work	1041

ARTISTIC CRAFTS

Engraving on Metal	331
Engraving on Glass	1056
Stained Glass Work	325
Silver Work (Making Claret Jug)	1439
China and Pottery Decoration	1234
Pewter Modelling	861
Modelling in Metal	367
Oriental Lacquer Work	441
Bronzing Plaster Cast	1130
Making Lamp Shades	495
Stencilling	138, 270, 470

HOBBIES

Useful Photographic Printing Box	1073
Notes on Infra-red Photography	1461
X-ray Photography	1515
Making Lantern Slides	1521

GAMES AND AMUSEMENTS

How to Play Billiards	42, 280
Care of Billiards Table	39
Various Billard Table Games	517
Party Games and Tricks	335
Making a Hard Tennis Court	469
Care of Tennis Racket	446
Tennis Net Preservative	1163
Restringing Tennis Racket	1162
Making Tennis Table Top	364
Making Folding Card Table	990
Golfing Games for the Garden	1086
Care of Cricket Bats	1359
Painting a Ball	366
Care of Skates	571
Making a Toboggan	1375
Making Greyhound Racing Track	843
Making Small Roundabout	1049
Building Small Boats	1002
Maintenance and Repair of Small Boats	828
Making a Magic Lantern	958
Making a Projection Screen	1252
How to Make a Zoetrope	989
Pepper's Ghost	980

MODELS

Model Glider	1457
Cardboard Modelling	1171
Building Model Boats	1221
Making a Doll's House	304, 535
Installing Model Electric Railway	1324

THINGS TO MAKE

Monk's Bench	1448
Chemical Weather Forecaster	1459
Mercury Barometer	950
Grandfather Clock	382
Curtain-covered Shelves	3

FOR THE LIVING-ROOM
Fireside.

Modern Mantelpiece	60
Old World Ingle Nook	1195

	PAGE
Leather Work	1151
Making Papier Maché Bowls	1272
Waxing Paper Flowers	1054
Glass Blowing	1329
Bookbinding in Leather	1568
Lettering	637
Printing on Fabrics	1208
Making Chair Covers	261
Raffia Work	299
Sealing Wax Craft	361, 1451
Book Repairs	266
Home-made Christmas Cards	352
Fixing Frost Flowers	768

AMATEUR'S WORKSHOP

Building the Workshop	509
Permanent Workshop Fittings	541
Tools for the Workshop	572
Power Drives and Machine Tool Installation	606
Adjusting Iron Planes	1323
Practical Notes on Using a Lathe	1426
Renovating Rusty Tools	1168

GENERAL

Rudiments of Painting	1518
Camera Lucida and Obscura	1555
Keeping Rabbits	1294
Care of Birds	1465
Collecting Butterflies and Moths	1199
Beekeeping	817
Aquariums	1027, 1467
Making a Simple Microscope	798
Making a Simple Telescope	831

CYCLING

Bicycle Repair and Adjustment	1006
Cycle Support	539

MOTORING

How to Clean a Car	357
Designs for Garages	527
Lighting a Garage	922
Making a Luggage Hold-all	922
Painting and Preserving Garages	1436
Building Trailer Caravan	1214
Making Gauntlet Gloves	458
Simple First Aid	250
Garage Door Opener	1578

(See also "Useful Crafts" and "Artistic Crafts.")

Brick Fireplace	1387
Fire Blower	1374
Sheet Iron Ashpans	1022
Electric Firescreen Radiator	217
Plywood Firescreen	154
Tiled Curb	552
Fire-iron Hanger	1048
Fireguard	235
Coal Cabinet	1087
Briquettes	1408

CLASSIFIED KEY

Books.
	PAGE
Attractive Bookshelves	3
Expanding Bookcase	176
Hanging and Standing Bookcases	1277
Trolley Bookcase	285
Bookcase from Old Drawers	469
Useful Reading Rest	430
Useful Reading Case	501
Pair of Book Ends	634
Paper Weights	630

Music.
Gramophone Record Filing Cabinet	887
Wireless Cabinet and Bookcase	1363
Radio-Gramophone Cabinet	1253
Clock Case Wireless Set	917
Combined Bookcase, Wireless and Lamp Stand	477
Radio Lounge Chair	1083

Seats.
Cosy Occasional Chair	446
Modern Easy Chair	880
Folding Armchair	598
Divan	80
Settee from Motor Seat	1204
Window Seat	314
Footstools	332
Rush-top Stool	895
Seat-box	939

Tables.
Wagon Tea-table	152
Useful Tea Wagons	997
Coffee Table	796
Folding Wall Table	181
Folding Card Table	990
Wall Desk	1434

Lamps.
Adjustable Pendant Light	534
Flickering Pillar Lamp	858
Lamp Shades	495
Anti-Glare Shades	114

Miscellaneous.
Tubular Steel Furniture	1368
Carved Chest	984
Needlework Cabinet Screen	57
Lady's Workbox	1213
Portable Workbasket	1389
Imitation Leaded Lights	1040
Sun Blinds	1441
Fog-Excluder for Windows	457
Sliding Sash	825
Ventilator for Door or Cupboard	454
Electric Fan	1454
Shelves for Flat Dwellers	256

FOR THE DINING-ROOM
Sideboards	782
Gate-Leg and Draw-Leaf Tables	321
Hatchway to Kitchen	961
Christmas Table Decorations	313

FOR THE KITCHEN
Furniture.
Gate-Leg and Draw-Leaf Tables	321
Collapsible Table	926
Emergency Table	1416
Kitchen Cabinet Table	1063
Tiled Table Top	380
Folding Table Leaf	827
Hatchway to Dining-room	961

	PAGE
Kitchen Cabinet	1137
Welsh Dresser	1189
Ice Chest	1183
Revolving Cupboard Fitment	1024

The Linen.
Washing Machine	1166
Copper Circulator	727
Improvised Copper Lid	955
Useful Ironing Cabinet	223
Linen Cupboards	376
Portable Ironing Board	405
Clothes Horses	87
Novel Use for Clothes Horse	622
Simple Clothes Airers	1180

Scullery.
Removable Draining Boards	110
Water Filter	1055
Domestic Water Softener	877
Semi-sliding Door for Shelves	927
Plate Shelves	3
Plate and Saucepan Rack	928
Saucepan Shelf	5, 700
Saucepan Tip	894
A Simple Trivet	492
Wire Handles	827
Heat-resisting Handles	1283

Miscellaneous.
Domestic Refrigerator	1543
Improvised Anvil	652
Improvised Thumb-Screw	718
Hayboxes	1131
Flypapers	1108
String Holder	239
Nail and Screw Box	1378
Chopper Shaft Lock	969
Broom Holder	1050
Vacuum Cleaner Holder	298
Electric Stirrer	1516

FOR THE LANDING
Linen Cupboards	371
Table Top	1266

FOR BEDROOMS AND BATHROOMS
Bedrooms.
Cabinet Bedstead	1382
Divan	80
Padded Top Ottoman	76
Eiderdown	553
Ultra-violet Ray Lamp	1176
Medical Coil	1011
First Aid Cabinet	540
Wardrobe	714
Bedside Table	493
Curtain-covered Shelves	3
Frameless Mirrors	8
Chair Trouser Press	1116
Compact Shoe Rack	52
Handy Tie Holder	239
Tie Press	1300
Safety-pin Holder	429

Bathroom.
Imitation Tiles	983
Adjustable Mirror	780
Toilet Compact	1099
Sponge Rack	207
Glass Holder	405

	PAGE
Tidy and Stool	445
Seats	693

FOR THE NURSERY
Furniture	1309
Fireside Settee	446
Doll's House	304, 535
Stand for Christmas Tree	239
Sand Tray	1447
Child's Motor-car	1398
Child's Scooter	268

FOR THE WORKSHOP
Home-made Equipment	1245
Building a Workshop	507
Permanent Workshop Fittings	541
Simple Cabinet Workbenches	757
Pole Lathe	1149
Bench Grips	1415
Inexpensive Saw Clamps	1422
Small Drills	1096
Toolbox Tray Lifter	1010
Bunsen Burner	489
Blow Lamp	1338
Soldering Iron Cover	406
Wood Panel Cutting Device	1178
Beading Tool	1168
Measuring Device	1135
Inexpensive Bar Bender	1435
Picture Framing Clamp	1355
Glue Pot	781
Syphon	396

FOR THE GARDEN
Decoration.
Sundial	128, 814
Ornamental Pond	897
Rockery	1347
Ornamental Fountain	1051
Concrete Steps	1165
Concrete Ornaments	953
Concrete Roller	970
Rustic Decorations	169
Trellis Fence and Door	353
Dwarf Brick Wall	126
Brick Wall	993
Gates	1243
Aviary	1462
Simple Stonework	1529

Buildings.
Summer-house Pavilion	1112
Triangular Summer House	1238
Greenhouses	865
Glass House	200
Small Poultry House	97
Tool Sheds	417
Bicycle Shed	615
Brick Coal House	551
W.C.	1335

Miscellaneous.
Storage Bin	26
Plant Propagation	736
Efficient Sprayer	218
Zinc Trays for Greenhouses	852
Dog Kennel	1306
Dog Exercising Track	1453
Wooden Coal Bunker	661
Heating Apparatus for Sand Pit	1068
Incinerator	1146
Chicken Brooder	1351
Poultry Run	666

CLASSIFIED KEY

	PAGE
A Swing	1119
Improvised Crowbar	405
Home-made Tools	1097
Barrow	935
Three-foot Rule	366
Clothes Post	651
Metal Tent Peg	1152
Hammock	1066
Tents and Shelters	1332
Pail Tilter	934
Helter-Skelter	1531

GENERAL
Building Brick Wall	993
Hiding Places for Valuables	1179
Pair of Steps	1460
Flight of Wood Stairs	1229
Floor Sander	1132
Finger Plates for Doors	374
Paperhanging Board	1319
Spray Painting Outfit	1033
Screen out of Clothes Horse	622
Battery Charger	840
House Telephones	435
Private Loudspeaking Telephone Installation	1398
Electric Motor	1106
Knife Grinder	1124
Lightning Conductor	709
Weather Indicator	681
Wind Vane	735
Useful Duplicator	986
Pantagraph	1354
Microscope	798
Telescope	831
Cherry-Stone Chains	1240
Sculling Exerciser	1547
Kites	1560

(*See also* " Hobbies," " Useful Crafts " and " Artistic Crafts.")

THE GARDEN

LAYOUT
	PAGE
Suggested Layouts	1232
Trench Garden	938
Bricks and their Uses	126
Improvised Level	652
Construction of Garden Paths	220
Laying Crazy Paving	187, 278
Rapid Hardening Concrete	816
Inlaying Concrete with Coloured Strips	830
Measuring Up Concrete	366
Uses for Broken Glass	700
Sinking a Small Well	977
Setting Up a Flagstaff	405
Tapered Post Sockets	630

Outdoor Wall Hooks	87
Beekeeping	817

UPKEEP
Hints on Watering	1258
Stopping a Leaky Can	1310
Care of Wooden Barrels	1188
Painting Rain Water Barrels	894
Lawns	1185
Lawn Mowers	462
Renovating Grass Shears	44
When to Plant	719
Rockery Plants	1350
Training Loganberries	1120
Horticultural Preparations, Fertilisers and Manures	1424
Weed Killers	846
Destroying Tree Roots	576
Use for Old Shovel Handle	1423
A Bonfire Hint	271
Leaks in Fish Ponds	492
Tightening Slack Wire Netting	446
Reinforcing Wood Posts	15
Capping Garden Posts	181
Repairs to Fences, Gates and Sheds	762
Repairing Conservatory Roof	1402
Painting a Greenhouse	236
Repairing Tool Handles	160

(*See also* " Things to Make " and " Hobbies.")

METAL WORK

METHODS OF WORKING
	PAGE
Useful Metal Working Hints	1164
Notes on Riveting	1111
Working Metal-faced Plywood	1121
Making Tubular Steel Furniture	1368
Lining Box with Metal	1031
Soft Soldering	211

Hard Soldering	13
Soldering Aluminium	1438
Making Killed Spirits of Salts	630
Taking Dents out of Thin Metal	1416
How to Shape Wire	1286
Sheet Metal Ornaments	506
Relief Modelling in Metal	367
Engraving on Metal	331
Two File Hints	717
Metal Screw Threads	1038
Useful Clip	955
Uses of Corrugated Iron	25

TIME, LABOUR AND MONEY-SAVING IDEAS

	PAGE
Uses for Old Razor Blades	230
Razor Blades (keeping)	181
Using the Loft	894
Use for Old Umbrella	271
Cleaning Chimney	271
Stopping Chimney Fire	181
Keeping Milk in Hot Weather	1242
Preventing Wine Turning Sour	350
Packing Bottles	239
Removing a Cork	340

Spitting Kettles	340
Removing Stamps	718
Fountain Pen Repair	487
Flannelette Duster	446
Picture Frame Tips	473
Glass Cutting	1423
Drilling Holes in Glass	199, 544
Making Loose Screws Hold	1293
Simple Marking Gauge	700
Holding Round Pieces for Sawing	566
Safe Wood Chopping	405
Hammer Improvement	110
Concealing Ugly Tiles	446
Fixing Weatherboard	30
Spring Catches	44
Whipping a Rope End	87
Waterproofing Matches	534
Removing Stubborn Nut	231
Uses for Inner Tubes	1019

INDEX

Acid,
  accumulator, 710
  etching, 331
Accumulator,
  charger, making, 840
  faults, wireless, 711
  radio, charging, 205
  repairs, wireless, 711
A.C. receiver, 1523
Aerial, wireless, 1320
Afternoon tea-table, 796
Air lock, curing, 618
Airing
  cupboards, 376, 683
  shoes, 52
Alabaster,
  cement for, 446
  cleaning, 781
All-in system, 356
Allotment sheds, 417
Aluminium,
  cleaning, 135
  electro-plating, 672
  leaf, applying, 1216
  paint, 1216, 1409, 1413
  soldering, 211, 1436
  surfaces, etching, 331
  tinning, 1431
Amateur's workshop, 509, 541, 572, 606
American
  cloth, 103
  whitewood, staining, 508
Ammonia, 680
  fuming, 416
Anaglypta, 292, 513
Ancient lights, 755
Angle brackets, fixing, 697
Annealing
  glass, 1329
  wire, 1286
Annuities, post office, 1538
Anti-glare shades, 114
Antimacassars, 1265
Antique
  appearance for metal, 369
  furniture, cleaning, 215
  silvering, 379
Animals, how to hold, 1072
Aquarium,
  cements, 271
  making, 1027
Archimedian drill, 590, 1397
Architect's plans, 738
Architraves, door, 875
"Ark Royal," 1221
Armature, 634, 1106
Armchair,
  folding, making, 598
  tubular steel, 1371
Asbestos
  covered garage, 531
  sheets for bath panels, 75
  sheets for garage, 533
  sheeting, 1381
  string, 550, 1283
  wall board, 659
Ash pans, sheet iron, 1022
Assessment, income tax, 345
Assessments, 1514
Assurance, life, 1549
Atmospheric pressure, 950

Attaché cases, repairs to, 203
Attic,
  insulation, 656
  using, 537
  wallboards, 654, 656
Auction sales, 750
Austrian oak, 449
Automatic regulators, 1559
Aviary,
  constructing, 1462
  law-regarding, 756
Awning 1441, 1443
Axes, sharpening, 591
Azol, 397

Back iron, 481
Backing,
  book, 1304
  picture, 473
Bacon fat, removing, 704
Bakelite, 101
Ball
  catches, 287
  cock, leaky, repair of, 19
  painting, 366
  valve, cistern, 838
Balmain's paint, 264
Bar bender, making, 1435
Barbola work, 1468
Barometer, mercury, 950
Barn paints, 1413
Barrel, making chair of, 446
Basket work, 1041
Bath,
  care of, 128
  enamelling, 27
  panelling, 75, 373,
  stains, 1440
  tablets, effervescent, 1408
  taps, remaking joints, 785
Bats, cricket, 1359
Battens, floor, 452, 664, 915
Battery,
  charger, constructing, 840
  for plating, 669
  receiver, 1524
Beading, 680
  sash, window, 644
  tool, home-made, 1168
Beads, window, 108
Beating up, 505
"Beatrice" stove, 200
Bed,
  lights, 806, 855, 856
  spring, squeaky, 1423
"Bedchester," 604
"Bedinet," 605
Bedrooms, 4, 855, 1310
Bedside table, making, 493
Bedstead,
  cabinet, making, 1382
Bee-keeping, 817
Bees' wax, 18
Bell,
  assembly, telephone, 438
  door, clockwork, 103
  electric, operating, 206
    repairing, 1509
  installation, 248
  transformers, 1490
  wire, rubber insulated, 48
  wire, saving, 672

Bench,
  grips, 1416
  hook, 523
  metal working, 759
  seat, rustic, 170
Bevelled rebates, 1372
Bicycle,
  lining, 1070
  repair, 1006
  shed, making, 615
  support, 539
Billiards,
  playing, 42, 280
  table, 40
  variations from, 517
Bill of exchange, 1536
Bill of sale, 1536
Binder, 432
Binding,
  book, re-colouring, 267
  books, 1303
Bird
  bath, 340, 954
  haven, rustic, 171
Birds, 1072, 1465
Bit, soldering, 212
Bits, twist, 726
Bitumen,
  felt, 941
  macadam, 220
  wood preservation, 167
Bituplastic, 596
Blackberry jelly, 1157
Blacklead stains, 92
Blank, key, 196
Block,
  flooring, 915
  plane, 486
  printing, 1208
  wood, 690
Blood stains, 1542
Blooming, 675, 967
Blow-lamps, 66, 563, 1338
Blower, fire, 1374
Blowholes, filling, 1164
Board,
  fitting, 214
  ironing, making, 224
Boats,
  model, building, 1221
  model, power-driven, 1227
  small, building, 1002
  small, maintenance, 828
Bobbin; transformer, 1493
Bodying-in grain, 33
Boiler,
  faults and remedies, 546
  gas, 682
  hot water, fitting, 1089
  independent, 682
  pipes, testing, 201
  types of, 545
Boilers, slow combustion, 1556
Bonding, brick, 1575
  bricks, 551, 996
Bone-black polish, 576
Bonfire hint, 271
Book
  binding, 1301
  ends, 634, 679
  match case, 1501

Book
  muslin, 500
  repairs, 266
  rest, making, 430
  shelves, 3
Bookbinding, 1568
Bookcase,
  and wireless cabinet, 1363
  designs, 1277
  expanding, making, 176
  for storing records, 265
  from drawers, 469
  trolley, making, 285
Book-keeping, 1566
Books, gilding on, 234
Boot
  dubbin, 952
  repairing, 743, 978
Borax, 13
Border, decorating, 1546
Bordering paper, 1475
Borders,
  basket, 1043
  laying, 515
Boring tools, 572, 1395
Borrowing money, 744
Bosting-in, 413
Bow saw, 521
Bowls, papier mâché, 1272
Bottles, packing, 239
Box,
  hingeless, 214
  light, doorway, 114
  lining with metal, 1031
  mattress, 1265
  nail and screw, 1378
  stool, making, 333
Box kite, 1560
Brace, using, 1395
Bradawl, 581, 1395
Brass,
  articles, bronzing, 317
  bronzing solution for, 1268
  cleaning, 135
  softening, 1164
  turning, 1431
Brawn recipe, 1237
Brazing, 14
Brick
  cleaning, 1456
  cutting, 127, 996
  laying, 126
  paths, 872
  wall, building, 993
  walls, cracks in, 490
Bricklaying tools, 993
Brickwork,
  curing deposits on, 110
  fixing wall boards to, 657
  plugging, 696
  pointing, 1001
Brine tank, 878
Briquettes, making, 1408
"Broadwell" centrifugal pump, 1053
Broken glass, use for, 700
Bronze powder,
  applying, 443
  for Gesso, 621
  stencilling with, 270
Bronzing
  brass articles, 317

1591

INDEX

Bronzing
  plaster cast, 1130
  solution, 1268
  steel, 1164
Brooch, pewter, 864
Broom, holder, 1050
Brooms, care of, 465
Brown hide, 1264
Brunswick black, 795
Brush,
  cement, preparing, 43
  graining, 111
  hand, 1048
  handles, protecting, 700
  hook, 652
  rack, 6
Brushes,
  care of, 906
  electric motor, 1107
  hair, stiffening, 516
  varnish, 968
Brushing, cellulose, 1154
Buckram, 567, 789
Builder, payments to, 740
Builder's estimates, 739
Building
  a bungalow, 1569
  regulations, local, 738
  society, investing with, 1538
  loan, 744, 1534
Buildings,
  cracks in, 490
  bye-laws regarding, 756
"Bulgin" distant wireless control, 50
Bull-nose plane, 486
Bungalow,
  building, 1569
  electric wiring for, 1476
  how to pebble-dash, 1345
Bunsen burner, making, 489
Burglary, safeguards against 309, 338, 491,
Burners,
  blow-lamp, cleaning, 563
  gas, 229, 1339, 1342
  oil lamp, 1115
  stove, 1417
Burning off, 66, 565
Burning, poker work, 1499
Burnishing, 218, 692
Burns, 251
Burst water pipes, 143, 609
Bush, making, 1433
Business, starting, 1562
Butt
  hinge, door, fitting, 733
  joint, 31, 387
  jointed wood, planing, 486
Butterflies, 1199
Buttons, sewing, 1241

Cabinet
  doors, hinges for, 733
  screen, needlework, 57
  workbenches, making, 757
Cake stands, rustic, 172
Calendar, making, 1451
Camel hair mops, 906, 907
Camera
  lucida, 1555
  obscura, 1555

Can, leaky, stopping, 1310
Candle stains, removing, 704
Candles, electric, 295, 853
Cane baskets, making, 1041
Caning, 1045
Canister lid, tight, 298
Canvas,
  flexible paint for, 214
  shelter, 1334
  shoes, 351
Carbon
  dioxide, 1030
  holders, 1177
  paper, 413
Caravan, trailer, 1214
Carborundum, 544, 577
Card table, folding, 990
Cardboard modelling, 1171
Carpet,
  holders, 1281
  old, use for, 446
  rejuvenation, 165
  selection and care, 389
  stains, removing, 92
  stair, laying, 1281
Carving
  knives, sharpening, 578
  picture moulding, 1142
  tools, 412
  wood, 412
Casement,
  curtains, 79
  sliding, making, 825
  window, 1540
  securing, 339
Castors,
  broken, 75
  damaged, replacing, 288
  sliding, fixing, 952
Caul, preparing, 1036
Caulking boat seams, 1004
Caustic soda, 877
Ceiling,
  blackened, 1450
  cracks, 490, 1219
  decoration, 292
  distempering, 11, 198
  guide lines, 277
  hook, squeaking, 1048
  marks on, 366
  paper, measuring, 272
  papering, 277
  papers, 292
  plywood, 932
  reliefs, 513
  stains, curing, 797
Cellofold, 567
Cellophane, uses for, 567
Celluloid
  accumulators, 712
  cements, 213
Cellulose
  lacquer, 117, 374, 455
  painting, 1153, 1413
Cement,
  wall, mixing, 1345
  waterproof, 190, 1028
Cementing
  cloth to wood, 15
  plugs, 699
Cements, useful, 901
Centre bit, 1396
Centre square, 718
Cesspools, 1367

Chains,
  cherry-stone, 1240
  cycle, 1008
Chair,
  beds, 603
  cane, making, 1044
  covers, loose, 257
  easy, 880
  frames, broken, 109
  lounge, radio, 1083
  occasional, making, 466
  repairs, 74
  trouser press, 1116
  upholstering, 1284
  writing-board, 1264
Chalk, use for, 239
Chamfering, 1373
Chamois leather, 1274
Change gears, lathe, 1433
Charger, battery, 840
Charges and income tax, 345
Chiaroscuro printing, 1317
Chatterton's compound, 669
Chest, carved, 984
Chest of drawers,
  modernising, 101
  repairing, 69
Chesterfield suite, 1264
Chicken
  brooder, 1351
  run, making, 666
Children and fireguards, 235
Chimney,
  cleaning, 271
  examining, 743
  fire, stopping, 181
  smoky, 1356
Chimneys, building, 1572
China,
  decoration, 1236
  marks, 1291
  repairing, 38, 134
  toughening, 1486
Chinese kite, 1560
Chisel,
  using, 724
  wood, 572, 581
Choking, 255
Chopper shaft lock, 969
Christmas
  cards, home-made, 352
  decorations, 313
  tree illumination, 295
  tree stand, 239
Chromium
  plating, 671
  plating, cleaning, 137
Chuck, self-centring, 1430
Church seat varnish, 966
Chutney recipes, 1394
Cider recipe, 1184
Ciment fondu, 816
Circular plug, 698
Cissing, varnish, 969
Cistern,
  flushing, 838
  incinerator, 1147
  loft, 539
  repair, 19, 163
  w.c., fixing up, 1337
"Claircolle," 11
Clamp,
  picture-framing, 1355
  saw, making, 1422

Claret,
  cup recipe, 1184
  jug, making, 1439
Clinker base, 220
Clock,
  adjusting beat of, 133
  case, wireless, 917
  cleaning, 129
  electric, 765, 918
  golf, 1086
  grandfather, making, 382
  with pewter case, 864
Clockwork door bell, 103
Clogged files, 717
Closet
  basin, 1337
  flush tank repair, 19
Clothes
  airers, useful, 1180
  horse, use for, 622
  post, making, 651
  renovations, 147
  shelves, lining, 102
Coal
  bunker, wooden, 661
  cabinet, making, 1087
  chest, utilising, 1408
  house, making, 551
  houses, law regarding, 756
  small, using up, 214
"Coborn" track, 728
Cobbler's wax, 718
Cocked beads, broken, 73
Coffee
  stains, removing, 704
  table, making, 796
Coffee stains, 1542
Cogged joint, 544
Coil, medical, 1011
Coiled door spring, 137
Cold
  bending, steel tube, 1369
  frame, making, 104
  glue, 388
  lacquer, 375
Colour
  combinations, 198
  effects, weaving, 506
  harmony, 225
  schemes, 226, 624, 974
  sketching, 1518
Coloured
  lacquer, 441
  lighting, 853
  oak moulding, 1143
  paints, 434
Colours, wallpaper, 53, 56
Collateral security, 1535
Comb case, 1500
Combing, 112
Commutator, 1107
Concrete,
  cleaning, 1456
  floors, waterproofing, 14
  inlaying, 830
  measuring up thicknesses of, 366
  mixing, 995, 1165
  rapid hardening, 816
Condenser,
  electrical, simple, 231
  for coil, 1012
Condensation
  channel, manhole, 1311

INDEX

Condensation on exposed pipes, 1450
Conduit, using pieces of, 781
Conservatory,
  designs for, 865
  roof, repairing, 1402
  sun blind, 1443
Constructing a bungalow, 1573
Cooker,
  gas, 229, 461, 1341
  haybox, 1131
Cookers, electric, repairing, 1508
Copal varnish, 966, 1414
Coping, making, 128
Copper,
  articles, oxidising, 480
    restoring, 827
  circulator, 727
  cleaning, 135
  lid improvement, 955
  plating, 670
  softening, 1164
  step, making, 704
  tape, 709
Coppers, care of, 1344
Cords,
  sash, 643
  venetian blind, 227
Cork grips, eyeglass, 428
Corks,
  old, use for, 894
  removing, 340
Corn bin, rat-proof, 26
Corrugated
  iron, uses of, 15, 25
  paper for record case, 265
Cot, use for, 446
Cotton reels, use for, 700
Countersink, 1397
Covers,
  book, loose, 266
  cushion, 1145
Cowl, chimney, 202
Cracks,
  buildings, 490
  ceilings, 743
  glass vessels, 214
  picture canvas, 182
  plaster, 7
  walls, 164, 274, 743
  water pipes, 609
Cramping large areas, 1246
Cramps
  for gluing, 388
  improvised, 826
Crayons, wax, 1440
Crazy
  music, playing, 650
  paving, laying, 187, 278
Creaky stairs, 934
Credit trading, 1273
Creosote
  as weed-killer, 846
  compounds, 88
Creosoted wood, 64
Cricket bats, care of, 1359
Cross-cut saws, 520
Crowbar, improvised, 405
"Croid" glue, 160, 385, 1029, 1171
Curb, tiled, making, 552

Curtains,
  draught-excluding, 884
  frills for, 82
  making, 786
  stretching, 775
  "swinging," 717
  types of, 79
Cushions,
  car, cleaning, 359
  covers for, 257, 264, 1145
  ideas for, 1144
  making, 301
Cutlets, lentil, 1397
Cut-out decorations, 276
Cut-outs, sealing-wax, 1482
Cutting
  angle, plane, 481
  gauge, veneer, 1100
  leather, 68
  threads, 1039
Cycle,
  lining, 1070
  repair, 1006
  shed, making, 615
  support, 537
Cyclostyle pen, 982
Cylinder locks, 193, 534

Dado, 1161
  decoration, 55
  painting band for, 492
Dais floor, 1197
Damp,
  course, brick, 996
  courses, 592
  piano, 1081
  -proof box, 1031
  stains, 790
  walls, 24, 161, 514, 592
"Dampro," use of, 595
D.C. receivers, 1527
Deal floor, 873
Decay, fence post, 89
Decayed woodwork, 162
Deck
  chair, broken, 142
  improved, 86
Deep framing, 1512
Demurrage, 993
Dents,
  furniture, 72, 446
  metal, removing, 1416
Desk,
  light, 114
  telephone, 440
  wall, making, 1434
"Devon" fireplace, 1389
"Dexbrine" paste, 514
"Deymel" chair, 605
Dies,
  solid, 1039
  split, 1039
Dining-room
  chair, re-upholstering, 155
  fireplace, 1158
  wallpapers, 55
Distemper
  brushes, 906
  making, 9
  removing, 10, 208
  washable, 11, 198, 294
Distempering, 9, 952

Distempers, 1412
Distilled water, 711
Distress, power of, 751
Divan, 605, 800, 1266
Dixon's compound, 549
Dog,
  exercising track, 1453
  kennel, making of, 1306
  tar on feet of, 1421
Doll's house,
  making, 304
  self-opening door for, 535
  wiring, 240
Domestic
  hot-water systems, 545
  tools, sharpening, 577
  water softener, making, 877
Door,
  badly shutting, 246, 718
  draughts, curing, 159
  hiding places, 1179
  hinges, loose, 246
  lining, fixing, 975
  noiseless, 366
  panels, shrunk, 487
  sagging, 125
  semi-sliding, making, 927
  shrunk, 246
  sliding, 728
  spring, coiled, fitting, 137
  stop, spring, 809
  swollen, 247
  varnishing, 140, 969
  ventilator, 454
  wrong-handed, 341
Doormat, well for, 665
Dovetail
  plug, double, 698
  joint, cutting, 725
  saw, 521
  setting out, 1133
Dowelled joints, making, 84
Dowels, 74, 84, 365, 445
Down draught, 1356
Drain,
  dirty, cleaning, 298
  leakage, testing, 837
  pipe materials, 834
  pipes, splashing, 700
  rods, 836
  testing, 743
Drainage,
  examination of, 164
  faults, 835
  lawn, 1188
  systems, 742, 833
Draining
  boards, removable, 110
Draught excluders, door, 732
Draught-excluding curtains, 884
Draughts, 159, 342
Draw-leaf table, making, 322
Draw tape, curtain, 83
Drawer,
  knobs, fixing, 197
  lock, secret, 699
  locks, 648
  rails, repairing, 70
  repairs, 72
  runner hint, 652
  stops, 894
  tight, curing, 226

Drawers, bookcase from, 469
Drawing-room,
  carpet, 390
  modern, 426
Drive, 433
Drill
  broken, removing, 1104
  press, 1247
Drilling,
  machines, 576
  notes on, 1431
  softwoods, 151
  stonework, 697
Drills, 1397
Drills, sharpening, 590
Drills, small, making, 1096
Dripping tap, 77, 289, 337
Driving
  brackets, 790
  staple, 699
Drop-in seats, 1504
Dropped gate, 762
Dry
  cleaning, 359, 701
  rot, 740, 808
Duplex paper transfer, 1069, 1072
Duplicator, useful, 981
"Durofix," 160
Dusty corners, 15
Duster,
  hanger for, 952
Dwarf brick wall, 126
Dwarf brick walls, greenhouses on, 1494
Dyed furs, 892
Dyeing mahogany, 680
Dyes,
  vegetable, 1251, 1376
  printing, 1210
Dynamo for plating, 669

Ear syringe, making, 1331
Earth terminal, 709
Easy chair, modern, 880
Eaves, weak joints at, 780
Ebonite finger plates, 375
Edge tools, protecting, 536
Edging, garden, 126, 220
Eiderdown,
  coverlet, using, 467
  making, 553
Electric
  appliances, repairing, 1505
  arc, 1176
  bell, installing, 1287
    operating, 206
  bells, sluggish, 637
  car, child's, 1398
  clock, 765, 918
  conduit, thread, 1038
  drive, 606
  evaporative refrigerator, 1545
  fan, making, 1454
  fire, imitation, 245
  fire, installing, 1159
  fire-screen radiator, 217
  heaters, 682
  immersion heater, 902
  iron, 507
  light, using, 853
    bulbs, colouring, 222

INDEX

Electric
  lock, 1578
  motor for workshop, 606
    handling, 1246
    constructing, 1106
  pump-fountain, 1051
  solderers, 212
  stirrer, 1516
  wires, defective, 507
Electrically operated door for doll's house, 535
Electricity,
  £ s. d. of, 357
  supply, burning off, 337
  supply, typical, 741
Electrolyte, 710
Electrolytes, plating, 670
Electro-plate,
  cleaning, 135
  distinguishing, 1393
Electro-plating, 668
Element, fitting a new, 1506
Elliptical hole, 1312
"Emdeca," 541
Emptying a pond, 900
Enamel
  brushes, storing, 907
  painting over, 1331
  paints, 1410, 1412
  using, 1249
Enamelling
  a bath, 27
  whitewood furniture, 117
Enamelware dish, 965
End grain, 677
End grain, chamfering, 1373
  planing, 486, 724
Endowment assurance, 1551
Endowment policy, 746
Engraving,
  on metal surfaces, 331
  wood, 688
Enlarger,
  pantograph, 1354
  photographic, 1073
Equation table, 815
"Erinoid," 101
Etching compounds, 331
Etchings, old, 1318
Ether solution, 1060
European lacquer, 444
Evaporative refrigerator, 1545
Eyeglass frames, 428
Examining a house, 161
Excavating, 995
Exchange, bill of, 1536
Exerciser, sculling, 1547
Expanding bookcase, 176
Expansion
  gap, floor, 874
  pipe, 545

Fabric
  ink, 1210
  printing on, 1208
  removing colour from, 1376
  transfers, 1071
  waterproofing, 1047
Fan, electric, making, 1454
Fanlight adjustment, 566
Fat stains, 1542
Feather bed, 475

Felt
  covering, roof, 941
  hats, cleaning, 703
  hats, old, using up, 1319
  to metal, cementing, 901
Female threads, 1039
Fences,
  liabilities for, 737
  old, treatment of, 91
  ownership of, 755
  preserving tops of, 181
  repairs to, 762
  rustic, 171
Fender stop, 940
Fermentation, wine, preventing, 350
Ferrocrete, 816
Fertilisers, 1424
Festoon kite, 1561
Fibre plug, 699
Field
  magnets, D.C. motor, 1106
  windings, 1454
Figured woods, 893
Files, 575, 717
Filing soft metals, 1164
Fillets, wood, 1380
Filling, 1250
  up, 849
Filter,
  infra-red, 1461
  rain water, 1055
Film packs, 400
Films, developing and printing, 397
Finger
  marks, 1542
  marks on wallpaper, 119
  plates for doors, 374
Finishing
  paints, 1410
  woodwork, 677
Fire,
  blower, making, 1374
  brick, repairing, 1343
  cement, 549
  electric, repairing, 1507
  gas, 1342
  guard, law regarding, 235
  guard, making, 235
  iron hanger, 1048
  lighters, 239
  lighting poker, 1026
  pillar, garden, 860
  screen, plywood, 154
  screen radiator, 217
Fireplace,
  brick, building, 1387
  dining-room, 1158
  mantels, 1129
  tiles, 198, 813
First aid
  cabinet, 540
  for the home, 250
"Fitzroy" barometer, 951
Fixed investment trusts, 1539
Flagstaff, setting up, 405
Flake white, 134
Flame,
  gas, 1339
  ring, stove, 1417
Flashed opal glass, 1074
Flashings, 945

Flat, choosing, 1217
Flexible stair tread nosing, 695
Flickering pillar lamp, 858
Floor,
  boards, 1092
  boards, raising, 45, 360, 809
  boards, shrunk, 45
  coloured concrete, 190
  construction, faulty, 593
  construction of, 908
  examining, 743
  oak, laying, 873
  old, 47
  parquet, laying, 449
  plywood, 158, 932
  polishes, 492
  polishing, 876
  removing tacks from, 391
  repairing, 916, 933
  sander, 1132
  springy, 47
  stain, 44
  tiling, 813
  tool shed, 418
  wiring under, 121
Flooring,
  batten, 915
  block, 915
  rubber, 1057
  poultry house, 98
"Florence" stove, 1417
Florescan colours, 270
Flowers, planting, 719
Flue pipe joints, 686
Flues,
  chimney, 1356
  geyser, 1343
Flush-pipe joint, leaky, 640
Flushing
  cisterns, 838
  water softener, 879
Fluter, using, 413
Fly
  cutter, 1248
  paper preparation, 1108
  trap, 1062
Focal length, 831
Focus, enlarger, 1073
Fog excluder, 457
Foreclosure, 746
Forks, repair of, 192
Footstools, making, 332
Foundation subsidence, 491
Foundations setting out, 1573
Fountain,
  garden, ornamental, 1051
  pen barrel, repairing, 487
Fox marks, 1542
Framework joint, 1139
Framing, pictures, 1140
Freehold, 737
French
  catch, fitting, 342
  door, curtains for, 81
  polish, cracked, 124
  polishes, 488
  polishing, 33, 216, 453, 679
Frieze,
  nursery, 1161
  wallpaper, 55

Frills,
  chair cover, 257, 264
  curtain, 82
Front door,
  painting, 65
Frosting glass windows, 44
Fuller's earth, 147
Fumigating a room, 334
Fuming, 416, 679
"Fur," 877
  boiler, 548
  cleaning, 264
  removing, 1559
Furniture,
  colouring, bruises on, 1274
  dents in, 446
  dual-purpose, 603
  for small house, 600
  legs, fractured, 116
  loft, 538
  made-to-measure, 601
  nursery, 1309
  old, repolishing, 215
  old, smartening up, 446
  polishes, 164
  reconditioning, 63
  repairing, 69
  revivers, 219
  steadiment, 87
  tubular steel, 1368
  upholstered, modern, 1264
  wallpapers to suit, 1161
  whitewood, enamelling, 117
  woods, 33
Furnishing
  a flat, 1217
  nursery, 1309
Furring, 7, 68, 164
Furs,
  care of, 889
  cleaning, 703
Fuse-box, 1268
Fuses, fitting up, 123
Futuristic fittings, 854

Galvanised
  iron, painting, 168
  sheets, 25
Games, party, 335
Garage,
  anti-burglar precautions for, 339
  designs for, 527
  door opener, 1578
  drives, 222
  law regarding, 754, 756
  lighting points in, 922
  painting, 1436
  power points in, 925
  preserving, 1436
Garden,
  barrow, 91, 935
  bricks, 126
  chair, improved, 86
  hammock making, 1066
  layouts, 1232
  ornaments, concrete, 953
  paths, constructing, 220
  pond, constructing, 897
  rockery, making, 1347
  roller, making, 970
  shears, sharpening, 578

INDEX

Garden,
  shed, repairing, 763
  sheds, 417
  shelters, making, 1334
  stonework, 1529
  sundial, 814
  swing, making, 1119
  tents, making, 1332
  tool handles, repairing, 160
  tools, home-made, 1097
  watering, 1258
Gas
  appliances, 1339
  boilers, 682
  consumption, 468
  cooker, care of, 229, 1341
  economiser, 1048
  fires, 1160, 1342
  leakage, detecting, 44
  pipes, holding, 1245
  poker, 1026
  solderers, 212
  stove, levelling, 461
  stove table, 1416
  supply, turning off, 337
Gate, dropped, 762
  leg table, making, 321
  types of, 1243
Gauge,
  limit, 1247
  marking, 700
German
  sausage recipe, 1237
  silver, 427
Gesso, 106, 619
Geysers, 214, 683, 1343
Gilding, 232, 1216
Gimlet, using, 1395
Gimp, 497
Glass,
  blowing, 1329
  canopy, making, 1181
  cements, 901
  cutting, 94, 330, 1403, 1422
  drilling, 93, 199, 544
  enamelled letters on, 732
  engraving on, 1056
  holder, 405
  house, 200
  houses, law regarding, 756
  indelible ink for, 1118
  mat, making, 301
  ornaments, 1331
  pane, broken, 107
  papering, 677
  sheets, coloured, 810
  shelves, fixing, 93
  tanks, cracked, 1030
  toughening, 1486
  transfers, 1071
  vessels, cleaning, 1263
  vessels, cracked, 214
Glazes, 294
Glazing
  aquarium panels, 1029
  putty, 237
" Glitto," 813
Glossary of terms, 1580
Gloss paints, 67
Gloves, 458, 1404
Glue, insoluble, 44

Glue,
  joints, 70
  pot, 385, 781
  size, 32
  washing, 703
Glued work, separating, 621
Gluing,
  broken china, 134
  preparing wood for, 32
  thin edges, 181
Gold,
  leaf, 443
  paints, 1413
  size, 232, 443, 1069
Golfing games, garden, 1086
Gouges, 413, 585, 726
Gnomon, 816
Grain, 33, 677
Graining, 111, 534, 1207
Gramophone,
  motor, cleaning, 115
  pick-up, mounting, 797
  record filing cabinet, 887
  records, making, 650, 1169
  records, storing, 265
  spring, replacing, 61
Grandfather clock, 382
Grass
  stains, 148
Grate, fitting a modern, 1552
  polish, liquid, 340
Grates, two-way, 1161
Grating, gully trap, 1415
Gratings, blocked, 161
Grease
  marks on prints, 183
  on whitewashed walls, 781
  spots on wallpaper, 119
Greasy bottles, cleaning, 249
Greenhouse
  designs for, 865, 1494
  roof, leaking, 1402
  shelves, zinc trays for, 852
Greyhound racing track, 843
Grinder, tool, 575
Grindstone, using, 174
Gross value, 1514
Grouting, 221
Grummet, 785
Gudgeon, 699
Guide lines, 277
Gullies, 835
Gully trap, unsanitary, 1415
Gutter, 851, 1109

Hairbrushes, stiffening, 516
Hair
  carpet, 389
  cutting a child's, 1298
Half-brick wall, 994
Half-joint, 31
Half-timbered wall, 1377
Halved joint, cutting, 725
Hammers, 110, 572
Hammock, garden, 1066
Hand-bags, repairs to, 569
Hand-brush, 1048
Hand-tools, 1427
Handle,
  cupboard, 700
  drawer, 101
  heat-resisting, 1283

Handle,
  loose, 581
  split chisel, 1450
  strap, 569
  using old shovel, 1423
  weighting tool, 298
  wire, 827
Hanger, fire iron, 1048
Hard
  soldering, 13
  tennis court, 409
  water, 877
Hardwood, 893, 1175
Hatchway, fitting a, 961
Hayboxes, 1131
Headers, 653
Hearths, 875
Heating,
  electric, 682
  gas, 682
  loft, 538
Hectograph, 983
Heels, 68, 979, 980
Helter-skelter, 1531
Henley wiring system, 120
Hero's fountain, 1051
Hiding-places, jewel, 1179
Hinged ventilator, 469
Hingeless box, 214
Hire purchase, 1273
Hock cup, 1184
Hoe, improved, 1098
Holdfast, 699
Home safes, 1537
Hooks, 591
Horizontal pump, 1051
Hose,
  garden, 1258
  rubber, 609
Hot
  bending, 1369
  lacquer, 375
  tap washer, 77
Hot-water
  boiler, fitting, 1089
  bottle cover, 1019
  pipe, repair, 610
  poor supply, 545
  radiators, 1160
  supply installation, 682
  systems, 545
  tank, faults, 550
House,
  distance of drains, 834
  drainage systems, 833
  equipping, 600
  examination of, 161
  having built, 737
  insurance, 1473
  painting inside of, 847
  planning restoration, 198
  points of law, 750
  practical points when building, buying, 737
  purchase, 743, 1534
  repairs, income tax allowances, 346
  simple colour schemes, 974
  subletting, 347
  when leaving, 337
  when moving, 303
Hydrometer, 710
Hypo, 397
Ice chest, 1183

Ice refrigerator, 1543
Imitation
  leaded lights, 1040
  stained glass work, 325
  tiles, 983
Immersion heater, 902
Incinerators, 1146
Income tax, 345, 1550
Infra-red photography, 1461
Injector, a simple, 146
Ink,
  marking, 181
  stains, 92
  wallpaper, on, 119
Inlay bandings, 1036
Inlaying
  concrete, 830
  marquetry, 1036
  polishing, 992
Inner tubes, uses for, 1019
Insulating boards, 654
Insulation, attic, 656
Insurance, 1473
Investing money, 1537
Investment corporation, 744
Invisible ink, 718
Iodine stains, 1475
Iron,
  cantilever, 1182
  cleaning, 136
  corbel, 911
  planes, adjusting, 1323
  rust, 139
Ironing board, 223, 405
" Ironite," 594
Ironmould, 1203
Irons, electric, 1505
Isinglass, 134
Ivory, cement for, 960

" J " hanger, 607
Jacks, 49
Jam stains, 1542
Jamb, cutting length of, 975
Jams, 1157, 1353
Janus cloth, 40
Jelly acid accumulator, 712
Jennings bit, 590
Joggles, 826
Joiner's cramp, 633
Joinery boards, 934
Joining glass, 1330
Joints,
  butt, 31
  dovetail, 1133
  dowelled, 84
  finding, in walls, 696
  garden shears, 580
  gluing, 32
  hot-water system, 547
  pipe, cement for, 405
  plywood, 929
  right-angle, 31
  secret, 32
  wire, 507
Joists, 908
  ceiling, 779
  ceiling, locating, 1219
  floor, 511
Jug, silver-mounted, 1439
Jumper, 77

Kapok, 939
Keene's cement, 7

INDEX

Kennels, designs for, 1306
Kettles, cure for spitting, 340
  electric, repairing, 1507
Key,
  cutting, 193
  water tap, 337
Keys, piano, cleaning, 1077
Kid, cleaning, 701
Killed spirits, 211, 630
Kitchen cabinet, 1136
  table, 1063
  cupboard, 1024
  ideas for, 827
  range, modernising, 1095
  table, collapsible, 926
  table for, 1416
Kitchenette,
  fitments in, 1218
  how to deal with a, 469
Kites, 1560
Kneeling mat, 1020
Knife-grinder, 1124
Knife, 191, 578
Knobs,
  bedstead, 279
  door, 1401
  drawer, 197
Knocking up, 692
Knots, 793
  treating, 113
  undoing, 1482

Lace, cleaning, 703
Lacquer,
  cleaning, 136
  work, simple oriental, 441
Lacquering, 218
Ladder from a plank, 340
  using, 847
Lagging, 904
Lamp,
  flickering pillar, 858
  guard, portable, 1148
  ultra-violet ray, 1176
Lampholder, 295
  connecting, 805
Lampshades,
  anti-glare, 114
  making, 313, 495, 856
Lampstand, combined book case, wireless set and, 477
Land, purchasing, 1570
Landing cupboards, 377
Lantern slides, 1521
Lap, tile, 776
Lathe, 543, 1149, 1426
Lath and plaster walls,
  fixing picture rail to, 559
  knocking hole in, 963
Laths, ceiling, 1220
Lawnmowers, 462
Lawns, 1185
Lead,
  cements for, 901, 1040
  gutter, 1110
  weights, 630
Leaded windows, 108
Lead-in, 1321
Leaks, air, 1421
Lean-to
  greenhouse, 869
  tool shed, 420
Leaseholds, 750

Leather binding, 1303
  recolouring, 267
  chamois, washing, 1274
  cleaning, 204, 267, 576
  handbag, 570
  reviver, 175
  upholstery, 92
Leatherwork, 1151
Leclanché cells,
  corroded, 533
  for H.T., 727
Lenses, 429, 831
Lens, focal length of, 831
Leroy's paste, 146
Lettering, 105, 631, 1070, 1305
Level,
  improvising a large, 652
  testing tiles for, 381
Levelling a lawn, 1185
Lewis bolt, 699
Life assurance, 1549
  and house purchase, 746
Light,
  additional switch, 613
  electric, 853
  orange, 1075
  wiring a bungalow, 1476
Lighting,
  additional points, 801
  coloured, 853
  fire, gas power for, 1026
  gas, 1339
Lightning conductor, 709
Lightwood, stain for, 1123
"Lignomur," 292, 513
Lime compound, 811
Limed oak, 36
Limewash, 1436
  making more durable, 827
Limited company, 1566
"Lincrusta," 513
Line,
  chalk, 697
  engravings, 690, 1317
Linen
  container, 1554
  cupboards, 376
Lining
  band, 1381
  bicycles, 1070
  door, 975
  strip, 830
Lino
  paint, 291
  print, 1208
Linoleum,
  covering a floor with, 291
  laying, 16
  repairing a hole in, 297
  restoring pattern, 366
Lintels, 1576
Lithographs, 1319
Loan, building society, 1534
Loans, 1536
  life assurance policy, 1549
Lock, electric, 1579
Locks, 193, 646, 699
Lockplate, 506
Loft-ladder, installing, 769
Loft, 537, 894
Loganberries, training, 1120
Looping-in, 924
Loose covers, 257

Loose
  knife handle, 192
  screws, 1293
Lounge-chair, radio, 1083
Luggage holdall for car, 318

Machine tools, 575
  installing, 606
Magic lantern, 958
Mahogany, 37, 1032
Main cock, 77
"Majority" K.N. diner, 605
Male threads, 1039
Manhole, 833, 1311
Mantelpiece, 60, 1129
Mantel registers, 1130
Manures, 1424
Marble,
  cement, 446
  cleaning, 1456
  painting over, 781
  renovating dull, 755
Marb-le-cote, 1091
Marking, 700, 725
Marquetry, 1035
Massage pad, 1012
Matches, waterproof, 534
Mattresses, 474, 1265
Meats, cooked, 1237
Medical coil, 1011
Meerschaum, cement, 901
Mercury barometer, 950
Meringues, 1257
Metal,
  cements for, 901
  ornamental shapes, 506
  polishes, 181
  screw threads, 1038
  taking dents out of, 1416
  teapot, cleaning inside, 446
  to line a box with, 1031
  wedges, 461
Metalwork,
  cleaning, 135
  soldering iron cover, 406
Metal-faced plywood, 1121
Metal-lined drawer, 1063
Metalworking hints, 1164
Methylated spirit, solid, 599
Microphone, 1169
  telephone, 437
Microscopes, 798
Milk in hot weather, 1242
Milliameter, use of, 106
Mirror,
  adjustable bathroom, 780
  re-silvering, 133
Mirrors, 1262, 1486
Mitres, 558
Model
  electric railway, 1324
  glider, 1457
Modelling
  book ends, 634
  cardboard, 1171
  copper, brass, or pewter, 367, 861
  paste, 634
Money
  methods of raising, 1533
  ways of investing and saving, 1537
Monk's bench, 1448

Mortar, 95, 993
Mortgage, 743, 1533
Mortise locks, 193, 646
Mortises, cutting, 725
Mosaic work, 1444
Motor,
  car, child's, 1398
  installing, 606
  seat, settee from, 1204
Moulded panels, 75
Moulder, 361
Moulding, 1372, 1143
  material for, 143
  rebated, 639
  replacing broken, 70
Moving, a hint when, 271
Mud stains, 1542, 1358
Muriatic acid, 630

Nail-box, 1378
Nail, 44, 46, 271, 559
Nailed courses, 776
Nailing, secret, 875
Name-plates,
  lettering for, 631
  metal, 367
  wood, 105
Name sign, illuminated, 524
Naphtha stains, 35
National Savings Certificates, 1537
Needle valve, 1033
Needlework cabinet 57
Neighbour, your, 754
"Neolite," 1529
Nest box, 98
Netting, tightening, 446
Newel post, light, 1267
Newspaper,
  for lining shelves, 102
  for protecting pipes, 289
  papier mâché bowls, 1272
Newspapers,
  for floors, 165
  some uses for old, 446
Nickel,
  cleaning, 136
  plating, 670
Nozzle, sprinkler, 1260
Nursery,
  furnishing, 1309
  picture design, 343
  wallpapers, 1161
Nut, removing, 231
Nuts, types of, 1040

Oak,
  colouring, 1032
  finish, 322
  floor, laying, 873
  polishing, 36
  posts, 91
  staining, 35
  varnish, 1414
Oars, making, 1004
Occasional chairs, 466, 1284
Ogee, 944
Oil,
  lamp burners, 1115
  painting, 1520
  paintings, care of, 182
  paints, 432, 1409, 1412

1596

INDEX

Oil,
  skin, effect, 1047
  staining, 35, 47
  stains, 1542
  stone, how to use, 174, 191, 214, 577, 1020, 1440
  stoves, care of, 1417
  treatment of walls, 576
  varnish, 140
Old-world ingle nook, 1195
Opal ceiling, fixing, 638
Ottoman, padded top, 76
Outbuildings,
  flight of stairs for, 1229
  permitted height of, 97
Outside W.C., making, 1335

Pads, 1145
Pail,
  filling, 952
  tilter, 934
Paint,
  aluminium, 1216
  brush scraper, 630
  brushes, care of, 143, 905
  burning off, 565
  cellulose, 1413
  enamel, 1410, 1412
  finishing, 1410
  flexible, 214
  for furniture, 63
  for spray painting, 1034
  lino, 291
  luminous, 264
  marks, removing, 298
  metallic, 1413
  mixing table, 807
  plastic, 199, 1381
  removers, 29, 44, 66, 849
  rust-preventing, 138
  selecting, 1409
  smell, removing, 827
  splashes, 340
  sprayer, making, 219
  stains, 148
  stencilling, 471
  table, 1411
  tinting, 1115
  undercoatings, 850, 1409
  varnishing, 67
  wall, plastic, 1380, 1381
  waterproof, 180
  white lead, 66, 432
Painted
  finger plates, 374
  surfaces, transfers for, 1071
Painting,
  ball, 366
  bathroom, 673
  bicycle, 1008
  boats, 828
  brasswork, 623
  cellulose, 1153
  cement or stone, 852
  china, 1236
  creosoted wood, 64
  equipment, 65
  front door, 65
  galvanised iron, 168
  garages, 1436
  glass, 325
  greenhouse, 236

Painting,
  interior woodwork, 705
  ironwork, 167
  kitchen, 208
  name plates, 105
  outfit, spray, 1033
  outside of house, 847
  outside W.C., 1338
  over enamel, 1331
  overglaze, 1236
  perambulator, 629
  plywood, 929
  rain-water barrels, 894
  rudiments of, 1518
  stucco, 850
  spray, 199, 1153
  steel furniture, 1371
  wall boards, 1380
  with sealing-wax, 1451
  wood, 456
Paintwork, cleaning 967
Panelling, 56, 199
  ceilings, 292
  in plywood, 560
  wallpaper, 276
Panels,
  plywood, 9
  wallboard, 654
Pantagraph, 1354
Paper
  cutter, 230
  flowers, waxing, 1054
  hanging, 272, 340
  hanging board, 1389
  removing stains, 1542
  rest, making, 430
Papier mâché bowls, 1272
Paradichlorbenzene, 1265
Parliament hinges, 526
Parquet floor, 449, 665
Parrot, 1466
" Parso-glaze," 294
Party
  games and tricks, 335
  walls, ownership of, 754
Passe partout, 1510
Paste,
  for wallpapering, 274
  modelling, 634
Pastel painting, 1520
  shades, 1380
Paths, 126, 220, 872
Patrasses, 924
Paved areas, 189
Pavilion, 1112
Paving, crazy, laying, 187
Pebble-dash, 1345
Pelmets, making, 789
Pendant light, 534
Pepper's ghost, 980
Perambulator, 627
Pergola, terraced, 1529
Permutits, 877
Personal security, loans on, 1536
Perspective, 1518
Perspiration stains, 148
Pests, garden, 1425
Petrol,
  cleaning clothes with, 147
  engine for workshop, 606
Pewter,
  cleaning, 136
  modelling, 861

Pewter solder, 211
Phenakistoscope, 989
Phenol solution, 846
Photo-mountant, 1171
Piano, repairing, 1077
Pianola faults, 1082
Pickle
  bath, mercury, 671
  recipes, 1394
Pick-up,
  connecting, 649, 651
  gramophone, 797
Picture
  framing, 182, 232, 473, 620, 1140, 1355
  rails, 55, 558, 1179
Pictures,
  arranging, 424
  attractive, making, 343
  notes on, 627
  renovating, 182
Pigeons, 1466
Pigment, 432
Pile, quality of, 391
Pillar
  drill, 1247
  lamp, flickering, 858
Pillars,
  brick, 127
  concrete, casting, 953
Pillows, 476
Pipe
  examination, 161
  jointing compound, 549
  joints, cement for, 405
Pipes,
  bending, 687
  boiler, furred, 549
  chair, 257, 263
  condensation on, 1450
  emptying, 290
  examining, 743
  freezing, 290
  hose, 1258
  materials for, 684
  mending, 464
  threads for, 1038
  water, burst, 143, 609
Pitch, screw thread, 1038
Planes, 572
  and planing, 481
  sharpening, 585
Planing
  end grain, 724
  support, 1246
Plank ladder, 340
Planning house, 737, 1569
Plans, submitting to local authority, 739
Planted rebates, 1373
Planting, 719
Plants,
  aquarium, 1030
  collars for, 396
Plaster,
  base, insulating board, 655
  cast, bronzing, 1130
  ceiling, remedying, 1219
  cracks in, 17
  cutting channel in, 122
  defects, hiding, 513
  filling, 33
  mouldings, cleaning, 1456
  of Paris, 106, 273, 508

Plastering, 1578
Plastic
  paint, 199, 1381
  wood, 46, 192, 291, 427, 559, 676
Plasticine squeeze, 636
Plate
  cloths, 1486
  glass, polishing, 15
  moulding, 562
  rack, making, 928
  shelves, 3
Plating vat, 669
Plugging walls, 696
Plugs, door lining, 975
  electric, 507
  patent, 697
Plum jam, 1157
Plumb line, 171
Plumbing tools, 685
Plywood,
  best uses of, 929
  firescreen, making, 154
  for fireplace, 1158
  for floors, 158
  panelling in, 560
  repair work, 933
  staining, 37
  surfaces, finishing, 932
  varnishing, 141
" Poilite " asbestos cement slates, 948
Pointing, 996
Poker,
  gas, 1026
  work on velvet, 1499
Policies, insurance, 1473
Policy, assurance, 1549
Polishes
  floor, 492
  french, 488
  furniture, 164
  metal, 181
Pond,
  fish, leaky, 492
  garden, making, 897
Porch
  lighting, 857
  sun blind, 1442
Portable
  buildings, 932
  lamp guard, 1148
  receiver, modern, 1013
Portland cement, 95, 187, 490, 551, 594, 640, 686, 994
  coloured, 190
  mixing coal with, 214
Post hint, 15
Post office
  annuities, 1537
  savings bank, 1537
Posters, 632
  use of, 627
Posts,
  fence, setting up, 354
  tapered sockets for, 630
Pot pourri recipe, 1212
Pottery
  decoration, 1234
  repairing, 38
Poultry-house,
  building, 97
  creosoting, 91

INDEX

Poultry-house,
    extensions, 99
    law regarding, 756
Poultry run, making, 666
Power
    drives for workshop, 606
    plug point, fitting, 806
    transformer, uses of, 205
Pram wheel, fitting tyres, 166
Primary
    colours, 225
    winding, 1011, 1490
Primers, cellulose, 1155
    paint, 1409
Priming, 66
    coat on plaster, 207
    paint, 167
    white lead, 236
Printing
    box, photographic, 827
Prints,
    cleaning, 183
    old, identifying, 1317
Projection
    lanterns, 958
    screen, making, 1252
" Pudlo," 596
Pulleys,
    sash cord, 645
    workshop, 608
Pulps, 272
Pumice powder, 444, 1117
Pumps, fountain, 1051
Punch tip, 44
Punt, making, 1004
" Purimachos," 549, 1343
Purlins, faulty, 778
Putty,
    facing, applying, 107
    glazing, 237
    softening, 565
    window, 87, 107
Pyrography, 1499
" Pyruma," 549

Quartering, veneer, 1104
Quirks, cleaning, 968
Quoin, 996, 1001

Rabbits, keeping, 1072
Rack rental value, 345
Radiator,
    electric fire-screen, 217
    enamels, 1412
    hot-water, screening, 1315
Radiators, electric, 1507
Radio-gramophone cabinet, making, 1253
Raffia-work, 299
Rafters, faulty, 777
Rag, putty joint, 640
Rainwater, 877
    and cesspools, 1367
    barrels, painting, 894
    drains, 833
    filter, 1055
    purifying, 271
Raising money, 1533
    for house purchase, 743
    paste, 442
Ratchet brace, 1395

Rateable value, 1514
Rates, 1514
Rawlplugs, 122, 698
Razor blade, uses for, 230
Razors, care of, 936
Reading case, making, 501
    rest, making, 430
Rebate plane, 486
Rebated moulding, 639
Rebating, 1372
Recesses, shelves in, 4
Records, care of, 888
    storing, 265, 887
Red cement, making, 469
    lead, 167
    paint, 411
    rugging, 475
Redemption, mortgage, 746
Reflecting surfaces, 854
Refrigerator, 1543
" Regentone " mains unit, 480
Reiming glass tube, 1329
Relay, closed circuit, 310
Relief
    decoration, 513, 627
    etching, 331
Reliefs, ceiling, 292
Remote control, 51
Rent, payment of, 751
Repair, law regarding, 751
Repairs and income tax, 346
Reshooting planes, 483
Resin, 212
Re-upholstering, 155
Rising butt hinges, 125
Rissoles, 1397
Riveting, 38, 1111
Road charges, 737
Rockery, building, 1347
Rodinal, 397
Roller
    blind, fitting, 189, 562
    concrete, garden, 970
Roll-top desk, making, 1483
Roman
    alphabet, 631
    mosaic, 1444
Roof,
    building, 1576
    conservatory, 1402
    corrugated iron, 25
    coverings, 94, 423
    cutting hole through, 1312
    examining, 743
    faults and remedies, 776
    flashings, faulty, 597
    garage, preserving, 1436
    gutter, repairing, 1109
    insulating board for, 656
    plywood, 931
    shed, repairing, 764
Room, fumigating, 334
Roots, tree, destroying, 576
Rope end, whipping, 87
Rough cast, 1578
Roughcast cement, 1377
Roundabout, making, 1049
Rubber
    carpets, 393
    flooring, 1057
    heels and soles, 980
    piping material, 159

" Ruberoid," 423, 948
Rug
    fastener, 366
    making, 21
Rule, garden, handy, 366
Running pipe joint, 612
Rush-top stool, making, 895
Rust
    on garden shears, 175
    preventing, 15, 110, 139, 700
Rustic work, garden, 169

Safety-pins, saving, 429
Safety razor blades, 181, 230, 938
Salad recipes, 1386
Sal-ammoniac solution, 533, 1509
Sale, bill of, 1536
Salt
    as anti-freezing device, 290
    preservatives, 92
Saltpetre, 576
Sand,
    buying, 993
    coloured, 1347
Sand tray, making, 1447
Sanding, 1155
Sand-pit, wood-lined, 1068
Sandwiches, recipes for, 1198
Sanitary papers, 208
Sanitation, 740
Sash
    tools, 905
    windows 339, 457, 643, 1540
Sawing round-pieces, 566
Saws and sawing, 298, 520, 587, 1422
Scaffolding, 1345
Scales, making, 1498
Scissors, 174, 578
Scooter, child's, making, 268
Scraper, 678, 727
Screen
    hinges, 734
    making, 622
Screw-cutting, 575, 1433
Screw-drivers, 581
Screw-driving hint, 271
Screw-plate, 109
Screw-threads, metal, 1038
Screws, 366
Sculling exerciser, 1547
Scumbles, 111
Scythe, 591, 1099
Sea-water stains, 149
Sealing-wax craft, 361
Seat-box, home-made, 939
Seat,
    bathroom, making, 693
    drop-in, mending, 1504
    home-made, 1486
Secondary
    colours, 225
    winding, 1011, 1493
Sectional book-case, 176
Secret
    drawer lock, 699
    dovetail, 1135
    nailing, 76, 875
" Secret screw joint," 32

Security for loans, 1533
Seed-sowing, 723
Self-centring chuck, 1429
Selector switch, making, 438
Self-closing door spring, 137
Sellers thread, 1038
" Serval," 945
Serviette ring, 567
" Set back " wall, 910
Set-screws, tank, 550
Settee,
    convertible, 604
    cover, 259
    from motor seat, 1204
    repairing, 1313
Sewage disposal, 1367
Sewer, 834
Sewing
    buttons to stay on, 1241
    carpets, 166
    leather, 457
    -machine maintenance, 348
Sharpening
    domestic tools, 577, 717
Shears, garden, 110, 175, 580
Shed,
    cycle, 615
    erected by tenant, 751
    lean-to, 420
    repairing, 763
    roof coverings, 991
Sheds, tool, 417
Sheffield plate, 1392
Shell bit, 1397
Shellac
    knotting, 113
    solution, 64
    varnish, 265
Shelters, garden, 1334
Shelves, 3
    book-case, 1277
    cupboard, lining, 102
    semi-sliding door for, 927
    tool shed, 419
Shingles, 654
Shiver, filling cracks with, 70
Shoe rack, compact, 52
Shoes,
    care of, 68, 351
Shovel handle, using, 1423
Shower-bath device, 1385
Shrunk
    door, 246, 487
    floor boards, 45
Shuttering, step, 1165
Sideboards, designs for, 782
Siemen's wiring system, 120
Sighting plane blade, 586
Silica fittings, 853
Silicate-resin solution, 597
Silk,
    dry cleaning, 701
    lampshades, 500
    taffeta, 553
Silver
    cleaning, 136
    effects in decoration, 1216
    hall-marks, 1275
    -plating,, 379 670
    tarnishing, 210
Silverwork, 1439
Sink
    pipe, choked, 557

INDEX

Sink
  tiles behind, 810
  trap, cleaning, 12
Site, selecting a, 1569
Sizing
  wallpaper, 344, 1035
  wood, 1035
Skates, care of, 571
Sketching, 1518
Skins, rabbit, 1297
Skirting, 395, 1072, 1450
Slag wool, 289
Slate, broken, replacing, 777
Slates, 948
  cement for, 366
Slating, 777
Sleeve board, making, 149
Slewing, 1043
Slide, lantern, 959
Sliding
  doors, 728
  sash, making, 825
Sludge in cistern, 284
Slump test, 1574
Smoky
  chimneys, 1356
  fireplace, 1159
Smoothing plane, 482, 483
Soap tray, 1099
Soft woods, 32, 151, 508
Softening
  putty, 565
  water, 877
Soil
  drains, 833
  removing, 188
Soldo, 211
Soldering, 13, 213
  aluminium, 1436
  soft, 211
Soleing, 978
Solenoid, 765, 1579
Solicitor's cost, 747
Solignum, 353
Sound
  proof partitions, 660
  recording, 1169
Spades, garden, 1098
Span-roof
  greenhouse, 1494
  tool shed, 421
Spatula, using, 363
Specific gravity, 710
Spirit-level, 461
Spirit varnish, 140
Spirits of salts, killed, 630
Splash-back, 75, 1263
Splicing, 795
  ladders, 847
  skirting board, 396
Splinters, removing, 781
Spokeshave, 587, 724
Sponge rack, making, 207
Spoon repairs, 192
Spray painting, 1033, 1153
Spring
  blinds, faults in, 184
  catches, 44
  steel, hole in, 1546
Springy, floors, 47
Sprinklers, garden, 1259
Squeegee, 1020
Stain, floor, 44, 46

Stained
  glass work, 325
  wood, polishing, 347
Staining, 199
Stair
  carpet holders, 992
  post, strengthening, 969
  tread nosing, flexible, 695
  treads, springy, 1021
Staircase
  carpets, 389, 393, 1281
  loft, 537
  table top over, 1261
Stairs,
  creaky, 934
  flight of, making, 1229
Stamps, removing, 718
Standing bookcase, 1277
Starting a business, 1562
Steel
  and iron, cleaning, 136
  tubes, bending, 1368
  turning, 1431
Stencilling, 138, 270, 470, 675, 982, 1056
  wallboards, 1381
Step, copper, 704
Steps,
  combined with seat and waste container, 1554
  garden, concrete, 1165
  pair of, making, 1460
  stone, 1530
  wood, making, 1229
Stucco, 655
Stile, 816
  swollen, 247
Stiles, sash, 825
Stiling border, 56
Stipple engravings, 1318
Stippler, 293, 294
Stippling, 12, 112
Stirrer, electric, 1516
Stockings, mending, 1248
Stocks, investment in Government, 1537
Stool,
  bathroom, making, 445
Stools, making, 332
Stone,
  cleaning, 1456
  cutting, 189
Stones, setting, 1316
Stoneware jars, 1237
Stonework, garden, 1529
Stopped rebates, 1373
Stopping, 1250
  up, 65, 67
  wood, 678
Stoves, oil, care of, 1417
Stoving lacquer, 375
Straps, hardening of, 940
Straw hat cleaner, 190, 703
Stretcher rails, 324
String
  cutter, 230
  holder, 239
Stripping, 142
  old papers, 273
  paint, 1154
Structural defects, 743
"Stuart" gas engine, 606
Stucco, painting, 850

Stuffing, 156, 1144, 1206
Sub-letting, 347
"Sugar Soap," 30
Suit, pressing, 149
Summer houses, 756
  pavilion, 1112
  triangular, making, 1238
Sulphate of magnesia, 110
Sulphation, 711
Sun blinds, making, 1441
Sundial, 1530
  brick, 128
  making, 814
Surface, levelling, 1573
Surrender
  value, 1536
  values, 1549
Sweating, 213
"Swinging" curtains, 717
Switch, additional, 613
Switches, electric, fixing, 122
Syphon,
  gas pipe, 1339
  making, 396

Table,
  bedside, making, 493
  draw-leaf, making, 322
  folding, making, 181
  gate-leg, making, 321
  lamp standard, 1427
  lamps, 857
  mats, 1020
  tennis top, making, 364
Tackle, lifting, 1246
Tallow, 212
Tally system, 1273
Tank support, 376
Tanks, leaky, 550
Tap faults, 78
Tar
  preservative, 1436
  stains, 148
Taxation at the source, 345
Tea
  stains, removing, 704
  wagon, making, 152, 997
Tea-cosy, making, 299
  tray, 679
Tee joint, 1371
Telephone installation, 1390
Telephones, house, 435
Telescope, making, 831
Temperature,
  readings, converting, 614
Tempering small drills, 1096
Template, 85, 607
Tenant's
  covenant, 751
  fittings, 754
Tennis
  racket gut reviver, 446
  restringing, 1162
Tent peg, metal, 1152
Terra-cotta, cleaning, 1191
Tesserae, 1444
Thawing pipes, 565
Therm, 468
Thermostat, 682, 904
Thinner, 433

Throated rebates, 1373
Thumb-screw, 718
Tidy, bath, making, 445
Tie
  holder, handy, 239
  press, making, 1300
Tiles,
  cleaning, 1456
  cutting, 380, 552
  how to fix, 810
  painting over, 781
  porous, 596
  ugly, concealing, 446
Tiling, rubber, 1059
  table top, making, 380
Timber, 677, 857, 893
Tin
  can covers, 1048
  surfaces, etching, 331
Tinmen's snips, 581
Tinning new bit, 212
Tinted paint, 434
Tinware, cleaning, 87, 136
Tobin's tube, 1357
Toboggan, 1375
Toilet, compact, useful, 1099
Tool
  handles, weighting, 298
  grinders, 575
  kits, 572
  rack, portable, 543
Tools, sharpening, 577
Towel rail, 371
Transfer
  decoration, 1069
  graining paper, 1207
Transfers, 680, 1108
Transformer, 1289
  for telephone, 438
  mains, 240, 248
  power, uses of, 205
  small, making, 1490
Trap
  intercepting, 1366
  sash window, 643
Trees, overhanging, 755
Trellis fence, erecting, 353
Trench garden, making, 938
Tricks, party, 336
Trimming, 909
  knife tip, 191
Trinket box, 363, 864
Tripoli, 755
Trivet, simple, 492
Trolley bookcase, 285
Try-square, 523
Trying plane, 483
Trusts, fixed investment, 1539
Tubs, shrinkage of, 298
Tumbler
  shelf, 1099
  switch, 243, 1340
Turning 1429
  large wheel, 1245
  metals, 1431
  tools, lathe, 1427
"Turnall" wall board, 659
Tusk tenon joint, 913
Twist
  bit, 726, 1395
  drills, sharpening, 590
"Tynecastle," 513

1599

INDEX

Ultra-violet ray lamp, 1176
Umbrella,
  old, use for, 271
  stand, making, 956
Undercutting, 7
Unions, hose pipe, 1258
Unit drive system, 606
Unspooling roll films, 398
Upholstered furniture, 1264
Upholstering chairs, 1284
Upholstery, cleaning, 1265
Upward shed, 505

Vacuum
  cleaner as air pump, 1034
    maintenance, 1419
    parts, holder for, 298
  pump, 836
Valuation, insurance, 1475
Varnish
  brushes, 905, 969
  remover, 214, 652
Varnished wallpaper, removing, 1486
Varnishes, 1414
  potting, unglazed, 1236
Varnishing, 966
  interior woodwork, 140
  paint, 67
  painted woodwork, 967
  wood, 679
Vegetable dyes, 1251, 1376
Veneer,
  repairing, 72
  ornaments, fixing, 57
Veneering, 934, 1100
Venetian blinds, 227
Vermin, destroying, 334
Vibration, damage by, 1219
Vice,
  bench, 572
  clamps for tubes, 1368
  disappearing, 757
  metal working, fitting, 759
  pipe, extemporised, 1245
View finding, 1518
Violin, one-string, 921
Vinegar, use for, 366
Vizor, grille, 596
Voltmeter, using, 710

Waling, 1043
Walls,
  arranging pictures on, 424
  blackened, 1450
  boards, 199, 653, 1379
  cupboard, 738
  examining, 161
  hooks, outdoor, 87
  ornament, design for, 413
  plugging, 696, 855
  sloping, 538
Wallpaper, 199
  calculating quantity, 272

Wallpaper
  cleaning, 408, 832
  for period furniture, 137
  hiding defects in, 118
  removing, 10, 208
  schemes, 53, 1161
  types of, 272
  using, 53, 885
  varnishing, 344
Walnut
  cabinet stain, 143
  polishing, 34
  staining, 34
Walpamur stainers, 625
Wardrobe,
  making, 714
  Victorian, converting, 1269
Warped timber, 677
Washer,
  manhole, 549
  tap, fitting, 77
Washing machine, making, 1166
Wasp trap, 1062
Watch cleaning, 1192
Water
  binding, 222
  butts, care of, 1118
  can, leaky, 1310
  cistern, cold, cleaning, 284
  colour decoration, 680
    drawings, restoring, 183
  keeper, brush, 906
  paints, 11, 516
  rusty, 549
  soluble salts, 88, 92
  stain for floor, 46
  system, typical, 742
  tank, mending, 1319
  turning off, 77
  wings, 1020
Water-colour painting, 1518
Waterfall, miniature, 1054
Waterproof
  cement, 190, 1028
  matches, 534
  paint, 180
  paper, 405
Waterproofing
  concrete floors, 14
  fabrics, 1047
  sailcloth, 15
  stone, 815
  walls, 594, 597
Water stains, 1542
Wax
  crayons, 1440
  filling for nail holes, 46
  polish, 454
  polishing with, 47
  stains, removing, 704
Waxed cambric, 553
Waxing
  paper flowers, 1054

Waxing
  stained glass, 330
  woodwork, 679
W.C., making, 1335
  trap, stoppage in, 835
Weatherboard, 30, 159, 763
Weatherboarding,
  garage, 530
  tool shed, 419
Weather-glass, 681, 1457
Weather vane, 735
Weaving, 503
Webbing, chair, 155, 882
Weed-killers, 846
Well,
  doormat, sinking, 665
  garden, 128
  small, sinking, 977
  water, 1055
Welsbach-Kern fire, 1343
Welsh dresser, making, 1189
Wet cell, making, 431
Wheel,
  large, turning, 1245
  of life, 989
Whipping rope end, 87
White
  enamel, cleaning, 15, 630
  paint, 66, 432
  priming, 236
Whitewash, ceiling, 277
Whitewood furniture, enamelling, 117
White wool, 475
"Whitney" electric pump, 1053
Will, how to make, 1276
Winding
  armature, 1107
  transformer, 1490
Window,
  cleaning preparations, 907
  converting sash to casement, 1540
  curtains, making, 786
  decoration, 79
  erecting, 1575
  faults and remedies, 643
  frames, rusting, 411
  leaded light, 1040
  leaks, 1025
  light, 700
  painting hint, 1280
  pane, replacing, 107
  safety device, 338
  putty, 87
  rattling, preventing, 894
  seat, making, 314
  sills, examining, 163
Wine,
  home-made, 350, 1487
Wiped pipe joint, 610
Wire,
  bent, straightening, 1164
  electric, defective, 507

Wire,
  netting, slack, 446
  shaping, 1286
Wireless
  cabinet and bookcase, combination, 1363
  fault-tracing chart, 144
  game, 649
  receiver, portable, 1013
  receivers "E.W.3," 1523
  set, clock case, 917
  set, novel uses for, 649
Wiring
  additional power and lighting points, 801
  house, extending, 120
Wood
  carving, 412
  chopping, safe, 405
  -cut, 688
  engravings, 688, 1317
  fillers, 33, 87
  panel-cutting device, 1178
  polishing, tip, 110
  preservation, 88, 169
  removing varnish, 652
  sizing, 1035
  screw, securing, 239
  surfaces, scoring, 87
  types of, 893
Wooden
  barrels, care of, 1118
  curtains, 792
  tanks, lead-lined, 284
Woodwork,
  imitation, 886
  joints, 31
Wool winder, 952
Woollen fabrics, 702
Workbasket, portable, 1389
Workbenches, cabinet, 757
Workbox, lady's, 1213
Workshop, 509, 534, 542, 572, 606, 1245
Wormholes
  in furniture, 146
  floor, 916
Worms, destroying, 1188
Writing
  board, chair, 1264
  case, making, 302

Xestobium, 146
X-ray photography, 1515
Xylophone, 1522

Yacht, model, building, 1223
Yale locks, 193

Zinc
  box lining, 1031
  chloride, 211
  cleaning, 136
  lining, ice chest, 1184
Zoetrope, making, 989

ERRATA

- e 16. Col. 1. 7 lines from foot. For "F" read "L."
- 17. Fig. 5. Standard lino knife has a curved hook.
- 124. Fig. 13. Caption. "switches" should read "fuses."
- 124. The accompanying diagram, showing the method of carrying the wiring to the light and to the switch, was omitted.

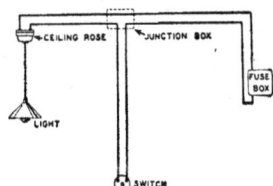

- 245. Fig. 23. The wiring of the left-hand bedroom fire should be wired in parallel and not in series.
- 411. Col. 2. 17 lines from foot of page. For "paint" read "paste."
- 487. Col. 2. 5 lines from foot of page. For "$\frac{5}{16}$" read "$\frac{3}{16}$."
- 669. Col. 3. Line 13. From "They should . . . supply" read "They should be connected in series to give about 8 volts pressure and in parallel groups to give from 2 to 6 amperes supply."
- 878. Col. 2. Lines 19 and 20. For "11 to 12" read "1," and for "60 to 70" read "$6\frac{1}{4}$."
- 896. Fig. 7. Knot shown is a thief, and not a reef, knot.
- 927. Col. 1. 22 lines from foot. For "less" read "more."
- 1027. Fig. 2. In sketch of cutting angle iron before bending, the angle should be 90°, and not 180°.
- 1039. Col. 1. Line 6. For "metre" read "metric."
- 1325. Fig. 5. Direction of arrows nearest rails should be reversed.
- 1363. Col. 3. In the list of timber required, for "20 × $28\frac{1}{2}$" read "20 × $30\frac{1}{4}$." The following pieces are also required: Two pieces laminated board $42\frac{1}{4}$ × 14 inches for sides of wireless cabinet; Two pieces laminated board $34\frac{1}{2}$ × 10 inches for sides of bookcase.
- 1408. Col. 3. Line 3. Proportions of coal dust and cement should be 6 to 9 of coal dust and 1 of cement.
- 1457. The thickness of the plywood should be $\frac{1}{32}$ inch.

www.ingramcontent.com/pod-product-compliance
Lightning Source LLC
Chambersburg PA
CBHW080835230426
43665CB00021B/2849